# INTRODUCTION TO PARALEGALISM

*Perspectives, Problems, and Skills*

## SIXTH EDITION

# The West Legal Studies Series

## Your options keep growing with West Legal Studies

Each year our list continues to offer you more options for every area of the law to meet your course or on-the-job reference requirements. We now have over 140 titles from which to choose in the following areas:

| | |
|---|---|
| Administrative Law | Family Law |
| Alternative Dispute Resolution | Federal Taxation |
| Bankruptcy | Intellectual Property |
| Business Organizations/Corporations | Introduction to Law |
| Civil Litigation and Procedure | Introduction to Paralegalism |
| CLA Exam Preparation | Law Office Management |
| Client Accounting | Law Office Procedures |
| Computer in the Law Office | Legal Research, Writing, and Analysis |
| Constitutional Law | Legal Terminology |
| Contract Law | Paralegal Employment |
| Criminal Law and Procedure | Real Estate Law |
| Document Preparation | Reference Materials |
| Environmental Law | Torts and Personal Injury Law |
| Ethics | Will, Trusts, and Estate Administration |

## You will find unparalleled, practical support

Each book is augmented by instructor and student supplements to ensure the best learning experience possible. We also offer custom publishing and other benefits such as West's Student Achievement Award. In addition, our sales representatives are ready to provide you with dependable service.

## We want to hear from you

Our best contributions for improving the quality of our books and instructional materials is feedback from the people who use them. If you have a question, concern, or observation about any of our materials, or you have a product proposal or manuscript, we want to hear from you. Please contact your local representative or write us at the following address:

West Legal Studies, 5 Maxwell Drive, P. O. Box 8007, Clifton Park, New York 12065

For additional information point your browser at

**www.westlegalstudies.com**

# INTRODUCTION TO PARALEGALISM

*Perspectives, Problems, and Skills*

## SIXTH EDITION

## William P. Statsky

**THOMSON**

**DELMAR LEARNING**

Australia Canada Mexico Singapore Spain United Kingdom United States

## WEST LEGAL STUDIES

INTRODUCTION TO PARALEGALISM
Perspectives, Problems, and Skills, Sixth Edition
by William P. Statsky

**Business Unit Executive Director:**
Susan L. Simpfenderfer

**Executive Production Manager:**
Wendy A. Troeger

**Executive Marketing Manager:**
Donna J. Lewis

**Senior Acquisitions Editor:**
Joan M. Gill

**Production Manager:**
Carolyn Miller

**Channel Manager:**
Wendy Mapstone

**Developmental Editor:**
Alexis Breen Ferraro

**Production Editor**
Betty L. Dickson

**Cover Design:**
Dutton and Sherman Design

**Editorial Assistant:**
Lisa Flatley

Printed in the United States
6 XXX 07

For more information contact Delmar,
5 Maxwell Drive, P.O. Box 8007
Clifton Park, NY 12065.

Or find us on the World Wide Web at
http://www.westlegalstudies.com

For permission to use material from this text or product, contact us by
Tel   (800) 730-2214
Fax   (800) 730-2215
www.thomsonrights.com

Library of Congress Cataloging-in-Publication Data

Statsky, William P.
    Introduction to paralegalism : perspectives, problems, and skills / William P. Statsky.--6th ed.
        p. cm -- (West Legal Studies series)
    Includes bibliographical references and index.
        ISBN 0-7668-3941-9
    1. Legal assistants--United States.   2. Legal assistants--Vocational guidance--United States.   I. Title.   II. Series.
    KF320.L4 S73 2002
    340'.023'73--dc21

                                                    2002025608

## NOTICE TO THE READER

*For Patricia Farrell Statsky,*
*whose wisdom, light, and love have*
*sustained more than she knows*

## BY THE SAME AUTHOR

*Case Analysis and Fundamentals of Legal Writing,* 4th ed. St. Paul: West Group, 1995 (with J. Wernet)

*Essentials of Paralegalism,* 2d ed. St. Paul: West Group, 1993

*Essentials of Torts,* 2d ed. Albany: Delmar Learning, 2001

*Family Law: The Essentials.* St. Paul: West Group, 1997

*Family Law,* 5th ed. Albany: Delmar Learning, 2002

*Inmate Involvement in Prison Legal Services: Roles and Training Options for the Inmate as Paralegal.* Chicago: American Bar Association, Commission on Correctional Facilities and Services, 1974

*Legal Desk Reference.* St. Paul: West Group, 1990 (with B. Hussey, M. Diamond, & R. Nakamura)

*The Legal Paraprofessional as Advocate and Assistant: Training Concepts and Materials.* New York: Center on Social Welfare Policy and Law, 1971 (with P. Lang)

*Legal Research and Writing: Some Starting Points,* 5th ed. Albany: Delmar Learning, 1999

*Legal Thesaurus/Dictionary: A Resource for the Writer and Computer Researcher.* St. Paul: West Group, 1985

*Legislative Analysis and Drafting,* 2d ed. St. Paul: West Group, 1984

*Paralegal Employment: Facts and Strategies for the 1990s,* 2d ed. St. Paul: West Group, 1993

*Paralegal Ethics and Regulation,* 2d ed. St. Paul: West Group, 1993

*Torts: Personal Injury Litigation,* 4th ed. Albany: Delmar Learning, 2001

*Rights of the Imprisoned: Cases, Materials, and Directions.* Indianapolis, Ind.: Bobbs-Merrill Company, 1974 (with R. Singer)

*What Have Paralegals Done? A Dictionary of Functions.* Washington, D.C.: National Paralegal Institute, 1973

The pain and the excitement of paralegalism, and indeed of the law itself, are that the problem we are given will often be smaller than the problem we find.

# CONTENTS IN BRIEF

# CONTENTS

## Part II
## THE SKILLS OF A PARALEGAL

# PREFACE

Five editions ago—in 1974—many were asking the question "What's a paralegal?" That day has long passed, although there is still a great deal of information that people need to have in order to appreciate the outstanding contribution paralegals have made in the delivery of legal services. This book seeks to provide that information and, at the same time, to introduce you to the fundamental skills needed to thrive in this still-developing career—a career whose members may one day outnumber attorneys in the traditional and untraditional law office. A great deal has happened since 1974. Yet the dominant themes of the field continue to be challenge, promise, and the opportunity to rethink the question of what is the most effective way to meet the legal needs of the public.

## CHANGES IN THE SIXTH EDITION

In addition to the updating material in the book on employment, salaries, roles, ethics, and regulation, a number of particular changes in the sixth edition should be mentioned:

- At the end of each chapter, there is a new feature called "On the Net," which specifies where additional material on the themes of the chapter can be found on the Internet.
- For most chapters, definitions of key terms are provided in the margins as well as in the body of the text and in the glossary.
- The discussion of the Internet as a job-search resource has been greatly expanded in Chapter 2.
- Examples of online job applications have been added in Chapter 2.
- Every major area of law listed in Chapter 2 (particularly in the section called "Paralegal Specialties: A Dictionary of Functions") is supplemented by one or more Internet sites for additional descriptions of that area of practice.
- Chapter 2 (in Appendix 2.A) now includes the Internet address of over 500 major law firms covering almost every state in the country; at these sites, the student will find descriptions of the firms, often including information on paralegal job openings.
- Chapter 2 (in Appendix 2.B) now includes the Internet address of every state department of personnel, which often contains links to online job descriptions of paralegal jobs in state government.
- More material has been added to Chapter 3 on the sometimes delicate relationship between paralegals and those legal secretaries who often perform paralegal tasks.

> Please note the Internet resources are of a time-sensitive nature and URL addresses may often change or be deleted.

xviPREFACE

- Chapter 4 now includes a more extended discussion of the distinction between giving legal advice and providing legal information in the important arena of the unauthorized practice of law. The discussion includes a major opinion on this distinction in a case involving paralegal participation in a program that provides assistance to victims of domestic violence.
- The most dramatic development in paralegalism since the fifth edition has been the California legislation on the definition of a paralegal and the requirements to be one. This legislation is extensively discussed in Chapter 4 and is reprinted in full in Appendix G.
- Chapter 4 also discusses new laws in the state of Washington that might lead to the creation of the first meaningful program of limited licensing for paralegals in the country.
- Chapter 5 includes a discussion of the multidisciplinary practice (MDP).
- Special problems of confidentiality in e-mail communications and the dangers of giving legal advice on the Internet are now covered in Chapter 5.
- Chapter 5 also analyzes the infamous case of the paralegal in the tobacco litigation who disclosed confidential client documents to the media, helping precipitate multi-billion-dollar awards and settlements.
- Chapter 5 includes a discussion (and illustration) of conflicts checking by computer.
- Chapter 6 contains more material on the common law and on the hierarchy of court systems.
- The role of IRAC in legal analysis receives expanded treatment in Chapter 7.
- A section on factor analysis (and how it differs from element analysis) has been added to Chapter 7.
- New material has been added on the difficult client (e.g., the client who lies) in Chapter 8, on legal interviewing.
- Chapter 9, on investigation, discusses the investigator's role in the Academy Award–winning motion picture *Erin Brockovich*.
- Chapter 9 also has expanded coverage of the resources available to conduct online factual investigation through commercial and free Internet sites.
- Chapter 10, on litigation, now includes material on e-filing in our state and federal courts.
- Chapter 10 also includes new material on paralegal roles in working with expert witnesses and in assisting with trial exhibits.
- Chapter 11, on legal research, covers the new citation rules of the Association of Legal Writing Directors (ALWD).
- Chapter 12 adds a new analytic tool called STOP as an aid in providing a counter-analysis in legal writing such as a memorandum of law.
- Chapter 13, on computers, has been re-written to reflect current developments in the role of computers in the practice of law.
- Chapter 14 offers an expanded discussion of how computers are used in the management of law offices.
- Chapter 14 also includes a new section on client trust accounts.
- The section on formal administrative advocacy in Chapter 15 has been re-written so that the hearing is now based on a social security dispute in which paralegals have federal authorization to provide administrative representation.
- Appendix F now includes definitions of a paralegal for those states that have adopted such a definition.
- Appendix G includes the full text of the new California law that specifies who can call themselves paralegals or legal assistants and who fits into the new category of legal document assistant (LDA).

## ANCILLARY MATERIALS
- **Instructor's Manual**—The *Instructor's Manual* is available both in print and online at www.westlegalstudies.com in the Instructor's Lounge under Resources. Written by the author of the text, the *Instructor's Manual* contains the following:

- Class ideas, such as lecture ideas and suggestions for using selected assignments
- Detailed competency lists for each chapter
- A test bank of over 500 questions, which includes a variety of questions in true/false, multiple choice, and essay format
- Transparency masters, containing approximately 50 exhibits from the text
- **Computerized Test Bank**—The Test Bank found in the *Instructor's Manual* is also available in a computerized format on CD–ROM. The platforms supported include Windows™ 1.3 and 95, Windows™ NT, and Macintosh. Features include:
  - Multiple methods of question selection
  - Multiple outputs—that is, print, ASCII, and RTF
  - Graphic support (black and white)
  - Random questioning output
  - Special character support
- **On-line Resource™**—The On-line Resource™ is a protected area that requires a user-name and password to gain access. You will find your username and password information below. You will need these to enter the protected area, and you must enter the username and password exactly as they appear below. The On-line Resource™ can be found at *www.westlegalstudies.com* in the On-line Resource™ section of the web site.
  Username:   s2t388
  Password:    883t2s
- **Student Study Guide and Workbook**—The Student Study Guide and Workbook are components of the On-line Resource™ and written by the author of the text. This supplement includes review questions, short writing exercises, and additional enrichment materials.
- **Westlaw®**—West's online computerized legal research system offers students "hands-on" experience with a system commonly used in law offices. Qualified adopters can receive 10 free hours of Westlaw®. Westlaw® can be accessed with Macintosh and IBM PCs and compatibles. A modem is required.
- **Strategies and Tips for Paralegal Educators**—This pamphlet by Anita Tebbe of Johnson County Community College provides teaching strategies specifically designed for paralegal educators. A copy of this pamphlet is available to each adopter. Quantities for distribution to adjunct instructors are available for purchase at a minimal price. A coupon on the pamphlet provides ordering information.
- **Survival Guide for Paralegal Students**—This pamphlet by Kathleen Mercer Reed and Bradene Moore covers practical and basic information to help students make the most of their paralegal courses. Topics covered include choosing courses of study and developing note-taking skills.
- **West's Paralegal Video Library**—West Legal Studies is pleased to offer the following videos at no charge to qualified adopters:
  - *The Drama of the Law II: Paralegal Issues Video* ISBN 0-314-07088-5
  - *"I Never Said I Was a Lawyer" Paralegal Ethics Video* ISBN: 0-314-08049-X
  - *The Making of a Case Video* ISBN 0-314-07300-0
  - *ABA Mock Trial Video—Anatomy of a Trial: A Contracts Case* ISBN: 0-314-07343-4
  - *ABA Mock Trial Video—Product Liability* ISBN: 0-314-07342-6
  - *Arguments to the United States Supreme Court Video* ISBN: 0-314-07070-2
- **Court TV Videos**—West Legal Studies is pleased to offer the following videos from Court TV for a minimal fee:
  - *New York, v. Ferguson—Murder on the 5:33: The Trial of Colin Ferguson* ISBN: 0-7668-1098-4
  - *Ohio v. Alfieri* ISBN: 0-7668-1009-2
  - *Flynn v. Goldman Sachs—Fired on Wall Street: A Case of Sex Discrimination?* ISBN: 0-7668-1096-8
  - *Dodd v. Dodd—Religion and Child Custody in Conflict* ISBN: 0-7668-1094-1
  - *In Re Custody of Baby Girl Clausen—Child of Mine: The Fight for Baby Jessica* ISBN: 0-7668-1097-6

- *Fentress v. Eli Lilly & Co., et al.—Prozac on Trial* ISBN: 0-7668-1095-X
- *Garcia v. Garcia—Fighting over Jerry's Money* ISBN: 0-7668-0264-7
- *Hall v. Hall—Irretrievably Broken—A Divorce Lawyer Goes to Court* ISBN: 0-7668-0196-9
- *Maglica v. Maglica—Broken Hearts, Broken Commitments* ISBN: 0-7668-0867-X
- *Northside Partners v. Page and New Kids on the Block—New Kids in Court: Is Their Hit Song a Copy?* ISBN: 0-7668-0426-7

## ACKNOWLEDGMENTS

It is difficult to name all the individuals who have provided guidance in the preparation of the six editions of this book. Looking back over the years, a number of people have played important roles in my initiation and growth as a student of paralegal education. I owe a debt to Jean and Edgar Cahn, founders of the Legal Technician Program at Antioch School of Law, where I worked; Bill Fry, Director of the National Paralegal Institute and a valued colleague since our days together at Columbia Law School, where he was my dean in one of the first paralegal training programs in the country, the Program for Legal Service Assistants; Dan Oran, who helped me plan the first edition; Michael Manna, Ed Schwartz; Bill Mulkeen; and finally, Juanita Hill, Willie Nolden, and Linda Saunders, some of my early students who taught me so much.

I wish to thank the following people at West Legal Studies, a division of Thomson Learning: Joan Gill, Senior Acquisitions Editor; Alexis Breen Ferraro, Developmental Editor; Betty Dickson, Production Editor; Carolyn Miller, Production Manager; and Lisa Flatley, Editorial Assistant.

Finally, a word of thanks to the reviewers who made valuable suggestions for improving the text:

Laura Barnard
Lakeland Community College, OH

Sarah Bartholomew
Valdosta State University, GA

Kathryn Clark Beachy
Tulane University, LA

Michele G. Bradford
Gadsden State Community
  College, AL

Toni Volza Esposito
Briarwood College, CT

Mimi K. Flaherty
RETS Tech Center, OH

Karl Freedman
Professional Career Development
  Institute, GA

Nancy L. Hart
Midland College, TX

Diana D. Juettner
Mercy College, NY

Kristine Mullendore
Grand Valley State University, MI

Kathryn L. Myers
Saint Mary of the Woods College, IN

H. Margaret Nickerson
William Woods University, MO

Virginia Noonan
Northern Essex Community
  College, MA

Gina-Marie Reitano
St. John's University, NY

James N. Sheperd
New Hampshire Technical College

Christine Thiltgen
American River College, CA

Cynthia Weishapple
Chippewa Valley Technical College,
  NY

Mary A. Whiting
Brooklyn College, NY

Andrea E. Williams
Central Florida Community College

- *[The] expanded use of well-trained assistants, sometimes called "paralegals," has been an important development. Today there are . . . double the number of . . . schools for training paralegals [as the number of schools for training attorneys]. . . . The advent of the paralegal enables law offices to perform high quality legal services at a lower cost. Possibly we have only scratched the surface of this development.*

Warren E. Burger, Chief Justice
of the United States Supreme Court, February 3, 1980

- *Paralegals are an absolutely essential component of quality legal services in the future.*

James Fellers, President,
American Bar Association, April 4, 1975

- *Paralegals are projected to rank among the fastest growing occupations in the economy through 2008.*

U.S. Department of Labor,
*Occupational Outlook Handbook, 2000–2001*

# How to Study Law in the Classroom and on the Job

## Outline

### A. Classroom Learning

The Two Phases of Legal Education
Rules and Skills
Prior Experience in the Law
Goals and Context of Assignments
Study Plan
An Additional 50 Percent
Distractions
Study Habits
Grammar, Spelling, and Composition
Study Groups
Research Skills
Definitions
Ambiguity
Note Taking
Memory Skills
Feedback
Speed Reading

### B. On-the-Job Learning: The Art of Being Supervised

"King's Clothes"
Repetition of Instructions
Instructions in Writing
Priority of Assignments
Priority of Tasks
Checklists
Manuals
Models
Independent Research
Office Mailing Lists for New Publications
Secretaries and Other Paralegals
Feedback
Training Programs
Evaluations

## Section A
# CLASSROOM LEARNING

Education does not come naturally to most of us. It is a struggle. This is all the more true for someone entering a totally new realm of training such as legal education. Much of the material will seem foreign and difficult. There is a danger of becoming overwhelmed by the vast quantity of laws and legal material that confronts you. How do you study law? How do you learn law? What is the proper perspective that a student of law should have about the educational process? These are our concerns in this introduction to the process of studying law. In short, our theme is training to be trained—the art of effective learning.

The first step is to begin with a proper frame of mind. Too many students have false expectations of what legal education can accomplish. This substantially interferes with effective studying.

### 1. Your Legal Education Has Two Phases. Phase I Begins Now and Ends When You Complete This Training Program. Phase II Begins When This Training Program Ends and is Not Completed Until the Last Day of Your Employment as a Paralegal.

You have entered a career that will require you to be a perpetual student. The learning never ends. This is true not only because the boundary lines of law are vast, but also because the law is changing every day. No one knows all of the law. Phase I of your legal education is designed to provide you with the foundation that will enable you to become a good student in phase II.

### 2. Your Legal Education Has Two Dimensions: The Content of the Law (the rules) and the Practical Techniques of Using That Content in a Law Office (the skills).

### Rules
There are two basic kinds of rules or laws:

Substantive Law: Those nonprocedural rules that govern rights and duties; for example, the requirements for the sale of land and the elements of battery;
Procedural Law: Those rules that govern the mechanics of resolving a dispute in court or in an administrative agency; for example, the number of days within which a party must respond to a claim stated in a complaint.

The law library contains millions of substantive and procedural laws written by courts (in volumes called *reporters*), by legislatures (in volumes called *statutory codes*), and by administrative agencies (in volumes called *administrative codes*). A great deal of the material in these volumes is also available on the Internet, as we will see. A substantial portion of your time in school will involve study of the substantive and procedural law of your state, and often of the federal government as well.

### Skills
By far the most important dimension of your legal education will be the skills of using rules. Without the skills, the content of the law is close to worthless. Examples of legal skills include:

- How to interview a client (see chapter 8).
- How to investigate the facts of a case (see chapter 9).
- How to draft a complaint, the document that initiates a lawsuit (see chapter 10).
- How to digest or summarize documents in a case file (see chapter 10).
- How to do legal research in a law library (see chapter 11).

The overriding skill that, to one degree or another, is the basis for all others is the skill of legal analysis (see chapter 7). Some make the mistake of concluding that legal analysis is the exclusive domain of the attorney. Without an understanding of at least the fundamentals of legal analysis, however, paralegals cannot understand the legal system and cannot intelligently carry out many of the more demanding tasks they are assigned.

### 3. You Must Force Yourself to Suspend What You Already Know About the Law in Order to be Able to Absorb (a) That Which is New and (b) That Which Conflicts With Your Prior Knowledge and Experience.

Place yourself in the position of training students to drive a car. Your students undoubtedly already know something about driving. They have watched others drive and maybe have even had a lesson or two from friends. It would be ideal, however, if you could begin your instruction from point zero. There is a very real danger that the students have picked up bad habits from others. This will interfere with their capacity to *listen* to what you are saying. The danger is that they will block out anything you say that does not conform to previously learned habits and knowledge. If the habits or knowledge is defective, your job as a trainer is immensely more difficult.

The same is true in studying law. Everyone knows something about the law from government or civics courses as a teenager and from the various treatments of the law in the media. Some of you may have been involved in the law as a party or as a witness in court. Others may have worked, or currently work, in law offices. Will this prior knowledge and experience be a help or a hindrance to you in your future legal education? For some, it will be a help. For most of us, however, there is a danger of interference.

This is particularly so with respect to the portrayal of the law on TV and in the movies. Some of the older dramas could easily give viewers the impression that most legal problems are solved by dramatically tricking a hostile witness on the stand into finally telling the truth. Not so. The practice of law is not an endless series of confessions and concessions that are pried loose from opponents. Nor are most of the more recent TV programs much more realistic. Every attorney does not spend all day engaged in the kind of case that makes front page news. Not long ago, a high-rated lawyer drama on TV was the series *L.A. Law*. One of its fans was a New Jersey paralegal who left her job with a sole practitioner to take another paralegal position with a firm that she thought was going to be like *L.A. Law*. Three months later she begged her old boss to take her back. She discovered that there was a great gap between reality and *L.A. Law*.

Another potentially misleading portrayal of the law came in the O.J. Simpson criminal and civil trials, which captivated the nation from 1995 to 1997. Very few parties to litigation have teams of attorneys, investigators, and experts ready to do battle with each other. The overwhelming number of legal disputes is never litigated in court. Most are either settled or simply dropped by one or both parties. Of the small number that are litigated, the vast majority involve no more than two opposing attorneys and several witnesses. In short, it is rare for the legal system to become the spectacle—some would say the circus—that the occasional high-profile case leads us to believe is common in the practice of law.

While excitement and drama can be part of the legal system, they are not everyday occurrences. What is dominant is painstaking and meticulous hard work. This reality is almost never portrayed in the media.

Therefore, it is strongly recommended that you place yourself in the position of a stranger to the material you will be covering in your courses, regardless of your background and exposure to the field. Cautiously treat everything as a new experience. Temporarily suspend what you already know. Resist the urge to pat yourself on the back by saying "I already knew that" or "I already know how to do that." For many students, such statements lead to relaxation. They do not work as hard once they have convinced themselves that there is nothing new to learn. No problem exists, of course, if these students are right. The danger, however, is that they are wrong or that they are only partially right. Students are not always the best judge of what they know and of what they can do. Do not become too comfortable. Adopt the following healthy attitude: "I've heard about that before or I've already done that, but maybe I can learn something new about it." Every new teacher, every new supervisor, every new setting is an opportunity to add a dimension to your prior knowledge and experience. Be open to these opportunities. No two people practice law exactly the same way. Your own growth as a student and as a paralegal will depend in large part on your capacity to listen for, explore, and absorb this diversity.

### 4. Be Sure That You Know the Goals and Context of Every Assignment

Throughout your education, you will be given a variety of assignments: class exercises, text readings, drafting tasks, field projects, research assignments, etc. You should ask yourself the following questions about each one:

- What are the goals of this assignment? What am I supposed to learn from it?
- How does this assignment fit into what I have already learned? What is the context of the assignment?

Successfully completing an assignment depends in part on understanding its goals and how these goals relate to the overall context of the course.

Keeping an eye on the broader picture will also be important on the job. Each assignment should prompt you to ask yourself a series of questions: What is the goal of this assignment? Why am I being asked to perform the task in this way? Has it always been done this way? Are there more efficient ways? After you have performed the task a number of times, can you eventually propose a more effective *system* of handling the task?

Of course, there is a danger of going to the opposite extreme. You cannot be so preoccupied with purpose, context, and systems that you fail to complete the immediate job before you. Timing is important. Often the office will have no tolerance for suggestions for improvement until immediate deadlines have passed. This simply means that you must always be operating at two levels. First, the *now* level: mobilize all of your resources to complete the task as efficiently as possible under the present work environment. Second, the *systems* level: keep your mind open, and challenge your creativity to identify steps and procedures that might be taken in the future to achieve greater efficiency in accomplishing the task.

### 5. Design a Study Plan

Make current *lists* of everything that you must do. Update them regularly. Divide every list into long-term projects (what is due next week or at the end of the semester) and short-term projects (what is due tomorrow). Have a plan for each day. Establish the following norm for yourself: every day you will focus in some way on *all* of your assignments. Every day you will review your long-term and short-term lists. Priority, of course, will be given to the short-term tasks. Yet some time, however small, will also be devoted to the long-term tasks. For example, on a day that you will be mainly working on the short-term projects, try to set aside 5 percent of your time for a long-term project by doing some background reading or by preparing a very rough first draft of an outline. It is critical that you establish *momentum* toward the accomplishment of *all* your tasks. This is done by never letting anything sit on the back burner. Set yourself the goal of making at least *some* progress on everything every day. Without this goal, the momentum may be very difficult to sustain.

Once you have decided what tasks you will cover on a given study day, the next question is: In what *order* will you cover them? There are a number of ways in which you can classify the things you must do—for example: (a) easy tasks that will require a relatively short time to complete, (b) complex tasks requiring more time, (c) tasks with time demands that will be unknown until you start them. At the beginning of your study time, spend a few seconds preparing an outline of the order in which you will cover the tasks that day and the approximate amount of time that you will set aside for each task. You may want to start with some of the easier tasks so that you can feel a sense of accomplishment relatively soon. Alternatively, you may want to devote early study time to the third kind of task listed above (c) so that you can obtain a clearer idea of the scope and difficulty of such assignments. The important point is that you establish a *schedule*. It does not have to be written in stone. Quite the contrary—it is healthy that you have enough flexibility to revise your day's schedule so that you can respond to unfolding realities as you study. Adaptation is not a sign of disorganization, but the total absence of an initial plan often is.

### 6. Add 50 Percent to the Time You Initially Think You Will Need to Study a Subject

You are kidding yourself if you have not set aside a *substantial* amount of time to study law outside the classroom. The conscientious study of law takes time—lots of it. It is true that some students must work and take care of family responsibilities. You cannot devote time that you do not have. Yet the reality is that limited study time leads to limited education.

Generally, people will find time for what they want to do. You may *wish* to do many things for which there will never be enough time. You will find the time, however, to do what you really *want* to do. Once you have decided that you want something badly enough, you will find the time to do it.

How much of each work hour do you spend in *productive* time? For most of us, the answer is about 20 minutes. The rest of the hour is spent worrying, relaxing, repeating ourselves, socializing, etc. One answer to the problem of limited time availability is to increase the amount of *productive* time that you derive out of each work hour. You may not be able to add any new hours to the clock, but you can add to your net productive time. How about moving up to 30 minutes an hour? Forty? You will be amazed at the time that you can "find" simply by making a conscious effort to remove some of the waste. When asked how a masterpiece was created, a great sculptor once responded: "You start with a block of stone and you cut away everything that is not art." In your study habits, start with a small block of time and work to cut away everything that is not productive.

There are no absolute rules on how much time you will need. It depends on the complexity of the subject matter you must master. It is probably accurate to say that most of us need to study more than we do—as a rule of thumb, about 50 percent more. You should be constantly on the alert for ways to increase the time you have available or, more accurately, to increase the productive time that you can make available.

Resolving time-management problems as a student will be good practice for you when you are confronted with similar (and more severe) time-management problems as a working paralegal. Many law offices operate at a hectic pace. One of the hallmarks of a professional is a pronounced reverence for deadlines and the clock. Time is money. An ability to find and handle time effectively can also be one of the preconditions for achieving justice in a particular case.

Soon you will be gaining a reputation among other students, teachers, supervisors, and employers. You should make a concerted effort to make sure you acquire a reputation for hard work, punctuality, and conscientiousness about the time you devote to your work. In large measure, success follows from such a reputation. It is as important, if not more important, than raw ability or intelligence. Phrased another way, your legal skills are unlikely to put bread on the table if you are casual about the clock.

### 7. Create Your Own Study Area Free from Distractions

It is essential that you find study areas that are quiet and free from distractions. Otherwise, concentration is obviously impossible. It may be that the worst places to study are at home or at the library unless you can find a corner that is cut off from noise and people who want to talk. Do not make yourself too available. If you study in the corridor, at the first table at the entrance to the library, or at the kitchen table, you are inviting distraction. You need to be able to close yourself off for two to three hours at a time. It is important for you to interact with other people—but not while you are studying material that requires considerable concentration. You will be tempted to digress and to socialize. You are in the best position to know where these temptations are. You are also the most qualified person to know how to avoid the temptations.

### 8. Conduct a Self-Assessment of Your Prior Study Habits and Establish a Program to Reform the Weaknesses

If you were to describe the way you study, would you be proud of the description? Here is a partial list of some of the main weaknesses of attitude or practice that students have about studying:

- They have done well in the past with only minimal study effort. Why change now?
- No one else in the class appears to be studying very much. Why be different?
- They learn best by listening in class. Hence, instead of studying on their own, why not wait until someone explains it in person?
- They simply do not like to study; there are more important things to do in life.

- They can't concentrate.
- They study with the radio on or with other distractions.
- They get bored easily. "I can't stay motivated for long."
- They do not understand what they are supposed to study.
- They skim read.
- They do not stop to look up strange words or phrases.
- They study only at exam time—they cram for exams.
- They do not study at a consistent pace. They spend an hour here and there and have no organized, regular study times.
- They do not like to memorize.
- They do not take notes on what they are reading.

What other interferences with effective studying can you think of? Or, more important, which of the above items apply to you? How do you plead? In law, it is frequently said that you cannot solve a problem until you obtain the facts. What are the facts in the case of your study habits? Make your personal list of attitude problems, study patterns, or environmental interferences. Place these items in some order. Next, establish a plan for yourself. Which item on the list are you going to try to correct tonight? What will the plan be for this week? For next week? For the coming month? What specific steps will you take to try to change some bad habits? Do not, however, be too hard on yourself. Be determined but realistic. The more serious problems are obviously going to take more time to correct. Improvement will come if you are serious about improvement and regularly think about it. If one corrective method does not work, try another. If the fifth does not work, try a sixth. Discuss techniques of improvement with other students and with teachers. Prove to yourself that change is possible.

### 9. Conduct a Self-Assessment on Grammar, Spelling, and Composition. Then Design a Program to Reform Weaknesses.

The legal profession lives by the written word. Talking is important for some activities, but writing is crucial in almost every area of law. You cannot function in this environment without a grasp of the basics of spelling, grammar, and composition. A major complaint made by employers today is that paralegals are consistently violating these basics. The problem is very serious. Here are eight steps that will help solve it:

#### Step One

Take responsibility for your training in grammar, spelling, and composition. Do not wait for someone to teach you these basics. Do not wait until someone points out your weaknesses. You must make a personal commitment to train yourself. If English courses are available to you, great. It is essential, however, that you understand that a weekly class may not be enough.

#### Step Two

Raise your consciousness about the writing around you. When you are reading a newspaper, for example, you should be conscious of the use of semicolons and paragraph structure in what you are reading. At least occasionally you should ask yourself why a certain punctuation mark was used by a writer. You are surrounded by writing. You read this writing for content. Begin a conscious effort to focus on the structure of the writing as well. This dual level of observation exists in other aspects of our lives. When people come out of the theater, for example, they often comment about how impressive the acting was. In addition to following the story or content of the play or movie, they were aware of its form and structure as well. These levels of consciousness (content and form) should also be developed for everything you read.

#### Step Three

Commit yourself to spending 10 minutes a day, five or six days a week, on improving your grammar skills. For a total of about an hour a week, drill yourself on the fundamentals of our language. Go to any general search engine on the Internet such as:

www.google.com
www.altavista.com

Type "English grammar" in the search box of the engine you use. Do some surfing to find grammar sites that not only give basic rules but also provide examples of the application of the rules and practice drills to allow you to test yourself on what you know. Avoid sites that charge fees or that are geared to citizens of other countries. Here are some examples of sites you might find useful:

www.edufind.com/english/grammar
ccc.commnet.edu/grammar
newark.rutgers.edu/~jlynch/Writing
englishplus.com/grammar
www.tnellen.com/cybereng/32.html

Sites such as these may provide links to comparable sites. Try several. Ask fellow students what sites they regularly use.

How do you know what areas of grammar you should study? Begin at the beginning. Start with the most basic instruction offered on the site you choose. If you consistently give correct answers to the exercises on a particular area of writing, move on to another area on the site.

One way to test your progress is to try the exercises at different sites. Suppose, for example, that you are on a site studying the distinction between *that* clauses and *which* clauses. After you finish the that/which exercises at this site, go to another grammar site and find its section on that/which. Read the examples and do the exercises at this site. Are you reinforcing what you learned at the first site, or are the examples and exercises at the second site making you realize that you need more work understanding this area of grammar? Using more than one site in this way will help you assess how well you are grasping the material.

### Step Four

Improve your spelling. Use a dictionary often. Begin making a list of words that you are spelling incorrectly. Work on these words. Ask other students, relatives, or friends to test you on them by reading the words to you one by one. Spell the words out loud or on paper. You can drill yourself into spelling perfection, or close to it, by this method. When you have the slightest doubt about the spelling of a word, check the dictionary. Add difficult words to your list. Again, the more often you take this approach now, the less often you will need to use the dictionary later.

Use the Internet as a resource. Type "spelling help" in a search engine. You will be led to many sites that will provide guidance. Examples include:

nv.essortment.com/spellinghelp_yyd.htm
www.spelling.hemscott.net

As we will see in chapter 13 on computers, many word processing programs have "spell checkers" that not only identify words you may have misspelled but also provide suggested corrections. Does this new technology mean that your spelling problems have been solved forever? Hardly. Spell checkers can catch many spelling blunders, but they can be very misleading. First of all, they cannot tell you how to spell many proper names such as the surnames of individuals (unless you add these names to the base of words being checked). An even more serious problem is that spell checkers do not alert you to improper word choices. Every word in the following sentence, for example, is incorrect, but a spell checker would tell you that the sentence has no spelling problems:

"Its to later too by diner."

Here is what should have been written:

"It's too late to buy dinner."

Since the first sentence has no misspellings, you are led—misled—to believe that you have written a flawless sentence.

### Step Five
Enroll in English and writing courses. Find out if drop-in help labs or remedial centers are available to you. Check offerings at local schools like adult education programs in the public schools or at colleges.

### Step Six
Find out which law courses in your curriculum require the most writing from students. If possible, take these courses—no matter how painful you find writing to be. In fact, the more painful it is, the more you need to place yourself in an environment where writing is demanded of you on a regular basis.

### Step Seven
Simplify your writing. Cut down the length of your sentences. Often a long-winded sentence can be effectively re-written into two shorter sentences. How can you tell if your sentences are too long? There are, of course, no absolute rules that will answer this question. Yet there is a general consensus that sentences formed by a legal mind tend to be too long.

Several writing scholars have devised readability formulas that allow you to measure sentence length. Among the most popular are the Gunning Fog Index, the Flesch Reading Ease Score, and the Flesch-Kincaid Grade Level Score. You can find them described on many Internet sites such as:

tech-head.com/fog.htm
www.logan.lib.ut.us/bridgerland/TutorTips
isu.indstate.edu/bminnick/asbe336/PowerPoint/fog-index.htm
www.nightscribe.com/Education/eschew_obfuscation.htm

Some states require certain kinds of legal contracts to use these readability formulas. See, for example, the Arkansas statute on insurance policies:

www.state.ar.us/insurance/rulesandregs/legal_rnr29.html

Try a readability formula on your own writing. It will take only a few minutes to apply. Find out if the word processor you use (e.g., Word, WordPerfect) has a formula built into the program that is ready to use every time you write something.)

Readability formulas are no more than rough guides. Use them to help raise your consciousness about your writing. As you review sentences you have written, you should be asking yourself self-editing questions such as "Would I have been clearer if I had made that sentence shorter?" The conscientious use of readability formulas will help you ask such questions.

### Step Eight
Prepare a self-assessment of your weaknesses. Make a list of what you must correct. Then set a schedule for improvement. Set aside a small amount of time each day to work on your writing weaknesses. Be consistent about this time. Do not wait for the weekend or for next semester when you will have more time. The reality is that you will probably never have substantially more time than you have now. The problem is not so much the absence of time as it is an unwillingness to dig into the task. Progress will be slow and you will be on your own. Hence there is a danger that you will be constantly finding excuses to put it off.

### 10. Consider Forming a Student Study Group, But be Cautious
Students sometimes find it useful to form study groups. A healthy exchange with your colleagues can be very productive. One difficulty is finding students with whom you are compatible. Trial and error may be the only way to identify such students. A more serious

concern is trying to define the purpose of the study group. It should not be used as a substitute for your own individual study. It would be inappropriate to divide a course into parts, with members of the group having responsibility for preparing notes on and teaching the assigned parts to the remainder of the group.

The group can be very valuable for mutual editing on writing assignments. Suppose, for example, that you are drafting complaints in a course. Photocopy a complaint that one member of the group drafts. The group then collectively comments upon and edits the complaint according to the standards discussed in class and in the course materials. (Be sure to check with your teacher in advance if group editing on such assignments is allowed.) Similarly, you could try to obtain copies of old exams in the course and collectively examine answers prepared by group members. Ask your teacher for fact situations that could be the basis of legal analysis memos (see chapter 7) or other drafting assignments. Make up fact situations of your own. The student whose work is being scrutinized must be able to take constructive criticism. The criticism should be intense if it is to be worthwhile. Students should be asked to rewrite the draft after incorporating suggestions made. The rewrite should later be subjected to another round of mutual editing. Do not hesitate to subject your writing to the scrutiny of other students. You can learn a great deal from each other.

### 11. Use Your Legal Research Skills to Help You Understand Components of a Course That Are Giving You Difficulty

The law library is more than the place to go to find law that governs the facts of a client's case. A great deal of the material in the law library consists of explanations/summaries/overviews of the same law that you will be covering in your courses. You need to learn how to gain access to this material as soon as possible. In chapter 11, a series of techniques is presented on doing background research through texts such as legal dictionaries, legal encyclopedias, treatises, annotations, etc. (See exhibit 11.19 in chapter 11.) You should become acquainted with these kinds of law books. They will prove invaluable as outside reading to help resolve conceptual and practical difficulties you are having in class.

### 12. Organize Your Learning Through Definitions or Definitional Questions

Among the most sophisticated questions an attorney or paralegal can ask are these: What does that word or phrase mean? What's the definition? To a very large extent, the practice of law is a probing for definitions of key words or phrases in the context of facts that have arisen. Can a five-year-old be liable for negligence? (What is *negligence?*) Can the government tax a church-run bingo game? (What is the *free exercise of religion?*) Can attorneys in a law firm strike and obtain the protection of the National Labor Relations Act? (What is a *covered employee* under the labor statute?) Can one spouse rape another? (What is the definition of *rape?*) Can a citizen slander the president of the United States? (What is a *defamatory statement*, and what are the definitions of the defenses to a slander action?) Etc.

For every course that you take, you will come across numerous technical words and phrases in class and in your readings. Begin compiling a list of these words and phrases for each class. Try to limit yourself to what you think are the major ones. When in doubt about whether to include something on your list, resolve the doubt by including it.

Then pursue definitions. Find definitions in class lectures, your textbook, a legal dictionary, or other secondary sources such as legal encyclopedias (see exhibit 11.10 in chapter 11 for a list of secondary sources) and on the Internet. Ask your teacher for guidance in finding definitions.

For some words, you may have difficulty obtaining definitions. Do not give up your pursuit. Keep searching. Keep probing. Keep questioning. For some words, there may be more than one definition. Others may require definitions of the definitions.

Of course, you cannot master a course simply by knowing the definitions of all the key words and phrases involved. Yet these words and phrases are the *vocabulary* of the course and are the foundation and point of reference for learning the other aspects of the course. Begin with vocabulary.

Consider a system of three-by-five or two-by-three cards to help you learn the definitions. On one side of the card, place a single word or phrase. On the other side, write the definition with a brief page reference or citation to the source of the definition. Using the cards, test yourself periodically. If you are in a study group, ask other members to test you. Ask a relative to test you. Establish a plan of ongoing review.

### 13. Studying Ambiguity—Coping With Unanswered Questions

Legal studies can be frustrating because there is so much uncertainty in the law. Legions of unanswered questions exist. Definitive answers to legal questions are not always easy to find, no matter how good your legal research techniques are. Every new fact situation presents the potential for a new law. Every law seems to have an exception. Furthermore, advocates frequently argue for exceptions to the exceptions. As indicated, when terms are defined, the definitions often need definitions. A law office is not always an easy environment in which to work because of this reality.

The study of law is in large measure an examination of ambiguity that is identified, dissected, and manipulated.

The most effective way to handle frustration with this state of affairs is to be realistic about what the law is and isn't. Do not expect definitive answers to all legal questions. Search for as much clarity as you can, but do not be surprised if the conclusion of your search is further questions. A time-honored answer to many legal questions is "It depends!" Become familiar with the following equation, since you will see it used often:

If "X" is present, then the conclusion is "A," but if "Y" is so, then the conclusion is "B," but if "Z" is . . .

The practice of law may sometimes appear to be an endless puzzle. Studying law, therefore, must engage you in similar thinking processes. Again, look for precision and clarity, but do not expect the puzzle to disappear.

### 14. Develop the Skill of Note Taking

Note taking is an important skill. You will regularly be told to "write it down" or "put it in a memo." Effective note taking is often a precondition to being able to do *any* kind of writing in the law.

First, take notes on what you are reading for class preparation and for research assignments. Do not rely exclusively on your memory. After reading hundreds of pages (or more), you will not be able to remember what you have read at the end of the semester, or even at the end of the day. Copy what you think are the essential portions of the materials you are reading. Be sure to include definitions of important words and phrases as indicated in guideline 12 above.

To be sure, note taking will add time to your studying. Yet you will discover that it was time well spent, particularly when you begin reviewing for an exam or writing your memorandum.

Second, take notes in class. You must develop the art of taking notes while simultaneously listening to what is being said. On the job, you may have to do this frequently—for example, when:

- Interviewing a client
- Interviewing a witness during field investigation
- Receiving instructions from a supervisor
- Talking with someone on the phone
- Attending a deposition
- Listening while a witness is giving testimony at trial

A good place to begin learning how to write and listen at the same time is during your classes.

Most students take poor class notes. This is due to a number of reasons:

- They may write slowly.
- They may not like to take notes; it's hard work.

- They may not know if what is being said is important enough to be noted until after it is said—when it is too late because the teacher has gone on to something else.
- They do not think it necessary to take notes on a discussion that the teacher is having with another student.
- They take notes only when they see other students taking notes.
- Some teachers ramble.

A student who uses these excuses for not taking comprehensive notes in class will eventually be using similar excuses on the job when precise note taking is required for a case. This is unfortunate. You must overcome whatever resistances you have acquired to the admittedly difficult task of note taking. Otherwise, you will pay the price in your schoolwork and on the job.

Develop your own shorthand system of abbreviations for note taking. Here are some commonly used abbreviations in the law:

| | | | |
|---|---|---|---|
| a/r | assumption of the risk | pf | prima facie |
| b/p | burden of proof | Q | question |
| cz | cause | rsb | reasonable |
| cl | common law | § | section |
| © | consideration | §§ | sections |
| k | contract | std | standard |
| dmg | damages | s/l | statute of limitations |
| Δ | defendant | sl | strict liability |
| L | liable, liability | $ | suppose |
| n | negligence | θ | third party |
| o | owner | t | tort |
| π | plaintiff | wd | wrongful death |

If you are participating in class by talking with the teacher, it will obviously be difficult for you to take notes at the same time. After class, take a few moments to jot down some notes on what occurred during the discussion. Then ask someone else who was in class to review these notes for accuracy and completeness. Sometimes you will have to begin taking notes at the moment the person starts talking rather than wait until the end of what he or she is saying. Try different approaches to increasing the completeness of your notes.

## 15. Studying Rules—The Role of Memory.

Memory plays a significant role in the law. Applicants for the bar, for example, are not allowed to take notes into the exam room. An advocate in court or at an administrative hearing may be able to refer to notes, but the notes are of little value if the advocate does not have a solid grasp of the case. Most of the courses you will be taking have a memory component. This is true even for open-book exams, since you will not have time to go through all the material while responding to the questions.

Students often make two mistakes with respect to the role of memory:

- They think that memorizing is beneath their dignity.
- They think that because they understand something, they know it sufficiently to be able to give it back in an examination.

Of course, you should not be memorizing what you do not understand. Rote memorization is close to worthless. This is not the case for important material that you comprehend. Yet simply understanding something does not necessarily mean that you have a sufficient grasp of it for later use.

Many systems for memorizing material can be effective:

- Reading it over and over
- Copying it
- Writing questions to yourself about it and trying to answer the questions
- Having other students ask you questions about it

- Making summaries or outlines of it
- Etc.

If you do not have a photographic mind, you must resort to such techniques. Try different systems. Ask other students for tips on how they memorize material.

You will have to find out from your teacher what material you will be expected to know for the course. You can also check with other students who have had this teacher in the past. It may not always be easy to find out how much a teacher expects you to know from memory. Teachers have been known to surprise students on examinations! Some teachers do not like to admit that they are asking their students to memorize material for their courses, yet they still give examinations that require considerable memorization.

### 16. Studying Skills—The Necessity of Feedback

Memory is most important when you are studying the basic principles of substantive and procedural law. Memory plays a less significant role in learning the skills of interviewing, investigation, legal analysis, drafting, coordinating, digesting, and advocacy. These skills have their own vocabulary that you must know, but it is your judgmental rather than your memory faculties that must be developed in order to become competent and excel in these skills.

They are developed primarily by *doing*—practice drills or exercises are essential. The learning comes from the feedback that you obtain while engaged in the skill exercises. What are the ways that a student obtains feedback?

- Evaluations on assignments and exams
- Role-playing exercises that are critiqued in class
- Comparisons between your work (particularly writing projects) and models that are provided by the teacher or that you find on your own in the library
- Critiques that you receive from students in study groups

You must constantly be looking for feedback. Do not wait to be called on. Do not wait to see what feedback is planned for you at the end of the course. Take the initiative immediately. Seek conferences or e-mail contact with your teachers. Find out who is available to read your writing or to observe your performance in any of the other skills. Set up your own role-playing sessions with your fellow students. Seek critiques of your re-writes even if re-writing was not required. Look for opportunities to critique other students on the various skills. Ask other students for permission to read their graded examinations so that you can compare their papers with your own. Create your own hypotheticals for analysis in study groups. (A *hypothetical* is simply a set of facts invented for the purpose of discussion and analysis.) Do additional reading on the skills. Become actively involved in your own skills development.

### 17. The Value of Speed-Reading Courses in the Study of Law.

In the study of law, a great deal of reading is required. Should you, therefore, take a speed-reading course? No, unless the course helps you *slow down* the speed of your reading! This advice may be quite distasteful to advocates (and salespersons) of speed-reading courses. The reality, however, is that statutes, regulations, and court opinions cannot be speed-read. They must be carefully picked apart and read word for word, almost as if you were translating from one language into another. If you are troubled by how long it takes you to read, do not despair. Do not worry about having to read material over and over again. Keep reading. Keep re-reading. The pace of your reading will pick up as you gain experience. Never strive, however, to be able to fly through the material. Strive for comprehensiveness. Strive for understanding. For most of us, this will come through the slow process of note taking and re-reading. It is sometimes argued that comprehension is increased through speed. Be careful of this argument. Reading law calls for careful thinking about what you read—and taking notes on these thoughts. There may be no harm in rapidly reading legal material for *the first time*. At your second, third, and fourth reading, however, speed is of little significance.

Section B

# On-the-Job Learning: The Art of Being Supervised

A great deal of learning will occur when you are on the job. Some of it may come through formal in-house office training and by the study of office procedure manuals. Most of the learning, however, will come in day-to-day interaction with your supervisors as you are given assignments. The learning comes through *being* supervised. Here are some guidelines to assist you in this important dimension of your legal education.

### Don't Play "King's Clothes" With the Instructions That You Receive.

Recall the story of the king's (or emperor's) clothes. The king was naked, but everybody kept saying what a beautiful wardrobe he had on. As new people arrived, they saw that he had no clothes, but they heard everyone talking as if he were fully dressed. The new people did not want to appear stupid, so they, too, began admiring the king's wardrobe. When paralegals are receiving instructions on an assignment, they play "king's clothes" when they pretend that they understand all the instructions but in fact do not. They do not want to appear to be uninformed or unintelligent. They do not want to give the impression that they are unsure of themselves. For obvious reasons, this is a serious mistake.

Whenever you are given an assignment in a new area—that is, an assignment on something that you have not done before—there should be a great deal that you do not understand. This is particularly true during your first few months on the job, when just about everything is new! Do not pretend to be something you are not. Constantly ask questions about new things. Do not be reluctant to ask for explanations. Learn how to ask for help. *It will not be a sign of weakness.* Quite the contrary. People who take steps to make sure that they fully understand all their instructions will soon gain a reputation for responsibility and conscientiousness.

### Repeat the Instructions to Your Supervisor Before You Leave the Room

Once your supervisor has told you what he or she wants you to do, do not leave the room in silence or with the general observation "I'll get on that right away." Repeat the instructions back to the supervisor *as you understand them.* Make sure that you and your supervisor are on the same wavelength by explaining back what you think you were told to do. This will be an excellent opportunity for the supervisor to determine what you did or did not understand and to provide you with clarifications where needed.

Supervisors will not always be sure of what they want you to do. By trying to obtain clarity on the instructions, you are providing them with the opportunity to think through what they want done. In the middle of the session with you, the supervisor may change his or her mind on what is to be done.

### Write Your Instructions Down

Never go to your supervisor without pen and paper. Preferably, keep an instructions notebook, diary, or journal in which you record the following information:

- Notes on what you are asked to do
- Whether the tasks in the assignment are billable
- The date you received the assignment
- The date by which the supervisor expects you to complete all or part of the assignment
- The date you actually complete the assignment
- Comments made by supervisors or others on what you submit

The notes will serve as your memory bank. Whenever any questions arise about what you were supposed to do, you have something concrete to refer to.

Exhibit A contains an assignment checklist on which you can record this kind of data for every major assignment you receive.

| EXHIBIT A | Checklist for Major Assignments |
| --- | --- |

Name of supervisor for the assignment:

What you have been asked to do:

Specific areas or tasks you have been told *not* to cover, if any:

Format supervisor expects, e.g., rough draft, final copy ready for supervisor's signature:

Date you are given the assignment:

Expected due date:

Is the task billable to a client? If so, to what account?

Location of samples or models in the office to check as possible guides:

Possible resource people in the office you may want to contact for help:

Practice manuals or treatises in the library that might provide background or general guidance:

Dates you contacted supervisor or others for help before due date:

Date you completed the assignment:

Positive, negative, or neutral comments from supervisor or others on the quality of your work on the assignment:

Things you would do differently the next time you get an assignment of this kind:

### Insist on a Due Date and on a Statement of Priorities

You need to know when an assignment is due. Ask for a due date *even if the supervisor tells you to "get to it when you can."* This phrase may mean "relatively soon" or "before the end of the month" to your supervisor, but not to you. If the supervisor says he or she does not know when it should be done, ask for an approximate due date. Tell the supervisor you want to place the assignment on your calendar so that it will not slip through the cracks because of all the other assignments. Also ask what priority the assignment has. Where does it fit in with your other assignments? If you have more than enough to fill the day, you need to know what takes priority. If you do not ask for a priority listing, the supervisor may assume you are under no time pressures.

### If The Instructions Appear to be Complicated, Ask Your Supervisor to Separate and Prioritize the Tasks

As you receive instructions, you may sometimes feel overwhelmed by all that is being asked of you. Many supervisors do not give instructions in clear, logical patterns. They may talk in a rambling, stream-of-consciousness fashion. When confronted with this situation, simply say:

> OK, but can you break that down for me a little more so that I know what you want me to do first? I think I will be able to do the entire assignment, but it would help if I approach it one step at a time. Where do you want me to start?

### As Often as Possible, Write Your Instructions and What You Do in the Form of Checklists

A methodical mind is one that views a project in "do-able" steps and that tackles one step at a time. You need to have a methodical mind in order to function in a busy law office. One of the best ways to develop such a mind is to think in terms of checklists. Attorneys love checklists. A great deal of the practice material published by bar associations, for example, consists of page after page of detailed checklists of things to do and/or to consider when completing a project for a client. Attorneys want to be thorough. An unwritten rule of law practice seems to be that you cannot be thorough without a checklist.

A checklist is simply a chronological sequencing of tasks that must be done in order to complete an assignment. Convert the instructions from your supervisor into checklists. In the process of actually carrying out instructions, you go through many steps—all of which could become part of a detailed checklist. The steps you went through to complete the task become a checklist of things to do in order to complete such a task in the future. To be sure, it can be time-consuming to draft checklists. Keep in mind, however, that:

- The checklists can be invaluable for other employees who are given similar assignments in the future.
- The checklists will be a benefit to you in organizing your own time and in assuring completeness.

You will not be able to draft checklists for everything that you do. Perhaps you will not be able to write more than one checklist a week. Perhaps you will have to use some of your own time to write checklists. Whatever time you can devote will be profitably spent so long as you are serious about writing and using the checklists. They may have to be rewritten or modified later. This should not deter you from the task, since most things that are worth doing require testing and reassessment.

Once you have a number of checklists, you have the makings of a how-to-do-it manual that you have written yourself.

### Find Out What Manuals and Checklists Already Exist in Your Office

It does not make sense to reinvent the wheel. If manuals and checklists on the topic of your assignment already exist in your office, you should find and use them. (Also check in computer databases where the office may store frequently used forms and instructions.) The problem is that how-to-do-it information is usually buried in the heads of the attorneys, paralegals, and secretaries of the office. No one has taken the time to write it all down. If this is *not* the case, you should find out where it is written down and try to adapt what you find to the assignment on which you are working.

### Ask for a Model

One of the best ways to make sure you know what a supervisor wants is to ask whether he or she knows of any models that you could use as a guide for what you are being asked to do. Such models may be found in closed case files, manuals, form books, practice texts, etc. Care must be applied in using such material. Every new legal problem is potentially unique. What will work in one case may not work in another. A model is a guide, a starting point—and nothing more. (See also exhibit 10.11 in chapter 10 on how to avoid abusing a standard form.)

### Do Some Independent Legal Research on the Instructions You Are Given

Often you will be told what to do without being given more than a cursory explanation of why it needs to be done that way. But all the instructions you are given have some basis in the law. A complaint, for example, is served on an opposing party in a designated way because the law has imposed rules on how such service is to be made. You may be asked to serve a complaint in a certain way without being told what section of the state code (or of your court rules) *requires* it to be served in that way. It would be highly impractical to read all the law that is the foundation for an assigned task. It is not necessary to do so and you would not have time to do so.

What you can occasionally do, however, is focus on selected instructions for an assignment and do some background legal research to gain a greater appreciation for why the instructions were necessary. (See the checklist on doing background research in exhibit 11.18 in chapter 11.) You will probably have to do such legal research on your own time unless the assignment you are given includes doing some legal research. Research can be time-consuming, but you will find it enormously educational. It can place a totally new perspective on the assignment and, indeed, on your entire job.

### Get on the Office Mailing Lists for New Publications

A law office frequently buys publications for its law library that are relevant to its practice. The publications often include legal treatises and legal periodicals (to be discussed later, in chapter 11). Before these publications are shelved in the library, they are often routed to the attorneys in the office so that they can become acquainted with current legal writing that will be available in the library. Each attorney usually keeps the publication for a few hours or a few days for review before passing it on to the next person on the mailing list.

Ask to be included in these mailing lists. The publications are often excellent self-education opportunities, particularly the articles in legal periodicals.

### Ask Secretaries and Other Paralegals for Help

Secretaries and paralegals who have worked in the office for a long period of time can be very helpful to you if you approach them properly. Everybody wants to feel important. Everybody wants to be respected. When someone asks for something in a way that gives the impression he or she is *entitled* to what is being sought, difficulties usually result. Think of how you would like to be approached if you were in the position of the secretary or paralegal. What would turn you off? What would make you want to go out of your way to cooperate with and assist a new employee who needs your help? Your answers (and sensitivity) to questions such as these will go a long way toward enabling you to draw on the experience of others in the office.

### Obtain Feedback on an Assignment Before the Date it is Due

Unless the assignment you are given is a very simple one, do not wait until the date that it is due to communicate with your supervisor. If you are having trouble with the assignment, you will want to check with your supervisor as soon as possible and as often as necessary. It would be a mistake, however, to contact the supervisor only when trouble arises. Of course, you want to avoid wasting anyone's time, including your own. You should limit your contacts with a busy supervisor to essential matters. You could take the following approach with your supervisor:

> Everything seems to be going fine on the project you gave me. I expect to have it in to you on time. I'm wondering, however, if you could give me a few moments of your time. I want to bring you up to date on where I am so that you can let me know if I am on the right track.

Perhaps this contact could take place on the phone or during a brief office visit. Suppose that you have gone astray on the assignment without knowing it? It is obviously better to discover this before the date the assignment is due. The more communication you have with your supervisor, the more likely it is that you will catch such errors before a great deal of time is wasted.

### Ask to Participate in Office and Community Training Programs

Sometimes a law office conducts training sessions for its attorneys. You should ask that you be included. Bar associations and paralegal associations often conduct all-day seminars on legal topics relevant to your work. They are part of what is called continuing legal education (CLE). Seek permission to attend some of these sessions if they are held during work hours. If they are conducted after hours, invest some of your own time to attend. If your employer won't pay the enrollment fee, ask if part of the fee could be paid. Even if you must pay the entire cost, it will be a worthwhile long-term investment.

### Ask to be Evaluated Regularly

For a number of reasons, evaluations may not be given or may not be helpful when they are given:

- Evaluations can be time-consuming.
- Evaluators are reluctant to say anything negative, especially in writing.
- Most of us do not like to be evaluated: it's too threatening to our ego.

Go out of your way to let your supervisor know that you want to be evaluated and that you can handle criticism. If you are defensive when you are criticized; you will find that the evaluations of your performance will go on behind your back! Such a work environment is obviously very unhealthy. Consider this approach that a paralegal might take with a supervisor:

> I want to know what you think of my work. I want to know where you think I need improvement. That's the only way I'm going to learn. I also want to know when I'm doing things correctly, but I'm mainly interested in your suggestions on what I can do to increase my skills.

If you take this approach *and mean it*, the chances are good that you will receive some very constructive criticism and gain a reputation for professionalism.

### Proceed One Step at a Time.

Perhaps the most important advice you can receive in studying law is to concentrate on what is immediately before you. Proceed one step at a time. What are your responsibilities in the next 15 minutes? Block everything else out. Make *the now* as productive as you can. Your biggest enemy is worry about the future: worry about the exams ahead of you, worry about your family, worry about the state of the world, worry about finding employment, etc. Leave tomorrow alone! Worrying about it will only interfere with your ability to make the most of what you must do now. Your development in the law will come slowly, in stages. Map out these stages in very small time blocks—begining with the time that is immediately ahead of you. If you must worry, limit your concern to how to make the next 15 minutes a more valuable learning experience.

## SUMMARY

Legal education is a lifelong endeavor; a competent paralegal never stops learning about the law and the skills of applying it. A number of important guidelines will help you become a good student in the classroom and on the job. Do not let the media blur your understanding of what the practice of law is actually like. To avoid studying in a vacuum, be sure that you know the goals of an assignment and how it fits into the other assignments. Organize your day around a study plan. Since the time demands on you will probably be greater than you anticipated, it is important that you design a system of studying. Step one is to assess your own study habits, such as how you handle distractions or how you commit things to memory. Then promise yourself that you will do something about your weaknesses.

Increase your proficiency in the basics of writing. How many of the rules about the comma can you identify? Do you know when to use *that* rather than *which* in your sentences? How many of your paragraphs have topic sentences? Are there zero spelling errors on every page of your writing? You have entered a field where the written word is paramount.

You must take personal responsibility—now—for the improvement of your grammar, spelling, and composition skills.

Use the law library to help you understand difficult areas of the law. But don't expect absolute clarity all the time. Seek out evaluations of your work. Become a skillful note taker. Get into the habit of looking for definitions.

These suggestions also apply once you are on the job. Don't pretend you understand what you don't. Repeat instructions back to your supervisor before you begin an assignment. Ask for due dates and priorities if you are given several things to do. Write down your instructions in your own notebook or journal. Find out if an assignment has been done by others in the past. If so, seek their help. Try to find a model and adapt it as needed. Be prepared to do some independent research. Get on internal office mailing lists for new publications. Participate in training programs at the law office and in the legal community. Ask to be evaluated regularly. Seek feedback before an assignment is due.

# Part I

# THE PARALEGAL IN THE LEGAL SYSTEM

## Contents

# Chapter 1

# INTRODUCTION TO A NEW CAREER IN LAW

## Chapter Outline

## Section A
# LAUNCHING YOUR CAREER

Welcome to the field! You probably fall into one or more of the following categories:

- You have never worked in a law office.
- You are or once were employed in a law office and now want to upgrade your skills.
- You have not made up your mind about whether to become an attorney and see the paralegal career as a way to learn more about the legal profession.

As you begin your legal education, you probably have a large number of questions:

- What is a paralegal?
- Where do paralegals work?
- What are the functions of a paralegal?
- How do I obtain a job?
- What is the difference between an attorney and a paralegal?
- What is the difference between a paralegal and the clerical staff of a law office?
- What problems do paralegals encounter on the job, and how can these problems be resolved?
- How is the paralegal field regulated? Who does the regulating and for what purposes?
- What are the ethical guidelines that govern paralegal conduct?

Some of these questions, particularly those involving regulation, do not have definitive answers. The paralegal field is still evolving, even though it has been a part of the legal system for about 40 years. All of the boundary lines of paralegal responsibility, for example, have not yet been fully defined. Consequently, you are about to enter a career that you can help shape. To do so, you will need a comprehensive understanding of the opportunities that await you and the challenges that will require your participation. Our goal in this book is to provide you with this understanding.

It is an exciting time to be working in the law. So many aspects of our everyday lives have legal dimensions. The law plays a dominant role in a spectrum of issues that range from the status of the unborn to the termination of life support systems. Eighty million lawsuits are filed every year, about 152 every minute.[1] One study concludes that 52 percent of Americans have a legal problem; one out of three will need the advice of an attorney in the next 12 months.[2] The news media are preoccupied with laws that have been broken, laws that no longer make sense, and laws that need to be passed in order to create a more just society. Caught up in the whirlwind of these debates is the attorney. And, as we will see, paralegals are essential members of the attorney's team.

## Section B
# DO YOU KNOW WHAT TIME IT IS?

Perhaps you're wondering what working in the law will be like. One of the hallmarks of legal work is its diversity. In five years, if you meet the person sitting next to you now in class and compare notes on what your workdays are like as paralegals, you will probably be startled by the differences. Of course, there will also be similarities.

One way to gauge what working in a law office might be like is to answer a particular question. Stop what you are doing for a moment and answer this question:

Do you know what time it is?

Depending on when you are reading this book, you probably will look at your watch or the clock on the wall and answer 9:45 A.M., 1:30 P.M., 3:32 P.M., 11:28 P.M., etc. There are hundreds of possible answers. But if you answered in this manner, you've made your first mistake in the study and practice of law. Look at the question again. Read it slowly. You were *not* asked, *What time is it?* You were asked, *Do you know* what time it is? There are *only* two possible answers to this question: *yes* or *no*.

Welcome to the law! One of the singular characteristics of the field you are about to enter is its *precision* and *attention to detail*. Vast amounts of time can be wasted answering the wrong question.[3] In fact, attorneys will tell you that one of the most important skills in the law is the ability to identify the question—the issue—that needs to be resolved.

Developing this sensitivity begins with the skill of *listening*—listening very carefully. It also involves *thinking before responding*, noting distinctions, noting what is said and what is not said, being aware of differences in emphasis, being aware that slight differences in the facts can lead to dramatically different conclusions.

To a large extent, the study of law is the study of definitions. Attorneys are preoccupied with questions such as "What does that clause mean?" and "What definition did the legislature intend?" Entire court opinions have turned on the meaning of a semicolon in a sentence. A dramatic example of controversy generated by a definition occurred during a famous grand jury hearing that was videotaped and later played on national television. The witness giving testimony under oath was a graduate of the Yale Law School and a former constitutional law professor. In testimony that will probably live in infamy, he said that his answer to a particular question would depend on what the "definition of 'is' is" in the question. The attorney giving this testimony was President Bill Clinton.

In short, you have a great deal ahead of you in the study of law; it's going to be a fascinating adventure.

## Section C
# MAJOR PLAYERS: THE BIG FIVE

During this course, we will meet many organizations. Five in particular have had a dramatic influence on the development of paralegalism. These five (not necessarily listed in order of influence) are as follows:

- National Federation of Paralegal Associations (NFPA) *www.paralegals.org*
- National Association of Legal Assistants (NALA) *www.nala.org*
- American Bar Association Standing Committee on Legal Assistants (SCOLA) *www.abanet.org/legalservices/legalassistants/home.html*
- Your state bar association (see Internet addresses in appendix C)
- Your local paralegal association (see postal and Internet addresses in appendix B)

These organizations will be covered in some detail throughout the remaining chapters of the book, but a brief word about each will be helpful at this point.

### NATIONAL FEDERATION OF PARALEGAL ASSOCIATIONS (NFPA)

The NFPA is an association of over 60 state and local paralegal associations throughout the country—representing more than 15,000 paralegals. (See appendix B.) Individual paralegals cannot be members of the NFPA. From its national headquarters in Kansas City, Missouri, the NFPA promotes paralegalism through **continuing legal education (CLE)** programs and political action. As we will see in chapter 4, the NFPA has a voluntary certification exam for *advanced* paralegals called PACE—Paralegal Advanced Certification Exam. The NFPA opposes certification for *entry-level* paralegals, i.e., those with no paralegal experience. This is a major difference between the NFPA and the other important national association of paralegals, the National Association of Legal Assistants (NALA), which has a certification exam for individuals with no paralegal experience.

**continuing legal education (CLE)** Training in the law (usually short-term) that a person receives after completing his or her formal legal training.

### NATIONAL ASSOCIATION OF LEGAL ASSISTANTS (NALA)

NALA is primarily an association of individual paralegals, although ninety state and local paralegal associations are affiliated with the organization. (See appendix B.) More than 18,000 paralegals in the country are represented by NALA; most of them have passed NALA's voluntary certification exam for *entry-level* paralegals called the CLA (Certified Legal Assistant) exam. NALA has a separate certification exam for advanced paralegals. From

Voting at the annual convention of the National Federation of Paralegal Associations. 21 National Paralegal Reporter 28 (Fall 1996). Used by permission of the National Federation of Paralegal Associations.

its national headquarters in Tulsa, Oklahoma, NALA is equally active in the continuing legal education and political arenas.

Over the years, NALA and the NFPA have carried on a lively debate on major issues such as whether there should be entry-level certification. This debate has contributed greatly to the vitality of the field. Both associations can be reached by their "snail" mail street addresses (see appendix B) and on the Internet (see exhibit 1.1).

### AMERICAN BAR ASSOCIATION (ABA)

The ABA is a voluntary association of attorneys; no attorney must be a member. Yet it is a powerful entity because of its resources, prestige, and the large number of attorneys who have joined. The ABA has a Standing Committee on Legal Assistants that has had a significant impact on the growth of the field. The role of the ABA has included the publication of research on paralegals, the establishment of a voluntary program of approving paralegal schools, and the creation of an associate membership category for paralegals. The latter development was not initially welcomed by everyone, as we will see in chapter 4.

### STATE BAR ASSOCIATION OF YOUR STATE

Every state has at least one bar association that plays a major role in regulating attorneys under the supervision of the state's highest court. (See appendix C.) Most of the state bar associations have taken formal positions (in guidelines or ethical opinions) on the use of paralegals by attorneys. (Go to appendix F to find out if your state or local bar association has taken positions on the use of paralegals by attorneys.) Some of these bar associations have followed the lead of the ABA and allow paralegals to become associate members. Whenever a paralegal issue arises, you will inevitably hear people ask, "What has the bar said about the issue?"

### YOUR LOCAL PARALEGAL ASSOCIATION

There are three main kinds of local paralegal associations: statewide, county or regionwide, and citywide. In appendix B, you will find a list of every local association in the country with an indication of whether it is affiliated with NFPA, affiliated with NALA, or not affiliated with any national association. A great many paralegals in the country have found major career support and inspiration through active participation in their local paralegal association.

**EXHIBIT 1.1** Reaching the Major National Paralegal Associations (NFPA and NALA) on the Internet.

## Welcome to NALA!

The National Association of Legal Assistants is the leading professional, national association for legal assistants and paralegals, providing continuing education and professional development programs. Incorporated in 1975, NALA is an integral part of the legal community, working to improve the quality and effectiveness of the delivery of legal services.

The National Association of Legal Assistants is composed of over 18,000 paralegals, through individual members and through its 90 state and local affiliated associations. This web site includes information about the paralegal career field, and about the programs and services of NALA.

Visit the site map for navigation help and a detailed listing of the pages of this site. This site is best viewed with Internet Explorer. Click here to download this (free) if you do not have it already.

For more info click the links in the menu bar above or visit:

Site Map
Association Info
Education Programs
Paralegal Profession
Member Notices
Guest Register
Career Net
NALA Net
Links
NALA Campus
NALA Store

National Association of Legal Assistants, Inc.
1516 S. Boston, Suite 200
Tulsa, OK 74119 913.587.6828
Fax 918.582.6772

www.nala.org

## Paralegals.org

Legal Resources
Getting Started
Career Center
Calendar
Industry Resources

Membership
PACE
Networking
CLE
Profession Development

What's New
Consumer Education

Publications ★ Pro Bono ★ International ★ Guest Registry ★
Search ★ Welcome Video ★ Marketing ★

### National Federation of Paralegal Associations

Post Office Box 33108
Kansas City, Missouri 64114
Telephone: 816.941.4000
Facsimile: 816.941.2725
Email: info@paralegals.org
Technical: webmaster@paralegals.org

www.paralegals.org

---

### Assignment 1.1

It is not too early to begin learning about and communicating with important associations.

**a.** Go to the Internet addresses of NFPA, NALA, SCOLA, your state bar association, and your local paralegal association. (If your local association does not have an Internet address, go to the closest paralegal association that has an Internet address.) On each of these sites:

  **(i)** Find an e-mail address where you may be able to write for additional information about the organization.

  **(ii)** Quote any sentence on the site that pertains to paralegal careers. Following the quote, give the citation to the site. Citations to Internet pages should include the name of the site, the date you visited the site, and the Internet address, e.g., National Association of Legal Assistants (visited May 2, 2002), www.nala.org.

**b.** Fill out and mail the forms at the end of this book: "Paralegal Associations: Local" and "Paralegal Associations: National."

---

Although NFPA, NALA, SCOLA, your state bar association, and your local paralegal association will dominate our discussion of paralegalism, we will also be referring to other important groups, such as:

- Legal Assistant Management Association (LAMA): an association of paralegal supervisors of other paralegals in large law offices (*www.lamanet.org*);
- American Association for Paralegal Education (AAfPE): an association of paralegal schools (*www.aafpe.org*); and
- Association of Legal Administrators (ALA): an association of individuals (mostly nonattorneys) who administer or manage law offices (*www.alanet.org/home.html*).

## Section D
# Job Titles

For convenience, this book uses the title *paralegal*. An equally common title is *legal assistant*. For the most part, they are synonymous, just as the titles *attorney* and *lawyer* are synonymous. Yet the titles *paralegal* and *legal assistant* have been the source of some confusion and debate. For example, legal assistant positions in some state governments are attorney positions, and a number of legal secretaries have changed their titles to legal assistant without significantly changing their job responsibility.

Several reasons account for the lack of uniformity on titles. First, there are no national standards regulating the paralegal field. Every state is free to regulate or to refuse to regulate a particular occupation. Second, most states have not imposed the kind of regulation on paralegals that would lead to greater consistency on titles within a particular state. For example, most states have not imposed minimum educational requirements or licensing. Hence few restrictions exist on who can call themselves paralegals, legal assistants, or related titles. Although there are some major exceptions in states such as California and Maine, for the most part, the field is unregulated.

**traditional paralegal**
A paralegal who is an employee of an attorney.

**independent contractor**
One who operates his or her own business and contracts to do work for others who do not control the details of how the work is performed.

To begin sorting through the maze, we examine two broad categories of paralegals: those who are employees of attorneys (often called **traditional paralegals**) and those who are **independent contractors.** In general, independent contractors are self-employed individuals who control the *details* or method of performing tasks; the *objectives* or end products of what they do are controlled by those who buy their services. We will be examining two kinds of paralegals who are independent contractors: those who sell their services to attorneys (a relatively small group) and those who sell their services to the public without attorney supervision (a larger and more controversial group).

Within these categories, you will find considerable diversity (and overlap) in the titles that are used:

## 1. EMPLOYEES OF ATTORNEYS

The vast majority (over 95 percent) are employees of attorneys. They may be called:

| | |
|---|---|
| paralegal | legal service assistant |
| legal assistant | paralegal specialist |
| certified legal assistant | paralegal assistant |
| lawyer's assistant | legal analyst |
| attorney assistant | legal technician |
| lawyer's aide | legal paraprofessional |

They are all traditional paralegals because they are employees of attorneys. Most are full time employees. Some, however, are temporary employees who work part-time or who work full-time for a limited period when a law firm needs temporary help, usually from paralegals with experience in a particular area of the law.

If a law firm has a relatively large number of paralegals, it might call its entry-level people:

| | |
|---|---|
| paralegal I | legal assistant clerk |
| project assistant | paralegal clerk |
| document clerk | case clerk |
| project clerk | legal aide |

Large law firms may also have individuals who help recruit, train, and supervise all paralegals in the office. This supervisor might be called:

| | |
|---|---|
| paralegal supervisor | director of legal assistants |
| legal assistant supervisor | director of practice support |
| supervising legal assistant | paralegal coordinator |
| paralegal manager | senior legal assistant |
| manager of paralegal services | legal assistant coordinator |
| legal assistant manager | case manager |
| director of paralegal services | paralegal administrator |
| director of legal assistant services | legal assistant administrator |

As indicated earlier, these individuals have their own association, the Legal Assistant Management Association (LAMA). For more on entry-level and supervisory paralegals, see the discussion of career ladders later in the chapter.

All of the titles listed thus far are generic in that they do not tell you what the person's primary skills are or in what area of the law he or she specializes. Other employee job titles are more specific:

| | |
|---|---|
| litigation assistant | real estate paralegal |
| litigation practice support specialist | bankruptcy paralegal |
| | water law paralegal |
| corporate paralegal | international trade paralegal |
| family law paralegal | workers' compensation paralegal |
| probate specialist | |

Other examples include the *conflicts specialist*, who helps the office determine whether it should refrain from taking a case because of a conflict of interest with present or prior clients (see chapter 5), and *depo summarizer*, who summarizes pretrial testimony, particularly depositions (see chapter 10).

Some law firms divide their paralegals into two broad categories: litigation and transactional. Litigation paralegals work on cases in litigation, particularly in the pretrial stages of litigation. A **transactional paralegal** provides assistance to attorneys whose clients are engaged in a large variety of transactions that involve contracts, leases, mergers, incorporations, estate planning, patents, etc.

**transactional paralegal**
A paralegal who helps an attorney provide legal representation in client transactions such as contracts and incorporations.

Occasionally, when an office wants its paralegal to perform more than one job, hybrid titles are used. For example, an office might call an employee a *paralegal/investigator,* a *paralegal/librarian,* or a *paralegal/legal secretary.*

Perhaps the strangest—and thankfully the rarest—hybrid title you may see is *attorney/paralegal.* A California law firm placed an ad in a Los Angeles legal newspaper looking for an individual who would work under this title. What's going on? The legal job market fluctuates. Depending on the state of the economy, jobs for attorneys might be abundant or scarce. In lean times, parts of the country could be flooded with unemployed attorneys, many of whom are recent law school graduates. Occasionally, these attorneys apply for paralegal jobs. An article in the *American Bar Association Journal,* taking note of the plight of unemployed attorneys, was entitled *Post–Law School Job May Be as Paralegal.*[4] Some law firms are willing to hire a desperate attorney at a paralegal's salary because the firm can charge clients a higher billing rate for an attorney's time than for a paralegal's time. Most law firms, however, think it is unwise to hire an attorney for a paralegal's position. The two fields are separate employment categories, and the firms know that the attorneys are not interested in careers as paralegals. Yet there will continue to be attorneys available for paralegal positions and law firms willing to hire them, particularly when the firms need temporary legal help.

There is a small category of attorneys who *frequently* seek work as paralegals. An attorney who has been disbarred or suspended from the practice of law may try to continue working in a law office by taking a job as a paralegal until he or she can reapply for full admission. Such work is highly controversial because of the temptation to go beyond paralegal work and continue to practice law. Consequently, some states forbid disbarred or suspended attorneys from working as paralegals. In other states, however, it is allowed, as we will see in chapter 5 and in appendix F.

## 2. SELF-EMPLOYED INDIVIDUALS WORKING FOR ATTORNEYS

Independent contractors who sell their services to attorneys perform many different kinds of tasks. For example, they might draft an estate tax return for a probate attorney or digest (i.e., summarize) pretrial documents for a litigation attorney. Some work out of a home office or in office space that they rent. Others do their work in the law offices of the attorneys for whom they work. (See exhibit 2.2 in chapter 2 for the internet site of an independent paralegal and appendix J on setting up an independent business.) An independent contractor might work primarily for one law firm, although most work for different firms around town. Even though independent contractors are not employees, the attorneys who use their services are still obligated to supervise what they do. (In chapter 5, we will study the ethical problem that can arise because of the difficulty of supervising a nonemployee. In addition, we will cover the conflict-of-interest danger that can exist when an independent contractor works for more than one attorney.) There is no uniform title that these self-employed individuals use. Here are the most common:

| | |
|---|---|
| independent paralegal | contract paralegal |
| freelance paralegal | legal technician |
| freelance legal assistant | |

## 3. SELF-EMPLOYED INDIVIDUALS SERVING THE PUBLIC

Finally, we examine those independent contractors who sell their services directly to the public. They do not work for (and are not supervised by) attorneys. They may have special authorization to provide limited services, as when a statute allows them to assist clients in social security cases.

Here are the most common titles these independent contractors use:

| | |
|---|---|
| independent paralegal | paralegal |
| freelance paralegal | contract paralegal |

To find out what titles they use in your area, check the Yellow Pages under entries such as *paralegal, legal, divorce,* and *bankruptcy.* For the most part, independent paralegals have been unregulated. Anyone can start advertising himself or herself as a paralegal.

Controversy over these paralegals has come from three main sources. First, a few of their disgruntled clients have filed complaints against them that have resulted in state prosecution for the **unauthorized practice of law (UPL).** Second, the organized bar has instigated similar UPL charges on the ground that the public needs protection from independent paralegals, particularly those who lack formal training. The bar also complains that the public might be confused into thinking that anyone called a paralegal works for an attorney. An unstated reason for opposition from the bar is the unwelcome competition that independent paralegals give to some practicing attorneys. Third, a significant number of traditional paralegals resent the use of the paralegal title by independent contractors. Most traditional paralegals have been through a rigorous training program and are subject to close attorney supervision on the job. These traditional paralegals resent anyone being able to use the paralegal title without similar training and supervision.

In most states, this formidable opposition has not put independent paralegals out of business. In fact, their numbers are growing. Yet a few states have imposed increased regulation on them. In California, for example, independent contractors cannot call themselves paralegals or legal assistants unless they work under attorney supervision. If a California attorney is not responsible for their work, they must call themselves *legal document assistants (LDAs)*. If they provide landlord-tenant help, they must be called *unlawful detainer assistants (UDAs)*. At the federal level, even greater restrictions have been placed on individuals who provide bankruptcy assistance. In every state, they must be called *bankruptcy petition preparers (BPPs)*. Later, in chapters 4 and 5, we will more closely examine the controversy generated by these independent contractors.

**unauthorized practice of law (UPL)** Engaging in acts that require either a license to practice law or other special authorization by a person who does not have the license or special authorization.

## Section E
# Definitions of a Paralegal

Different definitions of a paralegal exist, although there is substantial similarity among them. Definitions have been written by:

- State legislatures and state courts
- State bar associations
- Local bar associations
- The American Bar Association
- The national paralegal associations: NFPA and NALA
- Local paralegal associations

By far the most important definitions are those written by state legislatures and courts. Not every state has definitions written by their legislature or courts, but the number of states that have them is steadily growing. If the legislature or courts in your state have not adopted a definition, your state or local bar association probably has. You need to find out as soon as possible whether the legislature, courts, or bar association in your state has adopted a definition. (See appendix F, which collects many definitions from across the country.) The definitions proposed by the American Bar Association and by paralegal associations have been influential, but they are not controlling if the legislature, court, or bar association in your state uses its own definition.

Here is an example of a definition enacted by a state legislature—the Illinois State Legislature. This definition is typical of the definitions used in many states:

> "Paralegal" means a person who is qualified through education, training, or work experience and is employed by a lawyer, law office, governmental agency, or other entity to work under the direction of an attorney in a capacity that involves the performance of substantive legal work that usually requires a sufficient knowledge of legal concepts and would be performed by the attorney in the absence of the paralegal. 5 Illinois Compiled Statutes Annotated § 70/1.35 (2001).

In these definitions, the term *paralegal* always includes the term *legal assistant*. In addition, the definitions are usually interpreted to include independent contractors who sell their services to attorneys.

Here are the characteristics that are common to definitions in most states. A paralegal:

- Has special qualifications due to education, training, or on-the-job experience,
- Works under attorney supervision, and
- Performs substantive legal work that the attorney would have to perform if the paralegal was not present (substantive work refers to nonclerical work).

What about independent contractors who sell their services directly to the public? Some states specifically include them in their definition. For example, note the last clause in the following definition adopted by the Montana State Legislature:

> "Paralegal" or "legal assistant" means a person qualified through education, training, or work experience to perform substantive legal work that requires knowledge of legal concepts and that is customarily but not exclusively performed by a lawyer and who may be retained or employed by one or more lawyers, law offices, governmental agencies, or other entities *or who may be authorized by administrative, statutory, or court authority to perform this work.* Montana Code Annotated § 37-60-101 (12) (2000) (emphasis added).

The clause in italics at the end of the definition covers those paralegals who are not supervised by attorneys but who have special authority to provide limited legal assistance to the public (see chapter 4).

As we have seen, a few states such as California limit the title of paralegal (or legal assistant) to individuals who work under attorney supervision. Those who provide assistance directly to the public must call themselves something else in these states.

The American Bar Association and the two national paralegal associations (NALA and NFPA) have recommended definitions of a paralegal. Some of these definitions have been adopted, with or without modification, by state legislatures, state courts, and state bar associations. (See exhibit 1.2.)

---

**EXHIBIT 1.2**    **Definitions Recommended by the American Bar Association and the Two National Paralegal Associations**

**American Bar Association**
A legal assistant or paralegal is a person qualified by education, training or work experience who is employed or retained by a lawyer, law office, corporation, governmental agency or other entity and who performs specifically delegated substantive legal work for which a lawyer is responsible.

**National Federation of Paralegal Associations**
A paralegal is a person qualified through education, training or work experience to perform substantive legal work that requires knowledge of legal concepts and is customarily, but not exclusively, performed by a lawyer. This person may be retained or employed by a lawyer, law office, governmental agency or other entity or may be authorized by administrative, statutory or court authority to perform this work.

**National Association of Legal Assistants**
NALA had its own definition until 2001 when it decided to adopt the definition of the American Bar Association. This was not a major change, since the NALA definition was very similar to that of the ABA.

---

Section F

# PARALEGAL FEES AND THE TASK-SPECIFIC DEFINITION OF A PARALEGAL

The most common kinds of fees that attorneys charge are hourly fees and contingent fees. Hourly fees are determined, in the main, by how much time is spent on a client's case. In general, hourly attorney fees are due regardless of whether the client wins or loses. (In chapters 8 and 14, we will examine variations on this kind of fee.) A **contingent fee** is dependent on the outcome of the case. For example, in a personal injury case, the client may agree to pay one-third of whatever the attorney wins from a court judgment or settlement; no attorney fees are paid if the client recovers nothing. (Special costs such as filing fees and witness fees, however, are usually paid by the client in both hourly fee and contingent fee cases, regardless of the outcome.)

In most states, the client pays for attorney time *and for paralegal time* in cases where the office charges by the hour. In such states, the work of a paralegal can be separately charged to the client. These charges are called **paralegal fees**. (Of course, paralegals themselves do not charge or receive these fees; the fees are paid to the law office that employs the paralegals.) Paralegal work is not considered part of **overhead,** which includes the cost of insurance, utilities, and other everyday needs of a business. A client who hires a law firm is not charged for a share of the electricity the firm uses when it helps the client. Clerical salaries are also overhead. Paralegals are not clerical employees and, therefore, are not part of overhead.

In most cases, attorney and paralegal fees are paid by the firm's clients. There are, however, special categories of cases *in which the losing side in litigation pays the fees of the winning side*. Examples include employment discrimination, antitrust, and environmental cases. In these areas, special statutes give the judge authority to order the losing party to pay the winning party's attorney and paralegal fees. Cases applying these special statutes are often called **statutory fee cases.** Paralegal fees in such cases can be substantial. Here, for example, are the total paralegal fees (calculated at $85 per hour) claimed by the winning side in a 1999 water distribution case:

### Fees Claimed for Paralegals

| Name | Hrs. | Rate | |
| --- | --- | --- | --- |
| Sonia Rosenberg | 935 | $85 | $ 79,475 |
| Ronald Horne | 614.2 | $85 | $ 52,207 |
| Michael Gershon | 88.9 | $85 | $  7,556.50 |
| Total hours claimed | 1,638.1 | | $139,238.50[5] |

One of the main reasons paralegalism has blossomed as a new profession is the ability of a law firm to collect paralegal fees from its own clients in most cases and from a losing opponent in special statutory fee cases. Care is needed, however, in exercising the right to receive paralegal fees. Although paralegals are not clerical employees, they sometimes perform clerical functions in the office. This is not unusual, since attorneys themselves perform clerical functions on occasion, particularly when the office is shorthanded, facing a deadline, or trying to respond to a crisis in a client's case. When a paralegal performs a purely clerical task, such as filing letters in an office folder or ordering supplies for the copy machine, paralegal fees should not be charged. There is nothing wrong or unethical about a paralegal filing letters or ordering supplies. A good team player does whatever is needed at the time. When, however, paralegals perform such tasks, their boss should not be trying to collect paralegal fees for such tasks. Furthermore, it *is* unethical for an attorney to claim that a paralegal performed paralegal work when in fact the paralegal was performing clerical work. (See chapter 5 on ethics.)

So, too, an attorney should not charge attorney rates for performing tasks that should have been delegated to someone else in the office, such as a paralegal. One court phrased the problem this way: "Routine tasks, if performed by senior partners in large firms, should not be billed at their usual rates. A Michelangelo should not charge Sistine Chapel rates for painting a farmer's barn."[6] In short, the dollar value of a task is not enhanced simply because an attorney performs it.[7] The same is true of tasks that paralegals perform. Numerous court opinions have been written in which judges reduce or disallow statutory fees

**contingent fee** A fee that is dependent on the outcome of the case. (The fee is also called a contingency.)

**paralegal fee** A fee that an attorney can collect for the nonclerical work of his or her paralegal on a client case.

**overhead** The operating expenses of a business (e.g., office rent, furniture, insurance, clerical staff) for which customers or clients are not charged a separate fee.

**statutory fee case** A case applying a special statute that gives a judge authority to order the losing party to pay the winning party's attorney and paralegal fees.

for attorneys performing paralegal tasks and for paralegals performing secretarial or clerical tasks. (See appendix F to find out if such cases exist in your state.)

It is quite remarkable that law firms are being challenged in court for improperly delegating tasks among attorneys, paralegals, and secretaries in fee-dispute cases. Part of the difficulty is that the line between paralegal tasks and clerical tasks is not always easy to draw once we get beyond tasks that are obviously clerical.

What is a paralegal task? This question must be answered to avoid litigation over the collectability of paralegal fees, particularly in statutory fee cases. Paralegals perform a wide variety of tasks. (See "Paralegal Specialties" in chapter 2.) Which ones qualify for paralegal fees? The definitions of a paralegal that we discussed earlier are not always helpful in answering this question. In describing what paralegals do, most of the definitions use vague phrases such as "substantive legal work." What is meant by substantive? In statutory fee cases, in which an attorney asks for paralegal fees, the opponent often argues against the award of these fees on the ground that much of what the paralegal did was secretarial work. To resolve such controversies, judges need more guidance than the distinction between substantive work and clerical work.

This need has led some states to create task-specific definitions of a paralegal. For example, notice the detail in the following definition enacted by the Florida State Legislature:

> "[L]egal assistant" means a person, who under the supervision and direction of a licensed attorney engages in legal research, and case development or planning in relation to modifications or initial proceedings, services, processes, or applications; or who prepares or interprets legal documents or selects, compiles, and uses technical information from references such as digests, encyclopedias, or practice manuals and analyzes and follows procedural problems that involve independent decisions. Florida Statutes Annotated § 57.104 (2001).

In appendix F, you will see the full range of definitions that exist across the country. Many of these definitions simply refer to "substantive legal work." Others are task-specific like Florida's.

Regardless of which definition is used in a particular state, paralegals must keep detailed time sheets covering precisely what they did. Their supervising attorney may need to enter these time sheets into evidence in order to justify the award of paralegal fees in statutory fee cases. Furthermore, courts want to be convinced that attorneys are not using paralegals as an excuse for obtaining higher fees. Here is an example of what one court requires attorneys to demonstrate in their petition for paralegal fees:

> The petition must set forth the hours spent, the qualifications of the paralegal, the work performed and the hourly rate. In addition the petition should provide the court with assurance that the amount requested for the . . . services of the attorney and paralegal combined do not exceed the amount appropriate if the attorney had provided the services without the paralegal's assistance.[8]

Before we leave the topic of paralegal fees and the definition of a paralegal, there is one other issue we need to discuss. In a statutory fee case, assume the court is convinced that the tasks performed by the paralegal are genuinely paralegal tasks for which an award of paralegal fees is justified. The question then becomes, How much should be awarded? How much is a paralegal's time worth? Two possibilities exist:

- Prevailing market rate for paralegals: The market rate is the amount, on average, that law firms in the community charge their own clients for paralegal time (e.g., $60 per hour).
- Actual cost to the law firm: Actual cost is the amount that a law firm must pay to keep its paralegal (e.g., $30 per hour to cover the paralegal's salary, fringe benefits, office space, and other overhead costs related to maintaining any employee).

Of course, the winning side in a statutory fee case will argue that it should receive the market rate for paralegal time, while the losing side wants an actual-cost standard. In 1989, the United States Supreme Court in the landmark case of *Missouri v. Jenkins* resolved the issue in favor of using market rates.

## *Missouri v. Jenkins*

### United States Supreme Court
### 491 U.S. 274, 109 S. Ct. 2463, 105 L. Ed. 2d 229 (1989)

Justice BRENNAN delivered the opinion of the Court.

This is the attorney's fee aftermath of major school desegregation litigation in Kansas City, Missouri. [One of the issues we need to resolve is] should the fee award compensate the work of paralegals and law clerks by applying the market rate for their work.

This litigation began in 1977 as a suit by the Kansas City Missouri School District (KCMSD), the school board, and the children of two school board members, against the State of Missouri and other defendants. The plaintiffs alleged that the State, surrounding school districts, and various federal agencies had caused and perpetuated a system of racial segregation in the schools of the Kansas City metropolitan area. They sought various desegregation remedies. . . . After lengthy proceedings, including a trial that lasted 7½ months during 1983 and 1984, the District Court found the State of Missouri and KCMSD liable. . . .

The plaintiff class has been represented, since 1979, by Kansas City lawyer Arthur Benson and, since 1982, by the NAACP Legal Defense and Educational Fund, Inc. (LDF). Benson and the LDF requested attorney's fees under the Civil Rights Attorney's Fees Awards Act of 1976, 42 U.S.C. § 1988.* Benson and his associates had devoted 10,875 attorney hours to the litigation, as well as 8,108 hours of paralegal and law clerk time. . . . [T]he District Court awarded Benson a total of approximately $1.7 million and the LDF $2.3 million. [On appeal, the defendant now argues] that the District Court erred in compensating the

work of law clerks and paralegals (hereinafter collectively "paralegals") at the market rates for their services, rather than at their cost to the attorney. While Missouri agrees that compensation for the cost of these personnel should be included in the fee award, it suggests that an hourly rate of $15—which it argued below corresponded to their salaries, benefits, and overhead—would be appropriate, rather than the market rates of $35 to $50. . . .

[T]o bill paralegal work at market rates . . . makes economic sense. By encouraging the use of lower cost paralegals rather than attorneys wherever possible, permitting market-rate billing of paralegal hours "encourages cost-effective delivery of legal services and, by reducing the spiraling cost of civil rights litigation, furthers the policies underlying civil rights statutes." *Cameo Convalescent Center, Inc. v. Senn*, 738 F.2d 836, 846 (CA7 1984).**

Such separate billing appears to be the practice in most communities today.*** In the present case, Missouri concedes that "the local market typically bills separately for paralegal services," Transcript of Oral Argument 14, and the District Court found that the requested hourly rates of $35 for law clerks, $40 for paralegals, and $59 for recent law graduates were the prevailing rates for such services in the Kansas City area. . . . Under these circumstances, the court's decision to award separate compensation at these rates was fully in accord with § 1988 [of the Civil Rights Attorney's Fees Awards Act].

---

*Section 1988 provides in relevant part: "In any action or proceeding to enforce a provision of . . . the Civil Rights Act of 1964 [42 U.S.C. § 2000d], the court, in its discretion, may allow the prevailing party, other than the United States, a reasonable attorney's fee as part of the costs."

**It has frequently been recognized in the lower courts that paralegals are capable of carrying out many tasks, under the supervision of an attorney, that might otherwise be performed by a lawyer and billed at a higher rate. Such work might include, for example, factual investigation, including locating and interviewing witnesses; assistance with depositions, interrogatories, and document production; compilation of statistical and financial data; checking legal citations; and drafting correspondence. Much such work lies in a gray area of tasks that might appropriately be performed either by an attorney or a paralegal. To the extent that fee applicants under § 1988 are not permitted to bill for the work of paralegals at market rates, it would not be surprising to see a greater amount of such work performed by attorneys themselves, thus increasing the overall cost of litigation.

Of course, purely clerical or secretarial tasks should not be billed at a paralegal rate, regardless of who performs them. What the court in *Johnson v. Georgia Highway Express, Inc.*, 488 F.2d 714, 717 (CA5 1974), said in regard to the work of attorneys is applicable by analogy to paralegals: "It is appropriate to distinguish between legal work, in the strict sense, and investigation, clerical work, compilation of facts and statistics and other work which can often be accomplished by non-lawyers but which a lawyer may do because he has no other help available. Such non-legal work may command a lesser rate. Its dollar value is not enhanced just because a lawyer does it."

***Amicus National Association of Legal Assistants reports that 77 percent of 1,800 legal assistants responding to a survey of the association's membership stated that their law firms charged clients for paralegal work on an hourly billing basis. Brief for National Association of Legal Assistants as Amicus Curiae 11.

The *Jenkins* case involved a Missouri desegregation suit under § 1988 of a civil rights act. The lower court awarded the winning party $40 an hour for paralegal time, which was the market rate for paralegals in the late 1980s in the Kansas City area. On appeal, the losing party argued that it should pay no more than $15 an hour, which was the actual cost to the law firm of having a paralegal in the office. In addition to paralegal fees, the case concerned the award of fees for law clerks, who are students still in law school or law school graduates who have not yet passed the bar. Like paralegals, law clerks are nonattorneys. As you can see from the opinion, the Supreme Court rejected an actual-cost standard for these employees.

---

### Assignment 1.2

Justice Brennan in *Missouri v. Jenkins* says that using a market rate for paralegals will help reduce the "spiraling cost of civil rights litigation." How can forcing a losing party to pay more for paralegals reduce the cost of litigation?

---

Keep in mind that *Missouri v. Jenkins* is a federal case involving one federal statute—a civil rights act. The following categories of cases are *not* required to adopt the conclusion of *Jenkins:*

- Federal cases interpreting other federal statutes
- State cases interpreting state statutes

It is quite possible for a *state* court to refuse to award paralegal fees or, if it awards paralegal fees, to calculate them at actual cost rather than at the prevailing market rate. A state court, for example, could deny paralegal fees on the ground that paralegal costs are part of overhead that is already accounted for in the attorney's fee. Nevertheless, *Missouri v. Jenkins* has been quite persuasive. The vast majority of federal and state courts have adopted its reasoning for allowing paralegal fees at market rates in statutory fee cases. This is the reason *Missouri v. Jenkins* is a landmark case.

---

## Section G
## CAREER LADDERS IN LARGE LAW OFFICES

There is no career ladder for paralegals working in a small law office that consists of several attorneys, a secretary, and a paralegal. In an office with more than three paralegals, career ladders may exist. One of the more experienced paralegals, for example, might become the paralegal coordinator or manager, with duties such as:

- Recruiting and screening candidates for paralegal positions
- Orienting new paralegals to office procedures
- Training paralegals to operate software used in the office
- Training paralegals to perform certain substantive tasks, such as digesting (i.e., summarizing) pretrial testimony
- Coordinating assignments of paralegals among the different attorneys in the office to help ensure that paralegals are given assignments they are able to perform and that they complete them on time

Many law offices in the country have 50 or more paralegals. As indicated earlier, paralegal managers have formed their own national association, the Legal Assistant Management Association (*www.lamanet.org*).

The more paralegals in an office, the greater the likelihood that a career ladder exists for them in that office. The structure of the ladder might be fairly simple. For example, Paralegal I might be the entry-level position; Paralegal II, the intermediate position; and Paralegal III, the senior or supervisory position. Not all offices with career ladders, however, use the same titles, as we have seen. (The Web sites of some large firms refer to their career ladders. For a list of Web sites of the largest law firms in the country, see appendix 2A at the end of chapter 2.) Here are the career titles recommended by the Legal Assistant Management Association (alternative titles are listed in brackets):

- Legal Assistant Clerk [Paralegal Clerk]
  Performs clerical tasks such as numbering documents, labeling folders, filing, and completing other tasks that do not require substantive knowledge or litigation skills; legal assistant clerks may be supervised by legal assistants.
- Legal Assistant [Paralegal]
  Performs factual research, document analysis, cite checking, drafting pleadings, administering trusts and estates, and handling other substantive tasks that do not require a law degree.
- Senior Legal Assistant [Senior Paralegal]
  Supervises or trains other legal assistants. May be a specialist in a particular area.
- Supervising Legal Assistant [Supervising Paralegal]
  Spends approximately half time working on cases as a legal assistant and half time supervising other legal assistants.
- Case Manager
  Coordinates or directs legal assistants on large projects such as major litigation or corporate transaction.
- Legal Assistant Manager [Paralegal Manager, Paralegal Administrator, Director of Paralegal Services]
  Recruits, interviews, and hires legal assistants; helps train legal assistants and monitors their assignments; and helps administer budget and billing requirements of all legal assistants.[9]

---

**Assignment 1.3**

In this assignment, we explore what the world thinks a paralegal or legal assistant is. Much will depend on what the public has heard about this field. More and more television programs about attorneys feature law offices that include paralegals in their scripts. The same is true of mystery fiction about court cases. Yet some claim that a good deal of confusion still exists about what a paralegal is. As late as 2001, one veteran paralegal complained that "[m]ost people don't know what a paralegal is."[10] To gauge whether this is true in your community, contact the following individuals in your area. Ask each of them the question: "What is a paralegal or legal assistant?"

(a) A neighbor or friend who does not work in a law office and who has probably never been in a law office.
(b) A neighbor or friend who does not work in a law office but who has hired an attorney at least once in his or her life.
(c) A legal secretary.
(d) An attorney who has never hired a paralegal.
(e) An attorney who has hired a paralegal.
(f) A working paralegal who is not now in school.
(g) A high school student.
(h) A student in a law school studying to be an attorney.
(i) A police officer.
(j) A person who runs a small business.
(k) A clerk in a local court.
(l) A local judge.

Take careful notes on their answers to the question. Compare the answers.

- What common ideas or themes did you find in the definitions?
- What two definitions were the most different? List the differences.
- Do you think that your survey raises any problems about the perception of paralegals in your area? If so, what are these problems, and how can they be solved?

## Section H
## PARALEGAL SALARIES

How much do paralegals make? Although some data are available to answer this question, there is no definitive answer because of the great variety of employment settings. Here are some relevant statistics for the years indicated:

- According to a 2002 survey of over 2,100 paralegals by the National Association of Legal Assistants, the national average salary of paralegals was $43,002 with an average annual bonus of $2,909. On average, the paralegals surveyed had 16 years of experience. Here is a further breakdown of average salaries correlated with years of experience:
  - $31,993: 1–5 years of experience
  - $38,222: 6–10 years of experience
  - $41,431: 11–15 years of experience
  - $42,724: 16–20 years of experience
  - $44,721: 21–25 years of experience[11]
- According to a 2000 survey by the Legal Assistant Management Association:
  - the mean salary of a legal assistant was $38,077
  - the mean salary of a legal assistant clerk was $26,825
  - the mean salary of a senior legal assistant was $52,124
  - the mean salary of a legal assistant manager was $75,481[12]
- According to a 2001 survey by the National Federation of Paralegal Associations:
  - the average paralegal salary was $41,742
  - entry-level paralegals earned between $14,000 and $32,000
  - the highest paid paralegal in the survey earned $114,000
  - the average bonus received by paralegals was $2,468[13]
- According to a 2003 study by The Affiliates, a major legal staffing firm, the salary range for paralegals/case clerks with 0–2 years of experience was:
  - $25,550–$31,750 in law firms with 75 or more attorneys
  - $25,000–$29,500 in law firms with between 35 and 75 attorneys
  - $23,750–$28,000 in law firms with between 10 and 35 attorneys
  - $22,000–$26,500 in law firms with between 1 and 10 attorneys
  - $26,000–$31,500 in corporate law offices[14]
- According to a 2001 study by the United States Department of Labor:
  - the mean hourly earnings of full-time legal assistants was $17.46 (for attorneys, it was $38.77)
  - the mean weekly hours worked by full-time legal assistants was 38.5 (for attorneys, it was 38.8)[15]

Experienced paralegals do very well. If they have good résumés and have developed specialties that are in demand, they usually improve their financial picture significantly.

A number of other generalizations can be made about salaries across the country:

- Paralegals who work in the law departments of corporations (banks, insurance companies, other businesses) tend to make more than those who work in private law firms.
- Paralegals who work in large private law firms tend to make more than those who work in smaller private law firms.
- Paralegals who work in large metropolitan areas (over a million in population) tend to make more than those who work in rural areas.
- Paralegals who work for the government in civil service positions tend to make less than those who work for large private law firms or corporations. (See appendix 2.B at the end of chapter 2 for state government salaries in every state.)
- Paralegals who work in legal aid or legal service offices that are funded by government grants and charitable contributions tend to make less than all other paralegals.

- Paralegals who work for attorneys who understand the value of paralegals tend to make more than those working for attorneys who have a poor or weak understanding of what paralegals can do.
- Paralegals who work in an office where there is a career ladder for paralegals, plus periodic evaluations and salary reviews, tend to make more than those who work in offices without these options.
- Paralegals who are career-oriented tend to make more than those less interested in a long-term commitment to paralegal work.

In addition to the payment of bonuses, other fringe benefits must be considered (e.g., vacation time, health insurance, parking facilities). A comprehensive list of such benefits will be presented in chapter 2. (See exhibit 2.13.)

One final point to keep in mind about salaries: once a person has gained training *and experience* as a paralegal, this background may be used to go into other law-related positions. For example, a corporate paralegal in a law firm might leave the firm to take a higher-paying position as a securities analyst for a corporation, or an estates paralegal at a law firm might leave for a more lucrative position as a trust administrator at a bank. An extensive list of these law-related jobs will be given at the end of chapter 2. (See exhibit 2.16.)

## Section I
# FACTORS INFLUENCING THE GROWTH OF PARALEGALISM

In the late 1960s, most attorneys would draw a blank if you mentioned the words *paralegal* or *legal assistant*. According to Webster's *Ninth New Collegiate Dictionary*, the earliest recorded use of the word *paralegal* in English occurred in 1971. Today, the situation has changed radically. Most law offices either have paralegals or are seriously considering their employment. (A major exception to this trend is the one- or two-attorney office in which the only staff member is a secretary who often performs paralegal tasks.) Some surveys show that there is one paralegal for every four attorneys in law firms and one paralegal for every two attorneys in the law departments of corporations. It has been estimated that the number of paralegals may eventually exceed the number of attorneys in the practice of law. The United States Bureau of Labor Statistics has projected that paralegals will constitute one of the fastest growing fields in the country, with a growth of 62 percent between 1998 and 2008 (see exhibit 1.3).

| EXHIBIT 1.3 | The 10 Fastest Growing Occupations, 1998–2008 | | |
|---|---|---|---|

| | Numbers Employed | | Percentage |
| | 1998 | 2008 | Increase |
|---|---|---|---|
| Computer engineers | 299,000 | 622,000 | 108% |
| Computer support specialists | 429,000 | 869,000 | 102% |
| Systems analysts | 617,000 | 1,194,000 | 94% |
| Database administrators | 87,000 | 155,000 | 77% |
| Desktop publishing specialists | 26,000 | 44,000 | 73% |
| **Paralegals and legal assistants** | **136,000** | **220,000** | **62%** |
| Personal care and home health aides | 746,000 | 1,179,000 | 58% |
| Medical assistants | 252,000 | 398,000 | 58% |
| Social and human service assistants | 268,000 | 410,000 | 53% |
| Physician assistants | 66,000 | 98,000 | 48% |

*Source:* U.S. Department of Labor, Bureau of Labor Statistics, Employment Projections, Table 3b, *at* stats.bls.gov/news.release/ecopro.t06.htm (visited August 29, 2001).

What has caused this dramatic change? The following factors have been instrumental in bringing paralegalism to its present state of prominence:

1. The pressure of economics.
2. The call for efficiency and delegation.
3. The promotion by bar associations.
4. The organization of paralegals.

### 1. THE PRESSURE OF ECONOMICS

Perhaps the greatest incentive to employ paralegals has been arithmetic. Law firms simply add up what they earn without paralegals, add up what they could earn with paralegals, compare the two figures, and conclude that the employment of paralegals is profitable. There "can be little doubt that the principal motivation prompting law firms to hire legal assistants is the economic benefit enjoyed by the firm."[16] The key to increased profits is **leveraging.** Leverage, often expressed as a ratio, is the ability to make a profit from the income-generating work of others. The higher the ratio of paralegals to partners in the firm, the more profit to the partners or owners of the firm (assuming everyone is generating income from billable time). The same is true of associates in the firm. The higher the ratio of associates to partners, the greater the profit to the partners/owners.

In the best of all worlds, some of this increased profit will result in lower fees to the client. For example, Chief Justice Warren Burger felt that some attorneys charge "excessive fees for closing real-estate transactions for the purchase of a home. A greater part of that work can be handled by trained paralegals, and, in fact, many responsible law firms are doing just that to reduce costs for their clients."[17] If the state requires an attorney to be present at a closing, then, of course, the law would have to be changed to allow paralegals to do what Chief Justice Burger suggests. We will discuss such changes in chapter 4.

Exhibit 1.4 provides an example of the economic impact of using a paralegal. In the example, a client comes to a lawyer to form a corporation.[18] We will compare (a) the economics of an attorney and secretary working on the case, assuming a fee of $2,500, and (b) the economics of an attorney, secretary, *and* paralegal working on the same case, assuming a fee of $2,000. As you can see, with a paralegal added to the team, the firm's profit is increased about 16 percent in spite of the lower fee, and the attorney has more billable time to spend elsewhere. Some studies have claimed an even higher profit increase because of the effective use of paralegals.

The example assumes that the attorney's fee is $250 per hour and that the attorney billed the client $60 per hour for the paralegal's time. According to a 2000 survey:

- The average billing rate attorneys charged clients for paralegal time was:
  - $58 per hour in law firms with 6 to 8 attorneys
  - $76 per hour in law firms with 51 to 55 attorneys
  - $91 per hour in law firms with 91 to 95 attorneys
- On billable hours:
  - 6 percent of paralegals said they were expected to bill 21 to 25 hours per week
  - 32 percent of paralegals said they were expected to bill 31 to 35 hours per week
  - 20 percent of paralegals said they were expected to bill 36 to 40 hours per week[19]

A 2001 study of 6,000 paralegals at 399 large law firms concluded that the average number of annual billable hours worked by paralegals was 1,400.[20] (Later, in chapter 14, on law office management, we will further examine the implications of these statistics.) In many firms, paralegals are expected to turn in a minimum number of billable hours per week, month, or other designated period. This is known as a **billable hours quota.**

When a law firm bills clients for paralegal time, the paralegal becomes a *profit center* in the firm. In such cases, paralegals are not simply part of the cost of doing business reflected in the firm's overhead, they generate revenue (and, therefore, profit) for the firm. To calculate the amount of profit, the **rule of three** is sometimes used as a general guideline. To be profitable, a paralegal must bill three times his or her salary. Of the total revenue brought in through paralegal billing, one-third is allocated to salary, one-third to overhead, and one-third to profit. Phrased another way, when the gross revenue generated

---

**leveraging** Making profit from the income-generating work of others.

**billable hours quota** A minimum number of hours expected from a timekeeper on client matters that can be charged (billed) to clients per week, month, year, or other time period.

**rule of three** A general guideline used by some law firms to identify budget expectations from hiring paralegals: gross revenue generated through paralegal billing should equal three times a paralegal's salary.

| EXHIBIT 1.4 | The Profitability of Using Paralegals |
| --- | --- |

## TASK: TO FORM A CORPORATION

### a. Attorney and Secretary

| | Time | |
| --- | --- | --- |
| **Function** | *Attorney* | *Secretary* |
| 1. Interviewing | 1.0 | 0.0 |
| 2. Advising | 1.0 | 0.0 |
| 3. Gathering information | 1.0 | 0.0 |
| 4. Preparing papers | 2.0 | 4.0 |
| 5. Executing and filing papers | 1.0 | 1.0 |
| | 6.0 | 5.0 |

Assume that the attorney's hourly rate is $250 per hour and that the overhead cost of maintaining a secretary is $25 per hour.

| | |
| --- | --- |
| Attorney (6 × $250) | $1,500 |
| Secretary (5 × $25) | 125 |
| Total cost | $1,625 |

| | |
| --- | --- |
| Fee | $2,500 |
| Less cost | 1,625 |
| Gross profit | $ 875 |

### b. Attorney, Secretary, *and* Paralegal

| | Time | | |
| --- | --- | --- | --- |
| **Function** | *Attorney* | *Paralegal* | *Secretary* |
| 1. Interviewing | 0.5 | 0.5 | 0.0 |
| 2. Advising | 1.0 | 0.0 | 0.0 |
| 3. Gathering information | 0.0 | 1.0 | 0.0 |
| 4. Preparing papers | 0.5 | 1.5 | 4.0 |
| 5. Executing and filing papers | 0.5 | 0.5 | 1.0 |
| | 2.5 | 3.5 | 5.0 |

Assume a paralegal hourly rate of $60 per hour.

| | |
| --- | --- |
| Attorney (2.5 × $250) | $625 |
| Paralegal (3.5 × $60) | 210 |
| Secretary (5 × $25) | 125 |
| Total cost | $960 |

| | |
| --- | --- |
| Fee | $2,000 |
| Less cost | 960 |
| Gross profit | $1,040 |

### COMPARISON

| | | |
| --- | --- | --- |
| Fee: | a. Attorney and Secretary | $2,500 |
| | b. Attorney, Secretary, and Paralegal | $2,000 |
| Saving to client | | $500 |
| Increased profitability to attorney ($1,040 vs. $875) | | $165 |

By using a paralegal on the case, the attorney's profit increases about 19% over the profit realized without the paralegal. Furthermore, the attorney has 3.5 hours that are now available to work on other cases, bringing in additional revenue of $875 (3.5 × the attorney's hourly rate of $250).

through paralegal billing equals three times the paralegal's salary, the firm has achieved its minimum profit expectations.

For example:

| | |
| --- | --- |
| Paralegal's salary: | $30,000 |
| Paralegal rate: | $35 per hour |
| Billings the firm hopes this paralegal will generate: | $90,000 |
| Rule-of-three allocation: | |
| —paralegal salary: | $30,000 |
| —overhead for this paralegal: | $30,000 |
| —profit to the law firm: | $30,000[21] |

---

### Assignment 1.4

(a) In the example given in exhibit 1.4, how many billable hours per year would this paralegal have to produce in order to generate $30,000 per year in profits for the firm? Is this number realistic? If not, what must be done?

> **(b)** Assume that a paralegal seeks a salary of $25,000 a year and that the law firm would like to be able to pay this salary. Using the "rule of three," if this person is able to generate 1,400 billable hours per year, at what hourly rate must this paralegal's time be billed in order for the attorney and the paralegal to be happy?

Of course, the rule of three is not an absolute gauge for determining profit expectations from using paralegals. Other factors affect the profitability of paralegals to an office. A high turnover of paralegals in the office, for example, often means that the office will have substantially increased overhead costs in recruiting and orienting new paralegals. A recent survey concluded that "an 11%-to-25% annual attrition rate for paralegals is now the norm at a majority of law firms."[22] Another factor that can offset the rule of three is the extent to which attorneys have more billable time because of a paralegal's performance of nonbillable tasks. Some paralegals perform many tasks that cannot be billed to clients. Examples include recruiting new employees, helping to maintain the law library, organizing the office's closed case files, and doing most of the work on certain kinds of cases that an attorney would normally do for free (e.g., probating the estate of the attorney's brother-in-law). The more nonbillable tasks such as these that a paralegal performs, the less time he or she will have available to devote to billable tasks. This, however, does not mean that the paralegal is a drain on profits. A nonbillable task that a paralegal performs is often a task that the attorney does *not* have to perform. This, of course, enables the attorney to direct more of his or her efforts to fee-generating (i.e., billable) matters.

## 2. THE CALL FOR EFFICIENCY AND DELEGATION

Attorneys are overtrained for a substantial portion of the tasks that they perform in a law office. This is one of the major reasons that traditional law offices are charged with inefficiency. Paralegals have been seen as a major step toward reform. The results have been quite satisfactory, as evidenced by the following comments from attorneys who have hired paralegals:[23]

> A competent legal assistant for several years has been effectively doing 25% to 35% of the actual work that I had been doing for many years prior to that time.

> The results of our 3 attorney–3 paralegal system have been excellent. Our office's efficiency has been improved and our clients are receiving better service.

> It has been our experience that clients now ask for the legal assistant. Client calls to the attorneys have been reduced an estimated 75%.

It has taken a *very* long time for attorneys to realize that something was wrong with the way they practiced law. The following historical perspective presents an overview of how attorneys came to this realization.[24]

During the American colonial period, the general populace distrusted attorneys because many of them sided with King George III against the emerging independent nation. Some colonies tolerated the existence of attorneys but established roadblocks to their practice. In 1641, for example, the Massachusetts Bay Colony prohibited freemen from hiring attorneys for a fee:

> "Every man that findeth himself unfit to plead his own cause in any court shall have libertie to employ any man against whom the court doth not except, to help him, Provided he gave him noe fee or reward for his pains."[25]

Furthermore, almost anyone could become an attorney without having to meet rigorous admission requirements.

Up until the nineteenth century, the attorney did not have assistants other than an occasional apprentice studying to be an attorney himself. The attorney basically worked alone. He carried "his office in his hat."[26] A very personal attachment and devotion to detail were considered to be part of the process of becoming an attorney and of operating a practice. In the early nineteenth century, George Wythe commented:

> It is only by drudgery that the exactness, accuracy and closeness of thought so necessary for a good lawyer are engendered.[27]

The same theme came from Abraham Lincoln in his famous *Notes for a Law Lecture:*

> If anyone . . . shall claim an exemption from the drudgery of the law, his case is a failure in advance.[28]

Attorneys would be somewhat reluctant to delegate such "drudgery" to someone working for them, according to this theory of legal education.

During this period, attorneys often placed a high premium on the personal relationship between attorney and client. As late as 1875, for example, Clarence Seward and his partners "would have none of the newfangled typewriters" because clients would "resent the lack of personal attention implied in typed letters."[29] The coming of the Industrial Revolution, however, brought the practice of law closer to industry and finance. Some law offices began to specialize. As attorneys assumed new responsibilities, the concern for organization and efficiency grew. To be sure, large numbers of attorneys continued to carry their law offices "in their hats" and to provide an essentially one-to-one service. Many law offices in the 1850s, however, took a different direction.

Machines created new jobs. The typewriter introduced the typist. Librarians, investigators, bookkeepers, office managers, accountants, tax and fiduciary specialists, and research assistants soon found their way into the large law office. Although nonattorneys were hired primarily to undertake clerical or administrative responsibilities, they soon were delegated more challenging roles. As one study of a law firm noted with respect to several female employees who had been with the firm a number of years:

> In addition, these women were given considerable responsibility in connection with their positions as secretary or head bookkeeper. The head bookkeeper acted as assistant secretary to the partner-secretary of certain charitable corporations the firm represented. In this capacity, she recorded minutes of director's meetings, issued proxy statements, supervised the filing of tax returns for the organization and attended to other significant administrative matters.[30]

In this fashion, attorneys began delegating more and more nonclerical duties to their clerical staff. This was not always done in a planned manner. An employee might suddenly be performing dramatically new duties as emergencies arose on current cases and as new clients arrived in an already busy office. In such an environment, an attorney may not know what the employee is capable of doing until the employee does it. Despite its haphazard nature, the needs of the moment and OJT (on-the-job training) worked wonders for staff development.

By the 1960s, attorneys started to ask whether a new category of employee should be created. Instead of expanding the duties of a secretary, why not give the new duties to a new category of employee—the paralegal? A number of studies were conducted to determine how receptive attorneys would be to this idea on a broad scale. The results were very encouraging. The conclusion soon became inevitable that attorneys can delegate many tasks to paralegals without sacrificing quality of service. Today, this theme has become a dominant principle of law office management. Many attorneys no longer ask, "Can I delegate?" Rather they ask, "Why *can't* this be delegated?" Or "How can the delegation be effectively managed?" It is a given that substantial delegation is a necessity.

This is not to say, however, that all attorneys immediately endorse the paralegal concept with enthusiasm. Many are initially hesitant, as demonstrated by the following report on the hiring of legal assistants within the California Department of Health, Education, and Welfare (HEW):

> When the legal assistant program began in early 1977 in HEW, it was met with some skepticism, especially in offices in cities other than Sacramento. There was concern that the quality of the work might be diminished by legal assistants. However, team leaders and deputies are not only no longer skeptical, they are now enthusiastic supporters of the legal assistant program. The attorneys feel that the work product is at least as good, and more thorough, than that provided by attorneys, mainly because the legal assistants have developed an expertise in a narrow area of the law and the work is more stimulating to the legal assistants than it was to the attorneys. The legal assistants processed 152 cases in fiscal year 1977/78 and 175 cases in 1978/79. It was estimated that legal assistants are as efficient as attorneys in processing the preliminary phase of these cases. As a result, a legal assistant in this instance produces as many pleadings as a deputy attorney general would have produced in the same amount of time. For this reason the section has been able to provide a faster turnaround time for the client agencies.[31]

A call for more cost-effective methods of practicing law by the government came from the Council for Citizens Against Government Waste (the "Grace Commission"), which recommended that the United States Department of Justice increase the ratio of paralegals to attorneys in order to achieve a savings of $13.4 million over three years. Soon thereafter, legislation was proposed in Congress to establish an Office of Paralegal Coordination and Activities in the Department of Justice to work toward the increased use of paralegals in the department.[32] Although Congress did not pass this proposal, the effort is typical of the momentum toward paralegal use throughout the practice of law.

### 3. THE PROMOTION BY BAR ASSOCIATIONS

The bar associations assumed a large role in the development of paralegals. This has given great visibility to the field. In 1968, the House of Delegates of the American Bar Association established a Special Committee on Lay Assistants for Lawyers (subsequently renamed the Standing Committee on Legal Assistants) and resolved:

> (1) That the legal profession recognize that there are many tasks in serving client's needs which can be performed by a trained, non-lawyer assistant working under the direction and supervision of a lawyer;
>
> (2) That the profession encourage the training and employment of such assistants. . . .[33]

Most of the state bar associations now have committees that cover the area of paralegal utilization. As we will see in chapter 5 and in appendix F, many of these committees have established guidelines for the use of paralegals in a law office. Some bar associations, including the American Bar Association, have allowed paralegals to become associate members of their association. The real impact on the growth of paralegalism, however, has come from those bar association committees that deal with legal economics and law office management. Such committees have sponsored numerous conferences for practicing attorneys. These conferences, plus articles in bar association journals, have extensively promoted paralegals.

Although the role of bar associations in the development of paralegalism has been and continues to be of critical importance, their involvement has not been without controversy. Some have questioned whether the organized bar has a conflict of interest in regulating paralegals in light of the profit motive attorneys have in using paralegals. We will examine this issue in chapter 4.

### 4. THE ORGANIZATION OF PARALEGALS

Paralegals have been organizing. There are approximately 200 paralegal organizations throughout the country. (See the list in appendix B.) This has greatly helped raise everyone's consciousness about the potential of paralegalism. As indicated earlier, the two major national associations are the National Federation of Paralegal Associations (NFPA) and the National Association of Legal Assistants (NALA). We will be examining the work, impact, and value of these associations in the next several chapters. It is no longer true that attorneys are the sole organized voice speaking for paralegals and shaping the development of the field.

### NOTE ON ROLES FOR NONATTORNEYS IN THE DELIVERY OF LEGAL SERVICES IN OTHER COUNTRIES

#### England

The English legal profession has two main branches, consisting of solicitors and barristers. The *solicitor* handles the day-to-day legal problems of the public but has only limited rights to represent clients in certain lower courts. The bulk of litigation in the higher courts is conducted by the *barrister*. When representation in such courts is needed, the solicitor arranges for the barrister to enter the case. Solicitors often employ one or more *legal executives*, who are the equivalent of the American paralegal. Legal executives are delegated many responsibilities under the supervision of the solicitor. They undergo extensive training programs and take rigorous examinations at the Institute of Legal Executives. Once qualified, the legal executive obtains Fellowship in the Institute and is entitled to use the letters "F.Inst.L.Ex." after his or her name. There is also an Institute of Legal Executives in Australia.

### Canada

"Legal assistants became a part of the legal community in Canada more than 60 years ago, practicing first in Montreal, then in Toronto. . . . Although no exact figures are available, there are an estimated 3,000 legal assistants in Canada today. Among the first were former legal executives from England. . . . The ratio of legal assistant to lawyer ranges from 1:1 in small specialist firms to 10:1 or more in the large firms where legal assistants are often departmentalized. . . . The term 'legal assistant' is emerging as the most commonly used title in Canada and the term is recognized by the Law Society of British Columbia and the Canadian Bar Association. A unique situation exists in Ontario where the Law Society of Upper Canada requires legal assistants to be designated as law clerks. . . ." The word "paralegal" commonly refers to a nonlawyer who offers certain services to the public for a fee and who does *not* work under the supervision of a Canadian lawyer. Hence legal assistants who work for lawyers generally do not call themselves paralegals.[34] For the addresses of paralegal associations in Canada see appendix B.

### Japan

Attorneys *(bengoshi)* are not the only providers of legal services in Japan. A separate category of workers called *judicial scriveners (shihoo shoshi)* has special authority to assist the public in preparing legal documents such as contracts and deeds. The granting of this authority is conditioned on the successful completion of an examination.

### Cuba

In Cuba, legal assistants work with attorneys in law offices or collectives called *bufetes*. The assistants draft legal documents, interview clients, conduct legal research, file papers in court, negotiate for trial dates, etc.

### Russia

Attorneys-at-law in Russia are organized in lawyers' colleges. Membership in the colleges is granted to three kinds of individuals: first, graduates from university law schools; second, individuals with legal training of six months or more, with experience in judicial work, or at least one year as a judge, governmental attorney, investigator, or legal counsel; and third, persons without legal training but with at least three years' experience. There are also nonlawyer notaries who prepare contracts and wills for the public.

### Finland

In Finland, only members of the Finnish Bar Association can use the title of advocate. Advocates, however, do not enjoy an exclusive right of audience in the courts. Litigants can plead their own case or retain a representative who does not have to be an advocate.

### Germany

The main providers of legal services in Germany are the lawyer *(Rechtsanwalt)* and the notary *(Notar)*. The notary provides assistance in drafting contracts, wills, and other legal documents. To become a notary, an individual must be an attorney who has been in practice at least 10 years. "A third type of individual providing legal services is the *Rechtsberater*, which means 'legal assistant.' " While *Rechtsberaters* often operate like American paralegals, they are "also permitted under German law to operate independently of attorney supervision. *Rechtsberaters* can open their own offices and provide legal services to the public in a limited range of areas. . . . This includes small claims matters, no-contest domestic matters, etc." A *Rechtsberater* must pass a licensing exam and maintain liability insurance.[35]

### Egypt

In Egypt, there is a nonattorney who sells legal services directly to the public. He is called *ard haal-gy*, which roughly means someone who explains the situation. He sits outside the courts with his briefcase. Clients flock to the *ard haal-gy* for help with their court cases. He provides this help by drafting complaints, writs, and other legal documents that do not require the signature of an attorney. *Ard haal-gy* do not have formal liberal arts or legal training. But they are masters of the Egyptian language, largely because of their study of the Koran. Many are present or former sheiks who can recite up to a third of the Koran from memory. This gives them excellent skills in writing and speaking, which they use in drafting legal documents. They charge relatively modest fees, around $1.50 to $3.00 per case, and can earn up to $400 a month, a large sum considering their low overhead. Many *ard haal-gy* have their own assistants who help them handle cases. *Ard haal-gy* are probably practicing law illegally, but they are so entrenched by tradition and custom that no one challenges them.

## Section J
# CONCLUSION

Since its inception, the paralegal career in America has been an integral part of the legal profession's challenge of defining the practice of law in the twenty-first century. In a recent keynote address, Robert Stein, executive director of the American Bar Association, said that the four most important areas affecting the practice of law in the future were diversity, globalization, electronic contracts, and the growth of paralegals. "The paralegal profession," he said, "is undergoing a remarkable transformation as the value of a well trained paralegal is recognized by more and more law firms, corporations and governments as a means of providing cost effective services in an era of rising expenses and complex litigation."[36] These are some of the themes we will be exploring as you now begin the journey of becoming a "well trained paralegal."

# CHAPTER SUMMARY

The law has a wide-ranging impact on our society. Precision and attention to detail are critical attributes of anyone working in the law. Among the most important organizations in paralegalism are the National Federation of Paralegal Associations (NFPA), the National Association of Legal Assistants (NALA), the American Bar Association, your state bar association, and your local paralegal association. The titles *paralegal* and *legal assistant* are synonymous. While some states have laws that restrict the use of specific titles, most states do not. Paralegals are either employees of attorneys or independent contractors who sell their services to attorneys or who have authorization to sell limited services directly to the public.

Independent contractors who work without attorney supervision are sometimes charged with the unauthorized practice of law. They must call themselves bankruptcy petition preparers if they work in bankruptcy. In California, other independents must be called legal document assistants or unlawful detainer assistants.

Definitions of a paralegal have been written by legislatures, courts, bar associations, and paralegal associations. The most common characteristics of the definitions are that the paralegal has special qualifications due to education, training, or on-the-job experience; works under attorney supervision; and performs substantive (i.e., nonclerical) legal work that the attorney would have to perform if the paralegal was not present. The most important definitions are those written by the legislatures or courts.

In most states, attorneys can charge their clients paralegal fees in addition to fees for attorney time. In statutory fee cases, the losing side in litigation can be forced to pay the attorney fees of the winning side. These fees can include separate fees for paralegal tasks. Under the landmark civil rights case of *Missouri v. Jenkins* (which has been followed by many state courts and by many federal courts in non–civil right cases), paralegal fees are determined by market rate. The court must decide which paralegal tasks qualify for an award of paralegal fees. To make this decision, the court may need a more precise definition of a paralegal. This need has led to the creation of task-specific definitions of a paralegal. Paralegals must keep detailed time sheets that indicate what tasks they performed.

Paralegal salaries are influenced by a number of factors: experience, level of responsibility, kind of employer, geographic area, the employer's understanding of the paralegal's role, and the extent to which the paralegal is committed to the field as a career. One rough measure of paralegal profitability to a firm is the rule of three. This guideline states that gross revenue generated through paralegal billing should equal three times a paralegal's salary.

Bar associations and paralegal associations have promoted the value of paralegals extensively. The economic impact they have had on the practice of law is the major reason the paralegal field has flourished and grown so rapidly. In a properly leveraged firm, paralegals can be a "profit center" without any sacrifice in the quality of the service delivered by the firm. Also, a paralegal can help attorneys redirect some of their energies from nonbillable to billable tasks.

## KEY TERMS

continuing legal education (CLE)

traditional paralegal

independent contractor

transactional paralegal

unauthorized practice of law (UPL)

contingent fee

paralegal fee

overhead

statutory fee case

leveraging

billable hours quota

rule of three

## ON THE NET: MORE ON THE NEW CAREER IN LAW

### Definitions of a Paralegal

www.nala.org/terms.htm

www.paralegals.org/Development/pl_defin.htm

www.paralegals.org/Development/statedif.htm

### Paralegal Fees

www.paralegals.com/Development/fees.html

### *Missouri v. Jenkins* (full text of opinion)

caselaw.lp.findlaw.com/scripts/getcase.pl?navby=case&court=us&vol=491&page=274

### Overview of Paralegal Development and Roles

www.nala.org/HRBrochure.htm

www.legalassistanttoday.com/profession

### Occupational Outlook Handbook (Bureau of Labor Statistics)

stats.bls.gov/oco/ocos114.htm

## ENDNOTES

1. Gary Lockwood, *Seeking Cover in the Age of Litigation*, 9 Business Lawyer Today 10 (September/October 2001).
2. American Bar Association, *Findings of the Comprehensive Legal Needs Study* (1994).
3. See Jane Cracroft, *Developing Effective Witnesses*, The Legal Investigator, August 1991, at 7.
4. H. Samborn, *Post–Law School Job May Be as Paralegal*, 81 A.B.A. J. 14 (March 1995).
5. *Rural Water System No. 1 v. City of Sioux Center, Iowa*, 38 F. Supp. 2d 1057, 1061 (N.D. Iowa 1999).
6. *Ursic v. Bethlehem Mines*, 719 F.2d 670, 677 (3d Cir. 1983).
7. *Johnson v. Georgia Highway Express, Inc.*, 488 F.2d 714, 717 (5th Cir. 1974).
8. Local Rules for the Superior Court of California, County of Fresno, Probate Rules, Rule 84.2(D).
9. Ernst & Young, *Legal Assistant Managers and Legal Assistants* 388 (3d ed. 1989).
10. Korrie Price, *LAT (Legal Assistant Today) Forum* (www.legalassistanttoday.com/lat-forum), July 27, 2001.
11. NALA, *2002 National Utilization and Compensation Survey Report*, tbl. 4.7 (2002).
12. How LAMA Data Can Help You Retain Your Paralegals, in *IOMA's Report on Compensation and Benefits for Law Offices* 1 (April 2001).
13. NFPA, *2001 Paralegal Compensation and Benefits Report* (2001).
14. The Affiliates, *2003 Salary Guide* 13 (2003) (www.affiliates.com).
15. Bureau of Labor Statistics, U.S. Department of Labor, *National Compensation Survey: Occupational Wages in the United States, 2001*, tbl. 3 (August 2002).
16. Subcommittee on Legal Assistants, New York State Bar Association, *The Expanding Role of Legal Assistants in New York State* 7 (1982).
17. *U.S. News & World Report*, February 22, 1982, at 32.
18. Adapted from Jespersen, *Paralegals: Help or Hindrance?*, The Houston Lawyer, (March/April 1977), at 114–16.
19. NALA, *2000 National Utilization and Compensation Survey Report*, tbls. 3.2 & 3.7 (2000).
20. Altman Weil, Inc., *2001 Survey of Law Firm Economics* (www.altmanweil.com/products/surveys/slfe/annual.cfm).

21. Adapted from State Bar of Texas, *Attorneys' Guide to Practicing with Legal Assistants*, VI(3) (1986).

22. How LAMA Data Can Help You Retain Your Paralegals, in *IOMA's Report on Compensation and Benefits for Law Offices* 1 (April 2001).

23. Legal Assistants Committee, Oregon State Bar, *Legal Assistant Survey* (1977).

24. The research for part of the section on the historical background of paralegalism was conducted by the author and subsequently used with his permission in Lester Brickman, *Expansion of the Lawyering Process through a New Delivery System: The Emergence and State of Legal Paraprofessionalism*, 71 Columbia Law Review 1153, 1169 *ff* (1971).

25. Body of Liberties, cited in R. Warner, *Independent Paralegal's Handbook* 8 (1986).

26. Lee, *Large Law Offices*, 57 American Law Review 788 (1923).

27. Lewis, ed., George Wythe, in 1 *Great American Lawyers: A History of the Legal Profession in America* 55 (1907).

28. John Nicolay & John Hay, eds., Notes for a Law Lecture, in *Complete Works of Abraham Lincoln* 142 (1894). See also Paul Frank, *Lincoln as a Lawyer* 3 (1961).

29. Robert Swaine (1948), *The Cravath Firm and Its Predecessors: 1819–1947*, at 365, 449.

30. Emily Dodge, *Evolution of a City Law Office*, 1955 Wisconsin Law Review 180, 187.

31. Management Analysis Section, California Department of Justice, *Study of Paralegal Utilization in the California Attorney General's Office* 23 (December 1980).

32. H.R. 5107, 99th Cong., 2d Sess. (1986) A Bill to Increase Government Economy and Efficiency Regarding the Increased Use of Paralegals.

33. *Proceedings of the House of Delegates of the American Bar Association*, 54 A.B.A. J. 1017, 1021 (1968).

34. Patricia Hicks, *The Legal Assistant in Canada*, 8 The LAMA Manager 5 (October 1992).

35. Robert Loomis, *Practicing Law in Germany*, 11 WSPA Findings and Conclusions 6 (Washington State Paralegal Ass'n, January 1995).

36. Robert Stein, *Practice of Law in the New Century* (American Bar Association, 1999).

# Chapter 2

# PARALEGAL EMPLOYMENT

## Chapter Outline

A. The Job Market

B. Where Paralegals Work

C. Paralegal Specialties: A Dictionary of Functions

D. Finding a Job: Employment Strategies

E. The Job Hunting Notebook

F. Your Second Job

Appendix 2.A.    Paralegal Employment in Selected Large Law Offices

Appendix 2.B.    Summary Chart—Survey of State Government Job Classifications for Paralegals

## Section A
# The Job Market

The paralegal job market goes through cycles. (The same is true for attorneys.) There are periods when law offices are desperate for people to hire; at other times, offices are flooded with job applications. Don't be surprised if the job market on the day you begin your paralegal training program is not the same as the market on the day you graduate. Geography also plays an important role. In general, a large metropolitan area will present more employment prospects than rural areas simply because cities have more attorneys seeking paralegal help. In light of this reality, the safest course is to be prepared for competition when you begin to apply for employment. A central theme of this chapter, therefore, is the job-search strategy that will be needed in a market where there will be more applicants than available jobs.

It is important to make the distinction between jobs for entry-level paralegals and jobs for experienced paralegals. Almost always, your first job will be the toughest to obtain. A very large number of law offices are seeking paralegals with one, two, three, or more years of law office experience, often in a particular area of the law. Once you have proven your worth as a practicing paralegal, numerous opportunities open up to you, as we will see later in the chapter. Those looking for their first paralegal job may have a tougher time. Don't be discouraged, however, because there are many things you can do now to increase your chances of finding the job that is right for you.

Competition for paralegal jobs is likely to come from several sources:

- Other recent graduates from paralegal training programs
- Secretaries and clerks now working in law offices who want to be promoted into paralegal positions
- Paralegals with a year or more of experience who are seeking a job change
- People with no legal training or experience who walk into an office "cold" seeking a job
- People with no legal training or experience but who have connections (a friend of an important client, a relative of a partner)

How long will it take for you to find a paralegal job? Of course, no one can accurately answer this question. Many variables are involved, including your competence and the record you establish in paralegal school. According to a guideline used by one veteran legal recruiter (a guideline that applies to good nonlegal jobs as well), for every $10,000 in salary you hope to earn, you will need to set aside one month of search time. "So if you want $25,000 per year, your search should take about two and one-half months. But do not be disappointed if it takes longer."[1] Some graduates obtain jobs very quickly. Be prepared, however, for a competitive job market.

In this environment, the two keys to success are *information* about the employment scene and *techniques* to market yourself. With these objectives in mind, we turn now to the following themes:

- Places where paralegals work
- Paralegal specialties
- Effective job-finding strategies
- Alternative career options

## Section B
# Where Paralegals Work

There are 9 major locations where paralegals work. They are summarized in exhibit 2.1, along with the approximate percentage of paralegals working in each location.

In general, the more attorneys in a law firm, the greater the likelihood that significant numbers of paralegals will be working there. Where do attorneys work? Appendix 2.A at the end of this chapter identifies some of the large employers of attorneys in the country.

| EXHIBIT 2.1 | Where Do Paralegals Work and in What Percentages? |

I. Private law firms
  A. Small firm—1–10 lawyers (28%)
  B. Medium firm—11–50 lawyers (16%)
  C. Large firm—over 50 lawyers (30%)
II. Government
  A. Federal government (4%)
  B. State government (2%)
  C. Local government (1%)
III. Legal service/legal aid offices (civil law) (3%)
IV. Law departments of corporations, banks, insurance companies, and other businesses (8%)

V. Special interest groups or associations (1%)
VI. Criminal law offices
  A. Prosecution (1%)
  B. Defense (1%)
VII. Freelance or independent paralegals (1%)
VIII. Service companies/consulting firms (1%)
IX. Related fields (3%)
  A. Law librarian
  B. Paralegal teacher
  C. Paralegal supervisor/office administrator
  D. Miscellaneous

## 1. PRIVATE LAW FIRMS

Almost 75 percent of paralegals work for **private law firms**. Although the need for paralegals may be just as great in the other categories, private law firms have been doing most of the hiring. A private law firm is simply one that generates its income primarily from the fees of individual clients. In 1996, there were 24 paralegals for every 100 attorneys in private law firms; in 2000, the ratio was 27 paralegals per 100 attorneys.[2]

Traditionally, private law firms engaged in general practice, meaning that they handled a wide variety of legal problems presented by clients. Most law firms still fall into this category. There are, however, a number of smaller firms that concentrate on one area of law, e.g., environment, employment discrimination, or immigration. Such firms are often called **boutique law firms**. The number of such firms has been steadily growing in recent years.

Paralegals working for private law firms, particularly the larger ones in metropolitan areas, have the following characteristics:

- They are among the highest paid paralegals.
- They tend to experience more law office management and personnel problems than other paralegals.
- They tend to specialize more and hence have less variety in their work assignments.
- They have been the most politically active paralegals in forming associations and in dealing with the bar associations.
- They are predominantly women.

**private law firm** A law firm that generates its income from the fees of individual clients.

**boutique law firm** A firm that specializes in one area of the law.

## 2. GOVERNMENT

The civil service departments of federal, state, and local governments have established standards and classifications for many different kinds of government paralegals. These paralegals work in four main areas of government:

- In the office of the chief government attorney (e.g., attorney general, city attorney) for an entire jurisdiction (e.g., state, county, city)
- In the office of the chief attorney (often called the general counsel) for individual government agencies
- In the office of the chief attorney (again often called the general counsel) for units within an individual government agency (e.g., civil rights division, enforcement bureau)
- In the office of individual legislators, legislative committees, legislative counsel, or the legislative drafting office of the legislature

### Federal Government

Thousands of paralegals work for the federal government in the capital (Washington, D.C.) and the main regional cities of the federal government (Atlanta, Boston, Chicago,

**paralegal specialist** The major civil service job classification for paralegals who work for the federal government and for some state governments.

Dallas, Denver, Kansas City, New York, Philadelphia, San Francisco, and Seattle). The most important job classification for this position is the **paralegal specialist**. The occupational code for this position is GS-950. (GS means general schedule, the main pay scale in the federal government.) The word *specialist* does not necessarily mean that federal government paralegals work only in narrow areas of the law. The paralegal specialist performs "legal support functions which require discretion and independent judgment," according to the U.S. Office of Personnel Management (OPM), the federal agency in charge hiring standards within the federal government:

### Paralegal Specialist GS 0950

This series covers a variety of positions that involve legal work which is usually ancillary to the work of attorneys. . . . Duties may include examining case files to determine issues and sufficiency of evidence or documentation; searching for legal precedents, analyzing their applicability, and preparing digests of points of law involved; drafting briefs, other litigation papers, or advisory opinions for review and approval of attorneys; analyzing legal issues involved in requests for agency records; analyzing subpoenaed documents for possible patterns and trends relevant to litigation; initiating additional factfinding by agency personnel in other offices; developing and justifying recommendations for agency action on legal issues; analyzing appellate records to isolate facts pertinent to distinct legal issues; interviewing and evaluating potential witnesses; preparing for hearings and court appearances by briefing attorneys or administrative law judges on the issues and by assembling and arranging case files, documents, and exhibits; attending court sessions or hearings to be informed on progress, the development of new issues, issues that have been resolved, and areas that need more emphasis; and testifying in court concerning exhibits prepared.[3]

Paralegal specialists are found throughout the federal government, particularly at the Departments of Justice, Health and Human Services, Treasury, Transportation, and Interior. (For a list of federal agencies, see appendix D at the end of the book.) They are also extensively employed within the U.S. court system (see exhibit 6.3 in chapter 6).

Paralegal specialists are not the only individuals using special legal skills in the federal government. The following law-related occupations, filled mainly by nonattorneys, should be considered:

| | |
|---|---|
| Legal Clerk | Clerk of Court |
| Legal Technician | Social Services Representative |
| Immigration Specialist | Equal Employment Opportunity |
| Civil Rights Analyst | Specialist |
| Claims Examiner | Equal Opportunity Assistant |
| Hearings and Appeals Officer | Legislative Analyst |
| Legal Instruments Examiner | Legal Documents Examiner |
| Public Utilities Specialist | Land Law Examiner |
| Tax Law Specialist | Copyright Examiner |
| Internal Revenue Agent | Copyright Technician |
| Patent Advisor | Railroad Retirement Claims Examiner |
| Patent Examiner | Intelligence Analyst |
| Patent Technician | Internal Revenue Officer |
| Contract Administrator | Environmental Protection Specialist |
| Contract Specialist | Security Specialist |
| Contract Representative | Freedom of Information Act Specialist |
| Contracts Examiner | Estate Tax Examiner |
| Labor Relations Specialist | Fiduciary Accounts Examiner |
| Employee Relations Specialist | Workers' Compensation Claims |
| Wage and Hour Compliance | Examiner |
| Specialist | Unemployment Compensation Claims |
| Mediation Specialist | Examiner |

Mediator
Investigator
Regulatory Analyst
Foreign Affairs Analyst/Officer
Import Specialist

Unemployment Insurance Specialist
Corrections Assistant
Utilities Industry Analyst

Here are some Internet sites that can provide more extensive information about the federal government and about legal positions within its different units:

- *United States Government Manual* (*www.access.gpo.gov/nara/nara001.html*) descriptions of all agencies and courts of the federal government
- United States Office of Personnel Management (OPM) *www.opm.gov* (the federal agency that oversees hiring standards within the federal government)
- USAJobs *www.usajobs.opm.gov* (current paralegal specialist job openings with job descriptions, qualifications, and pay scales; type "paralegal" in the search box)

**State Government**

When looking for work as a paralegal in the *state* government, find out if your state has established civil service classification standards for paralegal positions. See appendix 2.B (at the end of this chapter) for some of this information. In addition, locate a directory of agencies, commissions, boards, or departments for your state, county, and city governments. You want to find a list of all (or most of the major) government offices. Many local public libraries will have a government directory. Alternatively, check the offices of state and local politicians, such as the governor, mayor, commissioner, alderman, representative, or senator. They will probably have such a directory. Finally, check your local phone book for the sections on government offices. Contact as many of them as you can to find out whether they employ paralegals. If you have difficulty obtaining an answer to this question, find out where their attorneys are located. Sections or departments that employ attorneys will probably be able to tell you about paralegal employment opportunities. In your search, include a list of all the courts in the state. Judges and court clerks may have legal positions open for nonattorneys.

In addition to the statewide personnel departments listed in appendix 2.B, many government offices have their own personnel department that will list employment openings. Also, whenever possible, talk with attorneys and paralegals who already work in these offices. They may know of opportunities that you can pursue.

Here are some Internet sites that can provide more extensive information about paralegals in state government:

- About Jobs in State Government *www.usgovinfo.about.com/blstjobs.htm* (job listings in every state)
- National Association of State Personnel Executives *www.naspe.net/Links/links.htm* (provides the Internet site of the civil service/personnel department in every state)

Do not limit your search to paralegal or legal assistant positions. Legal jobs for nonattorneys may be listed under other headings, such as research assistant, legal analyst, administrative aide, administrative officer, executive assistant, examiner, clerk, and investigator. As we have seen, this is also true for employment in the federal government.

## 3. LEGAL SERVICE/LEGAL AID OFFICES (CIVIL LAW)

Community or neighborhood legal service offices and legal aid offices exist throughout the country. They obtain most of their funds from the government, often in the form of yearly grants to provide legal services to **indigents**—those without funds to hire an attorney. The clients do not pay fees. These offices make extensive use of paralegals with titles such as:

Administrative Hearing
    Representative
Bankruptcy Law Specialist

Information and Referral Specialist
Legal Assistant
Legislative Advocate

**Indigent** A person who is without funds to hire legal counsel, who is impoverished.

| Case Advocate | Paralegal |
| Community Law Specialist | Paralegal Coordinator |
| Disability Law Specialist | Paralegal Supervisor |
| Domestic Relations Specialist | Public Benefits Paralegal |
| Food Stamp Specialist | Social Security Specialist |
| Housing/Tenant Law Specialist | Tribal Court Representative |
| Immigration Paralegal | Veterans Law Advocate |

As we will see in chapter 4 many administrative agencies permit nonattorneys to represent citizens at hearings before those agencies. Legal service and legal aid offices take advantage of this authorization. Some of their paralegals undertake extensive agency representation. The distinction between attorneys and paralegals in such offices is less pronounced than in many other settings. Unfortunately, however, these paralegals are among the lowest paid because of the limited resources of the offices where they work.

Here are some examples of the duties of a public benefits paralegal in a legal service office:

- Interview clients for eligibility for free legal services.
- Investigate claims of discrimination
- Represent clients at SSI (supplemental security income) hearings
- Help prepare information leaflets on poverty law topics for distribution in the community
- Assist attorneys to prepare for an appeal of denial of benefits
- Assist the office to collect data needed for quarterly reports to funding source

**Pro bono** Performed for the public good without fee or compensation (*pro bono publico*).

Legal service or legal aid offices are not the only way the government helps provide legal services to indigents. Many cities and counties have "volunteer lawyer" organizations that recruit private attorneys to provide **pro bono** (i.e., free) legal services. These organizations often employ paralegals.

In addition, there are several other settings in which paralegals have important roles:

- Paralegals may work in special institutions such as mental health hospitals or prisons.
- Paralegals who are senior citizens may provide legal services to senior citizens at nursing homes, neighborhood centers, and similar locations.

For further information on the kind of work performed by law offices that serve the poor and on paralegal job opportunities within them, check:
- Legal Services Corporation (LSC)
  *www.lsc.gov.*
  (LSC is a federal agency that funds many legal services programs)
- Examples of Legal Services Programs
  *www.ptla.org/links.htm*
  *www.legal-aid.org*
  *www.centralcallegal.org*
  *www.law.emory.edu/PI/ALAS*
  *www.neighborhoodlaw.org*
- Important Organizations
  *www.povertylaw.org/index.htm*
  *www.nlada.org*
- Job Opportunities for Attorneys and Nonattorneys
  *www.nlada.org/jobop.htm*
  *www.equaljustice.org*
- Pro Bono Programs in the Country
  *www.abanet.org/legalservices/probono/directory.html*

## 4. LAW DEPARTMENTS OF CORPORATIONS, BANKS, INSURANCE COMPANIES, AND OTHER BUSINESSES

Not every corporation or business in the country uses a law firm to handle all of its legal problems. Many have their own in-house law department under the direction of an attorney who is often called the **general counsel** or the corporate counsel. The attorneys in this department have only one client—the corporation or business itself. Fees are not involved; the department is funded from the corporate treasury. Examples of businesses and other institutions that often have law departments include manufacturers, retailers, transportation companies, publishers, general insurance companies, real estate and title insurance companies, estate and trust departments of large banks, hospitals, universities, etc. In increasing numbers, paralegals are being hired in these settings. The average corporate law department employs 5 paralegals and 17 staff attorneys. Paralegal salaries are relatively high because the employer (like the large private law office) can often afford to pay good wages.

For information about corporate law departments, check:

- American Corporate Counsel Association *www.acca.com*
- Federation of Defense and Corporate Counsel *www.thefederation.org*
- American Bar Association Business Law Section *www.abanet.org/buslaw/home.html*

Paralegals who work for law departments are often members of national and local paralegal associations. There are, however several specialty associations devoted to the interests of in-house paralegals:

- Metroplex Association of Corporate Paralegals *www.macp.net*
- SFPA, Corporate Practice Section *www.sfpa.com/a-ps.htm*

### 5. SPECIAL INTEREST GROUPS OR ASSOCIATIONS

Many **special interest groups** exist in our society: unions, business associations, environmental protection groups, taxpayer associations, consumer protection groups, trade associations, citizen action groups, etc. Examples of such groups include:

- American Bankers Association *www.aba.com/default.htm*
- National Foundation for Credit Counseling *www.nfcc.org*
- National Association of Home Builders *www.nahb.com*
- National Organization for Women *www.now.org*
- PFLAG: Parents, Families, and Friends of Lesbians and Gays *www.pflag.org*

Larger groups may have their own offices, libraries, and legal staff, including paralegals. The legal work often involves monitoring legislation, lobbying, preparing studies, etc. Direct legal services to individual members of the groups are usually not provided. The legal work relates to the needs (or a cause) of the organization as a whole. Occasionally, however, the legal staff will litigate test cases of individual members that have a broad impact on the organization's membership.

A different concept in the use of attorneys and paralegals by such groups is **group legal services.** Members of unions or groups of college students, for example, pay a monthly fee to the organization for which they are entitled to designated legal services, such as preparation of a will or **uncontested** divorce representation. The members pay *before* the legal problems arise. Group legal service systems are a form of legal insurance that operates in a manner similar to health insurance. Designated services are provided *if* the need for them arises. The group legal service office will usually employ paralegals. Here are some sources of information about group legal services:

- American Bar Association Group and Prepaid Legal Services
  *www.abanet.org/legalservices/prepaid/home.html*
- American Prepaid Legal Services Institute *www.aplsi.org*
- Hyatt Legal Plans *www.legalplans.com*

### 6. CRIMINAL LAW OFFICES

Criminal cases are brought by government attorneys called prosecutors, district attorneys, or attorneys general. Defendants are represented by private attorneys if they can afford the fees. If they are indigent, they might be represented by **public defenders,** who are attorneys working full-time in a special office funded by the government to represent the poor in criminal cases. Public defenders are usually government employees. Another option is the use of **assigned counsel,** who are private attorneys who work on individual

**general counsel** The chief attorney in a corporate law department; also called corporate counsel.

**special interest group** An organization that serves a particular group or cause.

**group legal services** A form of legal insurance in which members of a group pay a set amount on a regular basis, for which they receive designated legal services.

**uncontested** Unchallenged; without opposition.

**public defender** A government attorney who represents indigent people charged with crime.

**assigned counsel** A court-appointed attorney who will represent an indigent person.

cases by court appointment. The use of paralegals in the practice of criminal law is increasing, particularly due to the encouragement of organizations such as the National District Attorneys Association and the National Legal Aid & Defender Association. Sources of information on work in criminal justice include:

- National Legal Aid & Defender Association (NLADA) *www.nlada.org*
- National District Attorneys Association *www.ndaa.org*
- National Association of Attorneys General *www.naag.org*
- National Association of Criminal Defense Lawyers *www.criminaljustice.org*
- Criminal Defense Attorney Directory *www.criminal-attorneys-us.com*
- American Bar Association Criminal Justice Section *www.abanet.org/crimjust/home.html*
- Web Cites for Federal Defenders *www.rashkind.com*
- Prosecution Links *www.co.eaton.mi.us/ecpa/ProsList.htm*
- National Criminal Justice Reference Service *www.ncjrs.org* (click "search" and type "paralegal")

## 7. FREELANCE PARALEGALS

**freelance paralegal** (1) A self-employed paralegal who works as an independent contractor for one or more attorneys. (2) A self-employed paralegal who sells law-related services directly to the public.

As we learned in chapter 1, most **freelance paralegals** are self-employed independent contractors who sell their services to attorneys. They are also called *independent paralegals* and *contract paralegals*. They perform their services in their own office or in the offices of the attorneys who hire them for special projects. Often they advertise in publications read by attorneys, such as legal newspapers and bar association journals. Such an ad might look something like this:

> Improve the quality and
> ****cost-effectiveness****
> of your practice with the help of:
> Lawyer's Assistant, Inc.

In addition, these paralegals will usually have a flyer or brochure that describes their services. Here is an excerpt from such a flyer:

> Our staff consists of individuals with formal paralegal training and an average of five years of experience in such areas as estates and trusts, litigation, real estate, tax, and corporate law. Whether you require a real estate paralegal for one day or four litigation paralegals for one month, we can provide you with reliable qualified paralegals to meet your specific needs.

Many similar ads appear on the Internet e.g., (*www.paralegalserv.com*). To find them, type "paralegal services" or "independent paralegal" in any search engine such as Yahoo (*www.yahoo.com*) or Google (*www.google.com*). (For an example of a freelance paralegal service site on the Internet, see exhibit 2.2.) The attorneys in a law firm may be convinced of the value of paralegals but not have enough business to justify hiring a full-time paralegal employee. A freelance paralegal is an alternative.

For an overview on how to start a freelance business, see appendix J.

As we saw in chapter 1, there are also self-employed paralegals who sell their services directly to the public. They, too, are sometimes called freelance paralegals, although the terms *legal technician* and *independent paralegal* are more common. In California, however, individuals selling law-related services directly to the public are not allowed to call themselves paralegals or legal assistants. The legally accepted title for them is legal document assistant (LDA) or, if they work with evictions, unlawful detainer assistant (UDA). The titles *paralegal* and *legal assistant* in California (and in a few other states) are limited to those who work under attorney supervision. (See appendix G for the California law establishing these requirements.) Here are sources of information on this area of work:

- California Association of Legal Document Assistants *www.calda.org*
- Nolo *www.nolo.com* (click "search" and type "paralegal" in the search box)

| EXHIBIT 2.2 | Example of a Freelance Paralegal Service Site on the Internet |
|---|---|

**PARALEGAL ON ASSIGNMENT:** www.paralegalonassignment.com

- Home
- Services for Attorneys
- Notary Page
- Contact Us
- Biography
- Paralegal and Notary FAQs
- Legal Resources
- Legal Research and Forms
- Links and Articles
- Beneficial Websites
- TGIF !
- Help Find Florida's Missing Children
- National Federation of Paralegal Associations
- Bookstore

**Welcome to Paralegal On Assignment!**

We are a Florida freelance paralegal service providing attorneys with professional, affordable paralegal assistance on an as-needed contract basis. We also provide secretarial services and notary services.

**Attorneys:  Our Affordable Services Can Save You and Your Clients Money!**

Attorneys are frequently under pressure to provide quality professional services to their clients while minimizing the clients' costs. The use of an experienced contract paralegal, without the overhead expenses of an additional full-time employee, can bring substantial benefit to the client while providing the attorney a positive profit margin. We at Paralegal On Assignment have the experience and training necessary to provide the services you need at an affordable cost. We look forward to serving your paralegal needs.

NO BENEFITS TO PAY
NO OVERTIME
NO WORKSPACE DILEMMAS
NO PERSONNEL HASSLES

Just reliable quality work, custom tailored to your individual requirements. Our paralegals provide services to individual attorneys, corporate legal departments, and government entities. We will work as independent contractors with you and your staff to solve your critical needs.

**SERVICES OFFERED:**

Legal Transcription
Attend Initial Conference with Attorney and Client
File Organization
Database Input for Document Management
Document Imaging/OCR
Draft Correspondence and Pleadings
Interview Client and Others to Gather Background Information
Draft Discovery Requests and Responses
Investigate Factual Matters
Site Inspections and Photography
Prepare Reference Materials for Experts
Prepare Deposition Summaries
Prepare Medical Summaries and Chronologies
Conduct Legal Research and Internet Research
Locate and Interview Witnesses
Conduct Records Searches
Courthouse Searches, Document Retrieval
Prepare Trial Notebooks
Assist in Preparing Witnesses for Trial
Arrange for Blow-Ups and Visual Aids
Attend and Assist at Trial
Prepare Bankruptcy Documents - Best Case Solutions Software
Paralegal On Assignment also provides legal secretarial services and mobile notary services.

PARALEGAL ON ASSIGNMENT
Julie (Judy) Chandler, RP
115 N. Seminole Avenue
Inverness, FL 34450
jjchan@paralegalonassignment.com
352-860-1650

For the Florida  consumer, we also offer assistance in the preparation of Florida Supreme Court approved forms for divorce, modification of support, alimony, custody and /or visitation, stepparent adoption, paternity, grandparent visitation, name changes, and we prepare Chapter 7 bankruptcy documents.

*Disclaimer:* Paralegal On Assignment and staff are not attorneys and cannot give you advice regarding your legal situation. We cannot assist you in making a legal decision or represent you in a court of law. Nothing on this website is to be construed as the giving of legal advice.

We will be examining freelance paralegals, LDAs, and other independent contractors in greater detail in chapter 4.

## 8. SERVICE COMPANIES/CONSULTING FIRMS

Service companies and consulting firms sell special services to attorneys. Some individual freelance paralegals also do so, but usually on a less sophisticated level. Examples of services provided by established service companies and consulting firms include:

- Designing litigation graphics
- Selecting a computer system for a law office
- Designing and managing a computer-assisted document control system for a large case
- Helping a law firm establish a marketing strategy
- Designing a filing or financial system for the office
- Incorporating a new company in all 50 states
- Conducting a trademark search
- Digesting discovery documents
- Undertaking a UCC (Uniform Commercial Code) search and filing in all 50 states

To accomplish such tasks, these service companies and consulting firms recruit highly specialized staffs of management experts, accountants, economists, former administrators, etc. More and more paralegals are joining these staffs as employees; many of them are paralegals with prior law office experience, particularly computer experience.

Here are some examples of service companies and consulting firms on the Internet:

- Directed Decions (litigation consulting) *www.directeddecisions.com/index-html*
- Blum Shapiro (forensic accounting) *www.blumshapiro.com/litigation*
- Deposition Digests (digesting discovery documents) *www.depositiondigests.com*
- Law Marketing Portal (law firm marketing services) *www.LawMarketing.com*

A special category of consultant with medical training is the legal nurse consultant (LNC). This person is a nurse who provides a wide range of support services to attorneys in the medical aspects of medical malpractice, products liability, environment, and labor cases. For example, they have a large role in obtaining, summarizing, and interpreting medical records. Legal nurse consultants have formed their own association, the American Association of Legal Nurse Consultants (AALNC) *www.aalnc.org*. The AALNC considers LNCs to be a specialty practice of the nursing profession rather than a special category of paralegals. Not everyone, however, agrees with this position. A growing number of legal nurses consider themselves to be full-fledged paralegals.

## 9. RELATED FIELDS

Experienced paralegals have also been using their training and experience in a number of nonpractice legal fields. Many are becoming law librarians at firms. Paralegal schools often hire paralegals to teach courses and to work in administration. Law offices with large numbers of paralegals have hired paralegal administrators or supervisors to help recruit, train, and manage the paralegals. Some paralegals have become legal administrators or office managers with administrative responsibilities throughout the firm. It is clear that we have not seen the end of the development of new roles for paralegals within the law firm or in related areas of the law. At the end of the chapter, a more extensive list of such roles will be provided. (See exhibit 2.16).

---

### Assignment 2.1

Find want ads for any seven categories or subcategories of employment mentioned in exhibit 2.1. Cut each ad out and tape it on a sheet of paper. Beneath the ad, state where it was published, the date, and the page of the publication. You can use general circulation newspapers, legal newspapers, magazines, newsletters, the Internet, etc.

Section C

# PARALEGAL SPECIALTIES: A DICTIONARY OF FUNCTIONS

We now examine 45 areas of specialty work throughout the nine categories of paralegal employment just discussed. Paralegals often work in more than one of these specialties, and there is considerable overlap in the functions performed. The trend, however, is for paralegals to specialize. This follows the pattern of most attorneys.

For each specialty, you will find a listing of some of the major duties performed by paralegals. For most of the specialties, comments from paralegals or their supervisors about the paralegal's work in the specialty are included. For the six specialties where most paralegals work (corporate law, estate law, family law, litigation, real estate law, and tort law), you will also find excerpts from want ads to give you an idea of what employers are looking for when hiring for those specialties. For all of the specialties, you are given an Internet address where you will find more information about the kind of law involved in the specialty. For a general overview of paralegal responsibilities in many areas of law, see also:

- *www.paralegals.org/Development/responsibilities.html*
- *www.lectlaw.com/files/pap01.htm*
- *www.lawcost.com/paras.htm*
- *www.CAPAralegal.org/duties.html*

**Paralegal Specialties**

1. Administrative law
2. Admiralty law
3. Advertising law
4. Antitrust law
5. Banking law
6. Bankruptcy law
7. Civil rights law
8. Collections law
9. Communications law
10. Construction law
11. Contract law
12. Corporate law
13. Criminal law
14. Employee benefits law
15. Entertainment law
16. Environmental law
17. Estates, trusts, and probate law
18. Ethics and professional responsibility
19. Family law
20. Government contract law
21. Immigration law
22. Insurance law
23. Intellectual property law
24. International law
25. Judicial administration
26. Labor and employment law
27. Landlord and tenant law
28. Law librarianship
29. Law office administration
30. Legislation
31. Litigation (civil)
32. Military law
33. Municipal finance law
34. Oil and gas law
35. Parajudge
36. Pro bono work
37. Public sector
38. Real estate law
39. Social security law
40. Tax law
41. Tort law
42. Tribal law
43. Water law
44. Welfare law (public assistance)
45. Worker's compensation law
Note: Paralegal in the White House

---

***Assignment 2.2***

From the list above, pick a specialty that interests you, at least preliminarily.

**(a)** Explain why you might want to work in this area of the law.

**(b)** Find two Internet sites that provide explanations of any aspect of the substantive or procedural law in this area. (Start by checking the Internet sites presented in the text for that specialty under the heading "More on This Area of the Law on the Net.") What sites did you select? Quote at least two sentences from each site on any aspect of the law it covers.

(c) In appendix 2.A, at the end of the chapter, there are many Internet addresses of law firms. Find one firm that practices this specialty. (Click "areas of practice" or "services" on the site.) Quote at least two sentences from this firm's site on what it does in this specialty.

(d) Find a want ad for this area of the law. (Check your local newspaper, available legal newspapers, the Internet, etc.) Attach the ad to your report.

---

## 1. Administrative Law

I. Government Employment

Many paralegals work for specific administrative agencies. (See also Appendix 2.B for a list of paralegal functions in state agencies.) They might:

A. Handle questions and complaints from citizens.
B. Draft proposed regulations for the agency.
C. Perform legal research.
D. Provide litigation assistance in the agency and in court.
E. Represent the government at administrative hearings where authorized.
F. Manage the law office.
G. Train and supervise other nonattorney personnel.

II. Representation of Citizens

Some administrative agencies authorize nonattorneys to represent citizens at hearings and other agency proceedings. (See also *immigration law, pro bono work, public sector, social security law,* and *welfare law*.)

A. Interview client.
B. Conduct investigation.
C. Perform legal research.
D. Engage in informal advocacy at the agency.
E. Represent the client at agency hearing.
F. Draft documents for submission at hearing.
G. Monitor activities of the agency—for example, attend rulemaking hearings to take notes on matters relevant to particular clients.
H. Prepare witnesses, reports, and exhibits designed to influence the drafting of regulations at the agency.

● *Comment on Paralegal Work in This Area:*

We "have a great deal of autonomy and an opportunity to develop expertise in particular areas." We have our "own caseloads, interview clients and then represent those clients at administrative hearings." Georgia Ass'n of Legal Assistants, *Sallye Jenkins Sapp, Atlanta Legal Aid; Sharon Mahaffey Hill, Georgia Legal Services,* 10 ParaGraph 5.

When I got my first case at a hearing before the State Department of Mental health, I was "scared to death!" But the attorneys in the office were very supportive. "They advised me to make a good record, noting objections for the transcript, in case of future appeal. Making the right objections was scary." Milano, *New Responsibilities Being Given to Paralegals,* 8 Legal Assistant Today 27, 28.

● **More on This Area of the Law on the Net:**
- *findlaw.com/01topics/00administrative/index.html*
- *www.abanet.org/adminlaw/home.html*
- *www.law.cornell.edu/topics/administrative.html*
- *www.law.fsu.edu/library/admin*

## 2. Admiralty Law

This area of the law, also referred to as *maritime law,* covers accidents, injuries, and death connected with vessels on navigable waters. Special legislation exists in this area, such as the Jones Act. (See also *international law, litigation,* and *tort law*.)

I. Investigation
A. Obtain the facts of the event involved.
B. Arrange to board the vessel to photograph the scene of the accident.
C. Collect facts relevant to the seaworthiness of the vessel.
D. Take statements from witnesses.

II. Legal Research
A. Research liability under the applicable statutes.
B. Research special procedures to obtain compensation.

III. Subrogation
A. Handle small cargo subrogation files
B. Prepare status reports for clients.

IV. Litigation
A. Draft complaints and other pleadings.
B. Respond to discovery requests.
C. Monitor all maritime files needed to keep track of discovery deadlines.
D. Coordinate projects by expert witnesses.
E. Provide general trial assistance.

● *Comment on Paralegal Work in This Area:*

Jimmie Muvern, CLA (Certified Legal Assistant), works for a sole practitioner in Baton Rouge, Louisiana, who specializes in maritime litigation: "If there is a doubt regarding the plaintiff's status as a Jones Act seaman, this issue is generally raised by a motion for summary judgment filed well in advance of trial, and it is good practice for the legal assistant who may be gathering facts regarding the client's accident to also gather facts from the client and from other sources which might assist the attorney in opposing summary judgment on the issue of the client's status as a Jones Act seaman." J. deGravelles & J. Muvern, *Who Is a Jones Act Seaman?* 12 Facts & Findings 34 (NALA).

- **More on This Area of the Law on the Net:**
  - *www.admiraltylawguide.com/index.html*
  - *findlaw.com/01topics/39admiralty*
  - *www.law.cornell.edu/topics/admiralty.html*

### 3. Advertising Law

(See also *administrative law* and *intellectual property law*.)

I.  Compliance Work
A.  *Advertising*: Review advertising of company products to identify claims made in the advertising about the product. Collect data needed to support the accuracy of the claims pursuant to regulations of the Federal Trade Commission, state laws, and company guidelines.
B.  *Labels*: Review labels of company products to ensure compliance with the regulations on deception of the Federal Trade Commission. Monitor compliance with the Food & Drug Administration and company policy on:
    1. Product identity,
    2. Weight statement,
    3. Ingredient list,
    4. Name and address of manufacturer/distributor, and
    5. Nutrition information.
C.  *Product promotions*: Review promotions for company products (coupons, sweepstakes, bonus packs, etc.) to ensure compliance with Federal Trade Commission guidelines, state laws, and company policy.

II.  Inquiries and Complaints
A.  Keep up to date on government regulations on advertising.
B.  Help company attorney respond to inquiries and complaints from the public, a competitor, the Federal Trade Commission, the Food & Drug Administration, the state's attorney general, etc.

- *Comment on Paralegal Work in This Area*
  "On the surface, my job certainly does not fit the 'traditional' paralegal role. [Years ago, if] a fortune teller had ever read my coffee grounds, I might have learned that my paralegal career would include being part of the production of commercials and labels for household products I had grown up with." "My employer, the Procter & Gamble Company, is one of the largest consumer product companies in the United States." Its "Legal Division consists of forty attorneys and nine paralegals. Advertising law is challenging. It requires ingenuity, fast thinking and mastery of tight deadlines." Kothman, *Advertising Paralegal Finds Own Label*, National Paralegal Reporter 12 (NFPA).

- **More on This Area of the Law on the Net:**
  - *www.hg.org/advert.html*
  - *www.lawpublish.com*

### 4. Antitrust Law

(See also *administrative law, corporate law, criminal law,* and *litigation*.)

I.  Investigation/Analysis
A.  Accumulate statistical and other technical data on a company or industry involved in litigation. Check Securities & Exchange Commission (SEC) filings, annual reports, advertising brochures, etc.
B.  Prepare reports on economic data.
C.  Obtain data from government bodies.
D.  Find and interview potential witnesses.

II.  Administrative Agency
A.  Monitor the regulations and decisions of the Federal Trade Commission.
B.  Prepare drafts of answers to requests for information from the Federal Trade Commission.

III.  Litigation
A.  Assist in drafting pleadings.
B.  Request company witness files and other documents in preparation for deposition.
C.  Schedule depositions.
D.  Draft interrogatories.
E.  Prepare special exhibits.
F.  Organize, index, and digest voluminous records and lengthy documents.
G.  Prepare trial notebook.
H.  Attend trial and take notes on testimony of witnesses.
I.  Cite check briefs of attorneys.
J.  Provide general trial assistance.

- *Comment on Paralegal Work in This Area:*
  When Mitchell became a permanent employee at the firm, "he was given three days' worth of files to read in order to familiarize himself with the [antitrust] case. At this point in the case, the firm had already gone through discovery of 27,000 documents. Mitchell analyzed and summarized documents with the other ten paralegals hired to work on the case. With a major case such as this one, paralegals did not have a regular nine to five work day. Mitchell frequently worked seventy hours a week (for which he was paid overtime). In January, Mitchell and his team were sent across the country to take depositions for the case. His air transportation, accommodations, and meals were all 'first class,' but this was not a vacation; he worked around the clock." R. Berkey, *New Career Opportunities in the Legal Profession* 47 (Arco).

- **More on This Area of the Law on the Net:**
  - *www.findlaw.com/01topics/01antitrust*
  - *www.usdoj.gov/atr/index.html*
  - *www.jurist.law.pitt.edu/cour_pgs.htm*

### 5. Banking Law

Paralegals employed by banks often work in the bank trust department. They also work in the bank's legal department, where they become involved with litigation, real estate, bankruptcy, consumer affairs, and securities law. In addition to banks, paralegals work for savings and loan institutions and other commercial lenders. Finally, some paralegals are employed in law firms that specialize in banking law. The following overview of duties is limited to the paralegal working for the legal department of a bank. (See also *administrative law, corporate law, estates law*, and *municipal finance law*.)

I. Claims
Assist legal staff in assessing bank liability for various claims, such as negligence and collection abuse.

II. Compliance Analysis
Determine whether the bank is complying with the regulations and statutes that regulate the banking industry.

III. Monitoring
Keep track of the rulemaking and other activities of the various banking regulatory agencies and the bill-drafting activities of the legislative committees with jurisdiction over banks.

IV. Litigation
Assist attorneys litigating claims.

V. Miscellaneous
A. Draft and/or review loan applications and accompanying credit documents.
B. Perform document analysis on:
   1. Financial statements,
   2. Mortgages,
   3. Assignments, and
   4. Security agreements.
C. Conduct UCC (Uniform Commercial Code) searches.
D. Assemble closing documents.
E. Arrange for and attend loan closings.
F. Notarize documents.
G. Monitor recordation.
H. Act as liaison among the supervising attorney at the bank, the loan officer, and the customer.
I. Perform routine legal research and analysis for the Compliance Department.

● *Comment on Paralegal Work in This Area:*
   Ruth Sendecki is "the first legal assistant" at Merchants National Bank, one of the Midwest's largest bank holding companies. Most paralegals employed at banks today work in the trust department; Ruth, however, works with "general banking" at Merchants. Before this job, she worked at a bank, but not in a legal capacity. "You don't have to limit yourself to a law firm. You can combine being a legal assistant with other interests." Her "primary responsibility is in the commercial loan department. . . . She also serves the mortgage loan, correspondent banking and the international banking departments." According to her supervisor at the bank, "She is readily accessible for the

benefit of the attorney, the loan officer and the customer to facilitate completion of the arrangements for both sides." Furthermore, she "is expanding her knowledge base, and other departments are drawing on her knowledge." Kane, *A Banker with the $oul of a Legal Assistant*, 5 Legal Assistant Today 65.

● **More on This Area of the Law on the Net:**
   ■ *www.law.cornell.edu/topics/banking.html*
   ■ *guide.lp.findlaw.com/01topics/02banking/index.html*
   ■ *www.occ.treas.gov*
   ■ *www.fdic.gov/index.html*

**6. Bankruptcy Law**

Paralegals in this area of law may be employed by a law firm that represents the debtor (e.g., an individual, a business); a creditor (e.g., a bank-mortgagee); or the trustee in bankruptcy. (A trustee in bankruptcy does not have to be a lawyer. Some paralegals with bankruptcy experience have in fact become trustees.) A few paralegals work directly for a bankruptcy judge as a clerk or deputy in Bankruptcy Court. (Someone who provides bankruptcy assistance as an independent contractor, rather than as an employee of an attorney, is called a *bankruptcy petition preparer*, a position we will examine in chapter 4.) The following overview assumes the paralegal works for a firm that represents the debtor. (See also *banking law, collections law, contract law*, and *litigation*.)

I. Interviewing/Data Collection
A. Help client fill out an extensive questionnaire on assets and liabilities. May visit client's place of business to determine the kinds of records kept there.
B. Help client assemble documents:
   1. Loan agreements,
   2. Deeds of trust,
   3. Security agreements,
   4. Creditor lists,
   5. Payables lists,
   6. Employment contracts,
   7. Financial statements,
   8. Leases, etc.

II. Investigation
A. Confirm amounts of indebtedness.
B. Identify secured and unsecured claims of creditors.
C. Check UCC (Uniform Commercial Code) filings at the secretary of state's office and at the county clerk's office.
D. Check real property records in the clerk's office in the county where the property is located.
E. Verify taxes owed; identify tax liens.
F. Identify exempt property.

III. Asset Control
A. Open bankruptcy file.
B. Prepare inventories of assets and liabilities.
C. Arrange for valuation of assets.

IV. Creditor Contact

A. Answer inquiries of creditors on the status of the case

B. Request documentation from creditors on claims

V. Drafting

A. Original bankruptcy petition.

B. Schedule of liabilities.

C. Statement of affairs.

D. Status reports.

E. Final account.

VI. Coordination

A. Serve as liaison with trustee in bankruptcy.

B. Coordinate meeting of creditors.

C. Prepare calendar of filing and other deadlines.

● ***Comment on Paralegal Work in This Area***

"As a legal assistant, you can play a major role in the representation of a Chapter 11 debtor. From prefiling activities through confirmation of the plan of reorganization, there are numerous duties which you can perform to assist in the successful reorganization of the debtor." Morzak, *Organizing Reorganization*, 5 Legal Assistant Today 33.

"Bankruptcy work is unusual in a number of ways—extremely short statutes of limitation, for example.... The field is one in which there's lots of opportunity for paralegals. The paralegal does everything except sign the papers. . . . Most attorneys do not like bankruptcy, but if you do all the legwork for them, you can make a lot of money for them." Johnson, *The Role of the Paralegal/Legal Assistant in Bankruptcy and Foreclosure*, AALA News 7 (Alaska Ass'n of Legal Assistants).

● **More on This Area of the Law on the Net:**
  ■ *www.abiworld.org*
  ■ *guide.lp.findlaw.com/01topics/03bankruptcy/index.html*
  ■ *www.agin.com/lawfind*

## 7. Civil Rights Law

(See also *labor and employment law, pro bono work*, and *public sector*.)

I. Government Paralegal

A. Help identify and resolve discrimination complaints (based on sex, race, age, disability, etc.) made by government employees against the government.

B. Help government attorneys litigate discrimination complaints (based on sex, race, age, disability, etc.) brought by citizens against the government, against other citizens, or against companies.

II. Representation of Citizens

Assist law firms representing citizens in their discrimination complaints filed against the government, other citizens, or companies:

A. In court.

B. In special agencies created to hear discrimination cases, such as the Equal Employment Opportunity Commission or the Human Rights Commission.

● ***Comment on Paralegal Work in This Area:***

"One aspect that Matthews likes is that each case is a different story, a different set of facts. 'There is a lot of interaction with people in the courts and with the public. We do a great deal of civil rights litigation, everything from excessive police force to wrongful termination. Sometimes there are as many as 60 witnesses. The lawyers depend on me to separate the witnesses out and advise them which ones would do best in the courtroom. A lot of time the lawyer does not know the witness and has not seen the witness until the person is in the courtroom testifying.' For one case, Matthews reviewed more than 1,000 slides taken in a nightclub, looking for examples of unusual or rowdy behavior. The slides include everything from male strippers to people flashing. Autopsy and horrible injury photographs are also part of the job." *Broadening into the Paralegal Field*, 39 The Docket 7 (NALS).

● **More on This Area of the Law on the Net:**
  ■ *www.law.cornell.edu/topics/civil_rights.html*
  ■ *www.usdoj.gov/crt/crt-home.html*
  ■ *guide.lp.findlaw.com/01topics/36civil/index.html*
  ■ *www.aclu.org*

## 8. Collections Law[4]

(See also *banking law, bankruptcy law, contract law*, and *litigation*.)

I. Acceptance of Claims

A. Open file.

B. Prepare index of parties.

C. Prepare inventory of debts of debtor.

II. Investigation

A. Conduct asset check.

B. Verify address.

C. Verify filings at secretary of state's office and county clerk's office (e.g., UCC filings).

D. Contact credit bureau.

E. Verify information in probate court, registry of deeds, etc.

III. Litigation Assistant (Civil Court, Small Claims Court, etc.)

A. Draft pleadings.

B. Arrange for witnesses.

C. File documents in court.

D. Assist in settlement/negotiation of claim.

E. Assist in enforcement work, such as:
  1. Wage attachment (prejudgment attachment),
  2. Supplementary process,
  3. Execution, and
  4. Seizure of personal property.

- ***Comment on Paralegal Work in This Area:***

"O.K.—So, [collections work] is not the nicest job in the world, but somebody has to do it, right? If the attorney you work for does not want to do it, there are plenty more in town who will. For a paralegal working in this area, there is always something new to learn. . . . It is sometimes difficult to see the results of your labor right away in this kind of work, as very few files are paid in full and closed in a short period of time. It is disheartening to go through many steps and possibly spend a great deal of time just trying to get someone served or to locate someone, and then end up with nothing. I will admit that collections can be very frustrating, but boring they are not!" Wexel, *Collections: Persistence Pay$ Off*, The Paraview (Metrolina Paralegal Ass'n).

"I currently have responsibility for some 400 collection cases. My days are spent on the phone talking to debtors, drafting the necessary pleadings, executing forms, and hopefully depositing the money collected. The exciting part of collection is executing on a judgment. We were successful in garnishing an insurance company's account for some $80,000 when they refused to pay a judgment that had been taken against them. We have also gone with the Sheriff to a beer distributorship two days before St. Patrick's Day to change the locks on the building housing gallons and gallons of green beer. The debtor suddenly found a large sum of money to pay us so that we would release the beer in time for St. Patrick's Day." R. Swoagerm, *Collections Paralegal*, The Citator 9 (Legal Assistants of Central Ohio).

- **More on This Area of the Law on the Net:**
  - *www.nacm.org*
  - *www.consumerlaw.org*

## 9. Communications Law

(See also *administrative law* and *entertainment law*.)

I. Government Paralegal

Assist attorneys at the Federal Communications Commission (FCC) in regulating the communications industry—for example, help with rulemaking, license applications, and hearings.

II. Representation of Citizens or Companies
A. Draft application for licenses.
B. Prepare compliance reports.
C. Prepare exemption applications.
D. Prepare statistical analyses.
E. Monitor activities of the FCC.
F. Assist in litigation:
  1. Within the FCC and
  2. In court.

- ***Comment on Paralegal Work in This Area:***

The current specialty of Carol Woods is the regulation of television and radio. "I am able to do work that is important and substantive, and am able to work independently. I have an awful lot of contact with clients, with paralegals at the client's office, and with government agencies. One of the liabilities of private practice for both attorneys and paralegals is that there is so much repetition and you can get bored. A lot of times as a paralegal you can't call the shots or know everything that goes into the planning of a project. However, when you can participate in all facets of a project, it's great!" A. Fins, *Opportunities in Paralegal Careers* 84 (Nat'l Textbook Co.).

- **More on This Area of the Law on the Net:**
  - *www.fcc.gov*
  - *guide.lp.findlaw.com/01topics/05communications/index.html*
  - *www.law.cornell.edu/topics/communications.html*

## 10. Construction Law

(See also *contract law, litigation,* and *tort law.*)

I. Claims Assistance
A. Work with engineering consultants in the preparation of claims.

II. Data Collection
A. Daily manpower hours.
B. Amount of concrete poured.
C. Change orders.

III. Document Preparation
A. Prepare graphs.
B. Prepare special studies—for example, compare planned with actual progress on construction project.
C. Prepare documents for negotiation/settlement.
D. Help draft arbitration claim forms.

IV. Assist in Litigation

- ***Comment on Paralegal Work in This Area***

"Because of the complex factual issues that arise with construction disputes, legal assistants are critical in identifying, organizing, preparing, and analyzing the extensive relevant factual information. In many cases, whether a party wins or loses depends on how effectively facts are developed from documents, depositions, interviews, and site inspections. Thus, a successful construction litigation team will generally include a legal assistant skilled in organization and management of complex and voluminous facts. . . . Construction litigation also provides legal assistants with a very distinctive area for expertise and specialization." M. Gowen, *A Guide for Legal Assistants* 229 (Practicing Law Institute).

- **More on This Area of the Law on the Net:**
  - *guide.lp.findlaw.com/01topics/40construction/index.html*
  - *www.constructionlaw.com*
  - *www.constructionweblinks.com*

## 11. Contract Law

The law of contracts is involved in a number of different paralegal specialties. (See *advertising law, antitrust law, banking law, bankruptcy law, collections law, construction law, corporate law, employee benefits law, entertainment law, family law, government contract law, insurance law, intellectual property law, international law, labor and employment law, landlord and tenant law, municipal finance law, oil and gas law, real estate law,* and *tax law.*)

I. Contract Review
A. Review contracts to determine compliance with terms.
B. Investigate facts involving alleged breach of contract.
C. Do legal research on the law of contracts in a particular specialty.

II. Litigation Assistance

III. Preparation of Contract Forms
A. Separation agreements.
B. Employment contracts.
C. Contracts for sale, etc.

● ***Comment on Paralegal Work in This Area:***

"The . . . paralegal also assists two attorneys in drafting, reviewing, researching, revising and finalizing a variety of contracts, including Entertainment, Participant and Operational Agreements. Much of the . . . paralegal's time is spent studying existing contracts looking for provisions that may answer any inquiries or disputes. With hundreds of agreements presently active, researching, reviewing, amending, terminating, revising and executing contracts is an everyday activity for [the] . . . Legal Department." Miquel, *Walt Disney World Company's Legal Assistants: Their Role in the Show*, 16 Facts and Findings 29.

"Initially, my primary job was to review contracts, and act as Plan Administrator for the 401(k). I was also involved in the negotiation and development of a distributor agreement to market SPSS software to the Soviet Union. Most contract amendments were to software license agreements. The pace picked up when I was promoted to Manager of Human Services, while retaining all of my previous responsibilities." Illinois Paralegal Ass'n, *Spotlight on . . . Laurel Bauer*, 20 Outlook 21.

● **More on This Area of the Law on the Net:**
  ■ *www.law.cornell.edu/topics/contracts.html*
  ■ *www.law.cornell.edu/topics/commercial.html*
  ■ *guide.lp.findlaw.com/01topics/07contracts/index.html*
  ■ *guide.lp.findlaw.com/01topics/04commercial/index.html*

## 12. Corporate Law

Paralegals involved in corporate law mainly work in one of two settings: law firms that represent corporations and legal departments of corporations. (See also *banking law, employee benefits law, insurance law, labor and employment law, real estate law,* and *tax law.*)

I. Incorporation and General Corporate Work
A. Preincorporation.
  1. Check availability of proposed corporate name and, if available, reserve it.
  2. Draft preincorporation subscriptions and consent forms for initial board of directors where required by statute.
  3. Record Articles of Incorporation.
  4. Order corporate supplies.
B. Incorporation.
  1. Draft and file articles of incorporation with appropriate state agency for:
    a. Subchapter S corporation,
    b. Close corporation, or
    c. Nonprofit corporation.
  2. Draft minutes of initial meetings of incorporators and directors.
  3. Draft corporate bylaws.
  4. Obtain corporate seal, minutes book, and stock certificate book.
  5. Prepare necessary documents to open a corporate bank account.
C. Directors meetings.
  1. Prepare and send out waivers and notices of meetings.
  2. Draft minutes of directors meetings.
  3. Draft resolutions to be considered by directors:
    a. Sale of stock,
    b. Increase in capitalization,
    c. Stock split,
    d. Stock option,
    e. Pension plan,
    f. Dividend distribution, or
    g. Election of officers.
D. Shareholders meetings (annual and special)
  1. Draft sections of annual report relating to business activity, officers, and directors of company.
  2. Draft notice of meeting, proxy materials, and ballots.
  3. Prepare agenda and script of meeting.
  4. Draft oath, report of judge of elections, and other compliance documents when required.
  5. Maintain corporate minutes books and resolutions.
E. Draft and prepare general documents:
  1. Shareholder agreement,
  2. Employment contract,
  3. Employee benefit plan,
  4. Stock option plan,
  5. Trust agreement,
  6. Tax return, and
  7. Closing papers on corporate acquisition.

8. See also drafting tasks listed above for directors and shareholders meetings.

## II. Public Sale of Securities

A. Compile information concerning officers and directors for use in Registration Statement.
B. Assist in research of blue sky requirements.
C. Closing:
   1. Prepare agenda,
   2. Obtain certificates from state agencies with respect to good standing of company and certified corporate documents, and
   3. Prepare index and organize closing binders.

## III. Research

A. Monitor pending legislation that may affect office clients.
B. Extract designated information from corporate records and documents.
C. Assemble financial data from records on file at SEC and state securities regulatory agencies.
D. Undertake short- and long-term statistical and financial research on companies.
E. Perform legal research.

## IV. General Assistance

A. Maintain tickler system (specifying, for example, dates of next corporate meeting, shareholder meeting, upcoming trial, appellate court appearance).
B. Monitor the daily law journal or legal newspaper in order to identify relevant cases on calendars of courts, current court decisions, articles, etc., and forward such data in the journal or newspaper to appropriate office attorneys.
C. Act as file managers for certain clients: index, digest, and monitor documents in the file, prepare case profiles, etc.
D. Maintain corporate forms file.

## V. Miscellaneous

A. Prepare documents for qualification to do business in foreign jurisdictions.
B. Prepare filings with regulatory agencies.
C. Provide assistance in processing patent, copyright, and trademark applications.
D. Coordinate escrow transactions.
E. Work on certificates of occupancy.
F. Prepare documents needed to amend bylaws or Articles of Incorporation.
G. Prepare interrogatories.
H. Digest deposition testimony.
I. Perform cite checks.

● ***Comment on Paralegal Work in This Area:***

"When the majority of people describe a legal assistant or a paralegal, they often think of courtroom battles, million dollar lawsuits and mountains of depositions. For those of us in the corporate area, these sights are replaced with board room battles, million dollar mergers and mountains of prospectuses. Some of us have NEVER seen the inside of a courtroom or have never touched a pleading. I guess it can be said that 'we don't do windows, we don't type, and we don't do litigation.' A corporate paralegal is never without a multitude of projects that offer excitement or anxiety. This isn't to say, however, that the corporate field is without its fair share of boredom. . . . The future is only limited by your imagination. Not every paralegal wants the drama of a landmark case. Some of us are quite content seeing a client's company written up in the *Wall Street Journal* for the first time!" D. Zupanovich, *The Forming of a Corporate Paralegal*, 2 California Paralegal 4.

"The company I work for is a major worldwide producer of chemicals. . . . I recently had to obtain some technical information about the computer system at a hotel in a foreign country in order to set up documents on a diskette that would be compatible with the computer system in that country before one of the attorneys went there for contract negotiations." "One of the most thrilling experiences I have had since working for the company was that of working on the closing of a leveraged buyout of a portion of our business in Delaware. To experience first-hand the intensity of the negotiating table, the numerous last-minute changes to documents, the multitudinous shuffle of papers, and the late, grueling hours was both exhausting and exhilarating." Grove, *Scenes from a Corporate Law Department*, The Paraview 2 (Metrolina Paralegal Ass'n).

"Even 'dream jobs' have their moments of chaos. After only two months on the job [at Nestle Foods Corporation] Cheryl had to prepare for a Federal Trade Commission Second Request for Production of Documents relating to an acquisition. She suddenly was thrown into the job of obtaining and organizing over 6,000 documents from around the world, creating a document database and managing up to 10 temporary paralegals at a time. Of course, this preparation included weekends and evenings for a six-week period. Cheryl calls December the 'lost month.' " Scior, *Paralegal Profile: Corporate Paralegal*, Post Script 14 (Manhattan Paralegal Ass'n).

● ***Quotes from Want Ads:***

Law firm seeks paralegal for corporate work: "Ideal candidate is a self-starter with good communications skills and is willing to work overtime." "Ability to work independently is a must." Paralegal needed to assist corporate secretary: "Analytical, professional attitude essential. Knowledge of state and/or federal regulatory agencies required." "Ability to work under pressure." "All candidates must possess excellent writing and drafting skills." "Ideal candidate is a self-starter with good communication/research skills and is willing to work overtime." "Candidates having less than three years experience in general corporate legal assistance need not apply." Position requires "word processing experience and ability to manage multiple projects." Position requires "intelligent, highly motivated individual who can work with little supervision." "Great opportunity to learn all aspects of corporate business transactions." Position requires "career-minded paralegal with excellent organizational and communications skills, keen analytical ability and meticulous attention to detail." Position requires "an experienced paralegal with a strong blue-sky background, particularly in public and private real estate syndication." Applicant must have "excellent academic credentials, be analytical, objective, and dedicated to performing thorough quality work and to displaying a professional attitude to do whatever it takes to get the job done and meet deadlines."

- **More on This Area of the Law on the Net:**
  - *www.law.cornell.edu/topics/corporations.html*
  - *www.sec.gov*
  - *www.acca.com*
  - *guide.lp.findlaw.com/01topics/08corp/index.html*
  - *guide.lp.finlaw.com/01topics/34securities/index.html*

### 13. Criminal Law[5]

(See also *litigation* and *military law*.)

I. Paralegal Working for Criminal/Civil Division Prosecutor
A. Log incoming cases.
B. Help office screen out cases that are inappropriate for arrest, cases that are eligible for diversion, etc.
C. Act as liaison with police department and other law enforcement agencies.
D. Prepare statistical caseload reports.
E. Interview citizens who are seeking the prosecution of alleged wrongdoers; prepare case files.
F. Help the Consumer Fraud Department resolve minor consumer complaints—for instance, contact the business involved to determine whether a settlement of the case is possible without prosecution.
G. Conduct field investigations as assigned.
H. Prepare documents for URESA (Uniform Reciprocal Enforcement of Support Act cases).
I. Monitor status of URESA cases.
J. Help office maintain its case calendar.
K. Act as liaison among the prosecutor, the victim, and witnesses while the case is being prepared for trial and during the trial.
L. Act as general litigation assistant during the trial and the appeal.
II. Paralegal Working for Defense Attorney
A. Interview defendants to determine eligibility for free legal defense (if the paralegal works for a public defender).

B. Conduct comprehensive interview of defendant on matters relevant to the criminal charge(s).
C. Help the defendant gather information relevant to the determination of bail.
D. Help the defendant gather information relevant to eligibility for diversion programs.
E. Conduct field investigations; interview witnesses.
F. Help obtain discovery, particularly through police reports and search warrants.
G. Act as general litigation assistant during the trial and the appeal.

- *Comment on Paralegal Work in This Area:*

"Ivy speaks with an obvious love for her current job in the State Attorney's office. In fact, she said she would not want to do anything else! She also said there is no such thing as a typical day in her office, which is one of the many aspects of her job she enjoys. She not only helps interview witnesses and prepare them for trial, but she often must locate a witness, requiring some detective work! Ivy assisted in a case involving an elderly woman who was victimized after the death of her husband. The woman was especially vulnerable because of her illiteracy. Through the help of the State Attorney's office, the woman was able to recover her money and get assistance with housing and learning to read. Ivy continues to keep in touch with the woman and feels the experience to be very rewarding." Frazier, *Spotlight on Ivy Hart-Daniel*, JLA News 2 (Jacksonville Legal Assistants, Inc.).

"Kitty Polito says she and other lawyers at McClure, McClure & Kammen use the firm's sole paralegal not only to do investigations but 'to pick cases apart piece by piece.' Polito credits legal assistant Juliann Klapp with 'cracking the case' of a client who was accused by a co-defendant of hitting the victim on the back of the head. At trial, the pathologist testified that the victim had been hit from left to right. Klapp passed a note to the attorneys pointing out that such a motion would have been a back-handed swing for their right-handed client. Thus it was more likely that the codefendant, who is left-handed, was the one who hit the victim. The defendant won." Brandt, *Paralegals' Acceptance and Utilization Increasing in Indy's Legal Community*, 1 The Indiana Lawyer 1.

- **More on This Area of the Law on the Net:**
  - *www.law.cornell.edu/topics/criminal.html*
  - *guide.lp.findlaw.com/01topics/09criminal/index.html*
  - *www.fbi.gov*

### 14. Employee Benefits Law[6]

Employee benefits paralegals work in a number of different settings: in law firms, banks, large corporations, insurance companies, or accounting firms. The following overview of tasks covers a paralegal working for a law firm. (See also *contract law, corporate law, labor and employment law, social security law,* and *worker's compensation law.*)

I.  Drafting of Employee Plans
A.  Work closely with the attorney, the plan sponsor, the plan administrator, and the trustee in preparing and drafting qualified employee plans, such as:
1.  Stock bonus plans,
2.  Profit-sharing plans,
3.  Money purchase pensions,
4.  Other pension plans,
5.  Trust agreements,
6.  Individual retirement account (IRA) plans,
7.  Annuity plans,
8.  HR-10 or Keogh plans,
9.  Employee stock ownership plans,
10. Life and health insurance plans,
11. Worker's compensation plans, and
12. Social Security plans.

II.  Document Preparation and Program Monitoring
A.  Gather information.
B.  Determine eligibility for participation and benefits.
C.  Notify employees of participation.
D.  Complete input forms for document assembly.
E.  Assemble elections to participate.
F.  Determine beneficiary designations.
G.  Record elections to contribute.
H.  Allocate annual contributions to the individual participant accounts.
I.  Prepare annual account statements for participants.
J.  Identify potential discrimination problems in the program.

III.  Government Compliance Work Pertaining to:
A.  Tax requirements for qualifications, amendment, and termination of plan.
B.  Department of Labor reporting and disclosure requirements.
C.  Insurance requirements.
D.  Welfare and Pension Plans Disclosure Act requirements.
E.  ERISA (Employee Retirement Income Security Act) requirements.
F.  Pension Benefit Guaranty Corporation requirements.

IV.  Miscellaneous
A.  Help draft summary plan descriptions for distribution to employees.
B.  Help prepare and review annual reports of plans.
C.  Continue education in current law of the field—for instance, study to become a Certified Employee Benefit Specialist (CEBS).

● *Comment on Paralegal Work in This Area:*
   "Michael Montchyk was looking to use his undergraduate degree in statistics. . . . He now works for attorneys specializing in employee benefits, where understanding numbers and familiarity with the law are key skills." Lehren, *Paralegal Work Enhancing Careers of Many*, Philadelphia Business Journal 9B.
   "This area is not for everybody. To succeed, you need considerable detail orientation, solid writing skills, self-

motivation, the ability to keep up with a legal landscape that is never the same, and a knack for handling crisis situations which arise when least expected." Germani, *Opportunities in Employee Benefits*, SJPA Reporter 7 (South Jersey Paralegal Ass'n).

● **More on This Area of the Law on the Net:**
   ■ *www.ifebp.org/iclinks.asp*
   ■ *www.weblocator.com/attorney/ca/law/b21.html*
   ■ *www.benefitslink.com*
   ■ *www.pensionrights.org*

**15.  Entertainment Law**

(See also *contract law, corporate law, and intellectual property law*.)

I.  Types of Client Problem Areas
A.  *Copyright and trademark law*: Apply for government protection for intellectual property, such as plays, films, video, music, and novels.
B.  *Contract Law*: Help negotiate and draft contracts, and ensure their enforcement.
C.  *Labor law*: Assist a client to comply with the contracts of unions or guilds.
D.  *Corporate law*:
1.  Assist in formation of business organizations.
2.  Work on mergers.
3.  Maintain compliance with federal and state reporting laws and regulations.
E.  *Tax law*: Planning and compliance.
1.  Report passive royalty income, talent advances, residuals, etc.
2.  Allocate expenditures to specific projects.
F.  *Family Law:* Assist with prenuptial agreements, divorces, child custody, etc.

II.  Miscellaneous Tasks
A.  Register copyrights.
B.  Help a client affiliate with his or her guild.
C.  Monitor remake and sequel rights to films.
D.  Prepare documents to grant a license to use client's music.
E.  Check title registrations with the Motion Picture Association of America.
F.  Read scripts to determine whether clearances are needed for certain kinds of material and references.
G.  Apply for permits and licenses.
H.  Calculate costs of property rights.

● *Comment on Paralegal Work in This Area:*
   "I am a paralegal in the field of entertainment law, one of the fastest growing, and, to me, most exciting areas of the paralegal profession, and one whose duties are as varied as the practices of the lawyers for whom we work. . . . I started in a very large Century City firm whose entertainment practice covers everything from songwriters to financing of major motion pictures, and from major recording stars and producers to popular novelists. . . . My specialty (yes, a specialty within a

specialty) is music. . . . My husband is also an entertainment paralegal who works for 20th Century Fox. . . . Never, ever a dull moment!" Birkner, *Entertainment Law: A Growing Industry for the Paralegal*, 2 California Paralegal Magazine 7.

- **More on This Area of the Law on the Net:**
  - *dir.yahoo.com/Government/law/entertainment*
  - *guide.lp.findlaw.com/01topics/12entertainsport/index.html*
  - *www.ascap.com*

## 16. Environmental Law[7]

(See also *legislation, litigation, oil and gas law, real estate law,* and *water law*.)

I. Research

A. Research questions pertaining to the environment, land use, water pollution, and the National Environmental Policy Act.
   1. Locate and study pertinent state and federal statutes, case law, regulations, and law review articles.
   2. Obtain secondary materials (maps, articles, books) useful for broadening the information base.
   3. Contact, when appropriate, government officials or other informants for data or answers.
   4. Obtain and develop personality profiles of members of Congress, members of relevant bureaucracies, and other political figures.
   5. Help prepare memoranda of findings, including citations and supporting documents.

B. Develop research notebooks for future reference. When new topics arise in environmental law, prepare notebooks to facilitate future research on similar topics.

C. Prepare bibliographies on environmental topics.

II. Drafting

A. Draft memoranda regarding new federal and state laws, regulations, or findings of research.

B. Draft memoranda discussing pertinent issues, problems, and solutions regarding public policy developments.

C. Draft narrative histories of legislation regarding political impulses, the impact of administrative and court rulings, and substantive and technical differences between drafts of legislation or results of amendments.

D. Draft and edit articles on coastal management programs and problems, conservation, water pollution, and the National Environmental Policy Act.

E. Edit environmental impact statements.

F. Assist in the preparation of briefs.
   1. Check citations for pertinence and accuracy.
   2. Develop table of contents, list of authorities, and certificate of service.

III. Hearing Participation

A. Locate and schedule witnesses.

B. Gather pertinent research materials (including necessary local documents, maps, and specific subject matter).

IV. Litigation: Provide General Trial Assistance

- *Comment on Paralegal Work in This Area:*

  Mary Peterson's firm has made a specialty of environmental and land use law. In a recent major hazardous waste case, "we will try to prove that the paint companies, dry cleaning stores and even the federal government, which used the property to build aircraft during the war" are responsible. "Some of the toxic waste dumped there were cited by federal agencies even back to 1935." Her job is to investigate the types of hazardous wastes and, with the help of the Freedom of Information Act, gather all available evidence. Then she studies it, duplicates, indexes, and writes summaries, which she distributes to the partners and associates. It's a case that has taken eight months so far and may go on for several years "because you don't know what you will uncover tomorrow. The toxins and pollutants could be different. There is no standard, just a constantly changing picture." Edwards, *The General Practice Paralegal*, 8 Legal Assistant Today 49.

- **More on This Area of the Law on the Net:**
  - *www.epa.gov*
  - *guide.lp.findlaw.com/01topics/13environmental/index.html*
  - *www.eli.org*

## 17. Estates, Trusts, and Probate Law

(See also *banking law, collections law, employee benefits law, family law,* and *social security law*.)

I. Estate Planning

A. Collect data (birth dates, fair market value of assets, current assets and liabilities, etc.).

B. Using computer-generated forms, prepare preliminary drafts of wills or trusts.

C. Perform investment analysis in order to provide attorney who is fiduciary of estate with information relevant to investment options.

II. Office Management

A. Maintain tickler system.

B. Maintain attorney's calendar.

C. Open, index, monitor, and keep current all components of the office file on the client's trust and estate case.

D. Using computer programs, manage the accounting aspects of trusts and estates administered by the office.

E. Act as office law librarian (keeping loose-leaf texts up to date, etc.).

F. Train secretaries and other paralegals in the system used by the office to handle trusts, estates, and probate cases.

G. Selectively discard certain mail and underline significant parts of other mail.

III. Estate of Decedent

**A.** Assets phase.
1. Collect assets (such as bank accounts, custody accounts, insurance proceeds, social security death benefits, safety deposit box contents, and apartment contents).
2. Assist in the valuation of assets.
3. Maintain records (for example, wills and trusts, vault inventories, powers of attorney, property settlements, fee cards, bill-payment letters).
4. Record and file wills and trusts.
5. Notify beneficiaries.
6. Prepare profiles of wills and trusts for attorney review.

B. Accounting phase.
1. Prepare preliminary drafts of federal and state death tax returns.
2. Apply the income-principal rules to the estate.
3. Organize data relevant to the tax implications of estates.
4. Prepare accountings: final and accounts current (for example, set up a petition for a first and final accounting).

C. Termination-distribution phase.
1. Apply for the transfer of securities into the names of the people entitled.
2. Draw checks for the signature of executors.
3. Monitor legacies to charitable clients.
4. File and prepare tax waivers.
5. Assist with the closing documents.
6. Calculate distributable net income.
7. Follow up on collection and delivery.

IV. Litigation
1. Perform legal research.
2. Conduct factual research (investigation)—for instance, track down the names and addresses of all possible claimants and contact them.
3. Prepare sample pleadings.
4. Digest depositions (review, condense, point out inconsistencies, etc.).
5. Prepare drafts of interrogatories.
6. Prepare drafts of answers to interrogatories.
7. Notarize documents.
8. Act as court witness as to decedent's signature and other matters.
9. Assist with litigation.

● *Comment on Paralegal Work in This Area:*
"What I like best about estate planning is that you work with people on a very individual basis. I don't

think that in many other areas of law you get that one-on-one contact with the client. . . . You're working with people while they are thinking about the most important things in their lives—their families, their wealth and how to distribute it, and what they want to happen after they pass on. A lot of the clients contact me directly with their questions for the attorneys. Some of the widows especially are more comfortable calling me with their questions. They seem to think their questions might be 'stupid' and they're embarrassed to ask the attorneys directly. I can take their questions and see that the attorneys respond to them promptly." Bassett, *Top Gun Patricia Adams: Legal Assistant of the Year*, 6 Legal Assistant Today 70.

"The position can be very stressful. But it is seldom boring. My typical day involves responding to many telephone inquiries from clients, dictating memos, or letters requesting additional information concerning life insurance policies, valuation of assets, or simply sending notice of an upcoming hearing 'to all persons entitled,' etc. I draft virtually all documents needed in the administration of an estate, beginning with the initial petition for probate. . . . The decedent may have had an interest in a closely-held business, or leave minor or handicapped children, or leave a spouse with no knowledge of the family assets; these all require additional attention. Every case is different. Probate paralegals to some extent must be 'snoopy,' because you do learn a great deal about people, both deceased and living. In most cases your client is facing a difficult time with trepidation and it is your role to provide confidence. The end results are very rewarding." Rose, *Still a Probate Paralegal*, 12 The Journal 5 (Sacramento Ass'n of Legal Assistants).

● *Quotes from Want Ads:*
Law firm seeks someone with "good communication and organizational skills, [who] is self-motivated, relates well with attorneys, clients, and staff, is detail oriented, has a teamwork attitude, a pleasant personality, and is a nonsmoker." Bank has opening for "trust tax administrator, with emphasis on personal and trust planning." Paralegal must have "technical understanding of wills and estate plans and terminology. Must be self-starter." "This is a full-time position with extensive responsibility for both court-supervised and noncourt-supervised estates and trusts." Position requires a person who "enjoys writing and proofreading, and who has excellent grammatical skills." Job is "for individual who enjoys the complexity and detail of accounting and bookkeeping in a legal environment." "Applicants must be prepared to handle tax work."

● **More on This Area of the Law on the Net:**
■ *www.actec.org*
■ *www.abanet.org/rppt/home.html*
■ *www.law.cornell.edu/topics/estates_trusts.html*
■ *guide.lp.findlaw.com/01topics/31probate/index.html*

## 18. Ethics and Professional Responsibility

Paralegals in this area work in two main settings: (1) in large law firms as a conflicts specialist (also called a conflicts technician), helping the firm determine whether conflicts of interest exist between prospective clients and current or former clients, and (2) in state disciplinary agencies that investigate complaints against attorneys for unethical behavior.

I. Law Firm (*Conflicts Specialist*)
A. Research
   1. Identify all persons or companies with a personal or business relationship with the prospective client.
   2. Determine whether the firm has ever represented the prospective client and/or any of its related parties.
   3. Determine whether the firm has ever represented an opponent of the prospective client and/or any of its related parties.
B. *Reports:* Notify attorney of data indicating possible conflict of interest.
C. *Database work:* Update information in client database on current and past clients for purposes of future conflicts checks.

II. Disciplinary Agency
A. Screen incoming data on new ethical complaints against attorneys.
B. Help investigate complaints.
C. Provide general litigation assistance to disciplinary attorneys during the proceedings at the agency and in court.

● ***Comment on Paralegal Work in This Area:***
Jane Palmer "does all the research on every prospective client, identifying all the related parties." Her computerized database tells her if the firm has ever represented a party on either side, or been adverse to them. "The most valuable thing has been my experience with the firm, developing somewhat of a corporate memory. The job takes extreme attention to detail. You may not always have all the information you need, so you have to be a detective. Quick response is important; so is making sure to keep things confidential." Sacramento Ass'n of Legal Assistants, *New Responsibilities Given to Paralegals*, The Journal 5.

● **More on This Area of the Law on the Net:**
  ■ *www.legalethics.com/index.law*
  ■ *www.abanet.org/cpr/home.html*
  ■ *guide.lp.findlaw.com/01topics/14ethics/index.html*

## 19. Family Law[8]

(See also *contract law, employee benefits law, estates law, litigation, pro bono work,* and *public sector.*)

I. Telephone Screening of Clients

II. Commencement of Action

A. Interview client to obtain initial information for pleadings.
B. Prepare initial pleadings, including petition, summons and waiver of service, affidavit as to children, and response.
C. Draft correspondence to be sent to clients, courts, and other attorneys.
D. Arrange for service of process.

III. Temporary Orders
A. Prepare motions for temporary orders or temporary injunctions.
B. Draft notice and set hearings.
C. Assist in settlement negotiations.
D. Draft stipulations for temporary orders after negotiations.

IV. Financial Affidavits
A. Help clients gather and compile financial information.
B. Analyze income and expense information provided by client.
C. Work with accountants, financial advisors, brokers, and other financial experts retained by client.
D. Retain appraisers for real estate, business, and personal property.
E. Prepare financial affidavits.

V. Discovery
A. Prepare discovery requests.
B. Help clients organize documents and data to respond to discovery requests.
C. Help prepare responses to discovery requests.
D. Organize, index, and summarize discovered materials.

VI. Settlement Negotiations
A. Assist attorney in analysis of proposed settlements.
B. Research legal questions and assist in drafting briefs and memoranda.
C. Assist in drafting separation agreements.

VII. Hearings
A. Help prepare for hearings on final orders.
B. Research legal questions and assist in drafting briefs and memoranda.
C. Assist in the preparation of trial exhibits and trial notebooks.
D. Arrange for expert witnesses and assist in preparing witnesses and clients for trial.
E. Attend hearings.
F. Prepare decree.

VIII. Post-Decree
A. Prepare documents for transfers of assets.
B. Arrange to file and record all transfer documents.
C. Review bills for tax-deductible fees and help prepare opinion letter to client.
D. Draft pleadings for withdrawal from case.

IX.  Special Projects
A.  Develop forms for gathering information from clients.
B.  Maintain files on separation-agreement provisions, current case law, resource materials for clients, and experts in various fields (e.g., custody, evaluation, and business appraisals).

● *Comment on Paralegal Work in This Area:*

Karen Dunn, a family law paralegal, "draws considerable satisfaction from a divorce case where the client was a woman in her sixties whose husband had left her, a situation which created predictable distress, notably during discussion of financial aspects. She was able to tell me things she couldn't tell the attorney. I found out she had a thyroid condition, so she was able to get more money in the end. I worked with her on the financial affidavit and drafted temporary orders to provide child support and spousal maintenance until the decree was entered." Edwards, *The General Practice Paralegal*, 8 Legal Assistant Today 49.

"As the only paralegal in a one-attorney family law practice, my job responsibilities are numerous. I work for an attorney who believes her paralegal should handle nearly all the legal functions she does, with the exception of appearing in court on behalf of clients, taking depositions and giving legal advice. My skills are used to the maximum, as I gather and organize all case information, allowing the attorney to prepare for court and be more cost-effective. I am the liaison person between clients and the attorney. I am able to deal with the human, emotional aspects of our clients, and not just the technical aspects of the law. As each person is different, so is every case, which makes this job a continuing challenge." Lenihan, *Role of the Family Law Paralegal*, 10 Paragram 6 (Oregon Legal Assistants Ass'n).

● *Quotes from Want Ads:*

Position is "excellent for a highly motivated person with excellent organizational skills and the ability to interface with clients." "Two swamped attorneys need reliable paralegal to work in fully computerized office. Must have excellent research and writing skills." Applicant must be "self-motivated, well-organized person who has initiative and can assume responsibility." Position requires "ability, experience, and attention to detail." "Looking for very professional applicants."

● **More on This Area of the Law on the Net:**
  ■ *www.law.cornell.edu/topics/divorce.html*
  ■ *guide.lp.findlaw.com/01topics/15family/index.html*
  ■ *www.divorcecentral.com*
  ■ *www.abanet.org/family/home.html*
  ■ *patriot.net/~crouch/fln.html*

## 20.  Government Contract Law[9]

(See also *administrative law, construction law, contract law, litigation, and water law.*)

I.  Calendar
A.  Maintain calendar for court and appeals board appearances.
B.  Record dates briefs are due, etc.

II.  Claims
A.  Gather, review, summarize, and index client files.
B.  Assist in drafting contract claims.
C.  Conduct preliminary research on selected legal issues.

III.  Appeals
A.  Draft and answer interrogatories and requests for production of documents.
B.  Summarize and index answers to discovery.
C.  Assist in drafting appeal.
D.  Prepare questions for witnesses and summarize their prior testimony.
E.  Maintain documents during hearing.

IV.  Post-Hearing Briefs
A.  Summarize and index transcripts.
B.  Assist with analysis of government's brief.
C.  Conduct preliminary research on selected issues.
D.  Assist in drafting the post-hearing brief.

● **More on This Area of the Law on the Net:**
  ■ *www.law.cornell.edu/topics/government_contracts.html*
  ■ *guide.lp.findlaw.com/01topics/18govcontracts/index.html*

## 21.  Immigration Law

(See also *administrative law, family law, international law, labor and employment law,* and *public sector.*)

I.  Problem Identification
A.  Help individual who has difficulty in obtaining:
    1.  Visa,
    2.  Permanent residency based on occupation,
    3.  Nonimmigrant status, or
    4.  Citizenship status.
B.  Help individuals who are faced with deportation proceedings.

II.  Providing Information on:
A.  Visa process,
B.  Permanent residency process,
C.  Nonimmigrant status process,
D.  Registration process,
E.  Citizenship process, or
F.  Deportation process.

III.  Investigation
Assist the individual in obtaining data and documentation on birth, travel, residency, etc.

IV.  Referral
Refer individuals to foreign consulates, nationality organizations, government officials, etc, for assistance concerning their immigration status.

V. Applications/Forms

Assist the individual in filling out visa applications, permanent residency applications, etc.

VI. Monitor Consular Processing Procedure

● ***Comment on Paralegal Work in This Area:***

"This is not a specialty for the faint-hearted or the misanthrope. The immigration paralegal may deal with much more than the timely filing of paperwork. One distinguishing feature of immigration work is our knowledge of intensely personal aspects of the client's life. We know his criminal record, the success and failure of his personal life, how much money he makes, and his dreams and aspirations. . . . Some clients have a very laissez-faire attitude towards perjury, and may invite the paralegal to participate without a blush. In America, [said one client] you lie *to* your attorney. In my country, you cook up the lie *with* your attorney." Myers & Raman, *Sweet-Talking Clients and Intransigent Bureaucrats*, 15 National Paralegal Reporter 4 (NFPA).

● **More on This Area of the Law on the Net:**
  ■ *www.wave.net/upg/immigration/resource.html*
  ■ *guide.lp.findlaw.com/01topics/20immigration/index.html*
  ■ *www.aila.org*

**22. Insurance Law**

Paralegals in this area work for law firms that represent insurance companies who are defendants in litigation, often personal injury (PI) litigation. They also work for insurance companies themselves. The following overview covers the latter. (See also *corporate law, employee benefits law, litigation, social security law*, and *worker's compensation law*.)

I. Compliance

A. Analyze government regulations on the insurance industry.

B. Prepare applications for new insurance products to obtain approval from Department of Insurance.

II. Claims

A. Assist in processing disputed claims.

B. Provide trial assistance by coordinating activities of company attorneys with outside counsel to represent the company.

III. Monitoring and Research

A. Monitor regulations of agencies and statutes of the legislatures that affect the insurance industry, particularly the committees of the legislature with jurisdiction over the industry.

B. Provide factual and legal research on inquiries that come into the office from agents and brokers.

● ***Comment on Paralegal Work in This Area:***

"Compliance is an insurance industry term which refers to keeping the company and its products in compliance with state and federal law, and procuring licenses for the company in unlicensed states. Compliance is a good field for paralegals because there is opportunity to work autonomously and also to advance within most companies." I am a "Senior Compliance Analyst" at a life insurance company. "I have met many paralegals who are compliance analysts, compliance specialists, and compliance managers." Maston, *Insurance*, The Citator 8 (Legal Assistants of Central Ohio)

● **More on This Area of the Law on the Net:**
  ■ *www.law.cornell.edu/topics/insurance.html*
  ■ *guide.lp.findlaw.com/01topics/44insurance/index.html*

**23. Intellectual Property Law**

Paralegals in this area work on copyrights, patents, and trademarks. (See also *contract law* and *entertainment law*.)

I. Copyrights

A. Application

  1. Help client apply for registration of a copyright for a novel, play, or other work with the Copyright Office.
  2. Help client apply for protection in foreign countries.
  3. Collect data, such as nature of the work, date completed, name of creator/author, name of the work, owner, etc., for application.
  4. Help identify the classification for the copyright.
  5. Examine accuracy of certificate-of-copyright registration.

B. Marketing

  1. Identify potential users/licensees of the copyright.
  2. Help prepare contracts.

C. Infringement

  1. Conduct investigations to determine whether an infringement exists—for example, compare the copyrighted work with the alleged infringing work.
  2. Provide general litigation assistance.

II. Patent

A. Application

  1. Help the inventor apply for a patent with the U.S. Patent and Trademark Office.
  2. Help the inventor describe the invention—for example, assemble designs, diagrams, and notebooks.
  3. Conduct a patent search. Check technical libraries to determine the current state of the art.
  4. Determine filing fees.
  5. Help the client apply for protection in foreign countries.
  6. Monitor the responses from government offices.
  7. Examine certificate of patent for accuracy.

B. Marketing the invention

  1. Help identify licensees. Solicit bids, conduct financial checks, study the market, etc.
  2. Help prepare contracts.

C. Infringement
  1. Conduct investigation on products that may have violated the patent.
  2. Provide general litigation assistance.

III. Trademarks
A. Registration
  1. Research trademark files or order search of trademark or trade name preliminary to an application before the U.S. Patent and Trademark Office.
  2. Examine indexes and directories.
  3. Conduct investigations to determine when the mark was first used, where, on what products, etc.
  4. Prepare foreign trademark applications.
  5. Respond to official actions taken by government offices.
  6. Examine the certificate of trademark for accuracy.
  7. Maintain files for renewals.
B. Infringement
  1. Conduct investigations into who else used the mark, when, where, in what market, etc.
  2. Provide general litigation assistance.

- **Comment on Paralegal Work in This Area:**
  "With the right training, trademark paralegals can find richly rewarding experiences waiting for them, whether they remain in paralegal work or go on to build careers in some other facet of trademark law. Trademark work is very dynamic." Wilkinson, *The Case for a Career in Trademark Law*, 7 Legal Professional 29.

  "Paula Rein was a trademark paralegal before such a job title was even invented. Her career has spanned over 19 years, leading her to some of the biggest corporations and law firms in New York City. Her extensive knowledge of trademark administration has made her one of the most resourceful trademark paralegals in her occupation. In her current 'diversified position,' at a law firm that specializes in intellectual property, she works on the cases of clients in the food and service industries and professional associations. Paula thrives in her current position." Scior, *Paralegal Profile*, Postscript 13 (Manhattan Paralegal Ass'n).

- **More on This Area of the Law on the Net:**
  - *www.loc.gov/copyright*
  - *www.uspto.gov*
  - *www.patents.com*
  - *guide.lp.findlaw.com/01topics/23intellectprop/index.html*

### 24. International Law

Example: a paralegal working on a "dumping" case in international trade.

I. Investigation
A. Examine the normal behavior in the industry or market affected by the alleged dumping.
B. Do statistical research (cost and price data).
C. Prepare profiles of domestic competitors.

II. Preparation of Documents
A. Help prepare for presentation before the Commerce Department.
B. Help prepare for presentation before the Court of International Trade.

III. Accounting Research

IV. Coordination of data from:
A. Members of Congress,
B. Foreign embassies,
C. State Department, and
D. U.S. Special Trade Representative.

- **Comment on Paralegal Work in This Area:**
  Steven Stark works "40–50 hours a week, specializing in international legal assisting, a hot area, while the Japanese are busy buying up American properties. [Steve became the liaison for the firm's Tokyo branch office. He originally expected to stay at the firm only three years but found that] the longer you're here, the more they value you. New things still come up. You work with the constant tension of everyone being expected to perform at a very high level, at all times. This is a high-stakes game, with million and billion dollar deals. It's a peaked, emotional atmosphere, with long hours." Milano, *Career Profiles*, 8 Legal Assistant Today 35.

- **More on This Area of the Law on the Net:**
  - *www.abanet.org/intlaw/home.html*
  - *www.law.cornell.edu/topics/international.html*
  - *www.law.cornell.edu/topics/foreign_relations.html*
  - *guide.lp.findlaw.com/01topics/24international/index.html*

### 25. Judicial Administration

Most courts have clerks to help with the administrative aspects of deciding cases. In addition, a few courts have paralegals that work for the court. They perform some of the functions of the administrative clerks, such as determining whether the parties have been properly notified of trial dates, checking filings and proposed orders from attorneys to determine whether anything appears inappropriate or premature, or obtaining additional information for a judge.

- **Comment on Paralegal Work in This Area:**
  "The Shreveport City Court has employed me as its paralegal in the civil department for the past six years. The Baton Rouge City Court employs several paralegals." We handle many matters such as determining if the legal delays for pleading have expired "before initialing the pleading and passing it on to the clerk or judge for signature. The most important task is the handling of default judgments. I must certify that proper service has been made. Perhaps I could be called a "nitpicker" about these cases, but the judge acts on my certificate that everything is in order. It is

always challenging to stay informed on our constantly changing procedural laws; I must keep a set of the Civil Procedure [laws] at my desk." Waterman, *The Court's Paralegal*, 3 NWLPA News 5 (Northwest Louisiana Paralegal Ass'n).

- **More on This Area of the Law on the Net:**
  - *www.law.cornell.edu/topics/judicial_administration.html*
  - *www.ncsconline.org*

### 26. Labor and Employment Law

(See also *civil rights law, contract law, employee benefits law,* and *worker's compensation law.*)

I. Investigation

Look into:
A. Sexual harassment.
B. Wrongful discharge.
C. Violation of occupational safety and health laws.
D. Violation of labor laws involving collective bargaining, union organization, grievance and arbitration procedures.
E. Violation of Civil Rights Act protecting against discrimination on the basis of race, national origin, sex, or physical handicap.
F. Violation of Age Discrimination in Employment Act.
G. Violation of Americans with Disabilities Act.

II. Compliance

Assist companies in the design and implementation of policies on:
A. Drug and alcohol testing.
B. AIDS in the workplace.
C. Race, sex, disability, and age discrimination.

III. Litigation Assistance
A. Help handle labor disputes before the National Labor Relations Board, State Labor Relations Board, Civil Service Commission, Human Rights Board, and the courts.
B. Perform a variety of tasks:
  1. Maintain the files.
  2. Digest and index data in files.
  3. Arrange for depositions.
  4. Help draft petition and other pleadings.
  5. Maintain tickler system of due dates.
  6. Prepare exhibits.
  7. Prepare statistical data.
  8. Help prepare appeal.

- *Comment on Paralegal Work in This Area:*
  "My experience in the labor and employment area has proven to be both diverse and unique. It is diverse because of the various labor-related issues accessible to me as a paralegal. It is unique because it is an area of specialty which involves very few paralegals in my part of the state." Batke, *Labor and Employment Paralegal*, The Citator 3 (Legal Assistants of Central Ohio).

"In the labor law area, I was responsible for doing background research, preparing witnesses and drafting arbitration briefs. I also assisted with the drafting of revised language during contract negotiations with unions." Diebold, *A Paralegal of Another Kind*, 16 Facts and Findings 38 (NALA).

- **More on This Area of the Law on the Net:**
  - *guide.lp.findlaw.com/01topics/27labor/index.html*
  - *www.abanet.org/labor/home.html*
  - *www.law.cornell.edu/topics/labor.html*
  - *www.law.cornell.edu/topics/employment.html*

### 27. Landlord and Tenant Law

Paralegals in real estate law firms occasionally become involved in commercial lease cases, such as a dispute over the interpretation of the lease of a supermarket at a large shopping mall. Such landlord-tenant cases, however, are not as common as the cases that arise between landlords and tenants who live in the apartments they rent. For example, a landlord of a small apartment seeks to evict a tenant for non-payment of rent. Many of these cases are handled by publicly funded legal service or legal aid offices that do not charge fees. (See *public sector, oil and gas law,* and *real estate law.*)

- *Comment on Paralegal Work in This Area:*
  "The Legal Action Center is the largest non-governmental social service agency in the state. As a paralegal, Virginia Farley handles all eviction calls to the landlord-tenant unit. Three afternoons a week are designated intake times. She screens all eviction cases, determines whether the applicant is eligible for free assistance according to the Center's guidelines, recommends a plan once a case is accepted and assists in carrying out the plan under an attorney's supervision. [After arriving in the city], Virginia made a commitment to work directly with the poor and started serving as a volunteer in five organizations until a job opened up for her at the Legal Action Center." Roche, *Paralegal Profile*, 4 Findings and Conclusions 5 (Washington Ass'n of Legal Assistants).

- **More on This Area of the Law on the Net:**
  - *www.law.cornell.edu/topics/landlord_tenant.html*
  - *www.hg.org/landlord.html*

### 28. Law Librarianship

There is a separate degree that a law librarian can obtain. This degree, however, is not a requirement to be a law librarian. A number of small or medium-sized law offices are hiring paralegals to perform library chores exclusively or in combination with paralegal duties on cases. (See also *law office administration* and *litigation.*)

I. Administration
A. Order books for law library.
B. File loose-leaf material and pocket parts in appropriate volumes.

C. Pay bills of library vendors.
D. Test and recommend computer equipment, software, and services for the law library.
E. Prepare budget for library.

II. Cite Checking
A. Check the citations in briefs, speeches, articles, opinion letters, and other legal documents to determine the accuracy of quoted material.
B. Check the citations to determine the accuracy of citation format according to the Uniform System of Citation (the Bluebook), local court rules, or other citation guidelines required by the office.

III. Research
A. Perform factual research.
B. Perform legal research.

IV. Training
A. Train office staff in traditional legal research techniques.
B. Train office staff in computer research, for example, WESTLAW, LEXIS.
C. Train office staff in cite checking.

● *Comment on Paralegal Work in This Area:*
"I suppose my entry into the law librarianship profession might be considered unorthodox because I had no formal educational courses in librarianship. My experience was that of working first as a legal secretary and later evolving into a legal assistant. My job in a small general practice firm included taking care of the office library such as filing supplements and pocket parts (because no one else would do it!!); doing the bookkeeping and paying the bills." I did some legal research "as an extension of legal drafting." "In all my working years (and they are many) I had the greatest satisfaction from my work as a law librarian because each day I learned new things." Lewek, *The Legal Assistant as Law Librarian*, 17 Facts & Findings 28 (NALA).

● **More on This Area of the Law on the Net:**
 ■ *www.aallnet.org/index.asp*
 ■ *www.washlaw.edu/subject/law.libraries.html*

**29. Law Office Administration**

At the beginning of chapter 14, you will find a detailed job description of the legal administrator and of the legal assistant manager. (See exhibits 14.2 and 14.3.) Some experienced paralegals move into management positions at a law office. This might involve helping to administer the *entire* office, or *one component* of it, such as the administration of all the legal assistants in the office or the administration of the legal assistants and other support personnel working on a large case. As we saw in Chapter 1, paralegals who supervise other paralegals in large offices have formed a national association, LAMA, the Legal Assistant Management Association. In many

smaller offices, paralegals perform office management duties along with paralegal duties. (See also *law librarianship* and *litigation*.)

● *Comment on Paralegal Work in This Area:*
In 1984, the partners at the firm decided to upgrade their legal assistant program and needed a nonlawyer to run it. They offered Linda Katz the new position. "The firm is segmented into practice areas, with legal assistants dispersed throughout the areas. They report to supervising attorneys for work assignments each day. I serve as administrative supervisor, assuring consistency in how legal assistants are treated and utilized, and what opportunities they have for benefits and advancement." Milano, *Career Profiles*, 8 Legal Assistant Today 35.
"A good paralegal litigation manager [in a large document case] has both strong paralegal skills and strong management skills. Such a manager must be able to analyze the case's organizational needs, develop methods to cope with them effectively, and often must act as paralegal, office manager and computer expert—all in a day's work." Kaufman, *The Litigation Manager*, 6 Legal Professional 55.

● **More on This Area of the Law on the Net:**
 ■ *www.abanet.org/lpm/default.shtml*
 ■ *www.soholawoffice.com*
 ■ *www.ioma.com*
 ■ *www.lamanet.org*

**30. Legislation**

I. Monitoring
Keep track of all events, persons, and organizations involved in the passing of legislation relevant to the clients of the firm.

II. Legislative History
Compile the legislative history of a statute.

III. Drafting of Proposed Legislation

IV. Lobbying
A. Prepare reports and studies on the subject of proposed legislation.
B. Arrange for and help prepare witnesses who will testify at legislative hearings.

● *Comment on Paralegal Work in This Area:*
Margo Horner "is a legislative analyst for the Nat'l Federation of Independent Business (NFIB). With paralegal training and a masters degree in history, her job is research, creating legislative strategy, working with [legislators] and their staffs to produce legislation favorable to [NFIB]. Margo likes the frenetic tempo of her life." Smith, *Margo*, 1 Legal Assistant Today 14.

● **More on This Area of the Law on the Net:**
 ■ *www.law.cornell.edu/topics/legislation.html*
 ■ *www.state.ak.us/local/akpages/ADMIN/apoc/lobstadx.htm*

## 31. Litigation (Civil)

Civil litigation involves court disputes in every area of the law other than a case where the government is charging (prosecuting) someone for the commission of a crime. Hence civil litigation can potentially involve every specialty other than criminal law.

I. File Monitoring
A. Index all files.
B. Write case profile based on information in the files.
C. Read attorney briefs to check accuracy of the information in the litigation file.
D. Organize, index, and digest documents obtained through answers to interrogatories, depositions, and other discovery devices.
E. Code documents into a computer database.

II. Investigation
A. Gather documents:
   1. Medical records,
   2. Police records,
   3. Birth and death records,
   4. Marriage records,
   5. Adoption and custody records,
   6. Incorporation records, etc.
B. Research records. For example:
   1. Prepare a profit history report of a company.
   2. Identify the corporate structure of a parent company and its subsidiaries.
   3. Trace UCC (Uniform Commercial Code) filings.
   4. Find out from court dockets if a particular merchant is being sued, has sued before, etc. Does any pattern exist?
   5. Identify the "real owner" of an apartment building.
   6. Check housing code agency to find out if a landlord has other building code violations against it on record.
C. Gather facts (other than from documents). In a wide range of cases (such as real estate, corporate, divorce, and custody), the investigator substantiates facts, follows leads for possible evidence in connection with litigation, etc.

III. Discovery
A. Draft interrogatories.
B. Draft answers to interrogatories.
C. Draft deposition questions.
D. Prepare witnesses for deposition.
E. Prepare witness books for deposition.
F. Arrange time and place of deposition.
G. Draft requests for admissions.
H. Draft answers to requests for admissions.
I. Draft requests for production of documents.
J. Draft answers to requests for production of documents.
K. Index and digest discovery data.
L. Work with computer programmer in designing a system to manage discovery documents.

IV. Filings/Serving
File and/or serve documents in court, at agencies, on parties, on attorneys, etc.

V. General Assistance
A. Arrange for clients and others to be interviewed.
B. Arrange for expert witnesses to appear in court or at depositions.
C. Reconstruct (from a large collection of disparate records and other evidence) what happened at a particular time and place.
D. Assist clients in completing information questionnaire, especially in class-action cases.
E. Help organize the trial notebook containing items the attorney will need during the trial, such as charts and tables to be used as exhibits at trial.
F. Sit at counsel's table at trial to take notes and suggest questions for attorney to ask witnesses.
G. Attend (and report on) hearings in related cases.
H. Supervise document encodation on a computer project related to a case in litigation.
I. Prepare and evaluate prospective jurors from jury book and during voir dire.
J. Help prepare appeal documents—for example, the notice of appeal.

VI. Legal Research
A. Shepardize cited authority; perform cite check.
B. Write preliminary memos and briefs.
C. Prepare bibliographies of source materials related to a case in litigation.

VII. Pleadings
Write preliminary draft of pleadings using standard forms and/or adapting other pleadings written by attorneys on similar cases.

VIII. Expert Analysis
Assist in obtaining expert opinions for attorneys on:
A. Taxation.
B. Accounting.
C. Statistics.
D. Economics (e.g., calculation of damages).

IX. Court Witness.
A. Act as witness as to service of process.
B. Act as witness as to data uncovered or photographed (e.g., the condition of an apartment building).

● *Comment on Paralegal Work in This Area:*
"There are boxes and boxes with an infinite number of documents to be indexed. There are depositions to be summarized. There are cases whose cites need checking. There are trips to the courthouse downtown. There is red-lining of documents to determine changes between two documents. There is Bates-stamping of documents. And there are the exciting trips to visit clients." Lasky,

*Impressions of a New Paralegal*, 17 Reporter 5 (Los Angeles Paralegal Ass'n).

"I organized. I tabbed and tagged, listed and labelled, hoisted and hole-punched, folded and filed, boxed and Bates-stamped, indexed and itemized, sorted and summarized." Klinkseick, *Aim High*, 16 On Point 4 (Nat'l Capital Area Paralegal Ass'n).

"Initially, it was overwhelming with the number of files and the names to learn and things to remember, but with help, I learned skills and techniques and polished them day after day as each new case brought with it new quirks and new challenges. I've attended depositions, PTO shaft inspections, and pig farm operations. I've calculated medical expenses, reviewed medical records, and been baffled at how salesmen keep time records! But the ultimate of all experiences, I have to admit, are the trials. You prepare and prepare and hope that you haven't missed any of the details. Then before you know it, the jury has been selected and you're off! The trials keep your adrenaline flowing. They frazzle your patience. They show you your limitations. They elevate you when you win. They shake your confidence when you lose." Riske, *In the Limelight*, 7 Red River Review 4 (Red River Valley Legal Assistants, North Dakota).

"For almost six years now . . . , I've experienced the variety (and the drudgery) of preparing civil cases for trial. I've spent countless hours photocopying documents never read by any judge or jury, or worst of all, by anyone else. I've tracked down witnesses and encouraged them to talk only to find out that they know nothing about the case. In this business of endless paper where no two cases are alike, I've come to understand . . . that flexibility is essential and a sense of humor is invaluable in dealing with people, be they stressed out attorneys or reluctant witnesses." Vore, *A Litigation Recipe*, 16 On Point 4 (Nat'l Capital Area Paralegal Ass'n).

Rebecca McLaughlin tells of a particularly memorable event during her experience as a paralegal. "It was a few minutes after 12:00 noon on Friday, and presiding Judge Barbour always recesses court at precisely 12:30 on Fridays. The Government's star witness was on the stand and denied he had ever seen a certain letter. One of the trial attorneys motioned me to counsel table and asked if we had any proof that the witness had, in fact, seen this letter." Since there were well over 900 defense exhibits, almost 300 Government exhibits, and well over 40 file cabinets filled with supporting documents, Rebecca felt little hope for success [in finding out quickly]. "She hurried across the street to the office, found the witness' original copy of the letter with his handwritten notes in the margin, and returned to the courtroom with a BIG SMILE. The witness was impeached with his own document minutes before recess." "Later, Rebecca received a well-deserved standing ovation from the attorneys, and all the trial team

members. It was the highlight of her career." Johnson, *MALA Spotlight: Rebecca McLaughlin*, 8 The Assistant 17 (Mississippi Ass'n of Legal Assistants).

● **Quotes from Want Ads:**

"Excellent writing skills and attention to detail are absolute requirements." "Plaintiff's medical malpractice firm seeks non-smoker with word processing abilities." Position requires "extensive writing, document summarizing, and medical records research." Must have an ability "to work independently in handling cases from inception through trial preparation; familiarity with drafting law motions pleadings is essential." High-energy candidate "needs to be assertive and should have an excellent academic background." "Wanted: a sharp, take-charge litigation paralegal." "Knowledge of computerized litigation support is a plus; good communications and organizational skills are a must." "Applicant must possess a thorough working knowledge of all phases of trial work." "Successful candidate will be professional, prompt, pleasant and personable. No egomaniacs or job hoppers, please." "Overtime flexibility required." "Defense litigation paralegal needed. Must be a self-starter with the ability to accept unstructured responsibility." "Applicant must have a thorough knowledge of state and federal court procedures." Position requires an ability "to organize and manage documents in large multi-party litigation." "Applicants must possess strong supervisory, analytic, writing, and investigative skills, and an ability to perform under pressure." "Position requires good analytical and writing skills, and the ability to organize and control several projects simultaneously." "Deposition summarizer needed; work in your own home on your own computer." "Part-time proofreader for deposition summaries needed."

● **More on This Area of the Law on the Net:**
   ■ *www.abanet.org/litigation*
   ■ *www.atlanet.org*
   ■ *www.dri.org*

## 32. Military Law

In the Navy, a nonattorney who assists attorneys in the practice of law is called a **legalman**. Depending upon the assignment, the legalman can work in a large variety of areas of the law—for example, admiralty law, contracts, and military justice. The following job functions, however, are not limited to any particular branch of the armed services.

I. Military Proceedings
A. Assist in processing the following proceedings:
   1. Special court-martial.
   2. General court-martial.
   3. Courts of inquiry.
   4. Line-of-duty investigations.
   5. Reclassification board proceedings.

B. Prepare all special orders designating membership of special and general courts-martial and courts of inquiry.
C. Assure that charges are properly prepared and that specifications are completed and accurate.
D. Make initial determination on jurisdiction of court, status of accused, and subject matter of offenses.
E. Examine completed records of investigations and other records requiring legal review to ensure that they are administratively correct.
F. Prepare court-martial orders promulgating sentence.
G. Assure that records of court-martial are correct and complete before disposing of case.
H. Transmit bad-conduct discharge court-martial cases to appropriate officials.

II. Claims against the Government
A. Conduct examinations.
B. Process claims against the United States, e.g., federal tort claims.
C. Manage claim funds.
D. Undertake research on FLITE (Federal Legal Information Through Electronics).
E. Write briefs.

III. Administrative Duties
A. Maintain control records of all court-martial and claims cases within command.
B. Maintain law library.
C. Examine and distribute incoming correspondence, directives, publications, and other communications.
D. Supervise cataloging and filing of books, periodicals, newsletters, etc.
E. Maintain records of discipline within command.
F. Administer office budget.
G. Orient new personnel and monitor their training.

IV. Court Reporting
A. Use the steno-mask for recording legal proceedings.
B. Prepare charges to the jury.
C. Mark exhibits as they are entered into evidence.
D. Transcribe and assemble records of the proceeding.

● *Comment on Paralegal Work in This Area:*
"I have been working for the Office of the Staff Judge Advocate (SJA) at Fort Ord, California. The SJA is the Army's lawyer. We serve a military community of just over 90,000 people. Staff within the SJA consists of a combination of military and civilian attorneys, paralegals, legal clerks and court reporters. I am responsible for claims filed against the federal government under the Federal Tort Claims Act. I am responsible for discovery and investigative efforts, determining legal issues, writing memorandums of law and recommending settlement or denial. Job satisfaction for paralegal professionals is high in the U.S. government. I know that, should I desire to re-enter the civilian work sector, my experience and knowledge of the

government legal systems will uniquely qualify me to work for any firm which deals with the government." Richards, *Marching to a Different Drummer: Paralegal Work in the Military*, 2 California Paralegal Magazine 8.

● **More on This Area of the Law on the Net:**
■ *www.court-martial.com*
■ *www.law.cornell.edu/topics/military.html*
■ *guide.lp.findlaw.com/01topics/45military/index.html*

### 33. Municipal Finance Law[10]

(See also *banking law* and *corporate law*.)

I. Document Preparation
A. Basic documents:
  1. Prepare first drafts of basic documents, including bonds, indentures of trust, financing agreements, and all other related documents.
  2. Attend drafting sessions and note changes required to initial drafts.
  3. Prepare second and subsequent drafts by incorporating revisions.
B. Closing documents
  1. Prepare first drafts of all closing documents.
  2. Prepare second and subsequent drafts by incorporating revisions and red-line changes.
C. Draft official statement/private offering memorandum:
  1. Prepare first drafts.
  2. Attend drafting sessions.
  3. Perform due diligence to verify the information and data contained in the offering document.
  4. Prepare second and subsequent drafts by incorporating revisions and red-line changes.

II. Coordination
A. Establish timetable and list of participants.
B. Distribute documents to participants.
C. Coordinate printing of bonds and offering documents.
D. File all documents as required.
E. Coordinate publication of notices of meetings and elections, ordinances, public hearing notices, etc.

III. Closing
A. Prepare checklist.
B. Arrange and assist in preclosing and closing.
C. File any documents necessary to be filed prior to closing.
D. Secure requisite documents to be prepared or furnished by other participants.
E. Perform all post-closing procedures.
  1. File all documents or security agreements.
  2. Supervise preparation of closing binders, etc.

IV. Formation of Special Districts
A. Prepare documents necessary to organize the district.
B. File documents with municipality or county and district court.

C. Prepare documents for organizational meeting of district.

V. Elections (Formation of District or for Bond Election)

Draft election documents and obtain all necessary election materials.

VI. Develop and Maintain Research Files
A. IDB procedures for municipalities.
B. Home rule charters.
C. Demographic and economic statistics.
D. Memoranda noting statutory changes.
E. Interoffice research memoranda.
F. Checklists for each type of financing.

- **More on This Area of the Law on the Net:**
  - *www.quarles.com/prac_mun.asp*
  - *www.law.cornell.edu/topics/local_government.html*
  - *www.abanet.org/statelocal/home.html*

## 34. Oil and Gas Law

Some paralegals who work in the area of oil and gas law are referred to as *land technicians* or *landmen*. (See also *real estate law*.)

I. Collect and analyze data pertaining to land ownership and activities that may affect the procurement of rights to explore, drill for, and produce oil or gas.

II. Help acquire leases and other operating rights from property owners for exploration, drilling, and producing oil, gas, and related substances.

III. Monitor the execution of the leases and other operating agreements by ensuring that contract obligations are fulfilled (e.g., payment of rent).

IV. Help negotiate agreements with individuals, companies, and government agencies pertaining to the exploration, drilling, and production of oil or gas.

V. Assist in acquiring oil and gas producing properties, royalties, and mineral interests.

VI. Process and monitor the termination of leases and other agreements.

VII. Examine land titles.

- *Comment on Paralegal Work in This Area:*
  "As an oil and gas paralegal, my practice encompasses many different areas of law including real estate, litigation, bankruptcy, and securities, as well as contact with various county, state, and federal government agencies. I frequently spend time searching real estate records in counties ... for information on leases to determine such things as who has been assigned an interest in the lease. I have worked in mechanic's lien foreclosures, partition actions, and bankruptcy cases. While researching such things as regulatory information and oil prices, I have obtained information from the

Federal Energy Regulatory Commission offices in Washington. The variety of work requires a working knowledge of several areas of law, and is always challenging and interesting." Hunt, *Oil and Gas*, The Citator (Legal Assistants of Central Ohio).

- **More on This Area of the Law on the Net:**
  - *www.washlaw.edu/oilgaslaw.html*
  - *www.hg.org/natres.html*

## 35. Parajudge

In many states, the judge presiding in certain lower courts does not have to be an attorney. Such courts include justice of the peace courts and local magistrates courts.

Administrative agencies often hold hearings conducted by hearing officers, referees, or administrative law judges (ALJ). Frequently, these individuals are not attorneys, particularly at state and local agencies.

- **More on This Area of the Law on the Net:**
  - *www.fjc.gov/ALTDISRES/adrsource/connecti.html*

## 36. Pro Bono Work

Pro bono work refers to services provided to another person at no charge. Law firms often give their attorneys time off so they can take pro bono cases—for example, to defend a poor person charged with a crime. Paralegals are also encouraged to do pro bono work. This is done on their own time or on law firm time with the permission of their supervisor. The following are examples of the variety of pro bono work performed by paralegals:

I. Abused Women
A. Draft request for protective order.
B. Draft divorce pleadings.

II. AIDS Patients
A. Interview patients and prepare a memorandum of the interview for the pro bono attorney on the case.
B. Assist patients with guardianship problems.
C. Draft powers of attorney.

III. Homeless
A. Handle Supplemental Security Income (SSI) claims
B. Make referrals to shelters and drug programs.

- *Comment on Paralegal Work in This Area:*
  "Asked to share her favorite pro bono experience, Therese Ortega, a litigation paralegal, answered that to choose was too difficult; any time her efforts result in a benefit to the client, 'I get a warm glow.' One occasion she obviously cherishes was the fight on behalf of some low-income kidney dialysis patients whose eligibility for transportation to and from treatment was threatened. 'Perseverance and appeals paid off,' she says. Rides were re-established through the hearing process, then by information conferences. Finally, the cessation notices

stopped." *Spotlight on Therese Ortega*, 13 The Journal 3 (Sacramento Ass'n of Legal Assistants).

- **More on This Area of the Law on the Net:**
  - *www.abanet.org/legalservices/probono.html*
  - *www.scbar.org/public_pro_bono.htm*

### 37. Public Sector

A paralegal in the *private sector* works in an office whose funds come from client fees or from the budget of the corporate treasury. Every other setting is generally considered the *public sector*. More specifically, the latter refers to those law offices that provide civil or criminal legal services to the poor for free. Often, the services consist of helping clients obtain government benefits such as public housing, welfare, or medical care. Such services are referred to as *public benefits*, and providing such assistance is called practice of public benefits law. Some of the paralegals who are employed by these offices are called public benefits paralegals. The offices operate with government grants, charitable contributions, and the efforts of volunteers. The offices are called Legal Aid Society, Legal Services Office, Office of the Public Defender, etc. For examples of the kinds of functions performed by paralegals in these offices, see *administrative law, bankruptcy law, civil rights law, criminal law, family law, landlord and tenant law, litigation, pro bono work, social security law, welfare law, and worker's compensation law*.

- ***Comment on Paralegal Work in This Area:***
"If someone asked me what I disliked most about my job, I would have to answer: the size of my paycheck. That is the only drawback of working for a nonprofit law firm—[the Community Legal Aid Society which represents elderly and handicapped persons]. Everything else about my job is positive." For example, to "be an integral part of a case where a landlord is forced by the Courts to bring a house up to code and prevent a tenant from being wrongfully evicted is a great feeling." The positive aspects of the job "more than compensate for the size of the paycheck." Hartman, *Job Profile*, Delaware Paralegal Reporter 5 (Delaware Paralegal Ass'n).

"Mr. Watnick stressed that the organization doesn't have the luxury of using paralegals as "xeroxers" or errand runners. Staff paralegals have their own caseloads and represent clients before Administrative Law Judges—with a dramatically high rate of success." Shays, *Paralegals in Human Service*, Postscript 16 (Manhattan Paralegal Ass'n).

- **More on This Area of the Law on the Net:**
  - *www.povertylaw.org/links/links.htm*
  - *guide.lp.findlaw.com/01topics/17govbenefit/index.html*
  - *www.hud.gov*
  - *www.law.cornell.edu/topics/food_stamps.html*
  - *www.law.cornell.edu/topics/medicaid.html*

### 38. Real Estate Law

(See also *banking law, contract law,* and *landlord and tenant law.*)

I. General
Assist law firms, corporations, and development companies in transactions involving land, houses, condominiums, shopping malls, office buildings, redevelopment projects, civic centers, etc.
A. Research zoning regulations.
B. Prepare draft of the contract of sale.
C. Title work:
   1. If done outside, order title work from the title company; arrange title insurance.
   2. If done in-house:
      a. Examine title abstracts for completeness;
      b. Prepare a map based on a master title plat or the current government survey map;
      c. Help construct a chain of title noting defects, encumbrances, liens, easements, breaks in the chain, etc.
      d. Obtain releases of liens, payoff statements for existing loans, etc.
      e. Help draft a preliminary title opinion.
D. Mortgages:
   1. Assist in obtaining financing.
   2. Review mortgage application.
   3. Assist in recording mortgage.
E. Closing:
   1. Arrange for a closing time with buyer, seller, brokers, and lender. Obtain letter confirming date of closing.
   2. Collect the data necessary for closing. Prepare checklist of expenses:
      a. Title company's fee,
      b. Lender's fee,
      c. Attorney's fee,
      d. Taxes and water bills to be prorated,
      e. Tax escrow, discharge of liens, etc.
   3. Prepare and organize the documents for closing:
      a. Deed,
      b. Settlement statement,
      c. Note and deed of trust,
      d. Corporate resolutions,
      e. Performance bond,
      f. Waivers, etc.
   4. Check compliance with the disclosure requirements of the Real Estate Settlement Act.
   5. Arrange for a rehearsal of the closing.
   6. Attend and assist at the closing—for example, take minutes, notarize documents.
F. Foreclosure:
   1. Order foreclosure certificate.
   2. Prepare notice of election and demand for sale.
   3. Compile a list of parties to be notified.
   4. Monitor publication of the notice.

5. Assist with sale documents—for example, prepare bid letter.

G. Eminent domain:
1. Photograph or videotape the property taken or to be taken by the state.
2. Prepare inventory of the property taken.
3. Help client prepare business records pertaining to the value of the property.
4. Arrange for appraisals of the property.
5. Order and review engineering reports regarding soil.
6. Review tax appeal records on values claimed by the property owner.
7. Mail out notice of condemnation.

H. Office management:
1. Maintain office tickler system.
2. Maintain individual attorney's calendar.
3. Be in charge of the entire client's file (opening it, keeping it up to date, knowing where parts of it are at all times, etc.).
4. Train other staff in the office system of handling real estate cases.

II. Tax-exempt Industrial Development Financing

A. Undertake a preliminary investigation to establish facts relevant to:
1. Project eligibility,
2. The local issuer, and
3. Cost estimates of the financing.

B. Prepare a formal application to the issuer.

C. Prepare a timetable of approvals, meetings, and all other requirements necessary for closing.

D. Prepare a preliminary draft of portions of the proposal memorandum (relating to the legal structure of the financing) that is submitted to prospective bond purchasers.

E. Obtain confirmation from the Treasury Department that the company is in compliance with the financing covenants of current external debt instruments.

F. Obtain insurance certificates.

G. Write the first draft of the resolutions of the board of directors.

H. Write the preface and recital of documents for the legal opinion of the company.

I. Contact the bank to confirm the account numbers, amount of money to be transferred, and investment instructions.

J. Prepare a closing memorandum covering the following documents:
1. Secretary's certificate including resolutions of the board of directors, the certified charter and bylaws of the company, and the incumbency certificate;
2. UCC-1 financing statements;
3. Requisition forms;
4. Certificate of authorized company representative;
5. Deed;
6. Legal opinion of the company;

7. Transfer instruction letter; and
8. Officer's certificate.

K. Confirm that the money has been transferred to the company's account on the day of closing.

L. Order an updated good-standing telegram.

M. Send a copy of the IRS election statement.

N. Assemble, monitor, and distribute documents to appropriate departments.

● *Comment on Paralegal Work in This Area:*

"Although it may look boring to the untrained eye, and sound boring to the untrained ear, for those of us whose livelihoods depend upon it, real estate law is *interesting* and *exciting*. There is always something new to learn or a little flaw to resolve. What can be better than having clients come to you and thank you for your assistance in what would have been a complete disaster without your knowledge and expertise to get them through? I call that total job satisfaction. I am now capable of doing everything in a real estate settlement from opening the file to walking into the settlement room and disbursing the funds. It is not uncommon for me to receive calls from attorneys in the area asking me how certain problems can be solved. That boosts my ego more than any divorce case ever could!" Jaeger, *Real Estate Law Is a Legal Profession Tool*, 14 On Point 9 (Nat'l Capital Area Paralegal Ass'n).

At a paralegal conference, Virginia Henderson made a seminar presentation on her duties as a paralegal. Her "candor and energetic enthusiasm concerning her profession were encouraging and motivating. She was very explicit about her duties as a commercial real estate paralegal, explaining that attorney supervision is lessened once the paralegal assumes more responsibility and exhibits initiative as far as his/her duties are concerned. It was refreshing to listen to a veteran of the paralegal profession speak so optimistically about the profession's limitless potential. Here's to having more paralegals as seminar speakers!" Troiano, *Real Estate*, Newsletter 12 (Western New York Paralegal Ass'n).

"As a foreclosure legal assistant, one of my worst fears is to have a client call and say, 'Remember the Jones property you foreclosed for us last year? Well, we're trying to close on this and it seems there's a problem with the title. . . .' Oh no, what *didn't* I do! Mortgage foreclosure litigation is fraught with all kinds of pitfalls for the inexperienced and the unwary. An improper or faulty foreclosure could not only be disastrous for the client, it can also be a malpractice nightmare for the law firm." Hubbell, *Mortgage Foreclosure Litigation: Avoiding the Pitfalls*, 16 Facts and Findings 10 (NALA).

● *Quotes from Want Ads:*

"Ideal candidate must possess exceptional organization, communication, writing and research skills and be willing to work overtime." "We need a team player with high energy." Position requires an ability to work independently on a wide variety of matters and to meet deadlines." "Experience in retail real estate or real estate financing a must." "Should be assertive and have excellent analytical skills." Position requires a "self-motivated person. We seek a TIGER who can accomplish much with a minimum of supervision." "Knowledge of state and federal securities law a plus." "Must be flexible and possess high integrity." Position requires a "self-starter able to deal effectively with executive management, outside counsel, escrow and title companies, brokers, leasing agents, and clients."

● **More on This Area of the Law on the Net:**
■ *www.law.cornell.edu/topics/real_estate.html*
■ *www.law.cornell.edu/topics/real_property.html*
■ *www.law.cornell.edu/topics/mortgages.html*
■ *library.lp.findlaw.com/propertyrealestate.html*
■ *guide.lp.findlaw.com/01topics/33property/index.html*

## 39. Social Security Law

(See also *administrative law*, *public sector*, and *welfare law*.)

I. Problem Identification
Identify whether:
A. Person is denied benefits.
B. Recipient is terminated from disability payments.
C. Recipient is charged with receiving overpayment.
D. Medicare waivers/appeals are involved.

II. Case Preparation
A. Investigate relevant facts.
B. Perform legal research.
C. Engage in informal advocacy with Social Security employees.

III. Representation
A. Represent clients at administrative hearings regarding SSI (Supplemental Security Income).
B. Represent clients at administrative hearings regarding SSD (Social Security Disability).

IV. Appeal
A. Help attorney prepare a court appeal of the Social Security Administration's decision.

● *Comment on Paralegal Work in This Area:*
"Paralegal representation of a claimant in a Social Security Disability hearing is the closest to a judicial setting that a paralegal may expect to become involved in. For the paralegal, this can be a very complex and challenging field. It can also be extremely rewarding, bringing with it the satisfaction of successfully representing a claimant in a quasi-judicial setting." Obermann, *The Paralegal and Federal Disability Practice in Maine*, MAP Newsletter (Maine Ass'n of Paralegals).

● **More on This Area of the Law on the Net:**
■ *www.ssa.gov*
■ *www.naela.com*

## 40. Tax Law

(See also *corporate law, employee benefits law, estates law,* and *real estate law*.)

I. Compile all necessary data for the preparation of tax returns:
A. Corporate income tax,
B. Employer quarterly tax,
C. Franchise tax,
D. Partnership tax,
E. Sales tax,
F. Personal property tax,
G. Individual income tax,
H. Estate tax, and
I. Gift tax.

II. Miscellaneaous Tasks
A. Communicate with client to obtain missing information.
B. Compile supporting documents for the returns.
C. Draft extensions-of-time requests for late filings.
D. Make corrections in the returns based upon new or clarified data.
E. Compute the tax liability or transfer client information to computer input sheets for submission to a computer service that will calculate the tax liability.
F. Organize and maintain client binder.
G. Compute cash flow analysis and other calculations needed for proposed real estate syndication.
H. Compile documentation on the valuation of assets.
I. Maintain the tax law library.
J. Read loose-leaf tax services and other periodic tax data to keep current on tax developments. Bring such developments to the attention of others in the office.
K. Supervise and train other nonattorney staff within the tax department of the office.

● *Comment on Paralegal Work in This Area:*
"A legal assistant with the firm for the past thirteen years, Pat [Coleman] spends a lot of time in her office. She is surrounded by her work, and one gets the idea that Pat knows exactly what is in every file and could put her hand on any information that is needed. Notes are taped next to the light switch; the firm's monthly calendar highlighting important meetings is readily available, and helps her track her many deadlines. Pat is an *Enrolled Agent* (which permits her to practice before the Treasury Department), has a lot of tax background, and is competent in that area as well as bookkeeping. One of her least favorite tax forms is the 990 required of not-for-profit organizations. The 990 tax form is second only to private foundation returns when it comes to being pesky and tricky." Howard, *Patricia Coleman of Chicago Creates Her Niche in Taxes, Trusts and ERISA*, 3 Legal Assistant Today 40.

- **More on This Area of the Law on the Net:**
  - *www.taxsites.com*
  - *www.irs.ustreas.gov/prod/index.html*
  - *guide.lp.findlaw.com/01topics/35tax/index.html*

## 41. Tort Law

A *tort* is a civil wrong that has injured someone. Paralegals who work on *PI* (personal injury) cases are mainly litigation assistants. The major torts are negligence, defamation, strict liability, and misrepresentation. Paralegals in this area are also often involved in worker's compensation cases for injuries that occur on the job. (See *admiralty law, litigation,* and *worker's compensation.*)

- **Comment on Paralegal Work in This Area:**
  "Personal injury/products liability cases can be fascinating, challenging, and educational. They also can be stressful, aggravating and very sad. I have been involved in a great many cases in my career, on both sides of the plaintiff/defendant fence. Some of the cases seemed frivolous and somewhat 'ambulance chasing' in nature. Others were significant cases in which the plaintiff had wrongfully suffered injury. There are many talents a good personal injury/products liability paralegal must have. He or she must be creative, tenacious, observant and able to communicate well with people." Lee, *Personal Injury/Products Liability Cases,* 11 Newsletter 7 (Dallas Ass'n of Legal Assistants).

  "Recently, Mary Mann, a paralegal who works on product liability litigation, was asked by her attorney to track down a specific medical article [on a subject relevant to a current case]. The attorney only had a vague description of the article, a possible title, and the name of the organization that might have published it. In her search Mary spoke by phone to people in New York, Atlanta, Washington, and finally to a doctor in Geneva, Switzerland, who spoke very little English. In her effort to make herself understood by the doctor, Mary continued to speak louder and louder in very simplistic and basic English phrases, as people tend to do when confronted by a language barrier. She is sure her efforts to maintain a professional demeanor were humorous to those passing by her office. However, she did succeed in getting the article and in the process gained a friend in Switzerland!" Fisher, *Spotlight: Mary Mann,* 7 The Assistant 14 (Mississippi Ass'n of Legal Assistants).

  "Asbestos litigation . . . opened up in the late 1970's with the lawsuits initiated against the Johns-Mansville Corporation. In 1982 Mansville filed a Chapter 11 bankruptcy to protect its assets from the thousands of claims being filed against it." Huge numbers of paralegals were employed in this litigation. For those paralegals working *for* Johns-Mansville on the defense team, "the question of morality arose. I get asked about the morality of my job constantly. For me, personal moral judgment does not enter into it. Our legal system is based on the availability of equal representation for both sides. I think I play a small part in making that system work." Welsh, *The Paralegal in Asbestos Litigation,* 10 Ka Leo O'H.A.L.A. 6 (Hawaii Ass'n of Legal Assistants).

- **Quotes from Want Ads:**
  "Medical malpractice law firm seeks paralegal who is a self-starter, has good communication skills, is organized and detail-oriented." Position in PI [personal injury] firm requires "a take-charge person to handle case details from beginning to end." "Prefer person with experience in claims adjustment, medical records, or nursing." Position requires "dynamic, highly-motivated individual who will enjoy the challenge of working independently and handling a wide variety of responsibilities." "Excellent writing skills a must." "Should be able to perform under pressure." Manufacturer of consumer products "seeks paralegal with engineering background." Must be mature enough to handle "heavy client contact." Position requires "ability to read and summarize medical records."

- **More on This Area of the Law on the Net:**
  - *www.cpsc.gov*
  - *guide.lp.findlaw.com/01topics/22tort/index.html*
  - *www.toxlaw.com/bookmarks/laws.html*
  - *www.productslaw.com*

## 42. Tribal Law

Tribal courts on Indian reservations have jurisdiction over many civil and criminal cases in which both parties are Native Americans. Parties are often represented by tribal court advocates who are nonattorney Native Americans. In addition, the judges are often nonattorneys. (See *litigation.*)

- **More on This Area of the Law on the Net:**
  - *www.law.cornell.edu/topics/indian.html*
  - *guide.lp.findlaw.com/01topics/21indian/index.html*

## 43. Water Law[11]

(See also *administrative law* and *real estate law.*)

I. Water Rights
Investigate and analyze specific water rights associated with property:
A. Do research at Department of Water Resources regarding decrees, tabulations, well permits, reservoirs, diversion records, maps, and statements.
B. Communicate in writing and orally with Department of Water Resources personnel regarding status of water rights and wells.
C. Communicate in writing and orally (including interviews) with District Water Commissioners regarding status of water rights and wells, historic use, and use on land.
D. Communicate in writing and orally (including interviews) with property owners and managers,

ranch managers, ditch company personnel, etc. regarding status of water rights and wells, historic use, and use on land.

E. Do research at other agencies and offices (such as the Bureau of Land Management, state archives, historical societies, public libraries).

F. Prepare historic use affidavits.

G. Prepare reports regarding investigation and analysis of the status of water rights and wells, historic use and use on land.

H. Prepare maps, charts, diagrams, etc. regarding status of water rights and wells, historic use, and use on land.

II. Real Estate Transactions

A. Draft documents for the purchase and sale, encumbrance, or lease of water rights and wells.

B. Perform standup title searches in county clerk and recorder's offices.

C. Perform due diligence investigations.

D. Prepare for and assist at closings.

III. Well Permit Applications

A. Prepare well permit documents for filing—applications, land ownership affidavits, statements of beneficial use, amendments to record, extensions of time.

B. Coordinate and monitor the well permitting and drilling process.

C. In writing and orally, communicate with Department of Water Resources personnel, well drillers, and client.

IV. Water Court Proceedings—
Certain district courts have special jurisdiction over water right proceedings. Proceedings are governed by the Rules of Civil Procedure for District Courts and by local water court and district court rules.

A. Prepare water court documents for filing—applications, statements of opposition, draft rulings and orders, stipulations, withdrawals of opposition and affidavits.

B. Maintain diligence filing tickler system. Work with client to record and maintain evidence of diligence.

C. Review, route, and maintain a file of water court resumes.

D. Review, route, and maintain file of term day notices and orders. Prepare attorneys for term day and/or attend term day.

V. Monitor Publications
Read *Reporter*, water court resumes, and register for new water law cases and Department of Water Resources regulations.

● **More on This Area of the Law on the Net:**
  ■ *www.washlaw.edu/subject/water.html*
  ■ *www.hg.org/natres.html*

## 44. Welfare Law (Public Assistance)

(See also *administrative law, pro bono work, public benefits, and social security law.*)

I. Problem Identification

A. Perform preliminary interview:
  1. Identify nonlegal problems for referral to other agencies.
  2. Open a case file or update it.
  3. Using a basic fact sheet (or form), record the information collected during the interview.
  4. Determine next appointment.
  5. Instruct client on what to do next such as obtain medical and birth records, etc.
  6. Arrange for client to see office attorney.

B. Categorize problems.
  1. Help client learn what benefits exist in programs such as:
    a. Public Assistance (TANF)
    b. Social Security
    c. Medicare
  2. Help client fill out application forms.
  3. Deal with client who objects to home visits by case-workers or attempts by department to force him or her to take a job or enter a training program.
  4. Help client when department wants to reduce the amount of client's check or terminate public assistance altogether.

II. Problem Resolution

A. Consult with attorney immediately:
  1. Summarize facts for the attorney.
  2. Submit the case record to the attorney.
  3. Obtain further instructions from attorney.

B. Refer nonlegal problems to other agencies:
  1. Search for an appropriate agency.
  2. Contact agency for the client.

C. Investigate
  1. Verify information (call caseworker, visit department office, etc.).
  2. Search for additional information.
  3. Record relevant facts.
  4. Consult with attorney on difficulties encountered.

D. Analyze laws:
  1. Check office poverty law manual.
  2. Consult with office attorneys.
  3. Contact legal service attorneys outside office.
  4. Do research in law library.

E. Be an informal advocate (to determine if the problem can be resolved without a hearing or court action).
  1. Make sure everyone (department, client, etc.) understands the issue.
  2. Provide missing information.
  3. Pressure the department (with calls, letters, visits, etc.).
  4. Maintain records such as current and closed files.

F. Be a formal advocate:
1. Prior hearing (administrative review)
   a. Determine if such hearing can be asked for and when request must be made.
   b. Draft letter requesting such hearing.
   c. Prepare for hearing (see "Fair Hearing" below).
   d. Conduct hearing (see "Fair Hearing" below).
   e. Follow up (see "Fair Hearing" below).
2. Fair Hearing
   a. Determine if the hearing can be asked for and when request must be made.
   b. Draft letter requesting the hearing.
   c. Prepare for the hearing:
      i. In advance of hearing, request that the department send you the documents it will rely on at the hearing.
      ii. In advance of hearing, make sure that everyone (department representatives, client, etc.) is going to the hearing on the same issues.
      iii. Organize other relevant documents such as canceled check stubs.
      iv. Find witnesses.
      v. Prepare all witnesses (for example, explain what hearing will be about; conduct a brief role-playing experience to acquaint them with the format and what you will be seeking from the witnesses).
      vi. Map out a preliminary strategy to use in conducting the hearing.
      vii. Make a final attempt to resolve the issues without a hearing.
      viii. Make sure client and other witnesses will appear (e.g., give address of the hearing, take them to the hearing on the date of the hearing).
   d. Conduct the hearing:
      i. Make sure the name, address, and title of everyone present are identified for the record.
      ii. Make opening statement summarizing client's case.
      iii. Ask for a postponement if the client has not appeared or if an emergency has arisen requiring more time to prepare.
      iv. Clearly state what relief the client is seeking from the hearing.
      v. If confusion exists on the issues, fight for a statement of the issues most favorable to the client.
      vi. Take notes on the opening statement of the department representative.
      vii. Complain if department failed to provide sufficient information in advance of the hearing.
      viii. Present the client's case:
         a. Submit documents.

         b. Conduct direct examination of the client's witnesses, including the client.
         c. Conduct re-direct examination of witnesses (if allowed).
         d. Cite the law.
      ix. Rebut case of department:
         a. Raise objections to their documents and their interpretation of the law.
         b. Cross-examine their witnesses.
         c. Re-cross-examine their witnesses (if allowed).
      x. Make closing statement summarizing the case of the client and repeating the result the client is seeking.
   e. Follow up:
      i. Urge the hearing officer to reach a result without undue delay.
      ii. Request a copy of the transcript of the hearing.
      iii. When a result is reached, pressure the department to abide by it.
      iv. Consult with attorney to determine whether the hearing result should be appealed in court.
3. Court
   a. Assist the attorney in gathering the documents for appeal; interview the witnesses, etc.
   b. Prepare preliminary draft of the legal argument to be made to trial court handling the appeal.
   c. Be a general assistant for the attorney at court proceedings.
   d. File papers in court.
   e. Serve the papers on opponents.
G. Miscellaneous
1. Train other paralegals.
2. Write pamphlets on public assistance law for distribution in the community.
3. Organize the community around poverty issues.

● **More on This Area of the Law on the Net:**
   ■ *www.law.cornell.edu/topics/welfare.html*
   ■ *www.welfarelaw.org*

### 45. Worker's Compensation Law

(See also *administrative law, labor and employment law*, and *litigation*.)

I. Interviewing
A. Collect and record details of the claim (date of injury, nature and dates of prior illness, etc.).
B. Collect or arrange for the collection of documents, such as medical records and employment contract.
C. Schedule physical examination.

II. Drafting
A. Claim for compensation.
B. Request for hearing.
C. Medical authorization.

D.  Demand for medical information in the possession of respondent or insurance carrier.

E.  Proposed summary of issues involved.

III.  Advocacy

A.  Informal: Contact (call, visit, write a letter to) the employer and/or the insurance carrier to determine whether the matter can be resolved without a formal hearing or court action.

B.  Formal: Represent claimant at the administrative hearing.

IV.  Follow-up

A.  Determine whether the payment is in compliance with the award.

B.  If not, draft and file statutory demand for proper payment.

C.  If such a statutory demand is filed, prepare a tickler system to monitor the claim.

● *Comment on Paralegal Work in This Area:*

"I have been working as a paralegal in this area for more than seven years. This is one of the areas of the law [in this state] in which a paralegal can perform almost all of the functions to properly process a Workers' Compensation claim. A Workers' Compensation practice must be a very high volume in order to be [profitable]. Thus paralegal assistance in handling a large case load is an absolute necessity. An extensive volume of paperwork is processed on a daily basis. Client contact is a major portion of a paralegal's responsibilities. With a large case load, it is physically impossible for an attorney to communicate with each and every client on a regular basis. It is not unusual for a paralegal in this field to work on several hundred files each week." Lindberg, *Virtually Limitless Responsibilities of a Workers' Compensation Paralegal*, Update 6 (Cleveland Ass'n of Paralegals).

"The Company's two worker's compensation paralegals are responsible for reviewing each claimant's file, preparing a summary of medical reports, outlining the issues, and reviewing with the adjusters any questions or circumstances of the case before the claimant's deposition. In addition, they draft any necessary subpoenas, witness lists and settlement stipulations for their respective attorneys, and collect information and draft letters to the Special Disability Trust Fund outlining the Company's theory of reimbursement for second injury cases." Miquel, *Walt Disney World Company's Legal Assistants: Their Role in the Show*, 16 Facts and Findings 29 (NALA).

● **More on This Area of the Law on the Net:**
  ■  *www.law.cornell.edu/topics/workers_compensation. html*
  ■  *www.dol.gov/dol/esa/public/owcp_org.htm*

## A Paralegal in the White House

Meg Shields Duke

New Roles in the Law Conference Report 93 (1982)

[After working as a paralegal on the Reagan-Bush Campaign Committee], I'm a paralegal in the White House Counsel's office. I believe I'm the first paralegal in this office, in the White House. They've had law clerks in the past, but never have they hired a paralegal. There's one paralegal to nine attorneys at the moment. I think that's ridiculous and I hope we'll change that in the next several months to a year. But my responsibilities here are varied. Everybody is still trying to determine what their turf is. But for the first couple of months I've worked on a lot of transition matters, which might be expected. I was the coordinator for our transition audit (congressional transition audit), from the Hill which just ended a few weeks ago. I have engaged in drafting correspondence concerning the use of the president's name, the use of his image; our policy on gift acceptance by public employees; drafting standards of conduct for public employees in the White House, job freeze litigation, those few controversial things. The last few weeks of my time have been devoted to the Lefever nomination. It's all been fascinating. Anyway, there are a number of areas that we also get involved in, the ethics of government act, for example. It's the first time it has been applied across the board to a new administration. It has been very, very time consuming for all our staff. I've been assisting in that, reviewing each individual file for high level government employees. As I said, I'm in the counsel's office now and intend to stay for a couple of years. But I would like to start my own paralegal firm. I have a close friend who started her own paralegal firm in Florida and we've talked often in the past of expanding it to Washington and a few other cities West where we'd like to spend some time. We're investigating the possibilities of reopening another firm here in Washington D.C. at some point, maybe in the next year and a half. But I think there is a place for more paralegals in the public sector, at least in the White House area, and I understand the Department of Justice of course has many, but I'd like to see it expanded and I'd also like to see more people branching out and trying this independent approach because I think it's fun. It's risky, but it's worth it.

## Section D
# Finding a Job: Employment Strategies

There are many different strategies for finding employment. The strategies discussed in this section are primarily for individuals who have had very little or no employment experience with attorneys. Many of the strategies, however, are also relevant to people who have worked in law offices as secretaries or who are paralegals seeking other employment opportunities in the field.

### GENERAL STRATEGIES FOR FINDING EMPLOYMENT
1. Begin now.
2. Start compiling a Job Hunting Notebook.
3. Organize an employment workshop.
4. Locate working paralegals.
5. Go on informational interviews.
6. Locate potential employers.
7. Surf the Internet.
8. Prepare a résumé, cover letter, and writing sample(s).
9. Prepare for the job interview.

### Strategy 1: Begin Now
You should begin preparing for the job hunt on the first day of your first paralegal class. Do *not* wait until the program is almost over. Although your school will provide you with guidance and leads, you should assume that obtaining a job will be your responsibility. For most students, the job you get will be the job *you* find.

While in school, your primary focus should be on compiling an excellent academic record. *In addition*, you must start the job search now. It is not too early, for example, to begin compiling the lists called for in the Job Hunting Notebook that we will examine later. When school is over, be prepared to spend a substantial amount of additional time looking for employment, particularly if your part of the country is currently a "buyers market," where there are more applicants than available jobs.

*Being* a paralegal requires determination, assertiveness, initiative, and creativity. *Finding* paralegal work may require these same skills. This is not a field for the faint of heart who are easily discouraged.

It may be that you are still very uncertain about the kinds of employment options that exist. How can you begin looking for a job if you don't yet know what kind of job you would like to have? First of all, many of the suggested steps in this chapter will be helpful regardless of the kind of job you are pursuing. More important, however, the very process of going through these steps will help you clarify your employment objectives. As you begin seeking information and leads, the insights will come to you. At this point, keep an open mind, be conscientious, and begin now.

### Strategy 2: Begin Compiling a Job Hunting Notebook
Later in this chapter, you will find an outline for a Job Hunting Notebook that you should start preparing now. (See exhibit 2.14.) Following the outline, there are sample pages for the various sections in the Notebook.

### Strategy 3: Organize an Employment Workshop
Exhibit 2.1, at the beginning of this chapter, gave you a list of the major categories (and subcategories) of paralegal employment. As a group project, your class should begin organizing an employment conference or workshop consisting of a panel of paralegals from as many of the categories and subcategories of paralegals as you can locate in your area. Try to find at least one paralegal to represent each category and subcategory. The guest paralegals could be asked to come to an evening or Saturday session to discuss the following topics:

- What I do (what a typical day consists of)
- How I obtained my job
- My recommendations for finding work

■ Dos and don'ts in the employment interview
■ What were the most valuable parts of my legal education, etc.

Although you could ask a teacher or the director of the program at your school to help you organize the workshop, it is recommended that you make it a student-run workshop. It will be good practice for you in taking the kind of initiative that is essential in finding employment. You might want to consider asking the nearest paralegal association to co-sponsor the workshop with your class. (See question 5 in the form letter found at the end of the index of this book.)

Have a meeting of your class and select a chairperson to help coordinate the event. Then divide up the tasks of contacting participants, arranging for a room, preparing an agenda for the workshop, etc. You may want to invite former graduates of your school to attend as panel speakers or as members of the audience. The ideal time for such a workshop is a month or two after you begin your coursework. This means that you need to begin organizing immediately.

### Strategy 4: Locate working paralegals

Perhaps the most significant step in finding employment is to begin talking with paralegals who are already employed. They are the obvious experts on how to find a job! They are probably also very knowledgeable about employment opportunities in their office and in similar offices in the area. (See Job Hunting Notebook, p. 104.)

Attend paralegal association meetings. See appendix B for a list of paralegal associations. Contact the one nearest you and ask about joining. There may be special dues for students.

Ask if the association has a **job bank** service. Here is what a paralegal who used this service had to say:

> I gained access to an opening to a wonderful job at a law firm exclusively listed in the Minnesota Association of Legal Assistants (MALA) Job Bank. . . . I would never have heard about the position if I hadn't been a member of MALA.[12]

Not all associations have job bank services, however, and those that do have them may not make them available to students. (See question 4 in the form letter found at the end of the index of this book.)

Try to obtain copies of current and past issues of the monthly or bimonthly newsletters of all the local paralegal associations in your area. Some of these newsletters give listings of job openings that mention specific employers. If so, try to contact the employers to determine if the position is still open. If it is no longer open, ask if you could send your résumé to be kept on file in the event a position becomes available in the future. Also, try to speak to the paralegal who filled the position in order to ask for leads to openings elsewhere. When you are told that the position is filled, simply ask, "Is there a chance that I could speak for a moment on the phone to the person who was hired? I'd like to get a general idea about working in this area of the law." If the person is hesitant to grant this request, say, "Would you be kind enough to give this paralegal my name and number and ask him (or her) to give me a call so that I could ask a few brief questions? I would really appreciate it."

Ask the local paralegal association if it has a *job-finding manual* for paralegals in your area. The manual may have been created for an employment workshop conducted by the association. Ask the association if such a manual—or any other handouts—is still available from a prior workshop. Also find out if the association has scheduled a future workshop on employment that you can attend.

Try to attend a general session of the association. Many associations meet once a month. Become a participant. The more active you are as a student member, the more contacts you will make. If there is no paralegal association near you, organize one—beginning with your own student body and past graduates of your school.

Paralegal newsletters often announce **continuing legal education** (CLE) conferences and seminars for practicing paralegals. Similar announcements are found in the newsletters of the two major national paralegal associations:

■ *National Paralegal Reporter* National Federation of Paralegal Associations *www.paralegals.org/Publications/home.html*

---

**job bank** A service that lists available jobs, usually available only to members of an organization.

**continuing legal education (CLE)** Training in the law (usually short-term) that a person receives after completing his or her formal legal training.

■ *Facts & Findings* National Association of Legal Assistants
  *www.nala.org/Facts_Findings.htm*

Employed paralegals attend these events in large numbers. Hence they are excellent places to meet experienced paralegals.

Paralegals sometimes attend CLE sessions for attorneys conducted by local bar associations, particularly those bar associations where paralegals are allowed to become associate members. You should also find out if there are associations of legal secretaries and of legal administrators in your area. If so, they might conduct workshops or meetings that you can attend. At such meetings and elsewhere, try to talk with individual legal secretaries and legal administrators about employment opportunities for paralegals where they work.

### Strategy 5: Go on Informational Interviews

**informational interview** An interview whose primary purpose is to find out information about a particular kind of employment.

An **informational interview** is an opportunity for you to sit down with someone, preferably where he or she works, to learn about a particular kind of employment. Unlike a job interview, where you are the one interviewed, *you* do the interviewing in an informational interview. You ask questions that will help you learn what working at that kind of office is like.

> If, for example, you are a real "people" person who finds antitrust theory fascinating, you should listen to antitrust paralegals discussing their day-to-day work. You may hear that most of them spend years in document warehouses with one lawyer, two other paralegals and a pizza delivery man as their most significant personal contacts. That information may influence your decision about antitrust as a career path.[13]

Do *not* try to turn an informational interview into a job interview. While on an informational interview, it is inappropriate to ask a person for a job. Toward the end of the interview, you can delicately ask for leads to employment and you can ask how the person obtained his or her job, but these inquiries should be secondary to your primary purpose of obtaining information about the realities of work at that kind of office. Do not use an informational interview as a subterfuge for a job interview that you are having difficulty obtaining.

The best people to interview are employed paralegals whom you have met through the steps outlined in Strategy 4. While some attorneys and legal administrators may also be willing to grant you informational interviews, the best people to talk to are those who were once in your shoes. Simply say to a paralegal you have met, "Would it be possible for me to come down to the office where you work for a brief informational interview?" If he or she is not familiar with this kind of interview, explain its limited objective. Many will be too busy to grant you an interview, but you have nothing to lose by asking, even if you are turned down. As an added inducement, consider offering to take the paralegal to lunch. In addition to meeting this paralegal, try to have at least a brief tour of the office where he or she works. Observing how different kinds of employees interact with each other and with available technology in the office will be invaluable. If it is not possible to go to an office, go to paralegal association meetings and look for paralegals who work in areas of the law in which you may have an interest. Simply say to them, "Can I ask you about the work you do?" In effect, you can conduct informational interviews of paralegals wherever you find them.

Here are some of the questions you should ask in an informational interview.

- What is a typical day for you in this office?
- What kinds of assignments do you receive?
- How much overtime is usually expected? Do you take work home with you?
- How do the attorneys interact with paralegals in this kind of practice? Who does what? How many different attorneys does a paralegal work with? How are assignment priorities set?
- How do the paralegals interact with secretaries and other support staff in the office?

- What is the hierarchy of the office?
- What kind of education best prepares a paralegal to work in this kind of office? What courses are most effective?
- What is the most challenging aspect of the job? The most frustrating?
- How are paralegals perceived in this office?
- Are you glad you became this kind of paralegal in this kind of office? Would you do it over again?
- What advice would you give to someone who wants to become a paralegal like yourself?

Several of these questions are also appropriate in a job interview, as we will see later.

One final word of caution. Any information you learn at the office about clients or legal matters must be kept confidential, even if the person you are interviewing is casual about revealing such information to you. This person may not be aware that he or she is acting unethically by disclosing confidential information. Carelessness in this regard is not uncommon.

### Strategy 6: Locate Potential Employers

There are a number of ways to locate attorneys:

a. Placement office
b. Personal contacts
c. Ads
d. Other paralegals
e. Employment agencies
f. Directories and other lists of attorneys
g. Courts and bar association meetings

(See Job Hunting Notebook, page 105).

For every attorney that you contact, you want to know the following:

- Has the attorney hired paralegals in the past?
- If so, is the attorney interested in hiring more paralegals?
- If the attorney has never hired paralegals before, might he or she consider hiring one?
- Does the attorney know of other attorneys who might be interested in hiring paralegals?

The last point is particularly important. Attorneys from different firms often talk with each other about their practice, including their experiences with paralegals or their plans for hiring paralegals. Hence always ask about other firms. If you obtain a lead, begin your contact with the other firm by mentioning the name of the attorney who gave you the lead. You might say, "Mary Smith told me that you have hired paralegals in the past and might be interested in hiring another paralegal," or "John Rodriguez suggested that I contact you concerning possible employment at your firm as a paralegal." If you do not have the name of a contact to mention, you might simply say, "I'm going to be finishing my paralegal training soon [or I've just completed my paralegal training] and I was wondering whether your office employs paralegals." If the response is not encouraging, be sure to ask, "Do you have any suggestions on other offices where I might check?"

**a. Placement Office**   Start with the placement office of your paralegal school. Talk with staff members and check the bulletin board regularly (e.g., daily). If your school is part of a university that has a law school, you might want to check the placement office of the law school as well. While paralegal jobs are usually not listed there, you may find descriptions of law firms with the number of attorneys and paralegals employed. (See also appendix 2.A at the end of this chapter.) It might be useful for you to identify the major resources for obtaining *attorney* jobs, such as special directories, lists or ads in bar publications, legal newspapers, etc. In particular, try to find the following resource used by unemployed attorneys and law students:

*National Directory of Legal Employers* National Association for Law Placement *www.nalp.org*

This directory is available as a pamphlet and online through LEXIS–NEXIS. (Contact the central *public* library where you live to find out if it has this directory in its careers section.) Many of the hundreds of law offices in the directory indicate how many attorneys *and paralegals* they employ. Hence it may provide leads on offices to contact about paralegal employment.

**b. Personal Contacts**    Make a list of attorneys who fall into the following categories:

- Personal friends
- Friends of friends
- Attorneys you have hired
- Attorneys your relatives have hired
- Attorneys your former employers have hired
- Attorneys your friends have hired
- Attorneys your church has hired
- Teachers
- Politicians
- Neighbors
- Etc.

You should consider contacting these attorneys about their own paralegal hiring plans as well as for references to other attorneys. Don't be reluctant to take advantage of any direct or indirect association that you might have with an attorney. Such contacts are the essence of **networking,** which simply means establishing contacts with people who may be helpful to you now or in the future. We will have more to say about the critical importance of networking in chapter 3.

**networking** Establishing contacts with people who might become personal or professional resources.

**c. Ads**    You should regularly check the classified pages of your daily and Sunday newspaper as well as the legal newspaper for your area. (See exhibit 2.3 for some of the common abbreviations used in ads.) If you are seeking employment in another city, the main

| EXHIBIT 2.3 | Classified Ad Abbreviations | | |
|---|---|---|---|
| **ABBREVIATION** | **TRANSLATION** | **ABBREVIATION** | **TRANSLATION** |
| 2+ | plus means "or more" (years of experience) | gd | good |
| | | immed | immediate |
| acctg | acounting | inq | inquire |
| advc | advancement | k | thousands (usually |
| agcy | agency | | annual salary in |
| appt | appointment | | dollars) |
| asst | assistant | LLC | Limited Liability |
| atty | attorney | | Company |
| begnr | beginner | loc | location or located |
| bkpg | bookkeeping | mfg | manufacturing |
| bnfts | benefits | mgmt | management |
| clk | clerk | ofc | office |
| co | company (mjr co means major company) | opty | opportunity |
| | | ovtm | overtime |
| | | pd vac | paid vacation |
| col grad | college graduate | p/t | part-time |
| col | college | pub | public |
| dept | department | refs | references |
| dict | dictation | secty | secretary |
| DOE | depending on experience | | |
| EOE | Equal Opportunity Employer | sr | senior (usually means experienced) |
| eves | evenings | w/ | with (w/wo means |
| exp nec | experience necessary | | with or without) |
| exp pfd | experience preferred | wkend | weekend |
| f/pd | fee paid | wpm | words per minute |
| f/t | full-time | yr | year |

**Source:** *Finding a Job in the Want Ads* (New Mexico SOICC).

branch of your public library and the main library of large universities in your area may have out-of-town newspapers. Find out if these newspapers are online by checking the following sites:

- *www.newspapers.com*
- *newslink.org*
- *www.n-net.com*

Online newspapers may include their classified ads. If you have friends in these other cities, they might be willing to send you clippings from the classified ads of their newspapers. Occasionally, *national* legal newspapers have paralegal employment ads. Check:

- *National Law Journal*
  *www.nlj.com*
- *American Lawyer*
  *www.americanlawyer.com*
- *Corporate Counsel*
  *www.corpcounsel.com*

Law libraries often subscribe to such newspapers. They will also subscribe to local legal newspapers that may have paralegal ads.

Look for ads under the headings "Paralegal" and "Legal Assistant." For example:

| PARALEGAL TRUST ACCOUNTANTS For details see our ad in this section headed: ACCOUNTANT | PARALEGAL (CORPORATE) Large downtown Boston law firm seeks expd Corporate Paralegal. Opportunity for responsibility and growth. Must have strong academic background. Computer literacy a plus. Salary commensurate with exp. Send résumé in confidence to: X2935 TIMES | LEGAL ASSISTANT Large West Palm Beach, Florida firm wishes to employ legal assistant with immigration/naturalization experience, in addition to civil litigation, research & pleading abilities. Knowledge of Germanic languages helpful. Full fringe benefits/profit sharing. Salary negotiable. Contact . . . |
|---|---|---|
| PARALEGALS Fee Pd. Salary Open. Corporate & Real Estate positions. Superior writing ability is a necessity. Must be able to work under pressure. Superior opportunities. Contact . . . | | |

Look for "buzzwords" in the ads. These are key words or phrases that indicate what the employer is looking for (e.g., "computer literacy" "work under pressure," "writing," "immigration"). Later, when you write your résumé and cover letter in response to an ad, you should try to use (indeed, emphasize) these buzzwords. For detailed quotes from want ads for a variety of different kinds of paralegal jobs, see section C in this chapter on paralegal specialties.

The ad may not give the name and address of the employer seeking the paralegal. Instead, it will direct interested parties to an intermediary, such as a newspaper, which forwards all responses to the employer. Such ads are called **blind ads**. Some ads are placed by private employment agencies that specialize in legal placements.

You will find that most want ads seek paralegals with experience in a particular area of practice. Hence, if you are a recent graduate of a paralegal school who is looking for a beginning or entry-level position, you may not meet the qualifications sought in the ads. (See section F in this chapter, where we discuss the Catch-22 dilemma of no-experience/no-job faced by graduates seeking their first paralegal job.) Should you answer ads that specify qualifications such as experience that you do not have? Suppose, for example, that an ad seeks a corporate paralegal with two years of experience." You might consider answering such an ad as follows:

> I am responding to your ad for a corporate paralegal. I do not have the experience indicated in the ad, but I did take an intensive course on corporate law at my paralegal school, and I'm wondering whether I could send you my résumé so that you can consider what I have to offer.

**blind ad** A classified ad that does not give the name and address of the prospective employer.

Or, phrased more positively:

> I am responding to your ad for a corporate paralegal. I feel that I qualify for the position even though I don't have the experience indicated in the ad. I took an intensive course in corporate law in my paralegal school. Could I send you my résumé and writing sample so that you can consider what I have to offer?

If the answer is no, you can certainly ask for leads to anyone else who might be hiring individuals like yourself.

When reading want ads, do not limit yourself to the entries for "Paralegal" and "Legal Assistant." Also look for headings for positions that may be law related, such as "Research Assistant," "Legislative Aide," or "Law Library Assistant." For example:

---

RESEARCH ASSISTANT
IMMEDIATE POSITION
Social Science Research Institute in downtown looking for coder/editor of legal survey instruments. Post Box L3040.

---

PROOFREADER
Leading newspaper for lawyers has an immediate opening for a proofreader of manuscripts and galleys. Attention to detail, some night work. Past experience preferred. Low teens. Call Nance, 964-9700, Ext. 603.

---

LEGISLATIVE ASSISTANT/ SECRETARY—Good skills essential, dwntwn location, send résumé/sal. requirements to Post Box M 8341.

---

RECRUITMENT COORDINATOR
Local office of national law firm seeks individual to coordinate the attorney recruiting and the paralegal program. B.A. required and 1–3 years' personnel, recruitment, or paralegal experience preferred. Salary commensurate with experience. E.O.E. Please send résumé and salary requirements to Box 9-24-2101.

---

LEGISLATIVE ASSISTANT/ ADMINISTRATOR—If you are looking for that foot in the door, on CAPITOL HILL, here's the job for you. Newsmaking Congressman seeks dedicated indiv to handle challenging & rewarding duties. Track legislation, handle corresp & mailing. Get involved in the world of Capitol Hill. Good typg. Call Tues–Fri 8:30–4.

LIBRARY/CLERICAL— permanent, full-time pos. at lge law firm library. Duties include loose-leaf filing, processing new books & current periodicals, shelving books, and some typing. Exper. w/loose-leaf filing pref. Good benefits and excel. leave policy. Respond to Box No. M8272.

---

ADMINISTRATOR—LAW
Medium-size established law firm seeks manager with administrative, financial & personnel experience to supervise all non-legal office activities. Salary will be commensurate with experience. EOE. Applicants should send résumés with salary requirements to Box 9-17-2085.

---

Of course, some of the above jobs may not be what you are looking for. They may not be directly related to your legal training and experience. Nevertheless, you should read such ads carefully. Some might be worth pursuing.

On most classified pages, you will find many ads for legal secretaries, docket clerks, and word processors. You might want to respond to such ads as follows:

I saw your ad for a legal secretary. I am a trained paralegal and am wondering whether you have any openings for paralegals. If not, I would greatly appreciate your referring me to any attorneys you know who may be looking for competent paralegals.

What about *applying* for a clerical position in a law office? Many paralegals take the view that this would be a mistake. In a tight employment market, however, some paralegals believe that a secretarial or typing job would be a way to "get a foot in the door," and hope that they will eventually be able to graduate into a position in the office that is commensurate with their paralegal training. Such a course of action is obviously a very personal decision that you must make on your own. Clerical staff *do* sometimes get promoted to paralegal positions in a firm, but people also can get stuck in clerical positions.

Should you ever respond to want ads *for attorneys*? Such ads regularly appear in legal newspapers and magazines. Of course, a paralegal cannot claim to be an attorney. But any office that is looking for attorneys obviously has a need for legal help. Hence, consider these possible reasons for responding to such ads, particularly when they give the name and address of the office seeking the attorney:

- Perhaps the office is *also* looking for paralegal help but is simply not advertising for it (or you have not seen the want ad for paralegals).
- Perhaps the office is having difficulty finding the attorney it is seeking and would consider hiring a paralegal for a temporary period of time to perform paralegal tasks *while* continuing the search for the attorney.
- Perhaps the office has never considered hiring a paralegal *instead of* an attorney but would be interested in exploring the idea.

Many of these employers may be totally uninterested in a response by a paralegal to an ad for an attorney. Yet none of the possibilities just described is irrational. The effort might be productive. Even if you receive a flat rejection, you can always use the opportunity to ask the person you contact if he or she knows of any other offices that are hiring paralegals.

Finally, a word about want ads placed *by a paralegal* seeking employment. Should you ever place an ad in a publication read by attorneys, such as the journal of the bar association or the legal newspaper for your area? Such ads can be expensive and are seldom productive. Nevertheless, if you have a particular skill—for example, if you are a nurse trained as a paralegal and are seeking a position in a medical malpractice firm, an ad might strike a responsive chord.

**d. Through Other Paralegals**   In Strategy 4 mentioned earlier, we discussed methods to contact working paralegals. Once you talk with a paralegal, you can, of course, obtain information about contacting the employing attorney of that paralegal.

**e. Employment Agencies**   There have always been employment agencies for the placement of attorneys. Many of these agencies also handle placements for full-time and temporary paralegal positions. Recently, a number of agencies have been opened to deal primarily with paralegal placement. To find these agencies on the Internet, see exhibit 2.6, More Employment Resources on the Internet, later in the chapter. In this exhibit, check the heading "Temporary Legal Staffing." Many employers will hire temporary workers with the goal of hiring them full-time if they fit in and perform well. (This arrangement is referred to as temp-to-hire.) One placement agency recently used the ad at the top of page 76 in a newspaper.

Look for such ads in the classified pages of general circulation and legal newspapers. Paralegal association newsletters and special paralegal magazines such as *Legal Assistant Today* (*www.legalassistanttoday.com*) may also have this kind of ad. Check your Yellow Pages under "Employment Agencies." If you are not sure which of the listed agencies cover legal placements, call several at random and ask which agencies in the city handle paralegal placement or legal placement in general. Caution is needed in using such agencies, however. Some of them know very little about paralegals, in spite of their ads claiming to place paralegals. You may find that the agency views a paralegal as a secretary with a little extra training.

| Help Wanted |
|---|
| **Paralegal Agency**                                        **Fee Paid**<br>**Paralegal Placement Experts Recognized by**<br>**Over 200 Law Firms and Corporations**<br>**PENSIONS**<br>Outstanding law firm seeks 1+ yrs pension paralegal exper. Major responsibilities, quality clients & liberal benefits. Salary commensurate w/exper.<br>**LITIGATION**<br>SEVERAL positions open at LAW FIRMS for litigation paralegals. Major benefits incl bonus.<br>**MANAGING CLERK**<br>Midtown law firm seeks 1+ yrs exper as a managing clerk. Work directly w/top management. Liberal benefits. |
| These are just a few of the many paralegal positions we have available. Call us for professional career guidance. |

All agencies charge a placement fee. You must check whether the fee is paid by the employer or by the employee hired through the agency. Read the agency's service contract carefully before signing. Question the agency about the jobs they have available—for instance, whether evening work is expected or what typing requirements there are, if any.

Most employment or staffing agencies that work with paralegals can place them in temporary or part-time positions. Law firms and corporate law departments may prefer temporary paralegals because of the low overhead costs involved, the availability of experienced people on short notice for indefinite periods, and the ability to end the relationship without having to go through the sometimes wrenching experience of terminating permanent employees. Some agencies are able to handle every aspect of part-time paralegal placement, including payroll. The paralegal might be an employee of the agency. The fee paid to such an agency by the law office will include the cost of paying the paralegal and all administrative aspects of the placement.

**f. Directories and Other Lists of Attorneys**     Find a directory or list of attorneys. Ask a librarian at any law library or general library in your area. Your Yellow Pages will also list attorneys, often by specialty.

Also check with a librarian about national directories of attorneys. Two of the major directories are:

- *Martindale-Hubbell Law Directory*
  - available in bound volumes
  - available free on the Internet (*www.martindale.com*)
  - available for a fee at LEXIS–NEXIS
- *West's Legal Directory*
  - available free on the Internet (*directory.findlaw.com*)
  - available for a fee at WESTLAW

For an excerpt from the pages of the bound *Martindale-Hubbell Law Directory*, see exhibit 2.4. *Martindale-Hubbell* gives descriptions of law firms by state and city or county. For each firm, you are given brief biographies of the attorneys (listing bar memberships, college attended, etc.) as well as the firm's areas of practice. (As we will see in chapter 11, *Martindale-Hubbell* also includes a law digest that summarizes the law of every state and many foreign countries.) For an excerpt from *West's Legal Directory* at its findlaw site, see exhibit 2.5. (We will examine WESTLAW and LEXIS–NEXIS in greater detail in chapters 11 and 13.)

In addition to these broad-based legal directories, you should try to locate specialty directories of attorneys. Examples include criminal law attorneys, corporate counsel, bankruptcy attorneys, black attorneys, and women attorneys, etc. Here are examples of these associations on the Internet:

- National Bar Association (African-American Attorneys) *www.nationalbar.org*
- Hispanic National Bar Association *www.hnba.com*
- National Asian Pacific American Bar Association *www.napaba.org*
- Hellenic Bar Association *www.hellenicbarassociation.com*
- American Association of Nurse Attorneys *www.taana.org*

Read whatever biographical data is provided on the attorneys. If you have something in common with a particular attorney (for example, you were both born in the same small town or you both went to the same school), you might want to mention this fact in a cover letter or phone conversation.

| EXHIBIT 2.4 | Excerpt from a Page in Martindale-Hubbell Law Directory |
| --- | --- |

### YARBROUGH & ELLIOTT, P.C.
*1420 WEST MOCKINGBIRD LANE*
*SUITE 390, LB115*
**DALLAS, TEXAS 75247**
*Telephone: 214-267-1100*
*Fax: 214-267-1200*
*URL: http://www.yarbroughandelliott.com*

*Corporate Law, Partnership, Real Estate, Civil Litigation, Estate Planning, Family Law.*

**GEORGE M. YARBROUGH, JR.,** born Memphis, Tennessee, January 22, 1953; admitted to bar, 1978, Texas. *Education:* University of Mississippi (B.B.A., with honors, 1975); Southern Methodist University (J.D., 1978). Phi Eta Sigma; Phi Kappa Phi; Beta Gamma Sigma; Omicron Delta Kappa. President, Associated Student Body, University of Mississippi, 1974-1975. Member, Student Bar Association Executive Council, 1975-1976. *Member:* Dallas and American Bar Associations; State Bar of Texas (Member, Compensation and Employee Benefits Committee, 1986-1988). *PRACTICE AREAS:* Buying and Selling of Businesses; Limited Liability Company Law; Family Business Law.

**NANCY GAIL ELLIOTT,** born Corpus Christi, Texas, January 17, 1954; admitted to bar, 1985, Texas. *Education:* University of Texas (B.S., 1975; M.Ed., 1977); Texas Tech University (J.D., 1984). Phi Theta Kappa; Kappa Delta Pi; Phi Delta Phi. *Member:* Dallas Bar Association; State Bar of Texas. *PRACTICE AREAS:* Mechanics Liens; Asset Protection; Estate Planning; Guardianship; Contested Wills.

**g. Courts and Bar Association Meetings**     You can also meet attorneys at the courts of your area—for example, during a recess or at the end of the day. Bar association committee meetings are sometimes open to nonattorneys. The same may be true of continuing legal education (CLE) seminars conducted for attorneys. When the other strategies for contacting attorneys do not seem productive, consider going to places where attorneys congregate. Simply introduce yourself and ask if they know of paralegal employment opportunities at their firms or at other firms. If you meet an attorney who practices in a particular specialty, it would be helpful if you could describe your course work or general interest in that kind of law. If you are doing some research in that area of the law, you might begin by asking for some research leads before you ask about employment.

**h. Miscellaneous**     Look for ads in legal newspapers in which an attorney is seeking information about a particular product involved in a suit that is contemplated or underway. Or read feature stories in a legal newspaper on major litigation that is about to begin. If the area of the law interests you, contact the law firms involved (using the directories just described) to ask about employment opportunities for paralegals. Many firms hire additional paralegals, particularly for large cases.

Find the bar journal of your local or state bar association in the law library. The articles in the journal are often written by attorneys from the state. If the subject of an article interests you, read it and call or write the author. Ask a question or two about the topic of the article and the area of the law involved. Then ask about employment opportunities for paralegals in that area.

**EXHIBIT 2.5**  West's Legal Directory on Findlaw.com (www.directory.findlaw.com)

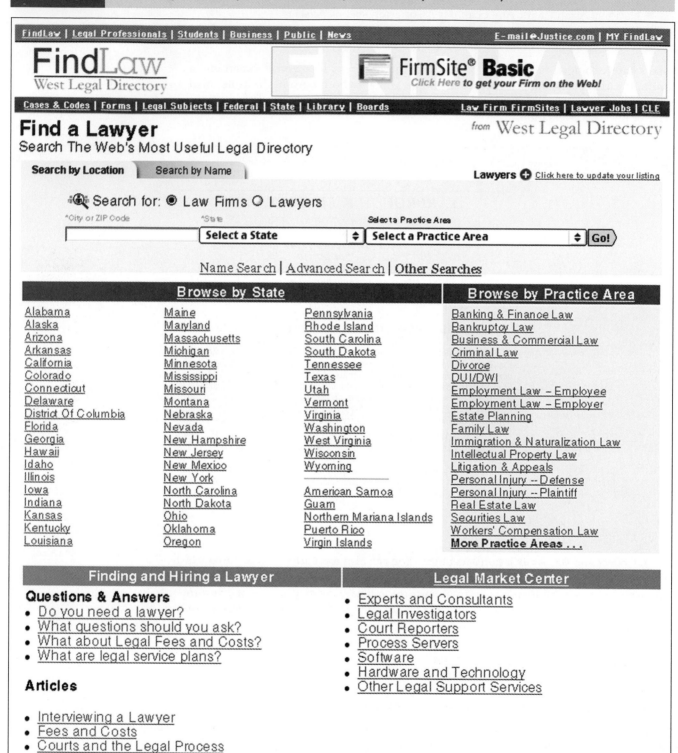

FindLaw | Legal Professionals | Students | Business | Public | News          E-mail@Justice.com | MY FindLaw

# FindLaw
## West Legal Directory

FirmSite® **Basic**
*Click Here to get your Firm on the Web!*

Cases & Codes | Forms | Legal Subjects | Federal | State | Library | Boards     Law Firm FirmSites | Lawyer Jobs | CLE

# Find a Lawyer
Search The Web's Most Useful Legal Directory          *from* West Legal Directory

**Search by Location** | Search by Name          Lawyers ⊕ Click here to update your listing

🔍 Search for: ● Law Firms ○ Lawyers

*City or ZIP Code         *State         Select a Practice Area

[                ]  [ Select a State ▾ ]  [ Select a Practice Area ▾ ]  [ Go! ]

Name Search | Advanced Search | Other Searches

### Browse by State

| | | |
|---|---|---|
| Alabama | Maine | Pennsylvania |
| Alaska | Maryland | Rhode Island |
| Arizona | Massachusetts | South Carolina |
| Arkansas | Michigan | South Dakota |
| California | Minnesota | Tennessee |
| Colorado | Mississippi | Texas |
| Connecticut | Missouri | Utah |
| Delaware | Montana | Vermont |
| District Of Columbia | Nebraska | Virginia |
| Florida | Nevada | Washington |
| Georgia | New Hampshire | West Virginia |
| Hawaii | New Jersey | Wisconsin |
| Idaho | New Mexico | Wyoming |
| Illinois | New York | |
| Iowa | North Carolina | American Samoa |
| Indiana | North Dakota | Guam |
| Kansas | Ohio | Northern Mariana Islands |
| Kentucky | Oklahoma | Puerto Rico |
| Louisiana | Oregon | Virgin Islands |

### Browse by Practice Area

Banking & Finance Law
Bankruptcy Law
Business & Commercial Law
Criminal Law
Divorce
DUI/DWI
Employment Law – Employee
Employment Law – Employer
Estate Planning
Family Law
Immigration & Naturalization Law
Intellectual Property Law
Litigation & Appeals
Personal Injury -- Defense
Personal Injury -- Plaintiff
Real Estate Law
Securities Law
Workers' Compensation Law
**More Practice Areas . . .**

### Finding and Hiring a Lawyer

**Questions & Answers**
- Do you need a lawyer?
- What questions should you ask?
- What about Legal Fees and Costs?
- What are legal service plans?

**Articles**

- Interviewing a Lawyer
- Fees and Costs
- Courts and the Legal Process

### Legal Market Center

- Experts and Consultants
- Legal Investigators
- Court Reporters
- Process Servers
- Software
- Hardware and Technology
- Other Legal Support Services

Click here to find out how to list your firm.

### Strategy 7: Surf the internet

Thus far in the chapter, we have mentioned resources on the Internet a number of times. Exhibit 2.6 presents additional resources available in cyberspace.

---

#### Assignment 2.3

(a) Use some of the Internet sites in exhibit 2.6 to find a job opening for a paralegal in a city where you hope to work. If you can't find an opening in that city, check openings for the entire state. Where did you find this information on the Internet?

(b) Use any of the Internet sites mentioned in exhibit 2.6 to locate a law firm in your state that employs more than 10 attorneys. State the name, address, and phone number of this firm. How many attorneys does it have? What kind of law does it practice? Where did you find this information on the Internet?

---

### Strategy 8: Prepare your résumé, cover letter, and writing samples

The cardinal principle of résumé writing is that you *target* the résumé to the job you are seeking. Hence you must have more than one résumé, or you must rewrite your résumé for each particular employer to whom you send it. A targeted résumé, for example, should contain the buzzwords used in the ad for the job you are seeking (e.g., "litigation management," "office systems"). Word processors make it relatively easy for you to cut and paste whatever portions of the résumé you need for a particular employer.

A résumé is an *advocacy* document. You are trying to convince someone (a) to give you an interview and ultimately (b) to offer you a job. You are not simply communicating information about yourself. A résumé is *not* a summary of your life or a one-page autobiography. It is a very brief *commercial* in which you are trying to sell yourself as a person who can make a contribution to a particular prospective employer. Hence the résumé must stress what would appeal to *this* employer. You are advocating (or selling) yourself effectively when the form and content of the résumé have this appeal. Advocacy is required for several reasons. First, there may be more applicants than jobs available. Second, most prospective employers ignore résumés that are not geared to their particular needs.

Before examining sample résumés, we need to explore some general guidelines that apply to *any* résumé.

#### Guidelines on drafting an effective résumé

1. Be concise and to the point. Generally, the résumé should fit on one page. A longer résumé is justified only if you have a unique education or experience that is directly related to law or to the particular law firm or company in which you are interested.

2. Be accurate. Studies show that about 30 percent of all résumés contain inaccuracies. Recently, a legal administrator felt the need to make the following comment (to other legal administrators) about job applicants: "I'm sure we have all had experiences where an applicant has lied on an application about experience, previous salary scales, length of time with previous employers, training, skills, and anything else they can think of that will make them appear more attractive."[14] While you want to present yourself in the best possible light, it is critical that you not jeopardize your integrity. All of the data in the résumé should be verifiable. Prospective employers who check the accuracy of résumés usually do so themselves, although some use outside organizations such as the National Credential Verification Service. (For an example of an online verification service, see *www.myreferences.com.*)

3. Include personal data—that is, name, street address, zip code, e-mail address, and phone (with area code) where you can be reached. (If someone is not always available to take messages while you are away, invest in an answering machine.) Do not include a personal photograph or data on your health, height, religion, or political party. You do not have to include information that might give a prospective employer a basis to discriminate against you illegally, such as your marital status or the names and ages of your children. Later we will discuss how to handle such matters in a job interview.

| EXHIBIT 2.6 | More Employment Resources on the Internet |
| --- | --- |

For the first five categories of sites in the following list, find out:

- whether specific paralegal jobs are posted (type "paralegal" or "legal assistant" in the search boxes provided on these sites, even for those sites that appear to be focused primarily on attorneys),
- whether you can post your résumé on the site for prospective employers to examine,
- whether the service charges a fee, and
- whether guidance is available (directly or through links) on résumé writing and job-interview strategies.

### PARALEGAL JOB SEARCH SITES
- www.lawjobs.com
- www.paralegalclassifieds.com
- www.lamanet.org/Resources/jobbank.cfm
- www.legalstaff.com
- www.paralegals.org/Center/home.html
- www.nala.org/careernet.htm

### GENERAL LEGAL SEARCH SITES
(for attorneys, paralegals, and other legal staff)

- www.legalemploy.com
- jobs.lawinfo.com
- www.careers.findlaw.com
- www.complaw.com/joblist.html
- www.lawforum.net/index.html
- www.specialcounsel.com/Home.asp

### GENERAL SEARCH SITES
(can be used for paralegal searches)

- www.monster.com
- www.hotjobs.com
- www.headhunter.net
- www.careerpath.com
- www.careerweb.com
- www.iccweb.com

### FEDERAL GOVERNMENT EMPLOYMENT
- www.usajobs.opm.gov
- www.ajb.dni.us/index.html
- www.fedworld.gov/jobs/jobsearch.html
- www.uscourts.gov

### TEMPORARY LEGAL STAFFING
- www.affiliates.com
- www.specialcounsel.com/Home.asp
- www.gregoryandgregory.com
- www.cambridgestaff.com
- www.accessnyc.com/legal.cfm
- www.strategiclegal.com
- www.theassociatesinc.com
- www.juristaff.com
- www.lawcorps.com
- www.staffwise.com
- www.bickertongordon.com
- www.colemanlegal.com
- www.stonelegal.com
- www.clausman.com
- www.exclusivelylegal.com
- www.contractcounsel.com
- www.gibsonarnold.com

### SALARY INFORMATION
- www.salary.com
- www.infirmation.com/shared/insider/payscale.tcl

### RÉSUMÉ AND INTERVIEWING PREPARATION RESOURCES
- www.hg.org/employment.html
- www.bc.edu/bc_org/svp/carct/resume.html
- resumes.yahoo.com
- www.quintcareers.com

### FINDING INFORMATION ABOUT LAW FIRMS
- www.washlaw.edu/washlaw/lawfirms.html
- www.directory.findlaw.com
- www.martindale.com
- www.infirmation.com/shared/lss
- See the Internet sites of law firms in appendix 2A

4. Provide a concise statement of your career objective at the top of the résumé. (It should be pointed out, however, that some people recommend that this statement be included in the cover letter rather than in the résumé.) The career objective should be a quick way for the reader to know whether your goal fits the needs of the prospective employer. Hence *the career objective should be targeted to a particular employer* and therefore needs to be rewritten just about every time you send out a résumé to a different employer. An overly general career objective gives the unfortunate effect of a "mass-mailing résumé." Suppose, for example, you are applying for a position as a litigation paralegal at a 40-attorney law firm that is looking for someone to help with scheduling and document handling on several cases going on simultaneously.

Don't say:  **Career Objective**—A position as a paralegal at an office where there is an opportunity for growth.

Do say:          **Career Objective**—A position as a litigation paralegal at a medium-sized law firm where I will be able to use and build on the organizational skills I developed in my prior employment and the case management skills that I have learned to date.

The first statement is too flat and uninformative. Its generalities could fit just about *any* paralegal job. Even worse, its focus is on the needs of the applicant. The second statement is much more direct. While also referring to the needs of the applicant, the second statement goes to the heart of what the employer is looking for—someone to help create order out of the complexity of events and papers involved in litigation.

5. Next, state your prior education and training if you have not had any legal work experience. If you *have* worked in a law office before, particularly as a paralegal, the next section of the résumé should be work experience, followed by education and training. (See Job Hunting Notebook, pages 101 ff.) List each school or training institution and the dates attended. Use a reverse chronological order—that is, start the list with the most current and work backward. Do not include your high school unless you attended a prestigious high school, you have not attended college, or you are a very recent high school graduate. When you give your legal education:

a. List the major courses.
b. State specific skills and tasks covered in your courses that are relevant to the job for which you are applying. Also state major topic areas covered in the courses that demonstrate a knowledge of (or at least exposure to) material that is relevant to the job. For example, if you are applying for a corporate paralegal job, relevant courses could be stated as follows:

**Corporate Law:**     This course examined the formation of a corporation, director and shareholder meetings, corporate mergers, and the dissolution of corporations; we also studied sample shareholder minutes and prepared proxy statements. Grade received: B+.

**Legal Research:**     This course covered the basic law books relevant to researching corporate law, including the state code. We also covered the skills of using practice books, finding cases on corporate law through the digests, etc. Grade received: A—.

c. List any special programs in the school, such as unique class assignments, term papers, extensive research, moot court, internship, or semester projects. Give a brief description if any of these programs are relevant to the job you are seeking.
d. State any unusually high grades; give overall grade point average (GPA) only if it is distinctive.

List any degrees, certificates, or other recognition that you earned at each school or training institution. Include high aptitude or standard test scores. If the school or institution has any special distinction or recognition, mention this as well.

6. State your work experience. (See Job Hunting Notebook, pages 99 ff.) List the jobs you held, your job title, the dates of employment, and the major duties that you performed. (Do not state the reason you left each job, although you should be prepared to discuss this if you are granted an interview.) Again, work backward. Start with the most current (or your present) employment. The statement of duties is particularly important. If you have legal experience, emphasize specific duties and tasks that are directly relevant to the position you are seeking—for example, include that you drafted corporate minutes or prepared incorporation papers. Give prominence to such skills and tasks on the résumé. Nonlegal experience, however, can also be relevant. Every prior job says something about you as an individual. Phrase your duties in such jobs in a manner that will highlight important personality traits. (See page 100.) In general, most employers are looking for people with the following characteristics:

■ Emotional maturity
■ Intelligence

- Willingness to learn
- Ability to get along with others
- Ability to work independently (someone with initiative and self-reliance who is not afraid of assuming responsibility)
- Problem-solving skills
- Ability to handle time pressures and frustration
- Ability to communicate—orally, on paper, online
- Loyalty
- Stability, reliability
- Energy

As you list duties in prior and current employment settings, do *not* use any of the language just listed. But try to state duties that tend to show that these characteristics apply to you. For example, if you had a job as a camp counselor, state that you supervised 18 children, designed schedules according to predetermined objectives, prepared budgets, took over in the absence of the director of the camp, etc. A listing of such duties will say a lot about you as a person. You are someone who can be trusted, you know how to work with people, you are flexible, etc. These are the kinds of conclusions that you want the reader of your résumé to reach. Finally, try to present the facts to show a growth in your accomplishments, development, and maturity.

7. Use *action verbs* throughout the résumé. Note that the examples just given used the verbs mentioned in the following lists:

**Action verbs to use**[15]

| Creative skills | Financial skills | Management skills | Technical skills |
|---|---|---|---|
| conceptualized | administered | administered | assembled |
| created | analyzed | analyzed | built |
| designed | balanced | coordinated | calculated |
| established | budgeted | developed | designed |
| fashioned | forecast | directed | operated |
| illustrated | marketed | evaluated | overhauled |
| invented | planned | improved | remodeled |
| performed | projected | supervised | repaired |

| Helping skills | Research skills | Clerical skills | Communication skills |
|---|---|---|---|
| assessed | clarified | arranged | arranged |
| coached | evaluated | catalogued | addressed |
| counseled | identified | compiled | authored |
| diagnosed | inspected | generated | drafted |
| facilitated | organized | organized | formulated |
| represented | summarized | processed | persuaded |
| | | systematized | |

**Non-action verbs to avoid**

| | |
|---|---|
| was involved in | had a role in |
| was a part of | was related to |

Non-action verbs are vague. They give the impression that you are not an assertive person.

8. State other experience and skills that do not fall within the categories of education and employment mentioned above. (See Job Hunting Notebook, page 100.) Perhaps you have been a homemaker for 20 years, raised 5 children, worked your way through college, and were the church treasurer, a Cub Scout volunteer, etc. In a separate category on the résumé called "Other Experience," list such activities and state your duties in the same manner mentioned above to demonstrate relevant personality traits. Hobbies can be included (without using the word "hobby") when they are distinctive and illustrate special talents or achievement.

9. State any special abilities (for example, that you can design a database or speak a foreign language), awards, credentials, scholarships, membership associations, leadership positions, community service, publications, etc. that have not been mentioned elsewhere on the résumé.

10. No one has a perfect résumé. There are facts about all of us that we would prefer to downplay or avoid (e.g., sudden change in jobs, school transfer because of personal or family difficulties, low aptitude test scores). There is no need to point out these facts, but in a job interview, you must be prepared to discuss any obvious gaps or problems that might be evident from your résumé. Thus far we have been outlining the format of a **chronological résumé**, which presents your education, training, and experience in a chronological sequence, starting with the present and working backward. (See exhibit 2.8). Later we will examine how a **functional résumé** might be more effective than a chronological résumé in handling difficulties such as sudden changes or gaps in employment. (See exhibit 2.9.) Although we will focus on these two résumé formats, others exist. On the Internet site *resumes.yahoo.com*, for example, you will find ten different résumé styles presented as **templates** that you can adapt. (A template is a formula created to help you perform a task—here, writing a résumé.)

11. At the end of the résumé, say, "References available on request." On a separate sheet of paper, type the names, work addresses, and phone numbers of people who know your abilities and who could be contacted by a prospective employer. If the latter is seriously considering you for a position, you will probably be asked for the list. This will most likely occur during a job interview. Generally, you should seek the permission of people you intend to use as references. Phone or e-mail them and ask if you can list them as references in your job search.

12. Do not include salary requirements or your salary history on the résumé. Leave this topic for the interview. If you are responding to an ad that asks for this history, include it in the cover letter.

13. The résumé should be neatly typed, grammatically correct, and readable. Be sure that there are no spelling errors or smudge spots from erasures or fingerprints. In this regard, if you can't make your résumé *perfect*, don't bother submitting it. Avoid abbreviations except for items such as street, state, degrees earned, etc. Do not make any handwritten corrections; retype or reprint the résumé after you make the corrections. Proofread carefully. Also ask someone else to proofread the résumé for you to see if you missed anything.

You do not have to use complete sentences in the résumé. Sentence fragments are adequate as long as you rigorously follow the grammatical rule on parallelism. This rule requires that you use a consistent (i.e., parallel) grammatical structure when phrasing logically related ideas in a list. Specifically, be consistent in the use of words ending in *ing, ed,* and *tion*. Similarly, be consistent in the use of infinitives, clauses, personal pronouns, and the active voice. For example, say "researched securities issues, drafted complaints, served papers on opposing parties." Do not say, "researched securities, drafting complaints, and I served papers on opposing parties." This sentence suddenly changes an "ed" word to an "ing" word and uses the personal pronoun ("I") with only one of the verbs in the list. Also, avoid jumping from past tense to present tense, or vice versa. Do not say "prepared annual budgets and manages part-time personnel." Say "prepare budgets and manage part-time personnel" or "prepared budgets and managed part-time personnel."

Leave generous margins. Cluster similar information together and use consistent indentation patterns so that readers can easily scan the résumé and quickly find those categories of information in which they are most interested.

The résumé should have a professional appearance. If you do not have your own word processor, have your résumé typed on quality paper (with matching envelopes) by a commercial printing company or word processing service. Obtain multiple copies of your résumé. Avoid submitting a résumé that was obviously reproduced on a poor-quality photocopy machine at a corner drugstore. The résumé is often the first contact that a prospective employer will have with you. You want to convey the impression that you know how to write and organize data. Furthermore, it is a sign of respect to

**chronological résumé** A résumé that presents biographical data on education and experience in a chronological sequence, starting with the present and working backward.

**functional résumé** A résumé that clusters skills and experience regardless of when they were developed or occurred.

**template** A formula designed to help you perform a task.

the reader when you show that you took the time and energy to make your résumé professionally presentable. Law offices are *conservative* environments. Attorneys like to project an image of propriety, stability, accuracy, and order. Be sure that your résumé also projects this image.

14. Again, the résumé concentrates on those facts about you that show you are particularly qualified *for the specific job you are seeking*. The single most important theme you want to convey in the résumé is that you are a person who can make a contribution to *this* organization. As much as possible, the reader of the résumé should have the impression that you prepared the résumé for the particular position that is open. In style and content, the résumé should emphasize what will be pleasing to the reader and demonstrate what you can contribute to a particular office. (See exhibit 2.7).

The last guideline is very important. You cannot comply with it unless you have done some *background research* on the law office where you are applying and, if possible, on the person who will be receiving the résumé. How do you do this background research? First and foremost, whenever practical, try to contact employees, particularly paralegals, who work there now or who once worked there. That's why Strategy 4, outlined above, on ways to locate working paralegals is so important.

The Internet is an excellent source of information about any relatively large law firm or corporation:

- See the Internet sites in exhibit 2.6 on finding information about specific law firms.
- See the Internet sites in appendix 2.A at the end of the chapter.
- Type the name of the firm in the search box of any general search engine (e.g., *www.google.com*) or legal search engine (e.g., *www.hg.org*).
- Use any of the major people and business finding sites (e.g., *www.switchboard.com* or *www.theultimates.com*) to locate law firms or businesses.

Ask a librarian at your local public library (particularly the central public library in your city or county) what book or online resources you can use to find information about a particular law firm or business. Good Internet sites to obtain information about companies include:

- *www.hoovers.com*
- *www.business.com*
- *www.llrx.com/features/co_research.htm*

Here is a partial checklist of information you want to obtain through background research on a prospective employer or job (see also page 95, guideline 18):

- What kind of law is practiced at the office? What are its specialties?
- If the office is the law department of a corporation, what are the company's main products or services?
- Why has the office decided to hire a paralegal now? What needs or problems prompted this decision?
- How is the office structured and governed? By management committee?
- How old is the office? Has it expanded recently? If so, in what areas?
- What kinds of clients does the office have? A variety of small clients? Several large clients that provide most of the fees?

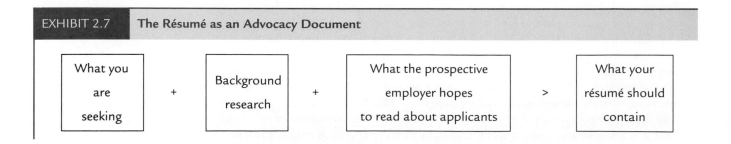

| EXHIBIT 2.7 | The Résumé as an Advocacy Document |
| --- | --- |

What you are seeking + Background research + What the prospective employer hopes to read about applicants > What your résumé should contain

- How many attorneys are in the office?
- How many paralegals? What kind of work do they do? Does the office understand the role of paralegals? What kinds of complaints have the paralegals had about the office? What are the advantages and disadvantages of working in the office?
- Has the office had personnel problems? High turnover?
- Does the office operate through systems? If not, how does it feel about developing such systems?

If you do your homework on a prospective employer, you will have begun collecting answers to such questions so that you can tailor your résumé to these answers. You will select those aspects of your prior employment or education, for example, that suggest or demonstrate you are able to handle the demands of the job.

Of course, for many jobs, you will *not* be able to obtain answers to these questions, no matter how much background research you do. All you may be able to find is general information about the firm or company. If so, you must do the best you can to predict what the "correct" answers are and structure your résumé, cover letter, and writing sample(s) accordingly.

The main point, however, is that a lot of preparation is needed before you approach a prospective employer. Much time and energy must be expended. A conscientious and organized job search will be good preparation for the career ahead of you. *The same kind of motivation, creativity, and aggressiveness that is needed to find a good job is also needed to perform effectively as a paralegal and to advance in this field.* The cornerstone of achievement and success is a heavy dose of old-fashioned hard work.

Exhibit 2.8 is an example of a *chronological résumé*, the traditional format and the one most commonly used by applicants today. As indicated earlier, this résumé presents your education, training, and work history in reverse chronological sequence, beginning with the most recent events and working backward.

A *functional résumé* clusters certain skills or talents together regardless of the period in which they were developed. See exhibit 2.9. This style of résumé can be particularly useful when you want to downplay large gaps in education, when you are making a radical change of careers, or when your skills were not gained in paralegal education, training, or employment. The functional résumé should not, however, ignore the chronological sequence of the major training and work events of your life, since a prospective employer will want to know what this sequence is. Note that the functional résumé in exhibit 2.9 has a skill cluster early in the résumé, followed by the historical overview in reverse chronological order.[16] Using this format puts the emphasis of the résumé on the skills or abilities highlighted at the beginning.

Finally, some employers will allow you to submit an online or electronic résumé over the Internet. See, for example, exhibit 2.10, containing an application for a litigation paralegal position at Proskauer & Rose. Filling in this application produces a résumé in the format preferred by this particular employer. Other employers may allow you to e-mail your résumé, usually as an attachment. If so, you will be typing your résumé on a blank screen (like a blank sheet of paper), rather than using preformatted questions such as those used in exhibit 2.10. For the résumé to be readable, your e-mail software must be compatible with the e-mail software of the recipient. If any difficulties occur, the recipient should be able to tell you what you need to do to make the connection work. Before sending the e-mail to the employer, send it to yourself or to a friend. This will allow you to see how it appears on the screen after it arrives, perhaps suggesting some changes in the way you initially typed or formatted it. Maintain proper formality in your e-mail submission. Do not be familiar. Do not address anyone by his or her first name or sign off by using your first name alone.

**Cover Letter**   The **cover letter** should state how you learned about the office. It should also highlight and amplify those portions of the résumé that are relevant to the position you are seeking. Without repeating the résumé unduly, explain how you are qualified for the job. Repeat any buzzwords that you picked up from the want ad or from background research you have been able to do on why the office is seeking a paralegal. Like the résumé itself, the cover letter should give the impression that you are a

**cover letter** A letter that accompanies and that makes reference to an enclosed document such as a résumé.

| EXHIBIT 2.8 | Sample Chronological Résumé |
|---|---|

**John J. Smith**
**43 Benning Road SE**
**Salem, Maryland 21455**
**(701) 456–0427**

**CAREER OBJECTIVE**
Position as a paralegal at a small law firm working in the area of probate, trusts, and estates.

**EDUCATION**
Jan. 1999–Jan. 2000, Maynard Paralegal Institute
Courses:
Trusts and Estates:
- overview of probate procedure in Maryland
- client interview to identify facts needed to prepare the federal 105 short form

Tax I:
- the basics of estate taxation
- introduction to personal income taxation
- fundamentals of accounting
- valuation of personal and real property

Other Courses:
Introduction to Law, Family Law, Litigation, Legal Research

Internship: Donaldson & Fry, L.L.P. (8/99 to 12/99)
Tasks performed under supervision of Alex Fry, Esq.:
- drafted answers to interrogatories in a divorce case
- maintained the firm's tickler system
- coded discovery documents
- cite checked an appellate brief

Sept. 1997–June 1999 Jefferson Community College
Courses:
Business Law; English I, II; Sociology; Creative Writing; French I; Introduction to Psychology

**EMPLOYMENT**
1995–1998   Teller, Salem National Bank
            Responsibilities: Received deposit and withdrawal requests; trained new tellers; supervised note
            department in the absence of the assistant manager.
1990–1994   Driver, ABC Biscuit Company

**HONORS**
1995 Junior Achievement Award for Outstanding Marketing

**ASSOCIATIONS**
Financial Secretary, Salem Paralegal Association; Regional Representative, National Federation of Paralegal
Associations; Member, National Association of Legal Assistants

**REFERENCES**
Available on request.

professional. It is also important that you communicate a sense of enthusiasm about the position.

Note that the cover letter in exhibit 2.11 is addressed to a specific person. Try to avoid sending a "To Whom It May Concern" letter unless you are responding to a blind ad. Whenever possible, find out the exact name of the person to whom the résumé should be sent. If you are not sure, call the office and ask. Also check the firm's Internet site to see if it gives the name of the person at the firm in charge of recruitment.

| EXHIBIT 2.9 | Sample Functional Résumé |
| --- | --- |

**Jane Doe**
**18 East 7th Avenue**
**Denver, Colorado 80200**
**303–555–1198**

## BRIEF SUMMARY OF BACKGROUND

Bachelor of Arts and Bachelor of Science (Education) with major in English and minor in Library Science. Taught creative writing and communications to high school juniors and seniors; worked several years as research and index assistant in records and research department of large international organization; worked part-time on a volunteer basis in schools and libraries as librarian and reading tutor.

## PROFESSIONAL SKILLS

### Communication Skills
- taught creative writing to high school seniors
- conducted workshops on library service to employees
- co-led workshops on literacy training
- served as Circulation Representative for *USA Today*

### Research Skills
- guided library patrons in use of basic reference materials
- used Internet to obtain sites for county resource manual
- recommended subscription purchases for general circulation library

### Organization Skills
- managed all phases of school library
- planned budget requests for library
- supervised paid and volunteer library staff

## EMPLOYMENT HISTORY

| | |
| --- | --- |
| 9/94–Present | Lincoln Elementary School (Denver): Teacher's Aide (part-time) |
| 6/86–6/94 | International Church Center |
| | Executive Department, Records and Research Section (Boston): Research and Index Assistant |
| 4/94–6/94 | Latin Preparatory School (Dorchester): School Librarian (substitute) |
| 2/93–6/94 | James P. O'Reilly Elementary School (Boston): School Librarian (volunteer) |
| 9/84–6/85 | Roosevelt High School (St. Paul): English Teacher Aide |

## EDUCATION

| | |
| --- | --- |
| 1993–1994 | University of Massachusetts, Boston Campus |
| | Special courses included: Library and Urban Children; Design Management |
| 1989–1990 | Harvard Extension, Problems in Urban Education |
| 1979–1983 | University of Minnesota, Minneapolis, B.S., *Major:* English *Minor:* Library Science |

## SCHOOL ACTIVITIES

National Honor Society, Dramatic Club, Creative Writing Club, YWCA, Minnesota Dance Company.

## REFERENCES

Available on request.

---

One final, critically important point about the cover letter: it must be grammatically correct and contain no spelling errors. Do you see any problem with the following sentence from a cover letter?

The description of responsibilities in the want ad fit my experience.

This sentence alone might cause a prospective employer to throw the letter, and its accompanying résumé, in the trash can. The subject and verb don't agree. The sentence should read:

The description of responsibilities in the want ad fits my experience.

| EXHIBIT 2.10 | Example of an Online Résumé/Application |
|---|---|

## Staff Recruiting

**Proskauer Rose LLP**

**Application For Employment**

POSITION APPLIED FOR: `Legal Assistant/Litigatio`
DATE:

Name:

_____ Last _____ First _____ M.I.

Social Security No.:

Present Address:

_____ No. _____ Street

_____ City _____ State _____ Zip

Apartment No.: ___ Telephone No.: ( ___ ) ___
_____ Area Code

Referred By:

Are you under 18 years of age? ○ Yes ○ No
If under 18, state your age: ___

Do you want to work ○ Full Time ○ Part Time
If part-time, specify days and hours:

Date you can start: ___ Salary desired: ___

Have you ever been employed by us? ○ Yes ○ No
If yes, when?

Have you ever been convicted of a crime, excluding traffic convictions?
○ Yes ○ No
If so, please describe:

A conviction record will not necessarily be a bar to employment. Factors such as age at time of offense, date, seriousness and nature of the offense, and rehabilitation will be taken into account.

Do you have the legal right to work in the United States?
○ Yes ○ No

Proof of your right to work in the United States will be required to be provided within 3 days of hire, if an offer of employment is made.

RECORD OF EDUCATION

| High School: | Course of Study: |
|---|---|

| Check Last Year Completed ○ 1 ○ 2 ○ 3 ○ 4 | Did you Graduate? ○ Yes ○ No | Diploma/Degree: |
|---|---|---|

| College: | Course of Study: |
|---|---|

| Check Last Year Completed ○ 1 ○ 2 ○ 3 ○ 4 | Did you Graduate? ○ Yes ○ No | Diploma/Degree: |
|---|---|---|

| Other/Specify: | Course of Study: |
|---|---|

| Check Last Year Completed ○ 1 ○ 2 ○ 3 ○ 4 | Did you Graduate? ○ Yes ○ No | Diploma/Degree: |
|---|---|---|

MILITARY SERVICE RECORD

Have you ever served in the U.S. Armed Forces? ○ Yes ○ No
List duties in the Service, including special training:

SKILLS (if relevant to position being applied for.)
Shorthand ○ Pitman ○ Gregg ○ Other ___ WPM ___
Word Perfect 7.0 ___
Operate dictating equipment ___
Other W/P Software ___
Are there are any other experiences, skills or qualifications which you feel would especially qualify you for work with our firm?

PRIOR WORK HISTORY (LIST IN ORDER, LAST OR PRESENT EMPLOYER FIRST)

There must be no lapses in your grammar and spelling. Your standard must be perfection. While this is also true of the résumé, it is particularly true of the cover letter. When the envelope is opened, the first thing that is read is the cover letter. The vast majority of us are *unaware of how poor our grammar is.* We have been lulled into a sense of security because readers of what we write—including teachers—seldom complain unless we make an egregious error. In the section on studying at the beginning of this book, there are suggestions for improving your writing skills. In the meantime, proofread, proofread, proofread; and then find others to proofread everything that you intend to submit in writing to a prospective employer. An additional technique used by careful writers is to read your cover letter (and résumé) *backward*—word by word, punctuation mark by punctuation mark. Of course, when you do this, you are not reading for meaning. You are isolating everything in the sentence in order to force yourself to ask whether anything might be in need of a dictionary or grammar check. Reading backward might help reveal glaring spelling or punctuation errors that you have been glossing over.

EXHIBIT 2.10    Example of an Online Résumé/Application—*continued*

| Dates | | Name, Address, Telephone Number of Employer | Rate of Pay | |
|---|---|---|---|---|
| From | To | | Start | Finish |
| | | | | |

| Supervisor's Name and Title | Reason for Leaving |
|---|---|
| | |

| Dates | | Name, Address, Telephone Number of Employer | Rate of Pay | |
|---|---|---|---|---|
| From | To | | Start | Finish |
| | | | | |

| Supervisor's Name and Title | Reason for Leaving |
|---|---|
| | |

| Dates | | Name, Address, Telephone Number of Employer | Rate of Pay | |
|---|---|---|---|---|
| From | To | | Start | Finish |
| | | | | |

| Supervisor's Name and Title | Reason for Leaving |
|---|---|
| | |

**BUSINESS REFERENCES**
Please list at least 3 references. Include the following for each: Name; Occupation; Dates Known; Address; Phone Number.

```
1.
2.
3.
```

If you have a personal resumé that you wish to append, please paste it into the field

below.

Continue

---

*Assignment 2.4*

Find a want ad from a law office seeking an entry-level paralegal. Try to locate an ad as detailed as possible in terms of what the employer is looking for.

(a) Prepare a résumé for this job. Make it a real résumé except for the following information, which you can make up:

■ You can assume that you have already had course work in the areas involved in the job.

- You can assume that you once had a part-time summer position with an attorney, but it was in an area of the law that is different from the area practiced in the law office seeking the paralegal.
Attach a copy of the ad to the résumé you hand in, and indicate where you obtained it.
(b) Prepare a cover letter to go with this résumé. You can make up identifying information the ad may not provide (e.g., the name and address of the person to whom you will be sending the résumé and letter). Assume that you called to obtain this information.

**Writing samples**    You should be constantly thinking about writing samples based upon the course work you do and any legal employment or internship experiences you have had. (If your writing sample comes from a prior job or internship, be sure that the confidentiality of actual parties is protected by "whiting out" or changing plaintiff and defendant names, addresses, case numbers, and any other identifying information.) In addition, consider preparing other writing samples *on your own*. For example:

- A brief memorandum of law on the application of a statute to a set of facts that you make up (see chapter 12)
- A pleading such as a complaint (see chapter 10)
- A set of interrogatories (see chapter 10)

---

| EXHIBIT 2.11 | Cover Letter |
|---|---|

43 Benning Road SE
Salem, Maryland 21455
701/456-0427
June 23, 2001

Linda Stenner, Esq.
Stenner, Skidmore & Smith
438 Bankers Trust Bldg
Suite 1200
Salem, Maryland 21458

Dear Ms. Stenner:

Michael Diamond, Esq. told me that your firm may have an opening for a trusts and estates paralegal. I am enclosing my résumé for your consideration. I am very interested in working in the field of probate, trusts, and estates. The course work that I did at Maynard Institute and my prior work at the Salem National Bank provided me with an appreciation of the complexity of this area of the law. I find the field fascinating.

I am fully aware of the kind of attention to detail that a paralegal in this field must have. If you decide to check any of my references, I am confident that you will be told of the high level of discipline and responsibility that I bring to the tasks I undertake.

I have two writing samples that may be of interest to you: a draft of a will that I prepared in my course on trusts and estates, and a memorandum of law on the valuation of stocks. These writing samples are available on request.

I would appreciate the opportunity to be interviewed for the paralegal position at your firm. I feel confident that my training and experience have prepared me for the kind of challenge that this position would provide.

Sincerely,

John J. Smith

- Articles of incorporation and bylaws for a fictitious corporation
- An analysis of a recent court opinion (see chapters 7 and 11)
- An intake memorandum of law based on an interview that you role-play with another student (see chapter 8)
- An annotated bibliography on a particular topic (see chapter 11)
- A brief article that you write for a paralegal newsletter on an aspect of your legal education or work experience as a paralegal (see appendix B)

Prepare a file or portfolio of all your writing samples. (See Job Hunting Notebook, page 104.) If possible, try to have a teacher, practicing attorney, or paralegal review each sample. Rewrite it based on their comments. You must take the initiative in preparing writing samples and in soliciting feedback from knowledgeable contacts that you make. You need to have a large pool of diverse writing samples from which to choose once you begin the actual job hunt. Start preparing these samples now.

### Strategy 9: The Job Interview

Once you have overcome the hurdles of finding a prospective employer who will read your cover letter and résumé, the next problem is to arrange for a job interview. In your cover letter, you may want to add the following sentence at the end: "Within the next two weeks, I will give you a call to determine whether an interview would be possible." This strategy does not leave the matter entirely up to the prospective employer as to whether there will be further contact with you. You must be careful, however, not to appear too forward. Some may resent this approach. On the other hand, you have little to lose by trying it several times to see what response you obtain.

### Job Interview Guidelines

(See Job Hunting Notebook, page 105)

Attired in your best interviewing suit, you nervously navigate your way to the reception area of what you hope will be your future employer's office. You are a comfortable ten minutes early. Upon arrival you are directed to the office of the interviewer, whom you greet with a smile and pleasant handshake. She offers you a cup of coffee, which you wisely refuse, since you may spill it. She then looks you in the eye and poses her first question. "Why are you interested in working for this firm?" [Suddenly you go blank!] all thoughts leave your mind as you pray for the ability to speak.[17]

1. Be sure you have the exact address; room number, and time of the interview. Give yourself sufficient time to find the office. If the area is new to you, be sure you have precise directions. It would be unfortunate to start your contact with the office by having to offer excuses for being late. Arrive at least ten minutes early. You will probably be nervous and will need to compose yourself before the interview. It is important that you be as relaxed as possible.
2. Try to find out in advance who will be interviewing you. (Don't be surprised, however, if the person who greets you is a substitute for the person originally scheduled to conduct the interview.) A number of different kinds of people might conduct the interview depending upon the size of the office: the law office manager, the managing attorney, the supervising attorney for the position, the paralegal supervisor, a staff paralegal, or a combination of the above if you are interviewed by different people on the same day or on different days. The style of the interview may be quite different depending on who conducts it. Someone with management responsibility might stress the interpersonal dimensions of the position, whereas a trial attorney might give you the feeling that you are being cross-examined. Try to determine whether you are being interviewed by the person who has the final authority to hire you. In many offices, you will be interviewed by someone whose sole task is to screen out unacceptable applicants. If you make it through this person, the next step will usually be an interview with the ultimate decision-maker. Whenever you know or suspect that you will be interviewed by an attorney, try to obtain his or her professional biography through

*West's Legal Directory* (see exhibit 2.5), *Martindale-Hubbell Law Directory* (see exhibit 2.4), or other directories. You might be lucky enough to talk with someone who has been interviewed by this person before (such as a paralegal now working at the office, another job seeker, or someone at the local paralegal association) so that you can obtain a sense of what to expect.

3. Although relatively uncommon, you may have to face a group interview, in which several interviewers question you at once.

4. Make sure that you are prepared for the interview. Review the guidelines discussed above on writing your résumé. In the résumé and in the interview, you are trying to sell yourself. Many of the principles of résumé writing apply to the interview. Know the kinds of questions you will probably be asked. Rehearse your responses. Write down a series of questions (tough ones), and ask a friend to role-play an interview with you. Have your friend ask you the questions and critique your responses. Also take the role of the interviewer and question your friend so that you can gauge both perspectives. Be prepared to handle a variety of questions. See exhibit 2.12. Keep in mind, however, that no matter how much preparation you do, you may still be surprised by the course the interview takes. Be flexible enough to expect the unexpected. If you are relaxed, confident, *and prepared*, you will do fine. (For an example of an online mock paralegal interview that you can take, see *interview.monster.com/ virtualinterview/paralegal*.)

5. You are not required to answer potentially illegal questions—for instance, "Are you married?" Some employers use the answers to such irrelevant questions to practice illegal sex discrimination. You need to decide in advance how you will handle them if they are asked. You may want to ask why the question is relevant. Or you may simply decide to steer the interview back to the qualifications that you have and the commitment that you have made to a professional career. A good response might be, "If you're concerned that my marital status may affect my job performance, I can assure you that it will not." Follow this up with comments about dedication and job commitment. It may be the perfect time to offer references.[18] Whatever approach you take, be sure to remain courteous. One commentator suggests the following response to an illegal question: "Gee, that's interesting. I haven't been asked that question before in a job interview."[19] Then continue talking about what makes you a dependable worker without allowing the question to control your response.

6. Avoid being critical of anyone. Do not, for example, "dump on" your prior employer or school. Criticizing or blaming other organizations, even if justified, is likely to give the interviewer the impression that you will probably end up blaming *this* organization if you get the job and difficulties arise.

7. What about being critical of yourself? You will be invited to criticize yourself when you are asked the seemingly inevitable question, "What are your weaknesses?" You may want to pick a *positive* trait and express it as a negative. For example: "I tend to get frustrated when I'm not given enough to do. My goal is not just to collect a paycheck. I want to make a contribution." Or "I think I sometimes have expectations that are too high. There is so much to learn, and I want it all now. I have to pace myself, and realize that the important goal is to complete the immediate task, even if I can't learn every conceivable aspect of that task at the present time." Or "I get irritated by carelessness. When I see someone turn in sloppy work, or work that is not up to the highest standards, it bothers me." If you use any of these approaches, be sure that you are able to back them up when you are asked to explain what you mean.

8. If you have done the kind of background research on the office mentioned earlier, you will have a fairly good idea what the structure and mission of the office are. Interviewers are usually impressed by applicants who demonstrate this kind of knowledge during the interview. It will be clear to them which applicants have done their homework. A major goal of the interview is to relate your education and experience to the needs of the office. To the extent possible, you want to know what these needs are before the interview so that you can quickly and forcefully demonstrate that you are the person the office is looking for. Most offices decide to hire someone because they have a problem—for example, they need someone with a particular skill, they need someone

| EXHIBIT 2.12 | The Six Categories of Job Interview Questions |
| --- | --- |

- Open-Ended Questions (which are calculated to get you to talk, giving the listener an idea of how you organize your thoughts)
    - (1) Tell me about yourself
    - (2) What do you know about our firm?
    - (3) What kind of position are you seeking?
    - (4) What interests you about this job?
- Closed-Ended Questions (which can be answered by one or two words)
    - (5) When did you receive your paralegal certificate?
    - (6) Did you take a course in corporate law?
- Soft-Ball Questions (which should be fairly easy to answer if you are prepared)
    - (7) What are your interests outside of school and work?
    - (8) What courses did you enjoy the most? Why? Which were least rewarding? Why?
    - (9) Do your grades reflect your full potential? Why or why not?
    - (10) Why did you leave your last job?
    - (11) How have you grown or developed in your prior jobs? Explain.
    - (12) How were you evaluated in your prior jobs?
    - (13) What are your strengths as a worker?
    - (14) Describe an ideal work environment. What would your "dream job" be?
    - (15) What factors make a job frustrating? How would you handle these factors?
    - (16) What do you hope to be doing in 10 years? What are your long-term goals?
    - (17) If you are hired, how long are you prepared to stay?
    - (18) Are you interested in a job or a career? What's the difference?
    - (19) Why did you become a paralegal?
    - (20) What problems do you think a paralegal might face in a busy law office? How would you handle these problems?
    - (21) Can you work under pressure? When have you done so in the past?
    - (22) How flexible are you in adapting to changing circumstances? Give examples of your flexibility in the last year.
    - (23) How do you feel about doing routine work?
    - (24) Do you prefer a large or a small law office? Why?
    - (25) What accomplishment in your life are you most proud of? Why?
    - (26) What salary expectations do you have? What was your salary at your last position?
    - (27) What other questions do you think I should ask in order to learn more about you?
    - (28) What questions would you like to ask me about this office?
- Tension Questions (which are calculated to put you on the spot to see how you handle yourself)
    - (29) No one is perfect. What are your weaknesses as a worker?
    - (30) Have you ever been fired from a position? Explain the circumstances.
    - (31) Why have you held so many jobs?
    - (32) Are you a competitive person? If not, why not? If you are, give some examples over the last six months that demonstrate this characteristic.
    - (33) Is there something in this job that you hope to accomplish that you were not able to accomplish in your last job?
    - (34) Do you type? If not, are you willing to learn? What is your typing speed?
    - (35) Do you smoke? If so, how would you handle a work environment that is totally smoke-free, including the wash rooms?
    - (36) Where else have you interviewed for a job? Have you been turned down?
    - (37) Why wouldn't you want to become an attorney now?
    - (38) Everyone makes mistakes. What is the biggest mistake that you made in any of your prior jobs and how did you handle it?*
    - (39) No job is perfect. What is the least appealing aspect of the job you are seeking here?
    - (40) There are over 50 applicants for this position. Why do you think you are the most qualified?
    - (41) If you are offered this position, what are the major concerns that you would have about taking it?
    - (42) What would make you want to quit a job?
    - (43) Give some examples of when you have shown initiative over the last six months in school or at your last job.

| EXHIBIT 2.12 | The Six Categories of Job Interview Questions—*continued* |
|---|---|

■ **Hypothetical Questions** (in which you are asked how you would handle a stated fact situation)
  (44) If you were told, "This isn't any good, do it again, and get it right this time," what would you do?
  (45) If you find out on Friday afternoon that you're expected to come in on Saturday, what would you do?**
  (46) Assume that you are given the position here and that you work very closely on a day-to-day basis with an attorney. After a six-month period, what positive and negative comments do you think this attorney would make about you as a worker?
  (47) Name some things that would be unethical for an attorney to do. What would you do if you found out that the attorney supervising you was doing these things?
  (48) Suppose that your first assignment was to read through and summarize 4,000 documents over an eight-month period. Could you do it? Would you want to do it?
  (49) Assume that two airplanes crash into each other and that your firm represents one of the passengers who was killed. What kind of discovery would you recommend?

■ **Potentially Illegal Questions** (because the questions are not relevant to the candidate's fitness and ability to do most jobs)
  (50) Are you married? Do you plan to marry?
  (51) Do you have any children? If so, how old are they? Who takes care of your children?
  (52) If you do not have any children now, do you plan to have any in the future?
  (53) How old are you?
  (54) What is your religion?
  (55) What is your political affiliation?

*Moralez, *Sample Interview Questions*, 11 Paragram (Oregon Legal Assistant Ass'n, May 1988).
**Wendel, *You the Recruiter*, 5 Legal Assistant Today 31 (September/October 1987).

to help them expand, or they need someone who can get along with a particularly demanding supervising attorney. If you are not sure, ask the interviewer directly why the office has decided to add a paralegal. The success of the interview is directly related to your ability to identify the problem of the office and to demonstrate how you can solve it for them.

9. If the paralegal job is in a certain specialty, such as probate or corporate law, you may be asked questions designed to assess your familiarity with the area. Prior to the interview, spend some time reviewing your class notes. Skim through a standard practice book for that area of the law in the state. Be sure that you can back up anything you said in your résumé about prior involvement with the area in your school or work experience. Such discussions are always an excellent opportunity for you to present writing samples in that field of the law.

10. Dress traditionally. There is, however, a caveat to this recommendation. "A red, wool crepe suit could work well for a professional woman in Los Angeles, Atlanta, Dallas, and Chicago but might seem too flashy in the financial districts of New York or traditional businesses in Boston or Milwaukee. An interview wardrobe is mostly built in solid colors, which offer a more elegant feeling. Both men and women are advised to dress conservatively for the first interview." Suit up for the interview even if the office is having a casual dress day. "The most important thing to remember is that law firms are generally conservative. . . . Most firms want to see candidates dressed in traditional, conservative 'Brooks Brothers' looks."[20] You want interviewers to remember what you said, not what you wore.

11. Be sure that you project yourself positively. Take the initiative in greeting the interviewer. A firm handshake is recommended. Maintain good posture and consistent eye contact. Remember that everything you do will be evaluated. The interviewer will be making mental notes on your body language. Avoid appearing ill at ease or fidgety. Many feel that the practice of law is a battlefield. The interviewer will be forming an opinion of whether you "fit in."

12. Try to avoid the topic of salary until the end of the interview when you have completed the discussion of the job itself. Preferably, let the interviewer raise the issue. Think through how you will handle the topic, but try to avoid discussing it until the appropriate time arises. If asked what salary you are seeking, give a salary range rather than a single rigid figure. Always relate salary to the specific skills and strengths that you would be able to bring to the office. You need to know what the "going rate" is—check recent salary surveys of local and national paralegal associations—so that the salary range you seek is realistic. (See "Salary Information" in exhibit 2.6 and the data in the section on paralegal salaries in chapter 1.) But avoid using the going rate as the first and sole reason for your position on salary.

13. Be an active participant in the interview even though you let the interviewer conduct the interview. Help keep the discussion going.

14. Be enthusiastic, but not overly so. You want to let the office know that you really want the job, not because you are desperate but because you see it as a challenge offering professional development. You are qualified for the job, and you feel that the office is the kind of place that recognizes valuable contributions from its workers.

15. Be yourself. Do not try to overwhelm the interviewer with your cleverness and charm.

16. Be prepared to leave the following documents with the interviewer: extra copies of your résumé, a list of references, and writing samples. Bring copies of the transcript of your school grades if they are impressive.

17. Ask the interviewer if you can have an opportunity to talk with one or more paralegals currently working at the office. It will be another sign of your seriousness.

18. Ask your own questions of the interviewer. In effect, you are interviewing the office as much as the other way around. Come with a written list and don't be afraid to let the interviewer see that you have a checklist of questions that you want to ask. It is a sign of an organized person. There is a great deal of information about the job that you could inquire about. From your background research about the job, you should already have some of this information, but you can now verify what you know. You want to ask pertinent and intelligent questions that will communicate to the interviewer that you are serious about the paralegal field, that you are prepared, and that you grasp what the interviewer has been telling you about the job and the office.

   Below are some topics you could cover in your own questions. See also exhibit 2.13 for more ideas for questions.

- What type of person is the office seeking to hire?
- What prompted the office to seek this type of person?
- Is there a difference between a paralegal and a legal assistant in the office?
- What are some examples of paralegal responsibilities? Will the paralegal specialize in certain tasks or areas of the law? (Ask for a description of a typical workday of a paralegal at the firm.)
- What skills will the paralegal need for the job? Digesting? Investigation? Research? Drafting? Interviewing?
- How many attorneys are in the firm? Is the number growing, declining, remaining constant?
- How is the firm managed or governed? Managing partner? Management committees? Legal administrator? Is there a policy manual for the firm?
- How many paralegals are in the firm? Is the number growing, declining, remaining constant? Are all the paralegals at the firm full-time? Does the firm use part-time or freelance paralegals? Does the firm have (or has it considered hiring) a paralegal coordinator?
- Is there a career ladder for paralegals in the firm?
- How long has the firm used paralegals? What is the average length of time a paralegal stays with the firm? What are the feelings of firm members on the value of paralegals to the firm? Why is this so? How would firm members describe an ideal

| EXHIBIT 2.13 | Checklist of Possible Paralegal Fringe Benefits |
| --- | --- |

**Compensation**
— Salary Increase Policy (amount or range? criteria for determining? frequency of review? who reviews?)
— Overtime (frequency? method or compensation?)
— Bonus (method for determining? frequency)
— Cost-of-Living Adustment (frequency? method for determining?)
— Pension/Retirement Plan (defined benefit? defined contribution? other?)
— Tax-Deferred Savings Plan
— Other Investment Plan

**Insurance:**
— Basic Medical (full coverage? partial?)
— Major Medical (full coverage? partial?)
— Dependent Medical Insurance (fully paid? partially paid?)
— Supplemental Medical (fully paid? partially paid?)
— Dental (full coverage? partial?)
— Maternity Leave (full coverage? partial?)
— Eye Care/Glasses (full coverage? partial?)
— Life Insurance (fully paid? partially paid?)
— Physical Disability (short term? long term? full coverage? partial?)
— Sick Days (number? carryover of unused sick leave allowed?)

**Professional Activities**
— Time Off for Association Events
— Association Dues Paid (full? partial?)
— Professional Magazine Subscription Paid (e.g., *Legal Assistant Today*)
— Association Dinner Events Paid
— Tuition Reimbursement for Paralegal Classes
— Tuition Reimbursement for Law School

**Other:**
— Vacation (number of days? carry over of unused vacation allowed?)
— Personal Leave Days (number allowed?)
— Child Care Assistance
— Paid Holidays (number?)
— Parking (fully paid? partially paid?)
— Mileage Allowance
— Club Membership
— Fitness Center
— Refreshments on the Job
— Sports Tickets
— Entertainment Allowance
— Free Legal Advice and Representation by the Firm on Personal Matters

**Comparability:**
— Paralegal Fringe Benefits Similar/Dissimilar to Those of New Attorneys?
— Paralegal Fringe Benefits Similar/Dissimilar to Those of Secretaries?

paralegal employee? Do all members of the firm feel the same about paralegals? What reservations, if any, do some members of the firm have about paralegals?

■ What other personnel does the firm have (secretaries, computer staff, library staff, clerks, messengers, part-time law students, etc.)? How many of each are there? What relationship does the paralegal have with each?

■ What kind of supervision does a paralegal receive? Close supervision? From one attorney? Several?

- Will the paralegal work for one attorney? Several? Is there a pool of paralegals available to many attorneys on a rotating basis as needed?
- What kind of client contact will the paralegal have? None? Phone? Meetings? Interviews? Document inspection at client's office?
- What kind of writing will the paralegal be doing? Memos? Letters that the paralegal will sign? Letters for attorney to sign?
- What opportunities does a paralegal have for further learning? Office training programs? (Do paralegals attend new-attorney training sessions?) Does the firm encourage outside training for paralegals, e.g., from paralegal associations, bar associations, area schools?
- Will the paralegals be attending staff meetings? Strategy sessions with attorneys?
- How are paralegals evaluated in the office? Written evaluations? Oral? How often?
- Are paralegals required to produce a set number of billable hours? Per day? Per week? Per month? Annually? Is there a **billable hours quota**? What is the hourly rate at which a paralegal's time is billed to a client? Do different paralegals in the office bill at different rates? If so, what determines the difference?
- How often are paralegals required to record their time? Daily, hourly, in 10-minute segments, etc.
- What secretarial assistance is available to the paralegal? None? A personal secretary? Secretary shared with an attorney? Use of a secretarial pool? Will the paralegal do any typing? Light typing? His or her own typing? Typing for others?
- Does the job require travel?
- What equipment will the paralegal be using? Computer, fax machine, copier, dictaphone? What software does the firm use for its major tasks? Word processing? Database management? Litigation support?
- Office space for the paralegal? Private office? Shared office? Partitioned office?
- Compensation and benefits—see exhibit 2.13. Checklist of Possible Paralegal Fringe Benefits.

**billable hours quota** A minimum number of hours expected from a timekeeper on client matters that can be charged (billed) to clients per week, month, year, or other time period.

19. Don't contaminate the law firm! Later, in chapter 5, when you study conflict of interest, you will learn that a new employee can contaminate an entire office by creating a conflict of interest. This could occur if a prospective employee once worked or volunteered at an office that represented a client who is an opponent of a current client of the office where the paralegal is seeking employment. Hence before an office hires an experienced paralegal (or an experienced attorney or secretary), the office needs to know the names of clients at offices where he or she has worked or volunteered. When you are seeking employment as a paralegal, therefore, you must be prepared to provide these names if you have had prior legal experience. This disclosure, however, usually does not need to occur until it is clear that the office is very interested in you and asks for a list of such clients. Never volunteer to show the list to anyone. The names of clients are confidential. But limited disclosure will be needed to avoid a disqualification due to a conflict of interest.

20. After you have thoroughly explored the position during the interview, if you still want the job, ask for it. Be sure that you make a specific request. Some interviewers go out of their way to stress the difficult aspects of the job in order to gauge your reaction. Don't leave the interviewer with the impression that you may be having second thoughts if in fact you still want the job after you have had all your questions answered.

**Follow-Up letter** After the interview, always send a letter to the person who interviewed you. In a surprising number of cases, the follow-up letter is a significant factor in obtaining the job. In the letter:

- Thank the person for the interview.
- Tell the person that you enjoyed the interview and the opportunity to learn about the office.
- State that you are still very interested in the position.
- Briefly restate why you are qualified for the position.

- Clarify any matters that arose during the interview.
- Submit references or writing samples that may have been asked for during the interview.

Keep a copy of all such letters. In a notebook, maintain accurate records on the dates you sent out résumés, the kinds of résumés you sent, the dates of interviews, the names of people you met, your impressions, the dates when you made follow-up calls, etc. (See page 106).

If you are turned down for a job, find out why. Call the office to try to obtain more information than is provided in standard rejection statements. Politely ask what could have improved your chances. Finally, use the occasion to ask for any leads to other prospective employers.

### Class Exercise 2.A

Role-play an interview in class. The instructor will decide what kind of job the interview will be for and will select students to play the role of interviewer and interviewee. The interviewer should ask a variety of questions such as those presented above in the guidelines for handling a job interview. The interviewee can make up the answers within the guidelines provided by the instructor. The rest of the class will evaluate the performance of the interviewee. What mistakes did he or she make? How should he or she have dealt with certain questions? Was he or she confident? Overconfident? Did he or she ask good questions of the interviewer? Were these questions properly timed? What impressions did the interviewee convey of himself or herself? Make a list of do's and don'ts for such interviews.

## Section E
# THE JOB HUNTING NOTEBOOK

Purchase a large three-ring, loose-leaf notebook for your Job Hunting Notebook. Include in it the outline of sections presented in exhibit 2.14. Following the outline, create at least one page for each section.

| EXHIBIT 2.14 | Outline of Job Hunting Notebook |
| --- | --- |

**Part I. Résumé and Writing Sample Preparation**
1. Prior and Current Nonlegal Employment—Analysis Sheet
2. Prior and Current Legal Employment—Analysis Sheet
3. Prior and Current Volunteer Activity—Analysis Sheet
4. Other Life Experiences—Analysis Sheet
5. Nonlegal Education and Training—Analysis Sheet
6. Legal Education and Training—Analysis Sheet
7. Notes on Résumé Writing
8. Draft of General Résumé
9. Drafts of Specialized Résumés
10. Writing Samples

**Part II. Contacts for Employment**
11. Contacts—Attorneys You Already Know or with Whom You Have Any Indirect Association
12. Contacts—Employed Paralegals
13. Contacts and Tasks—General

**Part III. Legwork in the Field**
14. Job Interview Checklist
15. Job interview—Analysis Sheet
16. Record Keeping

There are a number of purposes for the Notebook:
- To help you identify your strengths based on past legal or nonlegal employment, training, and other life experience.
- To help you organize this data for your résumés.
- To provide you with checklists of contacts that you should start making immediately.
- To help you prepare for job interviews.
- To provide a place to store copies of résumés, cover letters, writing samples, follow-up letters, notes on job leads and strategies, personal impressions, etc.
- To keep a calendar on all aspects of the job search.

The Notebook is your own personal document. No one else will see it unless you choose to share its contents with others.

1. **PRIOR AND CURRENT NONLEGAL EMPLOYMENT—ANALYSIS SHEET**
2. **PRIOR AND CURRENT LEGAL EMPLOYMENT—ANALYSIS SHEET**
3. **PRIOR AND CURRENT VOLUNTEER ACTIVITY—ANALYSIS SHEET**

We begin by analyzing your experience in these three areas: (1) in nonlegal jobs (e.g., cashier, truck driver); (2) in legal jobs (e.g., legal secretary, investigator); (3) and in volunteer activity (e.g., church sale coordinator, political campaign assistant). Make a list of these jobs and volunteer activities. Start a separate sheet of paper for each entry on your list, and then do the following:
- State the name, address, and phone number of the place of employment or location of the volunteer work.
- State the exact dates you were there.
- State the names of your supervisors there. (Circle the names of supervisors who had a favorable impression of you. Place a double circle around the name of each supervisor who would probably write a favorable recommendation for you, if asked.)
- Make a list of every *major* task you performed there. Number each task, starting with number 1. (As you write this list, leave a three-inch *left-hand margin* on the paper. In front of the number for each task, place all of the following letters that apply to that task. When an explanation or description is called for, provide it on attached sheets of paper.)

B    The task required you to conform to a *budget*. (Briefly describe the budget, including its size and who prepared it.)
C    There was some *competition* in the office about who was most qualified to perform the task. (Briefly describe why you were the most qualified.)
E    You were *evaluated* on how well you performed the task. (Briefly describe the evaluation of you.)
EI    To perform the task, you occasionally or always had to *exercise initiative*; you did not just wait for detailed instructions. (Briefly describe the initiative you took.)
ET    You occasionally or frequently had to devote *extra time* to perform the task. (Briefly describe the circumstances.)
J/C    It was not a mechanical task; you had to exercise some *judgment* and/or *creativity* to perform it. (Briefly describe the kind of judgment or creativity you exhibited.)
M    *Math* skills were involved in performing the task. (Briefly describe what kind of math you had to do.)
OD    *Others depended* on your performing the task well. (Briefly describe who had to rely on your performance and why.)
OT    You always or regularly performed the task *on time*.
OW    To perform the task, you had to coordinate your work with *other workers*; you did not work alone. (Briefly describe the nature of your interaction with others.)

P    You had some role in *planning* how the task would be performed; you were not simply following someone else's plan. (Briefly describe your planning role.)

PI    You did not start out performing the task; you were formally or informally *promoted into* it. (Briefly describe what you did before being asked to perform this task and the circumstances of the promotion.)

PP    You are *personally proud* of the way you performed the task. (Briefly describe why.)

R    You made *recommendations* on how the task could be more efficiently performed or better integrated into the office. (Briefly describe the recommendations you made and what effect they had.)

RR    You *received recognition* because of how well you performed the task. (Briefly describe the recognition you received and from whom.)

SE    To perform the task, you had to operate *some equipment* such as computers or motor vehicles. (Briefly describe the equipment and the skills needed to operate it.)

SO    To perform the task, you had to *supervise others* or help supervise others. (Briefly describe whom you supervised and what the supervision entailed.)

T    You also *trained* others to perform the task. (Briefly describe this training.)

TP    You had to work under *time pressures* when you performed the task; you didn't have forever to perform it. (Briefly describe these pressures.)

W    Performing the task involved some *writing*. (Briefly describe what kind of writing you did.)

Include other characteristics of the task that are not covered in this list.

## 4. OTHER LIFE EXPERIENCES—ANALYSIS SHEET

Circle *each* of the following experiences that you have had. Do not include experiences that required schooling, since these experiences will be covered elsewhere in the Notebook. Do not include experiences that involved volunteer work unless you have not already included them elsewhere in the Notebook. Attach additional sheets as indicated and where more space is needed.

- Raised a family alone
- Helped raise a family
- Traveled extensively
- Read extensively in a particular field on your own
- Learned to operate computer programs on your own
- Learned a language on your own
- Learned a craft on your own, such as weaving or fixing cars
- Learned an art on your own, such as painting or sculpture
- Developed a distinctive hobby requiring considerable skill
- Other life experiences (list each)

Attach a separate sheet of paper for *each* of the life experiences or activities that you listed above. Write the activity at the top of the sheet. Answer the following questions for each activity:

a.  How long did you engage in this activity?

b.  Have you ever tried to teach this activity to someone else? If so, describe your efforts.

c.  Do you think you could teach this activity to others? Explain your answer.

d.  Which of the following characteristics do you think are necessary or very helpful in being able to perform the activity competently? Do not focus at this point on whether you possess these characteristics. Simply compile a list of what would be helpful or necessary.

| | | |
|---|---|---|
| Intelligence | Compassion | Patience |
| Creativity | Responsibility | Dependability |
| Perseverance | Punctuality | Determination |
| Drive | Self-confidence | Stamina |

| | | |
|---|---|---|
| Independence | Poise | Self-control |
| Talent | Efficiency | Grace |
| Understanding | Skill | Dexterity |
| Cleverness | Competitiveness | Sophistication |
| Spirit | Congeniality | Stick-to-itiveness |
| Conviction | Judgment | Will power |
| Fortitude | Strength | Zeal |
| Ambition | Know-how | Experience |
| Ability to work with others | Imagination | Others? (list) |

e. Ask *someone else* (whom you trust and who is familiar with you) to look at the list. Ask this person if he or she would add anything to the list. Then ask him or her to identify which of these characteristics apply to *you* for this activity.

f. Now it's your turn. Which of these characteristics do *you* think apply to you for this activity?

g. If there are any major differences in the answers to (e) and (f) above, how do you explain the discrepancy? Are you too hard on yourself? Do you tend to put yourself down and minimize your strengths?

## 5. NONLEGAL EDUCATION AND TRAINING—ANALYSIS SHEET

On a separate sheet of paper, list every school or training program *not* involving law that you have attended or are now attending (whether or not you completed it), starting with the most recent. Include four-year colleges, two-year colleges, vocational training schools, weekend seminars, work-related training programs, internships, church training programs, hobby training programs, self-improvement training, etc. Include everything since high school.

Devote a separate sheet of paper to each school or training program, writing its name at the top of the sheet and answering the following questions for it. If more than one course was taught, answer these questions for two or three of the most demanding courses.

a. What were the exact or approximate dates of attendance?

b. Did you complete it? What evidence do you have that you completed it? A grade? A certificate? A degree? A transcript?

c. Were you required to attend? If so, by whom? If not, why did you attend?

d. How did you finance your attendance?

e. What requirements did you meet in order to attend? Was there competition to attend? If so, describe in detail.

f. Describe the subjects taught. What was the curriculum?

g. How were you evaluated?

h. What evidence of these evaluations do you have? Could you obtain copies of the evaluations? Do you have a transcript of your record?

i. Describe in detail any writing that you had to do, such as exams or reports. Do you have copies of any of these written items? If not, could you obtain copies?

j. What skills other than writing did you cover, such as organization, research, computer use, speaking, reading, operating equipment, managing or supervising people?

k. What evidence do you have or could you obtain that shows you covered these skills and how well you did in them?

l. Did you receive any special award or distinction? If so, describe it and state what evidence you have or could obtain that you received it.

m. Make a list of every favorable comment you can remember that was made about your work. What evidence of these comments do you have or could you obtain?

n. Was the experience meaningful in your life? If so, explain why. How has it affected you today?

o. What, if anything, did you do that called for extra effort or work on your part beyond what everyone else had to do?

p. Have you ever tried to teach someone else what you learned? If so, describe your efforts. If not, could you? Describe what you could teach.

q. List each teacher who knew you individually. Circle the name of each teacher who would probably write you a letter of recommendation if asked.

r. Would any other teacher or administrator be able to write you a letter of recommendation based on the records of the school or program? If so, who?

s. Does the school or program have a reputation for excellence? If so, describe its reputation.

## 6. LEGAL EDUCATION AND TRAINING—ANALYSIS SHEET

On a separate sheet of paper, list every *legal* course or training program that you have ever taken—formal or informal. Include individual classes, seminars, internships, etc. at formal schools, on the job, or through associations. Devote a separate sheet of paper to each course or program, writing its name at the top of the sheet and answering the following questions for it.

a. What were the exact dates of attendance?

b. Did you complete it? What evidence do you have that you completed it? A grade? A certificate?

c. What requirements did you meet in order to attend? Was there competition to attend? If so, describe in detail.

d. What text(s) did you use? Photocopy the table of contents in the text(s) and circle those items that you covered.

e. Attach a copy of the syllabus and circle those items in the syllabus that you covered.

f. Make two lists: a list of the major themes or subject areas that you were required to *know* or understand (content) and a list of the things that you were asked to *do* (skills).

g. Make a detailed list of everything that you were asked to write for the course or program, such as exams, memos, research papers, other reports. For every written work product other than exams, give the specific topic of what you wrote. Describe this topic in at least one sentence.

h. Which of these written work products could you now *rewrite* as a writing sample? Whom could you ask to evaluate what you rewrite to ensure that it meets high standards?

i. Describe in detail everything else you were asked to do other than mere reading assignments. Examples: role-play a hearing, visit a court, verbally analyze a problem, interview a client, evaluate a title abstract, search a title, operate a computer, find something in the library, find something on the Internet, investigate a fact.

j. How were you evaluated? What evidence do you have or could you obtain of these evaluations? Do you have a transcript of your record?

k. Did you receive any special award or distinction? If so, describe it and state what evidence you have or could obtain that you received it.

l. Make a list of every favorable comment you can remember that was made about your work. What evidence of these comments do you have or could you obtain?

m. What, if anything, did you do that called for extra work or effort on your part beyond what everyone else had to do?

n. Describe the most valuable aspect of what you learned.

o. Have you ever tried to teach anyone else what you learned? If so, describe your efforts. If not, could you? Describe what you could teach.

p. Describe every individual who evaluated you. Could you obtain a letter of recommendation from these individuals?

## 7. NOTES ON RÉSUMÉ WRITING

It is important that you have an open mind about résumés. There is no perfect format. Different people have different views. In the best of all worlds, you will be able to do some background research on the law office where you are applying for work and will learn what kind of résumé (in form and content) that office prefers. When this type of research is not possible, you must do the best you can to predict what kind of a résumé will be effective.

On this page in the Notebook, you should collect ideas about résumés from a wide variety of people such as:

| | |
|---|---|
| Teachers | Program administrators |
| Working paralegals | Unemployed paralegals |
| Paralegal supervisors | Legal administrators |
| Fellow students | Attorneys whom you know |
| Personnel officers | Authors of books and articles on |
| Placement officers | finding employment |
| Legal secretaries | Others? |

You want to collect different points of view on questions such as:

- What is an ideal résumé?
- What are the major mistakes that a résumé writer can make?
- What is the best way to phrase a career objective?
- How long should the résumé be?
- In what order should the data in the résumé be presented?
- How detailed should the résumé be?
- What kind of personal data should be included and omitted?
- How do you phrase educational experiences to make them relevant to the job you are seeking?
- How do you phrase employment experiences to make them relevant to the job you are seeking?
- How do you show that nonlegal experiences (school or work) can be relevant to a legal job?
- How do you handle potentially embarrassing facts, e.g., frequent job changes, low course grades?
- What should the cover letter for the résumé say?

## 8. DRAFT OF GENERAL RÉSUMÉ

Prepare a general résumé and include it here. We are calling it general because it is not directed or targeted at any specific job. It should be comprehensive with no page limitation. Use the guidelines, questions, and checklists in this Notebook to help you identify your strengths. The résumé you write for actual job searches will be shorter, specialized, and tailored to the job you are seeking. Before you write specialized résumés, however, you should write a general one that will be your main point of reference in preparing these other résumés. The general résumé will probably never be submitted anywhere. Take at least one full day to compile the general résumé after carefully thinking about the data needed for it.

## 9. DRAFTS OF SPECIALIZED RÉSUMÉS

Every time you write a résumé that is tailored to a specific job, include a copy here. Also include several practice copies of specialized résumés. While taking a course in corporate law, for example, write a résumé in which you pursue an opening at a law office for a corporate paralegal. For each résumé that you write (practice or real), solicit the comments of teachers, administrators, other students, working paralegals, attorneys, etc. Include these comments in this section of the Notebook.

## 10. WRITING SAMPLES

The importance of collecting a fairly large pool of writing samples cannot be overemphasized. Even if you eventually use only a few of them, the value of preparing them is enormous. The following characteristics should apply to *each* writing sample:

- It is your own work.
- It is clearly and specifically identified. The heading at the top tells the reader what the writing is.

- It is typed (handwritten work should be typed).
- There are no spelling or grammatical errors in it.
- Its appearance is professional.
- Someone whom you respect has evaluated it before you put it in final form.
- You feel that it is a high-quality product.
- It does not violate anyone's right to privacy or confidentiality. (If the sample pertains to real people or events, you have disguised all names or other identifying features.)

There are two main kinds of writing samples: those that are assigned in school or at work and those you generate on your own.

**Examples of required work that you could turn into a writing sample**

- A memorandum of law
- A legal research report or memo
- An answer to a problem in a textbook
- An exam answer
- An intake memorandum of law
- A complaint
- An answer to a complaint
- A motion
- A set of interrogatories
- Answers to a set of interrogatories
- An index to discovery documents
- A digest of one or more discovery documents
- Other memos, studies, or reports
- Articles of incorporation and bylaws

Any of these writing samples could be generated on your own if they are not required in your coursework. Ask your teachers or supervisors to help you identify written pieces that you could create. Also consider writing an article for one of the many newsletters of paralegal associations (see appendix B). The article could cover an aspect of your education or work experience. You could write about why you want to become a paralegal. You might write a response or reaction to someone else's article in a paralegal newsletter or magazine. Even if what you write is not published in a newsletter, it might still become a writing sample if it meets the criteria listed above.

## 11. CONTACTS—ATTORNEYS YOU ALREADY KNOW OR WITH WHOM YOU HAVE ANY INDIRECT ASSOCIATION

Make a list of attorneys as described in Strategy 6 in this chapter, page 71. Include their names, street and e-mail addresses, and phone numbers. Not only do you want to know whether any of these attorneys are interested in hiring paralegals, but equally important, you want to know if they can give you any leads to other employers who might be interested in hiring.

## 12. CONTACTS—EMPLOYED PARALEGALS

You want to talk with as many employed paralegals as you can to obtain leads to possible positions, as well as general guidelines for the job search. Make a list of the names, street and e-mail addresses, and phone numbers of all the paralegals that you contact. Include notes on what they told you. If they have nothing useful to say at the present time, ask them if you could check back with them in several months and if you could leave your name and number with them in the event that they come across anything in the future. See page 69 for ideas on how to locate employed paralegals for this kind of networking.

## 13. CONTACTS AND TASKS—GENERAL

Below you will find a general checklist of contacts and tasks that you should consider in your job search. Take notes on the results of these contacts and tasks and include these notes here if they are not included elsewhere in the Notebook. Your notes should include what you did, when, whom you contacted, their street and e-mail addresses and phone numbers, what was said, what follow-up is still needed, etc.

- Attorneys with whom you already have a direct or indirect association
- Employed paralegals
- Other paralegals searching for work; they may be willing to share leads that were unproductive for them, especially if you do likewise
- Contacts provided by your placement office
- Want ads in general circulation newspapers
- Want ads in legal newspapers
- Want ads and job bank openings listed in paralegal newsletters
- General directories of attorneys, such as *Martindale-Hubbell* and *West's Legal Directory*
- Special directories of attorneys, such as the *Directory of Corporate Counsel*
- Information from placement offices of local law schools
- Employment agencies specializing in paralegal placement
- Legal staffing agencies specializing in support staff and paralegal placement
- Employment agencies specializing primarily in attorney placement
- Bar association meetings open to the public
- Legal secretaries who may have leads
- Legal administrators who may have leads
- Local attorneys who have written articles in bar journals
- Stories in legal newspapers on recent large cases that are in litigation or are about to go into litigation (page 77)
- Local and national politicians who represent your area
- Service companies and consulting firms (page 38)

## 14. JOB INTERVIEW CHECKLIST

1. Exact location of interview
2. Time of arrival
3. Professional appearance in dress
4. Extra copies of résumé
5. Extra copies of writing samples
6. Copies of your transcripts
7. Name of person(s) who will conduct interview
8. Background research on the firm or company so that you know the kind of law it practices, why it is considering hiring paralegals, etc.
9. Role-playing of job interview in advance with a friend
10. Preparation for difficult questions that might be asked, such as why you left your last job so soon after starting it
11. Preparation of questions that you will ask regarding:
    Responsibilities of position
    Skills needed for the position
    Methods of supervision
    Office's prior experience with paralegals
    Career ladder for paralegals
    Relationship among paralegals, secretaries, and other clerical staff
    Client contact
    Opportunities for growth
    Methods of evaluating paralegals
    Continuing education
    Billable hours expected of paralegals
    Availability of systems

Working conditions (typing, photocopying, office, etc.)
Travel
Overtime
Computers and other equipment use
Compensation and fringe benefits (see exhibit 2.13)
12. Follow-up letter

### 15. JOB INTERVIEW—ANALYSIS SHEET
Write out the following information *after* each job interview that you have.
1. Date of interview
2. Name, address, and phone number of firm or company where you interviewed
3. Name(s) and phone number(s) of interviewer(s)
4. Kind of position that was open
5. Date you sent the follow-up letter
6. What you need to do next (send list of references, send writing samples, provide missing information that you did not have with you during the interview, etc.)
7. Your impressions of the interview (how you think you did, what surprised you, what you would do differently the next time you have an interview)
8. Notes on why you were not offered the job
9. Notes on why you turned down the job offered

### 16. RECORD KEEPING
You need a system to keep track of the steps taken to date. See exhibit 2.15 (Record Keeping and the Job Search). In addition, keep a calendar where you record important future dates, such as when you must make follow-up calls, when the local paralegal association meets, etc.

| EXHIBIT 2.15 | Record Keeping and the Job Search |
|---|---|

PERSON/OFFICE CONTACTED

HOW CONTACTED (PHONE, LETTER)

DATE OF CONTACT

ADDRESS

NOTES ON THE CONTACT

DATE FURTHER CONTACT NEEDED

DATE RÉSUMÉ SENT/DELIVERED

DATE WRITING SAMPLE SENT/DELIVERED

DATE OF INTERVIEW

NOTES ON INTERVIEW

DATE THANK YOU NOTE SENT

DATE FURTHER CONTACT NEEDED

(Fill out one card per contact; file alphabetically.)

## Section F
# YOUR SECOND JOB

If you examine want ads for paralegals, you will find that most prospective employers want paralegals with experience. The market for such individuals is excellent. But if you are *new* to the field, you are caught in the dilemma of not being able to find a job without experience and not being able to get experience without a job. How do you handle this classic Catch-22 predicament?

- You work even harder to compile an impressive résumé. You make sure that you have collected a substantial writing-sample file. Such writing samples are often the closest equivalent to prior job experience available to you.
- When you talk to other paralegals, you seek specific advice on how to present yourself as an applicant for your first job.
- You consider doing some volunteer work as a way to acquire experience for your résumé. Legal service offices and public interest law firms often encourage volunteer (i.e., pro bono) work. A recent law school graduate struggling to start a practice may be another option.
- Find out from legal staffing and employment agencies (see exhibit 2.6) if there are any temporary or part-time positions available that match your qualifications.
- Contact four or five law firms and offer to perform "runner" services for them at low or no cost, e.g., delivery of documents, filing, service of process.
- You may have to reassess what you will accept for your first job. Perhaps you can eventually turn the first job into a more acceptable position. You may simply use it to gain the experience necessary for landing a better second job.

Once you have had several years of experience and have demonstrated your competence, you will find many more employment options available to you. You will find it substantially easier to negotiate salary and articulate your skills in a job interview. You can also consider other kinds of employment where your legal training, skills, expertise, and experience are valuable. It is not uncommon for a paralegal to be recruited by former or active clients of a first employer. Numerous business contacts are made in the course of a job; these contacts could turn into new careers. In exhibit 2.16 you will find a list of some of the types of positions that paralegals have taken after they demonstrated their ability and acquired legal experience.

In short, you face a different market once you have acquired a record of experience and accomplishment. You are in greater demand in law firms and businesses. Furthermore, your legal skills are readily transferable to numerous law-related positions.

# CHAPTER SUMMARY

Someone once said that finding a job is a job in itself. The first step is to become informed about where paralegals work and what they do at those locations. The first part of this chapter was designed to provide you with this information. The major employers of paralegals are private law firms, the government, legal service offices, corporations, and other businesses. While other settings also exist, these are the largest. After examining these settings, we looked at approximately 45 specialties such as bankruptcy and criminal law. Our focus was the identification of paralegal functions in the specialties and a paralegal perspective of what life is like in each. For the specialties where most paralegals work—corporate law, estates, family law, litigation, real estate, and tort law—quotations from job ads identified traits and skills employers want.

In the second half of the chapter, we turned to strategies for finding employment. The strategies addressed the following questions: When should you begin the search? How do you compile a job hunting notebook? How do you organize an employment workshop? How do you locate working paralegals in order to obtain leads to employment? How do you arrange an informational interview? How can you use local paralegal associations as

| EXHIBIT 2.16 | Positions for Experienced Paralegals |
|---|---|

- Paralegal supervisor
- Law office administrator (legal administrator)
- Law firm marketing administrator
- Paralegal consultant
- Freelance/independent paralegal
- Law librarian/assistant
- Paralegal teacher
- Paralegal school administrator
- Placement officer
- Bar association attorney referral coordinator
- Court administrator
- Court clerk
- Sales representative for legal publisher/vendor
- Investigator
- Customs inspector
- Compliance and enforcement inspector
- Occupational safety and health inspector
- Lobbyist
- Legislative assistant
- Real estate management consultant
- Real estate specialist
- Real estate portfolio manager
- Land acquisitions supervisor
- Title examiner
- Independent title abstractor
- Abstractor
- Systems analyst
- Computer analyst
- Computer sales representative
- Bank research associate
- Trust officer (trust administrator)
- Trust associate
- Assistant loan administrator
- Fiduciary accountant
- Financial analyst/planner

- Investment analyst
- Assistant estate administrator
- Enrolled agent
- Equal employment opportunity specialist
- Employee benefit specialist/consultant
- Pension specialist
- Pension administrator
- Compensation planner
- Corporate trademark specialist
- Corporate manager
- Securities analyst
- Securities compliance officer
- Insurance adjustor
- Actuarial associate
- Claims examiner
- Claims coordinator
- Director of risk management
- Environmental specialist
- Editor for a legal or business publisher
- Recruiter, legal employment agency
- Personnel director
- Administrative law judge
- Arbitrator
- Mediator
- Internal security inspector
- Evidence technician
- Demonstrative evidence specialist
- Fingerprint technician
- Polygraph examiner
- Probation officer
- Parole officer
- Corrections officer
- Politician
- Etc.

a resource? How do you locate potential employers? How do you do background research on potential employers? What should your résumé contain? What is an effective cover letter? What kinds of writing samples should you prepare, and when should you start preparing them? How should you prepare for a job interview? What kinds of questions should you anticipate? What kinds of questions should you ask? How can you organize all of the contacts, events, and pieces of paper that are involved in a comprehensive job search?

Finally, we examined alternative career opportunities for paralegals, particularly for those who have gained paralegal experience on the job.

## KEY TERMS

| | |
|---|---|
| private law firm | group legal services |
| boutique law firm | uncontested |
| paralegal specialist | public defender |
| indigent | assigned counsel |
| pro bono | freelance paralegal |
| general counsel | informational interview |
| special interest group | job bank |

continuing legal education (CLE)
networking
blind ad
chronological résumé

functional résumé
template
cover letter
billable hours quota

## ENDNOTES

1. Andrea Wagner, *Tips & Traps for the New Paralegal*, 8 Legal Assistant Today 78 (March/April 1991).
2. Altman Weil, Inc., Press Release (August 14, 2000), *available at* www.altmanweil.com/news/release.cfm?PRID=4.
3. U.S. Office of Personnel Management, General Schedule Position Classification Standards, *available at* www.opm.gov/fedclass/html/gsseries.htm.
4. See Commercial Law League of America, *A Paralegal Approach to the Practice of Commercial Law* (November 14, 1975).
5. See J. Stein & B. Hoff, *Paralegals and Administrative Assistants for Prosecutors* (Nat'l District Attorneys Ass'n 1974); J. Stein, *Paralegals: A Resource for Defenders and Correctional Services* (1976).
6. Rocky Mountain Legal Assistants Association, *The Use of the Legal Assistant* (1975).
7. Colorado Bar Association Legal Assistant Committee. These tasks have been approved by the Committee, not by the Board of Governors of the Colorado Bar.
8. See endnote 7.
9. C. Berg, *Annual Survey* (San Francisco Ass'n of Legal Assistants. Dec 19, 1973).
10. See endnote 7.
11. See endnote 7.
12. *Merrill Advantage* (Spring 1990).
13. Gainen, *Information Interviews: A Strategy*, Paradigm (Baltimore Ass'n of Legal Assistants, November/December 1989).
14. Jacobi, *Back to Basics in Hiring Techniques*, The Mandate 1 (Ass'n of Legal Administrators, San Diego Chapter, October 1987).
15. U.S. Department of Labor, *Tips for Finding the Right Job* 17 (1991).
16. See Rocky Mountain Legal Assistant Association, *Employment Handbook for Legal Assistants* (1979).
17. Cunningham, *A Planned Approach to Interviewing*, 5 The LAMA Manager 1 (Legal Assistants Management Association, Fall 1989).
18. Reitz, *Be Steps Ahead of Other Candidates: Understand the Interview Game*, 5 Legal Assistant Today 24, 84 (March/April 1988).
19. Michelle Cottle, *Too Personal at the Interview*, New York Times, April 25, 1999, at BU10.
20. Chere Estrin & Stacey Hunt, *The Successful Paralegal Job Search Guide* 204–5 (2001).

# Appendix 2.A

# PARALEGAL EMPLOYMENT IN SELECTED LARGE LAW OFFICES

After the name of the law firms in this list, you will find two numbers separated by a slash (/). The first number is the number of attorneys employed by the office in the city indicated or in all the cities where the firm practices. The number to the right of the slash is the number of paralegals employed by the office. Some of the names of the offices have been shortened to the first two partner names; commas between names have been omitted. You will also find the Internet site of the offices. Go to these sites to find out what kind of law the office practices (click "Practice Areas," "Practice Groups," or "Services"). The site may also tell you whether the office is currently seeking to hire paralegals (click "Recruitment" or "Opportunities"). If a search box exists on the site, type "paralegal" or "legal assistant" in the box to try to learn more about nonattorneys at the office. Some firms have special paralegal links (e.g., *www.whitecase.com/lgl_assistants.html*). If there is a "Contact Us" option, you might want to send an e-mail inquiring about employment opportunities for paralegals at the office. (You may find that most of the firms on this list seeking paralegals are looking for paralegals with specified experience.) For additional information about specific law firms, see "Finding Information about Law Firms" in exhibit 2.6.

## Alabama (Birmingham)
Balch Bingham: 116/17 (www.balch.com)
Bradley Arant Rose: 163/42 (www.barw.com)
Johnston Barton Proctor: 56/13 (johnstonbarton.com)
Maynard, Cooper: 93/20 (www.mcglaw.com)

## Arizona (Phoenix)
Brown & Bain: 71/17 (www.brownbain.com)
Bryan Cave: 51/10 (www.bryancave.com)
Fennemore Craig: 134/21 (www.fennemorecraig.com)
Gallagher Kennedy: 82/13 (www.gknet.com)
Gammage Burnham: 29/11 (www.gblaw.com)
Jennings Strouss Salmon: 76/13 (www.jsslaw.com)
Jones Skelton: 60/20 (jshfirm.wld.com)
Lewis Roca: 124/41 (www.lrlaw.com)
Osborn Maledon: 37/14 (www.osbornmaledon.com)
Quarles Brady: 42/14 (www.quarles.com)
Snell Wilmer: 179/29 (www.swlaw.com)
Squire Sanders: 57/14 (www.ssd.com)
Steptoe Johnson: 36/9 (www.steptoe.com)

## California (Los Angeles)
Arter Hadden: 97/15 (www.arterhadden.com)
Brobeck Phleger: 78/15 (www.brobeck.com)
Gibson Dunn: 215/33 (www.gdclaw.com)
Jackson Lewis: 314/31 (www.jacksonlewis.com)
Latham Watkins: 246/46 (www.lw.com)
Loeb Loeb: 134/23 (www.loeb.com)
Manatt Phelps: 142/25 (www.manatt.com)
Mitchell Silberberg: 113/20 (www.msk.com)
Munger Tolles: 123/26 (www.mto.com)
Orrick Herrington: 61/15 (www.orrick.com)
Pillsbury Winthrop: 102/18 (pillsburywinthrop.com)
Quinn Emanuel: 89/18 (www.quinnemanuel.com)
Riordan McKinzie: 67/16 (www.riordan.com)
Sheppard Mullin: 160/19 (www.smrh.com)
Sidley Austin: 113/20 (www.sidley.com)
Skadden Arps: 133/32 (www.skadden.com)

## California (San Diego)
Gray Cary: 147/38 (www.gcwf.com)
Latham Watkins: 82/16 (www.lw.com)
Luce Forward: 179/29 (www.luce.com)

Pillsbury Winthrop: 36/9 (pillsburywinthrop.com)
Seltzer Caplan: 62/20 (www.scmv.com)

### California (San Francisco)
Brobeck Phleger: 189/55 (www.brobeck.com)
Cooley Godward: 121/41 (www.cooley.com)
Farella Braun: 88/32 (www.fbm.com)
Folger Levin: 46/18 (www.flk.com)
Gordon Rees: 113/25 (www.gordonrees.com)
Hancock Rothert: 75/34 (www.hrblaw.com)
Heller Ehrman: 173/69 (www.hewm.com)
Howard Rice: 103/30 (www.howardrice.com)
Jackson Lewis: 314/31 (www.jacksonlewis.com)
Latham Watkins: 77/22 (www.lw.com)
McCutchen Doyle: 167/17 (www.mccutchen.com)
Morrison Foerster: 263/18 (www.mofo.com)
O'Melveny Myers: 277/70 (www.omm.com)
Orrick Herrington: 163/47 (www.orrick.com)
Pillsbury Winthrop: 211/42 (pillsburywinthrop.com)
Thelen Reid: 134/36 (www.thelenreid.com)
Townsend Townsend: 71/23 (www.townsend.com)

### Colorado (Denver)
Brownstein Hyatt: 87/28 (www.bhf-law.com)
Holland Hart: 114/15 (www.hollandhart.com)
Holme Roberts: 136/30 (www.hro.com)
Leboeuf Lamb: 44/9 (www.llgm.com)
Sherman Howard: 124/22 (www.sah.com)
Wheeler Trigg: 31/19 (www.wtklaw.com)

### Connecticut (Hartford)
Bingham Dana: 75/15 (www.bingham.com)
Day Berry: 133/36 (dbh.com)
Jackson Lewis: 314/31 (www.jacksonlewis.com)
Murtha Cullina: 85/17 (www.murthalaw.com)
Pepe Hazard: 64/17 (pepehazard.com)
Robinson Cole: 104/18 (www.rc.com)
Shipman Goodwin: 114/29 (www.shipman-goodwin.com)
Updike Kelly: 61/12 (www.uks.com)

### Connecticut (New Haven)
Bergman Horowitz: 26/10 (taxlawyers.com)
Tyler Cooper: 69/16 (www.tylercooper.com)
Wiggin Dana: 123/38 (www.wiggin.com)

### Delaware (Wilmington)
Morris James: 49/18 (www.morrisjames.com)
Morris Nichols: 73/10 (www.mnat.com)
Potter Anderson: 62/14 (attys.pacdelaware.com)
Richards Layton: 94/14 (www.rlf.com)
Skadden Arps: 50/18 (www.skadden.com)
Young Conaway: 65/28 (www.ycst.com)

### District of Columbia
Akin Gump: 279/57 (www.akingump.com)
Arent Fox: 243/50 (www.arentfox.com)
Arnold Porter: 366/131 (www.arnoldporter.com)
Baach Robinson: 32/16 (www.barole.com)
Covington Burling: 302/103 (www.cov.com)
Crowell Moring: 212/62 (www.crowell.com)
Dickstein Shapiro: 233/50 (www.dsmo.com)
Finnegan Henderson: 153/51 (www.finnegan.com)
Hogan Hartson: 609/74 (www.hhlaw.com)
Howrey Simon: 272/53 (www.howrey.com)
Kilpatrick Lockhart: 108/32 (www.kl.com)
McDermott Will: 183/50 (www.mwe.com)
Morgan Lewis: 287/51 (www.morganlewis.com)
Skadden Arps: 184/64 (www.skadden.com)
Wilmer Cutler: 256/66 (www.wilmer.com)

### Florida (Jacksonville)
Fisher Tousey: 13/8 (www.fishertousey.com)
Foley Lardner: 47/9 (www.foleylardner.com)
Holland Knight: 58/12 (www.hklaw.com)
McGuire Woods: 32/8 (www.mwbb.com)

### Florida (Miami)
Akerman Senterfitt: 266/26 (www.akerman.com)
Carlton Fields: 54/12 (www.carltonfields.com)
Fowler White Burnett: 50/13 (www.fowler-white.com)
Greenberg Traurig 395/86 (www.gtlaw.com)
Holland Knight: 107/24 (www.hklaw.com)
Jackson Lewis: 314/31 (www.jacksonlewis.com)
Morgan Lewis: 40/9 (www.morganlewis.com)
Shutts Bowen: 122/21 (www.shutts-law.com)
Stearns Weaver Miller: 63/13 (www.stearnsweaver.com)
Steel Hector Davis: 110/13 (www.steelhector.com)
White Case: 51/8 (www.whitecase.com)

### Florida (Tampa)
Annis Mitchell Cockey: 71/22 (www.annislaw.com)
Carlton Fields: 79/21 (www.carltonfields.com)
Fowler White Gillen: 162/53 (www.fowlerwhite.com)
Holland Knight: 92/16 (www.hklaw.com)
Piper Marbury: 18/8 (www.piperrudnick.com)
Trenam Kemker Scharf: 62/13 (www.trenam.com)

### Georgia (Atlanta)
Alston Bird: 364/51 (www.alston.com)
Arnall Golden: 119/25 (www.agg.com)
Holland Knight: 64/10 (www.hklaw.com)
Hunton Williams: 85/21 (www.hunton.com)
Jackson Lewis: 314/31 (www.jacksonlewis.com)
Jones Day: 99/18 (www.jonesday.com)
Kilpatrick Stockton: 422/110 (www.kilstock.com)
King Spalding: 335/80 (www.kslaw.com)
Long Aldridge: 147/24 (www.lanlaw.com)

Morris Manning: 136/29 (www.mmmlaw.com)
Paul Hastings: 90/15 (www.phjw.com)
Powell Goldstein: 255/33 (www.pgfm.com)
Rogers Hardin: 42/16 (www.rh-law.com)
Smith Gambrell: 145/19 (www.sgrlaw.com)
Sutherland Asbill: 146/30 (www.sablaw.com)
Swift Currie: 64/15 (www.taglaw.com/Swift.html)
Troutman Sanders: 240/36 (www.troutmansanders.com)

## Hawaii (Honolulu)
Ashford Wriston: 27/5 (www.ashfordwriston.com)
Cades Schutte: 68/12 (www.cades.com)
Goodsill Anderson: 68/12 (www.goodsill.com)

## Idaho (Boise)
Holland Hart: 15/3 (www.hollandhart.com)
Stoel Rives: 16/2 (www.stoel.com)

## Illinois (Chicago)
Altheimer Gray: 182/23 (www.altheimer.com)
Baker McKenzie: 185/37 (www.bakerinfo.com)
Chapman Cutler: 183/17 (www.chapman.com)
Foley Lardner: 94/15 (www.foleylardner.com)
Freeborn Peters: 88/22 (www.freebornpeters.com)
Gardner Carton: 192/25 (www.gcd.com)
Jackson Lewis: 314/31 (www.jacksonlewis.com)
Jenner Block: 324/39 (www.jenner.com)
Katten Muchin: 330/41 (www.kmz.com)
Kirkland Ellis: 377/66 (www.kirkland.com)
Latham Watkins: 102/14 (www.lw.com)
Lord Bissell: 269/42 (www.lordbissell.com)
Mayer Brown: 478/80 (www.mayerbrown.com)
McDermott Will: 276/43 (www.mwe.com)
Neal Gerber: 130/27 (www.ngelaw.com)
Piper Marbury: 293/51 (www.piperrudnick.com)
Sachnoff Weaver: 106/24 (www.sachnoff.com)
Schiff Hardin: 214/35 (www.schiffhardin.com)
Seyfarth Shaw: 237/14 (www.seyfarth.com)
Sidley Austin: 438/104 (www.sidley.com)
Skadden Arps: 114/21 (www.skadden.com)
Sonnenschein Nath: 206/26 (www.sonnenschein.com)
Vedder Price: 157/28 (www.vedderprice.com)
Wildman Harrold: 188/24 (www.whad.com)
Winston Strawn: 381/79 (www.winston.com)

## Indiana (Indianapolis)
Baker Daniels: 168/26 (www.bakerdaniels.com)
Barnes Thornburg: 152/26 (www.btlaw.com)
Bose McKinney: 76/13 (www.boselaw.com)
Ice Miller: 198/29 (www.imdr.com)
Sommer Barnard: 53/5 (www.sommerbarnard.com)

## Iowa (Des Moines)
Belin Lamson: 32/9 (www.taglaw.com/Belin.html)

## Kansas (Wichita)
Husch Eppenberger: 5/3 (www.husch.com)

## Kentucky (Louisville)
Brown Todd: 124/41 (www.browntodd.com)
Greenbaum Doll: 85/15 (www.gdm.com)
Ogden Newell: 39/6 (www.ogdenlaw.com)
Stites Harbison: 67/20 (www.stites.com)
Wyatt Tarrant: 104/37 (www.wyattfirm.com)

## Louisiana (Baton Rouge)
Jones Walker: 45/9 (www.joneswalker.com)
Kean Miller: 106/26 (www.keanmiller.com)
Taylor Porter: 65/14 (www.taylorporter.com)

## Louisiana (Lafayette)
Jeansonne Remondet: 22/19 (www.jeanrem.com)
Onebane Bernard: 37/14 (www.onebane.com)

## Louisiana (New Orleans)
Chaffe McCall: 62/14 (www.chaffe.com)
Jones Walker: 190/38 (www.jwlaw.com)
Liskow Lewis: 84/29 (www.liskow.com)
Phelps Dunbar: 103/27 (www.phelpsdunbar.com)
Stone Pigman: 52/11 (www.stonepigman.com)

## Maine (Portland)
Drummond Woodsum: 34/5 (www.dwmlaw.com)
Pierce Atwood: 8/11 (www.pierceatwood.com)

## Maryland (Baltimore)
Gordon Feinblatt: 80/30 (www.gfrlaw.com)
Miles Stockbridge: 178/25 (www.milesstockbridge.com)
Ober Kaler: 109/26 (www.ober.com)
Piper Marbury: 176/32 (www.pipermar.com)
Venable Baetjer: 124/18 (www.venable.com)

## Massachusetts (Boston)
Bingham Dana: 302/45 (www.bingham.com)
Bromberg Sunstein: 33/11 (www.bromsun.com)
Brown Rudnick: 106/36 (www.brownrudnick.com)
Choate Hall: 181/19 (www.choate.com)
Fish Richardson: 64/15 (www.fr.com)
Foley Hoag: 187/26 (www.fhe.com)
Goldstein Manello: 49/10 (www.gmlaw.com)
Goodwin Procter: 366/65 (www.goodwinprocter.com)
Goulston Storrs: 140/24 (www.goulstorrs.com)
Hale Dorr: 304/77 (www.haledorr.com)
Hill Barlow: 116/27 (www.hillbarlow.com)
Holland Knight: 92/18 (www.hklaw.com)
Hutchins Wheeler: 120/17 (www.hutch.com)
Jackson Lewis: 314/31 (www.jacksonlewis.com)
Mintz Levin: 224/43 (www.mintz.com)

Nixon Peabody: 114/17 (www.nixonpeabody.com)
Nutter McClennen: 137/25 (www.nutter.com)
Palmer Dodge: 181/38 (www.palmerdodge.com)
Ropes Gray: 320/46 (www.ropesgray.com)
Skadden Arps: 34/17 (www.skadden.com)
Sullivan Worcester: 128/22 (www.sandw.com)

**Michigan (Detroit)**
Bodman Longley: 75/11 (www.bodmanlongley.com)
Butzel Long: 100/18 (www.butzel.com)
Clark Hill: 103/14 (www.clarkhill.com)
Dickinson Wright: 91/21 (www.dickinson-wright.com)
Dykema Gossett: 116/22 (www.dykema.com)
Honigman Miller: 161/26 (www.honigman.com)
Jaffe Raitt: 85/10 (www.jafferaitt.com)
Miller Canfield: 111/18 (www.millercanfield.com)

**Minnesota (Minneapolis)**
Briggs Morgan: 138/23 (www.briggs.com)
Dorsey Whitney: 302/59 (www.dorseylaw.com)
Faegre Benson: 239/35 (www.faegre.com)
Fredrikson Byron: 141/23 (www.fredlaw.com)
Gray Plant: 123/29 (www.gpmlaw.com)
Jackson Lewis: 314/31 (www.jacksonlewis.com)
Leonard Street: 145/30 (www.leonard.com)
Lindquist Vennum: 119/17 (www.lindquist.com)
Maslon Edelman: 70/17 (www.maslon.com)
Merchant Gould: 74/19 (www.merchant-gould.com)
Oppenheimer Wolff: 144/21 (www.oppenheimer.com)
Robins Kaplan: 123/43 (www.rkmc.com)
Winthrop Weinstine: 75/17 (www.winthrop.com)

**Mississippi (Jackson)**
Baker Donelson: 23/10 (www.bakerdonelson.com)
Phelps Dunbar: 44/12 (www.phelpsdunbar.com)
Watkins Ludlam: 54/20 (www.watkinsludlam.com)

**Missouri (Kansas City)**
Blackwell Sanders: 171/28 (www.blackwellsanders.com)
Bryan Cave: 80/30 (www.bryancavellp.com)
Husch Eppenberger: 41/16 (www.husch.com)
Lathrop Gage: 202/35 (www.lathropgage.com)
Morrison Hecker: 110/19 (www.moheck.com)
Polsinelli Shalton: 113/35 (www.pswlaw.com)
Shook Hardy: 277/61 (www.shb.com)
Sonnenschein Nath: 51/9 (www.sonnenschein.com)
Spencer Fane: 89/13 (www.spencerfane.com)
Stinson Mag: 114/16 (www.stinson.com)

**Missouri (St. Louis)**
Armstrong Teasdale: 143/19
   (www.armstrongteasdale.com)
Blackwell Sanders: 81/20 (www.bspmlaw.com)
Bryan Cave: 223/33 (www.bryancavellp.com)

Gallop Johnson: 74/143 (www.gjn.com)
Husch Eppenberger: 92/28 (www.husch.com)
Lewis Rice: 134/18 (www.lrf.com)
Thompson Coburn: 276/52
   (www.thompsoncoburn.com)

**Montana (Billings)**
Holland Hart: 10/4 (www.hollandhart.com)

**Nebraska (Omaha)**
Kutak Rock: 101/15 (www.kutakrock.com)

**Nevada (Las Vegas)**
Lionel Sawyer: 57/13 (www.lionelsawyer.com)

**New Hampshire (Concord)**
Orr Reno: 34/7 (www.orr-reno.com)
Sulloway & Hollis: 39/15 (www.sulloway.com)

**New Hampshire (Manchester)**
Devine Millimet: 65/21 (www.dmb.com)
McLane Graf: 80/27 (www.mclane.com)
Sheehan Phinney: 60/80 (www.sheehan.com)
Wiggin Nourie: 38/11 (www.wiggin-nourie.com)

**New Jersey (Morristown)**
Jackson Lewis: 314/31 (www.jacksonlewis.com)
Pitney Hardin: 153/33 (www.phks.com)
Porzio Bromberg: 56/64 (www.pbnlaw.com)
Riker Danzig: 153/35 (www.riker.com)

**New Jersey (Newark)**
Carpenter Bennett: 80/14 (www.carpben.com)
Gibbons Del Deo: 151/29 (www.gibbonslaw.com)
Leboeuf Lamb: 47/7 (www.llgm.com)
McCarter English: 223/50 (www.mccarter.com)
Sills Cummis: 155/38 (www.sillscummis.com)

**New Mexico (Albuquerque)**
Modrall Sperling: 69/16 (www.modrall.com)

**New York (Albany)**
Harris Beach: 174/42 (www.harrisbeach.com)
Whiteman Osterman: 49/11 (www.woh.com)

**New York (Buffalo)**
Damon Morey: 56/14 (www.damonmorey.com)
Harris Beach: 174/42 (www.harrisbeach.com)
Hodgson Russ: 121/54 (www.hodgsonruss.com)
Phillips Lytle: 96/32 (www.phillipslytle.com)

**New York (New York City)**
Anderson Kill: 107/40 (www.andersonkill.com)
Baker McKenzie: 66/76 (www.bakerinfo.com)
Cadwalader Wickersham: 307/65 (www.cadwalader.com)
Chadbourne Parke: 237/67 (www.chadbourne.com)
Cleary Gottlieb: 318/72 (www.cgsh.com)
Cravath Swain: 366/133 (www.cravath.com)
Davis Polk: 473/74 (www.dpw.com)
Debevoise Plimpton: 341/55 (www.debevoise.com)
Dewey Ballantine: (366/50) (www.deweyballantine.com)
Fried Frank: 300/89 (www.ffhsj.com)
Harris Beach: 174/42 (www.harrisbeach.com)
Kaye Scholer: 255/78 (www.kayescholer.com)
Leboeuf Lamb: 237/54 (www.llgm.com)
Milbank Tweed: 253/41 (www.milbank.com)
Morgan Lewis: 266/56 (www.morganlewis.com)
Orrick Herrington: 202/48 (www.orrick.com)
Paul Weiss: 350/78 (www.paulweiss.com)
Proskauer Rose: 351/63 (www.proskauer.com)
Schulte Roth: 243/47 (www.srz.com)
Shearman Sterling: 474/80 (www.shearman.com)
Sidley Austin: 284/61 (www.sidley.com)
Simpson Thacher: 537/129 (www.simpsonthacher.com)
Skadden Arps: 657/315 (www.skadden.com)
Stroock Stroock: 243/56 (www.stroock.com)
Sullivan Cromwell: 522/131 (www.sullcrom.com)
Wachtell Lipton: 159/42 (www.wlrk.com)
Walter Conston: 62/15 (www.wcag.com)
Weil Gotshal: 405/75 (www.weil.com)
White Case: 327/63 (www.whitecase.com)
Willkie Farr: 301/67 (www.willkie.com)

**North Carolina (Charlotte)**
Alston Bird: 122/14 (www.alston.com)
Cadwalader Wickersham: 29/15 (www.cadwalader.com)
Kennedy Covington: 124/32 (www.kclh.com)
Kilpatrick Stockton: 422/110 (www.kilstock.com)
Moore Van Allen: 112/36 (www.mvalaw.com)
Parker Poe: 94/23 (www.parkerpoe.com)
Robinson Bradshaw: 86/21 (www.rbh.com)
Smith Lewis: 84/18 (www.shmm.com)
Womble Carlyle: 46/11 (www.wcsr.com)

**North Carolina (Raleigh)**
Kilpatrick Stockton: 422/110 (www.kilstock.com)
Poyner Spruill: 47/14 (www.poynerspruill.com)
Smith Helms: 37/11 (www.shmm.com)
Womble Carlyle: 43/16 (www.wcsr.com)

**North Carolina (Winston-Salem)**
Kilpatrick Stockton: 422/110 (www.kilstock.com)
Womble Carlyle: 155/141 (www.wcsr.com)

**Ohio (Cincinnati)**
Dinsmore Shohl: 156/43 (www.dinshohl.com)
Frost Jacobs: 140/32 (www.frostbrowntodd.com)

Graydon Head: 63/11 (www.graydon.com)
Keating Muething: 82/26 (www.kmklaw.com)
Strauss Troy: 43/12 (www.strauss-troy.com)
Taft Stettinius: 128/26 (www.taftlaw.com)
Thompson Hine: 79/8 (www.thompsonhine.com)

**Ohio (Cleveland)**
Baker Hostetler: 159/15 (www.bakerlaw.com)
Calfee Halter: 176/12 (www.calfee.com)
Hahn Loeser: 82/20 (www.hahnlaw.com)
Jones Day: 230/39 (www.jonesday.com)
McDonald Hopkins: 60/14 (www.mhbh.com)
Squire Sanders: 162/29 (www.ssd.com)
Thompson Hine: 149/31 (www.thf.com)

**Ohio (Columbus)**
Bricker Eckler: 115/16 (www.bricker.com)
Kegler Brown: 63/12 (www.kbhr.com)
Porter Wright: 155/24 (www.porterwright.com)
Schottenstein Zox: 93/9 (www.szd.com)
Squire Sanders: 82/15 (www.ssd.com)
Vorys Sater: 284/40 (www.vssp.com)

**Oklahoma (Oklahoma City)**
Crowe Dunlevy: 81/28 (www.crowedunlevy.com)
McAfee Taft: 91/16 (www.mcafee-taft.com)

**Oklahoma (Tulsa)**
Crowe Dunlevy: 27/6 (www.crowedunlevy.com)
Gable Gotwals: 52/10 (www.gablelaw.com)
Hall Estill: 82/16 (www.hallestill.com)
Rhodes Hieronymus: 25/12 (www.rhodesokla.com)

**Oregon (Portland)**
Ball Janik: 38/8 (www.balljanik.com)
Banner Witcoff: 77/8 (www.bannerwitcoff.com)
Bullivant Houser: 75/18 (www.bullivant.com)
Davis Wright: 81/19, (www.dwt.com)
Miller Nash: 91/18 (www.millernash.com)
Schwabe Williamson: 113/18 (www.schwabe.com)
Stoel Rives: 168/35 (www.stoel.com)
Tonkon Torp: 60/11 (www.tonkon.com)

**Pennsylvania (Philadelphia)**
Ballard Spahr: 194/37 (www.ballardspahr.com)
Blank Rome: 263/41 (www.blankrome.com)
Cozen O'Connor: 202/49 (www.cozen.com)
Dechert Price: 257/95 (www.dechert.com)
Drinker Biddle: 167/29 (www.dbr.com)
Duane Morris: 165/33 (www.duanemorris.com)
Fox Rothchild: 213/44 (www.frof.com)
Klett Lieber: 102/17 (www.klettlieber.com)
Montgomery McCracken: 160/23 (www.mmwr.com)
Morgan Lewis: 234/60 (www.morganlewis.com)

Pepper Hamilton: 201/49 (www.pepperlaw.com)
Saul Ewing: 235/36 (www.saul.com)
Schnader Harrison: 145/33 (www.schnader.com)
Wolf Block: 237/42 (www.wolfblock.com)
Woodcock Washburn: 56/26 (www.woodcock.com)

### Pennsylvania (Pittsburgh)
Buchanan Ingersoll: 170/32 (www.bipc.com)
Eckert Seamans: 123/22 (www.escm.com)
Jackson Lewis: 314/31 (www.jacksonlewis.com)
Kilpatrick Lockhart: 212/69 (www.kl.com)
Pepper Hamilton: 40/11 (www.pepperlaw.com)
Reed Smith: 169/34 (www.rssm.com)
Thorp Reed: 89/19 (www.thorpreed.com)

### Rhode Island (Providence)
Partridge Snow: 33/13 (www.psh.com)

### South Carolina (Greenville)
Jackson Lewis: 314/31 (www.jacksonlewis.com)
Leatherwood Walker: 49/14 (www.lwtmlaw.com)
Wyche Burgess: 28/13 (www.wyche.com)

### South Dakota (Sioux Falls)
Davenport Evans: 30/6 (www.dehs.com)

### Tennessee (Nashville)
Baker Donelson: 46/12 (www.bakerdonelson.com)
Bass Berry: 108/32 (www.bassberry.com)
Boult Cummings: 82/18 (www.bccb.com)
Harwell Howard: 37/17 (www.h3gm.com)
Stites Harbison: 42/10 (www.stites.com)
Waller Lansden: 115/23 (www.wallerlaw.com)

### Texas (Austin)
Akin Gump: 195/23 (www.akingump.com)
Brobeck Phleger: 42/13 (www.brobeck.com)
Brown McCarroll: 60/15 (www.brownmccarroll.com)
Clark Thomas: 85/23 (www.ctw.com)
Fulbright Jaworski: 49/20 (www.fulbright.com)
Jackson Walker: 47/17 (www.jw.com)
McGinnis Lochridge: 55/15 (www.mcginnislaw.com)

### Texas (Dallas)
Akin Gump: 146/33 (www.akingump.com)
Andrews Kurth: 57/17 (www.andrews-kurth.com)
Baker Botts: 116/37 (www.bakerbotts.com)
Baron Budd: 59/132 (www.baronbudd.com)
Fulbright Jaworski: 72/17 (www.fulbright.com)
Gardere Wynne: 180/32 (www.gardere.com)
Haynes Boone: 201/31 (www.haynesboone.com)
Hughes Luce: 115/18 (www.hughesluce.com)

Jackson Lewis: 314/31 (www.jacksonlewis.com)
Jenkins Gilchrist: 232/58 (www.jenkens.com)
Jones Day: 148/21 (www.jonesday.com)
Locke Liddell: 226/45 (www.lockeliddell.com)
Strasburger Price: 167/38 (www.strasburger.com)
Thompson Coe: 69/22 (www.thompsoncoe.com)
Thompson Knight: 237/41 (www.tklaw.com)
Vial Hamilton: 106/22 (www.vialhamilton.com)
Vinson Elkins: 99/25 (www.vinson-elkins.com)
Winstead Sechrest: 260/38 (www.winstead.com)

### Texas (Houston)
Akin Gump: 156/16 (www.akingump.com)
Andrews Kurth: 133/20 (www.andrews-kurth.com)
Baker Botts: 229/146 (www.bakerbotts.com)
Bracewell patterson: 175/30 (www.bracepatt.com)
Fulbright Jaworski: 257/52 (www.fulbright.com)
Gardere Wynne: 85/18 (www.gardere.com)
Locke Liddell: 142/23 (www.lockeliddell.com)
Mayor Day: 102/32 (www.mdck.com)
Susman Godfrey: 34/14 (www.susmangodfrey.com)
Vinson Elkins: 346/86 (www.vinson-elkins.com)

### Utah (Salt Lake City)
Leboeuf Lamb: 25/3 (www.llgm.com)
Parr Waddoups: 46/7 (www.pwlaw.com)
Parsons Behle: 120/23 (www.pblutah.com)
Snell Wilmer: 30/4 (www.swlaw.com)

### Vermont (Burlington)
Downs Rachlin: 50/11 (www.drm.com)

### Virginia (Richmond)
Hunton Williams: 234/109 (www.hunton.com)
Mays & Valentine: 132/24 (www.maysval.com)
McGuire Woods: 220/74 (www.mwbb.com)
Sands Anderson: 55/19 (www.sandsanderson.com)
Williams Mullen: 115/23 (www.wmcd.com)

### Washington State (Seattle)
Davis Wright: 153/29 (www.dwt.com)
Foster Pepper: 130/28 (www.foster.com)
Garvey Schubert: 62/16 (www.gsblaw.com)
Heller Ehrman: 70/17 (www.hewm.com)
Jackson Lewis: 314/31 (www.jacksonlewis.com)
Lane Powell: 136/75 (www.lanepowell.com)
Perkins Coie: 255/67 (www.perkinscoie.com)
Preston Gates: 140/37 (www.prestongates.com)
Riddell Williams: 67/23 (www.riddellwilliams.com)
Williams Kastner: 72/187 (www.wkg.com)

## Washington State (Spokane)
Paine Hamblen: 60/16 (www.painehamblen.com)

## West Virginia (Charleston)
Bowles Rice: 55/22 (www.bowlesrice.com)
Jackson Kelly: 89/33 (www.jacksonkelly.com)
Spilman Thomas: 43/10 (www.spilmanlaw.com)

## West Virginia (Huntington)
Huddleston Bolen: 45/30 (www.huddlestonbolen.com)

## Wisconsin (Milwaukee)
Davis Kuelthau: 62/11 (www.daviskuelthau.com)
Foley Lardner: 226/35 (www.foleylardner.com)

Godfrey Kahn: 119/27 (www.gklaw.com)
Michael Best: 224/22 (www.mbf-law.com)
Quarles Brady: 207/35 (www.quarles.com)
Reinhart Boerner: 155/27 (www.rbvdnr.com)
Whyte Hirschboeck: 92/14 (www.whdlaw.com)

## Wyoming (Cheyenne)
Holland Hart: 14/4 (www.hollandhart.com)

*Sources: West's Legal Directory;* www.infirmation.com/shared/lss; National Law Journal, *The NLJ 250 Largest Law Firms* (www.ilrg.com/nlj250/index.html); National Association of Legal Placement, *Directory of Legal Employers;* and independent checking.

| APPENDIX 2.B | Summary Chart—Survey of State Government Job Classifications for Paralegals | | | |
|---|---|---|---|---|
| **GOVERNMENT** | **POSITION** | **RESPONSIBILITIES** | **QUALIFICATIONS** | **SALARY** |
| **Alabama**<br>Personnel Dept.<br>300 Folsom Admin. Bldg<br>Montgomery, AL 36130<br>334-242-3389<br>www.personnel.state.al.us | Legal Assistant<br>(11503) | • Perform legal research<br>• Draft pleadings<br>• Interview witnesses in preparation for trial<br>• Conduct routine investigations<br>• Assist attorney at depositions<br>• Digest laws and cases<br>• Write draft of Attorney General opinions<br>• Perform office administrative duties | Certificate from accredited college with minimum of 30 semester hours or 50 quarter hours in Legal Assistant Studies with courses in investigation, legal bibliography, evidence, criminal procedure, civil litigation and trial preparation, court management, and paralegalism | $23,917–$36,348 per year |
| Other position to check in Alabama: Docket Clerk (11501). | | | | |
| **Alaska**<br>Dept. of Administration<br>Div. of Personnel<br>Pouch C<br>P.O. Box 110201<br>Juneau, AK 99811<br>907-465-4430<br>800-587-0430<br>notes.state.ak.us | Paralegal<br>Assistant 1<br>(7105-13) | • Interview clients<br>• Assess severity of problem<br>• Obtain statements and affidavits<br>• Conduct investigations<br>• Coordinate witness scheduling<br>• Represent clients at hearings | Certificate from a state paralegal training program<br>OR<br>Associate of Arts program with a major in paralegal, criminal justice, or law studies; or a bachelor's degree or equivalent in social studies or behavioral sciences<br>OR<br>3 years of experience as legal secretary, court clerk, etc. | $37,732–$51,616 per year |
| Other positions to check in Alaska: Paralegal Assistant II (7106-16); Investigator II (7767); Latent Fingerprint Examiner (7756). | | | | |
| **Arizona**<br>Dept. of Administration<br>Human Resources Div.<br>1831 West Jefferson St.<br>Phoenix, AZ 85007<br>602-542-8373<br>www.hr.state.az.us | Legal Assistant<br>(32201) | • Perform legal research<br>• Write drafts of routine legal documents<br>• Interview complainants or witnesses<br>• Perform legal research | 4 years of full-time paralegal experience<br>OR<br>Associate's degree in paralegal studies<br>OR<br>Associate's degree in any area PLUS paralegal certification through an accredited program | $22,259–$40,611 per year |
| Other positions to check in Arizona: Legal Assistant II (32202); Legal Assistant III (32203); Legal Assistant Project Specialist (322040; Process Server (32206). | | | | |

*continued*

| APPENDIX 2.B | Summary Chart—Survey of State Government Job Classifications for Paralegals—*continued* |
|---|---|

| GOVERNMENT | POSITION | RESPONSIBILITIES | QUALIFICATIONS | SALARY |
|---|---|---|---|---|
| **Arkansas**<br>Office of Personnel Management<br>P.O. Box 3278,<br>1509 West 7th St.<br>Little Rock, AR 72203<br>501–682–1507<br>501–682–5094<br>www.state.ar.us/dfa/opm<br>www.state.ar.us/dfa/opm/classcodes/R177.txt | Legal Assistant (R177) | ● Perform legal research<br>● Check court files to inform attorneys of status of cases<br>● Maintain law library<br>● Prepare summaries of documents<br>● File documents in court | The formal education equivalent of 1 year of law school<br>OR<br>1 year of "para-legal" experience<br><br>(Other job-related education and/or experience may be substituted for all or part of the requirements.) | $18,699–$36,727 per year |
| **California**<br>Dept. of Personnel Administration<br>1515 S. St.<br>North Bldg.<br>Sacramento, CA 94814<br>916–324–0455<br>www.dpa.ca.gov<br>www.spb.ca.gov | Legal Assistant (JY66, 1820) | ● Assist in reviewing legal documents to determine if they comply with the law<br>● Do preliminary analysis of proposed legislation<br>● Digest and index opinions, testimony depositions, and other trial documents<br>● Perform research of legislative history<br>● Assist in drafting complaints and other pleadings<br>● Help answer inquiries on legal requirements | 6 units of paralegal or undergraduate legal courses (3 of which are in legal research)<br>AND<br>2 years of experience in state gov't in legal clerical or other law-related position<br>OR<br>3 years as a law clerk or legal secretary in a law office (Post-high school education can substitute for some of the experience requirement. 2 years of paralegal education can substitute for 1 year of experience.)<br>*Applicants must sit for an examination.* | $3,013–$3,663 per month |
|  | Legal Analyst (JY62, 5237) | ● Investigate and analyze facts involved in litigation<br>● Coordinate witnesses<br>● Draft interrogatories and answers to interrogatories<br>● Draft pleadings<br>● Summarize discovery documents | 2 years of gov't experience as a legal assistant<br>AND<br>6 units of paralegal or other legal courses (3 of which are in legal research)<br>OR<br>2 years of experience as a paralegal in a law firm or elsewhere<br>AND<br>12 units of paralegal or other legal courses OR equivalent to graduation from college | $3,418–$4,155 per month |

| | | | | |
|---|---|---|---|---|
| **APPENDIX 2.B** | **Summary Chart—Survey of State Government Job Classifications for Paralegals—*continued*** | | | |
| **GOVERNMENT** | **POSITION** | **RESPONSIBILITIES** | **QUALIFICATIONS** | **SALARY** |
| Colorado<br>Dept. of Personnel<br>General Support Services<br>State Centennial Bldg.<br>1313 Sherman St. Rm. 122<br>Denver, CO 80203<br>303-866-2323<br>www.gssa.state.co.us | Legal Assistant<br>(H5E1XX) | • Conduct legal research<br>• Take notes at depositions<br>• Conduct interviews<br>• Identify legal issues<br>• Review documents for legal sufficiency<br>• Monitor status of cases<br>• Provide information on legal procedures | Bachelor's degree and certificate from approved paralegal studies program | $2,651–$3,840 per month |
| Other position to check in Colorado: Legal Assistant II (H5E2XX). | | | | |
| Connecticut<br>Personnel Div.<br>Dept. of Administration Services<br>165 Capital Ave.<br>Hartford, CT 06106<br>800-452-3451<br>860-713-5000<br>860-713-5205<br>www.das.state.ct.us | Paralegal<br>Specialist 1<br>(6140) | • Act as liaison between legal and clerical staff<br>• Perform legal research<br>• Assist in drafting legal documents<br>• Maintain tickler systems<br>• Present written and oral argument at administrative hearings<br>• Maintain records | 2 years of experience working for a lawyer (A paralegal degree or certificate may substitute for this experience.) | $35,072–$42,201 per year |
| Other positions to check in Connecticut: Paralegal Specialist 2 (6141); Legal Office Director (5373). | | | | |
| Delaware<br>State Personnel Office<br>Townsend Bldg.<br>401 Federal St.<br>Dover, DE 19901<br>800-345-1789<br>302-739-4195<br>www.state.de.us/spo | Paralegal I<br>(93101) | • Conduct fact investigation<br>• Do minimal legal research<br>• Provide information to the public about cases<br>• Act as liaison for supervisor | Enough education and/or experience to demonstrate knowledge of (1) legal research, (2) interviewing, (3) record keeping, and (4) document maintenance. Also must have an ability to communicate effectively. | $26,094–$39,142 per year |
| Other positions to check in Delaware: Paralegal II (93102); Judicial Assistant I (12355). | | | | |
| District of Columbia<br>D.C. Office of Personnel<br>441 4th St. NW<br>Wash, DC 20001<br>202-727-6406<br>202-442-9600<br>www.dcop.dcgov.org/main.asp | Paralegal<br>Specialist<br>(DS-950) | • Similar to Paralegal Specialist positions in the federal government. (See page 32.) | | $36,604–$47,152 per year (grade 11) |
| Florida<br>Dept. of Management Services | Paralegal<br>Specialist<br>(7703) | • Conduct initial client interview<br>• Take affidavits from victims and witnesses<br>• Perform legal research | Completion of legal assistant (or related legal) training course | $1,844–$2,776 per month |

*continued*

**APPENDIX 2.B     Summary Chart—Survey of State Government Job Classifications for Paralegals—*continued***

| GOVERNMENT | POSITION | RESPONSIBILITIES | QUALIFICATIONS | SALARY |
|---|---|---|---|---|
| **Florida—continued**<br>Bureau of Personnel<br>Management<br>4050 Esplanade Way<br>Tallahassee, FL 32399<br>904–488–5823<br>904–487–9877<br>www.state.fl.us/dms.htm | | ● Maintain case files and<br>  tickler system<br>● Perform notary functions<br>● Prepare case summaries<br>● Draft pleadings | OR<br>Bachelor's degree with major<br>in allied legal services<br>OR<br>4 years of experience as a<br>paralegal or legal secretary | |

Other positions to check in Florida: Appeals Coordinator/Clerk (Public Employees Relations Commission) (7704); Legal Trainee (7706).

| GOVERNMENT | POSITION | RESPONSIBILITIES | QUALIFICATIONS | SALARY |
|---|---|---|---|---|
| **Georgia**<br>State Merit System of<br>   Personnel<br>   Administration<br>200 Piedmont Ave. SE<br>Atlanta, GA 30334<br>404–656–5636<br>www.gms.state.ga.us | Paralegal<br>(95412) | ● Draft legal documents<br>  for review<br>● Assist in scheduling<br>● Enter case data into<br>  computer<br>● Perform legal research | Completion of a program<br>of paralegal studies<br>OR<br>2 years of experience as a<br>litigation paralegal or<br>judicial clerk. | $25,895–<br>$45,453 per<br>year |

Other position to check in Georgia: Legal Assistant (95406).

| GOVERNMENT | POSITION | RESPONSIBILITIES | QUALIFICATIONS | SALARY |
|---|---|---|---|---|
| **Hawaii**<br>Dept. of Human<br>   Resources Development<br>235 S. Beretania St.<br>Honolulu, HI 96813<br>808–587–1100<br>808–587–0977<br>www.state.hi.us/hrd | Legal Assistant<br>II (2.141) | ● Prepare drafts of legal<br>  documents<br>● Perform legal research<br>● Summarize laws<br>● Establish evidence and<br>  develop cases | 4 years of legal experience<br>OR<br>Graduation from an<br>accredited legal assistant<br>training program. | $2,445–<br>$2,463<br>per month |

Other position to check in Hawaii: Legal Assistant III (2.142).

| GOVERNMENT | POSITION | RESPONSIBILITIES | QUALIFICATIONS | SALARY |
|---|---|---|---|---|
| **Idaho**<br>Personnel Commission<br>700 West State St.<br>Boise, ID 83720<br>208–334–2263<br>800–554–5627<br>www.dhr.state.id.us/<br>   employees.asp<br>www.dhr.state.id.us/specs/<br>   05910.asp | Legal Assistant<br>(05910) | ● Identify legal issues<br>● Perform legal research<br>● Draft legal documents<br>● Answer inquiries<br>● Conduct investigative<br>  interviews<br>● Assist in discovery<br>● Assist in trial preparation | Good knowledge of legal<br>research method, the court<br>system, court procedures,<br>and legal ethics.<br>Experience interpreting<br>and analyzing<br>laws, preparing legal<br>documents, tracking<br>documents on a computer<br>database, etc. | $26,956–<br>$45,011 per<br>year |
| **Illinois**<br>Dept. of Central<br>   Management Services<br>Bureau of Personnel<br>500 Stratton Office Bldg. | Paralegal<br>Assistant<br>(1887, 30860)<br>(RC–062–12) | ● Write legal memoranda<br>  and other documents<br>for attorneys<br>● Analyze hearing<br>  transcripts | Completion of 4 years of<br>college with coursework in<br>areas such as prelegal,<br>medical, English, and<br>statistics | $2,488–<br>$3,485 per<br>month |

| APPENDIX 2.B | Summary Chart—Survey of State Government Job Classifications for Paralegals—*continued* |
|---|---|

| GOVERNMENT | POSITION | RESPONSIBILITIES | QUALIFICATIONS | SALARY |
|---|---|---|---|---|
| **Illinois—continued**<br>Springfield, IL 62706<br>217–782–3379<br>www.state.il.us/cms<br>www.state.il.us/cms/<br>    persnl/default.htm | | • Excerpt data from<br>  transcripts<br>• Prepare statistical<br>  reports | OR<br>Equivalent training and<br>experience | |
| Other position to check in Illinois: Legal Research Assistant (23350) (MC–02) (RC–028–13). | | | | |
| **Indiana**<br>State Personnel Dept.<br>402 W. Washington St.<br>IGCS, Rm. W161<br>Indianapolis, IN 46204<br>317–232–3059<br>www.state.in.us<br>www.IN.gov/jobs | Legal Assistant<br>(22015/1VA5) | • Perform legal research<br>• Verify citations to be<br>  used in memos and<br>  decisions<br>• Maintain files<br>• Schedule hearings<br>• Respond to requests<br>  for subpoenas<br>• Supervise clerical staff<br>• Respond to inquiries<br>  from attorneys on<br>  current hearings<br>• Assist attorneys at<br>  depositions | 3 years of full-time paralegal<br>experience in law office.<br>(Accredited college training<br>in paralegal studies, political<br>science, business<br>administration, prelaw, or<br>a related area can substitute<br>for 2 years of experience.) | $19,656–<br>$30,940 per<br>year |
| **Iowa**<br>Dept. of Personnel<br>Grimes State Office Bldg.<br>E. 14th St. & Grand Ave<br>Des Moines, IA 50319<br>515–281–3351<br>515–281–3087<br>www.state.ia.us/idop | Paralegal<br>(15004)<br>(45004)<br>(95004) | • Prepare drafts of<br>  pleadings and<br>  motions<br>• Conduct fact<br>  investigations<br>• Perform legal research<br>• File legal documents | Graduation from an<br>accredited paralegal program<br>OR<br>Experience equal to 2 years<br>of full-time work as a<br>paralegal or in a similar<br>support capacity under the<br>supervision of a practicing<br>attorney. | $30,451–<br>$43,160<br>per year |
| **Kansas**<br>Dept. of Administration<br>Div. of Personnel Services<br>Landon State Office Bldg.<br>900 Jackson, Rm. 951S<br>Topeka, KS 66612<br>913-296-4278<br>da.state.ks.us<br>da.state.ks.us/ps/<br>    documents/specs/<br>    4093d3.htm | Legal Assistant<br>(4093D3) | • Perform legal research<br>• Investigate facts for<br>  attorneys<br>• Maintain calendar system<br>• Prepare standard<br>  motions, pleadings,<br>  standard discovery<br>  documents<br>• Provide<br>  paraprofessional<br>  trial assistance | Minimum requirements:<br>job knowledge at an entry<br>level in legal support. | $972–$1,303<br>biweekly |
| **Kentucky**<br>Personnel Cabinet<br>200 Fair Oaks Lane<br>Frankfort, KY 40601<br>502–564–4460 | Paralegal I<br>(9856) | • Conduct analytical<br>  research<br>• Investigate cases<br>• Interview complainants<br>  and witnesses | Bachelor's degree in<br>paralegal science<br>OR<br>Post-baccalaureate certificate<br>in paralegal studies | $1,776–<br>$2,353 per<br>month |

*continued*

| APPENDIX 2.B | Summary Chart—Survey of State Government Job Classifications for Paralegals—*continued* |

| GOVERNMENT | POSITION | RESPONSIBILITIES | QUALIFICATIONS | SALARY |
|---|---|---|---|---|
| **Kentucky—continued**<br>502-564-8030<br>personnel.ky.gov | | ● Draft documents<br>● Provide general<br>  assistance to attorneys<br>  in litigation | OR<br>Bachelor's degree with a<br>minor in paralegal studies<br>OR<br>Completion of a 2-year<br>program in paralegal studies<br>(Paralegal experience can<br>substitute for some of the<br>education.) | |

Other positions to check in Kentucky: Paralegal II (9857); Paralegal III (9858); Law Clerk (9801).

| GOVERNMENT | POSITION | RESPONSIBILITIES | QUALIFICATIONS | SALARY |
|---|---|---|---|---|
| **Louisiana**<br>Dept. of State Civil Services<br>1201 Capitol Access Rd.<br>DOTD Annex Bldg.<br>Baton Rouge, LA 70802<br>504-342-8534<br>www.dscs.state.la.us | Paralegal I<br>(165650)<br>(C1 PA) | ● Perform legal research<br>● Draft pleadings<br>● Interview potential trial<br>  witnesses<br>● Compose briefs and<br>  memoranda<br>● Collect delinquent<br>  payments<br>● Index legal opinions<br>● Maintain law library | Completion of a paralegal/<br>legal assistant studies<br>program at a 4-year college,<br>at a junior college, or at an<br>otherwise approved school<br>(Possession of a CLA<br>certification from National<br>Association of Legal<br>Assistants will substitute<br>for the education<br>requirement.) | $1,778–<br>$2,933 per<br>month |

Other positions to check in Louisiana: Paralegal 1 (165640); Paralegal 2 (113470).

| GOVERNMENT | POSITION | RESPONSIBILITIES | QUALIFICATIONS | SALARY |
|---|---|---|---|---|
| **Maine**<br>Bureau of Human<br>  Resources<br>State Office Bldg.<br>4 State House Station<br>Augusta, ME 04333<br>207-287-3761<br>207-624-7761<br>www.state.me.us/bhr | Paralegal<br>Assistant<br>(0016)<br>(CFA8015101)<br>(0994) | ● Summarize documents<br>  that affect land titles<br>● Perform legal research<br>● Assist attorney at<br>  hearings<br>● Conduct investigations<br>● Prepare legal<br>  documents | 4 years of college and 1<br>year of paralegal experience<br>OR<br>Graduation from an<br>approved paralegal course<br>(Relevant experience may<br>substitute for education<br>requirement.) | $22,872–<br>$38,251<br>per year |

Other positions to check in Maine: Paralegal (0884) (CFA8015103); Senior Paralegal (0880) (FA8015102); Legal Researcher (0018, 02045, 0979, 20E); Law Clerk (secretarial position with paralegal duties) (0061, 41255, 202.362–014, 0380, 0880, 18R); Workers Compensation Assistant (036900).

| GOVERNMENT | POSITION | RESPONSIBILITIES | QUALIFICATIONS | SALARY |
|---|---|---|---|---|
| **Maryland**<br>Office of Personnel<br>  Services and Benefits<br>State Office Bldg. #1<br>301 W. Preston St.<br>Baltimore, MD 21201<br>410-767-4715<br>800-705-3493<br>www.dbm.state.md.us | Paralegal I<br>(0884)<br>(6459) | ● Perform legal research<br>● Conduct investigations<br>● File pleadings<br>● Prepare witnesses | High school diploma or<br>certificate and 2 years of<br>legal experience<br>(One year of paralegal<br>education can substitute for<br>the experience.) | $25,286–<br>$39,002 per<br>year |

Other positions to check in Maryland: Legal Assistant (209, 13); Legal Assistant II (1292); Para-Legal I (e.g., Howard County Office of State's Attorney)

| APPENDIX 2.B | Summary Chart—Survey of State Government Job Classifications for Paralegals—*continued* |
|---|---|

| GOVERNMENT | POSITION | RESPONSIBILITIES | QUALIFICATIONS | SALARY |
|---|---|---|---|---|
| **Massachusetts**<br>Dept. of Personnel<br>  Administration<br>One Ashburton Pl.<br>Boston, MA 02108<br>617-727-1556<br>617-727-3777<br>www.state.ma.us/hrd | Paralegal<br>Specialist<br>(10-R39)<br>(Group 31) | • Answer inquiries on agency rules<br>• Analyze statutes<br>• Digest the law<br>• Prepare briefs and answers to interrogatories<br>• Interview parties<br>• Evaluate evidence<br>• Develop case tracking systems<br>• Schedule appointments | 2 years of experience in legal research or legal assistant work. (An associate's degree or a higher degree with a major in paralegal studies or one year of law school can be substituted for the required experience.) | $35,607–<br>$51,446 per<br>year |
| Other positions to check in Massachusetts: Legal Assistant I (1291); Legal Assistant II (1292). | | | | |
| **Michigan**<br>Dept. of Civil Service<br>Capitol Commons Center<br>400 South Pine St.<br>P.O. Box 30002<br>Lansing, MI 48909<br>517-373-3020<br>www.michigan.gov/mdcs | Paralegal 8<br>(8020403) | • Perform legal research<br>• Conduct investigations<br>• Draft legal documents<br>• Prepare interrogatories<br>• Digest and index laws<br>• Serve and file legal papers | Associate's degree in a paralegal or legal assistant program | $14.52–<br>$17.50 per<br>hour |
| Other positions to check in Michigan: Paralegal 9 (8020404); Paralegal E10 (8020405); Paralegal 11 (8031106). Note: The Legal Assistant 1 position requires a law degree. | | | | |
| **Minnesota**<br>Dept. of Employee<br>  Relations<br>200 Centennial Bldg.<br>658 Cedar St.<br>St. Paul, MN 55101<br>612-296-8366<br>www.doer.state.mn.us | Legal<br>Technician<br>(1541) | • Perform legal research<br>• Prepare legal documents<br>• Collect information from clients for attorney | Certification from a paralegal or legal assistant program<br>OR<br>4-year college degree with a major in prelaw, paralegal, or legal assistant<br>OR<br>2 years of varied paralegal experience<br>OR<br>1 year of law school | $32,239–<br>$45,310 per<br>year |
| Other positions to check in Minnesota: Paralegal (3611); Legal Analyst (2957). | | | | |
| **Mississippi**<br>State Personnel Board<br>301 N. Lamar St.<br>Jackson, MS 39201<br>601-359-2704<br>601-359-1406<br>www.spb.state.ms.us | Paralegal<br>Specialist<br>(1848) | • Interpret and explain laws to staff<br>• Assist in preparing legal documents<br>• Review reports<br>• Assist in referring cases for prosecution | Bachelor's degree in paralegal studies or a related field and 1 year of legal experience<br>OR<br>High school or GED plus 5 years related experience | $24,467–<br>$39,318<br>per year |

*continued*

| APPENDIX 2.B | Summary Chart—Survey of State Government Job Classifications for Paralegals—*continued* |
| --- | --- |

| GOVERNMENT | POSITION | RESPONSIBILITIES | QUALIFICATIONS | SALARY |
| --- | --- | --- | --- | --- |
| **Mississippi—continued** | | • Train and supervise staff in reference work techniques<br>• Perform research | (of which 1 year is *directly* related) | |

Other position to check in Mississippi: Legal Clerk I (1962) (clerical position with some paralegal duties).

| **Missouri**<br>Office of Administration<br>Div. of Personnel<br>Truman State Office Bldg.,<br>　4th Fl.<br>Jefferson City, MO 65102<br>573-751-4162<br>www.oa.state.mo.us/pers | Paralegal or legal assistant positions are not found under the Missouri Merit System. Individual agencies not covered by the Merit System, however, may have such positions under the paralegal (9730 class). For example, the Missouri Office of the State Public Defender has a Paralegal Investigator I position. Duties include records retrieval, review of pleadings and transcripts, and investigation of factual claims. Qualifications include graduation from a paralegal program plus two years of paraprofessional experience OR graduation from a four-year institution with a major in criminal justice or paralegal studies. The position pays $2,011 per month. | | | |

| **Montana**<br>Dept. of Administration<br>Personnel Div.<br>Mitchell Bldg., Rm. 130<br>P.O. Box 200127<br>Helena, MT 59620<br>406-444-3871<br>www2.state.mt.us/doa<br>　/spd/css/default.asp | Paralegal<br>Assistant I<br>(119004)<br>(249110) | • Perform legal research<br>• Compile citations and references; check cites<br>• Assemble exhibits<br>• Explain laws<br>• Arrange interviews and depositions<br>• File pleadings<br>• Supervise clerical staff | Graduation from an approved paralegal training program plus 3 years of experience as a paralegal assistant or equivalent in a law practice<br>OR<br>2 years toward a bachelor's degree with courses in business or public administration plus 3 years of experience as a paralegal assistant or equivalent in a law practice<br>OR<br>6 years of experience as a paralegal assistant or equivalent in a law practice | Grade 11<br>$21,773–<br>$30,689 per year |

Other positions to check in Montana: Paralegal Assistant II (119005); Agency Legal Services Investigator (168155).

| **Nebraska**<br>State Personnel Div.<br>Dept. of Administrative<br>　Services<br>P.O. Box 94905<br>Lincoln, NE 68509<br>402-471-2075<br>www.wrk4neb.org | Paralegal I<br>(A311131) | • Interview witnesses<br>• Take sworn statements<br>• Summarize depositions<br>• Draft interrogatories<br>• Draft pleadings<br>• Act as law librarian | 2-year associate's degree from business school<br>OR<br>4-year bachelor's degree<br>OR<br>post-college course of a paralegal institute (Formal training has no preference over experience and can be freely substituted.) | $27,080–<br>$39,200 per year |

Other positions to check in Nebraska: Paralegal II (V311132); Legal Aide I (C318131); Legal Aide II (C318132)

| APPENDIX 2.B | Summary Chart—Survey of State Government Job Classifications for Paralegals—*continued* |

| GOVERNMENT | POSITION | RESPONSIBILITIES | QUALIFICATIONS | SALARY |
|---|---|---|---|---|
| **Nevada**<br>Dept. of Personnel<br>209 E. Musser St.<br>Capitol Complex<br>Carson City, NV 89710<br>800-992-0900<br>775-684-0150<br>www.dop.nv.gov | Legal Assistant<br>(2.159) | • Digest information in files<br>• Explain status of case to clients or to the public<br>• Offer advice on procedures<br>• Interview clients and witnesses<br>• Schedule depositions<br>• Organize and prepare exhibits | 3 years of experience as a legal secretary (or 1 year as a Legal Secretary I in Nevada State service)<br>OR<br>Completion of 1 year of a 2-year paralegal course plus 1 year of legal secretary experience or completion of classes in typing and office management<br>OR<br>Any equivalent combination of education and experience | $30,902–$43,305 per year |

Other positions to check in Nevada: Legal Assistant II (2.159); Legal Research Assistant (7.750).

| GOVERNMENT | POSITION | RESPONSIBILITIES | QUALIFICATIONS | SALARY |
|---|---|---|---|---|
| **New Hampshire**<br>Div. of Personnel<br>State House Annex<br>25 Capitol St.<br>Concord, NH 03301<br>603-271-3261<br>www.state.nh.us/hv | Paralegal I<br>(6793-16) | • Maintain docket control and file organization<br>• Conduct investigations<br>• Review complaints of alleged violations<br>• Help assess credibility of potential witnesses<br>• Examine legal documents to ensure compliance with law | 2 years of experience in law or a related field<br>AND<br>An associate's degree<br>OR<br>A paralegal certificate from a certified paralegal program or 2 years of college with a major study in law<br>(Substitutions are allowed.) | $25,798–$34,515 per year |

Other positions to check in New Hampshire: Paralegal II (6792-19); Legal Coordinator and Contracts Monitor (5668-22); Legal Research Assistant (5676-23); Legal Research Aide I (5670-16); Legal Research Aide II (5671-18); Legal Aide (5660-14).

| GOVERNMENT | POSITION | RESPONSIBILITIES | QUALIFICATIONS | SALARY |
|---|---|---|---|---|
| **New Jersey**<br>Dept. of Personnel<br>3 Station Plaza, CN317<br>44 S. Clinton Ave.<br>Trenton, NJ 08625<br>609-292-4144<br>www.state.nj.us/personnel | Paralegal Technician 2<br>(30461) | • Perform legal research<br>• Investigate facts<br>• Prepare documents used in briefs, pleadings, appeals, and other legal proceedings<br>• Proofread legal documents | Completion of an approved course of paralegal training<br>AND<br>2 years of experience as a paralegal in a law office | $32,145–$43,836 per year |

Other positions to check in New Jersey: Paralegal Technician 1 (30462); Paralegal Technician Assistant (30459).

| GOVERNMENT | POSITION | RESPONSIBILITIES | QUALIFICATIONS | SALARY |
|---|---|---|---|---|
| **New Mexico**<br>State Personnel Office<br>2600 Cerrillos Rd.<br>Santa Fe, NM 87505<br>505-476-7777 | Legal Assistant I<br>(1330) | • Provide help in legal research<br>• Prepare affidavits and exhibits<br>• Serve legal papers | Education and legal experience equaling 4 years. The experience can be gained as a paralegal. An associate's degree in | $18,383–$27,577 per year |

*continued*

| APPENDIX 2.B | Summary Chart—Survey of State Government Job Classifications for Paralegals—*continued* | | | |
|---|---|---|---|---|
| GOVERNMENT | POSITION | RESPONSIBILITIES | QUALIFICATIONS | SALARY |
| New Mexico—continued<br>505-827-8120<br>www.state.nm.us/spo | | ● Prepare and maintain records<br>● Handle routine legal correspondence | paralegal studies can substitute for 3 years of experience. | |
| Other position to check in New Mexico: Legal Assistant II (1331). | | | | |
| New York<br>Dept. of Civil Service<br>State Campus, Bldg. 1<br>1220 Washington Ave.<br>Albany, NY 12239<br>518-457-3701<br>518-457-9374<br>800-833-4344<br>www.cs.state.ny.us | Legal Assistant I<br>(2522210) | ● Schedule witnesses<br>● Assemble exhibits<br>● Negotiate and propose preliminary settlements of fines as directed or authorized by the attorney<br>● Cite check legal documents<br>● Answer routine questions from the public | Associate's degree in paralegal studies<br>OR<br>Certificate of satisfactory completion in general practice legal specialty training from an approved school<br>OR<br>Law school graduation | $30,570–$43,320 per year |
| Other positions to check in New York: Legal Assistant Trainee I (2522230); Legal Assistant II (2522220) | | | | |
| North Carolina<br>Office of State Personnel<br>116 West Jones St.<br>Raleigh, NC 27603<br>919-733-7108<br>www.ncgov.com/asp/basic/employee.asp | Paralegal I<br>(NC 1422)<br>(INCAC 8G.0402) | ● Draft legal instruments<br>● Prepare routine opinions on agency<br>● Handle complaints and inquiries from the public<br>● Administer the law office<br>● Perform legal research | Graduation from a certified paralegal school and 1 year of paralegal experience | $24,761–$39,789 per year |
| Other positions to check in North Carolina: Paralegal II (NC 1423); Paralegal III (NC 1424) | | | | |
| North Dakota<br>Central Personnel Div.<br>Office of Management & Budget<br>600 E. Boulevard Ave., 14th Fl.<br>Bismarck, ND 58505<br>701-328-3290<br>www.state.nd.us/cpers | Legal Assistant I<br>(0701) | ● Draft legal documents<br>● Maintain case files<br>● Answer letters seeking information on laws<br>● Maintain law library<br>● File documents in court<br>● Assist attorneys in litigation | Completion of 2 years of college in legal assistance or prelaw<br>AND<br>2 years of experience in legal research analysis | $1,614–$2,690 per month |
| Other position to check in North Dakota: Legal Assistant II (0702). | | | | |
| Ohio<br>Dept. of Administrative Services<br>Div. of Personnel<br>30 E. Broad Street<br>Columbus, OH 43266 | Paralegal/Legal Assistant<br>(63810) | ● Perform legal research<br>● Review corporate filings<br>● Prepare responses to legal inquiries<br>● Prepare case summaries<br>● Negotiate settlements | Completion of paralegal certification program<br>OR<br>Other evidence showing you have the legal knowledge and skills required | $28,330–$33,280 per year |

| APPENDIX 2.B | Summary Chart—Survey of State Government Job Classifications for Paralegals—*continued* |
| --- | --- |

| GOVERNMENT | POSITION | RESPONSIBILITIES | QUALIFICATIONS | SALARY |
| --- | --- | --- | --- | --- |
| **Ohio—continued**<br>614-466-3455<br>www.state.oh.us/das | | • File documents in court<br>• Schedule hearings | OR<br>Completion of 1 year of law school | |
| **Oklahoma**<br>Office of Personnel<br>Management<br>2101 N. Lincoln Blvd.<br>Oklahoma City, OK 73105<br>405-521-2177<br>800-522-8122<br>www.state.ok.us/~opm | Legal Research<br>Assistant<br>(K101 FC: K10)<br>(E30A) | • Perform legal research<br>• Conduct investigations<br>• Assist attorneys in litigation<br>• File pleadings<br>• Maintain law library | Completion of approved legal research assistant program<br>OR<br>Completion of bachelor's degree in legal studies<br>OR<br>Completion of 18 semester hours of law school | $22,105–$36,843 per year |

Other positions to check in Oklahoma: Child Support Specialist (#30); Legal Assistant l; Legal Assistant II (Office of the Municipal Counselor, Oklahoma City).

| GOVERNMENT | POSITION | RESPONSIBILITIES | QUALIFICATIONS | SALARY |
| --- | --- | --- | --- | --- |
| **Oregon**<br>Dept. of Admin. Services<br>Human Resource Services<br>Div.<br>155 Cottage St. NE<br>Salem, OR 97310<br>503-378-8344<br>www.dashr.state.or.us | Paralegal<br>Specialist<br>(1526) (1622G) | • Organize complex facts<br>• Communicate with experts<br>• Analyze cases<br>• Assist attorneys in litigation<br>• Arrange for case settlements<br>• Answer interrogatories | 3 years of experience in a technical or professional field like real estate or accounting<br>AND<br>2 years of subparalegal experience as a legal secretary or in an administrative job in court, OR a 1-year certificate program in paralegal studies<br>OR<br>An equivalent combination of training and experience | $2,784–$3,870 per month |

Other positions to check in Oregon: Paralegal 1 (1523); Paralegal 2 (1524); Paralegal 3 (1525); Investigator (C1031); Special investigator (X 1032); Legal Assistant (C0680).

| GOVERNMENT | POSITION | RESPONSIBILITIES | QUALIFICATIONS | SALARY |
| --- | --- | --- | --- | --- |
| **Pennsylvania**<br>Office of Administration<br>Bureau of State<br>    Employment<br>517 Finance Bldg.<br>Harrisburg, PA 17120<br>717-787-5703<br>www.bse.state.pa.us | Legal<br>Assistant 1<br>(07010) | • Review work of field personnel for possible legal implications<br>• Summarize cases<br>• Review files<br>• Prepare reports | 3 years of progressively responsible clerical, auditing, enforcement, or investigative experience<br>OR<br>Any equivalent combination of experience and training | $25,624–$38,201 per year |

Other positions to check in Pennsylvania: Legal Assistant 2 (07020); Legal Assistant Supervisor (07030); Legal Assistant Manager (07040).

| GOVERNMENT | POSITION | RESPONSIBILITIES | QUALIFICATIONS | SALARY |
| --- | --- | --- | --- | --- |
| **Rhode Island**<br>Office of Personnel<br>    Administration<br>1 Capitol Hill | Paralegal Aide<br>(02461300) | • Perform legal research<br>• Conduct investigations<br>• Answer questions by interpreting laws | Completion of an approved paralegal training program<br>OR<br>Paraprofessional experience | $26,937–$29,261 per year |

*continued*

| GOVERNMENT | POSITION | RESPONSIBILITIES | QUALIFICATIONS | SALARY |
|---|---|---|---|---|
| **Rhode Island—continued**<br>Providence, RI 02908<br>401-277-2160<br>www.info.state.ri.us/<br>  admin.htm | | ● Assist in litigation<br>● Maintain files | in an extensive legal service program | |
| Other position to check in Rhode Island: Legal Assistant. | | | | |
| **South Carolina**<br>Budget and Control Board<br>Div. of Budget and<br>  Analyses<br>Office of Human<br>  Resources<br>1201 Main St.<br>Columbia, SC 29201<br>803-737-0900<br>www.state.sc.us/jobs | Administrative Assistant (AA75) [The Paralegal Assistant classification was combined with about 30 other job titles to create the Administrative Assistant position.] | ● Help perform legal research<br>● Draft legal documents<br>● Proofread legal documents | A high school diploma and work experience that is directly related to the area of employment (The employing agency may impose other requirements. Example: 2 years as a paralegal/legal assistant OR a high school diploma and 1 year of training under the supervision of a South Carolina attorney) | $21,679–$40,108 per year |
| **South Dakota**<br>Bureau of Personnel<br>500 E. Capitol<br>Pierre, SD 57501<br>605-773-3148<br>www.state.sd.us/bop | Legal Assistant (11205) | ● Conduct legal research<br>● Perform investigations<br>● Summarize discovery documents<br>● Draft correspondence and pleadings<br>● Index trial materials<br>● Act as client liaison<br>● Attend depositions, hearings, and trials | An equivalent combination of education and experience will be used to qualify applicants. Graduation from a college or university with an associate's degree in paralegal studies or a related field. | $11.07–$16.61 per hour |
| **Tennessee**<br>Dept. of Personnel<br>505 Deaderick St.<br>Nashville, TN 37243<br>800-221-7345<br>615-741-4841<br>www.state.tn.us/personnel | Legal Assistant (02350) | ● Help attorney prepare for trial<br>● Summarize laws and regulations<br>● Maintain law library<br>● Answer routine inquiries on laws and regulations | Associate's degree in paralegal studies, or bachelor's degree in paralegal studies, or a paralegal certificate, or 1 year of law school<br>OR<br>High school graduation (or equivalent) or 2 years of full-time experience in researching legal issues and documenting findings to assist in building case files, settling legal disputes, and/or providing legal counsel to clients | $2,009–$3,225 per month |

| APPENDIX 2.B | Summary Chart—Survey of State Government Job Classifications for Paralegals—*continued* | | | |
|---|---|---|---|---|
| **GOVERNMENT** | **POSITION** | **RESPONSIBILITIES** | **QUALIFICATIONS** | **SALARY** |
| **Texas**<br>State Auditor's Office<br>P.O. Box 12067<br>419 Reagan State<br>  Office Bldg.<br>206 East 9th St., Ste. 1900<br>Austin, TX 78711<br>512-479-4700<br>www.hr.state.tx.us<br>www.sao.state.tx.us | Legal Assistant<br>(3570) | • Perform legal research<br>• Check citations and<br>  references<br>• Schedule meetings and<br>  depositions<br>• Screen calls for attorneys<br>• Help prepare legal<br>  documents<br>• File pleadings in court | Graduation from a 4-year<br>college or university with<br>major coursework in law or<br>a related field<br>AND<br>Should have some<br>experience in paralegal work | $25,632–<br>$34,308 per<br>year |
| Other positions to check in Texas: Legal Assistant II (3572); Legal Assistant III (3574); Legal Assistant IV (3576); Administrative Technician II (Office of Attorney General). | | | | |
| **Utah**<br>Dept. of Human<br>  Resources Management<br>2120 State Office Bldg.<br>Salt Lake City, UT 84114<br>801-538-3080<br>www.dhrm.state.ut.us | Paralegal<br>(85305) | • Perform directed legal<br>  research<br>• Conduct investigations<br>• Maintain document<br>  control in litigation<br>• Draft routine legal<br>  documents | Certificate of paralegal<br>studies from an approved<br>institution<br>AND<br>1 year of paid experience<br>performing the duties of<br>the position | $11.27–<br>$16.93 per<br>hour |
| Other positions to check in Utah: Paralegal II (85306); Legal Assistant—Unemployment Insurance (85010). | | | | |
| **Vermont**<br>Agency of Administration<br>Dept. of Personnel<br>110 State St., Drawer 20<br>Montpelier, VT 05620<br>802-828-3491<br>www.state.vt.us/pers | Paralegal<br>Technician I<br>(081800)<br>(CLS 18) | • Assist attorneys in<br>  litigation<br>• Conduct investigations<br>• Interview parties<br>• Perform legal research<br>• Audit records<br>• Interpret laws<br>• Draft briefs and legal<br>  documents<br>• Advise parties of their<br>  rights | 4 years of experience at or<br>above senior clerical level,<br>including 1 year of<br>investigatory, analytical,<br>research, or paralegal duties<br>(30 college credits in legal<br>or paralegal studies can<br>substitute for general<br>experience requirement; a<br>JD degree is considered<br>qualifying.) | $13.45–<br>$20.79 per<br>hour |
| Other positions to check in Vermont: Paralegal Technician (08230); State Investigator—Civil Rights. | | | | |
| **Virginia**<br>Dept. of Human Resource<br>  Management<br>101 N. 14th St.<br>Richmond, VA 23219<br>804-225-2131<br>jobs.state.va.us | Legal Assistant<br>(21521) | • Perform legal research<br>• Keep track of cases<br>• Prepare witnesses<br>  for trial<br>• Manage law library<br>• Prepare exhibits of<br>  physical evidence | Graduation from high<br>school or equivalent<br>Paralegal coursework or<br>training preferred.<br>AND<br>Experience in judicial and<br>quasi-judicial systems and<br>in the application of legal<br>principles | $29,444–<br>$41,908 per<br>year<br>(For northern<br>Virginia: 9.6%<br>higher) |
| **Washington, D.C. (See District of Columbia)** | | | | |
| **Washington State**<br>Dept. of Personnel<br>521 Capitol Way S | Paralegal 1<br>(46610) | • Organize litigation files<br>• Enter data into<br>  computer databases | 2 years of experience as<br>paralegal<br>OR | $29,616–<br>$37,608 per<br>year<br>*continued* |

| APPENDIX 2.B | Summary Chart—Survey of State Government Job Classifications for Paralegals—*continued* |

| GOVERNMENT | POSITION | RESPONSIBILITIES | QUALIFICATIONS | SALARY |
|---|---|---|---|---|
| **Washington State—continued** P.O. Box 47500 Olympia, WA 98504 206-586-0194 hr.dop.wa.gov/home.html | | • Conduct investigations • Prepare responses to interrogatories • Prepare deposition questions • Prepare trial notebook • Negotiate claims | Graduation from 2-year paralegal course OR 4-year college degree plus 9-month paralegal program or 1 year of paralegal experience OR 3 years of legal secretarial experience plus 30 quarter hours of paralegal college courses | |
| Other positions to check in Washington: Paralegal 2 (46620); Paralegal 3 (46630). | | | | |
| **West Virginia** Div. of Personnel 1900 Kanawha Blvd. East Charleston, WV 25305 304-558-3950 www.state.wv.us/admin/   personnel | Paralegal (9500) | • Perform legal research • Summarize evidence • Supervise clerical staff • Maintain case calendar of attorneys • Compose routine correspondence • Monitor pending legislation | Completion of a paralegal assistant training program OR 2 years of paid experience in a legal setting performing legal research, reading and interpreting laws, and preparing legal documents under attorney supervision | $19,392– $35,892 per year |
| Other positions to check in West Virginia: Child Advocate Legal Assistant (9501); Lead Paralegal (9502). | | | | |
| **Wisconsin** Dept. of Employment   Relations 137 East Wilson St. P.O. Box 7855 Madison, WI 53707 608-266-9820 der.state.wi.us/static | Legal Assistant (19201) | • Help an attorney prepare for trial • Collect and compile data • Conduct preliminary witness interviews • Perform legal research • Provide information to public • Draft routine legal documents • Represent the agency at administrative hearings | The qualifications required will be determined on a position-by-position basis at the time of recruitment. Hiring will be based on an analysis of the education, training, work, or other life experiences that provide reasonable assurance that the knowledge and skills required for the position have been acquired. | $15.54– $18.94 per hour |
| Other positions to check in Wisconsin: Legal Assistant Entry (19201); Legal Assistant—Confidential (19211; 19212); Paralegal (15001) (15010) (15020). | | | | |
| **Wyoming** Personnel Management   Div. Dept. of Administration   and Information 2001 Capitol Ave. Cheyenne, WY 82002 307-777-6713 personnel.state.wy.us | Administrative Specialist 2 (ADO2) | • Perform legal research • Help establish form files • Help attorneys prepare for trial • Help in discovery • Draft pleadings • Perform docket control and file maintenance duties | Any combination of training and experience equivalent to an associate degree in paralegal studies or prelaw | $1,596– $2,953 per month |

# Chapter 3

# ON-THE-JOB REALITIES: ASSERTIVENESS TRAINING FOR PARALEGALS

## Chapter Outline

A. The Ideal

B. Communication

C. Expectations

D. The Environment of a Law Office

E. Office Politics

F. Self-Assessment and Employer Evaluations

G. Characteristics of Some Attorneys

H. Assertive/Nonassertive/Aggressive Behavior

I. Keeping a Diary and a Career Development File

J. The "Swoose Syndrome"

K. Paralegal CLE

L. Responsibilities of Supervisors

M. Relationship with Secretaries

N. Sexual Harassment

O. Working with Systems

P. Career Ladders

Q. Your Next Job

R. Paralegal Associations and Networking

## Section A
# The Ideal

The practice of law is not for the faint of heart. In this chapter, we will explore some of the major techniques needed to survive and thrive in the practice of law. Before doing so, we pause to examine the ideal.

What is a "perfect" paralegal job? Perhaps it is impossible to describe perfection in its fullest sense, but if we made the attempt, what would the description contain? Exhibit 3.1 presents such an attempt: it identifies 75 factors of an ideal paralegal job environment. The factors are not of equal importance, and some of them overlap. Nor would every paralegal agree that all 75 are needed. In general, however, these are the factors (not necessarily listed in order of priority) that must be considered according to many working paralegals.

---

*Assignment 3.1*

**(a)** Do you think that any of the 75 factors in exhibit 3.1 are *not* important for job satisfaction? Why?

**(b)** Select what you feel are the 15 most important factors. Write out your list and make a copy. Indicate whether you have ever had any law office work experience as a secretary, a paralegal, etc.

**(c)** Give the copy of your list to a person in the class whom your instructor will designate as the statistician. The latter will collect all the copies from the students and make the following tabulations: (1) which factors received the most votes on the "top 15" list by the students who have had prior law office experience; (2) which received the most votes from the other students.

In class, discuss the results of these tabulations. Are there significant differences in the opinions of the two groups? Can you explain the differences or similarities?

---

We move now to the *reality* of paralegal employment. The 75 factors obviously do not exist in every paralegal job. While most paralegals are satisfied with the career they have chosen, problems can arise in any occupation. Our focus in this chapter will be to identify some of these problems and to suggest resolution strategies. It should be pointed out that many of the problems we will be discussing are not peculiar to paralegalism. Sexism, for example, and the hassles of worker coexistence are certainly not unique to the law office. Indeed, this chapter is probably as much about human nature as it is about the paralegal career.

---

| EXHIBIT 3.1 | Seventy-Five Factors That Can Affect Paralegal Job Satisfaction |
|---|---|

1. Your pay is satisfactory.
2. You receive satisfactory bonuses.
3. Your fringe benefits are satisfactory (e.g. health plan, life insurance, pension, see exhibit 2.13
4. Your compensation is fair in relation to that of attorneys, other paralegals, and secretaries.
5. You are part of the professional staff in that you do not receive overtime pay for the extra hours you work.
6. You are part of the support staff in that you do receive overtime pay for the extra hours you work.
7. You are given financial support and time off to participate in activities of paralegal associations.
8. You are given financial support and time off to attend training sessions outside the office at paralegal schools, paralegal associations, bar associations, etc.
9. Adequate supplies are readily available.
10. Your hours are satisfactory.
11. You have your own office.
12. You have adequate access to secretarial help.
13. You have adequate access to word processing and other computer programs.
14. You have your own business card.
15. You are challenged by your job.
16. You like your job.
17. Your privacy is respected.
18. No sexism or racism exists.
19. People in the office share the same basic values.
20. The office has high standards of performance; there are many good role models.

| EXHIBIT 3.1 | Seventy-Five Factors That Can Affect Paralegal Job Satisfaction—*continued* |
|---|---|

21. You are respected.
22. You are not taken advantage of.
23. You are not unduly pressured to meet a billable-hours quota.
24. You are not unduly pressured to work evenings or weekends.
25. You are encouraged to develop new skills.
26. Your paralegal training is being used by the office.
27. Occasionally or frequently, you have meaningful client contact.
28. Your name is in the office directory and web site.
29. You do not feel isolated; there are few or no "attorney only" social events.
30. The office politics are manageable.
31. The secretaries, clerks, and other support personnel understand your job and accept your role in the office.
32. Your supervisors are not afraid of delegating tasks to paralegals.
33. The attorneys in the office understand your job and accept your role.
34. You are not in competition with anyone else in the office.
35. You have good rapport with other paralegals in the office.
36. You respect others in the office.
37. The office functions as a team; employees are not obsessed with a niche or territory that they are protecting.
38. People in the office are willing to compromise on personnel methods and procedures.
39. The office follows high standards of ethics and moral responsibility.
40. There is a career ladder in the office for paralegals.
41. You are not constantly relegated to someone else's deadline; it is recognized that you have deadlines of your own to which others must be sensitive.
42. People in the office know how to listen; employees do not simply *talk at* everyone else.
43. You feel you are making a contribution to the office.
44. You have the feeling that your office is offering a social service; it is not "just a business."
45. There is an adequate flow of communication in the office; you know what is going on because the office makes it known. The grapevine is not the main source of information.
46. There is a clear line of authority; you know who your supervisors are.
47. The importance of profit is never emphasized at the expense of people's lives.
48. At all times, you know which people you can go to for help and you are encouraged to seek this help.
49. You are adequately supervised by attorneys and other senior personnel.

50. You are encouraged to do self-evaluations, which are given serious consideration.
51. You are regularly evaluated in a constructive manner.
52. You are given credit for the contributions you make.
53. The roof does not cave in if you disagree with your supervisors.
54. If you make a mistake, it is not the end of the world.
55. You attend regular staff meetings.
56. You are allowed to participate in office training programs for new attorneys.
57. You attend strategy meetings for cases to which you are assigned.
58. You are not constantly being asked why you do not become an attorney.
59. There is low turnover in your office; people feel comfortable enough about the office to make a long-term commitment to it.
60. You are not the first paralegal in the office, the office has had experience working with paralegals.
61. You are not constantly interrupted with new assignments, new priorities, new crises; you are not the dumping ground for everyone else's problems.
62. You are kept busy all the time without feeling overburdened; "the time flies by."
63. You are permitted to see the end product of your work; for example, you occasionally have contact with a case from beginning to completion.
64. You are encouraged to make use of the law library.
65. Office manuals or procedure guides are available on many assignments.
66. A personnel manual clearly spells out critical employee policies.
67. You are encouraged to give your opinion on law office management issues.
68. You are encouraged to give your opinion on case strategy.
69. You have some independence; there are opportunities to work alone in the office.
70. You are given authority.
71. You are encouraged to make decisions within your competence, and someone will back you up on these decisions.
72. There is reasonable variety in your assignments.
73. You are given a reasonable amount of time to complete your assignments.
74. You are not given assignments beyond your present capacity.
75. You are given reasonable time and training to learn new areas.

Some of the discussion will be directed at attorneys and what they must do to solve a particular employment problem. Yet a major concern of this chapter is what the *paralegal* can do to overcome difficulties, even that appear to be beyond the control of the paralegal. According to Beth King, president of the Oregon Legal Assistant Association:

> Job satisfaction is one of life's most important assets. As such, it is something we should cherish and cultivate. We may blame a lack of job satisfaction on our employer or those with whom we work. In truth, satisfaction with our jobs lies within our control.[1]

## Section B
# COMMUNICATION

A busy law office is often a charged environment, particularly if the office is engaged in litigation or has a large caseload with a relatively high turnover.

> It is difficult to explain to outsiders the pressures of a law firm environment. Client demands [seem] never ending, equipment failures send staff into a frenzy, messengers run throughout the city like maniacs, . . . receptionists cannot find various personnel because they did not check in or out, the accounting [department] is complaining about time and billing, and priorities change every minute.[2]

When large projects or huge sums of money are at stake, careers are on the line. Attorneys, not known for their lack of ego, can at times have unrealistic expectations of those around them. In this atmosphere, communication can occasionally break down. According to a recent survey published by the journal *Legal Management,* "14 percent of each 40-hour workweek is wasted due to poor communication between staff and managers—amounting to a stunning seven weeks a year."[3] Here is an example:

> A senior partner thinks he told his paralegal to take care of an important filing. In actuality, all he told the paralegal to do was to *draft* the necessary documents to make the filing. The paralegal drafts the documents and puts them in the senior partner's in-box for his review. The filing deadline is missed. The senior partner blames his paralegal. The worst part of this scenario is that the paralegal is never told what happened or that she is being blamed. Perhaps the senior partner wishes to avoid a confrontation; perhaps he fears being told that the problem is not only his responsibility, but also his fault. In any event, the paralegal's reputation is smeared among the professional staff.[4]

**Source:** Sheila Swanson, 14 At Issue 8 (San Francisco Ass'n of Legal Assistants).

In a case such as this, trying to establish the truth—what actually happened—can sometimes be fruitless. People may simply be in no mood for "explanations."

The need, of course, is to *prevent* miscommunication. Be aware of the standard factors that contribute to communication problems:

- Distractions
- Time pressures
- Work overload
- Embarrassment over asking for clarification
- Personality conflicts
- Equipment breakdown
- Physical impairment (e.g., hearing difficulty, defective eyeglasses)
- Etc.

You can take specific steps to help avoid miscommunication. For example, you can keep an assignment notebook, diary, or daily journal in which you write down precisely what you are asked to do. You can repeat an assignment back to your supervisor immediately after receiving it. For lengthy or complex assignments, you could send your supervisor a brief note or e-mail message in which you confirm what you have been asked to do and when it is due. Perhaps most important of all is to have a constant awareness of the potential for miscommunication in a busy law office. The danger can be quite high. If you are constantly aware of the danger, you'll be in a better position to help avoid a communication breakdown. It is a little like crossing the street. The busier the intersection, the more caution you must use to avoid an accident. Most law offices are very busy intersections.

## Section C
# EXPECTATIONS

A fair amount of paralegal frustration on the job can result from unrealistic expectations about the career in general and about a particular job. Frustration is mainly generated by surprise: "I never thought the job would be like this!" For example, most paralegal programs spend a good deal of time teaching students to do legal research. In many law offices, however, paralegals do not do extensive legal research. Research courses are important in your curriculum because of the understanding they give you about the legal system and the language of the law. Although you may eventually be given research assignments, do not enter your first paralegal job expecting to spend a great deal of time in the law library.

One of the objectives of this book is to provide you with information that will help prevent surprise. You need a candid account of what you might find. Chapter 2 outlined steps on doing background investigation on a potential employer *before* you accept a job, such as talking with paralegals who have worked or who still work at the office. Following these steps, whenever possible, should give you a more accurate picture of what lies ahead if you take the job.

In a seller's market, where there are more applicants than jobs, you may be so anxious to obtain a job that you will overlook its potential negative aspects. This is unfortunate. It is essential that you walk into a job, or any situation, with open eyes. Not only will accurate information help reduce any frustration that may eventually develop, but also the information will be the foundation for corrective steps you can begin taking as soon as possible.

You need a lot of information. In the best of all possible worlds, you would have information relevant to each of the 75 factors listed in exhibit 3.1 that affect potential job satisfaction. (At a minimum, you would like information on the 15 factors that you identified as most important in assignment 3.1.) Of course, there are limitations on what you can learn now. Furthermore, even the information you receive can at best be a guide to your own prediction of how these factors might apply to you as an individual once you are on the job. This should not deter you, however, from going after whatever information is available about the paralegal field in your area and about particular prospective employers.

Whether the information you are able to gather is extensive or minimal, the healthiest attitude is to expect the unexpected. Be prepared for surprises about what supervisors think you are capable of doing, the level and quantity of assignments you are given, how secretaries and other paralegals in the office respond to you, who in the office will become the major influences on your growth and success as a paralegal, etc. This is not to say that everything you encounter will be a surprise. But it may not be a bad idea to proceed as if it will be. In short, be careful of your preconceptions about what is going to happen. Do not let them block the challenges waiting for you.

## Section D
# THE ENVIRONMENT OF A LAW OFFICE

When you walk into a law office, your first impression is likely to be that:

- The office is very formal and organized.
- The people here know what they are doing and are set in their ways.

These impressions can be very misleading. A law office is in a state of perpetual *becoming*. The environment is always changing. New people are added, new clients come in, old clients are lost, new ways of doing things are developed, personality conflicts arise—numerous factors interact to produce an office that is in constant transition. Furthermore, *you* go through a process of change along with everyone else as the office continues to grow. On the surface, the office may appear to be a model of stability, but underneath all the layers of order and permanence, there is a *live* office that is in motion.

The consequences of this reality for the new paralegal are twofold:

- Do not be deceived by appearances.
- Recognize your own responsibility and *power* to help create the environment in which you are working.

If you become dissatisfied with your job, avoid being passive or defeatist. Everyone else in the office is trying to mold the environment to his or her own needs. Join the club! You may not succeed the first time. You may not succeed the fifth time. You may not even be aware of when your advocacy for yourself is having an impact. *Yet you must assert yourself and do so regularly.* Change usually does *not* occur within the timetable of the person trying to bring about the change. Occasionally, you will get the impression that everyone is resisting what you feel is right. You must be prepared to lose on some points. But you must stick with it. The person who wins is often the person who outlasts the others. The losers are those who demand instant success—whether or not there is justice behind their positions.

Three things must happen before change can occur:

- You convince yourself that you have the power to create change.
- Your mind generates 10 to 15 ways of creating the change.
- You have the stamina and perspective to live through the unsuccessful attempts until you finally hit upon the strategy that produces the change.

What kind of changes are we talking about? They could involve any of the following:

- Salary
- Workload/billable hour expectations
- Secretarial help
- Career ladders
- In-house training
- Equipment needs
- How the office treats clients
- How the office treats vendors
- Office procedures
- Ethical irregularities
- Etc.

If you are the type of person who wants every possible change made in every area in need of change, and you want all the changes made *now*, you may not have the temperament needed to survive and thrive in a busy law office. Change is possible, and you can play a major role in creating it as long as you are not impatient and you keep looking for new ways to try to bring it about.

## Section E
# OFFICE POLITICS

Few people like office politics. Most of us want to work where office politics does not exist. If this is not possible, our instinct is to blame others. We do what is right; others play politics.

These attitudes are illusions and interfere with your chances of bringing about change. "There are three things in life you can always count on: death, taxes, and the inevitability of office politics."[5] Whenever two people work together, politics is involved. When 50 people work together, politics is the order of the day. The "people you work with become your second family, complete with squabbles and jealousies. It is not possible to completely avoid confrontations or politics."[6] People often disagree about minor and major matters. As a result, conscious or unconscious *negotiation* becomes the mechanism by which things get done. Bargaining takes place all the time. More to the point, bargaining in the context of egos takes place all the time. There is simply no alternative to this process.

If there is harmony in an office, it is because people are engaged in *effective* office politics. People are trading what others want. Disharmony usually results from the fact that people are not responding to each other's needs. A cardinal principle of human relations is that you cannot get anyone to do anything well until you have found a way of making them happy or at least satisfied about doing it. Coercion and management-by-might have within them the seeds of their own defeat. They may work for a while, but at great cost. People generally want to do their jobs well, but this will not happen unless they strive hard to help *other* people do *their* jobs well.

The following dimensions of office politics may at first appear to be unpleasant to some paralegals:

- You must make sure that the decision-makers in the office learn about your work.
- You must make sure that everyone in the office with whom you work has a good opinion of you.

Such behavior is distasteful to some who say good work should speak for itself and be its own reward. Why make a campaign about it?

Unfortunately, there is a danger, particularly in a large firm, of the paralegal getting lost in the shuffle. The remedy is to be constantly looking for ways to sell yourself without appearing to do so. This goes against the grain of many paralegals. They don't like to sell themselves, especially after they have been at an office for a while. They want to settle in and not be obsessed with getting ahead. Yet you can't have it both ways. You can't complain about conditions of employment and refuse to assert your most valuable asset—yourself. This means establishing credibility and making sure that people know your worth.

> Blow your own horn: let the attorney know how you saved the client thousands of dollars, how you found the hard-to-locate witness, how you organized a huge file in mere hours, how the information you gathered helped win the case, etc. (Attorneys do this all the time.) Make sure your colleagues know of your special areas of expertise. For example, perhaps you are a good photographer, know everything there is to know about stocks and bonds, or speak several languages. (One paralegal I know dabbles in handwriting analysis; her firm found out and now she is a "handwriting expert.") Show an interest in other matters your firm is handling. Compliment an attorney with whom you are not presently working when you hear he/she won in court, closed a complicated big dollar deal, negotiated brilliantly, etc. . . . Be a real team player.[7]
>
> Ignoring, or worse, denying the ever-present politics of legal environments can be hazardous to your employment. You must be in-tune with the un-spoken; listen to your intuition and the

grapevine. Stay out of gossip groups, keeping your ears open and your mouth shut. Watch how the attorneys interact with each other. Monitor power plays and coalitions. Make an effort to understand each of the attorneys you work with on an individual basis, and by that I mean: writing style, organizational preferences, demeanor. *You* must adapt to each attorney. . . . Strategize yourself when possible: work with other attorneys in your firm, or with outside co-counsel; assist baby lawyers without a demeaning attitude. (Remember that baby lawyers grow up to be associates and associates grow up to be partners.) Enlist help within and without your firm—usually persons you have no control over. You must appeal to them and win them over to help you. But be genuine! Everyone can spot a fake.[8]

What do you think of the following advice from another successful paralegal? "Set your goals and aim for them. Open your mouth and let people know that you're headed up. Search out greater responsibility. Work your tail off—and let everyone know about it."[9] Too extreme? Too risky? People really don't get ahead this way? You don't have to advertise talent because it will eventually be discovered without self-promotion? Maybe. Talk with successful and satisfied paralegals around you. Make inquiries. Take a long look at people you respect in a competitive environment. Try to assess whether their abilities might have gone untapped without a healthy, effective, measured dose of self-assertiveness.

## Section F
# SELF-ASSESSMENT AND EMPLOYER EVALUATIONS

None of the techniques and strategies discussed in this chapter can ever be a substitute for your own competence as a paralegal. The techniques and strategies are designed to combat unrecognized and unrewarded competence.

Are you competent? To answer this question, you must evaluate yourself and receive the evaluations of others. Here are some suggestions for making both kinds of evaluations more meaningful, now and on the job.

- Carefully read the evaluation form in exhibit 3.2.[10] First, note the standards used to earn a "Superior" rating and a "Very Good" rating in the eight categories being evaluated. These standards should be the day-to-day employment goals of every paralegal. Second, apply the form *now* to your present job or to any of your prior jobs, regardless of the kind of work involved. What ratings would you give yourself in the

| EXHIBIT 3.2 | **Legal Assistant Evaluation Form** |
| --- | --- |

### Personal and Confidential

Legal Assistant _____     Hire Date _____
Review Period _____     Department _____
Evaluating Attorney _____

A. **CONTACT.** Indicate the contact you have had with the legal assistant during the review period.
 — *Substantial* Regular, daily, or weekly contact. (Included in most attorney briefing/strategy meetings.)
 — *Occasional* Specific assignments and routine maintenance work requiring occasional personal instruction.
 — *Infrequent.* Limited contact.
B. **WORK PERFORMED,** Describe the work performed by the legal assistant for you, listing some examples. Specify the degree of difficulty and expertise required.

_____

_____

_____

_____

_____

| EXHIBIT 3.2 | Legal Assistant Evaluation Form—*continued* |
|---|---|

C. **PERFORMANCE EVALUATION.** Evaluate the legal assistant in each of the following eight areas. Check the blank to the left of the rating description that best summarizes the legal assistant's performance. Use the space on the back of the last page for additional comments.

    1. **Work Product.** (Consider the legal assistant's ability to understand what is required and to provide a work product that is both thorough and complete. Consider the speed and efficiency with which the work product is returned.)

      — *Superior.* In most cases, needs little instruction. Takes initiative in asking questions if aspects of the task are unclear. Is resourceful in developing more efficient ways to complete projects. Demonstrates ability to consider factors not indicated by attorney that make the work product more useful.

      — *Very good.* Needs instruction once or twice. Legal assistant completes task thoroughly and keeps attorney informed as to work progress.

      — *Good.* Sometimes needs to do a task several times before he or she feels comfortable. Substantial attorney supervision is necessary during first attempts at a project. Once legal assistant is comfortable with the job requirements, he or she does a through and complete work product.

      — *Marginal.* Has difficulty understanding what kind of work product is required. Sometimes does an incomplete job and takes more time than should be needed.

      — *Unacceptable.* Seldom masters what is required, and hence cannot do a thorough and complete work product.

      — *No opportunity to form an opinion.*

    2. **Efficient Management of Workload.** (Consider the volume of work produced and the efficient use of time in order to meet deadlines.)

      — *Superior.* Highly efficient. Completes all assignments successfully, on time, and without prompting.

      — *Very good.* Efficient. Most assignments completed successfully. Rarely misses deadlines.

      — *Good.* Basically efficient. Assignments are generally completed successfully within a reasonable amount of time.

      — *Marginal.* Needs to improve efficiency. Assignments sometimes go uncompleted. Needs substantial attorney supervision.

      — *Unacceptable.* Inefficient. Deadlines are rarely met. Assignments often uncompleted.

      — *No opportunity to form an opinion.*

    3. **Ability to Work Well under Pressure.** (Consider the ability of the legal assistant to make sound judgments and to organize work under pressure.)

      — *Superior.* Nearly always works well under pressure. Maintains organization and control over assignments; continues to make sound judgments.

      — *Very good.* In most cases works well under pressure; rarely makes unsound judgments or becomes disorganized.

      — *Good.* Generally works fairly well under pressure; sometimes makes judgments that are not carefully considered or becomes slightly disorganized.

      — *Marginal.* Frequently fails to work well under pressure. Tends to become disorganized and to exercise poor judgment.

      — *Unacceptable.* Rarely works well under pressure. Allows pressure to interfere with effective management of assignments and often uses poor judgment.

      — *No opportunity to form an opinion.*

    4. **Analytical Skill.** (Consider the legal assistant ability to digest and analyze the facts of a particular case or assignment and the thoroughness of performing factual research.)

      — *Superior.* Is exceptionally thorough in gathering facts and quick to master the facts. Depth of understanding is evidenced by a high-quality work product.

      — *Very good.* Is thorough in gathering information. Masters facts quickly and uses them well in preparation of work product.

      — *Good.* Generally thorough in gathering information. Masters facts over an acceptable period of time. Sometimes needs attorney direction in developing the information required for work product.

      — *Marginal.* Sometimes misses essential information during factual investigation. Knowledge of facts is incomplete. Needs substantial attorney direction in order to analyze facts correctly.

| EXHIBIT 3.2 | Legal Assistant Evaluation Form—*continued* |
|---|---|

— *Unacceptable.* Often misses essential information during factual investigation. Knowledge of facts is seriously deficient. Work product needs substantial revision in order to ensure completeness. Sometimes careless in presentation of facts to attorney.

— *No opportunity to form an opinion.*

5. **Professionalism.** (Consider the extent to which the legal assistant is personally involved in his or her work; the extent to which he or she takes the job requirements seriously; and the extent to which he or she demonstrates responsibility for high-quality work in all instances.)

— *Superior.* Exhibits exceptionally high level of personal involvement in assignments and is extremely responsible. Takes initiative.

— *Very good.* Highly involved in assignments. Demonstrates strong commitment to his or her work. Very dependable.

— *Good.* Generally dependable and involved in assignments. Demonstrates average commitment to his or her work.

— *Marginal.* Frequently appears to lack interest in assignments. Needs substantial follow-up by attorney as to both deadlines and quality of work.

— *Unacceptable.* Unwilling to assume the necessary responsibility.

— *No opportunity to form an opinion.*

6. **Ability to Work Independently.** (Consider the legal assistant's ability to exercise good judgment by making well-reasoned choices and then to maintain necessary communication with attorney.)

— *Superior.* Considers all options and makes good decisions. Always keeps attorney well informed.

— *Very good.* In most cases makes good decisions. Occasionally needs attorney assistance in defining options. Keeps attorney well informed.

— *Good.* Usually considers options before making a decision. May not recognize the need to request attorney assistance in defining options.

— *Marginal.* Has difficulty making well-reasoned choices after options are defined. Fails to cover necessary material with attorney and does not readily call upon attorney for assistance or explanation.

— *Unacceptable.* Is not able to make reasonable choices after options are defined. Rarely keeps attorney informed and lacks understanding as to appropriate area of legal assistant work as defined by attorney.

— *No opportunity to form an opinion.*

7. **Quality of Written Work.** (Consider the ability of the legal assistant to express himself or herself in clear, precise language; thoroughness; organization; accuracy and neatness; grammar.)

— *Superior.* Exceptionally clear, precise, and thorough work that is neat and free from errors.

— *Very good.* In most cases, precise, clear, and thorough.

— *Good.* Generally acceptable but occasionally needs improvement.

— *Marginal.* Frequently lacking in one or more respects.

— *Unacceptable.* Work product is almost always lacking in one or more respects.

— *No opportunity to form an opinion.*

8. **Outside Contact.** (Consider the extent to which the legal assistant is required to work with persons outside the firm, such as co-counsel, clients, state and federal agencies, state and federal court personnel.)

— *Superior.* Consistently demonstrates ability to readily gain the cooperation and confidence the assignment requires. Establishes excellent working relationships.

— *Very good.* Generally gains cooperation and confidence. Establishes cooperation and confidence.

— *Good.* Needs occasional assistance but is able to gain the necessary cooperation and confidence.

— *Marginal.* Unable to handle outside assignments without substantial attorney assistance. Has difficulty developing necessary confidence and cooperation.

— *Unacceptable.* No understanding of what is required in order to gain necessary cooperation and confidence. Complaints received with regard to legal assistant's behavior.

— *No opportunity to form an opinion.*

**COMMENTS.** On the back of this form, space is provided to allow for elaboration of any of the ratings checked under the preceding categories. You are encouraged to provide additional comments on the legal assistant's performance: strengths, weaknesses, and suggestions for improvement.

eight categories? What ratings do you think your supervisor would give you? (If you have never worked in a law office, simply substitute the word *supervisor* every time the word *attorney* is used in the form.)

■ When you become a paralegal, the ideal will be for you and your supervisor to design an evaluation form *together*. The goal is to have a form that is specifically geared to the tasks you perform in the office. Even if the office already has an evaluation form, think about ways to adapt it more closely to you as an individual. Make notes on what you would like to see in such a form. Discuss it with your supervisor. Your initiative in this regard will be much appreciated, especially if you make clear that your goal is to use the evaluation to improve communication and to find ways to increase your skills and productivity.

■ Start preparing for your evaluation on the first day of your employment *and* on the day after your last evaluation. Do not wait until a few days before the evaluation itself.[11]

■ When you work on large projects, ask for a "project evaluation" at the conclusion of the project. This evaluation should be in *addition* to any regularly scheduled evaluations you receive.

■ Before a regularly scheduled evaluation, write a pre-evaluation memo and submit it to your supervisor. The memo should list the major cases or projects you have worked on since the last evaluation, your functions on each, names of your supervisors and co-workers on each, special accomplishments, events showing initiative (such as weekend work), written or oral quotations from individuals commenting on your work, etc.[12]

■ Before an evaluation, review the criteria by which you will be evaluated, if available.

■ Before an evaluation, review your job description. If your duties have been slowly changing, rewrite your job description to reflect these changes. Submit the revision to your supervisor for approval.

■ If this is your first formal evaluation by a particular supervisor, try to talk with others in the office who have been evaluated by this supervisor before. Find out what you might expect from this person.

■ After an evaluation, set some *measurable* goals. Do not simply pledge that you will "work harder." Establish goals that are much more concrete. For example:
  • "Before January, attend a bar-association seminar or a paralegal-association conference covering an aspect of my job."
  • "For the next ten weeks, spend a minimum of ten minutes a day studying paragraph structure in grammar/writing books."
  • "Once a month for the next six months, go to lunch with a paralegal whose professionalism I respect in order to brainstorm techniques for improvement."
  • "Within five weeks, reread the word-processing software manual from cover to cover."

  Note that each of these goals can be placed on a calendar. You can determine whether each has been met. Of course, you should also commit yourself to broader goals, like learning how to digest interrogatories or improving your research skills. Yet be sure to include more objective, short-term, self-measurable goals as well.

■ If you receive a negative evaluation, ask for a follow-up evaluation *before* your next regularly scheduled evaluation in order to determine whether you have made any progress on what was considered negative.

■ Suppose you work in an office that does not have regularly scheduled performance evaluations. It never uses formal written evaluations. Employees are evaluated, but not on an organized, consistent, written basis. You need to become an advocate for a more structured system of evaluation. You will be successful if you can convince your supervisor of two things: structured evaluations have value and will not take too much of the supervisor's time. To save time, use evaluation forms such as the one in exhibit 3.2. Or design your own evaluation form, as suggested earlier. Ask a busy supervisor to give you a brief oral evaluation, making sure that your strengths and weaknesses are covered. Take detailed notes. Then write out your notes in the form of a memo. Give it to the supervisor and ask if it accurately reflects what the supervisor said.

■ When your supervisor sees that you are not threatened by criticism and that you are not defensive when you receive it, you will be more likely to receive constructive criticism. It is better to have something negative said directly to you than to have it whispered behind your back. Here are some suggestions on taking criticism:[13]

  • Listen to all comments without trying to influence or criticize the critic.
  • Be sure you understand the complaint.
  • Admit when you are wrong; it is a sign of strength.
  • Agree with the truth.
  • Admit that you do not know.
  • Ask for clarification.
  • Ask for instructions or advice; be someone who is teachable.
  • Think of ways you can put the advice into action.

We will have more to say about evaluations later when we discuss ways to support a request for a salary increase.

## Section G
# CHARACTERISTICS OF SOME ATTORNEYS

The personality of a particular attorney has a great deal to do with the effectiveness of a paralegal-attorney working relationship. Many paralegals speak in glowing terms about their attorney-supervisor. Not only is the attorney easy to work with, but also he or she provides a challenging environment within which the paralegal can grow. Other attorneys, however, fall short of this standard; they do not function well as the leader of a team. According to two experts on the practice of law, a number of characteristics common to many attorneys do not encourage effective team-building:[14]

> *Autonomy.* Attorneys are less likely to collaborate than people in other occupations. Often they adhere to their preferred approach even when another is equally desirable.
> *Critical.* The successful attorney is highly critical. Typically, the focus of the attorney is on what is wrong with an idea. The merits of the idea are often ignored.
> *Competitive.* Like the very nature of the legal system, the attorney is competitive and adversarial. In policy questions and in personal relationships, progress and truth are achieved through varying degrees of confrontation.

Similarly, Dr. Martin Seligman, professor of psychology, studied 20 professions for optimism and reached the following conclusion:

> [O]nly one profession demonstrated that success was correlated with pessimism, not optimism—the law. . . . Lawyers are trained to look for negative possibilities, for disasters, for unusual catastrophes. We want them to be diligent for our wills, our companies, our divorces, our contracts. . . . [L]awyers are trained to look for loopholes. This is why they cannot always be reflective listeners. They are listening to find something wrong with your logic. Sometimes they can't be sensitive listeners either because they are listening for the rational logic that affects the content.[15]

It may not be easy to work with attorneys who fit these characteristics. The key to survival is assertiveness. According to one expert, many attorneys "prefer to work with assertive paralegals who are competent and knowledgeable. If you are not assertive with attorneys, they will lose confidence in you, and you may find yourself burdened with problems [including] . . . boring work, poor raises, and poor working conditions."[16]

Thus far in the chapter, we have referred to the importance of initiative and assertiveness several times. We now turn to a closer examination of this topic.

## Section H
# ASSERTIVE/NONASSERTIVE/AGGRESSIVE BEHAVIOR

Of the three behaviors discussed here, nonassertive behavior is the easiest to define. It is passiveness or undue silence. A nonassertive person rarely, if ever, complains to a person causing or contributing to a problem.

Aggressive behavior is at the other extreme; it is constant complaining. An aggressive person is a negative person who cannot express dissatisfaction without depressing someone else. Aggressive people may be right in many of the things they are saying, but they are so unpleasant that supervisors and co-workers seldom listen to them.

In between these two extremes is assertive behavior. Assertive people:

- Are competent and display competence.
- Are prepared.
- Show initiative; do not always wait to be told what to do.
- Act like they belong in the office.
- Are always willing to learn.
- Respect the competence of others.
- Are problem-solvers.
- Know that one of the best ways to help others solve problems is to provide them with options.
- Appreciate the value of timing; know that "now" is not always the best time to resolve a problem.
- Act like professionals.
- Do not shy away from office politics.
- Know the difference between griping and negotiating.
- Understand the necessity of compromise.
- Know the difference between little concerns and major ones; do not treat every problem as a crisis.
- Know when and how to lose gracefully.
- Advocate with resolve, not fanfare.
- Are self-assured enough to give credit to subordinates.
- Are willing to help others do their job well.
- Are secure enough to be able to say *no*.
- Are not offensive.
- Can express an opinion without putting someone down.

Assertive paralegals make themselves known. The backbone of assertiveness is competence—you know that you are capable. The trump card of assertiveness is timing—you watch for the right moment to come forward. The foundation of assertiveness is preparation—you have collected all the facts that support your position.

Suppose, for example, you feel that you are not earning what you are worth. What do you do? You can take one of a number of approaches.

### Nonassertive

You hope that things will get better, but you don't want to rock the boat. After all, your salary isn't *that* bad; it could be worse. You talk with fellow paralegals about your salary, and you are very frank with your aunt when the two of you talk on the phone about your work. But there's no sense in trying to get the firm to pay you more. The firm probably doesn't earn that much. And Mr. Smith, the head of the firm, is very pleasant to work with. Money isn't that important. Maybe next year will be better.

### Aggressive

Three weeks after you begin your job, you tell your supervisor that your salary is ridiculous. "With inflation, how do you expect me to live on this salary?" When your supervisor is not responsive, you send a memo to all the attorneys in the firm demanding that "something be done about paralegal salaries." When you walk the corridors of the firm, you are always visibly angry.

**Assertive**

- You prepare a fact sheet of paralegal salaries in your area after you talk with paralegals at other firms and examine salary surveys conducted by local and national paralegal associations, such as the following:
  - *National Utilization and Compensation Survey Report* published by the National Association of Legal Assistants
  - *Paralegal Compensation and Benefits Report* published by the National Federation of Paralegal Associations
  - *Legal Assistant Managers and Legal Assistant Compensation* published by the Legal Assistant Management Association
- You make sure that your supervisors have evaluated you regularly in writing. You summarize these evaluations and add them to the fact sheet.
- You make a list of the various projects you have worked on. You highlight special projects, such as helping design part of the office manual or training a new paralegal or attorney.
- You make sure that the decision-makers in the firm know who you are and what you have accomplished.
- You add up your billable hours over a designated period. The total is added to the fact sheet.
- You make note of every nonbillable task you performed that freed an attorney to devote more of his or her time to billable tasks.
- You discuss strategies for seeking a raise with other paralegals in the firm, with other paralegals in the area, and perhaps with some attorneys in the firm with whom you have developed considerable rapport.
- When others make a favorable comment about your work, you ask them to put it in writing so that it can go into your personnel file.
- You select the right time to meet with your supervisor. You decide to wait until the supervisor is not hassled with a difficult case.
- You may adopt a two-part strategy: you first ask for a meeting with your supervisor to discuss ways of increasing your contribution and productivity. At a follow-up meeting, you bring up the topic of a salary increase.
- Months before you ask for a raise, you ask your supervisor to identify those factors that will be taken into consideration in evaluating your overall performance and in recommending a salary level. In the months that follow, you make sure that you organize your efforts and your notes in accordance with the criteria the supervisor initially identified.
- You let your supervisor know what increase you are requesting, phrasing it as a range rather than as a single rigid figure.
- If you are unsuccessful in obtaining the amount you are seeking, you have a fall-back position ready—for example, you seek a performance bonus in lieu of a raise; additional insurance, educational tuition reimbursement, or other fringe benefits; perhaps a different office setting; or flex time.

If you ask successful paralegals about their secret of success (see exhibit 3.3), one message will come through loud and clear: *Seize the initiative*. No one is going to hand you anything simply because you are smart or because you have a certificate. You must prove yourself. You must be assertive.

## Section I
# Keeping a Diary and a Career Development File

Keep a *daily diary* or journal in which you record:

- The assignments you are given.
- The dates the assignments are given and the due dates for completion.
- The dates when the assignments are actually completed.

| EXHIBIT 3.3 | Taking the Initiative: Recommendations of Successful Paralegals |
|---|---|

**Tami Coyne:**

I have heard this tired refrain many times: "I am a hard worker and just don't get the recognition or the responsibility I deserve." This attitude gets you nowhere. If you believe that it is up to your employer to pick you out of the crowd and reward you just because you do your job, you will be sorely disappointed. In order to advance as a paralegal, you must prove that you are capable of taking on greater responsibility by performing your present duties exceptionally well. Show your initiative by anticipating the next stage of any assignment and completing it before you are asked to do it. Do not wait for recognition or feedback. You must be the one to initiate a feedback discussion after you have completed an assignment.[17]

**Renee Sova:**

Volunteer to draft the next document. Say, "I can do that; will you let me try?" Patience is a virtue. If the lawyer doesn't accommodate your first request, keep asking. Upon receiving and ultimately completing the assignment, there is nothing wrong with asking: "What could I have done differently to make it better?" This shows you truly care about your work product. Always do more than is expected. Few professionals became successful [by leaving] their careers to fate.[18]

**Laurie Roselle:**

If you feel like a second-class citizen, that's the way you will be treated—and that's how you should be treated. However, if you want respect in this profession, you must command it. To command this respect, you must be an intelligent professional willing to take on responsibility without having to be asked. Find ways to make yourself even more valuable than you already appear to be. Don't sit and complain about the way things are. Take charge and change them.[19]

**Carol Musick:**

Stay current on file status. Don't wait to be told to do something. Attorneys don't have time to spoon feed their paralegals. Stay current and find out "what comes next" on your own initiative.[20]

**Marian Johnson:**

The greatest key to success is something no one can give you—a good attitude! Enthusiasm has nothing to do with noise; it has more to do with motivation. It deals with our attitude. An attitude is something you can do something about. I can choose to be enthusiastic or I can choose not to be. Excitement is infectious. It's sort of like a case of the measles. You can't infect someone unless you have the real thing![21]

**Chere Estrin:**

Be assertive. Take an attorney to lunch![22]

- Favorable and unfavorable comments (written or oral) that have been made about your work.
- Total billable hours per day attributable to your work.
- The dates when you work evenings and weekends.
- The dates when you work on something at home.
- The dates you were late, were absent, or had to leave early.
- The dates when you came in early or worked through lunch hour.
- The names of any clients you referred to the firm.
- The amount of time you spent doing your own typing or photocopying.
- The time you spend in courses, seminars, or other ventures to improve your skills.

You need to have the facts of your employment at your command. The diary is your personal record; you keep it to yourself for use as needed. Not only will the facts be valuable when you are making an argument for a raise, but also they might be essential when misunderstandings arise about what you have or have not done.

The diary may be burdensome for you at first, and you may not make use of it for a while. It is worth the burden and the wait. A law firm respects someone who has the facts, particularly with dates!

In addition, start a *career development file* that contains everything that is relevant to your employment and growth as a paralegal. It should include:

- *Résumés.* A copy of every résumé you have written, including a current one that you should update every two or three months.
- *Job history.* A record of the dates you were hired in previous and current jobs; who hired you; who supervised you; a copy of your job descriptions; starting salary; amounts and dates of raises, bonuses, and other benefits received; dates and reasons you left.
- *Work accomplishments.* A copy of every written evaluation; letters received from clients commenting on your work; verbal comments made about your work by supervisors that you later wrote down.
- *Professional activities.* Evidence of your involvement with paralegal associations; attendance at conferences, seminars, and classes (including names of major teachers, copies of syllabi, etc.); speaking engagements; articles you have written for paralegal newsletters.
- *Conflict-of-interest data.* A list of the cases on which you worked, including the exact names of all clients, opposing parties, and opposing attorneys; a brief description of your role in each case; the dates of your involvement in these cases. (These data may be needed when you seek employment with another law office that wants to avoid being disqualified from a case because of your involvement with a particular party at a prior job. See chapter 5).

Now you are ready. If the job you are waiting for opens up, you have almost everything ready to present to the prospective employer; or you are armed and ready to sit down with management to show you deserve the raise you have been so patiently waiting for; or you are prepared to show your supervisor you are ready to take on that new case that just came into the firm.[23]

Section J
# The "Swoose Syndrome"

Is a paralegal part of the clerical staff or part of the professional staff? In most offices, the answer is both. If someone is part swan and part goose, he or she is experiencing the *swoose syndrome.*[24] A paralegal has also been referred to as a "tweener": one who performs both clerical and attorney tasks and hence falls somewhere in *between* these two employment categories.[25]

A cynic once said: "The person who asked a simple question and received a simple answer, did not ask a lawyer." The question "Is a paralegal a professional?" is a simple question. The answer is *yes* in some respect and *no* in others. Exhibit 3.4 presents some of the main differences that exist between professional and clerical employees. The factors listed

"Good morning Mr. Davis. Here is the deposition summary I worked on till midnight, plus your coffee and danish."

| EXHIBIT 3.4 | Factors Affecting Professional vs. Clerical Status |
| --- | --- |

| FACTORS THAT TEND TO INDICATE A PARALEGAL HAS PROFESSIONAL STATUS | FACTORS THAT TEND TO INDICATE A PARALEGAL HAS CLERICAL STATUS |
| --- | --- |
| 1. Does not do typing for anyone else | 1. Does typing for others |
| 2. Has own office | 2. Does not have own office |
| 3. Has own computer (used primarily for database management) | 3. Has own computer (but used primarily for word processing) |
| 4. Does not do own photocopying | 4. Photocopies for others |
| 5. Has secretarial help | 5. Does not have secretarial help |
| 6. Has a business card | 6. Does not have a bussiness card |
| 7. Has name printed on letterhead of firm | 7. Does not have name printed on letterhead |
| 8. Is paid a bonus rather than overtime | 8. Is usually paid overtime rather than given a bonus |
| 9 After considerable experience as a paralegal, is often paid a salary that is comparable to that of attorneys recently hired out of law school | 9. Is paid a salary comparable to that of secretaries and other clerical staff |
| 10. Frequently attends strategy meetings on cases | 10. Never or only occasionally attends strategy meetings on cases |
| 11. Is often given financial support and time off to attend association meetings and training sessions. | 11. Occasionally is given financial support or time off to attend association meetings and training sessions |
| 12. Can become an associate member of a bar association | 12. Is not eligible to become an associate member of a bar association |
| 13. Clients can be separately billed for time | 13. Clients cannot be separately billed for time; services are part of overhead |

in the exhibit do not apply to every office, but they give a general idea of the distinctions that often exist. Later, in chapter 4, we will discuss the controversial question of whether paralegals are entitled to overtime compensation. In general, professionals do not receive overtime; their extra efforts are recognized by the office in the form of a bonus.

## Section K
## Paralegal CLE

Elsewhere in this book we have stressed the reality that your legal education never ends. There is always something to learn. This is true for attorneys, and it is certainly true for paralegals. Education after employment is referred to as **continuing legal education (CLE).** CLE is offered mainly by bar associations and by paralegal associations. It usually consists of relatively short seminars that take place on a workday afternoon at a downtown hotel or over a two- or three-day weekend in another city. (You can also take CLE courses online. See the sites listed under "Continuing Legal Education" in "On the Net" at the end of the chapter.) CLE is often significantly different from the paralegal education you initially received. Since CLE occurs while you are employed, you are able to select seminars that directly and immediately relate to your day-to-day job responsibilities. Here is an example of this reality from Felicia Garant, a paralegal in Maine:

> I had an experience where I attended a half-day title insurance seminar and passed around a memo to attorneys in my section of the firm summarizing what I had learned there. A few minutes after I circulated the memo, an attorney flew out of his office exclaiming, "There's a new law on this subject?" He asked me to help him get a copy of the law since he had a case at that time that would be directly affected. You are the attorney's extra pair of eyes and ears, and you may pick up something at these seminars which will be new to the attorney. Your attendance at seminars, educating yourself, then passing the information on to the attorney not only increases your qualification as a legal assistant, but also makes you a valuable employee.[26]

**continuing legal education (CLE)** Training in the law (usually short term) that a person receives after completing his or her formal legal training.

CLE is not limited to substantive law topics. According to a recent survey of legal staff, the top CLE subjects were as follows:[27]

> 68% software training
> 59% time management
> 57% getting along with difficult people
> 42% effective use of e-mail
> 29% electronic filing of court documents

Often, but not always, the employer is willing to pay all or part of your expenses in attending such seminars and to give you time off if they occur during work hours. (See exhibit 2.13 in chapter 2 for an overview of fringe benefits some paralegals receive.) Even if your employer refuses to pay for them, you should go on your own time and at your own expense. Few things are more important to the professional development of a paralegal than CLE.

In almost every state, attorneys must attend a designated number of CLE hours per year as a condition of maintaining their license to practice law. As we will see in chapter 4, CLE is required of all paralegals in California. The failure to comply with California's mandatory CLE requirement can lead to a fine and imprisonment! Mandatory CLE for paralegals, however, does not exist in most states.

The voluntary certification programs of the two national paralegal associations (NALA and NFPA) require a designated number of CLE hours to maintain the certification earned after passing their examination. (See exhibit 4.6 in chapter 4.)

## Section L
# RESPONSIBILITIES OF SUPERVISORS

What is good attorney supervisor? The checklist in exhibit 3.5 lists the factors that constitute effective supervision. You might cautiously consider showing this checklist to your supervisors so that they might evaluate themselves as supervisors. Do not do this, however, until you are well established in your job. Considerable tact is needed when suggesting that a supervisor might be less than perfect.

"I'm headed out for a show tonight, and tomorrow I'll be at the golf tournament. I know the report is due tomorrow. I'll ask Helen, my paralegal, to do the report. She needs something to do."

## Section M
# RELATIONSHIP WITH SECRETARIES

At one time, many secretaries, particularly those in smaller law offices, resented the hiring of paralegals. This friction arose for a number of reasons, as the following overview points out:

Historically, the legal secretary was "queen" of her territory. The more competent she was, the more control she had over her immediate environment—how the office looked, how the work was done, how the clients were handled, and for that matter, how the lawyer was trained. The longer she worked with one lawyer, the more responsibility she was given, and the better she got at her job. In the office of the sole practitioner, the practice could go on smoothly even if the lawyer was in court or out of town. She was just about as indispensable as one person could be. There was a relationship of mutual trust and respect between the legal secretary and the lawyer that was practically impenetrable. Then along came the legal assistant, intruding on the legal secretary's territory, doing many of the things that the legal secretary had been doing for years. To add insult to injury, the legal secretary was expected to perform secretarial work for the legal assistant![28]

Fortunately, this problem is less prevalent today. In most law firms, secretaries and paralegals work together smoothly. Yet tension can occasionally surface, particularly over the issue of titles.

| EXHIBIT 3.5 | Checklist for Effective Supervision of Paralegals |
|---|---|

(Grade each factor on a scale of 1 to 5 with a 5 indicating that the supervisor is excellent in this factor and 1 indicating an unsatisfactory rating)

| FACTOR | RATING (on a scale of 1–5) |
|---|---|
| a. You give clear instructions to the paralegal on assignments. | a. ―― |
| b. You do not overburden the paralegal with assignments. Before you give a new assignment, you determine what the paralegal already has to do. If the demands on a paralegal are great, you consider alternatives such as hiring temporary paralegal help. | b. ―― |
| c. You provide reasonable deadlines on assignments, with adequate time built in for review and redrafting where appropriate. | c. ―― |
| d. You take affirmative steps to inquire about the paralegal's progress on assignments to determine if you should offer more guidance or if deadline extensions are needed. You do not simply wait for the paralegal to come to you with problems. | d. ―― |
| e. You provide adequate training for each assignment given. You take the time to make sure the paralegal can perform the task. | e. ―― |
| f. You are not afraid to delegate tasks to the paralegal. | f. ―― |
| g. You delegate meaningful tasks, not just routine tasks. | g. ―― |
| h. You make sure that the paralegal has some variety in his or her work. | h. ―― |
| i. You are supportive when the paralegal makes a mistake; your corrective suggestions for the future are constructive. | i. ―― |
| j. You permit paralegals to experience the end product of cases on which they are working—for example, you give them a copy of the finished product, or you invite them to your court presentation. | j. ―― |
| k. You include the paralegal in strategy meetings on cases. | k. ―― |
| l. You encourage the paralegal to use the law library in order to increase his or her knowledge and to appreciate the legal context of a case. | l. ―― |
| m. You use the paralegal's skills and regularly look for ways the paralegal can increase his or her skills. | m. ―― |
| n. You encourage paralegals to give their opinion on cases and on office policy. | n. ―― |
| o. You design systems with instructions, checklists, forms, etc., for the performance of tasks involving paralegals. | o. ―― |
| p. You encourage the paralegal to help you write these systems. | p. ―― |
| q. You regularly evaluate the paralegal, informally and in writing. | q. ―― |
| r. You encourage the paralegal to help you design a relevant paralegal evaluation form. | r. ―― |
| s. You encourage the paralegal to evaluate you as a supervisor. | s. ―― |
| t. You give credit to the paralegal where credit is due. | t. ―― |
| u. You make sure others in the firm know about the contribution of the paralegal. | u. ―― |

| EXHIBIT 3.5 | Checklist for Effective Supervision of Paralegals—*continued* |
|---|---|

(Grade each factor on a scale of 1 to 5 with a 5 indicating that the supervisor is excellent in this factor and 1 indicating an unsatisfactory rating)

| FACTOR | RATING (on a scale of 1–5) |
|---|---|
| v. You lobby with other attorneys who do not use paralegals or do not appreciate their value in order to change their attitude. | v. —— |
| w. You make yourself aware of any tension that may exist among paralegals, secretaries, and other staff members in the office in order to help end the tension. | w. —— |
| x. You back the paralegal's reasonable requests on salary and working conditions. | x. —— |
| y. You introduce your clients to the paralegal, explain the latter's role, and express your confidence in your employee. | y. —— |
| z. You do not pressure the paralegal about producing a quota of billable hours. | z. —— |
| aa. You make sure the paralegal has suitable office space, supplies, secretarial support, access to word processing etc. | aa. —— |
| bb. When changes are made in office procedures that affect paralegals, you let them know in advance so that they can make suggestions about the changes. | bb. —— |
| cc. You support the paralegal's need for financial help (and time off) to attend outside training programs (CLE). | cc. —— |
| dd. You support the paralegal's need for financial help (and time off) to participate in the activities of paralegal associations. | dd. —— |
| ee. You recognize that the paralegal, like any employee, will need reasonable time off to attend to pressing personal matters. | ee. —— |
| ff. You consider letting the paralegal have reasonable time off to do some pro bono work (e.g., time donated to poverty law offices or public interest law firms). | ff. —— |
| gg. You don't assume that the paralegal is happy about his or her job simply because you have no complaints and the paralegal hasn't expressed dissatisfaction; you take the initiative to find out what is on the paralegal's mind. | gg. —— |
| hh. You treat the paralegal as an individual. | hh. —— |
| ii. You treat the paralegal as a professional. | ii. —— |

There are secretaries who perform paralegal tasks. Some of these secretaries prefer to be called paralegals (or legal assistants) even though they have not had formal paralegal training. In chapter 4, we will see that secretaries in California cannot do this unless they meet the education and CLE requirements for paralegals. In states other than California, attorneys might encourage secretaries to call themselves paralegals in order to be in a better position to collect paralegal fees for the nonclerical tasks that the secretaries perform. Some formally trained paralegals, however, are not happy about secretaries who call themselves paralegals simply because they perform a few paralegal tasks.

The confusion is based in part on the fact that there is an overlap of functions in many law offices. There are attorneys who perform paralegal tasks, secretaries who perform paralegal tasks, and paralegals who perform attorney tasks. On paper, the three roles are distinct, but in practice, there can be considerable overlap, particularly in smaller law offices. Furthermore, computers on every desk make it possible for individuals to increase the variety of tasks that they perform. In times of pressure (e.g., during a trial or when a large commercial transaction must be completed before a looming deadline), everyone tends to pull together by doing whatever it takes to accomplish the task at hand. During a crisis, you rarely hear anyone say, "That's not my job."

In light of this reality, it is understandable that some legal secretaries are ambivalent about their title. As we have seen, the paralegal occupation grew out of the legal secretary occupation. Before paralegal training programs became commonplace, most paralegals came from the ranks of legal secretaries. Many secretaries were members of NALS, the National Association of Legal Secretaries (*www.nals.org*). It administers two certification exams: the ALS (Accredited Legal Secretary) exam for individuals with one year of general office experience and the PLS (Professional Legal Secretary) exam for those with three years of legal experience. As the paralegal field grew, paralegals started forming their own associations. In fact, the National Association of Legal Assistants (NALA) was initially formed as a breakaway association from NALS. Both associations are still headquartered in Tulsa, Oklahoma. NALS, however, does *not* consider itself to be a secretaries-only association. Recently, it changed its name from the National Association of Legal Secretaries to the Association of Legal Professionals.

Clearly, the relationship between paralegals and legal secretaries is still evolving.

It is highly unlikely, however, that you will experience turf battles with secretaries. When problems arise, they most likely will be due to normal interoffice tension in a busy environment. On those occasions when you are allowed to have the assistance of a secretary, consider the following recommendations for a smooth working relationship.[29]

- Give the secretary accurate, detailed instructions along with a reasonable timetable for completion.
- Make sure your written instructions are legible.
- Avoid waiting until the last minute to assign work that you know about beforehand.
- Don't pawn off undesirable chores that are rightly yours.
- Limit interruptions.
- Make yourself available to discuss problems or questions that arise during the performance of a task.
- Provide all the tools necessary to complete a job.
- Look for ways to recognize the contribution of secretaries. (The Rhode Island Paralegal Association, for example, conducts an annual secretary-appreciation luncheon.) "Remember that a pat on the back is just a few vertebrae removed from a kick in the pants, but miles ahead in results."[30]
- A cheerful demeanor can go a long way toward making your relationship more pleasant. Treat your secretary the way you wish to be treated, and don't forget basic courtesies, such as saying "good morning" and "have a nice evening."

Paralegals sometimes complain that attorneys do not treat paralegals with respect. How ironic that an insensitive paralegal could become subject to this same criticism.

## Section N
## SEXUAL HARASSMENT

There are two major kinds of sexual harassment:

**Quid Pro Quo Harassment:** Submission to or rejection of unwelcome sexual conduct is made an explicit or implicit basis for employment decisions such as promotion or other job-related benefits.

**Hostile Environment Harassment:** Pervasive unwelcome sexual conduct or sex-based ridicule unreasonably interferes with an individual's job performance or creates an intimidating, hostile, or offensive working environment, even if no tangible or economic consequences result.

An example of the latter would be an office that is significantly pervaded by sexual commentary, dirty jokes, offensive pictures, or generalized sexual conduct even if there is no direct trading of sexual favors for employment benefits.[31]

An employer must actively combat sexual harassment by:

- Establishing a written policy against sexual harassment and distributing it throughout the office,
- Investigating all accusations of sexual harassment promptly,
- Establishing appropriate sanctions for employees who commit sexual harassment,

- Informing employees of their right to raise a charge of sexual harassment under Title VII of the Civil Rights Act of 1964, and
- Informing employees how to raise a charge of sexual harassment under Title VII.

It is not a defense for an employer to say he or she did not know that one of the employees engaged in sexual harassment of another employee or that the harassment took place in spite of an office policy forbidding it. If the employer *should have known of the harassing conduct,* the employer must take immediate and appropriate corrective action, beyond merely telling all employees not to engage in sexual harassment.

Studies indicate that the harassment can come from a superior, a colleague, or a client of the law office. See exhibit 3.6. Here are some concrete examples:

> The paralegal . . . told of one incident in which a partner placed his hand on her knee and asked if she had thought about her future with the firm. "Harassment of women lawyers is only the tip of the iceberg," according to the paralegal. "The support staff has it much, much worse."[32]
>
> Recently a female paralegal began working with an insecure male lawyer who was a first year associate at the firm. He started "making the moves" on her by constantly asking if she was dating anyone. One day he called her in his office, closed the door, dialed a number on the phone, and handed the receiver to the paralegal. "What I heard was an obscene recording. I laughed, opened the door, and left." She did not believe in pursuing office relationships. Resentment developed when they began working on the same case together. He falsely accused the paralegal of lying and of not completing assignments on time. He made derogatory comments to her co-workers. When she confided in a female lawyer at the firm, she was told that the associate acts that way with all the women at the firm, that the paralegal supervisor and the associate are very good friends, and that the partner in charge "sticks to this associate like glue" and does not want to be bothered by "petty personnel problems."[33]

When something of this nature happens, make detailed notes on who said and did what. Do this immediately after the incident. Should you do anything more? A passive response would be to ignore the problem and hope that it will go away. Another response would be to blame yourself. Phyllis Schlafly told the Senate Labor and Human Resources Committee that "men hardly ever ask sexual favors of women from whom the certain response is *no*."[34] It is highly unlikely, however, that blaming yourself is either correct or productive.

For isolated and less serious problems, all that may be needed is a firm comment to the offender such as:

> Mr. Smith, you know that I respect your ability and authority in the firm. But I want you to know that I do not appreciate the comment you made at that meeting about women. I did not think it was appropriate or professional.

| EXHIBIT 3.6 | Incidents of Sexual Harassment in Law Offices |
| --- | --- |

**PERCENTAGE OF RESPONDENTS WHO REPORT HAVING EXPERIENCED VARIOUS TYPES OF SEXUAL HARASSMENT ON THE JOB**

| Incident | By Superior | By Colleague | By Client |
| --- | --- | --- | --- |
| Unwanted sexual teasing, jokes, remarks, or questions | 36 | 30 | 32 |
| Unwanted pressure for dates | 8 | 6 | 10 |
| Unwanted letters, telephone calls, or materials of a sexual nature | 4 | 3 | 4 |
| Unwanted sexual looks or gestures | 21 | 11 | 16 |
| Unwanted deliberate touching, learning over, cornering, or pinching | 14 | 6 | 9 |
| Unwanted pressure for sex | 6 | 3 | 4 |
| Unwanted pressure for sex in return for promotions or business | 1 | 0 | 1 |
| Actual or attempted rape or assault | 1 | 0 | 0 |

**Source:** *National Law Journal/West Group Survey on Women and Law,* National Law Journal S2 (December 11, 1989).

Unfortunately, this approach may be inadequate when the problem becomes more complicated and persists. Clearly, all possible internal avenues for resolving the problem should be attempted. Hopefully, *somebody* in a position of responsibility will lend a sympathetic ear. Local paralegal associations should be a source of ideas and support. Speak with officers of the association. Go to general meetings. Ask for advice. It is highly likely that you will find others who have had similar experiences and who can provide concrete suggestions.

If all else fails, you have a powerful weapon at your disposal: the law. Harassment on the basis of sex is a violation of Title VII of the Civil Rights Act of 1964. The federal **Equal Employment Opportunity Commission (EEOC)** (*www.eeoc.gov*) as well as state departments of civil rights are available to enforce the law.

In 1994, the legal community was shocked by a jury award of $6.9 million in punitive damages against the world's largest law firm, Baker & McKenzie, because of sexual harassment by one of its partners against his legal secretary. With other damages, the award came to $7.1 million. The court later reduced the award to about $3.5 million. The partner dumped candy in the front pocket of the secretary's blouse and fondled her breast. At a luncheon, he grabbed her hips and asked her repeatedly, "What is the wildest thing you have done?" The jury found that the firm was negligent in the way it responded to her allegations against the partner. It was not enough for the firm to transfer the employee to another attorney when she complained of his behavior. The court was not persuaded by the argument that the partner simply had an "overactive imagination." After the trial, her attorney said that the case should substantially affect law firms across the country. And the chairman of Baker & McKenzie's executive committee said the firm will handle any future complaints of sexual harassment from its employees very differently.[35]

> **Equal Employment Opportunity Commission (EEOC)** The federal agency that investigates employment discrimination that violates federal law.

## Section O
# WORKING WITH SYSTEMS

Some paralegal employment problems are attributed to the fact that the firm has not carefully examined how paralegals can be effectively used in the office. Paralegals should be part of an attorney-paralegal-secretary team. The difficulty, however, is that the office may not have done the necessary planning to design the *system* that the team will execute.

A system is simply an organized way of accomplishing a task. All participants are supposed to perform those functions that they are capable of handling and for which they are not overtrained. Here is how many systems are created:

- Select the task that is to be systematized. It will usually be a task that the office performs regularly, such as incorporating a business, probating an estate, filing for divorce, engaging in discovery. (According to some studies, attorneys perform over 75 percent of their tasks more than once.)
- Carefully study the task to identify its various components. What are the pieces that must always be performed? What facts must always be obtained? What letters must always be sent? What forms must always be prepared?
- Prepare a systems or procedural manual containing a description of the task, instructions or checklists of things to be done, standardized letters, pleadings, forms, and other documents that are customarily used for that task. The manual might be placed in a three-ring notebook and/or on a computer.
- Place photocopies of statutes, court rules, or other laws frequently used to perform the task in a special section of the manual, often in the appendix.
- Delegate the performance of the components of the task to various members of the team.

It takes considerable sophistication to *design* a system. Even more sophistication is sometimes needed to *implement* the system and make it work. The participants must believe in the system and ideally have had a role in its design if it requires changes in their work habits. Many attorneys are notoriously resistant to change, particularly if they believe that the system fails to recognize the role of professional judgment. If you have been doing something the same way for 15 years, you tend to be suspicious of suggestions that more efficient ways are possible. Furthermore, in the transition from blueprint to operation, the system may have to be modified to work out the "bugs." In short, a precondition for success is a willingness and a determination of the participants to make the new system work.

When paralegals walk into an office for the first time, they may confront any one of a number of situations:

- There are no systems; everybody practices law in his or her own individualistic way:
- There is talk of systemization, but no one has yet done any serious design work.
- An ineffective system is in place.
- A system is in place, but the participants do not believe in it.
- A system exists on paper, but no one has expended the time and energy to make the system work:

All these environments can make life difficult for the paralegal. A disorganized office can be very frustrating.

One of the most valuable things a paralegal can do is to observe an effective system in place. One or more may exist in other parts of the firm where you work. It may be possible for you to visit other firms in the area. Formbooks, practice guides, and legal periodical literature describe manual and computer systems, but these descriptions are no substitute for seeing the real thing.

Don't be reluctant to try to design your own system. You might want to begin with a system for a portion of one of your tasks. Start out on a small scale by writing instructions or checklists for functions that you regularly perform. Write the system so that a new paralegal would be able to read it and know what to do. Here is an example of how a project led to the creation of a system:

> Diedre Wilton's organizational skills were really put to the test during a recent assignment which required her to file fictitious business name statements for a client in every county in California. "Almost every county had a different form!" lamented Diedre. "And I had to arrange for publication in fifty-eight different newspapers." She is creating an extensive file on the project so that . . . when the filings come up for renewal, the next person won't have to start from scratch.[36]

Supervisors will be *very* impressed by such efforts to create systems. A paralegal with this much initiative will soon become a prized member of the office.

## Section P
# Career Ladders

In the early days of the paralegal movement, a common complaint among paralegals was the absence of career ladders. Once a paralegal demonstrates competence by making a significant contribution to the office, what comes next? Higher salaries, a better office, more variety in assignments—these are all helpful, but they are not the same as *promotion*. Yet what can a paralegal be promoted to? The only next step was lawyerdom. But going to law school is a rather drastic step. Taking this step means, of course, leaving the field of paralegalism entirely. Hence, in those early days, the only way up was out!

Although some progress has been made in developing career ladders, the progress has been primarily limited to law offices that employ relatively large numbers of paralegals. Most of the paralegals in small offices still have no career ladder. For this and related reasons, surveys show that between 10 and 15 percent of working paralegals today say that they intend to go to law school—eventually.

Yet other paralegals resent the following question put to them by attorneys: "So when are you going to law school?" or "Why don't you become an attorney?" Here is another example of this mentality:

ever, the Department has consistently taken the position that they are *not* exempt and hence are entitled to overtime compensation.

This position was challenged in the 1994 federal trial court case of *Secretary of Labor v. Page & Addison*.[52] Page & Addison is a Texas law firm that employed 23 paralegals over a three-year period and did not pay them overtime compensation. When one left, she sued for back pay, claiming the firm was wrong in treating its paralegals as exempt. Most of the paralegals who remained at the firm disagreed with her. They did *not* want overtime compensation; they preferred to be treated as part of the exempt staff. Nevertheless, the Department of Labor investigated and concluded that none of the paralegals were exempt. The case then went to the United States District Court in Texas. Here is part of the judge's instruction to the jury:

> To prove this exemption is applicable, the Defendant [the Page & Addison law firm] must prove plainly and unmistakably that: 1) the employee's primary duty 2) requires the exercise of discretion and independent judgment 3) in the performance of office or non-manual field work. . . . "Discretion and independent judgment" involve the comparison and evaluation of possible courses of conduct and acting or making a decision after the various possibilities have been considered. An employee exercises discretion and independent judgment if that employee has the authority or power to make an independent choice, free from immediate direction and supervision and with respect to matters of significance. An employee who merely applies his knowledge in following prescribed procedures or determining which procedures to follow is not exercising discretion and independent judgment. The discretion and independent judgment exercised must be real and substantial, that is, they must be exercised with respect to matters of consequence. The fact that an employee's work is subject to approval and possible rejection by a supervisory employee does not mean that the employee does not exercise discretion and independent judgment. . . . The employee's job title is of little or no assistance in determining the employee's exempt or non-exempt status.

Note that the Court said that someone can be exempt even if he or she is supervised by someone else. Hence a paralegal does not cease to be exempt simply because an attorney has an ethical obligation to supervise the work of that paralegal. The key is the presence or absence of independent judgment. This determination depends in part on whether the paralegal acts "free from *immediate direction and supervision* and with respect to matters of significance" (emphasis added).

The jury came to the conclusion that the paralegals at Page & Addison *did* exercise discretion and independent judgment. Therefore they were exempt and not entitled to overtime compensation. This was a fairly dramatic conclusion. It was the first time a court had addressed the question so directly.

Is the issue now settled? No. "[F]ar from providing any clearcut direction, the case has only fueled the controversy about overtime pay for paralegals."[53] One national salary survey showed that 56 percent of paralegals were treated as exempt by their employers, while 44 percent were treated as nonexempt. The trend is toward classifying more and more paralegals as exempt, but there is still a great deal of diversity on the issue. Differences can be found even within a particular law firm. An example is Page & Addison, the law firm that won the case in *Secretary of Labor v. Page & Addison*. After the case was over, the firm set up a three-tiered system of paralegals: junior paralegal, paralegal, and senior paralegal. The firm treats its junior position, for starting paralegals, as nonexempt. "The paralegal position, for experienced paralegals who work independently, is exempt from overtime, as is the senior paralegal position, designed for legal assistants who supervise others."[54] The U.S. Department of Labor decided not to appeal *Secretary of Labor v. Page & Addison*, which, as indicated, was a trial court case. Hence we don't have the benefit of a higher court's view of the issue. This will change as the law in this area continues to evolve. In the meantime, the Department of Labor is free to investigate other law firms to determine whether *their* paralegals are exempt. In spite of *Secretary of Labor v. Page & Addison*, the Department is inclined to the view that paralegals are not exempt.

---

> ### Assignment 4.12
>
> **(a)** If you had a choice, would you want to receive overtime compensation as an entry-level paralegal?
> **(b)** Surveys have shown that a large number of *nonexempt* paralegals today do *not* receive overtime compensation. Can you explain this fact?

---

## Section G
## TORT LIABILITY OF PARALEGALS

Thus far we have discussed a number of ways that paralegal activities are or could be regulated.

- Criminal liability for violating the statutes on the unauthorized practice of law
- Special authorization rules on practice before administrative agencies and other tribunals
- Licensing
- Self-regulation
- Labor laws

**tort** A civil wrong (other than a breach of contract) that causes injury or other damage for which our legal system deems it just to provide a remedy such as compensation.

Finally, we come to **tort** liability, which is another method by which society defines what is and is not permissible. A tort action is brought when someone has allegedly caused injury or other damage by committing a civil wrong other than a breach of contract. While a tort is different from a breach of contract and a crime, the same conduct that constitutes a breach of contract or a crime can also constitute a tort.[55]

**vicarious liability** Being responsible (liable) solely because of what someone else has done or failed to do.

Two questions need to be kept in mind. First, when are paralegal employees *personally liable* for their torts? Second, when are employers *vicariously liable* for the torts of their paralegal employees? (As we will see, **vicarious liability** simply means being liable because of what someone else has done or failed to do.) The short answer to the first question is: *always*. The short answer to the second question is: *when the wrongdoing by the paralegal was within the scope of employment.* After covering both questions, we will then examine the separate question of when malpractice insurance will pay for such liability.

Several different kinds of wrongdoing are possible. The paralegal might commit:

- The tort of negligence
- An intentional tort, such as battery
- An act that is both a crime (such as embezzlement) *and* an intentional tort (such as conversion)

A client who is injured by any of these torts can sue the paralegal in the same manner that a patient in a hospital can sue a nurse. Paralegals are not relieved of liability simply because they work for, and function under the supervision of, an attorney. Every citizen is *personally* liable for the torts he or she commits. The same is true of criminal liability. Employees who commit crimes can be prosecuted by the district attorney. It is not a defense that they engaged in criminal conduct on behalf of their boss.

**respondeat superior** Let the master (boss) answer. An employer is responsible (liable) for the wrongs committed by an employee within the scope of employment.

**scope of employment** That which is done by an employee in furtherance of the business of the employer.

Next we turn to the employers of paralegals. Are they *also* liable for wrongdoing committed by their paralegals? Assume that the supervising attorneys did nothing wrong themselves. For example, the attorney did not commit the tort or crime as an active participant with the paralegal, or the attorney was not careless in selecting and training the paralegal. Our question is: Can an attorney be liable to a client solely because of the wrongdoing of a paralegal? As we noted, such *vicarious liability* exists when one person is liable solely because of what someone else has done or failed to do. The answer to our question is found in the doctrine of **respondeat superior**, which makes employers responsible for the torts of their employees or agents when the wrongdoing occurs within the **scope of employment**.[56]

Hence, if a paralegal commits a tort within the scope of employment, the client can sue the paralegal or the attorney, or both. This does not mean that the client recovers twice; there can be only one recovery for a tort. The client is simply given a choice in bringing the suit. In most cases, the primary target of the client will be the employer, who is the so-called **deep pocket**, meaning the one who has resources from which a judgment can be satisfied.

Finally, we need to examine what is meant by "scope of employment." Not every wrongdoing of a paralegal is within the scope of employment simply because it is employment related. The test is as follows: Paralegals act within the scope of employment when they are furthering the business of their employer, which for our purposes is the practice of law. Slandering a client for failure to pay a law firm bill certainly furthers the business of the law firm. But the opposite is probably true when a paralegal has an argument with a client over a football game and punches the client during their accidental evening meeting at a bar. In the latter example, the client could not sue the paralegal's employer for the intentional tort of battery under the doctrine of respondeat superior because the battery was not committed while furthering the business of the employer. Only the paralegal would be liable for the tort under such circumstances.

The most common tort committed by attorneys is **negligence**. This tort is committed when the defendant's failure to use reasonable care causes harm. When a member of an occupation or profession is charged with negligence, reasonable care is determined by the knowledge and skill commonly possessed by members of that occupation or profession in good standing. Attorney negligence is the failure to exercise the reasonable care expected by an attorney in good standing. An attorney is not an insurer, however. Every mistake will not lead to negligence liability even if it causes harm to the client. The harm must be due to an *unreasonable* mistake, such as forgetting to file an action in court before the statute of limitations runs out.

When a *traditional paralegal* commits negligence for which the attorney becomes liable under respondeat superior, the same standard applies. Since the work product of this paralegal blends into the work product of the supervising attorney, the attorney becomes as fully responsible for what the paralegal did as if the attorney had committed the negligence. Unreasonableness is measured by what a reasonable attorney would have done, not by what a reasonable paralegal would have done.

An *independent paralegal* (also called a legal technician), however, who does not work under the supervision of an attorney, *is* held to the standard of a reasonable independent paralegal. The standard will be the knowledge and skill commonly possessed by independent paralegals in good standing. If such a paralegal is charged with negligence, he or she will not be held to the standard of a reasonable attorney—unless the paralegal led the client to believe he or she was an attorney or worked under an attorney's supervision. (See also Formal Opinion 1988–103, found on page 179, which discussed the standard of care owed by a paralegal who represents clients at worker's compensation hearings.)

There have not been many tort cases in which paralegals have been sued for wrongdoing in a law office. Yet as paralegals become more prominent in the practice of law, more are expected to be named as defendants. Michael Martz, General Counsel of the Mississippi Bar Association, makes the unsettling point that the prominence of paralegalism means there will be more suits against them. "As paralegals become more and more professional and proficient, they . . . will become better targets for disgruntled clients looking for someone to sue."[57] The most common kinds of cases involving paralegals have occurred when the paralegal was a notary and improperly notarized signatures under pressure from the supervising attorney.

**deep pocket** Someone who has resources with which to pay a judgment. The opposite of shallow pocket.

**negligence** Harm caused by the failure to use reasonable care.

---

*Assignment 4.13*

Mary Smith is a paralegal at the XYZ law firm. One of her tasks is to file a document in court. She negligently forgets to do so. As a result, the court enters a default judgment against the client. What options are available to the client?

### Assignment 4.14

Digests are short-paragraph summaries of court opinions. Their primary function is to allow you to find court opinions. (See Chapter 11.) Go to the *American Digest System* (a national digest), to any regional digest (covering a cluster of states), or to any individual state digest. Find the cases listed in (a) and (b). Summarize what the digest tells you about each case. Try to limit yourself to cases written by any state or federal court sitting in your state or in a surrounding state.

(a) Cases dealing with the negligence of attorneys in the hiring and supervision of legal secretaries, law clerks, investigators, and paralegals. Summarize each case (if there are many, select any three cases.)

(b) Cases dealing with the negligence of doctors and/or hospitals in the hiring and supervision of nurses, paramedics, and other medical technicians. Summarize each case. (If there are many, select any two cases.)

## Section H
## MALPRACTICE INSURANCE

**malpractice** Professional misconduct or wrongdoing such as an ethical violation, crime, negligence, battery, or other tort.

Legal **malpractice** generally refers to wrongful conduct by an attorney for which an injured party (the attorney's client) can receive damages. Just as doctors purchase malpractice insurance against suits by their patients, so, too, attorneys can buy such insurance to cover suits against them by their clients for alleged errors and omissions. (See exhibit 4.8) We need to examine how paralegals fit into this picture.

Until the 1940s, not many attorneys bought malpractice insurance because suits by clients were relatively rare. Today, the picture has changed radically; cautious attorneys do not practice law without such insurance against their own malpractice. "Statistically, the new attorney will be subjected to three claims before finishing a legal career."[58] Hence very few attorneys are willing to **go bare**—that is, practice without insurance. This change has been due to a number of factors. As the practice of law becomes more complex, the likelihood of error increases. Furthermore, the public is becoming more aware of its right to sue. In spite of disclaimers by attorneys that they are not guaranteeing any results, client expectations tend to be high, and hence clients are more likely to blame their attorney for an unfavourable result. And attorneys are increasingly willing to sue each other. In fact, some attorneys have developed a legal malpractice specialty in which they take clients who want to sue other attorneys. As malpractice awards against attorneys continue to rise, the market for malpractice insurance has dramatically increased. And so has the cost. In some cities, the premium for insurance can be between $5,000 and $15,000 per year per attorney.

**go bare** To engage in an occupation or profession without malpractice (liability) insurance.

**occurrence policy** Insurance that covers all occurrences (e.g., a negligent error or omission) during the period the policy is in effect, even if the claim is not filed until after the policy expires.

Two kinds of professional liability insurance policies cover attorney malpractice: occurrence policies and claims-made policies. An **occurrence policy** covers all occurrences (such as negligent error or omission) during the period the policy is in effect, even if the claim on such an occurrence is not actually filed until after the policy expires. Insurance companies are reluctant to write such policies because of the length of time it sometimes takes to uncover the existence of the negligent error or omission. Here's an example: An attorney makes a careless mistake in drafting a will that is not discovered until the person who hired the attorney dies many years later. Under an occurrence policy, the attorney is covered if the mistake occurred while the policy was in effect, even if the actual claim was not filed in court until after the policy terminated. The most common kind of policy sold by insurance companies today is the **claims-made policy** under which coverage is limited to claims actually filed (made) during the period in which the policy is in effect.[59]

**claims-made policy** Insurance that covers only claims actually filed ("made") during the period in which the policy is in effect.

Malpractice policies usually cover all the attorneys *and* the nonattorney employees of the law office. One policy, for example, defines the individuals covered—"the insured"—as follows:

> The insured includes the firm, all lawyers within the firm, and all non-lawyer employees, as well as former partners, officers, directors and employees solely while they acted on behalf of the insured firm.[60]

| EXHIBIT 4.8 | Professional Liability Claims Against Law Firms by Error Group |
|---|---|

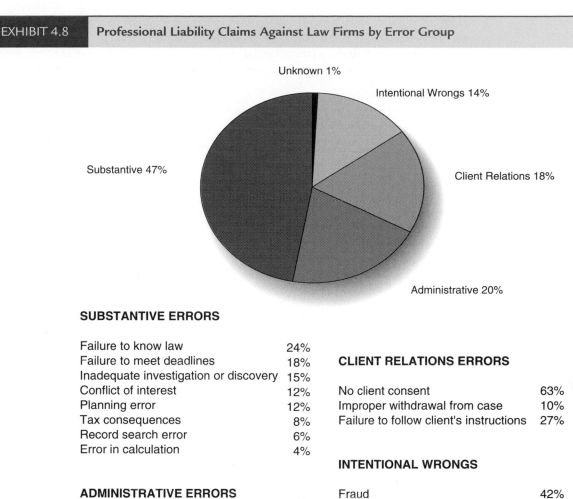

Unknown 1%

Intentional Wrongs 14%

Substantive 47%

Client Relations 18%

Administrative 20%

**SUBSTANTIVE ERRORS**

| | |
|---|---|
| Failure to know law | 24% |
| Failure to meet deadlines | 18% |
| Inadequate investigation or discovery | 15% |
| Conflict of interest | 12% |
| Planning error | 12% |
| Tax consequences | 8% |
| Record search error | 6% |
| Error in calculation | 4% |

**CLIENT RELATIONS ERRORS**

| | |
|---|---|
| No client consent | 63% |
| Improper withdrawal from case | 10% |
| Failure to follow client's instructions | 27% |

**INTENTIONAL WRONGS**

| | |
|---|---|
| Fraud | 42% |
| Civil rights | 16% |
| Malicious prosecution | 34% |
| Libel or slander | 9% |

**ADMINISTRATIVE ERRORS**

| | |
|---|---|
| Failure to file | 50% |
| Procrastination | 22% |
| Failure to calendar | 12% |
| Failure to react | 9% |
| Clerical error | 4% |
| Lost file | 2% |

*(Source: St. Paul Fire and Marine Insurance Company; due to rounding, figures don't add up to 100%)*

Such inclusion of employees is not always automatic, however. The policies of some insurance companies do not include paralegals or secretaries unless the law firm specifically requests coverage for them and pays an additional premium for their inclusion. Paralegals should therefore ask their employers if their malpractice policy explicitly covers paralegals.

What about independent or freelance paralegals who sell their services to attorneys? Although they may not be considered employees of the firm, they will usually be covered under the firm's policy in the same manner as full-time, in-house paralegal employees. So long as the employing attorney supervises and is responsible for the conduct of the paralegal, the malpractice policy usually provides coverage. In the language of one widely used policy, coverage is provided for "any other person for whose acts, errors or omissions the insured is legally responsible,"[61] which would include independent or freelance paralegals. A sophisticated paralegal would make sure that this is so before undertaking work for an attorney.

Independent or freelance paralegals who do not work for attorneys need to purchase their own liability policy if they want protection. Several insurance companies offer policies for such paralegals. One company, for example, offers "Paralegal Professional Indemnity Insurance" that provides $250,000 in coverage for $1,800 a year. Not many policies, however, are sold. Many paralegals prefer to "go bare."[62]

As we saw earlier in the chapter, legal document assistants (LDAs) in California are required to purchase a bond in the amount of $25,000. It costs approximately $500 a year.

---

## ■ CHAPTER SUMMARY

Criminal prosecution may result from violating statutes on the unauthorized practice of law. In general, they prohibit nonattorneys from appearing for another in a representative capacity, drafting most legal documents, and giving legal advice. Nonattorneys can sell forms and other legal materials but cannot give individual help in using them. They can provide (and even sell) legal information, but they cannot give legal advice.

There are some major exceptions to the prohibitions on nonattorney conduct. In a very limited number of circumstances, nonattorneys are authorized to do what would otherwise constitute the unauthorized practice of law. For example:

- In most states, a real estate broker can draft sales contracts.
- Several specialized courts allow nonattorneys to represent clients in court, although this is rare.
- A few states allow paralegals to appear in court to request a continuance or a new date for the next hearing in a case.
- An inmate can "practice law" in prison—for example, he or she can draft court documents for and give legal advice to another inmate if the prison does not offer adequate alternative methods of providing inmates with legal services.
- Many administrative agencies, particularly at the federal level, allow nonattorneys to represent clients before the agencies.

A number of states have considered broad-based licensing (which would cover all activities of all paralegals) and limited licensing (which would cover specified activities of those paralegals who are not supervised by attorneys). To date, neither kind of licensing has been enacted. Broad-based licensing for traditional paralegals is generally considered unnecessary because the public is sufficiently protected by attorney supervision. In California, however, the titles *paralegal* and *legal assistant* can be used only by individuals who work under attorney supervision, meet minimum educational requirements, and attend a designated number of hours of continuing legal education (CLE). Independent contractors who work without attorney supervision are called legal document assistants (LDAs) or unlawful detainer assistants (UDAs). They are subject to strict regulation, as are bankruptcy petition preparers (BPPs), who can provide limited assistance to citizens undergoing bankruptcy. Washington State may create new limited-licensing positions in the future similar to the position it has already created, the limited practice officer (LPO). NALA opposes limited licensing; NFPA favors it if it will expand the scope of tasks paralegals are able to carry out.

To address the problem of underrepresentation, some of the reforms in the practice of law have included pro bono programs, simplified forms, self-help centers, prepaid legal services, attorney advertising, publicly funded legal services, and the use of paralegals.

A number of bar associations allow paralegals to become associate or affiliate members. For example, the American Bar Association has a membership category called legal assistant associate.

There are two national certification programs. NALA offers an entry-level CLA (Certified Legal Assistant) exam and an advanced CLAS (Certified Legal Assistant Specialist) exam. NFPA offers Tiers I and II of PACE (Paralegal Advanced Certification Exam), both of which require paralegal work experience to take. Four states have state-specific certification exams: California, Florida, Louisiana, and Texas.

The Fair Labor Standards Act requires employers to pay overtime compensation to employees unless the latter are exempt. Paralegal managers are exempt. The United States Department of Labor believes that all other paralegals are not exempt, although a one trial court case in Texas came to the opposite conclusion. Exemption depends in part on the extent to which the paralegal exercises discretion and independent judgment on the job.

If a paralegal commits a tort, such as negligence, he or she is personally liable to the defendant. Under the theory of respondeat superior, the supervising attorney is also liable for the wrong committed by a traditional paralegal if it occurred within the scope of employment. Most attorneys have a claims-made malpractice insurance policy that covers their employees.

## KEY TERMS

| | |
|---|---|
| unauthorized practice of law | document preparer |
| practice of law | scrivener |
| regulation | legal technician |
| accreditation | limited practice officer |
| approval | legal document assistant (LDA) |
| certification | unlawful detainer assistant (UDA) |
| code | bankruptcy petition preparer (BPP) |
| ethics | pro bono work |
| guideline | prepaid legal service |
| licensure | attorney attestation |
| limited licensure | Certified Legal Assistant (CLA) |
| registration | Paralegal Advanced Certification Exam |
| statement of principles | (PACE) |
| pro se | Certified Legal Assistant Specialist |
| continuance | (CLAS) |
| jailhouse lawyer | Fair Labor Standards Act (FLSA) |
| adversarial | tort |
| Administrative Procedure Act | vicarious liability |
| registered agent | respondeat superior |
| enrolled agent | scope of employment |
| administrative law judge (ALJ) | deep pocket |
| Supremacy Clause | negligence |
| traditional paralegal | malpractice |
| continuing legal education (CLE) | go bare |
| independent contractor | occurrence policy |
| page 52 debate | claims-made policy |

## ON THE NET: MORE ON THE REGULATION OF PARALEGALS

**Paralegal Involvement with Bar Associations**
www.paralegals.org/Development/bar.html

**Report of ABA Commission on Nonlawyer Practice**
www.paralegals.org/Development/nonlawyer.html

**ABA Standing Committee on Legal Assistants (SCOLA)**
www.abanet.org/legalassts

**Model Act for Paralegal Licensure (NFPA)**
www.paralegals.org/regulation.html

**Washington State Limited Practice Board**
www.courts.wa.gov/board/1pb
www.courts.wa.gov/board/1pb/pdf/apr12.pdf

**Regulation Issues**
www.paralegals.org/Development/Regulations/home.html

**California Association of Legal Document Assistants**
www.calda.org

**What to Do If Your State Proposes Regulation**
www.paralegals.org/Development/activity.html

**Overtime Compensation (Exempt vs. Nonexempt)**
www.ewin.com/articles/salary.htm
www.dol.gov/dol/topic/wages/overtimepay.htm

**List of Self-Help Legal Books**
www.legalities.com
www.nolo.com

**Malpractice Avoidance**
www.hornbook.com

## ENDNOTES

1. The same distinction applies to someone who prepares documents to be filed in bankruptcy court. Congress calls such an individual a *bankruptcy petition preparer*. This is a person, other than an attorney or an employee of an attorney, who prepares for compensation a bankruptcy petition or other document for filing by a debtor in a United States Bankruptcy Court or a United States District Court. These individuals can type the documents; if they do much more, they are subject to substantial fines. 11 U.S.C. § 111. See also *In re Bachmann* 113 Bankruptcy Reporter 769 (S.D. Fla. 1990).
2. Legal Information vs. Legal Advice, *at* (www.abanet.org/legalservices/publicinfo.html) (visited August 14, 2001).
3. Peoples & Wertz, *Update: Unauthorized Practice of Law*, 9 Nat'l Paralegal Reporter 1 (Nat'l Federation of Paralegal Associations, February 1985).
4. Rule 10–2.1(a), Rules Regulating the Florida Bar (2001). See also *The Florida Bar*, 591 So. 2d 594 (Fla. 1991); *Florida Bar News* 12 (August 1, 1989).
5. District of Columbia Rules of Court, D.C. Court of Appeals Rule 49(c)(11) (2001); *Bar Report* (August/September 1993).
6. *Lassiter v. Dep't of Social Services*, 452 U.S. 18, 29, 101 S. Ct. 2153, 2161, 68 L. Ed. 2d 640, 651 (1981).
7. Winter, *No Contempt in Kentucky*, 7 Nat'l Paralegal Reporter 8 (Nat'l Federation of Paralegal Associations, Winter 1982).
8. 37 C.F.R. § 1.31. (2001).
9. 31 C.F.R. § 10.0 (2001); 26 U.S.C. § 7521 (2001).
10. Rose, *Representation by Non-Lawyers in Federal Administrative Agency Proceedings* (Administrative Conference of the United States 1984); Vom Baur, *The Practice of Non-Lawyers before Administrative Agencies*, 15 Federal Bar Journal 99 (1955).
11. ABA Standing Committee on Lawyers' Responsibility for Client Protection, *Report of 1984 Survey of Nonlawyer Practice before Federal Administrative Agencies* (October 19, 1984).
12. Office of Hearings and Appeals, Office of Policy Planning and Evaluation, Social Security Administration, *Highlights for Fiscal Year 1993* Tbls. 1, 2 (November 30, 1993).
13. Elaine Tackett, *Paralegal Representation of Social Security Claimants*, 16 Journal of Paralegal Education and Practice 67 (2000).
14. 42 U.S.C. § 406(b)(1)(A) (2001).
15. Commission on Nonlawyer Practice, American Bar Association, *Nonlawyer Activities in Law-Related Situations* 146 (1995).
16. Committee on Legal Assistants, New York County Lawyers' Association, *Committee Report* (October 14, 1993).
17. 373 U.S. 379, 388, 83 S. Ct. 1322, 1327, 10 L. Ed. 2d 428 (1963).
18. North Carolina State Bar Association, *Report of the Special Committee on Paralegals* 3 (1980).
19. Supreme Court of New Jersey, Press Release (May 18, 1999), *available at* (www.judiciary.state.nj.us/pressrel/admpara.htm).
20. West's Annotated California Business & Professions Code § 6450 (2000).
21. *Id.* at § 6455(a).
22. Sharlean Perez, *The New Law of the Paralegal Land*, 20 LAPA Reporter 1 (Los Angeles Paralegal Ass'n, October 2000).
23. *Legislative Report: AB 1761 FAQs*, Recap 7 (California Alliance of Paralegal Associations, Winter 2001).
24. Bob LeClair, AAFPE Listserv message (September 19, 2000).
25. *LAMA Position Paper on Legal Assistant Regulation* (October 9, 1996).
26. Nancy Ritter, *N.J. State Bar Savs No*, 16 Legal Assistant Today 16 (March/April 1999).
27. *In the Spirit of Public Service: A Blueprint for Rekindling of Lawyer Professionalism* 52 (ABA, Comm'n on Professionalism, 1986). See 112 F.R.D. 243 (1986)—the Federal Rules Decisions reporter.
28. Commission on Nonlawyer Practice, American Bar Association, *Nonlawyer Activity in Law-Related Situations* 175 (1995).
29. Mike France, *Bar Chiefs Protect the Guild*, The National Law Journal, August 7, 1995, at A1, A28.
30. ABA, *Nonlawyer Activity*, supra note 28, at 177.
31. Mark Curriden, *The ABA Nonlawyer Practice Report*, 13 Legal Assistant Today 89 (November/December 1995).
32. Mark Curriden, *The ABA Has Spoken: Will the Nonlawyer Practice Report Make a Difference?*, 14 Legal Assistant Today 62 (January/February 1996).
33. Washington State Supreme Court Rule 12(a), *available at* (www.courts.wa.gov/board/lpb).
34. National Association of Legal Assistants, *Statement to . . . State Bar of California* (1991).
35. Judge William Hogoboom, quoted in Harry Krause, *Family Law* 734 (3rd ed. 1990).
36. West's Annotated California Business & Professions Code §§ 6400–6450 (2000).
37. *In re Moore*, 232 Bankruptcy Reporter 1, 13 (D. Maine 1999).
38. 11 U.S.C.A. § 110 (2001).
39. Illinois State Bar Association and Chicago Bar Association, *Illinois Legal Needs Study* 5 (1989).
40. New York State Bar Association, *New York Legal Needs Study: Draft Final Report* 196 (1989).
41. Whelen, *An Opinion: Bar Association's Paralegal Non-Voting Membership*, 15 At Issue 9 (San Francisco Ass'n of Legal Assistants, May 1987).
42. *NFPA Findings*, 8 The Journal 3 (Sacramento Ass'n of Legal Assistants, January 1986).
43. Heller, *Legal Assistant Associate Membership in the ABA*, 14 On Point 1, 14 (Nat'l Capital Area Paralegal Ass'n, August 1988).
44. Anderson, *ABA Associate Membership: A Different Perspective*, 3 Findings and Conclusions 7 (Washington Ass'n of Legal Assistants, August 1987).
45. (www.michbar.org/sections/legalassist).
46. ABA Standing Committee on Legal Assistants, *Position Paper on the Question of Legal Assistant Licensure or Certification*, 5 Legal Assistant Today 167 (1986).
47. *The Member Connection*, 14 Facts & Findings 7 (NALA, June 1988).
48. *The Membership Responds*, 9 The ParaGraph (Georgia Ass'n of Legal Assistants, September/October 1987).
49. Acosta, *Let's Talk about Overtime!*, 10 Ka Leo O' H.A.L.A. 6 (Hawaii Ass'n of Legal Assistants, August/September 1987).
50. 29 U.S.C.A. §§ 201 et seq. (1976).
51. The Professional Employee Exemption:
    - Primary duty consists of work requiring knowledge of an advanced type in a field customarily acquired by a prolonged course of specialized intellectual instruction and study. (Such course of study means at least a baccalaureate degree or equivalent.)
    - Work requires the consistent exercise of judgment and discretion.
    - Work is predominantly intellectual and varied in character, as opposed to routine mental or physical work.

    The Administrative Employee Exemption:
    - The employee's primary duty consists of work related to management policies or general business operations.

■ The employee regularly exercises discretion and independent judgment.

The Executive Employee Exemption:

■ The employee's primary duty consists of the management of the enterprise.

■ The employee regularly supervises two or more other employees. 29 C.F.R. part 541 (1983).

52. U.S. District Court, Northern District, Texas, March 9, 1994.

53. Shari Caudron, *Overtime Pay*, 13 Legal Assistant Today 50, 53 (January/February 1996).

54. Id. at 51, 55.

55. See William Statsky, *Torts: Personal Injury Litigation* (4th ed. 2001).

56. We are talking here of vicarious *civil* liability or, more specifically, the tort liability of employers because of the torts committed by their employees. In general, employers are not subject to vicarious *criminal* liability. If a paralegal commits a crime on the job, only the paralegal goes to jail (unless the employer actually participated in the crime).

57. Michael Martz, *Ethics, Does a Paralegal Need Insurance?* The Assistant 13 (Mississippi Ass'n of Legal Assistants, Fall 1993).

58. R. Mallen & J. Smith, *Legal Malpractice* 2 (3d ed. 1989).

59. It is possible for a claims-made policy to cover a negligent error or omission that took place *before* the effective date of the policy, but most companies exclude coverage for prepolicy claims that the attorney knows about or could have reasonably foreseen at the time the policy is applied for.

60. Home Insurance Companies, Professional Liability Insurance.

61. American Home Assurance Company, Lawyers Professional Liability Policy.

62. As we saw earlier, most enrolled agents are nonlawyers who are authorized to provide certain tax services to the public. The National Association of Enrolled Agents offers a "Professional Liability Insurance Plan" through the St. Paul Fire and Marine Insurance Company. The Association's brochure says, "You can now secure protection against an unexpected lawsuit or penalty for damages arising from services you provide as an Enrolled Agent." Attorneys are not eligible to purchase this insurance.

# Chapter 5

# ATTORNEY ETHICS AND PARALEGAL ETHICS

## Chapter Outline

## Section A
# Introduction

As you know from the media, the legal profession is under attack. The general public does not have a favorable opinion of attorneys. Elsewhere in this book, we examine some of the reasons for this hostility. (See, for example, the beginning of chapter 8.) Here in chapter 5, we confront one of the main reasons: the perception that attorneys are not very ethical, or, more cynically, the perception that attorneys are ethical only when it doesn't cost them anything.

The organized bar has responded to this problem in different ways. Every law school must offer a required course in legal ethics. Many state bar associations require practicing attorneys to attend annual **continuing legal education (CLE)** courses or seminars on ethical themes. And state disciplinary bodies have hired more attorneys (and paralegals) to investigate claims of ethical violations by practicing attorneys.

Of course, attorneys are not the only individuals under attack for ethical misconduct. Some commentators claim that the problem is rampant throughout society. Our focus here, however, is the legal profession.

As paralegals, you are about to enter a very special work environment. You will meet many different kinds of attorneys: those whose ethical behavior is beyond reproach, those who engage in blatantly unethical behavior, and those who sometimes walk a thin line between ethical and unethical behavior. Which of these categories of attorneys will one day be your employers and supervisors? The short answer, of course, is that you don't know. The central question then becomes, How do you prepare yourself for any work environment?

When it comes to ethics, *you should be a conservative.* Our goal in this chapter is to provide you with the tools that will enable you to become an ethical conservative. We begin by presenting an overview of some of the most important ethical guidelines that we will study in this chapter. Carefully read—indeed, memorize—the summary in exhibit 5.1. In your career, the paramount question must always be "What is the right thing to do?" Answering this question will not always be easy, particularly if you are ever forced to make a choice between your ethics and your job.

**continuing legal education (CLE)** Training in the law (usually short term) that a person receives after completing his or her formal legal training.

## Section B
# Enforcing Ethics

### 1. ETHICS AND SANCTIONS

**Ethics** are rules that embody standards of behavior to which members of an organization must conform. The organization is often an association of individuals in the same occupation—for example, attorneys, paralegals, stockbrokers, or accountants. The ethical rules of some organization are enforced by **sanctions**. A sanction is any penalty or punishment imposed for unacceptable conduct, e.g., the sanction of a fine or expulsion from the organization because of fraud. (A very different meaning of sanction is permission or approval, e.g., the motion could not be filed without the sanction of the court.).

All of the major national paralegal associations have adopted ethical rules, as we will see later, in exhibit 5.4. *None,* however, are enforced by meaningful sanctions. A paralegal association might occasionally throw someone out of the association because of misconduct, but it is highly unlikely that the expulsion would interfere with his or her ability to work as a paralegal. Phrased another way, there are no jobs that require a paralegal to be a member in good standing of a paralegal association. This is not to say, however, that paralegal misconduct will go unnoticed. Such conduct may lead to sanctions by employers and the state, as we will see.

Attorneys, on the other hand, *are* subject to enforceable ethical rules that can affect whether they are allowed to continue practicing law. Attorney ethics are backed by sanctions. The rules attempt to govern everything an attorney does in the practice of law from adding clients to withdrawing from representing clients.

**ethics** Rules that embody standards of behavior to which members of an organization are expected to conform.

**sanction** (1) Penalty or punishment imposed for unacceptable conduct. (2) Permission or approval.

| EXHIBIT 5.1 | Paralegal Ethics: A Summary of Major Guidelines |
| --- | --- |

1. Study the ethical rules governing attorneys, including those on the ethical use of paralegals by attorneys. Read the rules. Re-read them. Attend seminars on ethics conducted by bar associations and paralegal associations. If you understand when attorneys are vulnerable to charges of unprofessional conduct, you will be better able to assist them in avoiding such charges.

2. Assume that people outside your office do not have a clear understanding of what a paralegal or legal assistant is. Make sure that everyone with whom you come in contact (clients, prospective clients, attorneys, court officials, agency officials, the public) understands that you are not an attorney.

3. Never tell anyone who is not working on a case anything about that case. This includes your co-workers, your spouse, your best friend, and your mother!

4. Know what legal advice is. When you are asked questions that call for legal advice, refuse to be coaxed into providing it, no matter how innocent the question appears to be, no matter how clear it is that you know the correct answer, and no matter how confident your supervisor is that you can handle such questions on your own.

5. Never make contact with an opposing party in a legal dispute, or with anyone closely associated with that party, unless you have the permission of your supervising attorney *and* of the attorney for the opposing party, if the latter has one.

6. Don't sign your name to anything if you are not certain that what you are signing is 100 percent accurate and that the law allows a paralegal to sign it. If you are asked to witness someone's signature, for example, be sure that the document you are witnessing is signed in your presence.

7. Never pad your time sheets by recording time that was not in fact spent on a client matter. Insist that what you submit be 100 percent accurate.

8. Disclose your inexperience. Let your supervisor know if all or part of an assignment is new to you and that you may need additional training and supervision to undertake it competently.

9. Know the common rationalizations for misrepresentation and other unethical conduct:

   ■ It's always done.
   ■ The other side does it.
   ■ The cause of our client is just.
   ■ If I don't do it, I will jeopardize my job.

   Promise yourself that you will not allow any of these rationalizations to entice you to participate in unethical conduct.

10. If what you are asked to do doesn't feel right, don't proceed until it does. Adhere to rigorous standards of professional ethics, even if those standards are higher than those followed by attorneys, paralegals, and others around you.

One of the things an attorney does is employ paralegals. Hence there are rules on how an attorney can use a paralegal ethically. Unethical use of paralegals by an attorney can subject the attorney to sanctions. We will spend considerable time in this chapter examining this reality.

## 2. ATTORNEY CODES

In most states, the regulation of attorneys is primarily under the control of the highest court in the state (often called the Supreme Court), which determines when an attorney can be granted a license to practice law and under what conditions the license will be taken away or suspended because of unethical conduct. The state legislature may also exert some regulatory authority over attorneys, and disputes occasionally arise over which branch of government can control a particular aspect of the practice of law. The judiciary often wins this dispute and becomes the final authority. In practice, however, the judicial branch and the legislative branch usually share regulatory jurisdiction over the practice of law. The day-to-day functions of regulation, however, are delegated to an entity such as a state bar association and a disciplinary board or grievance commission.

There are four kinds of bar associations:

■ National (for example, American Bar Association, Association of Trial Lawyers of America, Hispanic National Bar Association)

■ State (for example, Illinois State Bar Association, State Bar of Montana)
■ Local (for example, Boston Bar Association, New York County Bar Association, San Diego County Bar Association)
■ Specialty (for example, Academy of Matrimonial Attorneys, Association of Trial Lawyers of America, National Association of Women Lawyers)

**integrated bar association**
A state bar association to which an attorney must belong in order to practice law in the state.

**registration** The process by which individuals (or sometimes institutions) list their names on a roster kept by an agency of government or by a nongovernmental organization.

All national, local, and specialty bar associations are voluntary; no attorney is required to be a member. The majority of *state* bar associations in the country, however, are *integrated*, which simply means that membership is required as a condition of practicing law in the state. (**Integrated bar associations** are also referred to as *mandatory* or *unified* bar associations.) There is a state bar association in every state. Most, but not all, are integrated.

Under the general supervision of the state's highest court, the state bar association has a large role in regulating most aspects of the practice of law. For example, dues charged by integrated bar associations are used to fund the state's system of enforcing ethical rules. States that do not have integrated bar associations often have a **registration** requirement. Each attorney in the state registers to practice law and pays a registration fee that is used to fund that state's system of enforcing the ethical rules. A registration state will also have a state bar association. While attorney membership in it is voluntary, the association nevertheless has considerable influence over the regulation of attorneys. Given this dominant role of bar associations, the method of regulating attorneys in America is essentially that of self-regulation: attorneys regulating attorneys. This is true even in those states that allow nonattorney citizens to serve on boards or commissions that help regulate the legal profession.

There is no national set of ethical rules that applies to every state. Each state can adopt its own state code to regulate the attorneys in that state. The state code may have different names such as code of ethics, canons of ethics, code of professional responsibility, model rules. Yet the rules that the states have adopted are quite similar. The reason for this similarity is the influence of the American Bar Association.

The American Bar Association is a voluntary national bar association; no attorney must belong to it. Yet approximately 55 percent of the attorneys in America do belong to the ABA. It publishes ethical rules but does *not* discipline attorneys for unethical conduct. The role of the ABA in this area is to write ethical rules and to *propose* to the individual states that they be accepted. A state is free to adopt, modify, or reject the rules. The current recommendation of the ABA is found in a document called the *Model Rules of Professional Conduct*. This document has been very influential throughout the country. Many states adopted it with relatively minor changes. The *Model Rules* is a revision of the ABA's *Model Code of Professional Responsibility*, which a number of states still follow.

Exhibit 5.2 presents an overview of the major ethical codes governing attorney conduct. Most of these codes include provisions that are directly relevant to paralegals and other nonattorneys who work for attorneys. (See the last column of exhibit 5.2.) Later in the chapter, we will be examining these provisions more closely.

## 3. ACCUSATION OF UNETHICAL CONDUCT

When an attorney is charged with unethical conduct, the case is investigated by a disciplinary body appointed by the state's highest court. The name for this body differs from state to state, e.g., the Grievance Commission, the Attorney Registration and Disciplinary Commission, the Committee on Professional Conduct, the Board of Professional Responsibility.

A hearing is held to determine whether unethical conduct was committed by the accused attorney. The commission, committee, or board then makes its recommendation to the state's highest court, which makes the final determination of whether to accept this recommendation. A number of sanctions can be imposed by the court. As you can see from exhibit 5.3, they can range from relatively mild slaps on the wrist (reprimand, admonition) to expulsion from the legal profession itself (disbarment). Some states require attorneys to attend a day of special ethics training (the equivalent of traffic school) as part of the discipline imposed for violating the state's ethical code.

| EXHIBIT 5.2 | Ethical Codes Governing Attorney Conduct | | | | |
|---|---|---|---|---|---|
| **NAME OF DOCUMENT** | **DATE** | **AUTHOR** | **STATUS** | **STRUCTURE** | **PARALEGALS** |
| *Model Rules of Professional Conduct* | 1983 | American Bar Association | Current. The *Model Rules* replaces the *Model Code* (see below). The *Model Rules* is not binding on attorneys unless a state has adopted it. Forty-two states and the District of Columbia have adopted the *Model Rules* in whole or with changes. | There are eight main rules in the *Model Rules*. All of the rules are followed by interpretative comments. | Rule 5.3 of the *Model Rules* covers the ethical use of paralegals by attorneys and Rule 5.5 covers the unauthorized practice of law. (We will discuss both later in this chapter.) |
| *Model Code of Professional Responsibility* | 1969 | American Bar Association | The *Model Code* is an earlier version of the *Model Rules*. The *Model Code* is not binding on attorneys unless a state has adopted it. While the ABA now recommends the *Model Rules*, about seven states still follow their version of the *Model Code*. These states never adopted the *Model Rules*. | There are nine main canons in the *Model Code*. Within each canon are Disciplinary Rules (DR), which are mandatory statements or rules, and Ethical Considerations (EC); which are behavioral guidelines. | DR 3–101 of the *Model Code* covers the unauthorized practice of law. EC 3–6 covers the proper delegation of tasks to paralegals. (We will discuss DR-3-101 and EC-3-6 later in this chapter.) |
| State Codes | Varies | The state codes are written by the highest state court in the state. In addition, the state legislature may also pass statutes governing attorney ethics. | This is the code that is binding on every practicing attorney in the state. Most states have based their code on the ABA *Model Rules*. Some, however, still follow their version of the ABA *Model Code*. | Varies. If the state code is based on the *Model Rules*, the state code may have the same structure as the *Model Rules* (eight rules plus comments). If the state code is based on the *Model Code*, the state code may have the same structure as the *Model Code* (DRs and ECs). | Varies. May have Rule 5.3 (if the state code is based on the *Model Rules*) or may have DR 3–101 and EC 3–6 (if based on the *Model Code*). |
| Special Codes | Varies | A separate city, state, regional, or national bar association | These special bar associations often have their own code of ethics. For example, the code of the American Academy of Matrimonial Lawyers is called the *Bounds of Advocacy/Standards of Conduct*. | Varies. | Seldom specifically refer to paralegals. |

| EXHIBIT 5.3 | Attorney Sanctions for Unethical Conduct |
| --- | --- |

**Disbarment:**

The revocation or termination of the right to practice law. The disbarment can be permanent or temporary. If it is temporary, the attorney will be allowed to apply for reinstatement after a designated period.

**Suspension:**

The removal of an attorney from the practice of law for a specified minimum period, after which the attorney can apply for reinstatement. An *interim suspension* is a temporary suspension pending the imposition of final discipline. The attorney may be required to notify clients of the suspension. Sometimes the sanction of suspension is imposed but does not go into effect, i.e., the suspension is stayed. The attorney can continue to practice law while operating under a stayed suspension so long as he or she does not commit any further ethical violations.

**Reprimand:**

A public declaration that the attorney's conduct was improper. This does not affect his or her right to practice. A reprimand is also called a *censure, a public censure,* or *a public reproval.*

**Admonition:**

A nonpublic declaration that the attorney's conduct was improper. An admonition is the mildest from of punishment that can be imposed. It does not affect the attorney's right to practice. An admonition is also known as a *private reprimand* or a *private reproval.*

**Probation:**

Allowing the attorney to continue to practice but under specified conditions, such as submitting to periodic audits of client funds controlled by the attorney or making restitution to a client whose funds were wrongly taken by the attorney. He or she may also be asked to attend additional ethics training and/or to retake the Professional Responsibility portion of the bar exam.

Later in the chapter, we will cover one of the most contentious issues in this area: can a disbarred or suspended attorney continue working in a law office as a paralegal? As we will see, some states say no. The risk is too great that the disciplined attorney will continue to practice law under the guise of being a paralegal. Other states, however, allow it but may do so with restrictions, such as forbidding the attorney/paralegal from having any client contact.

## 4. PARALEGAL CODES AND GUIDELINES

Thus far we have been discussing attorney codes of ethics. Can a *paralegal* be sanctioned for violating these codes? Not directly. With one exception that we will discuss in a moment, the codes apply to attorneys only. Since paralegals cannot join a bar association as full members, they cannot be sanctioned by a bar association or by any other entity set up to monitor attorney conduct. Serious paralegal wrongdoing, however, can lead to severe consequences: the paralegals might be fired by their employer, they might be sued for negligence, they might face criminal prosecution, their supervising attorney might face ethical charges because of the paralegal's wrongdoing, etc. But the paralegals themselves cannot be punished for unethical conduct by the entity that regulates attorneys.

As indicated, there is an exception to the rule that attorney codes apply to attorneys only. Recently, there has been considerable debate over whether the legal profession should allow attorneys and nonlegal professionals to form a **multidisciplinary practice (MDP)**. This is a partnership between attorneys and groups such as accountants, doctors, therapists, economists, scientists, and environmental consultants that delivers legal and nonlegal services. In such a partnership, the nonattorney partner *would* be governed by the ethical code that governs attorneys. Only a few states allow such partnerships, although many are studying the possibility of allowing them. These entities would be a major departure from the rule that attorneys must not form a partnership with (or share fees with)

**multidisciplinary practice (MDP)** A partnership consisting of attorneys and nonlegal professionals that offers legal and nonlegal services.

nonattorneys. Critics warn that MDPs will lead to a loss of attorney control over the practice of law. The big fear is that companies such as Sears Roebuck and H&R Block will be able to start offering legal services in direct competition with traditional law firms. Proponents argue that MDPs will open up new markets for law firms, particularly in a global economy where large American law firms often compete in countries that authorize MDPs for their own attorneys.

If MDPs ever become widespread in the United States, they will probably not have a significant effect on paralegals. The goal of an MDP is to allow a law firm to expand its scope of business by partnering with individuals who have nonlegal skills and expertise. There is nothing nonlegal about paralegals! They are an intimate part of the attorney's legal team. While it is possible that a state might one day allow an attorney to form an MDP with a paralegal, the likelihood of this happening is relatively small.

Now we turn to **paralegal codes**. These are sets of rules and guidelines devoted exclusively to issues of paralegal ethics. There are two kinds of paralegal codes: those written by attorneys and those written by paralegals. See exhibit 5.4 for an overview of both.

**paralegal code** Rules and guidelines covering ethical issues involving paralegals.

| EXHIBIT 5.4 | Paralegal Codes and Guidelines |
| --- | --- |

| NAME OF DOCUMENT | DATE | AUTHOR | COMMENTS |
| --- | --- | --- | --- |
| **A. Those Written by Attorneys** | | | |
| *Model Guidelines for the Utilization of Legal Assistant Services* | 1991 | American Bar Association | A series of ethical guidelines recommended by the ABA for adoption by the states on the ethical use of paralegals by attorneys. (See www.abanet.org/legalassts/modguide.html.) States are free to adopt, amend, or reject these guidelines. |
| *State Codes and Guidelines* | Varies | State Bar Association | About half the states have adopted rules and guidelines on ethically practicing law with paralegals. To find out what exists in your state (and what you can find online), see appendix F. |
| **B. Those Written by Paralegals** | | | |
| *Model Code of Ethics and Professional Responsibility* | 1993 | National Federation of Paralegal Associations | The enforcement provisions of NFPA's *Model Code* are found in its *Model Disciplinary Rules* (1997). See www.paralegals.org/Development/modelcode.html. NFPA recommends the adoption of both the *Model Code* and *Model Disciplinary Rules* by every member association of NFPA. |
| *Code of Ethics and Professional Responsibility* | 1975 1995 | National Association of Legal Assistants | All members of NALA must agree to abide by its *Code of Ethics*. This code is elaborated upon in NALA's *Model Standards and Guidelines for Utilization of Legal Assistants* (1991). See www.nala.org/stand.htm. |
| Special Codes | Varies | Local, state, or regional paralegal associations | Other paralegal associations have written ethical codes to govern their membership. For example, here are some ethics you can read online ■ Houston Legal Assistants Association, *Code of Ethics* (www.hlaa.net/membership/codeofethics.html) ■ Kansas Paralegal Association *Code of Ethics and Professional Responsibility* (www.state.ks.us/public/ksparalegals/ethics.html) |

### Codes Written by Attorneys

The ABA has issued the *Model Guidelines for the Utilization of Legal Assistant Services*. Like the ABA's *Model Rules* and *Model Code* (see exhibit 5.2), the *Model Guidelines* are recommendations to the states. The ABA itself does not discipline anyone for violating the *Model Guidelines*. (Later in this chapter, you will find a discussion of every major guideline or rule contained in the *Model Guidelines*.) To date, about half the states have their own state paralegal codes that are similar to the *Model Guidelines*. Most were adopted by the state bar association or by the committee of the bar association that covers paralegals. Some have been formally approved and adopted by the state's highest court. The *Model Guidelines* and the state paralegal codes are primarily directed to attorneys who use paralegals in their practice. Hence, if there are violations by paralegals, it is the supervising attorney who may be subject to sanctions by the state entity that regulates attorney ethics. (For a summary of state guidelines for your state, see appendix F.)

### Codes Written by Paralegals

The two national paralegal associations, NFPA and NALA, have also written paralegal codes. (See exhibit 5.4 for the titles of these codes and where you can read them online.) As indicated earlier, these codes are not enforced by meaningful sanctions. The associations might terminate a paralegal's membership in the association for ethical improprieties, but this is rarely done. The associations simply do not have the resources or clout to implement a system of enforcement. This does not mean, however, that the paralegal codes are unimportant. Their main value is to reinforce the critical importance of ethics in the practice of law.

Paralegals are on the front line. *One of their primary responsibilities is to help an attorney avoid being charged with unethical conduct.* A recent seminar conducted by the Los Angeles Paralegal Association was entitled "Law Firm Ethics: How to Keep Your Attorneys Off '60 Minutes'!" Hence the paralegal must be intimately familiar with ethical rules. Our goal in this chapter is to provide you with that familiarity.

## Section C
# ETHICAL RULES

We turn now to an overview of specific ethical rules that apply to attorneys. The overview is based on the ABA's *Model Rules of Professional Conduct*. (See exhibit 5.2.) The rule numbers used in the discussion (such as Rule 1.5) refer to the *Model Rules*. Since not all states have adopted the *Model Rules*, we will occasionally refer to the ABA's *Model Code of Professional Responsibility*, which some states still follow.

Where appropriate, the discussion will include a *paralegal perspective* based on the ABA's *Model Guidelines* and the other paralegal codes mentioned in exhibit 5.4. In appendix F of the book, you will also find a state-by-state breakdown of important ethical rules.

One final note before we begin: Most ethics charges are brought by disgruntled clients who claim to have been harmed by the attorney's alleged unethical behavior. For example, the client's case was dismissed because the attorney carelessly forgot to file a pleading in court. We need to emphasize, however, that a person who initiates a charge of unethical conduct does *not* have to prove he or she suffered actual harm thereby. Suppose, for example, an attorney represents a client with whom the attorney has a clear conflict of interest. The attorney should never have taken the case. Representing the client in the case is unethical even if the attorney wins the case for the client! Proof of harm is not necessary to establish a violation of the ethical rules, although such harm is usually present.

### 1. COMPETENCE

**competent** Using the knowledge and skill that are reasonably necessary to represent a particular client.

*An attorney shall provide competent representation to a client.* **Model Rule 1.1**

A **competent** attorney is one who uses the *knowledge* and *skill* that are reasonably necessary to represent a particular client. What is reasonably necessary depends on the complexity of the case. A great deal of knowledge and skill, for example, will be needed when representing a corporate client accused of complicated antitrust violations.

How do attorneys obtain this knowledge and skill? They draw on the general principles of legal analysis and legal research learned in law school. But more important, they take the time needed to *prepare* themselves. They spend time in the law library. They talk with their colleagues. In some instances, they formally associate themselves with more experienced attorneys in the area. Attorneys who fail to take these steps are acting unethically if their failure means that they do not have the knowledge and skill reasonably necessary to represent a particular client.

Some attorneys have so many clients that they could not possibly give proper attention to each. Always looking for more lucrative work, they run the risk of neglecting the clients they already have. As a consequence, they might miss court dates or other filing deadlines, lose documents, fail to determine what law governs a client's case, etc. Such an attorney is practicing law "from the hip"—incompetently and unethically.

> **Example:** Mary Henderson, Esq. has a large criminal law practice. She agrees to probate the estate
> of a client's deceased son. She has never handled such a case before. Five years go by. No progress
> is made in determining who is entitled to receive the estate. If some minimal legal research had
> been done, Henderson would have been able to close the case within six months of taking it.

Henderson has probably acted unethically. The failure to do basic research on a case is a sign of incompetence. The need for such research is clear in view of the fact that she has never handled a probate case before. Either she must take the time to find out how to probate the estate, or she must contact another attorney with probate experience and arrange to work with this attorney on the case. Not doing either is unethical.

The vast majority of graduates of law schools need considerable on-the-job study and guidance before they are ready to handle cases of any complexity. A law school education gives new attorneys a good theoretical understanding of the law. This is different from the *practical* knowledge and skill needed to work on real cases. Many law schools have **clinical education** programs in which students receive credit for working on actual cases under the supervision of attorneys. For example, the school might operate its own tax clinic for senior citizens or might assign students to work several hours a week on different kinds of cases at a local legal aid office. Although these clinical programs provide practical experience, they are not a major part of the law school curriculum of every law school. Most new attorneys (including those with clinical experience), therefore, are quite nervous when they face their first client on their first job. The nervousness is based on the fact that they are acutely aware of how much they *don't* know. This doesn't necessarily mean they are incompetent to practice law. It simply means they must take the time to prepare themselves and to draw on the assistance of others where needed.

Continuing legal education (CLE) is another vehicle used by attorneys to achieve competence. Most states require attorneys to participate in a designated number of hours of CLE per year as a condition of maintaining their license to practice law. (This requirement is called *mandatory CLE*.) CLE sessions are designed to keep busy practicing attorneys current in their areas of practice. The sessions are often conducted by a CLE institute affiliated with the bar association. Throughout the year, and particularly during bar conventions, attorneys have the opportunity to attend relatively short CLE sessions, e.g., an afternoon.

If an attorney is incompetent, he or she can be sanctioned for being unethical. In addition, the incompetence may have other consequences. The client might try to sue the attorney for negligence in a legal malpractice case. (Such suits were discussed in chapter 4.) If the client is a criminal defendant who was convicted, he or she may try to appeal the conviction on the ground that the attorney's incompetence amounted to a denial of the effective "Assistance of Counsel" guaranteed by the Sixth Amendment of the U.S. Constitution.

**clinical education** A training program in which students work on real cases under attorney supervision.

### Paralegal Perspective:

■ It is unethical for an attorney to assign a task to a paralegal without making sure that the paralegal has the training or experience needed to perform that task competently. While the attorney has this supervisory responsibility, paralegals also have a responsibility to maintain their own competence.

- If you are given assignments that are beyond your knowledge and skill, let your supervisor know. Either you must be given training with close supervision, or you must be given other assignments. A "lawyer should explain to the legal assistant that the legal assistant has a duty to inform the lawyer of any assignment which the legal assistant regards as beyond his capability."[1]

- Be careful of the attorney who has so much confidence in your competence that he or she uses your work product with little or no checking. This is extremely dangerous, particularly for paralegals who work for very busy attorneys. The danger is that you will make a mistake that will not be caught until damage is done to the client. No matter how much experience you develop in an area of the law, unique problems often arise. Unless someone is reviewing your work, how will you know whether you have missed one of these problems? Your ego will appreciate the confidence your supervisor expresses in you by delegating so much responsibility, but the attorney still has an ethical obligation to supervise your work. Your competence is not a substitute for this supervision.

- After you complete an assignment, look for an opportunity to ask your supervisor how you could have improved your performance on the assignment. Do not wait for a year-end evaluation to learn what you can do to become a more competent paralegal.

- Find out which attorneys, administrators, paralegals, and secretaries in the office have a reputation for explaining things well. Try to spend time with such individuals even if you do not work with them on a daily basis. Take them to lunch. Find time to sit with them on a coffee break. Ask lots of questions. Let them know you respect high-quality work and appreciate anything they can tell you to help you increase your competence.

- Invest in CLE. Take the initiative in continuing your training after your formal education is over. Do not wait for someone to suggest further training. Ask if you can attend CLE sessions for attorneys in the areas of law that are relevant to your case assignments. (Check the Internet site of your local bar association in appendix C, and find the CLE link to your state at *www.aclea.org*, the site of the Association of Continuing Legal Education.) National and local paralegal associations also have afternoon and weekend CLE programs available to you. (Check the Internet sites of the paralegal associations listed in appendix B.) Find the time to attend CLE sessions, even if you must pay for them yourself. Because the law often changes, you need to use resources like CLE to keep current.

    As we saw in chapter 4, continuing legal education is not optional in California. Paralegals and legal document assistants (LDAs) in that state have mandatory CLE requirements. (See appendix G on California regulation.) Also, paralegals who have passed the CLA test of NALA or the PACE test of NFPA are required to attend a designated number of CLE hours to maintain their CLA or PACE status. State certification may also mandate CLE. (See exhibits 4.6 and 4.7.)

- Review the section in chapter 4 on malpractice insurance. No matter how competent you are, you could be a defendant in a negligence suit brought against a law firm by a disgruntled client. Before you are hired by a firm, find out if the firm has a malpractice policy, whether it covers paralegal employees, whether certain kinds of errors are excluded, and whether you need to obtain your own professional liability insurance.

## 2. DILIGENCE/UNWARRANTED DELAY

*Causing unwarranted delay in representing a client is unethical. The attorney must act with reasonable diligence and promptness.* **Model Rule 1.3**

*Reasonable efforts must be taken to expedite litigation.* **Model Rule 3.2**

Angry clients often complain that attorneys take forever to complete a case and keep clients in the dark about what is happening. "He never answers my calls." "It took months to file the case in court." "She keeps telling me that everything is fine, but nothing ever gets done." Such complaints do not necessarily indicate unethical behavior by the attorney. Events may be beyond the control of the attorney. For example, the court calendar is crowded or the other side is not responding. Yet this does not excuse a lack of regular communication with clients to keep them reasonably informed about the status of their case.

Other explanations for a lack of diligence and promptness, however, are more serious:

- The attorney is disorganized. The law office has not developed adequate systems to process cases. The delays are due to careless mistakes and a lack of skill.
- The attorney is taking many more cases than the office can handle. Additional personnel should be hired to do the needed work, or new cases should not be accepted.

Often the failure to use reasonable diligence and promptness causes harm to the client. For example, the attorney neglects to file a suit before the statute of limitations has run against the client. Unreasonable procrastination, however, can be unethical even if such harm does not result.

Another problem is the attorney who intentionally causes numerous delays in an effort to wear the other side down. It is unethical to engage in such dilatory practices. Attorneys must use reasonable efforts to expedite litigation, consistent with protecting the interests of their clients.

### Paralegal Perspective:

- An overloaded attorney probably works with an overloaded paralegal. Successful paralegals often take the initiative by asking for additional work. But reason must prevail. If you have more work than you can handle, you must let your supervisor know. Otherwise, you might find yourself contributing to the problem of undue delay.
- Learn everything you can about office systems, particularly for tasks that the office performs on a regular basis. Find out how systems are created. (See chapter 3.) After you have gained some experience in the office, you should start designing systems on your own initiative. Effective office systems substantially reduce the risk of unethical delays in client representation.
- When a busy attorney is in court or cannot be disturbed because of pressing work on another case, someone in the office should be available to communicate with clients who want to know the status of their case. In many offices, the paralegal is in a position to provide this information. This role can be delicate. In addition to asking about the status of their case, clients often ask questions that call for legal advice. Giving such advice may constitute the unauthorized practice of law. Later we will examine in greater depth the temptations and pressures on a paralegal to give legal advice.

### 3. FEES

*Fees for legal services must be reasonable.* **Model Rule 1.5(a)**

There is no absolute standard to determine when a fee is excessive and therefore unreasonable. A number of factors must be considered: the amount of time and labor involved, the complexity of the case, the customary fee in the locality for the same kind of case, the experience and reputation of the attorney, etc. In one case, a court ruled that $500 an hour was excessive in a simple battery case in which there was no trial (the accused pled guilty) and there were no unusual issues to be resolved. In another case, a court concluded that a fee of $22,500 was excessive in an uncomplicated real estate case involving very little attorney time. The case was settled through the efforts of someone other than the attorney.

A fee is not necessarily excessive simply because it is large. Cases exist in which courts have approved fees of hundreds of millions of dollars. An example is the tobacco litigation of the 1990s, in which attorneys brought suits that resulted in multibillion-dollar settlements and judgments. Prior to this time, the tobacco industry had remarkable success in winning personal injury suits brought by sick smokers and by the estates of deceased smokers. In assessing the reasonableness of a fee, a court will consider the odds against winning and the uniqueness of the issues raised in the litigation. By these standards, the at-

**retainer** The contract between an attorney and a client that covers the scope of services, fees, expenses, and costs of legal services. (The word also means an amount of money or other property paid by a client as a deposit or advance against future fees, expenses, and costs of legal services.)

torneys who won the cases against the tobacco industry were entitled to very high fees. When they began, few thought they had much chance of winning anything, let alone winning billions. (Later in the chapter, we will discuss the infamous role of a paralegal, Merrill Williams, in the tobacco litigation.)

The basis of the fee should be communicated to the client before or soon after the attorney starts to work on the case. This is often done in the contract hiring the attorney, called a **retainer**. (See exhibit 8.1 in chapter 8 for an example of a retainer. Kinds of fees are also discussed in greater detail in chapter 14.)

In exhibit 5.2, we outlined the major attorney codes of ethics. Many bar associations write formal and informal opinions that interpret sections of their code. Attorneys can submit questions to the bar's ethics committee. (To preserve confidentiality, attorneys submit these questions without client names or other identifying information, e.g., "If an attorney represents client A in a case against a local merchant, would it be ethical to . . .?") The questions selected are sometimes published as formal or informal opinions so that the entire legal community can benefit from the bar's interpretive advice. For example, in Formal Ethics Opinion 93-379, the American Bar Association addressed the issue of excessive fees through the following three fact situations:

> **Case I**. John Smith, Esq. (who bills by the hour) has two clients who happen to have separate cases in the same court on May 9, 2002, each requiring relatively minor attention from the attorney. If the attorney had gone to court on two separate days, each client could have been billed for three hours. On May 9, however, Smith was able to handle both cases. He spent a total of three hours in court. Can he bill each client three hours for the time spent on May 9, since he would have been able to do so if he went on separate days?
>
> *Answer*: No. Smith did not earn six billable hours on May 9. Billing more than one client for the same time is unreasonable. Savings resulting from scheduling must be passed on to clients.
>
> **Case II**. Mary Jones, Esq. (who bills by the hour) charges a client five hours transportation time to travel by airplane to a meeting with the client in another city. While on the plane, she skips the in-flight movie in order to spend two hours drafting a motion for a different client on another case. Can she bill the first client five hours and the second client two hours to cover the total of five hours on the plane?
>
> *Answer*: No. Jones has not earned seven billable hours. Billing more than one client for the same time is unreasonable. Savings resulting from being able to do two things simultaneously (traveling and drafting a motion) for different clients must be passed on to clients.
>
> **Case III**. George Harris, Esq. (who bills by the hour) bills a client for 10 hours to research a problem and draft a memorandum of law covering the issues in the case. Several days later he uses the same memorandum on a different case for another client who happens to have the same legal problem as the earlier client. Can he bill the second client 10 hours for the memorandum?
>
> *Answer*: No. Harris has not earned 20 billable hours. Billing more than one client for the same work product (a research memorandum) is unreasonable. Savings resulting from being able to reuse a work product must be passed on to clients.

As you can see, ethical opinions such as Formal Ethics Opinion 93-379 can be very helpful in interpreting the rules of ethics. The opinions help give the rules a concrete context. Later we will cover the steps you need to take to locate ethical opinions of the American Bar Association and of state bar associations. (Ethics opinions involving paralegals in your state are summarized in appendix F.)

At one time, bar associations published a list of "recommended" minimum fees that should be charged for designated kinds of services. A fee below the minimum was considered unethical. These **minimum-fee schedules** have now been prohibited by the United States Supreme Court. They constitute illegal price fixing by the bar in violation of the antitrust laws.

**Contingent fees** can sometimes present ethical problems. A contingent fee is a fee that is dependent on the outcome of the case.

> **Example:** An attorney signs a retainer to represent a client in an automobile negligence case. If the jury awards the client damages, the attorney will receive 30 percent of the award. If the client loses the case, the attorney receives no fee.

This is a contingent fee because it is dependent on the outcome of the negligence case.

**minimum-fee schedule** A bar association list of the lowest fees an attorney can charge for specific kinds of legal services.

**contingent fee** A fee that is dependent on the outcome of the case (the fee is also called a contingency).

The benefit of a contingent fee is that it provides an incentive for an attorney to take the case of a client who does not have funds to pay hourly fees while the case is pending. But contingent fees are not ethical in every case, even if the amount to be received by the successful attorney is otherwise reasonable. A contingent fee in a criminal case, and in most divorce cases, for example, is unethical.

> **Example:** Gabe Farrell is a client of Sam Grondon, Esq. in a criminal case. Gabe is charged with murder. Gabe agrees to pay Grondon $100,000 if he is found innocent. Grondon will receive nothing if Gabe is convicted of any crime.

This fee agreement is unethical. Contingent fees are not allowed in criminal cases. Note the pressures on Grondon. He arguably has no incentive to try to negotiate a guilty plea to a lesser charge, e.g., manslaughter, because such a plea would mean a conviction and, hence, no fee. In such a situation, the attorney's own personal interest (obtaining the $100,000) could conflict with the interest of the client (receiving a lesser penalty through a negotiated plea). Similar pressures can arise in family law cases:

> **Example:** To obtain a divorce from his wife, a client hires an attorney. The fee is $25,000 if the divorce is granted.

As the case develops, suppose a glimmer of hope arises that the husband and wife might reconcile. Here, again, the attorney's interest (obtaining the $25,000) could conflict with the interest of the client (reconciling). This might lead the attorney to discourage the reconciliation or to set up roadblocks to it. Reconciliation obviously removes the possibility of the contingency—obtaining the divorce—from occurring. In family law cases, therefore, contingent fees are unethical if the fee is dependent on securing a divorce, on the amount of alimony obtained, on the amount of support obtained, or on the amount of a property settlement in place of alimony or support. This is so even if the terms of the contingent fee are otherwise reasonable.[2]

One final theme should be covered: **fee splitting**. The splitting or division of a fee refers to a single client bill covering the fees of two or more attorneys who are not in the same firm. Sometimes one attorney will pay another a **forwarding fee** (also called a referral fee) for referring the case. (The forwarding attorney often does no actual work on the case.) Or attorneys from different firms may simply join forces to work on the case.

**fee splitting** A single client bill covering the fees of two or more attorneys who are not in the same firm.

**forwarding fee** A fee received by one attorney from another to whom the first attorney referred a client.

> **Example:** John Jones, Esq. is hired by a singer who is charging her record company with copyright infringement and breach of contract. Jones calls in Randy Smith, Esq., a specialist in copyright law from another firm. Both work on the case. They share (split) the fees paid by the singer, who receives one bill for the work of both attorneys even though they work for different law firms.

The attorneys are splitting or dividing the fee between them. This arrangement is proper under certain conditions. The total fee must be reasonable, and the client must be told about the participation of all the attorneys and not object. The share of the fee received by each attorney must be in proportion to his or her work on the case unless each attorney agrees to joint malpractice responsibility for the case.

Suppose, however, that the attorney splits a fee with a nonattorney.

> **Example:** Frank Martin is a freelance investigator. He refers accident victims to a law firm. For every client he refers to the firm, he receives 25 percent of the fee collected by the firm.

> **Example:** Helen Gregson is a chiropractor. She refers medical malpractice cases to a law firm, which compensates her for each referral.

These are improper divisions of fees with nonattorneys—even if the amount of the division is reasonable and the clients brought in by Martin or Gregson consent to their receiving a part of the fee. An attorney cannot share with a nonattorney a portion of a fee *paid by particular clients*. The rationale behind this prohibition is that the nonattorney might exercise some control over the attorney and thereby jeopardize the attorney's independent judgment.

For the same reason, an attorney cannot form a partnership with a nonattorney if any of the activities of the partnership consist of the practice of law. If the office practices law as a corporation, a nonattorney cannot own any interest in the company or be a director or officer. As we saw earlier, however, if a state allowed the formation of a multidisciplinary practice (MDP), nonattorneys would be allowed to become partners of the firm and thereby share fees.

When a client has a serious dispute with an attorney over a fee, the client will sometimes dismiss the attorney and ask for a return of the client's file, which may contain many documents such as correspondence, complaints, other pleadings, exhibits, and reports of experts. This file is the property of the client and must be surrendered by the attorney when the client requests it, even if there are unpaid bills for fees and costs. If the attorney has a claim for payment, the remedy is to sue the client for breach of contract; it is unethical for the attorney to hold the file hostage to ensure payment. The attorney can copy the file before turning it over, but at the attorney's own expense. (For more on an attorney's client-file responsibilities at the close of a case, see chapter 14.)

### Paralegal Perspective:

- Paralegals who work for law firms receive salaries. This does not constitute the unethical sharing of fees with nonattorneys, even though the firm pays salaries out of revenue generated by fees. So long as there is no advance agreement to pay a paralegal all or part of *particular* legal fees, there is no ethical impropriety. Suppose that a paralegal is eligible to become part of the firm's retirement plan, which has a profit-sharing component. Or suppose that the firm has a bonus plan for its paralegals. In most states, the same rule applies. Retirement plans and bonuses are ethical so long as there is no sharing or splitting of a particular client's fees. There is a major difference between:
  - A law firm agreeing to pay a paralegal 10 percent of whatever fees are collected in the Davis v. Kelly automobile negligence case on which the paralegal has done good work (unethical in all states) and
  - A law firm giving this paralegal a bonus because the firm appreciates the paralegal's good work on all of the negligence cases that resulted in high fees during the year (ethical in most states).

  Although the latter is ethical in most states, there are some states that disagree. See, for example, Indiana's Guideline 9.8 (printed in appendix F), which provides that a "legal assistant's compensation may not be contingent, by advance agreement, upon the profitability of the attorney's practice."

- A related restriction in many states is that an attorney cannot give a paralegal any compensation for referring business to the attorney.

- Paralegals occasionally speak with prospective clients before an attorney does. The paralegals are not allowed to set fees. Nor can they accept or reject cases. These are all attorney-only functions. While some states may allow a paralegal to tell a prospective client what standard fees an attorney charges for particular services, the discussion of fees is most often left to the attorney.

- Attorneys may charge clients fees for paralegal work on their cases (referred to as paralegal fees, as we saw in chapter 1). Paralegals record their time on time sheets that become the basis of the bills sent to clients. The amount that an attorney bills for paralegal time must be reasonable. Reasonableness is determined by a number of factors, such as the experience of the paralegal, the nature of the tasks the paralegal undertakes, and the market rate for paralegals in the area. Many retainers state the amount a client will be charged for a paralegal's time. (See exhibit 8.1.) The fact that the client agrees to a fee, however, does not prove that the fee is reasonable. Factors such as experience and market rate must still be used to determine whether the fee is reasonable. Furthermore, the fees must be for the performance of paralegal tasks. It is unethical to claim such fees for time the paralegal spent performing clerical duties such as photocopying. (See appendix F for summaries of court cases in which attorneys have been criticized for trying to bill paralegal rates for secretarial tasks performed by paralegals.)

In special **statutory fee cases**, the losing side can be forced to pay the attorney fees of the winning party in litigation. In addition to attorney fees, paralegal fees must also be paid. The same guidelines apply: the paralegal fees must be reasonable and cannot cover nonparalegal tasks. Some states ask attorneys to submit an affidavit to support the amount claimed for the paralegal's time. The affidavit must give a detailed statement of the time and services rendered by the paralegal, a summary of the paralegal's qualifications, etc.

- Your time records should be contemporaneous, that is, made at approximately the same time as the events you are recording. Try to avoid recording time long after you perform tasks that require time records.
- Avoid **double billing**. It is fraudulent to charge a client twice for the same service.

**Example:** Charles is a litigation paralegal in a law firm. One of his tasks is to digest (i.e., summarize) a deposition. The firm bills the client 20 hours for this task at the paralegal's rate ($65 per hour). The firm also bills the client 10 hours of Attorney Bedford's time for digesting the same deposition at the attorney's rate ($150 per hour).

The client is being double billed, a grossly unethical practice. It would be proper for an attorney to charge a client for time spent *supervising* a paralegal's work but not for *performing* the work of the paralegal. The related offense of **padding** is also fraudulent. It occurs when you add hours to your time sheet that were not in fact spent on the client's case.

**Example:** It takes Charles, the litigation paralegal, 12 hours to digest a deposition. His time sheets, however, say he spent 20 hours on the task.

Padding is a serious problem in the practice of law. Here is what one attorney observed:

I was routinely told to double and triple bill my time.… The lawyers are engaged in pervasive deception of clients, pretending to be doing work that they are not doing, pretending to spend more time than they are spending, pretending that work needs to be done which in fact does not need to be done. The delivery of legal services is conceptualized principally as a billing opportunity to be manipulated and expanded.[3]

Unfortunately, paralegals can find themselves under a similar pressure, which, of course, must be resisted.

One of the most common temptations that can corrupt a paralegal's ethics is to inflate billable hours, since there is often immense pressure in law firms to bill high hours for job security and upward mobility. Such "creative billing" is not humorous; it's both morally wrong and illegal. It's also fraudulent and a plain and simple case of theft.[4]

Paralegals claim that questionable billing is among the most common unethical practice attorneys ask them to perform. [One commentator] reported incidents where paralegals were ordered to double bill and bill for time they did not spend working.[5]

When you are employed as a paralegal, will you face such pressure? Yes, or at least very probably, if you work in an office where income is generated through hourly fees. The office wants high billings to increase its income. The paralegal wants high billings to demonstrate to the office that he or she is financially valuable to the office. This does not mean that everyone submits fraudulent time sheets and billings. But the pressure to do so is real.

A veteran paralegal recently made the following dramatic and troublesome comments about this problem:

The economic benefits [of using paralegals] to the client are receiving greater attention. From my experience, however, there has been more abuse than benefit. The client is billed for a task traditionally performed by a secretary, doublebilled for redoing a task because it was poorly delegated and is being billed at an attorney's rate for "routine tasks" which can be best handled by a qualified paralegal.[6]

The following case of *Brown v. Hammond* involves a paralegal, Cynthia Brown, who complained about the improper billing practices of her law firm. Like most nonunion employees

**statutory fee case** A case applying a special statute that gives a judge authority to order the losing party to pay the winning party's attorney and paralegal fees.

**double billing** Fraudulently charging a client twice for the same service.

**padding** Adding something without justification; adding unnecessary material in order to make something larger.

**at-will employee** An employee who can quit or be terminated at any time and for any reason; an employee who has no contract protection.

in the private sector, Brown was an **at-will employee**. The rule governing such employees is that they can be terminated (or they can quit) at any time for any reason. There are, however, some narrow public policy exceptions to this rule. The question in the *Brown* case was whether any of the exceptions applied.

## Brown v. Hammond

### 810 F. Supp. 644
### United States District Court, Eastern District, Pennsylvania (1993)

WALDMAN, District Judge.

Plaintiff [Cynthia Brown] is an employee of defendant attorney [Robert Hammond] and his law firm. She is suing for wrongful discharge after having "blown the whistle" on the defendants' allegedly improper billing practices. Jurisdiction is based on diversity of citizenship.* Defendants have moved to dismiss the complaint for failure to state a claim upon which relief can be granted, pursuant to Fed.R.Civ.P. [Federal Rule of Civil Procedure] 12(b)(6).

### I. LEGAL STANDARD

The purpose of a Rule 12(b)(6) motion is to test the legal sufficiency of a complaint.... In deciding a motion to dismiss for failure to state a claim, the court must "accept as true all the allegations in the complaint and all reasonable inferences that can be drawn therefrom, and view them in the light most favorable to the non-moving party." See *Rocks v. Philadelphia*, 868 F.2d 644, 645 (3d Cir. 1989). Dismissal is not appropriate unless it clearly appears that plaintiff can prove no set of facts in support of his claim which could entitle him to relief. See *Hishon v. King & Spalding*, 467 U.S. 69, 73, 104 S. Ct. 2229, 2232, 81 L. Ed. 2d 59 (1984).... A complaint may be dismissed when the facts pled and the reasonable inferences drawn therefrom are legally insufficient to support the relief sought....

### II. FACTS

The pertinent factual allegations in the light most favorable to plaintiff are as follows. From November 4, 1990 to April 4, 1991, plaintiff was employed by defendants at-will as a paralegal and secretary. The time she spent on client matters was billed to clients as "attorney's time" without any notice to such clients that the work was done by a non-lawyer. Her supervisors directed her at times to bill her work directly as attorney's time despite her protests that the practice was improper. She then informed various authorities and affected clients of this practice. Plaintiff does not

allege that she had any responsibility for overseeing the firm's billing practices.

Defendants responded by imposing new work rules with respect to hours of employment which applied only to and discriminated against plaintiff. She was subsequently terminated.

In count I, plaintiff asserts that she was terminated in violation of public policy for reporting the wrongful actions of defendants. In count II, she asserts that she was terminated in violation of public policy for refusing to perform wrongful actions....

### III. DISCUSSION

It is well established under Pennsylvania law that "absent a statutory or contractual provision to the contrary...either party [may] terminate an employment relationship for any or no reason." *Geary v. United States Steel Corp.*, 456 Pa. 171, 175–176, 319 A.2d 174 (1974). An employer may determine, without any fair hearing to an at-will employee, that the employer simply wishes to be rid of him. *Darlington v. General Electric*, 350 Pa. Super. 183, 210, 504 A.2d 306 (1986). An employer's right to terminate an at-will employee has been characterized as "virtually absolute." *O'Neill v. ARA Services, Inc.*, 457 F. Supp. 182, 186 (E.D. Pa. 1978).

Pennsylvania law does recognize, however, a nonstatutory cause of action for wrongful discharge from employment-at-will, but only in the quite narrow and limited circumstance where the discharge violates a significant and recognized public policy. *Borse v. Piece Goods Shop*, 963 F.2d 611, 617 (3d Cir. 1992); *Geary*, supra; *Darlington*, supra. Such a public policy must be "clearly mandated" and of a type that "strikes at the heart of a citizen's social right, duties and responsibilities." *Novosel v. Nationwide Insurance Co.*, 721 F.2d 894, 899 (3d Cir. 1983). *Geary* signals a "narrow rather than expansive interpretation of the public policy exception." *Bruffett v. Warner Communications. Inc.*, 692 F.2d 910, 918 (3d Cir. 1982). Public policy exceptions "have been recognized in only the most limited of circumstances." *Clay v. Advanced Computer Applications, Inc.*, 522 Pa. 86, 89, 559 A.2d 917 (1989).

While courts generally look to constitutional or legislative pronouncements, some courts have found

* Plaintiff is a citizen of Texas, and defendants are citizens of Pennsylvania. The amount in controversy exceeds $50,000.

an expression of significant public policy in professional codes of ethics. See *Paralegal v. Lawyer*, 783 F. Supp. 230, 232 (E.D. Pa. 1992); *Cisco v. United Parcel Services*, 328 Pa. Super. 300, 476 A.2d 1340 (1984)....

The court in [the] *Paralegal* [*v. Lawyer* case] found that the Pennsylvania Rules of Professional Conduct as adopted by the Pennsylvania Supreme Court pursuant to state constitutional powers, Pa. Const. art. 5, § 10(c), could provide the basis for a public policy exception to the at-will employment rule. See *Paralegal [v. Lawyer]*, 783 F. Supp. at 232 (finding public policy against falsifying material facts and evidence from rules 3.3(a)(1), 3.4(a), and 3.4(b)). In that case, a paralegal whose employer was being investigated by the state bar was terminated after she learned that the attorney-employer had created a false record to exculpate himself and so informed the lawyer who was representing the employer in disciplinary proceedings.

Taking plaintiff's allegations as true, defendants would appear to have violated the Pennsylvania Rules of Professional Conduct by misrepresenting to clients who had performed work for which they were paying or by effectively permitting the unauthorized practice of law by a non-lawyer. See Rule 1.5 (regulating fees); Rule 5.5(a) (prohibiting aiding non-lawyers in unauthorized practice of law); Rule 7.1 (prohibiting false or misleading communications about lawyer's services); 8.4(c) (defining "professional misconduct" to include dishonesty, fraud, deceit or misrepresentation).

Based upon pertinent precedent and persuasive authority, the court must distinguish between gratuitous disclosure of improper employer conduct and disclosures by persons responsible for reporting such conduct or for protecting the public interest in the pertinent area. See *Smith v. Calgon Carbon Corp.*, 917 F.2d 1338, 1345 (3d Cir. 1990)...(discharged chemical company employee not responsible for reporting improper emissions or spills); *Field v. Philadelphia Electric Co.*, 388 Pa. Super. 400, 565 A.2d 1170 (1989) (nuclear safety expert discharged for making statutorily required report to federal agency). See also *Hays v. Beverly Enters.*, 766 F. Supp. 350 (W.D. Pa.), aff'd, 952 F.2d 1392 (3d Cir. 1991) (physician's duty does not extend to plaintiff nurse); *Gaiardo v. Ethyl Corp.*, 697 F. Supp. 1377 (M.D. Pa. 1986). aff'd, 835 F.2d 479 (3d Cir. 1987) (plaintiff not supervisor or responsible for quality control).

The court concludes that plaintiff's termination for gratuitously alerting others about defendants' improper billing practice does not violate the type of significant, clearly mandated public policy required to satisfy the new narrow exception to Pennsylvania's rigid at-will employment doctrine.

By her own characterization what plaintiff did was to "blow the whistle" on wrongful conduct by her employer. The Pennsylvania Whistleblower Law, 43 Pa. C.S.A. [Consolidated Statutes Annotated] § 1421 et seq., protects from retaliatory adverse employment action employees of public bodies or entities receiving public appropriations who report wrongdoing.* That Law, which excludes from its protection wholly private employment, has been found not to codify any previously existing legal right or privilege and held not to constitute an expression of clearly mandated public policy in the context of private at-will employment.† See *Smith*, 917 F.2d at 1346; *Cohen v. Salick Health Care, Inc.*, 772 F. Supp. 1521, 1531 (E.D. Pa. 1991) (employee discharged for alerting employer's prospective contractee of inflated financial projections); *Wagner v. General Electric Co.*, 760 F. Supp. 1146, 1155 (E.D. Pa. 1991) (employee discharged after expressing criticism of employer's product to customers).

On the other hand, courts are less reluctant to discern important public policy considerations where persons are discharged for refusing to violate the law themselves. See *Smith*, 917 F.2d at 1344; *Woodson v. AMF Leisureland Centers, Inc.*, 842 F.2d 699 (3d Cir. 1988) (refusal to sell liquor to intoxicated patron); *Shaw v. Russell Trucking Line, Inc.*, 542 F. Supp. 776, 779 (W.D. Pa. 1982) (refusal to haul loads over legal weight); *McNulty v. Borden, Inc.*, 474 F. Supp. 1111 (E.D. Pa. 1979) (refusal to engage in anti-trust violations). No employee should be forced to choose between his or her livelihood and engaging in fraud or other criminal conduct. To the extent that plaintiff appears to allege that she was also terminated for refusing herself to engage directly in fraudulent billing, her action may proceed....

An appropriate order will be entered.

## ORDER

AND NOW, this 12th day of January, 1992, upon consideration of defendants' Motion to Dismiss Plaintiff's Complaint, consistent with the accompanying memorandum, IT IS HEREBY ORDERED that said Motion is GRANTED in part and DENIED in part in that [count 1] of plaintiff's complaint [is] DISMISSED.

---

* While the Whistleblower Law protects covered employees who report impropriety to outside authorities, it does not authorize such employees to voice complaints directly to clients of a public or publicly funded entity.

† Because of the special nature of the attorney-client relationship, an attorney's misrepresentation about the source, quality, nature or cost of work performed is arguably more reprehensible than such misrepresentation to clients and customers by other suppliers of goods and services. It is not, however, sufficiently different in kind therefrom to satisfy the narrow public policy exception to Pennsylvania's stringent at-will employment doctrine.

---

*Assignment 5.1*

(a) Who won this case? What happens next? In the next proceeding in the case, what does the paralegal have to prove?

(b) Do you think a paralegal has an obligation to report unethical conduct? Should there be a "snitch rule"? If so, to whom should the report be made? See the discussion later in the chapter (p. 254) on an attorney's duty to report misconduct of another attorney. Should paralegals have a similar duty?

(c) Go to Genna H. Rosten, *Wrongful Discharge Based on Public Policy Derived from Professional Ethics Codes*, 52 A.L.R. 5th 405 (1997). You can find A.L.R. 5th in a law library or online if you have access to WESTLAW (see Chapter 11). Does this annotation discuss any decisions written by state courts in your state on the issue of firing someone in circumstances similar to those of Cynthia Brown? If so, summarize these cases—up to a maximum of three.

---

## 4. CRIME OR FRAUD BY AN ATTORNEY

*An attorney must not engage in criminal or fraudulent conduct.* **Model Rule 8.4**

Sadly, there are attorneys who are charged with criminal conduct, such as theft of client funds, securities fraud, falsification of official documents, or tax fraud. Because such conduct obviously affects the attorney's trustworthiness and fitness to practice law, sanctions for unethical conduct can be imposed in addition to prosecution in a criminal court. Once an attorney is convicted of a serious crime in court, a separate disciplinary proceeding is often instituted to suspend or disbar the attorney for unethical conduct growing out of the same incident.

If an attorney misappropriates a client's funds, the client may be able to receive compensation from a client security fund that some states have established for this purpose.

### Paralegal Perspective:

■ Value your integrity above all else. A paralegal in Oklahoma offers the following advice: "Insist on the highest standards for yourself and for your employer. One small ethical breach can lead to a series of compromises with enormous" disciplinary and "legal malpractice consequences."[7]

■ If your supervisor is charged with criminal conduct, the chances are good that you will be questioned by prosecutors, and you might become a suspect yourself.

■ In the highly charged, competitive environment of a law office, some attorneys may be willing to violate the law in the interest of winning. Be sensitive to the overt and subtle pressure on you to participate in such violations. If you are subjected to this pressure, talk with other paralegals who have encountered this problem. Don't sit in silence. If there is no one in the office with whom you can frankly discuss the elimination of these pressures, you must consider quitting. (See section E of this chapter.)

■ Paralegals who are also notaries are sometimes asked by their supervisors to notarize documents that should *not* be notarized. In fact, paralegals "are most often named as defendants for false notarization of a signature."[8] Assume that a law office is sued and the paralegal is named as one of the defendants. If the plaintiff wins, who pays the judgment? As we saw in chapter 4, the office may have a malpractice insurance liability policy that will pay judgments against it and its employees. These policies often exclude intentional acts of misconduct, however. (False notarization is usually an intentional act.) Hence, the losing defendants—including the paralegal—must pay the judgments out of their personal pockets. In short, be extremely cautious of what you are asked to sign. The same is true of documents you are asked to witness even if no formal notarization is involved. Don't sign a clause saying you witnessed something being performed or executed (called an **attestation clause**) unless you *actually* witness it.

**attestation clause** A clause saying that a person saw someone sign a document.

- Be extremely careful about using any information you learn involving a corporation whose stock is likely to change in value as a result of an event that is not yet known to the public. Assume that Company X is planning to merge with Company Y. The news is not yet public. When it does become public, the value of the stock in Company X is expected to rise dramatically. You work at a law firm that represents Company X, and you find out about the planned merger while at work. If you buy stock in Company X before the announcement of the merger, you would benefit from the increased value of the stock that would result after the announcement. This might be an illegal use of inside information, called **insider trading**. In a dramatic case, a paralegal who worked at a securities law firm in Boston was charged with insider trading by the Securities and Exchange Commission (SEC). While working on a case involving a proposed merger, she learned certain information, which she gave to outside investors who used it to make illegal profits in the stock market. The story made national news. One headline read, "SEC Says Boston Paralegal Gave Tip Worth $823,471." Soon after the incident, she was fired. All employees of law firms must be extremely careful. Innocently buying stock as a personal investment could turn into a nightmare. One attorney "recommends that any paralegal who would like to buy or sell securities should check first with a corporate attorney in the firm to see if the firm represents the issuer or a company negotiating with the issuer. If it does, an accusation of 'insider trading' might later be made."[9] The same caution applies when a member of the paralegal's immediate family buys or sells such securities.

- Another problem area is the use of so-called **pirated software**. Some businesses buy or lease one copy of computer software and then copy it so that other employees in the office can use it on other terminals. If the software manufacturer has not authorized such copying as part of the original purchase or lease agreement, the copying is illegal and can subject violators to criminal penalties and civil damages.

- In all aspects of your career as a paralegal, adopt the motto "If it doesn't feel right, it probably isn't." (See guideline 10 in exhibit 5.1 at the beginning of this chapter.)

**insider trading** Improperly using material, nonpublic information to trade in the shares of a company.

**pirated software** Software that has been placed ("loaded") in a computer that is not authorized by the terms of the purchase or lease of the software.

## 5. CRIME OR FRAUD BY A CLIENT

*If an attorney knows that future conduct of a client would be criminal or fraudulent, the attorney must not advise the client to engage in the conduct nor otherwise assist the client in engaging in it.* **Model Rule 1.2(d)**

The client hires the attorney and controls the purpose of the attorney-client relationship. Furthermore, the client is entitled to know the legal consequences of any action he or she is contemplating. This does not mean, however, that the attorney must do whatever the client wants.

> **Example:** The president of a corporation hires Leo Richards, Esq. to advise the company on how to dump toxic waste into a local river.

Note that the president has not asked Richards *if* the dumping is legal. It would be perfectly ethical for Richards to answer such a question. In the example, the president asks *how* to dump. If Richards feels that the dumping can legally take place, he can so advise the president. Suppose, however, that it is clear to Richards that the dumping would violate the federal or state criminal code. Under such circumstances, it would be unethical for Richards to advise the president on how to proceed with the dumping. The same would be true if the president wanted help in filing an environmental statement that misrepresented the intentions of the company. Such an application would be fraudulent, and an attorney must not help someone commit what the attorney knows is fraudulent conduct.

When attorneys are later charged with unethical conduct in such cases, their defense is often that they did not know the conduct proposed by the client was criminal or fraudulent. This defense can be successful. If the law applicable to the client's case is unclear, an attorney can make a good-faith effort to find a legal way for the client to achieve his or her objective. The point at which the attorney crosses the ethical line is when he or she *knows* the client is trying to accomplish something criminal or fraudulent.

### Paralegal Perspective:

■ An attorney will rarely tell paralegals or other staff members that he or she knows the office is helping a client do something criminal or fraudulent. But you might learn that this is so, particularly if there is a close, trusting relationship between you and your supervising attorney. You must let this attorney or some other authority in the office know you do not feel comfortable working on such a case.

## 6. FRIVOLOUS LEGAL POSITIONS

*An attorney must not bring a frivolous claim or assert a frivolous defense.* **Model Rule 3.1**

**adversarial system** A method of resolving disputes based on the principle that justice and truth have a greater chance of being achieved when the parties to a dispute appear (alone or through an advocate) before a neutral judge who will resolve the dispute after hearing their conflicting positions.

We often say that we have an **adversarial system** of justice. This means that our method of resolving a legal dispute is to have opposing sides fight it out before an impartial decision maker. We believe that truth and fairness are more likely to emerge when each side has an equal chance to present its case forcefully. Within this system, a client has a right to hire an attorney to be a vigorous advocate. Otherwise, there could be an imbalance in the arguments presented to the decision maker.

But there are limits on how vigorous an advocate can be. It is unethical, for example, for an attorney to assert **frivolous positions** as claims or defenses. A position is frivolous if the attorney is unable to make a good-faith argument that existing law supports the position or that existing law should be changed or reversed to support the position. A position is not necessarily frivolous simply because the attorney thinks the client will probably lose. The key is whether there is a good-faith argument to support the position. If the attorney can think of no rational support for the position, it is frivolous. Because the law is often unclear, however, it is difficult to establish that an attorney is acting unethically under the test of good faith.

**frivolous position** A position taken on behalf of a client that the attorney cannot support by a good-faith argument based on existing law or on the need for a change in existing law.

Closely related to asserting frivolous positions is the unethical practice of asserting positions for the purpose of harassing or maliciously injuring someone.

A charge of unethical conduct is not the only consequence for asserting a frivolous position. Under Rule 11 of the Federal Rules of Civil Procedure, for example, whenever an attorney in a federal case submits a motion or pleading to the court, he or she certifies that "it is not being presented for any improper purpose, such as to harass or to cause unnecessary delay or needless increase in the cost of litigation" and that "the claims, defenses, and other legal contentions therein are warranted by existing law or by a nonfrivolous argument for the extension, modification, or reversal of existing law or the establishment of new law." Violating Rule 11 can lead to sanctions by the court (e.g., a fine) in addition to a charge of unethical conduct. Many states have their own version of Rule 11 for state court cases.

### Paralegal Perspective:

■ In the heat of controversy, tempers can run high. Attorneys do not always exhibit the detachment expected of professionals. They may so thoroughly identify with the interests of their clients that they lose perspective. Paralegals working for such attorneys may get caught up in the same fever, particularly if there is a close attorney-paralegal working relationship on a high-stakes case that has lasted a considerable time. The momentum is to do whatever it takes to win. While this atmosphere can be exhilarating, it can also create an environment where less and less attention is paid to the niceties of ethics.

## 7. SAFEKEEPING PROPERTY

*An attorney shall hold client property separate from the attorney's own property.*
**Model Rule 1.15**

A law office often receives client funds or funds of others connected with the client's case—for example, attorneys receive money in settlement of a case or as trustees or escrow agents. Such funds should be held in a **client trust account**. General operating funds of the office should be kept in a separate account. There must be no **commingling** of client funds and office funds. It is unethical to place everything in one account. This is so even if the firm maintains accurate records on what amounts in the single account belong to which clients and what amounts belong to the firm. In a commingled account, the danger is too great that client funds will be used for nonclient purposes.

It is also improper for an office to misuse funds on retainer. Clients sometimes deposit funds with an office to cover future fees and expenses. The office should not draw on these fees before they are earned or withdraw the funds for expenses not yet incurred. This is so even if the funds were never commingled when deposited by the client.

**client trust account** A bank account controlled by an attorney that contains client funds that may not be used for office operating expenses or for any personal purpose of the attorney.

**commingling** Mixing general law firm funds with client funds in a single account.

### Paralegal Perspective:

■ Use great care whenever your responsibility involves client funds, such as receiving funds from clients, opening bank accounts, depositing funds in the proper account at a bank, and making entries in law firm records on such funds. It should be fairly obvious to you whether an attorney is violating the rule on commingling funds. It may be less clear whether the attorney is improperly using client funds for unauthorized purposes. Attorneys have been known to "borrow" money from client accounts and then return the money before anyone discovers what was done. They might even pay the account interest while using the money. Elaborate bookkeeping and accounting gimmicks might be used to disguise what is going on. Such conduct is unethical even if the attorney pays interest and eventually returns all the funds. In addition, the attorney may eventually be charged with theft or criminal fraud. Of course, anyone who knowingly assists the attorney could be subject to the same consequences.

## 8. FALSE STATEMENTS AND FAILURE TO DISCLOSE

*(1) An attorney must not knowingly make a false statement of an important or material fact to a court or other tribunal;*

*(2) An attorney must not knowingly cite incorrect or invalid law to a court or other tribunal;*

*(3) An attorney must not offer evidence he or she knows is false;*

*(4) An attorney must tell a court or other tribunal about a material fact when the attorney knows that silence about that fact would assist the client to commit fraud or a crime such as perjury;*

*(5) If an attorney knows of a law that goes against the claims of his or her own client, the attorney must tell a court or other tribunal about that law if he or she knows that opposing counsel has not done so, usually due to carelessness or incompetence.* **Model Rule 3.3**

One of the reasons the general public holds the legal profession in low esteem is the perception that attorneys seldom comply with the above rules. Our adversarial system does not always encourage the participants to cooperate in court proceedings. In fact, quite the opposite is often true. In extreme cases, attorneys have been known to lie to the court, to offer knowingly false evidence, etc. Under Model Rule 3.3, such conduct is unethical.

The argue-against-yourself requirement of Rule 3.3 (see the last provision) is particularly startling.

**Example:** Karen Singer and Bill Carew are attorneys who are opposing each other in a bitter trial involving a large sum of money. Singer is smarter than Carew. Singer knows about a very damaging but obscure case that goes against her client. But because of sloppy research, Carew does not know about it. Singer never mentions the case, and it never comes up during the trial.

It is certainly understandable why Singer does not want to say anything about the case. She does not want to help her opponent. But she must pay a price for her silence. She is subject to sanctions for a violation of her ethical obligation of disclosure under Model Rule 3.3.

Another controversial part of Model Rule 3.3 that has the effect of forcing an attorney to turn against his or her own client is the requirement that the attorney disclose facts that are needed to avoid assisting the client commit fraud or a crime (see the fourth provision). Because this raises issues of confidentiality, we will discuss such disclosures later when we cover confidentiality.

### Paralegal Perspective:

■ Be aware that an attorney who justifies the use of deception in one case will probably repeat such deceptions in the future on other cases. To excuse the deception, the attorney will often refer to the necessity of protecting the client or to the alleged evilness of the other side. Deceptions are unethical despite such justifications.

■ Chances are also good that employees of such an attorney will be pressured into participating in deception—for example, give a false date to a court clerk, help a client lie (commit perjury) on the witness stand, help an attorney alter a document to be introduced into evidence, or improperly notarize a document.

■ Do not compromise your integrity no matter how much you believe in the cause of the client, no matter how much you detest the tactics of the opposing side, no matter how much you like the attorney for whom you work, and no matter how important this job is to you.

## 9. WITHDRAWAL

*An attorney must withdraw from a case: if the client fires the attorney, if continuing on the case violates ethical rules or other laws, or if competent representation is jeopardized because of the attorney's physical or mental health. Withdrawal for these reasons is required unless a court or other tribunal orders the attorney not to withdraw.* **Model Rule 1.16**

Attorneys are not required to take every case. Furthermore, once they begin a case, they are not obligated to stay with the client until the case is over. If, however, the case has already begun in court after the attorney has filed a notice of appearance, withdrawal is usually improper without the permission of the court.

In some circumstances, an attorney *must* withdraw from a case that has begun:

■ The client fires the attorney. An attorney is an agent of the client. Clients are always free to dismiss their agents.

■ Representation of the client would violate ethical rules—for example, the attorney discovers that he or she has a conflict of interest with the client that cannot be **cured** or remedied even with the consent of the client.

■ Representation of the client would violate the law—for example, the client insists that the attorney provide advice on how to defraud the Internal Revenue Service.

■ The attorney's physical or mental health has deteriorated to the point where the attorney's ability to represent the client has been materially impaired. This may be due to alcohol or drug abuse, marital problems, etc.

These are examples of when the attorney *must* withdraw from the case. There may be other circumstances that do not require withdrawal but that are serious enough to give the attorney the option of withdrawing without being charged with unethically walking away from the client. This option exists, for example, if the client insists on an objective that the attorney considers repugnant or imprudent. Similarly, the attorney has the

**cure** To correct or overcome.

option of withdrawing if the attorney is experiencing an unreasonable financial burden because of the failure of the client to pay attorney fees.

Withdrawal, if allowed, must be done reasonably. An attorney should not abruptly withdraw on the eve of an important hearing or on the day before the client's cause of action dies because of the expiration of the statute of limitations. The client will need time to find other representation. The attorney should send the client a **letter of disengagement** (also called a declination letter or, pejoratively, a "kiss-off" letter). It formally notifies the client that the attorney will no longer be representing the client. The letter confirms the termination of the attorney-client relationship. It should provide the reason for the withdrawal, a summary of the scope of the representation that was attempted, and a statement of the disposition of funds, if any, remaining in the client's account. (See also chapter 8 for a discussion of the **letter of nonengagement**, which should be sent to someone the attorney has never represented if the attorney declines a request for representation.)

### Paralegal Perspective:

- When you have a close working relationship with an attorney, particularly in a small law office, you become aware of his or her professional strengths and personal weaknesses. Bar associations around the country are becoming increasingly concerned about the impaired attorney, someone who is not functioning properly due to substance abuse or similar problems. A paralegal with such an attorney for a supervisor is obviously in a predicament. Seemingly small problems have the potential of turning into a crisis. If it is not practical to discuss the situation directly with the attorney involved, you need to seek the advice of others in the firm.

### 10. CONFIDENTIALITY OF INFORMATION

*An attorney must not disclose information relating to the representation of a client unless (a) the client consents to the disclosure or (b) the attorney reasonably believes the disclosure is necessary to prevent a client from committing a criminal act that is likely to result in imminent death or substantial bodily harm.* **Model Rule 1.6**

Information is **confidential** if others do not have a right to receive it. When access to information is restricted in this way, the information is considered privileged. After we cover ethics and confidentiality, we need to examine the related topics of the attorney-client privilege and the attorney work-product rule.

### Ethics and Confidentiality

The ethical obligation to maintain confidentiality applies to all or almost all information that relates to the representation of a client, whatever its source. One court has said, "[V]irtually any information relating to a case should be considered confidential…even unprivileged client information."[10] Note also that the obligation is broader than so-called secrets or matters explicitly communicated in confidence. Confidentiality has been breached in each of the following examples:

- At a party, an attorney tells an acquaintance from another town that the law firm is representing Jacob Anderson, whose employer is trying to force him to retire. (The identity of a client is confidential.)
- At a bar association conference, an attorney tells an old law school classmate that a client named Brenda Steck is considering a suit against her brother over the ownership of property left by their deceased mother. (The identity of a client and what lawsuits she is considering are confidential.)
- A legal secretary carelessly leaves a client's file open on his desk where a stranger (e.g., another client) briefly reads parts of it. (The contents of a client file are confidential.)

The rule on confidentiality is designed to encourage clients to discuss their case fully and frankly with their attorney, including embarrassing and legally damaging information. Arguably, a client would be reluctant to be open with an attorney if he or she had to worry

**letter of disengagement** A letter sent to a client formally notifying him or her that the law office will no longer be representing the client.

**letter of nonengagement** A letter sent to a prospective client that explicitly says that the law office will not be representing him or her.

**confidential** That which should not be revealed; pertaining to information that others do not have a right to receive.

about whether the attorney might reveal the information to others. The rule on confidentiality makes it unethical for attorneys to do so. Yet this rule is not absolute. There are some important exceptions.

**consent** To waive a right; to agree.

A client can always **consent** to an attorney's disclosure about the client—*if* the client is properly consulted about the proposed disclosure in advance. Furthermore, sometimes the client implicitly authorizes disclosures because of the nature of his or her case. In a dispute over alimony, for example, the attorney would obviously have to disclose certain financial information about the client to a court or to opposing counsel during the settlement negotiations.

Disclosure can also be ethically permissible in cases involving future criminal conduct.

> **Example:** An attorney represents a husband in a bitter divorce action against his wife. During a meeting at the law firm, the husband shows the attorney a gun and says he is going to use it to kill his wife later the same day.

Can the attorney tell the police what the husband said? Yes. It is not unethical for an attorney to reveal information about a crime if the attorney reasonably believes that disclosure is necessary to prevent the client from committing a criminal act that could lead to someone's imminent death or substantial bodily harm.

Finally, some disclosures can be proper in suits between attorney and client. Suppose, for example, the attorney later sues the client for nonpayment of a fee or the client sues the attorney for malpractice. In such proceedings, an attorney can reveal information about the client if the attorney reasonably believes disclosure is necessary to present a claim against the client or to defend against the client's claim.

### Attorney-Client Privilege

**attorney-client privilege** A client and an attorney can refuse to disclose communications between them whose purpose was to facilitate the provision of legal services for the client.

The **attorney-client privilege** serves a function similar to that of the ethical rule on confidentiality. The two doctrines overlap. The attorney-client privilege is an *evidentiary* rule that applies to judicial and other proceedings in which an attorney may be called as a witness or otherwise required to produce evidence concerning a client. Under the attorney-client privilege, the attorney can refuse to disclose communications with his or her client if the purpose of the communication was to facilitate the provision of legal services for the client. The privilege also applies to paralegals and other employees of an attorney. Here is an example of a statute that extends the attorney-client privilege to paralegal employees of an attorney:

## *Who May Not Testify without Consent*

### Colorado Revised Statutes § 13-90-107(1)(b) (1996)

An attorney shall not be examined without the consent of his client as to any communication made by the client to him or [as to] his advice given thereon in the course of professional employment; nor shall an attorney's secretary, paralegal, legal assistant, stenographer, or clerk be examined without the consent of his employer concerning any fact, the knowledge of which he has acquired in such capacity.

The *ethical* rule on confidentiality tells us when sanctions can be imposed on attorneys when they (or their employees) disclose confidential client information to anyone outside the law office. The *attorney-client privilege* tells us when attorneys (or their employees) can refuse to answers questions pertaining to confidential client information.

### Attorney Work-Product Rule

Suppose that, while working on a client's case, an attorney prepares a memorandum or other in-house document that does *not* contain any confidential communications. The memorandum or document, therefore, is *not* protected by the attorney-client privilege. Can the other side force the attorney to provide a copy of the memorandum or document?

Is it **discoverable**, meaning that an opposing party can obtain information about it during discovery at the pretrial stage of a lawsuit? This question leads us to the **attorney work-product** rule.

Under this rule, the *work product* of an attorney is considered confidential. Work product consists of notes, working papers, memoranda, or similar documents and tangible things prepared by the attorney in anticipation of litigation. An example is an attorney's interoffice memorandum that lays out his or her strategy in litigating a case. Attorneys do not have to disclose their work product to the other side. It is not discoverable.[11] To the extent that such documents are not discoverable, they are privileged. (The work-product rule is sometimes referred to as the work-product privilege.)

### Inadvertent Disclosure of Confidential Material

The great fear of law office personnel is that the wrong person will obtain material that should be protected by ethics, by the attorney-client privilege, or by the work-product rule. This can have devastating consequences. For example, if a stranger overhears a confidential communication by a client to the attorney or to the attorney's paralegal, a court might rule that the attorney-client privilege has been waived. At a recent paralegal conference, a speaker told a stunned audience that a paralegal in her firm accidentally "faxed" a strategy memo on a current case to the opposing attorney! The paralegal punched in the wrong phone number on the fax machine! This could just as easily have occurred by sending an e-mail message or attachment to the wrong address.

### Paralegal Perspective:

■ Attorneys must take reasonable steps to guard against a breach of confidentiality by their paralegals or other nonattorney employees. This includes instruction on the obligation not to disclose information relating to the representation of a client. When you are hired, the firm may ask you to sign a formal confidentiality agreement in which you promise not to divulge client information to anyone who is not working on the client's case. The agreement is simply a device to stress the importance of confidentiality. You, of course, are bound to maintain confidentiality even if your employer does not ask you to sign such an agreement.

■ As we shall see later, the two major national paralegal associations also stress the ethical obligation of confidentiality in their own ethical codes (see exhibit 5.4):
  • "A legal assistant must protect the confidences of a client and must not violate any rule or statute now in effect or hereafter enacted controlling the doctrine of privileged communications between a client and an attorney." Canon 7. National Association of Legal Assistants, *Code of Ethics and Professional Responsibility*.
  • "A paralegal shall preserve all confidential information provided by the client or acquired from other sources before, during, and after the course of the professional relationship." " 'Confidential information' means information relating to a client, whatever its source, that is not public knowledge nor available to the public." Section 1.5. National Federation of Paralegal Associations, *Model Code of Ethics and Professional Responsibility*.

■ Paralegals face *many* temptations to violate confidentiality. For example, a paralegal inadvertently reveals confidential information:
  • while networking with other paralegals at a paralegal association meeting;
  • during animated conversation with another paralegal at a restaurant or on an elevator;
  • after returning home from work during casual discussions with a relative, spouse, or roommate about interesting cases at the office.
  Some paralegals make the mistake of thinking that the rule applies only to damaging or embarrassing information or that the rule simply means you should not reveal things to the other side in the dispute. Not so. The rule is much broader. Virtually all information relating to the representation of a client must not be revealed to *anyone* who is not working on the case in the office.

■ In Missouri, the obligation of silence is even broader. The paralegal must not disclose information—"confidential or otherwise"—relating to the representation of the

---

**discoverable** Obtainable through one of the devices of pretrial discovery such as interrogatories or deposition.

**attorney work-product** Notes, working papers, memoranda, or similar documents and tangible things prepared by the attorney in anticipation of litigation are not discoverable.

client.[12] In Texas, confidential information includes both privileged information and unprivileged client information. An attorney must "instruct the legal assistant that all information concerning representation of a client (indeed even the fact of representation, if not a matter of public record) must be kept strictly confidential."[13] In Philadelphia, paralegals are warned that it is "not always easy to recognize what information about your firm's clients or office is confidential. Moreover, a client of your office might be offended to learn that a…firm employee has discussed the client's business in public, even if the information mentioned is public knowledge. The easiest rule is to consider *all* work of the office to be confidential: do not discuss the business of your office or your firm's clients with any outsider, no matter how close a friend, at any time, unless you are specifically authorized by a lawyer to do so."[14] Under guidelines such as these, there is very little that paralegals can tell someone about their work!

- During the war, sailors were told that "loose lips sink ships." The same applies to law firms. One law firm makes the following statement to all its paralegals: "Throughout your employment, you will have access to information that must at all times be held in strictest confidence. Even the seemingly insignificant fact that the firm is involved in a particular matter falls within the orbit of confidential information. Unless you have attorney permission, do not disclose documents or contents of documents to anyone, including firm employees who do not need this information to do their work."[15]

- If you attend a meeting on a case outside the law office, ask your supervisor whether you should take notes or prepare a follow-up memorandum on the meeting. Let the supervisor decide whether your notes or the memo might be discoverable.[16]

- Be *very* careful when you talk with clients in the presence of third persons. Overheard conversations might constitute a waiver of the attorney-client privilege. Cellular phones can sometimes cause problems. The signal in mobile communications is transmitted by frequency over airwaves. Therefore, outsiders can listen to conversations with relative ease. If you are on a cellular phone with a client, warn him or her that confidential information should not be discussed.[17]

- Do not listen to your messages on a phone answering machine when others in the room can hear the messages as well. Clients often leave messages that contain confidential information. When using speaker phones, intercoms, or paging systems, don't broadcast confidential information. Assume that many people will be hearing you on these public systems and that most of them are not entitled to hear what you are saying.

- Make sure your door is closed when discussing a client's case.

- When working on your computer, try to position the monitor so that others cannot read the screen, especially when you need to leave your desk. Computers have programs that automatically make the screen go dark or that add a design graphic after a designated period of time when there is no typing. The screen then reappears when you continue typing. Be sure that this screen saver program is installed on your computer.

- Use a shredding machine when throwing away papers containing confidential information. When erasing confidential files from a computer, using the delete key or button may not be enough. Also delete whatever may still be retrievable in recycle or trash bin folders.

- E-mail messages on the Internet are considered sufficiently secure; it is not a violation of confidentiality to send client information by e-mail. The messages do not have to be **encrypted**. Clients, however, should be warned that e-mail communication is not foolproof. Furthermore, when highly sensitive information is to be sent, clients should be asked to state their preferred method of communication. Confidential information should never be sent through open formats such as bulletin boards and listservs because strangers are easily able to read what is sent over them.

- Find out if anyone other than the client has access to the client's e-mail. If others have such access and read messages to and from the law firm, the attorney-client privilege might be considered waived.

**encrypted** Converted into a code that renders it incomprehensible until it is reconverted to a readable format by an authorized recipient.

■ E-mail messages are sometimes sent to the wrong persons. To put unintended recipients on notice that the mistake does not mean that the message is no longer confidential, law firms routinely include notices at the bottom of every e-mail message, such as the following:

> This message is for the intended individual or entity and may contain information that is privileged. If the reader of this message is not the intended recipient, you are hereby notified that any copying, forwarding, or other dissemination of this message is strictly prohibited. If you have received this communication in error, please notify the sender immediately by e-mail or telephone, and delete the original message immediately.

■ When using vendors such as outsider printers (e.g., a company that prints appellate briefs) and copying services, make sure that they sign confidentiality agreements stating that they will not disclose the contents of any of the documents on which they will be working.

■ Use a stamp marked *privileged* on protected documents.

■ During a job interview, do not use writing samples that contain confidential information, such as the position of a particular client at a law office where you worked or volunteered in the past. Before using writing samples from actual cases, obtain the consent of your former supervisor. If the interviewer asks you about cases you worked on, don't reveal anything confidential. Your lack of professionalism in carelessly referring to confidential information during the interview will probably destroy your chances of getting the job. What about the identity of clients you worked for in prior jobs? As we will see later, prospective employers *will* need this information. It will help them determine whether hiring you could disqualify the office from representing a particular client because your prior work presents a conflict of interest as to that client.

■ One of the most dramatic legal stories of the twentieth century was the tobacco litigation of the 1990s. The cases led to billions of dollars in settlements, judgments, and attorney fees. The litigation is still going on today. A critical event in this drama was a breach of confidentiality by a paralegal. Merrell Williams was a paralegal who once worked at Wyatt, Tarrant & Combs, the largest law firm in Kentucky. The firm represented Brown & Williamson (B&W), maker of Kool and Viceroy. As a $9-an-hour paralegal, Williams was assigned to work on the numerous documents involved in the litigation. "He was sickened by what he read, as document after document showed the lengths to which the tobacco company executives had gone to cover-up the risks of smoking."[18] He secretly photocopied and distributed confidential internal memos, letters, and other documents exchanged by the law firm and its client. The documents demonstrated that the tobacco manufacturer knew about the danger of smoking but tried to cover it up. The news media made extensive use of this material. No one doubted that Williams had produced the "smoking gun" against the tobacco industry. Here is how a *Los Angeles Times* article described the impact of what Williams had done:

> Big tobacco is known as a formidable legal adversary, skilled and even ruthless in the courtroom. Yet the industry is being undone by its former secrets....Disclosure of documents [containing these secrets], many dating back forty years, has done enormous damage, outraging citizens and forcing once-helpful politicians to climb on the anti-tobacco bandwagon....The ground shifted in 1994, when an obscure paralegal, who had secretly stolen thousands of pages of documents from a [law firm representing] B&W, leaked the purloined papers to Congress and the media. The documents were an instant sensation. In one 1963 memo, for example, the [tobacco] company's former general counsel declared, "We are, then, in the business of selling nicotine, an addictive drug."...Now the blood was in the water, and so were the sharks. For 1994 also marked the formation of a powerful alliance of product liability lawyers and state attorneys general, who began filing immense new claims against the industry.[19]

Wyatt, Tarrant & Combs obtained an injunction against Merrell Williams (no longer an "obscure paralegal") to prevent him from continuing to reveal what he learned at the firm. The firm says, "Williams broke his employment contract which requires confidentiality, and stole photocopies of documents from the law office." An ex-smoker himself, Williams has undergone quadruple bypass surgery and has "threatened to seek damages for injuries allegedly caused by smoking and by his exposure during the course of his employment to information that had induced psychological suffering." *Brown & Williamson Tobacco Corp. v. Williams*, 62 F. 3d 408, 411 (D.C. Cir. 1995).

This remarkable saga raises some critical issues. Clearly, Williams violated client confidentiality. Indeed, it is difficult to think of a violation that has had a greater impact. Yet was his violation justified on moral grounds? Tobacco causes the death of thousands every year in this country and hundreds of thousands around the world. Until Williams committed his act, the tobacco industry was all but invulnerable in the legislatures and in the courts of this country. The disclosure of the documents turned the tide. Was Williams a hero or a common thief? Of course, few paralegals during a job interview will tell an interviewer that Williams is one of their heroes. Such an acknowledgment would probably frighten off any potential employer. Furthermore, the Williams case is complicated by allegations that the attorney to whom Williams gave the documents provided Williams with a home, cars, and cash, either outright or as loans. This raised the further ethical and legal issue of whether stolen evidence was being paid for and received. Nevertheless, the question remains: Was Merrell Williams engaged in an act of civil disobedience for which anyone who cares about public health should be grateful?

## 11. CONFLICT OF INTEREST

*An attorney should avoid a conflict of interest with his or her client.*

**conflict of interest** Divided loyalty that actually or potentially places a person at a disadvantage even though you owe that person undivided loyalty.

Three words strike dread in the heart of a practicing attorney: **conflict of interest**. Why? Because if it exists, it can lead to the disqualification of the attorney (and his or her entire law firm) from representing the particular client with whom the conflict exists—even if the attorney is in the middle of the representation of this client! A conflict of interest means serving two masters. More precisely, it is divided loyalty that actually or potentially places a person at a disadvantage even though you owe that person undivided loyalty. The conflict does not have to lead to actual harm; all that is needed is the *potential* for harm or disadvantage.

Conflicts of interest are not limited to law. They can exist in many settings:

**Example**: Bill Davenport is a salesman who does part-time work selling the same type of product manufactured by two competing companies.

Davenport has a conflict of interest. How can he serve two masters with the same loyalty? Normally, a company expects the undivided loyalty of people who work for it. How can Davenport apportion his customers between the two companies? There is an obvious danger that he will favor one over the other. The fact that he may try to be fair in his treatment of both companies does not eliminate the conflict of interest. A *potential* certainly exists that one of the companies will be disadvantaged. It may be that both companies are aware of the problem and are not worried. This does not mean that there is no conflict of interest; it simply means that the affected parties have consented to take the risks involved in the conflict.

Let's look at another example of how widespread these conflicts can be:

**Example**: Frank Jones is the head of the personnel department of a large company. Ten people apply for a job, one of whom is Frank's cousin.

Frank has a conflict of interest. He has loyalty to his company (pressuring him to hire the best person for the job) and a loyalty to his cousin (pressuring him to help a relative). There is a potential that the company will be disadvantaged because Frank's cousin may not be the best qualified for the job. The conflict exists even if the cousin *is* the best qualified, and even if Frank does *not* hire his cousin for the job, and even if the company *knows* about the relationship but still wants Frank to make the hiring decision. For conflict of interest to exist, all you need is the potential for disadvantage due to *divided loyalties*; you do not have to show that harm or disadvantage actually resulted.

In legal settings, conflict of interest is a major concern. To understand why, we need to examine the following topics:

(a) Business transactions with a client
(b) Loans to a client
(c) Gifts from a client
(d) Sex with a client
(e) Personal bias
(f) Multiple representation
(g) Former client/present adversary
(h) Law firm disqualification
(i) Switching jobs and "the Chinese wall"
(j) Conflicts checks

As we examine each of these topics, one of our central concerns will be whether the independence of the attorney's professional judgment is compromised in any way because of conflicting interests.

### (a) Business Transactions with a Client

Attorneys sell professional legal advice and representation. When they go beyond such services and enter a business transaction with the client, a conflict of interest can arise.

> **Example**: Janet Bruno, Esq. is Len Oliver's attorney. Oliver owns an auto repair business for which Bruno has done legal work. Oliver sells Bruno a 30 percent interest in the repair business. Bruno continues as Oliver's attorney.

Serious conflict-of-interest problems may exist here. Assume that the business runs into difficulties and Oliver considers bankruptcy. He goes to Bruno for legal advice on bankruptcy law. Bruno has dual concerns: to give Oliver competent legal advice and to protect *her own* 30 percent interest in the business. Bankruptcy may be good for Oliver but disastrous for Bruno's investment. How can an attorney give a client independent professional advice when the advice may go against the attorney's own interest? Bruno's concern for her investment creates the potential that Oliver will be placed at a disadvantage. Divided loyalties exist.

This is not to say, however, that it is always unethical for an attorney to enter a business transaction with a client. If certain strict conditions are met, it can be proper.

> *An attorney can enter a business transaction with a client if*:
>
> *(i) the terms of the business transaction are fair and reasonable to the client and are fully disclosed to the client in understandable language in writing, and*
>
> *(ii) the client is given reasonable opportunity to seek advice on the transaction from another attorney who is not involved with the transaction or the parties, and*
>
> *(iii) the client consents to the business transaction in writing.* Model Rule 1.8(a)

In our example, Oliver must be given the chance to consult with an attorney other than Bruno on letting Bruno buy a 30 percent interest in the business. Bruno would have to give Oliver a clear, written explanation of their business relationship. And the relationship must be fair and reasonable to Oliver.

In the 1990s, many start-up companies, particularly dot.com businesses, offered attorneys stock for legal services in lieu of or in addition to a cash fee. This practice is ethical as long as the requirements we have discussed are met.

### (b) Loans to a Client

An attorney, like all service providers, wants to be paid. Often a client does not have the resources to pay until *after* the case is over.

> **Example**: Harry Maxell, Esq. is Bob Smith's attorney in a negligence action in which Smith is seeking damages for serious injuries caused by the defendant. Since the accident, Smith has been

out of work and on welfare. While the case is pending, Maxell agrees to lend Smith living expenses and court-filing fees.

A debtor-creditor relationship now exists between Smith and Maxell in addition to their attorney-client relationship. The loan covering *living expenses* creates a conflict of interest. Suppose that the defendant in the negligence case makes an offer to settle the case with Smith. Should he accept the offer? There is a danger that Maxell's advice on the offer will be colored by the fact that he has a financial interest in Smith—he wants to have his loan repaid. The amount of the offer to settle may not be enough to cover the loan. Should he advise Smith to accept the offer? Accepting the offer may be in Smith's interest but not in Maxell's own interest. Such divided loyalty is an unethical conflict of interest. Model Rule 1.8(e).

The loan covering *litigation expenses*, such as filing fees and other court costs, is treated differently. Such loans can be ethical. In our example, Maxell's loan to cover the cost of the filing fees is proper.

### (c) Gifts from a Client

Clients sometimes make gifts to their attorneys or to the spouse or relative of their attorneys. Such gifts rarely create ethical problems except when a document must be prepared to complete the gift.

> **Example**: William Stanton, Esq. has been the family attorney of the Tarkinton family for years. At Christmas, Mrs. Tarkinton gives Stanton a television set and tells him to change her will so that Stanton's 10-year-old daughter would receive funds for a college education.

If a document is needed to carry out the gift, it is unethical for the attorney to prepare that document. Its preparation would create a conflict of interest. In our example, the gift of money for college involves a document—Mrs. Tarkinton's will. Note the conflict. It would be in Mrs. Tarkinton's interest to have the will written so that the executor of her will retained considerable flexibility when questions arise on how much to pay for the college education. (For example, is there to be a maximum amount? Is room and board included?) And flexibility is needed on the effect of contingencies, such as a delay or an interruption in going to college. (What happens if the daughter does not go to college until after she marries and raises her own children?) Other questions could arise as well. Stanton, of course, would want the will drafted so that his daughter received the most money possible; he does not want any contingencies in the will that might threaten receipt of the funds. It is in his interest to prepare the will so that Mrs. Tarkinton's executor has very little flexibility.

Because of this conflict, an attorney cannot prepare a document such as a will, trust, or contract that results in any substantial gift from a client to the attorney or to the attorney's children, spouse, parents, or siblings. If a client wants to make such a gift, *another* attorney who is not part of the same law firm must prepare the document. There is, however, one exception. If the client-donor is *related* to the person receiving the gift, the attorney can prepare the document. Model Rule 1.8(c).

There does not appear to be any ethical problem in taking the gift of the television set from Mrs. Tarkinton. No documents are involved.

### Paralegal Perspective:

- Can a paralegal accept a gift from a client, e.g., a Christmas present, a trip, or other bonus from a client who just won a big judgment? First of all, never consider accepting gifts from clients unless your supervising attorney approves. Considerations of which you are unaware may make the gift inappropriate. Suppose, however, it is approved, but the gift involves the preparation of a document, which the attorney prepares. Though technically not the same as the attorney preparing the document for a gift to his or her spouse or children, the similarities certainly create an appearance of impropriety. The attorney will probably want to prepare the document to achieve the maximum advantage for his or her employee. This may not be in the best interest of the client—the giver of the gift.

## (d) Sex with a Client

One of the more dramatic examples of a conflict of interest is the attorney who develops a romantic relationship with a current client, particularly a sexual relationship. Clients often come to an attorney when they are most vulnerable. Under such circumstances, it is unconscionable for the attorney to take advantage of this vulnerability. An attorney with a physical or emotional interest in a client will be looking for ways to increase that interest and to inspire a reciprocal interest from the client. Needless to say, this may not be what the client needs. But the attorney's own need could well cloud his or her ability to put the client's welfare first. The only way to maintain professional independence is for attorneys—and their paralegals and other employees as well—to avoid these kinds of relationships with current clients. When the case is over and they cease being clients, such relationships are less likely to constitute a conflict of interest.

The ABA prohibits sexual relations between attorney and client, even if consensual, unless the sexual relationship began before the attorney-client relationship began. Model Rule 1.8. Surprisingly, however, only a few states specifically mention this subject in their codes of ethics. And those that do are hesitant to impose prohibitions. In Rule 4-8.4 of the Florida code, for example, sexual conduct is prohibited only if it can be shown that the conduct "exploits the lawyer-client relationship." In Rule 3-120 of the California code, a member of the bar shall not:

(B) (1) Require or demand sexual relations with a client incident to or as a condition of any professional representation; or

(2) Employ coercion, intimidation, or undue influence in entering into sexual relations with a client; or

(3) Continue representation of a client with whom the member has sexual relations if such sexual relations cause the member to perform legal services incompetently....

(C) Paragraph (B) shall not apply to...ongoing consensual sexual relationships which predate the initiation of the lawyer-client relationship.

## (e) Personal Bias

Do you think the attorneys in the following cases have a conflict of interest?

- A homosexual attorney represents a parent seeking to deny custody to the other parent because the latter is gay.
- An attorney who believes abortion is immoral works on a case where the client is Planned Parenthood.
- An attorney whose father was murdered 10 years ago represents a client charged with murdering his wife.
- An attorney who is opposed to the death penalty is the prosecutor on a case where the state has asked for the death penalty.

These attorneys have a **bias**, which is an inclination or tendency to think and to act in a certain way. This inclination or tendency creates a danger of prejudgment. The opposite of a biased person is an objective or **disinterested** person.

In our adversarial system, as indicated earlier, clients are entitled to vigorous representation within the bounds of law and ethics. If an attorney or paralegal has strong personal feelings that go against what a client is trying to accomplish, there is a likelihood—not a guarantee—that the feelings will interfere with the ability to provide that representation. If there is interference, it is unethical to continue. (We will return to the topic of bias in chapter 8 on interviewing (See page 345.)

## (f) Multiple Representation

Rarely can a client receive independent professional counsel and vigorous representation in a case of **multiple representation** (also referred to as common representation), where the same attorney represents both sides in a dispute.

**Example:** Tom and Henry have an automobile accident. Tom wants to sue Henry for negligence. Both Tom and Henry ask Mary Franklin, Esq. to represent them in the dispute.

**bias** An inclination or tendency to think and to act in a certain way. A danger of prejudgment.

**disinterested** Not working for one side or the other in a controversy; not deriving benefit if one side of a dispute wins or loses; objective.

**multiple representation** Representing more than one side in a legal matter or controversy.

Franklin has a conflict of interest. How can she give her undivided loyalty to both sides? Tom needs to prove that Henry was negligent; Henry needs to prove that he was not negligent, and perhaps that Tom was negligent himself. How can Franklin vigorously argue that Henry was negligent and at the same time vigorously argue that Henry was not negligent? How can she act independently for two different people who are at odds with each other? Since Tom and Henry have **adverse interests**, she cannot give each her independent professional judgment. (Adverse interests are simply opposing purposes or claims.) The difficulty is not solved by Franklin's commitment to be fair and objective in giving her advice to the parties. Her role as attorney is to be a partisan advocate for the client. It is impossible for Franklin to play this role for two clients engaged in a dispute where they have adverse interests. An obvious conflict of interest would exist. In *every* state, it would be unethical for Franklin to represent Tom and Henry in this case.

**adverse interests** Opposing purposes or claims.

Furthermore, client consent would *not* be a defense to the charge of unethical conduct. Even if Tom and Henry agree to allow Franklin to represent both of them, it would be unethical for her to do so. The presence of adverse interests between the parties makes it unethical for an attorney to represent both sides with or without their consent.

Suppose, however, that the two sides do *not* have adverse interests. Certain cases must go before a court even though the parties are in agreement about everything.

> **Example:** Jim and Mary Smith are separated, and both want a divorce. They have been married only a few months. There are no children and no marital assets to divide. George Davidson, Esq. is an attorney that Jim and Mary know and trust. They decide to ask Davidson to represent both of them in the divorce.

Can Davidson ethically represent both sides here? A few states *will* allow him to do so, on the theory that there is not much of a conflict between the parties. Jim and Mary want the divorce, there is no custody battle, and there is no property to fight over. All they need is a court to decree that their marriage is legally over. Hence the potential for harm caused by multiple representation in such a case is almost nonexistent. Other states, however, disagree. They frown on multiple representation in so-called friendly divorces of this kind.

There is no absolute ban on all multiple representation in the Model Rules, although such representation is certainly discouraged:

> *If two persons have adverse interests, it would be a conflict of interest for an attorney to represent both of them unless two conditions are met. First, the attorney must reasonably believe that representing one will not adversely affect the other. Second, both persons must consent to the multiple representation after the risks of such representation are explained to them.* **Model Rule 1.7**

In the Smith example, both conditions can probably be met. Such a divorce is little more than a paper procedure; there is no real dispute between the parties. Hence Davidson would be reasonable in believing that his representation of Jim would not adversely affect Mary, and vice versa. Davidson can represent both sides so long as Jim and Mary consent to the multiple representation after Davidson explains what risks might be involved.

Nevertheless, attorneys are urged *not* to engage in multiple representation even if it is ethically proper to do so. The case may have been "friendly" at the outset, but years later, when everything turns sour, one of the parties inevitably attacks the attorney for having had a conflict of interest. Cautious attorneys *always* avoid multiple representation.

### (g) Former Client/Present Adversary

As indicated earlier, clients are encouraged to be very open with their attorney. To be able to evaluate the legal implications of a case, the attorney needs to know favorable and unfavorable information about the client. The more trust that exists between them, the more frank the client will usually be. Assume that such a relationship exists and that the case is eventually resolved. Months later another legal dispute arises between the same parties, but this time the attorney represents the other side!

**Example:** Helen Kline, Esq. represented Paul Andrews in his breach-of-contract suit against Richard Morelli, a truck distributor. Andrews claimed that Morelli failed to deliver five trucks that Andrews ordered. A court ruled in favor of Morelli. Now, a year later, Andrews wants to sue Morelli for slander. After accidentally meeting at a conference, they started discussing the truck suit. Morelli allegedly called Andrews a liar and a thief. In the slander suit, Andrews hires Michael Manna, Esq. to represent him. Morelli hires Helen Kline, Esq.

A former client is now an adversary. Kline once represented Andrews; she is now representing a client (Morelli) who is an adversary of Andrews. Without the consent of the former client (Andrews), it is unethical for Kline to switch sides and represent Morelli against him. Model Rule 1.9(a). Consent is needed (a) *when the second case is the same as the first one or when the two are substantially related* and (b) *when the former client and the present client have adverse interests in the current case.* The slander suit is substantially related to the breach-of-contract suit, since they both grew out of the original truck incident. Furthermore, in the current slander case, Andrews and Morelli clearly have adverse interests.

If the cases are the same or are substantially related, the likelihood is strong that the attorney will use information learned in the first case to the detriment of the former client in the second case. Kline undoubtedly found out a good deal about Andrews when she represented him in the breach-of-contract case. She would now be in a position to use that information *against* him while representing Morelli in the slander case.

Kline had a **duty of loyalty** when she represented Andrews. This duty does not end once the case is over and the attorney fees are paid. The duty continues if the same case arises again or if a substantially related case arises later—even if the attorney no longer represents the client. A conflict of interest exists when Kline subsequently acquires a new client who goes against Andrews in the same case or in a substantially related case. Her duty of undivided loyalty to the second client would clash with her *continuing* duty of undivided loyalty to the former client in the original case.

Suppose, however, that an attorney *can* take the second case against a former client because the second case is totally unrelated to the first. There is still an ethical duty to refrain from using any information relating to the representation in the first case to the disadvantage of the former client in the second case. There is no ethical ban on taking the case, but if the office has any information relating to the first case, that information cannot be used against the former client in the second case. Although this duty might exist, it is not easy to enforce. Think of how difficult it might be to prove that the attorney in the second case used information obtained solely from the first case.

**duty of loyalty** The obligation to protect the interests of a client without having a similar obligation to anyone else that would present an actual or potential conflict.

### (h) Law Firm Disqualification

If an attorney is disqualified from representing a client because of a conflict of interest, every attorney in the *same law firm* is also disqualified unless the client being protected by this rule consents to the representation.

**Example:** Two years ago, John Farrell, Esq. of the law firm of Smith & Smith represented the stepfather in a custody dispute with the child's grandmother. The stepfather won the case, but the grandmother was awarded limited visitation rights. The grandmother now wants to sue the stepfather for failure to abide by the visitation order. John Farrell no longer represents the stepfather. The grandmother asks John Farrell to represent her. He declines because of a conflict of interest but sends her to his law partner, Diane Williams, Esq., down the corridor at Smith & Smith.

The *stepfather* would have to consent to the representation of the grandmother by Williams. There would certainly be a conflict of interest if John Farrell tried to represent the grandmother against the stepfather. The custody dispute and the visitation dispute are substantially related. Once one attorney in a firm is disqualified because of a conflict of interest, every other attorney in that firm is also disqualified. This is known as **imputed disqualification** or vicarious disqualification. The entire firm is treated as one attorney. The disqualification of any one **tainted** attorney in the office contaminates the entire firm. Farrell's partner (Williams) is disqualified because Farrell, the tainted attorney, would be disqualified. Model Rule 1.10. Someone is tainted (also called infected) if he or she brings a conflict of interest to a law office, which thereby becomes contaminated.

**imputed disqualification** All attorneys in the same firm are ineligible to represent a client because one of the attorneys or other employees in the firm has a conflict of interest with that client.

**tainted** Having or causing a conflict of interest.

### (i) Switching Jobs and "the Chinese Wall"

Finally, we need to consider the conflict-of-interest problems that can arise from changing jobs. We just saw that there can be an imputed disqualification of an entire law firm because one of the attorneys in the firm has a conflict of interest with a client. If that attorney now goes to work for a *new* firm, can there be an imputed disqualification of the new firm because of the same conflict of interest?

> **Example:** Kevin Carlson, Esq. works at Darby & Darby. He represents Ajax, Inc., in its contract suit against World Systems, Inc. The latter is represented by Polk, Young & West. Carlson quits his job at Darby & Darby and takes a job at Polk, Young & West.

While Carlson was at Darby & Darby, he obviously acquired confidential information about Ajax. Clearly, he cannot now represent World Systems in the contract litigation against Ajax. Blatant side-switching of this kind is highly unethical. But what about other attorneys at Polk, Young & West? Is the *entire* firm contaminated and hence disqualified from continuing to represent World Systems because of the hiring of Carlson? If other attorneys at Polk, Young & West are allowed to continue representing World Systems against Ajax, there would be pressures on Carlson to tell these attorneys what he knows about Ajax. Must Polk, Young & West, therefore, withdraw from the case?

The same question can be asked about **tainted paralegals** and other nonattorney employees who switch jobs:

> **Example:** Ted Warren is a paralegal who works for Mary Winter, Esq. Winter represents Apple in the case of Apple v. IBM. Ted has substantial paralegal responsibilities on this case. While the case is still going on, Ted switches jobs. He goes to work for Quinton & Oran, which represents IBM in the litigation with Apple.

Ted is tainted. He brings a conflict of interest to the firm of Quinton & Oran. While Ted worked for Mary Winter, he obviously acquired confidential information about Apple. There are pressures on him to tell the attorneys at Quinton & Oran what he knows about Apple so that they can use the information to the advantage of their client, IBM, in the litigation against Apple. Is the entire firm of Quinton & Oran, therefore, contaminated so that it must now withdraw from the case?

There are two main ways that contaminated law offices *try* to avoid imputed disqualification due to tainted attorneys or tainted paralegals whose job switching creates a conflict of interest: consent and screening.

**Consent**   The cleanest way a contaminated law office can avoid imputed disqualification is to try to obtain the consent of the party who has the most to lose—the party whose confidentiality is in jeopardy. In most cases, the consent of this person will avoid disqualification.

> **In our example of the tainted attorney:** Kevin Carlson, Esq. once represented Ajax at Darby & Darby in the litigation against World Systems. Carlson now works for Polk, Young & West, which represents World Systems. Ajax could be asked to consent to the continued representation of World Systems by Polk, Young & West even though Carlson now works for Polk, Young & West.
>
> **In our example of the tainted paralegal:** Ted Warren once worked for the law office of Mary Winter, Esq. who represents Apple in the litigation against IBM. Warren now works for Quinton & Oran, which represents IBM. Apple could be asked to consent to the continued representation of IBM by Quinton & Oran even though Warren now works for Quinton & Oran.

It is unlikely that clients will give their consent in such situations. Their current attorney will probably advise them that the risks are too great that the tainted employee will share (or has already shared) confidential information with the new employer. This is true even if the new employer swears that no such information was shared and promises that it will screen the tainted employee (see discussion of the Chinese Wall below) from the ongoing litigation.

**Screening**   The contaminated law office will often try to avoid imputed disqualification by screening the tainted employee from the case in question. As we will see, however, it is not always successful. The screening is known as a **Chinese Wall** (sometimes called an eth-

---

**tainted paralegal** A paralegal who brings a conflict of interest to a law firm because of the paralegal's prior work at another law firm.

**Chinese Wall** Steps taken to prevent a tainted employee (e.g., attorney or paralegal) from having any contact with the case of a particular client in the office with whom that employee has a conflict of interest; a tainted employee shielded by a Chinese Wall becomes a quarantined employee.

ical wall or a cone of silence) that is built around the tainted employee who brought the conflict of interest into the office. He or she becomes the **quarantined** employee. The components of the Chinese Wall are outlined in exhibit 5.5.

**quarantined** Isolated; kept away from information that would disqualify the firm.

We said that consent is a clear way to avoid imputed disqualification. What about screening? Can it avoid disqualification if consent cannot be obtained? In this discussion, we are assuming that the tainted employee has not already communicated confidential information to the new employer. If this has happened, screening will not prevent disqualification. Hence, in our examples, if Kevin Carlson tells attorneys at Polk, Young & West anything significant he knows about Ajax, the Polk firm will be disqualified from continuing to represent World Systems. If Ted Warren tells attorneys at Quinton & Oran anything significant he knows about Apple, the Quinton firm will be disqualified from continuing to represent IBM. Screening will never prevent disqualification if the damage has already been done by improper disclosures from the tainted employee. The purpose of the screening is to *prevent* such disclosures.

Suppose that there have been no disclosures. The office discovers that one of its employees is tainted. It then offers to quarantine this employee by building a Chinese Wall around him or her. Will this prevent disqualification in the absence of consent? Not all states answer this question in the same way, and the answer may differ if the tainted employee is an attorney as opposed to a paralegal or other nonattorney.

---

| EXHIBIT 5.5 | Components of a Chinese Wall |
|---|---|

The following are the most effective guidelines a law office can follow to screen a tainted employee (e.g. attorney, paralegal, investigator, secretary) who brings a conflict of interest to the office. The goal is to avoid imputed disqualification by isolating the employee from the case in which he or she has the conflict of interest.

1. The screening begins as soon as the tainted employee arrives at the office.
2. The tainted employee signs a statement promising not to discuss what he or she knows about the case with anyone in the office.
3. Those working on the case in the office promise not to discuss it with, or in the presence of, the tainted employee.
4. There is a written policy notifying everyone in the office that the screening mechanisms are in place and that violations will result in sanctions.
5. If there are several attorneys working in the office, the tainted employee will not be assigned to work with any untainted attorney handling the case in question.
6. Others not working on the case in the office are told that if they learn anything about the case, they must not discuss it with the tainted employee.
7. The receptionist and mail handlers are instructed not to forward anything about the case to the tainted employee.
8. The tainted employee works in an area that is physically segregated from work on the case in the office. This area is designed to avoid inadvertent access to the case file.
9. The file in the case is locked in cabinets or other storage facilities so that the tainted employee will have no access to the file.
10. Colored labels or "flags" are placed on each document in the file to indicate it is off limits to the tainted employee. For example, a sticker might say, "ACCESS RESTRICTED."
11. If any office files are located on a central computer system to which everyone has access, either the file in question is removed and placed in a separate database to which the tainted employee does not have access and/or the tainted employee is not given the password that grants a user access to the restricted file in the central system.
12. The tainted employee will not directly earn any profit from, participate in the fees of, or obtain any other financial gain from the case.
13. The firm documents all of the above steps that are taken. This documentation will become evidence, if ever needed, to rebut the presumption that the tainted employee had any communication or other involvement with anyone working on the case at the firm.

**Tainted Attorneys** In some states, a Chinese Wall will *not* avoid imputed disqualification. These states doubt that the tainted attorney will be able to resist the pressure to disclose what he or she knows in spite of the screening mechanisms of the Wall. "Whether the screen is breached will be virtually impossible to ascertain from outside the firm."[20]

Other states, however, do not automatically impose the extreme sanction of disqualification. These states consider three main factors in deciding whether to disqualify. First, how soon did the office erect the Wall around the tainted attorney? Courts like to see the Wall in place at the outset of the employment transfer. They are more suspicious if the Wall was not built until the other side (i.e., the former employer of the tainted attorney) raised the conflict-of-interest objection. Second, how effective was the Wall in preventing the tainted attorney from having contact with the case at the new firm? Courts like to see comprehensive screening devices that are scrupulously enforced. (See exhibit 5.5.) And, third, how involved was the tainted attorney in the case while at the previous firm? If the involvement was relatively minor, the court is less likely to be concerned.

**Tainted Paralegals** Courts are more sympathetic to tainted paralegals—so long as they have not actually revealed confidential information to their new employer and are effectively quarantined by a Chinese Wall. Here are some of the major developments in this area:

- In *Phoenix Founders, Inc. v. Marshall*, 887 S.W.2d 831 (Tex. 1994), a paralegal worked on a case at one firm and then switched jobs to work for opposing counsel on the same case. The court said that if a paralegal does any work on a case, there is a conclusive presumption that he or she obtained "confidences and secrets" about that case. There is also a presumption that the paralegal shared this information with her new firm, *but this presumption is not conclusive*; it can be rebutted by showing that the new firm took "sufficient precautions…to guard against any disclosure of confidences" through a Chinese Wall. At the new firm, "the newly-hired paralegal should be cautioned not to disclose any information relating to the representation of a client of the former employer. The paralegal should also be instructed not to work on any matter on which the paralegal worked during the prior employment, or regarding which the paralegal has information relating to the former employer's representation. Additionally, the firm should take other reasonable steps to ensure that the paralegal does not work in connection with matters on which the paralegal worked during the prior employment." In some circumstances, however, disqualification will always be required unless the former client consents to allow the paralegal to continue working at the new firm: "(1) when information relating to the representation of an adverse client has in fact been disclosed, or (2) when screening would be ineffective or the nonlawyer necessarily would be required to work on the other side of a matter that is the same as or substantially related to a matter on which the nonlawyer has previously worked…." In effect, there will be disqualification if there is proof the paralegal made actual disclosures of confidential information to the new firm or if there is little chance the screening of the Chinese Wall would be effective.[21]
- What's it like to work behind a Chinese Wall? Calling it a "deadly cone of silence," a Los Angeles paralegal described the experience of being quarantined this way: "I was a problem….I was put behind an ethical wall, and could hardly walk anywhere in the firm without having to shut my eyes and ears or look the other direction."[22]
- Many paralegals change jobs frequently. The market for experienced paralegals is outstanding. Bar associations realize that an overly strict disqualification rule could severely hamper the job prospects for such paralegals. In Informal Opinion 88-1526, the American Bar Association said:

  > It is important that nonlawyer employees have as much mobility in employment opportunity as possible consistent with the protection of clients' interests. To so limit employment opportunities that some nonlawyers trained to work with law firms might be required to leave the careers for which they are trained would disserve clients as well as the legal profession. Accordingly, any restrictions on the nonlawyer's employment should be held to the minimum necessary to protect confidentiality of client information.

Although such statements are comforting, the reality is that tainted paralegals are in a very vulnerable position. Many contaminated offices *terminate* the tainted paralegal who caused the contamination. Rather than take the risk that a Chinese Wall built around this paralegal will be judged too little and too late, the office will take the safer course and let the paralegal go.

■ In one dramatic case, a contaminated paralegal caused a San Francisco law firm to be disqualified from representing nine clients in asbestos litigation involving millions of dollars. The sole reason for the disqualification was that the firm hired a paralegal who had once worked for a law firm that represented the opponents in the asbestos litigation. Soon after the controversy arose, the disqualified firm laid off the tainted paralegal who brought this conflict to the firm. He was devastated when he found out that he was being let go. "I was flabbergasted, totally flabbergasted." He has not been able to find work since.[23] The case was widely reported throughout the legal community. A front-page story in the *Los Angeles Daily Journal* said that it "could force firms to conduct lengthy investigations of paralegals and other staffers before hiring them."[24]

■ A court rule in one state provides as follows:

> Rule 20-108. A lawyer is responsible to ensure that no personal, social or business interest or relationship of the legal assistant impinges upon, or appears to impinge upon, the services rendered to the client. *Comment.* If a lawyer accepts a matter in which the legal assistant may have a conflict of interest, the lawyer will exclude that legal assistant from participation in any services performed in connection with that matter. Furthermore, the lawyer must specifically inform the client that a nonlawyer employee has a conflict of interest which, was it the lawyer's conflict, would prevent further representation of the client in connection with the matter. The nature of the conflict should be disclosed. The lawyer will caution the legal assistant to inform the lawyer of any interest or association which might constitute or cause such a conflict, or which might give the appearance of constituting or causing such a conflict. In addition, no interest or loyalty of the legal assistant may be permitted to interfere with the lawyer's independent exercise of professional judgment. New Mexico Rules of Court.

■ One law firm makes the following statement to all its paralegals: "If you or a temporary legal assistant working under your supervision were formerly employed by opposing counsel, this could be the basis for a motion to disqualify" this law firm. "So also could personal relationships such as kinship with the opposing party or attorney or dating an attorney from another firm. Make your attorney aware of such connections."[25]

■ If you have worked (or volunteered) for an attorney in the past in *any* capacity (as a paralegal, as an investigator, as a secretary, etc.), you should make a list of all the clients and cases with which you were involved. When you apply for a new job, your list will be relevant to whether the law firm will be subject to disqualification if you are hired. You must be careful with the list, however. Do not attach it to your résumé and randomly send it around town! Until employment discussions have become serious, do not show it to the prospective employer. Furthermore, try to notify prior attorneys with whom you have worked that you are applying for a position at a law firm where its "conflicts check" on you must include knowing what cases you worked on with previous attorneys. Giving them this notice is not always practical and may not be required. Yet it is a safe procedure to follow whenever possible.

■ Freelance or independent paralegals who work for more than one law office on a part-time basis are particularly vulnerable to conflict-of-interest charges. For example, in a large litigation involving many parties, two opposing attorneys might unknowingly use the same freelance paralegal to work on different aspects of the same case or might use two different employees of this freelance paralegal. Another example is the freelance paralegal who worked on an earlier case for a client and now works on a different but similar case in which that client is the opponent. Attorneys who use freelance or independent paralegals, therefore, must be careful. The attorney cannot simply turn over work and be available to answer questions. At a minimum, the attorney must make inquiries about this paralegal's prior client casework for other attorneys in order to determine whether there are any conflicts.[26]

### (j) Conflicts Checks

**conflicts check** A determination of whether a conflict of interest exists that might disqualify a law firm from representing a client or from continuing the representation.

A prospective client walks in the door or someone makes a referral of a prospective client. How does the office determine whether any of its attorneys, paralegals, or other nonattorney employees have a conflict of interest with this prospect? A **conflicts check** must be undertaken. To perform this check, the office needs a comprehensive database containing information such as the following about every former and present client of the office:

- Names of clients (plus any aliases or earlier names before marriage)
- Names of spouses of clients
- Names of children of clients
- Names of key employees of clients (including the chief executive officers and directors of corporate clients)
- Names of major shareholders in companies in which the client has an interest
- Names of parent and subsidiary corporations affiliated with the client, plus their chief executive officers and directors
- Names of members of small associations the client controls or is a member of[27]

**conflicts specialist** A law firm employee, often a paralegal, who helps the firm determine whether a conflict of interest exists between prospective clients and current or former clients.

It is often an arduous job to find and check this information to determine whether any possible conflict exists. Some offices have hired paralegals to go through the office's computer files to try to identify conflict problems that must be addressed by senior attorneys in the office. (These paralegals are sometimes called **conflicts specialists** or conflicts technicians.) Unfortunately, however, many offices perform conflicts checks carelessly or not at all.

Similar information is needed when the office is thinking about hiring a new attorney or paralegal from another office (called a **lateral hire**). To determine whether they might contaminate the office, the names of the parties in their prior casework must be checked against the office's current and prospective clients.

**lateral hire** An attorney, paralegal, or other employee who has been hired from another law firm.

When a law office applies for malpractice insurance, the insurance carrier will often inquire about the system the office uses for conflicts checks. See exhibit 5.6 for examples of questions asked by one of the major liability insurance companies.

Some categories of information are sometimes difficult for the office to obtain. For example:

- Whether an employee in the office holds stock in the company of the adversary of a prospective client
- Whether a spouse, relative, or intimate friend of an employee in the office is employed by or holds stock in the company of the adversary of a prospective client
- Whether an employee in the office is related to or has had a romantic relationship with the adversary of a prospective client
- Whether an employee in the office is related to or has had a romantic relationship with anyone in the law office that represents the adversary of a prospective client

To discover this kind of information, the office usually must rely on its employees to come forward and reveal such connections.

Most litigation support software (see chapters 10 and 13) has conflicts-checking functions that enable a law firm to comb through the law firm's database(s) to find possible conflicts. See exhibit 5.7 for an example.

### 12. COMMUNICATION WITH THE OTHER SIDE

*If an opposing party is represented by an attorney, the permission of the party's attorney is needed to communicate with that party concerning the subject of the case.* **Model Rule 4.2**

*An unrepresented opposing party must not be misled into thinking that you are neutral or uninvolved in the case. The only advice you can give an unrepresented opposing party is to obtain his or her own attorney.* **Model Rule 4.3**

| EXHIBIT 5.6 | Questions on Malpractice Insurance Application about Conflict-of-Interest Avoidance |
|---|---|

### ADMINISTRATIVE SYSTEMS AND PROCEDURES—CONFLICT OF INTEREST

| | Yes | No |
|---|---|---|
| 22. Do you have a written internal control system for maintaining client lists and identifying actual or potential conflicts of interest? | ☐ | ☐ |
| 23. How does the firm maintain its conflict of interest avoidance system? ☐ Oral/Memory  ☐ Single Index Files  ☐ Multiple Index Files  ☐ Computer | | |
| 24. Have the firm members disclosed, in writing, all actual conflicts of interest and conflicts they reasonably believe may exist as a result of their role as director, officer, partner, employee or fiduciary of an entity or individual other than the applicant firm? | ☐ | ☐ |
| 25. Do firm members disclose to their clients, in writing, all actual conflicts of interest and conflicts they reasonably believe may exist? | ☐ | ☐ |
| 26. Upon disclosure of actual or potential conflicts, do firm members always obtain written consent to perform ongoing legal services? | ☐ | ☐ |
| 27. Has the firm acquired, merged with or terminated a formal business relationship with another firm within the last three years? | ☐ | ☐ |
| 28. Does the firm's conflict of interest avoidance system include attorney-client relationships established by predecessor firms, merged firms and acquired firms? | ☐ | ☐ |

**Source**: The St. Paul Fire and Marine Insurance Company, Professional Liability Insurance Application for Lawyers.

The ethical concern here is that an attorney will take unfair advantage of the other side.

> **Example**: Dan and Theresa Kline have just separated and are thinking about a divorce. Each claims the marital home. Theresa hires Thomas Farlington, Esq. to represent her. Farlington calls Dan to ask him if he is interested in settling the case.

It is unethical for Farlington to contact Dan about the case if Farlington knows that Dan has his own attorney. Farlington must talk with Dan's attorney. Only the latter can give Farlington permission to communicate with Dan. If Dan does not have an attorney, Farlington can talk with Dan, but he must not allow Dan to be misled about Farlington's role. Farlington works for the other side; he is not *disinterested*. Dan must be made to understand this fact. The only advice Farlington can give Dan in such a situation is to obtain his own attorney.

### Paralegal Perspective:

- The ethical restrictions on communicating with the other side apply to the employees of an attorney as well as to the attorney. "The lawyer's obligation is to ensure that the legal assistants do not communicate directly with parties known to be represented by an attorney, without that attorney's consent, on the subject of such representation."[28] You must avoid improper communication with the other side. If the other side is a business or some other large organization, do not talk with anyone there unless your supervisor tells you that it is ethical to do so. Never call the other side and pretend you are someone else in order to obtain information.
- If your office allows you to talk with someone who is not represented by an attorney, you cannot give this person any advice other than the advice to secure his or her own attorney.

| EXHIBIT 5.7 | Example of Conflicts Checking by Computer |
|---|---|

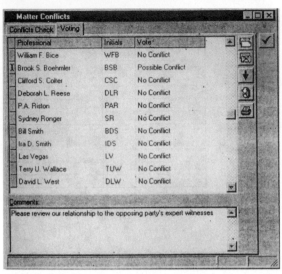

**Source:** ProLaw Software (www.prolaw.com)

## 13. SOLICITATION

There are two main ways that attorneys seek to be hired by prospective clients:

(a) *Live solicitation in person or on the phone.* Such solicitation is never ethical unless the attorney already has a family or professional relationship with the prospective client or unless the attorney's main goal is not to earn fees. Model Rule 7.3

(b) *Written or recorded solicitation in the mail or on the phone.* Such solicitation is always ethical unless the solicitation constitutes harassment or duress or unless the attorney already knows that the prospective client does not want to be solicited. Model Rule 7.3

People in distress are sometimes so distraught that they are not in a position to evaluate their need for legal services. They should not be subjected to pressures from an attorney who shows up wanting to be hired, particularly if the attorney is not a relative or has never represented them in the past. Such in-person **solicitation** of clients is unethical, if the attorney has a monetary goal such as generating fees.

> **Example:** Rachael Winters, Esq. stands outside the police station and gives a business card to any individual being arrested. The card says that Winters is an attorney specializing in criminal cases.

Winters is obviously looking for prospective clients. Doing so in this manner is referred to as **ambulance chasing**, which is a pejorative term for aggressively tracking down anyone who probably has a legal problem in order to drum up business. (An unkind member of Congress recently told an audience, "If you want to meet a trial lawyer, follow an ambulance."[29]) There is no indication that Winters is related to any of the people going into the police station or that she has any prior professional relationship with them (for example, they are *not* former clients). Winters appears to have one goal: finding a source of fees. Hence her conduct is unethical. Direct, in-person, or live telephone solicitation of clients in this way is not allowed. The concern is that an attorney who approaches strangers in trouble may exert undue influence on them. This is less likely to occur if the solicitation comes in the mail or through a prerecorded phone message, even though it is directed at individuals known to need legal services.

> **Example:** An attorney obtains the names of homeowners facing foreclosure and sends them the following letter: "It has come to my attention that your home is being foreclosed. Federal law may allow you to stop your creditors and give you more time to pay. Call my office for legal help."

While critics claim that such solicitation constitutes "ambulance chasing by mail," the technique is ethical in most states as long as it is truthful and not misleading. *In-person* (i.e.,

**solicitation** A request; a step taken to obtain something.

**ambulance chasing** Approaching accident victims (or others with potential legal claims) to encourage them to hire a particular attorney.

face-to-face) *or live telephone* solicitation, however, is treated differently because of the obvious pressure that it imposes. It is "easier to throw out unwanted mail than an uninvited guest."[30]

Although truthful direct-mail solicitations cannot be prohibited, they can be regulated by the state. For example, the state may require the attorney to print the phrase "Advertising Material" on the outside of the envelope and may prohibit all solicitations to victims and their relatives for a designated number of days after the accident or disaster for which the attorney is offering legal services. Some federal laws impose additional restrictions. For example, Congress has passed the Aviation Disaster Family Assistance Act, which provides that in the event of an air carrier accident:

> [N]o unsolicited communication concerning a potential action for personal injury or wrongful
> death may be made by an attorney or any potential party to the litigation to an individual injured
> in the accident, or to a relative of an individual injured in the accident, before the 30th day following
> the date of the accident. 49 U.S.C. § 1136 (g)(2).

In extreme cases, client solicitation can constitute the crime of **barratry** in some states. For example, in 1990, three attorneys and an employee of a law firm were indicted in Texas. They were charged with illegally seeking clients at hospitals and funeral homes soon after 21 students were killed and 69 others were injured in a school bus accident.[31]

**barratry** The crime of stirring up quarrels or litigation; persistently instigating lawsuits, often groundless ones. The illegal solicitation of clients.

### Paralegal Perspective:

- An unscrupulous attorney may try to use a paralegal to solicit clients for the office.

  **Example:** Bill Hill is a senior citizen who lives at a home for senior citizens. Andrew Vickers, Esq. hires Bill as his "paralegal." His sole job is to contact other seniors with legal problems and to refer them to Vickers.

Andrew Vickers is engaging in unethical solicitation through Bill Hill. Attorneys cannot hire a paralegal to try to accomplish what they cannot do themselves. Nor can they use a **runner**—an employee or independent contractor who contacts personal injury victims or other potential clients in order to solicit business for an attorney. If this person uses deception or fraud in the solicitation, he or she is sometimes called a *capper* or a *steerer*. An example would be someone who arranges for an unsuspecting motorist to be involved in a crash with another vehicle, whose driver (by prearrangement with the capper) flees after the collision. The capper then solicits the motorist to hire an attorney for purposes of filing an insurance claim.

**runner** Someone who solicits clients, usually personal injury clients for an attorney.

- See also the earlier discussion of fees in which we covered the related topics of unethically splitting fees with a nonattorney and paying someone to recommend the services of an attorney (page 225)

## 14. ADVERTISING

***Attorneys may advertise in the newspaper, on television, on the Internet, or through other media so long as the advertisements are truthful and do not mislead the public such as by creating unjustified expectations of the results the attorney will be able to obtain.* Model Rule 7.2**

At one time, almost all forms of advertising by attorneys were prohibited. Traditional attorneys considered advertising to be highly offensive to the dignity of the profession. In 1977, however, the United States Supreme Court stunned the legal profession by holding that truthful advertising cannot be completely banned.[32] The First Amendment protects such advertising. Furthermore, advertising does not pose the same danger as in-person or live telephone solicitation by an attorney. A recipient of advertising is generally under very little pressure to buy the advertised product—in this case, an attorney's services. Hence attorneys can ethically use truthful, nonmisleading advertising to the general public in order to generate business.

Studies have shown that more than one-third of all attorneys in the country engage in some form of advertising. Most of it consists of listings in the Yellow Pages. The use of other marketing tools is also on the rise. Attorneys spend almost $200 million every year on television advertising alone. Former United States Chief Justice Warren Burger commented that some attorney ads "would make a used-car dealer blush with shame." Proponents of attorney advertising, however, claim that it has made legal services more accessible to the public and has provided the public with a better basis for choosing among available attorneys.

Many law firms today have Internet pages on the World Wide Web (see appendix 2A at the end of chapter 2). They are designed to provide the public with general information about the firm, particularly the kind of legal services they offer. In addition, some of the firms' web pages go into detail about an aspect of the law that is relevant to their practice. For example, a family law attorney might have several pages that list the grounds for divorce in the state or the steps to take to establish paternity. Large law firms may have elaborate web pages that include pictures of attorneys in the firm and the names and e-mail addresses of its attorneys and paralegals. To avoid the charge that a law firm is practicing law on the Internet, a disclaimer will often be printed on the home page that tells readers that the site is not intended to establish an attorney-client relationship or to provide legal advice. The goal is to make clear that the site is simply advertising the firm. As such, it must meet the ethical requirements for advertising, e.g., be truthful and not misleading. The disclaimer should also warn viewers that the law of each state may differ; that the firm makes no representation, warranty, or claim that the information on the site is current or accurate; and that viewers should not rely on the information provided on the site without consulting local attorneys. There will often be an e-mail address on the site that a viewer or prospective client can use to contact the firm. Care must be taken in responding to such e-mail messages that no legal advice is given, particularly to individuals outside the state where the attorneys in the firm are licensed to practice law. The sender should be told that the firm cannot maintain the confidentiality of any communications sent through the web site and that, until a conflicts check is made, the firm cannot agree to represent anyone. One law firm concludes its disclaimer with this blunt statement: "You are not the client of this firm simply because you send us an e-mail message."[33]

### Paralegal Perspective:

- In California, the titles *paralegal* and *legal assistant* cannot be used by freelancers (independent contractors) who do not work under the supervision of attorneys. In their advertising, they must call themselves legal document assistants (LDAs) or unlawful detainer assistants (UDAs). (See chapter 4 and appendix G.)
- Bankruptcy petition preparers are not allowed to use the word *legal* or any similar term in their advertising. Some courts have concluded that they cannot use the word *paralegal*. (See chapter 4.)

## 15. REPORTING PROFESSIONAL MISCONDUCT

*Attorneys with knowledge that another attorney has violated the ethical rules must report this attorney to the appropriate disciplinary body if the violation is serious enough to cast substantial doubt on the attorney's trustworthiness or fitness to practice law.*
**Model Rule 8.3**

Attorneys may pay a price for remaining silent when they become aware of unethical conduct. The failure of an attorney to report another attorney may mean that both attorneys can be disciplined for unethical behavior. This is known as the "rat rule," the "snitch rule," or, more euphemistically, the "whistleblower rule." Not every ethical violation must be reported, however. The ethical violation must raise a substantial question of the attorney's trustworthiness or fitness to practice law.

### Paralegal Perspective:

- Suppose that a paralegal observes his or her supervising attorney commit fraud, steal from client funds, or use perjured testimony. Clearly, the paralegal has an obligation to avoid participating in such conduct. Such assistance could subject the paralegal to criminal and civil penalties. The problem is real; sooner or later unethical attorneys will probably ask or pressure their paralegals to participate in the unethical conduct.

But is the paralegal under an ethical obligation to report the offending attorney to the bar association or other disciplinary body? The National Federation of Paralegal Associations (NFPA) thinks so. In its *Model Code of Ethics and Professional Responsibility*, the obligation is stated as follows in EC-1.2(f):

> A paralegal shall advise the proper authority of non-confidential knowledge of any dishonest or fraudulent acts by any person pertaining to the handling of the funds, securities or other assets of a client. The authority to whom the report is made shall depend on the nature and circumstances of the possible misconduct, (e.g., ethics committees of law firms, corporations and/or paralegal associations, local or state bar associations, local prosecutors, administrative agencies, etc.). Failure to report such knowledge is in itself misconduct and shall be treated as such under these rules.

As pointed out earlier, ethical rules written by paralegals are not binding in the sense that they affect the paralegal's right to work as a paralegal. A paralegal who violates EC.-1.2(f) by failing to report his or her attorney to the bar association might be kicked out of the paralegal association that has adopted NFPA's *Model Code*, but it is highly unlikely that this will affect his or her employment prospects.

What then should a conscientious paralegal do? Here are some guidelines. First and foremost, do not participate directly or indirectly in the unethical conduct. Second, consult with fellow paralegals in the office and in your local paralegal association. Without naming names and without breaching client confidentiality, find out how others have handled similar predicaments on the job. Third, go to a senior officer at the firm, e.g., a partner, and let him or her know that the conduct you have observed is troubling you. You may need to confront the offending attorney himself or herself. Whomever you approach, be sure to have your facts straight! What appears to you to be an ethical violation may simply be aggressive or zealous advocacy that is on the edge but still within the bounds of propriety.

Should you go to the bar association or to a law enforcement agency? This is obviously a very tough question. The answer may depend on whether you have exhausted available routes within the office to resolve the matter to your satisfaction and, more important, whether you think this is the only way to prevent serious harm to a client. (See also An Ethical Dilemma: Your Ethics or Your Job! later in the chapter.)

If you do report an attorney in your office and you are fired or retaliated against in some other way, do you have any recourse? Review the case of *Brown v. Hammond* earlier in the chapter (page 228).

## 16. APPEARANCE OF IMPROPRIETY

How would you feel if you were told that, even though you have not violated any rule, you are still going to be punished because what you did *appeared* to be improper? That would be the effect of an obligation to avoid even the appearance of professional impropriety. In some states, it is unethical for attorneys to engage in such appearances. The ABA *Model Rules*, however, does not list appearance of impropriety as an independent basis for determining unethical conduct. To be disciplined in states that have adopted the *Model Rules*, an attorney must violate one of the specific ethical rules. Yet even in these states, conservative attorneys are as worried about apparent impropriety as they are about specific, actual impropriety.

## 17. UNAUTHORIZED PRACTICE OF LAW

*An attorney shall not assist a nonattorney in the unauthorized practice of law (UPL).* **Rule 5.5(b)**

In chapter 4, we saw that it is a crime in many states for a nonattorney to engage in the **unauthorized practice of law**. Our main focus in chapter 4 was the nonattorney who works for an office other than a traditional law office. An example would be an in-

**unauthorized practice of law** Engaging in acts that require either a license to practice law or other special authorization by a person who does not have the license or special authorization.

dependent paralegal who owns a do-it-yourself divorce office that sells kits and typing services. Now our focus is the nonattorney who works under the supervision of an attorney in a law office. We want to explore the ways in which attorneys might be charged with unethically assisting *their own paralegals* in engaging in the unauthorized practice of law. For example, an attorney might allow a paralegal to give legal advice, to conduct depositions, or to sign court documents. These areas will be discussed below along with an overview of other major ethical issues involving paralegals.

## 18. PARALEGALS

We turn now to a more direct treatment of when attorneys can be disciplined for the unethical use of paralegals. We will cover the following topics:

    (a) Paralegals, the ABA *Model Code*, and the ABA *Model Rules*
    (b) Misrepresentation of paralegal identity or status
    (c) Doing what only attorneys can do
    (d) Absentee, shoulder, and environmental supervision

### (a) Paralegals, the ABA *Model Code*, and the ABA *Model Rules*

The first major statement by the American Bar Association on the ethical use of paralegals by attorneys came in its *Model Code of Professional Responsibility:*

> DR 3-101(A): A lawyer shall not aid a nonlawyer in the unauthorized practice of law.
>
> EC 3-6: A lawyer often delegates tasks to clerks, secretaries, and other lay persons. Such delegation is proper if the lawyer maintains a direct relationship with his client, supervises the delegated work, and has complete professional responsibility for the work product. This delegation enables a lawyer to render legal services more economically and efficiently.

The following 1967 opinion elaborated on these standards:

---

### *Formal Opinion 316*
**American Bar Association, 1967**

A lawyer can employ lay secretaries, lay investigators, lay detectives, lay researchers, accountants, lay scriveners, non-lawyer draftsmen or non-lawyer researchers. In fact, he may employ non-lawyers to do any task for him except counsel clients about law matters, engage directly in the practice of law, appear in court or appear in formal proceedings as part of the judicial process, so long as it is he who takes the work and vouches for it to the client and becomes responsible for it to the client. In other words, we do not limit the kind of assistance that a lawyer can acquire in any way to persons who are admitted to the Bar, so long as the non-lawyers do not do things that lawyers may not do or do the things that lawyers only may do.

---

From these documents we learn that an attorney can hire a paralegal and is responsible for what the paralegal does. There are two levels of this responsibility: civil liability for malpractice and ethical liability for violation of ethical rules. In chapter 4, we discussed civil liability for malpractice under the topic of respondeat superior and negligence. Here in chapter 5 our primary focus is on ethical violations by attorneys based on what their paralegals do or fail to do.

> **Example:** The law firm of Adams & Adams represents Harold Thompson in his negligence suit against Parker Co. At the firm, Elaine Stanton, Esq. works on the case with Peter Vons, a paralegal whom she supervises. Peter neglects to file an important pleading in court and carelessly gives confidential information about Thompson to the attorney representing Parker. All of this causes Thompson great damage.

Stanton is fully responsible to the client, Thompson, who might decide to bring a malpractice suit in court against her. She cannot hide behind the fact that her paralegal was at fault.

(See the discussion of malpractice liability and respondeat superior in chapter 4. See also appendix F for examples of attorney negligence in supervising staff.)

What about ethics? Can Stanton be reprimanded, suspended, or disbarred because of what her paralegal did? Responsibility to a client for malpractice often raises separate issues from responsibility for unethical conduct. The two kinds of responsibility can be closely interrelated because the same alleged wrongdoing can be involved in the malpractice suit and in the disciplinary case. Yet the two proceedings are separate and should be examined separately.

As we saw in exhibit 5.2, the ABA replaced the *Model Code of Professional Responsibility* with its *Model Rules of Professional Conduct*. The *Model Rules* are more helpful in telling us when attorneys are subject to ethical sanctions because of their paralegals. This is done in **Model Rule 5.3**, covering paralegals. All attorneys in the law firm are not treated the same in Rule 5.3. As you read this rule, note that different standards of ethical responsibility are imposed on the following three categories of attorneys:

- A partner in the firm—see section (a)
- An attorney in the firm with direct supervisory authority over the paralegal—see section (b)
- Any attorney in the firm—see section (c)

**Model Rule 5.3** The rule in the ABA *Model Rules of Professional Conduct* governing the responsibility of different categories of attorneys for the misconduct of paralegals and other nonattorney assistants in a law firm.

## Model Rules of Professional Conduct, Rule 5.3. Responsibilities Regarding Nonlawyer Assistants

**American Bar Association, 1983**

With respect to a nonlawyer employed or retained by or associated with a lawyer:

(a) a partner in a law firm shall make reasonable efforts to ensure that the firm has in effect measures giving reasonable assurance that the person's conduct is compatible with the professional obligations of the lawyer (such efforts must also be made by other lawyers in the firm who have managerial responsibilities that are comparable to those of a partner);

(b) a lawyer having direct supervisory authority over the nonlawyer shall make reasonable efforts to ensure that the person's conduct is compatible with the professional obligations of the lawyer; and

(c) a lawyer shall be responsible for conduct of such a person that would be a violation of the Rules of Professional Conduct if engaged in by a lawyer if:

(1) the lawyer orders or ratifies the conduct involved; or

(2) the lawyer is a partner in the law firm in which the person is employed, or has direct

supervisory authority over the person, and knows of the conduct at a time when its consequences can be avoided or mitigated but fails to take reasonable remedial action.

**Comment:**

Lawyers generally employ assistants in their practice, including secretaries, investigators, law student interns, and paraprofessionals. Such assistants, whether employees or independent contractors, act for the lawyer in rendition of the lawyer's professional services. A lawyer should give such assistants appropriate instruction and supervision concerning the ethical aspects of their employment, particularly regarding the obligation not to disclose information relating to representation of the client, and should be responsible for their work product. The measures employed in supervising nonlawyers should take account of the fact that they do not have legal training and are not subject to professional discipline.

Let us analyze Rule 5.3 in detail by applying it to Elaine Stanton, Esq. in our example. First of all, under Rule 5.3(c)(1), *any* attorney in the firm who "orders" the paralegal to commit the wrongdoing in question is ethically responsible for that conduct. The same is true if the attorney "ratifies" (that is, approves or endorses) the wrongdoing after the paralegal commits it. There is no indication in the example that Stanton or any other attorney in the firm told Peter not to file the pleading in court or told him to give confidential information about Thompson to the other side. Nor is there any indication that an attorney ratified (approved of) Peter's conduct after it occurred. Therefore, Rule 5.3(c)(1) does not apply.

We need to know whether Stanton is a partner in the firm or is an attorney with managerial responsibilities that are comparable to those of a partner. If so, she has an ethical obligation under Rule 5.3(a) to "make reasonable efforts to ensure that the firm has in effect measures giving reasonable assurance" that the paralegal's conduct "is compatible with the professional obligations of the lawyer." Hence a partner (or comparable manager) cannot completely ignore office paralegals in the hope that someone else in the firm is monitoring them. Reasonable steps must be taken by *every partner* (or comparable manager) to establish a system of safeguards. Here are some examples:

- Make sure that all paralegals in the firm are aware of the ethical rules governing attorneys in the state. Have all paralegals sign a statement that they have read the rules.
- Make sure that all paralegals in the firm are aware of the importance of deadlines in the practice of law and of the necessity of using manual or computer date-reminder (tickler) techniques.

In the example, Peter Vons is supervised by Elaine Stanton, Esq. Hence she is an attorney with "direct supervisory authority" over Peter. Rule 5.3(b) governs the conduct of such attorneys. This section requires her to "make reasonable efforts to ensure" that the paralegal's conduct "is compatible with the professional obligations of the lawyer."

Assume that Stanton is charged with a violation of Rule 5.3(b) because her paralegal, Peter, failed to file an important pleading in court (raising the ethical issue of competence) and disclosed information about a client (raising the ethical issue of confidentiality). At Stanton's disciplinary hearing, she would be asked a large number of questions about how she supervised Peter. For example:

- How do you assign tasks to Peter?
- How do you know if he is capable of handling an assignment?
- How often do you meet with him after you give him an assignment?
- How do you know if he is having difficulty completing an assignment?
- Has he made mistakes in the past? If so, how have you handled them?

Peter might be called as a witness in her disciplinary hearing and be interrogated extensively. For example:

- Why didn't you file the court document on time?
- Describe the circumstances under which you revealed confidential information to the opponent in the Thompson case.
- How were you trained as a paralegal?
- What kinds of assignments have you handled in your paralegal career?
- How long have you worked for Elaine Stanton?
- How does she evaluate your work?
- What do you do if you have a question on an assignment but she is not available in the office?

The purpose of asking these questions of Stanton and of Peter would be to find out if Stanton made "reasonable efforts" to ensure that Peter did not violate ethical standards. Note that attorney supervisors do *not* have to guarantee that a paralegal will act ethically. They simply have to "make reasonable efforts" that this will occur. The preceding questions are relevant to whether Stanton exerted such efforts with respect to Peter.

Another basis of ethical liability is Rule 5.3(c)(2). Both a partner and a supervisory attorney can be subject to discipline if they knew about the paralegal's misconduct yet failed to take reasonable corrective steps at a time when such steps would have avoided or minimized ("mitigated") the damage. At their disciplinary hearing, a partner and/or a supervising attorney would be asked such questions as:

- When did you first find out that Peter did not file the court document?
- What did you do at that time? Why didn't you act sooner?
- When did you first find out that Peter spoke to the opposing attorney?
- What did you do at that time? Why didn't you act sooner?

Peter, too, might be asked questions at the hearing relevant to when his supervising attorney (Stanton) or any partner in the firm found out about what he had done—and what they did when they found out.

### (b) Misrepresentation of Paralegal Identity or Status

Attorneys know that paralegals working for them are not members of the bar, but it is unwise to assume that everyone else knows. Anyone outside the firm who comes in contact with such paralegals must not think that they are attorneys. To learn how to avoid a misrepresentation of status, intentionally or accidentally, we will examine the following issues:

- Titles
- Disclosure of status
- Business cards
- Letterhead
- Signature on correspondence
- Advertisements, announcement cards, signs, lists, and directories
- Name on court documents

**What Title Can be Used?**  In most states, there are no ethical problems with the title *paralegal* or *legal assistant*. No one is likely to think that persons with such titles are attorneys. Some bar associations prefer titles that are even more explicit in communicating nonattorney status—for example, *lawyer's assistant* and *nonattorney assistant*. Yet they are seldom used because of the widespread acceptance and clarity of the titles *paralegal* and *legal assistant*. Some years ago the Philadelphia Bar Association said that the titles *paralegal* and *legal assistant* should be given only to employees who possessed "the requisite training and education." California is one of the few states that impose restrictions on the use of titles. In that state, only individuals who work under the supervision of attorneys (and meet specified educational requirements) can call themselves paralegals or legal assistants. (See chapters 1 and 4 and appendix G.)

It is unethical to call a paralegal an "associate" or to refer to a paralegal as being "associated" with a law firm. The title *paralegal associate*, for example, should not be used. The common understanding is that an associate is an attorney. In Iowa, similar problems exist with the title *certified legal assistant*, as we shall see shortly.

**Note on Disbarred or Suspended Attorney as Paralegal**  When attorneys have been disbarred or suspended from the practice of law for ethical improprieties, they may try to continue to work in the law as paralegals for attorneys willing to hire them. Some states will not allow this because it shows disrespect for the court that disciplined the attorney and because the individual is highly likely to engage in the unauthorized practice of law by going beyond paralegal duties. Other states are more lenient but might impose other restrictions, such as not allowing a disbarred or suspended attorney to have any client contact while working as a paralegal.

**Should Paralegals Disclose their Nonattorney Status to Clients, Attorneys, Government Officials, and the General Public?**  Yes, this disclosure is necessary. The more troublesome questions are: What kind of disclosure should you make, and when must you make it? Compare the following communications by a paralegal:

- "I work with Ward Brown at Brown & Tams."
- "I am a paralegal."
- "I am a legal assistant."
- "I am not an attorney."

The fourth statement is the clearest expression of nonattorney status. The first is totally unacceptable because you have said nothing about your status. For most contacts, the second and third statements will be ethically sufficient to overcome any misunderstanding about your nonattorney status. Yet some members of the public may be confused about what a paralegal or legal assistant is. If there is any possibility of doubt, use the magic words "I am not an attorney." Do not assume that a person with whom you come in contact for the first time knows you are not an attorney; the safest course is to assume the opposite!

**May a Paralegal Have a Business Card?**    Every state allows paralegals to have their own *business cards* as long as their nonattorney status is clear. (See exhibit 5.8. For other examples of business cards, see appendix H.) At one time, some states wanted the word "nonlawyer" used along with the paralegal's office title. This is rarely required today.

Because paralegals are not allowed to solicit business for their employer, the card may not be used for this purpose. The primary focus of the card must be to identify the paralegal rather than the attorney for whom the paralegal works. Finally, there must be nothing false or misleading printed on the card. In most states, a paralegal who is a *certified legal assistant (CLA)* (see exhibit 4.6 in chapter 4) can include the CLA status on his or her card. In Iowa, however, this is not permitted, as we will see when we discuss signatures on correspondence. The concern in Iowa is that the CLA designation is too confusing. (See exhibit 5.9.)

| EXHIBIT 5.8 | Paralegal Business Card |
| --- | --- |

**HINCKLEY, ALLEN & SNYDER LLP**
*Attorneys at Law*

**DAWN E. OSTIGUY**
Legal Assistant

1500 FLEET CENTER
PROVIDENCE, RI 02903-2393
401 274-2000
FAX: 401 277-9600

E-MAIL: dostiguy@haslaw.com

Ethically proper in every state.

| EXHIBIT 5.9 | Paralegal Business Card |
| --- | --- |

## John Simpson, CLA
PARALEGAL

| PHONE | JONES, DAY, OVERTON & DAVIS, P.C. |
| --- | --- |
| (319) 456-9103 | 8262 PRESTWICK DR. |
| | WATERLOO, IA 50702 |

Ethically proper in every state *except* Iowa

**May the Letterhead of Law Firm Stationery Print the Name of a Paralegal?**    States differ in their answer to this question, although most now agree that nonattorneys' names can be printed on *law firm letterhead* if their title is also printed so that their nonattorney status is clear. (See exhibit 5.10.) Before 1977, almost all states did *not* allow attorney stationery to print the names of nonattorney employees. The concern was that the letterhead would be used as a form of advertising by packing it with names and titles to make the office look impressive. This concern evaporated in 1977, however, when the Supreme Court held that all forms of attorney advertising could not be banned.[34] After this date, most states withdrew their objection to the printing of paralegal names on attorney letterhead as long as no one would be misled into thinking that the paralegals were attorneys. In Michigan, it was recommended, but not required, that attorney and nonattorney names be printed on different sides of the stationery to "enhance the

| EXHIBIT 5.10 | Example of Attorney Letterhead with Paralegal Name |
|---|---|

## HOLLAND & HART LLP
### ATTORNEYS AT LAW

DENVER • ASPEN
BOULDER • COLORADO SPRINGS
DENVER TECH CENTER
BILLINGS • BOISE
CHEYENNE • JACKSON HOLE
SALT LAKE CITY
WASHINGTON, D.C.

SUITE 3200
555 SEVENTEENTH STREET
DENVER, COLORADO 80202-3979
MAILING ADDRESS
P.O. BOX 8749
DENVER, COLORADO 80201-8749

TELEPHONE (303) 295-8000
FACSIMILE (303) 295-8261
www.hollandhart.com

CAROL J. LEFFLER
LEGAL ASSISTANT
(303) 295-8551
(303) 713-6223 Fax
cleffler@hollandhart.com

clarification that the paraprofessional is not licensed to practice law." A few states adhere to the old view that only attorney names can be printed on law firm letterhead. Yet, to the extent that this view is still based on a prohibition of attorney advertising, it is subject to challenge. Though ethically permissible in most states, it should be pointed out that not many law firms in the country print nonattorney names on their law firm letterhead.

**May a Paralegal Write and Sign Letters on Attorney Stationery?**   There is never an ethical problem with a paralegal writing a letter that will be reviewed and signed by an attorney. Suppose, however, that the attorney wants the paralegal to sign his or her own name to the letter. Most states will permit this if certain conditions are met. For example, a title must be used that indicates the signer's nonattorney status, and the letter must not give legal advice.

The following formats are proper:

| Sincerely, | Sincerely, | Sincerely, |
|---|---|---|
| Leonard Smith<br>Paralegal | Pauline Jones<br>Legal Assistant | Jill Strauss<br>Legal Assistant for the Firm |

The following formats, however, pose difficulties:

| Sincerely, | Sincerely, | Sincerely, |
|---|---|---|
| William Davis | John Simpson, CLA | Mary Page<br>Certified Legal Assistant |

The first format is ethically improper. The lack of a title could mislead the reader into thinking that William Davis is an attorney. In most states, using the designation "CLA" or "Certified Legal Assistant" is also proper. In Iowa, however, they cannot be used. "A reader might think that CLA was a legal degree"; and if "Certified Legal Assistant" is used, "the public might be misled about his or her nonlawyer status." Hence, the second and third formats just shown cannot be used in Iowa. Presumably this also applies to a business card with the CLA designation. (See exhibit 5.9.) This is an extreme view and has not been followed elsewhere.

In most states, there are no limitations on the persons to whom a paralegal can send letters. Yet, in a few states (such as New Jersey), only an attorney can sign a letter to a client, to an opposing attorney, or to a court. A very minor exception to this rule would be "a purely routine request to a court clerk for a docket sheet." A paralegal can sign such a letter. This also is an extreme position. So long as the paralegal's nonattorney status is clear, and so long as an attorney is supervising the paralegal, restrictions on who can be the recipient of a paralegal-signed letter make little sense. Most states impose no such restrictions.

**May an Attorney Print the Name of a Paralegal in an Advertisement, an Announcement Card, a Door Sign, an Outdoor Sign, a Law Directory or Law List, an Office Directory, or a Telephone Directory?**    Attorneys communicate to the public and to each other through advertisements, law directories or lists (that print the names of practicing attorneys), office directories, general telephone directories, door signs, outdoor signs, and announcement cards (that announce that the firm has moved, opened a new branch, merged with another firm, taken on a new partner, etc.). It is relatively rare that an attorney will want to print the name of his or her paralegal in one of these vehicles of communication. In a small city or town, however, a solo practitioner or small law firm might want to do so. Although several states will not allow attorneys to do this, most states that have addressed the issue say it is ethically permissible if nothing false or misleading is said about the paralegal and the latter's nonattorney status is clear.

**May an Attorney Print the Name of a Paralegal on a Court Document?**    Formal documents that are required in litigation, such as appellate briefs, memoranda supporting a motion, complaints, or other pleadings, must be signed by an attorney representing a party in the dispute. With rare exceptions, the document cannot be signed by a nonattorney, no matter how minor the formal document may be. In most states, a paralegal can sign a letter on a routine matter to a clerk or other nonjudge, but formal litigation documents require an attorney's signature.

Suppose, however, that the attorney wishes to print on a document the name of a paralegal who worked on the document *in addition to* the attorney's name and signature. The attorney may simply want to give a measure of recognition to the efforts of this paralegal. Most states permit this as long as there is no misunderstanding as to the paralegal's nonattorney status and no attempt is made to substitute a nonattorney's signature for an attorney's signature.

Occasionally, a court opinion will recognize the contribution of a paralegal. Before the opinion begins, the court lists the names of the attorneys who represented the parties. The name of a paralegal might be included with these attorneys. Here, for example, is the list of attorneys that includes the name of a paralegal (Becky M. Strickland, who is a CLA or certified legal assistant) in the case of *United States v. Sanders*, 862 F.2d 79 (4th Cir. 1988):

Michael W. Patrick (Haywood, Denny, Miller, Johnson, Sessoms & Patrick, Durham, N.C., on brief), for defendant-appellant.

John Warren Stone, Jr., Asst. U.S. Atty. (Robert H. Edmunds, Jr., U.S. Atty., Greensboro, N.C., Becky M. Strickland, CLA Paralegal Specialist, on brief), for plaintiff-appellee.

Before PHILLIPS and WILKINSON, Circuit Judges, and BOYLE, District Judge for the Eastern District of North Carolina, sitting by designation.

## (c) Doing What only Attorneys can do

There are limitations on what attorneys can ask their paralegals to do. We just examined one such limitation: paralegals should never be asked to sign court documents. The failure to abide by these limits might subject the attorney to a charge of unethically assisting a nonattorney to engage in the unauthorized practice of law. The areas we need to examine are as follows:

- Legal advice
- Nonlegal advice
- Drafting documents
- Real estate closings
- Depositions
- Executions of wills
- Settlement negotiations
- Court appearances
- Counsel's table
- Administrative hearings

**practice of law** Using legal skills to assist a person in resolving his or her specific legal problem.

**May a Paralegal Give Legal Advice?**    The **practice of law** is the use of legal skills to assist a person to resolve his or her specific legal problem. According to one court:

It is neither necessary nor desirable to attempt the formulation of a single, specific definition of what constitutes the practice of law. Functionally, the practice of law relates to the rendition of services for others that call for the professional judgment of a lawyer. The essence of the professional judgment of the lawyer is his educated ability to relate the general body and philosophy of law to a specific legal problem of a client....Where this professional judgment is not involved, non-lawyers, such as court clerks, police officers, abstracters, and many governmental employees, may engage in occupations that require a special knowledge of law in certain areas. But the services of a lawyer are essential in the public interest whenever the exercise of *professional judgment* is required.[35]

(See appendix F for the definition of the practice of law in your state.) The major way that an attorney communicates this professional judgment is through **legal advice**. The attorney tells a particular person how "the general body and philosophy of law" govern that person's "specific legal problem." Unfortunately, this definition is not always easy to apply. Review the discussion in chapter 4, for example, on the distinction between providing legal information and giving legal advice. The scope of what is allowed is not always clear. If, however, a paralegal crosses the line and gives legal advice, he or she is engaging in the unauthorized practice of law.

A number of paralegals have pointed out how easy it is to fall into the trap of giving legal advice:

> Legal assistants should be alert to all casual questions [since your answers] might be interpreted as legal advice.[36]
>
> Most of us are aware of the obvious, but we need to keep in mind that sometimes the most innocent comment could be construed as legal advice.[37]
>
> A...typical scenario, particularly in a small law office where legal assistants have a great deal of direct client contact, is that the clients themselves will coax you to answer questions about the procedures involved in their cases, and lead you into areas where you would be giving them legal advice. Sometimes this is done innocently—because the attorney is unavailable and they are genuinely unaware of the difference between what you can do for them and what their legal counsel [must] do....They will press you for projections, strategy, applicable precedents—in short, legal advice. Sometimes you are placed in situations where you are not adequately supervised and your own expertise may be such that you know more about the specialized area of law than the attorney does anyway....We have all walked the thin line between assisting in the provision of legal services and actually practicing law.[38]

An attorney who permits a paralegal to give legal advice or who fails to take the preventive steps required by Model Rule 5.3 is aiding the paralegal in the unauthorized practice of law—and hence is acting unethically.

The consequences can be extremely serious. In addition to the sanctions described in exhibit 5.3, insurance problems may exist. Suppose a client sues and alleges that the firm's paralegal gave legal advice. Will the firm's malpractice insurance policy cover this suit? No, according to the General Counsel of the Mississippi Bar Association. "No available insurance policy will cover judgments resulting from a civil suit brought by an angry client based on the theory that a paralegal gave the client legal advice. In fact, if the paralegal gives legal advice, the predominant rule is that coverage is void for such act. Therefore, the paralegal is warned not to give the client advice (even if the paralegal knows the answer) even though it may be an emergency situation. Why? Giving legal advice constitutes the unauthorized practice of law, and the unauthorized practice of law is not covered."[39]

There are a number of situations, however, in which a paralegal *can* give legal advice. First, a paralegal can tell a client precisely what the attorney tells the paralegal to say, even if the message constitutes legal advice. The paralegal, however, cannot elaborate on, interpret, or explain this kind of message from the attorney. Second, the paralegal may be working in an area of the law where nonattorneys are authorized to represent clients, such as social security hearings. (See chapter 4.) In such areas, the authorization includes the right to give legal advice.

**May a Paralegal give a Client Nonlegal Advice?**   Yes. An attorney may allow a paralegal to render specialized advice on scientific or technical topics. For example, a qualified paralegal can give accounting advice or financial advice. The danger is that the nonlegal advice might also contain legal advice or that the client might reasonably interpret the nonlegal advice as legal advice.

**legal advice** The application of laws and legal principles to the facts of a particular person's legal problem.

**May a Paralegal Draft Legal Documents?**    Yes. A paralegal can draft any legal document as long as an attorney supervises and reviews the work of the paralegal. Some ethical opinions say that the document must lose its separate identity as the work of a paralegal and must leave the office as the work product of an attorney. In West Virginia, for example, "anything delegated to a nonattorney must lose its separate identity and be merged in the service of the lawyer." The key point is that an attorney must stand behind and be responsible for the document.

**May a Paralegal Attend a Real Estate Closing?**    The sale of property is finalized at an event called a real estate closing. Many of the events at the closing are formalities, such as signing and exchanging papers. Occasionally, however, some of these events turn into more substantive matters where negotiation, legal interpretation, and legal advice are involved.

In most states, paralegals are allowed to attend closings in order to assist their attorney-supervisor. The real question is whether they can attend *alone* and conduct the closing themselves. Chicago has one of the most liberal rules. There, paralegals can conduct the closing without the attorney-supervisor being present if no legal advice is given, if all the documents have been prepared in advance, if the attorney-supervisor is available by telephone to provide help, and if the other attorney consents. In some states, additional conditions must be met before allowing paralegals to act on their own. For example, the closing must take place in the attorney-supervisor's law office with the attorney readily accessible to answer legal questions. It must be noted, however, that this is a minority position. Most states would say that it is unethical for an attorney to allow a paralegal to conduct a real estate closing alone regardless of where the closing is held.

**May a Paralegal Conduct a Deposition?**    No. Paralegals can schedule depositions, can assist in preparing a witness who will be deposed (called the deponent), can take notes at the deposition, and can summarize deposition transcripts, but they cannot conduct the deposition. Asking and objecting to deposition questions are attorney-only functions.

**May a Paralegal Supervise the Execution of a Will?**    In Connecticut, the execution of a will must be supervised by an attorney. A paralegal can act as a witness to the execution, but an attorney must direct the procedure. Most other states would probably agree, although few have addressed this question.

**May a Paralegal Negotiate a Settlement?**    A few states allow a paralegal to negotiate with a nonattorney employee of an insurance company, such as a claims adjuster, as long as the paralegal is supervised by an attorney. Most states, however, limit the paralegal's role to exchanging messages from the supervising attorney and do not allow any actual give-and-take negotiating by the paralegal.

**May a Paralegal Make a Court Appearance?**    In the vast majority of courts, a paralegal cannot perform even minor functions in a courtroom, such as asking a judge to schedule a hearing date for an attorney. As we saw in chapter 4, very few exceptions to this rule exist. Only attorneys can act in a representative capacity before a judge. There are, however, a small number of specialized courts, like the small claims courts of some states, where you do not have to be an attorney to represent parties. This exception, however, is rare. And, as mentioned earlier, a paralegal should not sign a formal court document that is filed in litigation.

**May a Paralegal Sit at Counsel's Table during a Trial?**    In many courts, only attorneys can sit at counsel's table during a trial. Yet, in some courts, a paralegal is allowed to sit with the attorneys if permission of the presiding judge is obtained. The paralegal does not take an active role in the trial. He or she provides general assistance (e.g., note taking, organizing trial documents) for the attorney. While at the table, the paralegal is sometimes said to be sitting in the **second chair**. This phrase, however, is more accurately used to refer to another attorney who assists the lead attorney, who is in the "first chair." When a nonattorney such as a paralegal is allowed to sit at counsel's table, it might be more accurate to refer to him or her as being in the "third chair."

**second chair** A seat at the counsel's table in the courtroom used by an assistant to the trial attorney during the trial.

**May a Paralegal Represent Clients at Administrative Hearings?**   Yes, when this is authorized at the particular state or federal administrative agency. (See chapter 4, appendix E, and appendix F.)

### (d) Absentee Supervision, Shoulder Supervision, and Environmental Supervision

It is difficult to overestimate the importance of attorney supervision in the arena of ethics. According to the supreme court of one state, "Without supervision, the work of the paralegal clearly constitutes the unauthorized practice of law."[40] Almost every ethical opinion involving paralegals (and almost every attorney malpractice opinion involving paralegals) stresses the need for effective supervision. The justification for the very existence of perhaps 95 percent of paralegal activity is this supervision. Indeed, one of the main reasons many argue that paralegal licensing is not necessary is the protective cover of attorney supervision.

What is meant by supervision? The extremes are easy to identify. *Absentee supervision* refers to the attorney who is either never around or seldom available. Once tasks are assigned, paralegals are on their own. At the other extreme is *shoulder supervision*, practiced by attorneys who are afraid to delegate. When they do get up enough courage to delegate something, they constantly look over the shoulder of the paralegal, who is rarely left alone for more than two-minute intervals. Such attorneys suffer from *delegatitis*, the inordinate fear of letting anyone do anything for them.

Both kinds of supervision are misguided. If you work for an attorney who practices absentee supervision, disaster is just around the corner. You may feel flattered by the confidence placed in you; you may enjoy the challenge of independence; you may be highly compensated because of your success. But you are working in an office that is traveling 130 miles per hour in a 50 mile-per-hour zone. Any feeling of safety in such an office is illusory. Shoulder supervision, on the other hand, provides safety at the expense of practicality. Perpetual step-by-step surveillance will ultimately defeat the economy and efficiency motives that originally led the office to hire paralegals.

Perhaps the most effective kind of supervision is *environmental supervision*, or what might be called *holistic supervision*. It is far broader in its reach than the immediate task delegated to a paralegal. It addresses this essential question: what kind of environment will lead to a high-quality paralegal work product without sacrificing economy or ethics? The components of this kind of supervision are outlined in exhibit 5.11. Environmental supervision requires *hiring* the right people, *training* those people, *assigning* appropriate tasks, *providing* the needed resources, *monitoring* the progress, *reviewing* the end product, and *rewarding* competence.

Unfortunately, many law offices do *not* practice environmental supervision as outlined in exhibit 5.11. The chart represents the ideal. Yet you need to know what the ideal is so that you can advocate for the conditions that will help bring it about.

Thus far, our discussion on supervision has focused on the traditional paralegal who works full-time in the office of an attorney. We also need to consider the freelance or independent paralegal who works part-time as an independent contractor for one attorney or for several attorneys in different law firms. Very often this freelancer works in his or her own office at home. (See appendix J and exhibit 2.2 in chapter 2.) How can attorneys fulfill their ethical obligation to supervise such paralegals?

> **Example:** Gail Patterson has her own freelance business. She offers paralegal services to attorneys who hire her for short-term projects, which she performs in her own office.

Arguably, attorneys who hire Gail often do not provide the same kind of supervision that they can provide to a full-time paralegal who works in their office. We saw earlier that Model Rule 5.3(c)(2) says that an attorney has the responsibility to take steps to avoid the consequences of an ethical violation by a paralegal and, if a violation occurs, to mitigate the consequences. Suppose that Gail commits an ethical impropriety—for example, she reveals confidential communications. Because she works in her own office, the attorney who hired her may not learn about this impropriety in time to avoid or mitigate its consequences. Conflict of interest is another potential problem. Gail

| EXHIBIT 5.11 | "Environmental Supervision": The Ethical Ideal |
| --- | --- |

1. Before paralegals are hired, the office undertakes a study of its practice in order to identify what tasks paralegals should perform and what levels of ability will be required to perform those tasks.
2. As part of the interview process, the office conducts background checks on applicants for paralegal jobs in order to insure that competent people are hired who already have the needed skills or who are trainable so that they can acquire these skills on the job.
3. A program of orientation and training is created to introduce paralegals to the office and to prepare them for the tasks ahead.
4. Before the paralegal is hired, the office conducts a "conflicts check" to determine whether he or she might have a conflict of interest with any current client of the office. These conflicts might result from the paralegal's prior legal work as well as from his or her family and business connections with anyone who might oppose current clients. Once hired, a similar conflicts check is conducted for every new client or prospective client.
5. Paralegals are given a copy of the ethical rules governing attorneys in the state. In addition to reading these rules, they are given training on the meaning of the rules.
6. Paralegals are told what to do if they feel that an ethical problem exists. Lines of authority are identified if the paralegal needs to discuss the matter with someone other than, or in addition to, his or her immediate supervisor.
7. The office does not assume that every attorney knows how to supervise paralegals. Paralegals are assigned to attorneys who have the required supervisory sensitivity and skill. Furthermore, the office is always looking for ways to increase this sensitivity and skill.
8. An attorney reviews all paralegal work. Although paralegals may be given discretion and asked to exercise judgment in the tasks assigned, this discretion and judgment are always subjected to actual attorney review.
9. No task is assigned that is beyond the capacity of the paralegal. Specialized instruction always accompanies tasks the paralegal has not performed before.
10. Once a task is assigned, the paralegal is told where to receive assistance if the immediate supervisor is not available. This lack of availability, however, is relatively rare.
11. For tasks that the office performs on a recurring basis, there are manuals, office procedures, checklists, or other written material available to the paralegal to explain how the tasks are performed and where samples or models can be found. If such *systems* material does not currently exist, the office plans to create such material.
12. To cut down on misunderstanding, every paralegal assignment includes the following information:
    - A *specific due date*. ("Get to this when you can" is unacceptable and unfair.)
    - A *priority assessment*. ("Should everything else be dropped while I do this assignment?")
    - A *context*. ("How does this assignment fit into the broader picture of the case?") and
    - A *financial perspective*. ("Is this billable time?" "What resources can be used, e.g., fee-based online research?" "What support services will be available, e.g., the secretary?")
13. At reasonable times before the due date of selected assignments, the supervisor monitors the progress of the paralegal to insure that the work is being done professionally and accurately.
14. A team atmosphere exists at the office among the attorneys, paralegals, secretaries, and other employees. Everyone knows each other's functions, pressures, and potential as resources. A paralegal never feels isolated.
15. Evaluations of paralegal performance are constructive. Both the supervisor and paralegal act on the assumption that there will always be a need and opportunity for further learning.
16. The office sends the paralegal to training seminars conducted by paralegal associations and bar associations to maintain and to increase the paralegal's skills.
17. The office knows that an unhappy employee is prone to error. Hence the office makes sure that the work setting of the paralegal encourages personal growth and productivity. This includes matters of compensation, benefits, work space, equipment, and advancement.

works for many different attorneys and hence many different clients of those attorneys. It is possible that she could accept work from two attorneys who are engaged in litigation against each other without either attorney knowing that the other has hired Gail on the same case. (See the earlier discussion of this problem on page 249.)

What kind of supervision is needed to prevent such problems? There is no clear answer to this question. It is not enough that the attorney vouches for, and takes responsibility for, the final product submitted by the freelance paralegal. Ongoing supervision is also needed under Model Rule 5.3. Not many states, however, have addressed this area of ethics. In the future, we will probably see the creation of new standards to govern this kind of paralegal.

## Section D
## ETHICAL CODES OF THE PARALEGAL ASSOCIATIONS

As indicated at the beginning of this chapter, there are no binding ethical rules published by paralegal associations. Yet the two major national associations—the National Federation of Paralegal Associations (NFPA) and the National Association of Legal Assistants (NALA)—have written ethical codes that you should know about. See exhibit 5.4 for an overview of the structure and functions of these codes.

## Model Code of Ethics and Professional Responsibility

### National Federation of Paralegal Associations

For the complete text of this *Code* (plus the NFPA's *Guidelines for Enforcement of the Code*), see *www.paralegals.org/Development/modelcode.html*. Here are some of the major provisions of the NFPA Code:

1.1 A Paralegal Shall Achieve and Maintain a High Level of Competence.

1.2 A Paralegal Shall Maintain a High Level of Personal and Professional Integrity.

1.3 A Paralegal Shall Maintain a High Standard of Professional Conduct.

1.4 A Paralegal Shall Serve the Public Interest by Contributing to the Improvement of the Legal System and Delivery of Quality Legal Services, Including Pro Bono Publico Services.

1.5 A Paralegal Shall Preserve All Confidential Information Provided by the Client or Acquired from Other Sources before, during, and after the Course of the Professional Relationship.

1.6 A Paralegal Shall Avoid Conflicts of Interest and Shall Disclose Any Possible Conflict to the Employer or Client, as Well as to the Prospective Employers or Clients.

1.7 A Paralegal's Title Shall Be Fully Disclosed.

1.8 A Paralegal Shall Not Engage in the Unauthorized Practice of Law.

## Code of Ethics and Professional Responsibility

### National Association of Legal Assistants

For the complete text of this *Code* (plus NALA's *Model Standards and Guidelines for Utilization of Legal Assistants*), see *www.nala.org/stand.htm*. Here are some of the major provisions of the NALA Code:

Canon 1. A legal assistant must not perform any of the duties that attorneys only may perform nor take any actions that attorneys may not take.

Canon 2. A legal assistant may perform any task which is properly delegated and supervised by an attorney, as long as the attorney is ultimately responsible to the client, maintains a direct relationship with the client, and assumes professional responsibility for the work product.

Canon 3. A legal assistant must not: (a) engage in, encourage, or contribute to any act which could constitute the unauthorized practice of law; and (b) establish attorney-client relationships, set fees, give legal opinions or advice or represent a client before a court or agency unless so authorized by that court or agency; and (c) engage in conduct or take any action which would assist or involve the attorney in a violation of professional ethics or give the appearance of professional impropriety.

Canon 4. A legal assistant must use discretion and professional judgment commensurate with knowledge and experience but must not render independent legal judgment in place of an attorney. The services of an attorney are essential in the public interest whenever such legal judgment is required.

Canon 5. A legal assistant must disclose his or her status as a legal assistant at the outset of any professional relationship with a client, attorney, a court or administrative agency or personnel thereof, or a member of the general public. A legal assistant must act prudently in determining the extent to which a client may be assisted without the presence of an attorney.

## Code of Ethics and Professional Responsibility

**National Association of Legal Assistants—*continued***

Canon 6. A legal assistant must strive to maintain integrity and a high degree of competency through education and training with respect to professional responsibility, local rules and practice, and through continuing education in substantive areas of law to better assist the legal profession in fulfilling its duty to provide legal service.

Canon 7. A legal assistant must protect the confidences of a client and must not violate any rule or statute now in effect or hereafter enacted controlling the doctrine of privileged communications between a client and an attorney.

Canon 8. A legal assistant must do all other things incidental, necessary, or expedient for the attainment of the ethics and responsibilities as defined by statute or rule of court.

Canon 9. A legal assistant's conduct is guided by bar associations' codes of professional responsibility and rules of professional conduct.

## Section E
# AN ETHICAL DILEMMA: YOUR ETHICS OR YOUR JOB!

Throughout this chapter, we have stressed the importance of maintaining your integrity through knowledge of and compliance with ethical rules. There may be times, however, when this is much easier said than done. Consider the following situations:

- You are not sure whether an ethical violation is being committed. Nor is anyone else in the office sure. Like so many areas of the law, ethical issues can be complex.
- You are sure that an ethical violation exists, and the violator is your supervisor!
- You are sure that an ethical violation exists, and the violators are everyone else in the office!

You face a potential dilemma (1) if no one seems to care about the ethical problem or, worse, (2) if your supervising attorney is the one committing the ethical impropriety or (3) if the entire office appears to be participating in the impropriety. People do not like to be told that they are unethical. Rather than acknowledge the fault and mend their ways, they may turn on the accuser, the one raising the fuss about ethics. (That is apparently what happened to Cynthia Brown, the paralegal who complained about unethical billing practices in her office. See the case of *Brown v. Hammond*, discussed earlier in the chapter.) Once the issue is raised, it may be very difficult to continue working in the office.

You need someone to talk to. In the best of all worlds, it will be someone in the same office. If this is not practical, consider contacting a teacher whom you trust. Paralegal associations are also an excellent source of information and support. A leader in one paralegal association offers the following advice:

> I would suggest that if the canons, discipline rules, affirmations, and codes of ethics do not supply you with a clear-cut answer to any ethical question you may have, you should draw upon the network that you have in being a member of this association. Getting the personal input of other paralegals who may have been faced with similar situations, or who have a greater knowledge through experience of our professional responsibilities, may greatly assist you in working your way through a difficult ethical situation.[41]

Of course, you must be careful not to violate client confidentiality during discussions with someone outside the office. Never mention actual client names or any specific information pertaining to a case. You can talk in hypothetical terms. For example, "an attorney working on a bankruptcy case asks a paralegal to...." Once you present data in this sterilized fashion, you can then ask for guidance on the ethical implications of the data.

If handled delicately, most ethical problems that bother you can be resolved without compromising anyone's integrity or job. Yet the practice of law is not substantially different from other fields of endeavor. There will be times when the clash between principle and the dollar cannot be resolved to everyone's satisfaction. You may indeed have to make a choice between your ethics and your job.

## Section F
# DOING RESEARCH ON AN ETHICAL ISSUE

1. At a law library, ask where the following two items are kept:
   - The code or rules of ethics governing the attorneys in your state (see exhibit 5.2)
   - The ethical opinions that interpret the code or rules
2. Contact your state bar association. Ask what committee or other body has jurisdiction over ethics. Ask if this committee has published any opinions, guidelines, or other materials on paralegals. Also ask if there is a special committee on paralegals. If so, find out what it has said about paralegals.
3. Do the same for any other bar associations in your area, such as city or county bar associations.
4. For a summary of what bar associations in your state have said about paralegals, see appendix F. You will need to update what appendix F says about your state by using the research steps outlined in this section.
5. At a law library, ask where the following two items are kept:
   - The ABA's *Model Rules of Professional Conduct*
   - The ethical opinions that interpret these *Model Rules*, as well as the earlier *Model Code of Professional Responsibility* of the ABA
6. Examine the *ABA/BNA Lawyers' Manual on Professional Conduct*. This is a loose-leaf book containing current information on ABA ethics and the ethical rules of every state.
7. Other material to check in the library:
   - C. Wolfram, *Modern Legal Ethics* (1986)
   - G. Hazard and W. Hodes, *The Law of Lawyering: A Handbook on the Model Rules of Professional Conduct* (2d ed. 1992)
   - L. Bierwat and R. Hunter, *Legal Ethics for Management and Their Counsel* (1999)
   - American Law Institute, *Restatement (Third) of the Law Governing Lawyers* (1998)
   - *National Reporter on Legal Ethics and Professional Responsibility* (1982– )
   - *The Georgetown Journal of Legal Ethics* (periodical)
   - *Lawyers' Liability Review* (newsletter)
8. Either WESTLAW or LEXIS–NEXIS will enable you to do computerized legal research on the law of ethics in your state. (See chapters 11 and 13.) Here, for example, is a query (question) you could use to ask WESTLAW to find cases in your state in which a paralegal was charged with the unauthorized practice of law:

   paralegal "legal assistant" /p "unauthorized practice"

   After you instructed WESTLAW to turn to the database containing the court opinions of your state, you would type this query at the keyboard in order to find out if any such cases exist. For many states, there are separate databases devoted to ethics.
9. Another way to find court opinions on ethics in your state is to go to the digest covering the courts in your state. Use its index to find cases on ethical issues.
10. For Internet sites on ethics and professional responsibility, see "On the Net" at the end of the chapter.

### Assignment 5.2

(a) What is the name of the code of ethics that governs attorneys in your state?
(b) To what body or agency does a client initially make a charge of unethical conduct against his or her attorney in your state?
(c) List the steps required to discipline an attorney for unethical conduct in your state. Begin with the complaint stage and conclude with the court that makes the final decision. Draw a flow chart that lists these steps.

### Assignment 5.3

Paul Emerson is an attorney who works at the firm of Rayburn & Rayburn. One of the firm's clients is Designs Unlimited, Inc. (DU), a clothing manufacturer. Emerson provides corporate advice to DU. Recently, Emerson made a mistake in interpreting a new securities law. As a consequence, DU had to postpone the issuance of a stock option for six months. Has Paul acted unethically?

### Assignment 5.4

(a) Three individuals in Connecticut hire a large New York law firm to represent them in a proxy fight in which they are seeking control of a Connecticut bank. They lose the proxy fight. The firm then sends these individuals a $358,827 bill for 895 hours of work over a one-month period. Is this bill unethical? What further facts would you like to have to help you answer this question?

(b) Victor Adams and Len Patterson are full partners in the law firm of Adams, Patterson & Kelly. A client contacts Patterson to represent him on a negligence case. Patterson refers the case to Victor Adams, who does most of the work. (Under an agreement between them, Patterson will receive 40 percent and Adams will receive 60 percent of any fee paid by this client.) Patterson does not tell the client about the involvement of Adams in the case. Any ethical problems?

(c) An attorney establishes a bonus plan for her paralegals. A bonus will be given to those paralegals who bill a specified number of hours in excess of a stated minimum. The amount of the bonus will depend on the amount billed and collected. Any ethical problems?

### Assignment 5.5

Mary works in a law firm that charges clients $225 an hour for attorney time and $75 an hour for paralegal time. She and another paralegal, Fred, are working with an attorney on a large case. She sees all of the time sheets that the three of them submit to the firm's accounting office. She suspects that the attorney is padding his time sheets by overstating the number of hours he works on the case. For example, he lists 30 hours for a four-day period when he was in court every day on another case. Furthermore, Fred's time is being billed at the full $75-an-hour rate even though he spends about 80 percent of his time typing correspondence, filing, and performing other clerical duties. Mary also suspects that her attorney is billing out Mary's time at the attorney rate rather than the paralegal rate normally charged clients for her time. Any ethical problems? What should Mary do?

### Assignment 5.6

Smith is an attorney who works at the firm of Johnson & Johnson. He represents Ralph Grant, who is seeking a divorce from his wife, Amy Grant. In their first meeting, Smith learns that Ralph is an experienced carpenter but is out of work and has very little money. Smith's fee is $150 an hour. Because Ralph has no money and has been having trouble finding work, Smith tells Ralph that he will not have to pay the fee if the court does not grant him the divorce. One day while Smith is working on another case involving Helen Oberlin, he learns that Helen is looking for a carpenter. Smith recommends Ralph to Helen, and she hires him for a small job. Six months pass. The divorce case is dropped when the Grants reconcile. In the meantime, Helen Oberlin is very dissatisfied with Ralph's carpentry work for her; she claims he didn't do the work he contracted to do. She wants to know what she can do about it. She tries to call Smith at Johnson & Johnson but is told that Smith does not work there anymore. Another attorney, Georgia Quinton, Esq. helps Helen. Any ethical problems?

*Assignment 5.7*

John Jones is a paralegal working at the XYZ law firm. The firm is handling a large class action involving potentially thousands of plaintiffs. John has been instructed to screen the potential plaintiffs in the class. John tells those he screens out (using criteria provided by the firm) in writing or verbally that "unfortunately, our firm will not be able to represent you." Any ethical problems?

*Assignment 5.8*

A paralegal quits the firm of Smith & Smith. When she leaves, she takes client documents she prepared while at the firm. The documents contain confidential client information. The paralegal is showing these documents to potential employers as writing samples.

(a) What is the ethical liability of attorneys at Smith & Smith under Model Rule 5.3?

(b) What is the ethical liability of attorneys at law firms where she is seeking employment under Model Rule 5.3?

(c) What is the paralegal's liability?

*Assignment 5.9*

(a) Mary Smith is a paralegal at the ABC law firm. She has been working on the case of Jessica Randolph, a client of the office. Mary talks with Ms. Randolph often. Mary receives a subpoena from the attorney of the party that is suing Ms. Randolph. On the witness stand, Mary is asked by this attorney what Ms. Randolph told her at the ABC law office about a particular business transaction related to the suit. Randolph's attorney (Mary's supervisor) objects to the question. What result?

(b) Before Helen became a paralegal for the firm of Harris & Derkson, she was a chemist for a large corporation. Harris & Derkson is a patent law firm where Helen's technical expertise in chemistry is invaluable. Helen's next-door neighbor is an inventor. On a number of occasions, he discussed the chemical makeup of his inventions with Helen. Now the government has charged the neighbor with stealing official secrets to prepare one of these inventions. Harris & Derkson represent the neighbor on this case. Helen also works directly on the case for the firm. In a prosecution of the neighbor, Helen is called as a witness and is asked to reveal the substance of all her conversations with the neighbor concerning the invention in question. Does Helen have to answer?

*Assignment 5.10*

Bob and Patricia Fannan are separated, and they both want a divorce. They would like to have a joint-custody arrangement in which their son would spend time with each parent during the year. The only marital property is a house, which they agree should be sold, with each to get one-half of the proceeds. Mary Franklin, Esq. is an attorney whom Bob and Patricia know and trust. They decide to ask Franklin to represent both of them in the divorce. Any ethical problems?

*Assignment 5.11*

George is a religious conservative. He works for a law firm that represents Adult Features, Inc., which runs an X-rated Internet site. The client is fighting an injunction sought by the police against its business. George is asked by his supervisor to do some research on the case. Any ethical problems?

### Assignment 5.12

Peter is a paralegal at Smith & Smith. One of the cases he works on is *Carter v. Horton*. Carter is the client of Smith & Smith. Peter does some investigation and scheduling of discovery for the case. Horton is represented by Unger, Oberdorf & Simon. The Unger firm offers Peter a job working in its law library and in its computer department on database management. He takes the job. While at the Unger firm, Peter can see all the documents in the *Carter v. Horton* case. At lunch a week after Peter joins the firm, he tells one of the Unger attorneys (Jack Dolan) about an investigation he conducted while working for Smith & Smith on the *Carter* case. (Jack is not one of the Unger attorneys working on *Carter v. Horton*.) Two weeks after Peter is hired, the Unger firm decides to set up a Chinese Wall around Peter. He is told not to discuss *Carter v. Horton* with any Unger employee, all Unger employees are told not to discuss the case with Peter, the files are kept away from Peter, etc. The Wall is rigidly enforced. Nevertheless, Smith & Smith makes a motion to disqualify Unger, Oberdorf & Simon from continuing to represent Horton in the *Carter v. Horton* case. Should this motion be granted?

### Assignment 5.13

Alice is a freelance paralegal with a speciality in probate law. One of the firms she has worked for is Davis, Ritter & Boggs. Her most recent assignment for this firm has been to identify the assets of Mary Steck, who died six months ago. One of Mary's assets is a 75 percent ownership share in the Domain Corporation. Alice learns a great deal about this company, including the fact that four months ago it had difficulty meeting its payroll and expects to have similar difficulties in the coming year.

Alice's freelance business has continued to grow because of her excellent reputation. She decides to hire an employee with a different specialty so that her office can begin to take different kinds of cases from attorneys. She hires Bob, a paralegal with four years of litigation experience. The firm of Jackson & Jackson hires Alice to digest a series of long deposition documents in the case of *Glendale Bank v. Ajax Tire Co.* Jackson & Jackson represents Glendale Bank. Peterson, Zuckerman & Morgan represents Ajax Tire Co. Alice assigns Bob to this case. Ajax Tire Co. is a wholly owned subsidiary of the Domain Corporation. Glendale Bank is suing Ajax Tire Co. for fraud in misrepresenting its financial worth when Ajax Tire Co. applied for and obtained a loan from Glendale Bank.

Any ethical problems?

### Assignment 5.14

Assume that you owned a successful freelance business in which you provided paralegal services to over 150 attorneys all over the state. How should your files be organized in order to avoid a conflict of interest?

### Assignment 5.15

Joan is a paralegal who works for the XYZ law firm, which is representing Goff in a suit against Barnard, who is represented by the ABC law firm. Joan calls Barnard and says, "Is this the first time that you have ever been sued?" Barnard answers, "Yes it is. Is there anything else that you would like to know?" Joan says *no* and the conversation ends. Any ethical problems?

### Assignment 5.16

Mary is a paralegal who is a senior citizen. She works at the XYZ legal service office. One day she goes to a senior citizens center and says the following:

> All of you should know about and take advantage of the XYZ legal service office where I work. Let me give you just one example why. Down at the office there is an attorney named Armanda Morris. She is an expert on insurance company cases. Some of you may have had trouble with insurance companies that say one thing and do another. Our office is available to serve you.

Any ethical problems?

### Assignment 5.17

(a) What restrictions exist on advertising by attorneys in your state? Give an example of an ad on TV or in the newspaper that would be unethical. On researching an ethical issue, see page 269.

(b) In *Bates v. State Bar of Arizona*, 433 U.S. 350 (1977), the United States Supreme Court held that a state could not prohibit all forms of lawyer advertising. Has *Bates* been cited by state courts in your state on the advertising issue? If so, what impact has the case had in your state? To find out, shepardize *Bates*. The specific techniques of Shepardizing a case are found in exhibit 11.30 in chapter 11.

### Assignment 5.18

Mary Jackson is a paralegal at Rollins & Rollins. She is supervised by Ian Gregory. Mary is stealing money from the funds of one of the firm's clients. The only attorney who knows about this is Dan Roberts, Esq., who is not a partner at the firm and who does not supervise Mary. Dan says and does nothing about Mary's actions. What ethical obligations does Dan have under Model Rule 5.3?

### Assignment 5.19

John Smith is a paralegal who works for the firm of Beard, Butler, and Clark. John's immediate supervisor is Viola Butler, Esq. With the full knowledge and blessing of Viola Butler, John Smith sends a letter to a client of the firm (Mary Anders). Has Viola Butler acted unethically in permitting John to send out this letter? The letter is as follows:

**Law Offices of**
**Beard, Butler, and Clark**
**310 High St.**
**Maincity, Ohio 45238**
**512–663–9410**

*Attorneys at Law*                                                      *Paralegal*
**Ronald Beard**                                                      **John Smith**
**Viola Butler**
**Wilma Clark**

                                                                       May 14, 1997

Mary Anders
621 S. Randolph Ave.
Maincity, Ohio 45238

Dear Ms. Anders:

Viola Butler, the attorney in charge of your case, has asked me to let you know that next month's hearing has been postponed. We will let you know the new date as soon as possible. If you have any questions, don't hesitate to call me.

Sincerely,

John Smith
Legal Intern

JS:wps

---

### Assignment 5.20
Under what circumstances, if any, would it be appropriate for you to refer to a client of the office where you work as "my client"?

---

### Assignment 5.21
John Jones is a paralegal who works for an attorney named Linda Sunders. Linda is away from the office one day and telephones John, who is at the office. She dictates a one-line letter to a client of the office. The letter reads, "I advise you to sue." Linda asks John to sign the letter for her. The signature line at the bottom of the letter reads as follows:

Linda Sunders
by John Jones

Any ethical problems?

---

### Assignment 5.22
Mary is a paralegal who works at the XYZ law firm. She specializes in real estate matters at the firm. Mary attends a real estate closing in which her role consists of exchanging documents and acknowledging the receipt of documents. Are there ethical problems in allowing her to do so? Answer this question on the basis of the following variations:

(a) The closing takes place at the XYZ law firm.
(b) The closing takes place at a bank.
(c) Mary's supervising attorney is not present at the closing.
(d) Mary's supervising attorney is present at the closing.
(e) Mary's supervising attorney is present at the closing except for 30 minutes, during which time Mary continued to exchange documents and acknowledge the receipt of documents.
(f) During the closing, the attorney for the other party says to Mary, "I don't know why my client should have to pay that charge." Mary responds: "In this state that charge is always paid in this way."

---

### Assignment 5.23
John is a paralegal who works for the XYZ law firm, which is representing a client against the Today Insurance Company. The Company employs paralegals who work under the Company's general counsel. One of these paralegals is Mary. In an effort to settle the case, Mary calls John and says, "We offer you $2,000.00." John says, "We'll let you know." Any ethical problems?

*Assignment 5.24*
John Smith is a paralegal who works for Beard, Butler, and Clark. He sends out the following letter. Any ethical problems?

**John Smith**
Paralegal
310 High St.
Maincity, Ohio 45238
512–663–9410

June 1, 1997

State Unemployment Board
1216 Southern Ave
Maincity, Ohio 45238

Dear Gentlepeople:

I work for Beard, Butler, and Clark, which represents Mary Anders, who has a claim before your agency. A hearing originally scheduled for June 8, 1997, has been postponed. We request that the hearing be held at the earliest time possible after the 8th.

Sincerely,
John Smith

JS:wps

*Assignment 5.25*
In section C of chapter 2, there is a long list of tasks that paralegals have performed and comments by paralegals working in the specialties covered. Identify any three tasks or paralegal comments that *might* pose ethical problems or problems of unauthorized practice. Explain why.

*Assignment 5.26*
Draft your own paralegal code as a class project. Use any of the material in Chapter 5 as a resource. Also consult the material in appendix F for your state and for other states. First, have a meeting in which you make a list of all the issues that you think should be covered in the code. Divide up the issues by the number of students in the class so that every student has roughly the same number of issues. Each student should draft a proposed rule on each of the issues to which he or she is assigned. Accompany each rule with a brief commentary on why you think the rule should be as stated. Draft alternative versions of the proposed rule if different versions are possible and you want to give the class the chance to examine all of them. The class then meets to vote on each of the proposed rules. Students will make presentations on the proposed rules they have drafted. If the class is not happy with the way in which a particular proposed rule was drafted by a student, the latter will redraft the rule for later consideration by the class. One member of the class should be designated the "code reporter," who records the rules accepted by the class by majority vote.

After you have completed the code, invite attorneys from the local bar association to your class in order to discuss your proposed code. Do the same with officials of the closest paralegal association in your area.

## ▌ CHAPTER SUMMARY

Ethics are the standards of behavior to which members of an organization must conform. Begin your paralegal career by committing yourself to become an ethical conservative.

Attorneys are regulated primarily by the highest court in the state, often with the extensive involvement of the state bar association. Because paralegals cannot practice law and cannot become full members of a bar association, they cannot be punished by the bar association for a violation of the ethical rules governing attorneys. The American Bar Association is a voluntary association; no attorney must be a member. The ABA publishes ethical rules that the states are free to adopt, modify, or reject.

The current rules of the ABA are found in its *Model Rules of Professional Conduct*. These ethical rules require attorneys to be competent, to act with reasonable diligence and promptness, to charge fees that are reasonable, to avoid conduct that is criminal and fraudulent, to avoid asserting claims and defenses that are frivolous, to safeguard the property of clients, to avoid making false statements of law and fact to a tribunal, to withdraw from a case for appropriate reasons, to maintain the confidentiality of client information, to avoid conflicts of interest, to avoid improper communications with an opponent, to avoid improper solicitation of clients, to avoid improper advertising, to report serious professional misconduct of other attorneys, to avoid assisting nonattorneys to engage in the unauthorized practice of law, and to supervise paralegal employees appropriately.

Ethical opinions or guidelines exist in almost every state on the proper use of a paralegal by an attorney. All states agree that the title used for this employee must not mislead anyone about his or her nonattorney status, and that the employee must disclose his or her nonattorney status when necessary to avoid misunderstanding. Rules also exist on other aspects of the attorney-paralegal relationship, but not all states agree on what these rules should be. The following apply in most states:

Under attorney approval and supervision, paralegals in most states:

- Can have their own business cards
- Can have their names printed on the law firm letterhead
- Can sign law firm correspondence
- Can give nonlegal advice
- Can draft legal documents
- Can attend a real estate closing
- Can represent clients at agency hearings if authorized by the agency

With few exceptions, paralegals in most states:

- Cannot give legal advice
- Cannot conduct a deposition
- Cannot sign formal court documents
- Cannot supervise the execution of a will
- Cannot make an appearance in court

Separate ethical rules and guidelines have been adopted by the National Association of Legal Assistants and by the National Federation of Paralegal Associations.

## KEY TERMS

| | |
|---|---|
| continuing legal education (CLE) | retainer |
| ethics | minimum-fee schedule |
| sanction | contingent fee |
| integrated bar association | fee splitting |
| registration | forwarding fee |
| disbarment | statutory fee case |
| suspension | double billing |
| reprimand | padding |
| admonition | at-will employee |
| probation | attestation clause |
| multidisciplinary practice (MDP) | insider trading |
| paralegal code | pirated software |
| competent | adversarial system |
| clinical education | frivolous position |

client trust account
commingling
cure
letter of disengagement
letter of nonengagement
confidential
consent
attorney-client privilege
discoverable
attorney work-product
encrypted
conflict of interest
bias
disinterested
multiple representation
adverse interests
duty of loyalty

imputed disqualification
tainted
tainted paralegal
Chinese Wall
quarantined
conflicts check
conflicts specialist
lateral hire
solicitation
ambulance chasing
barratry
runner
unauthorized practice of law
Model Rule 5.3
legal advice
second chair

## ON THE NET: MORE ON ETHICS AND PROFESSIONAL RESPONSIBILITY

### State-by-State Rules of Ethics

www.abanet.org/cpr/links.html

www.virtualchase.com/resources/ethics.shtml

www2.law.cornell.edu/cgi-bin/foliocgi.exe

### ABA Center for Professional Responsibility

www.abanet.org/cpr/home.html

### Directory of Lawyer Disciplinary Agencies

www.abanet.org/cpr/disciplinary.html

### ABA *Model Code* (complete text)

www2.law.cornell.edu/cgi-bin/foliocgi.exe/Mdlcpr?

### Proposed Changes in the ABA *Model Rules*

www.abanet.org/journal/may01/fcle.html

www.abanet.org/cpr/e2k-whole_report_home.html

### Advertising, Solicitation, and Marketing

www.abanet.org/adrules/home.html

### NFPA Ethics; NALA Ethics

www.paralegals.org/Development/modelcode.html

www.nala.org/stand.htm

www.nala.org/news.htm

### Other Resources on Legal Ethics (Often through Links)

www.legalethics.com/states.htm

www.law.cornell.edu/ethics

www.aprl.net

www.freivogelonconflicts.com

www.nobc.org

www.catalaw.com/topics/Ethics.shtml

www.marlenhill.com

## ENDNOTES

1. New Mexico Rules Governing the Practice of Law, §20–110, Committee Commentary (Judicial Pamphlet 16).

2. In some states, an exception exists in cases to collect *past due* child support payments. A contingent fee in such cases might be allowed so long as the divorce is already final. South Dakota Bar Association, Ethics Opinion 95–8.

3. Lisa Lerman, *Scenes from a Law Firm*, 50 Rutgers Law Review 2153, 2159 (1998).

4. Smith, *AAfPE National Conference Highlights*, 8 Legal Assistant Today 103 (January/February 1991).

5. Sonia Chan, *ABA Formal Opinion 93–379: Double Billing, Padding and Other Forms of Overbilling*, 9 Georgetown Journal of Legal Ethics 611, 615 (1996).

6. C. Paddelford, 7 RECAP 2 (California Alliance of Paralegal Associations, Fall 1992).

7. Tulsa Ass'n of Legal Assistants, *Hints for Helping Your Attorney Avoid Legal Malpractice*, TALA Times (August 1989).

8. Race, *Malpractice Maladies*, Paradigm 12 (Baltimore Ass'n of Legal Assistants, July/August 1989).

9. Shays, *Ethics for the Paralegal*, Postscript 15 (Manhattan Paralegal Ass'n, August/September 1989).

10. *Phoenix Founders, Inc. v. Marshall*, 887 S.W.2d 831, 834 (Tex. 1994).

11. An exception exists if the "party seeking discovery has substantial need of the materials in the preparation of the party's case" and is unable to obtain the substantial equivalent of the materials without undue hardship by other means. This test, however, is rarely met. Federal Rule of Civil Procedure 26(b)(3).

12. Missouri Bar Ass'n, *Guidelines for Practicing with Paralegals* (1987).

13. State Bar of Texas, *General Guidelines for the Utilization of the Services of Legal Assistants by Attorneys* (1981); Rule 1.01, *Texas Disciplinary Rules of Professional Conduct* (1990).

14. Professional Responsibility Committee of the Philadelphia Bar Ass'n, *Professional Responsibility for Nonlawyers* (1989) (emphasis added).

15. *Orientation Handbook for Paralegals* 2 (Lane, Powell, Moses & Miller, 1984).

16. Daniels, *Privileged Information for Paralegals*, 17 At Issue 15 (San Francisco Ass'n of Legal Assistants, November 1990).

17. Betty Reinert, *Cyberspacing around Cowtown*, 13 Cowtown Paralegal Reporter 10 (March/April 1995).

18. Adam Levy, ... *Demise of the Tobacco Settlement*, 2 Journal of Health Care Law and Policy 1, 9 (1998).

19. Myron Levin, *Years of Immunity and Arrogance Up in Smoke*, Los Angeles Times, May 10, 1998, at D1, D17.

20. C. Wolfram, *Modern Legal Ethics* § 7.6.4 (1986).

21. The court said we need to determine "whether the practical effect of formal screening has been achieved." To make this determination, several factors should be considered. They include "the substantiality of the relationship between the matter on which the paralegal worked at the old firm and the matter she worked on at the new firm; the time elapsing between the matters; the size of the firm; the number of individuals presumed to have confidential information; the nature of their involvement in the former matter; and the timing and features of any measures taken to reduce the danger of disclosure." *Phoenix Founders, Inc.*, 887 S.W.2d at 836.

22. Susan L. Order, *Beware of Deadly Cone of Silence*, 18 Precedents 25 (San Diego Ass'n of Legal Assistants, July/August 1994).

23. Motamedi, *Landmark Ethics Case Takes Toll on Paralegal's Career, Family*, 7 Legal Assistant Today 39 (May/June 1990); *In re Complex Asbestos Litigation*, 232 Cal. App. 3d 572, 283 Cal. Rptr. 732 (1991).

24. M. Hall, *S.F. Decision on Paralegal Conflict May Plague Firms*, Los Angeles Daily Journal, September 25, 1989, at 1, col. 2.

25. *Orientation Handbook for Paralegals* 3 (Lane, Powell, Moses & Miller, 1984).

26. See *In re Opinion No. 24*, 128 N.J. 114, 607 A.2d 962 (1992).

27. David Vangagriff, *Computing Your Conflicts*, 10 The Compleat Lawyer 42 (Fall 1993).

28. New Mexico Rules Governing the Practice of Law, Section 20–104, Committee Commentary (Judicial Pamphlet 16).

29. *Health Plans Depict Lawyers as Threat*, N.Y. Times, October 8, 1999, at A22.

30. Metzner, *Strategies That Break the Rules*, National Law Journal 16 (July 15, 1991).

31. *Four Said to Have Used Bus Crash to Get Business for Law Firm*, N.Y. Times, April 7, 1990, at 8.

32. *Bates v. State Bar of Arizona*, 433 U.S. 350, 97 S. Ct. 2691, 53 L. Ed. 2d 810 (1977).

33. See (www.montlick.com/contact/form.html).

34. *Bates v. State Bar of Arizona*, 433 U.S. 350, 97 S. Ct. 2691, 53 L. Ed. 2d 810 (1977).

35. Tennessee Supreme Court Rule 8, EC 3–5.

36. King, *Ethics and the Legal Assistant*, 10 ParaGram 2 (Oregon Legal Assistants Ass'n, August 1987).

37. DALA Newsletter 2 (Dallas Ass'n of Legal Assistants, December 1990).

38. Spiegel, *How to Avoid the Unauthorized Practice of Law*, 8 The Journal 8–10 (Sacramento Ass'n of Legal Assistants, February 1986).

39. Michael Martz, *Ethics: Does a Legal Assistant Need Insurance?*, The Assistant 13 (Mississippi Ass'n of Legal Assistants, Fall 1993).

40. *In re Opinion No. 24 of Committee on Unauthorized Practice of Law*. 128 N.J. 114, 121, 607 A. 2d 962, 965 (1992).

41. Harper, *Ethical Considerations for Legal Assistants*, Compendium (Orange County Paralegal Ass'n, April 1987).

# Chapter 6

## INTRODUCTION TO THE LEGAL SYSTEM

## Chapter Outline

A. Federalism, Checks and Balances, and Paralegals

B. Common Law and Our Adversarial System

C. Judicial Systems

D. Administrative Agencies

E. The Legislative Process

Section A
# Federalism, Checks and Balances, and Paralegals

What are the components of our legal system and what kind of laws do they produce? These are our concerns in this chapter as we continue to explore the role of the paralegal.

Our legal system consists of three levels of government: the federal government (also called the national government or the United States government), 50 state governments,[1] and a large variety of local governments (called counties, cities, and townships). Of these three levels, the most important are the federal government and the state governments. To a large extent, local governments are dependent on (even though, in many respects, they are separate from) state governments.

A division of powers exists between the federal government and the state governments. Only the federal government, for example, has the power to declare war, whereas only a state government has the power to issue a marriage license or a divorce decree. Some powers are shared among these levels of government. In the area of public assistance or welfare, for example, both the federal government and the state governments play major roles. The term **federalism** refers to the division of powers between the federal government and the state governments. Federalism simply means that we live in a society where some powers are exercised by the federal government, others by the state governments, and still others by both the federal and the state governments.

Within the federal, state, and local levels of government, there are three *branches:* one that makes laws (**legislative branch**), one that carries out laws (**executive branch**), and one that interprets laws by resolving disputes that arise under them (**judicial branch**). The categories of law that these three branches of government write are outlined in exhibit 6.1.

Here is an overview of our three levels of government and the three branches that exist at each level:

**Federal Government**
*Legislative branch:* The Congress
*Executive branch:* The President and the federal administrative agencies (see the chart in appendix D.)
*Judicial branch:* The U.S. Supreme Court the U.S. Courts of Appeals, the U.S. District Courts, and other federal courts (see exhibits 6.3 and 6.4)

**State Government**
*Legislative branch:* The state legislature
*Executive branch:* The governor and the state administrative agencies
*Judicial branch:* The state courts (see exhibit 6.2)

**Local Government**
*Legislative branch:* The city council or county commission
*Executive branch:* The mayor or county commissioner and the local administrative agencies
*Judicial branch:* The local courts (some local courts, however, are considered part of the state judiciary)

In addition to the division of power between the federal and state levels of government, there is a division of power among the three branches—legislative, executive, and judicial—within each level. This division is called the system of **checks and balances** and is designed to prevent any one branch from becoming too powerful. The system allocates governmental powers among the three branches. One branch is allowed to block, check, or review another branch so that a balance of powers is maintained among the branches. Let's look at an example.

The legislative branch has the primary responsibility for writing the law. By majority vote, the legislature creates what are called *statutes* (see exhibit 6.1). But there are significant checks on this power. First of all, the chief executive must give final approval to a proposed law before it can become a statute. He or she can veto (i.e., reject) the proposed law. The legislature, however, has another power that operates as a countercheck on the chief executive's power to veto proposed laws. The legislature can override (i.e., nullify) the

---

**federalism** The division of powers between the federal government and the state governments.

**legislative branch** The branch of government with primary responsibility for making or enacting the law.

**executive branch** The branch of government with primary responsibility for carrying out, executing, or administering the laws.

**judicial branch** The branch of government with primary responsibility for interpreting laws by resolving disputes that arise under them.

**checks and balances** An allocation of governmental powers whereby one branch of government can block, check, or review what another branch wants to do (or has done) in order to maintain a balance of power among the legislative, executive, and judicial branches.

**EXHIBIT 6.1** Kinds of Laws

| CATEGORY | DEFINITION | WHO WRITES THIS KIND OF LAW? | EXAMPLE |
|---|---|---|---|
| (a) Opinion | A court's written explanation of how it applied the law to the facts before it to resolve a legal dispute. Also called a *case*. (The word *case* has two other meanings: a pending matter on a court calendar and a client matter handled by a law office.) | Courts—the judiciary (The courts that write most of the opinions are courts of appeal, also called appellate courts.) | In the opinion *Jackson v. I.B.M.*, the court of appeals affirmed the trial court ruling that Jackson had not been fired because of his race. |
| (b) Statute | A law that declares, commands, or, prohibits something. Also called *legislation*. (An *act* is the official document that contains the statute.) | The legislature. Some states also allow a direct vote of the people by referendum. | § 200 of title 4 of the statutory code requires corporations to file biannual finance statements with the secretary of state. |
| (c) Constitution | The fundamental law that creates the branches of government and identifies basic rights and obligations. | Varies. Often a combination of the legislature and a vote of the people. Another option might be a constitutional convention. | § 7 of article I of the constitution provides that all bills for raising revenue shall originate in the House of Representatives. |
| (d) Administrative Regulation | A law designed to explain or carry out the statutes and executive orders that govern an administrative agency. Also called an *administrative rule*. | Administrative agency. | § 16 of the administrative code provides that all finance statements filed pursuant to § 200 of the statutory code shall be accompanied by a $75 filing fee. |
| (e) Administrative Decision | A resolution of a controversy between a party and an administrative agency involving the application of the regulations, statutes, or executive orders that govern the agency. Also called an *administrative ruling*. | Administrative agency. | In *SEC v. Forbes and Shelton*, the Securities and Exchange Commission brought an enforcement action charging that corporate officials had committed financial fraud. |
| (f) Charter | The fundamental law of a municipality or other local unit of government authorizing it to perform designated governmental functions. | Varies. The state legislature often writes charter provisions for cities in the state. | § 160 of the municipal charter provides that applicants for the position of city clerk with the three highest scores on the civil service test shall be interviewed within thirty days of the receipt of the test scores. |

| EXHIBIT 6.1 | Kinds of Laws—*continued* |

| CATEGORY | DEFINITION | WHO WRITES THIS KIND OF LAW? | EXAMPLE |
| --- | --- | --- | --- |
| (g) Ordinance | A law that declares, commands or prohibits something. (Same as a stature, but at the local level.) | The local legislature (e.g., City Council, County Commission). | § 10.5-1 of the revised municipal code provides that telecommunications companies must obtain a "private use permit" when seeking to use any public right of way within city limits. |
| (h) Rules of Court | The procedural laws that govern the mechanics of litigation (practice and procedure) before a particular court. Also called *court rules*. | Varies. The legislature and/or the highest court in the jurisdiction. | Superior Court Rule 9C provides that opposing counsel shall confer in advance of filing any motion in a good faith effort to narrow areas of disagreement pertaining to the motion. |
| (i) Executive Order | A law issued by the chief executive pursuant to specific statutory authority or to the executive's inherent authority to direct the operation of governmental agencies. | President (for U.S. government); Governor (for state government); Mayor (for local government). | Executive Order No. 22 directs the Department of Education to complete within six months a comprehensive review of all vendor contracts involving a payment of $5,000 or over. |
| (j) Treaty | An international agreement between two or more nations or sovereigns. Also called a *convention*. | The President makes treaties by and with the consent of the U.S. Senate. (If the President has the authority to enter the agreement without Senate approval, it is called an *executive agreement*.) | Article 9 of the Extradition Treaty between the United States and Mexico provides that neither country is bound to deliver up its own nationals, but that each country has the discretion to do so. |
| (k) Opinion of the Attorney General | Formal legal advice given by the chief law officer of the government to another government official or agency (Technically, this is *not* a category of law, but it is often relied on as a source of law.) | Attorney General (sometimes called legal counsel) | Attorney General Opinion #90-39 concluded that the phrase "teacher's contract" in § 65(c) of the statutory code did not apply to teachers hired for temporary Summer positions. |

**judicial review** The power of a court to determine the constitutionality of a statute or other law, including the power to refuse to enforce it if the court concludes that it violates the constitution.

chief executive's veto by a two-thirds vote. These are some of the ways that the legislative and executive branches check each other.

The judiciary branch has a similar function. Courts can check the legislative and executive branches through the power of **judicial review**. This is the power to refuse to enforce a law because it is in conflict with the *constitution*. In turn, the judicial branch can be checked by the other branches. For example, the legislature controls the budget of the courts, and the chief executive often nominates the persons who will be judges.

The result of all these checks and counterchecks is a *balance* of power among the three branches so that no one branch becomes too powerful.

How do paralegals fit within these levels and branches of government? First of all, many paralegals are civil service employees of government, particularly in federal, state, and local administrative agencies (see appendix 2.B in chapter 2). To a more limited extent, paralegals are also employees of legislatures and courts. Second, paralegals help attorneys solve the legal problems of clients by applying the different kinds of law outlined in exhibit 6.1 to the facts presented by client cases. A single client case can involve the laws of different levels and branches of government.

For example:

Linda Thompson applies for unemployment compensation benefits after being terminated from her job. Her former employer says the termination was due to a slowdown in business at the company. Linda believes she was let go because she is a woman and because she is HIV positive. You are a paralegal working for Sims & Sims, which represents her. Your supervisor may ask you to undertake a variety of tasks: interviewing, investigation, research, analysis, drafting, law office administration, etc. A central focus of everything the attorney and paralegal do on such a case is the application of laws to the facts of the case. The laws are written by different branches of government at the different levels of government. Here are some examples of laws that might apply to Linda Thompson's case:

- The Fourteenth Amendment of the United States Constitution guaranteeing equal protection of the law.
- Federal statutes on civil rights, sex discrimination, disability discrimination, evidence and civil procedure in federal courts, etc.
- Opinions of federal courts on civil rights, sex discrimination, disability discrimination, evidence, civil procedure in federal courts, etc.
- Administrative regulations on sex discrimination of the U.S. Equal Employment Opportunity Commission and other federal administrative agencies.
- The Equal Rights Amendment of the state constitution prohibiting sex discrimination.
- State statutes on unemployment compensation, civil rights, sex discrimination, evidence and civil procedure in state courts, etc.
- State court opinions on unemployment compensation, civil rights, sex discrimination, evidence and civil procedure in state courts, etc.
- Administrative regulations on unemployment compensation of the State Unemployment compensation Commission.

These, then, are the major laws and institutions involved in the practice of law. We can say that our legal system is an organized method of resolving legal disputes and achieving justice through the interpretation and enforcement of laws written by different levels and branches of government. To participate, paralegals need to have a basic understanding of the essential components of this process. The chapters in part II of this book are designed to provide this understanding.

---

### Assignment 6.1

Find a recent article in your local general newspaper that meets the following criteria: (a) it refers to more than one kind of law listed in exhibit 6.1, and (b) it refers to more than one level of government. The article will have no formal citations to laws, so do the best you can to guess what kinds of law and levels of government are involved. Clip out the article. In the margin, next to each reference to a law, place the appropriate abbreviation: FO (if you think the reference is to a federal court opinion); SO (if you think the reference is to a state court opinion); FS (federal statute); SS (state statute); FC (United States Constitution); SC (state constitution); FAR (administrative regulation of a federal agency); SAR (administrative regulation of a state agency). Make up your own abbreviations for any other kind of law listed in Exhibit 6.1. If the article refers to the same law more than once, make a margin note only the first time the law is mentioned. (We'll have an informal contest to see which student can find the article with the most different kinds of laws involving more than one level of government.)

## Section B
# Common Law and Our Adversarial System

Before examining the components of our judicial system, we need to understand two of its critical characteristics. First of all, the system is based on the **common law**. This phrase has at least four meanings, the last of which will be our primary concern in this book:

- At the broadest level, common law simply means case law—court opinions—as opposed to statutory law. In this sense, all case law develops and is part of the common law.
- Common law also refers to the legal system of England and the United States. Its counterpart is the **civil law system** of many Western European countries other than England. The origin of civil law includes the jurisprudence of the Roman Empire set forth in the Code of Justinian. Many civil codes in Europe (other than England) have been greatly influenced by the Code Napoléon of France. Both the common law system and the civil law system rely on statutory codes and on case law. The difference is primarily one of emphasis. In a common law system, the role of case law is greater than it is in a civil law system. On the other hand, in a civil law system, statutory or code law has greater prominence than it does in a common law system. Forty-nine states in the United States have a common law system. Louisiana is unique in that its law is largely based on the civil code due to the historical importance of France in that state.
- More narrowly, common law refers to all of the case law *and* statutory law in England and in the American colonies before the American Revolution. The phrase **at common law** often refers to this colonial period.
- The most prevalent definition of common law is judge-made law in the absence of controlling statutory law or other higher law.

Courts are sometimes confronted with disputes for which there is no applicable law. There may be no constitutional provisions, statutes, or administrative regulations governing the dispute. When this occurs, the court will apply—and if necessary, create—common law to resolve the controversy. Here, common law is used in the fourth sense given above. That is, it is made by judges to compensate for the lack of statutory and other law applicable to the case at hand. In creating the common law, the court relies primarily on the unwritten customs and values of the community from time immemorial. Very often these customs and values are described and enforced in old opinions that are heavily cited by modern courts in the continuing process of developing the common law.

The common law grows slowly, case by case. Radical changes are not encouraged and, therefore, are relatively rare. Once a court decides a case, it becomes a potential **precedent** that can be helpful for the resolution of similar cases that arise in the future. Under the doctrine of **stare decisis**, a court will decide similar cases in the same way (i.e., it will follow available precedents) unless there is good reason for the court to do otherwise. Courts are most comfortable when they can demonstrate that their decisions are rooted in precedent. Knowing this, attorneys and paralegals study precedents in order to try to predict how a court might resolve a current case.

Suppose, for example, that a law firm is representing a client who is being sued for battery, which is a common law **cause of action.** He took a baseball bat and forcefully hit the handle bars of a bicycle on which the plaintiff was riding at the time. The bat did not touch the plaintiff's body. This case raises the question of whether you can batter someone without making contact with his or her body. One of the steps the law firm will take in representing this client is to do legal research in order to try to find precedents for this kind of case. Assume that on the shelves of the law library (or in an online legal database), the attorney or paralegal finds the prior case of *Harrison v. Linner*. This case held the defendant committed a battery when he knocked over a plate being held by the plaintiff even though the defendant never touched any part of the plaintiff's body. Is *Harrison v. Linner* a precedent for the bicycle case? Is hitting a bicycle handle with a bat sufficiently similar to knocking a plate out of someone's hand? The law firm must predict whether a court will apply *Harrison v. Linner* to the bicycle case. Making

---

**common law** (1) Court opinions, all of case law. (2) The legal system of England and of those countries such as the United States whose legal system is based on England's. (3) The case law and statutory law in England and in the American colonies before the American Revolution. (4) Judge-made law in the absence of controlling statutory law or other higher law.

**civil law system** The legal system of many Western European countries (other than England) that place a greater emphasis on statutory or code law than do countries (such as England and the United States) whose common law system places a greater emphasis on case law.

**at common law** All the case law and statutory law in England and in the American colonies before the Revolution.

**precedent** A prior decision that can provide some guidance for the resolution of a current dispute before the court.

**stare decisis** Courts should decide similar cases in the same way unless there is good reason for the court to do otherwise. A reluctance to reject precedent—prior opinions.

**cause of action** A legally acceptable reason for suing. Facts that give a party the right to judicial relief.

such a prediction requires legal analysis, which we will be studying in chapter 7. For our purposes, the example illustrates how precedent is used in our common law system. When the bicycle case goes before the court, the attorneys for both sides will be spending a good deal of time trying to convince the court that *Harrison v. Linner* is or is not a precedent.

Note that the fourth definition of common law says judge-made law in the absence of controlling statutory law or other higher law. As we will learn in chapter 11, there is a hierarchy in the categories of law. Constitutional law, for example, is higher in authority than statutory law. So, too, statutory law is higher in authority than common law. Assume that the courts have created common law in an area where no controlling statutes existed. This does not mean that statutes can never play a role in this area. The legislature can now decide to step in and create statutes that change the common law in this area. Such statutes are said to be *in derogation of the common law*.

One of the best examples of the interplay between common law and statutory law can be found in the area of contracts. A great deal of contract law was created by the courts as common law. Centuries ago, for example, the courts created the principle that a contract was not enforceable unless it was supported by consideration. Over the years, statutes have been written to change many common law contract principles. In some kinds of contracts, for example, statutes have changed the common law of consideration. For commercial contracts, the greatest statutory changes were brought about by the Uniform Commercial Code. Many other contract statutes in derogation of the common law also exist. Today, contract law consists of a mix of statutes and those common law principles that have not been changed by legislatures or indeed by the courts themselves, who are always free to change their own common law. This evolution of the common law has been taking place for centuries and has given us what commentators call the "seamless web" of the common law.

The second critical characteristic of our judicial system is that it is **adversarial**. An adversarial system is a form of head-to-head combat. If a dispute arises, you get everyone in the same room and have them fight it out—in the open. This approach is based on the theory that justice and truth have a greater chance of being achieved when the parties to a controversy appear (on their own or through a representative or advocate) before a neutral judge to present their conflicting positions. We don't expect the judge to control the case by calling and questioning the witnesses. By and large, we leave this to the parties and their representatives. Ideally, the parties have an equal opportunity to present their case to the decision-maker.[2] Unfortunately, the system is often criticized for failing to live up to this ideal. In many disputes between a citizen and a corporation, for example, the citizen cannot afford the kind of representation available to the corporation.

**adversarial** Involving the presence of an opponent or adversary.

## Section C
# JUDICIAL SYSTEMS

The lifeblood of a court is its **jurisdiction**. After examining the nature of jurisdiction, our goal here will be to identify the major courts that exist and to explore how they are interrelated.

### 1. JURISDICTION

There are 50 state court systems and 1 main federal court system. Each court within a system is identified by its jurisdiction to **adjudicate** (i.e., resolve through litigation) a legal dispute brought before it. When referring to the courts, the word *jurisdiction* has two major meanings.

First, it refers to the power of the court over the persons or over the property involved in the litigation. Power over the person is called **personal jurisdiction** (also, in personam jurisdiction). If the court is not able to obtain personal jurisdiction over the defendant, it still may be able to make an order over a particular thing (called the *res*) located within the territory over which the court has authority. An example of a res would be land. The jurisdiction that a court needs to render a judgment over such a res is called **in rem jurisdiction**. Everyone with an interest in the res (e.g., anyone who claims to own all or a part

**jurisdiction** Power or authority to act.

**adjudicate** To use a court or other tribunal to resolve a legal dispute through litigation. The noun is *adjudication*; the adjective is *adjudicative*.

**personal jurisdiction** The court's power over a particular person.

**in rem jurisdiction** The court's power over a particular thing ('res') located within the territory over which the court has authority.

**subject matter jurisdiction**
The power of the court to resolve a particular category of dispute.

**limited jurisdiction** The power of a court to hear only certain kinds of cases. Also called special jurisdiction.

**general jurisdiction** The power of a court to hear any kind of civil or criminal case, with certain exceptions.

**state questions** Issues or questions that arise from or that are based on the state constitution, state statutes, state administrative regulations, state common law, or other state laws.

**federal questions** Issues or questions that arise from or that are based on the federal constitution, federal statutes, federal administrative regulations, or other federal laws.

**exclusive jurisdiction** The power of a court to hear a particular kind of case, to the exclusion of other courts.

**concurrent jurisdiction** The power of a court to hear a particular kind of case, along with other courts that could also hear it.

**original jurisdiction** The power of a court to hear a particular kind of case initially; a trial court.

**appellate jurisdiction** The power of a court to hear an appeal of a case from a lower tribunal (e.g., a lower court or administrative agency) to determine whether the lower tribunal committed any errors of law.

of it), and not just those over whom the court has personal jurisdiction, must obey the judgment of a court with in rem jurisdiction.[3]

Second, jurisdiction means the power that a court must have over the subject matter or over the particular kind of dispute that has been brought before it. Some of the more common classifications of **subject matter jurisdiction** are:

- Limited jurisdiction
- General jurisdiction
- Exclusive jurisdiction
- Concurrent jurisdiction
- Original jurisdiction
- Appellate jurisdiction

### a. Limited Jurisdiction

A court of **limited** (or special) subject-matter **jurisdiction** can hear only certain kinds of cases. A criminal court is not allowed to take a noncriminal case, and a small claims court is authorized to hear only cases in which the plaintiff claims a relatively small amount of money as damages from the defendant. (The maximum amount a small claims court can award is set by statute.)

### b. General Jurisdiction

A court of **general jurisdiction** can, with some exceptions, hear any kind of civil or criminal case. (Here, the word *civil* means pertaining to a private right or matter.) A state court of general jurisdiction can handle any case that raises **state questions** (i.e., questions arising from or based on the state constitution, state statutes, state regulations, state common law, or other state laws); a federal court of general jurisdiction can handle any case that raises **federal questions** (i.e., questions arising from or based on the federal constitution, federal statutes, federal regulations, or other federal laws).[4]

### c. Exclusive Jurisdiction

A court of **exclusive jurisdiction** is the only court that can handle a certain kind of case. For example, a juvenile court may have exclusive jurisdiction over all cases involving children under a certain age who are charged with acts of delinquency. If this kind of case is brought in another court, there could be a challenge on the ground that the court lacked jurisdiction over the case.

### d. Concurrent Jurisdiction

Sometimes two courts have jurisdiction over a case; the case could be brought in either court. In such a situation, both courts are said to have **concurrent jurisdiction** over the case. For example, a family court and a county court may have jurisdiction to enforce a child-support order.

### e. Original Jurisdiction

A court of **original jurisdiction** is the first court to hear a case. It is also called a trial court or a *court of first instance*. In addition, it is a court of limited jurisdiction (if it can try only certain kinds of cases), or of general jurisdiction (if it can try cases involving any subject matter), or of exclusive jurisdiction (if the trial can take place only in that court), or of concurrent jurisdiction (if the trial can take place either in that court or in another kind of court).

### f. Appellate Jurisdiction

A court with **appellate jurisdiction** can hear appeals from lower tribunals (e.g., a lower court, an administrative agency) to determine whether the lower tribunal committed any error of law. For example, at the federal level, the United States Supreme Court has appellate jurisdiction to review a decision of a United States Court of Appeals. Similarly, at the state level, the New York Court of Appeals has appellate jurisdiction to review a decision of a lower New York state court. The reexamination of what the lower tribunal has done is called a review. Sometimes a party who is dissatisfied with a lower court ruling can appeal as a matter of right to the appellate court (the court must hear the appeal); in other kinds of cases, the appellate court has discretion as to whether it will hear the appeal.

## 2. STATE COURT SYSTEMS

First, we examine jurisdiction in our state courts. See exhibit 6.2.

### a. Courts of Original Jurisdiction

A state will have one or more levels or tiers of trial courts (courts of original jurisdiction). These courts hear the dispute, determine the facts of the case, and make the initial determination or ruling. In addition, they may sometimes have the power to review cases that were initially decided by an administrative agency.

The most common arrangement is a two-tier system of trial courts. At the lower level are courts of limited or special jurisdiction, the so-called **inferior courts**. Local courts, such

**inferior court** A lower court of limited or special jurisdiction.

| EXHIBIT 6.2 | Hierarchy of State Judicial Systems | |
|---|---|---|
| **LEVEL OF COURT** | **NAME(S) OF COURT AT THIS LEVEL IN DIFFERENT STATES** | **FUNCTION OF COURT AT THIS LEVEL AND THE LINES OF APPEAL** |
| The court of final resort—the highest court in the state court system | Supreme Court, Supreme Judicial Court, Supreme Court of Appeals, Court of Appeals | ■ This court has appellate jurisdiction.<br>■ It hears appeals from lower courts in the state. If the state has intermediate appellate courts, appeals are heard from these courts. If intermediate appellate courts do not exist in the state, the highest state court hears appeals directly from trial courts. |
| Intermediate appellate courts (exist in about half the states) | Court of Appeals, Court of Civil Appeals, Court of Criminal Appeals, Appellate Court, Appeals Court, District Court of Appeals, Intermediate Court of Appeals, Court of Special Appeals, Appellate Division of Superior Court | ■ This court has appellate jurisdiction.<br>■ It hears appeals from trial courts in the state. If the state does not have intermediate appellate courts, appeals go directly from the trial court to the court of final resort. |
| Trial courts: tier I | Superior Court, Circuit Court, District Court, Court of Common Pleas (in New York, the trial court at this level is called the Supreme Court) | ■ This is a trial court of general jurisdiction.<br>■ Cases from these courts are appealed to the intermediate appellate courts in the state if the state has intermediate appellate courts. If the state does not have such courts, cases are appealed to the court of final resort. |
| Trial courts: tier II | Probate Court, Small Claims Court, Family Court, Municipal Court, County Court, District Court, Justice of the Peace Court, Police Court, City Court, Water Court (Trial courts at this level are sometimes called *inferior courts*) | ■ This is a trial court of limited jurisdiction. *Examples*: The Probate Court hears estate cases of deceased or incompetent persons; the Small Claims Court hears cases involving small amounts of money damages; the Family Court hears divorce, custody, and other domestic relations matters; the Municipal Court hears traffic cases and those involving petty crimes.<br>■ Cases from trial courts of limited jurisdiction are often appealed to trial courts of general jurisdiction. Some, however, are appealed to the intermediate appellate courts (if they exist) or to the court of final resort. |

as city courts, county courts, small claims courts, or justice of the peace courts, often fall into this category. These courts may have original jurisdiction over relatively minor cases, such as violations of local ordinances and lawsuits involving small sums of money. Also included in this category are special courts that are limited to specific matters, such as surrogate courts or probate courts that hear matters involving the estates of deceased or mentally incompetent persons.

Immediately above the trial courts of limited jurisdiction are the trial courts of general jurisdiction, which usually handle more serious cases, such as lawsuits involving large sums of money. The name given to the trial courts at this second level varies greatly from state to state. They are known as superior courts, courts of common pleas, district courts, or circuit courts. New York is especially confusing. There, the trial court of general jurisdiction is called the *supreme court*, a label reserved in most states for the court of final appeals, the highest court in the system.

Not all states have a two-tier trial system. Some states do not have inferior courts of limited jurisdiction; they have only one court of original jurisdiction. Moreover, the individual levels may be segmented into divisions. A court of general jurisdiction, for example, may be broken up into specialized divisions such as landlord-tenant, family, juvenile, and criminal divisions.

### b. Courts of Appeals

A court of appeals (also called an *appellate court*) has appellate jurisdiction. This allows it to review decisions of a lower tribunal in order to determine whether that lower tribunal committed any errors of law by incorrectly interpreting or applying the law to the facts of the dispute. In this review process, appellate courts do not make their own findings of fact. No new evidence is taken, and no witnesses are called. The court limits itself to an analysis of the trial court record (consisting of transcripts of testimony, copies of the various documents that were filed, etc.) to determine if that lower court made any errors of law. Attorneys submit **appellate briefs** containing their arguments on the correctness or incorrectness of what the lower court did.

An appellate court often consists of an odd number of justices, e.g., 5, 7, 9, 11, 15. This helps avoid tie votes. Some of these courts hear cases in smaller groups of judges, usually 3. These groups are called **panels.** Once a panel renders its decision, the parties often have the right to petition to the full court to hear the case **en banc**, meaning with the entire membership of the court.

Many states have only one level of appellate court to which trial court judgments are appealed. About half the states have two levels or tiers of appellate courts. The first level is the court of middle appeals, sometimes called an intermediate appellate court. The decisions of this court can in turn be reviewed by the court of final appeals. This latter court, often known as the supreme court, is the **court of final resort**. As indicated in exhibit 6.2, about half the states do not have intermediate appellate courts. Appeals from trial courts in such states go directly to the court of final resort.

**appellate brief** A document submitted by a party to an appellate court and served on the opposing party in which arguments are presented on why the rulings of a lower court should be approved, modified, or reversed.

**panel** A group of judges, usually three, who decide a case. (See the glossary for other meanings of *panel*.)

**en banc** By the entire court.

**court of final resort** The highest court within a judicial system.

---

### Assignment 6.2

(a) Redo exhibit 6.2 so that your chart includes all the state courts of your state. Identify each level of state court in your state using exhibit 6.2 as a guide. Give the complete name of each court you include and a one-sentence description of its subject matter jurisdiction. Indicate the lines of appeal among these courts. To find out what state courts exist in your state, check your state statutory code and your state constitution. This is the only way to obtain current information about your state court system. You may come across a chart written by someone else, but it may not reflect recent changes in the structure and names of your state courts.

(b) Select any state trial court of general jurisdiction in your state. State its name, address, and phone number. Include the e-mail address and the World Wide Web site if the court has either. Also state the name, phone number, and fax number of the chief clerk of this court.

(c) Give the name, address, and phone number of the court to which decisions of the trial court you selected are appealed. Include the e-mail address and the World Wide Web site if the court has either. Also state the name, phone number, and fax number of the chief clerk of this appellate court.

## 3. FEDERAL COURT SYSTEM

The federal court system, like the state systems, consists of two basic kinds of courts: courts of original jurisdiction (trial courts) and appellate courts. See exhibit 6.3.

### a. Courts of Original Jurisdiction

The basic federal court at the trial level is the **United States District Court.** There are districts throughout the country, at least one for every state, the District of Columbia, Guam, the Virgin Islands, and Puerto Rico. The District Courts exercise general, original jurisdiction over most federal litigation and also serve as courts of review for many cases initially decided by federal administrative agencies. In addition to the District Courts, several federal courts, such as the United States Court of Federal Claims, and the United States Bankruptcy Court, exercise original, limited jurisdiction over specialized cases.

**United States District Court** The main trial court in the federal judicial system.

### b. Courts of Appeals

The federal system, like almost half of the 50 state judicial systems, has two levels or tiers of appellate courts: intermediate appellate courts and the court of final resort. The primary courts at the intermediate appellate level are the **United States Courts of Appeals.** These courts are divided into 12 geographic circuits, 11 of them made up of groupings of various states and territories, with a 12th for the District of Columbia. Their main function is to review the decisions of the federal courts of original jurisdiction, primarily the

**United States Court of Appeals** The main intermediate appellate court in the federal judicial system.

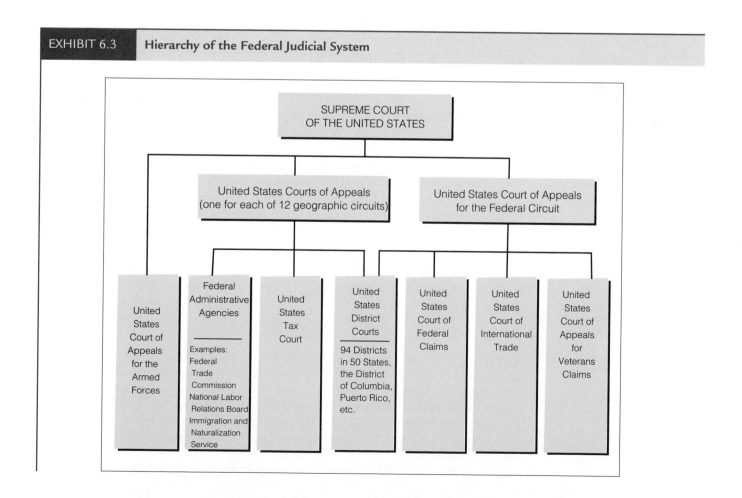

| EXHIBIT 6.3 | Hierarchy of the Federal Judicial System |

District Courts. In addition, decisions of certain federal agencies, notably the National Labor Relations Board, are reviewed directly by a Court of Appeals without first going to a District Court. Finally, there is a specialized Court of Appeals called the Court of Appeals for the Federal Circuit. This court reviews (a) decisions from the United States Court of Federal Claims, the United States Court of International Trade, and the United States Court of Appeals for Veterans Claims and (b) some decisions of the District Courts where the United States government is a defendant.[5]

**United States Supreme Court** The court of final resort in the federal judicial system.

The federal court of final resort is, of course, the **United States Supreme Court**, which provides the final review of the decisions of all federal courts and agencies. The Supreme Court may also review certain decisions of the state courts when these decisions raise questions involving the United States Constitution, a federal statute, or other federal law.

Exhibit 6.4 illustrates the division of the federal court system into 12 geographic circuits. Each circuit has its own United States Court of Appeals. The United States District Courts exist within these circuits.

---

### Assignment 6.3

(a) What is the complete name of the federal trial court that covers where you live? Give its address and phone number. Include the e-mail address and the World Wide Web site if the court has either. Also state the name, phone number, and fax number of the chief clerk of this court.

(b) What is the name of the Unites States Court of Appeals to which decisions of your federal trial court are appealed? Give its address and phone number. Include the e-mail address and the World Wide Web site if the court has either. Also state the name, phone number, and fax number of the chief clerk of this appellate court.

---

## Section D
# ADMINISTRATIVE AGENCIES

**administrative agency** A unit of government that carries out or administers the statutes of the legislature and the executive orders of the president, governor, mayor, or other chief executive of the executive branch.

An **administrative agency** is a unit of government whose primary mission is to carry out—or administer—the statutes of the legislature and the executive orders of the chief of the executive branch of government. At the federal level, the chief is the president; at the state level, it is the governor; and at most local levels, it is the mayor. As we will see in a moment, many agencies do more than carry out or execute the law; they also have closely related rulemaking and dispute-resolution responsibilities.

Administrative agencies can have a wide variety of names. Here are some examples:

- Fire Department
- Board of Licenses and Occupations
- Civil Service Commission
- Agency for International Development
- Department of Defense
- Office of Management and Budget

- Legal Services Corporation
- Bureau of Taxation
- Internal Revenue Service
- Division of Child Support and Enforcement
- Social Security Administration

Certain types of agencies exist at all three levels of government. For example, there is a separate tax collection agency in each of the federal, state, and local governments. Other agencies, however, are unique to one of the levels. For example, only the federal government has a Department of Defense (DOD) and a Central Intelligence Agency (CIA). Nothing comparable exists at the state and local levels of government. The latter have police departments and the highway patrol, but their role is significantly different from the DOD and CIA.

For a list of some of the most important federal agencies, see appendix D.

EXHIBIT 6.4 United States Courts of Appeals and United States District Courts

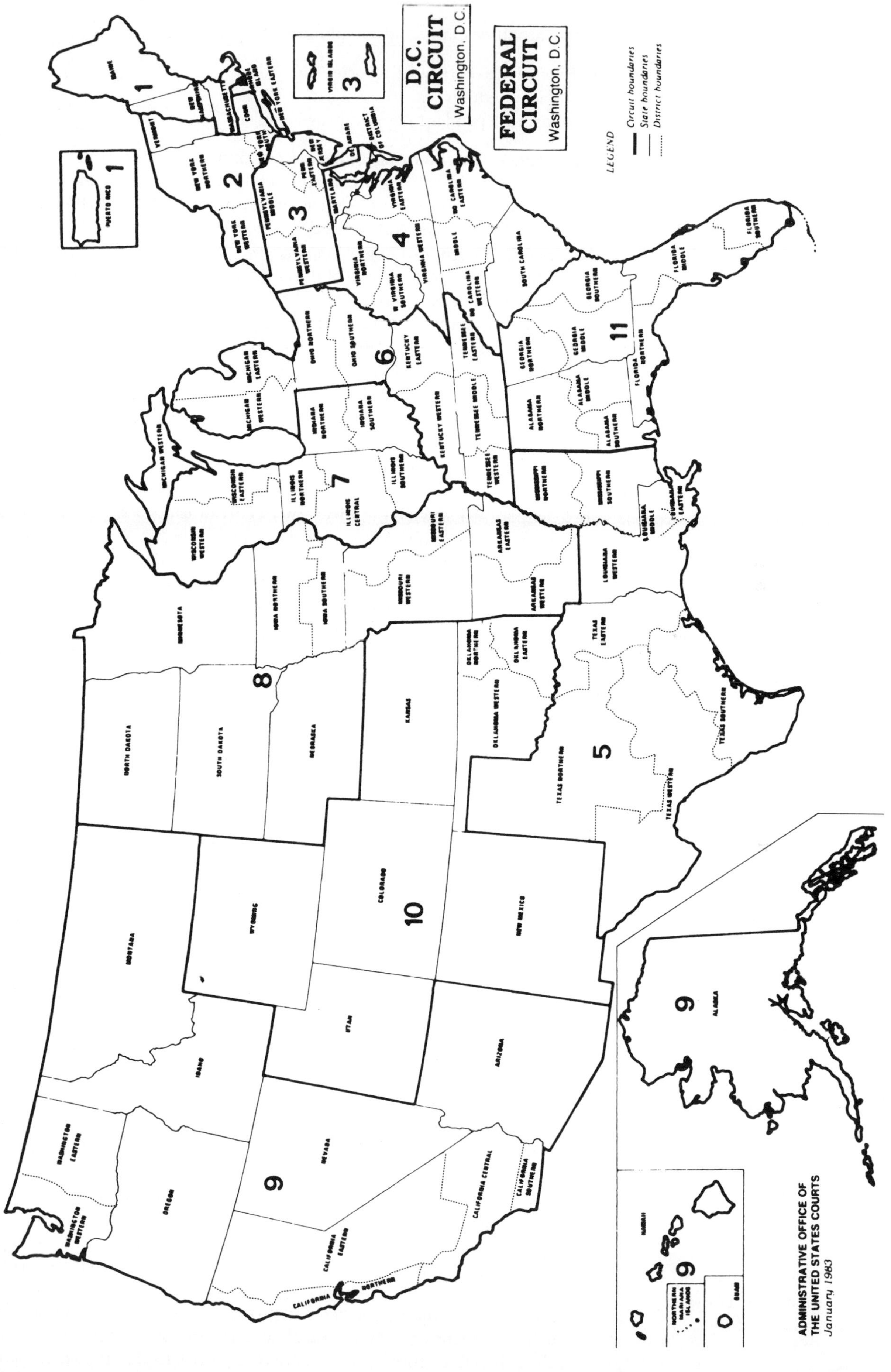
D.C. CIRCUIT
Washington, D.C.
FEDERAL CIRCUIT
Washington, D.C.
LEGEND
Circuit boundaries
State boundaries
District boundaries
ADMINISTRATIVE OFFICE OF
THE UNITED STATES COURTS
January 1983

There are three main kinds of administrative agencies:

- Executive department agencies
- Independent regulatory agencies
- Quasi-independent regulatory agencies

**executive department agency**  An administrative agency that exists within the executive branch of government, often at the cabinet level.

**Executive department agencies** exist within the executive branch of the government, often at the cabinet level. Examples include the Department of Agriculture and the Department of Labor. These agencies are answerable to the chief executive, who usually has the power to dismiss those in charge of them.

**independent regulatory agency**  An administrative agency that regulates an aspect of society. It often exists outside the executive branch of government.

**Independent regulatory agencies** exist outside the executive department and, therefore, outside the day-to-day control of the chief executive. Examples include the Securities and Exchange Commission and the Public Utilities Commission. Their function is usually to regulate an aspect of society—often a particular industry such as securities and public utilities. To insulate these agencies from politics, those in charge usually cannot be removed at the whim of the chief executive.

**quasi-independent regulatory agency**  An administrative agency that has characteristics of an executive department agency and an independent regulatory agency.

A **quasi-independent regulatory agency** is a hybrid agency, often with characteristics of the two kinds just described. It has more independence than an executive department agency, yet it might exist within the executive department. An example is the Federal Energy Regulatory Commission, which exists within the United States Department of Energy.

**government corporation**  An entity that is a mixture of a corporation and a government agency created to serve a predominantly business function in the public interest.

In a category all its own is the **government corporation**. This is an entity that has characteristics of a corporation and a government agency. It is designed to have considerable flexibility and independence in carrying out a predominantly business function in the public interest. Examples include the Tennessee Valley Authority, the United States Post Office, and the Corporation for Public Broadcasting. The government establishes this entity and usually provides its initial funding. Often, however, its ongoing budget comes from fees and private charitable giving. Members of the boards of directors of government corporations are usually appointed by the president and confirmed by the Senate.

Many administrative agencies have three functions: execution, rule making, and dispute resolution:

**quasi-legislation**  An administrative regulation enacted by an administrative agency that has some characteristics of the legislation (i.e., the statutes) enacted by the legislature.

- *Execution*. The primary function of the agency is to execute (i.e., carryout) the statutes governing the agency and the administrative regulations created by the agency itself. This is the agency's executive function.
- *Rule Making*. The agency often has the authority to write rules and regulations. (See exhibit 6.1 for a definition of administrative regulation.) In so doing, the agency is "making law" like a legislature. Indeed, such laws are often referred to as **quasi-legislation**.
- *Dispute Resolution*. The agency has the authority to interpret the statutes and regulations that govern it. Furthermore, it often has the authority to resolve disputes that arise over the application of such laws. It will hold administrative hearings and issue decisions. (See exhibit 6.1 for a definition of administrative decision.) In this sense, the agency is acting like a court when the latter adjudicates (i.e., resolves) disputes. The dispute-resolution power of the agency is therefore called a quasi-judicial power. The phrase **quasi-adjudication** refers to a written decision of an administrative agency that resolves a legal dispute in a manner that is similar to the way a court resolves such a dispute. An agency exercises its quasi-judicial power at several levels. At the first level is a *hearing*, which is similar to a trial in a court of original jurisdiction. The presiding agency official—known variously as hearing examiner, trial examiner, or **administrative law judge (ALJ)**—will, like the judge in a trial court, take testimony of witnesses and other evidence, determine the facts of the case, and apply the law to those facts in order to render a decision. In many agencies, the findings of fact and the decision of the hearing officer constitute only a recommendation to the director, commissioner, secretary, or other high official who will make the decision at this level. Like the courts, many agencies then provide a second, "appellate" level where a body such as a board or commission reviews the decision of the hearing examiner (or other official) to correct errors. After the parties to the dispute have used all these

**quasi-adjudication**  An administrative decision written by an administrative agency that has some characteristics of an opinion written by a court.

**administrative law judge (ALJ)**  A government official at an administrative agency who presides over a hearing to resolve a legal dispute.

avenues of redress within the agency, they have **exhausted administrative remedies** and may then appeal the final administrative decision to a court. (Later, in chapter 10, we will take a closer look at the dispute-resolution function of an agency.)

Here is an example of an agency using all three powers:

*Securities and Exchange Commission (SEC)*
- *Execution.* The SEC accepts filings of registration statements containing financial data on issuers of securities. This is done to carry out the statutes of Congress requiring such registration. When an agency carries out a statute, it is administering or executing that statute.
- *Rule Making.* The SEC writes regulations that provide greater detail on what the registration statements must contain.
- *Dispute Resolution.* The SEC holds a hearing to decide whether a corporation has violated the registration requirements laid out in the statutes and administrative regulations. The end product of the hearing is often an administrative decision.

**exhaust administrative remedies** To go through all dispute-solving avenues that are available in an administrative agency before asking a court to review what the agency did.

### Assignment 6.4
Give the name, street address, phone number, fax number, e-mail address, World Wide Web address, and function (stated briefly) of:

**(a)** Three federal agencies with offices in your state.
**(b)** Five state agencies in your state.
**(c)** Five city or county agencies with offices in your city or county.

## Section E
## THE LEGISLATIVE PROCESS

The legislative process consists of the steps that a bill must go through before it becomes a statute. (A **bill** is simply a proposed statute.) Exhibit 6.5 outlines these steps for the federal legislature—Congress. The chart in exhibit 6.5 assumes that the same idea for a bill is introduced simultaneously in both chambers of Congress, the House of Representatives and the Senate. It is, of course, also possible for a bill to be introduced in one chamber, go through all the steps for passage in that chamber, and *then* be introduced in the other chamber. The conference committee step outlined in the chart occurs only when both chambers have enacted their own version of the bill.

**bill** A proposed statute.

Congress is **bicameral**, meaning that it consists of two chambers, the House of Representatives and the Senate. In some state legislatures, the chambers have different names, such as the Assembly and the House of Delegates. Legislatures with only one chamber are called **unicameral**. The only state legislature that is unicameral is the Nebraska legislature. Local legislatures, however, such as city councils, are often unicameral.

**bicameral** Having two houses or chambers in the legislature.

The process of enactment can involve six major stages:

**unicameral** Having one house or chamber in the legislature.

- Proposal
- Initial committee consideration
- Floor debate
- Conference committee consideration
- Floor debate
- Response of the chief executive

The **legislative history** of a statute is what occurs at each of these stages.

(a) *Proposal* A member of the legislature must formally introduce the bill. Where do the ideas for proposed laws originate? There are many possible sources. The chief executive of the government (for example, the president or governor) may initiate the process by sending the legislature a message stating the reasons for a proposed law. Frequently, an administrative agency has made a study of a problem, which is the

**legislative history** All of the events that occur in the legislature before a bill becomes a statute.

**EXHIBIT 6.5**    **The Legislative History of a Federal Statute—How a Bill Becomes a Law**

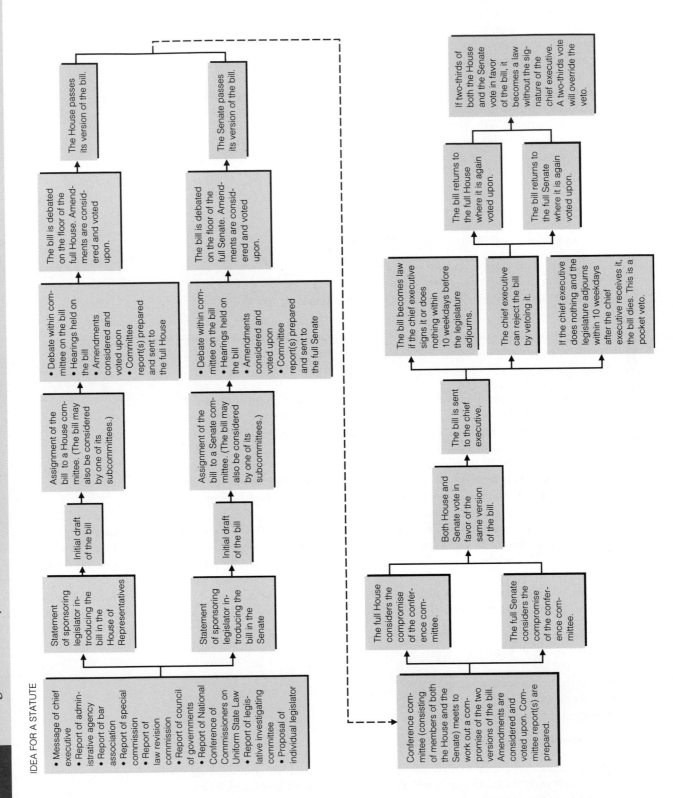

impetus for the proposal. The agency will usually be the entity with responsibility for administering the proposal if it is enacted into law. The bar association might prepare a report to the legislature calling for the new legislation. The legislature or chief executive may have established a special commission to study the need for changes in the law and to propose changes where appropriate. The commission might consist of members of the legislature and outside experts. Some states have ongoing law revision commissions that frequently make proposals for legislation. In many areas, a council of governments made up of neighboring governments studies problems and proposes legislative changes. The National Conference of Commissioners on Uniform State Laws (*www.nccusl.org*) is an organization with members from each state. The Conference makes proposals to the state legislatures for the enactment of uniform state laws where it deems uniformity to be desirable.

Finally, the idea for the legislation may come from within the legislature itself. One or both houses may have established an investigating committee to examine a particular problem and propose legislation where needed. Individual legislators can also propose bills. Can private citizens propose a bill? Usually not. They must convince an individual legislator to introduce or sponsor their idea for a bill.

(b) *Initial Committee Consideration.* When a member of the legislature introduces a bill, he or she usually accompanies it with a statement on why the bill should be enacted. As bills are introduced, they are assigned a consecutive number (e.g., S 250 is the 250th bill introduced in the Senate during the current session; HR 1753 is the 1753rd bill introduced in the House of Representatives during the current session).

Once the bill is introduced, it follows a similar procedure in each chamber. The bill is sent to the committee with responsibility over the subject matter of the bill—for example, a bill to change the criminal law might go to the Judiciary Committee. The initial draft of the bill might be considered by this committee and by one of its subcommittees. Hearings are held. Citizens and public officials give testimony for or against the bill. In some legislatures, this testimony is transcribed so that a word-for-word record is available. Legislators often propose amendments to the bill, which are voted on by the committee. The committee then issues a report summarizing why the bill is needed and what its major provisions are. If there is disagreement on the committee, a minority report is often prepared.

(c) *Floor Debate.* The bill with its accompanying report(s) then goes to the floor of the chamber of which the committee is a part. The bill is debated by the full chamber. During the debate, which will usually be recorded or transcribed, members ask questions about the meaning of certain provisions in the bill: what is covered and what is not. Amendments are often made from the floor and voted upon.

(d) *Conference Committee Consideration.* Because both chambers act independently of each other in considering the bill, it is rare that they both produce exactly the same bill. Inevitably, the amendment process leads to different versions of the proposed law. To resolve these differences, a *conference committee* is established, consisting of key members of both chambers, such as the chairpersons of the committees that initially considered the bill or the members who first introduced or sponsored the bill. A compromise is attempted in the conference committee. Amendments are considered and a final report of the conference committee is issued. Dissenting members of the committee might prepare a minority report. The majority report summarizes the major terms of the compromise and explains why it should be enacted by each chamber.

(e) *Floor Debate.* The conference committee compromise then goes back to the floor of each chamber where more debate, explanations, and amendments are considered. Again, everything is recorded or transcribed. If both chambers pass the same version of the bill, usually by a majority vote, it goes to the chief executive.

(f) *Response of Chief Executive.* There are three main ways for the bill to become law after it reaches the chief executive. First, he or she can sign it. Second, the chief executive can do nothing. If the legislature stays in session for at least 10 weekdays

**veto** An explicit rejection by the chief executive of a bill passed by the legislature.

**override** To supersede or change a result. To approve a bill over the veto of the chief executive.

**pocket veto** The chief executive's "silent" rejection of a bill by not acting on it within 10 weekdays of receiving it if the legislature adjourns during this period.

after he or she receives it, the bill automatically becomes law—without requiring a signature. Third, if the chief executive rejects or **vetoes** the bill, it can still become law if both chambers of the legislature **override** the veto by a two-thirds vote.

There are two main ways for the chief executive to reject a bill. First, he or she can explicitly veto the bill. It then goes back to the legislature, often with the chief executive's reasons for the rejection. Second, he or she can do nothing. If the legislature adjourns within 10 weekdays after the chief executive receives it, the bill automatically dies. This is known as a **pocket veto**. Because the legislature is no longer in session, the pocket veto deprives the legislature of the opportunity to override the veto.

---

### Assignments 6.5

(a) Redraw exhibit 6.5 so that your chart includes the steps needed for a bill to become a statute in your state legislature.

(b) Give the name, street address, phone number, e-mail address, and fax number of the chief legislator in each chamber of your legislature, e.g., Speaker of the House, President of the Senate. (If your state legislature is unicameral [Nebraska], answer these questions for the one chamber that exists.)

(c) What is the World Wide Web address of your state legislature? On this site, can you find current statutes in the code? Current bills in the legislature? Explain what is available.

(d) What is the full name of the legislative committee in each chamber (e.g., Judiciary Committee) with primary authority to consider laws that directly affect your state courts, such as procedural laws that govern the conduct of litigation? Give the name, political party, phone number, e-mail address, and fax number of the current chairperson of each of these committees.

(e) What is the name of the *local* legislature in your city or county? Give the name, street address, phone number, e-mail address, and fax number of the chief legislator of this body. (If you have both a city and a county legislature, answer this question for both.)

(f) What is the World Wide Web address of your local city legislature? Of your local county legislature? On these sites, can you find current ordinances or other laws in force? Current bills in the legislature? Explain what is available.

---

## ◼ CHAPTER SUMMARY

Our legal system consists of three levels of government (federal, state, and local) and three branches of government (executive, legislative, and judicial) within each level. Federalism is the division of powers between the federal or national government and the state governments. To keep any one branch from becoming too powerful, our system imposes checks and balances among the three branches.

There are 10 main categories of laws: opinions, statutes, constitutions, administrative regulations, administrative decisions, charters, ordinances, rules of court, executive orders, and treaties. (In a special category are opinions of the attorney general.) These laws are written by one of the three branches of government (legislative, executive, and judicial) that exist within the three levels of government (federal, state, and local).

Ours is a common law legal system. The main definition of common law is judge-made law in the absence of controlling statutory law or other higher law. The method of resolving legal disputes is adversarial. The opposing sides go before a neutral decision maker who listens to the arguments of each side before rendering a decision.

An understanding of jurisdiction is key to understanding our judicial system. To render a decision, a court must have jurisdiction over the persons (personal jurisdiction) or over the particular thing ('res') involved in the litigation (e.g., in rem jurisdiction). The court must also have subject matter jurisdiction, which specifies the kinds of cases over which a court can exercise its power. There are six main kinds of subject matter jurisdiction:

limited, general, exclusive, concurrent, original, and appellate. Courts of original jurisdiction are the trial courts. There may be two levels or tiers of trial courts within a judicial system. There may also be two levels or tiers of courts with appellate jurisdiction.

There are three kinds of administrative agencies: executive department agencies, independent regulatory agencies, and quasi-independent regulatory agencies. (Government corporations are special entities that are a mixture of corporation and government agency.) Agencies serve three main functions: to carry out statutes and executive orders, to write rules and regulations, and to resolve disputes that arise under laws for which the agency has responsibility.

The federal legislature (Congress) and most state legislatures are bicameral; that is, they consist of two chambers. For a bill to become a statute, it must go through approximately six stages. First, the bill is proposed by being introduced into one of the chambers of the legislature. It may be introduced into the other chamber simultaneously or at a later date. Second, a committee of each chamber gives the bill initial consideration. If the committee votes in favor of the bill, it goes to the next stage. Third, all of the members of one of the chambers debate and vote on the bill, and then all of the members of the other chamber debate and vote on the bill. Fourth, a conference committee usually made up of members of both chambers considers the bill. The role of this committee is to try to reconcile any differences in the two versions of the bill passed by each chamber. Fifth, the bill goes back to the full membership of each chamber for a vote on what the conference committee produced. Sixth, the chief executive signs or vetoes the bill. If he or she explicitly vetoes the bill, it can still become a statute if two-thirds of each chamber vote to override the chief executive. The legislative history of a statute consists of what happens during these six stages.

## KEY TERMS

| | |
|---|---|
| federalism | state questions |
| legislative branch | federal questions |
| executive branch | exclusive jurisdiction |
| judicial branch | concurrent jurisdiction |
| opinion | original jurisdiction |
| statute | appellate jurisdiction |
| constitution | inferior court |
| administrative regulation | appellate brief |
| administrative decision | panel |
| charter | en banc |
| ordinance | court of final resort |
| rules of court (court rules) | United States District Court |
| executive order | United States Court of Appeals |
| treaty | United States Supreme Court |
| opinion of the attorney general | administrative agency |
| checks and balances | executive department agency |
| judicial review | independent regulatory agency |
| common law | quasi-independent regulatory agency |
| civil law system | government corporation |
| at common law | quasi-legislation |
| precedent | quasi-adjudication |
| stare decisis | administrative law judge |
| cause of action | exhaust administrative remedies |
| adversarial | bill |
| jurisdiction | bicameral |
| adjudicate | unicameral |
| personal jurisdiction | legislative history |
| in rem jurisdiction | veto |
| subject matter jurisdiction | override |
| limited jurisdiction | pocket veto |
| general jurisdiction | |

## ON THE NET: MORE ON OUR LEGAL SYSTEM

**Understanding the Federal Courts**
www.uscourts.gov/about.html

**National Center for State Courts**
www.ncsconline.org

**How Our Laws Are Made (Congress)**
thomas.loc.gov/home/holam.txt

**How a Bill Becomes a Law (Example of State Legislation: Michigan)**
www.senate.state.mi.us/gop/resources/howabill.html

**How a Bill Becomes a Law (Example of County Ordinances: Baltimore)**
www.baltimorecountycouncil.org/howbill.htm

**Administrative Agency Links (Federal)**
www.firstgov.gov
www.abs-comptech.com/frn/agency.html
www.fedworld.gov

**Administrative Agencies (State and Federal)**
www.law.cornell.edu/topics/administrative.html

**State and Local Government on the Net**
www.statelocalgov.net

## ENDNOTES

1. Plus the District of Columbia, which has a special status but in some respects is treated as a state.
2. William Burnham, *Introduction to the Legal System of the United States* 78 (2d ed. 1999).
3. If a court's judgment is binding only on *designated* individuals who have an interest in the res (rather than on everyone with such an interest), the court had *quasi in rem jurisdiction* to render the judgment. The judgment is binding only on the designated individuals.

4. In this context, the word *federal* means United States. The United States government is the federal government, the United States courts are the federal courts, etc.
5. The United States Court of Appeals for the Federal Circuit also reviews cases from other special tribunals such as the United States Patent and Trademark Office and the International Trade Commission.

# Part II
# THE SKILLS OF
# A PARALEGAL

## Contents

# Chapter 7

# INTRODUCTION TO LEGAL ANALYSIS

## Chapter Outline

## Section A
# Introduction

Throughout society, people constantly apply rules to facts. For example:

> When Fred tells his soon-to-be 17-year-old daughter "we can't afford that car for you," he is applying rules to facts. In this instance, the rules are budgetary rules on how household funds are to be spent. The facts consist of his daughter's desire to have a particular car on the dealer's lot.
>
> When she responds, "But you allowed Tommy to have one like that when he turned 17," the discussion will probably heat up and focus on fairness rules that may or may not have been part of this family's history.

The vast majority of rule applications and rule conflicts in our society never enter the legal system. Most disputes are settled privately or are simply ignored. Fred and his daughter will not be resolving their car dispute in court. While our focus in this chapter will be those disputes that *do* enter the legal system, the method by which the law resolves such disputes is quite similar to the way in which rules are applied to facts in all kinds of conflict throughout society. There is no magic process of conflict resolution used in the law. The process that the law uses may at times be complicated, but it is remarkably similar to how every other segment of society identifies its rules and resolves its conflicts over them.

**legal analysis** The application of one or more rules of law to the facts of a client's case in order to answer a legal question that will help (1) keep a legal dispute from arising, (2) resolve a legal dispute that has arisen, or (3) prevent a legal dispute from becoming worse. Also called legal reasoning.

Attorneys become involved only when rules of law are applied to facts that raise *legal* disputes. In this arena, the heart of what the attorney does is called **legal analysis** or legal reasoning. It is the application of rules of law to facts in order to answer a legal question or issue. There are three interrelated goals of legal analysis: to keep a legal dispute from arising, to resolve a legal dispute that has arisen, and to prevent a legal dispute from becoming worse.

Paralegals need to study legal analysis for two main reasons. First, many paralegals are given assignments that in varying degrees call for legal analysis. Secondly, and perhaps more importantly, since attorneys talk the language of legal analysis all the time (issues, rules, elements, briefing, reasoning, etc.), a paralegal who knows the basics of legal analysis will be better equipped to understand and communicate with attorneys.

## Section B
# The Structure of Legal Analysis

The flow of legal analysis is demonstrated in the following chart containing a relatively simple example:

| RULE + | FACTS + | ISSUE + | CONNECTION (rule and facts) = | CONCLUSION |
|---|---|---|---|---|
| § 10. "Any business within the city must apply for and obtain a license to do business within the city limits." | Bill and his neighbors in the city have formed a food co-op through which members buy their food collectively from a wholesale company. All funds received by the co-op go for expenses and the purchase of more food to sell. | Is a food co-op a "business" within the meaning of § 10 requiring a license "to do business"? | The city argues that the co-op is a business in the city. The co-op concedes that it is in the city but argues that it does not "do business," since the co-op does not earn a profit. | The co-op has the better argument. § 10 was not intended to cover nonprofit ventures. Hence, the co-op does not have to have a license. |

Note the process:

- You start with a specific rule, such as a statute or regulation. (For the definition for these and other categories of rules of law, see exhibit 6.1 in chapter 6.) You quote the relevant language exactly.
- You state the major facts.
- You phrase the legal issue in terms of specific language in the rule and specific facts that raise a question or controversy.
- You draw the *connection* between specific language in the rule and specific facts. The substance of the analysis *is* this connection. Another term for connection is **application**—applying the rules to the facts.
- You reach a conclusion based on these steps.

Here is a more detailed statement of the analysis referred to as the "connection" in the chart.

Section 10 provides as follows:

> Any business within the city must apply for and obtain a license to do business within the city limits.

There are two main elements of § 10:

1. Any business
2. Within the city

When the facts fit within these two elements, the entity in question must apply for and obtain a license to do business. The consequence of the rule is the need to be licensed. This consequence is mandated once both elements apply to the facts.

1. *Any Business.* The city claims that the co-op is a business. It does not matter to the city that the co-op does not earn profits in the traditional sense. According to the city, the co-op members are "selling" goods to each other. A business is any entity that engages in any form of selling.

   The co-op, on the other hand, argues that § 10 was not intended to cover co-ops. A business is an enterprise that makes a profit over and above expenses. Nothing of this kind occurs in the co-op. Everything taken in by the co-op goes out in the form of food purchases and expenses. Hence, the co-op is not a business and does not have to have a license.
2. *Within the City.* There is no dispute between the parties on this element. The city and the co-op agree that the co-op operates within the city limits. The only dispute in this case concerns the first element: whether the co-op is a business.

If you had included legal research data on the meaning of § 10, the analysis might have contained:

- A discussion of court opinions, if any, that interpret § 10
- A discussion of administrative regulations, if any, that implement § 10
- A discussion of the legislative history, if available, of § 10
- A discussion of constitutional provisions, if any, that affect the applicability of § 10
- A discussion of secondary authority, if any, that interprets § 10, such as legal periodical literature and legal treatises

Later we will be examining opinions, regulations, legislative history, constitutional provisions, and secondary authority in greater detail, particularly in chapter 11.

The structure of legal analysis has four components. To remember them, use **IRAC** as a guide. IRAC is an acronym beloved of generations of attorneys who were introduced to IRAC during their first year of law school. (Watch the smile on the face of supervising attorneys when you tell them that you've studied IRAC.) The acronym IRAC stands for Issue, Rule, Application (or sometimes Analysis), and Conclusion:

| | |
|---|---|
| *Issue:* | Identify the legal issue to be resolved in the client's case. |
| *Rule:* | State the portion (element) of the rule that is at the center of the dispute. |

**application** Connecting facts to the elements of a rule in order to determine whether the rule applies to the facts. Explaining how the element of a rule applies or does not apply to the facts.

**IRAC** An acronym that stands for the components of legal analysis: issue (I), rule (R), application of the rule to the facts (A), and conclusion (C). A structure for legal analysis.

| Application: | Apply (connect) the rule to the facts of the client's case. Do this from the perspective of the client and from the perspective of the client's opponent. (The latter perspective is the *counteranalysis,* which is the position of the other side on how the rule applies to the facts.) |
| --- | --- |
| Conclusion: | State the conclusion on whether the rule applies to the facts. |

If a problem in the client's case involves more than one issue, each is "IRAC-ed" in the same manner.

**memorandum of law** A written explanation of how the law might apply to the fact situation of a client.

IRAC can be used in memos, in essay exam answers, or in your head—in short, whenever you are doing legal analysis. If you write out your analysis in a law office, you usually do so in a document called a **memorandum of law** (also called a *legal memorandum*) (see chapter 12). Often the memorandum of law (*memo* for short) is organized in four parts corresponding to the four components of IRAC. Some of the essay examinations you take in school can follow the same organizational format, although your examination answer may not be as formally structured as a memo. Even less formal will be the legal analysis you will do in your head. Whenever and wherever you do legal analysis, you can use the same analytical IRAC structure. Keep in mind, however, that IRAC is only a guide. There is no rigid formula for doing legal analysis. What is important is to make sure that you cover the essentials somewhere in your analysis. The essentials are issue, rule, application (connections), and conclusion.

Let us look at another example. Assume that a statute (§ 12) provides that additional punishment can be imposed "when a weapon is used by a defendant in the commission of a drug offense." John Smith is convicted of selling heroin to his brother. When John Smith was arrested, the police found a gun in his back pocket. The question is whether he can be subjected to additional punishment under § 12. Here is a skeleton overview of how this problem might be analyzed with IRAC as a guide in a memorandum of law. Before going through IRAC, note that we begin with a statement of the facts. Later, in chapter 12, we will cover some of the other components of a memorandum of law.

### FACTS

On December 12, 2002, John Smith was arrested at 465 East 8th Street, South Boston, at midnight. He was observed selling a substance to another adult, his brother Richard Smith. The substance was later determined to be heroin. When John Smith was arrested immediately after the sale, Officer Frank Doyle searched him and found a gun in his back pocket. Doyle was not aware of the presence of the gun until this search. At the trial, Smith was convicted of selling heroin. During sentencing, the prosecution asked for additional punishment because he used a weapon in the commission of a drug crime. Smith objected on the ground that he did not use the weapon under the applicable statute.

### ISSUE

Has a person "used" a weapon in committing a drug offense under § 12 when he is found with a gun in his back pocket at the time he is arrested for selling heroin even though the gun played no active role in the drug sale?

### RULE

Section 12 provides as follows:

A judge may impose additional punishment on a defendant when a weapon is used by the defendant in the commission of a drug offense. § 12.

### APPLICATION

There are three elements of § 12:

1. Weapon
2. Is used
3. In the commission of a drug offense

If these three elements apply, a judge can impose additional punishment on the defendant under § 12. There is no dispute between the parties on the first and third elements. Both

John and the prosecutor will agree that the gun found on John was a "weapon" and that selling heroin is the "commission of a crime." The question is whether John "used" this weapon in committing the crime.

The parties will disagree over the definition of "used." The prosecution will argue that it means having it in one's possession ready for employment as needed. Under this definition, Smith "used" the gun. A person with a gun in his pocket possesses the gun. Furthermore, Smith was in possession of the gun while Smith was selling heroin. Hence he used the weapon in the commission of a crime.

Smith, on the other hand, will argue that the prosecution's definition is too broad. When the legislature passed § 12, it intended "used" to mean actively employing a weapon in the actual commission of the drug offense for which the defendant was arrested. When Smith sold heroin to his brother, he never took out his gun. There is no evidence that his brother knew he was armed. John Smith never actively employed the gun by brandishing it, displaying it, striking anyone with it, or threatening to fire it. Hence he never "used" the gun. Merely possessing it is not enough under § 12. If the legislature had intended the word to mean mere possession, it could have used the verb *possessed* rather than *used*. If the weapon played no role in the commission of the drug offense, the legislature did not intend defendants to suffer additional punishment.

### CONCLUSION

Smith has the stronger argument. The word *used* suggests activity beyond passive possession.

---

If relevant court opinions existed that interpreted § 12, they would be included under the "A" component of IRAC to help us interpret the meaning of "used" in § 12 in the Smith case. Similarly, this section of the analysis might include:

■ A discussion of other rules (e.g., constitutional provisions), if any, that affect the applicability of § 12
■ A discussion of the legislative history, if available, of § 12
■ A discussion of secondary authority, if any, that interprets § 12, such as legal periodical literature and legal treatises

We will be returning to these themes later in the chapter as well as in chapters 11 and 12. Our goal here is simply to introduce you to the essential structure of legal analysis through IRAC.

We turn now to three skills that are very important to this structure:

■ *Element-identification skill*. This skill allows you to break any rule into its elements. The first step in identifying an issue is to identify the elements of the rule that will be applied.
■ *Issue-statement skill*. This skill allows you to identify which elements of a rule are in contention. The second step in identifying an issue is to identify which elements of the rule will be in contention. Each element in contention will be the basis of a separate issue.
■ *Definitions skill*. This skill allows you to determine if an element in contention can be defined broadly and narrowly. The application of the element will cover these competing definitions.

Mastering these three skills will go a long way toward equipping you to use IRAC in legal analysis.

## Section C
## THE ELEMENT-IDENTIFICATION SKILL

Step one in applying a rule is to break it down into its pieces or components. We call these components **elements**. Before the consequences of a rule can apply, you must demonstrate that all of the elements of that rule apply.

**element** A portion of a rule that is a precondition of the applicability of the entire rule.

Rules have different kinds of consequences. There are rules that:

- Impose punishments
- Require payments
- Require safety steps to be taken
- Institute procedures
- Make statements of policy
- Declare definitions of important concepts
- Etc.

The element-identification skill requires you to answer two questions: what is the consequence of the rule you are applying, and what must happen before this consequence will be imposed or go into effect? When you answer the second question, you will have identified the elements of the rule. An element is a portion of a rule that is a precondition of the applicability of the entire rule. If you can show that all of the elements of a rule apply to a fact situation, then the rule itself—and its consequence—applies. The failure of any *one* of the elements to apply means that the entire rule cannot apply.

When you are examining rules, you will find that they are rarely, if ever, already broken down into elements for you. Element identification is your responsibility. In our earlier discussion of the food co-op example (§ 10) and the weapon example (§ 12), the elements of the rules were relatively short. This is not always so. How long should an element be? This question has no absolute answer. The two main criteria to keep in mind are these: (1) each element must be a precondition to the consequence of the entire rule, and (2) you should be able to discuss each element separately with relative ease.

Let us examine some additional examples:

> **§ 971.22. Change of place of trial**. The defendant may move for a change of the place of trial on the ground that an impartial trial cannot be had in the county. The motion shall be made at the time of arraignment.

Step one is to break the rule into its elements. The effect or consequence of this rule is to change the place of the trial. Ask yourself what must happen before this consequence will follow. What conditions or preconditions must exist before the result will occur? The answer will provide you with the elements of the rule:

1. Defendant
2. May move for a change of the place of trial
3. On the ground that an impartial trial cannot be had in the county
4. The motion must be made at the time of the arraignment

Hence, there are four elements to § 971.22. All four must exist before the place of the trial will be moved.

Suppose you are analyzing the following statute:

> **§ 25–403**. A pharmacist must not sell prescription drugs to a minor.

Ask yourself what conditions must exist before § 25–403 applies. Your answer will consist of its elements:

1. Pharmacist
2. Must not sell
3. Prescription drugs
4. To a minor

No violation exists unless all four elements of the statute are established. If, for example, a pharmacist sells simple aspirin (a nonprescription drug) to a minor, he or she has not violated the statute. The third element cannot be established. Hence there is no violation because one of the elements (preconditions) cannot be met.

For a number of reasons, rules such as statutes and regulations can be difficult to break into elements. For example, the rule may be long or may contain:

- Lists
- Alternatives

■ Exceptions or provisos

Nevertheless, the same process is used. You must take the time to dissect the rule into its component elements. Examine the following rule as we try to identify its elements:

> **§ 5.** While representing a client in connection with contemplated or pending litigation, a lawyer shall not advance or guarantee financial assistance to his client, except that a lawyer may advance or guarantee court costs, expenses of investigation, expenses of medical examination, and costs of obtaining and presenting evidence provided the client remains ultimately liable for such expenses.

The elements of § 5 are:

1. A lawyer
2. Representing a client in connection with contemplated litigation or in connection with pending litigation
3. Shall not advance financial assistance to his client or guarantee financial assistance to his client, except that the following is proper:

   a. Lawyer advances or guarantees court costs, or
   b. Lawyer advances or guarantees expenses of investigation, or
   c. Lawyer advances or guarantees expenses of medical examination, or
   d. Lawyer advances or guarantees costs of obtaining and presenting evidence

   as long as the client remains ultimately liable for all expenses ("a"–"d").

When an element is stated in the alternative, list all the alternatives within the same element. Alternatives related to one element should be kept within the phrasing of that element. The same is true of exception or proviso clauses. State them within the relevant element when they are intimately related to the applicability of that element. In our § 5 example, the most complicated element is the third—(3). It contains lists, alternatives, an exception, and a proviso. But they all relate to the same point—the propriety of financial assistance. None of the subdivisions of the third element should be stated as a separate element.

Sometimes you must do some unraveling of a rule in order to identify its elements. This certainly had to be done with the third element of § 5. Do not be afraid to pick the rule apart in order to cluster its thoughts around unified themes that should stand alone as elements. Diagram the rule for yourself as you examine it.

If more than one rule is involved in a statute, regulation, constitutional provision, charter, ordinance, etc., treat one rule at a time. Each rule should have its own elements, and, when appropriate, each element should be subdivided into its separate components, as in the third element of § 5.

Once you have broken the rule down into its elements, you have the structure of the analysis in front of you. Each element becomes a separate section of your analysis. You discuss one element at a time, concentrating on those that pose the greatest difficulties.

Element identification has many benefits in the law, as demonstrated in exhibit 7.1. For example, knowing the elements of rules can help give direction to interviewing and investigation. While performing these tasks, you are often looking for relevant facts. How do you know which facts are relevant? One of the ways is to identify the elements of the potentially applicable rules that both sides may be arguing in the litigation. Facts are relevant if they help show that those elements apply or do not apply. As you can see from exhibit 7.1, element identification will also help identify issues, draft complaints and answers, conduct depositions, organize memos and exam answers, and even charge the jury.

To a very large extent, legal analysis proceeds by *element analysis*. A major characteristic of sloppy legal analysis is that it does not clearly take the reader (or listener) through the important elements of rules that must be analyzed.

---

### Assignment 7.1
Break the following rules into their elements:

(a) § 200. Parties to a child custody dispute shall attempt mediation before filing for a custody order from the court.

**(b)** § 75(b). A lawyer shall not enter into a business transaction with a client if they have differing interests therein and if the client expects the lawyer to exercise his or her professional judgment therein for the protection of the client.

**(c)** § 38. A person or agency suing or being sued in an official public capacity is not required to execute a bond as a condition for relief under this section unless required by the court in its discretion.

**(d)** § 1.2 A lawyer may not permit his or her legal assistant to represent a client in litigation or other adversary proceedings or to perform otherwise prohibited functions unless authorized by statute, court rule or decision, administrative rule or regulation, or customary practice.

**(e)** § 179(a)(7). If at any time it is determined that application of best available control technology by 1988 will not assure protection of public water supplies, agricultural and industrial uses, and the protection and propagation of fish, shellfish and wildlife, and allow recreational activities in and on the water, additional effluent limitations must be established to assure attainment or maintenance of water quality. In setting such limitations, *EPA (the Environmental Protection Agency)* must consider the relationship of the economic and social costs of their achievement, including any economic or social dislocation in the affected community or communities, the social and economic benefits to be obtained, and determine whether or not such effluent limitations can be implemented with available technology or other alternative control strategies.

---

**EXHIBIT 7.1    The Benefits of Element Identification**

- *Identifying Issues.* Once you identify the elements of a rule, the next step is to find the *elements* that are most likely to be in contention. These elements become the basis of legal issues (as we shall see in the next section).
- *Drafting a Complaint.* When drafting a legal complaint, you often organize your factual allegations around the *elements* of each important rule in the controversy. (The most important rule is called the *cause of action*, which is a legally acceptable reason for suing someone; negligence is an example.)
- *Drafting an Answer.* When drafting an answer to a complaint, you often state your defenses by alleging facts that support the *elements* of each defense. (Many *defenses*, such as the statute of limitations, are nothing more than rules designed to defeat the claims of another.)
- *Organizing an Interview of a Client.* One of the goals of interviewing a client is to obtain information on facts relevant to each of the *elements* of the potential causes of action and defenses in the case. Element analysis, therefore, helps you organize the interview and give it direction.
- *Organizing an Investigation.* One of the goals of investigation is to obtain information on facts relevant to each of the *elements* of the potential causes of action and defenses in the case. Element analysis, therefore, helps you organize the investigation and give it direction.
- *Conducting a Deposition.* During a deposition, many of the attorney's questions are designed to determine what facts the other side may be able to prove that support the *elements* of the potential causes of action and defenses in the case.
- *Organizing a Memorandum of Law.* One of the purposes of a memorandum of law is to tell the reader what rules might apply to the case, what *elements* of these rules might be in contention, and what strategy should be undertaken as a result of this analysis. As we saw earlier, a memo is often organized in an IRAC format. The "A" of IRAC consists of breaking a rule down into its elements and concentrating on those elements in contention.
- *Organizing an Examination Answer.* Many essay examinations in school are organized around the major *elements* of the rules that should be analyzed.
- *Charging a Jury.* When a judge charges (that is, instructs) a jury, he or she will go over each of the *elements* of the causes of action and defenses in the case in order to tell the jury what standard to use to determine whether facts in support of those elements have been sufficiently proven during the trial.

Section D
# THE ISSUE-STATEMENT SKILL

After you have broken a rule into its elements, the next step is to identify the **element in contention**. That element then becomes the basis of a **legal issue**. An element is in contention when you can predict that the other side in the controversy will probably not agree on the definition of the element, whether the facts fit within the element (i.e., within its definition), or both. If a rule has five elements and you anticipate disagreement over all of them, phrase five separate issues. If, however, only one of the five elements will probably be in contention, phrase only one issue. There is no need to waste time over elements that will most likely not be the basis of disagreement.

During informal discussions in a law office, you will often find that attorneys and paralegals phrase legal issues very broadly, almost in shorthand. For example:

- Was Tom negligent?
- Does § 12 apply?
- Can we use the trespass defense?

While broad issue statements such as these can be good starting points for discussion, you need to be able to provide a more *comprehensive* statement of the issue. This is done by including in your issue:

- A brief quote from the element in contention and
- Several of the important facts relevant to that contention

For example, suppose that you are analyzing the following rule and facts:

§ 92. The operator of any vehicle riding on a sidewalk shall be fined $100.
*Facts*: Fred rides his 10-speed bicycle on the sidewalk. He is charged with violating § 92.

The element breakdown and issue statement would be as follows:

*Elements of § 92*:

1. Operator
2. Any vehicle
3. Riding
4. On a sidewalk

*Issue*: Is a 10-speed bicycle a "vehicle" under § 92?

The parties will probably agree that Fred rode his bicycle on a sidewalk and that Fred was the operator of his bicycle. The first, third, and fourth elements, therefore, should not be made into legal issues. The only disagreement will be over the second element. Hence, it is the basis of an issue. Note the quotation marks around the element in contention (vehicle) and the inclusion of an important fact that is relevant to this contention (it was a 10-speed bicycle).

**element in contention** That portion of a rule about which the parties cannot agree. The disagreement may be over the definition of the element, whether the facts fit within the element, or both.

**legal issue** A question of law. A question of what the law is, or what the law means, or how the law applies to the facts.

---

*Assignment 7.2*

Provide a comprehensive phrasing of the legal issue or issues in each of the following situations:

(a) *Facts*: Tom owns a 1999 Ford. One day it stalls on a hill; the engine stops running. He wants to get the car off the street. He, therefore, pushes the car so that it glides off the street and onto the sidewalk. While pushing the car on the sidewalk, a police officer stops him.
*Statute*: § 92. The operator of any vehicle riding on a sidewalk shall be fined $100.

(b) *Facts*: Harry Franklin works for the XYZ Agency. In one of the Agency's personnel files is a notation that Paul Drake, another Agency employee, was once arrested for fraud. Harry obtains this information from this file and tells his wife about it. (She also knows Paul.) Harry is unaware that Paul has told at least three other employees about his fraud arrest.

*Regulation*: 20(d). It shall be unlawful for any employee of the XYZ Agency to divulge confidential material in any file of the Agency.

(c) *Facts*: Jones has a swimming pool in his backyard. The pool is intended for use by the Jones family members and guests who are present when an adult is there to supervise. One hot summer night, a neighbor's child opens an unlocked door of a fence that surrounds the Jones's yard and goes into the pool. (There is no separate fence around the pool.) The child knows that he should not be there without an adult. No one else is at the pool. The child drowns.

*Statute*: § 77. Property owners are liable for the foreseeable harm that occurs on their property.

(d) *Facts*: Dr. Carla Jones is the family physician of the Richardson family. After an appointment with Mary Richardson, age 16, Dr. Jones prescribes birth control pills. Mary tells Dr. Jones that she can't afford the pills and does not want her parents to know she is taking them. Dr. Jones says she will give her a supply of the pills at no cost in exchange for an afternoon of office clerical work at Dr. Jones's office.

*Statute*: § 25-403. A pharmacist must not sell prescription drugs to a minor.

---

## Section E
# THE DEFINITIONS SKILL

Language can frequently be defined broadly or narrowly. Assume that Jim meets a friend in a parking lot and says to him, "You can use my car." Jim is quite upset, however, when the friend returns five months later after driving the car through about 20 states. The friend asserts that he did nothing more than "use" the car. The question then becomes: What definition of "use" was intended and communicated?

> *Broad Definition*: Use means to operate or employ something for any purpose and for any length of time.
>
> *Narrow Definition*: Use means to operate or employ something for a reasonable purpose within a reasonable time.

The same dynamic is found when interpreting ambiguous language within elements in contention. Recall the bicycle example discussed in the preceding section:

> § 92. The operator of any vehicle riding on a sidewalk shall be fined $100.
> *Facts*: Fred rides his 10-speed bicycle on the sidewalk. He is charged with violating § 92.
> *Issue*: Is a 10-speed bicycle a "vehicle" under § 92?

This controversy may well turn on whether "vehicle" should be defined broadly or narrowly. Fred will argue that it should be interpreted narrowly, whereas the government will argue for a broad definition:

> *Broad Definition*: Vehicle means any method of transportation.
> *Narrow Definition*: Vehicle means any motorized method of transportation.

Whenever you have an element in contention that contains ambiguous language, you should put yourself in the shoes of each person in the controversy and try to identify what definition of the language each would propose. Think of a broad and a narrow definition, and state which side would argue which definition.

To help resolve a definition dispute, you would undertake some legal research—for example, you would try to find cases interpreting "vehicle" under § 92 and trace the legislative history of § 92. Often, however, you will *not* find the answer in the library. The precise question may never have arisen before. This is particularly true of recent statutes and regulations.

### Assignment 7.3

In each of the following problems, identify any ambiguous language in elements in contention. Give broad and narrow definitions of this language, and state which side would argue which definition. Do not do any legal research.

**(a)** *Facts*: Alice Anderson is nine months pregnant. A police officer gives her a ticket for driving in a car-pool lane in violation of § 101. The officer said he gave her the ticket because she was alone in the car at the time.
*Regulation*: § 101. Car-pool lanes can be used only by cars in which there is at least one passenger with the driver.

**(b)** *Facts*: Mary is arrested for violating § 55. She is charged as a felon. She forced open the lock on the driver's side of a van at 5 P.M. Mary didn't know that the door on the passenger side was unlocked. She went into the back of the van and fell asleep on the floor. The police arrested her after waking her up at 9 P.M. The owner of the van claims that a $20 bill is missing. Mary had a $20 bill on her, but she said it was her own.
*Statute*: § 55. A person who breaks and enters a dwelling at night for the purpose of stealing property therein shall be charged as a felon.

### Assignment 7.4

Analyze the problem in the following situations. Do not do any legal research. Simply use the facts and rules you are given. Be sure to include in your analysis what you have learned about elements, issues, and definitions. Use IRAC for each issue. As a guide, use the John Smith drug/weapon example on page 304.

**(a)** Susan is arrested for carrying a dangerous weapon. While in a hardware store, she got into an argument with another customer. She picked up a hammer from the counter and told the other customer to get out of her way. The customer did so, and Susan put the hammer back. She was later arrested and charged with violating § 402(b), which provides: "It is unlawful for anyone to carry a dangerous weapon."

**(b)** It is against the law in your state "to practice law without a license" (§ 39). Fred is charged with violating this law. He told a neighbor that a certain parking ticket received by the neighbor could be ignored because the police officer was incorrect in issuing the ticket. In gratitude, the neighbor buys Fred a drink. (Assume that what Fred told the neighbor about the ticket was accurate and that Fred is *not* an attorney.)

**(c)** Ted and Ann are married. Ted is a carpenter and Ann is a lawyer. They buy an old building that Ted will repair for Ann's use as a law office. Ted asks Ann to handle the legal aspects of the purchase of the building. She does so. Soon after the purchase, they decide to obtain a divorce. Ted asks Ann if she will draw up the divorce papers. She does so. Ted completes the repair work on the building for which Ann pays him a set amount. Has Ann violated § 75(b) that you found earlier in problem (b) of Assignment 7.1 on page 308?

## Section F
# FACTOR ANALYSIS

> **factor** One of the circumstances or considerations that will be weighed in making a decision, no one of which is usually conclusive.

Thus far we have concentrated on the analysis of elements in rules. Elements are preconditions to the applicability of the entire rule. If one element does not apply, the entire rule does not apply. We now turn to a closely related but different kind of analysis: *factor* analysis. A **factor** is simply one of the circumstances or considerations that will be weighed in making a decision, no one of which is usually conclusive.

Elements and factors are not limited to the application of rules to facts. Many of the important decisions we make in everyday life involve the equivalent of elements and factors, e.g., picking someone to marry, buying a car or a house. When people look for a house, they consider space, neighborhood, area schools, affordability, etc. If an item is essential, it is an element. Suppose, for example, that you will not buy a house with less than three bedrooms. Then this is a precondition to the entire purchase in the same manner as any single element of a rule is a precondition to the applicability of the entire rule. A house hunter may also want a large yard and a bus line within walking distance. But if these are not preconditions, they are simply factors to be considered, no one of which is necessarily dispositive or essential. If the bus line is a factor, the house hunter may decide to buy a particular house even though the bus line is not within walking distance. Why? Because this negative fact was examined in the light of everything else about the house (e.g., it had a very large yard, it was the right color) and, on balance, the decision was to make the purchase. The bus line problem did not outweigh all of the other factors.

Factors sometimes play an important role in legal analysis as well. Assume that § 107 provides that a quotation from a copyrighted work is not an infringement or violation of the copyright if the quotation constitutes "fair use." To determine whether "fair use" exists, § 107 says that a court will consider the following factors:

- The purpose and character of the use, including whether such use is of a commercial nature or is for nonprofit educational purposes;
- The nature of the copyrighted work;
- The amount and substantiality of the portion used in relation to the copyrighted work as a whole; and
- The effect of the use upon the potential market for or value of the copyrighted work.

These four considerations are factors that the court will assess to decide whether someone has made "fair use" of a copyrighted work. Because they are factors, no one of them will be conclusive or determinative. Each one will be considered and balanced against the others.

Assume that Mary O'Brien has a 3-page explanation of the energy crisis in the introduction to her 70-page copyrighted book that she sells. Ted Kelly decides to quote the entire explanation in a brochure that he compiles for a charity fundraising event for an environmental organization. He does not obtain the permission of O'Brien. Did Kelly infringe her copyright? We need to determine whether his quotation for the brochure constituted "fair use." This requires a factor analysis because § 107 tells us that "fair use" is determined by an assessment of factors.

The first factor is the purpose and character of the use. Kelly was not trying to sell anything. He was engaged in a nonprofit activity—raising funds for an environmental charity. The second factor is the nature of the copyrighted work. O'Brien's explanation of the energy crisis is in a book she sells; she is trying to earn a living from the book. The third factor is the amount used in the quote. Kelly used the entire explanation, consisting of 3 pages from O'Brien's 70-page book. The fourth factor is the effect of the use on the potential market of the copyrighted work. Here we must investigate whether the use of the quotation in the brochure hurt the sale of O'Brien's book containing her explanation of the energy crisis.

Some of the factors suggest that the use was fair, e.g., the brochure was not used for commercial purposes. Other factors suggest an unfair use, e.g., three pages from a short book is a fairly large percentage. No one factor is necessarily determinative. The court will balance all of these factors in order to determine whether Kelly made "fair use" of O'Brien's work. This is the nature of a factor analysis.

While every rule has elements, not every rule has factors. To determine whether factors are present in a rule, look for the word *factor* in the rule itself. (Section 107 in our example used this word.) If the word *factor* is not in the rule, look for words such as *consider, assess,* or *evaluate* preceded or followed by a list. For example:

§ 20. To determine whether the penalty will be waived, the agency shall consider the amount of the harm, the timing of the violation, and the extent to which the act was performed intentionally or accidentally.

The word *consider* in § 20 followed by a list suggests that a factor analysis is required. Be careful, however. There are no magic words that will always signal the need for a factor analysis. You must examine the rule carefully in order to determine whether you are being told that several items mentioned in the rule must be weighed in order to decide whether the rule applies.

Once you find factors in a rule, you simply examine the factors one at a time by connecting the facts you have (or must investigate) to each factor. Further investigation is often called for because of the large number of facts that are usually needed to assess each of the factors mentioned in the rule. One of the benefits of this kind of analysis is that it will help the office identify these investigation needs.

What is the relationship between elements and factors? As indicated, all rules have elements. Sometimes the applicability of an element is determined by the definition of that element. (See the definitions skill in the preceding section.) At other times, however, the applicability of an element is determined by factors. "Fair use" is one of the elements of § 107. But there is no traditional definition available for this element. Its applicability is determined by a factor analysis.

---

### Assignment 7.5

(a) Rachel Sanderson is running for mayor. In a campaign speech, she tells her audience that the city must not neglect the poor. She gives 10 examples of the kinds of poor families she means, each of which has experienced a different kind of poverty, e.g., poverty resulting from divorce, poverty resulting from illness. Harry Smith finds out that Sanderson's speech took numerous quotes from a short story he wrote for a college magazine some years ago. Smith is a mail carrier in the city where Sanderson is running for mayor. His story was entitled "The Faces of the Downtrodden." It contained 15 categories of families in distress. Sanderson used 10 of them in her speech. She used his labels for the 10 categories. He devoted two paragraphs to each category in his story. Sanderson's speech used at least one full paragraph, word for word, for each category from Smith's story. Was Sanderson's speech a "fair use" of Smith's story? Do a factor analysis on the applicability of § 107. In your analysis, you will need to identify further facts that should be investigated. State how such facts might be relevant to your factor analysis.

(b) Section 100 provides as follows: "Motorists shall be liable for the foreseeable harm or damage caused by their driving. To determine foreseeability, the court must consider road conditions, speed, weather, visibility, and any other circumstance that would affect the likelihood of the harm or damage occurring." Charles Wilson ran his truck into the side of a parked car when he came to an abrupt stop at an intersection. There was some oil on the road. Wilson's car skidded on the oil at the time of his attempt to stop. The incident occurred at 7 P.M., just after rush hour. Was the damage caused by Wilson foreseeable? Do a factor analysis on the applicability of § 100. In your analysis, identify further facts that you would need to investigate. State how such facts might be relevant to your factor analysis.

---

Section G
# BRIEFING COURT OPINIONS

The word *brief* has several meanings.

First, to **brief** a court opinion is to summarize its major components (e.g., key facts, issues, reasoning, disposition). Such a brief is your own summary of the opinion for later

**brief** A summary of the main or essential parts of a court opinion. (Brief also sometimes refers to a trial brief or to an appellate brief.)

**trial brief** An attorney's set of notes on the strategy he or she proposes to follow in conducting a trial.

**appellate brief** A document submitted by a party to an appellate court and served on the opposing party in which arguments are presented on why the rulings of a lower court should be approved, modified, or reversed.

**unoffical reporter** A collection of cases printed by a private or commercial printer/publisher without specific authority from the government.

**citation** A reference to any material printed on paper or stored in a computer database. A paper or online "address" where you can go to read something.

**appellant** The party bringing an appeal because of dissatisfaction with something the lower tribunal did. Sometimes called the petitioner.

use. This section of the chapter covers the skill of briefing opinions; the next section covers the more important skill of applying opinions. As you will see, you cannot apply an opinion unless you know how to brief it. Second, the word *brief* refers to a **trial brief** which is an attorney's set of notes on how he or she will conduct the trial. The notes (often placed in a trial notebook) will be on the opening statement, witnesses, exhibits, direct and cross-examination, closing argument, etc. This trial brief is sometimes called a trial manual or trial book. (Trial brief has other meanings as well. In some states, for example, when an attorney submits a written argument in support of a motion during a trial, the writing is called a trial brief.) Third, the **appellate brief** is the formal written argument to a court of appeals on why a lower court's decision should be approved, modified, or reversed. The focus of the appellate brief is on the claimed errors made "below." An appellate brief is submitted to the appellate court and served on the other side.

Here our concern is the first meaning of the word brief—a summarization of the essential components of a court opinion. (See exhibit 7.2 later in the chapter.) Before we examine these components, we will study an opinion as it might appear in a library reporter volume.

The circled numbers in the *Bruni* opinion below are explained after the opinion.

① The *California Reporter* is an **unofficial reporter** of state opinions in California. The "100" indicates the volume number of the reporter. An unofficial reporter is a collection of cases printed by a private or commercial printer/publisher without specific authority from the government. (Many of the terms covered in this overview will be examined again in greater detail in chapter 11.)

② The *Bruni* opinion begins on page 600. The **citation** of this opinion is *People v. Bruni*, 25 Cal. App. 3d 196, 100 Cal. Rptr. 600 (1972). The official cite is given at the top of the first column above the word PEOPLE.

③ When the *People* or the state brings an action, it is often a criminal law opinion. This is an appellate court decision. Trial court decisions are appealed to the appellate court. The **appellant** is the party bringing the appeal because of dissatisfaction with the ruling or decision of the lower court. The state of California brought the case as the plaintiff and prosecutor in the lower court (Superior Court, County of San Mateo) and is now the appellant in the higher court (Court of Appeal, First District, Division 1).

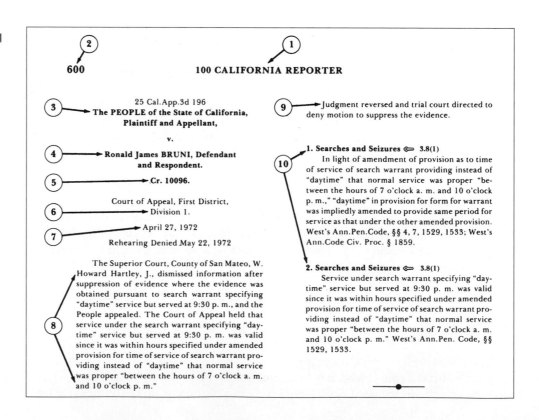

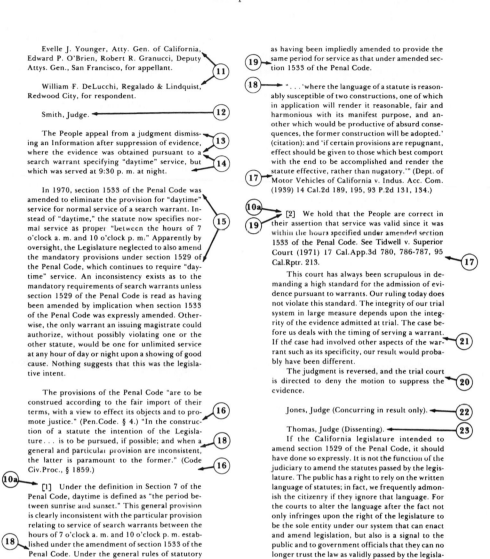

Evelle J. Younger, Atty. Gen. of California, Edward P. O'Brien, Robert R. Granucci, Deputy Attys. Gen., San Francisco, for appellant. (11)

William F. DeLucchi, Regalado & Lindquist, Redwood City, for respondent. (12)

Smith, Judge. ◄ (12)

The People appeal from a judgment dismissing an Information after suppression of evidence, (13) where the evidence was obtained pursuant to a search warrant specifying "daytime" service, but (14) which was served at 9:30 p. m. at night.

In 1970, section 1533 of the Penal Code was amended to eliminate the provision for "daytime" service for normal service of a search warrant. Instead of "daytime," the statute now specifies normal service as proper "between the hours of 7 o'clock a. m. and 10 o'clock p. m." Apparently by (15) oversight, the Legislature neglected to also amend the mandatory provisions under section 1529 of the Penal Code, which continues to require "daytime" service. An inconsistency exists as to the mandatory requirements of search warrants unless section 1529 of the Penal Code is read as having been amended by implication when section 1533 of the Penal Code was expressly amended. Otherwise, the only warrant an issuing magistrate could authorize, without possibly violating one or the other statute, would be one for unlimited service at any hour of day or night upon a showing of good cause. Nothing suggests that this was the legislative intent.

The provisions of the Penal Code "are to be construed according to the fair import of their terms, with a view to effect its objects and to promote justice." (Pen.Code. § 4.) "In the construction of a statute the intention of the Legislature... is to be pursued, if possible; and when a (18) general and particular provision are inconsistent, the latter is paramount to the former." (Code (16) Civ.Proc., § 1859.)

(10a)
[1] Under the definition in Section 7 of the Penal Code, daytime is defined as "the period between sunrise and sunset." This general provision is clearly inconsistent with the particular provision relating to service of search warrants between the hours of 7 o'clock a. m. and 10 o'clock p. m. estab-(18) lished under the amendment of section 1533 of the Penal Code. Under the general rules of statutory construction, we interpret "daytime" in the particular provisions of section 1529 of the Penal Code

(19) as having been impliedly amended to provide the same period for service as that under amended section 1533 of the Penal Code.

(18) "... 'where the language of a statute is reasonably susceptible of two constructions, one of which in application will render it reasonable, fair and harmonious with its manifest purpose, and another which would be productive of absurd consequences, the former construction will be adopted.' (citation): and 'if certain provisions are repugnant, effect should be given to those which best comport with the end to be accomplished and render the statute effective, rather than nugatory.'" (Dept. of (17) Motor Vehicles of California v. Indus. Acc. Com. (1939) 14 Cal.2d 189, 195, 93 P.2d 131, 134.)

(10a)
(19) [2] We hold that the People are correct in their assertion that service was valid since it was within the hours specified under amended section 1533 of the Penal Code. See Tidwell v. Superior Court (1971) 17 Cal.App.3d 780, 786-787, 95 (17) Cal.Rptr. 213.

This court has always been scrupulous in demanding a high standard for the admission of evidence pursuant to warrants. Our ruling today does not violate this standard. The integrity of our trial system in large measure depends upon the integrity of the evidence admitted at trial. The case before us deals with the timing of serving a warrant. If the case had involved other aspects of the war- (21) rant such as its specificity, our result would probably have been different.

The judgment is reversed, and the trial court is directed to deny the motion to suppress the (20) evidence.

Jones, Judge (Concurring in result only). ◄ (22)

Thomas, Judge (Dissenting). ◄ (23)
If the California legislature intended to amend section 1529 of the Penal Code, it should have done so expressly. It is not the function of the judiciary to amend the statutes passed by the legislature. The public has a right to rely on the written language of statutes; in fact, we frequently admonish the citizenry if they ignore that language. For the courts to alter the language after the fact not only infringes upon the right of the legislature to be the sole entity under our system that can enact and amend legislation, but also is a signal to the public and to government officials that they can no longer trust the law as validly passed by the legislative branch. Both results are intolerable.

I would affirm the judgment below.

④ Bruni was the defendant in the lower court because he was being sued or, in this case, charged with a crime. The appeal is taken against him by the People (appellant) because the lower court ruling was favorable to Bruni, to the dissatisfaction of the People. The party against whom a case is brought on appeal is called the **respondent**. Another word for respondent is *appellee*.

⑤ "Cr. 10096" refers to the *docket*, or calendar number of the case. "Cr." stands for *criminal*. (Docket numbers are not used in the citation of **reported** opinions. *Reported* here means printed in a traditional reporter. See number 7 below.)

⑥ Make careful note of the name of the court writing the opinion. As soon as possible, you must learn the hierarchy of state courts in your state. (See exhibit 6.2 in chapter 6). In many states, there are three levels of courts: trial level, middle appeals level, and supreme level. (Most opinions are appealed from the trial court to the middle appeals level and then to the supreme level.) Here, we know from the title of the court (Court of Appeal) that it is an appellate court. It is not the supreme court because in California the highest court is the California Supreme Court.

The name of the court is significant because of legal authority. If the court is the highest or supreme court of the state, then the opinion would be applicable throughout the state. A middle appeals court opinion, however, applies only in the area of the state over which it has jurisdiction. When you see that the opinion was written by a trial or middle appeals court, you are immediately put on notice that you must check to determine

**respondent** The party against whom an appeal is brought. Also called the appellee.

**reported** Printed in a traditional reporter.

whether the opinion was ever appealed subsequent to the date of the case. As we will learn in chapter 11, the two main systems for checking the subsequent history of an opinion are Shepard's Citations and KeyCite. (See exhibit 11.30 in chapter 11.)

⑦ When a reported opinion is being cited, only the year (here 1972) is used, not the month or day (April 27). (If the opinion has not yet been reported, the month, day, and year are used—along with the docket number.) Sometimes the text of the reported opinion will also give you the date of the hearing or rehearing as well as the date of the decision. The year of the decision is still the critical one for citation purposes.

⑧ Here the editors provide the reader with a summary of what the opinion says. The court did not write this summary; the editors did. It, therefore, is not an official statement of the law. It is merely an aid to the reader, who can quickly read this summary to determine whether the opinion covers relevant areas of law. This summary paragraph is often called the **syllabus**.

⑨ Here continues the unofficial summary, providing the reader with what procedurally must happen as a result of the April 27 opinion.

⑩ These are editor's **headnotes**, which are small-paragraph summaries of portions of the opinion. When the editors first read the opinion, they decide how many major topics or issues are covered in the opinion. Each of these topics is summarized in a headnote, all of which are then given consecutive numbers, here 1 and 2. These numbers correspond with the bracketed numbers [1] and [2] in the opinion itself. (See ⑩ₐ) If, for example, you wanted to read the portion of the opinion that was summarized in the second headnote of the opinion, you would go to the text of the opinion that begins with the bracketed [2].

The headnotes also have a **key number**, which consists of a topic and a number, here "Searches and Seizures ⌐ 3.8(1)." Each headnote will also be printed in the **digests** of West Group. Digests are volumes that contain nothing but the headnotes of court opinions. You can find out what other courts have said about the same or similar points by going to the digest volumes, looking up the key number of a headnote (e.g., Searches and Seizures ⌐ 3.8(1)), and reading summary paragraphs from many court opinions such as our opinion, *People v. Bruni*.

Caution is needed in reading the syllabus and headnotes of opinions. As indicated earlier, they are not written by the court and therefore should never be relied on or quoted. They are merely preliminary guides to what is in an opinion. To understand the opinion, you must carefully study the language of the opinion itself through the process called *briefing*.

⑪ Here are the attorneys who represented the appellant and respondent on appeal. Note that the attorney general's office represented the People. The attorney general or the district attorney's office represents the state in criminal cases.

⑫ The opinion begins with the name of the judge who wrote the opinion, Judge Smith. In this spot you will sometimes find the words *Per Curiam Opinion* or *Memorandum Opinion*. A per curiam opinion is a court opinion that does not mention the individual judge who wrote the opinion. Such opinions are usually short because they cover relatively simple issues. A memorandum opinion (mem.) also often does not name the judge who wrote the opinion. It will often briefly state the conclusion (holding) of the opinion or the disposition without providing reasons.

⑬ In reading or briefing an opinion, make note of the history of the litigation to date. The lower court rendered a judgment dismissing the information (similar to an indictment) against Bruni after certain evidence was suppressed and declared inadmissible. (This is the prior proceeding.) The People have now appealed the judgment. (This is the present proceeding.)

If the words *information* and *suppression* are new to you, look them up in a legal dictionary. Do this for every new word. (In this book, also check the definitions of such words in the glossary.)

⑭ It is critical to state the facts of the opinion accurately. Here the facts are relatively simple: A search warrant that said "daytime" service was served at 9:30 P.M., and evidence was taken pursuant to this search warrant. Defendant objected to the admission of this evidence at trial. In most opinions, the facts are not this simple. The facts may be given at

---

**syllabus** A one-paragraph summary of an entire court opinion, usually written by a private publisher rather than by the court.

**headnote** A small-paragraph summary of a portion of a court opinion, written by a private publisher.

**key number** A general topic (e.g., Searches and Seizures) and a number for one of its subtopics (e.g., 3.8(1)). Key numbers are used by West Group to organize millions of cases by topic in its digests.

**digest** Volumes that contain summaries of court opinions. (See glossary for other meanings of digest.)

the beginning of the opinion, or they may be scattered throughout the opinion. If you confront the latter situation, you must carefully read the entire opinion to piece the facts together. Ultimately, your goal is to identify the **key facts** of the opinion. A key fact is simply one that was essential or very important to the result or holding of the court.

(15) The next critical stage of reading an opinion is to state the issue (or issues) that the court was deciding. When phrasing an issue, you should make specific reference to the language of the rule in controversy (e.g., a statute) along with important facts that raise this controversy. The issue in *Bruni* is as follows: When § 1533 was amended to allow service up to 10 : 00 P.M., did the legislature impliedly also amend § 1529, which continues to require "daytime" service, so that evidence obtained pursuant to a warrant served at 9 : 30 P.M. can be admitted into evidence? See the discussion earlier in the chapter (section D) on phrasing issues, particularly phrasing them comprehensively.

(16) The court refers to other statutes to support the conclusion it will reach. Note the interrelationship of the statutory sections. One statute is interpreted by interpreting other statutes. Section 4 of the Penal Code ("Pen. Code") says that the sections of the Penal Code are to be interpreted ("construed") rationally in order to carry out their purpose or objective and to promote justice. Section 1859 of the Code of Civil Procedure ("Code Civ. Proc.") says that when a general and a particular section are inconsistent, the latter is preferred.

The interrelationship of the statutes in this opinion is as follows:

- Section 1529 of the Penal Code still says "daytime."
- Section 7 of the Penal Code defines daytime as sunrise to sunset.
- Section 1533 of the Penal Code, as amended, says between 7 : 00 A.M. and 10 : 00 P.M.
- Section 4 of the Penal Code and § 1859 of the Code of Civil Procedure provide principles of interpreting statutes that are inconsistent.

(17) In the same manner, a court will refer to other opinions to support its ruling. In this way, the court argues that the other opinions are **precedents** for the issues before the court. The court in *People v. Bruni* is saying that *Dept. of Motor Vehicles of California v. Indus. Acc. Com.* and *Tidwell v. Superior Court* are precedents for its own ruling. Precedent is important because of the principle of **stare decisis**, which means that courts should decide similar issues in the same way unless there is good reason to do otherwise.

(18) Here is the **reasoning** of the court to support its ruling: If there is a general statute (such as § 1529) and a specific statute (such as § 1533) that are inconsistent, the latter is paramount and is preferred. Hence the legislature probably intended to amend the more general statute—§ 1529—when it amended § 1533.

(19) The result, or **holding**, of the court's deliberation of the issue must then be identified. The holding is that § 1529 was impliedly amended to authorize service up to 10 : 00 P.M. The holding is also called the court's ruling.

(20) The consequences of the court's resolution of the issue are then usually stated, as here, toward the very end of the opinion. The judgment of the lower court is reversed. The lower court cannot continue to suppress (i.e., declare inadmissible) the evidence seized at the 9 : 30 P.M. search. This is the **disposition** of the court.

An appeals court could take a number of positions with respect to a lower court's decision. It could affirm it; modify it (reverse it only in part); or **remand** the case (send it back to the lower court) with instructions on how to proceed such as how to retry the case.

(21) In theory, a judge must be very precise in defining the issue before the court—and in resolving only that issue. The judge should not say more than *must* be said to decide the case. This theory, however, is sometimes not observed. This can make your job more difficult; you must wade through the language of the court to identify (1) the key facts, (2) the precise issues, (3) the precise holding, and (4) the precise reasoning. The worst tangent that a judge can stray into is called **dictum**. Dictum is a judge's or court's view of what the law is, or might be, on facts that are *not* before the court. Judge Smith indicated that the result of the case might be different if the warrant were not specific, e.g., if it did not name the individual to be searched or what the investigator was looking for. This was not the situation in *Bruni*; therefore, Judge Smith's commentary or speculation is dictum.

**key fact** A critical fact; a fact that is essential or very important to the conclusion or holding of a court.

**precedent** A prior decision or opinion that can be used as a standard or guide in a later similar case.

**stare decisis** Courts should decide similar issues in the same way unless there is a good reason for the court to do otherwise. In resolving an issue before it, the court should be reluctant to reject precedent—a prior opinion covering a similar issue.

**reasoning** An explanation of why the court resolved a legal issue the way it did— why it reached the particular holding for that issue.

**holding** A court's answer to a specific question or issue that arises out of the facts before the court. Also called a ruling.

**disposition** The order of a court reached as a result of its holding(s).

**remand** To send a case back to a lower tribunal with instructions from the appellate court on how to proceed.

**dictum** A statement made by a court that was not necessary to resolve the legal issues growing out of the specific facts before the court. A court's comments on the law that applies (or that might apply) to facts that are not before the court.

**majority opinion** The opinion whose result and reasoning are supported by at least half plus one of the judges on the court.

**concurring opinion** The opinion written by less than a majority of the judges on the court that agrees with result reached by the majority but not with all of its reasoning.

**dissenting opinion** An opinion of one or more judges that disagrees with the result and the reasoning of the majority.

⑳ On any court there may be several judges. They do not always agree on what should be done. The majority controls. In *Bruni*, Judge Smith wrote the **majority opinion**. A **concurring opinion** is one that votes for the result reached by the majority but for different reasons. In *Bruni*, Judge Jones concurred but specified that he accepted only the result of Judge Smith's opinion. Normally, judges in such situations will write an opinion indicating their own point of view. Judge Jones did not choose to write an opinion. He simply let it be known that he did not necessarily agree with everything Judge Smith said; all he agreed with was the conclusion that the warrant was validly served. To reach this result, Judge Jones might have used different reasoning, relied on different opinions as precedent, etc. If all the judges on the bench agree on the result and reasoning, the opinion is called a unanimous opinion.

㉓ A **dissenting opinion** disagrees with part or with all of the opinion of the majority. Dissenting opinions are sometimes heated. Of course, the dissenter's opinion is not controlling. It is often valuable to read, however, in order to determine what the dissenter thinks that the majority decided.

We turn now to the ten components found in a comprehensive brief of a court opinion (exhibit 7.2) followed by a 10-part brief of *Bruni* that conforms to the guidelines of briefing presented in exhibit 7.2. (You should keep in mind, however, that not everyone follows the same briefing format or uses the same labels for the different components of a brief.)

---

| EXHIBIT 7.2 | Comprehensive Brief of a Court Opinion |
|---|---|

**I. CITATION**
Where can the opinion be found? Provide a full *citation* to the opinion you are briefing, e.g., the volume number of the reporter, the abbreviation of the name of the reporter, the page on which the opinion begins, the date of decision.

**II. PARTIES**
Who are the *parties*? Identify the lead parties, their relationship to each other, their litigation status when the case began (e.g., defendant), and their litigation status now (e.g., appellant).

**III. OBJECTIVES OF PARTIES**
When the litigation began, what were the parties seeking? State the ultimate objectives of the parties in terms of the end result they want from the litigation. At this point, do not focus on tactical or procedural objectives.

**IV. THEORIES OF THE LITIGATION**
What legal theories are the parties using? At the trial level of a civil case, name the cause of action (e.g., negligence, breach of contract, violation of § 65) and the main defenses. In a criminal case, state what the prosecution was for and the response of the defendant. If the opinion is now on appeal, briefly state the main theory of each party. Where relevant, always refer to specific rules.

**V. HISTORY OF THE LITIGATION**
What happened below—what are the prior proceeding(s)? For each *prior proceeding*, briefly state the nature of the proceeding, the party initiating it, the name of the court or agency involved, and the result of the proceeding. For the *present proceeding*, briefly state the nature of the proceeding, who initiated it, and the name of the court or agency involved.

**VI. FACTS**
What are the facts? Specifically, state the facts that were very important or key to the holding(s) reached by this court. This is one of the most significant parts of the brief. For each holding, identify the facts that were most important to the court. Note the facts that the court emphasized by repetition or by the use of adjectives such as material, crucial, or critical. You know you have identified a key fact if you can say that the holding would probably have been different if that fact had not been in the opinion.

**VII. ISSUE(S)**
What are the questions of law now before the court? Provide a comprehensive statement of each *issue* by making specific reference to the language of the rule in controversy (e.g., a statute) along with important facts that raise this controversy.

**VIII. HOLDING(S)**
What are this court's answers to the issues? If you have stated each issue comprehensively, its holding will be a simple YES or NO response.

**IX. REASONING**
Why did the court answer the issues the way it did? State the reasons for each holding.

**X. DISPOSITION**
What order did this court enter as a result of its holding(s)? State the consequences of the court's resolution of the issue(s).

---

**Comprehensive Brief of *People v. Bruni***

| | |
|---|---|
| CITATION: | *People v. Bruni*, 25 Cal. App. 3d 196, 100 Cal. Rptr. 600 (1972). |
| PARTIES: | People of California/prosecution/plaintiff below/appellant here |
| | v. |
| | Bruni/accused/defendant below/respondent here |
| OBJECTIVES OF PARTIES: | The people want to convict and punish Bruni for criminal conduct. Bruni wants to avoid conviction and punishment. |
| THEORIES OF THE LITIGATION: | 1. TRIAL: The People sought to prosecute Bruni for the alleged commission of a crime. (The opinion does not tell us which crime. The legal theory that justifies the bringing of the prosecution is the alleged commission of a crime.) Because Bruni is resisting the prosecution, we can assume that the basis and theory of his case is simply that he did not commit the crime. At the trial this was probably his main defense.<br>2. APPEAL: Bruni says that the state violated § 1529 when the search warrant was served at 9:30 P.M. The People say § 1529 was impliedly amended by § 1533, which allows service up to 10:00 P.M. |
| HISTORY OF THE LITIGATION Prior Proceeding: | 1. TRIAL: A criminal prosecution was brought by the People (the state) in the Superior Court (San Mateo). RESULT: Judgment for Bruni dismissing the information after the court granted a motion to suppress the evidence obtained from the search warrant. |
| Present Proceeding: | 2. APPEAL: The People now appeal the dismissal of the information to the Court of Appeals (First District). |
| FACTS: | A search warrant that said "daytime" service was served at 9:30 P.M. Evidence was obtained during this search, which the People unsuccessfully attempted to introduce during the trial. |
| ISSUE: | When § 1533 was amended to allow service up to 10:00 P.M., did the legislature impliedly also amend § 1529, which continues to require "daytime" service, so that evidence obtained pursuant to a warrant served at 9:30 P.M. can be admitted into evidence? |
| HOLDING: | YES. |
| REASONING: | If there is a general statute (such as § 1529) and a specific statute (such as § 1533) that are inconsistent, the specific statute is paramount and is preferred. Hence the legislature probably intended to amend the more general statute—§ 1529—when it amended § 1533. |
| DISPOSITION: | The trial court's judgment dismissing the information is reversed. When the trial resumes, the court must deny the motion to suppress the evidence based on the time of the service. |

---

At the end of your brief, you should consider adding some notes that cover the following topics:

■ What has happened to the opinion since it was decided? Has it been overruled? Has it been expanded or restricted by later opinions? You can find the history of an opinion and its treatment by other courts by Shepardizing or KeyCiting the opinion (see exhibit 11.30 in chapter 11).

- Summary of concurring opinions, if any.
- Summary of dissenting opinions, if any.
- Interesting dicta in the majority opinion, if any.
- Your own feelings about the opinion. Was it correctly decided? Why or why not?

A *thumbnail brief* is, in effect, a brief of a brief. It is a shorthand version of the 10-part comprehensive brief. A thumbnail brief includes abbreviated versions of six of the components (citation, facts, issues, holdings, reasoning, disposition) and leaves out four of the components (parties, objectives, theories, history of the litigation). By definition, you must know how to do a comprehensive brief before you can do a shorthand one. Many students fall into the trap of doing *only* shorthand briefs. It takes considerable time to do a comprehensive brief. It is highly recommended, however, that early in your career you develop the habit and skill of preparing briefs comprehensively. Without this foundation, your shorthand briefs will be visibly superficial. Shorthand briefs are valuable time savers when communicating with colleagues, but they are not substitutes for comprehensive briefs.

---

**Thumbnail Brief of *People v. Bruni***

| | |
|---|---|
| CITATION: | *People v. Bruni,* 25 Cal. App. 3d 196, 100 Cal. Rptr. 600 (1972) |
| FACTS: | A "daytime" search warrant served at 9:30 P.M. uncovers evidence that the People unsuccessfully attempt to introduce during the trial. |
| ISSUE: | Did § 1533 (which allows service up to 10:00 P.M.) impliedly amend § 1529 (which requires "daytime" service), so that evidence obtained from a 9:30 P.M. search warrant is admissible? |
| HOLDING: | Yes |
| REASONING: | A specific statute (§ 1533) is preferred over an inconsistent general one (§ 1529). |
| DISPOSITION: | Dismissal of the information is reversed; motion to suppress the 9:30 P.M.–obtained evidence must be denied. |

---

*Assignment 7.6*

Prepare a comprehensive and a thumbrial brief of each of the following three opinions:

(a) *United States v. Kovel*, printed below.
(b) *Quinn v. Lum*, printed below. (You do not need to give the citation of this opinion. It is an actual opinion but was not reported in a traditional reporter.)
(c) *Brown v. Hammond*, on page 228 in chapter 5.

---

## *United States v. Kovel*

### United States Court of Appeals Second Circuit, 296 F. 2d 918 (1961)

FRIENDLY, Circuit Judge.

This appeal from a sentence for criminal contempt for refusing to answer a question asked in the course of an inquiry by a grand jury raises an important issue as to the application of the attorney-client privilege to a non-lawyer employed by a law firm.

Kovel is a former Internal Revenue agent having accounting skills. Since 1943 he has been employed by Kamerman & Kamerman, a law firm specializing in tax law. A grand jury in the Southern District of New York was investigating alleged Federal income tax violations by Hopps, a client of the law firm; Kovel was subpoenaed to appear on September 6, 1961. The law firm advised the Assistant United States Attorney that since Kovel was an employee under the direct supervision of the partners, Kovel could not disclose any communications by the client or the result of any work done for the client, unless the latter consented; the Assistant answered that the attorney-client privilege did not apply to one who was not an attorney.

On September 7, the grand jury appeared before Judge Cashin. The Assistant United States Attorney informed the judge that Kovel had refused to answer "several questions ... on the grounds of attorney-client privilege"; he proffered "respectable authority ... that an accountant even if he is retained or employed by a firm of attorneys, cannot take the privilege." The judge answered "You don't have to give me any authority on that." A court reporter testified that Kovel, after an initial claim of privilege had admitted receiving a statement of Hopps' assets and liabilities, but that, when asked "what was the purpose of your receiving that," had declined to answer on the ground of privilege "Because the communication was received with a purpose, as stated by the client"; later questions and answers indicated the communication was a letter addressed to Kovel. After verifying that Kovel was not a lawyer, the judge directed him to answer, saying "You have no privilege as such." The reporter then read another question Kovel had refused to answer, "Did you ever discuss with Mr. Hopps or give Mr. Hopps any information with regard to treatment for capital gains purposes of the Atlantic Beverage Corporation sale by him?" The judge again directed Kovel to answer reaffirming "There is no privilege—You are entitled to no privilege, as I understand the law."

Later on September 7, they and Kovel's employer, Jerome Kamerman, now acting as his counsel, appeared again before Judge Cashin. The Assistant told the judge that Kovel had "refused to answer some of the questions which you had directed him to answer." A reporter reread so much of the transcript heretofore summarized as contained the first two refusals. The judge offered Kovel another opportunity to answer, reiterating the view, "There is no privilege to this man at all." Counsel referred to New York Civil Practice Act, § 353, which we quote in the margin.*

Counsel reiterated that an employee "who sits with the client of the law firm ... occupies the same status ... as a clerk or stenographer or any other lawyer ..."; the judge was equally clear that the privilege was never "extended beyond the attorney." The court held [Kovel] in contempt, sentenced him to a

year's imprisonment, ordered immediate commitment and denied bail. Later in the day, the grand jury having indicted, Kovel was released until September 12, at which time, without opposition from the Government, I granted bail pending determination of this appeal.

Here the parties continue to take generally the same positions as below—Kovel, that his status as an employee of a law firm automatically made all communications to him from clients privileged; the Government, that under no circumstances could there be privilege with respect to communications to an accountant. The New York County Lawyers' Association as *amicus curiae* has filed a brief generally supporting appellant's [Kovel's] position.

Decision under what circumstances, if any, the attorney-client privilege may include a communication to a nonlawyer by the lawyer's client is the resultant of two conflicting forces. One is the general teaching that "The investigation of truth and the enforcement of testimonial duty demand the restriction, not the expansion, of these privileges," 8 Wigmore, *Evidence* (McNaughton Rev. 1961), § 2192, p. 73. The other is the more particular lesson "That as, by reason of the complexity and difficulty of our law, litigation can only be properly conducted by professional men, it is absolutely necessary that a man ... should have recourse to the assistance of professional lawyers, and ... it is equally necessary ... that he should be able to place unrestricted and unbounded confidence in the professional agent, and that the communications he so makes to him should be kept secret ...," Jessel, M. R. in *Anderson v. Bank*, 2 Ch.D. 644, 649 (1876). Nothing in the policy of the privilege suggests that attorneys, simply by placing accountants, scientists or investigators on their payrolls and maintaining them in their offices, should be able to invest all communications by clients to such persons with a privilege the law has not seen fit to extend when the latter are operating under their own steam. On the other hand, in contrast to the Tudor times when the privilege was first recognized, the complexities of modern existence prevent attorneys from effectively handling clients' affairs without the help of others; few lawyers could now practice without the assistance of secretaries, file clerks, telephone operators, messengers, clerks not yet admitted to the bar, and aides of other sorts. "The assistance of these agents being indispensable to his work and the communications of the client being often necessarily committed to them by the attorney or by the client himself, the privilege must include all the persons who act as the attorney's agents. 8 Wigmore *Evidence*, § 2301; Annot, 53 A.L.R. 369 (1928).

---

* "An attorney or counselor at law shall not disclose, or be allowed to disclose, a communication, made by his client to him, or his advice given thereon, in the course of his professional employment nor shall any clerk, stenographer or other person employed by such attorney or counselor ... disclose, or be allowed to disclose any such communication or advice."

## United States v. Kovel

### United States Court of Appeals Second Circuit, 296 F. 2d 918 (1961)—*continued*

Indeed, the Government does not here dispute that the privilege covers communications to non-lawyer employees with "a menial or ministerial responsibility that involves relating communications to *an attorney*." We cannot regard the privilege as confined to "menial or ministerial" employees. Thus, we can see no significant difference between a case where the attorney sends a client speaking a foreign language to an interpreter to make a literal translation of the client's story; a second where the attorney, himself having some little knowledge of the foreign tongue has a more knowledgeable non-lawyer employee in the room to help out; a third where someone to perform that same function has been brought along by the client, and a fourth where the attorney, ignorant of the foreign language, sends the client to a non-lawyer proficient in it with instructions to interview the client on the attorney's behalf and then render its own summary of the situation, perhaps drawing on his own knowledge in the process, so that the attorney can give the client proper legal advice. All four cases meet every element of Wigmore's famous formulation, § 2292, "(1) Where legal advice of any kind is sought (2) from a professional legal advisor in his capacity as such (3) the communications relating to that purpose, (4) made in confidence (5) by the client, (6) are at his instance permanently protected (7) from disclosure by himself or by the legal advisor, (8) except the protection be waived," ... Section 2301 of Wigmore would clearly recognize the privilege in the first case and the Government goes along to that extent, § 2301 would also recognize the privilege in the second case and § 2301 in the third unless the circumstances negated confidentiality. We find no valid policy reason for a different result in the fourth case, and we do not read Wigmore as thinking there is. Laymen consulting lawyers should not be expected to anticipate niceties perceptible only to judges—and not even to all of them.

This analogy of the client speaking a foreign language is by no means irrelevant to the appeal at hand. Accounting concepts are a foreign language to some lawyers in almost all cases, and to almost all lawyers in some cases. Hence the presence of an accountant, whether hired by the lawyer or by the client, while the client is relating a complicated tax story to the lawyer, ought not destroy the privilege, any more than would that of the linguist in the second or third variations of the foreign language theme discussed above; the presence of the accountant is necessary, or at least highly useful, for the effective consultation between the client and the lawyer which the privilege is designed to permit. By the same token, if the lawyer has directed the client, either in the specific case or generally, to tell his story in the first instance to an accountant engaged by the lawyer, who is then to interpret it so that the lawyer may better give legal advice, communications by the client reasonably related to that purpose ought fall within the privilege; there can be no more virtue in requiring the lawyer to sit by while the client pursues these possibly tedious preliminary conversations with the accountant than in insisting on the lawyer's physical presence while the client dictates a statement to the lawyer's secretary or is interviewed by a clerk not yet admitted to practice. What is vital to the privilege is that the communication be made *in confidence* for the purpose of obtaining *legal* advice *from the lawyer*. If what is sought is not legal advice but only accounting service, or if the advice sought is the accountant's rather than the lawyer's, no privilege exists. We recognize this draws what may seem to some a rather arbitrary line between a case where the client communicates first to his own accountant (no privilege as to such communications, even though he later consults his lawyers on the same matter, *Gariepy v. United States*, 189 F.2d 459, 463 (6th Cir. 1951)),‡ and others, where the client in the first instance consults a lawyer who retains an accountant as a listening post, or consults the lawyer with his own accountant present. But that is the inevitable consequence of having to reconcile the absence of a privilege for accountants and the effective operation of the privilege of client and lawyer under conditions where the lawyer needs outside help. We realize also that the line we have drawn will not be so easy to apply as the simpler positions urged on us by the parties—the district judges will scarcely be able to leave the decision of such cases to computers; but the distinction has to be made if the privilege is neither to be unduly expanded nor to become a trap.

The judgment is vacated and the cause remanded for further proceedings consistent with this opinion.

---

‡We do not deal in this opinion with the question under what circumstances, if any, such communications could be deemed privileged on the basis that they were being made to the accountant as the client's agent for the purpose of subsequent communication by the accountant to the lawyer; communications by the client's agent to the attorney are privileged, 8 Wigmore, *Evidence*, § 2317-1.

# Quinn v. Lum and Cronin, Fried, Sekiya & Kekina

Civ. No. 81284
Hawaii Court of Appeals

On January 25, 1984, Richard K. Quinn, Attorney at Law, a Law Corporation, filed suit against Rogerlene Lum, a member of the Hawaii Association of Legal Assistants (HALA) and formerly legal secretary with the Quinn firm, for injunctive relief based on the allegation that Mrs. Lum possesses confidential client information from her work as Quinn's legal secretary, which information would be transmitted to the codefendant, Mrs. Lum's new employer, Cronin, Fried, Sekiya & Kekina, Attorneys at Law, if she were to begin her employment with the Cronin firm as a legal assistant.

On or about January 3, 1984 Mrs. Lum notified Quinn that she had accepted a position as a paralegal with the Cronin firm. Quinn subsequently discussed and corresponded with Mr. Cronin regarding the hiring of Mrs. Lum, who was scheduled to begin work with the Cronin firm on January 30, 1984. Mr. Cronin repeatedly refused Quinn's request that she not be hired by the Cronin firm.

On January 26, a hearing on the application for a temporary restraining order was heard by Judge Philip T. Chun of the Circuit Court of the First Circuit, State of Hawaii. The application was denied.

Quinn alleges in the pleadings filed with the Court in Civil No. 81284 that Mrs. Lum's employment with the Quinn firm from December 1, 1982 to January 17, 1984, and as Mr. Quinn's secretary from April 25, 1983 to January 17, 1984, included attendance at the firm's case review committee meetings. Confidential discussions occurred concerning case evaluation, settlement evaluation, strategy and tactics between Quinn, his associates, and their clients.

Cronin et al. are attorneys of record for the plaintiffs in *Firme v. Honolulu Medical Group and Ronald P. Peroff, M.D.* Quinn's firm represents the defendants. The case was set for trial on March 19, 1984. According to exhibits attached to the records filed in the instant case, Mr. Cronin recognized the *Firme* situation and agreed that Mrs. Lum would not be involved in the *Firme* case in her new employment nor would his firm "[ever] seek to obtain any information from her concerning cases with which she was involved while in [Quinn's] office, nor would we have her work on any while here." Mr. Cronin goes on to say in his January 24 letter to Quinn that Quinn should consult with his clients in the *Firme* case as to whether Quinn's "attempt ... to stop Mrs. Lum from working for [the Cronin firm] is with their approval."

Quinn also alleges that while his firm is known in the Honolulu legal community as one which represents hospitals, doctors and other health care providers, the Cronin firm is known as a plaintiff medical malpractice firm. Quinn lists in several pleadings that on more than one occasion, these firms found themselves adversaries in the same cases.

[Quinn contends] that this action was brought not to "bar Lum from working as a legal secretary or even as a paralegal, since that would be ludicrous given the size of Hawaii's legal community." In fact, Quinn states he would have "no objection to Lum's working for any other law firm in Hawaii other than one which specializes in medical malpractice plaintiffs' work, like [Cronin's]."

A subsequent hearing on the original complaint for injunctive relief was then held in Judge Ronald Moon's court on February 6. Plaintiff's motion for a preliminary injunction that would bar such employment "for at least two years" was denied, with the judge noting *Quinn v. Lum* as a case of first impression.

The Court explained its decision in light of the standards to be met before a preliminary injunction could be issued, as dealt with in depth by Mrs. Lum's attorney, David L. Fairbanks, who is also the current President of the Hawaii State Bar Association.

The standards which must be met in order to obtain a preliminary injunction, as listed by Judge Moon, follow:

1. The Court did not feel there was a substantial likelihood that plaintiff would prevail on the merits. If an injunction were to be issued, it would:
   "[E]ssentially prevent a paralegal or legal secretary, [or] attorney from joining any law firm that may have had some case in the past, ... cases pending at the present time, or potential cases which may be worked on in the future" (Transcript of the Hearing, page 82).
2. The evidence is lacking regarding irreparable damage to Richard Quinn's clients.
3. The public interest would not be served by issuing such an injunction.

When an attorney enters practice in the State of Hawaii, he or she agrees to abide and be governed by the Hawaii Code of Professional Responsibility. This code does not attempt to govern the ethical actions of the non-attorneys. While Canon 37 of the American Bar Association's Code of Professional Responsibility, adopted pre-1971, states that a lawyer's em-

## Quinn v. Lum and Cronin, Fried, Sekiya & Kekina

Civ. No. 81284
Hawaii Court of Appeals—*continued*

ployees have the same duty to preserve client confidences as the lawyer, this Canon is not included in the Hawaii code. Compliance, therefore, with the same rules of ethics guiding the Hawaii attorney is currently left to the discretion—and conscience—of the non-attorney.

If an attorney in Hawaii breaches the Code of Professional Responsibility, the office of Disciplinary Counsel may choose to investigate the matter and may pass the matter on to the Disciplinary Board and possibly to the Hawaii Supreme Court for adjudication.

If an employee of a law office becomes suspect of some breach of ethics or acts of omission, the employing attorney becomes responsible for the em-

ployee's deeds. For example, if a legal secretary fails to file the complaint the day the Statute of Limitations expires thinking the next day would suffice, it is the attorney who is responsible to the client. The attorney can fire the secretary "for cause" but the attorney, nevertheless, stands responsible. It appears the only way for an attorney to further censor the employee directly is via a civil suit for tortious damages.

Whether a permanent injunction can or will be granted has yet to be seen in this case. What is clear is that neither the office of Disciplinary Counsel nor the Hawaii Supreme Court would or could become involved; they have no jurisdiction over the non-attorney working in a law office.

---

Section H

# APPLYING COURT OPINIONS

Our next concern is as follows: how do you apply an opinion? Of course, an opinion is itself a court's application of rules of law to facts. (The *Bruni* opinion, for example, applied California statutes to the facts of a search warrant.) How do we apply an opinion to a new set of facts —those presented by a client or by a teacher's assignment? Phrased another way, how do we determine whether the opinion is **analogous** to your facts? An opinion is analogous if it is sufficiently similar to justify a similar outcome or result. Before covering this theme, we need to briefly examine the two main kinds of rules that courts apply in their opinions: enacted law and common law.

**Enacted law** is any law that is not created within litigation. Enacted laws include constitutions, statutes, administrative regulations, and ordinances. See exhibit 6.1 in chapter 6 for the definitions of these rules and who writes them. The verb *enact* means to pass or adopt a rule after someone has proposed it. The proposal is often debated by a deliberative body such as a legislature or council, commented on by the public and by experts, amended, and eventually voted up or down. Most enacted laws are intended to cover broad categories of people or entities (e.g., taxpayers, motorists, businesses). With few exceptions, the reach of an enacted law is **prospective**—it governs future events that will occur after the rule is enacted. A statute, for example, might provide that after a certain date, all motorcycle riders in the state must wear helmets.

**Common law** is significantly different. It is judge-made law in the absence of controlling statutory law or other higher law such as the constitution. Common law is created by the courts. It applies to and grows out of litigation involving specific parties; in the main, it covers events that have already occurred (e.g., an automobile accident, an allegedly discriminatory firing). Examples of common law include negligence, breach of contract, and self-defense. (See chapter 6 for other definitions of common law and for the relationship between statutes and the common law, particularly the power of a statute to change the common law.)

**analogous** Sufficiently similar to justify a similar outcome or result.

**enacted law** Any law that is not created within litigation. Law written by a deliberative body such as a legislature or constitutional convention after it is proposed and often debated and amended.

**prospective** Governing future events; effective in the future.

**common law** Judge-made law in the absence of controlling statutory law or other higher law.

Court opinions that you will be applying interpret enacted law, common law, or both. How do you apply such opinions?

Assume that you are in the law library researching the facts presented by a client or by your teacher in a school assignment. (We will refer to these facts as the problem facts.) You are looking for court opinions that might apply to the problem facts. When you find an opinion that looks promising, you carefully study and brief it (see exhibit 7.2). You identify its holdings—the answers of the court to the legal issues before it. You now want to know whether any of the holdings applies to the problem facts. To answer this question, you need to go through two separate comparisons:

- *Rule comparison.* First, you compare the rule (enacted law or common law) that was interpreted and applied in the opinion with the rule that you have uncovered elsewhere in your research (or the rule that you have been given) as potentially applicable to your problem facts.
- *Fact comparison.* Second, you compare the key facts of the opinion (i.e., those that were essential or very important to the holding) with your problem facts.

Let's look at these comparisons in greater detail.

## RULE COMPARISON

Suppose your client in the problem facts is charged with a violation of § 23(b) of the state code on the payment of certain taxes. One of your first steps is to go to the law library and find § 23(b). You want to know whether § 23(b) applies to your client. After a preliminary analysis of this statute on your own, you search for court opinions that interpreted and applied § 23(b). You would not try to find opinions that interpreted housing or pollution statutes. You focus on opinions that cover the *same* rule involved in the case of the client—here § 23(b). This is also true of the common law. If the client has a negligence case, for example, you search for opinions that interpret the law of negligence.

*Rule comparison* in the analysis of opinions, therefore, is fairly simple. The general principle is as follows: you compare the rule involved in your client's case (or school assignment) with the rule interpreted and applied in the opinion, and you proceed only if the rule is exactly the same. Although there are some exceptions, this principle will be sufficient to guide you most of the time.

## FACT COMPARISON

Here is the heart of the analysis. Before the holding of an opinion can apply, you must demonstrate that the key facts of the opinion are substantially the same as the problem facts. If the facts are exactly the same or almost exactly the same, the opinion is said to be **on all fours** with your facts. If so, then you will have little difficulty convincing someone that the holding of the opinion applies to your facts. It is rare, however, that you will find an opinion on all fours. Consequently, careful analysis of *factual similarities and differences* must be made. In general, if the facts are substantially similar, the ruling applies; if they are substantially different, it does not.

You must identify the *key facts* in the opinion because these facts alone are the basis of the comparison. As we saw when we studied the brief of an opinion, a key fact is one that was very important or crucial to the holding or conclusion reached by the court. In a divorce opinion, for example, it will probably not be key that a plaintiff was 33 years old. The court would have reached the same result if the plaintiff was 32 or 34. Age may have been irrelevant or of very minor importance to the holding. What *may* have been key is that the plaintiff beat his wife because without this fact the court might not have reached the conclusion (holding) that the ground of cruelty existed. You carefully comb the opinion to read what the judge said about the various facts. Did the court emphasize certain facts? Repeat them? Label them as crucial or important? These are the kinds of questions you must ask yourself to determine which facts in the opinion were key. (See "Facts" in exhibit 7.2, earlier in the chapter.)

**on all fours** Exactly the same, or almost so.

Let us assume that you have been able to identify the key facts of the opinion. Your next concern is *comparing* these facts and the facts of your own problem. For example:

| **Your Facts** | **The Opinion:** *Smith v. Apex Co.* |
|---|---|
| Client sees an ad in the paper announcing a sale at a local store. He goes to the back of the store and falls into a pit. There was a little sign that said *danger* near the pit. The client wants to sue the store owner, J. Jackson, for negligence in failing to use reasonable care in preventing his injury. The law office assigns a paralegal to research the case. The paralegal finds the case of *Smith v. Apex Co.* and wants to argue that it applies. | This case involved a man (Tom Smith) who is looking for an address. He is walking down the street. He decides to walk into an office building to ask someone for directions. While coming down the corridor, he slips and falls on a wet floor. There was a small sign in the corridor that said *wet floor*, which Smith saw. Smith sued the owner of the building (Apex Co.) for negligence. The court held that the owner was negligent for failure to exercise reasonable care for the safety of users of the building. The cite of the opinion is *Smith v. Apex Co.*, 223 Mass. 578, 78 N.E.2d 422 (1980). |

First, identify all factual similarities:

- The client was in a public place (a store). Smith was also in a public place (an office building).
- Both situations involved some kind of warning (the *danger* sign and the *wet floor* sign).
- The warning in both situations was not conspicuous (the *danger* sign was "little"; the *wet floor* sign was "small").

Next, identify all factual differences:

- The client was in a store, whereas Smith was in an office building.
- The client's case involved a hole or pit, whereas *Smith v. Apex Co.* involved a slippery surface.
- The client was there about a possible purchase, whereas Smith was looking for directions and therefore not trying to transact any business in the office building.

Next, identify any factual gaps:

- Smith saw the *wet floor* sign, but we do not know whether the client saw the *danger* sign.

Ninety percent of your legal analysis is complete if you have been able to make these three categories of fact identification: factual similarities, factual differences, and factual gaps. Many students either ignore the categories or do a superficial job of laying them out. They do not carefully pick apart the facts in order to identify similarities, differences, and gaps.

Once you have done this properly, you make your final arguments about the opinion:

- If you want the holding in the opinion to apply, you emphasize the similarities between your facts and the key facts in the opinion. If any of your facts differ from a fact in the opinion, you try to point out that this is not significant because the latter was not a key fact in the opinion.
- If you do not want the holding in the opinion to apply, you emphasize the differences between your facts and the key facts in the opinion. If any of your facts is similar to a fact in the opinion, you try to point out that this is not significant because there is still a dissimilarity with at least one of the key facts in the opinion.

*Factual gaps* sometimes pose a problem. If the factual gap is in the facts of your client's case, you simply go back to the client and ask him or her about the fact. In our negligence example, the paralegal asks the client whether he saw the "danger" sign. Suppose, however, that the factual gap is in the opinion itself. Assume that your client was running when he fell into the pit but that the opinion does not tell you whether Smith was running, walking, etc. You obviously cannot go to Smith or to the judge who wrote the opinion and ask.

You must make a guess of what the judge would have done in the opinion if Smith was running at the time he slipped on the corridor floor. You may decide that it would have changed the result or that this additional fact would have made no difference to the holding of the court.

We turn now to an overview of how *Smith v. Apex Co.* would be applied to the client's case in a memorandum of law. The latter, as we have seen, is simply a written analysis, or explanation of how the law might apply to a fact situation. In chapter 12, we will discuss the components of a memorandum of law in greater detail. For now, we concentrate on only three components: legal issue, facts, and analysis.

The client's case and the *Smith* opinion involve exactly the same rule—the law of negligence. Assume that the part of this rule that is in contention (the *element in contention*) between the client and the store owner, J. Jackson, is the requirement that "reasonable care" be used.

*Legal Issue*: Did the store use "reasonable care" for the safety of users of the store when the only warning of a pit in the store was a small *danger* sign near the pit?

*Facts*: The client saw an ad in the newspaper announcing a sale. He went to the back of the store and fell into a pit. There was a small sign that said *danger* near the pit.

*Analysis*: An opinion on point is *Smith v. Apex Co.*, 233 Mass. 578, 78 N.E.2d 422 (1980). In this opinion, the holding of the court was that the owner of an office building was liable for negligence when Smith slipped on a wet corridor floor in the building. There was a small *wet floor* sign in the corridor. This opinion is substantially similar to our own client's case. Both were in public buildings where owners can expect people to be present. In both situations, the warning was insufficient. The *wet floor* sign in the opinion was "small." The *danger* sign in our situation was "little." Because of all these important similarities, it can be argued that the holding in *Smith v. Apex Co.* applies.

It is true that in the opinion the judge pointed out that Smith saw the sign. Our facts do not state whether the client saw the *danger* sign in the store. This, however, should not make any difference. The judge in the opinion would probably have reached the same holding if Smith had not seen the *wet floor* sign. In fact, the case would probably have been stronger for Smith if he did *not* see the sign. The building was dangerous in spite of the fact that users of the building such as Smith could see the sign. Obviously, the danger would be considered even greater if such users could not see the sign. We should find out from our client whether he saw the *danger* sign, but I do not think that it will make any difference in the applicability of the holding in *Smith v. Apex Co.*

The store owner will try to argue that the opinion does not apply. The argument might be that a pit is not as dangerous as a wet floor because a pit is more conspicuous than a wet floor and hence not as hazardous. A user is more likely to notice a hole in the floor than to know whether a floor is slippery enough to fall on. Our client could respond by pointing out that the pit was in the back of the store where it may not have been very noticeable. Furthermore, the wet floor in the opinion was apparently conspicuous (Smith saw the *wet floor* sign), yet in the opinion the judge still found the defendant liable.

---

### Assignment 7.7
In the following situations, point out any factual similarities, differences, and gaps between the client facts and the facts of the opinion.

(a) *Client Facts*: Jim is driving his car 30 m.p.h. on a dirt road at night. He suddenly sneezes and jerks the steering wheel slightly, causing the car to move to the right and run into Bill's fence. Bill sues Jim for negligence.
*Opinion*: A pedestrian brings a negligence action against Mary. Mary is driving her motorcycle on a clear day. A page of a newspaper unexpectedly flies into Mary's face. Because she cannot see where she is going, she runs into a pedestrian crossing the street. The court finds for Mary, ruling that she did not act unreasonably in causing the accident.

(b) *Client Facts*: Helen is the mother of David, age four. The state is trying to take David away from Helen on the ground that Helen has neglected David. Helen lives alone with David. She works part-time and leaves David with a neighbor.

> Helen's job occasionally requires her to travel. Once she was away for a month. During this period, David was sometimes left alone because the neighbor had to spend several days at the hospital. When David was discovered alone, the state began proceedings to remove David from Helen on the ground of neglect.
>
> *Opinion*: The state charged Bob Thompson with the neglect of his twins, aged 10. The state wishes to place the twins in a foster home. Bob is partially blind. One day he accidentally tripped and fell on one of the twins, causing severe injuries to the child. Bob lives alone with the twins but refuses to hire anyone to help him run the home. The court ruled that Bob did not neglect his children.

Finally, we need to relate IRAC to our discussion of applying opinions. IRAC (covered at the beginning of the chapter) is an acronym for the structure of legal analysis: Issue, Rule, Application (sometimes called Analysis), and Conclusion. We said that when you are analyzing any rule such as a statute, you break it down into its elements, create issues out of the elements in contention, and connect the facts to those elements. We also said that if you found any court opinions in your research, you would include them in your analysis. Opinions are examined in the "A" component of IRAC. That is what we did in the example of the client who fell into a pit and sued the store owner for negligence. The element in contention was "reasonable care," which became the basis of this issue: did the store use "reasonable care" for the safety of users of the store when the only warning of a pit in the store was a small danger sign near the pit? To help answer this question, we applied *Smith v. Apex Co.* through the comparisons we have outlined. If other opinions were potentially relevant, they would have to be argued in the same manner.

---

### Assignment 7.8

(a) Before Helen became a paralegal for the firm of Harris & Derkson, she was a chemist for a large corporation. Harris & Derkson is a patent law firm where Helen's technical expertise in chemistry is invaluable. Helen's next-door neighbor is an inventor. On a number of occasions, he discussed the chemical makeup of his inventions with Helen. The neighbor is being charged by the government with stealing official secrets in order to prepare one of these inventions. Harris & Derkson represents the neighbor on this case. Helen also works directly on the case for the firm. In a prosecution of the neighbor, Helen is called as a witness and is asked to reveal the substance of all her conversations with the neighbor concerning the invention in question. Does Helen have to answer? Apply *United States v. Kovel* to this question. Do not do any legal research. Limit yourself to the application of this one opinion based on the guidelines of this section. For the text of *Kovel*, see page 320.

(b) Salem is a factory town of 500 inhabitants in Hawaii. The factory employs 95 percent of the workers in the town. The town has only two private attorneys: Ann Grote and Timothy Farrell. Forty of the employees have decided to sue the factory over a wage dispute. Ann Grote represents all these employees. She works alone except for her only employee, Bob Davis, a paralegal. In this litigation, the factory is represented by Timothy Farrell who has no employees—no secretaries and no paralegals. Grote and Farrell are young attorneys who have just begun their practices. Their only clients are the 40 employees and the factory, respectively. The litigation has become quite complicated. Several months before the case is scheduled to go to trial, Farrell offers Davis a job as a paralegal at double the salary he is earning with Grote. Davis accepts the offer. Grote goes to court seeking a preliminary injunction against Davis and Farrell, which would bar them from entering this employment relationship. Apply *Quinn v. Lum and Cronin, Fried, Sekiya & Kekina* to the facts of the case of *Grote v. Davis and Farrell*. Do not do any legal research. Limit yourself to the application of this one opinion based on the guidelines of this section. For the text of *Quinn*, see page 323.

**(c)** Anthony Bay is a paralegal who works for Iverson, Kelley, and Winters in Philadelphia. He is an at will employee. His supervising attorney is Grace Swenson. One day Bay notices that Swenson deposited a client settlement check in the general law firm account. Bay calls the bar association disciplinary committee and charges Swenson with commingling funds unethically. (Attorneys have an ethical obligation to keep client funds and general law firm funds in separate accounts. Commingling or mixing these funds in one account is unethical, as we saw in chapter 5.) Bay is fired for disloyalty. In the meantime, the bar investigates the charge of commingling and finds that the charge is accurate. Swenson is eventually disciplined. Can Bay sue Swenson and Iverson, Kelley, and Winters for wrongful dismissal? Apply *Brown v. Hammond* to answer this question. Do not do any legal research. Limit yourself to the application of this one opinion based on the guidelines of this section. For the text of *Brown*, see page 228.

# CHAPTER SUMMARY

Legal analysis is the process of connecting a rule of law to a set of facts in order to answer a legal question or issue for the purpose of avoiding or resolving a legal dispute or preventing it from becoming worse. IRAC presents the structure of legal analysis: Issue (a question that arises out of the facts of the problem), Rule (the statute, common law, or other rule that is being applied), Application (the connection of the facts to the rule), and Conclusion (a statement of which side has the better argument of how the rule applies to the facts).

An important skill in legal analysis is the ability to break a rule down into its elements. An element is simply a component or portion of a rule that is a precondition of the applicability of the entire rule. If all the elements apply to a fact situation, then the rule applies to the fact situation. If any one element does not apply, then the rule does not apply. A legal issue is often phrased to ask whether one of the elements applies to the facts. (This element is referred to as the element in contention.) The answer may depend on whether the element is to be interpreted broadly or narrowly.

Sometimes the applicability of a rule (or an element within a rule) will be determined by an assessment of factors. A factor is one of the circumstances or considerations that will be weighed, no one of which is usually conclusive.

To brief an opinion means to identify its 10 major components: citation, parties, objectives of the parties, theories of the litigation, history of the litigation, facts, issues, holdings, reasoning, and disposition. In addition, it is often essential to determine the subsequent history of the opinion.

A thumbnail brief is a shorthand brief of an opinion consisting of the citation, facts, issues, holdings, reasoning, and disposition.

Opinions interpret enacted law, common law, or both kinds of law. There are two main steps in applying an opinion to a set of facts from a client's case. First, you compare the rule (which will be either an enacted law or a common law) that was interpreted in the opinion with the rule you are considering in the client's case. With limited exceptions, the opinion cannot apply unless these two rules are the same. Second, you compare the key facts in the opinion with the facts of the client's case. In general, the opinion will apply if these facts are the same or are substantially similar.

## KEY TERMS

| | |
|---|---|
| legal analysis | legal issue |
| application | factor |
| IRAC | brief |
| memorandum of law | trial brief |
| element | appellate brief |
| element in contention | unofficial reporter |

citation
appellant
respondent
reported
syllabus
headnote
key number
digest
key fact
precedent
stare decisis
reasoning

holding
disposition
remand
dictum
majority opinion
concurring opinion
dissenting opinion
analogous
enacted law
prospective
common law
on all fours

## ON THE NET: MORE ON LEGAL ANALYSIS

### How to Brief a Case
lawschool.westlaw.com/studentcenter/brief.asp
www.lib.jjay.cuny.edu/research/brief.html
lessons.cali.org/web/LWR09/brief.htm
www.law.umkc.edu/faculty/profiles/glesnerfines/bateman.htm

### IRAC
www.lawnerds.com/guide/irac.html
www.dcl.edu/rwa/irac.pdf

### Legal Analysis on Examinations
lawschool.westlaw.com/studentCenter/writingexam.asp? appflag=16%2E5&site=PH
www.gilbertlaw.com/student/survival_writing.asp

# Chapter 8

# LEGAL INTERVIEWING

## Chapter Outline

## Section A
# Client Relations in an Era of Lawyer Bashing

Before beginning our study of interviewing, we need to examine some preliminary matters that often influence client relationships today.

You may be working with many clients who are hiring an attorney for the first time. Their image of the legal profession is often heavily influenced by the portrayal of attorneys in the media. Lately, the media have been very negative about attorneys. In a steady stream of commercials, cartoons, and jokes, attorneys have been held up to public ridicule. Indeed, there has been so much unfavorable publicity that many bar associations have accused the media of lawyer bashing and have urged their members to take affirmative steps to improve the image of the profession.

This may be the environment in which a paralegal comes into contact with clients. How they perceive you matters a great deal. The way you dress, how you communicate, and how you perform your job can reinforce the negativism or help reverse it. Whether you are interviewing the client or have roles that require no client contact, it is extremely important that you project yourself as a professional. There is no better way to combat negative stereotypes of attorneys than for everyone in the office to maintain a high level of integrity and competence.

You should act on the assumption that every large or small task you perform on a client's case is of critical importance. Even if you have only a small role in a particular client's case, you should assume that how you perform your role will help determine whether the client is satisfied with the services rendered by the entire office and whether he or she will readily recommend the office to relatives, friends, and business associates. This is particularly important because about 40 percent of a law office's new business comes from referrals and recommendations of satisfied clients.[1]

Admittedly, you cannot single-handedly correct the public's perception of attorneys. It is due to forces beyond your control. Attorneys sometimes take unpopular cases such as defending people charged with committing heinous crimes. When interviewed on TV or radio, these attorneys seldom generate much sympathy when they suggest that the accused is the victim. Attorneys are frequently injected into the middle of bitter disputes where they become lightning rods for underlying and overt hostility. Opponents often accuse the other attorney of causing the hostility or of setting up roadblocks to resolution in order to increase fees. Although you cannot eliminate these perceptions, you can perform your job in such a way that the client feels that his or her case is the most important case you are working on and that you are doing everything possible to help the office keep costs to a minimum. This kind of professionalism will be a significant step in the direction of correcting public misconceptions about the practice of law.

## Section B
# Hiring the Firm

**retainer** (1) A contract between an attorney and a client that covers the scope of services, fees, expenses, and costs of legal services. (2) An amount of money (or other property) paid by a client as a deposit or advance against future fees, expenses, and costs of legal services.

Once the prospective client decides to hire the firm and the firm agrees to provide representation, their relationship should be formalized in a contract called the **retainer**. It covers the scope of services, fees, expenses, and costs of the legal services to be provided. (See exhibit 8.1.) The word *retainer* also refers to an amount of money (or other property) paid by the client as a deposit or advance against future attorney fees, expenses such as travel, and costs such as court filing fees.

Suppose, however, the attorney decides *not* to accept the case. This may happen for a number of different reasons. There may be a conflict of interest because the law office once represented the opponent of the prospective client (see chapter 5). The attorney may feel that the case lacks merit because there is no legal justification for what the client wants to accomplish. More commonly, the attorney will refuse to take the case for economic reasons. The client may not be able to afford the anticipated legal fees, and the party the client wants to sue may not have enough cash or other resources to pay a winning judgment. (Such an opponent is said to lack a **deep pocket**.) Whatever the reason, it is very important for the

**deep pocket** An individual who has resources with which to pay a potential judgment (the opposite of a *shallow pocket*).

EXHIBIT 8.1    Sample Retainer Agreement

_____, 20 ____

## ATTORNEY-CLIENT FEE CONTRACT

This ATTORNEY-CLIENT FEE CONTRACT ("Contract") is entered into by and between _____ ("Client") and _____ ("Attorney")

1. CONDITIONS. This Contract will not take effect, and Attorney will have no obligation to provide legal services, until Client returns a signed copy of this Contract and pays the deposit called for under paragraph 3.

2. SCOPE AND DUTIES. Client hires Attorney to provide legal services in connection with _____. Attorney shall provide those legal services reasonably required to represent Client, and shall take reasonable steps to keep Client informed of progress and to respond to Client's inquiries. Client shall be truthful with Attorney, cooperate with Attorney, keep Attorney informed of developments, abide by this Contract, pay Attorney's bills on time, and keep Attorney advised of Client's address, telephone number, and whereabouts.

> Note that paragraph 2 is careful to state that "reasonable" steps will be taken. The attorney's standard of performance will be reasonableness. The office's obligation is to do what is reasonable, not to guarantee any specific results. This disclaimer is made more explicit in paragraph 10.

3. DEPOSIT. Client shall deposit $ _____ by _____. The sum will be deposited in a trust account, to be used to pay:
____ Costs and expenses only.
____ Costs and expenses and fees for legal services.
Client hereby authorizes Attorney to withdraw sums from the trust account to pay the costs or fees or both that Client incurs. Any unused deposit at the conclusion of Attorney services will be refunded.

4. LEGAL FEES. Client agrees to pay for legal services at the following rates: partners—$_____ an hour; associates—$_____ an hour; paralegals—$_____ an hour; law clerks—$_____ an hour; and for other personnel as follows:

If services to Client require extensive word processing work for documents in excess of 15 pages, Client will be charged $_____ a page.
Attorneys and paralegals charge in minimum units of 0.2 hours.

> Paragraph 4 makes clear that fees for paralegal services are separate and additional to fees charged by attorneys and law clerks. (The latter are individuals who are still in law school or who have completed law school and are awaiting bar examination results.)

5. COSTS AND EXPENSES. In addition to paying legal fees, Client shall reimburse Attorney for all costs and expenses incurred by Attorney, including, but not limited to, process servers' fees, fees fixed by law or assessed by courts or other agencies, court reporters' fees, long-distance telephone calls, messenger and other delivery fees, postage, in-office photocopying at $_____ a page, parking, mileage at $_____ a mile, investigation expenses, consultants' fees, expert witness fees, and other similar items. Client authorizes Attorney to incur all reasonable costs and to hire any investigators, consultants, or expert witnesses reasonably necessary in Attorney's judgment, unless one or both of the clauses below are initialed by Client and Attorney.
___ Attorney shall obtain Client's consent before incurring any cost in excess of $____
___ Attorney shall obtain Client's consent before retaining outside investigators, consultants, or expert witnesses.

6. STATEMENTS. Attorney shall send Client periodic statements for fees and costs incurred. Client shall pay Attorney's statements within _____ days after each statement's date. Client may request a statement at intervals of no less than 30 days. Upon Client's request, Attorney will provide a statement within 10 days.

7. LIEN. Client hereby grants Attorney a lien on any and all claims or causes of action that are the subject of Attorney's representation under this Contract. Attorney's lien will be for any sums due and owing to Attorney at the conclusion of Attorney's services. The lien will attach to any recovery Client may obtain, whether by arbitration award, judgment, settlement, or other means.

8. DISCHARGE AND WITHDRAWAL. Client may discharge Attorney at any time. Attorney may withdraw with Client's consent or for good cause. Good cause includes Client's breach of this Contract, Client's refusal to cooperate with Attorney or to follow Attorney's advice on a material matter; or any other fact or circumstance that would render Attorney's continuing representation unlawful or unethical.

| EXHIBIT 8.1 | Sample Retainer Agreement—*continued* |
| --- | --- |

Note that paragraph 9 does *not* say that the client cannot have his or her file back until all fees are paid. Such a condition would be unethical. See chapter 5.

9. CONCLUSION OF SERVICES. When Attorney's services conclude, all unpaid charges shall become immediately due and payable. After Attorney's services conclude, Attorney will, upon Client's request, deliver Client's file to Client, along with any Client funds or property in Attorney's possession.

10. DISCLAIMER OF GUARANTEE. Nothing in this Contract and nothing in Attorney's statements to Client will be construed as a promise or guarantee about the outcome of Client's matter. Attorney makes no such promises or guarantees. Attorney's comments about the outcome of Client's matter are expressions of opinion only.

11. EFFECTIVE DATE. This Contract will take effect when Client has performed the conditions stated in paragraph 1, but its effective date will be retroactive to the date Attorney first provided services. The date at the beginning of this Contract is for reference only. Even if this Contract does not take effect, Client will be obligated to pay Attorney the reasonable value of any services Attorney may have performed for Client.

"Attorney"

By: _____

"Client"

_____

Source: Pamela I. Everett, *Fundamentals of Law Office Management*, 196–7 (1994).

---

**letter of nonengagement** A letter sent to a prospective client that explicitly says that the law office will not be representing him or her.

office to document its rejection of a prospective client by sending him or her a letter explicitly stating that the office will not be representing him or her. The document is called a **letter of nonengagement**. Its purpose is to avoid any misunderstandings if the person later claims to have been confused about whether the office had agreed to take the case. This person may try to assert that he or she took no further action on the case because of the belief that the office was going to provide representation. The ultimate nightmare occurs when this person loses the case by default because no one showed up in court at a scheduled hearing. One way to avoid this predicament is by sending him or her an emphatic letter of nonengagement (sometimes humorously referred to in the office as the "Dear Not Client Letter"). The letter will often conclude with a statement such as the following: "While our office cannot represent you, we urge you to protect your rights by seeking other counsel."

## Section C
# The Context of Interviewing in Litigation

There are three main kinds of legal interviews:

- The initial client interview
- The follow-up client interview
- The investigation field interview of someone other than the client

In the initial client interview the attorney-client relationship is established and legal problems are identified as the fact collection process begins. Follow-up interviews occur after the initial interview. The client is asked about additional facts and is consulted on a variety of matters that require his or her attention, consent, and participation. The field interview is conducted during investigation; the interviewer, as investigator, will contact individuals outside the office in order to try to verify facts already known and to uncover new relevant facts. Investigation will be examined in the next chapter. Here our focus will be the initial client interview.

Interviewing is among the most important skills used in a law office. Many assume that this skill is relatively easy to perform (all you need is a person to interview [the in-

| EXHIBIT 8.2 | Interviewing in the Context of Litigation |
|---|---|

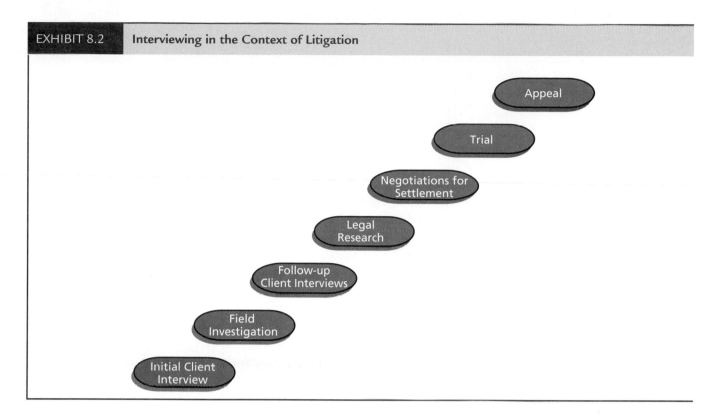

terviewee], a pleasing personality, and some time). Yet interviewing is much more than good conversation. To avoid incomplete and sloppy interviewing, the interviewer must establish a relationship with the client that is warm, trusting, professional, and goal-oriented. The focus of everything done in a law office, including the legal interview, is to identify legal problems and to help the client solve them.

Paralegals in different settings have varied duties and authority. In a private law office, an attorney will usually conduct the initial interview and may assign the paralegal the task of gathering detailed information from the client on a specific topic. For example, a paralegal may be asked to help a bankruptcy client obtain details on debts and assets by listing them all on a worksheet. On the other hand, in a government agency or in a government-funded legal service office, the paralegal's interviewing responsibilities can be extensive. For example, a paralegal might conduct the initial interview with a client and remain the primary office contact for the client throughout the resolution of the case.

The initial client interview is critical because it sets the foundation for the entire litigation process. (See exhibit 8.2) The facts obtained from this interview are further pursued through *field investigation*; subsequent or *follow-up client interviews* are often needed to clarify new facts and pursue leads uncovered during investigation; the laws governing the facts are *researched* in the law library; the facts and the governing law are informally argued between counsel for the parties in an effort to *settle* the case through *negotiation*; if there is no settlement, a *trial* is held in which the facts are formally established; finally, the process may end with an *appeal*. Everything begins with the facts obtained through the initial client interview. A poor job done at this stage can have major negative consequences throughout the remaining steps of the litigation process.

Section D

# THE FORMAT OF AN INTAKE MEMO

Before analyzing the interviewing process, we should look briefly at one of the end products of the interview—a document that is sometimes called the **intake memo**. It summarizes the interviewer's notes on the interview. The intake memo goes first to the supervisor and then into a newly opened case file on the client. The memo often has five parts:

**intake memo** A memorandum that summarizes the facts given by a client during the initial client interview.

1. *Heading*. The heading provides the following information at the top of the first page:
   - The name of the person who wrote the memo (you)
   - The supervisor in charge of the case to whom the memo is addressed
   - The date the memo was written
   - The date the interview was conducted
   - The name of the case
   - The office file number of the case
   - The kind of case (general area of the law)
   - The notation **RE**, which means concerning or in reference to. After RE, you state the general subject matter of the memo.

2. *Personal Data*.
   - Name of the client
   - Home address
   - Phone numbers where the client can be reached; e-mail address
   - Age of client
   - Marital status
   - Place of employment of the client
   - Etc.

3. *Statement of the Assignment*. The first paragraph of the memo should state the precise objective the paralegal was given in conducting the interview. It is a more detailed statement of what was listed under RE in the heading.

4. *Body of the Memo*. Here the facts are presented in a coherent, readable manner according to a number of possible organizational principles:
   - A chronological listing of the facts so that the events are unfolded as a story with a beginning, middle, and end
   - A categorizing of the facts according to the major topics or issues of the case (e.g., Background, Accident, Causation, Medical Expenses), each with its own subject heading under which the relevant facts are placed
   - Any other format called for by the supervisor

5. *Conclusion*. Here a number of things could be included:
   - A brief summary of the major facts listed in the body of the memo
   - The paralegal's impressions of the client, such as
     - how knowledgeable the client appeared to be
     - how believable the client appeared to be
   - A list of the next steps, for example:
     - What further facts should be sought through investigation
     - What legal research should be undertaken
     - Any other recommendations on what should be done on the case based on what was learned during the interview
   - A list of anything the paralegal told the client to do, for example:
     - Bring in specified documents relevant to the case
     - Check on further facts and call back
     - Return for another interview

Exhibit 8.3 shows a sample of the introductory parts of an intake memo.

---

Section E
# What Facts Do You Seek? Guides to the Formulation of Questions

Unless the paralegal knows what to accomplish in an interview, valuable time will be wasted. For example, suppose a client is being interviewed concerning the **grounds** for a divorce. The paralegal does not simply write down *all* the facts about the marriage and the client's problems in it. The facts must be clustered or arranged in categories that are relevant to grounds for divorce. Unless the paralegal has this objective in mind before and during the interview, he or she may end up with a confusing collection of facts and may

---

**RE** Concerning (*In re* in the title of a court opinion means "in the matter of." See chapter 11.)

**ground** A reason that is legally sufficient to obtain a remedy or other result.

| EXHIBIT 8.3 | Beginning of an Intake Memo |
| --- | --- |

**Intake Memo**

**To**: Ann Fuller, Supervisor
**From:** Jim Smith, Paralegal
**Date of Memo:** March 13, 2001
**Date of Interview:** March 12, 2001

**Case**: John Myers vs. Betsy Myers
**File Number:** 01–102
**Kind of Case:** Child Custody
**Re:** Intake Interview of John Myers

**Personal Data**
**Name of Client:** John Myers
**Address:** 34 Main Street, Salem, Massachusetts 01970
**Phone:** 966–3954 (H) 297–9700 (× 301) (W)
**E-mail:** jmyers@aol.com
**Age:** 37
**Marital Status:** Married but separated from his wife, Betsy Myers
**Employment:** ABC Construction Co., 2064 South Street, Salem, Massachusetts 02127

You asked me to conduct a comprehensive intake interview of John Myers, our client, in order to obtain a listing of his assets and the facts surrounding his relationship with his children.
   A. ASSETS
     John Myers owns . . .

have to conduct a second interview to go over matters that should have been covered initially. (As all-star Yankee catcher Yogi Berra once said, "If you don't know where you are going, when you get there you'll be lost.") This does not mean that the paralegal cannot talk about anything other than what is directly related to the objective, but it does mean that each interview must have a definite *focus*.

There are six major ways to achieve focus in the formulation of questions to be asked of a client:

- Instructions of the supervisor for the interview
- Checklists
- Legal analysis
- Fact particularization
- Common sense
- Flexibility

There methods are designed to help you avoid all the following examples of an *ineffective* interview:

- You fail to seek the information that the supervisor wanted you to obtain.
- You miss major relevant facts.
- You fail to obtain sufficient detail on the major relevant facts.
- You fail to ask questions about the extent to which the client was sure *or unsure* about the major facts the client gives you.
- You fail to pursue leads the client provides about other relevant themes or topics that may not have been part of the supervisor's explicit instructions or may not have been within the scope of your initial questions.

## INSTRUCTIONS OF THE SUPERVISOR FOR THE INTERVIEW

The instructions of the supervisor control what you do in the interview. You may be asked to do a limited interview or a comprehensive one. Be sure to write down what the supervisor wants from the interview. One concern that frequently arises is the amount of detail desired. Attorneys like facts. During three years of law school, they were constantly asked by their law professors, "What are the facts?" The likelihood is that the attorney for whom you work will want considerable detail from the interview. Even if you are told to limit yourself to obtaining the basic facts from the client, you may find that the supervisor wants a lot of detail about those basic facts. When in doubt, the safest course is to be detailed in your questioning. If possible, try to sit in on an interview conducted by your supervisor to observe his or her method of questioning and the amount of detail sought. Also, examine some closed or open case files that contain intake memos. Ask the supervisor if any of these memos is exemplary, and if so, why. Once you have a model, it can be very useful as a guide.

### CHECKLISTS

The office where you work may have checklists that are used in conducting interviews. For some kinds of cases, such as probate or bankruptcy, the checklists may be extensive. If such checklists are not available, you should consider writing your own for the kinds of cases in which you acquire experience.

Caution is needed in using checklists:

■ You should find out why individual questions were inserted in the checklist.
■ You should be flexible enough to ask relevant questions that may not be on the checklist.

By definition, a checklist is nothing more than a standard form. Use it as a guide that must be adapted to the case and client in front of you, rather than as a rigid formula from which there can be no deviation. (See exhibit 10.11 on How to Avoid Abusing a Standard Form in chapter 10.)

### LEGAL ANALYSIS

Extensive **legal analysis** does not take place while the interview is being conducted. Yet *some* legal analysis may be needed to conduct an intelligent interview. (See chapter 7 for an overview of legal analysis.)

Most of the questions you ask in the interview should be **legally relevant** or be reasonably likely to lead to something that is legally relevant. (As we will see in chapter 10, this is the standard of permissible questions that can be asked during pretrial discovery.) A question is legally relevant if the office needs the answer to determine whether a particular legal principle governs. At least a general understanding of legal analysis is needed to be able to apply the concept of legal relevance intelligently. It could be dangerous for the paralegal to be asking questions by rote, even if checklists are used. The question-and-answer process is a little like a tennis match—you go where the ball is hit or it passes you by.

Suppose that you are interviewing a client on an unemployment compensation claim. The state denied the claim because the client is allegedly not "available for work," as required by statute. You cannot conduct a competent interview unless you know the legal meaning of this phrase. From this understanding, you can formulate questions that are legally relevant to the issue of whether the client has been and is "available for work." You will ask obvious questions such as:

> Where have you applied for work?
> Were you turned down, and if so, why?
> Did you turn down any work, and if so, why?
> What is your present health?

Suppose that during the interview, the client tells you the following:

> There were some ads in the paper for jobs in the next town, but I didn't want to travel that far.

You must decide whether to pursue this matter by inquiring about the distance to the town, whether public transportation is available, the cost of such transportation, whether the client owns a car, etc. Again, legal analysis can be helpful. What did the legislature mean by the phrase "available for work"? As we saw in chapter 7, one of the central questions asked in legal analysis is how broadly or narrowly legal terms can be defined. Does "available for work" mean available anywhere in the county or state (broad), or does it mean available within walking distance or by easily accessible public transportation (narrow)? Is one *un*-available for work because of a refusal to make efforts to travel to an otherwise available job in another area? Questions such as these must go through your mind as you

**legal analysis** The application of one or more rules to the facts of a client's case in order to answer a legal question that will help (1) keep a legal dispute from arising, (2) resolve a legal dispute that has arisen, or (3) prevent a legal dispute from becoming worse.

**legally relevant** Contributing to the resolution of a legal problem or issue.

decide whether to seek more details about the ads for work in the other town. These are questions of legal analysis. *You must be thinking while questioning.* Some instant mental analysis should be going on all the time. This does not mean you must know the answer to every legal question that comes to mind while interviewing the client. But you must know something about the law and must be flexible enough to think about questions that should be generated by unexpected facts provided by the client.

When in doubt about whether to pursue a line of questions, check with your supervisor. If he or she is not available, the safest course is to pursue it. As you acquire additional interviewing experience in particular areas of the law, you will be better equipped to know what to do. Yet you will never know everything. There will always be fact situations that you have never encountered before. Legal analysis will help you handle such situations.

## FACT PARTICULARIZATION

**Fact particularization** is one of the most important concepts in this book. To *particularize a fact* means to ask an extensive series of questions about that fact in order to explore its uniqueness. Fact assessment is critical to the practice of law; fact particularization (FP) is critical to the identification of the facts that must be assessed. FP is a fact collection technique. It is the process of viewing every person, thing, or event as unique—different from every other person, thing, or event. Every important fact a client tells you in an interview should be particularized. You do this by asking a large number of follow-up questions once you have targeted the fact you want to explore. (See exhibit 8.4.)

**fact particularization** A fact-gathering technique used to generate a list of numerous factual questions that will help you obtain a specific and a comprehensive picture of all available facts that are relevant to a legal issue.

> **Example**: You are working on an automobile negligence case. Two cars collide on a two-lane street. They were driven by Smith and Jones. Jones is a client of your law office. One of the facts alleged by Jones is that Smith's car veered into Jones's lane moments before the collision. Your job is to particularize this fact by trying to obtain a much more detailed picture of the alleged veering. This is done by seeking a comprehensive elaboration of this fact. Using FP, you ask the following commonsense questions: who, what, where, how, when, and why.
>
> ■ What does Jones mean by veering into the other lane?
> ■ How much veering was done? An inch? A foot? Did the entire car come into the other lane? How much of an angle was there?
> ■ Who saw this happen? According to Jones, Smith's car veered. Did Jones see this happen himself? Who else saw it, if anyone? Any passengers in Jones's car? Any passengers in Smith's car? Were there any bystanders? Has the neighborhood been checked for witnesses, e.g., people who live or work in the area, people who frequently sit on public benches in the area?
> ■ Were the police called after the accident? If so, who was the officer? Was a report made? If so, what does it say, if anything, about the car veering into the other lane? Where is this report? How can you obtain a copy?
> ■ What time of day was it when it occurred?
> ■ Why did Smith's car veer according to Jones or anyone else who alleges that this occurred?
> ■ How fast was Jones's car going at the time of the veering? Why was Jones going at this speed? Who would be able to substantiate the speed? Who might have different views of how fast Jones was going?
> ■ How fast was Smith's car going at the time of the veering? Why was Smith going at this speed? Who would be able to substantiate the speed? Who might have different views of how fast Smith was going?
> ■ Have there been other accidents in the area? If so, how similar have they been to this one?

| EXHIBIT 8.4 | Fact Particularization (FP) |
|---|---|

You *particularize* a fact you already have:

1. by assuming that what you know about this fact is woefully inadequate,
2. by assuming that there is more than one version of this fact, and
3. by asking a large number of basic who, what, where, how, when, and why questions about the fact, which, if answered, will provide as specific and as comprehensive a picture of that fact as is possible at this time.

- What was the condition of the road at the time Smith started to veer? At the time of the collision?
- What was the weather at the time?
- How was visibility?
- What kind of a road is it? Straight? Curved at the area of the collision? Any inclines? Any hills that could affect speed and visibility?
- What kind of area is it? Residential? Commercial?
- Is there anything in the area that would distract drivers, e.g. potholes?
- Where is the nearest traffic light, stop sign, or other traffic signal? (Prepare a diagram.) How, if at all, did they affect traffic at the time of the accident?
- What is the speed limit of the area?
- What kind of car was Smith driving? Were there any mechanical problems with the car? Would these problems help cause the veering? What prior accidents has Smith had, if any?
- What kind of car was Jones driving? Were there any mechanical problems with the car? What prior accidents has Jones had, if any?
- Etc.

FP can be a guide in formulating factual questions that need to be asked in different settings:

- In a client interview (our focus in this chapter)
- In investigations (see chapter 9)
- In interrogatories (written questions sent to an opponent prior to trial) (see exhibits 10.9 and 10.10 in chapter 10)
- In a deposition (an out-of-court session in which questions are asked of an opponent or of a potential witness of the opponent prior to trial) (see exhibits 10.4 and 10.5 in chapter 10)
- In an administrative or court hearing (in which witnesses are formally questioned) (see chapters 10 and 15)

In legal interviewing, the starting point for the FP process is an important fact that the client has told you during the interview. Here are additional examples: "I tried to find work"; "the car hit me from the rear"; "the pain was unbearable"; "the company was falling apart"; "he told me I would get the ranch when he died"; "he fired me because I am a woman." Then you ask the client the basic who-what-where-how-when-and-why questions that we used in the Smith and Jones driving example. As a guide to help you organize these questions, exhibit 8.5 presents eight categories of questions that need to be asked in order to achieve competent FP.

| EXHIBIT 8.5 | Categories of Questions for Fact Particularization (FP) |
| --- | --- |

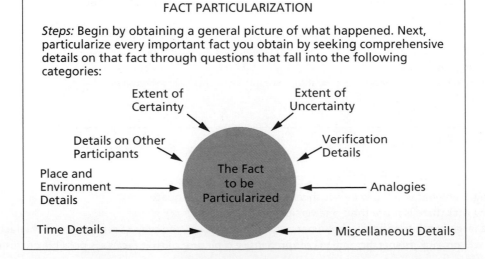

FACT PARTICULARIZATION

*Steps:* Begin by obtaining a general picture of what happened. Next, particularize every important fact you obtain by seeking comprehensive details on that fact through questions that fall into the following categories:

Extent of Certainty — Extent of Uncertainty — Details on Other Participants — Verification Details — Place and Environment Details — The Fact to be Particularized — Analogies — Time Details — Miscellaneous Details

The eight categories are not mutually exclusive, and all eight categories are not necessarily applicable to every fact that you will be particularizing. The questions need not be asked in any particular order as long as you are comprehensive in your search for factual detail. The point of FP is simply to get the wheels of your mind rolling so that you will think of a large number of questions and avoid conducting a superficial interview.

### Time Details

When did the fact occur or happen? Find out the precise date and time. The interviewer should be scrupulous about all dates and times. If more than one event is involved, ask questions about the dates and times of each. If the client is not sure, ask questions to help jog the memory and ask the client to check his or her records or to contact other individuals who might know. Do not be satisfied with an answer such as "It happened about two months ago." If this is what the client says, record it in your notes, but then probe further. Show the client a calendar and ask about other events going on at the same time in an effort to help him or her be more precise.

### Place and Environment Details

Be equally scrupulous about geography. Where did the event occur? Where was the thing or object in question? Where was the client at the time? Ask the client to describe the surroundings. Ask questions with such care that you obtain a verbal photograph of the scene. If relevant, ask the client to approximate distances between important objects or persons. You might want to have the client draw a diagram, or you can draw a diagram on the basis of what you are told and ask the client if the drawing is accurate. Ask questions about the weather or about lighting conditions. You want to know as much as you can about the environment or whatever the client could observe about the environment through the senses of touch, sight, hearing, and smell.

### Details on Other Participants

Who else was involved? Ask questions about who they were, their roles, their age, appearance, etc., if relevant. Where were they at the time? When did they act? Why did they act? Why did they fail to act? Could you have anticipated what they did or failed to do? Why or why not? Have they ever acted or failed to act in this way before? Ask questions designed to obtain a detailed picture of who these other participants were and their precise relationship to the fact being particularized.

### Extent of Certainty/Uncertainty

Everything the client tells you can be placed somewhere on the spectrum of certainty:

| Absolutely Certain | Substantially Certain | Fairly Certain | Have a Vague Certainty | Unsure | Only a Guess |
|---|---|---|---|---|---|
| \| | \| | \| | \| | \| | \| |

It would be a big mistake, for example, to record that the client said a letter was received two weeks ago when in fact the client said. "I think it came two weeks ago." Do not turn uncertainty into certainty by sloppy listening and sloppy recording in your intake memo of what the client said. Of course, it may be possible for a client to be uncertain about a fact initially but then become more certain of it with the help of your questioning. If so, record this transition by saying, "The client at first did not remember who else was present, but then said she was fairly certain that Fred was there."

At the outset, explain to the client how critical it is for you to obtain accurate information. Encourage the client to say, "I'm not sure" when that is the case. Not everyone wants to make such admissions, particularly about facts that are favorable to what they are trying to accomplish. Clients must be relaxed and unthreatened before they will be this honest and frank about what they know and, more important, about what they do not know. A lot depends on the attitude of the interviewer in asking questions and in reacting to answers. Let the client know that when you ask a question, you are looking for no more than the best of his or her recollection. Never be irritated or disappointed when a client cannot answer a question with absolute certainty. Do not keep saying "Are you sure?" after every client answer. Probing will often be necessary in order to find out where on the spectrum of certainty a fact falls. Yet this probing must be undertaken with tact and sensitivity.

### Verification Details

The fact that the client tells you something happened is *some* evidence that it happened. Verification details are *additional* evidence that supports what the client has said. Always pursue verification details. Ask yourself how you would establish the truth of what the client has said if the client suddenly disappeared and you had to rely exclusively on other sources. Inquire about documents (such as letters or check stubs) that support the client's statements. Inquire about other people who might be available to testify to the same subject. Ask the client questions that will lead you to such verification details. This approach does not mean that you do not trust the client or that you think the client is lying. It is simply a good practice to view a fact from many perspectives. You are always seeking the strongest case possible. This calls for probing questions about verification details.

### Analogies

Some facts that you are particularizing (e.g., "the pain was unbearable"; "I was careful"; "it looked awful"; "I was scared") are difficult to pin down. In the interview, you should ask the client to explain such statements. Sometimes it is helpful to ask the client to use **analogies** to describe what is meant. When you ask a client to use an analogy, you are simply asking him or her to explain something by comparing it to something else. For example:

analogy A comparison of similarities and differences.

> What would you compare it to?
> Was it similar to anything you have ever seen before?
> Have you observed anyone else do the same thing?
> Have you ever been in a similar situation?
> Did it feel like a dentist's drill?

First, you ask the client to compare the fact to something else. Then you ask about the similarities and differences. Through a series of directed questions, you are encouraging the client to analogize the fact he or she is describing to some other fact. This is done in a further attempt to obtain as comprehensive a picture as possible of what the client is saying.

### Miscellaneous Details

Here, you simply ask about any details that were not covered in the previous categories of questions. Include questions on anything else that might help in particularizing the fact under examination.

---

*Class Exercise 8.A*

In this exercise, FP will be role-played in class. One student will be selected to play the role of the client and another, the role of the paralegal interviewer. The rest of the class will observe and fill out the FP Score Card on the interview.

*Instructions to Interviewer.* You will not be conducting a complete interview from beginning to end. You will be trying to particularize a certain fact that is given to you. Go through all the categories of FP outlined in exhibit 8.5. Use any order of questioning you want. Probe for comprehensiveness. Your instructor will select one of the following facts to be used as the basis of the interview:

(a) "I was hit in the jaw by Mary."
(b) "He neglects his children."
(c) "I have not been promoted because I am a woman."

Your opening question to the client will be "What happened?" The client will make one of the three statements above. You then use the process of FP to particularize this statement.

*Instructions to Client.* The interviewer will ask you what happened. Simply make one of the three statements above as selected by the instructor. Then the interviewer will ask you a large number of questions about the statement. Make up the answers—ad lib your responses. Do not, however, volunteer any information. Answer only the questions asked.

*Instructions to Class.* Observe the interview. Use the following score card to assess how well you think the interviewer particularized the fact.

**FP Score Card**

| Precision in obtaining time details | 5 4 3 2 1 | Sloppiness in obtaining time details |

| Precision in obtaining place and environment details | 5 4 3 2 1 | Sloppiness in obtaining place and environment details |

| Precision in obtaining details on other participants | 5 4 3 2 1 | Sloppiness in obtaining details on other participants |

| Precision in finding out where the client's statements fall on the spectrum of certainty | 5 4 3 2 1 | Sloppiness in finding out where the client's statements fall on the spectrum of certainty |

| Precision in seeking verification details | 5 4 3 2 1 | Sloppiness in seeking verification details |

| Effectiveness in using analogies to obtain greater detail | 5 4 3 2 1 | Ineffectiveness in using analogies to obtain greater detail |

| Precision in obtaining miscellaneous details | 5 4 3 2 1 | Sloppiness in obtaining miscellaneous details |

Following the interview, put a check on the appropriate number for each of the preceding categories of assessment. A "5" score means you thought the interview was very precise or effective in fulfilling the goal of FP. A "1" score means the opposite. Also, make notes of questions you think the interviewer *should have asked*. These questions, and your scores, will be discussed in class after the interview.

## COMMON SENSE

Common sense is another major guide to determining what questions to ask, achieving comprehensiveness, and giving the interview a focus. Though law is full of legalisms and technicalities, good judgment and common sense are still at the core of the practice of law. It is common sense, for example, to organize an interview by having the client tell the relevant events chronologically in the form of a story with a beginning, middle, and end. It is common sense to follow up on a topic the client mentions with further questioning even though you had not anticipated the topic. If the client says something you do not understand, common sense dictates that you ask what the client means before continuing with the interview. At times, it may be common sense to stop the interview for a moment to obtain further guidance from your supervisor.

## FLEXIBILITY

In the previous discussion, the importance of flexibility was mentioned a number of times. You must expect the unexpected and you must be relaxed. Although you lead the interview and give it direction, you must be ready to go where the interview takes you. It would be potentially disastrous for you to block out topics that arise simply because they were not part of your game plan in conducting the interview or are not on your checklist. As with so many areas of the law, you may not know what you are looking for until you find it. In interviewing a client about incorporating a business, for example, you may stumble across a lead from something the client says that could involve fraud or criminal prosecution on a matter unrelated to the incorporation. Don't block this out. Pursue what appears to be reasonably related to the law office's relationship with the client. Check with your supervisor. Again, let common sense be your guide. Flexibility is one of the foundations of common sense.

## Section F
# WHAT DOES THE CLIENT WANT?

A number of points can be made about many clients, particularly new ones:

- They are not sure what they want.
- They change their minds about what they want.
- They are not aware of their legal and nonlegal options.
- The legal problem they tell you about involves other legal problems that they are not aware of and that even you may not be aware of at the outset.

Suppose a client walks into the office and says, "I want a divorce." The following observations *might* be possible about the client:

1. The client has an incorrect understanding of what a divorce is.
2. The client says she wants a divorce because she thinks this is the only legal remedy available to solve her problem.
3. If the client knew that other options existed (e.g., annulment, judicial separation, a restraining order, a support order), she would consider them.
4. What really troubles the client is that her husband beats the kids; a divorce is the only way she thinks she can stop it.
5. The client does not want a divorce. She is being pressured by her husband to institute divorce proceedings. He threatened her with violence if she refuses.
6. The client consciously or unconsciously wants and needs an opportunity to tell someone how badly the world is treating her, and if given this opportunity, she may not want to terminate the marriage.
7. If the client knew more about marriage or family counseling, she would consider using it before taking the drastic step of going to a law office for a divorce.

If any of these observations is correct, think of how damaging it would be for someone in the law office to take out the standard divorce forms and quickly fill them out immediately after the client says, "I want a divorce." This response would not be appropriate without first probing beneath the statement to determine what in fact is on the client's mind. Some clients who speak only of divorces and separation agreements are receptive to and even anxious for reconciliation. The danger exists that the client might be steered in the direction of a divorce because no other options are presented to her, because no one takes the time to help her express the ideas, intentions, and desires that are lurking beneath the seemingly clear statement, "I want a divorce."

This is not to say that you must psychoanalyze every client or that you must always distrust what the client tells you initially. It is rather a recognition of the fact that *most people are confused about the law and make requests based on misinformation about what courses of action are available to solve problems.* Common sense tells us to avoid taking all statements at face value. People under emotional distress need to be treated with sensitivity. We should not expect them to be able to express their intentions with clarity all the time in view of the emotions involved and the sometimes complicated nature of the law.

---

*Assignment 8.1*

During an interview, the client makes the following statements. What areas do you think need to be probed to make sure the office does not misunderstand what the client wants?

(a) I want to institutionalize my sick father.
(b) I want my boss arrested for assaulting me.
(c) I want to file for bankruptcy and go out of business.

---

Section G
# ASSESSING YOUR OWN BIASES

You need to be aware of how your personal feelings might affect your work on the case. Such feelings are the foundation of **bias**, which is an inclination or tendency to think and to act in a certain way. How would you answer the following question: "Am I objective enough that I can assist a person even though I have a personal distaste for what that person wants to do or what that person has done?" Many of us would quickly answer "yes" to this question. We all like to feel that we are levelheaded and not susceptible to letting our prejudices interfere with the job we are asked to accomplish. Most of us, however, have difficulty ignoring our personal likes and dislikes.

**bias** An inclination or tendency to think and to act in a certain way. A danger of prejudgment.

---

*Assignment 8.2*

In the following fact situations, to what extent might an individual be hampered in delivering legal services because of personal reactions toward the client? Identify potential bias.

(a) Mr. Smith, the client of your office, is being used by his estranged wife for custody of their two small children. Mr. and Mrs. Smith live separately, but Mr. Smith has had custody of the children during most of their lives while Mrs. Smith has been in the hospital. Mrs. Smith has charged that Mr. Smith often yells at the children, leaves them with neighbors and day care centers for most of the day, and is an alcoholic. Your investigation reveals that Mrs. Smith will probably be able to prove all these allegations in court.

(b) Mrs. Jones is being sued by Mr. Jones for divorce on the ground of adultery. Mrs. Jones is the client of your office. Thus far your investigation has revealed that there is considerable doubt over whether Mrs. Jones did in fact commit adultery. During a recent conversation with Mrs. Jones, however, she tells you that she is a prostitute.

(c) Jane Anderson is seeking an abortion. She is not married. The father of the child wants to prevent her from having the abortion. Jane comes to your office for legal help. She wants to know what her rights are. You belong to a church that believes abortion is murder. You are assigned to work on the case.

(d) Paul and Victor are a gay couple who want to adopt Sammy, a six-month-old baby whose parents recently died in an automobile accident. Sammy's maternal grandmother is not able to adopt him because of her age and health. She opposes the adoption by Paul and Victor because of their lifestyle. Your office represents Paul and Victor. You agree with the grandmother's position but have been assigned to work on the case.

(e) Tom Donaldson is a client of your office. His former wife claims that he has failed to pay court-ordered alimony payments and that the payments should be increased substantially because of her needs and his recently improved financial status. Your job is to help Tom collect a large volume of records concerning his past alimony payments and his present financial worth. You are the only person in the office who is available to do this record gathering. It is clear, however, that Tom does not like you. On a number of occasions, he has indirectly questioned your ability.

**objectivity** The state of being dispassionate; the absence of a bias.

Having analyzed the fact situations in assignment 8.2, do you still feel the same about your assessment of your own **objectivity**? Clearly, we cannot simply wish our personal feelings away or pretend that they do not exist. Nor are there any absolute rules or techniques that apply to every situation you will be asked to handle. Nor are the following admonitions very helpful: "Be objective," "be dispassionate," "don't get personally involved," "control your feelings." Such admonitions are too general, and when viewed in the abstract, they may appear not to be needed, since we want to believe that we are always objective, detached, and in control.

We must recognize that there are facts and circumstances that arouse our emotions and tempt us to impose our own value judgments. Perhaps if we know where we are vulnerable, we will be in a better position to prevent our reactions from interfering with our work. It is not desirable for you to be totally dispassionate and removed. A paralegal who is cold, unfeeling, and incapable of empathy is not much better than a paralegal who self-righteously scolds a client. It is clearly not improper for a paralegal to express sympathy, surprise, and perhaps even shock at what unfolds from the client's life story. If these feelings are genuine and if they would be normal reactions to the situation at a given moment, then they should be expressed. The problem is *how to draw the line* between expressing these feelings and reacting so judgmentally that you interfere with your ability to communicate with the client now and in the future. Again, there are no absolute guidelines. As you gain experience in the art of dealing with people, you will develop styles and techniques that will enable you to avoid going over that line. The starting point in this development is to recognize how easy it is to go over the line.

Some paralegals apply what is called the "stomach test." If your gut tells you that your personal feelings about the case are so intense that you may not be able to do a quality job for the client, you need to take action.[2] Talk with your supervisor. You may have some misunderstandings about the case that your supervisor can clear up. You may be able to limit your role in the case or be reassigned to other cases. Without breaching client confidentiality, contact your local paralegal association to try to talk with other paralegals who have handled similar situations. They may be able to give you some guidance.

Attorneys often take unpopular cases involving clients who have said or done things that run the gamut from being politically incorrect to being socially reprehensible. As professionals, attorneys are committed to the principle that *everyone* is entitled to representation. Paralegals need to have this same commitment. But attorneys and paralegals are human beings. No one can treat every case identically. In the final analysis, you need to ask yourself whether your bias is so strong that it might interfere with your ability to give the needs of the client 100 percent of your energy and skill. If such interference is likely, you have an obligation not to work on the case. As we saw in chapter 5, the failure to recognize the presence of this kind of bias can have ethical implications. It is unethical for you to be working on a case to which you cannot devote 100 percent of your professional skills. There should not be a conflict of interest between your personal feelings or belief system and the client's need for vigorous representation from every member of the legal team.

---

*Assignment 8.3*
Think about your past and present contacts with people who have irritated you the most. Make a specific list of what bothered you about these people. Suppose that you are working in a law office where a client did one of the things on your list. Could you handle such a case?

---

■ Section H
## COMMUNICATION SKILLS

### INTRODUCTION
You have probably been interviewed hundreds of times in your life. You may also have interviewed others frequently. The next assignment and the class exercise that follows it are designed to identify what you now know about interviewing in general.

*Assignment 8.4*

Write down your answers to the following questions. When you have finished this chapter, come back to what you have written and ask yourself whether your perspective has changed.

(a) List some of the times you have interviewed someone. List some of the times you have been interviewed by someone.

(b) Describe what you feel are the central ingredients of a good interview in any setting.

(c) Describe a bad interview. From your experience, what are some of the worst mistakes an interviewer can make?

(d) Describe what you think are some of your strong and weak points as an interviewer. What can you do to improve?

The following exercise involves an interview role-played in class. After watching this interview, you will be asked to deduce some principles of communication for interviewing.

*Class Exercise 8.B*

In this exercise, two students will role-play a legal interview in front of the class. The rest of the class will observe the interview and comment on it.

*Instructions to Client.* You will role-play the part of a client. A month ago you sprained your back while lifting a computer and carrying it from one room to another. You are an accountant. When you came to work that day, you found the computer on your desk. It did not belong there, and you did not know how it got there. You decided to move it to another desk. That was when you sprained your back.

You have come to the law office for legal advice. You have already seen an attorney in this office who has agreed to take your case. An interviewer has been assigned to conduct an interview with you to obtain a complete picture of what happened. This interview will now be role-played in front of the class.

The basic facts involve the accountant and the computer. You can make up all other facts to answer the interviewer's questions. Make up the name of the company for which you work, the details surrounding the accident, etc. You can create *any* set of facts as long as your answers are reasonably consistent with the basic facts given to you above.

*Instructions to Interviewer.* You will play the role of the interviewer in the case involving the sprained back. You are a paralegal in the office. All you know about the case thus far is that the office has agreed to represent the client and you have been assigned to interview the client for detailed information about the client and about the accident. Start off by introducing yourself and stating the purpose of the interview. Then proceed to the questions. Take notes on the client's answers.

You do not need to know any law in order to conduct the interview. Let common sense be your guide. Your goal is to compile a comprehensive picture of the facts as this client is able to convey them. Consult the material on fact particularization (FP) as you prepare and formulate questions. Be sure to listen carefully to the answers so that you can ask appropriate questions that seek more details on the facts contained in the answers.

The class will observe you in order to assess the manner and content of the interview. A good deal of constructive criticism may develop from the class discussion. As you listen to the criticism, try to be as objective as you can. It is difficult to conduct a comprehensive interview and probably impossible to conduct one flawlessly. For every question that you ask, there may be 20 observations on how you could have asked it differently. Hence, try not to take the comments personally.

*Instructions to Class.* You will be watching the interview involving the sprained back. You have two tasks:

1. Read through the LICS (Legal Interviewing Communications Score) form. Then close your book so that you will give your complete attention to the interview. After the interview, fill out the LICS form. The teacher will ask you to state the

total score you gave the interview or to submit this score to someone who will calculate the average score from all students' scores.

2. Identify as many dos and don'ts of interviewing as you can. If you were writing a law office manual on *How to Interview*, what would you include? What guidance would you give an interviewer on taking notes during the interview, asking follow-up questions, maintaining eye contact with the client, etc.? After you observe the interview, discuss specific suggestions on what an interviewer should or should not do. Ideas will also come to mind while you are filling out the LICS form.

## Legal Interviewing Communications Score (LICS)

**How to Score:**
You will be observing the role-playing of a legal interview and evaluating the interviewer on a 100-point scale. These 100 points will be earned in the four categories listed below. The score is not based on scientific data. It is a rough approximation of someone's oral communication skills in a legal interview. A score can be interpreted as follows:

90–100 Points: Outstanding Interviewer
80–89 Points: Good Interviewer
60–79 Points: Fair Interviewer
0–59 Points: A Lot More Work Needs to Be Done

(Of course, the LICS does *not* assess the interviewer's ability to *write* an intake memorandum of law for the file. See exhibit 8.3 and the discussion of the intake memo at the beginning of this chapter.)

**Category I: Role Identification**
On a scale of 0–5, how well did the interviewer explain his or her role and the purpose of the interview?
(A 5 score means the interviewer took time to explain clearly what his or her job was in the office and what he or she hoped to accomplish in the interview. A low score means the interviewer gave little or no explanation at all or mumbled an explanation without being sensitive to whether the client understood.)

**Category I Score:** ☐

**Category II: Factual Detail**
On a scale of 0–80, how would you score the interviewer's performance in asking enough questions to obtain factual comprehensiveness? How well was FP performed?
(An 80 score means the interviewer was extremely sensitive to detail in his or her questions. A low score means that the interviewer stayed with the surface facts, with little or no probing for the who-what-where-how-when-why details. The more facts you think the interviewer did not obtain, the lower the score should be.)

**Category II Score:** ☐

**Category III: Control**
On a scale of 0–10, how would you score the interviewer's performance in controlling the interview and in giving it direction?
(A 10 score means the interviewer demonstrated an excellent sense of control and direction. A low score means the interviewer rambled from question to question or let the client ramble from topic to topic.)

**Category III Score:** ☐

**Category IV: Earning the Confidence of the Client**
On a scale of 0–5 how would you score the interviewer's performance in gaining the trust of the client and in setting him or her at ease?
(A 5 score means the interviewer appeared to do an excellent job of gaining the trust and confidence of the client. A low score means the client seemed to be suspicious of the interviewer and probably doubted his or her professional competence. The more the interviewer made the client feel that he or she was genuinely concerned about the client, the higher the score. The more the client obtained the impression that the interviewer was "just doing a job," the lower the score.)

**Category IV Score:** ☐

**Total Score:** ☐

## ANALYSIS OF A LEGAL INTERVIEW

### Introduction

We will now examine portions of a **hypothetical** interview involving Sam Donnelly, who walks into the law office of Day & Day seeking legal assistance. Last month he was a passenger in a car that collided with a truck.

Our goal in this analysis is to identify guidelines that can help you conduct competent interviews. In particular, we want to increase your sensitivity to the large variety of factors that affect the quality of the communication between a client and an interviewer. Earlier in the chapter, we discussed fact particularization as an important technique in achieving factual comprehensiveness in the interview. Here our focus will be the broader context of interviewing and communication.

Assume that Mr. Donnelly is in the office of William Fenton, Esq., one of the partners of Day & Day. During their meeting, the law firm agrees to represent Mr. Donnelly. The arrangement is confirmed in the *retainer* that Mr. Donnelly signs. (See exhibit 8.1 for a sample retainer.) At the conclusion of the meeting, Mr. Fenton calls his paralegal, Jane Collins. He asks her to come to his office so that he can introduce her to Mr. Donnelly.

> **Attorney:** *[As the paralegal walks into Mr. Fenton's office, he says]* Mr. Donnelly, I want to introduce you to Jane Collins who will be working with me throughout the case. I have asked her to schedule an appointment with you to do a comprehensive interview that will cover the facts you and I began to discuss today. Jane will be an additional contact for you throughout the case. If at any time you can't reach me, let Jane know what concerns, questions, or needs you have. I will be reviewing all of Jane's work and will be meeting with her regularly. Jane is a trained paralegal. She is not an attorney and therefore can't give legal advice, but she can do many things to help me represent you.
>
> **Client:** Nice to meet you.
>
> **Paralegal:** *[Jane walks over to where Mr. Donnelly is sitting and, with a smile, extends her hand to offer a firm handshake.]* I'm very pleased to meet you, Mr. Donnelly. I look forward to working with you on the case. Let me give you one of my cards so that you'll know how to reach me.
>
> **Client:** Thank you.
>
> **Attorney:** I've already explained to Mr. Donnelly that you will be doing an in-depth interview with him on the case.
>
> **Paralegal:** Yes.... When would be a good time for me to call you to set up an appointment for the interview, Mr. Donnelly?

It is extremely important to note that the supervising attorney, Mr. Fenton, has taken the initiative to introduce the client to the paralegal. This sets the tone for the client-paralegal relationship. Many clients have little more than a general understanding of what a paralegal is. Here, the introduction by the supervising attorney is very specific in identifying Jane as a nonattorney who has been trained to help attorneys represent clients. She will also act as a liaison between the attorney and the client.

Note also the manner in which the paralegal treats the client. She walks toward the client to greet him with a firm handshake and a smile. She tells the client that she looks forward to working with him. She gives him her business card. (This is often appreciated because the client is probably meeting several new faces during the first few visits to the law office.) She is very deferential to the client in asking when she can call him for an appointment. These are signs of a paralegal who is willing to go out of her way to make the client feel important. Throughout the remainder of the chapter, we will examine additional techniques paralegals can use to set clients at ease.

### Preparing for the Interview

How do you get ready for an interview? Exhibit 8.6 lists some of the major steps you should take to prepare. The list assumes that this is one of the first legal interviews you have conducted.

In addition to the suggestions in exhibit 8.6, try to observe someone interview a client. Find out if anyone else in the office will be conducting an interview soon. If so, ask permission to sit in. Watching others interview can be very instructive. Another way to pre-

**hypothetical** Not actual or real but presented for purposes of discussion or analysis.

pare is to read some intake memos or other reports written after interviews in other cases. They can be found in the open or closed files of other clients. Pay particular attention to the amount and kind of information obtained in those cases.

Your mental attitude in preparing for the interview is very important. You need to approach each interview as if it is going to be a totally new experience for you. It is very dangerous for you to think that you know what the client is going to say, no matter how many times you have worked on a particular kind of case before. The danger is that you will not be listening carefully to what the client is saying. An interviewer who has an I've-heard-it-all-before attitude may block out what is unique about the facts of *this* client's case.

The hallmark of the *professional* is to view every client, every problem, and every incident as different and potentially unique. ("There's never been one like this before.") A professional interviewer, therefore, keeps probing for more facts to try to show that this case is not like all the rest. The goal of the professional is to find out what makes this case stand out. The trademark of the *bureaucrat*, on the other hand, is to see the similarities in clients, problems, and incidents. ("These cases are a dime a dozen.") The bureaucrat clusters things together into coherent groupings and patterns so that time can be saved and efficiency achieved. The bureaucrat feels that chaos could result if we viewed everything as potentially unique. An interviewer who has a bureaucratic attitude usually does not spend much time probing for facts; his or her goal is to fit this case into a category of similar cases handled in the past.

We all have within us professional and bureaucratic tendencies that are sometimes at war with each other.[3] Our bureaucratic self is very practical; our professional self can be a bit extreme in its search for uniqueness. When conducting legal interviews, however, or engaging in any task in the representation of a client, our goal is to try within reason to let our professional selves dominate.

| EXHIBIT 8.6 | Preparing for an Interview |
| --- | --- |

- Schedule the interview during a time when you will not be rushed or constantly interrupted.
- Schedule the interview at a location that will be private and convenient for the client.
- Find out from your supervisor if the client has any special needs such as wheelchair accessibility.
- Call or write the client in advance to confirm the date and place of the interview. Give an estimate of how long the interview will take. If the directions are complex, offer to send or fax a map (hand-drawn if necessary). Remind the client of anything you want him or her to bring to the interview, e.g., insurance policies, copies of tax returns.
- Anticipate and prepare for the client's comfort, e.g., a comfortable chair, a pad and pencil in case the client wants to take notes, a supply of tissues. Also, know where you can quickly obtain fresh water or coffee after offering them to the client early in the interview.
- If the office has already opened a file on the client, read everything in it before the interview. Bring any documents in the file that you may want to question the client about or have the client review during the interview.
- Have a final brief meeting with your supervisor to make sure you understand the goals of the interview.
- Find out if the office has any checklists you should use in asking questions. If none exist, prepare an outline of about a dozen major questions you will ask the client. You will have many more questions in the interview, but you can use this outline as a guide.
- Spend a little time in the law library doing some general background research in the area of the law involved in the client's case to obtain an overview of some of the major terminology and legal issues. This overview may suggest additional questions you will want to ask during the interview.
- Prepare any forms you may want to ask the client to sign during the interview, e.g., consent to release medical information, authorization to obtain employment history records.
- Have your own supplies ready for note taking. Some interviewers recommend using different colored pens so that you can switch colors when the client is telling you something you want to give particular emphasis in your notes.[4]
- Walk into the interview with the attitude that the client will be telling you a story that you have never heard before. Do not assume you know what the client is going to say even if you have handled many cases of this kind before.

## Environment

You need to consider the impact of the physical setting or environment in which you conduct the interview. It will usually take place in the office of the interviewer. If this office is not private enough, however, try to reserve the conference room or borrow an available office from someone else if it would be more private than your own. In our example, let us assume that Jane Collins's office is suitable for her interview with Sam Donnelly.

*[There is a knock at Jane Collins's door. She gets up from her chair, goes over to the door, opens it, and says, as she extends her hand].*

Paralegal: Hello, Mr. Donnelly. I'm Jane Collins, Mr. Fenton's paralegal. It's good to see you again. Won't you come in?…Did you have any trouble finding the office?

Client: No, I had to use the bus, but it worked out fine.

Paralegal: Let me take your coat for you. Please have a seat. *[The paralegal points the client toward a chair on the opposite side of the desk from where she sits. They face each other.]*

Note the seating arrangement the paralegal selects as illustrated in diagram A. ("I" stands for interviewer and "C" stands for client.)

### Diagram A

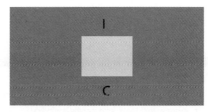

A number of other seating arrangements could have been used:

| Diagram B | Diagram C | Diagram D |
|---|---|---|

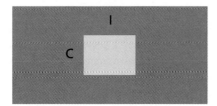  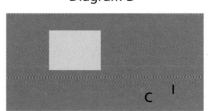

The chairs can be arranged so that the interviewer and the client sit on opposite sides of a desk (diagram A), diagonally across a desk (diagram B), on the same side of a desk (diagram C), or in another part of the room away from the desk altogether (diagram D). Seating arrangements are usually made at the convenience of the "owner" of the office. Rarely is enough thought given to how a particular arrangement may help or hurt the flow of communication. Sometimes the seating arrangement will create an austere and official atmosphere; other settings may be close and warm.

Of the four seating arrangements diagrammed above, which do you think would be most effective? Which would you feel most comfortable with? Which do you think the client would be most comfortable with? A number of factors can help you answer these questions. First, there is probably no single seating arrangement that will be perfect for all situations. The interviewer must be flexible enough to experiment with different arrangements. For most legal interviews, you will be taking extensive notes as the client answers your questions. If you are going to make any notes about the client that you may not want him or her to see (e.g., "appears reluctant to answer"), you will want to select a seating arrangement that does not allow the client to read what you are writing.

To some extent, seating arrangements can be a reflection of your personality. How do you want to project yourself? As an authority figure? If so, you might be inclined toward the seating arrangement in diagram A. Do you, on the other hand, want the client to feel closer to you and not to have the impression that you are hiding behind a desk? Do you think it would ever be wise to change a seating arrangement in the middle of an interview? If a particular arrangement is used for the initial interview, do you think a different arrangement might ever be appropriate for follow-up interviews with the same client? When clients look up, do you want them to be looking straight at you (diagram A) or do you think that it might be more comfortable for them to be able to face in other directions (diagram B) without appearing to scatter their attention?[5]

Of course, an office is much more than an arrangement of desks and chairs. Describe the potential benefits or disadvantages of the following:

- Numerous posters on the wall display political slogans, e.g., "Down with the Republicans!" or "Pro choice IS Pro Family."
- A copy of the latest issue of the Rush Limbaugh Newsletter is on the desk.
- The desk is cluttered with papers, books, and half-eaten food.
- A sign on the wall says, "Don't even think of smoking here."

You want the office to help you project a professional image of yourself. A messy desk usually suggests the opposite. Be careful about explicit messages around the room. Your political views may clash with those of the client. Do not broadcast your politics by having partisan literature on the walls or the desk. What do you think of the no-smoking sign? Courtesy would suggest a more friendly way of letting clients know that they should not smoke in your room, e.g., a sign that says, "Thank you for not smoking."

### Getting Started

Note that the paralegal, Jane Collins, went to the door to greet the client. Suppose that, instead, she had remained in her chair and called, "Come in," in a loud voice. Do you think it makes any difference whether the interviewer walks over to the client? When you walk into a room with someone, you are communicating the message "Come share my room with me." If, however, you are seated at your desk and call the visitor in, the message to the visitor is likely to be: "This is my room; I control it; you have my permission to enter." Although this is not necessarily an inappropriate message, it is not as friendly and warm as going to the door to escort the client in.

Notice, however, that the paralegal apparently did *not* go out to the front entrance of the law firm to greet the client. Here is what may have happened: the client came to the front door, was greeted by a receptionist, was told to wait in the reception area, and was then given directions to find the paralegal's office on his own. If this is what happened, it was a mistake. The paralegal should have left instructions with the receptionist to call her when the client arrived, and the paralegal then should have gone out to the reception area to greet the client and personally walk him back to her office. This would be the most courteous approach. Furthermore, you do not want clients roaming around offices—even if they know the way. A wandering client may overhear confidential conversations between other members of the firm or see open files of other clients on the desks of secretaries. It can be unethical for the law firm to allow outsiders to know *anything* about the cases of other clients. This danger is minimized if the paralegal escorts the client from the front door to her office.

Note that the paralegal reintroduced herself to the client: "Hello, Mr. Donnelly. I'm Jane Collins, Mr. Fenton's paralegal. It's good to see you again." She does not expect the client to remember who she is. It is a sign of courtesy to reintroduce yourself at the beginning of a second meeting. And never call a client by his or her first name unless expressly invited to do so by the client.

| | |
|---|---|
| Paralegal: | Thank you for coming in today, Mr. Donnelly. Are you ready for today's session? |
| Client: | Ready as I can be. |
| Paralegal: | Good.…How have you been? |
| Client: | Not bad considering all this mess. I can't believe all this is happening. |
| Paralegal: | Being involved in an accident can be very upsetting. It must be very hard for you.…Our office has handled cases like this before. While no one can predict how a case will turn out, you can rest assured that we will be doing everything possible to help lessen the burden on you. |
| Client: | Thank you. |
| Paralegal: | Let me ask you, Mr. Donnelly, is there anything that you want to cover now before we begin? |

Client:     This letter came in the mail this morning. It looks like the truck company has its lawyers on the case.

Paralegal:     *[She takes the letter from Mr. Donnelly and spends a few moments reading it.]* This is a letter from the attorney representing the truck company seeking information from you. They obviously don't know yet that we represent you. Once they know you are represented, it is improper for them to contact you directly. They need to go through your attorney. I'll let Mr. Fenton know about this letter right away. Why don't I photocopy it before you leave so that you can keep a copy for your records. After Mr. Fenton sees this, we'll let you know if there is anything you need to do about the letter. For now, let us take care of it.

Early on, the paralegal thanked the client: "Thank you for coming in today." Throughout the case, the office may ask the client to do many things such as come to meetings, sign documents, and collect information. Each time, you should express appreciation for doing what was asked. Never expect the client to thank *you*, although this may occur. You do not want the client to have the impression that you are doing the client a favor. The reverse is always true. Hence, constantly be appreciative.

Soon after inviting the client in, the paralegal asked, "Did you have any trouble finding the office?" And a little later, "How have you been?" It is a good idea to begin the interview at a personal level with some small talk about the weather, how the client is doing, or a recent sports event the client might know something about. This helps put the client at ease. The client may still be a bit nervous about the accident or whatever led to the conflict and the involvement of attorneys. Being a little lighthearted and personal for a few moments at the beginning of the interview may help break the ice.

When clients are particularly stressed or overwhelmed, you need to provide reassurance that the office will be actively working on the case and that the situation is manageable. The paralegal did that here when she told the client the office has handled similar cases in the past and would be doing everything possible to help lessen the burden on him. Comments such as these should help reassure the client. Of course, many clients want to be told they are going to win their cases. Avoid making any statement that could be interpreted as a promise or guarantee of success. Otherwise, the office could be sued for **breach of contract** if the case is not successful. Instead of telling a client "You've got a great case," say something like the following: "There is no way of telling how a case will turn out. You've got a lot of good points in your favor, and we're going to work as hard as we can for you."

The paralegal also told the client, "Being involved in an accident can be very upsetting. It must be very hard for you." Here, the paralegal is expressing understanding and empathy for the client's predicament. This is extremely important. The comment tells the client that the paralegal is *listening* to what the client is saying. Mr. Donnelly refers to the "mess" he is in and says, "I can't believe all this is happening." Rather than ignoring this comment, the paralegal lets the client know that she has heard what he said. This is comforting for clients. On the other hand, you don't want to be patronizing or condescending. A comment such as "You poor fellow" would obviously fall into this category.

Interviewers often learn a large number of highly personal facts about the client's life. Think of how you would feel if you were revealing such facts about yourself to a stranger. Think of how you would want this person to react to what you are revealing. At such a vulnerable time, clients need understanding and compassion. This does not mean that you should lose your objectivity. As indicated earlier, if it would be natural for you to express an emotion in response to what a client tells you, express the emotion. For example, "I'm very sorry to hear that" or "I can understand why you'd be angry." At the same time, you need to have an appropriate professional distance from the emotions and drama of the client's story.

Of course, never be judgmental of the client. Do not ask the client, "Why did you do that?" if your tone is one of suspicion or disbelief. Clients should not feel that they are required to justify their actions or inactions to you. This obviously would not encourage open communication between interviewer and client.

Also important was the paralegal's question "[I]s there anything that you want to cover now before we begin?" Early in the interview, find out if the client has any immediate concerns or questions on his mind. This should be done not only as a matter of

**breach of contract** A cause of action in which a party seeks a court remedy for the alleged failure of a party to perform the term(s) of an enforceable contract.

courtesy but also as a technique to make sure the client has your undivided attention. On the way into the law office, the client may have been thinking of several things he wants to ask about. He may be worried that he will forget them. Or he may be a little embarrrassed about asking his questions. Give the client a chance to express anything on his mind at the outset before you begin your barrage of questions. In our example, this technique worked. Mr. Donnelly did have something on his mind—the letter he received from opposing counsel.

| | |
|---|---|
| Paralegal: | Our goal today is to obtain a comprehensive statement of the facts of the accident. It will take at least an hour, maybe a little more. As Mr. Fenton told you, I'm not an attorney. I'll be able to help on the case in many ways, but I won't be able to give you legal advice. That will have to come from Mr. Fenton. If anything comes up today that calls for legal advice, I'll bring it to Mr. Fenton's attention so that we can get you the response you need. Since I work for an attorney, you should know that everything you tell me is protected by the attorney-client privilege. |
| Client: | Fine. |
| Paralegal: | Before we begin, Mr. Donnelly, you mentioned that you had to take the bus in. Is there a problem with your car? It wasn't involved in the accident with the truck, was it? |
| Client: | No, no….I let my brother borrow my car today. |
| Paralegal: | All right….I want to start by getting an overview of what happened on the day of the accident. Then we'll go back and fill in the details. I'll be taking detailed notes to make sure that I remember everything you say. . . . OK, what happened that day? |

This is the second meeting between the paralegal and Mr. Donnelly. Although the supervising attorney, Mr. Fenton, told Mr. Donnelly that Jane Collins was not an attorney, it is a good idea for the paralegal to reinforce this point herself. Paralegals who have a lot of contact with clients are often pressured by clients to give legal advice. Making it clear at the outset that this is inappropriate can cut down on this pressure, although, unfortunately, it will not eliminate it.

The paralegal also told the client that what he tells her "is protected by the attorney-client privilege." The client needs to know this, but *not* in this way. The phrase "attorney-client privilege" is legal **jargon**. It is technical language that does not have an everyday meaning. Avoid jargon unless the client needs to know it and you explain it in language the client can understand. When you use jargon or confusing terms, do not interpret the client's lack of questions to mean that the client understands the jargon. Do not wait for the client to ask you to explain unfamiliar terms. Take the initiative to provide explanations. In our example, it probably would have been sufficient to tell Mr. Donnelly that what he tells her will be confidential rather than using the more technical phrase, "attorney-client privilege."

Another useful technique for beginning an interview is to briefly state the major goal of the interview—here, to obtain a comprehensive statement of the facts of the accident. Give the client an overview of what you hope to accomplish and how long it may take.

Let the client know you will be taking notes so you will have an accurate record of what he says during the interview. As indicated earlier, the document that contains the detailed report of the interviewer is sometimes called the *intake memo* (see exhibit 8.3). Others in the office working on the case need to be able to read and rely on this report, since they all cannot interview the client.

Occasionally, your supervisor will want you to tape-record the interview. Be sure the client consents to the recording. At the beginning of the interview, say, "This is Jane Collins, a paralegal in the law office of Day & Day. Today's date is March 13, 2002. I am in our law office with Mr. Samuel Donnelly. Mr. Donnelly, have you agreed to have this interview tape-recorded?" The latter question and answer will help disprove any allegations that you secretly recorded the interview.

A good interviewer is always listening for clues to other legal or relevant nonlegal problems. There is always a danger that an interviewer will block out anything that does not fit within the topics scheduled for discussion. In our example, the paralegal said to Mr. Don-

**jargon** Technical language; words that do not have an everyday meaning.

nelly, "[Y]ou mentioned that you had to take the bus in. Is there a problem with your car?" While the car apparently has nothing to do with the case, it was worth inquiring into. Suppose, for example, the client is not driving because of injury to his eyes caused by an eye doctor. Or perhaps the client has had a contract dispute with an auto mechanic. It is a good idea to listen for suggestions or clues to other problems provided by a client. If you do not want to cover the matter immediately, make a note to raise it later in the interview at a more appropriate or convenient time.

The major techniques and guidelines for beginning an interview are summarized in exhibit 8.7.

### Kinds of Questions

One of the early questions the paralegal asked the client was "[W]hat happened that day?" This is known as an **open-ended question**. It is a broad, relatively unstructured question that rarely can be answered in one or two words. An open-ended question gives the client more control over the kind and amount of information to be provided in response. It also gives the interviewer an opportunity to size up the ability of the client to organize his or her thoughts in order to present a coherent response. Here are some other examples of open-ended questions: "What brings you in today?" "What led to the crisis at the bank?" One of the most frequently used categories of open-ended questions is the **overview question**, which asks for a summary of something such as an important event. For example, "What happened during your first year in college?" or Jane Collins's question, "[W]hat

**open-ended question** A broad, unstructured question that rarely can be answered in one or two words.

**overview question** A question that asks for a summary of an event or condition.

| EXHIBIT 8.7 | Beginning the Interview |
| --- | --- |

- Introduce yourself by name and title. If this is your second meeting with the client, reintroduce yourself.
- Do not call a client by his or her first name unless invited to do so by the client.
- Express appreciation each time the client does something the office asks, e.g., come in for an interview, read and sign a document.
- Make sure the client understands that you are not an attorney and cannot give legal advice.
- Start at a personal level (e.g., with some small talk) rather than launching right into the task at hand.
- Review the goals of the interview with the client (based on the assignment from your supervisor), and provide an estimate of how long the interview might take.
- Make the client feel that his or her case is special. Avoid giving the impression that you are engaged in anything boring or routine.
- Never tell a client how busy you are. It suggests to the client that he is bothering you and might give the impression that the office is disorganized.
- Express understanding and empathy for the client's predicament without being condescending.
- Do not be judgmental.
- Make sure the client understands that what he or she tells you is confidential.
- Find out if there are immediate concerns that the client wants to raise.
- Avoid legal jargon unless the client needs to become familiar with the jargon and you provide clear definitions and explanations.
- Let the client know you will be taking notes, and why.
- Listen for clues to other legal and relevant nonlegal problems that the office may need to explore.
- Begin new topics with open-ended questions. (See exhibit 8.8 on the kinds of questions an interviewer can ask.)
- Spend the first few minutes obtaining an overview/outline of the entire event or transaction. Then go back to obtain the details.
- Encourage the client to give you the facts chronologically as a story with a beginning, middle, and end. If more than one event is involved in the case, cover them separately in the same chronological way. Then go into how the events are interconnected.
- If the client appears overwhelmed or unusually distressed, try to provide reassurance by letting him or her know that the office is actively working on the case and is doing everything it can. Do not, however, promise results or say anything that a client could interpret as a promise or even as a prediction of what the outcome of the case will be.

happened that day?" An open-ended *request* (e.g., "Tell me about the problem") invites the same kind of broad response but is phrased as a request rather than as a question.

Open-ended questions (or requests) invite the person questioned to give a long and potentially rambling answer. Hence they should not be overused. These questions are often most effective when beginning a new topic in the interview.

**closed-ended question** A narrowly structured question that usually can be answered in one or two words. Also called a directed question.

At the opposite extreme is the **closed-ended question**, which is a narrowly structured question that usually can be answered in one or two words. Examples: "How old are you?" "What time did the accident occur?" "Did you receive the letter?" Closed-ended questions give the interviewer more control over the interview because they let the client know precisely what information is sought.

If the facts of a case are relatively complex, you should consider spending the first few minutes asking overview questions in order to obtain an outline of the entire event or transaction, and then going back to obtain the details. Once you have the big picture, you will be better able to see connections among the individual facts. The paralegal in our example took this approach when she said, "I want to start by getting an overview of what happened on the day of the accident. Then we'll go back and fill in the details." She followed this up with the open-ended overview question, "[W]hat happened that day?"

**chronological question** A question designed to encourage the interviewee to tell the story of what happened chronologically—step by step.

Both the request for an overview and the detailed questioning should be designed to encourage the client to tell the events of the case *chronologically*. The case may have many confusing aspects. The client may be inclined to talk about four or five things simultaneously—the accident, the hospitalization, the events leading up to the accident, the deceitfulness of the other side, etc. The best way to conduct an orderly interview is to help the client structure the case as a *story* with a beginning, middle, and end. Hence you should regularly ask **chronological questions** such as "What happened next?" or "What did you do then?" If the client says something substantially out of chronological sequence, politely say, "Could we get to that in a moment? First I want you to finish telling me what happened after. ..." Although you want to see the interconnections among the various events of the case, the discussion may become tangled and confusing unless you cover one topic at a time in the same methodical manner. In most instances, the most methodical way is chronologically.

**leading question** A question that suggests an answer within the question.

**corroborative question** A question designed to verify (or corroborate) facts by seeking information beyond what is provided by the interviewee.

In general, you should avoid asking **leading questions** in which the answer is suggested in the question. For example, "You didn't return the call, did you?" "You've forgotten everything that occurred during the meeting?" The danger of a leading question is that a nervous client or witness will simply give you the answer you appear to want. Leading questions might sometimes be useful when trying to challenge something that a hostile witness is saying, but this should not be the case with your own client. If a client is having difficulty remembering something (e.g., the weather on a particular day), a leading question might help jog the memory (e.g., "Was it raining that day?"). If a client needs constant prodding through leading questions, however, you may have reason to doubt the client's entire story.

Another category is the **corroborative question**, which seeks to verify (or corroborate) facts beyond the word of the client or witness. For example, "Were there any passengers in the car who will back that up?"

**combination question** A question that has more than one part.

**multiple-choice question** A question that asks the interviewee to choose among two or more options stated in the question.

In general, you should avoid **combination questions**—those with more than one part. They can confuse the person being interviewed. There are two kinds of combination questions: multiple-choice and add-on. A **multiple-choice question** asks the client or witness to choose among options presented by the interviewer. It is an "or" question. For example, "Did you personally review the balance sheet, *or* did you rely exclusively on what the accountant told the committee?" The interviewee may not remember both options and simply respond to the last part of the question. An **add-on question** is simply several questions phrased as one. It is an "and" question. For example, "When did you arrive in Boston, *and* how long did you stay there?" "What was your salary when you began work at the company, at the time of the accident, *and* on the date you were terminated?" Avoid add-on questions for the same reason you should avoid most multiple-choice questions; they can be confusing.

**add-on question** A question that stacks one or more additional questions within it.

There are some combination questions that are relatively simple. For example, "Was he driving a car *or* a truck?" "What is your husband's name, *and* where was he born?" Yet the danger of confusion still exists, and the better practice is to break all combination questions into individual questions that are asked separately.

See exhibit 8.8 for an overview of the major kinds of questions an interviewer can ask.

### Attentive Listening

Studies have shown that clients rate "evidence of concern" as being more significant than the results they obtain from a law office.[6] This is a remarkable conclusion. Of course, clients want to win their cases. Yet they are also desperate for a sympathetic ear. Being involved in a legal dispute is often traumatic for them. In addition to being treated competently as a plaintiff or defendant, clients want a law office that is genuinely concerned about them as persons.

One of the best ways to demonstrate concern is through **attentive listening**. This simply means that you take affirmative steps to let the client know that you have heard what he or she has said and that you consider every meeting with the client important. Exhibit 8.9 summarizes some of the major techniques of attentive listening.

Experienced paralegals often handle the same kind of case over and over. Clients, however, want to feel that their case deserves and will get *individual* attention; they do not want their cases handled in an assembly-line or mass-production manner. While they like having experienced attorneys and paralegals working for them, they are particularly pleased when they feel that the office is treating their case as special.

**attentive listening** Taking affirmative, ongoing steps to let an interviewee know that you have heard what he or she has said and that you consider the meeting with him or her to be important.

### Comprehensiveness

A major goal of most legal interviews is to achieve factual comprehensiveness; you want to obtain as many relevant facts as the client is able to give. The most important technique in accomplishing this goal is *fact particularization*, discussed earlier in the chapter. (See exhibits 8.4 and 8.5). Also important are *corroborative questions* that ask about documents

| EXHIBIT 8.8 | **Kinds of Questions** |
| --- | --- |

Here are some of the major categories of questions, some of which overlap:

- *Open-Ended Questions*. Those that are broad and relatively unstructured, allowing the client or witness to express what is on his or her mind. They rarely can be answered by one or two words. Examples: "What can we do for you today?" "Tell me what happened on the day of the accident?" What kind of a marriage did you have?"
- *Closed-Ended Questions*. Those that narrowly focus the attention of the client or witness and call for a very brief answer, often yes or no. Examples: "Are you seeking a divorce?" "Were you wearing your glasses when you saw the accident?" "Did your husband ever hit you?"
- *Overview Questions*. Those that seek a summary of a major event or condition. Examples: "Would you first give me a general picture of what happened?" "What are the major incidents that led to the dismissal?" "Could you start me off by giving a brief description of what happened at the party before the shooting?"
- *Chronological Questions*. Those designed to get the client or witness to tell the story of what happened chronologically—step by step. Examples: "Then what happened?" "What did he say after he saw the accident?" "What happened next?"
- *Leading Questions*. Those in which the answer is suggested in the question. Examples: "Where was the fender dented?" "The car wasn't damaged when you received it, was it?" "You were traveling 75 m.p.h?"
- *Corroborative Question*. Those designed to verity (or corroborate) facts by seeking information beyond the word of the client or witness. Examples: "Who else saw the accident?" "Were you the only one who complained?" "Do you have receipts?"
- *Combination Questions*. Those that contain more than one part. Examples: "Did you accept the offer, reject it, or ask for more time to respond?" (multiple choice) "What school does your child attend and are you satisfied with how well he is doing there?" (add on).

| EXHIBIT 8.9 | Attentive Listening |
|---|---|

- Make it obvious to the client that he or she has your full attention. If you know that there might be an interruption during the interview, alert the client and apologize in advance.
- Occasionally lean forward toward the client as he or she speaks.
- Avoid being fidgety or appearing nervous.
- Take notes. This is an obvious sign that you think what the client is saying is important.
- Maintain eye contact whenever you are not taking notes.
- As the client speaks, give frequent *yes* nods. Also say "ah hum" or "I see" when the client momentarily pauses while answering your questions. This will let the client know you are following what he or she is saying.
- Periodically let the client know he or she is providing useful information. Make comments such as "That could be very important" or "I'm glad you recall the event in such detail."
- In addition to listening to the words of the client, "listen" to the feelings the client is expressing through gestures and other body language. Words are not the only way a client lets you know that he or she is anxious, suspicious, worried, or in pain.
- At appropriate times, restate a feeling the client is trying to describe, e.g., "The stress you were under must have been overwhelming." You may want to do this in the form of a question, e.g., "You were really angry when you found out, weren't you?"
- Occasionally read something from your notes out loud to the client and ask if you have correctly recorded what he or she has said. At other times, paraphrase what the client says in your own words to encourage the client to provide further clarification or to confirm that you have understood what the client has said. ("Let me see if I understand what you've said....") This reinforces the value of precision in the practice of law as well as letting the client know how important this interview is.
- Ask spontaneous questions that occur to you while listening to an answer of the client. This helps demonstrate that you are not trying to fit the client's answers into your preconceived notions about the case. Rather, you are following the client's train of thought.
- Refer back to what the client said earlier, e.g., "When we were discussing the purchase, you said that your father wanted his brother to manage the property. Could you tell me what you meant?"
- Never express impatience, no matter how frustrated you are at the client's failure to answer what you feel is an easy question.
- While a client is answering a question, try to avoid interrupting unless he or she is rambling and you need clarification before the client moves to another point.
- Do not finish the client's sentences for him or her no matter how certain you are of what the client is trying to say. Finishing someone's sentences demonstrates your impatience and is condescending.

or other individuals who can support the version of the facts the client is relating. (See exhibit 8.8.)

Most clients want to tell you about the facts that support their case. You need to encourage them to tell you negative as well as positive facts. Tell them how important it is for the attorney to know *all* the facts. The attorney for the other side may find out about negative facts. Indeed, one of the preoccupations of the other side is to find the facts that will hurt the client. The client's attorney must know all the facts in advance so that he or she can prepare a response when these facts come out.

Clients are often opinionated. Probe beneath the opinions to obtain the underlying facts. If a client says, "He's a liar," or "The road is dangerous," probe beneath these opinions to get at the underlying facts that led the client to reach these opinions. Again, fact particularization will help you uncover them.

Earlier we said that checklists of questions can be helpful in preparing for an interview. Be careful in using checklists, however. Although they can provide guidance on what to cover in the interview, you must be flexible enough to deviate from the checklist when relevant topics come up that are not on the checklist. Use any checklist (whether written by others or prepared on your own) as no more than a starting point. Suppose, for example, you are interviewing a client about her financial assets. You are working from a checklist of questions on wages, real estate holdings, stocks, bonds, etc. During the interview, the client happens to mention an ailing grandparent who is very fond of the client. This suggests the possibility of another possible asset: inheritance from this grandparent. Suppose, however, the checklist contains no questions about future inheritances. Common sense (one of the guides to formulating questions discussed earlier in the chapter) should tell you to ask whether the client thinks she might be a beneficiary in someone's will.

Take accurate notes on the facts the client gives you. Recall that one of the components of fact particularization is to record the extent of the certainty/uncertainty a client expresses about a fact. Suppose the client tells you, "I'm not sure" how fast an approaching car was going, but then says it was "about 50 mph." Your final report based on your notes should say:

> When I asked the client how fast the other car was going, he said he was "not sure." Then he estimated "about 50 mph."

This lets the supervising attorney know that the client may be vulnerable as a witness in court if questioned about the matter of speed. An interviewer does not achieve the desired factual comprehensiveness unless he or she asks about and records the extent to which the client is certain or uncertain about the facts conveyed.

The techniques for obtaining factual comprehensiveness are summarized in exhibit 8.10.

### Ethical Concerns

Paralegal:   [*Telephone rings.*] Excuse me, Mr. Donnelly. "Yes, hello. How are you? . . . No, the Jackson case has been resolved. Mr. Jackson decided not to go through with his suit after McDonald's made its offer . . . . You're welcome." Sorry, Mr. Donnelly, let's get back to the . . . .

A legal interview must be conducted competently *and ethically*. Unfortunately, there are more than a few opportunities for an interviewer to run afoul of ethical rules.

Mr. Donnelly has just heard the paralegal discuss the Jackson case on the phone. This is a violation of the paralegal's ethical obligation to preserve the confidence of a client. Even though Mr. Donnelly may not have understood anything about the Jackson and McDonald case, he was not entitled to hear what he heard. He should not even know that Jackson or McDonald is a client of Day & Day. Revealing information about a client is a breach of confidentiality, whether it is done intentionally or carelessly. Mr. Donnelly may now have the impression that the paralegal will be as careless about discussing *his case* in front of strangers.

Client:   A friend of mine told me that if another car rams into you and commits a clear traffic violation, their negligence is automatic. Is that true?

Paralegal:   I'll take that question up with Mr. Fenton and get back to you. All legal questions like that need to be dealt with by an attorney.

Another major ethical danger that can arise during an interview is giving legal advice As we saw in chapters 4 and 5, legal advice consists of applying laws or legal principles to the facts of a particular client's case. The more contact a paralegal has with clients, the greater the likelihood the paralegal will be asked to give legal advice. This is especially true during legal interviews. Clients are often hungry for answers. Mr. Donnelly is no exception. He asked the paralegal whether a traffic violation makes one's negligence "automatic." Even general questions about the law could be interpreted as questions that call for legal advice. Mr. Donnelly is probably trying to understand how the courts will handle his case.

| EXHIBIT 8.10 | Achieving Factual Comprehensiveness |
| --- | --- |

- Apply the technique of fact particularization to all the major facts the client tells you and that you need to cover. (See exhibits 8.4 and 8.5).
- Ask corroborative questions. (See exhibit 8.8)
- Encourage the client to tell you about negative facts.
- Probe beneath client opinions to obtain the underlying facts.
- Follow available checklists of questions, but be prepared to ask questions not on the checklist if they pertain to relevant topics that come up during the interview.
- Ask questions to determine the extent to which the client is certain or uncertain about an important fact.

Suppose the paralegal knows the correct answer. Think of how tempting it would be for her to answer the question. It takes a lot of will power for her to refrain from answering. She wants to appear intelligent. We all want to show off what we know. Be conservative, however, about ethics. (See exhibit 5.1 in chapter 5.) When in doubt, avoid giving an answer. The paralegal told Mr. Donnelly that she would "get back" to him after consulting with Mr. Fenton. This is better than coldly saying, "I'm not allowed to answer that question." When she said, "All legal questions like that need to be dealt with by an attorney," she is also helping to train the client about the limitations inherent in the paralegal's role. This may cut down on pressures in the future from Mr. Donnelly's attempts to ask her for legal advice.

Some of the major areas of ethical concern are summarized in exhibit 8.11.

### Ending the Interview

The interview is over when you have accomplished the objectives of the interview or when the client is not able to provide you with any additional information. The client may need to check some of his records at home or contact a family member or business associate in order to answer some of your questions. Although much of the missing data can be communicated on the phone or through the mail, do not be reluctant to reschedule the interview if needed.

Give the client the opportunity to raise anything that *he* thinks should have been covered. For example, you could say, "Before we end today's session, let me ask you if there is anything you think we haven't covered or haven't covered enough." If the client raises anything, you may want to take some additional time now to go over the client's areas of concern, or you may have to tell the client that you'll get back to him on when you will be able to go over those concerns. The important point is to find out how the client feels about what was discussed during the interview and to respond to any of his concerns.

Often the client needs to sign documents that authorize the office to obtain confidential information about the client, e.g., a consent to release medical information. Be sure to explain the document clearly to the client and give him some time to read through what he is being asked to sign. Do not simply hand the client a document and say, "I'll need your signature on this form that will allow us to get your medical records." Here is a more appropriate approach:

Paralegal: *[Handing the document to him.]* Mr. Donnelly, I want you to take a look at this document. It's a consent to release medical information. We'll use it to ask doctors, hospitals, or other medical providers to give us information about your medical condition. Would you please take a moment to read through it and let me know if you have any questions about it. If not, there's a space at the end of the document for your signature.

Client: OK.

Paralegal: Once you sign it, I'll keep the original and get you a copy for your records.

---

**EXHIBIT 8.11 Avoiding Ethical Probelms during Interviews**

- If you cannot avoid phone interruptions or visits by others to your office during the interview, be sure that you do not discuss the facts of other clients' cases. Never mention the names of clients (or their opponents) in front of another client even if you are certain that the latter will not recognize these names. Excuse yourself and leave the room if you must discuss anything about other cases.
- While talking to the client, do not have open files of other clients on the desk.
- Do not let the client wander in the corridors of the office, e.g., to go to the coffeepot. You do not want the client to overhear conversations about other cases among attorneys, paralegals, secretaries, or other employees.
- Make sure the client understands you are not an attorney.
- Resist pressures from the client to give legal advice. When in doubt about whether a question you are asked calls for legal advice, do not answer. Refer the matter to your supervising attorney.
- If the client says anything during the interview that suggests the possibility of a conflict of interest (e.g., the client tells you that the opposing side's spouse once was represented by your law firm), stop the interview and check with your supervisor about whether you should continue.
- Never discuss fees with a client.

The client will want to know what is going to happen next—after the interview. Remind the client of any scheduled appointments, such as, doctor visits or depositions. If there are none, simply tell the client that you will be preparing a report for the attorney on the case and that the office will be getting back to the client. Also, summarize anything you asked the client to do during the interview, e.g., call you to provide the exact address of a former employer.

Begin preparing a draft of your intake memorandum soon after the interview is over, while the data and your notes are fresh in your mind. (See exhibit 8.3.) Do this even if you need to obtain additional facts to include in your memorandum by follow-up interviewing or investigation. Modern word processing makes it relatively easy to make additions to memos or other documents. (See chapter 13.) Do not wait until you have all the facts before you start writing.

Also, make a notation in the client's file that you conducted the interview, even before you complete the intake memo. If the file does not have a summary form on which events can be recorded, simply place a brief note in the file stating the date and place of the interview. Someone else in the office working on the case (e.g., supervising attorney, law clerk, secretary) should be able to pick up the file and tell what has been done to date.

For a summary of these and similar steps you need to take at the end of an interview, see exhibit 8.12.

### Personality Observations

After conducting an interview, you should formulate some preliminary observations about the client's personality. Here is how one attorney described this aspect of the interview:

> "Assess the client's personality" and whether you think the office "can work with this person."
> "Watch for red flags or danger signals, including the client who is emotionally distraught or vengeful; is inconsistent with the story or avoids answering questions; has unrealistic objectives; suggests use of improper influence or other unethical or illegal conduct; rambles, wanders off the subject, or constantly interrupts you"; tells the office "how to run the case; has already discharged or filed disciplinary complaints against other lawyers; has a personality disorder; or is flirtatious."[7]

In your intake memorandum to your supervisor, include your observations and assessments relevant to concerns such as these.

### Improving Your Interviewing Skills

There are many ways you can improve your interviewing skills. They are summarized in exhibit 8.13. Be a perpetual student of the law. Always be inquisitive. Never be totally comfortable with any of your skills. One of the fascinating aspects of working in a law office is the availability of infinite opportunities to grow and improve.

| EXHIBIT 8.12 | Ending the Interview |
| --- | --- |

- Ask the client to sign any standard forms needed by the office, e.g., consent to release medical information, authorization to obtain employment history records. Before doing so, clearly explain what the document is designed to do and give the client the opportunity to ask any questions about the document before he or she signs it.
- Ask the client if there is anything else on his or her mind that he or she would like to raise before the interview is concluded.
- Let the client know precisely what the next step will be in the office's representation of the client, e.g., the attorney will call the client, the paralegal will schedule a medical examination of the client.
- Remind the client how to reach you. Have additional copies of your business card on the desk.
- Thank the client for the interview.
- Start preparing a draft of your intake memorandum.
- In the client's file, make a brief note of the fact that you conducted the interview. Include the date and place of the interview.

| EXHIBIT 8.13 | Improving Your Interviewing Skills |
| --- | --- |

- There is a good deal of literature on legal interviewing. Check legal periodicals and legal treatises. Ask a law librarian for leads to such literature. See also exhibits 11.35 and 11.38 in chapter 11.
- Try to attend seminars that cover legal interviewing, e.g. CLE (Continuing Legal Education) seminars for attorneys conducted by bar associations or CLE seminars conducted by paralegal associations.
- Ask someone you respect in the office to observe you interview a client and then give you a critique. (You will need the advance permission of the client for this person to sit in.)
- Ask someone you respect in the office to read your intake memorandum and critique it. An experienced interviewer will be able to see if there appear to be any gaps in what you covered in your memorandum.
- Try to sit in when others in the office are interviewing clients. Read their memorandum on the interview and ask them questions about their interviewing techniques. (To observe someone else's interview, you will need the consent of the interviewer and of the client interviewee.)
- Ask attorneys and other paralegals about their interviewing experiences even if you are not able to watch them conduct an interview.

## THE "DIFFICULT" CLIENT

Most clients are relatively easy to work with. Occasionally, however, you will encounter clients who can be troublesome. Here are some examples.

### The Client Who Knows All the Law

Some clients are quick to tell the office that they know the law. They may have been in litigation before, have taken courses on law, have a close relative who is an attorney, or have read a good deal about the law on the Internet. The difficulty arises if such clients are always second-guessing the way the office is handling their case or are unduly critical of anyone trying to help them. Ultimately, the attorney in charge of the case must decide if the office can continue to work with such clients. All clients, of course, are entitled to their opinions about the legal system and about anyone trying to help them. The central question is whether a client is prepared to listen to the advice provided by the attorney. The client is not obligated to follow every recommendation, but there may be no point in continuing with the attorney-client relationship if the client does not trust the attorney's professional judgment. Paralegals working with such clients must be careful to avoid arguing with them or giving them legal advice. If a client starts lecturing a paralegal about the law, the best response is to listen respectfully and then respond by saying "I'll be sure to let the attorney know what you have said."

### The Angry Client

Some clients can be very angry. They may be feel outrage at the injustice someone has allegedly committed against them. It is important that such clients be given a chance to express themselves. At the very least, they need to know that the office they have hired understands what they have been through and how they feel. They need an opportunity to vent. If, however, they continue to be angry after they have had this opportunity, the office may have difficulty providing them with effective representation. As indicated earlier, it is important to show empathy for a client by making comments such as "This must be a very difficult time for you" or "I can understand why that would be upsetting." These comments can have a settling effect on clients without immersing the interviewer into the middle of an emotional thicket. You do not want to lose your professionalism by adopting the same pessimistic or hostile frame of mind as the client.

### The Demanding/Suspicious Client

Some clients have difficulty believing that everyone in the office is not preoccupied with their case. They demand instant attention and results. ("Why is it taking so long? I want this thing over!") They may interpret delays as a tactic by the office to run up fees. An obvious response is to explain that the courts and the legal system often work at a very slow pace unless an extreme emergency exists. Generally, it is not very helpful to point out that there are other clients who also need the attention of the attorneys and paralegals in the office. One possibly effective approach is to keep demanding clients constantly informed of the status of their case. Mail them copies of documents as these are prepared for them, and send them a periodic report on the status of their case. During the initial interview, the office needs to head off or offset any unrealistic client expectations about how much time the case will take by providing a time range such cases often take for completion. The client also needs to be told that complications (e.g., new counterdemands by the opponent) almost always create additional delays.

### The Client Who Lies

There is a difference between clients who give facts a favorable interpretation and clients who lie. Assume, for example, that an office represents a husband who is seeking sole custody of his children in a bitter divorce case. It is understandable that he will attempt to portray himself as a loving father. He may glowingly describe the positive effect he has had on his children by attending sports events with them and by helping them with their homework. Careful questioning and further investigation will help determine whether he has exaggerated his role. If he has, an experienced legal team will know how to present his case in a favorable light without compromising the truth. Suppose, however, that the father goes beyond exaggeration. For example, he may falsely claim that he does not use corporal punishment on the children, or he may deny that he takes illegal drugs in front of them in spite of evidence to the contrary. Of course, if any of these facts can reasonably be interpreted in the father's favor, the office has an obligation to present this interpretation to the court. Yet it may eventually become clear to the office that the client has a tendency to lie. Serious ethical problems can arise in such cases. As we saw in chapter 5, an attorney has an ethical obligation to avoid telling the court something that is not true and to avoid allowing a client to lie to the court when the attorney knows that this is what the client has done or is about to do. An attorney's withdrawal from a case is justified when continued representation of the client will cause the attorney to violate an ethical obligation. Furthermore, it may be impossible for the attorney to provide competent representation without knowing all available facts. The client must be told that the attorney cannot rebut negative facts without knowing what those facts are. The client cannot make those facts go away by lying about them or concealing them. If the office cannot convince the client of this reality, the likelihood of representing the client effectively and ethically is very low.

---

### *Class Exercise 8.C*

Form a circle of chairs with a single chair in the middle. The student sitting in the middle will play the role of the client. The students in the circle (numbering about 10) will be the interviewers, in rotation. The instructor will ask one of the students to begin the interview. As this student runs into difficulty during the interview, the student to his or her right picks up the interview, tries to resolve the difficulty in his or her own way, and then proceeds with the interview. If *this* student cannot resolve the difficulty, the student to his or her right tries, and so on. The objective is to identify as many diverse ways of handling difficulties as possible in a relatively short period. No interviewer should have the floor for more than a minute or two at any one time. The student playing the role of the client is given specific instructions about how to play the role. For example, sometimes he or she is asked to be shy; other times, demanding. The client should not overdo the role, however. He or she should respond naturally within the role assigned. Here are four sets of instructions to attempt this "interview in rotation."

(a) The interviewer greets the client and says, "I am a paralegal." The client is confused about what a paralegal is. The interviewer explains. The client is insistent upon a comprehensive definition that he or she can understand.

(b) The client comes to the law office because he or she is being sued for negligent driving. The interviewer asks the client if he or she must wear eyeglasses to drive. The answer is *yes*. The interviewer then asks if he or she was wearing eyeglasses during the accident. The client is very reluctant to answer. (In fact, the client was not wearing glasses at the time.) The client does not appear to want to talk about this subject. The interviewer persists.

(c) The client is being sued by a local store for $750.00 in grocery bills. The client has a poor memory and the interviewer must think of ways to help him or her remember. The client wants to cooperate but is having trouble remembering.

(d) The client wants to sue an auto mechanic. The client gives many opinions, conclusions, and judgments (such as "The mechanic is a crook," "I was their best customer," "The work done was awful.") The interviewer is having difficulty encouraging the client to state the facts underlying the opinions. The client insists on stating conclusions.

After each exercise, the class should discuss principles, guidelines, and techniques of interviewing.

---

### Class Exercise 8.D
Below are two additional role-playing exercises to be conducted in class.

(a) The instructor asks the class if anyone was involved, in any way, in a recent automobile accident. If someone says *yes*, this student is asked if he or she would be willing to be interviewed by another class member whose job is to obtain as complete a picture as possible of what happened. At the outset, the interviewer knows nothing other than that some kind of an automobile accident occurred. The interviewee can make up any sensitive facts if he or she wishes to keep some of the actual events confidential.

(b) The instructor asks the class if anyone has recently had trouble with any government agency (like the post office or sanitation department). If someone says *yes*, this student is asked if he or she would be willing to be interviewed by another class member whose job is to obtain as complete a picture as possible of what happened. The interviewer at the outset knows nothing other than the fact that the person being interviewed has had some difficulty with a government agency. The interviewee can make up any sensitive facts if he or she wishes to keep some of the actual events confidential.

---

### Class Exercise 8.E
When an office represents a debtor, one of the paralegal's major responsibilities may be to interview the client in order to write a comprehensive report on the client's assets and liabilities. Assume that your supervising attorney has instructed you to conduct a comprehensive interview of the client in order to write such a report. Assets are everything the client *owns* or has an interest in. Liabilities are everything *owed;* they are debts. These are the only definitions you need; you do not need any technical knowledge of law to conduct this interview. All you need is common sense in the formulation of questions.

Your instructor will role-play the client in front of the room. It will be a collective interview. Everyone will ask questions, but you will each write individual reports on the interview based on your own notes. Raise your hand to be recognized. Be sure to ask follow-up questions when needed for factual clarity and comprehensiveness. You can repeat the questions of other students if you think you might elicit a more detailed response. Any question is fair game as long as it is directly or indirectly calculated to uncover assets or liabilities. There may be information the client does not have at this time, such as bank account numbers. Help the client determine how such information can be obtained later. In your notes, state that you asked for information that the client did not have and state what the client said he or she would do to obtain the information. To achieve comprehensiveness, you must obtain factual detail. This means that you go after names, addresses, phone numbers, dates, relevant surrounding circumstances, verification data, etc. In short, we want fact particularization (FP). (See also exhibit 8.10.) Take detailed notes on the questions asked by every student (not just your own) and the answers provided in response. You will have to write your report based on your own notes.

The heading of your report will be as follows:

Inter-Office Memorandum

**To:** [name of your instructor]
**From:** [your name]
**Date:** [date you prepared the report]
**RE:** Comprehensive Interview of
_____

**Case File Number:** _____

(Make up the case file number.) The first paragraph of your report should state what your supervisor has asked you to do in the report. Simply state what the assignment is. Organization of the data from your notes is up to you. Use whatever format you think will most clearly communicate what you learned from the client in the interview.

## CHAPTER SUMMARY

Projecting competence and professionalism is an essential ingredient in performing any task on behalf of a client. The retainer establishes the scope of the attorney-client relationship. If the office decides not to represent the prospective client, it should send him or her a letter of nonengagement.

Interviewing is conversation for the purpose of obtaining information. In a law office, legal interviewing is designed to obtain facts that are relevant to the identification and eventual resolution of a legal problem. These facts are often reported in a document called an intake memo. Six major guides exist to the kinds of questions that should be asked during a legal interview. The most important is the instructions of the supervisor on the goals of the interview. Other guides include preprinted checklists for certain kinds of interviews, legal analysis to help you focus on relevance, fact particularization as a device to achieve comprehensiveness, and, finally, common sense and flexibility to help you remain alert and responsive as the interview unfolds.

Determining what the client wants often takes probing and presentation of options. Otherwise, the office might fail to identify client objectives. Most of us are not fully aware of how our prejudices affect our performance. Detecting interviewer bias may not be easy; it is sometimes difficult to distance our personal feelings from the client's objectives.

The supervising attorney helps set the tone for an effective interview by introducing the client to the paralegal and explaining the latter's role. The professional interviewer strives to uncover facts that make the case of each client unique. There are many ways to prepare for an interview such as scheduling the interview at a convenient time, reading everything in the file, having supplies available, and preparing initial questions. The seating arrangement should facilitate communication. The walls, desk, and overall appearance of the office should project a professional image. Go out to greet the client when he or she arrives at the reception desk.

Always be appreciative of what the client does. Some small talk at the beginning of the interview can help decrease client tension. Avoid making any promises of what the office can accomplish. Express empathy without being condescending or losing objectivity. Find out if there are any immediate concerns on the client's mind. Avoid legal jargon unless the client needs to know about it and clear explanations are given. Briefly restate the purpose of the interview for the client. Let the client know why you are taking notes. Listen for clues to other problems the office should know about.

The following are the major kinds of questions an interviewer can ask (some of which overlap): open-ended, overview, closed-ended, chronological, leading, corroborative, and combination. One of the most important ways of building a relationship with the client is through attentive listening techniques such as maintaining eye contact and repeating back what the client has told you. Factual comprehensiveness is achieved through fact particularization, corroborative questions, probing, etc. The interviewer must be alert to potential ethical problems such as breaching confidentiality and giving legal advice.

At the conclusion of the interview, ask the client to read and sign needed forms, find out if the client has any concerns not addressed during the interview, tell the client what next steps are planned, and make sure the client knows how to reach you. As soon as possible, make a note to the file that you conducted the interview. Begin writing the report or intake memo soon after the interview, making note of any personality characteristics relevant to working with the client that you observed. To improve your interviewing technique, read literature and attend CLE seminars on interviewing, seek the critique of others, try to observe others interview, etc.

Special sensitivity is needed when working with potentially difficult clients such as those who claim to know all the law, who are angry, who are demanding, or who lie. Every effort should be made to work with such clients while maintaining professionalism, but ultimately the office may have to decide whether continued representation is feasible or ethically appropriate.

## KEY TERMS

retainer

deep pocket

letter of nonengagement

intake memo

RE

ground

legal analysis

legally relevant

fact particularization

analogy

bias

objectivity

hypothetical

breach of contract

jargon

open-ended question

overview question

closed-ended question

chronological question

leading question

corroborative question

combination question

multiple-choice question

add-on question

attentive listening

## ON THE NET: MORE ABOUT INTERVIEWING

**Interviewing: Selected Articles**

www.rongolini.com/Interviewing.html

**Legal Interviewing: Difficult Clients**

www.law.cua.edu/faculty/barry/Articles/binder12.htm

**Resources on Client Interviewing**

www.dmulawsociety.btinternet.co.uk/clientinterviewing/reading.html

## ENDNOTES

1. Brent Roper, *Practical Law Office Management* 121 (1995).
2. Shari Caudron, *Crisis of Conscience*, 12 Legal Assistant Today 73, 75 (September/October 1994).
3. William P. Statsky & Philip C. Lang, *The Legal Paraprofessional as Advocate and Assistant: Roles, Training Concepts and Materials* (Center on Social Welfare Policy and Law, 1971).
4. Denise Clemens, *Client Interviewing*, 11 California Paralegal Magazine 12, 13 (October/December 1991).
5. See also White, *Architectural Suggestions for a Law Office Building*, 9 Practical Lawyer 66 (No. 8, 1956).
6. H. Freeman & H. Weihofen, *Clinical Law Training, Interviewing and Counseling* 13 (1972).
7. *The Initial Interview*, 12 Family Advocate 6 (Winter 1990).

# Chapter 9

# INVESTIGATION IN A LAW OFFICE

## Chapter Outline

## Section A
# THE NATURE AND CONTEXT OF INVESTIGATION

**legal investigation** The process of gathering additional facts and verifying presently known facts in order to advise a client about solving or avoiding a legal problem.

**Legal investigation** is the process of gathering additional facts and verifying known facts in order to advise a client about solving or avoiding a legal problem. Our study of investigation will focus on three main topics:

- The nature of investigation,
- The techniques of investigation, and
- Evidence law relevant to investigation.

In many law offices, paralegals "are often called upon by attorneys to track down important information that is relevant to a real estate transaction, a corporate transaction, a case that is in litigation or a case where litigation is anticipated."[1] Lana Clark, a litigation paralegal, says, "Many of us have been approached by our attorneys at the last minute to interview a witness and 'Find out what he knows.' "[2] For large cases, a law firm might use an outside licensed private investigator or perhaps an investigator with a specialty (e.g., a **forensic** accountant who will examine corporate records for evidence of fraud or embezzlement).

**forensic** Pertaining to the use of science to help resolve a legal question. Used in arguments or public debate.

In the movie *Erin Brockovich*, based on a true story, Julia Roberts won an Academy Award for her role as a nonattorney employee who was given a major investigation assignment in the law office where she worked. She investigated the link between a highly toxic antirust chemical agent (chromium-6) used by a major public utility and the life-threatening diseases suffered by residents in the area where the utility had dumped the agent. Their water supply had become contaminated. Brockovich's work led to a $333 million dollar settlement for the victims and, eventually, to a $1 million dollar bonus for herself from her grateful supervising attorney. Of course, most paralegal investigation assignments will not be this dramatic. Yet the movie certainly highlighted the importance of investigation and the critical role that nonattorneys can have in this arena of fact gathering.

In chapter 8, on legal interviewing, we examined six major guides to fact gathering:

- Instructions of the supervisor
- Checklists
- Legal analysis
- Fact particularization (FP)
- Common sense
- Flexibility

You should review these guides now because they are equally applicable to investigation. Fact particularization (FP) is especially important.

We begin our study of legal investigation with some general observations about its nature and context:

1. *Investigative techniques are often very individualistic.* Styles, mannerisms, and approaches to investigation are often highly personal. Through a sometimes arduous process of trial and error, the investigator develops effective techniques. Some of these techniques come from the suggestions of fellow investigators. Most, however, are acquired from on-the-job experience.
2. *It is impossible to overemphasize the importance of hustle, imagination, and flexibility.* If there is one characteristic that singles out the effective investigator, it is a willingness to dig. Many investigation assignments are relatively straightforward. For example:

   - Check court records to find out if a particular doctor has any other malpractice cases pending against him or her
   - Find out if someone has filed a worker's compensation claim

- Obtain a copy of an ambulance report
- Photograph the ceiling of a bathroom that a tenant claims is falling down

Other assignments are potentially more involved because they are open-ended (e.g., find out what property or other assets of the defendant may be available to pay a judgment). An extensive range of options and conclusions is possible in such assignments. The answer is not always there for the asking. For such assignments, investigators must be prepared to identify and pursue leads, be unorthodox, and let their feelings, hunches, and intuition lead where they will. In short, the formal principles of investigation must give way to hustle, imagination, and flexibility.

Good investigators are always in pursuit. They are on the offensive and do not wait for the facts to come to them. They know that legwork is required. They know that 50 percent of their leads will turn out to be dead ends. They are not frightened by roadblocks and therefore do not freeze at the first hurdle. They know that there are no perfect ways of obtaining information. They know that they must take a stab at possibilities and that it takes persistent thinking and imagination to come up with leads. At the same time, good investigators are not fools. They do not pursue blind alleys. After being on the job for a while, they have developed "a feel" for whether a possibility or lead is reasonable. They have been able to develop this feel because, when they first started investigating, they had open minds and were not afraid to try things out.

3. *Investigators may not know what they are looking for until they find it.* Investigation, like interviewing and legal research, sometimes takes on a life of its own, particularly in open-ended assignments where you may be walking into the unknown. You may not know what you are looking for until you find it. Suppose, for example, that the law firm has a client who is charging his employer with racial discrimination. In the process of working on the case, the investigator discovers that this employee had a managerial job at the company and that several of the workers under him have complained that *he* practiced racial discrimination against them. The investigator had no idea that she would uncover this until it was uncovered. In short, an open mind is key when undertaking an assignment.

4. *Investigation and interviewing are closely related.* The interviewer conducting the initial client interview has two responsibilities: to help identify legal problems and to obtain from the client as many relevant facts on those problems as possible. The starting point for the investigator is the report or intake memo (see exhibit 8.3) prepared by the interviewer on what the client said. The investigation needs may be clear from this report, or they may become clear only after the investigator and his or her supervisor have defined them more precisely.

The investigator should approach the interview report with a healthy skepticism. Thus far, all the office may know is what the client has said. The perspective of the office is therefore narrow. Without necessarily distrusting the client's word, the investigator's job is to verify the facts given during the interview and to determine whether new facts exist that were unknown or improperly identified during the interview. The interview report should not be taken at face value. New facts may be revealed or old facts may for the first time be seen in a context that gives them an unexpected meaning. The investigator must approach a case almost as if the office knows nothing about it or as if what the office knows is invalid. By adopting this attitude, the investigator will be able to give the case an entirely different direction when the product of the investigation warrants it.

5. *The investigator must be guided by goals and priorities.* It is one thing to say that the investigator must be open-minded enough to be receptive to the unexpected. It is quite another to say that the investigator should start in a void. The starting point is a set of instructions from the supervisor. How clear a supervisor is about an investigation assignment may vary with each assignment. For example:

- Supervisors may have a very definite idea of what they want.
- Supervisors may think they know what they want but are not sure.

- Whatever conception supervisors have about what they want, they are not effective in explaining it to the investigator.
- Supervisors have no idea what they want other than a desire to obtain as many facts about the case as possible.

The first responsibility of the investigator is to establish communication with the supervisor. With as much clarity as possible, determine what the supervisor wants to accomplish through the investigation.

6. *Investigation, negotiation, and trial are closely related.* There are two ultimate questions that should guide the investigator's inquiry into every fact being investigated:

- How will this fact assist or hurt the office in attempting to settle or negotiate the case without a trial?
- How will this fact assist or hurt the office in presenting the client's case at trial?

A large percentage of legal claims never go to full trial. Opposing counsel hold a number of bargaining sessions in which they attempt to hammer out a **settlement** acceptable to their clients. Very often they discuss the law that they think will be applicable if the case goes to trial. Even more often they present each other with the facts that they think they will be able to establish at trial. Here, the investigator's report becomes invaluable. As a result of this report, the attorney should be able to suggest a wide range of facts that could be used at trial ("we have reason to believe . . ." or "we are now pursuing leads that would tend to establish that . . ." etc.). The attorney's bargaining leverage is immeasurably increased by a thorough investigation report.

If negotiations do not produce a settlement, the investigator's report can help the attorney:

- Determine whether to go to trial
- Decide what witnesses to call
- Choose questions to ask of witnesses
- Decide how to **impeach** (i.e., contradict or attack the credibility of) opposing witnesses
- Anticipate how the other side might try to impeach your client and witnesses
- Determine what tangible or physical evidence to introduce
- Decide how to attack the tangible or physical evidence the other side will introduce

The investigator should be familiar with the standard, pretrial **discovery** devices: depositions, interrogatories, requests for admissions, medical examination reports, etc. (See exhibit 10.4 in chapter 10.) A **deposition** is a pretrial question-and-answer session conducted outside court, usually in the office of one of the attorneys. The attorney asks questions of the other party (or of a witness of the other party) in order to obtain facts that will assist in preparing for trial. Depositions are often transcribed so that typed copies of the session are available. **Interrogatories** are used for the same purpose, but differ in that the questions and answers are usually provided in writing rather than in person. An interrogatory is simply a question submitted by one party to another. A **request for admission** is a statement of fact submitted by one party to another. The latter is asked to admit or deny the statement. Statements that are admitted do not have to be proven at trial. A request for a medical examination will be granted by the judge when the examination will help resolve a medical issue in the trial.

Investigators can be of assistance during this discovery stage by helping the attorney decide what questions to ask in a deposition or in an interrogatory, what admissions to request, whether to ask for a medical examination, etc.

After the discovery devices have been used, the investigator should carefully study all the facts these devices disclose in order to:

- Cross-check or verify these facts, and
- Look for new leads (names, addresses, incidents) that could be the subject of future investigation.

**settlement** An agreement to end a dispute before it is resolved by all available agencies or courts.

**impeach** To challenge; to attack the credibility of.

**discovery** Compulsory pretrial disclosure of information by one party (and its prospective witnesses) to another party during litigation.

**deposition** A method of discovery by which parties and their prospective witnesses are questioned before trial. A pretrial question-and-answer session to help parties prepare for trial.

**interrogatories** A method of discovery consisting of written questions sent by one party to another to assist the sender to prepare for trial.

**request for admission** A method of discovery consisting of a statement of fact that the other side is asked to affirm or deny.

7. *It is important to distinguish between proof of a fact and evidence of a fact.* **Evidence** is anything that tends to prove or disprove a fact. **Proof** is enough evidence to establish the truth or falsity of a fact. Investigators are looking for evidence. They should not stop looking simply because they have not found proof. It is the role of the judge and jury to determine truth and falsity. The function of investigators is to identify reasonable options or fact possibilities. To be sure, they can speculate on whether a judge or jury would ever believe an alleged fact to be true. But the presence or absence of proof is not the test that should guide them in their investigations. The tests that an investigator should apply in determining whether to investigate a fact possibility are:

   ■ Am I reasonable in assuming that a particular fact will help establish the case of the client? Am I reasonable in assuming that the specific evidence of that fact I am investigating might be accepted as true by a judge, jury, or hearing officer?
   ■ Am I reasonable in assuming that a particular fact will help to challenge or discredit the case of the opposing party? Am I reasonable in assuming that the specific evidence of that fact I am investigating might be accepted as true by a judge, jury, or hearing officer?

   It is important to be able to approach the case from the perspective of the opponent, even to the point of assuming that you work for the other side! What facts will the opponent go after to establish its case? What is the likelihood that such facts will be accepted?

8. *The investigator must know some law.* Investigators do not have to be experts in every area of the law or in any particular area of the law in order to perform their job. For their field work to have a focus, however, they must have at least a general understanding of evidence, civil procedure, and the areas of the law governing the facts of the client's case. They must know, for example, what *hearsay* and *relevance* mean. They must understand basic procedural steps in litigation in order to see how facts can be used in different ways at different steps in the litigation process. Some substantive law is also needed. In a divorce case, for example, the investigator must know what the grounds for divorce are in the state. The same kind of basic information is needed for every area of the law involved or potentially involved in the client's case. Such knowledge can be obtained:

   ■ In paralegal courses or seminars
   ■ Through brief explanations from the supervisor
   ■ By talking to experienced attorneys and paralegals whenever they have time to give you an overview of the relevant law
   ■ By reading a chapter in a legal treatise or a section in a legal encyclopedia that provides an overview of the relevant law. (See exhibit 11.18 in chapter 11 on Techniques for Doing Background Research on a Topic.)

9. *The investigator must know the territory.* When you are on the job as an investigator, it is important to begin acquiring a detailed knowledge of the makeup of the city, town, or state where you will be working. Such knowledge should include:

   ■ The political structure of the area: Who is in power? Who is the opposition? In what direction is the political structure headed?
   ■ The social and cultural structure of the area: Are there racial problems? Are there ethnic groupings that are diffused or unified? Are there different value systems at play?
   ■ The contacts that are productive: If you want something done at city hall, whom do you see? What court clerk is most helpful? Does the director of a particular agency have any control over the staff? What agencies have "real services" available?

   It is usually very difficult for the investigator to acquire this knowledge in any way other than going out into the field and obtaining it through experience.

**evidence** Anything that tends to prove or disprove a fact.

**proof** Enough evidence to establish the truth or falsity of a fact.

Others can provide guidance, and often will. In the final analysis, however, you will probably discover that what others say is biased or incomplete. You must establish your own network of contacts and sources of information. First and foremost, you must establish your credibility in the community. People must get to know and trust you. Simply announcing yourself as an investigator (or presenting a printed card indicating title and affiliation) will not be enough to win instant cooperation from the community. You must *earn* this cooperation. If you gain a reputation as arrogant, dishonest, opportunistic, or insensitive, you will quickly find that few people want to deal with you. An investigator could be in no worse predicament.

Often the best way to learn about an area and begin establishing contacts is by being casual and unassuming. Have you ever noticed that insurance agents often spend time talking about the weather, sports, politics, the high cost of housing, etc., *before* coming to their sales pitch? Their intent is to relax you, to find out what interests you, to show you that they are human. Then they hit you with the benefits of buying their insurance. The investigator can use this approach not only in establishing contacts at agencies and in the community generally, but also in dealing with prospective witnesses on specific cases.

## Section B
# Fact Analysis: Organizing the Options

The process of structuring or organizing fact options may initially appear to be complex and cumbersome. But the process can become second nature to you once you understand it, try it out, evaluate it, modify it, and find it helpful. It is, of course, perfectly proper to adopt any process that you find effective. Whatever method you use, you need to develop the *discipline* of fact analysis as soon as possible.

A number of fundamental characteristics of facts should be kept in mind:

- Events take place.
- Events mean different things to different people.
- Different people, therefore, can have different versions of events.
- Inconsistent versions of the same event do not necessarily indicate fraud or lying.
- Although someone's version may claim to be the total picture, it probably will contain only a piece of the picture.
- In giving a version of an event, people usually mix statements of *why* the event occurred with statements of *what* occurred. Or worse, they may tailor their description of what happened to fit their version of why the event occurred.
- Whenever it is claimed that an event occurred in a certain way, one can logically expect that certain signs, indications, or traces (evidence) of the event can be found.

Given these truisms, the investigator should analyze the facts along the lines indicated in exhibit 9.1. It is possible for a single client's case to have numerous individual facts that are in dispute. Furthermore, facts can change, or people's versions of facts can change in the middle of a case. Each new or modified fact requires the same comprehensive process of fact analysis outlined in exhibit 9.1.

Of course, every fact will not necessarily have multiple versions. It is recommended, however, that you assume there will be more than one version until you have demonstrated otherwise to yourself. Obtaining different versions of a fact is sometimes difficult because the differences may not be clear on the surface. Undoubtedly, you will have to do some probing to uncover the versions that exist. Better to do so now than to be confronted with a surprise at trial or at an agency hearing.

People will not always be willing to share their accounts or versions of facts with you. If you are not successful in convincing them to tell their story, you may have to make assumptions of what their story is *likely* to be and then check out these assumptions.

| EXHIBIT 9.1 | Fact Analysis in Investigation |
|---|---|

**Starting Point:**

All the facts you currently have on the case:

- Arrange the facts chronologically.
- Place a number before each fact that may have to be established in a legal proceeding.

**State the Following Versions of Each Fact:**

Version I: The client's
Version II: The opponent's (as revealed to you or as assumed)
Version III: A witness's
Version IV: Another witness's
Version V: Any other reasonable version (e.g., from your own deductions)

**As to Each Version:**

- State precisely (with quotes if possible) what the version is.
- State the evidence or indications that tend to support the version according to persons presenting the version.
- State the evidence or indications that tend to contradict this version.
- Determine how you will verify or corroborate the evidence or indications.

## Section C
# Distortions in Investigation

Investigators are not mere newspaper reporters or photographers who simply report what they see, hear, or otherwise experience. You have a much more dynamic role. In a very significant sense, you sometimes have the power to influence what someone else says about the facts. This can have both positive and negative consequences.

Be alert to the danger of asking questions in such a manner that you are putting words into the person's mouth. The primary technique that can bring about this result is the **leading question**. A leading question is one that suggests an answer in the statement of the question. For example, "You were in Baltimore at the time, isn't that correct?" "You earn over $200 a week?" "Would it be correct to say that when you drove up to the curb, you didn't see the light?" (For more on the different kinds of questions that can be asked, see exhibit 8.8 in chapter 8.)

**leading question** A question that suggests an answer in the question.

Questions can intentionally or unintentionally manipulate someone's answer by including a premise that has yet to be established. It takes an alert person to say to such questions, "I can't answer your question (or it is invalid) because it assumes another fact that I haven't agreed to." In the following examples of questions and answers, the person responding to the question refuses to be trapped by the form of the question:

Q: How much did it cost you to have your car repaired after the accident?
A: It's not my car and it wasn't an accident; your client deliberately ran into the car that I borrowed.
_____

Q: Have you stopped beating your wife?
A: I never beat my wife!
_____

Q: Can you tell me what you saw?
A: I didn't see anything; my brother was there and he told me what happened.

The last leading question containing the unestablished premise can be highly detrimental. Suppose the question and answer went as follows:

Q: Can you tell me what you saw?
A: The car was going about 70 m.p.h.

In fact, the person answering the question did not see this himself; his brother told him that a car was traveling at this speed. This person may have failed to tell the investigator that he did not see anything first-hand for a number of reasons:

- Perhaps he did not hear the word "saw" in the investigator's question.
- He may have wanted the investigator to think that he saw something himself; he may want to feel important by conveying the impression that he is special because he has special information.
- He may have felt that correcting the investigator's false assumption was not important; he may have thought that the investigator was more interested in *what* happened than in *who* saw what happened.

Whatever the reason, the investigator has carelessly put himself or herself in the position of missing a potentially critical fact, namely, that the person is talking from hearsay. Before asking what the person "saw," the investigator should ask, "Were you there?" and if so, "Did you see anything?"

Also, be careful about the way you phrase a question. "Research indicates the wording of questions to witnesses significantly affects their recall. For example, more uncertain or 'don't know' responses are given if a witness is asked about an indefinite item (e.g., 'Did you see *a* knife?') than occurs when the question contains a definite article ('Did you see *the* knife?')."[3]

Communication is often blurred when the questioner concentrates on some themes to the exclusion of others. If you do not ask questions about certain matters, intentionally or otherwise, you are likely to end up with a distorted picture of a person's version of the facts. For example, assume that Smith and Jones have an automobile collision. The investigator, working for the attorney who represents Jones, finds a witness who says that she saw the accident. The investigator asks her to describe what she saw, but fails, however, to ask her where she was at the time she saw the collision. In fact, she was sitting in a park more than two blocks away and could see the collision only through some shrubbery. The investigator did not ask questions to uncover this information; it was not volunteered. The investigator, therefore, walks away with a potentially distorted idea of how much light this individual can shed on what took place. This is similar to the distortion that can result from the use of questions that contain an unestablished premise.

Yet, in some instances, these techniques may have beneficial results. First of all, a leading question can help jar someone's memory, making the person better able to recall the facts. If, however, this person constantly needs leading questions in order to remember, you have strong reason to suspect that, rather than being merely shy, inarticulate, or in need of a push now and then, the person knows little or nothing.

Suppose that the witness being questioned is uncooperative or has a version of the facts that is damaging to the client of the investigator's office. It may be that the techniques described in this section as normally improper can be used to challenge a version of the facts. A leading question with an unestablished premise, for example, may catch an individual off guard and give the investigator reasonable cause to believe that the person is not telling the truth.

If you have reason to doubt someone's willingness to tell you what he or she knows, a leading statement or question might be helpful in prompting communication:

> A technique I've found very successful is to ask a question I feel will evoke a factual answer. For example, I would ask Mr. John Doe, "Mr. Doe, you claim that you are a witness to the accident when, in fact, I understand you were not in a position to see everything that happened." Often, the person will respond with a defensive answer similar to, "I was in a position to see everything," and then continue to tell me their location and what they saw.[4]

Suppose that the person being questioned is not hostile but is neutral, or seemingly so. The way such individuals are questioned may help them emphasize certain facts as opposed to others. Once witnesses have committed themselves to a version of the facts, either completely on their own or with some subtle help from the questioner, there is a good chance that they will stick by this version because they do not want to appear to be vague, uncertain, or inconsistent later. An investigator who takes such a course of action must be extremely careful, however. You are taking certain risks, not because your conduct is illegal or unethical, but because a witness who needs subtle pressuring to state a version of the facts in a certain way is probably going to be a weak witness at trial or at an agency hearing. On cross-examination, the witness may fall apart.

## Section D
# Sources of Evidence/Sources of Leads

As we have seen, evidence is anything that tends to prove or disprove a fact. Two major categories of evidence are **parol evidence** (oral) and **tangible evidence** (physical). Exhibit 9.2 presents a partial checklist of some of the standard sources of parol and tangible evidence—or leads to such evidence. Of course, once evidence is identified, it often becomes its own lead to further evidence.

**parol evidence** Oral evidence.

**tangible evidence** Evidence that can be seen or touched; physical evidence.

| EXHIBIT 9.2 | Checklist of the Standard Sources of Evidence and Leads (For Internet leads, see On The Net at the end of the chapter.) |
|---|---|

- Statements of the client
- Documents the client brings or can obtain
- Information from the attorneys involved with the case in the past
- Accounts of eyewitnesses
- Hearsay accounts
- Interrogatories, depositions, other discovery devices; letters requesting information
- Pleadings (such as complaints) filed thus far in the case
- Newspaper accounts; interviews with news reporters (many public libraries have online media indexes you can check)
- Notices in the media requesting information
- General records of municipal, state, and federal administrative agencies
- Business records (such as canceled receipts)
- Employment records, including job applications
- Photographs
- Hospital records
- Informers or the "town gossip"
- Surveillance of the scene
- Reports from the police and other law enforcement agencies (see exhibit 9.3)
- Fingerprints
- School records
- Military records
- Information that may be voluntarily or involuntarily provided by the attorney for the other side

- Use of alias
- Bureau of vital statistics and missing persons
- Court records
- Workers' Compensation records
- Office of politicians
- Records of Better Business Bureaus and consumer groups
- Telephone book
- *Polk Directory*
- *Reverse Directory*
- Boat register
- Automobile registry (DMV)
- County assessor (for real property)
- Tax assessor's office
- County election records
- Post Office (record of forwarding addresses)
- Object to be traced (such as an auto)
- Credit bureaus
- Reports of investigative agencies
- Associations (trade, professional, etc.)
- *Who's Who* directories
- Insurance Company Clearing House
- Standard and Poor's *Register of Directors and Executives*
- Telling your problem to a more experienced investigator and asking for other leads
- Shots in the dark

## Section E
# Gaining Access to Records

Often the simplest way to obtain a record or other information is to ask for it. See, for example, the sample letter requesting information in exhibit 12.2 in chapter 12. Gaining access to some records, however, can sometimes be difficult. There are four categories of records you may need to examine:

1. Those already in the possession of a client or an individual willing to turn them over to you on request

2. Those in the possession of a governmental agency (for example, see exhibit 9.3) or of a private organization and available to anyone in the public
3. Those in the possession of a governmental agency or of a private organization and available only to the client or to the individual who is the subject of the records
4. Those in the possession of a governmental agency or of a private organization and claimed to be confidential except for in-house staff

Obviously, there should be no difficulty in gaining access to the first category of records unless they have been misplaced or lost, in which event the person who once had

---

| EXHIBIT 9.3 | Request for Copy of Peace Officer's Accident Report |
|---|---|

### REQUEST FOR COPY OF PEACE OFFICER'S ACCIDENT REPORT
### (PLEASE SUBMIT IN DUPLICATE)

Statistical Services                                        Date of Request _____
Texas Department of Public Safety
P.O. Box 15999                                              Claim or Policy No. _____
Austin, Texas 78761–5999

Enclosed is a (check)(money order) payable to the Texas Department of Public Safety in the amount of $ _____
for (check service desired):
☐ Copy of Peace Officer's Accident Report – $4.00 each
☐ Certified Copy of Peace Officer's Accident Report – $8.00 each
for the accident listed below:

---

Please provide as accurate and complete information as possible.

ACCIDENT DATE _____
             MONTH        DAY         YEAR

ACCIDENT LOCATION _____   _____   _____
                      COUNTY              CITY          STREET OR HIGHWAY

WAS ANYONE
KILLED IN THE ACCIDENT? _____ If So, Name of Deceased _____

INVESTIGATING AGENCY AND/OR OFFICER'S NAME (IF KNOWN)

| | DRIVER INFORMATION (If Available) | | |
|---|---|---|---|
| DRIVER'S FULL NAME | DATE OF BIRTH | TEXAS DRIVER LICENSE NO. | ADDRESS |
| 1. _____ | | | |
| 2. _____ | | | |
| 3. _____ | | | |

---

Texas Statutes allow the investigating officer 10 days in which to submit his report.
**Requests should not be submitted until at least 10 days after the accident date to allow time for receipt of the report.**

The Law also provides that if an officer's report is not on file when a request for a copy of such report is received, a certification to that effect will be provided in lieu of the copy and the fee shall be retained for the certification.

Mail To _____

Mail Address _____

City _____ State _____ Zip _____

Requested by _____ Phone # _____

possession would ask the source of the records to provide another copy. As to records in the latter three categories, the checklist in exhibit 9.4 should provide some guidelines on gaining access, including use of the **Freedom of Information Act** (FOIA) for government records. Before making a FOIA request, go to the Internet site of the federal or state agency that has the information you need. Find out if the site gives you any specific instructions on filing a FOIA request at the agency. For a list of FOIA contacts at federal agencies, for example, see *www.usdoj.gov/04foia/foiacontacts. htm.*

**Freedom of Information Act**
A statute that gives citizens access to certain information in the possession of the government.

| EXHIBIT 9.4 | Guidelines for Gaining Access to Records |
|---|---|

1. Write, phone, or visit the organization and ask for the record.
2. Have the client write, phone, or visit and ask for it.
3. Draft a letter for the client to sign that asks for it.
4. Have the client sign a form stating that he or she gives you authority to see any records that pertain to him or her and that he or she specifically waives any right to confidentiality with respect to such records.
5. Find out if one of the opposing parties has the record, and if so, ask his or her attorney to send you a copy.
6. Find out if others have it (such as a relative of the client or a co-defendant in this or a prior court case) and ask them if they will provide you with a copy.
7. For records available generally to the public, find out where these records are and go use them.
8. If you meet resistance (fourth category of records), make a basic fairness pitch to the organization as to why you need the records.
9. Find out (by legal research) if there are any statutes, regulations, or cases that arguably provide the client with the right of access to records kept by government agencies—for example, through the Freedom of Information Act (FOIA) of Congress covering federal agencies. (See exhibit 9.5.) Many states have their own FOIA for state agencies. Before making a FOIA request, go to the Internet site of the federal or state agency that has the information you need. Find out if the site gives you any specific instructions filing a FOIA request at that agency. For a list of FOIA contacts at federal agencies, for example, see *www.usdoj.gov/04foia/foiacontacts.htm.*
10. If the person who initially turns down the request for access is a line officer, appeal the decision formally or informally to his or her supervisor, and up the chain of command to the person with final authority.
11. Solicit the intervention of a politician or some other respectable and independent person in trying to gain access.
12. Let the organization know that your office is considering (or is preparing) a suit to establish a right to the record (when this is so).

## Section F
## EVALUATING EVIDENCE

At all times, you must make value judgments on the usefulness of the evidence that you come across. A number of specific criteria can be used to assist you in assessing the worth of what you have. The checklists in exhibits 9.6 and 9.7 may be helpful in determining this worth.

## Section G
## INTERVIEWING WITNESSES

Francis Ritter, a seasoned investigator, tells us that there are six parts to every conversation: three for the speaker and three for the listener. For the *speaker* they are:

- What the speaker wants to say
- What the speaker actually says, and
- What the speaker thinks he or she said.

The *listener* deals with:

- What the listener wants to hear,
- What the listener actually heard, and
- What the listener thinks he or she heard.[5]

| EXHIBIT 9.5 | Sample FOIA Letter |
| --- | --- |

Agency Head or FOIA Officer
Title
Name of Government Agency
Address of Agency
City, State, Zip

Re: Freedom of Information Act (FOIA) Request.

Dear _____

This is a request under the Freedom of Information Act. I request that a copy of the following documents [or documents containing the following information] be provided to me: [identify the documents or information as specifically as possible].

In order to help to determine my status for purposes of determining the applicability of any fees, you should know that I am [insert a suitable description of the requester and the purpose of the request; here are some sample descriptions of the requester:

– a representative of the news media affiliated with the _____ newspaper (magazine, television station, etc.), and this request is made as part of news gathering and not for a commercial use.
– affiliated with an educational or noncommercial scientific institution, and this request is made for a scholarly or scientific purpose and not for a commercial use.
– an individual seeking information for personal use and not for a commercial use.
– affiliated with a private corporation and am seeking information for use in the company's business.]

[Another alternative] I request a waiver of all fees for this request. Disclosure of the requested information to me is in the public interest because it is likely to contribute significantly to public understanding of the operations or activities of the government and is not primarily in my commercial interest. [Include specific details, including how the requested information will be disseminated by the requester for public benefit.]

[Optional] I am willing to pay fees for this request up to a maximum of $ _____. If you estimate that the fees will exceed this limit, please inform me first.

[Optional] I request that the information I seek be provided in electronic format, and I would like to receive it on a personal computer disk [or a CD–ROM].

[Optional] I ask that my request receive expedited processing because _____. [Include specific details concerning your "compelling need," such as being someone "primarily engaged in disseminating information" and specifics concerning your "urgency to inform the public concerning actual or alleged Federal Government activity."]

[Optional] I also include a telephone number at which I can be contacted during the hours of _____, if necessary, to discuss any aspect of my request.

Thank you for your consideration of this request.

Sincerely,

Name, Address, City, State, Zip Code, Telephone Number

Source: U. S. Congress, COMMITTEE ON GOVERNMENT REFORM AND OVERSIGHT, A CITIZEN'S GUIDE ON USING THE FREEDOM OF IN-FORMATION ACT AND THE PRIVACY ACT OF 1974 TO REQUEST GOVERNMENT RECORDS, 105th Congress, 1st Session (1997). (genesis.gsfc.nasa.gov/foia/citzguid.htm)

The following guidelines apply to all witness interviews:

1. *Know what image you are projecting of yourself.* In the minds of many people, an investigator is often involved in serious and dangerous undertakings. How would you react if a stranger introduced himself or herself to you as an investigator? This might cause many people to be guarded and suspicious, so you may not want to call yourself an investigator. You may want to say, "My name is _____, I work for (name of law office) and we are trying to get information on _____."

| EXHIBIT 9.6 | Checklist on Assessing the Validity of Parol (Oral) Evidence |
|---|---|

**CHECKLIST TO USE IF THE WITNESS IS SPEAKING FROM FIRST-HAND (EYEWITNESS) INFORMATION**

- How long ago did it happen?
- How good is the memory of this witness?
- How far from the event was the witness at the time?
- How good is the sight of the witness?
- What time of day was it and would this affect vision?
- What was the weather at the time and would this affect vision?
- Was there a lot of commotion at the time and would this affect vision or ability to remember?
- What was the witness doing immediately before the incident?
- How old is the witness?
- What was the last grade of school he or she completed?
- What is the witness's employment background?
- What is the reputation of the witness in the community for truthfulness?
- Was the witness ever convicted of a crime? Are any criminal charges now pending against him or her?
- Does the witness have technical expertise or other qualifications relevant to what he or she is saying?
- Is the witness related to, an employee of, or friendly with either side in the litigation? Would it be to this person's benefit, in any way, to see either side win?
- Does any direct evidence exist to corroborate what this witness is saying?
- Does any hearsay evidence exist to corroborate it?
- Is the witness willing to sign a statement covering what he or she tells the investigator? Is he or she willing to say it in court?
- Is the witness defensive when asked about what he or she knows?
- Are there any inconsistencies in what the witness is saying?
- How does the witness react when confronted with the inconsistencies? Defensively?
- Are there any gaps in what the witness is saying?
- Does the witness appear to exaggerate?
- Does the witness appear to be hiding or holding anything back?

**CHECKLIST TO USE IF THE WITNESS IS SPEAKING FROM SECOND-HAND (HEARSAY) INFORMATION**

- How well does the witness remember what was told to him or her by the other person (the declarant) or what the witness heard him or her say to someone else?
- How is the witness sure that it is exact?
- Is the declarant now available to confirm or deny this hearsay account of the witness? If not, why not?
- Under what conditions did the declarant allegedly make the statement (for example, was declarant ill)?
- Is there other hearsay testimony that will help corroborate this hearsay?
- Does any direct evidence exist to corroborate this hearsay?
- How old is the witness? How old is the declarant?
- What are the educational and employment backgrounds of both?
- What is their reputation in the community for truthfulness?
- Was either ever convicted of a crime? Are any criminal charges pending against either?
- Does the witness or the declarant have technical expertise or other qualifications relevant to what was said?
- Is the witness or the declarant related to, an employee of, or friendly with either side in the litigation? Would it be to the benefit of the witness or the declarant to see either side win?
- Is the witness willing to sign a statement covering what he or she tells the investigator? Is he or she willing to say it in court?
- Is the witness defensive when asked about what he or she was told by the declarant or what he or she heard the declarant say to someone else?
- Are there any inconsistencies in what the witness is saying?
- How does the witness react when confronted with the inconsistencies? Defensively?
- Are there any gaps in what the witness is saying?
- Does the witness appear to exaggerate?
- Does the witness appear to be hiding or holding anything back?

Can you think of different people who would respond more readily to certain images of investigators? The following is a partial list of some of the images that an investigator could be projecting by dress, mannerisms, approach, and language:

- A professional
- Someone who is just doing a job

| EXHIBIT 9.7 | Checklist on the Validity of Physical (Tangible) Evidence |
|---|---|

| CHECKLIST FOR WRITTEN MATERIAL | CHECKLIST FOR NONWRITTEN MATERIAL |
|---|---|
| ■ Who wrote it?<br>■ Under what circumstances was it written?<br>■ Is the original available? If not, why not?<br>■ Is a copy available?<br>■ Who is available to testify that the copy is in fact an accurate copy of the original?<br>■ Is the author of the written material available to testify on what he or she wrote? If not, why not?<br>■ Is there any hearsay testimony available to corroborate the authenticity of the writing?<br>■ Is there any other physical evidence available to corroborate the authenticity of the writing?<br>■ What hearsay or direct evidence is available to corroborate or contradict what is said in the writing?<br>■ Can you obtain sample handwriting specimens of the alleged author?<br>■ Who found it and under what circumstances? | ■ Where was it found?<br>■ Why would it be where it was found? Was it unusual to find it there?<br>■ Who is available to identify it?<br>■ What identifying characteristics does it have?<br>■ Who owns it? Who used it?<br>■ Who owned it in the past? Who used it in the past? Who has had possession?<br>■ Who made it?<br>■ What is its purpose?<br>■ Does it require laboratory analysis?<br>■ Can you take it with you?<br>■ Can you photograph it?<br>■ Is it stolen?<br>■ Is there any public record available to trace its history?<br>■ What facts does it tend to establish?<br>■ Was it planted where it was found as a decoy? |

■ Someone who is emotionally involved in what he or she is doing
■ A neutral bystander
■ A friend
■ A manipulator or opportunist
■ A salesperson
■ A wise person
■ An innocent and shy person

You must be aware of (a) your own need to project yourself in a certain way, (b) the way in which you think you are projecting yourself, (c) the way in which the person to whom you are talking perceives you, and (d) the effect that all this is having on what you are trying to accomplish.

Here is how one paralegal, Janet Jackson, describes her approach:

> [The] basic techniques are to approach the person as a friend, make him or her feel comfortable talking, and gain his or her trust. One simple way of doing this is using the principle that people respond to their names. I address the contact by name several times throughout the interview. I also use a friendly, soft, nonthreatening, inquisitive tone of voice. The first few moments . . . are always the most difficult and the most important. Usually in these few moments the contact makes the decision whether to talk. So, a strong opening is needed. I plan, write out, and practice my opening so I can deliver it smoothly and quickly in a friendly, confident voice. . . . I say, "Hello, Mr. Jones, my name is Janet Jackson and I work for the law firm of X, Y & Z. We have been retained by the T. Company to represent them in a lawsuit brought against them by Mr. John Smith. I would like to ask you a few questions about the lawsuit. . . ." I then identify myself as a legal assistant and explain that I am collecting information. Often I have found that saying that I am a legal assistant, not an attorney, causes people to relax and let down their guard.[6]

2. *There are five kinds of witnesses: hostile, skeptical, friendly, disinterested or neutral, and a combination of the above.* Hostile witnesses want your client to lose; they will try to set up roadblocks in your way. Skeptical witnesses are not sure who you are or what you want in spite of your explanation of your role. They are guarded and unsure

whether they want to become involved. Friendly witnesses want your client to win and will cooperate fully. **Disinterested** or neutral witnesses do not care who wins. They have information that they are usually willing to tell anyone who asks. Hostile and friendly witnesses have probably prejudged the case. They may be incapable of examining all the facts dispassionately; they are already inclined to think or act in a certain way. They have a **bias**.

If the hostile witness is the opposing party who has retained counsel, it is unethical for the investigator to talk directly with this person without going through his or her attorney (see chapter 5). If the opposing party is not represented by an attorney, check with your supervisor on how, if at all, to approach this party. Never do anything to give an unrepresented party the impression that you are disinterested.

To complicate matters, it must be acknowledged that witnesses are seldom totally hostile, skeptical, friendly, or neutral. At different times during the investigation interview, and at different times throughout the various stages of the case, they may shift from one attitude to another. Although it may be helpful to determine the general category witnesses fit into, it would be more realistic to view any witness as an individual in a state of flux in terms of what he or she is capable of saying and what he or she wants to say.

3. *The investigator must have the trust of the witness.* You have the sometimes difficult threshold problem of sizing up the witness from whom you are trying to obtain information. Here are some of the states of mind that witnesses could have:

- They want to feel important.
- They want to be "congratulated" for knowing anything, however insignificant, about the case.
- They want absolute assurance from you that they will not get into trouble by talking to you. They shy away from talk of courts, lawyers, and law.
- They are willing to talk only after you have given full assurance that you will never reveal the source of the information they give you.
- They are willing to talk to you only in the presence of their friends.
- If they know your client, they want to be told that you are trying to keep the client out of trouble.
- They want the chance to meet you first and then have you go away so they can decide whether they want to talk to you again.
- They are not willing to talk to you until you fulfill some of their needs—for example, listen to their troubles or act in a fatherly or motherly manner.

In short, the investigator must gain the trust of individuals by assessing their needs and by knowing when they are ready to tell you what they know. To establish communication, sensitivity to such undercurrents is often required. The most effective approach may not be to take out your notebook immediately upon introducing yourself.

4. *The investigator must assess how well the witness would do under direct examination and cross-examination.* As witnesses talk, ask yourself a number of questions:

- Would they be willing to testify in court? Whatever the answer to this question is now, are they likely to change their minds later?
- Would they be effective on the witness stand?
- Do they know what they are talking about?
- Do they have a reputation for integrity and truthfulness in the community?
- Are they defensive?
- Would they know how to say "I'm not sure" or "I don't understand the question," as opposed to giving an answer for the sake of giving an answer or to avoid being embarrassed?
- When they talk, are they internally consistent?
- Do they know how to listen as well as talk?
- Do they understand the distinction between right and wrong, truth and lying?

**disinterested** Not working for one side or the other in a controversy; not deriving benefit if one side of a dispute wins or loses; objective.

**bias** An inclination or tendency to think and to act in a certain way. A danger of prejudgment.

## Section H
# SPECIAL INVESTIGATIVE PROBLEMS: SOME STARTING POINTS

### JUDGMENT COLLECTION

**judgment creditor** The person to whom a court-awarded money judgment (damages) is owed.

The person who wins a money judgment in court is called the **judgment creditor**. Unfortunately, collecting that judgment can be a difficult undertaking. An investigator may be asked to assist the law firm in ascertaining the financial assets of a particular individual or corporation against whom the judgment was obtained, called the **judgment debtor**.

**judgment debtor** The person ordered by a court to pay a money judgment (damages).

One of the best starting points for such an investigation is government records. The following is a partial list of records available from the county clerk or court office:

- Real property records (check grantee and grantor indexes)
- Real and personal property tax assessments
- Filings made under the Uniform Commercial Code
- Federal tax liens
- Court dockets—to determine whether the judgment debtor has been a plaintiff or defendant in prior litigation (check the abstract-of-judgment index)
- Inheritance records—to determine whether the judgment debtor has inherited money or other property (determined by checking records of the surrogate's court or probate court, which handles inheritance and trust cases)

Such records could reveal a good deal of information on the financial status of the party under investigation. You might find out whether he or she owns or has an interest in valuable personal or business property. Even though tax records often undervalue the property being taxed, they are some indication of a person's wealth. Another indication is the existence of past suits against the party. If a party has been sued in the past, someone made a determination that he or she probably had a **deep pocket** at that time, meaning sufficient assets to satisfy a judgment.

**deep pocket** An individual who has resources with which to pay a potential judgment.

For corporations that are judgment debtors, check the records of state and federal government agencies (such as the state Secretary of State and the federal Securities and Exchange Commission) with whom the corporation must file periodic reports or disclosures on its activities and finances. You should also check with people who have done business with the corporation (customers or other creditors) as well as with its competitors in the field. These records and contacts could provide good leads.

A great deal of this information is now online so that it can be searched through computers. For resources available on the World Wide Web (paid and free), see "On The Net" at the end of the chapter. Here are some of the major databases and libraries available on WESTLAW and LEXIS-NEXIS, the two largest fee-based online commercial research services.

#### Westlaw
Here, for example, are some of the databases that can be searched on WESTLAW:

**Asset Locator (ASSET).** Identifies major property holdings of a person or business including real estate, stocks, aircraft, watercraft, business equipment, and inventory.

**Executive Affiliation Records (EA–ALL)** Provides name, title, business address, and phone number of millions of executives nationwide.

**Combined Uniform Commercial Code (UCC), Liens/Civil Judgment Filings (ULJ–ALL).** Provides

information on UCC filings, liens, and civil judgments relating to businesses and individuals.

**Dun & Bradstreet Business Records Plus (DUNBR).** Provides information on a company's history, operations, and financial performance as well as intracompany relationships for 20 million companies worldwide.

**Combined Corporate & Limited Partnership Records (CORP-ALL).** Provides abstracts of corporate, limited partnership, and limited liability company filing information.

**County Records (COU).** Provides abstracts of public information such as county-level UCC filings, lien filings, deeds, general execution dockets, assumed names, trade names, judgments, lis pendens, and other local court records.

**Combined Bankruptcy Records (BKR–ALL).** Provides abstracts of filings in U.S. bankruptcy courts. Includes business filings in all 50 states and personal filings in selected states.

### Lexis–Nexis

**ASSETS (ALLTOWN).** Provides data that will allow you to discover the location and assessed value of corporate and individual real estate, locate hidden assets, find elusive parties and witnesses, determine current tax mailing addresses for service of process, assess the collectibility of judgments, and locate property for judgment lien attachment.

**Bankruptcy (INSOLV) (ALLBKT).** Provides access to current business and consumer bankruptcy petitions, dismissal and discharge data under chapters 7, 11, 12, and 13 from most districts of the U.S. bankruptcy court in all 50 states.

**Business Filings (INCORP).** Provides access to state and local business filings, including corporate registrations, limited partnership registrations, limited liability company registrations, county d/b/a filings, and professional licenses.

**Business Reports (BUSRPT) (D&BRPT).** Provides business reports from Dun & Bradstreet and Experian that will help establish company existence, identify expert witnesses, assess financial performance, ascertain client solvency, and confirm company ownership for potential conflicts of interest.

**Courts (DOCKET).** Provides information from civil and criminal

**Lawsuits (LS).** Provides abstracts of civil lawsuits filed in selected state and local courts.

**Real Property Records, Liens & Judgments (RLJ).** Provides abstracts of federal, state, and county real property liens and judgments in selected counties.

**Dow Jones–All Plus Wires (ALLNEWS–PLUS).** Provides documents from all wires, newspapers, magazines, journals, newsletters, and transcripts as provided by Dow Jones & Company, Inc.

court indices and dockets from various local and federal jurisdictions, judgments and liens, bankruptcy petitions, EPA Civil Docket, and OSHA inspection reports.

**Liens (ALLUCC) (ALLIEN).** Provides information on Uniform Commercial Code liens, state and federal tax liens, and judgments from state courts. The data contain debtor names, addresses, secured parties, assignees, and types of collateral pledged.

**License (LICNSE).** Provides information on professional licenses, liquor licenses, driver licenses, pilots, and tax practitioners. This information allows you to locate self-employed individuals, verify their license status, locate business assets, and conduct due diligence research.

**Personal Property (P–PROP).** Provides information on personal property from boat, motor vehicle, and aircraft registrations.

**Verdicts and Settlements (ALLVER).** Provides information on recent civil verdicts and settlements from the databases of the Association of Trial Lawyers of America (ATLA); National Jury Verdict Review & Analysis (NTLREV); Verdicts, Settlement & Tactics (VERST); National Law Review Annual Review (NLJVR); and Medical Litigation Alert (MDALRT).

## MISSING PERSONS

An investigator may be asked to locate a missing heir, a relative of a client, a person who must be served with process in connection with current litigation, etc. A missing person is generally not difficult to locate—unless this person does not want to be found.

John Lehe, a legal investigator, suggests that you begin with the easily available resources: telephone books, directory assistance operators, and cross-reference directories. "In contacting directory assistance operators, ask for telephone numbers for anyone with the same last name on the street of the last-known address. It is possible for relatives to live on the same street and they may be able to provide the [missing person's] current address or place of employment."[7] Local neighborhood libraries often have a telephone reference section that should be checked. Find out if they have any old telephone directories available.

Your local library may have a cross-reference directory (sometimes called a reverse or criss-cross directory). If all you have is the address of a person, you may be able to use this resource to find out who lives at that address, plus his or her surrounding neighbors.

Try sending a registered letter to the person's last-known address, "return receipt requested," which asks the post office to send you back a notice with the signature of the person who signed to receive the letter.

**skiptracing** Efforts to locate individuals, particularly debtors, and their assets.

A number of effective locator or **skiptracing** services are available online. For Internet resources, see the section on "Finding People or Businesses" in "On The Net" at the end of the chapter. The commercial databases also have powerful finding tools:

WESTLAW: **People Finder (PEOPLE)**
LEXIS–NEXIS: **FINDER (EZFIND, P-TRAK, P-FIND, B-FIND, P-SEEK)**

The Social Security Administration will not give you personal information on recipients. Knowing the person's number, however, might provide a clue. The first three digits of a social security number indicate the state in which the card was issued. For example:

| | | |
|---|---|---|
| 545–573 California | 010–034 Massachusetts | 540–544 Oregon |
| 602–626 California | 362–386 Michigan | 159–211 Pennsylvania |
| 261–267 Florida | 468–477 Minnesota | 449–467 Texas |
| 589–595 Florida | 135–158 New Jersey | 627–645 Texas |
| 318–361 Illinois | 050–134 New York | 387–399 Wisconsin |
| 212–220 Maryland | 268–302 Ohio | |

People who "disappear" sometimes return to the state where they grew up—often the state where they obtained their social security card.

Other possible sources of information:

- Relatives and friends
- Former landlord, neighbors, mail carrier, and local merchants in the area of the last-known address
- Professional associations such as unions and other job-related groups (people often retain membership in local chapters as they move around the country)
- Local credit bureau
- Police department, hospitals
- References listed on employment applications
- Naturalization certificate, marriage record, driver's license, car registration
- Newspaper indexes (central and university libraries often keep such indexes; check obituary columns, local interest stories, etc.)

## BACKGROUND INVESTIGATIONS

Exhibit 9.8 presents a form used by a large investigative firm for its general background investigations on individuals. The first part of the form seeks information regarding identification of the subject. The antecedent data cover prior history.

| EXHIBIT 9.8 | Background Investigations |
|---|---|

## Identification of Subject

**1.** Complete Name _____ Age _____ SS# _____ Marital Status _____
Spouse's Name; Pertinent Info _____

Children's Names and Ages _____

**2.** Current Residence Address and Type of Neighborhood _____

How Long at Present Address—Prior Residence Info _____

**3.** Business Affiliation and Address, Position, Type of Bus. _____

## Antecedent History

**1.** Place & Date of Birth _____
Parents' Names & Occupations _____

Where Did They Spend Their Youth? _____

**2.** Education—Where, Which Schools, Dates of Attendance

Degree? What Kind? _____ Any Other Info Pertaining to Scholastic Achievement, Extracurric.
Activities _____

**3.** First Employer, to Present—F/T or P/T, Position or Title, Job Description, Exact Dates of Employment, Type
of Company _____

**4.** Relationship with Peers, Supervisors, Subordinates—Where Do Subj.'s Abilities Lie? Any Outside Activities?
Reputation for Honesty, Trustworthiness, Integrity? Does Subj. Work Well under Pressure? Anything
Derogatory? Reasons for Leaving? Would They Rehire? Salaries? Health? Reliability? Job Understanding?
Willingness to Accept Responsibility? _____

If Self-Employed—What Was the Nature of the Business? With Whom Did Subj. Deal? Corp. Name?

Date & Place of Incorporation _____
Who Were Partners, If Any? _____
What % of Stock Did Subj. Own? _____ Was Business Successful? _____ What Happened to it? _____
If Sold, to Whom? _____
Any Subsid. or Affiliates? _____

| EXHIBIT 9.8 | Background Investigations—*continued* |
|---|---|

**5.** What is Subj.'s Character or Personality Like? Did Informer Know Subj. Personally?

_____

Hobbies? _____

Family Life? _____

Even-Tempered? _____ Loner or Joiner? _____

Introverted, Extroverted? _____ Written or Oral Abilities? _____

Does Informer Know Anyone Else Who Knows Subj.? _____

_____

**6.** Credit Information _____

_____

_____

**7.** Subj.'s Involvement in Litigation _____ Civil _____ Criminal _____ Bankruptcy _____

State _____ Federal _____ Local _____

_____

_____

**8.** Banking—Financial: Bank _____

Types of Accounts—Average Bal. _____

How Long Did Subj. Have Accounts? _____ Any Company Accounts? _____

_____

Is Subj. Personally Known to Officers of the Bank? _____ Any Borrowing? _____

Secured or Unsecured? _____ If Secured, by What? _____

Do They Have Financial Statement on the Subj.? _____

What Is Net Worth of Subj.? _____ Other Assets? Real Estate _____

Stocks _____

Equity in Subj.'s Co., etc. _____

## AUTOMOBILE ACCIDENTS

### *Auto Accident Analysis*

**by Dale W. Felton 27 Trial Magazine 60 (February 1991)[8]**

Accidents don't just happen. Except in instances of mechanical failure or acts of God, vehicle collisions occur because of driver negligence. If a collision is properly investigated and analyzed, who was at fault can usually be determined. If the analysis reveals the defendant was negligent, demonstrative evidence can be used to show jurors how the defendant's negligence caused the collision.

Every law office handling vehicle-accident cases would benefit from learning effective methods of investigation and accident analysis. Many of these cases could be settled if insurance adjusters were shown definitive or scientific facts demonstrating that fault lies with the [defendant] insured and not with the plaintiff. Insurance adjusters—like jurors—are receptive to scientific analysis of liability. . . .

An analysis of negligence should not be attempted without first conducting a thorough investigation. It is important to investigate as quickly as possible. Accident scenes change, and witnesses move. Of course, you often do not get a case until months after the accident occurred. Even then, the investigation should be started immediately. Bits of evidence and many helpful facts may still be available.

#### Reports

Begin the investigation by getting a complete statement of facts from the client. Then, get a police report of the collision. [See exhibit 9.3.] This report will include the officer's estimate of the damage to each vehicle as well as the location of the damage. Often the report will list names, addresses, and telephone numbers of the witnesses and usually the statements that each party gave to the officer at the scene. The report will also show who was ticketed and why. Reports often include a sketch of the accident scene as well as the officer's analysis of the factors contributing to the collision.

Sometimes, however, these drawings may be inaccurate. The officer's analysis of contributing factors may not make sense. In fact, in most instances where an insurance company denies liability, it is because an investigating officer indicated that the plaintiff was in some way at fault. Here the law office must prove that the police officer's analysis was not correct.

In serious collisions, investigating police officers will often keep notes, take photographs, and make a scale drawing of the scene. You can obtain these by subpoena.

After obtaining a police report, take witness statements, being careful that each statement includes all facts the witness knows. [See exhibit 9.9.] The vehicles involved and the accident scene should be photographed as soon as possible because vehicles may be repaired quickly and accident scenes may change due to construction, resurfacing, installation of traffic control devices, etc. A full investigation also includes taking appropriate measurements and determining the point of impact from physical evidence at the scene, the police report, and the witness statements.

## Photographs

Law offices should own and know how to use a [good quality] camera, even if they employ full-time investigators or photographers. Many times, if you wait for someone else to take a photograph, the accident scene will have changed.

Know what photographs you need and make sure that the proper ones are taken. The only way to be sure to get the *right* photograph is to ensure that plenty are taken. The late Axel Hanson, one of the greatest investigators who ever lived, once said that he took 211 photographs of a vehicle involved in a fatality, and *one* proved to be the key to liability.

Photographers should move around the vehicle in a circle, taking photographs "every five minutes on the hands of a clock." Photographers should also take close-ups of damaged areas and use a flash to ensure that shadows do not obscure these areas.

Photographers should take shots from beneath the damaged part of the vehicle, an area that will often reveal the severity of the impact. Photographs taken while focusing straight down on the damaged area are needed because they will reveal the angle of impact. Photographers should carry ladders or, if they are allowed to, stand on the vehicle itself to get these shots. Downward shots of the vehicle involved in a collision can be matched to illustrate the angle at which the vehicles collided.

The photographer should also take pictures of any internal damage to the vehicle, including the speedometer and seats. In a rear-end collision the seats will often be bent backward or broken off at the frames. Jurors can readily understand that an impact

strong enough to break seats would be severe enough to injure a human being.

A 50 mm lens best approximates the view as seen by the human eye. To illustrate what each driver saw, photographers should work from as far back as 1,000 feet from the point of collision. (If drivers did not travel 1,000 feet on the road in question before impact, photos should be taken starting from the point where each driver entered the roadway.) Photographs should be taken every 100 feet until 300 feet from the collision site; then every 50 feet until 100 feet from the point of impact; then every 25 feet to the point of impact. Only in this way can photographs show what the driver of each vehicle could see when approaching the collision site.

In photographing a crash scene, the photographer should obtain the same types of vehicles that were in the actual accident from a used-car lot or car dealership. Measurements should be made to determine driver's-eye height. Photographers can set tripods at this height to take approach shots. If a bus or truck is involved, it will be necessary to measure driver's-eye height in the same type of vehicle. In these instances, photographers must use ladders to get eye-height shots of what the drivers could see as they approached the collision site. A foot or two can make a world of difference in what a driver can see. These photographs should show any obstructions to a driver's view.

Photographs should also be taken of all road signs, not only to show their wording but also to show their location. At the point of impact, photos should be taken of gouge marks, scrapes, and any other damage the vehicles caused to the road surface or surrounding area. Both distance and close-up shots should be taken to pinpoint the damage. For close-up shots, it is often advisable to include a ruler or a pencil in order to indicate the scale.

## Light Bulbs

Examining the light bulbs near a vehicle's damaged area will reveal whether they were operating at the time of the crash. During a collision, a heated light filament will stretch or break, while an inoperative cool filament will not. A bulb with a stretched or broken filament can easily be compared with a new bulb to show whether the bulb in question was functioning at the time of the collision. This principle applies to tail lights; brake lights; to turn indicators (front back, or side); and to headlights.

The person examining the vehicles should *always* consider whether lighting could have been a factor in the collision and, if so, examine the appropriate bulbs. For example, in all rear-end collisions at night, tail lights are a factor. Brake lights and turn signals

## Auto Accident Analysis—continued

may be factors day or night. If bulbs figured in the crash, they should be removed by an investigator and retained. It may be many months before the plaintiff's lawyer learns that the defendant is claiming that the plaintiff did not have the appropriate lights on or failed to give a turn signal.

Photographers should document the removal of bulbs, which should be placed in a padded, labeled box. It is important to indicate the vehicle they came from, their location on the vehicle, the person who removed them, and the date and time of removal. In *Golleher v. Herrera*, the court ruled that to introduce expert testimony concerning whether a vehicle's light bulb was functioning at the time of a collision, not only must the bulb be put into evidence but there must also be testimony that the bulb was the one that came from a particular location on one vehicle in the collision. 651 S.W. 2d 329, 333–34 (Tex. Ct. App. 1983).

### Skid Marks

Careful measurements of all skid marks at the scene are essential.* Before measuring them, the investigator should ensure that the skid marks were laid down in the collision in question. To avoid measuring the wrong marks, it is best to have someone who can definitely identify the marks—the client, a witness, or an ambulance driver—at the scene for the investigation. Of course, this also applies for measuring gouges, scrapes, and other physical damage at the accident site. Formulas can be used to determine the minimum speed of the vehicle before the driver applied the brakes.

*Straight-skid speed formula.* Often a vehicle traveling at a high rate of speed leaves only a few feet of skid marks because the brakes were not applied until the instant before impact. In those instances, determining the speed from skid marks may not be possible. But where skid marks were laid down over a long distance, the straight-skid speed formula may reveal that the colliding vehicle was traveling at excessive speed.

*Yaw mark formula.* A yaw mark is left on a road surface by the sideward motion of a tire when the driver turned the wheel sharply, usually to avoid a collision or to take a curve at excessive speed. A yaw mark will reveal the speed at the time the vehicle made the mark. A yaw mark should not be confused with a skid mark. It is a scuff mark made while the tire is rotating. It is easily identified by striations left on the roadway by the tire sidewall.

*Flip-vault formula.* If an object was thrown from either vehicle because of the impact, the investigator can calculate the minimum speed of the colliding vehicle if the exact point of impact of the vehicles and the exact point where the item first contacted the ground are known. The calculation is done using the flip-vault formula. Therefore, when examining the scene, the investigator should look for anything that may have been thrown from either vehicle.

For example, if a toolbox was thrown from the back of a truck and it can be determined exactly where it hit the ground, applying the flip-vault formula can determine the speed of the colliding vehicle at impact. In one case, a screwdriver with the driver's name taped to the handle was thrown from the colliding vehicle, and the screwdriver stuck blade-first into the ground many feet away from where the vehicles collided. The investigator applied the flip-vault formula to determine speed.

*Fall formula.* Investigators can use the fall formula to determine the speed of a vehicle that ran off an embankment. The investigator must measure the horizontal distance that the vehicle traveled before hitting the ground and then measure the vertical distance that the vehicle dropped. This formula can be helpful in proving whether a vehicle that went off an embankment was speeding.

### Drag Factor

Investigators cannot determine speed from skid marks or yaw marks unless they know the drag factor of the roadway. The drag factor is the coefficient-of-friction, plus or minus grade. It is that percentage of the weight of an object that is required to push or pull it along a surface. The grade takes into account whether or not the object was going uphill or downhill.

To determine speed from skid marks, investigators must measure the drag factor accurately. Many books and other publications give drag-factor ranges for dry concrete, wet concrete, dry asphalt, wet asphalt, gravel and ice.‡ These ranges are best used only to get a general idea of what might be expected for each surface. The drag factor can vary greatly, even on the same roadway. Speed from skid marks or a yaw mark can only be determined by conducting a

---

* J. Baker, *Traffic Accident Investigation Manual* 216–27 (1975).

‡ L. Fricke, *Traffic Accident Reconstruction* 62–14 (1990); "How to Use the Traffic Template and Calculator," Traffic Institute North-western University, at 19 (1984); R. Rivers, *Traffic Accident Investigators' Handbook* 157 (1980).

drag-factor test at the specific point where the marks were made. Just as important, the test must be conducted in the same direction that the vehicle was traveling to take into account the plus or minus grade.

## Measurements and Scale Drawings

In examining a collision scene, the investigator should take all measurements relative to a fixed reference point located close to the point of impact like a telephone pole or a corner of a building. The best method is to use a north-south, east-west grid and locate each distance measured north, south, east, or west of the reference point. Using this method, investigators can make an infinite number of measurements and plot each point on a scale drawing of the scene. Triangulation could also be used in measuring a scene, but it requires many times the number of measurement and is much more time-consuming. However, where the roadway is curved, roadway edges are uneven, or an object some distance off the roadway must be pinpointed, triangulation is the only method that will work. The grid method is simplest for most situations.

Besides the obvious distances that must be measured—such as the width of each roadway and the location of all traffic signs—the exact locations of any buildings or obstructions to clear view between the vehicles should be precisely determined.

A 1 : 20 scale is one scale to use for drawings in almost all these cases. The drawing helps in performing a time and distance analysis, as well as in seeing the entire collision process on paper. Along with minimum speed calculations, a scale drawing of the accident scene can be persuasive when presented to an insurance adjuster. If the case does not settle, a scale drawing can be used to prove a plaintiff's case at trial.

## Time and Distance Analysis

Once the investigation is complete and a scale drawing made, the collision can be analyzed.

Time and distance must be taken into account in every collision or vehicle-pedestrian accident. Every moving mass is traveling at a certain speed that converts to either miles per hour or feet per second. To determine the feet per second a vehicle was traveling, multiply miles per hour times 1.47. If you convert miles per hour to feet per second, you can work backward from the point of impact and place the vehicles at the various points on the scale drawing for each second or even one-tenth of a second before the collision occurred. With the scale drawing and the locations of each vehicle at different intervals before impact, you can see the view each driver had of the

scene and of each other, determine to what extent speed of each driver was a factor, and determine what action or actions could have been taken by either driver to avoid a collision.

Of course, the miles-per-hour figure may come from the testimony of the driver. In many instances, a defendant driver will say in deposition that the vehicle was going at a slower rate of speed than it actually was. The statement may hurt the defense because at the lower speed the defendant would have had more time to see plaintiff's vehicle and come to a stop or turn in order to avoid a collision.

Time and distance can also be used to refute contributory negligence on the part of the plaintiff. For example where the defendant pulled out in front of the plaintiff or made a left turn into the plaintiff's path, time and distance calculations can be used to show that the legal speed at which the plaintiff was traveling did not allow stopping before colliding with the defendant. In many instances, taking into account the judicially accepted three-quarters-of-a-second reaction time will show that the plaintiff did not even have time to apply the brakes.

A time and distance analysis is especially helpful in pedestrian cases. Pedestrians have a normal walking speed of about three miles per hour. At this speed it takes several seconds to walk just a few steps. It can usually be shown that in those several seconds the driver had more than ample time to avoid striking the pedestrian.

The flip-vault formula can also be applied in pedestrian cases. If the point of impact and the point where a pedestrian hit the ground after impact are known, the speed of the striking vehicle can be determined. Often, doing a time and distance analysis and applying the flip-vault formula will clearly demonstrate a driver's fault.

## Determining Negligence (See Examples on pages 390–91.)

In Example 1, the driver (S) was traveling at a speed (25 mph) that was safe for the circumstances (an uncontrolled intersection ahead with a view obstruction on the right). The driver looked to the right and as soon as an approaching vehicle (T) was observed, applied the brakes and yielded the right-of-way.

In Example 2, the driver (S) was traveling at a speed too great for existing conditions. At 35 miles per hour; even though the driver maintained a proper lookout and saw the approaching vehicle (T), he could not stop in time to avoid colliding with it.

In Example 3, the driver (S) was traveling at a safe speed (25 mph) but was not looking to see if a

## Auto Accident Analysis—*continued*

vehicle was approaching from the right. By the time she saw the approaching vehicle (T), it was too late. Failure to keep a proper lookout was the cause of the collision.

In Example 4, the driver (S) was traveling at a speed (25 mph) that was safe for conditions and kept a proper lookout. However, he chose the wrong evasive tactic. The driver tried to turn left in front of the approaching vehicle (T) rather than apply the brakes and yield the right-of-way to the vehicle.

In Example 5, the driver (S) was traveling at a safe speed (25 mph), kept a proper lookout, but did nothing to avoid the collision. She simply failed to apply the brakes.

Example 6 shows a combination of errors. The driver (S) was traveling at a greater speed (35 mph) than existing conditions permitted and failed to keep a proper lookout.

A similar analysis on your scale drawing will clearly illustrate to an insurance adjuster, a defense lawyer, and—if those two are hardheaded—a jury, precisely what the defendant did wrong. After seeing and understanding this type of accident analysis, jurors are less likely to fall for the defendant who testifies, "I don't know where he came from. He just came out of nowhere."

What about a rear-end collision? Where the rear-ended vehicle is stopped, the colliding driver may have been negligent in speed, lookout, or brakes application. But what about a rear-end collision that occurs as two cars are traveling down a roadway at about the same speed and the first car has to stop for some unexpected reason?

Alleging that speed caused the collision is faulty, because the first driver was traveling at the same rate of speed as the second. If the second driver testifies that the instant he saw the first driver's brake lights come on he slammed on his brakes, he is probably telling the truth. Usually this type of rear-end collision is not the result of negligent speed, lookout, or brakes application. It is the result of following too closely.

### Analysis Works

Accident analysis really works, but it will not work unless law offices put their best efforts into it. If they ensure that a proper investigation is done and perform an accident analysis in each case, the results will be rewarding.

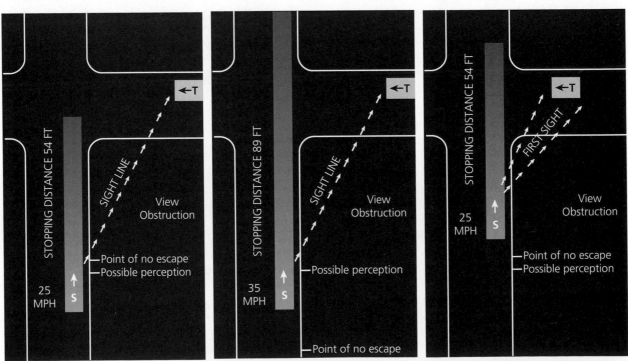

Example 1: Safe                    Example 2: Too Fast                    Example 3: Delayed Perception

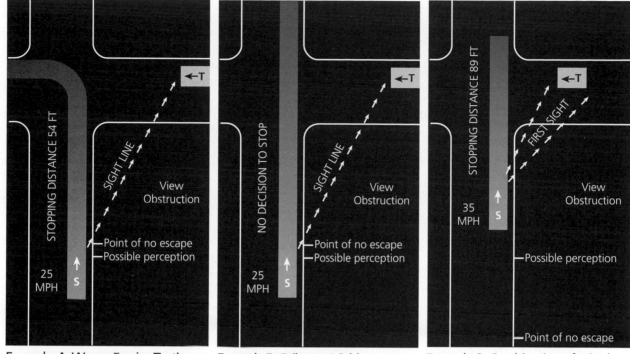

Example 4: Wrong Evasive Tactic        Example 5: Failure to Yield        Example 6: Combination of Mistakes

### Assignment 9.1

Which of the following statements do you agree or disagree with? Why? How would you modify the statements you disagree with to reflect your own view?

**(a)** There is a great difference between investigation conducted by the police and that conducted by a paralegal working for a law office.

**(b)** An investigator is an advocate.

**(c)** It is impossible for the investigator to keep from showing his or her own personal biases while in the field investigating.

**(d)** There is often a need for a separate investigation to verify the work of another investigation.

**(e)** A good investigator will probably be unable to describe why he or she is effective. There are too many intangibles involved.

**(f)** It is a good idea for an investigator to specialize in one area of the law, such as automobile negligence cases.

**(g)** If someone is willing to talk to and cooperate with an investigator, there is reason to suspect that this person has a bias.

### Assignment 9.2

If you were Tom in each of the following situations, what specific things would you do to deal with the situation?

**(a)** Tom teaches a second-grade class. It is the end of the school day on Friday and the bus is in front of the school ready to take his class home. If the students are not out in time for the bus, it will leave without them. It is 2 : 50 P.M., and the bus is scheduled to leave at 3 : 05 P.M. Tom discovers that his briefcase is missing from the top of his desk.

**(b)** Tom is the father of two teenagers, Ed and Bill. He comes home one day and finds a small package of marijuana in the front hall. He immediately suspects that Ed or Bill left it there. He turns around and goes out to look for them.

**(c)** Tom's son, Bill, has been accused of using abusive language in front of his teacher. Tom calls the teacher, who refuses to talk about it. The teacher refers

Tom to the principal. The principal refuses to talk about it and refers Tom to the assistant superintendent at the central office.

(d) Tom's sister is ill. She received a letter from a local merchant where she often buys goods on credit. The letter informs her that she owes $122.00 and that unless she pays within a week "legal proceedings will be instituted" against her. She calls Tom and tells him that she paid the bill by sending $122.00 in cash last week. She asks Tom to help her.

(e) Tom works for a local legal service office. The office has a client who wants to sue her landlord because the kitchen roof is falling down. Tom is assigned to the case.

(f) Sam owes Tom $50,000. When Tom asks for his money, Sam tells him that he is broke. Tom suspects differently.

(g) Tom's uncle once lived in Boston. After spending two years in the army, he started traveling across the country; he has not been heard from for five years. Tom wants to locate his uncle.

(h) A welfare department has told a client that it is going to terminate public assistance because the client's boyfriend is supporting her and her family. The client denies this. Tom is assigned to the case.

(i) A client has been to the office seeking help in obtaining custody of his children from their mother (to whom he is not married). He claims that she is not taking proper care of the children. Tom is assigned to the case.

---

*Assignment 9.3*

Using the suggestions covered in the chapter thus far, as well as the Internet resources listed in "On The Net" at the end of the chapter, how would you find the following information?

(a) The average life span of a lobster.
(b) The maiden name of the wife of the first governor of your state.
(c) The assessed property tax value of the tallest commercial building in your city in 1980.
(d) The weather in your state capital at noon on January 1 of last year.
(e) The number of vehicles using diesel fuel that drove in or through the state last month.
(f) The salary of the air traffic controller with the most seniority on duty on the day last year when the nearest airport experienced the largest rainfall of the year.

---

**Note on the Need for a License**

In some states, investigators must be licensed. What about paralegals who are assigned investigation tasks by their supervising attorneys? A literal reading of the licensing statute might lead to the conclusion that such paralegals must be licensed along with traditional, self-employed private investigators. Often, however, the legislature will make an exception to the licensing requirement for employees of attorneys who engage in investigation under the attorney's supervision. Paralegal associations have been successful in seeking these exemptions for paralegals. The main opposition to such exemptions has come from organizations of private investigators, who allegedly seek to impose roadblocks to paralegal investigation in order to secure more business for themselves.

---

Section I
# Evidence and Investigation

## INTRODUCTION

We turn now to a closer look at the relationship between investigation and the law of evidence. The major goal of investigation is to uncover and verify facts that will be admissible in court. Admissibility is determined by the law of evidence.

During a trial, each party attempts to establish its version of the facts. There are four main ways that this can be done:

- Admission
- Judicial notice
- Presumption
- Evidence

### Admission

Paula sues Dan for negligence following an automobile accident. Paula claims that Dan has prescription eyeglasses and that he was not wearing them at the time of the accident. Before the trial, Dan concedes that he has glasses but denies that he was not wearing them at the time of the accident. Dan's statement that he needs glasses is an **admission**—a voluntary acknowledgment of a fact that an opponent wants to prove. One of the ways in which such acknowledgments are made during discovery is through a *request for admission*. As we have seen, this is a discovery device that asks a party to affirm or deny the truth of a particular fact. Those admitted as true do not have to be proven in the trial. A less formal way to accomplish the same result is by **stipulation,** which is simply an agreement between the parties about a particular matter. For example, the parties can stipulate that there were no passengers in Dan's car at the time of the accident. (We will return to the topic of admission later when we discuss admission by a party opponent as an exception to the hearsay rule.)

### Judicial Notice

Some facts are so well accepted that the court can acknowledge them—i.e., take **judicial notice** of them—without requiring either party to prove those facts. An example is that water freezes at 32 degrees Fahrenheit or that there are 31 days in July.

### Presumption

A **presumption** is an assumption or inference that a certain fact is true once another fact is established. If a party proves that fact A exists, then fact B is established. For example, proof that a person has disappeared for seven years raises the presumption that he or she is dead. Also, proof that a letter was properly addressed and mailed raises the presumption that the addressee received it. Most presumptions are **rebuttable**, meaning that evidence to the contrary can be introduced. Because the presumption of death is rebuttable, for example, a court would accept evidence that someone using the missing person's social security number applied for a job in another state eight years after the disappearance. If the court will not consider evidence to the contrary, the presumption is **irrebuttable**. Presumptions that are irrebuttable pertain more to conclusions of law than to facts. For example, a child under seven years of age is presumed to be incapable of committing a crime. This is a conclusive presumption. Evidence that a six-year-old child has the intelligence of a teenager, therefore, would not be admitted.

### Evidence

Most facts are established by the introduction of evidence without the aid of admissions, judicial notice, or presumptions.

## EVIDENCE IN GENERAL

Evidence is anything that tends to prove or disprove a fact. **Admissible evidence** is evidence that the judge will permit the jury to consider. Admissible evidence does not mean that the evidence is true. It simply means that there are no valid objections to keep the evidence out. The jury is free to conclude that it does not believe the evidence that the judge ruled admissible. Two important categories of evidence can be admissable:

**Direct evidence** is evidence (based on personal observation or knowledge) that tends to establish a fact (or to disprove a fact) without the need for an inference.

**Circumstantial evidence** is evidence of one fact (not based on personal knowledge or observation) from which another fact can be inferred.

---

**admission** A voluntary acknowledgment of a fact that an opponent wants to prove.

**stipulation** An agreement between opposing parties about a particular matter.

**judicial notice** A court's acceptance of a well-known fact without requiring proof of that fact.

**presumption** An assumption or inference that a certain fact is true once another fact is established.

**rebuttable** Not conclusive; evidence to the contrary is admissible.

**irrebuttable** Conclusive; evidence to the contrary is inadmissible.

**admissible evidence** Evidence that the court will allow the trier of fact (usually the jury) to consider.

**direct evidence** Evidence (based on personal knowledge or observation) that tends to establish a fact (or to disprove a fact) without the need for an inference.

**circumstantial evidence** Evidence of one fact (not based on personal knowledge or observation) from which another fact can be inferred.

**Example:** The police officer says, "I saw skid marks at the scene of the accident." This statement is:

| Direct evidence | ■ that the police officer spoke these words. |
| | ■ that skid marks were at the scene of the accident. |
| Circumstantial evidence | ■ that the driver of the car was speeding (this is the inference that can be drawn from the officer's statement). |

Examples of *direct* evidence that someone was speeding would be an admission by the driver that he or she was speeding, radar results, and testimony of people who saw the car being driven.

### Investigation Guideline:

Direct evidence is preferred over circumstantial, although both kinds of evidence may be admissible. Identify the inference in the circumstantial evidence. Then try to find direct evidence of whatever was inferred.

## RELEVANCE

**relevant evidence** Evidence that has a reasonable relationship to the truth or falsity of a fact.

**Relevant evidence** is evidence that has a reasonable relationship to the truth or falsity of a fact. Phrased another way, evidence is relevant when it reasonably tends to make the existence of a fact more probable or less probable than it would be without that evidence. Relevancy is a very broad concept. It simply means that the evidence *may* be helpful in determining the truth or falsity of a fact involved in a trial. The test of relevancy is common sense and logic. If, for example, you want to know whether a walkway is dangerous, it is relevant that people have slipped on this walkway in the immediate past. Prior accidents under the same conditions make it more reasonable for someone to conclude that there is danger.

All relevant evidence is not necessarily admissible evidence, however. It would be highly relevant, for example, to know that the defendant told his attorney he was driving 80 m.p.h. at the time of the accident, yet the attorney-client privilege would make such a statement inadmissible. Also, relevant evidence is not necessarily conclusive evidence. The jury will usually be free to reject relevant evidence it does not believe. Relevancy is simply a *tendency* of evidence to establish or disestablish a fact. It may be a very weak tendency. Prior accidents may be relevant to show danger, but the jury may still conclude, in the light of all the evidence, that there was no danger.

### Investigation Guideline:

Let common sense be your main guide in pursuing relevant evidence. So long as there is some logical connection between the fact you are pursuing and a fact that must be established at trial, you are on the right track.

---

### Assignment 9.4

Examine the following four situations. Discuss the relevance of each item of evidence being introduced.

(a) Mrs. Phillips is being sued by a department store for the cost of a gas refrigerator. Mrs. Phillips claims that she never ordered and never received a refrigerator from the store. The attorney for Mrs. Phillips wants to introduce two letters: (1) a letter from Mrs. Phillips's landlord stating that her kitchen is not equipped to handle gas appliances and (2) a letter from another merchant stating that Mrs. Phillips bought an electric refrigerator from him a year ago.

(b) Phil Smith has been charged with burglary in Detroit on December 16, 1999. His attorney tries to introduce testimony into evidence that on December 7, 8, 11, 15, and 22, 1999, the defendant was in Florida.

(c) Al Neuman is suing Sam Snow for negligence in operating his motor vehicle. Al's attorney tries to introduce into evidence the fact that Snow currently has pending against him four other automobile negligence cases in other courts.

(d) Jim is on trial for the rape of Sandra. Jim's attorney wants to introduce into evidence (1) the fact that Sandra subscribes to *Cosmopolitan* magazine, (2) the fact that Sandra is a member of AA, and (3) the fact that Sandra is the mother of Jim's child, who was born three years ago when they were dating. They separated in bitterness five months after the birth and never married.

## COMPETENCE OF WITNESSES

A witness is **competent** to testify if the witness:

- understands the obligation to tell the truth,
- has the ability to communicate, and
- has knowledge of the topic of his or her testimony.

Children or mentally ill persons are not automatically disqualified. They are competent to testify if the judge is satisfied that the above criteria are met.

The competence of a witness must be carefully distinguished from the credibility of the witness. Once a court rules that a witness is competent, he or she is allowed to give testimony; competency is simply a ticket into the trial. The actual impact of the evidence given by a witness depends on the **credibility** or believability of the witness. Credibility goes to the *weight* of the evidence. This weight is assessed by the trier of fact—usually the jury. Competence goes to whether that witness will be allowed to testify at all, a decision made by the judge. The jury may decide that everything said by a competent witness has little weight and therefore is unworthy of belief.

## LAY OPINION EVIDENCE

An **opinion** is an inference from a fact. For example, after you watch George stagger down the street and smell alcohol on his breath, you come to the conclusion that he is drunk. The conclusion is the inference. The facts are the observation of staggering and the smell of alcohol on his breath. Technically, a lay witness should not give opinion evidence. He or she must state the facts and let the trier of fact form the opinions. (Under certain circumstances, expert witnesses *are* allowed to give opinions on technical subjects not within the understanding of the average layperson.) The problem with the lay opinion rule, however, is that it is sometimes difficult to express oneself without using opinions, as when a witness says it was a sunny day or the noise was loud. Courts are therefore lenient in permitting opinion testimony by lay witnesses when the witness is talking from his or her own observations and it would be awkward for the witness not to express the opinion. If people regularly use opinions when discussing the topic in question, it will be permitted.

> **Investigation Guideline:**
> Know when a person is stating an opinion. Even though an opinion may be admissible, you should assume that it will *not* be admissible. Pursue all of the underlying facts that support the inference in the opinion. In the event that the person is not allowed to testify by using the opinion, be prepared by having admissible evidence of the underlying facts the person relied on for the opinion.

---

*Assignment 9.5*

Make a list of the questions that you would ask in order to uncover the underlying facts that formed the basis of the following opinions:

(a) He was insane.
(b) She couldn't see.
(c) It was cold out.
(d) He was traveling very fast.

---

## HEARSAY

**Hearsay** is an out-of-court statement offered to prove the truth of the matter asserted in the statement.[9] There are four conditions to the existence of hearsay: (1) a witness in court gives testimony, (2) about a statement made out of court by a person (called the declarant), (3) in order to establish the truth of the matter in the statement, (4) so that

---

**competent** Allowed to give testimony because the person understands the obligation to tell the truth, has the ability to communicate, and has knowledge of the topic of his or her testimony. (See glossary for another meaning of competent.)

**credibility** The extent to which something is believable.

**opinion** An inference from a fact. (See glossary for other meanings of opinion.)

**hearsay** An out-of-court statement offered to prove the truth of the matter asserted in the statement.

the value of the statement depends on the credibility of the declarant.[10] If evidence is hearsay, it is inadmissible unless one of the exceptions to the hearsay rule applies.

**Example:** Sam, a witness in court, says, "Fred told me on Elm Street that he was speeding."

Note the four conditions for the presence of hearsay:

| | |
|---|---|
| *Testimony in court* | The witness, Sam, is on the stand. |
| *Statement made out of court* | The statement by Fred (the declarant) was made on Elm Street, not in court. |
| *Offered to assert the truth of the matter in the statement* | Assume that the purpose of the attorney questioning Sam is to show that Fred was speeding—that is, that the statement is true. |
| *The value of the statement depends on the credibility of the out-of-court declarant* | Fred is the out-of-court declarant. The value of the statement depends on how believable or credible Fred is. |

If the statement is not offered to prove the truth of the matter asserted in the statement, it is not hearsay. Suppose, for example, that the attorney wants to prove that Fred was alive immediately after the accident—that death was not instantaneous. The above statement would be admitted to prove that Fred actually said something, i.e., that Fred was alive enough to make a statement. If the testimony of the witness is offered to prove simply that the words were spoken by Fred rather than to prove that Fred was speeding, then the statement is not hearsay. The testimony that "Fred told me on Elm Street that he was speeding" would therefore be admissible. The jury would have to be cautioned to examine the testimony for the limited purpose for which it is offered and not to consider it evidence that Fred was speeding.

Conduct intended as a substitute for words (called assertive conduct) can also be hearsay. For example, the witness is asked "What did Fred say when you asked him if he was speeding?" The witness answers, "He nodded his head yes." This testimony is hearsay if it is offered to prove that Fred was speeding. Conduct—nodding the head—was intended as a substitute for words.

**Investigation Guideline:**
Know when hearsay exists so that you can try to find alternative, nonhearsay evidence to prove the truth of the assertions made in the hearsay. See also the second column of exhibit 9.6 for a checklist on assessing the validity of hearsay evidence.

---

### Assignment 9.6

Is hearsay evidence involved in the following situations? Examine the four conditions of hearsay in each.

**(a)** Tom is suing Jim for negligence. On the witness stand, Tom says, "Jim was speeding at the time he hit me."

**(b)** Tom is suing Jim for negligence. While Tom is on the stand, his attorney introduces into evidence a mechanic's bill showing that the repair of the car cost $178.

**(c)** Mary and George were passengers in Tom's car at the time of the collision with Jim. George testifies that just before the collision, Mary shouted, "Look out for that car going through the red light!"

**(d)** He told me he was God.

---

There are a number of exceptions to the hearsay rule that have the effect of making evidence admissible even though it fulfills all the conditions of hearsay. Here are some examples:

1. *Admission by Party Opponent.* An admission by a party opponent is an earlier statement by a party that is now offered in court by an opponent. Example: Mary sues Sam for negligence. While Mary is presenting her case, she introduces a statement that Sam made to Paul in which Sam said, "I screwed up big time." This statement is admissible as an admission by a party opponent—Sam. (Note, however, that many states and the federal rules declare such statements by party opponents to

be admissible because they are nonhearsay rather than as an exception to the hearsay rule.)

2. *Statement against Self-Interest.* A statement against self-interest is an out-of-court statement, made by a nonparty (who is now unavailable as a witness) that was against the financial interest of the declarant at the time it was made. Example: A nonparty tells a friend at a ball game, "I still owe the bank the money."

3. *Dying Declaration.* A dying declaration is an out-of-court statement concerning the causes or circumstances of death made by a person whose death is imminent. Example: Tom dies two minutes after he was hit over the head. Seconds before he dies, he says, "Linda did it." Many states limit the dying-declaration exception to criminal cases. Some states, however, would also allow it to be used in a civil case, such as in a civil battery or wrongful death case against Linda.

4. *Excited Utterance.* An excited utterance is an out-of-court statement relating to a startling event or condition made while the declarant was under the stress of excitement caused by the event or condition. Example: Fred says, "I heard John say, 'Oh my God, the truck just hit a child.' "

5. *Statement of Present Sense Impression.* A statement of present sense impression is an out-of-court statement describing or explaining an event or condition made while the declarant was perceiving the event or condition or immediately thereafter. Example: Janice says, "As the car turned the corner, a bystander turned to me and said, 'That car will never make it.' "

6. *Statement of Existing Physical or Mental Condition.* A statement of existing physical or mental condition is an out-of-court statement of a then-existing physical or mental condition. Example: Bob says, "A second before Sheila fell, she said to me, 'I feel dizzy.' "

7. *Declaration of Existing State of Mind.* A declaration of existing state of mind is an out-of-court statement made about the person's present state of mind. Example: Len says, "The manager said she knows about the broken railing and will fix it."

8. *Business Record.* A business record is a record kept in the course of a regularly conducted business activity. This also applies to nonprofit organizations such as universities. Example: A hospital record containing a description of a patient's condition upon entering the emergency room.

---

### Assignment 9.7

Smith is being sued for assaulting Jones, who later died. Smith is on the stand when the following exchange occurs.

*Counsel for Smith.* Did you strike the decedent, Jones?

*Smith*: Yes.

*Counsel for Smith*: Did Jones say anything to you before you struck him?

*Counsel for Jones's estate*: "Objection, your honor, on the grounds of hearsay. Smith cannot give testimony on what the decedent said, since the decedent is obviously not subject to cross-examination.

**(a)** If Smith is allowed to answer the last question, he will say, "Yes, Jones told me that he was going to kill me." Would this statement be hearsay?

**(b)** If so, under what circumstances, if any, can it be admissible?

### PRIVILEGE

A **privilege** in the law of evidence is the right to refuse to testify or the right to prevent someone else from testifying on a matter.

1. *Privilege against Self-Incrimination.* Under the privilege against self-incrimination, an accused person cannot be compelled to testify in a criminal proceeding or to answer questions that directly or indirectly connect the accused to the commission of a crime, i.e., incriminating questions.

2. *Attorney-Client Privilege.* Under the **attorney-client privilege**, a client and an attorney can refuse to disclose any communication between them if its purpose was to fa-

**privilege** A special benefit, protection, or right such as the right to refuse to testify or to prevent someone else from testifying.

**attorney-client privilege** A client and an attorney can refuse to disclose any communication between them whose purpose was to facilitate the provision of legal services for the client.

cilitate the provision of legal services for that client. The attorney cannot disclose the communication without the permission of the client. Closely related to the attorney-client privilege is the *work product privilege*. Under the latter, an attorney's work in preparation for litigation is privileged. With rare exceptions, the other side's request to be shown this work will be denied. Work in preparation for litigation includes notes, working papers, memoranda, and tangible things.

3. *Doctor-Patient Privilege*. Under the doctor-patient privilege, a patient and doctor can refuse to disclose any confidential (private) communications between them that relate to medical care. The doctor cannot disclose the communication without the permission of the patient.

4. *Clergy-Penitent Privilege*. Under the clergy-penitent privilege, a penitent and a member of the clergy can refuse to disclose any confidential (private) communications between them that relate to spiritual counseling or consultation. The minister, priest, or rabbi cannot disclose the communication without the permission of the penitent.

5. *Marital Communications*. A husband and wife can refuse to disclose confidential (private) communications between them during the marriage. One spouse can also prevent the other from making such disclosures. Both spouses must agree to the disclosure. The marital communications privilege does not apply, however, to litigation between spouses, e.g., divorce litigation.

6. *Government Information*. Some information collected by the government about citizens is confidential and privileged. Examples include most adoption and tax records. The privilege would not prevent use of the information to prosecute the citizen in connection with the citizen's duty to provide accurate information. It would, however, prevent third parties from gaining access to the confidential information.

**Investigation Guideline:**
When a privilege applies, look for alternative, nonprivileged sources of obtaining the information protected by the privilege.

## BEST EVIDENCE RULE

To prove the contents of a private (nonofficial) writing, you should produce the original writing unless it is unavailable through no fault of the person now seeking to introduce a copy of the original, e.g., it was destroyed in a sudden storm.

## AUTHENTICATION

Authentication is evidence that a writing (or other physical item) is genuine and that it is what it purports to be—for example, the testimony of witnesses who saw the document being prepared.

## PAROL EVIDENCE RULE

Oral evidence cannot be introduced to alter or contradict the contents of a written document if the parties intended the written document to be a complete statement of the agreement.

---

Section J
# TAKING A WITNESS STATEMENT

There are four major kinds of witness statements:

1. Handwritten statement
2. Recorded statement in question-and-answer format (on audio- or videotape)
3. Responses to a questionnaire that is mailed to the witness to answer
4. Statement taken in question-and-answer format with court reporters

The most common kind of statement is the first, which we shall consider here.

In a handwritten statement, the investigator writes down what the witness says, or the witness writes out the statement himself or herself. There is no formal structure to which the written statement must conform. The major requirements for the statement are clarity and accuracy.

Here is how one paralegal explains the process to the witness:

"What I'd like to do today is take a written statement from you. After we talk about what you recall about the accident, I'd like to write it down, then have you review it, verifying with your signature that this statement is indeed what you have said about the matter."[11]

From whom should you take a witness statement? "Many people feel that a witness can only be someone who has actually viewed the event or occurrence. Obviously, this is not true. Quite often the so-called **occurrence witness** cannot offer as significant a contribution in testimony as the **pre-occurrence witness** or **post-occurrence witness**. An alert, intelligent post-occurrence witness can shed a great deal of light upon the matter in dispute by testifying as to physical facts such as positions of cars or skid marks. He could also testify as to statements made immediately after the occurrence by a party to the lawsuit. The pre-occurrence witness can testify as to the condition of premises or machinery immediately before the accident. Therefore, the paralegal should be interested in interviewing witnesses who can set the stage for the scene of the accident, in addition to those who actually witnessed the occurrence."[12]

Suppose that a person says he or she knows nothing. Should a "witness" statement be taken of this person? Some recommend that you *should* take a "negative statement" to discourage this person from coming back later to claim "remembered information." Here's an example of such a statement:

"I was not at xxx address on xxx date and did not see a traffic accident at the time. I did not see anything happen at xxx location. I did not hear anything. I talked to no one about this accident nor did I hear anyone say anything about it."[13]

A written statement should begin by identifying (1) the witness (name, address, place of work, names of relatives, and other identifying data that may be helpful in locating the witness later); (2) the date and place of the taking of the statement; and (3) the name of the person to whom the statement is being made. See the example of a witness statement in exhibit 9.9.

Then comes the body of the statement, in which the witness provides information about the event or occurrence in question (an accident that was observed, what the witness did and saw just before a fire, where the witness was on a certain date, etc.). Be sure that the statement includes facts relevant to the ability of the witness to observe, e.g., amount of light available, weather conditions, obstructions. This lends credibility to the statement. It is often useful to have the witness present the facts in chronological order, particularly when many facts are involved in the statement.

At the end of the statement, the witness should say that he or she is making the statement of his or her own free will, without any pressure or coercion from anyone. The witness then signs the statement. The signature goes on the last page. Each of the other pages is also signed or initialed. If others have watched the witness make and sign the statement, they should also sign an **attestation clause**, which simply states that they observed the witness sign the statement.

---

**occurrence witness**
Someone who actually observed an event or incident.

**pre-occurrence witness**
Someone who did not observe an event or incident but who can give a first-hand account of what happened before the event or incident.

**post-occurrence witness**
Someone who did not observe an event or incident but who can give a first-hand account of what happened after the event or incident.

**attestation clause**   A clause stating that a person saw someone sign a document or perform other tasks related to the validity of the document.

---

| EXHIBIT 9.9 | Witness Statement |
|---|---|

**Statement of Patricia Wood**

I am Patricia Wood. I am 42 years old and live at 3416 34th Street, N.W., Nashua, New Hampshire 03060. I work at the Deming Chemical Plant at Region Circle, Nashua. My home phone is 966–3954. My work phone is 297–9700 × 301. My email address is pwood@pacbell.com. I am married to John Wood. We have two children, Jessica (fourteen years old) and Gabriel (eleven years old). I am making this statement to Rose Thompson, a paralegal at Fields, Smith and Farrell. This statement is being given on March 13, 2002 at my home, 3416 34th Street, NW.

On February 15, 2002, I was standing on the corner of . . .

Before the witness signs, he or she should read the entire statement and make any corrections that need to be made. Each correction should be initialed by the witness. Each page should be numbered with the total number of pages indicated each time. For example, if there are four pages, the page numbers would be 1 of 4, 2 of 4, 3 of 4, and 4 of 4. Each of these page numbers should be initialed and dated by the witness. The investigator should not try to correct any spelling or grammatical mistakes made by the witness. The statement should exist exactly as the witness spoke or wrote it. Just before the signature of the witness at the end of the statement, the witness should say (in writing), "I have read all ___ pages of this statement, and the facts within it are accurate to the best of my knowledge." The witness should also write the date next to his or her signature.

Investigators sometimes use tricks of the trade to achieve a desired effect. For example, if the investigator is writing out the statement as the witness speaks, the investigator may *intentionally* make an error of fact. When the witness reads over the statement, the investigator makes sure that the witness catches the error and initials the correction. This becomes added evidence that the witness carefully read the statement. The witness might later try to claim that he or she did not read the statement. The initialed correction helps rebut this position.

Try to make sure that every page of the witness statement (other than the last) ends in the middle of a sentence or somewhere before the period. This is to rebut a later allegation that someone improperly added pages to the witness statement after it was signed. The allegation is somewhat difficult to support if the bottom line of one page contains a sentence that is continued at the top of the next page.

Witness statements are generally not admitted into evidence at the trial. They might be admissible to help the attorney demonstrate that the pretrial statement of the witness is inconsistent with the testimony of this witness during the trial itself. The main value of witness statements is thoroughness and accuracy in case preparation. Trials can occur years after the events that led to litigation. Witnesses may disappear or forget. Witness statements taken soon after the event can sometimes be helpful in tracking down witnesses and in helping them recall the details of the event.

---

### Assignment 9.8

Select any member of the class and take a witness statement from this person. The statement should concern an accident of any kind (e.g., a serious mishap at work, a highway collision) in which the witness was a participant or an observer. (The witness, however, should not be a party to any litigation growing out of the accident.) You write out the statement from what the witness says in response to your questions. Do not submit a statement handwritten by the witness except for his or her signature, initials, or corrections, if any. Assume that you (the investigator-paralegal) work for the law firm of Davis and Davis, which represents someone else involved in the accident.

---

## Section K
# The Settlement Work-Up

**settlement work-up** A summary of the major facts in the case presented in a manner designed to encourage the other side (or its insurance company) to settle the case. Also called a settlement brochure.

One of the end products of investigation is the **settlement work-up**, which is a summary of the major facts obtained through investigation, client interviewing, answers to interrogatories, deposition testimony, etc. The work-up, in one form or another, is used in negotiation with the other side or with the other side's liability insurance company in an effort to obtain a favorable settlement in lieu of trial. In addition to the presentation of the facts of a case, the settlement work-up might also summarize the law that will govern those facts.

Exhibit 9.10 shows a memo containing data for a proposed settlement work-up.[14] Note its precision and attention to detail. Excellent FP (fact particularization, see exhibit 8.5 in chapter 8) had to be used as the basis of this report.

| EXHIBIT 9.10 | Draft of a Proposed Settlement Work-Up |
| --- | --- |

**Interoffice Memorandum**

To: Mary Jones, Esq
From: Katherine Webb, Paralegal
Date: October 12, 1995
Re: Joseph Smith vs. Dan Lamb
    Case Summary—Settlement Work-Up

### I. Facts of Accident

The accident occurred on September 6, 1993, in Orange, California. Joseph Smith was driving westbound on Chapman Avenue, stopped to make a left turn into a parking lot, and was rear-ended by the one-half-ton panel truck driven by Dan Lamb.

The defendant driver, Mr. Lamb, was cited for violation of Vehicle Code Sections 21703 and 22350, following too close, and at an unsafe speed for conditions.

### II. Injuries

Severe cervical and lumbar sprain, superimposed over pre-existing, albeit asymptomatic, spondylolisthesis of pars interarticulus at L5–S1, with possible herniated nucleus pulposus either at or about the level of the spondylolisthesis; and contusion of right knee.

Please see attached medical reports for further details.

### III. Medical Treatment

Mr. Smith felt an almost immediate onset of pain in his head, neck, back, and right knee after the accident and believes that he may have lost consciousness momentarily. He was assisted from his car and taken by ambulance to the St. Joseph Hospital emergency room, where he was initially seen by his regular internist, Raymond Ross, M.D.

Dr. Ross obtained orthopedic consultation with Brian A. Ewald, M.D., who reviewed the multiple X-rays taken in the emergency room and found them negative for fracture. Lumbar spine X-rays did reveal evidence of a spondylolisthesis defect at the pars interarticulus of L5, but this was not felt to represent acute injury. Dr. Ewald had Mr. Smith admitted to St. Joseph Hospital on the same day for further evaluation and observation.

On admission to the hospital, Mr. Smith was placed on complete bed rest, with a cervical collar and medication for pain. On September 10, neurological consultation was obtained with Michael H. Sukoff, M.D., who, although he did not find any significant objective neurological abnormality, felt that there might be a herniated disc at L4–L5, with possible contusion of the nerve roots.

Drs. Ewald and Sukoff followed Mr. Smith's progress throughout the remainder of his hospitalization. He was continued on bed rest, physiotherapy, and medication, and fitted with a lumbosacral support. He was ultimately ambulated with crutches and was discharged from the hospital on September 25, 1993, with instructions to continue to rest and wear his cervical collar and back brace.

On discharge from the hospital, Mr. Smith was taken by ambulance to the Sky Palm Motel in Orange, where his wife and children had been staying during his hospitalization. Arrangements were made for home physiotherapy and rental of a hospital bed. Mr. Smith was taken by ambulance on the following day to his residence in Pacific Palisades.

After returning home, Mr. Smith continued to suffer from headaches, neck pain, and severe pain in his lower back, with some radiation into both legs, especially the right. He was totally confined to bed for at least two months following the accident, where he was cared for by his wife. Daily physical therapy was administered by Beatrice Tasker, R.P.T.

Mr. Smith continued to receive periodic outpatient care with Dr. Ewald. By the end of December 1993, Mr. Smith was able to discontinue the use of his cervical collar and was able to walk, with difficulty, without crutches. At the time of his office visit with Dr. Ewald on December 21, he was noted to be having moderate neck discomfort, with increasingly severe low back pain. At the time, Dr. Ewald placed Mr. Smith on a gradually increasing set of Williams exercises and advised him to begin swimming as much as possible.

Mr. Smith continued to be followed periodically by Dr. Ewald through March 1994, with gradual improvement noted. However, Mr. Smith continued to spend the majority of his time confined to his home and often to bed, using a cane whenever he went out. In addition, he suffered periodic severe flareups of low back pain, which would render him totally disabled and would necessitate total bed rest for several days at a time.

| EXHIBIT 9.10 | Draft of a Proposed Settlement Work-Up—*continued* |
|---|---|

During this period of time, Mr. Smith also experienced headaches and blurred vision, for which Dr. Ewald referred him to Robert N. Dunphy, M.D. Dr. Dunphy advised that the symptoms were probably secondary to his other injuries and would most likely subside with time.

On April 1, 1994, Mr. Smith consulted Dr. Ewald with complaints of increased back pain following an automobile ride to San Diego. Dr. Ewald's examination at that time revealed bilateral lumbar muscle spasm, with markedly decreased range of motion. Due to his concern about the extremely prolonged lumbar symptoms, and suspecting a possible central herniated nucleus pulposus, Dr. Ewald recommended that Mr. Smith undergo lumbar myelography. This was performed on an inpatient basis at St. Joseph Hospital on April 4, 1994, and reported to be within normal limits.

Mr. Smith continued conservative treatment with Dr. Ewald, following the prescribed program of rest, medication, exercise, and daily physiotherapy administered by his wife. He was able to graduate out of his lumbosacral support by approximately October 1994, resuming use of the garment when he experienced severe flareups of low back pain.

In his medical report dated January 2, 1995, Dr. Ewald stated that he expected a gradual resolution of lumbar symptomatology with time. However, in his subsequent report, dated January 10, 1995, Dr. Ewald noted that since his original report, Mr. Smith had suffered multiple repetitive episodes of low back pain, secondary to almost any increase of activity. An an office visit on February 25, Mr. Smith was reported to have localized his discomfort extremely well to the L5-S1 level, and range of motion was found to have decreased to approximately 75%. Since his examination in February, Dr. Ewald has discussed at length with both Mr. Smith and his wife the possibility of surgical intervention, consisting of lumbar stabilization (fusion) at the L5–S1 level, secondary to the spondylolisthesis present at that level. Dr. Ewald has advised them of the risks, complications, and alternatives with regard to consideration of surgical stabilization, noting that surgery would be followed by a 6-to-9-month period of rehabilitation, and further warning that even if the surgical procedure is carried out, there is no guarantee that Mr. Smith will be alleviated of all of his symptomatology.

As stated in Dr. Ewald's medical report dated March 10, 1995, Mr. Smith is himself beginning to lean toward definite consideration with regard to surgery, although he is presently continuing with conservative management.

Dr. Ewald recommends that in the event Mr. Smith does choose to undergo surgery, a repeat myelogram should be performed in order to rule out, as much as possible, the presence of a herniated nucleus pulposus either above or at the level of the spondylolisthesis.

## IV. Residual Complaints

Mr. Smith states that his neck injury has now largely resolved, although he does experience occasional neck pain and headaches. However, he continues to suffer from constant severe pain in his low back, with some radiation of pain and numbness in the right leg.

Mr. Smith notes that his low back pain is worse with cold weather and aggravated by prolonged sitting, walking, driving, or nearly any form of activity. He finds that he must rest frequently and continues to follow a daily regimen of swimming, Williams exercises, pain medication, and physiotherapy administered by his wife. He has also resumed the use of his lumbosacral brace.

Mr. Smith was an extremely active person prior to the accident, accustomed to working 12 to 16 hours per day and engaging in active sports such as tennis. Since the accident, he has had to sell his business and restrict all activities to a minimum, because he has found that any increase in activity will trigger a flareup of low back pain so severe that he is totally incapacitated for several days at a time.

As stated by Dr. Ewald, Mr. Smith is now seriously considering the possibility of surgical stabilization, despite the risks and complications involved. He has always viewed surgery as a last resort but is now beginning to realize that it may be his only alternative in view of his prolonged pain and disability. However, he currently intends to delay any definite decision until after the summer, during which time he intends to increase his swimming activity and see if he can gain any relief from his symptomatology.

## V. Specials

(Copies of supporting documentation are attached hereto.)

### A. Medical

| | |
|---|---|
| 1. Southland Ambulance Service (9/6/93) | $937.00 |
| 2. St. Joseph Hospital (9/6/93–9/25/93) | 22,046.29 |
| 3. Raymond R. Ross, M.D. (Emergency Room, 9/6/93) | 2,025.00 |
| 4. Brian A. Ewald, M.D. (9/6/93–4/28/95) | 1,604.00 |

| EXHIBIT 9.10 | **Draft of a Proposed Settlement Work-Up—*continued*** |
| --- | --- |

 5. Michael H. Sukoff, M.D. (9/10/95–9/22/95) . . . . . . . . . . . . . . . . . . . . . . . . . . . . . . . . . . . . . . . . . . .    1,140.00
 6. Wind Ambulance Service (9/25/95) . . . . . . . . . . . . . . . . . . . . . . . . . . . . . . . . . . . . . . . . . . . . . . . . .     939.50
 7. Wind Ambulance Service (9/26/95) . . . . . . . . . . . . . . . . . . . . . . . . . . . . . . . . . . . . . . . . . . . . . . . . .     989.00
 8. Beatrice Tasker, R.P.T. (9/21/93–10/22/93) . . . . . . . . . . . . . . . . . . . . . . . . . . . . . . . . . . . . . . . .    1,825.00
 9. Abbey Rents (Rental of hospital bed and trapeze bar, 9/25/93–11/25/93) . . . . . . . . . . . . . . .     422.00
10. Allied Medical & Surgical Co. (Purchase of cane, 1/10/93) . . . . . . . . . . . . . . . . . . . . . . . . . . . .      30.45
11. Rice Clinical Laboratories (2/1/94) . . . . . . . . . . . . . . . . . . . . . . . . . . . . . . . . . . . . . . . . . . . . . . .     114.00
12. Robert N. Dunphy, M.D. (2/1/94–4/15/94) . . . . . . . . . . . . . . . . . . . . . . . . . . . . . . . . . . . . . . . .     895.00
13. St. Joseph Hospital (X-rays and lab tests, 2/9/94) . . . . . . . . . . . . . . . . . . . . . . . . . . . . . . . . . .     756.00
14. St. Joseph Hospital (Inpatient myelography, 4/23/94–4/24/94) . . . . . . . . . . . . . . . . . . . . . . . .     851.60
15. Medication . . . . . . . . . . . . . . . . . . . . . . . . . . . . . . . . . . . . . . . . . . . . . . . . . . . . . . . . . . . . . . . .   __1,357.70__
     Total Medical Expenses . . . . . . . . . . . . . . . . . . . . . . . . . . . . . . . . . . . . . . . . . . . . . . . . . . . . .   __$35,932.54__

**B. Miscellaneous Family Expenses**
(During plaintiff's hospitalization, 9/6/93–9/25/95.)

1. Sky Palm Motel (Lodging for wife and children) . . . . . . . . . . . . . . . . . . . . . . . . . . . . . . . . . . . .   $2,050.50
2. Taxicab (9/6/93) . . . . . . . . . . . . . . . . . . . . . . . . . . . . . . . . . . . . . . . . . . . . . . . . . . . . . . . . . . . .   __12.45__
Total Miscellaneous Expenses . . . . . . . . . . . . . . . . . . . . . . . . . . . . . . . . . . . . . . . . . . . . . . . . . . . .   __$2,062.95__

**C. Wage Loss**

At the time of the accident, Mr. Smith was employed as president and co-owner, with Mr. George Frost, of the Inter Science Institute, Inc., a medical laboratory in Los Angeles. As stated in the attached verification from Mr. Mamikunian, Mr. Smith was earning an annual salary of $48,000.00, plus automobile, expenses, and fringe benefits.

In a telephone conversation with Mr. Smith on May 6, 1995, he advised me that the Inter Science Institute had grossed $512,000.00 in 1993 and $700,000.00 in 1994. He further confirmed that prior to the accident of September 6, 1993, both he and Mr. Smith had been approached on at least two to three different occasions by companies, including Revlon and a Canadian firm, offering substantial sums of money for purchase of the business. On the basis of the foregoing, both Mr. Smith and Mr. Frost place a conservative estimate of the value of the business at $2,000,000.00.

Due to injuries sustained in the subject accident, Mr. Smith was unable to return to work or perform the necessary executive and managerial functions required in his position as president and part owner of the business. As a result, on or about October 26, 1993, while still totally incapacitated by his injuries, Mr. Smith was forced to sell his 50% stock interest in the Inter Science Institute for a total sum of $300,000.00.

On the basis of the prior estimated value of the business at $2,000,000.00, *Mr. Smith sustained a loss of $700,000.00 in the sale of his one-half interest in Inter Science Institute, Inc., in addition to the loss of an annual salary of $48,000.00, plus automobile, expenses, and fringe benefits.*

Even if one were to assume that the sale of his interest in the business was reasonable value, Mr. Smith has sustained a loss—in salary only—in the sum of *$84,000.00* to date, based on an annual salary of $48,000.00 up to October 12, 1995.

---

*Assignment 9.9*

Assume that the settlement work-up in exhibit 9.10 is not successful. The case must now go to trial. Prepare a report for the litigator of all the evidence that should be collected and considered for use at the trial.

**(a)** List all possible witnesses your side (representing Joseph Smith) might call and give a summary of what their testimony is likely to be.

**(b)** List all possible witnesses the other side (representing Dan Lamb) might call and give a summary of what their testimony is likely to be.

**(c)** List all possible physical evidence your side should consider using and give a summary of what each item might establish.

**(d)** List all possible physical evidence the other side is likely to consider using and give a summary of what each item might establish.

**(e)** What further facts do you think need to be investigated?

# ▋ Chapter Summary

The goal of investigation is to obtain new facts and to verify facts already known by the office. It is a highly individualistic skill where determination, imagination, resourcefulness, and openness are critical. A good investigator has a healthy suspicion of preconceived notions of what the facts are because such notions might interfere with uncovering the unexpected. In the search for the facts, the investigator is concerned with truth in the context of the evidence that will be needed to establish that truth in court. But the standard that guides the search is not truth or proof; the guideline of the investigator is to pursue whatever evidence that is reasonably available.

People often have different perspectives on what did or did not happen, particularly in regard to emotionally charged events. When different versions of facts exist, the investigator must seek them out.

Competent investigation requires a knowledge of the standard sources of information; an ability to use the techniques of gaining access to records, and an ability to evaluate the trustworthiness of both oral and physical evidence.

Investigators must be aware of the image they project of themselves, be prepared for witnesses with differing levels of factual knowledge, be ready for witnesses who are unwilling to cooperate, and be able to gain the trust of witnesses.

The law of evidence is an important part of the investigator's arsenal. This should include an understanding of the following: the four ways a version of the facts can be established at the trial (admission, judicial notice, presumption, evidence), admissibility, the distinction between direct evidence and circumstantial evidence, the nature of relevance, when a witness is competent to give testimony and to state an opinion, the nature of hearsay, and the major exceptions that allow hearsay to be admitted. Investigators need to understand the effect of the privilege against self-incrimination, the attorney-client privilege, the doctor-patient privilege, the clergy-penitent privilege, the privilege for marital communications, and the confidentiality of some government information. They must also understand the best evidence rule, the authentication of evidence, and the parol evidence rule.

Two important documents that are the products of competent investigation are a witness statement, which is taken to preserve the testimony of an important witness, and a settlement work-up, which is an advocacy document that compiles and organizes facts in an effort to encourage a favorable settlement.

## KEY TERMS

| | |
|---|---|
| legal investigation | stipulation |
| forensic | judicial notice |
| settlement | presumption |
| impeach | rebuttable |
| discovery | irrebuttable |
| deposition | admissible evidence |
| interrogatories | direct evidence |
| request for admission | circumstantial evidence |
| evidence | relevant evidence |
| proof | competent |
| leading question | credibility |
| parol evidence | opinion |
| tangible evidence | hearsay |
| Freedom of Information Act | privilege |
| disinterested | attorney-client privilege |
| bias | occurrence witness |
| judgment creditor | pre-occurrence witness |
| judgment debtor | post-occurrence witness |
| deep pocket | attestation clause |
| skiptracing | settlement work-up |
| admission | |

## ON THE NET: MORE ABOUT INVESTIGATION

### Overview of Factual Research on the Internet
www.virtualchase.com/legalresearcher/index.html
www.gao.gov/special.pubs/soi/soi_ch5.htm#PAGE187

### Finding People or Businesses
www.switchboard.com
www.bigbook.com
www.people.yahoo.com
www.whowhere.lycos.com
www.merlindata.com
www.555-1212.com

### Finding Assets
www.tracerservices.com
www.check-mate.com
www.members.tripod.com/proagency/ask8.html

### Finding Information about Businesses
www.hoovers.com
www.onesource.com
www.dnb.com
www.choicepoint.net

### Investigation Services
www.vitalrec.com/links6.html
www.ussearch.com
www.thepiregister.com
www.ottolabs.com

### Public Records
www.searchsystems.net
www.knowx.com
www.rapsheets.com
www.crimetime.com/online.htm
www.ancestry.com/search/rectype/military/main.htm
www2.genealogy.com/ssdi_cgi/gen_foot4.html
www.edgar-online.com
www.nass.org/sos/sos.html
www.census.gov
www.cdc.gov/nchs/howto/w2w/w2welcom.htm
www.vitalrec.com

### Expert Witness Directory
www.tasanet.com
www.juryverdicts.com/experts/index.html
www.idex.com
www.expertpages.com

### Freedom of Information
www.usdoj.gov/oip/foi-upd.htm
www.aclu.org/library/foia.html
www.tncrimlaw.com/foia_indx.html
www.sba.gov/foia/guide.html

## ENDNOTES

1. Massachusetts Paralegal Association, *Fact Finding for the Legal Assistant* (MCLE Seminar 1993.)

2. Lana Clark, *Developing a Strategy for Witness Interviews*, 10 Legal Assistant Today 65 (January/February 1993).

3. A. Daniel Yarmey, *The Psychology of Eyewitness Testimony* 9 (Free Press, 1979); (E. Loftus et al., *Powerful Eyewitness Testimony*, Trial Magazine 64–66 (April 1988).

4. Bryon Keith, *Dealing Smartly with Different Witnesses*, The Legal Investigator 38 (November 1991).

5. Francis Ritter, *The Art of Hearing between the Lines*, The Legal Investigator 9 (February 1992).

6. Janet Jackson, *Interviewing Witnesses*, At Issue 1 (San Francisco Ass'n of Legal Assistants, April 1994).

7. John Lehe, *Techniques for Locating Missing Parties*. 11 Legal Assistant Today 80, 81 (January/February 1994).

8. Reprinted with permission of Trial (February 1991) © copyright The Ass'n of Trial Lawyers of America.

9. Roger Haydock and John Sonsteng, *Trial* 209 (1991).

10. E. Cleary, ed., *McCormick's Handbook of the Law of Evidence* 584 (1972).

11. K. Wilkoff, *Writing Witness Statements That Win Cases*, 12 Legal Assistant Today 51, 52 (September/October 1994).

12. Yetta Blair, *Interviewing Witnesses and Securing Their Signed Written Statements*, 14 Points and Authorities 10 (San Joaquin Ass'n of Legal Assistants, May 1992).

13. Kathryn Andrews, *Interviews and Statements* 10 (Oregon Legal Assistant Ass'n, October 1988).

14. Prepared by Katherine Webb, Legal Assistant at Cartwright, Sucherman, Slobodin & Fowler, San Francisco, California.

# Chapter 10

# LITIGATION ASSISTANTSHIP

## Chapter Outline

## Section A
## Overview of Litigation

**litigation** The formal process of resolving a legal dispute through special tribunals such as courts; a lawsuit.

America is a litigious society. This means that we have a tendency to sue people. We engage in **litigation**—a lot. In 2000, over 91 million new cases were filed in state courts, and 322, 262 new cases were filed in federal courts.[1] Litigation is the formal process of resolving legal controversies through special tribunals. The main tribunals established for this purpose in our legal system are the courts. Administrative agencies can also resolve some legal disputes through the exercise of their quasi-judicial power. (Quasi-judicial means acting like or similar to a court. See chapter 6.)

Paralegals can perform many functions in assisting attorneys who are litigating cases. Before studying what these functions are, read the following overview of litigation, which will provide a context for understanding the roles of the attorney and paralegal. The overview is presented in the form of a story—the litigation woes of Michael Brown, who finds himself embroiled in a civil trial, a criminal trial, and an administrative dispute. At the end of the story, you will find most of this overview in outline form in exhibits 10.2 and 10.3.

There are two broad categories of litigated disputes: civil and criminal. A **civil dispute** consists of:

**civil dispute** A legal controversy in which (a) one private person or business sues another, (b) a private person or business sues the government, or (c) the government sues a private person or business for a matter other than the commission of a crime.

- One private person or business suing another (e.g., Jones sues his neighbor for trespass), or
- A private person or business suing the government (e.g., a senior citizen sues the Social Security Administration for denial of disability benefits), or
- The government suing a private person or business for a matter other than the commission of a crime (e.g., the state department of revenue sues a restaurant for failure to deduct state taxes from the wages of waiters).

A **criminal dispute** is a legal controversy in which the government alleges the commission of a crime.

**criminal dispute** A legal controversy in which the government alleges the commission of a crime.

### THE LEGAL ODYSSEY OF MICHAEL BROWN: AN ANATOMY OF THE LITIGATION PROCESS

Michael Brown is a truck driver for the Best Bread Company. Several years ago, as Brown was walking home from work, Harold Clay, an old friend from the past, stopped and offered him a ride. They had not seen each other since Clay had moved cross-country a number of years ago. They carried on an excited conversation as Clay drove. After a few blocks, a car driven by George Miller, a resident of a neighboring state, ran through a red light and struck Clay's car. All three individuals were seriously injured and were taken to a local hospital. Clay died two weeks later from injuries received in the crash.

Several days after the accident, Brown's boss, Frank Best, wrote Brown a letter. In it, Best said he had learned that the police had found about half an ounce of heroin under the front passenger seat of Clay's car and were planning to charge Brown with possession of narcotics with intent to distribute. Best also stated that several thefts had occurred at the company warehouse recently and that he now suspected Brown of having been involved in them. For these reasons, he decided to fire Brown, effective immediately.

At least three different legal disputes involving Brown could arise out of this fact situation:

1. A dispute among Brown, Miller, and Clay's estate regarding civil liability for the accident.
2. A dispute between Brown and the government regarding the criminal drug charge.
3. A dispute among Brown, the Best Bread Company, and the State Unemployment Compensation Board concerning Brown's entitlement to unemployment compensation benefits.

Each of these disputes could lead to a number of court decisions. The third dispute might involve an administrative decision, possibly followed by one or more court decisions, all concerning Brown's claim for unemployment compensation.

## 1. Civil Liability

Brown suffered substantial injury as a result of the crash. From whom could he collect *damages?* Who was *liable* for the accident? Was Miller at fault? Clay? Was each of them *jointly* and *severally* liable?

**Damages:** An award of money (paid by the wrongdoer) to compensate the person who has been harmed.

**Liable:** Legally responsible.

**Joint and several liability:** When two or more persons are jointly and severally liable, they are legally responsible, together and individually. Each wrongdoer is individually responsible for the entire judgment. The person who has been wronged can collect from one of them or from all of them until his or her award of damages is paid.

Brown hired Brenda Davis, Esq. to represent him. Once Brown signed the *retainer*, Davis would later enter an *appearance* and become the *attorney of record*.

**Retainer:** The contract that states the scope of services, fees, expenses, and costs of legal services. (Retainer also refers to an amount of money or other property paid by the client as a deposit or advance against future fees, expenses, and costs of legal services.)

**Appearance:** Going to court to act on behalf of a party to the litigation. The attorney usually appears by filing a *notice of appearance* in court, which is often accomplished through a *praecipe*. A praecipe is a formal request to the court (usually made through the court clerk) that something be done. Here, the request is that the attorney become the attorney of record.

**Attorney of record:** An attorney of record is the attorney who has filed a notice of appearance (through a praecipe or other means) and who is formally mentioned in court records as the official attorney of the party. Once this occurs, the attorney often cannot withdraw from the case without court permission.

The attorney explained that a number of factors had to be considered before deciding on the *forum* in which to sue Miller and Clay's *estate*. Brown might be able to bring the suit in a number of places: (a) in a state trial court where Brown lives, (b) in a state trial court where Miller lives, (c) in a state trial court where Clay's estate is located, (d) in the federal trial court sitting in Brown's state, (e) in the federal trial court sitting in Miller's state, or (f) in the federal trial court sitting in the state where Clay's estate is located. The reason Brown could sue in a federal court is the existence of *diversity of citizenship*. Davis advised Brown to sue in federal court. The suit would be brought in the U.S. District Court sitting in Brown's own state, since this would be the most convenient *venue* for Brown.

**Forum:** The court where the case is to be tried.

**Estate:** All the property left by a decedent (one who has died), from which any obligations or debts of the decedent must be paid. When we say that an estate is sued (or brings a suit), we are referring to the decedent's representative who is authorized to resolve claims involving the decedent's assets and debts.

**Diversity of citizenship:** A kind of jurisdiction giving a federal court the power to hear a case based upon the fact that (a) the parties to the litigation are citizens of different states and (b) the amount of money involved exceeds the amount specified by federal statute.

**Venue:** The place of the trial. In most judicial systems, there is more than one trial court. For example, there may be one for each county or district. The selection of a particular trial court within a judicial system is referred to as a *choice of venue*.

Having decided on a court, Davis was ready to begin the lawsuit. She instructed her paralegal, Ted Alexander, to prepare the first draft of the *complaint*, naming Brown as the *plaintiff* and *stating a cause of action* for negligence against Miller and Clay's estate as *codefendants*. The complaint was the first *pleading* of the case. In the complaint, Davis stated the facts she felt constituted a cause of action for negligence. Some of the factual *allegations* were based on Brown's personal knowledge, while others were based on *information and belief*. The prayer for relief in the complaint contained an *ad damnum* clause that asked for $100,000. When she finished drafting the complaint, Davis signed the pleading, attached a written demand for a *jury trial*, and instructed her paralegal to *file* both documents with the clerk of the court.

**Complaint:** A *pleading* (see definition below) filed by the plaintiff that tries to state a claim or *cause of action* (see definition below) against the defendant.

**Plaintiff:** The party initiating the lawsuit.

**Cause of action:** Facts that give a party the right to judicial relief. A legally acceptable reason for suing.

**Stating a cause of action:** Including in a *pleading* (see definition below) facts that, if proved at trial, would entitle the party to the judicial relief sought (assuming the other party does not plead and prove any defenses that would defeat the effort).

**Codefendants:** More than one defendant sued in the same civil case. More than one defendant prosecuted in the same criminal case.

**Pleading:** A formal document that contains allegations and/or responses of the parties in a trial. The major pleadings are the complaint and answer.

**Allegation:** A claimed fact; a fact that a party will try to prove at trial.

**Information and belief:** A standard legal term used to indicate that the allegation is not based on the firsthand knowledge of the person making the allegation but that the person, nevertheless, believes in good faith that the allegation is true.

**Ad damnum:** A statement in the complaint in which the plaintiff asks for a specified sum of money as damages. (See prayer for relief in exhibit 10.12 later in the chapter.)

**Jury trial:** A group of citizens who will decide the issues or questions of fact at the trial. The judge decides the issues or questions of law. If there is no jury at the trial, the judge decides both the questions of law and the questions of fact.

**File:** To deposit a pleading, motion, or other formal document with a court clerk or other court official. Often what is filed thereby becomes a public record.

*Service of process* came next. It was accomplished when a copy of the complaint, along with the *summons*, was served on both Miller and the legal representative of Clay's estate. Davis did not serve these parties herself. She used a *process server*, who then had to file with the court an *affidavit* of service indicating the circumstances under which service was achieved. Service was made before the *statute of limitations* on the negligence cause of action had run out. Once the defendants were properly served, the court acquired *in personam jurisdiction* over them.

**Service of process:** *Process* is the means used by the court to acquire or exercise its power or jurisdiction over a person. *Service of process* is the formal notification given to a defendant that a suit has been initiated against him or her and that he or she must respond to it. (The words *summons* and *process* are often used interchangeably.) The most common method of service of process is to place the complaint and summons in the hands of the defendant.

**Summons:** The formal notice from the court ordering the defendant to appear and answer the plaintiff's allegations. The summons is *served* on the defendant.

**Process server:** A person who charges a fee for serving process.

**Affidavit:** A written statement of fact in which a person (called the *affiant* swears that the facts in the statement are true.

**Statute of limitations:** The law establishing the period within which the lawsuit must be commenced. If it is not brought within that time, it can never be brought; it is *barred*.

**In personam jurisdiction:** The power of the court over the person of the defendant obtained in part by proper service of process. (It is also called **personal jurisdiction**.)

Both Miller and Clay's estate filed *motions to dismiss* for *failure to state a cause of action*. The motions were denied by the court.

**Motion to dismiss:** A request that the court decide that a party may not further litigate a claim—that is, that the claim be dropped.

**Failure to state a cause of action:** Failure of a party to allege enough facts that, if proved, would entitle the party to judicial relief. Even if the party proved every fact he or she alleges, the facts would not establish a cause of action entitling the party to recover against his or her opponent. The motion to dismiss for failure to state a cause of action is sometimes referred to as (a) a *demurrer* or (b) a *failure to state a claim upon which relief can be granted*.

Because the case had been filed in a federal court, the *procedural law* governing the case would be found in the *Federal Rules of Civil Procedure*. (The *substantive law* of the case would be the state law of negligence.) According to the Federal Rules of Civil Procedure, Miller and Clay's estate were each required to file an *answer* to Brown's complaint within 20 days. Miller filed his answer almost immediately. Since Clay was dead and unable to tell his attorney what had happened at the accident, the attorney for the estate had some difficulty preparing an answer and was unable to file it within the 20 days. To avoid a *default judgment* against the estate, the attorney filed a *motion* asking for an extension of 30 days within which to file the answer. The motion was granted by the court, and the answer was filed within the new deadline.

> **Procedural law:** The rules that govern the mechanics of resolving a dispute in court or in an administrative agency.
>
> **Federal Rules of Civil Procedure (Fed. R. Civ. P.):** The technical rules governing the manner in which civil cases are brought in and progress through the United States District Courts, which are the federal trial courts.
>
> **Substantive law:** The non procedural rules that define or govern rights and duties (such as the duty to use reasonable care) other than procedural rights and duties.
>
> **Answer:** The pleading that responds to or answers allegations of the complaint.
>
> **Default judgment:** An order of the court deciding the case in favor of the plaintiff because the defendant failed to appear or to file an answer before the deadline.
>
> **Motion:** A request made to the court, such as a motion to dismiss. The party making the motion is called the *movant*. The verb is *move*, as in "I move that the court permit the demonstration" or "I move that the case be dismissed."

The answer filed on behalf of Clay's estate denied all allegations of negligence and raised an *affirmative defense* of contributory negligence against Brown on the theory that if Clay had been partially responsible for the collision, it was because Brown had carelessly distracted him through his conversation in the car. Finally, the answer of Clay's estate raised a *cross-claim* against the codefendant Miller, alleging that the accident had been caused by Miller's negligence. The estate asked $1,000,000 in damages.

> **Defense:** A response to a claim of the other party, setting forth reason(s) why the claim should be denied. The defense may be as simple as a flat denial of the other party's factual allegations or may involve entirely new factual allegations. (In the latter situation, the defense is an *affirmative defense*.)
>
> **Affirmative defense:** A defense that is based on new factual allegations by the defendant not contained in the plaintiff's allegations.
>
> **Cross-claim:** Usually, a claim by one codefendant against another codefendant.

Miller's answer also raised the defense of contributory negligence against Brown and stated a cross-claim against Clay's estate, alleging that the accident had been caused solely by the negligence of Clay, or of Clay and Brown together. On this same theory (that Brown together with Clay had negligently caused the accident), Miller's answer also stated a *counterclaim* against Brown. Miller sought $50,000 from Brown and $50,000 against Clay's estate as damages.

> **Counterclaim:** A claim or a cause of action against the plaintiff stated in the defendant's answer:

For a time, Miller and his attorney considered filing a *third-party complaint* against his own automobile insurance company, since the company would be liable for any judgment against him. They decided against this strategy because they did not want to let the jury know that Miller was insured. If the jury knew this fact, it might be more inclined to reach a verdict in favor of the plaintiff and for a high amount of damages. The strategy was also unnecessary because there was no indication that Miller's insurer would *contest* its obligation to compensate Miller (within the policy limits of his insurance) for any damages that he might have to pay Brown or Clay's estate in the event that the trial resulted in an *adverse judgment* against him.

> **Third-party complaint:** A complaint filed by the defendant against a third party (that is, a person not presently a party to the lawsuit). This complaint alleges that the third party is or may be liable for all or part of the damages that the plaintiff may win from the defendant.

**Contest:** To challenge.

**Adverse judgment:** A judgment or decision against you.

At this point, five claims had been filed by the parties. A sixth, Miller's third-party claim against his insurer, had been considered but ultimately had not been filed. These claims and their relationship to each other are illustrated in exhibit 10.1.

| EXHIBIT 10.1 | Diagram of the Claims in the Brown/Miller/Clay's Estate Litigation |
| --- | --- |

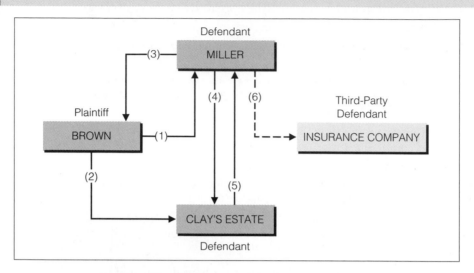

1. Plaintiff Brown's complaint for negligence against Miller and
2. Against Clay's Estate, as codefendants
3. Defendant Miller's counterclaim for negligence against plaintiff, Brown
4. Defendant Miller's cross-claim for negligence against his codefendant, the Estate
5. Defendant Estate's cross-claim for negligence against its codefendant, Miller
6. Third-party complaint that defendant Miller considered but ultimately decided *not* to file against his insurance company

Once the pleadings were filed, all three parties began to seek *discovery*. Each attorney first served *interrogatories* on the opposing parties. These were followed by *depositions* and *requests for admissions*. Miller was also served with a *subpoena duces tecum*, which ordered him to bring his driver's license and car registration to his attorney's office, where his deposition took place. He complied with this order. During the deposition, however, Miller refused to answer several questions. As a result, Brown's attorney had to file a discovery motion in court, seeking an *order* compelling Miller to answer. A *hearing* was subsequently held on the motion. After listening to arguments by all of the attorneys, the judge granted the motion in full, ordering Miller to answer the questions. Faced with the court's order, Miller answered the remaining questions.

Each party then filed a *motion for summary judgment*. The judge denied these motions, and the case was ready for trial.

**Discovery:** The pretrial devices that can be used by one party to obtain facts about the case from the other party in order to assist in preparing for trial. Discovery is the compulsory disclosure of facts related to litigation. The major discovery devices are *interrogatories, deposition, production of documents and things, physical or mental examination*, and *requests for admission*. (For an overview of all these devices, see exhibit 10.4 later in the chapter.)

**Interrogatories:** A discovery device consisting of written questions about the case submitted by one party to the other party. The answers to the interrogatories are usually given under oath—that is, the person answering the questions signs a sworn statement that the answers are true.

**Deposition:** A discovery device by which one party asks questions of the other party or of a witness for the other party. The person who is *deposed* is called the *deponent*. The deposition is conducted under oath outside the courtroom, usually in one of the attorneys' offices. A recording or transcript—a word-for-word account—is made of the deposition. (Most depositions consist of *oral* questions and answers. A deposition can be written, however.)

**Request for admission:** A statement of fact that the other side is asked to affirm or deny. Those facts that are affirmed will be treated by the court as having been established and need not be proven at the trial.

**Subpoena duces tecum:** A command that a witness appear at a certain time and place and bring specified things such as documents or records. (If ordered to give testimony, the subpoena would be called a *subpoena ad testificandum.*)

**Order:** An official command by the court requiring, allowing, or forbidding some act to be done.

**Hearing:** A proceeding in which the judge or presiding officer examines some aspect of the dispute. An *adversary hearing* exists when both parties are present at the hearing to argue their respective positions. An *ex parte hearing* exists when only one party is present at the hearing. Hearings occur in court as well as in administrative agencies.

**Motion for summary judgment:** A *summary judgment* is a judgment of the court that is rendered without a full trial because of the absence of conflict on any of the material facts. A motion for a summary judgment is a request by a party that a decision be reached on the basis of the pleadings alone without going through a full trial. A summary judgment is normally allowed only when there is no dispute between the parties as to any of the material or significant facts. Summary judgment can be granted on the entire case or on some of the claims raised within it. The word *summary* means done relatively quickly and informally without going through an entire adversary hearing or a full trial.

As the trial date neared, each of the attorneys received a notice asking them to appear before a *magistrate* for a *pretrial conference*. On the appointed day, the attorneys met with the magistrate to prepare the case for trial. During the conference, the magistrate, with the help of the attorneys, prepared a pretrial statement for the trial judge on the case. It contained a statement of the facts that had been *stipulated* by the attorneys and the facts that were still *in issue*. It also listed the *tangible evidence* and witnesses that each attorney intended to *introduce* at the trial.

**Magistrate:** A judicial officer having some but not all of the powers of a judge. In the federal trial courts (the United States District Courts), the magistrate may conduct many of the preliminary or pretrial proceedings in both civil and criminal cases.

**Pretrial conference:** A meeting between the judge (or magistrate) and the attorneys to go over preliminary matters before the trial begins. At this conference, the presiding officer often encourages the parties to settle the dispute on their own in order to avoid a trial.

**Stipulated:** Agreed to. Once the parties have reached a *stipulation* about a fact, neither side is required to offer evidence as to the existence or nonexistence of that fact at trial.

**In issue:** In question. If an *issue of fact* exists, then the existence or nonexistence of that fact must be established at trial. (An issue of fact is also called a factual issue, a factual question, or a question of fact.) If an *issue of law* exists, then the judge must rule on what the law is or on how the law applies to the facts. (An issue of law is also called a legal issue, a legal question, or a question of law.)

**Tangible evidence:** Physical evidence; evidence that can be seen or touched, such as letters, photographs, or skeletons.

**Introduce evidence:** To place evidence formally before a court or other tribunal so that it will become part of the record for consideration by the judge, jury, or other decision-maker.

After some delay, the case was finally *set for trial*. All of the parties and their attorneys assembled in the courtroom. The judge entered, took the bench, and ordered the *bailiff* to summon a *jury panel* for the trial. Once the potential or prospective jurors were seated in the courtroom, *voir dire* began. Several jurors were *challenged for cause* and dismissed—one because she worked for the insurance company that had issued the policy on Miller's car. The position as to this prospective juror was that she might be *biased*. Several other jurors were dismissed as a result of *peremptory challenges*. Twelve jurors plus two *alternates* were eventually *impaneled* and seated in the jury box.

**Set for trial:** To schedule a date when the trial is to begin.

**Bailiff:** A court employee who keeps order in the courtroom and renders general administrative assistance to the judge.

**Jury panel:** A group of citizens who have been called to jury duty. From this group, juries for particular trials are selected.

**Voir dire:** The oral examination of prospective jurors by the attorneys, by the judge, or by both the attorneys and the judge for the purpose of selecting a jury.

**Challenge for cause:** A request from a party to a judge that a prospective juror *not* be allowed to become a member of this jury because of specified causes or reasons.

**Bias:** An inclination or tendency to think and to act in a certain way. The potential for unfairness because of prior knowledge or involvement leading to possible preconceptions and a lack of open-mindedness.

**Peremptory challenge:** A request from a party to a judge asking that a prospective juror *not* be allowed to become a member of this jury without stating a reason for this request. Both sides are allowed a limited number of peremptory challenges, but they will be granted as many challenges for cause as they can establish.

**Alternate:** An extra juror who will take the place of a regular juror if one becomes incapacitated during the trial.

**Impaneled:** Selected and sworn in (referring to a jury) (also spelled empaneled).

When the jury was seated, Brown's attorney rose and told the judge that she wished to invoke the *rule on witnesses*. The judge nodded to the bailiff, who then led all of the witnesses (except for the parties themselves) out of the courtroom. Brown's attorney then began the trial with her *opening statement* to the jury. When she finished, Miller's attorney also delivered an opening statement. The attorney for Clay's estate, however, decided to reserve his opening statement until it was time for him to present the estate's case.

**Rule on witnesses:** A rule that requires certain witnesses to be removed from the courtroom until it is time for their individual testimony so that they will not be able to hear each other's testimony.

**Opening statement:** A speech or presentation made by each attorney to the jury summarizing the facts the attorney intends to try to prove during the trial.

Brown's attorney, whose client had the *burden of proof*, called her first witness, a 10-year-old boy who had seen the accident. Miller's attorney immediately rose and requested a *bench conference*. When all the attorneys had gathered around the bench, he stated that he *objected* to the witness on the basis of *competency*. The judge then *excused the jury* temporarily while he conducted a brief *examination* of the witness. The judge *overruled* the objection upon being satisfied that the boy was old enough to understand the obligation to tell the truth and had the ability to communicate what he knew.

**Burden of proof:** The responsibility of proving a fact at the trial. Generally, the party making the factual allegation has the burden of proof as to that allegation.

**Bench conference:** A discussion between the judge and the attorneys held at the judge's bench so that the jury cannot hear what is being said.

**Objection:** A formal challenge usually directed at the evidence that the other side is trying to pursue or introduce.

**Competency:** Legal capacity to testify.

**Excused the jury:** Asked the jury to leave the room.

**Examination:** Questioning, asking questions of.

**Overrule:** Deny. (The word *overrule* is also used when a court repudiates the holding of a prior opinion written by the same court.)

The jury was brought back into the courtroom, and Brown's attorney began her *direct examination*. After a few questions, Miller's attorney again objected, this time on the *ground* that the child's answer had been *hearsay*. The judge *sustained* the objection and, after instructing the jury to disregard the boy's answer, ordered it *stricken from the record*. Brown's attorney continued her examination of the witness for a few minutes before announcing that she had no further questions. The attorney for the estate then rose to conduct a brief *cross-examination* of the boy. He was followed by Miller's attorney, whose cross-examination was also brief. There was no *redirect examination*.

**Direct examination:** Questioning the witness first. Normally, the attorney who *calls* the witness to the stand conducts the direct examination.

**Ground:** Reason.

**Hearsay:** An out-of-court statement offered to prove the truth of the matter asserted in the statement.

**Sustain:** To affirm the validity of.

**Strike from the record:** To remove the testimony or evidence from the written record or *transcript* of the trial.

**Cross-examination:** Questioning the witness after the other side has completed the direct examination. Generally, the person conducting the cross-examination must limit himself or herself to the topics or subject matters raised during the direct examination of this witness by the other side.

**Redirect examination:** Questioning the witness after the cross-examination. The attorney who conducted the direct examination conducts the redirect examination.

Brown's attorney, Davis, called several other witnesses who had seen the accident occur. Each witness was examined and cross-examined in much the same fashion as the boy had been. Davis was about to call her fourth witness, Dr. Hadley, when the judge announced a brief recess for lunch. The judge admonished the jury not to discuss the case with anyone, even among themselves, and ordered everyone to be back in the courtroom by 2:00 P.M.

Dr. Hadley was called to the stand immediately after the lunch recess. Brown's attorney began her direct examination with a series of questions about the doctor's medical training and experience in order to *qualify* him as an *expert witness*. She then moved that Dr. Hadley be recognized as an expert witness. The *court*, with no objections by either defense counsel, granted the motion.

**Qualify:** To present evidence of a person's education and experience sufficient to convince the court that the witness has expertise in a particular area.

**Expert witness:** A witness who has been *qualified* as an expert and who, therefore, will be allowed to give his or her expert opinion to assist the jury in understanding technical subjects not within the understanding of the average layperson.

**Court:** Here refers to the judge trying the case.

Attorney Davis conducts direct examination of Dr. Hadley, the doctor who treated plaintiff Brown.

Brown's attorney then asked the doctor to testify as to the nature and extent of the injuries that the plaintiff, Brown, had suffered as a result of the accident. In addition to multiple cuts and bruises, the doctor stated that Brown had suffered a broken knee. The knee, in the doctor's opinion, had been permanently injured, and Brown would continue to suffer periodic pain and stiffness due to the injury. To show the expense that these injuries had cost Brown, the attorney produced the original copies of the bills that the doctor had sent to Brown. She handed the bills to the *clerk*, who marked them as plaintiff's *exhibit* number one. After allowing defense counsel to inspect the bills, Brown's attorney handed them to the doctor, who promptly identified them. The attorney then *moved the bills into evidence* and turned the witness over to defense counsel for cross-examination.

> **Clerk:** The court employee who assists the judge with record keeping at the trial and other administrative duties.
>
> **Exhibit:** An item of physical or tangible evidence offered to the court for inspection.
>
> **Move . . . into evidence:** To request that the items be formally declared *admissible*. This is not the same as declaring them to be true. Admissible means that the items will be admitted simply for consideration as to their truth or falsity.

It was late in the afternoon when Brown's attorney finished with her final witness, Brown himself. The judge did not want to recess for the day, however, until the attorneys for the defendants completed their cross-examination of Brown. After about an hour, all the defense attorneys completed their questioning of Brown, and Brown's attorney *rested her case*. The judge *adjourned* the trial until the following morning.

> **Rest one's case:** To announce formally that you have concluded the presentation of evidence (through the introduction of tangible evidence, through direct examination of your own witnesses, etc.). While the other side presents its case, however, you will be entitled to cross-examine its witnesses.
>
> **Adjourn:** To halt the proceedings temporarily.

On the following morning, the attorney for Clay's estate advised the judge that he had a preliminary matter to bring up before the jury was brought into the courtroom. He then proceeded to make a motion for a *directed verdict* in favor of the estate on Brown's claim of negligence. The judge listened to arguments by the attorneys on the motion. He decided that he would neither deny nor grant the motion but would *take it under advisement*. Miller's attorney also moved for a directed verdict on the negligence claim of Clay's estate against Miller. After hearing the arguments on this motion, the judge denied it because Clay's estate had introduced sufficient evidence to make out a *prima facie case* of Miller's negligence. Hence he would allow this claim of negligence to go to the jury.

> **Directed verdict:** An order by the court that the jury reach a verdict for the party making the motion for a directed verdict on the ground that the other side, which has just rested its case, has failed to produce enough convincing evidence to establish a cause of action.
>
> **Take under advisement:** To delay ruling on the motion until another time.
>
> **Prima facie case:** The party's evidence, if believed by the jury, would be legally sufficient to support a verdict in favor of that party—that is, the party has introduced evidence that, if believed, would include all the facts necessary to establish a cause of action. If the plaintiff *fails* to establish a prima facie case, the judge will decide the case in favor of the defendant without any further proceedings. If the judge finds that there *is* a prima facie case, the defendant will be allowed an opportunity to produce contrary evidence. The case will then go to the jury to decide which version of the facts meets the *standard of proof* (see definition below).

The jury was summoned into the courtroom and seated in the jury box for the second day of the trial. The attorney for the estate began his case by making an opening statement to the jury, reserved from the previous day. He then proceeded to call his witnesses. He had only a few witnesses and was able to conclude his case just before noon, at which time he introduced Clay's death certificate into evidence. The judge then declared a recess for lunch.

Miller's attorney began to present his case in the afternoon, and by late afternoon, he, too, had rested his case. The judge dismissed the jury until the following morning and told the attorneys to be prepared for *closing arguments* at that time. He also asked them to submit any *jury instructions* they would like to request so that he could review them. Brown's attorney requested an instruction that the codefendants had to overcome a *presumption* of negligence against them. The judge denied this request. Finally, he announced that he had decided to deny the estate's earlier motion for a directed verdict.

> **Closing argument:** The final statements by the attorneys summarizing the evidence they think they have established and the evidence they think the other side has failed to establish.
>
> **Jury instructions:** A statement of the guidelines and law given to the jury by the judge for use in deciding the issues of fact. The instructions to the jury are also referred to as the *charge* to the jury. The attorneys are usually allowed to submit proposed instructions for consideration by the judge.
>
> **Presumption:** An assumption or inference that a certain fact is true once another fact is established. A *rebuttable* presumption is an assumption that can be overcome or changed if the other side introduces enough facts to overcome it. If the other side does not rebut the presumption, then the assumption stands. An *irrebuttable* presumption cannot be overcome no matter how convincing the evidence of the other side against the assumption.

Closing arguments began late the following morning. Each attorney carefully reviewed the evidence for the jury and argued for a *verdict* in favor of his or her client. Following a brief recess for lunch, the judge thanked the alternate jurors for their time and dismissed them. He then began to instruct the remaining 12 jurors as to the law they were to follow in finding the facts and in reaching a verdict. He said that they, as jurors, were the finders of fact and were to base their decision solely upon the testimony and exhibits introduced during the trial. He explained the concept of burden of proof and stated which party had to carry this burden as to each of the various *elements* of negligence. Each element had to be proved by a *preponderance of the evidence*. This was the *standard of proof* for this kind of case. Finally, he described the manner in which they should compute the amount of damages, if any, suffered by the parties. The jury was then led out of the courtroom to deliberate on its verdict. The judge retired to his chambers, and the attorneys settled back with their clients to wait.

> **Verdict:** The final conclusion of the jury.
>
> **Elements:** Here, the components of a cause of action. (An element is a component or portion of a rule that is a precondition of the applicability of the entire rule.)
>
> **Preponderance of the evidence:** A standard of proof (used in many civil suits) that is met when a party's evidence on a fact indicates that it is "more likely than not" that the fact is as the party alleges it to be.
>
> **Standard of proof:** A statement of how convincing a version of a fact must be before the trier of facts (usually the jury) can accept it as true. The main standards of proof are proof *beyond a reasonable doubt* (in criminal cases only), proof *by clear and convincing evidence*, and proof by *preponderance of the evidence*.

After about an hour, the judge received a note from the foreman of the jury, asking that the jury be allowed to view several of the exhibits. The items requested consisted largely of the various medical bills allegedly incurred by Brown and Clay. The attorneys for Brown and for the estate took this as a good sign—the jury had probably decided the case against Miller and was now trying to compute damages.

A second note arrived in another hour, announcing that the jury had reached a verdict. The bailiff summoned everyone back to the courtroom, and the jury came in a few minutes later. At the clerk's request, the foreman rose to read the verdict. On Brown's original complaint against Miller for negligence, the jury found for Brown and against Miller, awarding Brown $30,000 in damages. However, on Brown's complaint against Clay's estate (the codefendant), the jury decided in favor of the estate, finding that Clay had not been negligent. The jury found for the estate on its cross-claim against its codefendant, Miller, awarding $750,000 in damages to the estate. Finally, the jury found against Miller on his own cross-claim against the estate, as well as on his counterclaim against Brown.

The judge entered a *judgment* against Miller in the amounts awarded by the jury. After denying a motion by Miller for a *judgment notwithstanding the verdict*, he thanked the jurors and dismissed them.

> **Judgment:** The final conclusion of a court. The judgment will resolve the legal dispute before the court or will indicate what further proceedings are needed to resolve it. Many judgments order the losing party to do something (such as pay damages) or to refrain from doing something. A *declaratory judgment* establishes the rights and obligations of the parties, but it does not order the parties to do or refrain from doing anything.

> **Judgment notwithstanding the verdict:** A judgment by the trial judge that is contrary to the verdict reached by the jury, in effect, overruling the jury. (Also referred to as *a judgment n.o.v.*)

Miller's attorney immediately made a *motion for a new trial*, arguing several possible grounds. When this motion was denied by the trial judge, he moved for a reduction of the verdict on the grounds that the amounts awarded were excessive. This motion was also denied, and the attorney announced his intention to *appeal*. The judge did, however, grant Miller a *stay* of the judgment, conditioned upon his filing a *timely notice of appeal* and posting the appropriate *bond*.

> **Motion for a new trial:** A request that the judge set aside the judgment and order a new trial on the basis that the trial was improper or unfair due to specified prejudicial errors that occurred.

> **Appeal:** To ask a court of *appellate jurisdiction* (a higher court within the same judicial system as the trial court) to *review* or examine the decision of the lower court on the basis that the lower court made error(s) of law in conducting the trial.

> **Stay:** To delay enforcement or *execution* of the court's judgment.

> **Timely:** On time, according to the time specified by law.

> **Notice of appeal:** A document announcing an intention to appeal, which is filed with the appellate court and served on the opposing party.

> **Bond:** A sum of money deposited with the court to ensure compliance with some requirement.

Miller asked his attorney what the $30,000 verdict against him meant. Since Brown had originally sued for $100,000, could Brown later sue Miller again for the rest of the amount he claimed? The attorney explained that, because of the stay granted by the judge, Miller would not have to pay anything until a decision on appeal had been reached. Furthermore, Brown could not sue Miller again on the same cause of action because Brown had received a *judgment on the merits* that would be *res judicata* and would *bar* any later suit based on the same facts. This would also be true of a later action by Clay's estate against Miller.

> **Judgment on the merits:** A decision on the substance of the claims raised. Normally, a judgment of dismissal based solely on a procedural error is not a judgment on the merits. A judgment that is not on the merits results in a *dismissal without prejudice*. A party who has received a judgment on the merits cannot bring the same suit again. A party whose case has been dismissed without prejudice can bring the same suit again so long as all procedural errors are cured (i.e., corrected) in the later action.

> **Res judicata:** The legal doctrine that a judgment on the merits will prevent the same parties from relitigating the same cause of action on the same facts; the parties have already had their day in court.

> **Bar:** Prevent or stop.

Miller's attorney filed his notice of appeal with the United States Court of Appeals and posted bond the following week. As attorney for the *appellant*, it was also his duty to see to it that the *record*, including *transcripts* and copies of exhibits, was transmitted to the Court of Appeals and that the case was *docketed* by the clerk of that court. Miller's attorney then had 40 days in which to draft and file his *appellate brief* with the Court of Appeals. He served copies of the brief on the attorneys for the *appellees*, Brown and Clay's estate, who in turn filed their appellate briefs concerning the *issues on appeal*.

> **Appellant:** The party initiating the appeal; the party who is complaining of error(s) made by the lower tribunal.

**Record:** The official collection of all the trial pleadings, exhibits, orders, and word-for-word testimony that took place during the trial.

**Transcript:** The word-for-word typed record of everything that was said during the trial. The court reporter prepares this transcription, which is paid for by the parties requesting it.

**Docket:** The court's official calendar of pending cases. Once all the necessary papers have been filed, the appeal is "docketed" by the clerk—that is, placed on the court's official calendar.

**Appellate brief:** A document submitted by a party to an appellate court and served on the opposing party in which arguments are presented on why the rulings of a lower court should be approved, modified, or reversed.

**Appellee:** The party against whom the appeal is brought (also called the *respondent*). Often, the appellee is satisfied with what the trial court did and wishes the appellate court to approve of or *affirm* the trial court's rulings.

**Issues on appeal:** The claimed errors of law committed by the trial judge below. The appellate court does not retry the case. No witnesses are called, and no testimony is taken by the appellate court. The court examines the record and determines whether errors of law were committed by the trial judge.

Several months passed before the attorneys finally received a notice from the clerk of the Court of Appeals that the appeal had been scheduled for *oral argument* before a three-judge *panel* of the court. The arguments were heard a few weeks later. Six months after oral argument, the attorneys received the decision of the court in its written *opinion*. By a vote of two to one (one judge *dissenting*), the court *affirmed* the judgments against Miller. The only error that the majority found was the admission of certain testimony offered through Brown's expert witness. However, because Miller's attorney had not objected to this testimony at trial, the opinion stated, he had *waived* this defect.

**Oral argument:** A spoken presentation before an appellate court on why the rulings of a lower tribunal were valid or invalid. The presentation is usually made by the attorneys for the appellant and appellee.

**Panel:** The group of judges, usually three, who decide a case. (For other meanings of *panel*, see the glossary at the end of the book.)

**Opinion:** A court's written explanation of how it applied the law to the facts to resolve a legal dispute. (An opinion is also called a case.) One case can contain several opinions: a majority opinion, a concurring opinion (see the definition that follows), and a dissenting opinion. Opinions are often collected in official and unofficial *reporters*.

**Dissent:** Disagree with the decision (the result and the reasons) of the *majority* on the court. If a judge agrees with the result reached by the majority but disagrees with the reasons the majority used to support that result, the judge would cast a *concurring* vote and might write a separate concurring opinion.

**Affirm:** To agree with or uphold the lower court judgment. If the appellate court *remanded* the case, it would be sending it back to the lower court with instructions to correct the irregularities specified in the appellate opinion. If the appellate court *reversed* the court below, it would have changed the result reached below.

**Waive:** To lose a right or privilege because of an explicit rejection of it or a failure to claim it at the appropriate time. Here, the court is referring to the rule that failure to object during trial is an implied waiver of the right to complain about the alleged error on appeal.

Miller, undaunted, *petitioned* for a *rehearing* by the court *en banc*. The petition was denied. Miller then discussed the possibility of further appeal with his attorney. The attorney explained that Miller could, if he desired, try to appeal to the United States Supreme Court. He cautioned Miller, however, that he could not *appeal as a matter of right* in this case but would be limited to a petition for a *writ of certiorari*. He advised Miller that it was extremely unlikely that the Supreme Court would grant the petition and that it probably would not be worth the expense. Miller agreed, and no further appeal was attempted. Shortly thereafter the Court of Appeals issued its *mandate*, and the case was returned to the District Court, where Miller, through his insurance company, *satisfied* the judgment.

**Petition:** To make a formal request; similar to a motion. (The word *petition* is sometimes synonymous with the word *complaint*, the plaintiff's pleading that attempts to state a cause of action.)

**Rehearing:** A second hearing by a court to reconsider the decision it made after an earlier hearing.

**En banc:** By the entire court. The *panel* of judges that heard the first appeal may have consisted of only three judges, yet the number of judges on the full court may be much larger.

**Appeal as a matter of right:** An appeal in which the appellate court has no discretion on whether to hear the appeal and thus is *required* to review the decision below.

**Writ of certiorari:** An order by an appellate court requiring a lower court to certify the record of a lower court proceeding and to send it up to the appellate court, which has decided to accept an appeal of the proceeding. The writ is used in a case in which the appellate court has discretion to accept or reject the appeal. If the writ is denied, the court refuses to hear the appeal, and, in effect, the judgment below stands unchanged. If the writ is granted, the lower court "sends up" the record and the appeal proceeds.

**Mandate:** The order of the court. Here, the mandate of the appellate court was to affirm the trial court's judgment.

**Satisfy:** To comply with a legal obligation (here, to pay the judgment award).

## 2. Criminal Liability

Brown was involved in a second legal dispute at the same time the negligence suit was under way. In addition to suing Clay's estate and Miller, Brown was defending himself in a criminal *prosecution* for possession of narcotics with intent to distribute.

**Prosecution:** The bringing and processing of legal proceedings against someone; usually a criminal proceeding, but the word includes civil proceedings as well. (The verb is *prosecute*.) The words *prosecution* and *prosecutor* also refer to the attorney who represents the government in a criminal case.

As Brown was leaving the hospital after having recovered from his injury, he was met at the door by two police officers. The officers produced a *warrant* and advised Brown that he was under arrest. After he was read his rights, he was taken to the police station.

**Warrant:** An order from a judicial officer authorizing an act such as the arrest of an individual or the search of property.

The following morning Brown was taken before a judge for his *initial appearance*. The judge advised Brown that he had been charged with a *felony*, possession of narcotics with intent to distribute. He then advised Brown of his rights, including his right to be represented by an attorney. Since Brown was unemployed and without adequate funds to pay an attorney, the judge asked him if he would like the court to appoint an attorney to handle the case. Brown said yes. An attorney was *assigned* to represent Brown. The judge, at the attorney's request, then agreed to give Brown a chance to confer with his new attorney before continuing the hearing.

**Initial appearance:** The first court appearance by the accused during which the court (a) informs him or her of the charges, (b) makes a decision on bail, and (c) determines the date of the next court proceeding.

**Felony:** A crime punishable by a sentence of one year or more. A *misdemeanor* is a crime punishable by a sentence of less than a year.

**Assigned:** Appointed. Assigned counsel is an attorney appointed by the court to represent an individual who is *indigent*, which means lacking funds to hire a private attorney. If the attorney is a government employee handling criminal cases, he or she is often called a *public defender*.

When the case was recalled, Brown and his court-appointed attorney again approached the bench and stood before the judge. The attorney handed the clerk a praecipe formally entering his name as attorney of record for Brown and advised the judge that he was prepared to discuss the matter of *bail*. He proceeded to describe for the judge the details of Brown's background—his education, employment record, length of residence in the city, etc. He concluded by asking that he be released on his own *personal recognizance*. The prosecutor was then given an opportunity to speak. He recommended a high bond, pointing out that the defendant was unemployed and had no close relatives in the area. These facts, he argued, coupled with the serious nature of a felony charge, indicated a very real risk that the defendant might try to flee. The judge nevertheless agreed to release Brown on his personal recognizance and set a date for a *preliminary hearing* the following week.

> **Bail:** A sum of money or other property deposited with the court in order to ensure that the defendant will reappear in court at designated times.
>
> **Personal recognizance:** The release of an accused solely on the basis of his or her promise to return at designated times. No bond or other bail is required.
>
> **Preliminary hearing:** A hearing during which the state is required to produce sufficient evidence to establish that there is *probable cause* (see definition below) to believe that the defendant committed the crimes charged.

The only witness at the preliminary hearing was the police officer who investigated the accident. The officer testified that when he helped pull Brown out of the car, he noticed a small paper sack sticking out from under the passenger's side of the front seat. Several glassine envelopes containing a white powdery substance, the officer said, had spilled out of the sack. The substance, totaling about one-half ounce, was tested and proved to be 80 percent pure heroin. Brown's attorney cross-examined the officer briefly, but little additional information came out. The judge found that there was *probable cause* to hold the defendant and ordered the case *bound over* for *grand jury* action. He continued Brown's release on personal recognizance.

> **Probable cause:** A reasonable basis to believe that the defendant is guilty of the crime(s) charged.
>
> **Bound over:** Submitted.
>
> **Grand jury:** A special jury whose duty is to hear evidence of felonies presented by the prosecutor to determine whether there is sufficient evidence to return an *indictment* (see definition below) against the defendant and cause him or her to stand trial on the charge(s).

Shortly after the preliminary hearing, Brown's attorney went to the prosecutor to see if he could work out an informal disposition of the charge. He tried to convince the prosecutor to enter a *nolle prosequi* on the charge, explaining that Brown had simply been offered a ride home and was not aware that the heroin was in the car. The prosecutor was unwilling to drop the charge. However, he was willing to "nolle" the felony charge of possession with intent to distribute if Brown would agree to *plead* guilty to the lesser offense of simple possession of a dangerous drug, a misdemeanor. The attorney said he would speak to his client about it.

> **Nolle prosequi:** A statement by the prosecutor that he or she is unwilling to prosecute the case. The charges, in effect, are dropped.
>
> **Plead:** To deliver a formal statement or response. In a criminal case, to *plead* means to admit or deny the charges made by the prosecutor.

He spoke to Brown that same afternoon, told him about the *plea bargaining* session, and advised him of the prosecutor's offer. Brown was not interested. He felt he was innocent and was unwilling to plead guilty, even to a misdemeanor.

> **Plea bargaining:** Negotiation between the prosecution and the defense attorney during which an attempt is made to reach a compromise in lieu of a criminal trial. Generally, the defendant agrees to plead guilty to a lesser charge in return for the state's willingness to drop a more serious charge. If the defendant is charged with multiple crimes, the agreement might be a plea of guilty to one or more of the charges in exchange for the dismissal of the others.

Several weeks went by before Brown's attorney was notified that the grand jury had returned an *indictment* against his client. The next step would be the *arraignment* on the following Monday. On this date, Brown and his attorney appeared before the judge, and Brown was formally notified of the indictment. He entered a plea of not guilty to the charge. The judge set a trial date 10 weeks from that day and again agreed to continue Brown's release on personal recognizance.

> **Indictment:** A formal document issued by a grand jury accusing the defendant of a crime. (If the state has no grand jury, the accusation is often contained in a document called an *information*.)

**Arraignment:** A court proceeding in which the defendant is formally charged with a crime and enters a plea. Arrangements are then made for the next proceeding, which is usually the trial.

The day for the trial arrived. Brown's attorney and the prosecutor announced that they were ready. Voir dire was held, and a jury was impaneled. The trial itself was relatively uneventful, lasting less than a day. The prosecutor, following a brief opening statement, presented only two witnesses: the police officer who had been at the scene and an expert from the police lab who identified the substance as heroin. He then rested his case. Brown's attorney made his opening statement and presented his only witness, Brown himself. The jury listened attentively as Brown, on direct examination, explained the events leading up to the accident and his subsequent arrest. Not only had he been unaware of the heroin, he testified, but he had never even seen it, since he had been knocked unconscious by the accident and had not revived until he was in the ambulance. Brown had a previous conviction for shoplifting, and the prosecutor on cross-examination attempted to use this conviction to *impeach* Brown's testimony. Brown's attorney successfully objected, arguing that the conviction, which had occurred eight years previously, was too remote to be *relevant*. The judge agreed and prohibited any mention of the prior conviction. After a few more questions, the prosecutor concluded his cross-examination, and the defense rested its case.

**Impeach:** To attack or discredit by introducing evidence that the testimony of the witness is not credible (believable).

**Relevant:** Having a reasonable relationship to the truth or falsity of an alleged fact; tending to prove or disprove a fact in issue.

Both sides presented their closing arguments following the lunch recess. The judge then instructed the jury; he described the elements of the offense and explained that the burden of proof in a criminal case is on the *government*. That burden, he continued, is to prove each element of the offense *beyond a reasonable doubt*. The jury took less than 45 minutes to reach its verdict. All parties quickly reassembled in the courtroom to hear the foreman announce the verdict *acquitting* Brown of the offense. A *poll* of the jury, requested by the prosecutor, confirmed the result, and the judge advised Brown that he was free to go.

**Government:** Here, the prosecutor.

**Beyond a reasonable doubt:** The standard of proof required for conviction in a criminal case. If any reasonable doubt exists as to any element of the crime, the defendant cannot be convicted. Reasonable doubt is such doubt as would cause prudent persons to hesitate before acting in matters of importance to themselves.

**Acquit:** Find not guilty; absolve of guilt.

**Poll:** To ask each member of a body (e.g., a jury) that has just voted how he or she individually voted. (*Poll* also means to seek a sampling of opinions.)

Generally, criminal cases in which the defendant is acquitted may not be appealed by the prosecutor. Hence, in this case, there was no appeal of the trial judgment. If a defendant is convicted, he or she is sentenced. A convicted defendant *does* have the right to appeal.

### 3. Administrative Dispute

The day after his indictment on the felony charge, Brown went down to the state unemployment office to apply for benefits. After being interviewed by a clerk, he filled out an application form. The clerk told Brown that he would receive a letter in about a week notifying him of the agency's initial determination of his eligibility. If he were eligible, his benefits would start in 10 days.

Brown received the letter a few days later. It advised him that, although he was otherwise eligible for benefits, a routine check with his former employer had disclosed that he had been fired for misconduct. For this reason, the letter stated, he would be deemed disqualified for a nine-week period. Moreover, the benefits due for those nine weeks would be deducted from the total amount he would otherwise have been entitled to receive. If he wished to appeal this decision, the letter went on, he could request an *administrative hearing* within 10 days.

> **Administrative hearing:** A proceeding at an administrative agency designed a to resolve a controversy. The hearing is usually conducted less formally than a court hearing or trial.

Brown felt that he needed some legal advice, but he was still out of work and broke. (The lawsuit in the civil action had not been filed yet—it would be well over a year before the case would be tried, the appeal completed, and the judgment award actually paid.) Brown, therefore, decided to obtain help from the local legal aid office. He explained his problem to a receptionist and was introduced to the paralegal who would be handling his case. The paralegal, an expert in unemployment compensation law, helped Brown fill out a form requesting a hearing and said he would let Brown know as soon as the date was set. Brown left and the paralegal, after consulting with his supervisor, began to research and draft a *memorandum* to submit to the *hearing examiner* on Brown's behalf.

> **Memorandum:** Here, a written presentation of a party's arguments on facts and legal issues in the case. (This memorandum is referred to as an external memorandum of law one addressed to someone outside the law office. See exhibit 12.3 in chapter 12.)

> **Hearing examiner:** A person who presides over the hearing and makes findings of fact and rulings of law, or who recommends such findings and rulings to someone else in the agency who will make the final decision. (The examiner is also called *administrative law judge, referee,* or *hearing officer.*)

In Brown's state, a claimant can have nonattorney representation at unemployment compensation hearings. Therefore, the paralegal at the legal aid office was allowed to represent Brown at his hearing. The only witnesses at the hearing were Brown and his former boss, Frank Best. Best told the examiner about Brown's arrest and about the thefts from the warehouse. Taken together, he argued, these events make it impossible for him to trust Brown on the job any longer. Brown, in turn, denied any participation in the thefts and maintained his innocence on the drug charge. (Brown had not yet been acquitted of the felony.) The hearing examiner, at the close of the proceedings, thanked the parties and promised a decision within a few days.

The hearing examiner's decision arrived shortly thereafter in a document labeled *Proposed Findings and Rulings.* The last paragraph contained the examiner's recommended decision. The hearing examiner agreed with Brown that his boss's mere suspicion that Brown was involved in the thefts was not enough to justify a finding of misconduct. However, the decision went on, the pending criminal charges for a drug-related offense did provide the employer with good cause to fire Brown, since drug involvement could affect his ability to operate a truck safely. The paragraph concluded by recommending a finding of misconduct and the imposition of a nine-week penalty period.

> **Proposed findings and rulings:** Recommended conclusions presented to someone else in the agency who will make the final decision.

A second letter arrived 10 days later containing the *administrative decision* of the agency. The letter, signed by the director of the local agency, adopted the recommended decision of the hearing examiner. This decision, the letter concluded, could be appealed within 15 days to the State Unemployment Compensation *Board of Appeals.* Brown immediately appealed.

> **Administrative decision:** A resolution of a controversy between a party and an administrative agency involving the application of the regulations, statutes, or executive orders that govern the agency. (See exhibit 6.1 in chapter 6) In this case, the decision refers to a determination by a superior of the hearing examiner adopting, modifying, or rejecting the recommended decision of the hearing examiner.

> **Board of appeals:** A nonjudicial administrative tribunal that reviews the decision made by the hearing officer or by the head of the agency. (If this tribunal is part of the administrative agency that rendered the initial administrative decision, the appeal is sometimes referred to as an intra-agency appeal. *Intra* means inside or within.)

Copies of the hearing transcript along with memoranda from both sides were filed with the Board of Appeals. The Board, exercising its *discretion*, refused to allow oral arguments before it and reversed the decision reached *below*. It issued a short administrative decision stating that, while Best may have had cause to be suspicious of Brown, there was not sufficient evidence of actual misconduct on Brown's part. The Board, in this final administrative decision, ordered the local office to begin paying benefits immediately, including back benefits to cover the period since Brown had first applied.

> **Discretion:** The power to choose among various courses of conduct based solely on one's reasoned judgment or preference.
>
> **Below:** The lower tribunal that heard the case before the appeal was brought.

Best decided to appeal this administrative decision in a state court. He was allowed to do so, since he had *exhausted* his *administrative remedies*. He filed a complaint in the county court seeking review of the Board's decision. He submitted the entire record from the proceedings below and asked the court for a *trial de novo*. Brown, now represented by an attorney from the legal aid office, filed his answer and immediately made a motion for summary judgment. The court, upon a review of the record and the pleadings, granted the motion and affirmed the judgment of the Board of Appeals. Best, after discussing the case at length with his attorney, decided against a further appeal of the case to the state court of appeals.

> **Exhausting administrative remedies:** Pursuing *all* available methods of resolving a dispute within the administrative agency before asking a court to review what the agency did. A court generally will not allow a party to appeal an administrative decision until administrative remedies are exhausted.
>
> **Trial de novo:** A totally new fact-finding hearing.

Many of the steps described in the litigation woes of Michael Brown, which you have just read, are outlined in exhibit 10.2 (overview of civil litigation) and in exhibit 10.3 (overview of criminal litigation).

| EXHIBIT 10.2 | Overview of Civil Litigation |
| --- | --- |

(Possible proceedings where administrative decisions, court rulings, and opinions could be written. The events and their sequence presented here are examples only.)

| EVENT | DEFINITIONS | DECISIONS, RULINGS, AND OPINIONS |
| --- | --- | --- |
| **I. Agency Stage**<br><br>1. Someone protests an action taken by the *administrative agency*<br>2. *Administrative hearing*<br>3. *Intra-agency appeal* to a commission, board of appeals, director, or secretary within the agency.<br><br>(If no agency is involved, the litigation begins in court at the pretrial stage.) | *Administrative agency:* a governmental body whose primary function is to carry out or administer statutes passed by the legislature, executive orders issued by the governor or other chief executive, and administrative regulations issued by the agency itself.<br>*Administrative hearing* a proceeding at an administrative agency presided over by a hearing officer (e.g., an administrative law judge) to resolve a controversy<br>*Intra-agency appeal:* a review by an agency of an earlier decision within the same agency to determine if the earlier decision was correct | A mid-level agency official (e.g., hearing examiner), writes a *recommended decision*.<br>The commission, board of appeals, director, or secretary writes an *administrative decision*. |

| EXHIBIT 10.2 | Overview of Civil Litigation—*continued* |
|---|---|

| EVENT | DEFINITIONS | DECISIONS, RULINGS, AND OPINIONS |
|---|---|---|
| **II. Pretrial Stage** <br><br> 4. Plaintiff files a *complaint* <br> 5. Court clerk issues a *summons* <br> 6. *Service of process* on defendant <br> 7. Defendant files an *answer* <br> 8. *Discovery* by *interrogatories* <br> 9. *Discovery* by *deposition* <br> 10. Other discovery <br> 11. Pretrial *motions* <br> 12. *Settlement* efforts <br> 13. *Voir dire* | *Complaint:* a pleading in which the plaintiff states claims or causes of action against the defendant <br> *Summons:* a court notice requiring the defendant to appear and answer the complaint <br> *Service of process:* a formal notification to a defendant that a suit has been instituted against him or her and that he or she must respond to it <br> *Answer:* a pleading in which the defendant gives a response to the plaintiff's complaint <br> *Discovery:* methods by which one party obtains information from the other party about the litigation before trial <br> *Interrogatories*: a method of discovery through written questions submitted by one party to another before trial <br> *Deposition:* a method of discovery in which parties and their prospective witnesses are questioned outside the courtroom before trial <br> *Motion:* a formal request to the court, such as a motion to dismiss <br> *Settlement:* a resolution of the dispute, making the trial unnecessary <br> *Voir dire:* selection of the jury (not all cases are tried by a jury) | The trial court often makes rulings concerning these events but rarely writes an opinion on any of the rulings. <br><br> Occasionally, a party may be allowed to appeal a pretrial ruling to an appeals court, which may write an opinion affirming, modifying, or reversing the ruling. Such an appeal is called an *interlocutory* appeal. It takes place before the trial court reaches a final judgment. |
| **III. Trial Stage** <br><br> 14. *Opening statement* of plaintiff <br> 15. *Opening statement* of defendant <br> 16. Plaintiff presents its case: <br>   **(a)** *evidence* introduced <br>   **(b)** *direct examination* <br>   **(c)** *cross-examination* <br> 17. *Motions* to dismiss <br> 18. Defendant presents its case: <br>   **(a)** *evidence* introduced <br>   **(b)** *direct examination* <br>   **(c)** *cross-examination* <br> 19. Closing arguments to jury by attorneys <br> 20. *Charge* to jury by judge <br> 21. *Verdict* of jury <br> 22. *Judgment* of court | *Opening statement:* a summary of the facts the attorney will try to prove during the trial <br> *Evidence:* that which is offered to help prove or disprove a fact involved in the dispute <br> *Direct examination:* Questioning a witness at a hearing by the side that called the witness. <br> *Cross examination:* Questioning a witness at a hearing by an opponent after the other side has conducted a direct examination of that witness. <br> *Charge* the judge's instructions to the jury an how it should go about reaching its verdict <br> *Verdict* the results of the jury's deliberation <br> *Judgment* the final conclusion of a court | The trial court often makes rulings concerning these events, but rarely writes an opinion on any of the rulings. <br><br> After the trial, the trial court delivers its judgment. Usually, no opinion (explaining the judgment) is written. <br><br> Several trial courts, however, such as federal trial courts (United States District Courts) and New York State trial courts, do sometimes write trial court opinions. |

| EXHIBIT 10.2 | Overview of Civil Litigation—*continued* |
|---|---|

| EVENT | DEFINITIONS | DECISIONS, RULINGS, AND OPINIONS |
|---|---|---|
| **IV. Appeal Stage**<br>23. Filing of *notice of appeal*<br>24. Filing of *appellant's appellate brief*<br>25. Filing of *appellee's appellate brief*<br>26. Filing of appellant's reply brief<br>27. Oral argument by attorneys<br>28. Judgment of court | *Notice of appeal:* a statement of the intention to seek a review of the trial court's judgment<br>*Appellant:* the party bringing the appeal because of dissatisfaction with the trial court's judgment<br>*Appellee,* the party against whom the appeal is brought<br>*Appellate brief:* A document submitted by a party to an appellate court and served on the opposing party in which arguments are presented on why the rulings of a lower court should be approved, modified, or reversed. | An opinion of the middle appeals court (intermediate appellate court) is often written.<br><br>This opinion of the middle appeals court might be further appealed to the highest court, in which event another opinion could be written.<br><br>[Note that in some states there is no middle appeals court; the appeal goes directly from the trial court to the highest state court. See exhibit 6.2 in chapter 6.] |
| **V. Enforcement Stage**<br>29. *Posttrial discovery*<br>30. *Execution* by the sheriff | *Posttrial discovery:* Steps taken after a trial to help the party who won a money judgment (called the *judgment creditor*) against the losing party who must pay such a judgment (called the *judgment debtor*). An example would be a deposition of the judgment debtor to help identify his or her assets.<br>*Execution:* Carrying out or enforcing a judgment. | Court opinions or rulings are not common at this stage unless the parties disagree about something that requires a decision from a judge. |

| EXHIBIT 10.3 | Overview of Criminal Litigation |
|---|---|

(Possible proceedings where court rulings, and opinions could be written. The events and their sequence presented here are examples only.)

| EVENT | DEFINITIONS | RULINGS AND OPINIONS |
|---|---|---|
| **I. Pretrial Stage**<br><br>1. *Arrest*<br>2. *Initial appearance* before a judge or a magistrate<br>3. *Preliminary hearing*<br>4. *Indictment* by grand jury<br>5. *Arraignment*<br>6. Discovery<br>7. Pretrial motions<br>8. *Voir dire* | *Arrest:* to take someone into custody in order to bring him or her before the proper authorities<br>*Initial appearance* the first court appearance by the accused during which the court (a) informs him or her of the charges (b) makes a decision on bail, and (c) determines the date of the next court proceeding.<br>*Preliminary hearing* a court proceeding during which a decision is made as to whether there is probable cause to believe that the accused committed the crime(s) charged. | The trial court often makes rulings concerning these events, but rarely writes an opinion on any of the rulings.<br><br>Occasionally, a party may be allowed to appeal a pretrial ruling immediately to an appeals court, which may write an opinion affirming, modifying, or reversing the ruling. This *interlocutory* appeal takes place before the trial court reaches a final judgment. |

| EXHIBIT 10.3 | Overview of Criminal Litigation—*continued* | |
|---|---|---|

| EVENT | DEFINITIONS | RULINGS AND OPINIONS |
|---|---|---|
| | *Indictment:* a formal charge issued by the grand jury accusing the defendant of a crime. (If no grand jury is involved in the case, the accusation is contained in a document called an *information.*)<br>*Arraignment:* a court proceeding in which the defendant is formally charged with the crime and enters a plea. Arrangements are then made for the next proceeding, which is usually the trial.<br>*Voir dire:* selection of the jury (not all cases are tried by a jury) | |

## II. Trial Stage

| EVENT | DEFINITIONS | RULINGS AND OPINIONS |
|---|---|---|
| 9. *Opening statements* of attorneys<br>10. Government presents its case against the defendant:<br>(a) *evidence* introduced<br>(b) *direct examination*<br>(c) *cross-examination*<br>11. Motions to dismiss<br>12. Defendant presents its case:<br>(a) *evidence* introduced<br>(b) *direct examination*<br>(c) *cross-examination*<br>13. Closing arguments to jury by attorneys<br>14. *Charge* to jury by judge<br>15. *Verdict* to jury<br>16. *Judgment* of court, including the sentence if defendant is convicted | *Opening statements:* a summary of the facts the attorney will try to prove during the trial<br>*Evidence:* that which is offered to help prove or disprove a fact involved in the dispute<br>*Direct examination:* Questioning a witness at a hearing by the side that called the witness.<br>*Cross-examination:* Questioning a witness at a hearing by an opponent after the other side has conducted a direct examination of that witness.<br>*Charge:* the judge's instructions to the jury on how it should go about reaching its verdict<br>*Verdict:* the results of the jury's deliberation<br>*Judgment:* the final conclusion of a court | The trial court often makes rulings concerning these events, but rarely writes an opinion on any of the rulings.<br>After the trial, the trial court delivers its judgment. Usually, no opinion (explaining the judgment) is written.<br>Several trial courts, however, such as federal trial courts (United States District Courts) and New York State trial courts, do sometimes write trial court opinions. |

## III. Appeal Stage

| EVENT | DEFINITIONS | RULINGS AND OPINIONS |
|---|---|---|
| 17. Filing of *notice of appeal*<br>18. Filing of *appellant's appellate brief*<br>19. Filing of *appellee's appellate brief*<br>20. Filing of appellant's reply brief<br>21. Oral argument by attorneys<br>22. Judgment of court | *Notice of appeal:* a statement of the intention to seek a review of the trial court's judgment.<br>*Appellant:* the party bringing the appeal because of dissatisfaction with the trial court's judgment<br>*Appellee:* the party against whom the appeal is brought<br>*Appellate brief:* A document submitted by a party to an appellate court and served on the opposing party in which arguments are presented on why the rulings of a lower court should be approved, modified, or reversed. | An opinion in the middle appeals court (intermediate appellate court) will often be written.<br>This opinion in the middle appeals court might be appealed to the highest court, in which event another opinion could be written.<br>[Note that in some states, there is no middle court; the appeal goes directly from the trial court to the highest state court. See exhibit 6.2 in chapter 6.] |

## Section B
# Alternative Dispute Resolution (ADR)

**alternative dispute resolution (ADR)** A formal method of resolving a legal dispute without litigating it in a court or administrative agency.

**arbitration** A method of ADR in which the parties submit their dispute to a neutral third person who renders a decision that resolves the dispute.

**rent-a-judge** A method of ADR in which the parties hire a retired judge to arbitrate their dispute.

**mediation** A method of ADR in which the parties submit their dispute to a neutral third person who helps the parties reach their own decision to resolve the dispute.

**med-arb** A method of ADR in which the parties first try mediation, and if it does not work, they try arbitration.

**neighborhood justice center (NJC)** A government or private center where disputes can be resolved by mediation or other method of ADR.

**summary jury trial** A method of ADR in which the parties present their evidence to an advisory jury, which renders a nonbinding verdict.

As you can see, litigation can be an involved and costly process. If the parties cannot resolve the dispute on their own, an increasingly popular option is **alternative dispute resolution (ADR)**. Many disputants try it before resorting to traditional litigation. In some kinds of cases, e.g., medical malpractice, disputants may be required to try ADR before being allowed to have a court trial. A few states require ADR to be attempted in all cases. There are several different kinds of ADR:

**Arbitration**. Both sides agree to submit their dispute to a neutral third person who will listen to the evidence and make a decision. They can also agree on whether the decision of the arbitrator will be binding or advisory. The arbitrator is usually a professional arbitrator hired through organizations such as the American Arbitration Association. An arbitration proceeding is not as formal as a court trial. Generally, the decision of an arbitrator is not appealable to a court. If a party is dissatisfied, he or she must go to court and start all over again rather than appealing a particular arbitration decision.

**Rent-a-Judge:** This is another form of arbitration. A retired judge is hired by both sides to listen to the evidence and to make a decision, which has no more or less validity than any other arbitrator's decision.

**Mediation:** Both sides agree to submit their dispute to a neutral third person who will help the disputants reach a negotiated settlement on their own. The mediator does not render a decision, although sometimes he or she may make suggestions or recommendations.

**Med-Arb:** First, mediation is tried. If it is not successful, the proceeding becomes an arbitration, and the mediator switches roles. He or she then makes a decision as an arbitrator.

**Neighborhood Justice Center (NJC):** In many localities, an NJC exists to offer mediation and arbitration services for disputes involving ongoing relationships in the community, such as between landlord and tenant or among neighbors. The NJC could be sponsored by the government, a foundation, or an existing community organization.

**Summary Jury Trial:** The parties use an advisory jury, which often comes from the regular pool of jurors in the county. The attorneys present their evidence to this jury in an abbreviated format. The jury deliberates and renders a nonbinding advisory verdict. Attorneys then question the jurors on the strengths and weaknesses of each side's presentation. The parties use all of this information in deciding whether they should settle, and if so, for what.

Paralegals have many roles in assisting attorneys who have cases in ADR. For example, a paralegal can organize files, schedule discovery and ADR itself, conduct investigations, summarize or digest data from discovery, help prepare the client for ADR, and assist the attorney during the ADR proceeding in much the same fashion as paralegals assist attorneys during regular trials. If ADR leads to a resolution of the case, paralegals can be involved in finalizing the settlement such as by preparing a draft of the document that lays out the terms of the agreements reached.

In addition, some paralegals have become arbitrators and mediators themselves. In most states, you do not have to be an attorney to conduct arbitration or mediation. Service companies are available that offer arbitration and mediation services to parties involved in disputes. A few of these companies hire people with paralegal training and experience to be arbitrators or mediators.

## Section C
# Litigation Assistantship: Pretrial Stage

For a list of paralegal functions in litigation, see "Paralegal Specialties: A Dictionary of Functions" in section C of chapter 2. Note the separate entry on litigation (page 57) as well as the trial and litigation tasks listed under many of the specialty entries. We turn now to a more detailed look at paralegal roles during litigation.

At the *pretrial* stage, we will examine paralegal tasks under the following topics:

1. Service of process and court filings
2. Data retrieval
3. Digesting and indexing
4. Calendar control and scheduling
5. Drafting interrogatories and answers to interrogatories
6. Drafting pleadings
7. Drafting the settlement work-up
8. Preparation of trial notebook
9. Expert witnesses
10. Interviewing
11. Investigation
12. Legal research

The remainder of this chapter will cover most of these tasks, particularly those at the beginning of the list. Some are also discussed in chapter 8 on interviewing, chapter 9 on investigation, chapter 11 on legal research, chapter 13 on computers in the law, and chapter 14 on law office administration.

## 1. SERVICE OF PROCESS AND COURT FILINGS

The lawsuit begins with service of process—the delivery of the complaint and summons to the defendant. This is often done in person, although there are circumstances when the law allows substituted service such as by registered mail. In addition, witnesses are often served with a **subpoena**, which is a command to appear at a certain time and place. (If the command is to bring documents or things, it is a **subpoena duces tecum**; if the command is to give testimony, it is a **subpoena ad testificandum**.) A paralegal may be asked to serve process or to serve a subpoena. Alternatively, the law firm may decide to hire a service company that is a professional process server. If so, a paralegal may have the responsibility of hiring and monitoring the company.

Completing a service yourself takes preparation and care. You have to know the local rules on how to serve someone properly. In addition, you need to anticipate the kinds of difficulty you might encounter "on the street." Here is how paralegal David Busch describes his first service assignment.

> "I was given a subpoena to serve on a lady for a hearing the next day. I rushed to the courthouse to pick up the subpoena and immediately proceeded to the address given to me by the attorney. I spent over an hour looking for the address when I realized that it was a bad address. I frantically found a pay phone and called the lawyer." He was in court. His secretary "gave me a work address. I rushed to the work address to find out that she was on vacation for two weeks beginning yesterday. . . . This was frustrating. This was my first service and I could not even find the lady." I realized that process serving is not as easy as handing someone a copy of a lawsuit.[2]

Filing documents in court also requires careful preparation:

> There are few things more frustrating to the legal assistant than getting something to the courthouse for filing, often on the very last day it is due, and having it returned, not filed, because of a technical error or oversight. Since the legal assistant is the "last checkpoint" for pleadings and other documents being sent to the courthouse, it falls on him or her to ensure those documents are complete and acceptable.

This observation is from litigation paralegal Erin Schlemme, who recommends the following basic steps for successful filings:[3]

- Know the correct address of the court where the filing must be made.
- Phone in advance to determine the exact hours when the clerk's office will be open to accept filings.

**subpoena** A command to appear at a certain time and place.

**subpoena duces tecum** A command that a witness appear at a certain time and place and bring specified things such as documents or records.

**subpoena ad testificandum** A command to appear at a certain time and place to give testimony.

- Place the correct court number on what you are filing (this may be the docket number or a special computer coding number provided by the court's file management system).
- Use the correct format including the proper size of paper, content of the cover sheet, etc.
- Have the correct fees (know whether the clerk can accept a personal check or will accept only cash or a law firm check).
- Obtain an official statement indicating that you have made the filing, e.g., a dated receipt or a copy of what you have filed that has the clerk's court stamp on it.

Similar care is needed when filing in courts that allow facsimile filing. Under this method, pleadings are "faxed" directly to the court, eliminating the need to go to the court yourself or to hire a delivery service. The special procedures instituted by the court to use this method of filing must be scrupulously followed.

**e-filing** Electronic filing of court pleadings and other documents.

The same is true of courts that allow electronic filing (referred to as **e-filing** or ECF, electronic case filing). Documents to be e-filed are converted into an image or digital format. The court may use an Internet service company such as CourtLink (*www.courtlink.com*) to facilitate the process. Once properly filed, the documents are then available on the Internet under rules established by the court. Paralegals must know the rules for proper e-filing. In one state, for example:

> "Any document that is electronically filed with the court after the close of business on any day shall be deemed to have been filed on the next court day. 'Close of business,' as used in this paragraph, shall mean 5 p.m. or the time at which the court would not accept filing at the court's filing counter, whichever is earlier."[4]

Futhermore, while a document that is filed electronically will often have the same legal effect as an original paper document, a printed form of the document (containing any required signatures) may have to be kept in the attorney's files and made available upon request by the court or any party involved in the litigation.

**PACER** Public Access to Court Electronic Records.

Public access to court records through the Internet is increasing dramatically. Many federal courts, for example, provide public access to docket information through **PACER** (Public Access to Court Electronic Records). PACER subscribers can obtain court information by dialing in to the court computer by modem, by using a computer terminal at the offices of the federal district court, or by accessing PACER through the Internet (*www.netside.net/usdcfls/pacer/pacer.htm*). Clearly, we are moving in the direction of the paperless (or almost paperless) courtroom.

## 2. DATA RETRIEVAL

Finding or retrieving data from a file can sometimes be a difficult task. As soon as a lawsuit starts, letters, memoranda, affidavits, and other documents are collected at a rather fast pace. The filing problems presented by this volume of documents can be substantial. A usable index system should exist to let everyone know what is in a file. Even with a good index, however, portions of an active file may be scattered throughout the office on the desks of different people working on the case.

Several basic guidelines should be part of the paralegal's standard practice when engaged in any data retrieval assignment:

- Have a comprehensive knowledge of the office's filing system. Be sure you know who in the office already has this knowledge so that they can be consulted. Is there an index system? Is there a cross-index system? Are file summaries available?
- Have a comprehensive knowledge of the different stages of litigation and the most common documents involved in each stage.
- If possible, find out who wrote the document that contains the data you are trying to retrieve. Ask him or her for leads.

- Determine whether the data you are seeking may be found in more than one document, and if so, look for each document.
- Recognize that data in a document may be contradicted by other data in other documents. To determine the most current status of data, start examining the most recent documents in the file and work back.

Computerization, as we will see in chapter 13, has dramatically changed the way law offices store, manage, and retrieve data from the large number of files that a case often generates. Entire documents can be placed into a computer database by typing them word by word or by "scanning" them in through a photocopy-type machine that can "lift" text from a sheet of paper directly into a computer database. Once the documents are in the computer, searching for data can be relatively easy. For example, you can ask the computer to locate every document in which the phrase "back pain" is found. A well-designed computer database can answer such a question in seconds.

### 3. DIGESTING AND INDEXING

To help a party prepare for trial, the following discovery devices are available:

- interrogatories
- deposition
- production of documents and things; entry on land for inspection and other purposes
- physical or mental examination
- request for admission

For a definition of these devices and an overview of the tasks paralegals perform for them, see exhibit 10.4.

Perhaps one of the most frequently performed discovery tasks is digesting or summarizing discovery documents, particularly depositions. Here is how Dana Nikolewski describes a recent experience with this seemingly never-ending task:

> It's Thursday and I'm on page 20 of a 300-page deposition, which I really should have finished summarizing last week. The phone rings and I relish the thought of this brief interruption, until I recognize the voice on the other end as none other than our local courier announcing the arrival of 200 more depositions which I know need to be summarized ASAP.[5]

Litigation paralegals do indeed spend a good deal of time digesting. Occasionally, you will see a want ad for paralegals to digest depositions full-time. Such individuals are sometimes called **depo summarizers**. While all paralegals do not perform the task full-time, the experience of Dana Nikolewski is not unusual.

Before digesting can occur, every page of a discovery document may have to be sequentially numbered. The digests will refer to specific page numbers in these documents. You will be inserting the page numbers. A variety of numbering formats are possible (e.g., 1, 2, 3, 4; or 0001, 0002, 0003, 0004, or ABC-1, ABC-2, ABC-3, ABC-4). You can combine names with numbers. The pages of the Jackson deposition, for example, might be numbered Jackson01, Jackson02, Jackson03, Jackson04, etc. Page numbering is often performed with a desk tool called a **Bates stamp**. Each time a page number is stamped using this tool, the number on the tool automatically advances so that the next page will be stamped with the next number. Whoever is inserting or stamping the page numbers does not have to advance the number on the Bates stamp manually. Numbering pages with this tool is referred to as Bates numbering.

To **digest** a document, you summarize it according to a given organizational principle. To **index** a document, you state where certain topics are covered in the document. The complexity of the task depends on the complexity of the case and the volume of paper generated before and during discovery.

---

**depo summarizer** An employee whose main job is digesting (summarizing) discovery documents, particularly depositions.

**Bates stamp** A desk tool used to place a sequential number on a page. After using the stamp on a page, it automatically advances to the next number, ready to stamp the next page.

**digest** A summary of something. (See glossary for other definitions).

**index** An alphabetical list of topics covered in a document with page or section number where those topics are covered in the document.

| EXHIBIT 10.4 | Paralegal Roles during Discovery | |
|---|---|---|

| DISCOVERY DEVICE | WHO MUST SUBMIT TO DEVICE? | ROLE OF LITIGATION ASSISTANT |
|---|---|---|
| **1. Interrogatories**<br><br>A method of discovery consisting of written questions sent by one party to another to assist the sender to prepare for trial.<br><br>(See Federal Rule of Civil Procedure, #33.) | Parties only. Nonparty witnesses do not have to answer and cannot send interrogatories | **a.** Prepare a draft of the interrogatories.<br>**b.** Prepare a draft of answers to interrogatories received from the other side.<br>**c.** Read all pleadings, interview reports, and investigation reports as background for the drafting tasks listed in (a) and (b) above.<br>**d.** Arrange conference with client to go over questions and answers.<br>**e.** Draft a motion to compel a response to interrogatories.<br>**f.** Draft a motion to have matters not answered be deemed admitted.<br>**g.** Index and digest interrogatories and answers for office file.<br>**h.** Enter due dates in office tickler to serve as reminders. |
| **2. Deposition**<br><br>A method of discovery by which parties and their prospective witnesses are questioned before trial in order to assist the party initiating the deposition to prepare for trial. Depositions usually take place outside the courtroom.<br><br>If the party being deposed (called the *deponent*) has not seen the questions before they are asked, the deposition is called a *deposition upon oral examination.* (Such questions are always asked by an attorney.) If the deponent is given the questions in writing, the deposition is called a *deposition upon written questions.* (Such questions are often asked by a stenographer or court reporter rather than by an attorney.)<br><br>(See Federal Rules of Civil Procedure, #30, 31.) | A deposition can be taken of a party to the suit. It is also possible to take the deposition of a nonparty witness. | **a.** Schedule time and place for the deposition.<br>**b.** Prepare any subpoenas needed for the deposition such as the *subpoena duces tecum* that requires the person subpoenaed to bring specified things (e.g., documents) with him or her.<br>**c.** Prepare a list of suggested questions for the attorney to ask the deponent. (This is done after reading everything in the file to date, e.g., complaint, answer, interview reports, investigation reports, and answers to interrogatories.)<br>**d.** Arrange for scheduling and payment of stenographer or reporter.<br>**e.** Order transcript of deposition.<br>**f.** Take notes at the deposition.<br>**g.** Prepare motion to force compliance by other side.<br>**h.** Prepare motion to have matters not answered deemed admitted.<br>**i.** Read transcript of deposition to index it, digest it, compare it to interrogatory answers, look for inconsistencies, etc.<br>**j.** Make entries in office tickler on due dates. |

| EXHIBIT 10.4 | Paralegal Roles during Discovery—continued | |
|---|---|---|

| DISCOVERY DEVICE | WHO MUST SUBMIT TO DEVICE? | ROLE OF LITIGATION ASSISTANT |
|---|---|---|
| **3. Production of documents and things; entry on land for inspection and other purposes**<br><br>A method of discovery by which a party can prepare for trial by forcing another party to produce documents or other things or to allow entry on land. This can be for purpose of copying, photographing, measuring, or otherwise inspecting the items designated.<br><br>(See Federal Rule of Civil Procedure #34.) | This device is directed at parties only. The party must be in possession or control of the document, thing or land in question. If you want a *nonparty* to turn over documents and other materials you can seek a deposition of this non-party and use a *subpoena duces tecum* to specify what should be brought to the deposition. | **a.** Prepare a draft of a request for production of documents, things, etc. specifying what you want to copy, inspect, or test, and when you want to do so.<br>**b.** Arrange who will do the inspecting, copying, etc., payment of costs involved, etc.<br>**c.** Draft a motion to compel the inspection, copying, etc.<br>**d.** File, digest, and index the report(s) based on the inspection, copying, etc.<br>**e.** Enter scheduled dates for inspection, copying, etc. in the officer tickler. |
| **4. Physical or mental examination**<br><br>A method of discovery by which a party can prepare for trial by obtaining a court-ordered independent examination of a person whose physical or mental condition is in controversy.<br><br>(See Federal Rule of Civil Procedure #35.) | Limited to parties only and to persons under the control of parties e.g., the child of a party. (In a few courts, the employees of a party can also be forced to undergo a physical or mental examination.) | **a.** Schedule doctor's appointment and payment.<br>**b.** Prepare court motion to order the examination.<br>**c.** Prepare court motion to have matters relevant to the examination be deemed admitted for failure to submit to examination.<br>**d.** Enter dates pertaining to the examination in office tickler. |
| **5. Request for admissions**<br><br>A method of discovery by which a party submits a statement of facts to another party who must affirm or deny the facts. Those facts that are admitted will be treated by the court as having been established and need not be proven at the trial.<br><br>A similar request may be made to admit the genuineness of certain documents or other things.<br><br>(See Federal Rule of Civil Procedure #36.) | Limited to parties only. | **a.** Read everything in the file (pleadings, interview and investigation reports, interrogatory answers, deposition transcript, etc.) in order to prepare a list of facts the other side will be requested to admit.<br>**b.** File, index, and digest the responses from the other side in the office file.<br>**c.** Enter due dates in office tickler. |

Some of the basic objectives of digesting and indexing include:

■ Creating order out of what might be hundreds or thousands of pages of data.
■ Providing ready access to selected topics in these pages once the summaries are correlated by subject matter. (For example, an index and digest of depositions and interrogatory answers might point out every time any witness referred to the quality of work performed by an employee who is alleging that she was fired because of sex discrimination.)

- Providing a way of comparing testimony, verifying facts, spotting inconsistencies, and identifying evidentiary holes that need to be filled by further interviewing, investigation, and discovery.
- Assisting the attorney in organizing the trial, particularly by suggesting questions to be used in the direct and cross-examination of witnesses on the stand. Such strategy considerations will often go into the attorney's *trial notebook* (see discussion below), which you may be asked to help prepare.

The starting point in *indexing* any document is to find out what topics in the document your supervisor wants you to index, such as leg injuries, medical payments, tax assessments, or wage history. Every time these topics appear in the document, you note the page number so that someone else can find these topics easily in that document. For an example of an index of a deposition, see exhibit 10.5.

| EXHIBIT 10.5 | Deposition Index |
| --- | --- |

### INDEX OF DEPOSITION OF IAN SMITH
### 3/13/01

| TOPIC | PAGES IN DEPOSITION |
| --- | --- |
| Leg injuries | 2, 24, 33, 35, 45 |
| Medical payments | 1, 7, 19 |
| Tax assessments | 40, 43, 50 |
| Wage history | 1, 2, 4, 7, 25, 29 |

The method of *digesting* or summarizing data is also fairly simple. Suppose, for example, the following material comes from page 65 of the transcript (word-for-word account) of a deposition of Mr. Smith:

| Line | page 65 |
| --- | --- |

1. Q. Could you tell me please exactly how long after the accident
2.    you first felt the pain in your leg?
3. A. Well, it's hard to say precisely because everything happened
4.    so fast and my head was spinning from....
5. Q. Was it an hour, a day, a week?
6. A. Oh, no, it wasn't that long. I'd say the pain started
7.    about ten minutes after the collision.

Depositions have two sets of numbers: the Bates numbers that you insert (65 in our example) and the line numbers inserted by the court reporter who typed the transcript of the deponent's testimony. Note that at the left margin, every line is sequentially numbered. The top line on every page will begin with the number "1." The transcript of Mr. Smith's testimony from page 65 of the deposition could be digested into:

Began feeling pain in leg about 10 min. after collision: page 65, lines 1–7

Alternatively, your supervisor might want you to present this digest in three columns in what is called a *page/line format*. For example:

| PAGE/LINE | SUMMARY | TOPIC |
|---|---|---|
| 65 : 1–7 | Began feeling pain in leg about 10 min. after collision | Injury, Leg Pain |

As you can see, considerable space can be saved by eliminating the question-and-answer format and focusing directly on the information sought. As a rule of thumb, every 10 pages can be summarized into 1 page unless you are instructed to include more detail in your summaries. The time needed to produce such summaries depends on the complexity of the material and your experience. In general, an experienced paralegal can digest 10–15 pages in one hour.

The summaries can be placed on small file cards under the heading "Injury" or on summary sheets that are categorized by such headings. You can then collate all statements made by the same witness on a particular topic. You can compare what this same deposition witness said about a particular topic in his or her answers to interrogatories. You can compare what other witnesses have said about the same topic. The possibilities are endless once you have prepared careful, readable summaries.

In large cases, discovery data can be entered into computer databases using specially designed software such as Discovery Manager and Summation. (Often such programs have online training programs for new users.) The computer makes the creation of digests and other reports considerably easier.

The computer has also affected the way in which deposition transcripts are received. When court reporters type transcripts of deposition testimony (or of trial testimony), they are usually able to provide attorneys with disk copies of the testimony so that the text of the testimony can be fed into the case management computer programs used by the office. In some courts, it is possible for attorneys to hook up their computer to the computer of the court reporter who is typing everything the witness is saying. The reporter's stenographic quotes are instantly translated into English so that the attorney can read on his or her laptop computer screen what the witness has just said. (This is called **real-time** transcript access).[6] Depositions can also be taken on video. Video synchronization allows the word-for-word text of what the deponent is saying to be scrolled on the monitor as he or she speaks. Depositions on the Internet are also possible. We will examine more of these developments in Chapter 13 on computers in the law.

For general guidelines on digesting, see exhibit 10.6.

There are two major kinds of digest summaries:

- Digest by person
- Digest by subject matter

### Digest by Person

In a **digest by person**, you focus on a particular witness, such as the person questioned in a deposition. Your instructions may be to provide a page-by-page summary of what the witness said. If so, you simply go through the entire document and summarize everything (see exhibit 10.7). Include a table of contents at the beginning of the report you prepare that provides the summary (see exhibit 10.8).

**real-time** Occurring now; happening as you are watching; able to respond immediately.

**digest by person** A summary of the information in a document organized around every mention of a particular person.

**EXHIBIT 10.6    Guidelines for Digesting Discovery Documents**

1. Obtain clear instructions from your supervisor. What precisely have you been asked to do? What have you expressly or by implication been told not to do? How much time do you have to complete the digest? It is a good idea to write down the supervisor's instructions. If you have never worked with a particular supervisor before, show him or her your work soon after you begin the assignment to make sure you have understood the instructions.

2. Know the difference between paraphrasing testimony and quoting testimony. To *paraphrase* is to phrase the testimony partly or entirely in your own words. To quote is to use the exact words of the witness even though you may leave out part of what the witness said. Supervisors may not want you to do any paraphrasing. They may want to do their own paraphrasing. Again, you need to know precisely what is expected.

3. Do not "editorialize," i.e., inject your personal comments. For example, do not say that the response of a witness whose testimony you are digesting is "unbelievable."

4. Know the case inside and out. You cannot digest something you do not understand. You must have a general understanding of the causes of action and the defenses so that you can grasp the context of the testimony. Read the client file, including interview and investigation reports, pleadings, interrogatory answers, other discovery documents, etc.

5. The answers given in a deposition often ramble. (The same may be true of some interrogatory answers.) Given this reality, act on the assumption that the same topic is covered in more than one place in the discovery document. Look for this diversity and record it in your summary by pointing out *each* time the same topic is mentioned.

6. Do not expect the answers to be consistent—even from the same witness. Do not consciously or unconsciously help the witness by blocking out potential inconsistencies. If on page 45 the witness said she saw a "car" but on page 104 said she saw a "van," do not blot out the distinction by saying she saw a "motor vehicle," or by failing to mention both. The danger of doing this is more serious than you think, particularly when you are reading hundreds of pages and are getting a little red in the eyes.

7. Always think in terms of categories as you summarize. Place your summaries into categories. The categories may be as broad as the name of a given witness. Other categories include:

   - Background information
   - Education
   - Past employment
   - Present employment
   - Medical history

   - Insurance
   - Prior claims
   - Pre-accident facts
   - Accident facts

   - Post-accident facts
   - Medical injuries from this accident
   - Damage to property
   - Prior statements made

   Your supervisor will usually tell you what categories or topics to use in organizing your summaries. If not, use your common sense and create your own.

8. Each summary should include the specific document you used (e.g., deposition) the page, and, for depositions, the lines on the page that are the basis of the summary.

9. Find out if the law firm has an office manual that gives you instructions on digesting. If not, check closed case files for samples of the kind of digesting and indexing that the film has done in the past. Ask your supervisor if you should use such samples as models.

10. Prepare summaries of your summaries whenever you have an extensive digesting assignment that requires the examination of numerous documents for numerous topics.

11. Update the summaries. After you finish your digest, more facts may become known through further investigation and discovery. Supplement your earlier summary reports by adding the new data.

12. Keep a list (or know where to find a list) of every piece of paper in a file. Some digesting/indexing assignments will require you to examine everything in the file.

**digest by subject matter** A summary of the information in a document organized around every mention of a particular topic.

### Digest by Subject Matter

In a **digest by subject matter**, you are asked to focus on a particular topic only. For example:

- Everything the witness said about the dismissal
- Everything that all the witnesses said about the condition of the car after the accident
- Everything that all the witnesses said about events after 6 P.M. on 5/30/02

| EXHIBIT 10.7 | Digest by Person | |
|---|---|---|

| PAGE/LINE | SUMMARY | TOPIC |
|---|---|---|
| 1:1–35 | John R. Smith, 12 Main St. Buffalo N.Y. 14202, 456-9103. | Personal Data |
| 1:36–40 | Mechanic, XYZ Factory, 3/13/83; became supervisor 3/97. | Employment |
| 2:1–28 | Met plaintiff 7/31/91 at factory; was plaintiff's superior; trained plaintiff to operate equipment. | Relationship to Plaintiff |
| 2:29–47 | Was working on date of accident (9/1/00); saw plank fall on plaintiff. | Accident |

| EXHIBIT 10.8 | Table of Contents for Digest by Person | |
|---|---|---|

### DIGEST OF DEPOSITION OF JOHN R. SMITH

**CASE:** Jones v. XYZ Factory     **OFFICE FILE NUMBER:** 01-341
**DEPONENT:** John R. Smith, supervisor of plaintiff     **COURT DOCKET NUMBER:** Civ. 2357-1
**DATE OF DEPOSITION:** 2/24/01     **ATTORNEY ON CASE:** Linda Stout
**DATE SUMMARY PREPARED:** 5/16/01
**SUMMARY PREPARED BY:** George Henderson, Paralegal

### TABLE OF CONTENTS

| Topic | Pages in Deposition |
|---|---|
| Background information | 1–4, 9 |
| Smith's Knowledge of Accident | 2–3, 5, 7–10 |
| Company Report Filed by Smith | 23 |
| Smith's Instructions to Plaintiff Just before Accident | 15–17 |

- All statements made to the police after the accident
- All references to the meeting of 7/23/01

The subject matter or topic can be limited to a particular discovery document, such as a deposition, or it can cover a large number of documents:

- The complaint
- The answer
- Interrogatory answers
- Deposition transcripts
- Responses to requests for admission
- Reports obtained via a motion to produce documents or other things
- Medical examination reports
- Other investigation reports
- Etc.

Hence one digest summary can pull together everything on a particular topic from all of the above sources so that comparisons, correlations, and commentaries can be made.

If the case involves a large number of events (e.g., arising out of a relatively complex personal injury or business dispute), the office may also want a **time line** summary, in which you present the sequence of events in careful chronological fashion. For example:

- 3/13/03. John Farrell (JF) notifies Lincoln Car Rental (LCR) about defect in steering wheel.
- 3/14/03. JF returns vehicle to LCR. Given replacement truck.

**time line** A chronological presentation of significant events, often organized in a straight line or linear arrangement.

- 3/15/03. Accident occurs on Rt. 52 outside Portsmouth, OH.
- Etc.

Time lines can also be effectively used in trial graphics. See, for example, the time line on the birth of an oxygen-deprived baby at the bottom of exhibit 10.13, later in the chapter.

### 4. CALENDAR CONTROL AND SCHEDULING

Here are five words that a paralegal (and everyone else in a law office) should never be heard saying: "Oh, was that due today?"[7] The clock is a dominant presence in every well-run law office. Calendars are filled with events such as dates for:

- Client meetings
- Filing a lawsuit before the statute of limitations expires
- Sending a demand letter to an insurance company setting out terms for a settlement
- Requesting a jury trial
- Filing interrogatories
- Filing requests for production of documents
- Responding to discovery requests from opposing parties
- Filing pretrial motions
- Hearings
- Etc.

Numerous events must take place according to specified deadlines, sometimes at the risk of losing important rights. One of the most common grounds for legal malpractice claims against attorneys, for example, is allowing the statute of limitations to run on a cause of action. The failure to file a lawsuit within the time allowed by law can result in the permanent loss of a client's right to assert a cause of action, no matter how good a case the client would have had.

**tickler** A system designed to provide reminders of important dates.

A major method of achieving calendar control is the office **tickler**, which is used to record important dates and to remind everyone to take appropriate action on these dates. Attorneys need constant reminders of due dates, particularly when they are working on more than one case or when more than one attorney is working on a single case.

Scheduling is often a secretarial responsibility, although in complex cases, paralegals can become involved. Arrangements must be made for expert witnesses to prepare reports and to give deposition and trial testimony; timely notifications of discovery events must be made; medical examinations must be arranged, etc.

Ticklers operate in different ways. One common system uses both paper forms and a computer scheduling program. Suppose, for example, that an attorney must conduct a deposition on May 23. Weeks before this date, the attorney's paralegal will enter this date on a specially designed, multipart form. One of the parts of the form is torn off and sent to the attorney as a reminder of the deposition. Another part will be torn off and sent to the attorney as a further reminder a few days before May 23. The paralegal also enters the date into a computer program that generates a weekly or monthly graphic calendar that is regularly updated. Sophisticated case management software can streamline the process. The computer might be programmed to send out e-mail reminders automatically as the day of the deposition approaches. Part of a paralegal's responsibility may be to monitor such calendars rigorously. As additional protection against missed deadlines, there may be a centralized calendar system for the entire office and an individual calender system for each attorney. Most attorneys carry their own daily planner or pocket calendar everywhere they go. The same is true of many litigation paralegals.

### 5. DRAFTING INTERROGATORIES AND ANSWERS TO INTERROGATORIES

Here are some sample interrogatories used in a personal injury case:

---

**Sample Interrogatories Covering Injuries and Damages**

1. State the name of each person for whom you claim damages for personal injuries.
2. Describe in detail all injuries and symptoms, whether physical, mental, or emotional, experienced since the occurrence and claimed to have been caused, aggravated, or otherwise contributed to by it.
3. As to each medical practitioner who has examined or treated any of the persons named in your answer to interrogatory 1, above, for any of the injuries or symptoms described, state:
   (a) The name, address, and specialty of each medical practitioner;
   (b) The date of each examination or treatment;
   (c) The physical mental, or emotional condition for which each examination or treatment was performed.
4. Has any person named in your answer to interrogatory 1, above, been hospitalized since the occurrence?
   (a) The name and location of each hospital in which each was confined;
   (b) The dates of each hospitalization;
   (c) The conditions treated during each hospitalization;
   (d) The nature of the treatment rendered during each hospitalization.
5. Have any diagnostic studies, tests, or procedures been performed since the accident? If so, state:
   (a) The nature thereof;
   (b) The name, address, and occupation of the person performing same;
   (c) The place where performed and, if in a clinic, laboratory, or hospital, the name and address thereof;
   (d) The name and present or last-known address of each party now in possession or control of any records prepared in connection with each study, test, or procedure.
6. Is any person named in your answer to interrogatory 1, above, still under the care of any medical practitioner? if so, state:
   (a) The name and address of each practitioner;
   (b) The nature of each condition for which care is being rendered;
   (c) Which of the conditions are related to the accident.
7. State as to each item of medical expense attributable to the accident:
   (a) The amount;
   (b) The name and address of the person or organization paid or owed therefore;
   (c) The date of each item of expense (attach copies of itemized bills).

---

Considerable skill is required in drafting interrogatories and in replying to or answering them. The tasks have opposite objectives: in drafting interrogatories, you want to obtain as much information as possible from the other side, while in responding to interrogatories you usually want to say as little as possible without being untruthful. Exhibits 10.9 and 10.10 present guidelines on drafting and answering interrogatories.

## 6. DRAFTING PLEADINGS

The major pleadings in litigation are the complaint and the answer. Very often you will use standard forms as the starting point in drafting pleadings. Closely examine the guidelines in exhibit 10.11 on using standard forms.

Here, we will concentrate on drafting a complaint through an examination of its basic structure:

- Caption
- Designation of the pleading
- Statement of jurisdiction
- Body
- Prayer for relief
- Subscription
- Verification

Not all complaints follow this format. You need to check the requirements in the statutes and court rules that govern the structure for complaints in the court where you are filing the action. Exhibit 10.12 presents a sample complaint[8] that follows the basic structure listed above.

| EXHIBIT 10.9 | Guidelines on Drafting Interrogatories |
|---|---|

1. Be sure that your office tickler states when the interrogatories must be filled.
2. Obtain general and specific instructions from your supervisor on the questions to be asked in the interrogatories.
3. Read all the documents on the case that have been prepared thus far (such as the client interview report [intake memo], field investigation report, complaint, and answer).
4. Look at drafts of other interrogatories that have been used in other cases that are similar to your case. Determine whether courts in your area have approved any standard-form interrogatories.
5. Recognize the need to adapt interrogatories from the files of other clients to the peculiar needs of your case.
6. Start out with request for basic data (name, address, age, occupation, etc.) from the person who will be answering the interrogatories—the respondent.
7. Try to avoid questions that call for simple *yes/no* answers unless you also ask follow-up questions about the factual basis for such answers.
8. Phrase the questions so as to elicit facts. Try to avoid questions that call for an opinion from the respondent unless the opinion is relevant or might provide leads to other facts.
9. Know what facts will be necessary to establish your client's case, and ask specific questions focusing on those facts. Know the elements of the causes of action and defenses in the case. Ask questions designed to uncover facts for each element.
10. As to each fact, ask questions calculated to elicit the respondent's ability to comment on the fact. (How far away was he or she? Does he or she wear glasses? Etc.)
11. Phrase the fact questions so that the respondent will have to indicate clearly whether he or she is talking from firsthand knowledge or hearsay.

| EXHIBIT 10.10 | Guidelines on Responding to Interrogatories |
|---|---|

1. Be sure that your office tickler states when the answers are due.
2. Obtain general and specific instructions from your supervisor on drafting the answers.
3. Check all the facts in proposed answers with the facts asserted in available documents (such as the client interview report [intake memo], field investigation report, complaint, and answer).
4. Do not volunteer information beyond the confines of the question unless necessary to clarify a position (when, for example, a simple answer would be damagingly misleading without the clarification).
5. When an answer to a question is not known, say so.
6. When asked questions that cannot be answered with precise facts, preface the answer by saying "to the best of my knowledge" or "as far as I can recall" in order to provide some leeway if the answer later proves to be incorrect.
7. Recognize that the other side will try to use the answers against you. For example, opposing counsel may try to get the client to say something on cross-examination that will contradict the answers given by the client to the interrogatories.
8. Recognize the kinds of improper questions that a party does not have to answer. For example:
   - Clearly irrelevant questions that are not likely to lead to admissible evidence
   - Unduly repetitive or burdensome questions
   - Questions inquiring into *attorney work product*, e.g., questions that ask for the attorney's strategy or that ask for copies of legal memoranda. (Work product consists of anything prepared by an attorney, or by his or her staff, in anticipation of litigation.)
   - Questions that expressly or implicitly call for a violation of the attorney-client privilege, e.g., "what did your attorney tell you?"
9. Prepare supplemental answers to prior answers where new facts are obtained after the initial interrogatories were answered and filed.

| EXHIBIT 10.11 | How to Avoid Abusing a Standard Form |
| --- | --- |

1. A standard form is an example of the document or instrument that you need to draft, such as a pleading, contract, or other agreement.
2. Standard forms are found in a number of places—for example, in formbooks, in manuals, in practice texts, in some statutory codes, and in some court rules. Many of these standard forms are available through a computer database either as stand-alone software or online. On the Internet, for example, see *www.USCourtForms.com* and the sites listed in On the Net at the end of the chapter.
3. Most standard forms are written by private attorneys. Occasionally, however, a standard form will be written by the legislature or by the court as the suggested or required format to use.
4. Considerable care must be exercised in the use of a standard form. Such forms can be deceptive in that they appear to require little more than filling in the blanks. The intelligent use of these forms usually requires much more.
5. The cardinal rule is that you must always *adapt* the form to the particulars of the client's case. You fit the form to the client's case, not the client's case to the form.
6. Do not be afraid of changing the printed language in the form if you have a good reason. Whenever you make such a change, be sure to alert your supervisor so that it can be approved.
7. You should never use a standard form unless and until you have satisfied yourself that you know the meaning of *every* word and phrase on the form. This includes *boilerplate*, which is standard language often used in the same kind of document. The great temptation of most form users is to ignore what they do not understand because the form has been used so often in the past without any apparent difficulty. Do not give in to this temptation. Find out what everything means by:
   - Using a legal dictionary (often a good starting point)
   - Asking your supervisor
   - Asking other knowledgeable people
   - Doing other legal research
8. You need to know whether the entire form or any part of it has ever been litigated in court. To find this out, do some legal research in the area of the law relevant to the form.
9. Once you have found a form that appears useful, look around for another form that attempts to serve the same purpose. Analyze the different or alternative forms available. Which one is preferable? Why? Keep questioning the validity and effectiveness of any form.
10. Do not leave any blank spaces on the form. If a question does not apply, make a notation to indicate this, such as N.A., meaning not applicable.
11. If the form was written for another state, be sure that the form can be adapted and is adapted to the law of your state. Often, however, an out-of-state form is simply unadaptable to your state because of the differences in the laws of the two states.
12. Occasionally, you may go to an old case file to find a document that might be used as a model for a similar document that you need to draft on a current case. All the above cautions apply to the adaptation of documents from closed case files.

## Caption of Complaint

A **caption** is the heading of a complaint (see top of exhibit 10.12). The caption of a complaint should contain the name of the court, the names of the parties, and the number assigned to the case by the court.

**caption** The beginning (usually the top) of a complaint that provides identifying information such as the names of the parties, the court in which the action is being brought, and the docket number assigned to the case by the court.

## Designation of the Pleading

The title of the pleadings should be clearly stated at the top. The pleading for our example in exhibit 10.12 is a Complaint for Negligence.

## Statement of Jurisdiction

If the court requires a statement of the court's **subject matter jurisdiction**, the citation to the statute or other law conferring this jurisdiction must be included. (This jurisdiction is the power or authority of the court to hear a particular category or kind of case.) Many state courts do not require a statement of subject matter jurisdiction in complaints.

**subject matter jurisdiction** The power of the court to resolve a particular category or kind of dispute.

**EXHIBIT 10.12**    **Structure of Complaint**

**Caption** ⎰

STATE OF _____ COUNTY OF _____
_____ COURT

John Doe, Plaintiff

v.                    Civil Action No. _____

Richard Roe, Defendant

**Designation of Pleading** →

COMPLAINT FOR NEGLIGENCE

Plaintiff alleges that:

**Statement of Jurisdiction** →

    1. The jurisdiction of this court is based on section _____, title _____ of the [State] Code.

    2. Plaintiff is a plumber, residing at 107 Main Street in the City of _____, _____ County, State of _____.

    3. Upon information and belief, defendant is a traveling salesman, residing at 5747 Broadway Street in the City of _____, County of _____, State of _____.

    4. On or about the second day of January, 2002 an automobile driven by defendant, on Highway 18 in the vicinity of the Verona intersection, struck an automobile being driven by the plaintiff on said highway.

**Body** ⎰

    5. Defendant was negligent in the operation of said automobile at the aforesaid time and place as to:

    a. Speed,

    b. Lookout,

    c. Management and control.

    6. As a result of said negligence of defendant, his automobile struck plaintiff's automobile and caused the following damage:

    a. Plaintiff was subjected to great pain and suffering.

    b. Plaintiff necessarily incurred medical and hospital expense.

    c. Plaintiff suffered a loss of income.

    d. Plaintiff's automobile was damaged.

**Prayer for Relief** →

    Wherefore plaintiff demands judgment in the amount of two hundred thousand dollars ($200,000), together with the costs and disbursements of this action.

**Subscription** →

_____
Plaintiff's Attorney
1 Main Street

_____ , _____

**Verification** ⎰

    John Doe, being first duly sworn on oath according to law, deposes and says that he has read the foregoing complaint and that the matters stated therein are true to the best of his knowledge.

_____
John Doe

Subscribed and sworn to before me on this_____ day of _____, 2000.

_____
Notary Public

My commission expires:

For purposes of determining **venue**—the place of the trial—the complaint may also have to allege the residence of the parties, where the accident or wrong allegedly occurred, etc.

**venue** The place of the trial.

### Body

The claims or causes of action of the plaintiff are presented (stated) in the *body* of the complaint. (A cause of action is a set of facts that gives a party the right to judicial relief; it is a legally acceptable reason for suing.) Every separate cause of action used by the plaintiff should be stated in a separate "count," e.g., Count I, Count II, or simply as First Cause of Action, Second Cause of Action, etc. The paragraphs should be consecutively numbered. Each paragraph should contain a single fact or a closely related grouping of facts.

With what factual detail must the complaint state the cause of action? There are two main schools of thought on this question: fact pleading versus notice pleading.

1. *Fact Pleading.* In **fact pleading**, there must be a statement of the *ultimate facts* that set forth the cause of action. Not every detail that the plaintiff intends to try to prove at trial is pleaded. The complaint need not contain a catalog of the evidence that the plaintiff will eventually introduce at the trial. Only the ultimate facts are pleaded. There is, however, no satisfactory definition of an ultimate fact. Generally, it is one that is essential to the establishment of an element of a cause of action.

   The complaint should *not* state conclusions of law, such as "Jones assaulted Smith" or "Jones violated section 23 of the state code." The problem, however, is that it is sometimes as difficult to define a conclusion of law as it is to define an ultimate fact. Some statements are mixed statements of fact and law—for example, "Jones negligently drove his car into . . ." As a matter of common sense and practicality, if the conclusion of law (here, "negligently") is also a convenient way of stating facts, it will be permitted.

   For guidance, check prior decisions of the courts in the state that have concluded what are proper and improper statements of fact in a complaint.

2. *Notice Pleading.* In federal courts under the Federal Rules of Civil Procedure and in states that have adopted the lead of the federal courts, the goal of the complaint is to say enough to notify or inform the defendant of the nature of the claims against him or her. This is the essence of **notice pleading**. There is no requirement that ultimate facts be alleged. The plaintiff must simply provide a short and plain statement of the claim showing the pleader is entitled to relief.

   It is not improper to fail to plead an ultimate fact. The critical point is that the complaint will not be thrown out if it *fails* to plead an ultimate fact or if it *includes* conclusions of law—as long as the complaint gives adequate notice of the nature of the claim. The technicalities of pleading facts, conclusions of law, etc., are unimportant in notice pleading.

   Notice pleading does not necessarily require a different kind of pleading from fact pleading; notice pleading is simply more liberal or tolerant in what is acceptable.

**fact pleading** A statement of every ultimate fact. A fact is ultimate if it is essential to establish an element of a cause of action.

**notice pleading** A short and plain statement of the claim showing the pleader is entitled to relief.

When the plaintiff lacks personal knowledge of a fact being alleged, the fact should be stated upon **information and belief**, as in the third paragraph of exhibit 10.12.

There are times when the law requires specificity in the pleading. For example, allegations of fraud must be stated with specificity or particularity. Also, when special damages are required in defamation cases, the facts must be pleaded with some specificity.

**information and belief** To the best of one's knowledge; a good-faith understanding.

### Prayer for Relief

In the **prayer for relief**, the complaint asks for a specific amount of damages or for some other form of relief such as an injunction against a nuisance. (If the prayer asks for damages, the clause requesting it is called the *ad damnum* clause.) In the event that the defendant fails to appear and answer the complaint, a default judgment is entered against

**prayer for relief** A request for damages or other form of judicial relief.

the defendant. The relief given the plaintiff in a default judgment cannot exceed what the plaintiff asked for in the prayer for relief.

### Subscription

A **subscription** is someone's signature. If an attorney prepared the complaint, his or her subscription is required. If the plaintiff wrote the complaint and is acting as his or her own attorney in the case, the plaintiff signs.

**subscription** A signature; the act of signing one's name.

### Verification

A **verification** is an affidavit that is submitted with the pleading. It is signed by a party on whose behalf the pleading was prepared, who swears that he or she has read the pleading and that it is true to the best of his or her knowledge. (Not all states require that complaints be verified.)

**verification** An affidavit stating that a party has read the pleading and swears that it is true to the best of his or her knowledge.

## 7. DRAFTING THE SETTLEMENT WORK-UP

Throughout the pretrial stage of litigation, the opposing attorneys often engage in efforts to negotiate a settlement of the case in order to avoid a trial. One of the formal documents the parties sometimes use during negotiations is the **settlement work-up**, also called a settlement brochure. It contains a summary of the major facts in the case presented in a manner designed to encourage the other side (or its liability insurance company) to settle the case. Paralegals often have a large role in helping draft this document. For a sample settlement work-up, see exhibit 9.10 in chapter 9.

**settlement work-up** A summary of the major facts in the case presented in a manner designed to encourage the other side (or its liability insurance company) to settle the case.

## 8. PREPARATION OF TRIAL NOTEBOOK

A **trial notebook**, also called a trial book, is a collection of documents, arguments, and strategies that an attorney plans to use during a trial. It is often organized in a looseleaf binder for easy use by the attorney. The notebook becomes the attorney's checklist for conducting the trial.

Not all trial notebooks are organized the same way. Litigation assistant Pam Robtoy cautions us that "[j]ust as each attorney has different preferences on how they want you to perform different tasks, each notebook you organize will be different, depending on which attorney will be utilizing the notebook and the particular requirements of the case. For example, a trial notebook for a medical malpractice case would likely contain a section for medical research regarding the surgical procedure, medication, etc. that is the focus of the case."[9] A trial notebook for a breach-of-contract case would not.

Many trial notebooks contain the following sections:[10]

**trial notebook** A collection of documents, arguments, and strategies that an attorney plans to use during a trial.

- Table of Contents
- Things to Do
- Trial Schedule/Deadlines
- Trial Team (street addresses, phone numbers, e-mail addresses)
- Case Outline
- Statement of Facts
- Pleadings
- Trial Briefs/Trial Memoranda (submitted to the court)
- Law
- Outline of Liability
- Our Exhibits
- Opposition Exhibits
- Our Witnesses
- Opposition Witnesses
- Witness Statements
- Requests for Production and Responses

- Requests for Admission and Responses
- Direct Examination Outline of Questions
- Anticipated Cross-Examination Questions
- Outline of Damages
- Motions
- Deposition Index and Outlines
- Voir Dire Questions
- Juror Information
- Jury Chart
- Records
- Opening Statements
- Plaintiff Testimony
- Requests for Jury Instructions
- Defendant Testimony
- Final Arguments

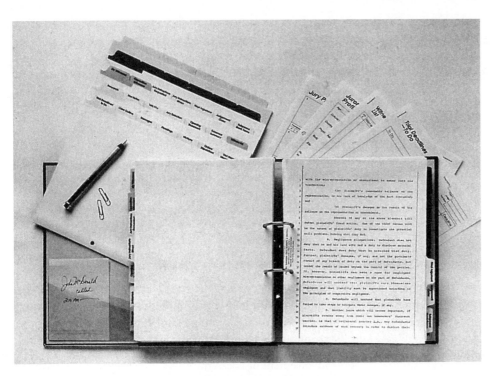

LawFiles Trial Notebook. Courtesy of Bindertek, Sausalito, California

It's often the paralegal's job to collect the material that will go into the notebook, organize it, keep it current, and help make it useful to the attorney as a vehicle for trial preparation and trial management. Specifically, the paralegal might:

- Prepare summaries of deposition testimony.
- Prepare a list of all parties and witnesses plus people who are expected to be mentioned during testimony; index this list to the rest of the trial notebook.
- Prepare sample questions to ask witnesses, particularly when needed to lay the foundation for evidence to be introduced.
- Prepare a summary description or log of all the exhibits to be used.
- Prepare an abstract of the contents of every document.
- State the location of documents and exhibits that will not be contained in the trial notebook itself.
- Cross-index material on particular witnesses or on legal theories.
- Summarize all information known about each juror from voir dire.
- Prepare end tabs for each section of the notebook.
- Color-code different kinds of documents and information, such as using blue sheets for citations to authorities supporting claims and yellow sheets for deposition testimony and other statements of the opposing party.

Of course, you need to adapt these tasks to the particulars of your case. One paralegal recently color-coded all the tabs (green for exhibits, orange for discovery data, etc.) before she discovered that the attorney using the trial notebook was color blind!

## 9. EXPERT WITNESSES

Paralegals often have an important role in working with expert witnesses that the trial attorney may want to use. The first task is to locate potential experts for consideration. Many can be located online. WESTLAW and LEXIS–NEXIS, for example, have extensive databases or libraries that provide detailed information on experts available for hire. (For more on these commercial services, see chapters 11 and 13.) The Internet is also an excellent resource for locating experts. See the sites in the "On the Net" section at the end of the chapter.

Once an expert is selected, he or she is sent a formal engagement letter. Patricia Gustin, a paralegal who has helped draft such letters, recommends that the letter include:[11]

- Confirmation of all past discussions (by phone, e-mail, letter, in-person meetings) about hiring the expert
- A summary of the case, including the case name and docket number, if the case has already been filed in court
- Anticipated dates for the expert's testimony at deposition, at trial, or at both
- The scope of the expert testimony to be provided
- A list of articles or documents enclosed in the letter that the expert should review
- Names of the primary contacts in the office that the expert should use
- A list of support people and available resources in the law office for the witness
- A summary of the financial terms for hiring the expert

Once an expert witness is hired, the paralegal might become the major contact person for the witness when he or she is not dealing directly with the trial attorney.

## Section D
# LITIGATION ASSISTANTSHIP: TRIAL STAGE

The role of paralegals at trials depends, in part, on the involvement that they have had with the case up to trial. If the involvement has been minimal, then they may not have much to do to assist the attorney at trial. If, on the other hand, they have been working closely with the attorney on the case all along, their role at trial could include a number of tasks:

- Monitoring all the files, documents, and evidence that the attorney will need to plan and to replan strategy as outlined in the trial notebook.
- Doing some spot legal research on issues that come up during the trial that require an answer fairly quickly.
- Preparing preliminary drafts of certain motions and other documents that are required during the course of the trial.
- Assuring the presence of witnesses; assisting the attorney in preparing them for direct examination and in anticipating what may be asked of them on cross-examination.
- Taking notes on the testimony of certain witnesses. The attorney may be able to use these notes in preparing for other segments of the trial (e.g., closing argument). A typed transcript of the testimony may not be available until after the trial.
- Making suggestions to the attorney on what questions to ask a witness based on the paralegal's close following of what has happened thus far in the trial and based on his or her involvement with the documents and files prepared during the pretrial stage.
- Assisting with trial exhibits.

Trial exhibits can include photographs, x-rays, medical illustrations, video presentations (e.g., a day in the life of the injured plaintiff), anatomical models, surgical appliances, etc. Some paralegals are able to design exhibits. See, for example, the graphic designed by Kathleen Young, a litigation paralegal, in exhibit 10.13. Notice that the graphic contains a time line that shows when significant events occurred in a birth case where the graphic was used. The head was delivered at 1:47 and the baby at 1:53, indicating a total of six minutes when the baby was deprived of oxygen. Time lines can help the jury visualize the impact of crucial facts. If the office hires a litigation consultant to create such graphics, the role of the paralegal might be to help monitor the work of the consultant. Computer graphics presentation programs such as Microsoft's Power-Point are available to help create graphics. They can generate slides that contain text, pictures, drawings, and maps. PowerPoint also allows videos or movies to be integrated into the presentation. (For more on these computer programs, see chapter 13.) To display exhibits at trial, the paralegal may have to obtain permission from clerks, the

| EXHIBIT 10.13 | Time Line Trial Graphic Designed by a Paralegal |

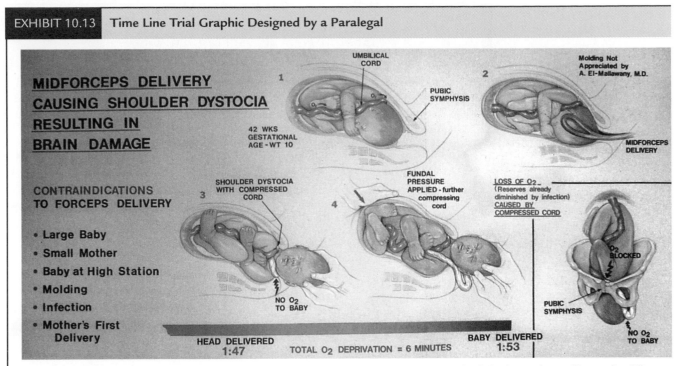

Time line illustration created by paralegal Kathleen Young, Litigation Visuals, Inc. (www.litvis.com) that helped win a $3.9 million verdict. "Illustrations really do help the jury know where they are going in calculating damages." 11 *Legal Assistant Today* 28 (November/December, 1993).

judge's secretary, or other court personnel for the in-court use of devices such as computers, overhead projectors, video players, magnetic boards, blackboards, and chart holders.

In some courtrooms, a judge will allow a paralegal to sit with the attorney at counsel's table during the trial. Here is how one attorney describes the benefits of this arrangement:

> At trial, the paralegal sitting with counsel can be extremely helpful. Paralegals should be trained to take notes while counsel is examining witnesses and to monitor the admission of exhibits. Thereafter, they can prepare a binder of all exhibits for subsequent trial days and can digest the transcripts. At the end of a day of trial, the file may be out of order, and paralegals can reorganize it for the next day. Finally, paralegals can assist the attorney by calling witnesses to arrange testimony, meeting witnesses in the hall, and talking with the client and his family. Generally, the attorney has so much to concentrate on in trial that paralegals can give the client the needed attention while providing a "buffer" between lawyer and client.[12]

For more on the role of the paralegal sitting "second chair" (or "third chair") during the trial, see page 264 in chapter 5.

If the office is about to begin a very important and potentially complex trial, it may decide to conduct a **shadow trial** first. A shadow trial is a mock (i.e., pretend) trial designed to give the participants "stand-up" practice and feedback. For example, the office might hire some strangers to play the roles of jurors and conduct part of the trial in front of them. Attorneys in the office would be assigned the roles of opposing counsel. "Jury" deliberations would take place in front of everyone. After the trial, there would be a freewheeling discussion of the strengths and weaknesses of the case. In effect, the shadow trial acts as a kind of focus group in preparation for the real trial. (Since actual opposing attorneys and witnesses are not involved, a mock trial is different from the summary jury trial discussed earlier under ADR—alternative dispute resolution.) Litigation paralegals often have a large role in helping organize shadow trials, e.g., hiring the jurors, holding an orientation session for them before the proceedings, acting as a nonvoting juror to keep the deliberations moving along and on track.

**shadow trial** A mock trial conducted by one side in order to give its attorneys practice and feedback from individuals playing the role of jurors.

## Section E
# LITIGATION ASSISTANTSHIP: APPEAL STAGE

Once the trial is over, the central question becomes whether to appeal. Both sides may have to make this decision, since neither party may have obtained everything it wanted at the trial. Attorneys must review all of the documents and testimony in the trial in order to identify grounds for an appeal. A paralegal may be asked to go back over the record and do the following:

- Make a list of every time I objected to something during the trial. Include the page number where my objection is found, a brief summary of what my objection was, and the ruling of the judge on my objection.
- Make a list of every time opposing counsel made reference to a particular topic, such as the plaintiff's prior involvement in other litigation.
- Make a list of every time the judge asked questions of witnesses.

Other paralegal tasks can include:

- Researching the legislative history of relevant statutes
- Shepardizing cases and conducting cite checking
- Reading appellate briefs to cross-check the accuracy of quoted testimony from the typed transcript of the trial
- Monitoring the typing, printing, and filing of appellate briefs

## Section F
# LITIGATION ASSISTANTSHIP: ENFORCEMENT STAGE

**judgment debtor** The person ordered by a court to pay a money judgment (damages).

**judgment creditor** The person to whom a court-awarded money judgment (damages) is owed.

**execution** Carrying out or enforcing a judgment.

If a money judgment was awarded to the client, considerable work may be required in collecting it from the **judgment debtor**, the party obligated by the court to pay the judgment. (The person who won the judgment and must be paid is the **judgment creditor.**) The paralegal can arrange for the sheriff to begin **execution**, which is the process of carrying out or enforcing a judgment. The judgment debtor may be ordered by the court to submit to an examination of what his or her assets are. Investigation work will probably be required to determine what assets exist, where they are, and how they might be reached (see chapter 9 on investigation). In some cases, the attorney may be able to petition the court for a contempt order against the judgment debtor for noncompliance. The paralegal can help by assembling the factual basis to support this charge and in drafting some of the court papers involved.

## CHAPTER SUMMARY

Civil litigation begins with the filing of a complaint, to which the defendant responds with an answer. In these pleadings, the parties state their causes of action and defenses. The next major event is discovery, which can include interrogatories, depositions, requests for admission, etc. If motions for summary judgment are denied, the trial proceeds. After voir dire and opening statements to the jury, the party with the burden of proof puts on its case through the introduction of evidence and the direct examination of witnesses. The latter can be cross-examined by the other party. When the first party rests, the other goes through the same steps. A motion for a directed verdict will be granted (thus ending the case) if there was a failure to establish a prima facie case. After closing statements to the jury and the instructions of the judge, the case goes to the jury. Its verdict (if accepted by the court) becomes the basis of the court's judgment.

If dissatisfied with the judgment, the appellant files a notice of appeal and an appellate brief. The appellee also files an appellate brief. After oral argument, the appellate court affirms, modifies, or reverses the judgment of the lower court. A further appeal to a higher appellate court might also be possible.

Criminal litigation often begins with an arrest warrant, followed by an initial appearance. Once the decision on bail is made, the prosecution proceeds to the preliminary hearing to determine whether probable cause exists. If so, the grand jury will then determine whether to issue an indictment. The arraignment is next. If plea bargaining is unsuccessful, the case goes to trial, where guilt must be established beyond a reasonable doubt. The criminal trial then proceeds in a manner similar to a civil trial: voir dire, opening statements, etc. The appeal process is also similar: notice of appeal, appellate briefs, etc.

In an administrative hearing, a hearing examiner makes a decision on the dispute within the agency. His or her decision will usually be in the form of a recommendation to a higher official or body within the agency. When a party has exhausted administrative remedies, he or she can appeal the agency's decision to a court.

Alternatives to litigation can include arbitration, rent-a-judge, mediation, med-arb, neighborhood justice centers, and summary jury trial.

Among the roles fulfilled by paralegals during litigation are the following: serving and filing documents, retrieving and organizing data from the files, indexing and digesting discovery documents, maintaining the calendar, drafting interrogatories and answers to interrogatories, drafting complaints and other pleadings, helping prepare the trial notebook, coordinating trial exhibits, working with expert witnesses, providing assistance as needed during the trial, retrieving and digesting facts in preparation for appeal, and providing general assistance in collecting a judgment.

## KEY TERMS

litigation
civil dispute
criminal dispute
damages
liable
joint and several liability
retainer
appearance
attorney of record
forum
estate
diversity of citizenship
venue
complaint
plaintiff
cause of action
stating a cause of action
codefendant
pleading
allegation
information and belief
ad damnum
jury trial
file
service of process
summons
process server
affidavit
statute of limitations
in personam jurisdiction

personal jurisdiction
motion to dismiss
failure to state a cause of action
procedural law
Federal Rules of Civil Procedure (Fed. R. Civ. P.)
substantive law
answer
default judgment
motion
defense
affirmative defense
cross-claim
counterclaim
thirty-party complaint
contest
adverse judgment
discovery
interrogatories
deposition
request for admission
subpoena duces tecum
order
hearing
motion for summary judgment
magistrate
pretrial conference
stipulated
in issue
tangible evidence

introduce evidence
set for trial
bailiff
jury panel
voir dire
challenge for cause
bias
peremptory challenge
alternate
impaneled
rule on witnesses
opening statement
burden of proof
bench conference
objection
competency
excused the jury
examination
overrule
direct examination
ground
hearsay
sustain
strike from the record
cross-examination
redirect examination
qualify (a witness)
expert witness
court
clerk
exhibit
move into evidence
rest one's case
adjourn
directed verdict
take under advisement
prima facie case
closing argument
jury instructions
presumption
verdict
elements
preponderance of the evidence
standard of proof
judgment
judgment notwithstanding the verdict
motion for a new trial
appeal
stay
timely
notice of appeal
bond
judgment on the merits
res judicata
bar
appellant
record

transcript
docket
appellate brief
appellee
issues on appeal
oral argument
panel
opinion
dissent
affirm
waive
petition
rehearing
en banc
appeal as a matter of right
writ of certiorari
mandate
satisfy
prosecution
warrant
initial appearance
felony
assigned
bail
personal recognizance
preliminary hearing
probable cause
bound over
grand jury
nolle prosequi
plead
plea bargaining
indictment
arraignment
impeach
relevant
government
beyond a reasonable doubt
acquit
poll
administrative hearing
memorandum
hearing examiner
proposed findings and rulings
administrative decision
board of appeals
discretion
below
exhausting administrative remedies
trial de novo
alternative dispute resolution (ADR)
arbitration
rent-a-judge
mediation
med-arb
neighborhood justice center (NJC)
summary jury trial

subpoena
subpoena duces tecum
subpoena ad testificandum
e-filing
PACER
depo summarizer
digest
index
Bates stamp
real-time
digest by person
digest by subject matter
time line
tickler
caption

subject matter jurisdiction
venue
fact pleading
notice pleading
information and belief
prayer for relief
subscription
verification
settlement work-up
trial notebook
shadow trial
judgment debtor
judgment creditor
execution

## ON THE NET: MORE ON CIVIL PROCEDURE AND LITIGATION

### State and Federal Courts
www.ncsconline.org/Information/Info_court_web_sites.html
www.uscourts.gov

### Alternative Dispute Resolution
www.adr.org
www.cpradr.org
www.cybersettle.com (online ADR)

### Rules of Procedure and Evidence in Federal Courts
www.law.cornell.edu/rules/frcp/overview.htm
www.law.cornell.edu/rules/fre/overview.html
www.law.ukans.edu/research/frcrimi.htm

### Court Forms
forms.lp.findlaw.com
www.USCourtForms.com
www.lectlaw.com/forma.htm

### Electronic Court Filing
www.legaldockets.com
www.courtlink.com
www.pacer.psc.uscourts.gov

### Internet Depositions
www.I-Dep.com

### Expert Witnesses
www.tasanet.com
www.juryverdicts.com/experts/index.html
www.idex.com
www.expertpages.com

### Request for Production of Documents (Tobacco Case)
www.uiowa.edu/~rclinton/clinton/CivPro/PMIRFP2.htm

### Famous Trials
www.law.umkc.edu/faculty/projects/ftrials/ftrials.htm
www.law.umkc.edu/faculty/projects/ftrials/Simpson/simpson.htm (O.J. Simpson)

### Michigan Cyber Court
www.michigancybercourt.net

## ENDNOTES

1. See the National Center for State Courts (www.nsconline.org) and the Federal Judiciary (www.uscourts.gov/judbus2000/contents.html).

2. David Busch, *A Job and an Adventure*, 12 AAPLA Advocate 3 (Alamo Area Professional Legal Assistants, October/November 1993).

3. Erin Schlemme, *Courthouse Etiquette*, 11 The TALA Times 4 (Tulsa Ass'n of Legal Assistants, February 1993).

4. California Civil Procedure Code § 1010.6(a).

5. Dana Nikolewski, *Just Call Me Dorothy*, 13 Newsletter 5 (Dallas Ass'n of Legal Assistants, April 1989).

6. Stacy Hunt, *Making Life Easier for All of Us*, 17 Legal Assistant Today 90 (September/October 1999).

7. Christofer French, *The Professional Paralegal Job Search* 18 (1995).

8. Adapted from MacDonald, Pick, DeWitt, and Volz, *Wisconsin Practice Methods* § 1530, at 239 (2d ed. 1959).

9. Pam Robtoy, *Preparing Trial Notebooks*, 14 Legal Paraphernalia 5 (St. Louis Ass'n of Legal Assistants, July/August 1994).

10. Hollins, *Assignment: Trial Prep*, 2 California Paralegal 30 (April/June 1990); Feder, *Translating Professional Competence into Performance Competence*, 15 Legal Economics 44 (April 1989).

11. Patricia Gustin, *Making the Expert Witness Part of the Legal Team*, 27 Facts & Finding 14 (November 2000).

12. Lynne Z. Gold-Bikin et al. *Use of Paralegals in a Matrimonial Practice*, 16 FAIR$hare 9 (September 1996).

# Chapter 11

# LEGAL RESEARCH

## Chapter Outline

Section A

# INTRODUCTION

This chapter does not cover every aspect of legal research, nor does it treat every conceivable legal resource that could be used in a law library. Rather, the chapter examines the major components of legal research with the objective of identifying effective starting points.

A great deal of information is provided in the pages that follow. You should first skim the chapter to obtain an overview and to see where some concepts are covered in more than one place. Then you should begin collecting the terminology called for in assignments 11.1 and 11.2. The best way to avoid becoming overwhelmed is to become comfortable with terminology as soon as possible.

When you walk into a law library, your first impression is likely to be one of awe. You are confronted with row upon row of books, most of which seem unapproachable; they do not invite browsing. To be able to use the law library, your first responsibility as a legal researcher is to break down any psychological barrier that you may have with respect to the books and other resources in it. This is done not only by learning the techniques of research but also by understanding the limitations of the law library.

A major misunderstanding about the law library is that it contains the answer to every legal question. In many instances, legal problems have no definitive answers. The researcher often operates on the basis of "educated guesses" of what the answer is. To be sure, your guess is supported by what you uncover through legal research. The end product, however, is only the researcher's opinion of what the law is, rather than the absolute answer. No one will know for sure what the "right" or final answer is until the matter is litigated in court. If the problem is never litigated, then the "right" answer will be whatever the parties accept among themselves through negotiation or settlement. The researcher will not know what answer carries the day for the client until the negotiation process is over.

Many simple problems, however, can be answered by basic (easy) legal research. Suppose, for example, you want to know the name of the government agency in charge of incorporating a business or the maximum number of weeks one can receive unemployment compensation. Finding the answer is not difficult if you know what books or other resources to go to and how to use their indexes or other points of access. Many legal research problems, however, are not this simple.

Perhaps the healthiest way to approach the law library is to view it not so much as a source of answers as a storehouse of ambiguities that are waiting to be identified, clari-

A paralegal in the law library

fied, manipulated, and applied to the facts of a client's case. You may have heard the story of a client who walked into a law office and asked to see a one-armed attorney. When asked why he required an attorney meeting such specifications, he replied that he was tired of presenting problems to attorneys and having them constantly tell him that "on the one hand" he should do this but "on the other hand" he should do that; he hungered for an attorney who would give him an answer. This concern is well taken. A client is entitled to an answer, to clear guidance. At the same time (or on the other hand), part of the attorney's job is to identify alternatives or options and to weigh the benefits and disadvantages of each option. Good attorneys are so inclined because they understand that our legal system is infested with unknowns and ambiguities. Good legal researchers also have this understanding. They are not frightened by ambiguities; they thrive on them.

In school, you will learn a good deal of law. Eventually, you will probably forget most of it. If you don't, you should! No one can know all of the law at any given time, even in a specialty. Furthermore, the law is always changing. Nothing is more dangerous than someone with out-of-date "knowledge" of the law. Law cannot be practiced on the basis of the rules learned in school. Those rules may no longer be valid by the time you try to use them in actual cases. Thousands of courts, legislatures, and administrative agencies spend considerable time writing new laws and changing or adapting old ones. In light of this reality, you need to focus on the *techniques* of doing legal research covered in this chapter. These techniques will remind you to distrust the law you think you know and will equip you to find out what the law is *today.*

The law library and the techniques of legal research are the indispensable tickets of admission to current law. School teaches you to think. *You teach yourself the law through the skill of legal research.* Every time you walk into a law library, you are your own professor. You must accept nothing less than to become an expert on the topic of your research, no matter how narrow or broad the topic. The purpose of the law library is to enable you to become an expert on the current law of your topic. Do not fall into the trap of thinking that you must be an expert in an area of the law to research it properly. The reverse is true. A major way for you to become an expert in an area is by discovering on your own what the law library can teach you about that area.

Never be reluctant to undertake legal research on a topic simply because you know very little about the topic. Knowing very little is often a beneficial starting point for the researcher! Preconceptions about the law can sometimes lead you away from avenues in the library that you should be traveling.

Becoming an expert through comprehensive legal research does not necessarily mean that you will know everything about a particular topic or issue. An expert has answers *and* knows how to *formulate the questions that remain unanswered even after comprehensive legal research*. An expert is someone who can say:

> This is what the current law says, and these are the questions that the law has not yet resolved.

Of course, you cannot know what is unresolved until you know what is resolved. The law library will help tell you both.

## Section B
# FRUSTRATION AND LEGAL RESEARCH

You are in the position of the king who sadly discovered that there is no royal road to geometry. If he wanted to learn geometry, he had to struggle through it like everyone else. Legal research is a struggle and will remain so for the rest of your career. The struggle will eventually become manageable and even enjoyable and exciting—but there is no way to avoid the struggle no matter how many shortcuts you learn. The amount of material in a law library is simply too massive for legal research to be otherwise, and the material is growing every day with new laws, new formats for law books, new technology, and new publishers offering new services that must be mastered.

Unfortunately, many cannot handle the pressure that the law library sometimes seems to donate in abundance. Too many attorneys, for example, stay away from the library and consequently practice law "from the hip." They act on the basis of instinct and bravado rather than on the basis of the most current law uncovered through comprehensive legal research. Such attorneys need to be sure that they have adequate malpractice insurance!

Legal research will be difficult for you at the beginning, but with experience in the law library and the right attitude, you will overcome the difficulties. The most important advice you can receive is *stick with it*. Spend a lot of time in the library. Be inquisitive. Ask a lot of questions of fellow students, teachers, librarians, attorneys, paralegals, legal secretaries, etc. Be constantly on the alert for tips and techniques. Take strange books from the shelf and try to figure out what they contain, what they try to do, how they are used, and how they duplicate or complement other law books with which you are more familiar. Do not wait to be taught how to use sets of books that are new to you. Strike out on your own.

The coming of computer technology to legal research is of some help, but computers cannot eliminate your need to learn the basics. The struggle does not disappear if you are lucky enough to study or work where computers are available. Intelligent use of computers requires an understanding of the fundamental techniques of legal research. Furthermore computer legal research can be expensive. A good deal of free legal information is now available on the Internet, but as we will see, it is not always as current or accurate as information available in traditional library volumes and in commercial (fee-based) computer research services.

At this stage of your career, most of the frustration will center on the question of how to *begin* your legal research of a topic. Once you overcome this frustration, the concern will then become how to *end* your legal research. After locating a great deal of material, you will worry about when to stop. In this chapter, our major focus will be the techniques of beginning. Techniques of stopping are more troublesome for the conscientious researcher. It is not always easy to determine whether you have found everything that you should find. Although guidelines do exist and will be examined (in section Y, later in the chapter), a great deal of experience with legal research is required before you can make the judgment that you have found everything available on a given topic. Don't be too hard on yourself. The techniques will come with time and practice. You will not learn everything now; you can only begin the learning that must continue throughout your career.

Keep the following "laws" of legal research in mind:

1. *The only books that will be missing from a shelf are those that you need to use immediately.*
2. *A vast amount of information on law books and research techniques exists, most of which you will forget soon after learning.*
3. *Each time you forget something, relearning it will take half the time it previously took.*
4. *When you have relearned something for the fourth time, you own it.*

At times, you will walk away from a set of law books that you have used and wonder what you have just done—even if you obtained an answer from the books. At times, you will go back to a set of books that you have used in the past and draw a blank on what the books are and how to use them again. These occurrences are natural. You will forget and you will forget again. Stay with it. Be willing to relearn. You cannot master a set of books after using them only a few times. Learning legal research is a little like learning to play a musical instrument: a seat is waiting for you in the orchestra, but you must practice. A royal road does not exist. Computers will help, but their availability requires you to know another "law" of legal research:

5. *The computer will become your best friend only when you have acquired the techniques of traditional book (i.e., paper) legal research that will allow you to find what you need without a computer.*

## Section C
# ORGANIZATION OF THE CHAPTER

This chapter has two main parts. The second half covers checklists and strategies for finding the 10 main categories of law that might be needed to resolve a legal issue that has arisen out of the facts of a client's problem. The 10 categories of law are:

| | |
|---|---|
| Opinions | Charters |
| Statutes | Ordinances |
| Constitutions | Rules of court |
| Administrative regulations | Executive orders |
| Administrative decisions | Treaties |

For definitions of these categories (plus a special 11th category—the opinions of the attorney general), see exhibit 6.1 in chapter 6.

Before we learn how to find these categories of law, we will do two things: cover some of the *basics* needed to perform any research task and study the major *research resources*. These will be our goals in the first half of the chapter.

### BASICS
The basics include the following topics:

- Terminology of legal research
- Kinds of legal authority
- Citation of legal authority
- Indexes

Once we have grasped these fundamentals, we turn to the research resources.

### RESEARCH RESOURCES
The major research resources we will use to find the law needed to resolve a legal issue are as follows:

| | |
|---|---|
| Catalogs | Legal periodicals |
| Digests | Legal encyclopedias |
| Annotations | Treatises |
| Shepard's | Phone and mail |
| Loose-leaf services | Computers |

Our approach in this chapter, therefore, will be as follows: first, we will cover the basics and the research resources; then, we will use this material to find the 10 major categories of law.

## Section D
# TERMINOLOGY OF LEGAL RESEARCH: TWO CHECKLISTS

This section contains two lists. The first is a list of essential research terms that you need to understand before you start doing any legal research (see exhibit 11.1 and assignment 11.1). The second is a more comprehensive list of terms that you need to understand by the time you finish studying legal research (see exhibit 11.2 and, assignment 11.2). All of the terms in the essentials list (exhibit 11.1) are also in the comprehensive list (exhibit 11.2). Do assignment 11.1 now. Assignment 11.2 should be completed by the end of the course. You need to learn the language of legal research as well as how to do legal research. Assignments 11.1 and 11.2 will help you start acquiring this language.

Do not be intimidated by the comprehensive list. You are not expected to grasp everything in it right away. Start collecting definitions now. When you start solving research problems in the library, the terms will have increased meaning for you.

Both lists contain numbers in parentheses after each entry. They are page numbers in the book where the terms are covered. Check the index for other pages where they are covered.

---

**EXHIBIT 11.1    The Terminology of Legal Research: A Checklist of Essentials**

1. act (469)
2. administrative regulation (281)
3. advance sheet (for reporters) (469)
4. *ALWD Citation Manual* (471, 516)
5. *American Jurisprudence* 2d (471, 584)
6. *American Law Reports* (471)
7. annotation (471, 556)
8. authority (506, 512)
9. bill (472)
10. *Bluebook: A Uniform System of Citation* (472)
11. brief of a case (472)
12. CARTWHEEL (539)
13. cause of action/defense (308)
14. CD-ROM (467)
15. cite/citation (480)
16. cite, parallel (480)
17. code, administrative (469)
18. code, statutory (501)
19. common law (284, 324)
20. constitution (281)
21. *Corpus Juris Secundum* (481, 585)
22. digests (for reporters) (482)
23. headnote (489)
24. holding (317, 511)
25. *Index to Legal Periodicals and Books* (489)
26. Internet (489, 678)
27. KeyCite (492)
28. key number (482)
29. KF call number (550)
30. legal encyclopedia (492)
31. legal periodical (492)
32. legal treatise (493)
33. legislative history (293, 598)
34. LEXIS (494, 667)
35. loose-leaf/loose-leaf service (467, 494)
36. online (467)
37. opinion (also called a case) (473)
38. ordinance (282)
39. parallel cite (480, 518)
40. pocket part (495, 539)
41. precedent (317, 509)
42. public law (493)
43. reporter (473)
44. rules of court (282, 496)
45. search engine (680)
46. section (§) (592)
47. session law (496)
48. shepardize (497, 561)
49. statute (281)
50. Westlaw (504, 667)

| EXHIBIT 11.2 | The Terminology of Legal Research: A Comprehensive Checklist |
|---|---|

1. abstract (469)
2. act (469)
3. administrative decision (281)
4. Administrative Procedure Act (176)
5. administrative regulation (281)
6. advance session law service/legislative service (470)
7. advance sheet (469)
8. *A.L.R. Bluebook of Supplemental Decisions* (472)
9. *A.L.R. Digest to 3d, 4th, 5th, Federal* (557)
10. *ALR Federal Tables* (557)
11. *ALR Index* (557)
12. (A.L.R.) *Permanent A.L.R. Digest* (557)
13. *A.L.R.2d Digest* (557)
14. *A.L.R.2d Later Case Service* (559)
15. *ALWD Citation Manual* (471, 516)
16. *American Digest System* (471)
17. *American Jurisprudence 2d* (471, 584)
18. *American Law Reports* (471)
19. amicus curiae brief (473)
20. analogous/on point (508)
21. annotated (471)
22. annotated bibliography (616)
23. annotated reporter (471)
24. annotated statutory code (471)
25. annotation (471, 556)
26. Annotation History Table (560)
27. annotation (superseded/supplemented) (560)
28. appellant (418)
29. appellee (respondent) (315)
30. *Atlantic Digest* (472, 486)
31. *Atlantic 2d* (472, 478)
32. authority (506)
33. authority (primary/secondary; mandatory/persuasive) (506, 512)
34. Auto-Cite (472)
35. *Bankruptcy Reporter* (477)
36. bill (472)
37. black letter law (585)
38. *Black's Law Dictionary* (472)
39. *Blue and White Book* (472, 520)
40. *Bluebook: A Uniform System of Citation* (472)
41. Boolean search/natural language search (669)
42. brief, appellate (472)
43. brief of a case (472)
44. Bulletin (473)
45. *California Reporter* (473)
46. CALR (466, 667)
47. caption (of a case) (519)
48. CARTWHEEL (539)
49. casebook (479)
50. case note (581)
51. case of first impression (514)

52. cause of action/defense (284, 308)
53. CD-ROM (467)
54. *Century Digest* (479, 484)
55. certiorari, writ of (420, 523
56. *C.F.R. Index and Finding Aids* (607, 608)
57. CFR Parts Affected (608)
58. charter (281)
59. citator (480, 677)
60. cite checking (533)
61. cite/citation (480)
62. cited material (564)
63. cite, parallel (480, 518)
64. citing material (564)
65. CLE materials (480)
66. code, administrative (469)
67. *Code of Federal Regulations* (481)
68. code, statutory (501)
69. codify (480)
70. committee report (602)
71. common law (284, 324)
72. conference committee (295)
73. conflicts of law (509)
74. Congressional Information Service (602)
75. *Congressional Record* (481)
76. consolidated litigation (522)
77. constitution (281)
78. construed/construction (596)
79. *Corpus Juris Secundum* (481, 585)
80. cumulative (481)
81. *Current Law Index* (482)
82. *Decennial Digest* (482, 484)
83. depository library, federal (462)
84. Descriptive Word Index (591)
85. deskbook (482)
86. dictum (plural: dicta) (317, 511)
87. digests (for A.L.R.) (557)
88. digests (for Martindale-Hubbell) (494)
89. digests (for reporters) (482, 485)
90. docket number (522)
91. enabling statute (579, 607)
92. enacted law (324, 507)
93. *Encyclopedia of Associations* (588)
94. et al. (522)
95. et seq. (577)
96. executive agreement (611)
97. executive order (282)
98. *Federal Claims Reporter* (477)
99. federalism (280)
100. *Federal Practice Digest 4th* (484)
101. *Federal Register* (488)
102. *Federal Reporter* (476, 488)
103. *Federal Rules Decisions* (488)
104. *Federal Supplement* (476, 488)
105. Freestyle (669)

| EXHIBIT 11.2 | The Terminology of Legal Research: A Comprehensive Checklist—*continued* |
|---|---|

106. full faith and credit (510)
107. *General Digest* (484, 488)
108. GlobalCite (480)
109. handbook/hornbook/practice manual/form book (484, 489, 493)
110. headnote (489)
111. historical note (of a statute) (592)
112. holding (317, 511)
113. hornbook (489)
114. hypertext (490, 678)
115. *Illinois Decisions* (479)
116. *Index Medicus/MEDLINE* (583)
117. *Index to Legal Periodicals and Books* (489)
118. In re (522)
119. interfiling (467)
120. Internet (489, 678)
121. interstate compact (490)
122. Jurisdictional Table of Cited Statutes and Cases (558)
123. KeyCite (492)
124. key number (482)
125. KF call number (550)
126. law directory (494)
127. law review/law journal (492)
128. legal dictionary (492)
129. legal encyclopedia (492)
130. legal newsletter (492)
131. legal newspaper (492)
132. legal periodical (492)
133. *Legal Resource Index* (583)
134. legal thesaurus (493)
135. LegalTrac (493)
136. legal treatise (493)
137. legislation (493)
138. legislative history (293, 598)
139. legislative intent (507)
140. LEXIS/LEXIS–NEXIS (494, 667)
141. Library of Congress (LC) Classification System (450)
142. Loislaw (467, 490, 679)
143. loose-leaf/loose-leaf service (467, 494)
144. *LSA: List of Sections Affected* (608)
145. *Martindale-Hubbell Law Directory* (494)
146. memorandum opinion (316)
147. microforms (microfiche/microfilm/ ultrafiche) (467)
148. *Military Justice Reporter* (477)
149. *National Reporter Blue Book* (472, 520)
150. National Reporter System (477)
151. *New York Supplement* (479)
152. nominative reporter (523)
153. *North Eastern 2d* (478, 494)
154. *North Western Digest* (486, 494)
155. *North Western 2d* (478, 494)

156. notes of decisions (471)
157. nutshell (494)
158. on all fours (325, 508)
159. online (467)
160. opinion (also called a case) (473)
161. opinion (concurring/dissenting/majority) (318)
162. opinion of the attorney general (282)
163. opinion (unpublished/unreported) (473)
164. ordinance (282)
165. outline (495)
166. overrule/reverse/override (296, 509, 566)
167. *Pacific Digest* (485, 495)
168. *Pacific Reporter 2d* (478, 495)
169. parallel cite (480, 518)
170. Parallel Table of Authorities and Rules (607)
171. pattern jury instructions (495)
172. per curiam opinion (316)
173. pinpoint cite (524)
174. Plaintiff/Defendant Table (in digests) (554)
175. pocket part (495, 539)
176. Popular Name Table (525, 597)
177. precedent (317, 509)
178. private law (493)
179. public domain (467)
180. public domain citation (524)
181. public law (493)
182. record (496)
183. regional digest (485)
184. regional reporter (477)
185. register (496)
186. remand (317)
187. reporter (regional, official/unofficial) (473)
188. restatements (496)
189. root expander (!) (670)
190. rules of court (282, 496)
191. search engine (680)
192. section (§) (592)
193. serial publication (551)
194. series (of a multivolume publication) (496)
195. session law (496)
196. shepardize (497, 561)
197. *Shepard's Case Name Citator* (520)
198. Shepard's (cited material/citing material) (497)
199. Shepard's (delta ▲) (565)
200. Shepard's (history of the case/treatment of the case) (566)
201. short-form cite (535)
202. slip law (498)
203. slip opinion (498)
204. *South Eastern Digest* (487, 498)
205. *South Eastern 2d* (478, 598)
206. *Southern 2d* (478, 598)
207. *South Western 2d* (478, 598)
208. special edition state reporter (477)

| EXHIBIT 11.2 | The Terminology of Legal Research: A Comprehensive Checklist—*continued* |
|---|---|

209. stare decisis (317, 509)
210. star paging (476)
211. statute (281)
212. statutes at large (501)
213. statutory history table (537)
214. superscript number in Shepard's (567)
215. *supra* (534)
216. Supremacy Clause (510)
217. *Supreme Court Reporter* (475, 502)
218. syllabus (in reporters) (316)
219. table of authorities (534)
220. Table of Courts and Circuits (558)
221. Table of Jurisdictions Represented (558)
222. Table of Key Numbers (555)
223. Table of Laws and Rules (586)
224. Table of Laws, Rules, and Regulations (557)
225. TAPP (544)
226. term of art (545)
227. thomas.loc.gov (491)
228. total client-service library (502)
229. treaty (282)
230. uniform state laws (502)

231. universal character (*) (670)
232. *U.S. Code* (502)
233. *U.S. Code Annotated* (502)
234. *U.S. Code Congressional and Administrative News* (502)
235. *U.S. Code Service* (503)
236. U.S. Court of Appeals (289)
237. U.S. District Court (289, 476)
238. *U.S. Law Week* (503)
239. *U.S. Reports* (475, 503)
240. *U.S. Supreme Court Bulletin* (476)
241. *U.S. Supreme Court Digest* (LEXIS Law Pub.) (484)
242. *U.S. Supreme Court Digest* (West Group) (484)
243. *U.S. Supreme Court Reports, Lawyers' Edition* (475, 504)
244. validation research (612)
245. *Veterans Appeals Reporter* (477)
246. West Group (471, 476)
247. Westlaw (504, 667)
248. *West's Legal Directory* (76)
249. World Wide Web (490, 678)
250. *Words and Phrases* (504)

### Assignment 11.1

For each of the words and phrases in exhibit 11.1, prepare a three-by-five-inch index card on which you include the following information:

- The word or phrase
- The pages in this text where the word or phrase is discussed (begin with the page number given in parentheses; then add other page numbers as the word or phrase is discussed elsewhere in the text, as well as in the glossary)
- The definition or function of the word or phrase
- Other information about the word or phrase that you obtain as you use the law library
- Comments by your instructor in class about any of the words and phrases

Some words and phrases may call for more than one card. You should strive, however, to avoid including too much information on the cards. Keep the cards in alphabetical order. The cards will become your own file system on legal research that you can use as a study guide for the course and as a reference tool when you do legal research in the library. Be sure to add cards for new words and phrases that you come across in class and in the library.

### Assignment 11.2

Do assignment 11.1 for the list in exhibit 11.2. Turn in this assignment when you complete your study of legal research.

## Section E
# FINDING LAW LIBRARIES

The availability of law libraries depends to a large degree on the area where you live, study, or work. Rural areas, for example, have fewer possibilities than larger cities or capitals.

Twelve different law library possibilities are listed below. Find out which ones exist in your area. You may need permission to use some of them. (This is certainly true of a private law firm's library.) Find out where the nearest **federal depository library** is located. This is a public or private library that receives free federal government publications to which it must admit the general public. If a private law school or university is a federal depository library, it must allow you to use the publications it receives free, but you may be denied access to the rest of the library's collection. (To find the depository library nearest to you, go to *www.access.gpo.gov/su_docs/locators/findlibs*.)

### Locations of Law Libraries

- Law school library
- General university library (may have a law section)
- Law library of a bar association
- State law library (in the state capital and perhaps in branch offices in counties throughout the state)
- Local public library (may have a small law section)
- Law library of the legislature or city council
- Law library of the city solicitor or corporation counsel
- Law library of the district attorney or local prosecutor
- Law library of the public defender
- Law library of a federal, state, or local administrative agency (particularly in the office of the agency's general counsel)
- Law library of a court
- Law library of a private law firm

You may need some ingenuity to locate these libraries and to gain access to them. Try more than one avenue of entry. Do not become discouraged when the first person you contact tells you that the library is for members or private use only. Some students adopt the strategy of walking into a library—particularly a library supported by public funds—and acting as if they belong. Rather than asking for permission, they wait for someone to stop them or to question their right to be there. Other students take the wiser course of seeking permission in advance. Yet, even here, some creativity is needed in the way that you ask for permission. The bold question "Can I use your library?" may be less effective than an approach such as "Would it be possible for me to use a few of your law books for a short period of time for some important research that I must do?"

Once you gain access to a law library, you may face another problem. Some library employees resent spending a great deal of time answering student questions. At a recent conference of the American Association of Law Libraries, an entire session was devoted to the theme of student paralegal requests for assistance that "can take a tremendous amount of the law librarian's time and energy." Even if an employee at the desk is willing to give you all the time you need, the *supervisor* of that employee may be opposed to the attention you are getting. Use your common sense in such situations. Keep your requests to a minimum, particularly if other students are seeking the same kind of help. Before you ask a question, re-read the textbook. Many questions can be answered on your own.

Another option is the **virtual** law library available on the **Internet**. In the computer age, something is virtual if it exists in a computer-generated environment. The Internet is a self-governing network of networks to which millions of computer users all over the world have access. Among the many kinds of information you can obtain on the Internet are court opinions, statutes, and administrative regulations. Hence the Internet serves as a virtual law library to anyone who has purchased the right equipment and connection to the Internet. (Most local public libraries offer free Internet access on the premises of the library.) Because the Internet is largely unregulated, however, you must be cautious about the currentness and accuracy of the information you find on what is called the information superhighway. As indicated earlier, you cannot rely on the free material obtained on the Internet to the same extent as you can on traditional library volumes and on the major commercial (fee-based) computer databases (e.g., Westlaw, LEXIS, Loislaw) that we will discuss in this chapter and in chapter 13. Nevertheless, the reliability of the Internet is increasing, particularly at the sites maintained by government bodies such as legislatures, courts, and administrative agencies. We will have a lot more to say about this dimension of legal research.

## Section F
# CATEGORIES OF RESEARCH MATERIALS

The research materials that you will use in your legal career fall into four categories based on their function:

- Materials that contain the full text of the law
- Materials that help you locate the law
- Materials that help you understand and interpret the law
- Materials that help you determine the current validity of the law

The four main columns of exhibit 11.3 classify research materials by these four functions. As we will see, some materials can serve more than one function. Legal periodicals, for example, can help you find the law as well as understand it. Exhibit 11.3 is our point of departure. All of the material mentioned in exhibit 11.3 will be examined in detail later in the chapter.

| EXHIBIT 11.3 | The Four Functions of Research Materials | | | |
|---|---|---|---|---|
| **Kind of Law** | **Materials That Contain the Full Text of This Kind of Law** | **Materials That Can Be Used to Locate This Kind of Law** | **Materials That Can Be Used to Help Understand This Kind of Law** | **Materials That Can Be Used to Help Determine the Current Validity of This Kind of Law** |
| (a) Opinions | Reports Reporters A.L.R., A.L.R. 2d, A.L.R.3d, A.L.R.4th, A.L.R.5th, A.L.R. Fed. Legal newspapers Loose-leaf services Slip opinions Advance sheets CD–ROM Westlaw LEXIS Loislaw Internet | Digests Annotations in A.L.R. A.L.R.2d, A.L.R.3d, A.L.R.4th, A.L.R.5th, A.L.R. Fed. Shepard's Legal periodicals Legal encyclopedias Legal treatises Loose-leaf services Words and Phrases | Legal periodicals Legal encyclopedias Legal treatises Legal newsletters Annotations in A.L.R., A.L.R.2d, A.L.R.3d, A.L.R.4th, A.L.R.5th, A.L.R. Fed. Loose-leaf services | Shepard's KeyCite GlobalCite Insta-Cite Auto-Cite |
| (b) Statutes | Statutory Code Statutes at Large Session Laws Compilations Consolidated Laws Slip Laws Acts & Resolves Laws Legislative Services CD–ROM Westlaw | Index volumes of statutory code Loose-leaf services Footnote references in other materials | Legal periodicals Legal encyclopedias Legal treatises Legal newsletters Annotations in A.L.R., A.L.R. 2d, A.L.R.3d, A.L.R.4th, A.L.R.5th, A.L.R. Fed. Loose-leaf services | Shepard's KeyCite |

| EXHIBIT 11.3 | The Four Functions of Research Materials—*continued* | | | |
|---|---|---|---|---|
| Kind of Law | Materials That Contain the Full Text of This Kind of Law | Materials That Can Be Used to Locate This Kind of Law | Materials That Can Be Used to Help Understand This Kind of Law | Materials That Can Be Used to Help Determine the Current Validity of This Kind of Law |
| (b) Statutes —continued | LEXIS Loislaw Internet | | | |
| (c) Constitutions | Statutory Code Separate volumes containing the constitution CD–ROM Westlaw LEXIS Loislaw Internet | Index volumes of statutory code Loose-leaf services Footnote references in other materials | Legal periodicals Legal encyclopedias Legal treatises Legal newsletters Annotations in A.L.R., A.L.R.2d, A.L.R.3d, A.L.R.4th, A.L.R.5th, A.L.R. Fed. Loose-leaf services | Shepard's KeyCite |
| (d) Administrative Regulations | Administrative Code Separate volumes containing the regulations of certain agencies Loose-leaf services CD–ROM Westlaw LEXIS Loislaw Internet | Index volumes of the administrative code Loose-leaf services Footnote references in other materials | Legal periodicals Legal treatises Legal newsletters Annotations in A.L.R., A.L.R.2d, A.L.R.3d, A.L.R.4th, A.L.R.5th, A.L.R. Fed. Loose-leaf services | Shepard's (for some agencies) List of Sections Affected (for federal agencies) KeyCite (for federal agencies) |
| (e) Administrative Decisions | Separate volumes of decisions of some agencies Loose-leaf services Westlaw LEXIS Loislaw Internet | Loose-leaf services Index to (or digest volumes for) the decisions Footnote references in other materials | Legal periodicals Legal treatises Legal newsletters Annotations in A.L.R., A.L.R.2d, A.L.R.3d, A.L.R.4th, A.L.R.5th, A.L.R. Fed. Loose-leaf services | Shepard's (for some agencies) |
| (f) Charters | Separate volumes containing the charter Municipal Code Register Bulletin State session laws Official journal Legal newspaper Internet | Index volumes to the charter or municipal code Footnote references in other materials | Legal periodicals Legal treatises Annotations in A.L.R., A.L.R.2d, A.L.R.3d, A.L.R.4th, A.L.R.5th, A.L.R. Fed. | Shepard's |

| EXHIBIT 11.3 | The Four Functions of Research Materials—*continued* | | | |
|---|---|---|---|---|
| **Kind of Law** | **Materials That Contain the Full Text of This Kind of Law** | **Materials That Can Be Used to Locate This Kind of Law** | **Materials That Can Be Used to Help Understand This Kind of Law** | **Materials That Can Be Used to Help Determine the Current Validity of This Kind of Law** |
| (g) Ordinances | Municipal code<br>Official journal<br>Legal newspaper<br>Internet | Index volumes of municipal code<br>Footnote references in other materials | Legal periodicals<br>Legal treatises<br>Annotations in A.L.R., A.L.R.2d, A.L.R.3d, A.L.R.4th, A.L.R.5th, A.L.R. Fed. | Shepard's |
| (h) Rules of Court | Separate rules volumes<br>Statutory code<br>Practice manuals<br>Deskbook<br>CD–ROM<br>Westlaw<br>LEXIS<br>Loislaw<br>Internet | Index to separate rules volumes<br>Index to statutory code<br>Index to practice manuals<br>Index to deskbook<br>Footnote references in other materials | Practice manuals<br>Legal periodicals<br>Legal treatises<br>Legal newsletters<br><br>Annotations in A.L.R., A.L.R.2d, A.L.R.3d, A.L.R.4th, A.L.R.5th, A.L.R. Fed.<br>Legal encyclopedias<br>Loose-leaf services | Shepard's<br>KeyCite |
| (i) Executive Orders | Federal Register<br>Code of Federal Regulations<br>Weekly Compilation of Presidential Documents<br>U.S. Code Congressional and Administrative News<br>U.S.C./U.S.C.A./ U.S.C.S.<br>Westlaw<br>LEXIS<br>Internet | Index volumes to the sets of books listed in the second column<br>Footnote references in other materials | Legal periodicals<br>Legal treatises<br>Legal newsletters<br>Annotations in A.L.R., A.L.R.2d, A.L.R.3d, A.L.R.4th, A.L.R.5th, A.L.R. Fed.<br>Loose-leaf services | Shepard's |
| (j) Treaties | Statutes at Large (up to 1949)<br>United States Treaties and Other International Agreements<br>Department of State Bulletin | Index within the volumes listed in second column<br>World Treaty Index<br>Current Treaty Index<br>Footnote references in other materials | Legal periodicals<br>Legal treatises<br>Legal newsletters<br>Annotations in A.L.R., A.L.R.2d, A.L.R.3d, A.L.R.4th, A.L.R.5th, A.L.R. Fed. | Shepard's |

| EXHIBIT 11.3 | The Four Functions of Research Materials—*continued* |
|---|---|

| Kind of Law | Materials That Contain the Full Text of This Kind of Law | Materials That Can Be Used to Locate This Kind of Law | Materials That Can Be Used to Help Understand This Kind of Law | Materials That Can Be Used to Help Determine the Current Validity of This Kind of Law |
|---|---|---|---|---|
| (j) Treaties —continued | International Legal Materials<br>Westlaw<br>LEXIS<br>Internet | | Legal encyclopedias<br>Loose-leaf services | |
| (k) Opinions of the Attorney General | Separate volumes containing these opinions<br>Westlaw<br>LEXIS<br>Internet | Digests<br>Footnote references in other materials | | |

## Section G
# FORMATS OF LEGAL RESEARCH

The legal community spends over $4 billion a year to be able to read the research materials listed in exhibit 11.3. A great deal of choice is available. You can read a court opinion or a statute, for example, in a book, online, on a disk, or on microform. Variety exists even within these media categories. Here is an overview of available formats:

**Legal Research Media**

1. Paper
   (a) Pamphlet
   (b) Hardcover, fixed pages
   (c) Hardcover, loose-leaf
2. Online (CALR)
   (a) Commercial
   (b) Public domain
3. CD–ROM
4. Microform
   (a) Microfilm
   (b) Microfiche
   (c) Ultrafiche

Of course, it can be very expensive for a law firm to purchase all of these media. Few, if any, law libraries in the country are comprehensive enough to provide access to all of them for every category of law. A cost-conscious law firm, therefore, must determine what media will be the most cost-effective. **CALR** (computer-assisted legal research), for example, is sometimes more expensive than using traditional library volumes; yet CALR often allows you to find something in a few minutes that might take a day or two using other media. A law firm may decide that it is more cost-effective to charge a client for computer costs than for the hours needed to use a slower method of research.

### PAPER
Traditional library books are pamphlets or hardcover volumes made of paper. Very often the pamphlets are considered temporary. They tend to contain recent legal research

material that will eventually be printed in more permanent hardcover volumes. When the latter become available, the law library throws away the pamphlets.

Most hardcover volumes contain pages that you cannot remove without ripping the book. A **loose-leaf**, book, in contrast, is a hardcover book with removable pages. It often has a three-ring binder structure that snaps open and shut for easy insertion and removal of pages. (**Interfiling** means inserting pages anywhere in a text rather than just at the end.) The great benefit of loose-leaf materials is that publishers can send subscribers new pages containing updated material along with instructions on what pages to remove because they contain outdated material.

Inserting pages into a loose-leaf book

### ONLINE (CALR)

**Online** has several meanings. The broadest definition is using a computer. For example, some software programs have built-in manuals that you can read on your computer screen without being connected to other computers. They are called online manuals. In legal research, the more common meaning of *online* (the one used in this book most of the time) is using a computer that *is* connected to other computers, usually through regular telephone lines hooked up by a modem. This connection allows you to do online computer-assisted legal research (CALR). Major fee-based (i.e., commercial) online services in the law include Westlaw, LEXIS, and Loislaw. Some online services, however, are in the **public domain**, meaning that they are accessible to anyone at no cost. Most of this material is on the constantly growing Internet.

### CD–ROM

**CD–ROM** (compact disk with read-only memory) is an optical information-storage system that operates much like a compact disk sold in music stores. Through your computer system, you gain access to the vast amount of information stored on the disk. Up to 60 large volumes of law books can be stored on one disk! Users cannot add any information to the disk: they can only read the information on it through their computer screen or monitor (hence the phrase *read only*). Unlike more traditional computer-assisted research systems, you do not need a modem to use CD–ROM.

Examples of CD–ROM products

### MICROFORM

**Microforms** are images or photographs that have been reduced in size. Among the materials stored on microforms are pages from reporters, codes, treatises, periodicals, etc. Vast amounts of material can be stored in this way. An entire volume of a 1,000-page law book can fit on a single plastic card. Special machines (*reader-printers* and *fiche readers*)

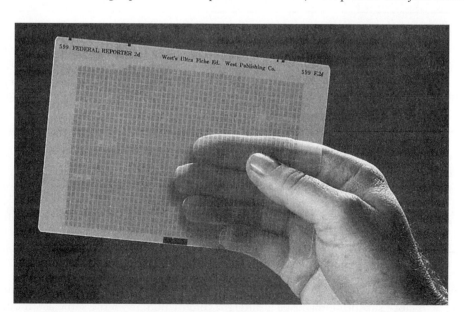

Example of ultrafiche (a microform) that contains an entire reporter volume (Federal Reporter, 2d, West's Ultra Fiche Ed. West Group)

magnify the material so that it can be read. These machines are sometimes awkward to use. The major value of microforms is the space savings that can result by storing (i.e., archiving) a large quantity of materials that no longer need to take up shelf space. In general, these are older materials that researchers do not use on a regular basis. Several kinds of microforms are available. (a) *Microfilm* stores the material on film reels or cassettes. (b) *Microfiche* stores the material on single sheets of film. (c) *Ultrafiche* is microfiche with a considerably greater storage capacity, providing a reduction factor of 100 or more.

---

### Section H
# GLOSSARY OF RESEARCH MATERIALS

We turn now to an overview of the major research terms and research materials that we will encounter throughout the remainder of the chapter. The overview is presented in the form of a glossary. At the end of the glossary, you will find a chart (exhibit 11.9 on page 504) that summarizes most of the materials introduced in the glossary. Later in the chapter, we will focus on how to *use* the materials listed in this glossary. At this stage, our goal is more modest: identifying what exists.

One final caution about definitions before we begin. There are standard definitions of most terms used in legal research, but there are a few dramatic exceptions. For example:

- The phrase *Supreme Court* means the highest court in our federal judicial system (the United States Supreme Court) and the highest state court in many state judicial systems (e.g., California Supreme Court). In New York, however, one of the main *lower* courts is called the Supreme Court.
- The word *digest* usually refers to a set of volumes that contain small-paragraph summaries of court opinions. In Minnesota, there is a digest that fits this definition—it gives small-paragraph summaries of Minnesota court opinions. There is another digest in Minnesota, however, called *Dunnell Minnesota Digest*, that is a legal encyclopedia rather than a traditional digest. Furthermore, we will see that the word *digest* can refer to other kinds of research materials as well.

Although standard definitions are generally available, you should be prepared to find variations.

---

### Assignment 11.3

The glossary on pages 468–504 contains over 80 photographs of books and pamphlets, not counting the photos of page excerpts. Some of the photos contain more than one volume. In this assignment, you are to go to the most comprehensive law library or libraries near you and find the books and pamphlets depicted in the photographs (or close substitutes). There are several reasons why you may not be able to find the exact book or pamphlet in one of the photos:

- The library may not have purchased or subscribed to the book or pamphlet.
- The library has the book or pamphlet, but not the volume number or issue depicted in the photo. (Some pamphlets, for example, are thrown away when bound volumes come out that include the material in the pamphlets.)
- The library has the book or pamphlet, but the one you want is simply not on the shelf. (It may be in use or have been misshelved.)
- The photograph is not clear enough to allow you to make out the volume number or other identifying information about the book or pamphlet in the photo.

If any of these reasons applies, try to find as close a substitute as possible in the law library. A close substitute might be a different volume number in the same set, a different title in the same category of book, or the same category of book but for a different state. Proceed as follows:

(a) Make a list of every book or pamphlet photographed in the glossary on pages 469–504 (not including photos of page excerpts). If more than one book or pamphlet is depicted in a photo, list each separately.

(b) Place a check mark (✔) in front of a book or pamphlet on the list if you found it *exactly* as pictured in the photograph, e.g., the same volume number. Include a one-sentence description of the kind of material found in that book or pamphlet.

(c) Place an (s), meaning substitute, in front of a book or pamphlet on the list if you substituted another book or pamphlet for the one in the photo for any of the reasons listed above. State why you had to use a substitute and make clear what your substitute is. Include a one-sentence description of the kind of material found in the book or pamphlet.

(d) Place an (x) in front of a book or pamphlet on the list if you were not able to find it or a substitute. State why this was so. Still include a one-sentence description of the kind of material found in the book or pamphlet you were seeking.

**Abstract**   An **abstract** is a summary of the important points made in a text; it is an overview. Summaries of opinions are sometimes called *abstracts* or *squibs*. One of the major places they are printed is in **digests**, which are volumes of small-paragraph summaries of opinions.

**Act**   An **act** is the official document that contains a statute passed by the legislature. A *bill* (which is a proposed statute) becomes an act once the legislature enacts it into law. It can be printed in several formats: as a **slip law** (which consists of a single act), in the *session laws* (which is a collection of every private and public act arranged chronologically), and in a *statutory code* (which is a collection of every public act arranged by subject matter). Session laws are also called Statutes at Large, Acts and Resolves, Laws, etc.

**Administrative Code**   An **administrative code** is a collection of the regulations of one or more administrative agencies. Generally, the regulations of state and local administrative agencies are poorly organized and difficult to find. Not so for the regulations of *federal* administrative agencies, as we will see when we cover the *Code of Federal Regulations*. A distinguishing feature of a code is that the material in it is organized by subject matter rather than chronologically. A subject matter organization would mean that all or most regulations on the environment, for example, are together in one place in the code. A chronological printing, however, would mean that laws on totally different subject matters could follow each other, depending on the order in which the laws were passed. The following sets of laws often have a subject matter organization: administrative codes (that print administrative regulations) and statutory codes (that print statutes).

**Advance**   In general, the word *advance* or **advance sheet** refers to a pamphlet that comes out prior to (in advance of) a thicker pamphlet or a bound volume. Very often the material in the advance publication is reprinted in the thicker pamphlet or hardcover volume so that the advance publication can be thrown away. Here are three examples of publications that have this advance feature:

1. Advance sheet for a reporter. A **reporter** is a publication that contains the full text of court opinions. A reporter advance sheet prints these opinions soon after they are written by the courts. Once several reporter advance sheets are available, the opinions in them are all printed in a hardcover volume so that all the advance sheets can be thrown away.

2. Advance sheet for *Shepard's Citations*. A *citator* is a publication (or online service) containing lists of citations that will allow you to assess the current validity of something and also give you leads to other relevant materials. The major citator is *Shepard's Citations*. The advance sheet supplement for Shepard's contains early citator information—the citations—which is later reprinted in larger supplement pamphlets and hardcover volumes. Once the library receives the larger publication, the advance sheet is thrown away.

Advance sheet for a reporter (here the *Supreme Court Reporter*). An advance sheet contains the full text of court opinions that will later be printed in a hardcover reporter volume (here the *Supreme Court Reporter*).

Advance sheet supplements for Shepard's (here the *Shepard's United States Citations*). The first photo is the advance sheet, the material from which is later reprinted in a thicker supplement pamphlet (middle photo) and finally in a hardcover volume (third photo).

3. Advance sheet for a statutory code. The most current statutes are often first published in a special pamphlet that may be called a **legislative service** or **advance session law service**. Most libraries throw these pamphlets away once they are published in hardcover session law volumes and (if they are public laws) in a bound statutory code.

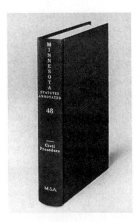

An advance session law service for Minnesota statutes. Many of the statutes in this pamphlet are later printed in the hardcover statutory code for the state, *Minnesota Statutes Annotated*.

As we will see later, the advance session law services for federal statutes are *USCS Advance* (for the *United States Code Service*) and *United States Code Congressional and Administrative News* (for the *United States Code Annotated*).

## A.L.R., A.L.R.2d, A.L.R.3d, A.L.R.4th, A.L.R.5th, A.L.R.Fed.

- A.L.R. (or A.L.R.1st): *American Law Reports, First Series*
- A.L.R.2d: *American Law Reports, Second Series*
- A.L.R.3d: *American Law Reports, Third Series*
- A.L.R.4th: *American Law Reports, Fourth Series*
- A.L.R.5th: *American Law Reports, Fifth Series*
- A.L.R. Fed.: *American Law Reports, Federal Series*

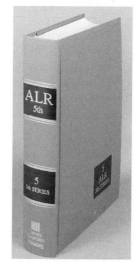

These six sets of books contain the complete text of *selected* court opinions along with extensive commentaries, which are, in effect, research papers on issues within the opinions selected. The research papers are called **annotations**. The sets of books are, therefore, called **annotated reporters** because they print the full text of opinions plus commentary on them. They are published by West Group. As we shall see later, annotations are excellent case finders. (Although the abbreviation *A.L.R.* refers primarily to the First Series, it also commonly refers to all six sets collectively.) Many annotations have been placed online so that they can now be found and read on a computer screen. The computer systems that provide online access to A.L.R. are Westlaw and LEXIS. More recent annotations are also available on CD–ROM.

Example of a volume of *American Law Reports, Fifth Series*. All A.L.R. volumes print several opinions plus extensive annotations on selected issues in these opinions.

**ALWD Citation Manual**    The citation guide published by the Association of Legal Writing Directors. It is the major competitor to *The Bluebook: A Uniform System of Citation.*

**American Digest System**    The American Digest System consists of three sets of digests that provide small-paragraph summaries of court opinions written by every federal and every state court that publishes its opinions. The three digests (published by West Group) are the *General Digest* (containing the most recent summaries), the *Decennial Digests* (containing summaries covering 10-year periods), and the *Century Digest* (containing summaries for cases written prior to 1897).

**American Jurisprudence 2d (Am.Jur.2d)**    Am. Jur. 2d is a national **legal encyclopedia** published by West Group. (Am. Jur. 2d is the second edition of Am. Jur. First.) A legal encyclopedia is a multivolume set of books that summarizes every major legal topic, arranged alphabetically. (Am. Jur. 2d is also available online through Westlaw and LEXIS.) The other major national legal encyclopedia is *Corpus Juris Secundum* (C.J.S.), also from West Group.

There are three main uses of national legal encyclopedias such as Am. Jur. 2d and C.J.S.: (1) they are useful as background reading before you begin legal research in a new area of the law, (2) they are good case finders because of their extensive footnotes to court opinions, and (3) they provide cross-references to other publications of West Group on whatever topic you are reading about in the encyclopedia. In addition to these two national encyclopedias, several states have state encyclopedias devoted to the law of one state (e.g., Florida and Michigan).

Example of a volume of *American Jurisprudence 2d*, a national legal encyclopedia

**American Law Reports (A.L.R.)**    *American Law Reports* is an annotated reporter. It prints the full text of selected opinions and extensive annotations based on issues in those opinions.

**Annotation**    An *annotation* is a set of notes or commentaries on something. The main volumes containing annotations are the six sets of *American Law Reports*: A.L.R., A.L.R.2d, A.L.R.3d, A.L.R.4th, A.L.R.5th, and A.L.R. Fed. The annotations are research papers that are based on selected court opinions in these volumes. When a supervisor asks you to "find out if there are any annotations," you are being sent to A.L.R., A.L.R.2d, etc.

The verb is **annotated**. If materials are annotated, they contain notes or commentaries. An **annotated statutory code** prints statutes by subject matter and includes research references such as notes of court opinions that have interpreted the statutes (often called **notes of decisions**. The abbreviation for annotated is Ann. (e.g., Del. Code Ann. for *Delaware Code Annotated*) or A. (e.g., U.S.C.A. for *United States Code Annotated*). An *annotated reporter*, such as A.L.R., prints court opinions along with notes or commentaries. An *annotated bibliography* contains a list of references along with a brief comment on each reference.

With rare exceptions, annotations are written by private publishers and authors. They are not official documents of courts, legislatures, or agencies.

**Atlantic Digest**    A digest that summarizes state court opinions in the *Atlantic Reporter*. See research link A and exhibit 11.6.

**Atlantic Reporter 2d (A.2d)**    A regional reporter that prints the full text of state court opinions in the atlantic region of the country. See exhibit 11.5.

Example of a bill introduced in the House of Representatives of Congress. A bill is a proposed statute.

Opinions in *Atlantic 2d* (A.2d)                    *Atlantic Digest*

### RESEARCH LINK A
Every opinion in the *Atlantic 2d* reporter written by the state courts in the atlantic region (Conn., Del., D.C., Me., Md., N.H., N.J., Pa., R.I., and Vt.) is digested (summarized) in *Atlantic Digest*.

**Auto-Cite**    **Auto-Cite** is an online program of LEXIS that will tell you whether an opinion you are checking is good law. For example, you will be told whether the opinion has been overruled or criticized by another opinion. Auto-Cite also provides parallel cites and other citing material. Auto-Cite is an online citator.

**Bill**    A **bill** is a proposed statute (one that has not yet been enacted into law). The steps a bill goes through before it becomes a law are known as its **legislative history**.

**Black's Law Dictionary**    A single-volume legal dictionary.

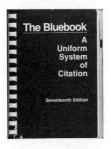

*The Bluebook: A Uniform System of Citation*, providing guidelines on proper citation form

**Blue Book**    The phrase **blue book** (sometimes spelled *bluebook*) usually refers to one of the following four books or sets of books:

■ *The Bluebook: A Uniform System of Citation*
  This is a small blue pamphlet published by the law reviews of several law schools. The pamphlet covers the "rules" of citation form. It is considered by many to be the bible of citation form, although as we will see, not everyone follows it and a competing bible (the *ALWD Citation Manual*) has recently emerged.
■ *National Reporter Blue Book*
  This set of books, published by West Group, enables you to find a *parallel cite* to a court opinion. A parallel cite is simply an additional reference to printed or online sources where you will be able to read the same material word for word. A parallel cite to an opinion would be a reference to another reporter that prints the entire text of the opinion. The *National Reporter Blue Book* covers every state. Some states have a *Blue and White Book*, which covers parallel cites for the opinions of one state only.
■ *A.L.R. Blue Book of Supplemental Decisions*
  This set of books allows you to update the annotations in *A.L.R. First Series*.
■ State directory. Many states have a directory or manual that gives names, addresses, telephone numbers, and e-mail addresses of their state agencies. They may also include information about the functions of each agency. Many of these directories are called *bluebooks*.

*National Reporter Blue Book*, providing parallel cites to court opinions

**Brief**    The word *brief* has several meanings in the law. First, the *brief of a case* is a summary of the major portions of a court opinion (e.g., key facts, issues, holdings, reasoning). (See exhibit 7.2 in chapter 7.) Second, a *trial brief* is an attorney's set of notes on how he or she will conduct a trial. (Occasionally, a written argument submitted to a trial court is also called a trial brief, although more commonly such a document is called a trial memorandum.) Third, an **appellate brief** is a document submitted by a party to an appellate court and served on the opposing party in which arguments are presented on why the rulings of a lower court should be affirmed (approved), modified, or reversed. If a nonparty receives permission to submit an appellate brief, it is called an **amicus curiae** (or friend-of-the-court) **brief**. For example, the American Civil Liberties Union (ACLU) might ask an appellate court (in a case in which the ACLU is not a party) to be allowed to submit an amicus curiae brief that supports the position of a racist organization that is being denied a city permit to march in a parade. (It is possible to locate appellate briefs in some large law libraries and online through LEXIS and Westlaw. For briefs on the Internet, see *www.briefreporter.com.*)

**Bulletin**    A bulletin is a publication issued on an ongoing or periodic basis (such as the *Internal Revenue Bulletin*).

**California Reporter (Cal.Rptr.)**    A court reporter containing selected California state cases.

Front cover of an appellate brief submitted to the United States Supreme Court. (An appellate brief asks a court of appeals to approve, modify or reverse what a lower court has done.)

**Cases**    The word *case* has three meanings. First, a case is a court **opinion**, which is a court's written explanation of how it applied the law to the facts before it to resolve a legal dispute. (See exhibit 6.1 in chapter 6.) Opinions are printed in volumes called reporters or reports. The words *case* and *opinion* are often used interchangeably. For example, you will hear researchers say that they "read a case" or that they "read an opinion." Second, *case* means a pending matter before a court—a matter that is still in litigation. (Every trial and appellate court, for example, has a **docket** that lists the cases on its calendar.) Third, *case* means any client matter in a law office, whether or not litigation is involved. (A large law office, for example, may have hundreds of cases in its active case file and thousands in its closed case files.)

The first meaning of case  an opinion—is our primary concern in this chapter. Every year over 130,000 opinions are written by more than 3,500 judges sitting in 600 different courts throughout the United States.[1] Our study of this vast array of law will focus on three major themes:

- Where can you read these opinions?
  (We will cover this theme now.)
- How do you find them?
  (We will cover this theme later, in section P of the chapter.)
- How do you read (i.e., brief) and apply them?
  (We cover these themes in chapter 7.)

For many opinions, there are 12 possible places where you can read them. They are outlined in exhibit 11.4. The most common is the unofficial reporter. (See the fourth option in exhibit 11.4.) An **official reporter** is a reporter printed under the authority of the government, often by a government printing office. An **unofficial reporter** is a reporter printed by a commercial publishing company without special authority from the government. As we will see, the West Group is the major publisher of unofficial reporters, particularly through its National Reporter System. Unofficial does not mean unreliable. In fact, West Group's unofficial reporters are so reliable that many states have discontinued their own official reporters. In such states, most people, including judges, rely almost exclusively on the unofficial reporter.

Courts do not formally publish every opinion they write. An **unpublished opinion** is one that the court does not deem to be important enough for general publication. Because publishers do not print such opinions in their traditional reporters, the opinion is called an **unreported opinion**. It may still be possible, however, to read an unpublished or unreported opinion, particularly in the online commercial databases of Westlaw and LEXIS. (West Group has a special reporter called *Federal Appendix* that prints unpublished federal opinions.) You may be able to read opinions in unpublished reporters, but you cannot rely on them to the same extent as reported opinions. Courts place severe limitations on when you can cite and rely on an unpublished opinion.

We turn now to an overview of the major reported opinions, focusing first on federal court opinions and then on state court opinions.

**Federal Court Opinions**    The opinions of the United States Supreme Court are printed in an official reporter, *United States Reports* (abbreviated U.S.), and in several unofficial

| EXHIBIT 11.4 | Twelve Possible Places to Read the Same Court Opinion |
| --- | --- |

| Category | Description | Currency (How soon is the opinion available in this format after the court writes it?) | Frequency of Use (How often do researchers read the opinion in this format?) | Editorial Enhancements (How many features are available in this format in addition to the text of the opinion?) |
| --- | --- | --- | --- | --- |
| 1. Slip Opinion | A single opinion printed by the court. | Very current | Seldom | Almost none |
| 2. Advance Sheet | A pamphlet (containing several opinions) printed in advance of a hardcover reporter volume. | Very current | Very often | Many (e.g., headnotes with key numbers) |
| 3. Reporter (official) | A hardcover volume containing many opinions. An official reporter is one printed under the authority of the government, often by the government itself. Official reporters are sometimes called *reports*. | Not very current | Not very often | Not many |
| 4. Reporter (unofficial) | A hardcover volume containing many opinions. An unofficial reporter is one printed by a commercial publishing company (e.g., West Group) without special authority from the government. | Fairly current | Very often | Many (e.g., headnotes with key numbers) |
| 5. Loose-leaf Service | A hardcover volume with removable pages often containing many opinions. | Very current | Fairly often | Many (e.g., suggestions on practicing law) |
| 6. Legal Newspaper | A newspaper (published daily, weekly, etc.) devoted to legal news; may print text of opinions of local courts. | Very current | Fairly often | Almost none |
| 7. Legal Newsletter | A special-interest publication (printed monthly, bimonthly, etc.) covering a particular area of law; may print text of opinions in that area. | Fairly current | Fairly often | Some |
| 8. Microforms (microfilm, microfiche, ultrafiche) | Images or photographs that have been reduced in size. | Very current | Not often | Many |
| 9. CD–ROM | An optical information storage system that operates much like a compact disk containing music. | Fairly current | Not very often (although increasing) | Many |

| EXHIBIT 11.4 | Twelve Possible Places to Read the Same Court Opinion—*continued* |

| Category | Description | Currency (How soon is the opinion available in this format after the court writes it?) | Frequency of Use (How often do researchers read the opinion in this format?) | Editorial Enhancements (How many features are available in this format in addition to the text of the opinion?) |
|---|---|---|---|---|
| 10. Online Commercial Database | Online companies sell access to legal materials (e.g., opinions) and law-related materials. The major companies are Westlaw and LEXIS. (See chapter 13 for an overview of these online services.) | Very current | Fairly often | Many |
| 11. Bulletin Boards | A local dial-in online service for the exchange of messages and information. Some courts have their own bulletin boards that print their opinions. | Very current | Not very often | Almost none |
| 12. Internet | A self-governing network of computers to which millions of computer users all over the world have access. Among the information available online through the Internet are court opinions | Very current | Not very often (although increasing) | Almost none |

reporters: the *Supreme Court Reporter* published by West Group (abbreviated S. Ct.) and *United States Supreme Court Reports, Lawyers' Edition*, published by LEXIS Law Publishing Co. (abbreviated L. Ed.).

When an opinion is printed in the *United States Reports*, it will also be printed word for word in S. Ct. and in L. Ed., the unofficial reporters—but not necessarily on the same page numbers. Suppose that you are reading an opinion in an unofficial reporter and you want to quote from it. The standard practice is to give the reference or citation to the quote as it appears in the *official* reporter. Suppose, however, that the latter is not available in your library, but one of the unofficial reporters is. How do you quote a page number in an of-

The three major reporters containing opinions of the United States Supreme Court

ficial reporter when all you have available is an unofficial reporter? You use a technique called **star paging**. While you are reading a page in an unofficial reporter, you will find a notation of some kind provided by the printer (an asterisk, a star, or other special notation) plus a page number. The latter is a reference to a page number of the same case in the official reporter. Star paging therefore enables you to determine on what pages the same court language can be found in official and unofficial reporters.

Example of star paging. This excerpt is from page 658 of a reporter. Note the special mark telling you where the same text will begin on page 378 of another reporter.

> **658**
> to determine which crimes have been punished too leniently, and which too severely. § 994(m). Congress has called upon the Commission to exercise its judgment about which $\perp_{378}$ types of crimes and which types of criminals are to be considered similar for the purposes of sentencing.

*Federal Reporter, Third Series* (F.3d). Currently contains the full text of the opinions written by the United States Courts of Appeals.

*Federal Supplement* (F. Supp.). Currently contains the full text of the opinions written by the United States District Courts.

As we will see later in the chapter, star paging will not be needed if each paragraph in an opinion is separately numbered as they are in vendor-neutral citation systems. The paragraph numbers will be the same regardless of what reporter you are using.

Two loose-leaf services also print the text of all U.S. Supreme Court opinions:

- *United States Law Week* (U.S.L.W.) published by Bureau of National Affairs (BNA)
- *United States Supreme Court Bulletin* (S. Ct. Bull.) published by Commerce Clearing House (CCH)

It is also possible to read U.S. Supreme Court opinions in electronic formats. They are all available online from the main computer services, LEXIS and Westlaw. Increasingly, the opinions are becoming available on the Internet. Finally, U.S. Supreme Court opinions are available on CD–ROM, an optical information-storage system.

We now turn to reporters for the *lower* federal courts, primarily the U.S. Courts of Appeals and the U.S. District Courts. (The latter are the main trial courts in the federal judicial system. See exhibit 6.3 in chapter 6). Two major reporters contain the full text of opinions from these lower federal courts:

- *Federal Reporter, First Series* (abbreviated F.)
- *Federal Reporter, Second Series* (abbreviated F.2d)
- *Federal Reporter, Third Series* (abbreviated F.3d)
- *Federal Supplement* (abbreviated F. Supp.)
- *Federal Supplement, Second Series* (abbreviated F. Supp. 2d)

The first three reporters in this list (F., F.2d, F.3d) primarily contain opinions written by the U.S. Courts of Appeals. The last two reporters (F. Supp., F. Supp. 2d) primarily contain opinions written by the U.S. District Courts. Both sets are unofficial reporters published by West Group.

In addition, West Group publishes several specialty or topical reporters that also cover federal courts. For example:

*Federal Rules Decisions (F.R.D.)*
- Contains opinions of the U.S. District Courts on the Federal Rules of Civil Procedure and the Federal Rules of Criminal Procedure, and also
- Contains articles, speeches, and conference reports on federal procedural issues

*Military Justice Reporter (M.J.)*
- Contains opinions of the United States Court of Appeals for the Armed Forces and selected opinions of other federal courts on military issues

*Bankruptcy Reporter (B.R.)*
- Contains opinions of the United States Bankruptcy Courts and selected bankruptcy opinions of other federal courts

*Federal Claims Reporter*
- Contains opinions of the United States Court of Federal Claims

*Veterans Appeals Reporter*
- Contains opinions of the United States Court of Veterans Appeals

In addition to these bound reporters, the opinions of lower federal courts are available online through LEXIS and Westlaw. Many are also accessible on the Internet.

**State Court Opinions**    At one time, all states had official reporters containing the opinions of their highest state courts. As indicated earlier, however, a large number of states have discontinued their official reports. For such states, the unofficial reporters are the main source for opinions of their state courts.

The major publisher of unofficial state reports is West Group through its *National Reporter System*. There are seven **regional reporters** in the System. (West Group's other reporters are also part of the National Reporter System.) A regional reporter is simply an unofficial reporter that contains state court opinions of several states within one of seven regions of the country. (See exhibit 11.5.)

If a law office subscribes to a regional reporter covering its own state, the office is also receiving opinions of other states in the same region. These other opinions may be of little practical value to the office. West Group, therefore, publishes special state editions for over half the states. These **special edition state reporters** (sometimes called *offprint re-*

Example of an official state reports volume

| EXHIBIT 11.5 | Seven Regional Reporters in the National Reporter system |
|---|---|

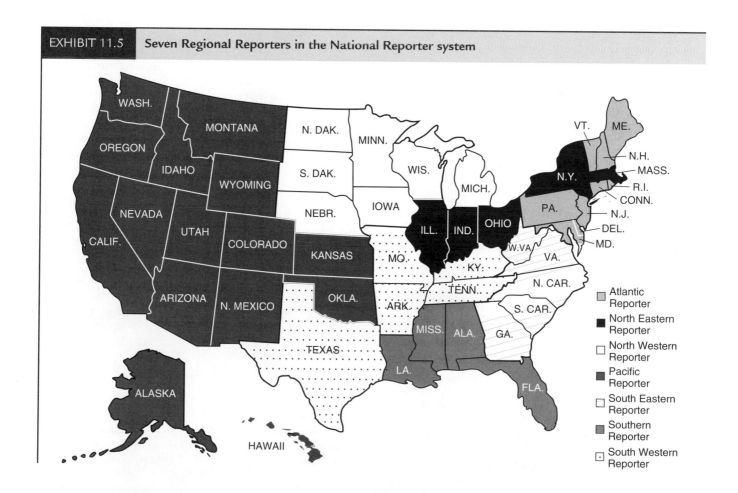

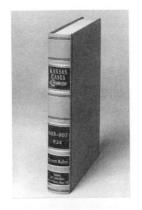

A volume of *Kansas Cases* (a special edition state reporter) containing all the Kansas opinions printed in *Pacific Reporter 2d*.

*porters*) contain only the opinions of an individual state that are also printed in the regional reporter. For example, the opinions of the highest court in Kansas are printed in the *Pacific Reporter*. A Kansas attorney who does not want to subscribe to the *Pacific Reporter* can subscribe to the special edition Kansas reporter, called *Kansas Cases*. (See research link B.)

Regional Reporter        Special Edition State Reporter

### RESEARCH LINK B

The seven regional reporters each contain the opinions of several states. If all of the opinions of one of these states are taken out and also printed in a separate reporter, the latter is called a special edition state reporter (or an offprint reporter).

**Regional Reporters:**

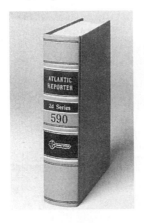

*Atlantic Reporter, Second Series* (A.2d). The opinions of state courts in Conn., Del., D.C., Me., Md., N.H., N.J., Pa., R.I., Vt.

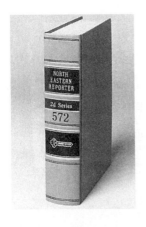

*North Eastern Reporter, Second Series* (N.E.2d). The opinions of state courts in Ill., Ind., Mass., N.Y., Ohio.

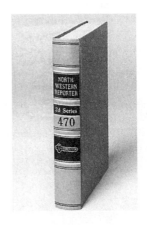

*North Western Reporter, Second Series* (N.W.2d). The opinions of state courts in Iowa, Mich., Minn., Neb., N.D., S.D., Wis.

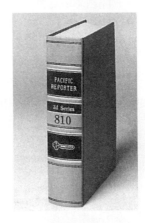

*Pacific Reporter, Second Series* (P.2d). The opinions of state courts in Alaska, Ariz., Cal., Colo., Haw., Idaho, Kan., Mont., Nev., N.M., Okla., Or., Utah, Wash., Wyo.

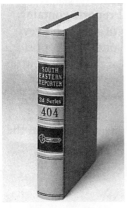

*South Eastern Reporter, Second Series* (S.E.2d). The opinions of state courts in Ga., N.C., S.C., Va., W. Va.

*Southern Reporter Second series* (So. 2d). The opinions of state courts in: Ala., Fla., La., Miss.

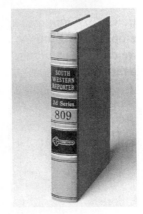

*South Western Reporter, Second Series* (S.W.2d). The opinions of state courts in Ark., Ky., Mo., Tenn., Tex.

Finally, West Group publishes three separate reporters containing state court opinions of New York, California, and Illinois:

- *New York Supplement* (N.Y.S.)
- *California Reporter* (Cal. Rptr.)
- *Illinois Decisions* (Ill. Dec.)

Each contains the opinions of the highest court in the state as well as selected opinions of its lower courts.

### Major Characteristics of West Group Reporters

- The reporters contain the full text of court opinions.
- The opinions are arranged in roughly chronological order according to the date of the decision; they are not arranged by subject matter. A murder case, for example, could follow a tax case.
- The reporters have advance sheets that come out before the hardcover volumes. When the hardcover reporter volume comes out, all the advance sheets are thrown away.
- A table of cases appears at the beginning of each reporter volume.
- Many reporters have a statutes table listing the statutes construed (i.e., interpreted) within an individual reporter volume.
- There is no traditional index to the opinions in a reporter volume. How then do you find opinions? Later we will see that digests are one of the major ways of locating what is in reporters. A digest is a separate set of volumes that contain small-paragraph summaries of opinions. In effect, the digest acts as an index to the opinions in reporter volumes.
- Each opinion is summarized in a series of small paragraphs called **headnotes**. They are written by West Group editors, not by the court. Headnotes are eventually printed in at least five places: first, just before the opinion begins; second, at the beginning of the advance sheet containing the opinion; third, at the end of the hardcover reporter volume containing the opinion; fourth, in West Group digests (again, it is this feature of digests that enables them to become indexes to court opinions); fifth, on Westlaw.

Where else is the full text of state court opinions found?

- Online through LEXIS and Westlaw
- On CD–ROM
- On ultrafiche, which is a single sheet of film containing material that has been reduced by a factor of 100 or more. West Group publishes an ultrafiche edition of the National Reporter System.
- Online on the Internet

For a summary of up to twelve places where you may be able to read the same opinion, see exhibit 11.4.

**Casebook**    A **casebook** is a law school textbook. It consists mainly of a collection of edited court opinions and other materials relating to a particular area of the law, e.g., Lockhart, Kamisar, Choper, and Shiffrin, *Constitutional Law: Cases, Comments, Questions.* Casebooks are not used for legal research; they are classroom texts.

**CD–ROM**    CD–ROM (compact disk with read-only memory) is an optical information–storage system. See the discussion of this medium in section G of this chapter. For the large number of CD–ROM products available in the law, see *Directory of Law-Related CD–ROMs* by Information Publishing (*www.infosourcespub.com.*)

**Century Digest**    The *Century Digest* is one of the three digests in the American Digest System published by West Group. The *Century Digest* contains small-paragraph summaries of court opinions written prior to 1897. The other two digests in the American Digest System are the *Decennial Digests* and the *General Digest.*

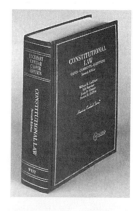

Example of a casebook used in a law school classroom

**CIS**  *CIS* is the abbreviation for the Congressional Information Service. It is one of the major publishers of information that will allow you to trace the legislative history of a federal statute.

**Citation**  A **citation** (also called a *cite*) is a reference to any material printed on paper or stored in a computer database, e.g., an opinion, statute, legal periodical article, legal treatise, or treaty. The citation is the "address" where you can locate and read the material. Most citations are to printed materials; such citations consist of information such as volume number, page number, and date. As we will see later in section J, there are citation guidelines for citing different kinds of legal materials. One of the major publications containing citation guidelines is *The Bluebook: A Uniform System of Citation*, which we saw earlier. Law school teachers and legal periodical publishers love the *Bluebook*. But many courts do not follow it: they may have their own official citation rules that must be followed. (In section J, we will also examine the *ALWD Citation Manual*, another citation guide that is a recent competitor to the *Bluebook*.)

A **parallel cite is** an additional reference to the *same* material. If, for example, there are two parallel cites to an opinion, you will be able to find the opinion, word for word, in two different reporters.

A new development in the arena of citations is the **public domain citation**. This is a citation that is medium-neutral, which means that the references in the citation are not to traditional volume and page numbers of commercial publishers. As we will see later, courts use paragraph numbering systems to create a public domain citation. Paragraph numbering eliminates the need for star paging.

**Citator**  A **citator is** a book, CD-ROM, or online service that contains lists of citations that can (1) help you assess the current validity of an opinion, statute, or other item and (2) give you leads to other relevant materials. It is an organized list of citations to legal materials that have referred to (i.e., cited) whatever you are checking. For example, if you are checking the validity of an opinion, the citator will tell you what the courts have said about that opinion and what legal periodical articles have mentioned it. The same is true if you want to check the validity of a statute, constitutional provision, administrative regulation, rule of court, etc. (see research link C). The two main reasons to use a citator are to assess the validity of what you are checking and to locate additional laws or other materials on the issues covered in what you are checking. The major citator in legal research is *Shepard's Citations*. You can find *Shepard's Citations* in a set of printed volumes (pamphlets and hardcover), on CD-ROM, and online in LEXIS. The other major online citators are KeyCite (found in Westlaw), Auto-Cite (found in LEXIS), and GlobalCite (found in Loislaw).

Citators (Shepard's)(KeyCite)(Auto-Cite) (GlobalCite) ⟩⟨ opinion, statute, constitutional provision, administrative regulation, rule of court, etc.

**RESEARCH LINK C**
A citator will help you determine the current validity of an opinion, statute, constitutional provision, administrative regulation, rule of court, etc. The citator will also lead you to additional relevant laws.

**CLE Materials**  **CLE materials** are continuing legal education texts, videos, or other materials prepared for attorneys after they have completed law school. Many states require attorneys to participate in a designated number of CLE hours per year. Materials for CLE programs often contain checklists, sample forms, and the full text of recent cases, statutes, and administrative regulations that would be of practical value to an attorney working in a particular specialty. For links to continuing legal education materials on the Internet for your state, see *www.aclea.org/orgs.html.*

**Code**  A **code** is a collection of laws or rules classified by subject matter regardless of when they were enacted. To **codify** something means to rearrange it by subject matter. *Uncodified* material is arranged chronologically by date of enactment; *codified* material is arranged by subject matter or topic regardless of when passed or enacted. When a statute or act is first passed by the legislature, it appears initially as a *slip law* which is a single act, often printed as a small pamphlet) and then is printed in uncodified books called Session Laws or Statutes at Large. Finally, statutes of general interest are later codified in statutory codes.

**Code of Federal Regulations (C.F.R.)** The C.F.R. is an administrative code in which many of the administrative regulations of federal agencies are organized by subject matter. The C.F.R. is printed by the United States government in a large number of pamphlets that are reissued each year in a different color. It is also possible to read the C.F.R. online on West-law and LEXIS. Finally, the C.F.R. is available free on the Internet at *www.access. gpo.gov/nara/cfr/index.html*. Before a federal administrative regulation is adopted and printed in the C.F.R., it must be proposed and printed in the daily *Federal Register* (Fed. Reg.) (see research link D).

Sample volumes of the *Code of Federal Regulations* (C.F.R.), which contain many administrative regulations of federal agencies

*Federal Register* (Fed. Reg.) ⟩⟨ *Code of Federal Regulations* (C. F. R.)

## RESEARCH LINK D

Before a federal administrative regulation is adopted and printed in the *Code of Federal Regulations* (C.F.R.), it is proposed in the daily *Federal Register* (Fed. Reg.).

**Congressional Record** The *Congressional Record* (Cong. Rec.) is an official collection of the day-to-day happenings of Congress, particularly on the floor of the House and Senate when Congress is in session. It is one source of legislative history for federal statutes. It also contains many relatively trivial items that are relevant only to the districts of individual legislators.

**Corpus Juris Secundum (C.J.S.)** *Corpus Juris Secundum* is a national legal encyclopedia published by West Group. (It is the second edition of *Corpus Juris*.) *A legal encyclopedia* is a multivolume set of books that summarizes every major legal topic, arranged alphabetically. (Parts of C.J.S. are also available online through Westlaw.) The other major national legal encyclopedia is Am. Jur. 2d, also from West Group. There are three main uses of national legal encyclopedias such as C.J.S. and Am. Jur. 2d: (1) they are useful as background reading before you begin legal research in a new area of the law, (2) they are good case finders because of their extensive footnotes to court opinions, and (3) they provide cross-references to other publications of West Group on whatever topic you are reading in the encyclopedia. In addition to these two national encyclopedias, several states have state encyclopedias devoted to the law of one state (e.g., Florida and Michigan).

Sample volumes of *Corpus Juris Secundum*, a national legal encyclopedia

**Cumulative** **Cumulative** means that which repeats earlier material and consolidates it with new material in one place. A cumulative supplement, for example, is a pamphlet or volume that repeats, updates, and consolidates all earlier pamphlets or volumes. Because of the repetition, the earlier pamphlets or volumes can be thrown away. Similarly, pocket parts (containing supplemental material at the end of a book) are often cumulative. When the most recent pocket part comes out, the old one can be thrown away. Here is an example of a cumulative pocket part in a statutory code:

> **UNITED STATES CODE ANNOTATED**
>
> Title 28
> Judiciary and Judicial Procedure
> §§ 171 to 1250
>
> Cumulative Annual Pocket Part
>
> *For Use in 2002*
>
> Replacing prior pocket part in back of volume

**Current Law Index**  *Current Law Index* (CLI) is the most comprehensive general index to legal periodical literature available. (The other major one is the *Index to Legal Periodicals and Books*.) The CLI comes out in three versions: a paper version (consisting of pamphlets and hardcover volumes), a CD–ROM version (called *LegalTrac*), and an online version (called *Legal Resource Index*). The online version is available on Westlaw and LEXIS.

**Decennial Digest**  The *Decennial Digest* is one of the three digests in the American Digest System published by West Group that contains small-paragraph summaries of court opinions written by every federal and state court that publishes its opinions. Each *Decennial Digest* covers a 10-year period. (Recent decennials are published in two five-year parts.) The other two digests in the American Digest System are the *Century Digest* and the *General Digest*.

**Deskbook**  A **deskbook** is a single-volume collection of the rules of procedure for one or more courts, usually in the same judicial system. These rules of procedure are called court rules or rules of court.

**Digests**  Our goals in this section are to define *digest*, to identify the major digests, and to explain the relationship between digests and reporters. Later in this book, we will cover the techniques of using digests in research (see section O).

Digests are volumes containing small-paragraph summaries of court opinions organized by subject matter. (These summaries are sometimes called *abstracts* or *squibs*). The primary purpose of digests is to summarize—to digest—case law. For this reason, digests serve as excellent case finders. The major publisher of digests, is West Group. The West Key Number System® is the organizational principle used to classify the millions of small-paragraph summaries in the digests. Here is how this principle works. West Group divides all of law into over more than 400 general topics such as Arson, Infants, Marriage, Negligence, and Obscenity. Each of these general topics is further classified into subtopics, and each subtopic is then assigned a number. The phrase **key number** refers to two things: the general topic and the number of the subtopic. Examine the following examples of subtopics under the general topic of Negligence:

---

**NEGLIGENCE**

🔑 305 Abnormally or Inherently Dangerous Activities and Instrumentalities

🔑 1032 Reasonable or Ordinary Care in General

🔑 1600 Defenses and Mitigating Circumstances

Examples of key numbers

---

The second key number in this example is referred to as "Negligence 1032." (It is *not* referred to as "1032 Reasonable or Ordinary Care in General.") The key number must include the general topic. You usually do not have to state what the subtopic is; giving the general topic and the number is enough. If a supervisor asks you to check Negligence 1032 in a West Group digest, you simply go to the N volume of the digest, where you will check number 1032 under Negligence.

Once you find a key number (consisting of a general topic and a number) that is relevant to your research problem, you will find summaries of court opinions under that key number. For example, the following excerpt from a digest contains opinions that are summarized (or digested) under key number Obscenity 1 and key number Obscenity 2:

**OBSCENITY**

🗝 1. **Nature and elements in general.**

III.App. 1973. Obscenity vel non is not constitutionally protected. People v. Rota, 292 N.E.2d 738.

**Iowa 1973.** Knowledge of obscene material is an essential element in obscenity prosecutions. I.C.A. § 725.5. State v. Lavin, 204 N.W.2d 844.

🗝 2. Power to Regulate; Statutory and Local Regulations.

**D.C.Md. 1972.** Although Maryland motion picture censorship statute did not provide disseminator of motion picture film with an adversary hearing before board of censors on issue of obscenity, disseminator was not constitutionally prejudiced in this regard because the statute requires an adversary judicial determination of obscenity with circuit court for Baltimore City exercising de novo review of the board's finding of obscenity, and with burden of proving that the film is unprotected expression resting on the board. Code Md. 1957, art. 66A, §§ 6(c, d), 19(a); 28 U.S.C.A. § 100. Star v. Preller, 352 F.Supp. 530.

Excerpt from a West Group digest containing small-paragraph summaries of opinions

Beneath each summary paragraph is a citation to the case being summarized. For example, see the citation for *People v. Rota* in the first paragraph listed.

Where do these summary paragraphs come from? They come from the *headnotes* of court opinions in West Group reporters. (For an example of two headnotes at the beginning of an opinion, see the *Bruni* opinion in section G of chapter 7.) As we saw earlier, a headnote is a summary of a portion of the opinion that is printed before the opinion begins.

We now turn to an overview of the following four kinds of West Group digests:

- A national digest covering most state and federal courts
- Federal digests covering only federal courts
- Regional digests covering the courts found in the regional reporters
- Digests of individual states

Most of these digests are called key number digests because they organize the case summaries within them according to the key number system.

**National Digest** West Group publishes one national digest: the American Digest System. This massive set (containing over 100 volumes) gives you small-paragraph summaries of the court opinions of most state and federal courts. The American Digest System has three main units:

- *Century Digest,* covering summaries of opinions written prior to 1897.
- *Decennial Digests,* covering summaries of opinions written during 10-year periods starting in 1897. The more recent Decennials are printed in two five-year parts. Part 1 of the Tenth Decennial, for example, covers the period from 1986 to 1991.

Part 2 covers 1991 to 1996. (Prior to the Ninth Decennial, all of the Decennial Digests were issued in one part only—covering the entire 10 years.)

■ *General Digests*, covering summaries of opinions written since the last Decennial was published. The *General Digest* volumes are kept on the shelf only until they are eventually consolidated (cumulated) into the next *Decennial Digest*. When the latter arrives, all of the *General Digest* volumes are thrown away.

Here are examples of volumes from each of the three units of the American Digest System:

Example of a *Century Digest* volume

Example of a *Decennial Digest* volume

Example of a *General Digest* volume

*Federal Practice Digest 4th.* Gives small-paragraph summaries of federal court opinions.

**Federal Digests Covering Only Federal Courts**    West Group publishes five large digests that cover the three main federal courts: the U.S. Supreme Court, the U.S. Courts of Appeals, and the U.S. District Courts. The five digests are:

■ *Federal Digest*
■ *Modern Federal Practice Digest*
■ *Federal Practice Digest 2d*
■ *Federal Practice Digest 3d*
■ *Federal Practice Digest 4th*

The last digest listed—*Federal Practice Digest 4th*—is the most important because it covers the most recent period; it digests federal cases from the mid-1980s to the present. The other four cover earlier time periods and are therefore used less frequently.

Finally, West Group publishes a number of special digests that cover specific federal courts or specific topics of federal law:

■ *West's Bankruptcy Digest*
■ *West's Education Law Digest*
■ *West's Military Justice Digest*
■ *West's Veterans Appeals Digest*
■ *U.S. Court of Appeals Digest for the Fifth Circuit*
■ *U.S. Court of Appeals Digest for the Eleventh Circuit*
■ *United States Supreme Court Digest* (West Group)

The *United States Supreme Court Digest* (West Group) covers opinions of the United States Supreme Court only. A competing digest is the *United States Supreme Court Digest, Lawyers' Edition*, published by LEXIS Law Publishing. Because it is not a West Group digest, it does not use the key number system to classify the small-paragraph summaries in it. It has its own system of organizing the small-paragraph summaries.

*United States Supreme Court Digest.* Published by West Group

*United States Supreme Court Digest, L. Ed.* Published by LEXIS Law Publishing

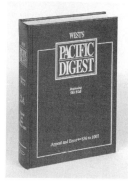

*Pacific Digest,* one of the regional digests. Gives small-paragraph summaries of opinions in the *Pacific Reporter.*

**Regional Digests**   A **regional digest** contains small-paragraph summaries of those court opinions that are printed in its corresponding regional reporter. The opinions in the *Pacific Reporter,* for example, are digested in the *Pacific Digest.* As we shall see in exhibit 11.6, only four of the seven regional reporters have corresponding regional digests. Those digests are *Atlantic Digest, North Western Digest, Pacific Digest,* and *South Eastern Digest* (see research link E). Regional digests for the other three regions either do not exist or have been discontinued.

| Four Regional Reporters: *Atlantic 2d* (A.2d), *North Western 2d* (N.W.2d), *Pacific 2d* (P.2d), *South Eastern* (S.E.2d) | Four Regional Digests: *Atlantic Digest, North Western Digest, Pacific Digest, South Eastern Digest* |
|---|---|

## RESEARCH LINK E

The opinions in four of the regional reporters (A.2d, N.W.2d, P.2d, and S.E.2d) are summarized (digested) in their corresponding regional digests.

**Digests of Individual States**   An individual state digest contains small-paragraph summaries of the opinions of the state courts within that state, as well as the opinions of the federal courts that are relevant to that state. Almost every state has its own digest. (The main exceptions are Delaware, Nevada, and Utah.)

To summarize, examine exhibit 11.6, where you will find a list of reporters, the names of the courts whose full opinions are currently printed in those reporters, and the names of the digests that give small-paragraph summaries of those opinions.

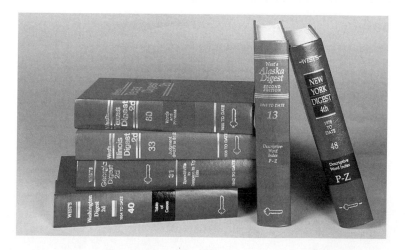

Examples of state digests

| EXHIBIT 11.6 | Reporters and Digests: A Checklist |
|---|---|

| Name of Reporter | The Courts Whose Opinions Are Currently Printed in Full in This Reporter | The Digests That Contain Small-Paragraph Summaries of the Opinions in This Reporter |
|---|---|---|
| *United States Reports* (U.S.) <br> *Supreme Court Reporter* (S. Ct.) <br> *United States Supreme Court Reports, Lawyers' Edition* (L. Ed.) <br> *United States Law Week* (U.S.L.W.) <br> *United States Supreme Court Bulletin* (CCH) (S. Ct. Bull.) | United States Supreme Court | American Digest System <br> *United States Supreme Court Digest* (West Group) <br> *United States Supreme Court Digest, L. Ed.* <br> *Federal Digest* <br> *Modern Federal Practice Digest* <br> *Federal Practice Digest 2d* <br> *Federal Practice Digest 3d* <br> *Federal Practice Digest 4th* <br> Individual state digest (for Supreme Court cases relevant to that state) |
| *Federal Reporter 2d* (F.2d) <br> *Federal Reporter 3d* (F.3d) | United States Courts of Appeals | American Digest System <br> *Federal Digest* <br> *Modern Federal Practice Digest* <br> *Federal Practice Digest 2d* <br> *Federal Practice Digest 3d* <br> *Federal Practice Digest 4th* <br> Individual state digest (for federal cases relevant to that state) |
| *Federal Supplement* (F. Supp.) <br> *Federal Supplement 2d* (F. Supp. 2d) | United States District Courts | American Digest System <br> *Federal Digest* <br> *Modern Federal Practice Digest* <br> *Federal Practice Digest 2d* <br> *Federal Practice Digest 3d* <br> *Federal Practice Digest 4th* <br> Individual state digest (for federal cases relevant to that state) |
| *Atlantic Reporter 2d* (A.2d) | State courts in Conn., Del., D.C., Me., Md., N.H., N.J., Pa., R.I., Vt. | American Digest System <br> *Atlantic Digest* <br> Individual state digest for Conn., D.C., Me., Md., N.H., N.J., Pa., R.I., Vt. |
| *North Eastern Reporter 2d* (N.E.2d) | State courts in Ill., Ind., Mass., N.Y., Ohio | American Digest System <br> Individual state digests for Ill., Ind., Mass., N.Y., Ohio <br> (There is *no* North Eastern Digest) |
| *North Western Reporter 2d* (N.W.2d) | State courts in Iowa, Mich., Minn., Neb., N.D., S.D., Wis. | American Digest System <br> *North Western Digest* <br> Individual state digests for Iowa, Mich., Minn., Neb., N.D., S.D., Wis. |

| | EXHIBIT 11.6 | Reporters and Digests: A Checklist—*continued* | |
|---|---|---|---|

| Name of Reporter | The Courts Whose Opinions Are Currently Printed in Full in This Reporter | The Digests That Contain Small-Paragraph Summaries of the Opinions in This Reporter |
|---|---|---|
| *Pacific Reporter 2d (P.2d)* | State courts in Alaska, Ariz., Cal., Colo., Haw., Idaho, Kan., Mont., Nev., N.M., Okla., Or., Utah., Wash., Wyo. | American Digest System *Pacific Digest* Individual state digests for Alaska, Ariz., Cal., Colo., Haw., Idaho, Kan., Mont., N.M., Okla., Or., Wash., Wyo. |
| *South Eastern Reporter 2d (S.E.2d)* | State courts in Ga., N.C., S.C., Va., W.Va. | American Digest System *South Eastern Digest* Individual state digests for Ga., N.C., S.C., Va., W.Va. |
| *Southern Reporter 2d (So. 2d or S.2d)* | The highest state court and some intermediate appellate courts in Ala., Fla., La., Miss. | American Digest System Individual state digests for Ala., Fla., La., Miss. (There is *no* Southern Digest) |
| *South Western Reporter 2d (S.W.2d)* | The highest state court and some intermediate appellate courts in Ark., Ky., Mo., Tenn., Tex. | American Digest System Individual state digests for Ark., Ky., Mo., Tenn., Tex. (There is *no* South Western Digest) |

**Digests in CD–ROM and Online** All of the digests we have been discussing are printed in hardcover volumes. West Group also provides two alternatives. First, some of its digests are available on CD-ROM. Second, most of the digests are available online through West-law. Earlier we looked at key numbers Negligence 1032, Obscenity 1, and Obscenity 2 as they would appear in a digest volume. One of the ways to find them on Westlaw is to use a special Westlaw "k" number assigned to each of over 400 general topics in the West Group digest system. For example, Negligence is k number 272 and Obscenity is k number 281. To, find Negligence 1032, Obscenity 1, and Obscenity 2 in Westlaw, you would type:

272k1032
281k1
281k2

If you are using hardcover digest volumes and want to look at the potentially thousands of cases summarized under Negligence 1032, you would go to the N volume of the digest and find number 1032 under Negligence. If, however, you are online on Westlaw, you would simply type 272k1032 at the keyboard after selecting the database you want. This would lead you to the potentially thousands of cases summarized under 272k1032. See research link F. Later we will cover both kinds of searches in greater depth.

West Group's digest volumes: key number

Westlaw (online): k number

**RESEARCH LINK F**
Every key number in a bound West Group digest volume (which allows you to find cases summarized under a particular topic) has a corresponding k number in Westlaw (which allows you to find the same cases summarized under that k number online).

**Federal Cases**   *Federal Cases* is the name of the West Group reporter that contains very early opinions of the federal courts (up to 1880), before F., F.2d, F.3d, F. Supp, and F. Supp. 2d came into existence.

**Federal Practice Digest 2d; Federal Practice Digest 3d; Federal Practice Digest 4th**   See exhibit 11.6.

**Federal Register (Fed. Reg.)**   The *Federal Register* is a daily publication of the federal government that prints proposed regulations of the federal administrative agencies; executive orders and other executive documents; and news from federal agencies, such as announcements inviting applications for federal grants. (The *Federal Register* is published by the United States government.) Many of the proposed regulations that are adopted by the federal agencies are later printed in the *Code of Federal Regulations* (C.F.R.). See research link D.

Examples of the *Federal Register* and the *Code of Federal Regulations*. The C.F.R. prints regulations that were first proposed in the Fed. Reg.

**Federal Reporter 2d; Federal Reporter 3d**   A West Group reporter currently containing opinions of the United States Courts of Appeals.

**Federal Rules Decisions (F.R.D.)**   A West Group reporter containing opinions of United States District Courts on issues of civil and criminal procedure, plus articles, speeches, and conference reports on federal procedural issues.

**Federal Supplement 2d (F. Supp. 2d)**   A West Group reporter currently containing opinions of the United States District Courts.

Example of a form book

**Form Book**   A **form book** is a collection of sample forms, often with practical guidance on how to use them. Form books are usually written by private individuals, although a court might issue its own set of required or recommended forms. A form book is sometimes called a practice manual.

**General Digest**   The *General Digest* is one of three digests within the American Digest System published by West Group. The other two are the *Century Digest* and the *Decennial Digests*. All three digests contain small-paragraph summaries of court opinions by every federal and state court that publishes its opinions. The *General Digest* covers opinions written since the date of the last *Decennial Digest*. Eventually, every *General Digest* volume will be thrown away, and the material in them will be consolidated into the next *Decennial Digest* (see research link G).

| General Digest | Decennial Digest |
|---|---|
| (the most recent digest of the American Digest System) | (the largest digest of the American Digest System) |

## RESEARCH LINK G

The *General Digest* is a multivolume digest that summarizes (digests) opinions of every state and federal court. All *General Digest* volumes will eventually be thrown away. The material in them will be printed in the next *Decennial Digest* covering a ten-year period, in two five-year parts.

**Headnote**     A *headnote* is a small-paragraph summary of a portion of an opinion, printed just before the opinion begins. Most headnotes are written by a private publisher such as West Group. (A few courts, however, ask one of their clerks or other employees to write them.) In West Group reporters, each headnote has two numbers. First is a consecutive number. In an opinion with four headnotes, for example, the headnotes will be numbered 1, 2, 3, and 4. (Later we will see that these consecutive numbers are important when shepardizing opinions.) Second, each headnote is assigned a key number, which consists of a general topic and a number. These headnotes with key numbers are also printed in digests. Here is an example of the third headnote from an opinion that has the key number "Libel and Slander 28":

> **3. Libel and Slander** 🔑 **28**
>
> One may not escape liability for defamation by showing that he was merely repeating defamatory language used by another person, and he may not escape liability by falsely attributing to others the ideas to which he gives expression.

The third headnote from an opinion in a West Group, reporter

For another example, see the headnotes at the beginning of the *self* opinion in exhibit 11.28 later in the chapter. Again, all headnotes from opinions in reporters are also printed in West Group digests that cover those reporters. See exhibit 11.6 for a checklist of what digests cover what reporters.

**Hornbook**     A **hornbook** is a legal treatise designed primarily for the law school student. The treatise summarizes an area of the law that is often covered within a single law school course.

**Index to Legal Periodicals and Books (ILP)**     *Index to Legal Periodicals and Books* (ILP) is one of the two major general indexes to legal periodical literature. (The other is the *Current Law Index*.) The ILP is available in three versions: paper (consisting of pamphlets and hardcover volumes), CD–ROM, and online.

**Internet**     The Internet is a self-governing network of networks to which millions of individual computer users all over the world have access. It is not run or controlled by any single government or organization. A *network* is a group of computers connected by telephone lines, fiber-optic cables, satellites, or other systems. The members of the network can communicate with each other to share information that is placed on the network. Vast quantities of data are available on the networks of the Internet, including legal information. Examples include court opinions, statutes, administrative regulations, treaties, court addresses, and directories of attorneys. Here, for example, is the online site where you can find New Jersey statutes, bills, names of state legislators, the current calendar of the New Jersey State legislature, etc.:

*www.njleg.state.nj.us*

Examples of hornbooks

At the federal level, a number of major Internet sites provide laws and information from and about Congress, federal courts, and federal administrative agencies. For example:

> *thomas.loc.gov* (see exhibit 11.7)
> *www.fedworld.gov* (see exhibit 11.7)

(We will cover such sites in greater detail later in Chapter 13) As indicated earlier, a great deal of the information you can obtain on these sites is free once you are connected to the Internet. Often, however, this information is not as current or accurate as the information available in traditional library volumes and on commercial (fee-based) databases such as Westlaw, LEXIS, and Loislaw.

One of the best ways to find information on the Internet is through the **World Wide Web**. The web allows you to gain access to other data through **hypertext**, which is a method of displaying and *linking* together information that is located in different places on the Internet. For example, if you are in a document that contains the court opinions of your state, you may be able to "click" the phrase *state statutes* to switch to another document or site that contains information on the statutes of your state.

Here, for example, is a description of a research resource available from Georgetown University Law Center. Note the extensive amount of material available by hypertext linking:

> We invite you to take a look at our web site (*www.ll.georgetown.edu*). It contains links to many sources of law and law-related information. State coverage, for example, is provided through a clickable list of links to the law of each state. In addition, an "A–Z Legal Topics" list will lead you to comprehensive materials on subjects as diverse as bankruptcy, civil rights, family law, legal ethics, and sexual orientation and the law.

Another major legal research benefit of the Internet is the **listserv**, which is a program that manages computer mailing lists (e-mail lists) automatically. When you join a listserv that relates to the law, you may be able to ask research questions that are read by potentially thousands of other members of the list. Here are examples of the kinds of legal and factual questions you are likely to find "posted" on (sent to) a legal listserv:

> I need a copy of the Air Force Instruction, which has replaced AF Regulation 126–7 (dated 28 August 1987). If you have it and can fax it to me, I would appreciate it. My fax number is . . .
>
> We have a case that involves a '92 Chev Cavalier in which during impact with a tree, the door-mounted seat belt failed, allowing the passenger to be thrown from the vehicle. Would anyone in cyberspace have dealt with a case involving GM and door-mounted seat belts? Or have web sites that I might check involving such? Any help would be appreciated.
>
> We are in need of the current cost of living figures for clerical workers in Boston, MA, Hartford and Stamford, CT. Do any of you know how to get this information? I would appreciate any leads.

Anyone on the list can read these questions and the answers given in response. After answers are posted, you will often find another message sent by the grateful person who posted the original question, exclaiming, "Thanks for saving my life!"

You need to distinguish the Internet from an **intranet**. The latter is a private network of computers within a particular company or organization that enable them to share information online, often using features similar to those on the World Wide Web. A law office with branch offices, for example, might have an intranet for sharing appellate briefs, legal memoranda, or other data. Unlike the Internet, the public at large does not have access to an intranet. If an office with an intranet allows selected outside individuals (e.g., clients) to connect to some of the data on its intranet, that part of the system is called an *extranet*.

**Interstate Compact**    An interstate compact is an agreement between two or more states governing a problem of mutual concern, such as the resolution of a boundary dispute. The compact is passed by the legislature of each state and is therefore part of the statutes of the states involved. Congress must give its approval. Hence the compact also becomes part of the statutes of Congress.

| EXHIBIT 11.7 | Examples of Legal Sites on the Internet |
|---|---|

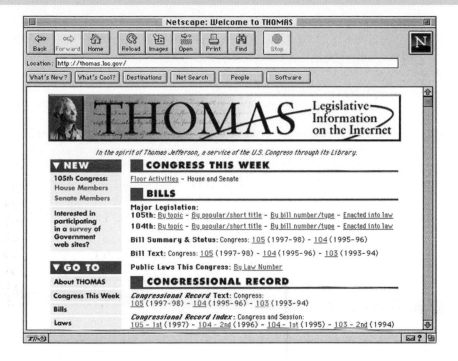

**Thomas**
thomas.loc.gov

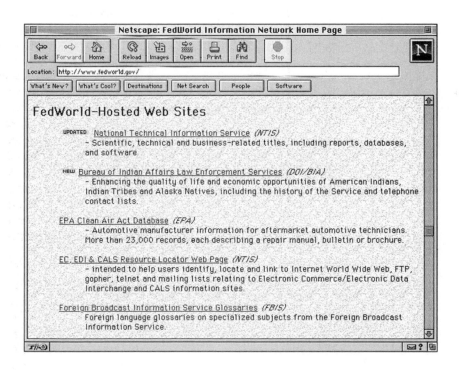

**Fedworld**
www.fedworld.gov

*West Group's*

*Black's Law Dictionary*

Example of a national legal
newspaper

Examples of academic legal
periodicals

**KeyCite**   **KeyCite** is online citation reserach service (available on Westlaw) that claims to be more comprehensive and current than the paper and online versions of Shepard's.

**Legal Dictionary**   A **legal dictionary** contains definitions of words and phrases used in the law. Examples include *Black's Law Dictionary* (West Group), *Ballentine's Law Dictionary* (West Group), and *Statsky's Legal Thesaurus/Dictionary* (West Group). The major multivolume legal dictionary is *Words and Phrases* from West Group. The definitions in this set consist of thousands of excerpts from court opinions that have treated the word or phrase. Hence this massive dictionary can also serve as an excellent case finder.

**Legal Encyclopedia**   A *legal encyclopedia* is a multivolume set of books that summarizes every major legal topic. It is valuable (a) as background reading for a research topic that is new to you and (b) as a case finder (due to its extensive footnotes). The two national encyclopedias are *American Jurisprudence 2d* (Am. Jur. 2d) and *Corpus Juris Secundum* (C.J.S.), both published by West Group. A number of states have their own encyclopedias covering the law of that state, e.g. *Florida Jurisprudence* and *Michigan Law and Practice*.

**Legal Newsletter**   Many private companies and public-interest groups publish **legal newsletters** that provide practical guidelines and current developments in very specific areas of the law. Examples: *Corporate Counsellor, Daily Tax Report, AIDS Policy & Law, Matrimonial Strategist*. Printed weekly, biweekly, or monthly, they are often quite expensive even though they tend to be relatively brief.

**Legal Newspaper**   There are two kinds of **legal newspapers:** local and national. Local legal newspapers are usually published weekly or every business day. They print court dockets (calendars), the full text of selected opinions of local courts, information on new rules of court, job announcements, etc. Most large cities have their own legal newspaper. Examples: *New York Law Journal, Chicago Daily Law Bulletin, San Francisco Daily Journal*. There are several national legal newspapers such as the weekly *National Law Journal*(see www.nlj.com). They cover more than one state on topics such as law firm mergers and dissolutions, salary surveys, careers of prominent attorneys, trends in federal areas of the law, etc.

**Legal Periodical**   In the broadest sense, a **legal periodical** is a pamphlet on a legal topic that is usually sold by subscription and issued at regular intervals—other than a pamphlet that simply updates or supplements another publication. All periodicals are first printed as pamphlets (called *issues*) and then are often placed in hardcover volumes if the law library considers them sufficiently important. This broad definition of legal periodical would include legal newspapers and legal newsletters. More commonly, however, the phrase legal periodicals refers to three categories of periodicals:

- Academic legal periodicals (often called *law reviews* or *law journals*) are published by law schools and hence are scholarly in nature. Law students are selected to do some of the writing and all of the editing for most academic legal periodicals. (It is a mark of considerable distinction for a student to be "on law review.") Most academic legal periodicals are general in scope, covering a wide variety of legal topics. Others are special-interest legal periodicals that concentrate on specific subject areas such as women's rights or environmental law.
- Commercial legal periodicals are published by private companies. They tend to be more practice-oriented, specialized, and expensive than the academic legal periodicals.
- Bar association legal periodicals are published by national, state, or local bar associations. Their focus is on practical articles and features of interest to the membership.

There are two major general indexes to legal periodical literature:

- *Current Law Index* (CLI)
- *Index to Legal Periodicals and Books* (ILP)

These indexes are available in different formats:

- Paper (pamphlets and hardcover volumes)
- CD–ROM (*LegalTrac* is the CD–ROM version of CLI; *Wilsondisc* is a CD–ROM version of ILP)
- Online (primarily through Westlaw and LEXIS).

See research link H. In addition to these general indexes, there are special indexes to legal periodical literature on topics such as tax law.

---

*Current Law Index* (CLI)
Three versions of CLI:
• Pamphlets and hardcover volumes
• CD–ROM: *LegalTrac*
• Online: Westlaw and LEXIS

*Index to Legal Periodicals and Books* (ILP)
Three versions of ILP:
• Pamphlets and hardcover volumes
• CD–ROM: *Wilsondisc*
• Online: Westlaw and LEXIS

Legal Periodicals
Examples: *Yale Law Journal, Marquette Law Review, Harvard Law Review, Ecology Law Quarterly, ABA Journal, Boston Bar Journal*

---

### RESEARCH LINK H

A great deal of literature exists in the three kinds of legal periodicals (academic, commercial, and bar association). The two major indexes to this literature are the *Current Law Index* (CLI) and the *Index to Legal Periodicals and Books* (ILP).

**Legal Thesaurus**    A **legal thesaurus** provides word alternatives for words used in legal writing. The thesaurus may also be helpful when you need word alternatives to form queries for computer-assisted legal research (see chapter 13). Example: Statsky's *Legal Thesaurus/Dictionary: A Resource for the Writer and Legal Researcher* (West Group).

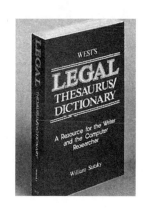

Statsky's *Legal Thesaurus/Dictionary*

**LegalTrac**    **LegalTrac** is a major general index to legal periodical literature. It is the CD–ROM version of the *Current Law Index*, the most comprehensive general index to legal periodical literature available.

**Legal Treatise**    A **legal treatise** (not to be confused with treaty) is any book written by a private individual (or by a public official writing as a private citizen) that provides an overview, summary, or commentary on a legal topic. The treatise will usually attempt to give an extensive treatment of that topic. Hornbooks, handbooks, and form books are also treatises. Some treatises (e.g. hornbooks) are designed primarily as study aids for students. Treatises are printed in single volumes, multivolumes, and loose-leafs.

**Legislation**    **Legislation** is the process of making statutory law by the legislature. The word *legislation* also refers to the statutes themselves. (Legislation sometimes refers to constitutions and treaties as well as to statutes. More commonly, however, legislation refers to statutes alone. For the definition of statute and other categories of primary authority, see exhibit 6.1 in chapter 6).

There are two main categories of statutes:

- **Public laws** (also called *public statutes*): statutes that apply to the general public or to a segment of the public and have permanence and general interest. Example: a statute defining a crime. Such statutes are published as slip laws, as session laws, and as codified laws.
- **Private laws** (also called *private statutes*): statutes that apply to specifically named individuals or groups and have little or no permanence or general interest. Example: a statute naming a bridge after a deceased senator. These statutes are published as slip laws and as session laws; they are not codified.

**LEXIS**    LEXIS is a legal research computer system owned by the Reed Elsevier company. It is part of Reed's broader computer service called LEXIS–NEXIS.) (See chapter 13.) LEXIS also refers to the LEXIS Publishing Company.

**Loose-Leaf Service**    The word *loose-leaf* refers to pages that can be inserted and removed easily, often using a three-ring binder. A legal **loose-leaf service** is a multipurpose collection of materials on a broad or narrow area of the law. As new material is written covering the subject matter of the loose-leaf text, it is placed in the binder, often replacing the pages that the new material has changed or otherwise supplemented. (As we saw earlier, inserting new pages anywhere in the text rather than just at the end of the text is called interfiling.) Loose-leaf updating can occur as often as once a week. Examples of loose-leaf services include *Environmental Reporter, Tax Management, Employment Practices Guide, Standard Federal Tax Reports, United States Law Week, Criminal Law Reporter, Family Law Reporter, Media Law Reporter, Sexual Law Reporter, Labor Relations Reporter.*

Examples of a loose-leaf service

**Maroon Book**    The maroon book is the citation guide formally called *The University of Chicago Manual of Legal Citation.* It is competitor of the more widely used citation guides, *The Bluebook: A Uniform System of Citation* and the *ALWD Citation Manual.*

**Martindale-Hubbell Law Directory**    The *Martindale-Hubbell Law Directory*, published by Reed Elsevier, is a multivolume set of books that serves three major functions by providing:

- An alphabetical listing of attorneys and law firms by state and city—this is the **law directory,** which is the main component of the set
- Short summaries of the law of all fifty states (in its separate Digest volume)
- Short summaries of the law of many foreign countries (in its separate Digest volume)

The *Martindale-Hubbell Law Directory* is also available on the Internet at the following site:

     *www.martindale.com*

Martindale-Hubbell Law Directory

**Microfiche**    *See* Microform in Section G.

**New York Supplement (N.Y.S.)**    A state reporter containing New York cases.

**North Eastern Reporter 2d (N.E.2d)**    A regional reporter that prints the full text of state court opinions in the northeastern region of the country. See exhibit 11.5.

**North Western Digest**    A digest that summarizes state court opinions printed in the *North Western Reporter. See* research link I and exhibit 11.6.

Opinions in *North Western 2d* (N.W.2d)      *North Western Digest*

**RESEARCH LINK I**

Every opinion in the *North Western 2d* reporter written by the state courts in the northwestern region (Iowa, Mich., Minn., Neb., N.D., S.D., and Wis.) is digested (summarized) in *North Western Digest.*

**North Western Reporter 2d (N.W.2d)**    A regional reporter that prints the full text of state court opinions in the northwestern region of the country. See exhibit 11.5.

**Nutshell**    A **nutshell** is a legal treatise written in pamphlet form. It summarizes a topic that is often covered in a law school course. Nutshells, therefore, are primarily used as study aids by law students. Nutshells are similar to hornbooks in function, although nutshells are usually smaller and are always printed as pamphlets. Nutshells are published by West Group.

Examples of nutshells (the two pamphlets) and hornbooks

**Outlines**    An outline, also called a *study outline*, is a pamphlet that summarizes and outlines a legal subject. Like the nutshell, the topic of an outline often parallels the subject matter of a law school course (e.g., contracts, torts). Some of the popular outlines include Gilbert (*www.gilbertlaw.com/index.asp*), Emanuel (*lawschool.lexis.com/emanuel*), and the Black Letter Series (*www.westgroup.com.*)

**Pacific Digest**    A digest that summarizes state court opinions printed in the *Pacific Reporter*. *See* research link J and exhibit 11.6.

Opinions in *Pacific 2d* (P.2d)                    *Pacific Digest*

## RESEARCH LINK J

Every opinion in the *Pacific 2d* reporter written by the state courts in the pacific region (Alaska, Ariz., Cal., Colo., Haw., Idaho, Kan., Mont., Nev., N.M., Okla., Or., Utah, Wash., and Wyo.) is digested (summarized) in *Pacific Digest*.

**Pacific Reporter 2d (P.2d)**    A regional reporter that prints the full text of state court opinions in the pacific region of the country. See exhibit 11.5.

**Pattern Jury Instructions**    Toward the end of a jury trial, the judge must give the jury *instructions* (also called the *charge*) on the law that will govern its deliberations. In some states and judicial systems, there are suggested instructions that can be adapted to the specifics of a particular trial. The instructions are called model jury instructions or, more commonly, **pattern jury instructions.** They are often printed in hardcover volumes and are widely used. See also, the *Online Civil Pattern Jury Instructions* at *courts.state.de.us/superior/pattern_online.htm*.

**Pocket Part**    A pocket part is a small pamphlet inserted into a special pocket built into the inside cover of a bound volume (usually the back cover). The pocket part is published after the bound volume is published. The purpose of a pocket part is to update the material in the bound volume. Pocket parts are critically important in legal research. You may be reading something in the bound volume without being aware that it is no longer valid. One of the ways to check its validity is to check the pocket part for that volume. (For a list of law books that often have pocket parts, see exhibit 11.15, later in the chapter.)

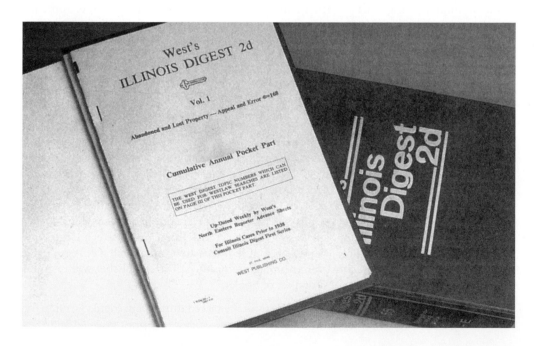

Example of a law book with a pocket part

**Record**    When referring to a trial, the **record** is the official collection of what happened during the trial. It includes a word-for-word transcript of what was said, the pleadings, and all the exhibits. *See also* Congressional Record.

**Regional Digest**    A digest that summarizes cases in a regional reporter. See exhibit 11.6. See also research links A, I, J, and L.

**Register**    A **register** is a set of books that contain administrative regulations, e.g., the *Federal Register*.

**Reporter**    A set of volumes containing the complete text of court opinions. An *official reporter* is a reporter published under the authority of the government, often by the government itself. (Official reporters are sometimes called Reports, e.g., *United States Reports*.) An *unofficial reporter* is a reporter printed by a private or commercial publisher without specific authority from the government. (There are also some sets of books called reporters that contain the complete text of administrative decisions.) See exhibits 11.5 and 11.6 for lists of reporters.

**Restatements**    Restatements are scholarly publications of the American Law Institute (ALI) (*www.ali.org*) that attempt to formulate (that is, restate) the existing law of a given area. Occasionally, the Restatements also state what the ALI thinks the law *ought* to be.

Examples of Restatements:

Example of a Restatement

*Restatement of Agency*          *Restatement of Property*
*Restatement of Conflicts of Law*    *Restatement of Restitution*
*Restatement of Contracts*        *Restatement of Security*
*Restatement of Foreign*          *Restatement of Torts*
  *Relations Law*                *Restatement of Trusts*
*Restatement of Judgments*

Because the Restatements are written by a private organization (ALI) rather than by an official government entity, they are not laws. However, because of their scholarly content, they have great prestige in the courts. Judges frequently rely on them in their opinions. One of the reasons this is so is the elaborate procedure the ALI follows before issuing one of its Restatements. First, a renowned scholar in the field prepares an initial draft of the Restatement. This draft is reviewed by a committee of advisors consisting of other scholars and specialists in the field. A special council of the ALI then reviews and revises the draft. This leads to a *tentative draft* that is considered by the ALI at one of its annual meetings. After further editing and revision, the final version is approved by the ALI. You can read the Restatements in bound volumes and online in Westlaw and LEXIS.

Examples of rules of court volumes

**Rules of Court**    **Rules of court,** also called *court rules,* are the laws of procedure that govern the conduct of litigation before a particular state or federal court. (For the definition of rules of law and other primary authorities, see exhibit 6.1 in chapter 6.) Rules of court are often found in the statutory code and in separate volumes or pamphlets, called *deskbooks.*

**Series**    A new **edition** is usually a revision of an earlier version of a book or set of books. A new **series,** in contrast, refers to a new numbering order for new volumes within the *same* set of books. Reporters, for example, come in series. *Federal Reporter, First Series* (F.) has 300 volumes. After volume 300 was printed, the publisher decided to start a new series of the same set of books—*Federal Reporter, Second Series* (F.2d). The first volume of F.2d is volume 1. F.2d has 999 volumes. After volume 999 was printed, the publisher decided to start a new series of the same set of books—*Federal Reporter, Third Series* (F.3d). After a large number of F.3d volumes are printed, we will undoubtedly see an F.4th, which will begin again with volume 1. There is no consistent number of volumes that a publisher will print before deciding to start a new series for a set of books.

**Session Law**    **Session laws** are uncodified statutes enacted during a particular session (often lasting two years) of the legislature. (Individual session laws are printed as *slip laws.*) Session laws are printed chronologically rather than by subject matter. Other names for this kind of law include Statutes at Large (e.g., *United States Statutes at Large*), Acts and Resolves, Laws, etc. The generic name *session laws* is often used to refer to all of them. Session laws contain both *public statutes*—also called *public laws* (which are statutes that apply to the general public or to a segment of the public and have permanence and general interest)—and *private statutes*—also called *private laws* (which are statutes that apply to specifically named individuals or groups and have little or no permanence or general interest). Public statutes or laws are later *codified*, which means they are placed in statutory codes and arranged by subject matter. See research link K.

> *Slip Law* (a single public or private statute)
> *Session Laws* (arranged by date)
> (public and private statutes)
>
> *Statutory Code* (arranged by subject matter)
> (public statutes only)

## RESEARCH LINK K
After public and private statutes are first printed as *slip laws*, they are printed in volumes of *session laws* where they are arranged chronologically (by date of enactment). The public statutes are then arranged by subject matter and printed in a *statutory code*.

**Shepard's**    Our goal here is to provide a brief overview of Shepard's and sheparding by identifying the major sets of Shepard's volumes that exist. Later, in section O of this chapter, we will learn how to use Shepard's—how to **shepardize.**

*Shepard's Citations* is a citator, which is a list of citations that can help you assess the current validity of an item and can lead you to other relevant materials. To *shepardize* an item means to use any of the three versions of *Shepard's Citations* (paper, CD-ROM, or online) to obtain validation and other data on whatever you are shepardizing. If, for example, you are shepardizing a case, you may be given the *parallel cite* of the case (another reporter where you will find the same case), the *history* of the case (such as citations to all the appeals within the same litigation as the case you are shepardizing), the *treatment* of the case (such as citations to other cases that have followed or criticized the case you are shepardizing and citations to legal periodical literature commenting on the case). If you are shepardizing a statute, you may be given the session law citation of the statute, amendments or repeals of the statute, cases that have interpreted the statute, legal periodical literature commenting on the statute, etc.

There are two main benefits of citators such as *Shepard's Citations*. First, they can help you determine the current validity of cases, statutes, or whatever you are shepardizing. Second, they can lead you to additional relevant laws. See research link C.

What can you shepardize? Here is a partial list:

Excerpt from a page in a Shepard's volume (For the online version of Shepard's, see www.shepards.com)

- Court opinions
- Statutes
- Constitutions
- Some administrative regulations
- Some administrative decisions
- Ordinances
- Charters

- Rules of court
- Some executive orders
- Some treaties
- Patents, trademarks, copyrights
- Restatements
- Some legal periodical literature

It is important to distinguish between **cited material** and **citing material** within Shepard's. The cited material is always what you are checking or shepardizing. Everything on the above list is cited material. It simply means that which is mentioned—cited—by something else. What do we call the materials that *do* the citing? Answer: *citing* materials. Here are some examples:

- Assume you are shepardizing *Smith v. Smith*, 100 N.E.2d 458 (Mass. 1980). You find out through Shepard's that this case was once mentioned by the case of *Jones v. Jones*, 105 N.E.2d 62 (Mass. 1982). What was cited? The *Smith* case. Therefore, it is the cited material. Who did the citing? The *Jones* case. Therefore, it is the citing material.

- Assume you are shepardizing section 100 of the state statutory code. You find out through Shepard's that this statute was once mentioned by the case of *Kiley v. New York*, 296 N.E.2d 222 (N.Y. 1982). What was cited? Section 100. Therefore, it is the cited material. Who did the citing? The *Kiley* case. Therefore, it is the citing material.

As you can see from the first example, an opinion can be the cited material—what you are shepardizing—and another opinion can be the citing material for what you are shepardizing.

In exhibit 11.8, there is an overview of some of the major items that can be shepardized, with the appropriate set of *Shepard's Citations* that you would use to do so.

**Slip Law**     A **slip law** is a single act passed by the legislature. It is printed separately, often in a small pamphlet. It is the first official publication of the act. All slip laws are later printed chronologically in volumes that may be called Session Laws, Acts, Statutes at Large, etc. Finally, if the slip law is a public law (public statute), it is also printed in a **statutory code,** where the arrangement is by subject matter.

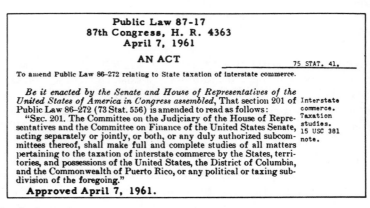

Example of a slip law

**Slip Opinion**     When a court first announces a decision, it is usually published in what is called a **slip opinion** or slip decision. It contains a single case in pamphlet form. The slip opinions are later printed in advance sheets for reporters, which in turn become hardcover reporters.

**South Eastern Digest**     A digest that summarizes state court opinions printed in the *South Eastern Reporter*. See research link L and exhibit 11.6.

Opinions in *South Eastern 2d* (S.E.2d)       *South Eastern Digest*

Example of a slip opinion

### RESEARCH LINK L

Every opinion in the *South Eastern 2d* reporter written by the state courts in the southeastern region (Ga., N.C., S.C., Va., and W.Va.) is digested (summarized) in *South Eastern Digest*.

**South Eastern Reporter 2d (S.E.2d)**     A regional reporter that prints the full text of state court opinions in the southeastern region of the country. See exhibit 11.5.

**Southern Reporter 2d (So. 2d)**     A regional reporter that prints the full text of state court opinions in several southern states. See exhibit 11.5.

**South Western Reporter 2d (S.W.2d)**     A regional reporter that prints the full text of state court opinions in the southwestern region of the country. See exhibit 11.5.

| EXHIBIT 11.8 | Overview of Major Items That Can Be Shepardized |
|---|---|

Assume that you want to shepardize an opinion of the United States Supreme Court:

Here is the set of Shepard's you use to shepardize an opinion of the United States Supreme Court:

Supreme
Court
Reporter

*Shepard's*
*United*
*States*
*Citations*

Assume that you want to shepardize opinions found in *Federal Reporter, 3d:*

Here is the set of Shepard's you use to shepardize an F.3d opinion:

*Federal*
*Reporter*
*3d* (F.3d)

*Shepard's*
*Federal*
*Citations*

Assume that you want to Shepardize opinions found in *Federal Supplement 2d:*

Here is the set of Shepard's you use to shepardize an F. Supp. 2d opinion:

*Federal*
*Supplement 2d*
(F. Supp. 2d)

*Shepard's*
*Federal*
*Citations*

| EXHIBIT 11.8 | Overview of Major Items That Can Be Shepardized—*continued* |

Assume that you want to shepardize a federal statute of Congress: a statute found in U.S.C.A. (*United States Code Annotated*) or in U.S.C.S. (*United States Code Service*) or in U.S.C. (*United States Code*):

Here is the set of Shepard's you use to shepardize a federal statute:

*United
States Code
Annotated
(U.S.C.A.)*

*Shepard's
Federal
Statute
Citations*

Assume that you want to shepardize a regulation of a federal agency found in C.F.R.:

Here is the set of Shepard's that will enable you to shepardize a regulation in C.F.R.:

*Code of
Federal
Regulations
(C.F.R.)*

*Shepard's
Code of
Federal
Regulations
Citations*

Assume that you want to shepardize opinions found within the following regional reporters:

    *Atlantic Reporter 2d*
    *Pacific Reporter 2d*
    *South Western Reporter 2d*
    *South Eastern Reporter 2d*
    *North Eastern Reporter 2d*

At the right are the sets of Shepard's that you use to shepardize the opinions in these regional reporters.

| EXHIBIT 11.8 | Overview of Major Items That Can Be Shepardized—*continued* |
|---|---|

Assume that you want to shepardize the following:

    A Rhode Island court opinion
    A Rhode Island statute
    A Rhode Island constitutional provision
    A New Hampshire court opinion
    A New Hampshire statute
    A New Hampshire constitutional provision

Here are the sets of Shepard's that you would use:

Note: Every state has its own set of Shepard's similar to *Shepard's Rhode Island Citations* and *Shepard's New Hampshire Citations* above.

**Statutes at Large**   An uncodified printing of statutes. Statutes at Large (abbreviated Stat.) are session laws.

**Statutory Code**   Statutes are first published as *slip laws*, then in *session law* volumes, and finally, if they are of general public interest, in a *statutory code*. A statutory code is a collection of statutes of the legislature organized by subject matter. For example, the statutes on murder are together, the statutes on probate are together, etc. An **official statutory code** is one printed under the authority of the government, often by the government itself. An **unofficial statutory code** is one printed by a commercial publishing company without special authority from the government. Statutory codes are often annotated (particularly unofficial codes), meaning that notes or commentaries accompany the full text of the statutes. The notes might include summaries of cases (often called *notes of decisions*) that have interpreted the statute and information on the legislative history of the statute, such as the dates of earlier amendments. Statutes are published in printed volumes, on CD-ROMs, online through fee-based services (e.g., Westlaw, LEXIS, and Loislaw), and online through free Internet sites that we will examine later.

Example of a state statutory code

    The three major *federal* statutory codes are:

U.S.C.—*United States Code* (published by the U.S. Government Printing Office) (official)
U.S.C.A.—*United States Code Annotated* (published by West Group) (unofficial)
U.S.C.S.—*United States Code Service* (published by LEXIS Law Publishing) (unofficial)

Updating: The *United States Code* is updated by:

  ■  Bound supplement volumes

The *United States Code Annotated* is updated by:

  ■  Pocket parts
  ■  Pamphlet supplements
  ■  *United States Code Congressional and Administrative News* (U.S.C.C.A.N.)

The *United States Code Service* is updated by:

  ■  Pocket parts
  ■  *U.S.C.S. Advance*

The three major federal statutory codes: U.S.C., U.S.C.A., U.S.C.S.

**Supreme Court Reporter (S. Ct.)**    An unofficial reporter that prints every opinion of the United States Supreme Court. It is published by West Group. Before the final volumes are printed, it comes out in pamphlet advance sheets and in hardcover *Interim Edition* volumes.

**Total Client-Service Library**    The **Total Client-Service Library** is the system by which West Group refers you to many of the books and other materials West Group publishes. For example, West Group publishes *American Law Reports* (A.L.R., A.L.R.2d, etc.). If you are reading an annotation on felony murder in one of the A.L.R. volumes, you will find a Total Client-Service Library reference section to other West Group publications (e.g., Am. Jur. 2d) on the same or similar felony murder issues.

**Ultrafiche**    *See* Microform in section G.

**Uniform State Laws**    **Uniform state laws** are statutes that cover areas of law where uniformity across state lines is deemed appropriate. Examples are the Uniform Consumer Credit Code and the Uniform Arbitration Act. One of the major organizations that writes and proposes uniform state laws is the National Conference of Commissioners on Uniform State Law (NCCUSL): *www.nccusl.org*. The proposals are submitted to every state legislature, which is free to adopt, modify, or reject them. To find out whether an individual state has adopted one of the proposed uniform state laws, you would check the index of the statutory code of that state. All of the uniform state laws are printed in a set of books called *Uniform Laws Annotated* (U.L.A.), published by West Group. The U.L.A. is also available online on Westlaw. Drafts of uniform state laws can be found on the Internet at *www.law.upenn.edu/bll.*

     Another major national organization that writes and proposes laws is the American Law Institute (ALI) (*www.ali.org*), which also publishes the Restatements that we examined earlier. Some of the ALI proposals are called "model acts," such as the Model Penal Code. Again, legislatures are free to adopt, modify, or reject what is proposed. Occasionally, the NCCUSL and the ALI will work together to jointly propose a law. A major example is the important Uniform Commercial Code (UCC).

**United States Code (U.S.C.)**    The official code published by the United States government containing federal statutes.

**United States Code Annotated (U.S.C.A.)**    An unofficial code published by West Group containing federal statutes.

**United States Code Congressional and Administrative News (U.S.C.C.A.N.)**    U.S.C.C.A.N., published by West Group will enable you to:

- Obtain the complete text of public laws or statutes of Congress before they are published in U.S.C./U.S.C.A./U.S.C.S.
- Obtain the complete text of some congressional committee reports (important for legislative history)

- Translate a Statute at Large cite into a U.S.C./U.S.C.A./U.S.C.S. cite (through Table 2)
- Obtain leads to the legislative history of federal statutes (primarily through Table 4)

**Table 4**
**LEGISLATIVE HISTORY**

Bill numbers in parentheses ( ) are companion bills reported either in the Senate or the House

| Public Law | | 84 Stat. Page | Bill No. | Report No. 91– | | Comm. Reporting | | Cong. Rec. Vol. 116 (1970) Dates of Consideration and Passage | |
|---|---|---|---|---|---|---|---|---|---|
| No. 91– | Date App. | | | House | Senate | House | Senate | House | Ser |
| 191 | Feb. 3 | 1 | S.J.Res. 121 | 819 | 185 | PA | PR | Jan. 20 | M |
| 192 | Feb. 4 | 4 | H.J.Res. | none | 647 | none | J | Jan. 26 | |
| 193 | | | | | *s | none | none | Feb. 7 | |
| | | | | | App | App | D* | | |
| | | | | | | | J | | |
| | | | | | | | Ap* | | |

- Obtain the complete text of some federal agency regulations (duplicating what is found in the *Federal Register*—Fed. Reg.—and in the *Code of Federal Regulations*—C.F.R.)
- Obtain the complete text of executive orders and other executive documents
- Obtain the complete text of all current *United States Statutes at Large* (see below)

**United States Code Service (U.S.C.S.)** An unofficial code published by LEXIS Law Publishing containing federal statutes.

**United States Law Week (U.S.L.W.)** U.S.L.W. is a loose-leaf service published by the Bureau of National Affairs (BNA) that prints the full text of every United States Supreme Court opinion on a weekly basis. It also prints other data on cases in the Supreme Court and summarizes important cases from other courts.

**United States Reports (U.S.)** An official reporter that prints every opinion of the United States Supreme Court. The advance sheets for *United States Reports* are called **preliminary prints.**

**United States Statutes at Large (Stat.)** The *United States Statutes at Large* (Stat.) contains the full text of every public law or statute and every private law or statute of Congress. (A private law or private statute applies to specifically named individuals or to groups and has little or no permanence or general interest, unlike a public law or public statute.) The statutes within Stat. are printed chronologically. See research link M. All current statutes at large are now also printed in *U.S. Code Congressional and Administrative News* as well as in separate Stat. volumes. (The public laws of general interest are later codified and printed in each of the three sets of codified federal statutes: U.S.C., U.S.C.A., and U.S.C.S.)

*United States Statutes at Large* (Stat.)
(public and private statutes of Congress arranged by date)

*United States Code* (U.S.C.)
(public statutes of Congress arranged by subject matter)

*United States Code Annotated* (U.S.C.A.)
(public statutes of Congress arranged by subject matter)

*United States Code Service* (U.S.C.S.)
(public statutes of Congress arranged by subject matter)

### RESEARCH LINK M
All public and private statutes of Congress are printed chronologically as session laws in *United States Statutes at Large* (Stat.). If they are public statutes, they are also codified and printed by subject matter in the three codes containing federal statutes: U.S.C. (official), U.S.C.A. (unofficial), and U.S.C.S. (unofficial).

*Words and Phrases*, a
multivolume legal dictionary

**United States Supreme Court Reports, Lawyers' Edition (L. Ed.)**   An unofficial reporter that prints every opinion of the United States Supreme Court. It is published by LEXIS Law Publishing.

**Westlaw**   Westlaw is a legal research computer system owned by West Group.

**Words and Phrases**   A multivolume legal dictionary. Most of the definitions in this dictionary are quotations from court opinions.

### OUTLINE
For a summary of many of the glossary entries we have been examining, see exhibit 11.9.

| EXHIBIT 11.9 | Major Legal Reference Materials: An Outline |
| --- | --- |

**BOOKS OF LAW**

Federal Statutes
- *U.S. Statutes at Large*
- *U.S. Code*
- *U.S. Code Annotated*
- *U.S. Code Service*

State Statutes
- Session laws
- State statutory codes

Federal Court Opinions

U.S. Supreme Court
- *U.S. Reports*
- *Lawyers' Edition 2d*
- *Supreme Court Reporter*
- *U.S. Law Week*
- *U.S. Supreme Court Bulletin* (CCH)

U.S. Courts of Appeals
- *Federal Reporter 3d*

U.S. District Courts
- *Federal Supplement 2d*

Specialty or Topical Reporters
- *Federal Rules Decisions*
- *Military Justice Reporter*
- *Bankruptcy Reporter*
- *Federal Claims Reporter*
- *Veterans Appeals Reporter*

State Court Opinions

Regional Reporters of the National Reporter System
- *Atlantic Reporter 2d*
- *North Eastern Reporter 2d*
- *North Western Reporter 2d*
- *Pacific Reporter 2d*
- *South Eastern Reporter 2d*
- *Southern Reporter 2d*
- *South Western Reporter 2d*

Others
- Official state reporters
- Special edition state reporters (offprint reporters)

| EXHIBIT 11.9 | Major Legal Reference Materials: An Outline—*continued* |

**BOOKS OF LAW (cont.)**

Federal & State Constitutions . . . . . . . . . . — Within statutory code

Federal Administrative Regulations . . . . . . . . . . . . . . . . . . . . . .
- *Federal Register*
- *Code of Federal Regulations*

State Administrative Regulations . . . . . . . . . . . . . . . . . . . . . .
- State register
- State administrative code

Charters & Ordinances . . . . . . . . . . . . . . — Municipal code

**BOOKS OF SEARCH AND/OR INTERPRETATION**

Digests . . . . . . . . . . . . . . . . . . . . . . . . . .
- American Digest System
  - *Century Digest*
  - *Decennial Digests*
  - *General Digests*
- U.S. Supreme Court digests
- Regional digests
- Individual state digests
- *Federal Practice Digest 4th*
- *Bankruptcy Digest*
- *Military Justice Digest*
- *Education Law Digest*
- *Veterans Appeals Digest*

Legal Encyclopedias . . . . . . . . . . . . . . . . .
- *American Jurisprudence 2d*
- *Corpus Juris Secundum*

Legal Periodicals . . . . . . . . . . . . . . . . . . .
- *Index to Legal Periodicals and Books*
- *Current Law Index*
- *LegalTrac*
- *Wilsondisc*

Annotations . . . . . . . . . . . . . . . . . . . . . .
- *American Law Reports*
- *American Law Reports 2d*
- *American Law Reports 3d*
- *American Law Reports 4th*
- *American Law Reports 5th*
- *American Law Reports Fed.*

Others . . . . . . . . . . . . . . . . . . . . . . . . . .
- Loose-leaf services
- Legal treatises
- Legal newsletters
- Legal newspapers

**COMPUTER RESEARCH** . . . . . . . . . . . . . . . . . . .
- Westlaw
- LEXIS
- Loislaw
- Internet

**CITATORS** . . . . . . . . . . . . . . . . . . . . . . . . . . . . .
- Shepard's
- KeyCite (Westlaw)
- Auto-Cite (LEXIS)
- GlobalCite (Loislaw)

| EXHIBIT 11.9 | Major Legal Reference Materials: An Outline—*continued* |
|---|---|

**PARALLEL**
**CITATION** . . . . . . . . . . . . . . . . . . . . . . . . . .
**TABLES**

⌐ *National Reporter Blue Book*
⌐ *Blue and White Book*

**LEGAL DICTIONARIES** . . . . . . . . . . . . . . . . . .

⌐ *Black's Law Dictionary*
| *Ballentine's Law Dictionary*
| *Statsky's Legal Theasurus/Dictionary*
⌐ *Words and Phrases*

**CITATION GUIDELINES** . . . . . . . . . . . . . . . . . .

⌐ *Bluebook: A Uniform System of Citation*
| *ALWD Citation Manual*
⌐ *Chicago Manual of Legal Citation*

Section I

# AUTHORITY IN RESEARCH AND WRITING

## 1. INTRODUCTION

The purpose of legal research is to find the law that will help a client solve a legal dispute, prevent such a dispute from arising, or prevent the dispute from getting worse. All three are accomplished by analyzing the facts of the client's case and by applying any existing *mandatory primary authority* to these facts. Our goal in this section is to identify what we mean by this kind of authority and to explore what must be done if such authority cannot be found. First, some definitions.

Authority is any source that a court can rely on in reaching its decision.

### Primary and Secondary Authority

**Primary authority** is any *law* that the court can rely on in reaching its decision. Examples include statutes, administrative regulations, constitutional provisions, executive orders, charters, ordinances, treaties, and other court opinions (see exhibit 6.1 in chapter 6).

**Secondary authority** is any *nonlaw* that the court can rely on in reaching its decision. Examples include legal and nonlegal periodical literature, legal and nonlegal encyclopedias, legal and nonlegal dictionaries, and legal and nonlegal treatises. (See exhibit 11.10, later in this section.)

As we study primary and secondary authority, keep in mind that it makes no difference whether this authority is in a printed pamphlet or book; on a CD-ROM; online through Westlaw, LEXIS, or the Internet; or on microform. Most primary and secondary authority can be found in a variety of media. (See section G on the formats of research materials that are available.) Here, we want to identify the variety of authority that a court might consider, regardless of the kind of format or media in which this authority could be read.

### Mandatory Authority and Persuasive Authority

**Mandatory authority** is whatever the court *must* rely on in reaching its decision. Only primary authority—such as another court opinion, a statute, or a constitutional provision—can be mandatory authority. A court is never required to rely on secondary authority, such as a legal periodical article or legal encyclopedia. Secondary authority cannot be mandatory authority.

**Persuasive authority** is whatever the court relies on when it is not required to do so. There are two main kinds of persuasive authority: (a) a prior court opinion that the court is not required to follow but does so because it finds the opinion persuasive and (b) any secondary authority that the court is not required to follow but does so because it finds the secondary authority persuasive.

### Nonauthority

**Nonauthority** is (a) any primary or secondary authority that is not on point because it is not relevant and does not cover the facts of the client's problem; (b) any invalid primary authority, such as an unconstitutional statute; or (c) any book that is solely a finding aid, such as *Shepard's Citations* or digests.

## 2. MANDATORY AUTHORITY

Courts *must* follow mandatory authority. There are two broad categories of mandatory authority: (a) **enacted law** such as a statute, a constitutional provision, an ordinance, or an administrative regulations, and (b) other court opinions. (See chapter 7 for a discussion of the meaning of enacted law.) Each category will be considered separately.

### Enacted Law as Mandatory Authority

Any enacted law is mandatory authority and must be followed if the following three tests are met:

- The enacted law is being applied in a geographic area over which the authors of the law have power or jurisdiction (e.g., a Florida statute being applied to an event that occurred in the state of Florida).
- It was the intention of the authors of the enacted law (e.g., the legislature that wrote the statute) to cover the kinds of facts that are currently before the court.
- The application of this enacted law to these facts does not violate some other law that is superior in authority (e.g., the statute does not violate the constitution).

If an enacted law such as a state statute meets these three tests, it is mandatory authority in every state court in the state.

For example, assume that § 14 of the Florida statutory code provides "It shall be a felony to break and enter a dwelling for the purpose of stealing property therein." Smith is charged with violating § 14 after being arrested for breaking down the door of a Miami apartment and taking jewelry from within. Is § 14 mandatory authority in a Florida criminal court where Smith is being prosecuted? Yes. The author of § 14 is the Florida legislature. The alleged crime occurred in Miami, a geographical area over which the Florida legislature clearly has power or jurisdiction. The first test is met. There is little doubt that an apartment is a "dwelling." Hence the legislature intended § 14 to cover stealing from an apartment. The second test is met. There is no indication that § 14 violates the state constitution or any other higher authority. Assuming there is no such violation, the third test is met. Therefore, § 14 is mandatory authority in the criminal trial of *Florida v. Smith*.

Suppose, however, that Smith is arrested for breaking into a *car* and stealing valuables from the glove compartment. Is § 14 mandatory authority in this case? We need to know whether a car is a "dwelling" for purposes of § 14. (In part, it might depend on whether the owner of the car ever slept in it.) To answer this question, we need to ask whether the Florida legislature intended to include motor vehicles within the meaning of "dwelling" in § 14. This is a question of **legislative intent.** If the statute was not intended to cover these facts, it is not applicable; it cannot be mandatory authority. In this instance, it would be nonauthority.

Furthermore, even if the enacted law *was* intended to cover the facts before the court, it is not mandatory authority if it violates some higher law. The authors of an administrative regulation, for example, may intend to cover a particular individual's activities, but if this regulation is inconsistent with the statute that the regulation is supposed to be carrying out, the regulation is not mandatory authority; it is invalid. Similarly, a statute may clearly cover a given set of facts but be invalid because the statute is unconstitutional. For example, a statute that prohibits marriage between the races is clearly intended to prevent interracial marriage, but the statute is not mandatory authority because it is in violation of the constitution.

*States* enacted law (e.g., a state statute, a state administrative regulation) is usually mandatory only in the state that enacted that law. Suppose, however, that a state court is considering a *federal* enacted law.

*Federal* enacted law (e.g., the United States Constitution, a federal statute, a federal administrative regulation) can sometimes be mandatory authority in *state* courts. The United States Constitution is the highest authority in the country. If a provision of this Constitution applies, it controls over any state law to the contrary. Federal statutes and the regulations of federal administrative agencies are also superior in authority to state laws in those areas entrusted to the federal government by the United States Constitution, such as interstate commerce, patents, bankruptcy, or foreign affairs. Federal statutes and regulations in these areas are mandatory authority in state courts.

### Court Opinions as Mandatory Authority

When is a court *required* to follow an opinion, so that the opinion is mandatory authority? Two conditions must be met:

- The opinion is **analogous.**
- The opinion was written by a higher court that is superior to the court currently considering the applicability of the opinion.

In general, a court opinion is **on point** if it raises or covers the same issue as the one before you in the client's case. When we say that an opinion is analogous, we mean that:

- There is a sufficient similarity between the **key facts** of the opinion and the facts of the client's case *and*
- There is a sufficient similarity between the rule of law (e.g., statute, common law principle) that was interpreted and applied in the opinion and the rule of law that must be interpreted and applied in the client's case.

A *key fact* is a fact that was essential or very important to the conclusion or holding of the court's opinion. The easiest case is when the opinion is **on all fours** with the facts of the client's case. This means that the key facts of the opinion are exactly the same or almost exactly the same as the facts of the client's case. (See chapter 7 for a more detailed discussion of the process of applying an opinion by comparing it to a client's case.)

If the opinion is not analogous because there is not sufficient similarity between the opinion and the client's case, the opinion cannot be mandatory authority.

The second condition for the existence of mandatory authority requires us to examine the relationship between the court that wrote the opinion and the court that is currently considering that opinion. We will briefly cover six variations:

1. The highest court in the judicial system is considering an opinion written by a lower court in the same judicial system.
2. A lower court is considering an opinion written by the highest court in the same judicial system.
3. A court is considering an opinion written in the past by the same court.
4. A state court is considering an opinion written by a court from another state.
5. A state court is considering an opinion written by a federal court.
6. A federal court is considering an opinion written by a state court.

In each of these six situations, a court is attempting to determine whether the conclusion or holding in a prior opinion is binding in the litigation currently before the court. Assume that the opinion is analogous: the facts currently before the court are sufficiently similar to the key facts in the opinion under consideration, and the rules of law are also the same or sufficiently similar.

1. *The highest court in the judicial system is considering an opinion written by a lower court in the same judicial system.*

   A higher court is never required to follow an opinion written by a lower court in the same judicial system, whether or not the opinion is analogous. The California Supreme Court, for example, does not have to follow the holding in an opinion written by a California Superior Court, one of the lower courts in the California judicial system. Similarly, the United States Supreme Court does not have to follow the holding in an opinion written by a United States District Court, the trial court in the federal judicial system. If the opinion is analogous, it can only be persuasive authority; the higher court can follow the holding if it chooses to do so.

2. *A lower court is considering an opinion written by the highest court in the same judicial system.*

   An opinion written by the highest court in a judicial system *is* mandatory on every lower court in the same judicial system—if the opinion is analogous. An analogous opinion by the Supreme Court of Montana, for example, must be followed by every lower state court in Montana.

3. *A court is considering an opinion written in the past by the same court.*

   Does a court have to follow its *own* prior opinions? If, for example, the Florida Supreme Court wrote an opinion in 1970, is the holding in that opinion mandatory authority for the Florida Supreme Court in 2002 if the opinion is analogous? No. A court is always free to **overrule** and in effect invalidate its own prior opinions. This, however, rarely happens. A court is reluctant to change holdings in prior opinions unless there are good reasons to do so. This reluctance is known as **stare decisis.** Stated more positively: if a **precedent** exists, a court will follow it in a later similar case unless there are good reasons for the court to change the precedent. A precedent is simply a prior decision that can be used as a standard in a later similar case. To maintain fairness and stability, stare decisis means that courts should decide similar cases in the same way unless there is good reason to do otherwise.

   The Florida example involved the highest state court considering an earlier opinion written by the same court. Suppose the opinion had been written by an intermediate or middle appeals court. Sometime later, this same court is asked to follow its own prior opinion because the previous opinion is analogous to the case currently before the court. Does it have to? No. Any court can later overrule itself and reach a holding that differs from the holding it reached in the earlier opinion.

4. *A state court is considering an opinion written by a court from another state.*

   A state court generally does not have to follow an opinion written by a state court in another state, no matter how similar or analogous the cases are. An Idaho court, for example, does not have to follow an opinion written by a Texas court.

   There are two main exceptions to the principle that an opinion of one state is not mandatory authority in another state. The first involves conflicts of law and the second, full faith and credit:

   ■ **Conflicts of law.** Suppose that an accident occurs in New York, but the negligence suit based on this accident is brought in a state court in Ohio, where the defendant lives. Assume that the Ohio court has **subject matter jurisdiction** over the dispute (meaning that the court has the power to hear this kind of dispute) and **personal jurisdiction** over the parties (meaning that the court has the power to render a decision that would bind these particular parties). What negligence law does the Ohio court apply? Ohio negligence law or New York negligence law? The negligence law of the two states may differ in significant respects. This is a conflicts-of-law problem, which arises whenever there is an inconsistency between the laws of two different, co-equal legal systems such as two states. Under the principles of the conflicts of law, a court of one state may be required to apply the law of another state. For example, the law to be applied may be the law of the state where the injury occurred or the law of the state that is at the center of the dispute. If this state is New York, then the Ohio court will apply New York negligence law. Analogous opinions of New York courts on the law of negligence will be mandatory authority in the Ohio court.

- **Full faith and credit.** The United States Constitution provides that "Full Faith and Credit shall be given in each State to the public Acts, Records, and judicial Proceedings of every other State" (art. IV, § 1). Suppose that Richards sues Davis for breach of contract in Delaware. Davis wins. Richards cannot go to another state and bring a breach-of-contract suit against Davis arising out of the same facts. If the Delaware court had proper jurisdiction (subject matter and personal) when it rendered its judgment, the Delaware opinion must be given full faith and credit in every other state. The case cannot be relitigated. The Delaware opinion is mandatory authority in every other state.

5 and 6.   *A state court is considering an opinion written by a federal court and vice versa.*

The general rule is that state courts have the final say on what the state law is and federal courts have the final say on what the federal law is. State courts do *not* have to follow opinions written by federal courts *unless* the issue before the state court involves a federal question—one arising out of the United States Constitution or out of a statute of Congress. (The clause in the United States Constitution that says federal law controls over state or local law whenever a federal question is raised is the **Supremacy Clause**.)

Federal courts do not have to follow state court opinions except to the extent that the federal court needs to know what the state law is on a given topic, and the state court opinions provide this information. When does a federal court need to know what the state law is on a given topic? Mainly in *diversity of citizenship* cases. (The parties must be citizens of different states, and the amount in controversy must exceed a designated amount.) Also, the case before the federal court must raise a state question rather than a federal question arising under the United States Constitution or statute of Congress. In a proper diversity case, a federal court will apply state law to resolve the controversy. In such cases, state court opinions will be mandatory authority in the federal court.

### 3. PERSUASIVE AUTHORITY

We turn next to persuasive authority, which is any law or nonlaw that a court decides to follow because of its persuasiveness rather than because of a mandate or duty to follow it. The most common categories of persuasive authority we need to consider are (1) other court opinions and (2) secondary authority.

#### Court Opinions as Persuasive Authority

Review the two conditions mentioned earlier on when an opinion is mandatory authority: The opinion must be analogous, *and* the opinion must have been written by a court that is superior to the court currently considering that opinion. If both these tests are not met, either the opinion is nonauthority, or it might be *persuasive authority*.

Suppose that you are reading an opinion that is analogous, but not mandatory because of one of the following:

- It was written by an inferior court and is now being considered by a court within the same judicial system that is superior to the court that wrote the opinion; or
- It was written by a court from a different judicial system such as a Texas court considering a Virginia opinion. (Assume that there are no conflict-of-interest or full-faith-and-credit issues.)

If either of these two situations exists, the court, as we have seen, does *not* have to follow the opinion; it is not mandatory authority. If, however, the opinion is analogous, the court would be free to adopt the opinion as persuasive authority.

A number of factors go into a court's determination of whether a prior opinion is persuasive enough to adopt. A judge is usually interested in knowing how many other courts have adopted the conclusion (the holding) of this opinion. Is there a "majority rule" or school of thought that has developed around that conclusion? Has the opinion been frequently cited with approval? (To find out, check citators such as Shepard's and KeyCite.) How well reasoned is the opinion? These considerations will help a judge decide whether to adopt an opinion as persuasive. Finally, it is human nature for judges to gravitate toward opinions that are most in tune with their personal philosophies and biases—although preferences on this basis are never acknowledged.

Finally, we need to consider **dictum** as persuasive authority. Dictum is a statement made by a court that was not necessary to resolve the narrow question or issue before the court. Assume that a tenant (Mr. Kiley) sued his landlord (ABC Properties, Inc.) for failing to repair the main elevator in the building. The landlord claimed the tenant should repair it. The court rendered its decision in the opinion of *Kiley v. ABC Properties, Inc.*, ruling in favor of the tenant. In the *Kiley* opinion, the court says, "Landlords have an obligation to maintain elevators as well as all common passageways in the rented premises." The court's statement about the elevator is its **holding;** its statement about common passageways, however, is dictum. (A holding is a court's answer to a specific question or issue that arises out of facts before the court.)

The narrow issue before the court was whether the landlord must repair the *elevator*. The court's answer to this issue is its holding. Everything else is dictum. There was no need for the court to tell us about the landlord's legal obligation concerning *passageways*. The law governing passageways should be resolved in a future case when the dispute before the court involves parties fighting over who must maintain passageways. To be sure, it was convenient for the court in the *Kiley* opinion to add its view about passageways; they seem to be similar in function to elevators. But in our legal system, we prefer that courts stick to the disputes arising from the facts before them. Occasionally, they don't, leading to dictum.

Now assume that, years later, another landlord-tenant case comes before the court. Jackson (the tenant) is being sued by Weber (the landlord) over repair of the passageway in the building where Jackson lives. Is *Kiley v. ABC Properties, Inc.*, mandatory authority? No. Jackson is very happy about the language in *Kiley* that says landlords must maintain passageway. But the *Kiley* opinion is not mandatory authority on the issue of a landlord's responsibility to maintain passageways because this issue was never before the *Kiley* court. The language about passageways in *Kiley* was dictum. Does this mean that the court in the Jackson/Weber case must ignore the dictum in *Kiley* on passageways? No. The court can decide to adopt the *Kiley* statement on passageways because it finds the statement persuasive. It is not required to follow the *Kiley* statement but may decide to do so as persuasive authority.

### Secondary Authority as Persuasive Authority

Secondary authority such as a legal treatise or a legal periodical article is not the law itself. It is not written by the legislature, a court, an agency, a city council, etc. Secondary authority can never be mandatory authority; it can only be persuasive. The chart in exhibit 11.10 provides an overview of the major kinds of secondary authority that a court could decide to rely on in reaching its conclusion.

Almost all secondary authorities quote from the law itself; they quote primary authority. For example, here is an excerpt from page 321 of the third edition of a 1990 legal treatise called *Administrative Law and Process in a Nutshell* by Ernest Gellhorn and Ronald M. Levin. Note that this excerpt quotes from § 553(b)(3)(B) of the Administrative Procedure Act (APA), which is within title 5 of the United States Code Annotated (U.S.C.A.):

> The final exemption to the APA's notice-and-comment procedures applies when "notice and public procedure . . . are impracticable, unnecessary, or contrary to the public interest." 5 U.S.C.A. § 553(b)(3)(B). In practice this exception applies primarily when delay in the issuance of the rule would frustrate the rule's purpose . . . Ernest Gellhorn & Ronald M. Levin, *Administrative Law and Process in a Nutshell* 321 (3d ed. 1990).

| EXHIBIT 11.10 | Categories of Secondary Authority | |
|---|---|---|
| **Kind** | **Contents** | **Examples** |
| **1a.** Legal Encyclopedias | Summaries of the law, organized by topic | *Corpus Juris Secundum*<br>*American Jurisprudence 2d* |
| **1b.** Nonlegal Encyclopedias | Summaries of many topics on science, the arts, history, etc. | *Encyclopaedia Britannica* |
| **2a.** Legal Dictionaries | Definitions of legal terms taken almost exclusively from court opinions | *Words and Phrases* |
| **2b.** Legal Dictionaries | Definitions of legal terms that come from a variety of sources | *Black's Law Dictionary*<br>*Ballentine's Law Dictionary*<br>*Statsky's Legal Thesaurus/Dictionary* |
| **2c.** Nonlegal Dictionaries | Definitions of all words in general use | *Webster's Dictionary* |
| **3a.** Legal Periodicals (academic) | Pamphlets (often later bound) containing articles on a variety of legal topics | *Harvard Law Review*<br>*Utah Law Review*<br>*Yale Journal of Law and Feminism* |
| **3b.** Legal Periodicals (commercial) | Pamphlets (often later bound) containing articles on a variety of legal topics | *Case and Comment*<br>*Practical Lawyer* |
| **3c.** Legal Periodicals (bar association) | Pamphlets (often later bound) containing articles on a variety of legal topics | *American Bar Association Journal*<br>*California Lawyer*<br>*Colorado Lawyer* |
| **3d.** Nonlegal Periodicals | Pamphlets (often later bound) containing articles on a variety of mainly nonlegal topics | *Newsweek*<br>*Foreign Affairs* |
| **4a.** Legal Treatises | Summaries of and commentaries on areas of the law | *McCormick on Evidence*<br>Johnstone and Hopson, *Lawyers and Their Work* |
| **4b.** Nonlegal Treatises | Summaries of and commentaries on a variety of mainly nonlegal topics | Samuelson, *Economics* |
| **5.** Form books, Manuals, Practice Books | Same as legal treatises with a greater emphasis on the "how-to-do-it" practical dimensions of the law | Dellheim, *Massachusetts Practice*<br>Moore's *Federal Practice*<br>*Am. Jur. Pleading and Practice Forms Annotated* |
| **6.** Loose-leaf Services | Collections of materials in ring binders covering current law in designated areas | *State Tax Guide* (CCH)<br>*Labor Relations Reporter* (BNA) |
| **7a.** Legal Newspapers | Daily or weekly information relevant to a law practice | *Chicago Law Bulletin*<br>*National Law Journal* |
| **7b.** Nonlegal Newspapers | General-circulation newspapers | *New York Times*<br>*Detroit Free Press* |
| **8.** Legal Newsletters | Weekly, biweekly, or monthly practical information on a specific area of the law | *Matrimonial Strategist*<br>*AIDS Policy & Law* |

If you want to quote § 553(b)(3)(B) in your memorandum or other writing, do not do it solely by quoting a secondary authority such as this legal treatise. Go directly to the current United States Code (using U.S.C., U.S.C.A., or U.S.C.S.) and quote from § 553(b)(3)(B) itself. Do not rely solely on the Gellhorn/Levin quotation of § 553(b)(3)(B). You may *also* want to cite the Gellhorn/Levin observation that includes the quote from § 553(b)(3)(B) but not as a substitute for a direct quote. As a general rule, *you should never use someone else's quotation of the law*. Quote *directly* from the primary authority. Use the secondary authority to bolster your arguments on the interpretation of the primary authority. This is one of the main functions of secondary authority: to help you persuade a court to adopt a certain interpretation of primary authority. You are on very dangerous ground when you use secondary authority as a substitute for primary authority.

Secondary authority frequently paraphrases or summarizes primary authority, e.g., a legal treatise or encyclopedia summarizes the law on a particular topic. (For an example, see the excerpt from the legal encyclopedia *Corpus Juris Secundum* in exhibit 11.36, later in the chapter.) You will be very tempted to use such summaries in your own writing. Generally, secondary authority is clearly written and quotable. It provides summaries of the law that often seem to fit very nicely into what you are trying to say. There are serious dangers, however, in relying on quotes containing these summaries. Although there are circumstances in which the summaries can be used (with appropriate citation to avoid the charge of **plagiarism**), you need to be aware of the five major dangers of doing so:

- The excerpts are secondary authority, and the goal of your writing is to use primary authority to support your arguments.
- The excerpts may contain summaries of several court opinions; these opinions should be individually analyzed before you use any of them in your writing. As indicated earlier, you need to go to the source, whether it be a statute, an opinion, or any other primary authority.
- The excerpts may be based on opinions from different states, and your legal writing must focus on the law of the state in which the client is litigating the case.
- The excerpts may contain summaries of opinions written by federal courts, and your case may be in a state court where there are no federal issues.
- The excerpts may contain summaries of opinions on state issues written by state courts, and your case may be in a federal court where there are no state issues.

In short, too much reliance on such excerpts from secondary authority amounts to laziness in legal research and analysis. It is sometimes difficult to find and apply primary authority. If someone else at least appears to have done all the work for you in secondary authority, why not use it? The answers to this question are the five dangers just mentioned.

Even if you never use secondary authority in your writing, it may still be of value to you. For example, the footnotes in a legal treatise, encyclopedia, or periodical might give you leads to the primary authority that you need to find and analyze. Furthermore, if you are doing research in an area of the law that is new to you, some background reading in a legal treatise, encyclopedia, or periodical often provides an excellent introduction to the area, as we will see later in exhibit 11.18. Armed with some basic definitions and a general understanding, you will be better equipped to launch your research and analysis into the specific issues before you.

Suppose you want to use an excerpt from a secondary authority in your legal writing. You may, for example, want to quote from a treatise to bolster your argument on the interpretation of a statute or other primary authority. As such, you are asking the court to accept the secondary authority as persuasive authority. What steps are necessary to do so properly? What is the proper foundation for the use of secondary authority in legal writing? Exhibit 11.11 presents this foundation.

Most well-written and comprehensively researched legal memoranda and appellate briefs make relatively few references to secondary authority. Experienced advocates know that judges are suspicious of secondary authority. It is true that some secondary authorities are highly respected, such as *Prosser on Torts* or any of the Restatements of the American Law Institute. Yet even these must be used with caution. The preoccupation of a court is with primary authority. Before you use secondary authority in your writing, you

| EXHIBIT 11.11 | The Foundation for Using a Quote from a Legal Treatise or Any Other Secondary Authority in Your Legal Writing as Possible Persuasive Authority |
|---|---|

1. The quote from the legal treatise (or other secondary authority) is not a substitute for a direct quote from the court opinion, statute, or other primary authority. When you need to tell the reader what the primary authority says, you do not do so solely through secondary authority.
2. The quote from the legal treatise (or other secondary authority) that you want to use does not contradict case law, statutory law, or any other primary authority that exists in the jurisdiction where the client is in litigation. Stated more simply, there must be no contrary mandatory authority.
3. If the quote from the legal treatise (or other secondary authority) *does* contradict case law, statutory law, or any other primary authority, you cannot use the quote unless you satisfy yourself:
   - That the court (before which the client is in litigation) has the power to invalidate or otherwise change the law that contradicts what the legal treatise (or other secondary authority) says and, in effect, to adopt a new interpretation of the law in the jurisdiction; and
   - That there is a reasonable likelihood that a court with such power is inclined to change the law.

must be sure that (a) the secondary authority is not used as a substitute for the primary authority; (b) the secondary authority is not unduly repetitive of the primary authority; (c) the secondary authority will be helpful to the court in adopting an interpretation of primary authority, particularly when there is not a great deal of primary authority on point; (d) you discuss the secondary authority after you have presented the primary authority; and (e) the foundation for the use of secondary authority (see exhibit 11.11) can be demonstrated if needed.

Suppose you find a quote in a legal treatise that not only does not contradict any law within the jurisdiction where the client is in litigation but also concisely states the law that does exist. In this instance, the treatise quote is, in effect, an accurate summary of the law. Although you are on much safer ground in using such a quote, you should provide some indication in your legal writing that such a parallel exists between the law and the treatise quote. At the very least, you should state in your writing that the quote from the secondary authority is consistent with the law of the jurisdiction and be prepared to back up this statement if it is later challenged or questioned by anyone.

Finally, you may find statements in secondary authority that neither contradict nor summarize the law of your jurisdiction. The issue being discussed in the secondary authority may simply have never arisen in your jurisdiction. Such issues are called issues of **first impression.** (A case raising such issues is called a *case of first impression*.) Again, you are on relatively safe ground in using such discussions in your legal writing. In fact, the use of secondary authority is usually most effective when it treats issues that have not yet been resolved in your jurisdiction. Courts are often quite receptive to adopting secondary authority as persuasive authority when novel questions or issues are involved.

---

### Assignment 11.4

Are the following statements true or false? If false, explain why.

(a) All primary authority is mandatory authority because primary authority consists of statutes, constitutional provisions, or other laws.
(b) Secondary authority can be mandatory authority.
(c) An invalid state statute can be persuasive authority if a court decides to follow the statute even though it does not have to.
(d) A federal administrative regulation can be mandatory authority in a state court.
(e) An opinion of the United States District Court can be mandatory authority for the United States Supreme Court.
(f) Because dictum is a comment by the court that was not necessary to resolve the issues before the court, dictum is nonauthority.

**(g)** An opinion in one state cannot be mandatory authority in the court of another state.

**(h)** A federal court can overrule an opinion of a state court.

**(i)** If your library does not have a copy of the statute you need to cite, you can cite the language of the statute that is printed in a scholarly analysis of the statute in a legal periodical article.

**(j)** A dissenting opinion can be persuasive authority.

---

### Assignment 11.5

Mary Franklin is pregnant in Missouri. The father, Bob Vinson, disappears before the baby is born. Mary agrees to let a Missouri couple adopt the baby. Bob was never notified of the adoption. When he finds out, he seeks to have the adoption nullified so that he can have full custody of the child.

Assume that each of the following authorities is relevant to the issue of whether Bob Vinson can invalidate the adoption and that you want to cite all of them in your memorandum of law. In what order would you cite them if you wanted to cite the most controlling first? Place them in ascending order of importance, starting with the most important.

**(a)** An administrative regulation of a Missouri agency

**(b)** A statute of the Missouri legislature

**(c)** A statute of Congress

**(d)** A *Harvard Law Review* article on parental consent to adoption

**(e)** An opinion of the highest state court in Missouri interpreting a statute of the Missouri legislature

**(f)** A provision of the Missouri Constitution

**(g)** A legal treatise on adoption written by a Missouri judge

**(h)** An opinion of the highest state court in New York

**(i)** A provision of the United States Constitution

---

## Section J
## Citation Form

A *citation*, or *cite*, is a reference to any material printed on paper or stored in a computer database. The cite gives you the "address" where you can go in the library to find whatever is cited.

Are there any consistent rules on citation form? If you pick up different law books and examine the citations of similar material within them, you will notice great variety in citation form. You will find that people abbreviate things differently, do not include the information in the same order in the cite, use parentheses differently, use punctuation within the cite differently, include different amounts of information in the same kind of cite, etc. There does not appear to be any consistency. Yet, in spite of this diversity and confusion, you are often scolded by supervisors for failing to use "proper citation form." What, you may well ask, is "proper"?

Start by checking the rules of court or statutes governing the court that will have jurisdiction over the problem you are researching. They may or may not contain *official citation rules*, (States that have their own official citation rules include California, Florida, Louisiana, Maine, Michigan, New Jersey, New York, Ohio, Pennsylvania, Tennessee, and Texas.) If official citation rules exist, they must obviously be followed no matter what any other citation guidebook may say. These are, in effect, citation *laws*.

Suppose, however, that there are no official citation laws in your state or that such laws do not cover the citation question that you have. In such circumstances, *ask your supervisor what citation form you should use*. You will probably be told, "Use the *Bluebook*." This is a reference to *The Bluebook: A Uniform System of Citation*, which we looked at earlier. It is a small blue pamphlet (although in earlier editions, white covers were used). The *Bluebook* is published by a group of law students on the law reviews of their law schools.

Caution is needed in using the *Bluebook*. It is a highly technical and sometimes difficult-to-use pamphlet because it packs so much information into a relatively small space. Primary users of the *Bluebook* are law schools that typeset their law reviews by using professional printers. What about those of us who use regular typewriters or word processors and do not typeset what we produce? While the *Bluebook* does cover many of our citation needs in its Practitioners' Notes, keep in mind that we are not the main audience of the *Bluebook*. Also, be aware that many courts do *not* follow the *Bluebook* even if there are no court rules on citation form for their courts. Judges often simply use their own "system" of citation without necessarily being consistent.

Until recently, the *Bluebook* had no serious competition. *The University of Chicago Manual of Legal Citation* (called the maroon book) tried to compete, but few institutions were willing to make the switch from blue to maroon. One of the complaints about the maroon book is that it is not as specific as the *Bluebook* in providing citation guidance. In 2000, a new competitor emerged, the *ALWD Citation Manual* by the Association of Legal Writing Directors and Darby Dickerson. Many schools have begun to adopt this alternative. It is difficult to determine what impact the ALWD guidebook will have. Most of your older attorney supervisors spent countless law school hours pouring over and applying the *Bluebook*. They may have little tolerance for anything new. Life without *Bluebook* rules is unimaginable for such attorneys. You may find, however, that some of the more recent graduates from law school have joined the ALWD bandwagon and expect their paralegals to be able to cite the ALWD way. Consequently, you must be prepared to use *Bluebook* and ALWD citation formats. Because the *Bluebook* is still dominant, all of the examples in this section will follow *Bluebook* format. Many of the major differences with ALWD will be noted in brackets [*ALWD:*].

Before we begin, review general citation guidelines in exhibit 11.12.

---

**EXHIBIT 11.12    General Citation Guidelines**

1. Find out if there are citation laws in the rules of court or in statutes that you must follow.
2. Ask your supervisor if he or she has any special instructions on citation form. What guidelines should you follow? *Bluebook? ALWD?* Others?
3. Consult the specific citation guidelines presented below (I–VIII). Most of these rules are based on the *Bluebook*. Where ALWD differs, the ALWD rule will be provided in brackets.
4. Remember that the *functional* purpose of a citation is to enable readers to locate your citation in a library. You must give enough information in the cite to fulfill this purpose. Courtesy to the reader in providing this help is as important as compliance with the niceties of citation form.
5. Often a private publisher of a book will tell you how to cite the book. ("Cite this book as. . . .") Ignore this instruction! Instead, follow guidelines 1–4 above.
6. When in doubt about whether to include something in a citation after carefully following guidelines 1–4 above, resolve the doubt by including it in the cite.

---

## SPECIFIC CITATION GUIDELINES

    I. Citing Opinions
   II. Citing Constitutions and Charters
  III. Citing Federal Statutes
  IV. Citing State Statutes
   V. Citing Administrative Regulations and Decisions
  VI. Citing Documents of Legislative History
 VII. Citing Secondary Authority
VIII. Citing Internet Sources

Our focus will be on providing complete or full citations for each of these categories. Later we will also learn how to provide a **short-form citation,** which is an abbreviated citation of an authority that you have already cited in full earlier in your memorandum or other writing.

### I. Citing Opinions

First, let's look at the components of a typical citation of an opinion. See exhibit 11.13. Not all opinions are cited in the same way, however. The citation format that you

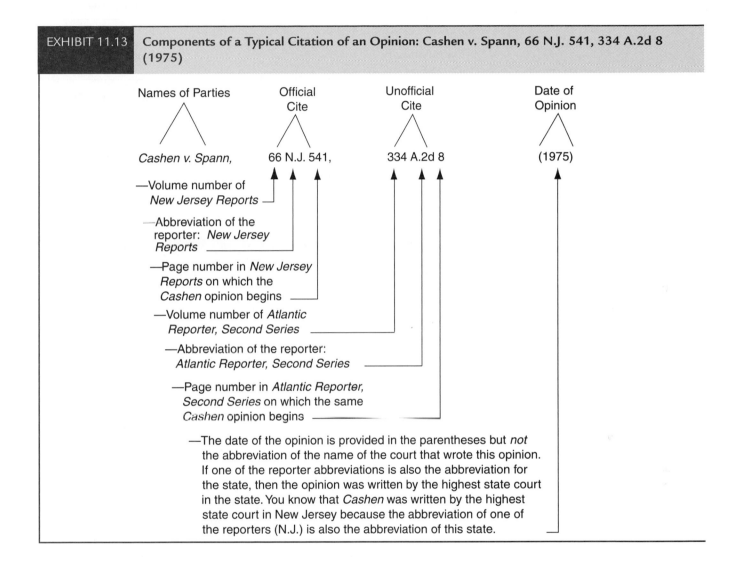

**EXHIBIT 11.13** Components of a Typical Citation of an Opinion: Cashen v. Spann, 66 N.J. 541, 334 A.2d 8 (1975)

use depends on the kind of court that wrote the opinion. Before examining the guidelines that explain these differences, here is an overview:

Example A: Format of a citation to an opinion of the highest federal court (the United States Supreme Court):

> *Taglianetti v. United States*, 394 U.S. 316 (1969)

Example B: Format of a citation to an opinion of a federal middle appeals court (the United States Court of Appeals for the Second Circuit):

> *Podell v. Citicorp Diners Club, Inc.*, 112 F. 3d 98 (2d Cir. 1997)

Example C: Format of a citation to an opinion of a federal trial court (the United States District Court for the District of Maryland):

> *United States v. Holland*, 59 F. Supp. 2d 492 (D. Md. 1998)

Example D: Format of a citation to an opinion of the highest state court (New Jersey Supreme Court):

> *Petlin Associates, Inc. v. Township of Dover*, 64 N.J. 327, 316 A.2d 1 (1974)

Example E: Format of a citation to an opinion of a lower state court (Connecticut Superior Court, Appellate Session):

> *Huckabee v. Stevens*, 32 Conn. Supp. 511, 338 A.2d 512 (Super. Ct. 1975)

Example F: Format of a public domain citation (Supreme Judicial Court of Maine)

> *Pine Ridge Realty, Inc. v. Massachusetts Bay Ins. Co.*, 2000 ME 106, ¶ 3, 752 A.2d 595, 599

Example G: Format of a citation to an administrative decision (National Labor Relations Board):

> *Standard Dry Wall Products, Inc.*, 91 N.L.R.B. 544 (1950).

Example H: Format of a citation to an opinion of the Attorney General:

> 40 Op. Att'y Gen. 423 (1945)

*Guidelines for Citing Opinions*

1. The names of the parties in a case should be *italicized* (if your printer has this capacity) or <u>underlined</u> (i.e., underscored). If you are able to use italics, an example would be as follows:

   *Steck v. Farrell*, 479 F.2d 1129 (7th Cir. 1990)

   If you cannot italicize the names of the parties, underline (underscore) them:

   <u>Steck v. Farrell</u>, 479 F.2d 1129 (7th Cir. 1990)

2. You will note that some of the citations in the above boxed examples have parallel cites (see examples D, E, and F) and some do not. Before examining the rules of providing parallel cites and the techniques of finding such cites, some basics need to be covered.

   The same opinion can be printed in more than one place. (See exhibit 11.4 for 12 possibilities in traditional reporters, CD–ROM, and online services.) A parallel cite is an additional reference to the same material; it is a second "address" for whatever is being cited. If there is a parallel cite to an opinion, you will be able to find that opinion (word for word) in at least two different reporters. Note that in example D, the *Petlin* opinion can be found in *New Jersey Reports* (abbreviated N.J.) and in *Atlantic Reporter 2d* (A.2d). Similarly, both the *Huckabee* opinion in example E and the *Pine Ridge* opinion in example F have a parallel cite. The other opinions cited in examples A, B, C, G, and H do not have parallel cites.

3. Do not confuse parallel cite with the "same case on appeal." Examine the citations of the following two opinions:

   *Jarrett v. Jarrett*, 64 Ill. App. 3d 932, 382 N.E.2d 12 (1978)
   *Jarrett v. Jarrett*, 78 Ill. 2d 337, 400 N.E.2d 421 (1979)

   - Note that each opinion has its own parallel cite. The first *Jarrett* opinion begins on page 932 of volume 64 of *Illinois Appellate Court Reports, Third Series* (Ill. App. 3d) *and* also on page 12 of volume 382 of *North Eastern Reporter, Second Series* (N.E.2d). The second *Jarrett* opinion begins on page 337 of volume 78 of *Illinois Reports, Second Series* (Ill. 2d) *and* also on page 421 of volume 400 of *North Eastern Reporter, Second Series* (N.E.2d).
   - The 1979 *Jarrett* opinion is the *same case on appeal* as the 1978 *Jarrett* opinion. In fact, the 1979 opinion reversed the 1978 opinion. "Same case on appeal" means that the opinions are part of the same litigation. The first *Jarrett* opinion is *not* a parallel cite of the second *Jarrett* opinion. Although part of the

same litigation, the 1978 opinion and the 1979 opinion are totally separate opinions, each of which has its own parallel cite.

- Assume that you wanted to cite the 1978 opinion. As we will see later, you need to tell the reader about anything significant that has happened to an opinion on appeal, such as a reversal. Here is how you would do this for the *Jarrett* opinions:

*Jarrett v. Jarrett*, 64 Ill. App. 3d 932, 382 N.E.2d 12 (1978), *rev'd*, 78 Ill. 2d 337, 400 N.E.2d 421 (1979)

**4.** There are six main techniques of finding a parallel cite. See Research Link N.

- Check the top of the caption. Go to the reporter that contains the opinion. At the beginning of the opinion, there is a *caption* giving the names of the parties, the name of the court that wrote the opinion, the date of the decision, and other information about the litigation that led to the opinion. See if there is a parallel cite at the top of the caption. This technique does not always work, but it is worth a try. It works primarily when you check the captions of the opinions printed in the seven regional reporters we examined in exhibit 11.5. Here is an example from the *North Western Reporter*, one of the seven regional reporters:

**728** Mich. 504 NORTH WESTERN REPORTER, 2d SERIES

200 Mich. App. 635
Farmer ASHER and Lucy Marie Asher,
His wife, Plaintiffs-Appellants,

v.

EXXON COMPANY, U.S.A., a Division
of Exxon Corporation, a Foreign
Corporation, Defendant-Appellee,

Court of Appeals of Michigan.
Submitted March 10, 1993, at Detroit.
Decided July 19, 1993, at 9.25 a.m.

Finding a parallel cite by checking the top of the caption. If you go to 504 N.W.2d 728 and check the top of the caption of *Asher v. Exxon Co., U.S.A.*, you will find that its parallel cite is 200 Mich. App. 635.

- Shepardize the case in the standard sets of *Shepard's Citations*, such as *Shepard's Southwestern Reporter Citations*. To *shepardize* a case means to obtain the validation and other data on that case provided by any of the three versions of *Shepard's Citations* (paper, CD-ROM, or online). Among the data provided for a court opinion are available parallel cites. The first cite in *Shepard's Citations* found in parentheses is the parallel cite. If you find no cite in parentheses, it means (a) that no parallel cite exists, (b) that the reporter containing the parallel cite has not been printed yet, or (c) that the parallel cite was given in one of the earlier volumes of Shepard's and was not repeated in the volume you are examining.

Using *Shepard's Citations* to find a parallel cite. If you shepardized the *E.I. DuPont* case (that begins on page —756—), you are told that its parallel cite is volume 280, page 477 of *Arkansas Reports* (280Ark477).

| — 756 — | 702SW910 |
| E. I. Du | 707SW²375 |
| Pont de | 707SW²392 |
| Nemours and | Cir. 8 |
| Co. v. Dillaha | d758F2d⁴1303 |
| 1983 | 789F2d²614 |
| | 909F2d²1155 |
| (280Ark477) | 923F2d⁵1289 |
| 669SW³464 | dPR¶ 10340 |
| 685SW⁴811 | PR¶ 10822 |
| 695SW⁵835 | PR¶ 10970 |
| 697SW⁴889 | |
| 699SW¹743 | |

■ Use the *Shepard's Case Names Citator*. Shepard's also has a separate set of citators called *Case Name Citators*. Their sole function is to give you parallel cites. Court opinions are listed alphabetically by party names along with the parallel cites.

| | |
|---|---|
| Using *Shepard's Case Names Citator* to find a parallel cite. The parallel cites for *Wilson v. Peters* are 343 Ill App 354 and 99 NE2d 150. | **Wil-Win**             **ILLINOIS CASE NAMES CITATOR** |

| Wil-Win | ILLINOIS CASE NAMES CITATOR |
|---|---|
| Wilson v. Parker 132 Ill App 2d 5, 269 NE2d 523 (1971)<br>Wilson v. Peters 343 Ill App 354, 99 NE2d 150 (1951)<br>Wilson, Renson v 335 Ill App.7, 80 NE2d 381 (1948) | Wilson v. Reeves Red-E-Mix Concrete Products 29 Ill App 3d NE2d 521 (1975)<br>Wilson & Tavridges Inc. v. Inductrial Commission 32 Ill 2d 355, 204 NE24 556 (1965)<br>Wilson Enterprises Inc., Thakkar v. 120 Ill App 34 878, 76 Ill Dec 331, 458 NE2d 95 (1983) |

■ Go to the *National Reporter Blue Book*, a set of books published by West Group. The *National Reporter Blue Book* will also tell you which official reporters have been discontinued. If your state has a *Blue and White Book*, you can also use it to try to find a parallel cite.

■ Check the table of cases in a digest. Go to every digest that gives small-paragraph summaries of court opinions for the court that wrote the opinion, e.g., the American Digest System. Go to the table of cases in these digests. See if there is a parallel cite for your case. In the following excerpt from a digest table of cases, you find two cites for *Ames v. State Bar*—106 Cal. Rptr. 489 and 506 P.2d 625:

Finding a parallel cite by checking the Table of Cases in digests

```
   ..an Tre..
 ..orp, TexCiv.
   App  &  E  79                          T.
   Costs 260(4);  S .es 181(11).          E
Ames v. State Bar  106 CalRptr 489,       an.
   506 P2d 625—Atty & C 32, 58, 12.;   Archer
   Const Law 230(2), 287.                 Const
Amherst, Town of, v. Cadorette, N.H.      ry 39,
   300 A2d 327.  See Town of Am-       Archuleta
   herst v. Cadorette.                    F2d 33—
Ammerman v. Bestline Products, Inc,       392.
   DCWis, 352 FSupp 1077—Courts 263    Argonaut
   (6);  ..nd Civ Proc ?.  .. 15.         SE2d
Am.·       T..                            ..e
```

■ Use commercial computer databases. When you call up your case on any of the major online, fee-based computer systems (e.g., Westlaw, LEXIS, and Loislaw), you will be given any parallel cites that exist.

5. If you are citing an opinion in your memorandum or other writing, are you required to give a parallel cite? For many opinions, there is:

■ An official cite to an *official reporter* (an official reporter is a reporter printed under the authority of the government, often by the government itself) and

Six Techniques for Finding a Parallel Cite of an Opinion:
• Top of the caption
• Shepardize
• *Shepard's Case Names Citator*
• *National Reporter Blue Book*
• Table of cases in digests
• Westlaw, LEXIS and Loislaw

Opinion (you have the cite to this opinion in one reporter)

### RESEARCH LINK N
You have the citation to one reporter where you can read an opinion. You now want a parallel cite so that you can read the same opinion—word-for-word—in another reporter. There are six major techniques you can use to try to find a parallel cite. For example, assume you know the cite of the *Smith* case in *New York Reports*, but you don't know its cite in the *North Eastern Reporter*. Use the six techniques to try to find the N.E.2d parallel cite.

- An unofficial cite to an *unofficial reporter* (an unofficial reporter is a reporter printed by a commercial printing company without special authority from the government)

When must you provide both the official cite and the unofficial cite of an opinion? Here are the guidelines to follow:

- For *federal* opinions, do not use parallel cites. See examples A B, and C at the beginning of the section covering the citation of the major federal courts. None of the citations to the federal cases in these examples has parallel cites.
- For *state* opinions, provide a parallel cite if the local rules of the court to which you are submitting a document (e.g., an appellate brief) require the use of parallel cites. (Later we will cover what to do if a state has adopted public domain citations.)
- If the local rules do not require parallel cites, it is generally sufficient to cite only the unofficial reporter.

Let's look more closely at citations with and without parallel cites. The following citation does not include a parallel cite:

*Nace v. Nace*, 790 P.2d 48 (Ariz. 2003)

Note the abbreviation Ariz. just before the date in the parentheses. This is an abbreviation of the court that wrote the opinion. When the abbreviation is the abbreviation of the state itself, you know that the opinion was written by the highest state court in the state. If you did not provide this abbreviation, someone looking at the cite would not know what court wrote it. The general rule is to provide an abbreviation of the court that wrote the opinion unless the identity of this court is unambiguously clear by looking at the abbreviation of any of the reporters in the cite. The reporter in this cite is *Pacific Reporter 2d* (P.2d). Looking at the cite of this reporter certainly does not tell you what court wrote *Nace*. (Many states are covered in P.2d. See exhibit 11.5 and research link J.) Hence you must abbreviate the court in the parentheses before the date.

Suppose, however, that you need to provide the parallel cite to the *Nace* case. Assume that the case begins on page 411 of volume 162 of *Arizona Reports* (abbreviated Ariz.), the official state reporter. Here is how you would cite the case:

*Nace v. Nace*, 162 Ariz. 411, 790 P.2d 48 (2003)

Note that there is no need to include the abbreviation of the court that wrote the opinion in the parentheses before the date. As we have seen, if the abbreviation of a reporter is the abbreviation of a state, you can assume that the case was written by the highest state court in that state. Hence there is no need to abbreviate the court in the parentheses with the date. You can tell by looking at the abbreviation of the official reporter (162 Ariz. 411) that the highest state court in Arizona wrote the case because Ariz is the abbreviation of the state.

6. When a parallel cite is required, the official cite goes first, as in the second *Nace* example above and in examples D and E at the beginning of the section.
7. Include only the last name of parties who are people. For example, if the parties are listed as "Frank Taylor v. Mary Smith" in the caption, your cite should list them as *Taylor v. Smith*.
8. When a party is a business or organization, you need to determine whether to abbreviate part of the party's name. There are eight words that are almost always abbreviated: and (&), Association (Ass'n), Brothers (Bros.), Company (Co.), Corporation (Corp.), Incorporated (Inc.), Limited (Ltd.), and Number (No.). The abbreviation of other words in a party's name depends on whether the citation is a stand-alone citation or is part of a sentence. Here is an example of a stand-alone citation:

*Erie R.R. Bldg. Preservation Ass'n v. Smith Co.,* 100. F.3d 23 (5th Cir. 1998)

Here is an example of the same citation that is part of a sentence:

In *Erie Railroad Building Preservation Ass'n v. Smith Co.*, 100 F.3d 23 (5th Cir. 1998), the court discussed the reversion doctrine.

Note that the words "Association" and "Company" are abbreviated in both examples. They are among the eight that are almost always abbreviated. The abbreviation of "Railroad" and "Building," however, differs in the examples. The *Bluebook* gives a list of words that you must abbreviate in stand-alone citations but not when you use them in a citation that is part of a sentence (which the *Bluebook* refers to as a citation "in a textual sentence"). The list includes words such as Authority (Auth.), Board (Bd.), Building (Bldg.), Committee (Comm.), Department (Dep't), Education (Educ.), Government (Gov't), Railroad (R.R.), and University (Univ.). The general rule is as this follows: abbreviate these words only in stand-alone citations.

*ALWD* and the *Bluebook* do not agree on some of these abbreviations. For example:

| | Bluebook | ALWD |
|---|---|---|
| Association | Ass'n | Assn. |
| Department | Dep't | Dept. |
| Government | Gov't | Govt. |
| University | Univ. | U. |

9. When the United States is a party, can you use the abbreviation U.S.? Yes, according to *ALWD*; no, according to the *Bluebook*. See examples A and C.

10. Assume that Maine is a party. Your cite should say "State" (rather than "State of Maine" or "Maine") *if and only if* the opinion was written by a Maine state court. Suppose, however, that Maine is a party in an opinion written by an Ohio court. In such a case, use "Maine" (not "State of Maine" or "State") in your cite as the name of this party. This same guideline applies for the words "Commonwealth" and "People." These words are used alone in a cite only if the court that wrote the opinion you are citing is in the same state referred to by the words "Commonwealth" and "People." Example: You are citing an opinion of the California Supreme Court, whose caption describes the parties as follows:

*People of California v. Gabriel S. Farrell*

Your cite of this opinion would be *People v. Farrell*.

11. When an opinion consolidates more than one litigation, it is referred to as a **consolidated litigation**. A supreme court, for example, may use one opinion to resolve similar issues raised in several different lower court cases. The caption of such an opinion will probably list all the parties from these different lower court cases. For example, the caption might say *A v. B; C v. D; E v. F*. When you cite this opinion, include only the *first* set of parties listed in the caption—here, *A v. B*. If the caption says **et al.** (meaning "and others") after the name of a party, do not include the phrase *et al.* in your cite.

12. Often the court will tell you the **litigation status** of the parties, such as plaintiff, defendant, appellant, or appellee. Do not include this information in your cite.

13. Titles of individual parties (such as administrator or secretary) should be omitted from your cite. One exception is the Commissioner of Internal Revenue. Cite this party simply as "Commissioner"—for example, *Jackson v. Commissioner*.

14. When the caption of an opinion contains the phrase *In re* (meaning "in the matter of"), include this phrase in your cite—for example, *In re Jones*.

15. Include the year of the decision at the end of the cite in parentheses. If more than one date is given in the caption of the opinion, use the year from the date the opinion was decided.

16. Do not include the **docket number** of the case in the cite unless the case is still pending. (The docket number is the number assigned to a case by the court.)

17. Once an opinion is written, two things can occur. First, it might be appealed one or more times, leading to more opinions that are part of the same litigation (all

referred to as the *same case on appeal*). What happens to an opinion on appeal is known as its *subsequent history* or the *history of the case*. Second, other opinions that are not part of the same litigation might agree with it and therefore follow it, or they might criticize it and therefore refuse to adopt its conclusions. How other opinions react to a particular opinion in any of these ways is known as the *treatment of the case* in the courts. When you give the citation of an opinion, you need not include any information about treatment of this kind. But, as indicated earlier, your citation *does* have to alert the reader to important subsequent history events. Here is an example:

*Herbert v. Lando*, 568 F.2d 974 (2d Cir. 1977), *rev'd*, 444 U.S. 111 (1979)

It would obviously be important to let the reader know that the *Herbert* case was reversed (*rev'd*) on appeal. In addition, you would want to let the reader know whether the case was affirmed (*aff'd*) on appeal and whether an appellate court accepted certiorari (*cert. granted*) or denied certiorari (*cert. denied*). (Certiorari refers to the **writ of certiorari.** This is an order by an appellate court requiring a lower court to certify the record of a lower court proceeding and to send the record "up" to the appellate court, which has decided to accept the appeal.) For older cases, a reader would usually not be interested in knowing whether an appellate court accepted or denied certiorari. Hence this information is included in your cite only if the case you are citing is less than two years old. If, however, you feel it is important for the reader to have this kind of information on the subsequent history of older cases, include it in the citation.

18. The reporter volumes that contain current opinions are conveniently arranged by volume number. All the volumes of the same set have the same name, e.g., *Atlantic Reporter 2d*. At one time, however, life was not this simple. Volumes of opinions were identified by the name of the individual person who had responsibility for compiling the opinions written by the judges. These individuals were called reporters. "7 Cush. 430," for example, refers to an opinion found on page 430 of volume 7 of Massachusetts cases when Mr. Cushing was the official reporter. When he ended his employment, Mr. Gray took over, and the cite of an opinion in the volume immediately after "7 Cush." was "1 Gray." By simply looking at the cover of the volume, you *cannot* tell what court's opinions are inside unless you happen to be familiar with the names of these individuals and the courts for which they worked. These volumes are called **nominative reporters** because they are identified by the name of the individual person who compiled the opinions for the court.

19. Assume that all you know are the names of the parties and the name of the court that wrote the opinion. How do you obtain the full cite so that you can find and read the opinion? Here are some techniques to use:

- Go to every digest that covers that reporter. See exhibit 11.6 for a list of what digests cover what reporters. Check the table of cases in the digests.
- Call the court clerk for the court that wrote the opinion. If it is a recent case, the clerk may be able to send you a copy. Occasionally, the clerk will give you the cite of the case. (It will help if you can tell the clerk the docket number of the case.)
- Go to the reporter volumes that cover the court that wrote the opinion. Because you do not have a volume number, you cannot go directly to the volume that has the opinion. If you can *approximate* the date of the case, however, you can check the table of cases in each reporter volume that probably covers that year. You may have to check the table of cases in 10 to 15 volumes before achieving success. The opinions are printed in the reporters in roughly chronological order.
- Use *Shepard's Case Names Citator* referred to (and excerpted) earlier.
- On the Internet, type the name of the case in a general or legal search engine. Or go directly to the site maintained by the court that wrote the opinion. (See exhibit 11.43, later in the chapter.) You may be led to the full text of the opinion.
- If you have access to fee-based online services (e.g., Westlaw, LEXIS, or Loislaw), enter the name of the case as a search query (see chapter 13) in the appropri-

ate database or file. This will lead you to the opinion with all available parallel cites.

20. When you are quoting specific language in an opinion or in a legal periodical article, you need to give two page numbers: first, the page number on which the opinion or legal periodical article begins; and second, the page number on which the quote is found. This is known as a **pinpoint cite,** or a *jump cite* which is a reference to material on a specific page in a document, as opposed to the page on which the document begins. The page on which the quote is found is the "pinpointed" number. For opinions, this number goes immediately after the page number on which the opinion begins, separated by a comma. Assume that you want to quote from an opinion that has a parallel cite. Hence your quote will be found in the opinion printed in both reporters, but on different page numbers. A pinpoint cite of this opinion would state the page number in each reporter where the opinion begins *plus* the page number in each reporter on which your quote is found. In the following example, the *Bridgeton* opinion begins on page 17 of *Maryland Reports* (Md.) and on page 376 of the *Atlantic Reporter 2d* (A.2d). The quote from the *Bridgeton case*, however, is found on page 20 and on page 379 of these reporters, respectively:

"Even though laches may not apply, one must use reasonable promptness when availing himself of judicial protection." *Bridgeton Educ. Ass'n v. Board of Educ.*, 147 Md. 17, 20, 334 A.2d 376, 379 (1975).

In some documents, all of the paragraphs are separately numbered. In such documents, the pinpoint can be to a paragraph number rather than to a page number.

21. Most opinions are read in reporters published by vendors such as West Group, e.g., *Supreme Court Reporter, North Western Reporter 2d.* For example, here is a cite to a South Dakota Supreme Court opinion that directs the reader to a quote on pinpoint page 332:

*Davis v. Cardiff*, 402 N.W.2d 327, 332 (S.D. 2001)

Because this cite relies on a volume number (402) and page numbers (327 and 332) that are assigned by the vendor (West Group), it is called a vendor-specific citation. Here is the citation to the same opinion as a **vendor-neutral citation:**

*Davis v. Cardiff*, 2001 SD 22, ¶ 74

*Davis* is the 22d opinion decided by the South Dakota Supreme Court in 2001. Every paragraph in the opinion is sequentially numbered. Our quote is in the 74th paragraph of the *Davis* opinion. Note the differences in the two formats. A vendor-neutral cite:

- Does not contain abbreviations of any reporters
- Uses a year instead of a volume number and places the year immediately after the names of the parties
- Tells you in what order the opinion was decided that year
- Does not tell you the page number on which the opinion begins
- Gives the pinpoint reference as a paragraph number rather than as a page number

The numbers in the vendor-neutral cite are assigned by the court rather than by a vendor. Hence the citation format is in the *public domain*, meaning that no one owns it. The format can be used by anyone at no cost. A vendor-neutral citation, therefore, is also called a *public domain citation.*

States with courts that have adopted vendor-neutral citations include Arizona, Colorado, Florida, Louisiana, Maine, Mississippi, Montana, New Mexico, North Dakota, Oklahoma, Pennsylvania, South Dakota, Utah, and Wisconsin. Many more are considering this option. The states that use vendor-neutral citations may differ somewhat in what is required, although the format described here contains most of the basics.

When a vendor-neutral citation is required, you should *also* provide the traditional vendor-specific cite if it is available. Hence our cite to the *Davis* opinion would be:

*Davis v. Cardiff*, 2001 SD 22, ¶ 74, 402 N.W.2d 327, 332

If no pinpoint reference is needed, the cite would be:

*Davis v. Cardiff*, 2001 SD 22, 402 N.W.2d 327

See also example F at the beginning of this section for another example of a vendor-neutral cite. For a report on the Internet that gives the details of vendor-neutral systems adopted by specific courts, see *www.aallnet.org/committee/citation*.

## II. Citing Constitutions and Charters

Constitutions and charters are cited to (a) the abbreviated name of the constitution or charter, (b) the article, and (c) the section.

U.S. Const. art. I, § 9
N.M. Const. art. IV, § 7

When citing constitutions and charters currently in force, do not give the date of enactment.

## III. Citing Federal Statutes

1. All federal statutes of Congress are collected in chronological order of passage as session laws in the *United States Statutes at Large* (abbreviated "Stat."). Session laws are statutes of the legislature that are organized chronologically by date of enactment rather than by subject matter. If the statute is of general public interest, it is also printed in *each* of three codes in which the statutes *are* organized by subject matter:

   ■ *United States Code* (U.S.C.)
   ■ *United States Code Annotated* (U.S.C.A.)—West Group.
   ■ *United States Code Service* (U.S.C.S.)—LEXIS Law Publishing

   The preferred citation format is to U.S.C., which is the official code. (In the following example, the number before the abbreviation of the code—42—is the title number. This is where title numbers are placed in all citations to federal statutes.)

   42 U.S.C. § 3412(a)(1970)
       or
   Narcotic Rehabilitation Act of 1966, 42 U.S.C. § 3412(a)(1970)

   Although it is not necessary to give the **popular name** of the statute (as in the second version of the above example), citing the popular name when known is often helpful.

2. A new edition of the U.S.C. comes out every six years. The date you use in citing a statute in U.S.C. is the date of the edition you are using unless your statute is found in one of the annual Supplements to the U.S.C., which come out in between editions. If your statute is in a Supplement, you cite the volume and year of this Supplement. Suppose your statute is found in the sixth Supplement published in 1983. Your cite would be as follows:

   29 U.S.C. § 169 (Supp. VI 1983)

   The date you use in citing a statute in U.S.C. is not the year the statute was enacted or passed by the legislature. Nor is it the year the statute became effective. The date you use is the date of the edition of the code or of the Supplement.

3. Although citation to U.S.C. is preferred, it is not uncommon to find citations to the other codes: U.S.C.A. and U.S.C.S. (There is never a need, however, to cite more than one of the three codes.) The format is as follows:

   29 U.S.C.A. § 169 (West 1983)
   29 U.S.C.S. § 169 (LEXIS 1982) or (LEXIS L. Publg. 1982) according to ALWD

In parentheses before the date, include the name of the publisher. Use the year that appears on the title page of the volume, or its latest copyright year, in this order of preference. If your statute is in one of the annual pocket parts of either of these two codes, include "Supp." and give the year of the pocket part—for example: (West Supp. 1998).

4. There is one instance in which you *must* cite to the *United States Statutes at Large* (Stat.) rather than to U.S.C. The rule is as follows: cite to the statute in *Statutes at Large* if (a) there is a difference in the language of the statute between Stat. and U.S.C. and (b) the statute in U.S.C. is in a title that has *not* been enacted into positive law by Congress.

    It is highly unlikely that you will find a difference in language between Stat. And U.S.C. Yet the conscientious researcher must check this out before relying on any statutory language. All the statutes in U.S.C. fall within one of 50 titles—for example, title 11 on Bankruptcy, title 39 on the Postal Service. If Congress goes through all the statutes in a particular title and formally declares that all of them are valid and accurate, then that title has been enacted into positive law. You can rely exclusively on the language of such statutes even if the language is different from the statute as it originally appeared in *Statutes at Large*. At the beginning of the first volume of U.S.C., you will be told which titles of the U.S.C. have been enacted into positive law.

5. A *Statute at Large* cite, when needed, should include:

    - The name of the statute if one exists; if one does not exist, include "Act of" and give the full date of enactment—month, day, and year
    - The Public Law (Pub. L.) number of the statute or its chapter number
    - The section of the statute you are citing
    - The volume number of the *Statutes at Large* used
    - The abbreviation "Stat."
    - The page number on which your statute is found in the Stat. volume
    - In parentheses, the year the statute was enacted or passed by the legislature. Do not include the year, however, if you used the "Act of" option referred to in the first bullet.

    Narcotic Addict Rehabilitation Act, Pub. L. No. 80-793, § 9, 80 Stat. 1444 (1966)

    Note again that the year in parentheses at the end of the cite is the year the statute was passed. Guideline 2 above said that you do not use the date of enactment when citing a statute in U.S.C. The rule is different when giving a Stat. cite.

    This example referred you to section number (§) 9 of this public law (Pub. L.). The statute might also have several title numbers. If so, § 9 would be found within one of these titles. Assume, for example, that § 9 is in title III of the public law. It is important to remember that these section and the title numbers are found in the original *session law* edition of the statute. When this statute is later printed in U.S.C. (assuming it is a public law of general interest), it will *not* go into § 9 of the third title. The U.S.C. has its own title and section number scheme. (For example, title III, § 9 of the above statute might be found in title 45, § 1075(b) of the U.S.C.) This can be very frustrating for the researcher new to the law. If you are reading a statute in its original session or public law form, you will not be able to find this statute under the same title and section number in U.S.C. You must translate the public law or Stat. cite into a U.S.C. cite. Phrased another way, you

| Session Law: | To find a session law in a code, check: |
|---|---|
| *United States Statutes at Large* (Stat.) | • Table III in the Tables volume of U.S.C./U.S.C.A./U.S.C.S.<br>• Table 2 in U.S.C.C.A.N. |

**RESEARCH LINK O**
If you have a federal statute with a Stat. (session law) cite and you want to read this statute in one of the three federal codes, you need a way to translate a Stat. cite into a U.S.C./U.S.C.A./U.S.C.S cite.

must translate the session law cite into a code cite. Later we will see that this is done by using one of two tables: Table III in a special Tables volume of U.S.C./U.S.C.A./U.S.C.S. or Table 2 in *U.S. Code Congressional and Administrative News* (U.S.C.C.A.N.). See research link O.

Rarely will you need to cite a session law when its codified cite is available. The latter is usually all that is needed. If, however, you need to cite a session law that has already been codified, let the reader know where it will found in the code, i.e., give both the session law *and* the codified cite. Here is an example:

Health Insurance Portability Act of 1996, Pub. L. No. 104–191, § 102, 110 Stat. 1936 (codified at 42 U.S.C.A. § 300gg (West Supp. 1997))

6. Of course, if the statute is a private law that is deemed to be of no general public interest, it will not be printed in the U.S.C. or the U.S.C.A. or the U.S.C.S. It will be found only in *Statutes at Large* (Stat.).

7. The *Internal Revenue Code* (I.R.C.) is within the *United States Code* (U.S.C.). Hence, to cite a tax statute, use the guidelines presented earlier on citing U.S.C./U.S.C.A./U.S.C.S.

26 U.S.C. § 1278 (1976)

There is, however, another option that is considered acceptable:

I.R.C. § 1278 (1976)

8. There is a special format for citing the Federal Rules of Civil Procedure, Federal Rules of Criminal Procedure, Federal Rules of Appellate Procedure, and Federal Rules of Evidence.

Fed. R. Civ. P. 15
Fed. R. Crim. P. 23
Fed. R. App. P. 3
Fed. R. Evid. 310

## IV. Citing State Statutes

1. Like federal statutes, the statutes of the various states are compiled in two kinds of collections: state *codes* (arranged by subject matter) and *session laws* (arranged in chronological order of enactment).

2. Citations to state codes vary from state to state. Exhibit 11.14 shows examples of standard *Bluebook* citation formats. If there are variations between the *Bluebook* and *ALWD* formats, the *ALWD* format is presented in brackets beneath the *Bluebook* citation. Use these as guides unless local rules of court dictate otherwise. The year at the end of the cite should be the year that appears on the spine of the volume, or the year that appears on the title page, or the latest copyright year—in this order of preference.

| EXHIBIT 11.14 | State Statutory Code Citation Formats |
| --- | --- |

These examples of state statutory code citations comply with the Bluebook (local rules, however, may require a different format). ALWD variations, if any, are noted in brackets beneath the Bluebook citation format.

| | |
| --- | --- |
| Alabama: | Ala. Code § 37–10–3 (1977) |
| Alaska: | Alaska Stat. § 22.10.110 (Michie 1962) |
| | [Alaska Stat. § 22.10.110 (LEXIS L. Publg. 1962)] |
| Arizona: | Ariz. Rev. Stat. § 44–1621 (1956) |
| | Ariz. Rev. Stat. Ann.§ 44–1621 (West 1956) |
| Arkansas: | Ark. Code Ann. § 20–316 (Michie 1968) |
| | [Ark. Code Ann. § 20–316 (LEXIS L. Publg. 1968)] |
| California: | Cal. Prob. Code § 585 (West 1956) |
| | Cal. Prob. Code § 585 (Derring 1956) |
| | [Cal. Prob. Code Ann. § 585 (West 1956)] |
| | [Cal. Prob. Code Ann. § 585 (LEXIS L. Publg. 1956)] |

| EXHIBIT 11.14 | State Statutory Code Citation Formats—*continued* |
|---|---|

| Colorado: | Colo. Rev. Stat. § 32–7–131 (1971) |
| | Colo. Rev. Stat. Ann. § 32–7–131 (West 1971) |
| Connecticut: | Conn. Gen. Stat. § 34–29 (1989) |
| | Conn. Gen. Stat. Ann. § 53a–135 (West 1972) |
| Delaware: | Del. Code Ann. tit. 18, § 2926 (1974) |
| District of Columbia: | D. C. Code Ann. § 16–2307 (1981) |
| Florida: | Fla. Stat. ch. 2.314 (1986) |
| | Fla. Stat. Ann. ch. 2.314 (Harrison 1985) |
| | Fla. Stat. Ann. § 1078 (West 1976) |
| | [Fla. Stat. § 2.314 (1986)] |
| Georgia: | Ga. Code Ann. § 110–118 (1973) |
| | Ga. Code Ann. § 22–1414 (Harrison 1977) |
| Hawaii: | Haw. Rev. Stat. § 431:19–107 (1988) |
| | Haw. Rev. Stat. Ann. § 431:19–107 (Michie 1988) |
| | [Haw. Rev. Stat. Ann. § 431:19–107 (LEXIS L. Publg. 1988)] |
| Idaho: | Idaho Code § 18–3615 (Michie 1987) |
| | [Idaho Code § 18–3615 (1987)] |
| Illinois: | 5 Ill. Comp. Stat. 100/5–80 (1993) |
| | 5 Ill. Comp. Stat. Ann. 100/5–80 (West 1993) |
| Indiana: | Ind. Code § 9–8–1–13 (1976) |
| | Ind. Code Ann. § 9–8–1–13 (Michie 1976) |
| | Ind. Code Ann. § 9–8–1–13 (West 1979) |
| | [Ind. Code Ann. § 9–8–1–13 (LEXIS L. Publg. 1983)] |
| Iowa: | Iowa Code § 455.92 (1958) |
| | Iowa Code Ann. § 94.14 (West 1984) |
| Kansas: | Kan. Stat. Ann. § 38–1506 (1986) |
| | Kan. Corp. Code Ann. § 17–6303 (West 1995) |
| | [Kan. Stat. Ann. § 9–8–1–13 (West 1995)] |
| Kentucky: | Ky. Rev. Stat. Ann. § 208.060 (Banks-Baldwin 1988) |
| | Ky. Rev. Stat. Ann. § 44.072 (Michie 1986) |
| | [Ky. Rev. Stat. Ann. § 208.060 (1988)] |
| | [Ky. Rev. Stat. Ann. § 44.072 (LEXIS L. Publg. 1986)] |
| Louisiana: | La. Rev. Stat. Ann. § 15:452 (West 1982) |
| | La. Code Civ. Proc. Ann. art. 3132 (West 1961) |
| | [La. Stat. Ann. § 15:452 (1981)] |
| Maine: | Me. Rev. Stat. Ann. tit. 36, § 1760 (West 1964) |
| | [36 Me. Rev. Stat. Ann. § 1760 (1964)] |
| Maryland: | Md. Code Ann., Fam. Law § 7–106 (1984) |
| | Md. Ann. Code art. 78, § 70 (1957) |
| | [Md. Fam. Law Code Ann. § 7–106 (1984)] |
| | [Md. Ann. Code art. 12, § 556 (1999)] |
| Massachusetts: | Mass. Gen. Laws ch. 106, § 2–318 (1984) |
| | Mass. Gen. Laws Ann. ch. 156, § 37 (West 1970) |
| | Mass. Ann. Laws ch. 123, § 15 (Law. Co-op. 1988) |
| | [Mass. Ann. Laws ch. 123, § 15 (LEXIS L. Publg. 1988)] |
| Michigan: | Mich. Comp. Laws § 550.1402 (1980) |
| | Mich. Comp. Laws Ann. § 211.27 (West 1986) |
| | Mich. Stat. Ann. § 28.1070 (Michie 1987) |
| | [Mich. Stat. Ann. § 28.1070 (LEXIS L. Publg. 1987)] |
| Minnesota: | Minn. Stat. § 336.1–101 (1988) |
| | Minn. Stat. Ann. § 104.08 (West 1987) |
| Mississippi: | Miss. Code Ann. § 19–13–57 (1972) |
| Missouri: | Mo. Rev. Stat. § 545.010 (1986) |
| | Mo. Ann. Stat. § 334.540 (West 1989) |
| | [Mo. Rev. Stat. Ann. § 334.540 (West 1989)] |

| EXHIBIT 11.14 | State Statutory Code Citation Formats—continued |
|---|---|

Montana:    Mont. Code Ann. § 37-5-313 (1989)
    Mont. Rev. Code Ann. § 37-5-313 (Smith 1989)

Nebraska:    Neb. Rev. Stat. § 44-406 (1983)
    Neb. Rev. Stat. Ann. § 44-406 (Michie 1995)
    [Neb. Rev. Stat. Ann. § 44-406 (LEXIS L. Publg. 1986)]

Nevada:    Nev. Rev. Stat. § 463.150 (1987)
    Nev. Rev. Stat. Ann. § 679B.180 (Michie 1986)
    [Nev. Rev. Stat. Ann. § 679B.180 (LEXIS L. Publg. 1986)]

New Hampshire:    N.H. Rev. Stat. Ann. § 318:25 (1984)

New Jersey:    N.J. Rev. Stat. § 40:62-127 (1961)
    N.J. Stat. Ann. § 14A:5-20 (West 1969)
    [N.J. Stat. Ann. § 14A:5-20 (1969)]

New Mexico:    N.M. Stat. Ann. § 31-6-2 (Michie 1978)
    [N.M. Stat. Ann. § 31-6-2 (1978)]

New York:    N.Y. Penal Law § 151.05 (McKinney 1988)
    N.Y. Penal Law § 115.05 (Consol. 1978)
    N.Y. Penal Law § 115.05 (Gould 1978)

North Carolina:    N.C. Gen. Stat. § 15A-1321 (1988)

North Dakota:    N.D. Cent. Code § 23-12-11 (1989)

Ohio:    Ohio Rev. Code Ann. § 2835.03 (Anderson 1979)
    Ohio Rev. Code Ann. § 2305.131 (West 1996)

Oklahoma:    Okla. Stat. tit. 42, § 130 (1979)
    Okla. Stat. Ann. tit. 21, § 491 (West 1983)

Oregon:    Or. Rev. Stat. § 450.870 (1987)
    [Or. Rev. Stat. Ann. § 450.870 (1987)]

Pennsylvania:    1 Pa. Cons. Stat. § 1991 (1972)
    18 Pa. Cons. Stat. Ann. § 3301 (West 1983)
    Pa. Stat. Ann. tit. 24, § 7-708 (West 1990)
    [1 Pa. Consol. Stat. Ann. § 1991 (1972)]
    [18 Pa. Consol. Stat. § 3301 (West 1983)]

Puerto Rico:    7 P.R. Laws Ann. § 299 (1985)
    [7 Laws P.R. Ann. § 299 (1985)]

Rhode Island:    R.I. Gen. Laws § 34-1-2 (1956)

South Carolina:    S.C. Code Ann. § 16-23-10 (Law. Co-op. 1976)
    [S.C. Code Ann. § 16-23-10 (1976)]

South Dakota:    S.D. Codified Laws § 15-6-54 (c) (Michie 1984)
    [S.D. Codified Laws § 15-6-64 (c) (1984)]

Tennessee:    Tenn. Code Ann. § 33-1-204 (1984)

Texas:    Tex. Penal Code Ann. § 19.06 (Vernon 1989)
    [Tex. Penal Code Ann. § 19.06 (1989)]

Utah:    Utah Code Ann. § 41-3-8 (1953)

Vermont:    Vt. Stat. Ann. tit. 19, § 708 (1987)

Virginia:    Va. Code Ann. § 18.2-265.3 (Michie 1950)
    [Va. Code Ann. § 18.2-265.3 (1950)]

Washington:    Wash. Rev. Code § 7.48A.010 (1987)
    Wash. Rev. Code Ann. § 11.17.110 (West 1967)

West Virginia:    W. Va. Code § 23-1-17 (1985)
    W. Va. Code Ann. § 23-1-17 (Michie 1985)

Wisconsin:    Wis. Stat. § 52.28 (1967)
    Wis. Stat. Ann. § 341.55 (West 1971)

Wyoming:    Wyo. Stat. Ann. § 26-18-113 (Michie 1977)
    [Wyo. Stat. Ann. § 26-18-113 (1977)]

## V. Citing Administrative Regulations and Decisions

1. Federal administrative regulations are published in the *Federal Register* (Fed. Reg.). Many of these regulations are later codified by subject matter in the *Code of Federal Regulations* (C.F.R.).

2. Federal regulations that appear in the *Code of Federal Regulations* are cited to (a) the title number in which the regulation appears, (b) the abbreviated name of the code—C.F.R., (c) the number of the particular section to which you are referring, and (d) the date of the code edition that you are using.

   29 C.F.R. § 102.60(a) (1975)

3. Federal regulations that have not yet been codified into the *Code of Federal Regulations* are cited to the *Federal Register* using (a) the volume in which the regulation appears, (b) the abbreviation "Fed. Reg.", (c) the page on which the regulation appears, and (d) the year of the *Federal Register* you are using. (*ALWD* requires the full date, not just the year.)

   27 Fed. Reg. 2092 (1962)
   [*ALWD*: 27 Fed. Reg. 2092 (March 13, 1962)]

4. Federal regulations are often divided into several parts in the *Federal Register*. If you are not citing the entire regulation, give the page in the *Federal Register* where the regulation begins *and* the page that contains the part to which you are referring.

   27 Fed. Reg. 2092, 2094 (1962)
   [*ALWD*: 27 Fed. Reg. 2092, 2094 (March 13, 1962)]

   Often the *Federal Register* will tell you where in the *Code of Federal Regulations* a particular regulation will also be found. If so, tell the reader by giving both the Fed. Reg. cite and the codified cite.

   58 Fed. Reg. 7185 (1996) (to be codified at 14 C.F.R. § 39.13)
   [*ALWD*: 58 Fed. Reg. 7185 (April 22, 1996) (to be codified at 14 C.F.R. § 39.13)]

5. On citing administrative decisions, see example G at the beginning of this section.

## VI. Citing the Documents of Legislative History

1. Legislative history consists of all the events that occur in the legislature before a bill is enacted into law. The main documents of legislative history are bills, reports and hearings of congressional committees, transcripts of floor debates, etc.

2. Bills are cited by reference to (a) the number assigned to the bill by the House of Representatives or Senate, (b) the number of the Congress during which the bill was introduced, and (c) the year of the bill.

   H.R. 3055, 94th Cong. (1976)
   S. 1422, 101st Cong. (1989)
   [*ALWD*: Sen. 1422, 101st Cong. (1989)]

3. Reports of congressional committees are cited by reference to (a) the abbreviation of the House (H.) or Senate (S. in the *Bluebook*, Sen. in *ALWD*) where the report was written, (b) the number of the Congress and the number of the report connected by a hyphen, (c) the page number of the report to which you are referring, and (d) the year in which the report was published. If the report is also printed in the set of books called *United States Code Congressional and Administrative News* (U.S.C.C.A.N.), include the volume number of U.S.C.C.A.N. (which will be a year), the page number in U.S.C.C.A.N. where the report begins, and the specific page number of the report to which you are referring.

   H.R. Rep. No. 92–238, at 4 (1979)
   S. Rep. No. 92–415, at 6 (1971), *reprinted in* 1971 U.S.C.C.A.N. 647, 682
   [*ALWD*: Sen. Rep. No. 92–415, at 6 (1971), *reprinted in* 1971 U.S.C.C.A.N. 647, 682]

4. Hearings held by congressional committees are cited by reference to (a) the title of the hearing, (b) the number of the Congress during which the hearing was held,

(c) the number of the page in the published transcript to which you are referring, and (d) the year in which the hearing was held.

*Hearings on H.R. 631 before the Subcomm. on Labor of the Senate Comm. on Labor and Public Welfare*, 92d Cong. 315 (1971)

5. The *Congressional Record* is issued on a daily basis and later collected into bound volumes. The *bound* volumes are cited by referring to (a) the number of the volume in which the item appears, (b) the abbreviation Cong. Rec., (c) the number of the page on which the item appears, and (d) the year. The *daily* volumes are cited in the same manner except that (a) the page number should be preceded by the letter "H" or "S" to indicate whether the item appeared in the House pages or the Senate pages of the volume, (b) the date should include the exact day, month, and year, and (c) the phrase "daily ed." should go before the date.

*Bound volumes:*
103 Cong. Rec. 2889 (1975)
*Daily volumes:*
122 Cong. Rec. S2395 (daily ed. Feb. 26, 1976)
132 Cong. Rec. H1385 (daily ed. Mar. 13, 1990)

## VII. Citing Secondary Authority

1. Legal *treatises* are cited to (a) the number of the volume being referred to (if part of a set), (b) the full name of the author, (c) the full title of the book as it appears on the title page, (d) the number of the section or page to which you are referring, (e) the edition of the book, if other than the first, and (f) the date of publication. The title of the book should be italicized or underscored. *ALWD* requires the name of the publisher in the parentheses at the end of the cite; the *Bluebook* almost never does. If the treatise has more than one volume, the volume number goes at the beginning of the cite (*Bluebook*) or after the name of the treatise (*ALWD*).

Alice W. Rand, *International Tribunals* 370 (2d ed. 1970)
[*ALWD*: Alice W. Rand, *International Tribunals* 370 (2d ed., Princeton U. Press 1970)]
6 Melvin M. Belli, *Modern Trials* § 289 (1963)
[*ALWD*: Melvin M. Belli, *Modern Trials* vol. 6, § 289 (West 1963)]

2. Legal periodical articles are cited by reference to (a) the full name of the author, (b) the title of the article, (c) the number of the volume in which the article appears, (d) the abbreviated name of the legal periodical, (e) the number of the page on which the article begins, and (f) the year of publication. The title of the article should be italicized or underscored.

Robert Catz & Susan Robinson, *Due Process and Creditor's Remedies*, 28 Rutgers L. Rev. 541 (1975)
William P. Statsky, *The Education of Legal Paraprofessionals: Myths, Realities, and Opportunities*, 24 Vand. L. Rev. 1083 (1971)

If you are referring to material on a specific page in an article, you need to add a pinpoint cite that will give the page number containing that material. The page number you are pinpointing goes immediately after the page number on which the article begins. Suppose, for example, that you were quoting from page 550 of the above *Rutgers Law Review* article. The cite would be:

Robert Catz & Susan Robinson, *Due Process and Creditor's Remedies*, 28 Rutgers L. Rev. 541, 550 (1975)

3. Legal periodical *notes* and *comments* written by law students are cited in the same manner as articles (see guideline 2) except that the or *Bluebook* requires the word *Note* or *Comment* to be placed after the author's name, whereas *ALWD* wants the phrase *Student Author* placed after his or her name.

4. Legal *encyclopedias* are cited by reference to (a) the number of the volume, (b) the abbreviated name of the encyclopedia, (c) the subject heading to which you are

referring—in italics or underscored, (d) the number of the section to which you are referring, and (e) the date of publication of the volume you are citing.

83 C.J.S. *Subscriptions* § 3 (1953)
77 Am. Jur. 2d *Vendor and Purchaser* § 73 (1975)

5. Restatements of the law published by the American Law Institute are cited by reference to (a) the title of the Restatement, (b) the edition being referred to (if other than the first edition), (c) the number of the section being referred to, and (d) the date of publication.
*Restatement (Second) of Agency* § 37 (1957)

6. Annotations in A.L.R., A.L.R.2d, A.L.R.3d, A.L.R.4th, A.L.R.5th, and A.L.R. Fed. are cited by (a) the full name of the author, if available, (b) the title of the annotation—in italics or underscored, (c) the volume number, (d) the abbreviation of the A.L.R. unit, (e) the page number where the annotation begins, and (f) the date of the volume. After the author's name, the *Bluebook* requires the word *Annotation*; ALWD does not.

James J. Watson, Annotation, *Attorney's Fees: Cost of Services Provided by Paralegals*, 73 A.L.R.4th 938 (1989)
[*ALWD*: James J. Watson, *Attorney's Fees: Cost of Services Provided by Paralegals*, 73 A.L.R.4th 938 (1989)]

### VIII Citing Internet Sources

When you do want to cite something on the Internet, the *Bluebook* requires that you provide (a) the name of the author, if given; (b) the title or top-level heading of the material you are citing; (c) the date of publication or the last modification date, or (if neither is available) the date you visited the site; and (d) the uniform resource locator (URL). The URL is the electronic address of material on the Internet. *ALWD* rules are similar except that *ALWD* requires the date visited to be placed at the end of the cite, the word *accessed* used in place of the word *visited*, and the URL address to be set off with <> notations.

National Federation of Paralegal Associations, *Informal Ethics and Disciplinary Opinion No. 96–2* (visited July 19, 1997), www.paralegals.org/Development/ethics96-2.html.
[*ALWD*: National Federation of Paralegal Associations, *Informal Ethics and Disciplinary Opinion No. 96–2* <www.paralegals.org/Development/ethics96-2.html> (accessed July 19, 1997)]

For an outstanding citation guide on the Internet, see:

Peter W. Martin, *Introduction to Basic Legal Citation* (visited August 1, 2001), www.law.cornell.edu/citation/citation.table.html.
[*ALWD*: Peter W. Martin, *Introduction to Basic Legal Citation* <www.law.cornell.edu/citation/citation.table.html> (accessed August 1, 2001)]

---

*Assignment 11.6*
Each of the following citations has one or more things wrong with it. Describe the errors and gaps in format. For example, a parallel cite is missing or something is abbreviated incorrectly. You do not have to go to the library to check any of these cites. Simply use the guidelines presented above. For some of the cites, you will need additional information to determine the accuracy of the format of the cite. For example, you may need to know where the cite will be used. If you need further information, state what you need and why you need it.

(a) *Smith v. Jones*, 135 Mass. 37, 67 N.E. 2d 316, 320 (1954).
(b) *Paul Matthews v. Edward Foley, Inc.*, 779 F. 2d 729 (W.D.N.Y., 1979).

(c) *Jackson v. Jackson*, 219 F.Supp. 1276, 37 N.E. 2d 84 (1980).

(d) *Davis v. Thompson, et al*, 336 P. 2d 691, 210 N.M. 432 (1976).

(e) *Washington Tire Company v. Jones*, 36 N.J. Super. 222, 351 A. 2d 541 (1976).

(f) *State of New Hampshire v. Atkinson*, 117 N.H. 830, 228 A. 2d 222 (N.H.Super., 1978).

(g) *Richardson v. U.S.*, 229 U.S. 220 (1975).

(h) American Law Institute, *Restatement of Torts* (2d ed 1976).

(i) U.S. Const. Art. III (1797).

(j) Smith, F., Products Liability (3rd ed. 1985).

(k) 42 USC 288 (1970).

(l) 17 U.S.C.A. 519 (1970).

(m) 40 Fed. Reg. § 277 (1976).

---

### Assignment 11.7

(a) For your state, check the state code and rules of court of the highest state court in the state to find out whether any special citation rules must be followed in documents submitted to the courts. If so, redo assignment 11.6 by stating which, if any, of the citations in (a) to (m) would have to be changed to conform to these special citation rules, and how.

(b) Find any court opinion written by the highest state court in your state. Locate this opinion by using the regional reporter for your state. (See exhibit 11.5.) Pick an opinion that is at least 10 pages long.

   (i)   Write down every citation in this opinion (up to a maximum of 25).

   (ii)  State whether these citations conform to the citation rules outlined in this section. Point out any differences.

   (iii) State whether these citations conform to the special citation rules, if any, you identified in answering question (a) above. Point out any differences.

---

Section K
# Cite Checking

When an assignment involves **cite checking,** you are given a document written by someone else and asked to check the citations provided by the author of the document. The assignment is quite common in law firms, particularly when the document to be checked is an appellate brief. Students on law review in law school also do extensive cite checking on the work of fellow students and outside authors.

Although our focus in this section will be cite checking documents written by others, the guidelines discussed here are in large measure equally applicable to your own writing. (Subjecting what you have written to your own criticism and review is what is known as self-editing.)

## GUIDELINES FOR CITE CHECKING

The first step is to obtain clear instructions from your supervisor on the scope of the assignment. Should you do a "light check" or a comprehensive one? Should you focus solely on citation format, or should you determine the accuracy of all quotes used by the writer of the document?

The following guidelines assume that you have been asked to undertake a comprehensive check.

1. Make sure that you have a *copy* of the document on which you can make comments. Avoid using the original.

2. If the pages of the document already have pencil or pen markings made by others (or by the author who made last-minute insertions), use a pencil or pen that is a different color from all other markings on the pages. In this way, it will be clear to any reader which corrections, notations, or other comments are your own. If you find that you do not have enough room to write in the margins of the pages,

use separate sheets of paper. You can increase the size of the margins by photo-copying the document on a machine that will reduce the size of what is copied.

3. If the document will be submitted to a court, be sure that you are using the official citation rules, if any, that must be followed for all citations in documents submitted to that court. If official citation rules do not exist, find out what rules or guidelines on citation format the supervisor wants you to use. The *Bluebook*? *ALWD*?

4. Before you begin, try to find a model. By going through the old case files of the office, you may be able to locate a prior document, such as an old appellate brief, that you can use as a general guide. Ask your supervisor to direct you to such a document. Although it may not cover all the difficulties you will encounter in your own document, you will at least have a general guide approved by your supervisor.

5. Check the citation form of *every* cite in the document written by the author of that document. This includes any cites in the body of the text, the footnotes, the appendix material, and the introductory pages of the document, such as the table of authorities at the beginning of a brief. (A **table of authorities** is a list of the primary and secondary authority the writer is using in an appellate brief or other document. The table will indicate on what page(s) in the document each authority is discussed or mentioned. See chapter 12.)

6. For longer documents, you need to develop your own system for ensuring the completeness of your checking. For example, you might want to circle every cite that you have checked and found to be accurate, and place a small box around (or a question mark next to) every cite that is giving you difficulties. You will want to spend more time with the latter, seeking help from colleagues and your supervisor.

7. When you find errors in the form of the citation, make the corrections in the margin of the pages where they are found.

8. For some errors, you will not be able to make the corrections without obtaining additional information, such as a missing date or a missing parallel cite. If you can obtain such data by going to the relevant library books (or available online resources), do so. Otherwise, make a notation in the margin of what is missing or what still needs correction.

9. Consistency in citation format is extremely important. On page 2 of the document, for example, the author may use one citation format, but on page 10, he or she may use a completely different format for the same kind of legal material. You need to point out this inconsistency and make the consistency corrections that are called for.

10. Often your document will quote from opinions, statutes, or other legal materials. Check the accuracy of these quotations. Go to the material being quoted, find the quote, and check it against the document line by line, word by word, and punctuation mark by punctuation mark. Be scrupulous about the accuracy of quotations.

11. Shepardize (or KeyCite) anything that can be sheparadized, such as opinions and statutes. Here are some examples of what you need to determine through shepardizing:

    ■ Whether any of the cited opinions has been overruled or reversed.
    ■ Whether any of the cited statutes has been repealed or amended by the legislature, or has been invalidated by a court.

12. Check the accuracy of all **supra** reference.

    The word *supra* means "above" or "earlier." It refers to something already mentioned (and cited) in the document you are cite checking. For example, assume that footnote 8 on page 23 of the document contains the following cite:

    [8]Robert G. Danna, *Family Law* 119 (1992).

    The particular reference is to page 119 of Danna's book. Now assume that 10 pages later—in footnote 17—the document again refers to Danna's book, this time to page 35. A full citation to this page would be as follows:

    [17]Robert G. Danna, *Family Law* 35 (1992).

But a full citation is not needed. You can use a *short-form citation*. This is an abbreviated citation of an authority that you use after you have already given a full citation of that authority earlier in the document. For the short-form citation of a legal treatise such as the Danna *Family Law* book, use the author's last name followed by the *supra* reference:

[17]Danna, *supra* note 8, at 35.

[*ALWD*: [17]Danna, *supra* n. 8, at 35.]

This means that the full cite of Danna's book was already given earlier (*supra*) in the document in footnote 8. There is no need to repeat the full cite. The cite checker must simply go to footnote 8 and make sure that the full cite of the book is provided there.

Finally, assume that Danna's book was cited in full in the body of the text of the document rather than in a footnote. A later footnote reference to the same book would be as follows:

[17]Danna, *supra*, at 35.

The accuracy of this reference is checked in the same way: make sure that the full cite of Danna's book is in fact provided earlier in the body of the text of the document.

Infra means "below" or "later" and refers to something that will come later in the document. In the same manner as you checked the *supra* references, you must determine whether the *infra* references are accurate.

13. Check the accuracy of all of short-form case citations.

Assume that the document you are cite checking gives the following reference early in the document:

*Sierra Club v. Sigler*, 695 F.2d 957, 980 (5th Cir. 1983).

The cite is to page 980 of the *Sierra Club* case, which begins on page 957 of the *Federal Reporter, Second Series*. Now assume that the author wants to refer to page 962 of the same case later in the document. Generally, there is no need to repeat the entire citation. The following short form may be used:

*Sierra Club*, 695 F.2d at 962.

To check the accuracy of this cite, you must go back in the document to make sure that *Sierra Club* has already been cited in full.

Do not, however, use *supra* when you are citing court opinions. *Supra* can be used for many items, such as legal treatises and legal periodicals. With rare exceptions, however, do not use it in citations to court opinions. When you wish to avoid repeating the full citation of an opinion, use the short-form case citation just discussed.

14. All **id.** references should also be checked. *Id.* means the same as something previously mentioned. Use *id.* when you are citing an authority that is also the *immediately preceding* authority cited in a footnote. (*Id.* is more specific than *supra*; the latter means above or earlier. *Id.*, however, means *immediately* above.) Assume, for example, that footnote 21 in the appellate brief you are cite checking says:

[21]*Kohler v. Tugwell*, 292 F. Supp. 978 (E.D. La. 1968).

And footnote 22 says:

[22]*Id.* at 985.

The *Id.* reference means that here in footnote 22 you are referring to the immediately preceding authority—the *Kohler* opinion in footnote 21.

Be careful about *id.* references. A writer cannot use *id.* if more than one authority is cited in the preceding footnote. Suppose, for example, that footnote 21 cited *Kohler* and another opinion:

[21]*Smith v. Harris*, 260 F.2d 601 (2d Cir. 1956); *Kohler v. Tugwell*, 292 F. Supp. 978 (E.D. La. 1968).

If footnote 22 wanted to cite *Kohler*, you could not use *id.* because there is more than one authority in footnote 21. Footnote 22 should use the short-form citation as follows:

[22]*Kohler*, 292 F. Supp. at 985.

### CITE-CHECKING SOFTWARE

Computer companies have developed two kinds of cite-checking software. First, there is *format* software, which tells you whether a particular citation conforms to *The Bluebook: A Uniform System of Citation* or to the *ALWD Citation Manual*, or to both. The developers have placed all the citation rules in one or both of these guidelines into the program so that it can recognize discrepancies between these rules and the citation format you used in your memorandum or other writing. In addition to pointing out citation errors, the program will refer you to specific citation rules you have violated. Two examples of such software are The Electronic Bluebook and CiteRite. The second kind of cite-checking software provides *validation* data on citations, meaning that you will be told if the law you are citing is still good law, i.e., is still valid. You will be told, for example, whether a particular court opinion has been overruled and whether a particular statute has been repealed. Two examples of such software are WestCheck, used in conjunction with Westlaw, and CheckCite, used in conjunction with LEXIS. Unlike the format cite-checking software, the validation programs are online and hence are used through a modem.

---

### Assignment 11.8

In chapter 5 on page 228 you will find the opinion of *Brown v. Hammond* by Judge Waldman. Assume that this opinion in chapter 5 is only the first draft of the judge's opinion. After writing it, Judge Waldman hands it to you and asks you to cite check it. Make sure all the citations are in proper form according to the guidelines presented in this section. Check the accuracy of every quote. Check other references as well. If, for example, the text cites an opinion and summarizes what is in the opinion, check whether the summary is accurate. If you cannot check some of the cites, point out why (e.g., the library you are using does not have whatever you need to check a particular cite).

---

### Section L
# Components of Many Law Books

Many law books are similar in structure. To be sure, some books, such as *Shepard's Citations*, are unique. In the main, however, the texts follow a pattern. The following components are contained in many:

1. *Outside Cover.* On the outside cover, you will find the title of the book, the author(s) or editor(s), the name of the publisher (usually at the bottom), the edition of the book (if more than one edition has been printed), and the volume number (if the book is part of a set or series of books). After glancing at the outside cover, you should ask yourself the following questions:
   - Is it a book *containing* law (written primarily by a court, a legislature, or an administrative agency), or is it a book *about* the law (written by a scholar who is commenting on the law)? Is the book a combination of both? (For an overview of the four main functions of books and other legal materials, see exhibit 11.3.)
   - Is this book the most current available? Look at the books on the shelf in the area where you found the book that you are examining. Is there a replacement volume for your book? Is there a later edition of the book? Check your book in the card or computer catalog to see if other editions are mentioned.
2. *Publisher's Page.* The first few pages of the book often include a page or pages about the publisher. The page may list other law books published by the same company.
3. *Title Page.* The title page repeats most of the information contained on the outside cover: title, author or editor, publisher. It also contains the date of publication.

4. *Copyright Page.* The **copyright page** (often immediately behind the title page) has a copyright mark © plus a date or several dates. The most recent date listed indicates the timeliness of the material in the volume. Given the great flux in the law, it is very important to determine how old the text is. If the book has a pocket part (see item 14 below), it has been updated to the date on the pocket part.

COPYRIGHT © 1979, 1983, 1989, 1994, 1998 WEST GROUP

COPYRIGHT © 2002

By

WEST GROUP

The dates on this copyright page indicate that the material in the book is current up to 2002, the latest copyright date. Caution, however, is needed in reaching this conclusion. Publishers like to have their books appear to be as current as possible. A book with a 2002 copyright date may in fact have been published *at the beginning* of 2002 or *at the very end* of 2001! A 2002 date does not necessarily mean that you are current up to December of that year. We will return to this concern later when we discuss pocket parts.

5. *Foreword and/or Preface.* Under such headings, you may find some basic information about the book, particularly material on how the book was prepared and guidance on how to use it.

6. *Summary Table of Contents.* On one or two pages, you may find the main topics treated in the book.

7. *Detailed Table of Contents.* When provided, the detailed table of contents can be very extensive. The major headings of the summary table of contents are repeated, and detailed subheadings and sub-subheadings are listed. Use this table as an additional index to the book.

8. *Table of Cases.* The **table of cases** lists, alphabetically, every opinion that is printed or referred to in the text, with the page(s) or section(s) where the opinion is found or discussed. This table is sometimes printed at the end of the book.

9. *Table of Statutes.* The **table of statutes** gives the page numbers or section numbers where every statute is interpreted or referred to in the text. This table is sometimes printed at the end of the book.

10. *List of Abbreviations.* The abbreviation list, if provided, is critical. A reader who is unfamiliar with law books should check this list immediately. It may be the only place in the book that spells out the abbreviations used in the body of the text. In *Shepard's Citations*, for example, abbreviations are found in the first few pages of the bound volumes and in most of its pamphlets.

| History of Case | |
|---|---|
| a (affirmed) | Same case affirmed on appeal. |
| cc (connected case) | Different case from case cited but arising out of same subject matter or intimately connected therewith. |
| D (dismissed) | Appeal from same case dismissed. |
| m (modified) | Same case modified on appeal. |
| r (reversed) | Same case reversed on appeal. |
| s (same case) | Same case as case cited. |
| S (superseded) | Substitution for former opinion. |
| v (vacated) | Same case vacated. |
| US cert den | Certiorari denied by U. S. Supreme Court. |
| US cert dis | Certiorari dismissed by U. S. Supreme Court. |
| US reh den | Rehearing denied by U. S. Supreme Court. |
| US reh dis | Rehearing dismissed by U. S. Supreme Court. |
| **Treatment of Case** | |
| c (criticised) | Soundness of decision or reasoning in cited case criticised for reasons given. |
| d (distinguished) | Case at bar different either in law or fact from case cited for reasons given. |
| e (explained) | Statement of import of decisions in cited case. Not merely a restatement of the facts. |
| f (followed) | Cited as controlling. |
| h (harmonized) | Apparent inconsistency explained and shown not to exist. |
| j (dissenting opinion) | Citation in dissenting opinion. |
| L (limited) | Refusal to extend decision of cited case beyond precise issues involved. |
| o (overruled) | Ruling in cited case expressly overruled. |
| p (parallel) | Citing case substantially alike or on all fours with cited case in its law or facts. |
| q (questioned) | Soundness of decision or reasoning in cited case questioned. |

Example of abbreviations used by Shepard's

11. *Statutory History Table.* Some texts, particularly statutory codes, may include a statutory history table that lists every statute cited in the book and indicates whether it has been repealed or whether it has a new section number and title. The

Example of a statutory
history table

### TABLE OF PRISON LAW SECTIONS

Showing the distribution of those sections of the former Prison Law in effect prior to the general amendment by L.1929, c. 243, which are contained wholly or in part in the Correction Law, or which have been omitted or repealed.

| Prison Law Section | Correction Law Section |
| --- | --- |
| 1 | 1 |
| 10–20 | 600–610 |
| 21 | Repealed |
| 22 L.1919, c. 12 | 611 |
| 22 L.1920, c. 933 | 612 |
| 23–32 | 613–622 |
| 40–50 | 40–50 |

legislature may have changed the entire name of the statutory chapter (from Prison Law to Correction Law, for instance) and renumbered all the sections. Without this table, the researcher can become lost. In the example below, note that former Prison Law sections 10–20 are now found in Correction Law sections 600–610. You may find a citation to a Prison Law section in a book that was published before the state changed to Correction Law sections. When you go to look up the Prison Law section, you will find nothing unless you have a way to translate the section into a Correction Law section. The *statutory history table* will be one way to do it.

12. *Body of the Text.* The fundamental characteristic of the body of many legal texts is that it is arranged according to units such as parts, subparts, divisions, subdivisions, chapters, subchapters, sections, subsections, etc. Often each unit covers a similar subject matter and is numbered or lettered in sequence. You should thumb through the entire book to obtain a feel for the numbering and classification system used by the author or editor.

13. *Footnotes.* Footnotes are very important in law books; researchers place great emphasis on them. They often give extensive citations to cases and other cross-references, and hence can be an excellent lead to additional law.

14. *Pocket Parts and Other Updating Features.* A unique and indispensable feature of many law books is the *pocket part*. It is a small booklet addition to the text, usually placed in a specially devised pocket built into the inside of the rear cover. The pocket part is published after the book is printed and is designed to bring the book up to date with the latest developments in the field covered by the book. Of course, a pocket part can also grow out of date. Normally, it is replaced once a year. On the front cover of the pocket-part booklet, there is a date telling you what period is covered. The title page (see item 3 above) may say that the last edition of the book was published in 1990, but the front page of the pocket part may say "for use during 2001–2002." Again, however, use caution in interpreting these dates. The publisher may have prepared this pocket part at the end of 2001 or at the beginning of 2002. You cannot assume that the material in the pocket part is current up to December of 2002.

Normally, the organization of the pocket part exactly parallels the organization of the main text. For example, to find out if there has been anything new in the area covered by chapter 7, part 2, section 714 of the main text, you go to chapter 7, part 2, section 714 of the pocket part. If you find nothing there, then nothing new has happened. If changes or additions have occurred, they will be found there. The changes may appear in different formats. <u>All new text might appear underlined.</u> ~~All old text might appear with a strikeout line through it.~~ Or you may be able to assume that any text that appears in the pocket part is new text.

Pocket parts are *cumulative* in that, whenever a pocket part is replaced by another pocket part, everything in the earlier pocket part is consolidated into the most recent one. The earlier pocket part is thrown away.

Not all law books have pocket parts. For an overview, see exhibit 11.15.

How is new material added to law books without pocket parts—the ones listed in the second column of exhibit 11.15? Shepard's is kept current by advance

| EXHIBIT 11.15 | Pocket Parts |
| --- | --- |

**LAW BOOKS THAT ALWAYS OR OFTEN HAVE POCKET PARTS:**

- State Statutory Codes (e.g., *Georgia Code Annotated*)
- Unofficial Federal Codes (e.g., U.S.C.A. and U.S.C.S.)
- Annotated Reporters (e.g., A.L.R. 5th)
- Legal Encyclopedias (e.g., C.J.S. and Am. Jur. 2d)
- State Digests (e.g., *Illinois Digest 2d*)
- Regional Digests (e.g., *Pacific Digest*)
- Federal Digests (e.g., *Federal Practice Digest 4th*)
- Legal Treatises Written for Practitioners (e.g., C.Z. Nothstein, *Toxic Torts*)

**LAW BOOKS THAT NEVER HAVE POCKET PARTS:**

- Shepard's (e.g., *Shepard's Federal Citations*)
- American Digest System (*Century Digest, Decennial Digests,* & *General Digests*)
- Loose-leaf Services (e.g., *United States Law Week*)
- West Group Reporters (e.g., regional reporters, S. Ct., F.3d, F. Supp. 2d)
- Session Laws (e.g., *United States Statutes at Large*)
- Legal Periodicals (e.g., *Boston College Law Review*)
- Legal Newspapers (e.g., *San Francisco Daily Journal*)
- Legal Newsletters (e.g., *The Guardian*)

sheets and supplemental pamphlets; the American Digest System by adding *General Digest* volumes, which are thrown away when the next *Decennial Digest* is published; loose-leaf services by inserting pages with new material into the binders and removing pages with outdated material (a process called interfiling). For the other items in the second column of exhibit 11.15—West Group reporters, session laws, etc.—new material is added simply by adding new volumes or issues.

Some sets of books use a variety of methods to bring them up to date: pocket parts, supplement pamphlets, supplement volumes, reissued volumes, revised volumes, etc. The newest method of updating is the Internet. At the beginning or end of a volume, you may be given a World Wide Web address where you can go for additional material on the book (often including an errata page listing errors that were not caught until after the volume was published).

15. *Appendix.* The text may include one or more appendixes at the end. Normally, they include tables, charts, or the entire text of statutes or regulations, portions of which are discussed in the body of the book.
16. *Glossary.* The book may include a glossary, which is a dictionary that defines a selected number of words used in the body of the book.
17. *Bibliography.* A brief or extended bibliography of the field covered by the book may be included at the end of each chapter or at the end of the book.
18. *Index.* The index is a critical part of the book. Unfortunately, some books either have no index or have a poorly prepared index. The index is arranged alphabetically and should refer the reader to the page number(s) or to the section number(s) where topics are treated in the body of the text. The index is found at the end of the book. If there are many volumes in the set, you may find more than one index. For example, there may be a *general index* for the entire set and a series of smaller indexes covering individual volumes.

## Section M
# THE CARTWHEEL

Most people think that using an *index* is a relatively easy task—until they start trying to use indexes of law books! These indexes are often poorly written because they are not comprehensive. To be comprehensive, an index might have to be as long as the text it is indexing. Hence publishers are reluctant to include such indexes.

Because of this reality, one of the most important skills in legal research is the creative use of indexes in law books. When you master this skill, 70 percent of the research battle is won. The **CARTWHEEL** is a word-association technique designed to assist you in acquiring the skill by giving you a method of generating words and phrases. See exhibit 11.16.

| EXHIBIT 11.16 | The CARTWHEEL: Using the Index of Law Book |
|---|---|

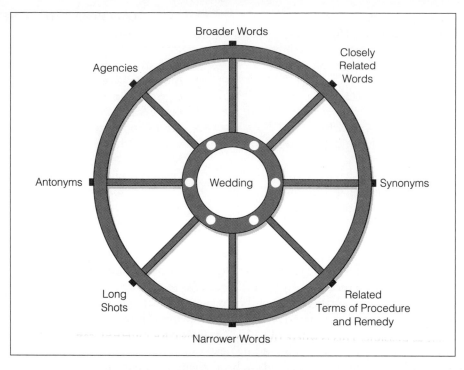

1. Identify all the *major words* from the facts of the client's problem, e.g., wedding (most of these facts can be obtained from the intake memorandum written following the initial interview with the client). Place each word or small set of words in the center of the CARTWHEEL.
2. In the index, look up all of these words.
3. Identify the *broader categories* of the major words.
4. In the index, look up all of these broader categories.
5. Identify the *narrower* categories of the major words.
6. In the index, look up all of these narrower categories.
7. Identify all *synonyms* of the major words.
8. In the index, look up all of these synonyms.
9. Identify all of the *antonyms* of the major words.
10. In the index, look up all of these antonyms.
11. Identify all words that are *closely related* to the major words.
12. In the index, look up all of these closely related words.
13. Identify all terms of *procedure* and *remedy* related to the major words.
14. In the index, look up all of these procedural and remedial terms.
15. Identify all *agencies*, if any, that might have some connection to the major words.
16. In the index, look up all of these agencies.
17. Identify all *long shots*.
18. In the index, look up all of these long shots.

**Note**: The above categories are not mutually exclusive.

(The skill can also be used when checking tables of contents and using online search engines.) Professor Roy Steele, a veteran teacher of legal research, made the following observation about new students:

> I think it is important for students to understand that they cannot just walk into a library and start pulling books off the shelf. That is the quickest way to become frustrated. Legal research requires thoughtful planning. A student must determine which resources will be checked. It is not enough that a student knows [that] a certain resource has an index or table of contents. The

student must know what he/she is looking for. This requires the student to develop a list of search terms. Some people would call the development of this list *brainstorming*. However, brainstorming is somewhat hit or miss; it lacks structure and organization. The CARTWHEEL is one of the most effective ways of systematically developing a list of search terms. [It is] a method of analyzing a legal problem and developing a list of descriptive words, which can be used to search indexes.

The objective of the CARTWHEEL can be simply stated: to develop the habit of phrasing every word involved in the client's problem *15 to 20 different ways!* When you go to the index (or to the table of contents) of a law book, you naturally begin looking up the words and phrases that you think should lead you to the relevant material in the book. If you do not find anything relevant to your problem, two conclusions are possible:

- There is nothing relevant in the law book.
- You looked up the wrong words in the index.

Although the first conclusion is sometimes accurate, nine times out of ten, the second conclusion is the reason you fail to find material that is relevant to the client's problem. The solution is to be able to phrase a word in as many different ways and in as many different contexts as possible—hence the CARTWHEEL.

Suppose the client's problem involved, among other things, a wedding. The first step would be to look up the word *wedding* in the index of any law book you are examining. Assume that you are not successful with this word, either because the word is not in the index or because the page or section references do not lead you to relevant material in the body of the book. The next step is to think of as many different phrasings and contexts of the word *wedding* as possible. This is where the 18 steps of the CARTWHEEL can be useful.

If you applied the steps of the CARTWHEEL to the word *wedding*, here are some of the words and phrases that you might check:

1. *Broader words:* celebration, ceremony, rite, ritual, formality, festivity, etc.
2. *Narrower words:* civil wedding, church wedding, golden wedding, proxy wedding, sham wedding, shotgun marriage, etc.
3. *Synonyms:* marriage ceremony, nuptial, etc.
4. *Antonyms:* alienation, annulment, divorce, separation, legal separation, judicial separation, etc.
5. *Closely related words:* license, blood test, contract, minister, matrimony, marital, conjugal, domestic, husband, wife, bride, anniversary, custom, children, pre-marital, spouse, relationship, family, home, consummation, cohabitation, sexual relations, betrothal, wedlock, oath, community property, name change, domicile, residence, etc.
6A. *Terms of procedure:* action, suit, statute of limitations, complaint, discovery, defense, petition, jurisdiction, court, superior court, county court, etc.
6B. *Terms of remedy:* damages, divorce, injunction, partition, rescission, revocation, specific performance, etc.
7. *Agencies:* Bureau of Vital Statistics, County Clerk, Department of Social Services, License Bureau, Secretary of State, Justice of the Peace, etc.
8. *Long shots:* dowry, common law, single, blood relationship, fraud, religion, illegitimate, remarriage, antenuptial, alimony, bigamy, pregnancy, gifts, chastity, impotence, incest, virginity, support, custody, consent, paternity, etc.

If the CARTWHEEL can generate this many words and phrases from a starting point of just one word (wedding), potentially thousands more can be generated when you subject all of the important words from the client's case to the CARTWHEEL. Do you check them all in the index volume of every code, digest, encyclopedia, practice manual, and treatise? No. You can't spend your entire legal career in the law library working on one case! Common sense will tell you when you are on the right track and when you are needlessly duplicating your efforts. You may get lucky and find what you are after in a few minutes. For most important tasks in any line of work (or play), however, being comprehensive is usually time-consuming.

As indicated in exhibit 11.16, the categories may overlap; they are not mutually exclusive. There are two reasons for checking antonyms: they might cover your topic, and they might give you a cross-reference to your topic. It is not significant whether you place a word in one category or another so long as the word comes to your mind as you comb through all available indexes. The CARTWHEEL is, in effect, a *word-association game* that should become second nature to you with practice. Perhaps some of the word selections seem a bit far-fetched. You will not know for sure, however, whether a word is fruitful until you try it. Be imaginative, and take some risks.

---

**Assignment 11.9**
CARTWHEEL the following words or phrases:

(a) Paralegal
(b) Woman
(c) Rat bite
(d) Rear-end collision
(e) Monopoly

---

Indexes and tables of contents are often organized into *headings, subheadings, sub-subheadings*, and perhaps even sub-sub-subheadings. Examine the following excerpt from an index. Note that "Burden of proof" is a sub-subheading of "Accidents" and a subheading of "Unavoidable accident or casualty." The latter is a subheading of "Accidents," which is the main heading of the index entry. If you were looking for law on burden of proof, you might be out of luck unless you *first* thought of looking up "accidents" and "unavoidable accident."

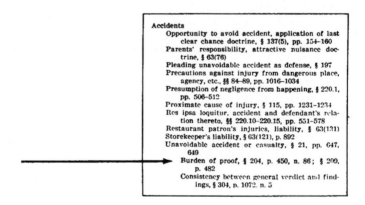

Suppose that you identify the following words to check in an index:

| minor | sale |
| explosion | warranty |
| car | damage |

The index may have no separate heading for "minor," but "minor" may be a subheading under "sale." If so, you would not find "minor" unless you first thought of checking "sale." Under each of the above six words, you should be alert to the possibility that the other five words may be subheadings for that word. Hence the process of pursuing these six words in an index (or table of contents) would be as follows: (The word in bold letters is checked first and then the five words *under it* are checked to see if any of them are subheadings.)

| Car | Damage | Explosion | Minor | Sale | Warranty |
|-----|--------|-----------|-------|------|----------|
| damage | car | car | car | car | car |
| explosion | explosion | damage | damage | damage | damage |
| minor | minor | minor | explosion | explosion | explosion |
| sale | sale | sale | sale | minor | minor |
| warranty | warranty | warranty | warranty | warranty | sale |

---

*Assignment 11.10*

One way to gain an appreciation for the use of indexes is to write one of your own. When you write an index for this assignment, be sure to use headings, subheadings, sub-subheadings, etc., in each index.

(a) Write a comprehensive index of your present job or the last job that you had.

(b) Pick one area of the law that you have covered in class or read about. Write your own comprehensive index on what you have learned.

(c) Write a comprehensive index of the following statute:

§ 132. Amount of force. The use of force against another for the purpose of effecting the arrest or recapture of the other, or of maintaining custody of him, is not privileged if the means employed are in excess of those which are reasonably believed to be necessary.

---

*Assignment 11.11*

Examine the index from a legal encyclopedia in exhibit 11.17. It is an excerpt from the heading of "Evidence." "Death" is the subheading of "Evidence." What sub-subheadings or sub-sub-subheadings of "Evidence" would you check to try to find material on the following:

(a) Introducing a death certificate into evidence.

(b) The weight that a court will give to the personal conclusions of a witness.

(c) Introducing the last words of a decedent into evidence.

(d) A statement by the person who died disclaiming ownership of land around which he or she had placed a fence.

## OTHER INDEX SEARCH SYSTEMS

The CARTWHEEL is not the only technique for using indexes (and tables of contents) effectively. Others include Descriptive Words and TAPP.

### Descriptive Words

West Group suggests a five-part descriptive word framework for generating search terms: Parties, Places or Things, Basis of Action or Issue, Defenses, and Relief Sought. By trying to identify terms that fall into these categories, you will be generating numerous words to check in the indexes (and tables of contents) of law books you are examining.

**Parties** Identify persons of a particular class, occupation, or relation involved in the problem you are researching (e.g., commercial landlords, children born out of wedlock, physicians, sheriffs, aliens, collectors). Include any person who is directly or indirectly necessary to a proper resolution of the legal problem.

**Places or Things** Identify all significant objects—those places and things perceptible to the senses that are involved in the problem being researched (e.g., automobiles, sidewalks, derricks, garages, office buildings). An object is significant if it is relevant to the cause of action or dispute that has arisen. (A cause of action is a set of facts that give a party a right to judicial relief; it is a legally acceptable reason for suing.)

**Basis of Action or Issue** Identify the alleged wrong suffered or infraction (e.g., negligence, loss of goods, assault, failure to pay overtime, sex discrimination).

**Defenses** Identify those reasons in law or fact why there arguably should be *no* recovery (e.g., assumption of the risk, failure of consideration, act of God, infancy).

**Relief Sought** Identify the legal remedy being sought (e.g., damages, injunction, annulment).

| EXHIBIT 11.17 | Excerpt from a Legal Encyclopedia Index (Corpus Juris Secundum) |
| --- | --- |

## EVIDENCE

**Dealers,**
   Securities, judicial notice, § 29, p. 890
   Value,
      Household goods, opinion evidence, § 546(121), p. 479, n. 95
      Property, § 546(115), p. 430
         Opinion evidence, § 546(122), p. 483
**Death,**
   Autopsy, generally, ante
   Best evidence rule, § 803, p. 136
   Book entries,
      Entrant, proof of handwriting, § 693, p. 942
      Supplemental testimony respecting entries by clerks and third persons, § 693, p. 939
      Supporting entries by deceased persons by oath of personal representative, § 684, p. 910
   Clerk or employee making book entries, § 692
   Copy of record, certification by state registrar, § 664, p. 865, n. 69
   Declaration against interest, death of declarant, § 218, p. 604
   Declarations, § 227, p. 624
      Death of declarant as essential to admission, § 230
   Dying declarations, generally, post
   Experiments, object or purpose, § 588(1)
   Former evidence, death of witness, § 392
   General reputation, § 1048
   Hearsay, § 227, p. 624
      Death certificates, § 194, pp. 561, 562; § 766, p. 66
      Death of declarant, § 205
      Impossibility of obtaining other evidence, § 204
   Letters, § 703, p. 976
   Maps and diagrams of scenes of occurrence, § 730(1), p. 1045
   Memorandum, § 696, p. 955
   Mortality tables, generally, post
   Newspaper announcement, § 227, p. 625
   Opinion evidence,
      Animals, § 546(68)
      Cause and effect, § 546(11), p. 129
      Effect on human body, § 546(97), p. 374
      Fixing time, § 546(91), n. 16
   Owners, admissions, § 327
      Personal property, § 334
   Parol or extrinsic evidence, rule excluding, action to recover for, § 861, p. 230
   Photographs, personal appearance or identity, § 710
   Presumptions, ancient original public records, official making, § 746, p. 37
   Prima facie evidence, record of, § 644
   Private documents, recitals, § 677
   Public records and documents, registers of, § 623
   Reputation, § 227, p. 626
   Res gestae, statements, § 410, p. 991
   Rumor, § 227, p. 625
   Self-serving declarations, effect of death of declarant, § 216, p. 591
   Services, value, opinion evidence in death action, § 546(124), p. 489, n. 96
   Statements, weight of evidence, § 266
   Value of service rendered by claimant, opinion evidence, § 546(125), p. 493, n. 41

**Death—Continued**
   Witness, unsworn statements, circumstances tending to disparage testimony, § 268
   Wrongful death,
      Admissions, husband and wife, § 363
      Admissions of decedent, privity, § 322, n. 96.5
      Declarations against interest, § 218, p. 607
      Loss of life, value, opinion evidence, § 546 (121), p. 473, n. 54
      Municipal claim, evidence of registry, § 680, n. 21
      Value of decedent's services, opinion evidence, § 546(124), p. 489, n. 96
**Death certificates,**
   Certified copies, § 651, p. 851
      Officer as making, § 664, p. 865, n. 69
      Prima facie evidence, § 773
   Church register, competency, § 727
   Conclusiveness, § 766, p. 64
   Expert testimony, supporting opinion, § 570
   Foreign countries, authenticated copies, § 675, p. 885
   Hearsay, § 194, pp. 561, 562; § 766, p. 66
   Kinship, § 696, p. 949, n. 2
   Official document, § 638, pp. 823, 824
   Prima facie case or evidence, post
   Debate, judicial notice, United States congress, § 43, p. 995
   Debs, judicial notice, § 67, p. 56, n. 17
   Debtor and creditor, admissions, § 336
   Debts. Indebtedness, generally, post
**Decay,**
   Judicial notice, vegetable matter, § 88
   Opinion evidence, buildings, § 546(73), p. 290
**Decedents' estates,**
   Judicial admissions, claim statements, § 310
   Judicial records, inferences from, § 765
   Official documents, reports and inventories of representatives, § 638, p. 818
   Value, opinion evidence, § 546(121), p. 478
**Deceit.** Fraud, generally, post
**Decisions,** judicial notice, sister states, § 18, p. 861
**Declaration against interest,** §§ 217–224, pp. 600–615
   Absence of declared from jurisdiction, § 218, p. 604
   Account, § 224
   Admissions, distinguished, § 217, p. 603
   Adverse character, § 222
   Affirmative proof as being best evidence obtainable, § 218, p. 604
   Apparent interest, § 219, p. 608
   Assured, § 219, p. 611
   Best evidence obtainable, necessity of, § 218, p. 604
   Boundaries, § 219, p. 611
   Coexisting, self-serving interest, § 221
   Contract, § 224
   Criminal prosecution, statement subjecting declarant to, § 219, p. 608
   Death action, § 218, p. 607
   Death of declarant, § 218, p. 605
   Dedication to public use, § 219, p. 611
   Deeds, § 224
   Disparagement of title § 219, p. 611
   Distinctions, § 217, p. 603
   Enrollment of vessel, § 224

**Example**    At a professional wrestling match the referee was thrown from the ring in such a way that he struck and injured the plaintiff, who was a front-row spectator. The following descriptive words for this problem should be checked:

    *Parties*—spectator, patron, arena owner, wrestler, referee, promoter
    *Places and things*—wrestling match, amusement place, theater, show
    *Basis of action or issue*—negligence, personal injury to spectator, liability
    *Defense*—assumption of risk
    *Relief sought*—damages

### TAPP

Lawyers Co-operative Publishing Company (part of West Group) suggests generating search terms by thinking of TAPP categories: Things, Acts, Persons, or Places involved in the problem you are searching.

    *Things*—automobile, pool, knife, blood, etc.
    *Acts*—swimming, driving, rescuing, accounting, etc.
    *Persons*—mother, pedestrian, driver, etc.
    *Places*—state freeway, residence, etc.

### Assignment 11.12

This assignment asks you to identify as many index (and table of contents) entries as you can that may cover designated topics. Use the CARTWHEEL, descriptive words, and TAPP systems. Go to the indexes (and tables of contents) in the sets of books indicated. Make a notation of *every* index (and table of contents) entry that appears to cover the topic. Try to find multiple entries in the indexes (and tables of contents) for the topic you are searching. In class, the teacher may call on you to indicate what entries you found that appeared to be successful so that others in the class can compare their entries with yours.

(a) Rape. Books to use: your state statutory code.
(b) Race discrimination. Books to use: the state digest that covers your state courts.
(c) Suicide. Books to use: *American Jurisprudence 2d*.
(d) Divorce. Books to use: *Corpus Juris Secundum*.
(e) Homosexuality. Books to use: *Index to Annotations*.

## Section N
# THE FIRST LEVEL OF LEGAL RESEARCH: BACKGROUND

There are three interrelated levels of researching a problem:
*Background Research.* Provides you with a general understanding of the area of law involved in your research problem.
*Specific Fact Research.* Provides you with primary and secondary authority that covers the specific facts of your research problem.
*Validation Research.* Provides you with information on the current validity of all the primary authority you intend to use in your research memorandum on the problem.

At times, all three levels of research go on simultaneously. If you are new to legal research, however, it is recommended that you approach your research problem in three separate stages or levels. Our concern in this section is the first level: background research. See exhibit 11.18. The other two levels are covered throughout the remainder of this chapter.

Let us assume you are researching a topic that is totally new to you. Where do you begin? What law books do you take off the shelves, or what computer databases or files do you start checking? More specifically:

■ Should you start looking for federal law or state law?
■ Should you begin looking for statutes or for court opinions?
■ Should you check constitutional law?
■ Should you check procedural law?
■ Should you check administrative law?
■ Should you check ordinances or other local laws?

By definition, you don't know the answers to such questions—we are assuming that you have never researched a problem like the one now before you. Of course, you will want to ask your supervisor for direction on where to begin. Also, you should try to seek out a colleague who may have some time to provide you with initial guidance. But suppose that such assistance is fairly minimal or is simply not available. Where do you begin?

Start with some of the 10 techniques for doing background research outlined in exhibit 11.18. Spend an hour or two (depending on the complexity of the problem) doing some reading in law books that will provide you with an overview and a general understanding of the area(s) of law involved in your research problem. You will then be in a better position to be able to identify the major **terms of art** you need to understand and the major questions or issues you need to address. (A legal term of art is a word or phrase that has a special or technical meaning in the law.) Of course, while doing this background research, you will probably also come up with leads that will be helpful in the second and third levels of research.

| EXHIBIT 11.18 | Techniques for Doing Background Research on a Topic |

### 1. Legal Dictionaries

Have access to a *legal dictionary* throughout your research. For example:

> *Black's Law Dictionary*
> *Ballentine's Law Dictionary*
> *Oran's Law Dictionary*
> Statsky's *Legal Thesaurus/Dictionary*
> *Words and Phrases*

Look up the meaning of all important terms that you come across in your research. These dictionaries are starting points only. Eventually you want to find primary authority that defines these terms. Legal dictionaries on the Internet include

- dictionary.lp.findlaw.com
- www.jurist.law.pitt.edu/dictionary.htm
- www.lectlaw.com/def.htm

### 2. Legal Encyclopedias

Find discussions of your topic in the major national *legal encyclopedias:*

> *American Jurisprudence 2d*
> *Corpus Juris Secundum*

Also check encyclopedias, if any, that cover only your state. Use the CARTWHEEL to help you use their indexes.

### 3. Legal Treatises

Find discussions of your topic in *legal treatises*. Go to your card or computer catalog in the library. Use the CARTWHEEL to help you locate treatises such as hornbooks, nutshells, handbooks, form books, practice manuals, scholarly studies, etc. Many of these books will have *KF call numbers*. If there are open stacks in the library, go to the KF section to browse through what is available on the shelves. Use the CARTWHEEL to help you use the indexes of these books.

### 4. Annotations

Find discussions of your topic in the *annotations* of A.L.R. (A.L.R. 1st), A.L.R.2d, A.L.R.3d, A.L.R.4th, A.L.R.5th, and A.L.R. Fed. Use the CARTWHEEL to help you find these discussions through indexes such as the *ALR Index*.

### 5. Legal Periodical Literature

Find discussions of your topic in *legal periodical* literature. The three main indexes to such literature are:

> *Index to Legal Periodicals and Books* (ILP)
> *Current Law Index* (CLI)
> *LegalTrac* (the CD–ROM version of CLI)

Use the CARTWHEEL to help you use these indexes to locate legal periodical literature on your topic.

### 6. Agency Reports/Brochures

If your research involves an administrative agency, call or write the agency. Find out what agency reports, brochures, or newsletters are available to the public. Such literature often provides useful background information.

| EXHIBIT 11.18 | Techniques for Doing Background Research on a Topic—*continued* |
|---|---|

### 7. Committee Reports

Many research projects involve one or more statutes. Before statutes are passed, committees of the legislature often write **committee reports** that comment on and summarize the legislation. (See exhibit 6.5 in chapter 6.) In addition to being good sources of legislative history on the statute, the reports are excellent background reading. If practical, contact both houses of the legislature to find out which committees acted on the statute. If the statute is fairly recent, they may be able to send you copies of the committee reports or tell you where to obtain them. If you live near the library of the legislature, you may be able to find committee reports there. The committee reports of many recent federal statutes are printed in *U.S. Code Congressional and Administrative News* (U.S.C.C.A.N.).

### 8. Reports/Studies of Special Interest Groups

There are *special interest* groups for almost every area of the law, e.g., unions, bar associations, environmental associations, tax associations, insurance and other business associations. They often have position papers and studies that they might be willing to send you. Although one-sided, such literature should not be ignored.

### 9. Martindale-Hubbell Digest

The Digest volume of *Martindale-Hubbell Law Directory* provides concise summaries of the law of the fifty states and many foreign countries.

### 10. Internet

Numerous directories and legal search engines (e.g., www.findlaw.com) and general search engines (e.g., www.google.com) exist on the Internet. Using the CARTWHEEL, try entering relevent words into these search engines. You may be led to general discussions of your topic that can be helpful as background research.

Most of this background research will be in secondary authority—legal dictionaries, legal encyclopedias, legal treatises, legal periodical literature, etc. Use these materials for the limited purposes of (1) doing background reading and (2) providing leads to primary authority—particularly through footnotes. You will not have time to use all of the 10 techniques of background research presented in exhibit 11.18. Usually, one or two of the techniques are sufficient for the limited purpose of providing an overview and getting you started.

Exhibit 11.19 illustrates the kind of information you should be able to derive from background research.

### Assignment 11.13

Fill out the checklist in exhibit 11.19 for the following research questions. Assume that the individuals involved in each of these questions live in your state.

(a) Can a woman agree to bear the child of another woman using in vitro fertilization?

(b) Can a doctor assist a patient to commit suicide?

(c) Can someone sell pornography on the internet?

(d) Can a church be forced to pay taxes on profits from its bingo games?

| EXHIBIT 11.19 | Checklist of Information to Try to Obtain Through Background Research |
|---|---|

**MAJOR AREAS OF LAW THAT MAY BE INVOLVED IN THE RESEARCH PROBLEM**
**(circle those that preliminarily seem applicable)**

| | | | |
|---|---|---|---|
| antitrust | criminal law | international | sports |
| bankruptcy | employment | labor relations | taxation |
| children | environment | landlord-tenant | torts |
| civil procedure | estates and probate | military | trademarks |
| civil rights | ethics | municipalities | transportation |
| commercial | evidence | partnership | women |
| communications | family | patents | other |
| constitutional law | fraud | public benefits | |
| consumer | gifts | real estate | |
| contracts | health | sales | |
| copyright | immigration | sea | |
| corporations | insurance | securities | |

---

JURISDICTIONS THAT MAY NEED TO BE CHECKED
(circle those that preliminarily seem applicable)

| Federal | State | Local | International |
|---|---|---|---|

---

PRIMARY AUTHORITY THAT MAY NEED TO BE CHECKED
(circle those that preliminarily seem applicable; see Exhibit 6.1 in chapter 6)

| | | |
|---|---|---|
| opinions | administrative decisions | executive orders |
| statutes | charters | treaties |
| constitutions | ordinances | |
| administrative regulations | rules of court | |

---

MAJOR CAUSES OF ACTION AND DEFENSES THAT NEED TO BE EXPLORED

---

MAJOR TERMS OF ART THAT APPEAR TO BE CRITICAL AND THAT NEED TO BE DEFINED

---

CITATIONS TO MAJOR STATUTES THAT MIGHT BE APPLICABLE

---

CITATIONS TO MAJOR ADMINISTRATIVE REGULATIONS THAT MIGHT BE APPLICABLE

---

CITATIONS TO MAJOR COURT OPINIONS THAT MIGHT BE APPLICABLE

## Section O
# CHECKLISTS FOR USING NINE MAJOR SEARCH RESOURCES

We have said that the main objective of legal research is to locate mandatory primary authority. There are three levels of government—federal, state, and local. Exhibit 11.20 presents an overview of their primary authority.

| EXHIBIT 11.20 | Kinds of Primary Authority |

| FEDERAL LEVEL OF GOVERNMENT | STATE LEVEL OF GOVERNMENT | LOCAL LEVEL OF GOVERNMENT (CITY, COUNTY, ETC.) |
| --- | --- | --- |
| U.S. Constitution | State constitution | Charter |
| Statutes of Congress | State statutes | Local ordinances |
| Federal court opinions | State court opinions | Local court opinions |
| Federal administrative regulations | State administrative regulations | Local administrative regulations |
| Federal administrative decisions | State administrative decisions | Local administrative decisions |
| Federal rules of court | State rules of court | Local rules of court |
| Executive orders of the president | Executive orders of the governor | Executive orders of the mayor |
| Treaties | | |

For definitions of these primary authorities (constitution, statute, opinion, etc.), see exhibit 6.1 in chapter 6.

How do you find the law outlined in exhibit 11.20? The main ways are to use the following search resources or tools:

- Catalogs
- Digests
- Annotations
- Shepard's
- Loose-leaf services
- Legal periodical literature
- Legal encyclopedias
- Legal treatises
- Phone and mail

A tenth resource is the computer. In the remainder of the chapter, we will continue to refer to research that can be performed on the Internet and on commercial services such as Westlaw and LEXIS. Most of our computer coverage, however, will occur in chapter 13 on computers in the law.

Because the nine search resources can often be used to find more than one category of primary authority, they are presented together here in section O. Later in the chapter, we will be referring back to this section often. In short, the search resources are extremely important. Indeed, they can be considered the foundation of legal research itself.

### TOPICS FOR SECTION O ASSIGNMENTS 11.14 TO 11.23

The following topics will be used for the assignments in section O. You will be referred back to these topics throughout our study of the nine search resources covered in this section. In each assignment, you are to assume that your legal research problem involves the topic indicated in (a) to (o) below. Use the CARTWHEEL to help you locate material in whatever search resources the assignment is asking you to check.

For these assignments, your instructor may require you to do all of the topics (a to o) or selected ones.

### TOPICS

(a) A local government uses its zoning laws to try to close a bar that features topless dancers.
(b) A minor daughter challenges the validity of a deceased parent's will that leaves everything to the parent's pet cat.

**(c)** A newspaper falsely prints that an individual had been convicted of child molestation.

**(d)** A client is angry at his attorney for revealing to the police that the client fantasized about killing the president of the United States.

**(e)** A civil suit against a homeowner is brought by a burglar for injuries received when the burglar fell because of a defective floor in the house being burglarized.

**(f)** A high school teacher is disciplined for using a Scientology workbook in class.

**(g)** A husband is arrested after his wife accuses him of raping her.

**(h)** A father wants to revoke the adoption of a child he did not know existed at the time of the adoption; the mother told him the baby died in childbirth.

**(i)** A man sues to prevent an abortion from being performed on the woman he impregnated; the woman is a mentally retarded, unmarried adult living with her parents, who are arranging the abortion.

**(j)** A lesbian sues the Girl Scouts organization that turned down her application to be a volunteer because of her sexual orientation.

**(k)** A parent seeks to invalidate the marriage of his 13-year-old daughter who married her first cousin, also 13 years old.

**(l)** A paralegal is charged with insider trading after buying stock in a company that is a client in the law firm where the paralegal works.

**(m)** A patient wants to prevent his doctor from telling an insurance company about the patient's AIDS status.

**(n)** A person wants to cancel a contract to buy a house because the seller failed to disclose that there had recently been a murder in the house.

**(o)** A patient is scheduled for surgery where her right arm is to be amputated; by mistake, the surgeon amputates the left arm.

## 1. CATALOGS

A well-organized catalog is one of the researcher's best friends. If the law library has not switched over to a completely computerized catalog, you need to learn some of the basics of the manual card catalog. Most law libraries use the *Library of Congress (LC) classification system*. Under this system, many law books have KF call numbers. Here is an example of a card from a card catalog:

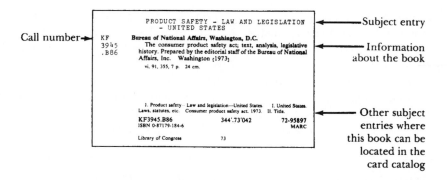

Most law libraries have open stacks, meaning that users are free to browse through all or some of the shelves. Take advantage of this opportunity when it exists. Go to the KF section to do some browsing. Here are some examples of topics (with their beginning KF call numbers) that you might want to explore to find out what your library has available on the shelves:

| | |
|---|---|
| Civil Procedure Law: KF 8810 | Marital Relations: KF 501 |
| Constitutional Law: KF 4501 | Paralegals: KF 320L |
| Corporate Law: KF 1384 | Real Property Law: KF 560 |
| Criminal Law: KF 9201 | Tort Law: KF 1246 |
| Ethics: KF 300 | Trials: KF 8910 |
| Lawyers: KF 297 | Wills and Trusts: KF 728 |

Exhibit 11.21 Presents guidelines on using the catalog effectively.

| EXHIBIT 11.21 | Checklist for Using the Catalog |
|---|---|

1. Find out what kind of catalog your library uses. A card (paper) catalog? Microfiche? Computer? Locate the description of how to use the catalog. (The how-to material for computerized catalogs may be online or available through a HELP key on the keyboard.) If the library still uses the card catalog, there may be more than one available. For example, one set of cards may alphabetize all books by author name, while another may be separately alphabetized by book title.

2. Select several entries from the catalog at random. Pick ones that appear to contain different kinds of information. Try to figure out why they are different. If you can't, ask a staff member of the library to briefly explain the differences.

3. Be sure you understand the information in the catalog that tells you where the books are located in the library. Some books may be on reserve, in special rooms, or in other buildings.

4. Select several KF entries at random, particularly on books housed in different locations within the same building. Try to find these books on the shelves. Ask for help if you cannot locate them.

5. Now try the reverse process. Select at random three different kinds of books from the library shelves (not the same books you looked at in step 4 above). Take these books to the catalog and try to find the entries for them. Your goal is to become as proficient in the structure and use of the catalog as possible. Steps 2–5 are designed to help you achieve this goal *before* you experience the pressure of actual research.

6. Ask a staff member what kinds of research material, if any, are *not* cataloged, such as microfilm, ultrafiche, appellate briefs, or old exams.

7. Ask a staff member what special lists of law books, if any, are in the library, such as a list of legal periodicals or a list of reserve books. These lists may be in notebooks on special tables or in folding "pages" attached to the wall.

8. Ask whether the library can obtain books for you at other libraries through interlibrary loan.

9. Some law books received by the library are serial subscriptions, e.g., a legal periodical, a loose-leaf service. The subscription can include units such as pocket parts, supplemental pamphlets, insert pages, and new hardcover volumes received throughout the year. When you use the library's catalog, are you told what is the most recent unit of the subscription received by the library? (Check any serial subscription at random.) If not, ask a librarian how you can find out. (Simply looking at what is on the shelf may not tell you since the latest unit may have been misshelved or may be in use.)

10. When using any catalog, the CARTWHEEL will help you think of words and phrases to check.

11. Never antagonize the employees of a law library. You are going to need all the help you can get! Do not abuse their availability. Do not ask any questions until you first try to find the answer on your own.

*Assignment 11.14*

Use the catalog of a law library to find the call number (e.g., a KF number) of one law book that might be helpful in researching each of the topics for the section O assignments (see page 549). Most of the law books you will select will be legal treatises or loose-leaf services, but you are not limited to these categories of books. You can use any law book so long as you locate it through the catalog. Pick one per topic. Give the citation of each book and place a check mark next to the citation to indicate that you were able to locate the book on the shelves of the library. (If you can't locate the book, pick a different one from the catalog.) If the title of the book you select does not indicate that the book probably covers the topic, give the heading of a chapter, section, or page in the book showing that the topic is probably covered in the book. At the top of your answer sheet, give the name and address of the law library you used.

## 2. DIGESTS

We have already examined the major digests and the names of reporters whose opinions are summarized (in small paragraphs) in the digests. You should review this material now. See exhibit 11.6. See also research links A, E, I, J, and L in section H on the relationship between regional reporters and regional digests.

Our focus here is on the digests of West Group. The thousands of opinions summarized in these digests are organized by the key number system. Every important issue examined in an opinion is summarized in a small paragraph (called a headnote) and assigned a topic and number (called a key number) by West Group editors. As we will see, these paragraphs are printed in several places, such as in the digests of West Group. Paragraphs with the same key number are printed together in the digests. This enables a researcher to find numerous opinions on the same point of law. For example, West Group assigns Searches & Seizures ☞ 81 to the topic of invalid warrants. You can go to any West Group digest, take down the "S" volume, find Searches & Seizures, and turn to number 81 to try to find a potentially large number of different opinions that covered this issue.

The beauty of the West Group digests is that once you know how to use one of the digests, you know how to use them all. To demonstrate this, we begin by following the journey of a court opinion (and its headnotes) from the time the opinion arrives at West Group. (See exhibit 11.22.)

Keep the following points in mind about exhibit 11.22:

■ The state court opinions printed in West Group's reporters from the other 49 states go through the process or journey outlined in the *first* column of exhibit 11.22 for California. Of course, different states have their own reporters and digests (see exhibit 11.6), but the process is the same.
■ All U.S. District Court opinions printed in *Federal Supplement* (F. Supp. 2d) go through the process or journey outlined in the *second* column of exhibit 11.22.
■ All U.S. Supreme Court opinions printed in *Supreme Court Reporter* (S. Ct.) go through the process or journey outlined in the *second* column of exhibit 11.22. (For additional digests that summarize all U.S. Supreme Court opinions, see exhibit 11.6.)

---

| EXHIBIT 11.22 | Journey of a Court Opinion and Its Headnotes |
|---|---|

**JOURNEY OF A STATE COURT OPINION, e.g., CALIFORNIA**

1. The California Supreme Court sends a copy of its opinion to West Group in Minnesota.
2. West Group editors write brief paragraph *headnotes* for the opinion. Each headnote is a summary of a portion of the opinion.
3. The headnotes are printed at the beginning of the full text of the opinion in the reporter—here, the *Pacific Reporter 2d* (P.2d). The editors assign each of these headnotes a key number, which consists of a topic and a number, e.g., Criminal Law ☞ 1064(5).
4. In addition to being printed at the beginning of the opinion in P.2d, the headnotes will also be printed at the beginning of the advance sheet for P.2d that contains the opinion and in the back of the bound P.2d volume that contains the opinion.
5. This headnote is also printed in the appropriate digests of West Group. The above example will go in the "C" volume of these digests where "Criminal Law" is covered. The headnote will be placed under key number 1064(5) of Criminal Law, along with summaries of other opinions on the same or similar areas of law. In what digests will such headnotes from a

**JOURNEY OF A FEDERAL COURT OPINION, e.g., A U.S. COURT OF APPEALS**

1. The U.S. Court of Appeals sends a copy of its opinion to West Group in Minnesota.
2. West Group editors write brief paragraph *headnotes* for the opinion. Each headnote is a summary of a portion of the opinion.
3. The headnotes are printed at the beginning of the full text of the opinion in the reporter—here, the *Federal Reporter 3d* (F.3d). The editors assign each of these headnotes a key number, which consists of a topic and a number, e.g., Appeal and Error ☞ 336.1.
4. In addition to being printed at the beginning of the opinion in F.3d, the headnotes will also be printed at the beginning of the advance sheet for F.3d that contains the opinion and in the back of the bound F.3d volume that contains the opinion.
5. This headnote is also printed in the appropriate digests of West Group. The above example will go in the "A" volume of these digests where "Appeal and Error" is covered. The headnote will be placed under key number 336.1 of Appeal and Error, along with summaries of other opinions on the same or similar areas of law. In what digests will such headnotes from

| EXHIBIT 11.22 | Journey of a Court Opinion and its Headnotes—*continued* |

**JOURNEY OF A STATE COURT OPINION, e.g., CALIFORNIA**

recent California opinion be printed? The list follows:

- All headnotes of P.2d cases go into the American Digest System. First, the headnote goes into a *General Digest* volume. After a ten-year period (in two five-year intervals), all the *General Digests* are thrown away, with the material in them printed in the next *Decennial Digest*.
- All headnotes of P.2d cases are also printed in its regional digest—the *Pacific Digest*.
- All headnotes of California cases in P.2d are also printed in the individual state digest—the *California Digest*.

6. Hence, the headnote from the opinion of the California Supreme Court will be printed:

- at the beginning of the P.2d advance sheet containing the opinion.
- at the beginning of the opinion in P.2d.
- at the end of the P.2d volume containing the opinion.
- in the American Digest System (first in the *General Digest* and then in the *Decennial Digest*).
- in the regional digest—*Pacific Digest*.
- in the individual state digest—*California Digest*.

In all the above digests, the headnote will be printed in the "C" volume for Criminal Law under number 1064(5), along with headnotes from other opinions on the same or similar area of the law.

7. Finally, West Group publishes all of these opinions and headnotes on Westlaw, its computer research system. (See research link F on the need to translate a digest key number into a Westlaw k number so that you can find cases digested online under the same topics.)

**JOURNEY OF A FEDERAL COURT OPINION, e.g., A U.S. COURT OF APPEALS**

a recent F.3d opinion be printed? The list follows:

- All headnotes of F.3d cases go into the American Digest System. First, the headnote goes into a *General Digest* volume. After a ten-year period (in two five-year intervals), all the *General Digests* are thrown away with the material in them printed in the next *Decennial Digest*.
- All headnotes of F.3d cases are also printed in the most current federal digest—the *Federal Practice Digest 4th*.
- If our F.3d case dealt with a particular state, the headnotes of the F.3d case will also be printed in the individual state digest of that state.

6. Hence, the headnote from the opinion of the U.S. Court of Appeals will be printed:

- at the beginning of the F.3d advance sheet containing the opinion.
- at the beginning of the opinion in F.3d.
- at the end of the F.3d volume containing the opinion.
- in the American Digest System (first in the *General Digest* and then in the *Decennial Digest*).
- in the *Federal Practice Digest 4th*.
- in a state digest if the F.3d case dealt with a particular state.

In all the above digests, the headnote will be printed in the "A" volume for Appeal and Error under number 336.1, along with headnotes from other opinions on the same or similar area of the law.

7. Finally, West Group publishes all of these opinions and headnotes on Westlaw, its computer research system. (See research link F in on the need to translate a digest key number into a Westlaw k number so that you can find cases digested online under the same topics.)

Assume that you are doing research on the right of a citizen to speak in a public park. You find that West Group's digests cover this subject under the following key number:

Constitutional Law ☞ 211

West Group publishes about 60 digests—state, federal, and national. (See exhibit 11.6.) You can go to the "C" volume of *any* of these 60 digests, turn to "Constitutional Law," and look for number "211" under it. Do you want only Idaho case law? If so, go to Constitutional Law ☞ 211 in the *Idaho Digest*. Do you want only case law from the states in the western

United States? If so, go to Constitutional Law ☞ 211 in the *Pacific Digest*. Do you want only current federal case law? If so, go to Constitutional Law ☞ 211 in the *Federal Practice Digest 4th*. Do you want only U.S. Supreme Court cases? If so, go to Constitutional Law ☞ 211 in the *U.S. Supreme Court Digest* (West Group).

Do you want the case law of *every* court in the country? If so, trace Constitutional Law ☞ 211 through the three units of the American Digest System:

- Go to Constitutional Law ☞ 211 in every *General Digest* volume.
- Go to Constitutional Law ☞ 211 in every *Decennial Digest*.
- Go to the equivalent number for Constitutional Law ☞ 211 in the *Century Digest*.

To **trace a key number** through the American Digest System means to find out what case law, if any, is summarized under its topic and number in every unit of the American Digest System. (For the *Century Digest*, you will need an equivalent number because there are no key numbers in the *Century Digest*. See step 8 in the checklist in exhibit 11.23).

---

| EXHIBIT 11.23 | Checklist for Using the Digests of West Group |
|---|---|

1. Locate the right digests for your research problem. This is determined by identifying the kind of case law you want to find. State? Federal? Both? Review figure 11.6 on the American Digest System, the four regional digests, the major federal digests, the two digests for U.S. Supreme Court cases (only one of which is a West Group digest), and the individual state digests. You must know what kind of case law is summarized in each of these digests.

2. Find key numbers that cover your research problem. There are hundreds of topics and subtopics in West's digests. How do you find the ones relevant to your research problem? There are eight techniques:

- Descriptive Word Index (DWI). Every digest has a **DWI**. Use the CARTWHEEL to help you locate key topics in the DWI.

- Table of Contents. There are over 400 main digest topics (e.g., Constitutional Law, Criminal Law), which are covered throughout the volumes of the digest you are using. At the beginning of each main topic, you will find a table of contents. If you can find one of these main topics in the general area of your research, you then use its table of contents to locate specific key numbers. These tables of contents have different names: "*Scope Note*," "*Analysis*," or "*Subjects Included*." Use the CARTWHEEL to help you locate key numbers in them.

- Headnote in West Group Reporter. Suppose that you already have an opinion on point. You are reading its full text in a West Group reporter. Go to the most relevant headnotes at the beginning of this opinion. (For example, see the husband-and-wife and negligence headnotes at the beginning of the *Self* opinion in exhibit 11.28, later in this chapter, and the search and seizure headnotes at the beginning of the *Bruni* opinion in chapter 7.) Each headnote has a key number. Use this key number to go to any of the digests to try to find more case law under that number.

- Table of Cases in the Digests. Suppose again that you already have an opinion on point. You are reading its full text in a West Group reporter. Go to the table of cases in the American Digest System or in any other digest that covers the reporter your opinion is in. Look up the name of the opinion in this table of cases. (If you can't find it, check this table in the pocket part of the volume you are using. Not all digest volumes, however, have pocket parts.) If you find your opinion in the table, you will be told what key numbers that opinion is digested under in the digest. Go to those key numbers in the body of the digest to find that opinion summarized, along with other opinions under the same key numbers. (Note: the table of cases in some West Group digests is called *plaintiff-defendant table* or *defendant-plaintiff table*, depending on which party's name comes first. The defendant-plaintiff table is useful if you happen to know only the name of the defendant or if you want many opinions where the same party was sued, e.g., General Motors. Defendant-plaintiff tables usually refer you back to the plaintiff-defendant table, where the key numbers are listed.)

- Library References in a West Group Statutory Code. After West Group prints the full text of statutes in the statutory codes it publishes, it also provides research references, such as historical note, cross references, library references, and notes of decisions. The library references give you key numbers on topics covered in the statutes. For an example, see

EXHIBIT 11.23    Checklist for Using the Digests of West Group—*continued*

exhibit 11.44 containing an excerpt from a statutory code (§ 146). After the text of the statute, there are library references to two key numbers: Prisons 13, and Reformatories 7. Hence a West Group statutory code has given you a lead to a key number, which you can take to any of the West Group digests to find case law.

- Leads in Legal Encyclopedias. Both of the national legal encyclopedias, *Corpus Juris Secundum* (C.J.S.) and *American Jurisprudence 2d* (Am. Jur. 2d), will include leads to key numbers of West Group digests on those topics.
- Leads in A.L.R. Annotations. Recent volumes of *American Law Reports 5th* and *American Law Reports Fed.* will give you leads to key numbers as part of the annotations in these volumes.
- Westlaw. One of the searches you can make on Westlaw is a digest field search, which will give you almost instant access to the millions of headnotes printed in West Group digests. (See research link F on the need to translate a digest key number into a Westlaw k number.)

3. Assume that while using the Descriptive Word Index (DWI) in any of the digests, you come across a key number that appears to be relevant to your research problem. But when you go to check that number in the body of the digest, you find no case law. The DWI has, in effect, led you to nonexistent case law. The editors are telling you that there are no cases digested under this key number *at this time*. Go to the table of contents for the main topic you are in. Check the "Analysis" or "Scope Note" there to see if you can find a more productive key number. Or, go to a different digest to see if you will have more luck with your original key number.

4. West Group editors occasionally add new topics and numbers to the key number system. Hence you may find topics and numbers in later digest volumes that are not in earlier digest volumes.

5. West Group digests obviously duplicate each other in some respects. The American Digest System, for example, contains everything that is in all the other digests. A regional digest will duplicate everything found in the individual state digests covered in that region. (See the chart in exhibit 11.6.) It is wise, nevertheless, to check more than one digest. Some digests may be more up to date than others in your library. You may miss something in one digest that you will catch in another.

6. Be sure you know all the units of the most comprehensive digest—the American Digest System: *Century Digest, Decennial Digests, General Digest*. These units are distinguished solely by the period of time covered by each unit. Know what these periods of time are: *Century Digest* (1658–1896), *Decennial Digests* (10-year periods, although since the *Ninth Decennial* they come in two 5-year parts), *General Digest* (the period since the last *Decennial Digest* was printed).

7. At the time the *Century Digest* was printed, West Group had not invented the key number system. Hence topics are listed in the *Century Digest* by *section* numbers rather than by key numbers. Assume that you started your research in the *Century Digest*. You located a relevant section number and you now want to trace this number through the *Decennial Digests* and the *General Digest*. To do this, you need a corresponding *key* number. There is a parallel table in volume 21 of the *First Decennial* that will tell you the corresponding key number for any section number in the *Century Digest*. Suppose, however, that you started your research in the *Decennial Digests* or the *General Digest*. You have a key number and now want to find its corresponding section number in the *Century Digest*. In the *First Decennial* and *Second Decennial*, there is a "see" reference under the key number that will tell you the corresponding section number in the *Century Digest*.

8. Tricks of the trade are also needed in using the *General Digest*, which covers the most recent period since the last *Decennial Digest* was printed. When the current 10-year period is over, all the *General Digest* volumes will be thrown away. The material in them will be consolidated or cumulated into the next *Decennial Digest* (which is issued in two 5-year parts beginning with the *Ninth Decennial*). When you go to use the *General Digest*, there may be 20 to 30 bound volumes on the shelf. To be thorough in tracing a key number in the *General Digest*, you must check *all* these bound volumes. There is, however, a shortcut. Look for the *Table of Key Numbers* within every 10th volume of the *General Digest*. This table tells you which *General Digest* volumes contain anything under the key number you are searching. You do not have to check the other nine *General Digest* volumes.

One final point: The headnotes and digests we are discussing are written by a private publishing company—West Group. You never quote headnotes or digests in your legal writing. They *cannot* be authority—primary or secondary. They are mere leads to case law.

---

### Assignment 11.15

Go to any West Group digest that covers cases of your state courts. (See exhibit 11.6) Find any two key numbers that might be helpful in researching each of the topics for the section O assignments (see page 549). Pick two per topic. Under both key numbers, find a case written by a state court in your state or by a federal court that sits in your state. If you cannot find a case written by such a court in either of the key numbers, select a different key number until you are able to find one. Give the key number, the citation of the case, and a statement of why you think the case might cover the problem. Also specify which digest you used.

---

### 3. ANNOTATIONS

An annotation is a set of notes or commentary on something. It is, in effect, a research paper. The most extensive annotations are those of West Group in the following six sets of books:

A.L.R. (A.L.R.1st)                   A.L.R.4th
*American Law Reports, First*         *American Law Reports, Fourth*
A.L.R.2d                             A.L.R.5th
*American Law Reports, Second*        *American Law Reports, Fifth*
A.L.R.3d                             A.L.R. Fed.
*American Law Reports, Third*         *American Law Reports, Federal*

All six sets are reporters in that they print opinions in full. They are *annotated reporters* in that notes or commentaries are provided with each opinion in the form of an annotation. Unlike the regional reporters of West Group, the annotated reporters contain only a small number of opinions. The editors select opinions raising novel or interesting issues, which then become the basis of an annotation. The following is an example of the beginning of an annotation found on page 1015 of Volume 91 of A.L.R.3d:

One of the joys of legal research is finding an annotation on point. A wealth of information is contained in annotations, such as a comprehensive, state-by-state survey of law on an issue. A single annotation often contains hundreds of citations to court opinions. Picture yourself having the capacity to hire your own team of researchers to go out and spend days finding just about all the case law that exists on a particular point of law. Though none of us is likely to have this luxury, we do have a close equivalent in the form of annotations in the six sets of *American Law Reports*. They are a gold mine of research references. There are hundreds of volumes in these six sets, so the chances are very good that you will find an annotation that is *on point*, i.e., that covers the issues of your research problem.

Most of the references in the annotations are to case law. Their primary service, therefore, is to act as a case finder. Because of this, the annotation system of Lawyers Co-op. is the major competitor of the other massive case finders—the digests of West Group. The competition has led to a rich source of material at our disposal. (The competition is expected to continue even though Lawyers Co-op. is now part of West Group.)

The annotations cover both federal and state law. A.L.R.1st, A.L.R.2d, and most of A.L.R.3d cover both state and federal law. The later volumes of A.L.R.3d and all of A.L.R.4th and A.L.R.5th cover mainly state law. A.L.R. Fed. covers only federal law. The annotations in these six sets do not follow any particular order. There may be an annotation on zoning, for example, followed by an annotation on defective wheels on baby carriages. The annotations in A.L.R.1st and A.L.R.2d are older than the annotations in the other sets, but this is not significant because all of the annotations can be updated.

We turn now to the two major concerns of the researcher:

- How do you find an annotation on point?
- How do you update an annotation that you have found?

As you will see, it is much easier to find and update annotations in A.L.R.3d, A.L.R.4th, A.L.R.5th, and A.L.R.Fed. than in the earlier A.L.R.1st and A.L.R.2d. This is not a major concern, however; the latter two sets are used fairly infrequently today because of the age of the annotations in them, even though these annotations can be updated to current law.

### Finding an Annotation on Point

The major ways of finding annotations on point are outlined in exhibit 11.24. These methods are most useful when you are at the very beginning of your search and have no leads. As you can see in exhibit 11.24, the six sets of A.L.R. do not have the same index system: the multivolume *ALR Index* covers all of the sets (except for A.L.R.1st), a Quick Index volume covers all of the sets (except for A.L.R.2d), and a LEXIS search or a Westlaw search will lead you to annotations in all the sets (except for A.L.R.1st). Finally, all six sets have digests that provide summaries of the annotations in them. Although more awkward to use, these digests can serve as indexes to the annotations in all the sets.

Exhibit 11.25 tells you what to do if you are further along in your research and already have an opinion (state or federal), a statute (state or federal), or a regulation (federal) that is on point, or potentially on point. Use the methods listed in the second column of exhibit 11.25 to try to find any annotations that discuss or mention that opinion, statute, or regulation.

Annotations are one of the "citing materials" in Shepard's. This simply means that the annotations have discussed or mentioned whatever you are shepardizing. Hence, if you shepardize the items in the first column of exhibit 11.25, you will be led to all annotations, if any, that have mentioned that item. If you have access to KeyCite (available on Westlaw) or to Auto-Cite (available on LEXIS), these computer services will tell you what annotations have mentioned your federal or state court opinion. *ALR Federal Tables* will do the same for federal opinions, statutes, and regulations. Finally, use the Table of Laws, Rules, and

---

| EXHIBIT 11.24 | **Finding Annotations When You Have No Leads** |
|---|---|

| INDEX SYSTEMS FOR A.L.R.1st | INDEX SYSTEMS FOR A.L.R.2d | INDEX SYSTEMS FOR A.L.R.3d, A.L.R.4th, A.L.R.5th | INDEX SYSTEMS FOR A.L.R. Fed. |
|---|---|---|---|
| ■ *ALR First Series Quick Index*<br>■ *Permanent ALR Digest* | ■ *ALR Index*<br>■ LEXIS<br>■ Westlaw<br>■ *ALR2d Digest* | ■ *ALR Index*<br>■ *ALR Quick Index 3d, 4th, 5th*<br>■ LEXIS<br>■ Westlaw<br>■ *ALR Digest to 3d, 4th, 5th, Federal* | ■ *ALR Index*<br>■ *ALR Federal Quick Index*<br>■ LEXIS<br>■ Westlaw<br>■ *ALR Digest to 3d, 4th, 5th, Federal* |

| EXHIBIT 11.25 | Finding Annotations When You Have a Lead |
|---|---|

| IF YOU ALREADY HAVE A CITATION TO: | USE THE FOLLOWING METHODS OF FINDING ANNOTATIONS THAT MENTION THAT CITATION: |
|---|---|
| A State Court Opinion | ■ Shepardize the opinion.<br>■ Check KeyCite (on Westlaw).<br>■ Check Auto-Cite (on LEXIS). |
| A Federal Court Opinion | ■ Shepardize the opinion.<br>■ Check KeyCite (on Westlaw).<br>■ Check Auto-Cite (on LEXIS).<br>■ Check the "Table of Cases" in the separate volume called *ALR Federal Tables*. |
| A State Statute | ■ Shepardize the statute.<br>■ Check KeyCite (on Westlaw)<br>■ Check Auto-Cite (on LEXIS)<br>■ Check the "Table of Laws, Rules, and Regulations" in the last volume of *ALR Index*. |
| A Federal Statute | ■ Shepardize the statute.<br>■ Check KeyCite (on Westlaw)<br>■ Check the "Table of Laws, Rules, and Regulations" in the last volume of *ALR Index*.<br>■ Check the separate volume called *ALR Federal Tables*. |
| A Federal Regulation | ■ Shepardize the regulation.<br>■ Check KeyCite (on Westlaw)<br>■ Check the "Table of Laws, Rules, and Regulations" in the last volume of *ALR Index*.<br>■ Check the separate volume called *ALR Federal Tables*. |

Regulations to find annotations on a federal statute (in U.S.C., U.S.C.A., or U.S.C.S.) or on a federal administrative regulation (in C.F.R.). This excellent table is located in the last volume of the *ALR Index*.

As indicated earlier, some of the annotations in the six sets are very long and comprehensive. How do you find the law of a *particular* state or court within an annotation without having to read the entire annotation? At the beginning of annotations in A.L.R.3d and A.L.R.4th, you will find a Table of Jurisdictions Represented, which will direct you to specific sections of the annotation that cover the law of your state. At the beginning of annotations in A.L.R. Fed., there is a Table of Courts and Circuits, which will direct you to sections of the annotation dealing with certain federal courts. (See top of page 559.) In addition to these tables, there will usually be other indexes or tables of contents at the beginning of the annotations.

The table at the beginning of annotations in A.L.R.5th is called Jurisdictional Table of Cited Statutes and Cases. (See top of page 559.) The state-by-state breakdown in this table includes full citations to the statutes and cases discussed in the annotation.

### Updating an Annotation

Suppose that you have found an annotation on point. It has led you to very useful law. This annotation, however, may be 10, 20, 30, or more years old. How do you update this annotation to find the most current law on the points covered in the annotation? Of course, any opinion or statute found within the annotation can be shepardized or KeyCited as a technique of finding more law. But our focus here is the updating systems within A.L.R. itself. Exhibit 11.26 outlines these systems.

If the annotation you want updated is in A.L.R.1st, start with the *A.L.R. Blue Book of Supplemental Decisions*. (Check each volume of this *Blue Book* because the volumes are noncumulative.) If the annotation you want updated is in A.L.R.2d, start with the *A.L.R.2d Later*

<table>
<tr><td>

**TABLE OF JURISDICTIONS REPRESENTED**
Consult POCKET PART in this volume for later cases

US: §§ 2[b], 3, 4[a], 5[b], 6[a], 7[a], 10[b]
Ala: §§ 2[b], 4[a], 6[a], 7[a], 8, 10[b]
Cal: §§ 4[a, b], 7[a, b], 10[b], 11
Fla: §§ 5[a]
Ga: §§ 3, 4[b], 5[b], 6[b], 10[a]
Ill: §§ 4[b], 5[a, b], 6[a, b], 10[a]
Ind: §§ 4[a], 5[b], 6[a], 7[a, b], 8, 9, 10[b]
Iowa: §§ 7[a], 8
Ky: §§ 3, 4[a], 5[b]
La: §§ 5[b], 7[a, b]
Me: §§ 5[b], 7[a], 10[b]
Md: §§ 4[b]
Mich: §§ 4[a], 10[b]

Miss: §§ 4[a]
Mo: §§ 4[a], 6[a], 10[b]
NH: §§ 3, 4[b]
NC: §§ 7[a]
Ohio: §§ 4[a, b], 6[a], 7[a, b], 10[b]
Or: §§ 4[a], 10[b]
Pa: §§ 4[a], 7[a], 10[b]
Tenn: §§ 4[a], 5[b], 6[a]
Tex: §§ 4[a], 7[a], 10[b]
Vt: §§ 9
Wash: §§ 6[a], 7[a], 8
Wis: §§ 7[a], 8, 10[b], 11

</td><td>

**TABLE OF COURTS AND CIRCUITS**
Consult POCKET PART in this volume for later cases and statutory changes

Sup Ct: §§ 2[a], 3[a], 5, b, 14
First Cir: §§ 5[b], 6[b], 15[b], 16[a], 18[a]
Second Cir: §§ 2[b], 3[a, b], 5[a], 12[a], 16[a], 18[a]
Third Cir: §§ 3[a], 5[a], 7, 11[b], 12[b], 13[a], 15[b]
Fourth Cir: §§ 2[b], 3[a], 4[b], 5[a, b], 8, 9, 10[b], 12[a, b], 13[b], 14, 15[a, b], 16[a], 17, 18[a]
Fifth Cir: §§ 3[a], 5[a, b], 8, 10[a], 11[a, b], 13[a], 15[a], 16[b], 18[b]

Sixth Cir: §§ 5[b], 6[b], 10[a, b], 12[a], 13[a], 15[b]
Seventh Cir: §§ 2[a], 4[b], 5[b], 10[b], 15[b]
Eighth Cir: §§ 3[a], 4[a, b], 5[a, b], 6[a], 12[a], 13[a], 15[b], 16[a], 17, 19
Ninth Cir: §§ 2[a, b], 3[a], 4[a], 5, a, 6[b], 7, 8, 10[a], 11[a, b], 12[a, b], 13[a, b], 15[a, b], 16[b], 17, 18[a, b]
Tenth Cir: §§ 2[b], 3[a], 5[a, b], 6[a, b], 9, 11[a, b], 12[a], 14, 17, 18[b]
Dist Col Cir: §§ 3[b], 5[b], 6[b], 10[a, b]
Ct Cl: § 16[a]

</td></tr>
</table>

---

### Jurisdictional Table of Cited Statutes and Cases

#### ALABAMA

A R Civ P, Rule 60(a). See §§ 4[a], 14[a]
Alabama R Civ P, Rule 60(a). See § 5[b]
Antepenko v Antepenko (1991, Ala Civ App) 584 So 2d 836—§ 4[a]
Cornelius v Green (1988, Ala) 521 So 2d 942—§ 5[b]
Merchant v Merchant (1992, Ala Civ App) 599 So 2d 1198—§ 14[a]

#### ARIZONA

16 A R S R Civ P, Rule 60(a). See § 10[b]
Harold Laz Advertising Co. v Dumes (1965) 2 Ariz App 236, 407 P2d 777—§ 10[b]

#### CALIFORNIA

Cal Code Civ Proc § 473. See §§ 6[a, b], 7[b], 10[a]
Cal Code Civ Proc § 579. See § 10[a]
Bastajian v Brown (1941) 19 Cal 2d 209, 120 P2d 9—§ 10[a]
Benway v Benway (1945) 69 Cal App 2d 574, 159 P2d 682—§ 4[a]

---

*Case Service.* (Check the volume that covers your annotation, plus the pocket part of this volume of the *Later Case Service.*) If the annotation you want updated is in A.L.R.3d, or in A.L.R.4th, or in A.L.R.5th, or in A.L.R. Fed., you check the pocket part of the volume containing the annotation.

There are no pocket parts to the volumes of A.L.R.1st and A.L.R.2d. Hence you must use the *Blue Book* and *Later Case Service* in order to perform needed updating. Thankfully, the volumes of A.L.R.3d, A.L.R.4th, A.L.R.5th, and A.L.R. Fed. *do* have pocket parts that can be used to update annotations in them. The existence of these pocket parts makes it much easier to update annotations in A.L.R.3d, A.L.R.4th, A.L.R.5th, and A.L.R. Fed. than to update annotations in A.L.R.1st or A.L.R.2d.

---

**EXHIBIT 11.26    How to Update an Annotation**

**UPDATING AN ANNOTATION IN A.L.R.1st**

- *A.L.R. Blue Book of Supplemental Decisions*
- Annotation History Table in the last volume of *ALR Index*

**UPDATING AN ANNOTATION IN A.L.R.2d**

- *A.L.R.2d Later Case Service*
- Annotation History Table in the last volume of *ALR Index*

**UPDATING AN ANNOTATION IN A.L.R.3d, A.L.R.4th, A.L.R.5th, AND A.L.R. Fed.**

- Pocket part of volume containing the annotation
- Annotation History Table in the last volume of *ALR Index*

Note: Any opinion or statute you find in an annotation can also be updated by shepardizing or KeyCiting that opinion or statute.

Of course, if you are reading an annotation online through Westlaw or LEXIS, you are automatically given the most current cases for the annotation. You do not have to check more than one computer screen to obtain the most updated version of the annotation.

One final updating feature must be covered: the Annotation History Table. Note that exhibit 11.26 lists this table as a further method of updating annotations in all six sets of A.L.R. The law in some annotations may become so outdated that it is replaced by another annotation. The outdated annotation is called a *superseded annotation*, which should no longer be read. If, however, an annotation is substantially updated but not totally replaced by another annotation, the older annotation is called a *supplemented annotation* which can be read along with the newer annotation. There are two ways to find out which annotations have been superseded or supplemented. Check the Annotation History Table found in the last volume of the *ALR Index*. Another way to find out is to check the standard method for updating annotations in A.L.R.1st (the *Blue Book*), in A.L.R.2d (*Later Case Service*), in A.L.R.3d (pocket parts), in A.L.R.4th (pocket parts), in A.L.R.5th (pocket parts), and in A.L.R. Fed. (pocket parts).

The techniques of finding and updating annotations are summarized in exhibit 11.27.

---

**EXHIBIT 11.27    Checklist for Finding and Updating Annotations**

1. Your goal is to use the six sets to find annotations on your research problem. The annotations are extensive research papers on numerous points of law.
2. The most current annotations available are in A.L.R.3d, in A.L.R.4th, in A.L.R.5th, and in A.L.R. Fed. Start with these sets. Then try to find annotations in A.L.R.2d and in A.L.R.1st. Use the CARTWHEEL to help you locate annotations in the following index resources:
   (a) To find annotations in A.L.R.3d, in A.L.R.4th, and in A.L.R.5th:
      - Use *ALR Index*
      - Use *ALR Quick Index 3d, 4th, 5th*
      - Use LEXIS or Westlaw
      - Use *ALR Digest to 3d, 4th, 5th, Federal*
   (b) To find annotations in A.L.R. Fed.:
      - Use *ALR Index*
      - Use *ALR Federal Quick Index*
      - Use LEXIS or Westlaw
      - Use *ALR Digest to 3d, 4th, 5th, Federal*
   (c) To find annotations in A.L.R.2d:
      - Use *ALR Index*
      - Use LEXIS or Westlaw
      - Use *ALR2d Digest*
   (d) To find annotations in A.L.R.1st:
      - Use *ALR First Series Quick Index*
      - Use *Permanent ALR Digest*
3. If you have already found a particular law (see list below) and you want to know if there is an annotation that mentions that law, check the following resources:
   (a) If you already have a state court opinion:
      - Shepardize the opinion
      - Check KeyCite (on Westlaw)
      - Check Auto-Cite (on LEXIS)

   (b) If you already have a federal court opinion:
      - Shepardize the opinion
      - Check KeyCite (on Westlaw)
      - Check Auto-Cite (on LEXIS)
      - Check the Table of Cases in *ALR Federal Tables*
   (c) If you already have a state statute:
      - Shepardize the statute
      - Check KeyCite (on Westlaw)
      - Check Auto-Cite (on LEXIS)
      - Check the Table of Laws, Rules, and Regulations in the last volume of *ALR Index*.
   (d) If you already have a federal statute:
      - Shepardize the statute
      - Check KeyCite (on Westlaw)
      - Check the Table of Laws, Rules, and Regulations in the last volume of *ALR Index*
      - Check *ALR Federal Tables*
   (e) If you already have a federal administrative regulation:
      - Shepardize the regulation
      - Check KeyCite (on Westlaw)
      - Check the Table of Laws, Rules, and Regulations in the last volume of *ALR Index*
      - Check *ALR Federal Tables*
4. Use the tables or other indexes at the beginning of the annotation to help you locate specific sections of the annotation. Section 1[a] of the annotation will give you the *scope* covered in the annotation. (Before you spend much time with the annotation, however, check the "Annotation History Table" to determine if it has been superseded or supplemented by another annotation. See step 6 below.)
5. Section 1[b] of the annotation may provide citations to related annotations and materials that

| EXHIBIT 11.27 | Checklist for Finding and Updating Annotations—*continued* |
|---|---|

you may want to check. In § 1[b] you might find a reference to annotations that are more relevant than (or as relevant as) the annotation you are about to examine.

6. Update all annotations that are on point.
   (a) To update an annotation in A.L.R.1st:
      ■ Check the *A.L.R. Blue Book of Supplemental Decisions*
      ■ Check the Annotation History Table in the last volume of *ALR Index*
   (b) To update an annotation in A.L.R.2d:
      ■ Check the *A.L.R.2d Later Case Service*
      ■ Check the Annotation History Table in the last volume of *ALR Index*

   (c) To update an annotation in A.L.R.3d, in A.L.R.4th, in A.L.R.5th, or in A.L.R. Fed.:
      ■ Check the pocket part
      ■ Check the Annotation History Table in the last volume of *ALR Index*

7. Within the six sets of annotations, *Lawyers Co-op.* will give you lists of its other publications (e.g., Am. Jur. 2d) that cover the same or similar topics in its annotations. The main vehicle used to provide these leads is the list called Total Client-Service Library References.

---

### Assignment 11.16

Find one annotation that might be helpful in researching each of the topics for the section O assignments (see page 549). Locate one per topic. In each annotation, find a case written by a state court of your state or by a federal court that sits in your state. If you cannot find a case written by such a court, select a different annotation that does contain one. Give the citation of the annotation and of the case that it cites.

---

### 4. SHEPARD'S

There have been four great research inventions in the law:

■ The key number system of the West Group digests
■ The annotations in A.L.R. (A.L.R.1st), A.L.R.2d, A.L.R.3d, A.L.R.4th, A.L.R.5th, and A.L.R. Fed
■ CALR (computer-assisted legal research), particularly Westlaw and LEXIS
■ Shepard's

We have just examined the first two. CALR is covered here in chapter 11 but primarily in chapter 13. We turn now to the fourth invention—Shepard's.

### Shepardize

The main meaning of the verb shepardize is to use the volumes (or CD–ROM or on-line version) of *Shepard's Citations* to obtain validation and other data on the primary authority you are checking. (You can also shepardize some secondary authorities, such as legal periodical articles, although this is not as common as shepardizing primary authority.) When you shepardize opinions, statutes, and other primary authorities, Shepard's will help you answer questions such as the following:

■ Is this opinion that I just found still good law? Is it still valid? Have other courts followed it or rejected it?
■ How can I find other opinions like it?
■ Is this statute that I found still good law? Is it still valid? Has it been changed by the legislature? How have the courts interpreted it?

Before we examine how Shepard's provides you with this kind of information, review exhibit 11.8 in section H, containing photographs of the major items that can be shepardized.

Shepard's is a citator, which is a book, CD–ROM, or online service that contains lists of citations that can help you assess the current validity of an item and can give you leads to other relevant materials. We will examine Shepard's as a citator through the following topics:

(a) The units of a set of Shepard's
(b) Determining whether you have a complete set of Shepard's
(c) The distinction between cited material and citing material
(d) Abbreviations in Shepard's
(e) Shepardizing a case (court opinion)
(f) Shepardizing a statute
(g) Shepardizing a regulation

We will limit ourselves to shepardizing cases, statutes, and regulations. Knowing how to shepardize these items, however, will go a long way toward equipping you to shepardize other primary authorities as well, such as constitutions, administrative decisions, charters, and rules of court.

### The Units of a Set of Shepard's

By "set of Shepard's," we mean the group of volumes of Shepard's that cover whatever you are trying to shepardize. Every set of Shepard's includes two main units: (a) *hardcover* or bound red volumes and (b) white, gold, blue, gray, yellow, or red *pamphlet* supplements. The hardcover volumes and the pamphlet supplements are sometimes broken into parts, e.g., Part 1, Part 2. The white pamphlet is the advance sheet that is later thrown away and *cumulated* (or consolidated) into a larger pamphlet. Eventually, all the pamphlets are thrown away and cumulated into hardcover or bound red volumes. The pamphlet supplements contain the most current shepardizing material.

Example of a set of
Shepard's citations

### Determining Whether You Have a Complete Set of Shepard's

*Shepard's Citations* comes in three formats: paper (pamphlets and hardcover or bound volumes), CD–ROM, and online (through LEXIS). The CD–ROM and online versions are the easiest to use. In most instances, you simply enter what you want to shepardize once in order to call up all available citing materials on the computer screen. Paper Shepard's, which most researchers use, is not as easy.

As indicated, Shepard's comes in sets, e.g., the set for Illinois, the set for federal statutes. For some sets, there may be 10 hardcover or bound volumes and 3 or 4 pamphlet supplements. Before you start shepardizing, you must determine whether you have a complete set in front of you on the shelf. To determine whether your set is complete, go through the following steps:

1. Pick up the most recently dated pamphlet supplement—usually the advance sheet—that the library has received for that set of Shepard's. The date is at the top of the supplement. Be careful, however; the pamphlet supplement you find on the shelf may *not* be the most recent; someone else may be using it, or it may have been misshelved. To determine the most recent Shepard's supplement received by the library, check the library's computer catalog. Type in the name of the set of Shep-

ard's. Among the information provided, the computer should tell you the most recent supplement received by the library. If it does not, ask a librarian how you can determine what is the most recent.

2. Once you are satisfied that you have the most recent unit, find the following statement on the front cover: WHAT YOUR LIBRARY SHOULD CONTAIN. This will tell you what is a complete set of Shepard's for the set you are using. Go down the list and make sure everything you are told should be on the shelf is indeed there. (The last entry on the list should be the pamphlet supplement that contains the list you are reading.)

Assume, for example, that today's date is January 2002. You want to shepardize a Wisconsin state case and a Wisconsin state statute. You go to *Shepard's Wisconsin Citations*. On the front cover of a January 2002 advance sheet for this set of Shepard's, you find the following:

---

**WHAT YOUR LIBRARY SHOULD CONTAIN**

1999 Bound Volumes 1 and 2, Cases*
1999 Bound Volume 3, Statutes*
1999 Bound Volume 4, Case Names*
*Supplemented with:*
—April, 2001 Annual Cumulative Supplement Vol. 90 No. 4
—January, 2002 Advance Sheet Vol. 91 No. 1

**DESTROY ALL OTHER ISSUES**

---

To be complete, therefore, the following units of *Shepard's Wisconsin Citations* should be on the shelf:

- a 1999 bound volume (vol. 1) of *Shepard's Wisconsin Citations* covering cases; and
- a 1999 bound volume (vol. 2) of *Shepard's Wisconsin Citations* covering cases; and
- a 1999 bound volume (vol. 3) of *Shepard's Wisconsin Citations* covering statutes; and
- a 1999 bound volume (vol. 4) of *Shepard's Wisconsin Citations* covering case names; and
- an April 2001 Annual Cumulative Supplement pamphlet (vol. 90, no. 4) of *Shepard's Wisconsin Citations* covering cases, statutes, and case names; and
- a January 2002 Advance Sheet pamphlet (vol. 91, no. 1) of *Shepard's Wisconsin Citations* covering cases, statutes, and case names.

The last item on the list is always the pamphlet that contains the list you are reading. Hence the above list is found on the January 2002 Advance Sheet (vol. 91, no. 1) of *Shepard's Wisconsin Citations*.

Occasionally, the list can become quite involved. For example, you may find two lists on the pamphlet. One list tells you what should be on the shelf before a certain bound Shepard's volume is received by the library, and a second list tells you what should be on the shelf after that bound volume is received by the library. Yet the same process is followed. Carefully go through the list (or lists) one unit at a time, checking to see if what the list says should be on the shelf is there.

Why do you need to take the time to be sure that the set of Shepard's you want to use is complete? Because the failure to do so might result in your missing vital information about what you are shepardizing. Assume you are in the library reading the case of *Smith v. Smith* decided in 1990. At the time you are reading this case, you are not aware that it was overruled in 1995. The reporter containing the opinion does not give you this information because the overruling occurred after the reporter volume was printed. Before you rely on a case, you must shepardize it. You go to the right set of Shepard's and check the *Smith* case in every bound volume and pamphlet supplement on the shelf. None of them, however, tells you that there are problems with the case. Unfortunately, the pamphlet that says *Smith* was overruled is not on the shelf. Someone else may be using it in another room of the library or it may have been misshelved. Careless researchers would not even know that the pamphlet was missing. Careful researchers, however, make it their business to know what should be on the shelf. They do this by checking the WHAT YOUR LIBRARY SHOULD CONTAIN list. When you do this, as a conscientious researcher, you realize that you cannot complete your shepardizing of *Smith* until you find the missing pamphlet. You go from table to table in the library looking for it. If this does not work, you ask a librarian for help in locating it.

It is also possible to use the Internet to find out what a complete set of Shepard's should contain. Go to Shepard's Internet site (*helpcite.shepards.com*), and click What Your Library Should Contain for whatever set of Shepard's you are using.

### The Distinction between Cited Material and Citing Material

- *Cited material* is whatever you are shepardizing, such as a case, statute, or regulation.
- *Citing material* is whatever mentions, treats, or discusses the cited material, such as another case, a legal periodical article, an annotation in A.L.R., etc.

Suppose you are shepardizing the case found in 75 F.3d 107 (a case that begins on page 107 of volume *75* of *Federal Reporter 3d*). While reading through the columns of Shepard's, you find the following cite: f56 S.E.2d 46. The *cited* material is 75 F.3d.107. The *citing* material is 56 S.E.2d 46, which followed (f) or agreed with the decision in 75 F.3d 107.

Suppose you are shepardizing a statute: 22 U.S.C. § 55.8 (section 55.8 of title 22 of the United States Code). While reading through the columns of Shepard's, you find the following cite: 309 U.S. 45. The *cited* material is 22 U.S.C. § 55.8. The *citing* material is 309 U.S. 45, which interpreted, treated, or mentioned 22 U.S.C. § 55.8.

Shepard's always indicates the cited material by the bold print along the top of every page of Shepard's and by the bold print numbers that are the volume or section numbers of the cited material. In the following excerpt, the cited material is 404 P.2d 460. The citing material follows the number –**460**–:

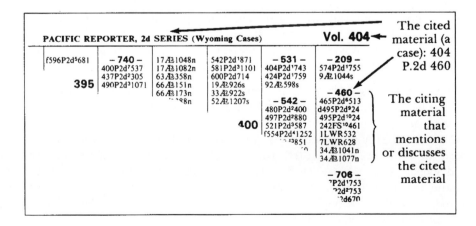

In the following excerpt, the cited material is a statute: § 37–31, which is in Article (Art.) 2 of the Wyoming Statutes. The citing material is indicated beneath § 37–31.

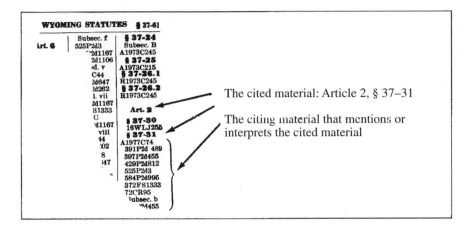

In recent sets of Shepard's the volume number or title number of the cited material is placed in a small box. In the following example, the cited material is 131 *Arizona Reports* 93. The citing material is the Ninth Circuit case, 106F3d[5]1475.

### ARIZONA REPORTS

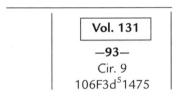

As we will see later, another change in recent sets of Shepard's is the addition of the actual names of the parties in the cited case.

### Abbreviation in Shepard's

Shepard's packs a tremendous amount of information (the cites) into every one of its pages. Each page contains up to eight columns of cites for the cited and the citing materials. For the sake of economy, Shepard's uses many abbreviations that are peculiar to Shepard's. For example:

FS → means *Federal Supplement*

A3 → means *American Law Reports 3d*

* → (asterisk) means that the year that follows the citing case is the year of the cited statute or regulation; it is not the year of the citing case

Δ → (delta symbol) means that the year that follows the citing case is the year of the citing case; it is not the year of the cited statute or regulation

You are not expected to know the meaning of every abbreviation and symbol used by Shepard's. *But you must know where to find their meanings.* There are two places to go:

- The abbreviations tables at the beginning of most units of Shepard's.
- The preface or explanation pages found at the beginning of most units of Shepard's.

Many researchers neglect the latter. Buried within the preface or explanation pages may be an interpretation of an abbreviation or symbol that is not covered in the abbreviation tables.

### Sheparding a Case (Court Opinion)

Almost every reporter has a corresponding set of Shepard's that will enable you to shepardize cases in that reporter (see exhibits 11.5 and 11.8 in section H). For example, if the case you want to shepardize is 40 N.Y.2d 100, you go to the set of Shepard's that covers cases in New York—*Shepard's New York Citations*. If the case you want to shepardize is 402 F.2d 1064, you go to the Shepard's that covers F.2d cases—*Shepard's Federal Citations*.

Of course, many cases have parallel cites—the case is found word for word in more than one reporter. You can shepardize most cases with parallel cites through either reporter. Assume you want to shepardize the following case:

*Welch v. Swasey*, 193 Mass. 364, 79 N.E. 745 (1907)

This case is found in two reporters: *Massachusetts Reports* and *North Eastern Reporter*. Hence you can shepardize the case and obtain similar citing material from two different sets of Shepard's: *Shepard's Massachusetts Citations* and *Shepard's Northeastern Citations*. A thorough researcher will shepardize his or her case by using *both* sets of Shepard's.

To shepardize a *case* means to obtain the following six kinds of information about the cited case (the case you are shepardizing):

1. The *parallel cite* of the case. The first entry in parentheses is the parallel cite.
2. The *history of the case*. Here, you will find all cases that are part of the same litigation, e.g., appeals, reversals.
3. The *treatment of the case*. Here, you will find all citing cases that have analyzed or mentioned the cited case, e.g., followed it, distinguished it, criticized it, or just mentioned it.
4. Citing legal periodical literature (law review article, case note, etc.) that has analyzed or mentioned the cited case.
5. Citing annotations in A.L.R. (A.L.R. 1st), A.L.R.2d, A.L.R.3d, A.L.R.4th, A.L.R.5th, or A.L.R. Fed. that have analyzed or mentioned the cited case.
6. Citing opinions of the attorney general that have analyzed or mentioned the cited case.

A *parallel cite* (item 1 above) is an additional reference where you will be able to read the same material word for word. There are two main reasons you may need a parallel cite. First, the rules of citation may require you to include a parallel cite (see section J). Second, the cite to a case you have may be to a reporter your library does not subscribe to; a parallel cite may lead you to a reporter your library does have.

The *history of the case* (item 2) gives you every case that was part of the same litigation as the case you are shepardizing. For example, you will be given abbreviations that tell you whether the case went up on appeal where it was affirmed (a), dismissed (D), modified (m), reversed (r), etc. Citations to each of these cases are provided. If one of the cases is so recent that its traditional citation is not yet available, Shepard's will give you the *docket number* of the decision. (A docket number is the consecutive number assigned to a case by the court when it is filed by the party bringing the litigation.) The most obvious reason you need the history of a case is that you do not want to cite a case that is no longer valid.

The *treatment of the case* (item 3) tells you how other cases in unrelated litigation have responded to (treated) the case you are shepardizing. For example, you will be given abbreviations that tell you whether the case has been criticized (c), questioned (q), explained (e), followed (f), overruled (o), etc., by other cases—the *citing cases*. You need to know how a case has been treated in order to assess how much weight it can be given. A case that has been ignored or criticized is obviously of less weight than one that other cases have cited with approval (followed—f).

Note that one of the history options is *reversed*, which should be distinguished from the treatment option of being *overruled*. To **reverse** an opinion means to change its holding on appeal in the same litigation. **Overrule** means to change its holding in different litigation.

As you can see, both the history and the treatment of a case help you perform the third level of legal research, validation research, which we introduced in section N and will examine again in section Y.

The great value of Shepard's as a case finder comes through items 3 to 5. If a citing case (item 3) analyzes or mentions the cited case (which you are shepardizing), the two cases probably deal with similar facts and law. All citing cases, therefore, are potential leads to more case law on point. Similarly, a citing legal periodical article (item 4) or a citing A.L.R. annotation (item 5) will probably discuss a variety of cases in addition to the cited case. Hence, again, you are led to more case law through Shepard's.

One final point before we examine an extended excerpt from a Shepard's page. Recall that opinions in reporters are broken down into headnotes at the beginning of the opinion. These headnotes, written by private publishers such as West Group, are small-paragraph summaries of portions of the opinion printed just before the text of the opinion begins.[2]

A case can involve many issues, only a few of which may be relevant to your research problem. Is it possible to narrow your shepardizing to those parts of the case that are most relevant to your research problem? Yes. It is possible to shepardize a portion of a case through its headnote numbers. In effect, you are shepardizing the headnote! Let's examine how this is done:

- Every headnote of the cited case has a consecutive number: 1, 2, 3, 4, etc.

  Assume, for example, that you are shepardizing the case of *Jackson v. Jackson* —the cited case— and that there are 10 headnotes to this case. But as you read *Jackson*, it is clear that you are interested in only the fifth headnote. The other 9 summarize parts of the case that are not relevant to your research problem.

- When the editors of Shepard's come across a *citing* case that deals with only one of the headnotes of the *cited* case, they include the number of this headnote as part of the reference to the *citing* case in the columns of Shepard's. The number is printed as a small raised, or elevated, number—called a **superscript** number—within the reference to the citing case. For example, the number 3 in the following cite is printed as a superscript number: 284 N.Y.$^3$ 487 (1965). You have seen superscript numbers before. Footnote numbers, for example, are almost always in superscript on a page.

  When you shepardize the *Jackson* case in our example, you find that many citing cases have analyzed or mentioned *Jackson*. It might take hours for you to read them all. Here are three citing cases that you find:

  102N.Y.$^3$34
  111N.Y.$^5$109
  116N.Y.21

  Two of these citing cases have superscript numbers. The second one is of particular interest to you because it dealt with the fifth headnote of the *Jackson* case. Though you do not ignore the other two, you concentrate on 111 N.Y.109. You leave Shepard's and go read this case in a reporter (or on CD–ROM or online). Be careful. It is easy to become confused. The superscript number refers to the headnote number of the *cited* case, not of the *citing* case, even though this number is printed within the reference of the citing case. The number 5 in the citing case, 111 N.Y. 109, refers to the fifth headnote of the *Jackson* case, It is not the fifth headnote of 111 N.Y. 109.

Let's look at another example. Assume that you are shepardizing *Welch v. Swasey*, 193 Mass. 364. In the columns of Shepard's, you find the following:

f196Mas$^8$476

The *citing* case is 196 Mass. 476. This case follows (f-agrees with) the *cited* case of *Welch v. Swasey*, 193 Mass. 364. Note the raised number 8—the superscript figure. This 8 refers to the eighth headnote of the *cited* case, *Welch v. Swasey*. The *citing* case dealt with that portion of *Welch* that was summarized in the eighth headnote of the *Welch* case. Again, do not make the mistake of thinking that the small raised number refers to a headnote in the citing case. It refers to a headnote number of the *cited* case.

A final example. Assume that you are researching the problem of whether a person can sue his or her spouse for negligence: are spouses immune from tort actions against each other? In your research, you come across the promising case of *Self v. Self*, which starts on

| EXHIBIT 11.28 | Excerpt from a Case: (*Self v. Self*) in *Pacific Reporter 2d* |

SELF V. SELF
Cite as 376 P.2d 65

Cal.

**65**

26 Cal.Rptr. 97
**Catherine SELF, Plaintiff and Appellant,**
v.
**Adrian SELF, Defendant and Respondent.**
**L.A. 26878.**

Supreme Court of California,
In Bank
Nov. 9, 1962

Action against husband by wife, whose arm allegedly was broken in course of unlawful assault by husband. The Superior Court, Los Angeles County, John F. McCarthy, J., granted the husband's motion for summary judgment and the wife appealed. The Supreme Court, Peters, J., held that wife could recover if husband broke her arm in course of unlawful assault.

Reversed.

Opinion, 20 Cal.Rptr. 781, vacated.

**1. Husband and Wife ⌐ 205(2)**
Rule of interspousal immunity for intentional torts is abandoned; one spouse may sue the other in tort where tort is intentional.

**2. Husband and Wife ⌐ 205(2)**
Wife could recover from husband if he broke her arm in course of unlawful assault; disapproving Peters v. Peters, 156 Cal. 32, 103 P. 219, 23 L.R.A., N.S., 699; Watson v. Watson, 39 Cal.2d 305, 246 P.2d 19. West's Ann.Civ.Code, §163.5.

**3. Negligence ⌐ 14**
Generally, in absence of statute or some other compelling reason of public policy, where there is negligence proximately causing injury, there should be liability.

———

Robert H. Lund and John R. Brunner, Long Beach, for plaintiff and appellant.

Wolver & Wolver and Eugene L. Wolver, Los Angeles, amici curiae, on behalf of plaintiff and appellant.

Baird, Mooney & Baird, C. Duane Mooney and Woodrow W. Baird, Long Beach, for defendant and respondent.

PETERS, Justice.

[1, 2] The sole problem involved in this case is whether California should continue to follow the rule of interspousal immunity for intentional torts first announced in this state in 1909 in the case of Peters v. Peters, 156 Cal. 32, 103 P. 219, 23 L.R.A., N.S., 699. Because the reasons upon which the Peters case was predicated no longer exist, and because of certain legislative changes made in recent years, we are of the opinion that the rule of the Peters case should be abandoned. In other words, it is our belief that the rule should be that one spouse may sue the other in tort, at least where that tort is an intentional one . . . .

page 65 of volume 376 of *Pacific Reporter 2d* (376 P.2d 65). The beginning of this case is excerpted in exhibit 11.28.
   Note the following characteristics of the case in exhibit 11.28:

- The case has three headnotes.
- The headnotes are numbered consecutively: 1, 2, 3.
- The headnotes also have key numbers consisting of a topic and a number [Husband and Wife ⌐ 205(2) for the first two headnotes and Negligence ⌐ 14 for the third].
- The headnotes summarize portions of the opinion that begin after the name of the judge who wrote the opinion (Justice Peters). The consecutive numbers of the headnotes correspond to the bracketed numbers in the opinion. For example, the first two headnotes summarize that portion of the opinion that begins with the bracketed numbers [1, 2] just below the justice's name. The third headnote summarizes the portion of the opinion that begins with the bracketed number [3] (not shown in exhibit 11.28).

   As indicated, you find this case promising in your research. You want to use this case in the memorandum of law that you will be submitting to your supervisor. But you are not ready to use this case—you haven't shepardized it yet. You must never rely on a case until you find out its history and treatment, as explained earlier. Shepard's will tell you.

To shepardize a case in the *Pacific Reporter 2d*, you use *Shepard's Pacific Reporter Citations*, as we saw in exhibit 11.8, earlier in the chapter. Exhibit 11.29 shows a sample page from *Shepard's Pacific Reporter Citations* that will enable you to start shepardizing the *Self v. Self* case. Let's examine this sample page closely.

Note the following characteristics of the Shepard's page in exhibit 11.29:

- There are six columns on this page.
- The names of the cases to be shepardized—the *cited cases*—are all given in full. Toward the bottom of the fifth column is the full name of the case you are shepardizing, *Self v. Self*. This is a recent feature of Shepard's. Earlier editions of Shepard's did not give the actual names of the parties of the cited case. You were simply given the numbers of its citation. Now you are given both. The first cited case shepardized on this page is the *Cocanougher* case near at the top of the first column; the last cited case is *Self*.
- Another recent feature is the date of the cited case printed just below its name. *Self* was decided in 1962.
- The volume number of the cited cases is placed in a box. See the top of the second column. All the cited cases following this box are in volume 376 of the *Pacific Reporter 2d*. All the cited cases before this box are in volume 375 of the *Pacific Reporter 2d*.
- The first page number of the cited cases is centered in the column between two long dashes. The first page of the *Cocanougher* case is 1014. The first page of the *Self* case is 65. (Look back at the actual text of the *Self* case in exhibit 11.28. You can confirm that this case begins on page 65 of volume 376 of the *Pacific Reporter 2d*. See the top right corner of exhibit 11.28.)
- Parallel cites are given in parentheses beneath the name and year of the case. There are two parallel cites to *Self v. Self*: (58C2d683) and (26CaR97). You are not expected to know what C2d, CaR, or any other abbreviation means. Check the abbreviations table and preface material in any Shepard's unit (other than the advance sheet) for the meaning of abbreviations. There we are told that C2d means *California Supreme Court Reports, Second Series* and that CaR means *California Reporter*. Hence the *Self* case can be found in three places: 376 P.2d 65, 58 C2d 683, and 26 CaR 97. (Note that the top of the caption in exhibit 11.28 gives us the *California Reporter* (Cal. Rptr.) parallel cite but not the C2d parallel cite. The C2d cite was not available at the time the *Pacific Reporter 2d* volume in exhibit 11.28 was printed.)
- There are a number of abbreviations that lead you to the *history of the cited case*. Small "s," for example, means same case at a different stage of the litigation. The *Self* case includes the following notation: s 20CaR781. If you went to volume 20 of the *California Reporter* and turned to page 781, you would find that something occurred (we are not told what) in the *Self* litigation. For example, the court might have denied a particular motion or rendered an opinion against one of the parties. To find out, you need to go to 20 CaR 781. There are other history notations on the sample page in exhibit 11.29. Find the "cc" reference for the *Cocanougher* case. This means connected case. The reference may be to a case involving the same parties, but in a different action.
- Most of the other references in exhibit 11.29 give you the *treatment of the cited case*. This is done by providing numerous citing cases that have analyzed or mentioned the cited case. The first citing case for *Self* is f 376P2d[1]71. This tells you that the cited case (*Self*) was followed (f) by the citing case found at 376 P.2d 71. Page 71 refers to the page number where the citing case makes specific reference to the cited case, *Self*. What does this citing case say about *Self*? We are not told other than that it followed (f) *Self*. To find out, you need to go to page 71 of volume 376 of the *Pacific Reporter 2d*. (In a moment, we will discuss the superscript number 1 before the page number: [1]71.)

**EXHIBIT 11.29**    Sample page from Shepard's Pacific Reporter Citations

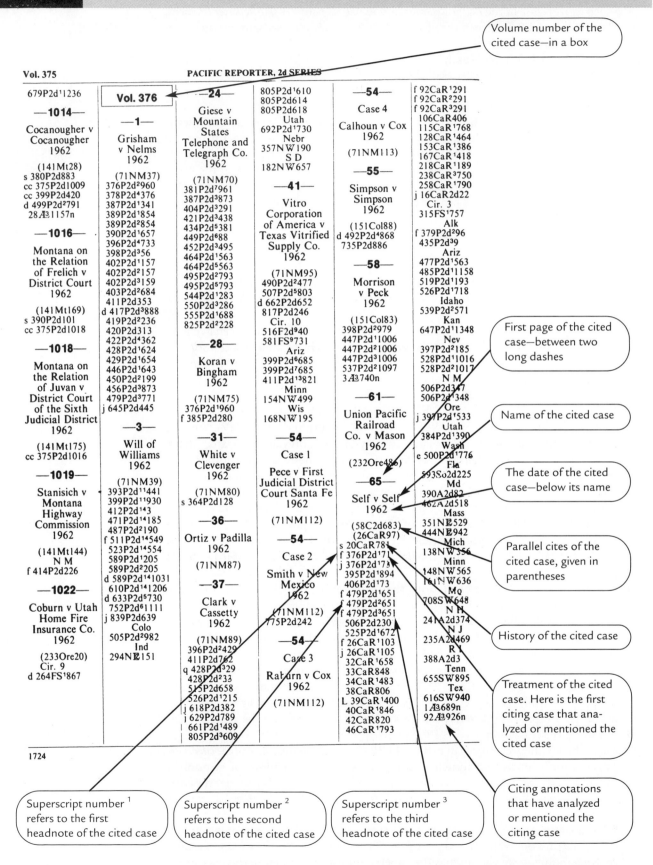

Volume number of the cited case—in a box

First page of the cited case—between two long dashes

Name of the cited case

The date of the cited case—below its name

Parallel cites of the cited case, given in parentheses

History of the cited case

Treatment of the cited case. Here is the first citing case that analyzed or mentioned the cited case

Citing annotations that have analyzed or mentioned the citing case

Superscript number [1] refers to the first headnote of the cited case

Superscript number [2] refers to the second headnote of the cited case

Superscript number [3] refers to the third headnote of the cited case

- Examine the other notations in front of the citing cases: "e" means the citing case explained the cited case; "L" means the citing case limited or restricted the application of the cited case; "j" means the cited case was analyzed or mentioned in a dissenting opinion of the citing case. Again, all these abbreviations are explained for you at the beginning of the Shepard's volume or pamphlet.

- The overwhelming number of citations for the *Self* case constitute the *treatment of the case* in which citing cases have analyzed or mentioned the cited case, *Self*. Note how these citing cases are clustered or grouped by court. The citing cases begin with the courts of the same state as the cited case—California for the *Self* case. Then you get the federal citing cases, if any, and the state citing cases, if any. There are many state citing cases for *Self* in the sixth column, beginning with Alaska state cases (Alk) and ending with Texas state cases (Tex).

- Citing annotations also analyze or mention the cited case. The references to these annotations, if any, are printed after the citing cases. There are two citing annotations for *Self*, the first in volume 1 and the second in volume 92 of *American Law Reports, Third Series*. (See the end of the the sixth column.)

- Finally, note the numerous superscript numbers within the citing cases: [1, 2, 3, 4, 5, 6,] etc. Although these numbers are found within the cites of citing cases, they refer to headnote numbers of the *cited* case. They tell you that the citing case dealt with the points of law that are summarized in that particular headnote number of the cited case. Of the many citing cases for *Self*, let's look at the following three in the fifth column:

  376P2d[1]71
  479P2d[2]651
  479P2d[3]651

These three citing cases analyzed or mentioned the cited case, *Self*. In particular, the first citing case dealt with the portion of *Self* that was summarized in the first headnote of *Self*. The next citing case dealt with the portion of *Self* that was summarized in the second headnote of *Self*. The last citing case dealt with the portion of *Self* that was summarized in the third headnote of *Self*.

- Look back at the *Self* excerpt in exhibit 11.28. Note again that there are three consecutively numbered headnotes: 1, 2, 3. These numbers correspond to the superscript numbers[1, 2, 3] in the citing cases for *Self* in the Shepard's excerpt in exhibit 11.29. Assume that when you read the *Self* case, you were particularly interested in the court's discussion of negligence because your research problem has negligence issues in it. Read the third headnote in exhibit 11.28. It specifically refers to negligence. Hence, when you shepardize *Self*, you want to give particular attention to any citing case that has a superscript number[3]. There are four of them in the fifth and sixth columns of the Shepard's excerpt in exhibit 11.29: 479P2d[3]651, 92CaR[3]291, 238CaR[3]750, and 435P2d[3]9. You may want to read all the citing cases, but these four will get your immediate attention because they are potentially more relevant to your research.

- Of course, when you shepardize a case, you need to check the cited case *(Self)* in every unit of Shepard's. See the earlier discussion on determining whether you have a complete set of Shepard's. In the other units of Shepard's you will use to Shepardize *Self*, you may find other citing cases containing the superscript[3].

- Note that some of the citing cases have no superscript numbers. This makes it a little more difficult to assess how they treated the cited case. Like all citing references, however (including those with superscript numbers), you must read the actual text of a citing case (in reporters, on CD–ROM, or online) to determine in what manner it analyzed or mentioned the cited case. Shepard's is only the first step in finding out.

- When shepardizing a case, you may find citing legal periodical literature that has analyzed or mentioned the cited case. The excerpt from Shepard's in exhibit 11.29, however, has no citing legal periodical literature for *Self*. (Nor do any of the other cited cases in the excerpt have any citing legal periodical literature.)

■ When shepardizing a case, you may find citing annotations that have analyzed or mentioned the cited case. The excerpt from Shepard's in exhibit 11.29 has two citing annotations for *Self* at the very bottom of the sixth column.

■ When shepardizing a case, you may find citing opinions of the attorney general that have analyzed or mentioned the cited case. The excerpt from Shepard's in exhibit 11.29, however, has no citing opinions of the attorney general for *Self*. (Nor do any of the other cited cases in the excerpt have any citing opinions of the attorney general.)

The techniques for shepardizing a case are summarized in exhibit 11.30.

| EXHIBIT 11.30 | Checklist for Shepardizing a Case |

1. You have a case you want to shepardize. In what reporter is this case found? Go to the set of Shepard's in the library that covers this reporter.

2. If the case you want to shepardize has a *parallel cite* that you already have, find out if the library has a set of Shepard's for the other reporter volumes in which the case is also printed. You may be able to shepardize the case through two sets of Shepard's. If so, shepardize the case twice. You may be able to find information about the cited case in one set of Shepard's that is not available in the set of Shepard's used to shepardize it through its parallel cite.

3. Know whether you have a complete set of Shepard's in front of you by reading the WHAT YOUR LIBRARY SHOULD CONTAIN list on the most recent pamphlet of that set. (To check this on the Internet, go to *helpcite.shepards.com*.)

4. The general rule is that you must check the cite of the case you are shepardizing (the cited case) in *every* unit of a set of Shepard's. With experience, you will learn, however, that it is possible to bypass some of the units of the set. There may be information on the front cover of one of the Shepard's volumes, for example, that will tell you that the date or volume number of the reporter containing your cited case is not covered in that Shepard's volume. You can bypass it and move on to other units of the set.

5. In checking all the units of Shepard's, it is recommended that you work *backward* by examining the most recent Shepard's pamphlets first so that you start with the latest *history* of the case and the latest citing materials in the *treatment* of the case.

6. Suppose that in one of the units of a set of Shepard's, you find nothing listed for the cited case. This could mean one of three things:
   (a) You are in the wrong set of Shepard's.
   (b) You are in the right set of Shepard's, but the Shepard's unit you are examining does not cover the particular volume of the reporter that contains your cited case. (See guideline 4 above.)
   (c) You are in the right set of Shepard's. The silence in Shepard's about your cited case

means that since the time of the printing of the last unit of Shepard's for that set, nothing has happened to the case—there is nothing for Shepard's to tell you.

7. Know the six kinds of information that you can try to obtain when shepardizing a case: parallel cites, history of the cited case, treatment of the cited case (found in the citing cases), citing legal periodical literature, citing annotations, and citing opinions of the attorney general.

8. The *history* of the case tells you what has happened in different stages of the same litigation involved in the cited case. If a decision in the litigation is very recent, Shepard might give you its docket number rather than its citation. (More information on docket numbers may be found at the end of the unit of Shepard's you are using.)

9. The page number listed for every citing case is the page on which the *cited* case is mentioned. It is not the page on which the *citing* case begins.

10. Use the abbreviations tables and the preface pages at the beginning of most units of Shepard's—and use them often.

11. A small "n" to the right of the page number of citing material (e.g., 23ALR198n) means the cited case is mentioned within an annotation. A small "s" to the right of the page number of citing material (e.g., 23ALR198s) means the cited case is mentioned in a supplement to (or pocket part of) the annotation.

12. You can also shepardize a case online through LEXIS. Online shepardizing is substantially easier than using the hardcover and pamphlet units of Shepard's. You simply enter the cite you want to shepardize (e.g., the cited case) in order to obtain all available citing materials. (For more on LEXIS, see chapter 13.)

13. For more information about Shepard's:
    ■ 800–899–6000 (product support line)
    ■ www.shepards.com

14. KeyCite is the major competitor to Shepard's. KeyCite is available only online through Westlaw. KeyCite will allow you to obtain citator references for cited cases.

*Assignment 11.17*

Pick any case that you found while doing any one of the parts of Assignment 11.15 or 11.16. Do questions (a)–(g) below on this case.

**(a)** What set of *Shepard's Citations* would you use to shepardize this case?

**(b)** Is this set of *Shepard's Citations* on the shelf complete? List everything that should be on the shelf. Place a check mark next to each unit that is on the shelf and an "x" next to each unit that is missing.

**(c)** List the parallel cites, if any, for this case provided by Shepard's.

**(d)** State the history of this case according to Shepard's. Give the meaning of abbreviations of all symbols that Shepard's uses to indicate this history. If there is no history of the case provided by Shepard's, redo this assignment until you find a case that does have such a history.

**(e)** In the treatment of the cited case, find a citing case written by a state court in your state. Give the meaning of abbreviations of all symbols, if any, that Shepard's uses to indicate this treatment. If there is no citing case written by a state court of your state, redo this assignment until you find a cited case that does have such a citing case. Give the citation of the citing case.

**(f)** Go to the reporter that prints the full text of the citing case you found in (e). Find the citing case in it and quote the sentence from the case that refers to the cited case.

**(g)** Question (a) asked you to identify a set of Shepard's that you would use to shepardize the case you selected, and question (c) asked you if the case had a parallel cite.

    (i)   If there is a parallel cite, is there another set of Shepard's that would allow you to shepardize your case? If so, what is the name of this set of Shepard's?

    (ii)  Go to this other set of Shepard's. Is it complete? Redo question (b) for this set.

    (iii) Can you find the same information in this set that you found when answering questions (c), (d), and (e) for the other set? If not, what is different?

## Sheypardizing a Statute

You shepardize a *statute* to try to find the following seven kinds of information:

1. A parallel cite of the statute (found in parentheses immediately after the section number of the statute). The parallel cite (if given) is to the session law edition of the statute.
2. The history of the statute in the legislature, such as amendments, added sections, repealed sections, renumbered sections, etc.
3. Citing cases that have analyzed or mentioned the statute, declared it unconstitutional, etc.
4. Citing administrative decisions, such as agency decisions that have analyzed or mentioned the statute.
5. Citing legal periodical literature, such as law review articles that have analyzed or mentioned the statute.
6. Citing annotations in A.L.R. (A.L.R.1st) A.L.R.2d, A.L.R.3d, A.L.R.4th, A.L.R.5th, and A.L.R. Fed. that have analyzed or mentioned the statute.
7. Citing opinions of the attorney general that have analyzed or mentioned the statute.

To learn how to shepardize a statute, you must first learn the distinction between a statute's session law cite and its codified cite. First, let's review some basics.

A statute is a law passed by the legislature declaring, commanding, or prohibiting something. The official document that contains the statute is called an act. There are two main kinds of statutes:

■ *Public laws*, which are statutes that apply to the general public or to a segment of the public and have permanence and general interest (example: a statute changing welfare eligibility)

- *Private laws*, which are statutes that apply to specifically named individuals or groups and have little or no permanence or general interest (example: a statute that names a Wyoming post office building after a recently deceased senator)

Statutes can be found in three major formats printed in the following order:

- *Slip law*: A single statute (public or private law) that is printed separately, often in a small pamphlet.
- *Session law*: A single statute (public or private law) that is printed in chronological order along with every other statute passed during a particular session of the legislature, usually lasting one or two years. (If, for example, the legislature passes a bankruptcy statute and a murder statute on the same day, they will be printed in the session laws one after the other.) Other names for session laws include *Acts, Laws,* and, most commonly, *Statutes at Large*. The major set of federal session laws is called *United States Statutes at Large* (abbreviated Stat.). The citation to a session law is called its **session law cite**.
- *Code*: A collection of statutes (public laws only) that are printed by subject matter regardless of when the legislature passed them. When we say a statute has been *codified*, we mean that it has been printed in a code where the rules or laws in it are printed by subject matter rather than chronologically. (For example, all of the bankruptcy statutes are printed together, and all of the murder statutes are printed together elsewhere in the code.) The citation to a statute in a code is called its **codified cite**.

Every private law will have only a session law cite because it will not be printed in a code. Every public law, however, will have both a session law cite *and* a codified cite. Here are examples of session law and codified law cites of a state statute (Ohio) and of a federal statute, both of which are public laws:

| Session Law Cite of a Statute | Codified Cite of the Same Statute |
|---|---|
| 1975 Ohio Laws, C. 508 ⟷ | Ohio Rev. Code Ann. § 45 (1978) |
| 87 Stat. 297 (1965) ⟷ | 34 U.S.C. § 18(c) (1970) |

Notice the totally different numbering system in the codified and session law cites—yet they are the same statutes. Section 45 of the Ohio Revised Code Annotated is found word for word in Chapter (C.) 508 of the 1975 session laws of Ohio. And section 18(c) of title 34 of the United States Code is found word for word in volume 87 of Statutes at Large (Stat.) on page 297. Notice also the different years for the same statute. The year in the session law cite is the year the legislature passed the statute. The year in the codified cite, however, is usually the year of the edition of the code.

Assume that you want to shepardize a statute. (The cited material will be a cited statute.) When do you shepardize a statute through its session law cite, and when do you shepardize through its codified cite?

There are two instances when you *must* shepardize the statute through its session law cite:

- If the statute will never be codified because it is a private law and therefore of no general public interest
- If the statute has not yet been codified because it is so recent (codification will come later)

If the statute *has* been codified, you must shepardize it through its latest codified cite. But suppose you know only the session law cite of the statute. How do you find its codified cite? Go to the current code that should contain your statute. Look for special tables at the beginning or end of the code. For federal statutes in the United States Code, for example, there is a *Tables volume* in which you will find Table III. (See research link O on page 526). Table III will enable you to translate a session law cite into a codified law cite. (A Tables volume also exists for U.S.C.A. and for U.S.C.S.) You can also make the translation through Table 2 in *United States Code Congressional and Administrative News* (U.S.C.C.A.N.).

Shepard's has its own abbreviation system for session laws. Suppose that you are shepardizing Kan. Stat. Ann. § 123 (1973)—a codified cite. Section 123 is the *cited statute*— what you are shepardizing. In the Shepard's columns for Kansas statutes, you might find:

§ 123

(1970C6)
A1972C23
Rp1975C45

The *parallel cite* in parentheses is 1970C6, which means chapter 6 of the 1970 Session Laws of the state of Kansas. The mention of a year in Shepard's for statutes usually refers to the session laws for that year. (You find the meaning of "C" by checking the abbreviations tables at the beginning of the Shepard's volume.)

Immediately beneath the parentheses in the above example for section 123 (the cited statute), you find two other references to session laws:

| | |
|---|---|
| A1972C23 This means that in chapter 23 of the 1972 Session Laws of Kansas, there was an amendment to section 123 (which is what "A" means, according to Shepard's abbreviations tables). | Rp1975C45 This means that in chapter 45 of the 1975 Session Laws of Kansas, section 123 was repealed in part (which is what "Rp" means, according to Shepard's abbreviations tables). |

You will note that Shepard's does *not* tell you what the amendment was or what was repealed in part. How do you find this out? Two ways. First, you go to the actual session laws if your library has them. Second, you go to the cited statute (§ 123) in the codified collection of the statutes (here the *Kansas Statutes Annotated*). At the bottom of the statute in the code, there may be historical or legislative history notes that will summarize amendments, repeals, etc. For an example of this kind of information on a New York statute, see exhibit 11.44, later in the chapter. (Be sure to check these notes for the cited statute in the pocket part of the code volume you are using.)

Other citing material given in Shepard's for a statute is less complicated. For example, there are cites to citing cases, citing legal periodical articles, etc., that follow a pattern very similar to that of the citing material for cases you are sheparizing.

Assume that you want to shepardize a federal statute in the *United States Code* (U.S.C.). The set of Shepard's you would use is *Shepard's Federal Statute Citations* (see exhibit 11.8 in section H). There are two major kinds of citing cases that analyze or mention a federal cited statute. Both kinds give you a year in front of the citing case, but the year can have two very different meanings:

- When there is an asterisk (*) in front of the year, Shepard's is telling you that the court that wrote the citing case specified the year of the U.S.C. in which the cited statute is found. The year following the asterisk is the year *of the U.S.C.* that contains the cited statute, not the year of the citing case. In an asterisk cite, you are not told the year of the citing case.
- When there is a delta (Δ) in front of the year, Shepard's is telling you that the court that wrote the citing case did *not* specify the year of the U.S.C. in which the cited statute is found. The year following the delta is the year *of the citing case*, not the year of the U.S.C. In a delta cite, you are not told the year of the U.S.C. that contains the cited statute.

Assume, for example, that the federal statute you are shepardizing—the cited statute—is section 2506 in title 22 of the *United States Code* (22 U.S.C. § 2506). Exhibit 11.31 contains an excerpt from one of the units of *Shepard's Federal Statute Citations* that you would use to shepardize this statute.

The first citing case is 37FedCl 426. The abbreviations tables at the beginning of Shepard's tell you that FedCl means the Federal Claims Court. On page 426 of volume 37 of this reporter, you will find that the court analyzed or mentioned the cited statute, 22 U.S.C. § 2506. Note the year 1997 following the delta. This means that the court that wrote

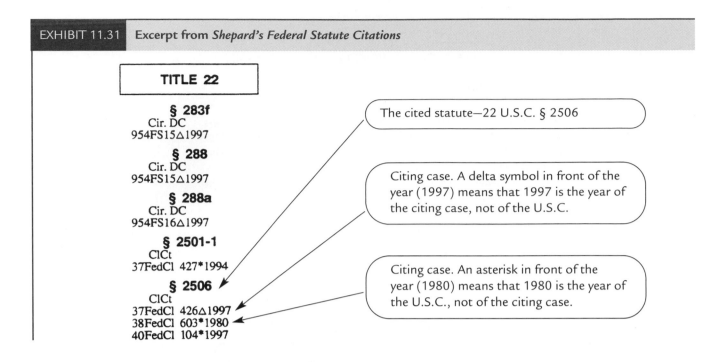

**EXHIBIT 11.31    Excerpt from *Shepard's Federal Statute Citations***

the citing case did not specify the year of 22 U.S.C. § 2506. Hence 1997 is the year of the citing case, 37FedCl 426; it is not the year of 22 U.S.C. § 2506.

The next citing case is 38FedCl 603. Again, the abbreviations tables tell you that this is a Federal Claims Court case. On page 603 of volume 38 of this reporter, you will find that the court analyzed or mentioned the cited statute, 22 U.S.C. § 2506. Note the year 1980 following the asterisk. This means that the court that wrote the citing case *did* specify the year of 22 U.S.C. § 2506. Hence 1980 is the year of 22 U.S.C. § 2506; it is not the year of the citing case, 38FedCl 603.

The techniques for shepardizing a statute are summarized in exhibit 11.32.

---

*Assignment 11.18*

(a) Go to your state statutory code. Pick any statute in this code that might be helpful in researching any *one* of the topics for the section O assignments. (See page 549.) Which topic did you select, (a) to (o)? Give the citation of the statute. Give a brief quote from this statute indicating that it might be relevant to the topic you selected.

(b) What set of *Shepard's Citations* would you use to shepardize this statute?

(c) Is this set of *Shepard's Citations* on the shelf complete? List everything that should be on the shelf. Place a check mark next to each unit that is on the shelf and an "x" next to each unit that is missing.

(d) According to Shepard's, have there been any amendments, or has the legislature taken any other action on this statute? If so, give the meaning of abbreviations of all symbols that Shepard's uses to indicate this action. (Be sure to check every unit of Shepard's for this set.)

(e) Find a citing case written by a state court in your state. Give the meaning of abbreviations of all symbols, if any, that Shepard's uses to indicate how this citing case treated the cited statute. If there is no citing case written by a state court of your state, redo this assignment until you find a cited statute that *does* have such a citing case. Give the citation of the citing case.

(f) Go to the reporter that prints the full text of the citing case you found in (e). Find the cited statute in it and quote the sentence from the case that refers to the cited statute.

| EXHIBIT 11.32 | Checklist for Shepardizing a Statute |
| --- | --- |

1. Go to the set of Shepard's that will enable you to shepardize your statute. For federal statutes, it is *Shepard's Federal Statute Citations*. (See exhibit 11.8 for a photo of this set.) For state statutes, go to the set of Shepard's for your state. This set of Shepard's may cover both state cases and state statutes in the same units or in different case and statute editions of the set.

2. If the statute has been codified, shepardize it through its latest codified cite. If all you have is the session law cite of the statute, translate it into a codified cite by using the tables in the current code. For federal statutes, go to Table III of the Tables volume of U.S.C./U.S.C.A./U.S.C.S. and Table 2 in *United States Code Congressional and Administrative News* (U.S.C.C.A.N.).

3. If the statute has not been codified, you can shepardize it through its session law cite.

4. Know whether you have a complete set of Shepard's in front of you by reading the WHAT YOUR LIBRARY SHOULD CONTAIN list on the most recent pamphlet of that set. (To check this on the Internet, go to *helpcite.shepards.com*.)

5. Check your cite in *every* unit of Shepard's. It is recommended that you work *backward* by examining the most recent Shepard's pamphlets first so that you obtain the latest history and citing material first.

6. At the top of a Shepard's page, and in its columns, look for your statute by the name of the code, year, article, chapter, title, or section. Repeat this for every unit of Shepard's.

7. Know the seven kinds of information you can try to obtain by shepardizing a statute: parallel cite (not always given), history of the statute in the legislature, citing cases, citing administrative decisions, citing legal periodical literature, citing annotations, and citing opinions of the attorney general.

8. The history of the statute in the legislature will give you the citing material in session law form, e.g., A1980C45. This refers to an amendment (A) printed in the 1980 Laws of the legislature, Chapter (C) 45. Another example: A34St.654. This refers to an amendment (A) printed in volume 34, page 654, of the *Statutes at Large*. If you want to locate these session laws, find out if your library keeps them. Also, check the historical note after the statute in the statutory code.

9. The notation *et seq* means "and following" (*et sequens*). The citing material may be analyzing more than one statutory section.

10. Find the meaning of abbreviations used by Shepard's in its tables and preface material at the beginning of most of the units of the set of Shepard's.

11. If your state code has gone through revisions or renumberings, read the early pages in the statutory code and in the Shepard's volumes to try to obtain an explanation of what has happened. This information may be of considerable help to you in interpreting the data provided in the Shepard's units for your state code.

12. You can also shepardize a federal statute (and many state statutes) online through LEXIS.

13. For more information about Shepard's:
    - 800-899-6000 (product support line)
    - www.shepards.com

14. The online alternative to Shepard's is KeyCite, available only on Westlaw. KeyCite will allow you to obtain citator references for cited statutes.

### Shepardizing a Regulation

You cannot shepardize administrative regulations of state agencies. No sets of Shepard's cover state regulations. You can, however, shepardize federal regulations in the *Code of Federal Regulations* (C.F.R.). This is done through *Shepard's Code of Federal Regulations Citations*. It will also allow you to shepardize presidential proclamations, executive orders, and reorganization plans.

To shepardize a C.F.R. regulation means to obtain the following three kinds of information about the *cited regulation* (the regulation you are shepardizing):

1. The history of the regulation in the courts—for example, citing cases that have invalidated or otherwise discussed the cited regulation.

2. Citing legal periodical literature that has analyzed or mentioned the cited regulation.

3. Citing annotations in A.L.R. (A.L.R.1st), A.L.R.2d, A.L.R.3d, A.L.R.4th, A.L.R.5th, and A.L.R. Fed. that have analyzed or mentioned the cited regulation.

The C.F.R. comes out in a new edition every year. All the changes that have occurred during the year are incorporated in the new yearly edition. (Each year is printed in a different color.) Two kinds of changes can be made:

- Those changes made *by the agency* itself, e.g., amendments, repeals, renumbering—this is the history of the regulation in the agency.
- Those changes forced on the agency *by the courts*, e.g., declaring a section of the regulation invalid—this is part of the history of the regulation in the courts.

Unfortunately, Shepard's will give you only the history of the regulation in the courts (plus references to the regulation in legal periodical literature and in annotations). The columns of Shepard's will *not* give you the history of the regulation in the agency. (As we will see later, to obtain the latter, you must check elsewhere, e.g., the CFR Parts Affected tables in the *Federal Register*.) The main value of Shepard's for C.F.R. is that it will lead you to what the courts have said about the regulation (plus the periodical and annotation references).

When shepardizing through *Shepard's Code of Federal Regulations Citations*, the cited material, of course, is the federal regulation—which we refer to as the cited regulation. Shepard's provides two categories of *citing* material:

- Citing cases, periodicals, and annotations that refer to the cited regulation *by year*, that is, by C.F.R. edition.
- Citing cases, periodicals, and annotations that refer to the cited regulation *without* specifying the year or edition of the regulation in the C.F.R.

To indicate the first kind of citing material, Shepard's prints on asterisk just before a given year. If, for example, the cited regulation you were sheparding is 12 C.F.R. § 218.111(j), you might find the following:

§218.111(j)
420F2d90*1965

The citing material is a citing case—420 F.2d 90. The asterisk means that this case specifically identified the year of the cited regulation—1965. This year is *not* the year of the citing case. It is the year of the cited regulation. We are not given the year of the citing case.

Now let us examine the second kind of citing material mentioned above. There may be citing material that mentions the regulation but does *not* tell us the specific year or edition of that regulation. Shepard's uses a delta (Δ) in such situations. If, for example, the cited regulation you were sheparding is 12 C.F.R. § 9.18(a)(3), you might find the following:

§9.18(a)(3)
274FS628Δ1967

The citing material is a citing case—274 F. Supp. 628. The delta means that the citing case did not refer to the year or edition of section 9.18(a)(3). When this occurs, the year following the delta is the year of the citing case and *not* the year of the cited regulation. The citing case of 274 F. Supp. 628 was decided in 1967.

The technique for sheparding a federal regulation are summarized in exhibit 11.33.

### 5. LOOSE-LEAF SERVICES

Loose-leaf refers to easily removable pages, often within a three-ring binder. The primary advantage of this structure is the ease of inserting updating material and the frequency with which updating can occur (e.g., weekly). Normally, the buyer of a loose-leaf pays for the initial volume(s) plus a subscription that consists of new pages that periodically come in the mail. New pages might simply be added to the end of the volume, or they might be interfiled. Interfiling means inserting pages anywhere within an existing text, not just at the end. The pages come with instructions telling the filer which pages to remove from the volume(s) and which to insert as replacements or additions. (This task, sometimes performed by paralegals, is called loose-leaf filing.)

Inserting pages into a loose-leaf service

---

**EXHIBIT 11.33**    **Checklist for Shepardizing a Federal Regulation**

1. Go to *Shepard's Code of Federal Regulations Citations.* (For a photo, exhibit 11.8.)
2. Know whether you have a complete set of Shepard's in front of you by reading the WHAT YOUR LIBRARY SHOULD CONTAIN list on the most recent pamphlet in that set. (To check this on the Internet, go to *helpcite.shepards.com.*)
3. Shepardize your regulation through every unit of this set of Shepard's.
4. Know the three kinds of information you can obtain when shepardizing a federal regulation: history of the regulation in the courts, citing legal periodical literature, and citing annotations.
5. An asterisk or a delta symbol will appear next to the year of all citing material: the citing cases, the citing periodical literature, and the citing annotations.
   (a) The asterisk means that the citing material referred to the specific year of the cited regulation. Hence the year is the year of the cited regulation, not of the citing material.
   (b) The delta symbol means that the citing material did not refer to the specific year of the cited regulation. Hence the year is the year of the citing material, not of the cited regulation.
6. The set of Shepard's for C.F.R. does not directly tell you what amendments, revisions, or other changes were made *by the agencies* to the

regulations. You are told only what *the courts* have said about the regulations. (To find out what the agencies have done to the regulations, you must check sources such as the CFR Parts Affected tables in the *Federal Register.*)
7. Check the meaning of abbreviations in the tables and preface at the beginning of most of the Shepard's units.
8. All regulations in C.F.R. are based on statutes of Congress. (A statute that is the basis or authority for the actions of an agency is called an **enabling statute**.) As we will see later, you can find out what statutes in U.S.C. are the authority for particular regulations in C.F.R. by checking the "authority" reference under many of the regulations in C.F.R. Once you know the statute that is the basis for the regulation, you might want to shepardize that enabling statute for more law in the area. (See exhibit 11.32 on shepardizing a statute.)
9. You can also shepardize a federal regulation online through LEXIS:
10. For more information about Shepard's:
    ■ 800-899-6000 (product support line)
    ■ www.shepards.com
11. The online alternative to Shepard's is KeyCite, available only on Westlaw. KeyCite will allow you to obtain citator references for cited federal regulations.

---

Several different kinds of legal materials are published as loose-leafs:

■ Legal treatises. Some loose-leafs are standard legal treatises that provide a comprehensive overview of a legal topic, perhaps along with checklists and forms. An example is *Larson's Workmen's Compensation Law.*

■ Reporters. Reporters are volumes containing court opinions. Although most reporters have a permanent binding with nonremovable pages, a few are loose-leafs. An example is *United States Law Week,* which contains every opinion of the United States Supreme Court.

■ Services. A loose-leaf service is a multipurpose collection of materials on a broad or narrow area of law. It might be called a guide, reporter, index, coordinator, library, etc. Examples include *Congressional Index, Employment Practices Guide,* and *AIDS Law and Litigation Reporter.*

For a comprehensive list of what is available, see *Legal Looseleafs in Print,* published by Infosources Publishing at *www.infosourcespub.com.*)

Our primary focus in this section is the third category—the loose-leaf service. There is no prescribed definition of a loose-leaf service. A publisher might use this phrase for any of its loose-leaf books. More commonly, however, the phrase refers to volumes containing a wide variety of legal materials. For example:

■ Recent court opinions or summaries of opinions
■ Relevant legislation—usually explained in some detail
■ Administrative regulations and decisions, or summaries of them (some of this material may not be readily available elsewhere)
■ References to relevant studies and reports
■ Practice tips

In short, loose-leaf services can be extremely valuable. The major publishers include Commerce. Clearing House (CCH) (*www.cch.com*) and the Bureau of National Affairs (BNA) (*www.bna.com.*) Loose-leaf services cover numerous areas of the law, e.g., criminal law, taxes, corporate law, and unions. You should assume that one or more loose-leaf services exist on the general topic of your research problem until you prove otherwise to yourself.

Unfortunately loose-leaf services are sometimes awkward to use. Occasionally, library users misfile pages that they take out for photocopying. There is no standard structure for a loose-leaf. You might find the following, for example:

- One volume or a multivolume set
- Organization by page number, organization by section number, organization by paragraph number, or a combination of these
- Different colored pages to indicate more recent material
- New pages inserted by interfiling, by addition to the end of one of the volumes, or a combination of both methods
- Indexes at the end, in the middle, or at the beginning of the volumes
- Bound volumes that accompany the three-ring volumes
- Transfer binders that contain current material

You should approach the structure of each loose-leaf service as a small puzzle sitting on the shelf waiting to be put together.

The techniques for finding and using loose-leaf services are summarized in exhibit 11.34.

---

**EXHIBIT 11.34    Checklist for Finding and Using Loose-Leaf Services**

1. Divide your research problem into its major topics, such as family law, tax law, antitrust law, etc. Assume that one or more loose-leaf services exist for these topics until you demonstrate otherwise to yourself.
2. Find out where the loose-leaf services are located in your library. Are they all together? Are they located in certain subject areas? Does the library have a separate list of them?
3. Check the library's card or online catalog. Look for subject headings on your topics to see if loose-leaf services are mentioned. Check the names of the major publishers of loose-leaf services, e.g., Commerce Clearing House and Bureau of National Affairs. (See exhibit 11.21 on using the catalog.)
4. Ask library staff members if they know of loose-leaf services on the major topics of your research.
5. Call other law libraries in your area. Ask the staff members there if they know of loose-leaf services on the major topics of your research. See if they can identify loose-leaf services that you have not yet found.
6. Speak to experts in the area of the law, e.g., professors. (See exhibit 11.39.) Ask them about loose-leaf services.
7. Once you have a loose-leaf service in front of you, you must figure out how to use it:

(a) Read any preface or explanatory material in the front of the volumes of the loose-leaf service.
(b) Ask library staff members to give you some help.
(c) Ask attorneys or paralegals who are experts in the area if they can give you a brief demonstration of its use.
(d) Ask a fellow student who is familiar with the service.
(e) Read any pamphlets or promotional literature by the publishers on using their loose-leaf services. For each loose-leaf service, you need to know the following:
- What it contains and what it does not contain
- How it is indexed
- How it is supplemented (updated)
- What its special features are
- How many volumes or units it has and the interrelationship among them

You obtain this information through techniques (a) to (e) above.

8. In your research memo, you rarely cite a loose-leaf service unless the material you found there does not exist elsewhere. Use the loose-leaf service mainly background research (see exhibit 11.18) and as a search tool for leads to find primary authority, such as cases, statutes, and regulations.

*Assignment 11.19*

Find one loose-leaf that might be helpful in researching each of the topics for the section O assignments (see page 549). Locate one per topic. In each loose-leaf, find a case written by a state court in your state or by a federal court that sits in your state. If you cannot find a case written by such a court, use a different loose-leaf until you find one. Give the citation of the loose-leaf and of the case.

## 6. LEGAL PERIODICAL LITERATURE

Legal periodical literature consists of the following:

- Lead articles and comments written by individuals who have extensively researched a topic
- **Case notes** that comment on recent court opinions
- Book reviews

There are three major publishers of periodicals: academic institutions, including almost all of the nation's law schools (where the students running the periodicals have the prestige of being "on law review"); commercial companies; and bar associations. Legal periodicals are either general, covering a wide variety of legal topics, e.g., *Harvard Law Review*, or specialized, e.g., *Family Law Journal*. The large number of legal periodicals that exist provide researchers with a rich source of material.

How can you locate legal periodical literature on point? What index systems will allow you to gain access to the hundreds of legal periodicals and the tens of thousands of articles, comments, case notes, book reviews, and other material in them? Two major general index systems exist:

- *Index to Legal Periodicals and Books* (ILP) published by H.W. Wilson Co.
- *Current Law Index* (CLI) published by Information Access Corporation

Of the two, the CLI is more comprehensive because it indexes more legal periodicals. Both are available in three different versions: a paper version (consisting of pamphlets and hardcover volumes), a CD–ROM version, and an online version. Few law libraries subscribe to all the legal periodicals indexed in the ILP and the CLI. Hence you may be obtaining leads to periodicals that your library does not have. If so, check other libraries in the area.

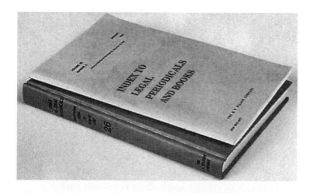

Examples of the paper versions of the *Index to Legal Periodicals and Books* (ILP) ■ and the *Current Law Index* (CLI). Both are also available online and on CD-ROM.

### Index to Legal Periodicals and Books (ILP)

- The ILP first comes out in pamphlets that are later consolidated (i.e., cumulated) into bound volumes.
- You must check each ILP pamphlet and each ILP bound volume for whatever years you want.
- The ILP regularly adds new periodicals that are indexed.
- Every recent ILP pamphlet and bound volume has four indexes:
    - (1) A Subject and Author Index
    - (2) A Table of Cases commented on
    - (3) A Table of Statutes commented on
    - (4) A Book Review Index
- Abbreviation tables appear at the beginning of every pamphlet and bound volume.
- The Subject and Author Index in the ILP is easy to use. You simply go to the topic on which you are seeking periodical literature, e.g. abortion, smoking. If you have the name of an author and want to know if he or she has written anything on the topic of your research, you simply check that author's last name in this index.
- Toward the end of every ILP pamphlet and hardcover volume is a Table of Cases. Suppose that elsewhere in your research you come across an important case, and you now want to know if that case was ever commented on (i.e., noted) in the legal periodicals. Go to the ILP pamphlet or hardcover volume that covers the year of the case and check the Table of Cases. (See research link P.)
- The Table of Statutes serves the same function for statutes. This table will tell you where you can find periodical literature commenting on certain statutes that are important to your research, e.g., the Pregnancy Leave Act. (See research link Q.)
- At the end of every pamphlet and hardcover ILP volume is a Book Review Index. If you are looking for a review of a law book you have come across elsewhere in your research, go to the ILP pamphlet or hardcover volume that covers the year of publication of the book for which you are seeking reviews.
- The ILP is also available:
    - (1) On WILSONLINE, the publisher's online research system
    - (2) On WILSONDISC, a CD–ROM system
    - (3) On Westlaw
    - (4) On LEXIS

### Current Law Index (CLI)

The CLI indexes more periodicals than the ILP. In fact, one of the reasons the CLI was created was the unwillingness of the publisher of the ILP (H.W. Wilson Co.) to expand the number and kind of periodicals it indexed.

- The CLI first comes out in pamphlets that are later consolidated (i.e., cumulated) into hardcover volumes.
- You must check each CLI pamphlet and each annual CLI issue for the years you want.
- There are four indexes within each CLI unit:
    - (1) A Subject Index
    - (2) An Author-Title Index
    - (3) A Table of Cases
    - (4) A Table of Statutes
- Abbreviation tables appear at the beginning of every CLI unit.
- The Subject Index gives full citations to periodicals under a topic (e.g., child welfare, zoning) and under an author's name.
- Book reviews are included under the Author-Title Index along with cites to periodical literature by the authors.
- The Table of Cases is valuable if you already know the name of a case located elsewhere in your research. To find out if that case was commented on, check the Table of Cases in the CLI unit that covers the year of the case. (See research link P.)
- The Table of Statutes is equally valuable. If you already have the name of a statute from your other research (such as the California Fair Employment Practices Act),

look for the name of that statute in the Table of Statutes for the CLI unit that covers the approximate time the statute was passed. (See research link Q.)

- The CLI began in 1980; it does not index periodicals prior to this date. The ILP must be used for the period before 1980.

**Legal Resource Index (LRI)**   The Legal Resource Index (LRI) is the online version of the *Current Law Index*. The LRI is available on Westlaw and LEXIS.

**LegalTrac**   LegalTrac is the CD–ROM version of the *Current Law Index*.

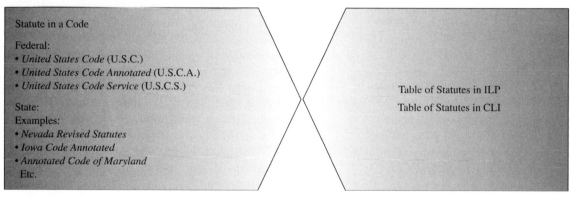

Case in a Reporter:
*Atlantic 2d* (A.2d), *North Eastern 2d* (N.E.2d), *North Western 2d* (N.W.2d), *Pacific 2d* (P.2d), *Southern 2d* (So.2d), *South Eastern 2d* (S.E. 2d), *South Western 2d* (S.W. 2d), *Unites States Reports* (U.S.), *Federal Reports 3d* (F.3d), *etc.*

Table of Cases in ILP

Table of Cases in CLI

## RESEARCH LINK P
If you have found a federal or state case in a reporter that is important to your research, find out if that case has been commented on in a case note in legal periodical literature. To find out, check the tables of cases in ILP and CLI.

Statute in a Code

Federal:
- *United States Code* (U.S.C.)
- *United States Code Annotated* (U.S.C.A.)
- *United States Code Service* (U.S.C.S.)

State:
Examples:
- *Nevada Revised Statutes*
- *Iowa Code Annotated*
- *Annotated Code of Maryland*
  Etc.

Table of Statutes in ILP

Table of Statutes in CLI

## RESEARCH LINK Q
If you have found a federal or state statute in a code that is important to your research, find out if that statute has been commented on in a legal periodical literature. To find out, check the tables of statutes in ILP and CLI.

### Other Index Systems
A number of other periodical index systems exist:

- Index to Federal Tax Articles
- Index to Foreign Legal Periodicals
- Index to Canadian Legal Periodical Literature
- Jones-Chipman Index to Legal Periodical Literature (covering periodical literature up to 1937 only)
- Index Medicus (covers medical periodicals—usually available only in medical libraries)
- MEDLINE (a computer search system for medical periodicals—available mainly in medical libraries). Free access to MEDLINE is possible through the Gateway of the National Library of Medicine at *gateway.nlm.nih.gov/gw/Cmd.*

### Legal Periodicals on the Internet
There is a great deal of legal periodical literature on the Internet. You can find lists (directories) of legal periodicals, as well as legal newsletters and magazines, some written solely online (*cyberjournals*). There are also extensive indexes to this literature that allow you to

do key word searches to find literature on a vast number of legal topics. Here are some of the Internet addresses to check, many of which have links to each other and to other legal resources on the Internet:

- www.lawreview.org
- www.hg.org/journals.html
- www.usc.edu/dept/law-lib/legal/journals.html
- stu.findlaw.com/journals (click "law reviews")

---

**EXHIBIT 11.35**     **Checklist for Finding Legal Periodical Literature**

1. Use legal periodical literature mainly for background research and for leads to primary authority, particularly through the extensive footnotes in this literature.
2. There are two major general index systems: *Index to Legal Periodicals and Books* (ILP) and *Current Law Index* (CLI). They are issued in pamphlets and hardcover volumes. (There are also CD-ROM versions and online versions, which are considerably easier to use. One of the most popular is LegalTrac, the CD-ROM version of CLI.)
3. The CARTWHEEL will help you locate material in ILP and CLI.
4. Both ILP and CLI also contain separate indexes. You should become familiar with all these internal index features.
5. Start with the subject indexes within ILP and CLI.
6. Identify the name and date of every important case that you have found in your research thus far. Go to the table of cases in ILP and in CLI to find out if any periodical literature has commented on these cases. (Go to the ILP and CLI units that would cover the year the case was decided. To be safe, also check their units for two years after the date of the case.) See research link P.
7. If you are researching a statute, find out if any periodical literature has commented on the

statute. (See research link Q.) This is done in two ways:
   (a) Check the tables of statutes in ILP and CLI.
   (b) Break your statute down into its major topics. Check these topics in the subject indexes of ILP and CLI to see if any periodical literature on these topics discusses your statute.
8. If you have the name of an author who is known for writing on a particular topic, you can also check for literature written by that author under his or her name in ILP and CLI.
9. Ask library staff members if the library has any other indexes to legal periodical literature, particularly in specialty areas of the law.
10. It is possible to shepardize some legal periodical literature. If you want to know whether the periodical article, note, or comment was ever mentioned in a court opinion, go to *Shepard's Law Review Citations*.
11. It is possible to search for legal periodical literature online in Westlaw, LEXIS, and WILSONLINE.
12. There are many sites on the Internet that allow you to obtain lists of legal periodicals and to find specific information within some of these periodicals.

---

*Assignment 11.20*

Find one legal periodical article that might be helpful in researching each of the topics for Section O the assignments (see page 549). Choose one per topic. In each article, scan the footnotes to find a case written by a state court in your state or by a federal court that sits in your state. If you cannot find a case written by such a court, choose a different legal periodical article until you find one. Give the citation of the article. Quote the sentence (or footnote) from the article that mentions this case.

### 7. LEGAL ENCYCLOPEDIAS

The major multivolume legal encyclopedias are *Corpus Juris Secundum* (C.J.S.), a dark blue set, and *American Jurisprudence 2d* (Am. Jur. 2d), a green set. Both are published by West Group. In many law libraries, they are the most frequently used volumes on the shelf because they are easy to use and are comprehensive. If you know how to use a general encyclopedia, you know how to use a legal encyclopedia. The volumes contain hundreds of alphabetically arranged topics on almost every area of the law. For each topic, you are given explanations of the basic principles of law and extensive footnote references supporting these principles. The vast majority of the references are to cases, although for certain topics, such as federal taxation, there are references to statutes as well. Legal encyclopedias have two main values. They are excellent as background research in a new area of the law. (See exhibit 11.18.) They are also valuable as leads to primary authority, particularly case law. In addition to the national legal encyclopedias, some states have state-specific encyclopedias devoted to the law of one state, e.g., *Florida Jurisprudence*.

For a sample page from C.J.S., see exhibit 11.36. Every section begins with a summary of that section in bold print. The phrase **black letter law** has come to mean any summary or overview that contains basic principles of law.

At the end of both C.J.S. and Am. Jur.2d is a huge *general index*. There are also extensive topic indexes within individual volumes. See exhibit 11.37.

---

**EXHIBIT 11.36** | **Excerpt from a Page in *Corpus Juris Secundum***

### §§ 22–23 BURGLARY

**c. Use of Instrument, Explosives, or Torch**

**In order to constitute burglary, entry need not be made by any part of accused's body, but entry may be made by an instrument, where the instrument is inserted for the purpose of committing a felony.**

In order to constitute a burglary, it is not necessary that entry be made by any part of the body; it may be by an instrument,[5] as in a case where a hook or other instrument is put in with intent to take out goods, or a pistol or a gun with intent to kill.[6] It is necessary, however, that the instrument shall be put within the structure, and that it shall be inserted for the

immediate purpose of committing the felony or aiding in its commission, and not merely for the purpose of making an opening to admit the hand or body, or, in other words, for the sole purpose of breaking.

A statute making it an offense to break and enter a building with intent to commit a crime, and defining "enter" as including insertion into the building of any instrument held in defendant's hand and intended to be used to detach or remove property, does not require that the offender intend the detachment or removal of property to occur at the moment of insertion only, and the intended detachment or removal relates to a later time as well...

**5.** Cal.—People v. Walters, 57 Cal.Rptr.484, 249 C.A.2d 547. Del.—Bailey v. State, 231 A.2d 469.
Me.—State v. Liberty, 280 A.2d 805.
N.J.—Corpus Juris Secundum quoted in State v. O'Leary, 107 A.2d 13, 16, 31 N.J. Super. 411.
N.M.—State v. Tixier, 551 P.2d 987, 89 N.M. 297.
Or.—Terminal News Stands v. General Cas. Co., 278 P.2d 158, 203 Or. 54.

Tenn.—State v. Crow, 517 S.W.2d 753.
Tex.—Tanner v. State, Cr., 473 S.W.2d 936.
Wyo.—Mirich v. State, 593 P.2d 590.
**6.** N.J.—Corpus Juris Secundum quoted in State v. O'Leary, 107 A.2d 13, 16, 31 N.J.Super. 411.
Pa.—Commonwealth v. Stefanczyk, 77 Pa.Super.27.
Tex.—Stroud v. State, 60 S.W.2d 439, 124 Tex.Cr. 56.

---

### Assignment 11.21

**(a)** Find one section in C.J.S. that might be helpful in researching each of the topics for the section O assignments (see page 549). Find one per topic. Within this section, find a case cited in the footnotes written by a state court in your state or by a federal court that sits in your state. If you cannot find a case written by such a court, choose a different section of C.J.S. until you find one. Give the citation of the C.J.S. section you used. Quote the sentence (or footnote) from the section that mentions this case.

**(b)** Find one section in Am. Jur. 2d that might be helpful in researching each of the topics for the section O assignments (see page 549). Find one per topic. Within this section, find a case cited in the footnotes written by a state court in your state or by a federal court that sits in your state. If you cannot find a case written by such a court, choose a different section of Am. Jur. 2d until you find one. Give the citation of the Am. Jur. 2d section you used. Quote the sentence (or footnote) from the section that mentions this case.

| EXHIBIT 11.37 | Checklist for Using Legal Encyclopedias |
| --- | --- |

1. Use the two national legal encyclopedias (Am. Jur. 2d and C.J.S.) for the following purposes:
   (a) For background research on areas of the law that are new to you.
   (b) For leads in their extensive footnotes to primary authority, such as cases and statutes.
2. Both legal encyclopedias have multivolume general indexes at the end of their sets. Use the CARTWHEEL to help you locate material in them. In addition to these general indexes, Am. Jur. 2d and C.J.S. have separate indexes in many of the individual volumes
3. Neither Am. Jur. 2d nor C.J.S. includes a table of cases.
4. Both Am. Jur. 2d and C.J.S. have a separate volume called *Table of Laws and Rules*. Check this table if you have found a relevant statute, regulation, or rule of

court from your other research that you want to find discussed in Am. Jur. 2d. or C.J.S.
5. Am. Jur. 2d and C.J.S. are published by West Group. Within these legal encyclopedias, the publisher provides library references to other research books that it publishes, e.g., annotations in A.L.R. (A.L.R. 1st), A.L.R. 2d, A.L.R.3d, A.L.R.4th, A.L.R.5th, and A.L.R. Fed.
6. Both encyclopedias also have references to key numbers, so that you can find additional case law in West Group digests.
7. Find out if your library has a *local* encyclopedia that is limited to the law of your state. States with such encyclopedias include California, Florida, Kentucky, Illinois, Maryland, Michigan, Minnesota, New York, Ohio, Pennsylvania, and Texas.
8. Am. Jur. 2d is available online through LEXIS and Westlaw.

## 8. LEGAL TREATISES

A legal treatise is any book written by private individuals (or by public officials writing in a private capacity) on a topic of law. Some treatises are scholarly; others are more practice oriented. The latter are often called hornbooks, handbooks, form books, and practice manuals. Treatises give overview summaries of the law, plus references to primary authority. There are single-volume treatises such as *Prosser on Torts*, as well as multivolume treatises such as *Moore's Federal Practice, Collier on Bankruptcy*, etc. See exhibit 11.38.

| EXHIBIT 11.38 | Checklist for Finding and Using Legal Treatises |
| --- | --- |

1. Always look for legal treatises on the topics of your research problem. Assume, until you prove otherwise to yourself, that three or four such treatises exist and are relevant to your problem.
2. Treatises are useful for background research and for leads to primary authority.
3. Many treatises are updated by pocket parts, supplemental volumes, and page inserts if the treatise is printed as a loose-leaf.
4. Start your search for treatises in the card or computer catalog (see exhibit 11.21 on using the catalog).
5. Check with experts in the area of law in which you are interested, e.g., teachers, for recommendations on treatises you should examine. See exhibit 11.39.
6. If your library has open stacks, find the treatise section. For example, go to the section of the stacks containing books with KF call numbers. Locate the section of the stacks containing treatises on your topic. Browse through the shelves to try to find additional treatises. Some treatises that you

need, however, may be on reserve rather than in the open stacks.
7. Once you have found a treatise, check that author's name in the *Index to Legal Periodicals and Books* (ILP) or the *Current Law Index* (CLI) to try to find periodical literature on the same topic by this author. You can also use these indexes to see if there are any book reviews on the treatises. (See exhibit 11.35 on finding legal periodical literature.)
8. Libraries do not always purchase subsequent editions of treatises. If a library has not purchased a later edition, its catalog will not tell you that a later edition exists. One way to find out if there is a later edition of a treatise you have found on the shelf is to check *Law Books & Serials in Print* or *Books in Print*.
9. If you know the name of a treatise, an online catalog (e.g., the Library of Congress at catalog.loc.gov) may give you some information about the treatise such as the name of its publisher. For a fee-based service that searches legal treatises for you, see www.indexmaster.com.

*Assignment 11.22*
Find one legal treatise that might be helpful in researching each of the topics for the section O assignments (see page 549). Find one per topic. The legal treatise you select must be different from any of the legal treatises you may have used in assignments 11.14 and 11.19. In each legal treatise, find a citation to a case written by a state court in your state or by a federal court that sits in your state. If you cannot find a case written by such a court, choose a different legal treatise until you find one. Give the citation of the legal treatise and of the case. Quote the sentence (or footnote) from the legal treatise that mentions this case.

## 9. PHONE AND MAIL—CONTACT THE EXPERTS
In law offices throughout the country, many attorneys and paralegals use the telephone and e-mail as a research tool. They contact colleagues and experts for leads. As students, you also can use this resource. With caution—and, if needed, with the approval of instructors or supervisors—you should consider contacting experts on the topics of your research. If you can get through to them and if you adopt a sufficiently humble attitude, they may give you leads to important laws and may even discuss the facts of your research problem. Many experts are quite willing to help you free of charge, as long as you are respectful and do not give the impression that you want more than a few moments of their time. You do not ask to come over to spend an afternoon!

Making contact through the mail is less likely to obtain a response unless you use e-mail rather than traditional "snail" mail. It takes very little effort—and no cost—for a prospective expert to respond to a brief question e-mailed from you. See exhibit 11.39.

---

**EXHIBIT 11.39    Checklist for Doing Phone and Mail Research**

1. Your goal is to contact someone who is an expert in the area of your research problem. You want to try to talk with him or her briefly on the phone. (As an alternative, try to e-mail your question to the expert. Some of the sources listed below that give names and addresses of experts may also give their e-mail addresses.)

2. Do not try to contact an expert until you have first done a substantial amount of research on your own. For instance, you should have already checked the major cases, statutes, regulations, legal treatises, legal periodical literature, annotations, etc., that are readily available in the library.

3. Prepare the questions you want to ask the expert. Make them short and to the point. For example, "Do you know of any recent case law on the liability of a municipality for . . . ?" "Could you give me any leads to literature on the doctrine of promissory estoppel as it applies to . . . ?" "Do you know of any good Internet sites I could check on . . . ?" "Do you know anyone I could contact who has done empirical research on the new EPA regulations?" "Do you know of anyone currently litigating § 307?" Do *not* recite all the facts of the research problem to the expert and say, "What should I do?" If the expert wants more facts from you, let him or her ask you for them. You must create the impression that you want no more than a few moments of the expert's time. If the expert wants to give your request more attention, he or she will let you know.

4. Introduce yourself as a student doing research on a problem. State how you got the expert's name (see the next guideline) and then state how grateful you would be if you could ask him or her a "quick question."

5. Your introductory comments should state how you came across the expert's name and learned of his or her expertise. For example, say, "I read your law review article on. . . ." "I saw your name as an attorney of record in the case of. . . ." "Mr./Ms. _____ told me you were an expert in this area and recommended that I contact you."

6. Where do you find these experts? A number of possibilities exist:
   (a) *Special interest groups and associations*
       Contact attorneys within groups and associations such as unions, environmental groups, and business associations. Ask

| EXHIBIT 11.39 | Checklist for Doing Phone and Mail Research—*continued* |
|---|---|

your librarian for lists of such groups and associations, for example, the *Encyclopedia of Associations*.

**(b)** *Government agencies*

Contact the law departments of the government agencies that would be involved in the area of your research.

**(c)** *Specialty libraries*

Ask your librarian for lists of libraries, such as the *Directory of Special Libraries and Information Centers*.

**(d)** *Law professors*

Ask a librarian if the library has the *AALS Law Teacher's Directory*, which lists teachers by name and courses taught.

**(e)** *Attorneys of Record*

If you have found a recent court opinion on point, the names of the attorneys for the case are printed at the beginning of the opinion (see exhibit 11.28). Try to obtain the phone number and address of the attorneys from *West's Legal Directory* (available on findlaw.com and Westlaw) or from the *Martindale-Hubbell Law Directory* (www.martindale.com). These attorneys

may be willing to send you a copy of appellate briefs on the case. Also ask them about any ongoing litigation in the courts.

Often you are permitted to go to the court clerk's office and examine pleadings, appellate briefs, etc., on pending cases. All of these documents will give the names and addresses of the attorneys of record who prepared them. Finally, don't forget to check the closed case files of your own office for prior research that has already been done in the same area as your problem.

**(f)** *Authors of legal periodical literature and of legal treatises*

Try to contact the author of a law review article or treatise that is relevant to your research. (See exhibits 11.35 and 11.38 on legal periodicals and legal treatises.) The author's business address can often be found in sources such as the *AALS Law Teacher's Directory*, *West's Legal Directory*, *Martindale-Hubbell*, etc. On locating individuals on the Internet, see chapter 13.

---

*Assignment 11.23*

Give the names, addresses, telephone numbers, and e-mail addresses of two experts you would try to contact because they might be helpful in researching each of the topics for the section O assignments (see page 549). Give two per topic. State why you think they might be helpful and where you obtained the information on how to contract them.

---

Section P
# FINDING CASE LAW

In chapter 7, we covered the structure of a court opinion, the briefing of an opinion, and the application of an opinion to a set of facts. Here, our focus is on *finding* these opinions in the library—finding case law.

In searching for case law, you will probably find yourself in one or more of the following situations:

■ You already have one case on point (or close to being on point), and you want to find additional ones. (Something is on point if it raises or covers the same issue as the one before you.) See exhibit 11.40.

■ You are looking for cases interpreting enacted laws such as a statute, constitution, charter, ordinance, court rule, or regulation that you already have. See exhibit 11.41.

■ You are starting from square one. You want to find case law when you do *not* have a case, statute, or other law to begin with. You may be looking for cases interpreting common law or for cases interpreting enacted law you have not found yet. See exhibit 11.42.

The search techniques in exhibits 11.40 to 11.42 are not necessarily listed in the order in which they should be tried. Your goal is to know how to use all of them. In practice, you can vary the order.

First, a reminder about doing the first level of legal research: background research. You should review the checklist for background research presented in exhibit 11.18. While doing this research, you will probably come across laws that will be of help to you on the specific facts of your problem (which is the second level of research). If so, you may already have some case law and now want to find more.

| EXHIBIT 11.40 | Techniques for Finding Case Law When You Already Have One Case On Point |
| --- | --- |

1. *Shepardize the case that you have.* (See exhibit 11.30 on shepardizing cases). In the columns of Shepard's, look for cases that have mentioned your case. Such cases will probably cover similar topics. (You can also shepardize a case online through LEXIS).

2. *Shepardize cases cited by the case you have.* Almost every court opinion discusses or at least refers to other opinions. Is this true of the case you already have? If so, shepardize every case your case cites that might be relevant to your research. (See exhibit 11.30 on shepardizing cases.)

3. *KeyCite your case.* If you have access to Westlaw, do a KeyCite check on the case you already have. KeyCite (like Shepard's) will lead you to any cases that have cited the case you have.

4. *Use the West Group digests.* There are two ways to do this:

   **(a)** Go to the Table of Cases in all the digests covering the court that wrote the case you already have, such as the Table of Cases in the American Digest System. The Table of Cases will tell you what key numbers your case is digested under in the main volumes of the digest. Find your case digested under those key numbers. Once you have done so, you may find other relevant case law under the same key numbers.

   **(b)** Go to the West Group reporter that contains the full text of the case you already have. At the beginning of this case in the reporter, find the headnotes and their key numbers. Take the key numbers that are relevant to your problem into any of West Group's digests to find more case law. (See exhibit 11.23 on using digests.)

5. *Find an annotation.* First identify the main topics or issues in the case you already have. Look up these topics in the *ALR Index* and in the other index systems for finding annotations in A.L.R. (A.L.R. 1st), A.L.R.2d, A.L.R.3d, A.L.R.4th, A.L.R.5th, and A.L.R. Fed. (For a description of these annotation index systems, see exhibit 11.27.) Another way to try to find annotations is by shepardizing the case you have. Annotations are among the citing materials of Shepard's. Once you find an annotation, you will be given extensive citations to more case law.

6. *Find a discussion of your case in the legal periodicals.* Go to the Table of Cases in the *Index to Legal Periodicals and Books* (ILP) and the *Current Law Index* (CLI). There you will be told if your case was analyzed (noted) in the periodicals. If so, the discussion may give you additional case law on the same topic. (See exhibit 11.35 on finding legal periodical literature. See also Research Link P in section O.)

7. *Go to Words and Phrases.* Identify the major words or phrases that are dealt with in the case you have. Check the definitions of those words and phrases in the multivolume legal dictionary called *Words and Phrases*. By so doing you will be led to other cases defining the same words or phrases.

---

*Assignment 11.24*

Go to the regional reporter that covers your state. (See exhibit 11.5 in section H). Pick any opinion in this reporter that meets the following criteria: it was decided by the highest state court of your state, it is at least 20 years old, and it has at least five head-notes in it. Assume that this case is relevant to your research problem. What is the citation of this case? Find *additional* cases by using the techniques in exhibit 11.40. Try to find one additional case through each technique. Describe each of the techniques you used. Explain how you used it and give the cite to the additional case it led you to. If you were not able to use any of the techniques, explain why (e.g., your library did not have the materials you needed for the technique).

Now let us assume that you already have a statute and you want case law interpreting that statute. The techniques for doing so (many of which are the same when seeking case law interpreting constitutions, regulations, etc.) are presented in exhibit 11.41.

| EXHIBIT 11.41 | Techniques for Finding Case Law Interpreating a Statute |
|---|---|

1. *Sheparadize the statute that you have.* (See exhibit 11.32 on sheparadizing statutes.) In the columns of Shepard's, look for cases that have mentioned your statute. (You can also sheparadize a statute online through LEXIS.)

2. *KeyCite your statute on Westlaw.* If you have access to KeyCite on Westlaw, do a KeyCite check on the statute you have. KeyCite (like Shepard's) will lead you to available case law interpreting your statute.

3. *Examine the Notes of Decisions for your statute in the statutory code.* At the end of your statute in the statutory code, there are paragraph summaries of cases (often called Notes of Decisions) that have interpreted your statute. (See exhibit 11.44 later in the chapter.) Look for these summaries in the bound volume of the code, in the pocket part of this volume, and in any supplemental pamphlets at the end of the code. (For federal statutes, the codes to check are U.S.C.A. and U.S.C.S. The U.S.C. will *not* have such case summaries.)

4. *Find an annotation on your statute.* There are several ways to find out if there is an annotation in A.L.R. (A.L.R. 1st), A.L.R.2d, etc., that mentions your statute. First, sheparadize that statute. Such annotations are among the citing materials of Shepard's. second, KeyCite your statute on Westlaw. You will be told if there are any annotations that mention your statute. Third, check the Table of Laws, Rules, and Regulations in the last volume of the *ALR Index.* See exhibit 11.27. Such annotations will probably lead you to more case law on the statute. (If the statute you have is a federal statute, you can also find annotations on that statute through a separate volume called *ALR Federal Tables.*)

5. *Find legal periodical literature on your statute.* Law review articles on statutes, for example, often cite cases that interpret the statutes. There are four ways to find such articles:

   (a) Sheparadize the statute. Citing material for a statute will include citing legal periodical literature.

   (b) KeyCite your statute on Westlaw. You will be told if there is any legal periodical literature that covers your statute.

   (c) Check the Table of Statutes in the *Index to Legal Periodicals and Books* (ILP) and in the *Current Law Index* (CLI). See research link Q.

   (d) Go to the subject indexes in ILP and CLI and check the topics of your statute. (See exhibit 11.35 on legal periodicals.)

6. *Go to loose-leaf services on your statute.* Find out if there is a loose-leaf service on the subject matter of your statute. Such services often give extensive cites to cases on the statute. (See exhibit 11.34 on loose-leaf services.)

7. *Go to legal treatises on your statute.* Most major statutes have treatises on them that contain extensive cites to cases on the statute. (See exhibit 11.38 on legal treatises.)

8. *Sheparadize or KeyCite any cases you found through techniques 1–7 above.* Once you have found one good case that interprets your statute, sheparadizing or KeyCiting that case may lead to additional cases interpreting the statute.

---

*Assignment 11.25*

Go to the state statutory code for your state. Pick any statute in this code that meets the following criteria: it is printed in the bound volume rather than in a pocket part or supplement, and there are at least 10 court opinions interpreting this statute summarized beneath the statute (Notes of Decisions). Assume that this statute is relevant to your research problem. What is the citation of this statute? Find cases interpreting this statute using the techniques in exhibit in 11.41. Try to find one case through each technique. Describe each of the techniques you used. Explain how you used it, and give the cite to the case it led you to. If you were not able to use any of the techniques, explain why (e.g., your library did not have the materials you needed for the technique).

---

Finally, in exhibit 11.42, we assume that you are starting from scratch. You are looking for case law, and you do not have a starting case or statute with which to begin. You may be looking for cases interpreting common law or for cases interpreting a statute or other enacted law you have not found yet.

---

*Assignment 11.26*

Go to today's general-circulation newspaper. Select any topic in any of the stories in the newspaper that interests you. Select one that you think is related to the law in some way. Assume that you want to do legal research on this topic, starting with case law. What topic did you select? Find cases on this topic by using the techniques in exhibit 11.42. Try to find one case through each technique. Describe each of the techniques you used. Explain how you used it and give the cite of the case it led you to. If you were not able to use any of the techniques, explain why (e.g., your library did not have the materials you needed for the technique). If the topic you selected has never been involved in court cases, select another topic from the newspaper after describing the steps you took with the techniques that were unsuccessful.

| EXHIBIT 11.42 | Techniques for Finding Case Law When You Do Not Have a Case or Statute to Begin With |
|---|---|

1. *West Group digests*. In the Descriptive Word indexes (DWI) of the West Group digests, try to find key numbers on the topics of your research. (See exhibit 11.23 on using the West Group digests.)

2. *Annotations*. Try to locate annotations on the topics of your research through the index systems for A.L.R. (A.L.R.1st), A.L.R.2d, A.L.R.3d, A.L.R.4th, A.L.R.5th, and A.L.R. Fed. (See exhibit 11.27 on finding annotations.)

3. *Legal treatises*. Try to find treatises on the topics of your research in the card or online catalog. (See exhibit 11.38 on finding treatises.)

4. *Loose-leaf services*. Find out if there are loose-leaf services on the topics of your research. (See exhibit 11.34 on finding loose-leaf services.)

5. *Legal periodical literature*. Try to find legal periodical literature on the topics of your research in the subject indexes of ILP and CLI. (See exhibit 11.35 on finding legal periodical literature.)

6. *Legal encyclopedias*. Go to the indexes for Am. Jur. 2d and C.J.S. Try to find discussions in these legal encyclopedias on the topics of your research. (See exhibit 11.37 on using legal encyclopedias.)

7. *Phone and mail research*. Find an expert. (See exhibit 11.39 on doing phone and mail research.)

8. *Words and Phrases*. Identify all the major words or phrases from the facts of your research problem. Look up these words or phrases in the multivolume legal dictionary *Words and Phrases*, which gives definitions from court opinions.

9. *Shepardizing and KeyCiting*. If techniques 1–8 led you to any good cases, shepardize or KeyCite that case to try to find additional cases. On Shepardizing cases, see exhibit 11.30.

10. *Internet*. Exhibit 11.43 presents Internet sites where you can try to find case law. For sites on this list that have search boxes, enter the topics of your research to try to find cases on those topics.

| EXHIBIT 11.43 | Case Law on the Internet |
|---|---|

The sites in this chart may provide access to (1) the full text of all or some cases, (2) the current docket of the court, (3) the court's rules of court, and (4) administrative information such as the address of the court, names of court personnel, filing instructions, etc.

**All Federal Courts**
www.uscourts.gov/links.html
www.loc.gov/law/guide/usjudic.html
guide.lp.findlaw.com/10fedgov/judicial/index.html
www.law.emory.edu/FEDCTS
www.washlaw.edu
www.pacer.psc.uscourts.gov
www.firstgov.gov (under "Agencies," click federal and state)

**All State Courts**
www.findlaw.com/11stategov
www.law.cornell.edu/opinions.html#state
www.ncsconline.org/Information/info_court_web_sites.html
www.hg.org/usstates.html
www.washlaw.edu/uslaw/statelaw.html

## Section Q
# Reading and Finding Statutes

Statutes are laws written by legislatures that declare, command, or prohibit something. Statutes are among the most important primary authorities you will research. The vast majority of court opinions interpret and apply one or more statutes or administrative regulations based on those statutes. Indeed, one of the reasons there are so many opinions is that people constantly disagree over the meaning of statutes.

In the hierarchy of laws, constitutional law is the highest form of primary authority. (For the definition of the categories of law, see exhibit 6.1. in chapter 6.) Next in the hierarchy are statutes. As long as a statute does not violate the constitution, the statute controls. Courts cannot change a statute, but they can declare it unconstitutional. Courts create common law, yet legislatures can change the common law by enacting statutes in derogation of the common law. In short, statutes play a central role in our legal system.

### READING STATUTES

In exhibit 11.44, there is an excerpt from a New York statutory code. It is an annotated statutory code which simply means that the statutes are organized by subject matter (rather than chronologically) and that a variety of research references are provided along with the text of the statutes. Here is an explanation of the circled numbers in Exhibit 11.44:

①This is the section number of the statute. The symbol "§" before "146" means section.

②This is a heading summarizing the main topic of the statute. Section 146 covers who can visit state prisons in New York. This summarization was written by the private publishing company, not by the New York state legislature.

③Here is the body of the statute written by the legislature.

④At the end of a statutory section, you will often find a reference to session laws which are statutes enacted during a particular session of the legislature and printed in chronological order rather than by subject matter. The reference to session laws will use abbreviations such as L. (laws), P.L. (Public Law), Stat. (Statutes at Large), etc. Here, you are told that in the Laws (L.) of 1962, chapter (c.) 37, § 3, this statute was amended. The Laws referred to are the session laws. See the Historical Note ⑥ below for a further treatment of this amendment.

⑤The amendment to § 146 was effective (eff.) on February 20, 1962. The amendment may have been passed by the legislature on an earlier date, but the date on which it became the law of New York was February 20, 1962. It is important to know the effective date of a statute. Attorneys sometimes take cases that involve facts that occurred prior to the effective date of an otherwise applicable statute. Unless the statute is retroactive, you must locate the earlier version of the statute, often available only as session laws. Although no longer in effect, the earlier version may be the statute that governs the client's case.

⑥The Historical Note provides the reader with some of the legislative history of § 146. First, the reader is again told that § 146 was amended in 1962. Note that early in the body of the statute, there is a reference to the title "commissioner of general services." The 1962 amendment simply changed the title from "superintendent of standards and purchase" to "commissioner of general services." The Historical Note was written by the private publisher, not by the New York state legislature.

⑦Also part of the Historical Note is the *Derivation* section. This tells the reader that the topic of § 146 of the Corrections Law was once contained in § 160 of the Prison Law, which dates back to 1847. In 1929, there was another amendment.

⑧The *Cross References* refer the reader to other statutes that cover topics related to § 146.

⑨The *Library References* refer the reader to other texts that address the topic of the statute. On the left-hand side, there are two key numbers (Prisons ☞ 13 and Reformatories ☞ 7) that can be used to find more case law in the digests of West Group. In the right column, the library reference is to specific sections of C.J.S. (*Corpus Juris Secundum*), a West Group legal encyclopedia.

| EXHIBIT 11.44 | Excerpt from a Statutory Code (New York State) |
|---|---|

**§ 146.    Persons authorized to visit prisons**

The following persons shall be authorized to visit at pleasure all state prisons:  The governor and lieutenant-governor, commissioner of general services, secretary of state, comptroller and attorney-general, members of the commission of correction, members of the legislature, judges of the court of appeals, supreme court and county judges, district attorneys and every minister of the gospel having charge of a congregation in the town wherein any such prison is situated.  No other person not otherwise authorized by law shall be permitted to enter a state prison except under such regulations as the commissioner of correction shall prescribe.  The provisions of this section shall not apply to such portion of a prison in which prisoners under sentence of death are confined.

As amended L.1962, c. 37, § 3, eff. Feb. 20, 1962.

**Historical Note**

L.1962, c. 37, § 3, eff..Feb. 20, 1962, substituted "commissioner of general services" for "superintendent of standards and purchase".

**Derivation.** Prior to the general amendment of this chapter by L.1929, c. 243, the subject matter of this section was contained in former Prison Law, § 160; originally derived from R.S., pt. 4, c. 3, tit. 3, § 159, as amended L.1847, c. 460.

**Cross  References**

Promoting prison contraband, see Penal Law, §§ 205.20, 205.25.

**Library References**

Prisons ☞13.
Reformatories ☞7.

C.J.S. Prisons §§ 18, 19.
C.J.S. Reformatories §§ 10, 11.

**Notes of Decisions**

**I.   Attorneys**

Warden of maximum security prison was justified in requiring that interviews of prisoners by attorney be conducted in presence of guard in room, in view of fact that attorney, who sought to interview 34 inmates in a day and a half, had shown no retainer agreements and had not stated purpose of consultations. Kahn v. La Vallee, 1961, 12 A.D.2d 832, 209 N.Y.S.2d 591.

Supreme court did not have jurisdiction of petition by prisoner to compel prison warden to provide facilities in prison which would not interfere with alleged violation of rights of prisoner to confer in private with his attorney.  Mummiani v. La Vallee, 1959, 21 Misc.2d 437, 199 N.Y.S.2d 263, affirmed 12 A.D.2d 832, 209 N.Y.S.2d 591.

Right of prisoners to confer with counsel after conviction is not absolute but is subject to such regulations as commissioner of correction may prescribe, and prisoners were not entitled to confer with their attorney privately within sight, but outside of hearing of a prison guard, when warden insisted on having a guard present in order to insure against any impropriety or infraction of prison rules and regulations during interview.  Id.

⑩The most important research resource in an annotated code is the Notes of Decisions. It includes a series of paragraphs that briefly summarize every court opinion that has interpreted or applied § 146. Of course, the opinions were decided before the code volume containing § 146 was published. For later opinions, the reader must look to the pocket part of this code volume and to any supplemental pamphlets that have been added to the code. (Another way to find more recent opinions interpreting the statute is to shepardize or KeyCite the statute.) The first opinion that you are given in exhibit 11.44 is *Kahn v. La Vallee*. Next is *Mummiani v. La Vallee*. At the end of the final paragraph, you will find *Id.*, which means that the paragraph refers to the case cited in the immediately preceding paragraph, the *Mummiani* case.

With this perspective of what a statute in an annotated code looks like, we turn to some general guidelines on understanding statutes:

1. *The organization of a statutory code is often highly fragmented because it contains a large number of units and subunits.* A statutory code can contain anywhere from 5 to 150 volumes. If you are unfamiliar with a code, you should examine the first few pages of the first volume. There you will usually find the subject matter arrangement of all the volumes.

    An individual subject in a code may be further broken down into titles, parts, articles, or chapters, which are then broken down into sections and subsections. Here is an example of a possible categorization for the state of "X" covering the topic of corporations:

> X State Code Annotated
> Title 1. Corporations
> Chapter 1. Forming a Corporation
> Section 1. Choosing a Corporate Name
> Subsection 1(a). Where to File the Name Application
> Subsection 1(b). Displaying the Name Certificate
> Subsection 1(c). Changing the Corporate Name
> Section 2 . . .
> Chapter 2 . . .
> Etc.

    Of course, each state uses its own classification terminology. What is called a chapter in one state may be called a title in another.

    You also need to be sensitive to the internal context of a particular statutory section. A section is often a sub-sub-subunit of larger units.

> Example: Examine § 1183 in exhibit 11.45.
> Note that § 1183 is within Part II, which is within Subchapter II, which is within Chapter 12, which is within Title 8.

    Each section (§) of a statute is part of several units. The meaning of specific statutory language in a section sometimes depends on what unit it is in. Often you will see introductory phrases in a section such as,

- For purposes of this Title, . . .
- As used in this Chapter, . . .
- For purposes of this Subchapter, . . .
- For purposes of this Part, . . .
- As used in this article, . . .

    This kind of language should alert you to the need to view the section in context. The legislature is telling you that the law contained in the section you are reading may be limited to the unit of which that section is a part.

    As indicated earlier, a legislature may completely revise its labeling system page 538. What was once "Prison Law," for example, may now fall under the topic heading of "Correction Law." What was once section 73(b) of "Corporations Law" may now be section 13(f) of "Business and Professions Law." If such a revision has occurred, you should be able to find out about it either in a transfer or conversion table at the beginning of one of the code volumes or in the Historical Note at the bottom of the section. One of the advantages of CARTWHEEL (see exhibit 11.16 in section M) is that you are less likely to miss such statutes in the index of the code; the CARTWHEEL forces you to think of synonyms and broader/narrower categories of every word you are checking in an index.

2. *Statutes on administrative agencies often follow a common sequence.* A large number of statutes in a code cover administrative agencies. In fact, statutes are carried out

**EXHIBIT 11.45  Sections, Parts, Subchapters, Chapters, and Titles in a Statutory Code**

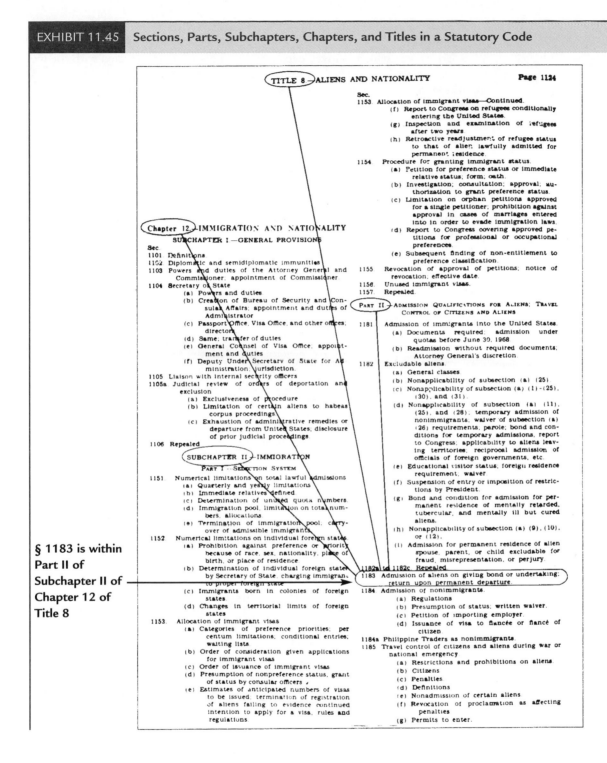

§ 1183 is within Part II of Subchapter II of Chapter 12 of Title 8

mainly by administrative agencies. These statutes are sometimes organized in the following sequence:

- The agency is created and named.
- The major words and phrases used in this cluster of statutes are defined.
- The administrators of the agency are given titles and powers.
- The budgetary process of the agency is specified.
- The method by which the public first comes into contact with the agency is established, such as applying for the benefits or services of the agency.
- The way in which the agency must act when a citizen complains about the agency's actions is established.

- How the agency must go about terminating a citizen from its services is established.
- The way in which a citizen can appeal to a court, if not satisfied with the way the agency handled his or her complaint, is established.

3. *All statutes must be based on some provision in the constitution that gives the legislature the power to pass the statute.* Legislatures have no power to legislate without constitutional authorization. The authorization may be the general constitutional provision vesting all legislative powers in the legislature; more often, it will be a specific constitutional provision such as the authority to raise revenue for designated purposes.

4. *Check to see if a statutory unit has a definition section.* At the beginning of a cluster of statutes, look for a definition section. If it exists, the section will define a number of words used in the remaining sections of the unit. Here is an example of such a definition section:

> **§ 31. Definitions.**—As used in this article, unless the context shall require otherwise, the following terms shall have the meanings ascribed to them by this section:
> 1. "State" shall mean and include any state, territory or possession of the United States and the District of Columbia.
> 2. "Court" shall mean the family court of the state of New York; when the context requires, it shall mean and include a court of another state defined in and upon which appropriate jurisdiction has been conferred by a substantially similar reciprocal law.
> 3. "Child" includes a step child, foster child, child born out of wedlock or legally adopted child and means a child under twenty-one years of age, and a son or daughter twenty-one years of age or older who is unable to maintain himself or herself and is or is likely to become a public charge.
> 4. "Dependent" shall mean and include any person who is entitled to support pursuant to this article.

5. *Find the statutes of construction.* Many codes have statutes that give you guidelines on how to interpret the statutes in the code. (**Construction** simply means interpretation.) For example, there may be a statute of construction on how to interpret a statute that contains a list of specific items followed by a general item. The rule of construction is that the general item should be construed (interpreted) as being of the same kind (**ejusdem generis**) as the specific items. Suppose § 100 of a statute prohibits "hunting, fishing, horse racing, and other public events." What does "other public events" mean? The ejusdem-generis statute of construction says you are to interpret a general item as being of the same kind as the specific items in the list. This would lead to the conclusion that "other public events" in § 100 means other *outdoor sporting* events, not any public event or even any sporting event. Why? Because all of the specific items in the list are outdoor sporting events. Hence, under this interpretation, § 100 would prohibit ocean swimming races but not necessarily indoor swimming races. Statutes of construction such as these can be very helpful in understanding statutes.

---

*Assignment 11.27*

Each of the following problems consists of a statute and a set of facts. Determine whether ejusdem generis is helpful in deciding whether the statute applies to the facts.

(a) *Statute.* § 88. An injunction can be obtained against any person who falsely claims to the the inventor of a product by circular, advertisement, or otherwise. *Facts:* George writes a letter to Sam falsely stating that he (George) invented the portable radio.

(b) *Statute:* § 608.7. Evidence of abandonment shall include exposure of the child in a street, field, or other place with the intent to leave the child there indefinitely. *Facts:* Roger took his infant child to the church rectory. When no one was looking, he left the child in a corner of the hallway and ran out.

6. *Statutes should be briefed.* A "brief" of a statute consists of answer to the following questions:
   (a) What is the citation of the statute? (On citing statutes, see exhibit 11.14)
   (b) What are the *elements* of the statute? (See discussion of elements in chapter 7.)
   (c) To whom is the statute addressed? Who is the audience? (Everyone? The director of an administrative agency? Citizens who want to apply for a permit? Etc.)
   (d) What condition(s) make the statute operative? (Many statutes have "when" or "if" clauses that specify condition(s) for the applicability of the statute.)
   (e) Is the statute mandatory or discretionary? A mandatory statute requires that something happen or be done ("must," "shall"). A discretionary statute permits something to occur but does not impose it ("may," "can").
   (f) What is the internal statutory context of the statute? To what other statutes, if any, does your statute refer?
   (g) What is the effective date of the statute?
   (h) Has the statute been amended in the past? (Check the Historical Notes that follow the statute. Briefly summarize major relevant changes.)
   (i) Has the statute been declared valid or invalid by the courts? (Check Notes of Decisions following the statute, and shepardize or KeyCite the statute.)
   (j) Do administrative regulations exist that interpret and carry out the statute? (On finding regulations based on statutes, see research link R later in the chapter. Give citations to any such regulations.)

7. *Statutory language tends to be unclear.* Seldom, if ever, is it absolutely clear what a statute means or how it applies to a given set of facts. For this reason, statutory language regularly requires close scrutiny and interpretation.

8. *Statutes are to be read line by line, pronoun by pronoun, punctuation mark by punctuation mark.* Statutes cannot be speed read. They should be read with the same care that you would use if you were translating a foreign language to English. Sentences sometimes appear endless. Occasionally, so many qualifications and exceptions are built into a statute that it appears incomprehensible. Do not despair. The key is perseverance and a willingness to tackle the statute slowly, piece by piece—through its elements.

## FINDING STATUTES

We turn now to techniques for finding statutes in traditional legal materials (exhibit 11.46) and on the Internet (exhibit 11.47) and the further research steps that should be taken before using or relying on a statute that you have found (exhibit 11.48).

| EXHIBIT 11.46 | Techniques for Finding Statutes |
| --- | --- |

1. Go to the statutory code in which you are interested. Some states have more than one statutory code. (See exhibit 11.14.) For federal statutes, there are the *United States Code* (U.S.C.), the *United States Code Annotated* (U.S.C.A.), and the *United States Code Service* (U.S.C.S.). Know how to use all available statutory codes that cover the same set of statutes. Although they contain the same statutes, the index and research features may differ.

2. Many university libraries in your area subscribe to the U.S.C. If these libraries are *federal depository libraries*, you must be given access to this set as well as to other subscriptions the library receives free from the federal government, e.g., the *Code of Federal Regulations* and the *Congressional Record*. If there is a university library that you want to use, call its reference desk and ask if it is a depository library. (There is an Internet list of depository libraries in every state that you can check. See www.lib.uidaho.edu/govdoc/otherdep.html.) On finding law libraries, see section E.

3. Read the explanation or preface pages at the beginning of the first volume of the statutory code. Also read the comparable pages at the beginning of the Shepard's volumes that will enable you to shepardize statutes in that code. These pages can be very helpful in explaining the structure of the code, particularly if there have been new editions, revisions, or renumberings.

4. Most statutory codes have general indexes at the end of the set as well as individual indexes for separate volumes. Use the CARTWHEEL to help you use these indexes. Also check any tables of contents that exist. Some statutes have popular names, such as the Civil Rights Act of 1964. If you know the popular name of a statute, you can find it in the statutory code through a Popular Name Table that often exists within the code itself.

EXHIBIT 11.46    Techniques for Finding Statutes—*continued*

5. While reading one statute in the code, you may be given a cross-reference to another statute within the same code. Check out these cross-references.

6. Update any statute that you find in the statutory code by checking the pocket part of the volume you are using; supplement pamphlets at the end of the code; bound supplement volumes; session law pamphlets; advance legislative services; online resources such as Westlaw, LEXIS, and the Internet; etc.

7. Loose-leaf services. Find out if there is a loose-leaf service on the topic of your research. Such services will give extensive references to applicable statutes. (See exhibit 11.34 on finding and using loose-leaf services.)

8. Legal treatises. Find out if there are legal treatises on the topics of your research. Such treatises will often give extensive references to applicable statutes. (See exhibit 11.38 on finding and using legal treatises).

9. Legal periodical literature. Consult the *Index to Legal Periodicals and Books* (ILP) and the *Current Law Index* (CLI). Use these indexes to locate periodical literature on the topics of your research. This literature will often give extensive references to applicable statutes. (See exhibit 11.35 on finding legal periodical literature.)

10. Annotations. Use the available index systems for A.L.R. (A.L.R. 1st), A.L.R.2d, A.L.R.3d, A.L.R.4th, A.L.R.5th, and A.L.R. Fed. to help you locate annotations. Annotations will sometimes refer you to statutes—particularly in A.L.R. Fed. for federal statutes. (See exhibit 11.27 on finding and updating annotations.)

11. Legal encyclopedias. Occasionally, legal encyclopedias such as Am. Jur. 2d and C.J.S. will summarize important statutes in the text and refer you to important statutes in the footnotes. (See exhibit 11.37 on using legal encyclopedias.)

12. Computers. State and federal statutes are available online through Westlaw and LEXIS. Many are also available on the Internet. See exhibit 11.47 for some of the most commonly used Internet sites for statutes. Finally, most statutes are available on CD–ROM.

13. Phone and mail research. Try to find an expert. (See exhibit 11.39 on doing phone and mail research.)

14. Occasionally, in your research, you will come across a statute that is cited in its session law form. To find this statute in the statutory code, you must translate the session law cite into the codified cite. This is done by trying to find transfer or conversion tables in the statutory code. For federal statutes, a session law or *Statutes at Large* cite is translated into a U.S.C./U.S.C.A./ U.S.C.S. cite by:

    (a) Checking Table III in the Tables volume of U.S.C./U.S.C.A./U.S.C.S.

    (b) Checking Table 2 in *U.S. Code Congressional and Administrative News* (U.S.C.C.A.N.) See research link O in section J. Some session laws, however, are never printed in the statutory code. Hence there is no codified cite for such statutes. You must go directly to the session laws in the library—if the library has them. (For federal statutes, the session laws are in *United States Statutes at Large*.)

Once you have found a statute that is relevant to your research problem, you need to do further research on the statute before you rely on it. See exhibit 11.48.

## Section R
# LEGISLATIVE HISTORY

In Chapter 6, we examined the six stages of the legislative process through which a bill becomes a statute. (See exhibit 6.5 in chapter 6.) The documents and events that occur during this process constitute the *legislative history* of a statute. Here, we consider two themes: the importance of legislative history and how to find it.

### WHY SEARCH FOR LEGISLATIVE HISTORY: ADVOCACY OBJECTIVES

To understand why researchers try to find the legislative history of a statute, let's look at an example:

In 1975, the state legislature enacts the Liquor Control Act. Section 33 of this Act provides that "[l]iquor shall not be sold on Sunday or on any day on which a local, state, or federal election is

| EXHIBIT 11.47 | **Finding Statutes on the Internet** |
|---|---|

The following Internet sites will lead you (directly or through links) to information about the legislature (e.g., names and addresses of individual legislators, steps on how a bill becomes a law). Many of the sites also allow you to enter search queries (questions) in order (a) to find the status of current bills pending in the legislature (important for monitoring legislation) or (b) to find statutes already enacted and part of the code. Not all of the sites, however, have the complete code online. For additional leads to the law of your state, check the general home page for your state; there you will often find links to a variety of state laws. Here is the address of the home page of most states (insert your state's abbreviation in place of the **xx**): **www.state.xx.us**

**UNITED STATES (federal statutes of Congress):**
www.access.gpo.gov/congress/cong013.html
thomas.loc.gov
www.uscode.house.gov/usc.htm
www4.law.cornell.edu/uscode
www.ilrg.com/codes.html
fedlaw.gsa.gov
www.lawresearch.com/v2/statute/statfed.htm

**ALL STATES (statutes of state legislatures; click the link to your state):**
www.findlaw.com/casecode/#state

www.findlaw.com/11stategov
www.llsdc.org/sourcebook/state-leg.htm
www.prairienet.org/~scruffy/f.htm
www.lcweb.loc.gov/global/state/stategov.html
www.washlaw.edu/uslaw/statelaw.html
www.piperinfo.com/state/index.cfm
www.law.cornell.edu/states/listing.html
www.ncsl.org/public/sitesleg.htm
www.lexnotes.com/sources/states/statutes.shtml
www.ilrg.com/codes.html

| EXHIBIT 11.48 | **Techniques for Further Research on Statutes You Have Found** |
|---|---|

1.  Make sure the statute is still valid:
    - Check your statute in the pocket part of the volume where you found the statute.
    - Check your statute in supplement pamphlets and in hardcover supplements that go with the code.
    - Shepardize the statute. (See exhibit 11.32 on shepardizing statutes).
    - Keycite the statute on Westlaw.
2.  Check all cross-references within the statute. If the statute refers to other statutes in the code, check them for their relevance to your research.
3.  Find cases interpreting the statute:
    - Check *notes of decisions* following the statute.
    - Shepardize the statute. Among the citing materials are cases that have analyzed or mentioned the statute. (See technique 1 above).
    - KeyCite the statute on Westlaw to find cases interpreting the statute.
4.  Find administrative regulations based on the statute. Many statutes are carried out by administrative regulations. The statute is considered the *authority* for such regulations. It is the enabling statute, which is a statute that is the basis or authority for what an agency does. To find the enabling statute for a federal regulation, check what is called the "Authority" reference

beneath the regulation in the *Code of Federal Regulations* (C.F.R.) or at the beginning of the cluster of regulations you are examining in the C.F.R. See research link R, later in the chapter.
5.  Find annotations on the statute.
    - If you shepardize the statute, the citing materials include annotations in A.L.R. (A.L.R. 1st), A.L.R. 2d, etc.
    - If you KeyCite the statute on Westlaw, you will find any annotations that cover the statute.
    - Check the Table of Laws, Rules, and Regulations found in the last volume of *ALR Index*. See exhibit 11.27.
    - For federal statutes, also check the separate volume called *ALR Federal Tables*.
6.  Find legal periodical comments or other periodical literature on the statute. Check the tables of statutes in the ILP and CLI. (See exhibit 11.35 and research link Q).
7.  Find out if there are any loose-leaf services that cover the statute. (See exhibit 11.34.)
8.  Find out if there are any legal treatises that cover the statute. (See exhibit 11.38.)
9.  Find a discussion of your statute in *Corpus Juris Secundum* or *American Jurisprudence 2d*. See the separate volume called *Table of Laws and Rules* that is part of C.J.S and Am. Jur. 2d. (See exhibit 11.37.)
10. Review the legislative history of the statute. See exhibits 11.49 and 11.50.

being held." The Fairfax Country Club claims that § 33 does not apply to the sale of liquor on Sunday or on election day *by membership clubs*; it applies only to bars that provide service to any customers that come in off the street. The question, therefore, is whether the legislature intended to include membership clubs within the restrictions of § 33. The state liquor board says that it did. The Fairfax Country Club argues that it did not.

How can the legislative history of § 33 help resolve this controversy? An advocate has two objectives when researching the legislative history of a statute:

- To determine whether the specific facts currently in controversy were ever discussed by the legislature when it was considering the proposed statute and
- To identify the broad or narrow purpose that prompted the legislature to enact the statute and to assess whether this purpose sheds any light on the specific facts currently in controversy

For example, when the legislature was considering § 33, was there any mention of country or membership clubs in the governor's message, in committee reports, in floor debates, etc.? If so, what was said about them? What was said about the purpose of § 33? Why was it enacted? What evil or mischief was it designed to combat? Was the legislature opposed to liquor on moral grounds? Did it want to reduce rowdyism that comes from the overuse of liquor? Did it want to encourage citizens to go to church on Sunday and to vote on election day? Were complaints made to the legislature about the use of liquor by certain groups in the community? If so, what groups? Answers to such questions might be helpful in formulating arguments on the meaning and scope of § 33. The advocate for the Fairfax Country Club will try to demonstrate that the legislature had a narrow objective when it enacted § 33: to prevent neighborhood rowdyism at establishments that serve only liquor. The legislature, therefore, was not trying to regulate the more moderate kind of drinking that normally takes place at membership clubs where food and liquor are often served together. The opponent, in contrast, will argue that the legislature had a broader purpose in enacting § 33: to decrease the consumption of liquor by all citizens on certain days. The legislature, therefore, did not intend to exclude drinking at a membership club.

### FINDING LEGISLATIVE HISTORY

In tracing legislative history, you are looking for documents such as bills, hearing transcripts, proposed amendments, and committee reports. It is often very difficult to trace the legislative history of *state* statutes. The documents are sometimes poorly preserved, if at all. See exhibit 11.49.

It is easier to trace the legislative history of a *federal* statute because the documents are generally more available. See exhibit 11.50.

| EXHIBIT 11.49 | Techniques for Tracing the Legislative History of State Statutes |
|---|---|

1. Examine the historical data beneath the statute in the statutory code (see exhibit 11.44). Amendments are usually listed there.
2. For an overview of codification information about your state, check the introductory pages in the first volume of the statutory code, or the beginning of the volume where your statute is found, or the beginning of the Shepard's volume that enables you to shepardize the statutes of that state.
3. Ask your librarian if there is a book (sometimes called a legislative service) that covers your state legislature. If one exists, it will give the bill numbers of statutes, proposed amendments, names of committees that considered the statute,

etc. If such a text does not exist for your state, ask the librarian how someone finds the legislative history of a current state statute in your state.
4. Check the Internet site of the state legislature. (See exhibit 11.47.) It may have links to sources of legislative history, such as an archives link or a legislative research link. A particularly useful site is that of the National Conference of State Legislatures (www.ncsl.org). It has links to every state legislature. (See also www.llrx.com/columns/roundup13.htm.) Some sites have an e-mail address to which you can send specific questions. If your state has such an address, send an e-mail asking for a lead to the legislative history of the statute you are researching.

| EXHIBIT 11.49 | Techniques for Tracing the Legislative History of State statutes—*continued* |

5. Contact the committees of both houses of the state legislature that considered the bill. The office of your local state representative or state senator might be able to help you identify these committees. If your statute is not too old, staff members on these committees may be able to give you leads to the legislative history of the statute. Ask if any committee reports (or committee prints) were written. Ask about amendments, etc.

6. Ask your librarian (or a local politician) if there is a law revision commission for your state. If so, ask a legislative reference librarian there for leads.

7. Is there a state law library in your area? If so, contact it for leads. (See appendix I.)

8. Check the law library and drafting office of the state legislature for leads.

9. Cases interpreting the statute sometimes give the legislative history of the statute, or portions of it. To find cases interpreting a statute, check the Notes of Decisions after the statute in the statutory code (see exhibit 11.44) and shepardize the statute (see exhibit 11.32 on shepardizing a statute).

10. You may also find leads to the legislative history of a statute in legal periodical literature on the statute (see exhibit 11.35), in annotations on the statute (see exhibit 11.27), in treatises on the statute (see exhibit 11.38), and in loose-leaf services on the statute (see exhibit 11.34). Phone and mail research might also provide some leads (see exhibit 11.39).

11. For an overview of state legislative history sources, check *State Legislative Sourcebook* by Lynn Hellebust or *Guide to State Legislative and Administrative Materials* by M. L. Fisher.

| EXHIBIT 11.50 | Techniques for Tracing the Legislative History of a Federal Statute |

1. Examine the historical data at the end of the statute in the *United States Code* (U.S.C.), in the *United States Code Annotated* (U.S.C.A.), and in the *United States Code Service* (U.S.C.S.).

2. You will also find the PL (Public Law) number of the statute at the end of the statute printed in U.S.C./U.S.C.A./U.S.C.S. This PL number will be important for tracing legislative history. (Note that each amendment to a statute will have its own PL number.)

3. Step one in tracing the legislative history of a federal statute is to find out if the history has already been compiled (collected) by someone else. There may be a list available telling you which area libraries have collected specific legislative histories.
   ▪ Ask your librarian.
   ▪ Check *Sources of Compiled Legislative Histories* by Nancy Johnson. This book will tell you where to locate already collected (compiled) legislative histories. Performing a similar service is *Federal Legislative Histories* by Bernard Reams.
   ▪ Contact the Library of Congress in Washington, D.C., if convenient. It collects legislative histories. (See its sourcebook on the Internet, www.llsdc.org/sourcebook/fed-leg-hist.htm.)
   ▪ If the statute deals with a particular federal agency, check with the library, law department, or legislative liaison office of that agency in Washington, D.C., or in one of its state or regional offices throughout the country. (Check your local phone directory listings under federal government and the Internet at www.firstgov.gov.) The agency may have compiled the legislative history and may give you access to it.
   ▪ Contact special interest groups or associations that are directly affected by the statute. (See *Encyclopedia of Associations* by Gale.) They may have compiled the legislative history.
   ▪ One question you can ask through phone and mail research is whether the expert knows if anyone has compiled the legislative history of the statute. See exhibit 11.39.

4. The *Congressional Record* gives you the transcript of the conversations between legislators on the floor while the bill is being debated. These conversations (though sometimes later altered—"amended"—by participating legislators) may cover the meaning of particular clauses in a bill. The conversations are often used by advocates when citing legislative history. The *Congressional Record* is published by Congress in daily pamphlets and later in permanent hardbound volumes.

5. The following materials are also useful in tracing the legislative history of federal statutes:
   ▪ *United States Code Congressional and Administrative News* (contains committee reports of important

bills; see its Table 4, which is a status table providing leads to legislative history). U.S.C.C.A.N. is a good place to begin your search for federal legislative history.

- *Monthly Catalog of U.S. Government Publications* (acts as an index to tell you which committee hearings have been published).
- *Congressional Index* from Commerce Clearing House (contains digest of bills, status tables, voting records, current news, etc.).
- The paper, CD–ROM, microform, and online products of CIS (Congressional Information Service) that contain reprints of legislative history documents, abstracts, indexes, and other finding tools. The CIS materials include:
  - *CIS/Annual Index to Publications of the United States Congress (CIS/index)*
  - *CIS/Annual Legislative Histories of U.S. Public Laws (CIS/Legislative Histories)*
  - *CIS/Annual Abstracts of Congressional Publications*
  - *Congressional Masterfile*
- *United States Serial Set* (committee reports, legislative studies, and other legislative documents).
- *Congressional Quarterly Weekly Report* (contains a legislative history table and a status table on current major bills).
- *Congressional Monitor* (contains a summary of daily events in Congress, lists of printed committee reports and other legislative documents).

6. Contact both committees of Congress that considered the legislation. They may be able to send you:
   - committee reports (summaries of the bill and a statement of the reasons for and against its enactment)
   - committee prints (a miscellaneous compilation of information prepared by committee staff members on a bill consisting of statistics, studies, reports, comparative analysis of related bills, etc.)

- hearing transcripts (a word-for-word account of the testimony given by a witness), etc.
- copies of the bill and amendments to it

If you have any difficulty, ask staff members in the office of your United States Senator and Representative for help in obtaining what you need from the relevant committees.

7. Cases interpreting the statute sometimes give the legislative history of the statute. To find cases interpreting the statute, check the Notes of Decisions after the statute in the U.S.C.A. and in the U.S.C.S. Also, shepardize the statute (see exhibit 11.32 on shepardizing a statute).

8. Find out if there is an annotation on the statute. See the Table of Laws, Rules, and Regulations in the last volume of *ALR Index*. For federal statutes, also check the volume called *ALR Federal Tables*. (See exhibit 11.27 on finding and updating annotations.)

9. You may also find leads to the legislative history of a statute in legal periodical literature (see exhibit 11.35), in legal treatises on the statute (see exhibit 11.38), in loose-leaf services on the statute (see exhibit 11.34).

10. To try to find a discussion of your statute in the C.J.S. or Am. Jur. 2d legal encyclopedias, check a separate volume called *Table of Laws and Rules*. (See exhibit 11.37.)

11. Examine your statute in its session law form in *United States Statutes at Large* for possible leads.

12. Check the Internet. Sites that can provide useful leads include:
    - www.lib.umich.edu/govdocs/legishis.html
    - www.access.gpo.gov/su_docs/legislative.html
    - www.llsdc.org/sourcebook
    - www.als.edu/lib/leghist.html

    Sites for finding current statutes may provide leads to sources for legislative history. See exhibit 11.47.

13. Check legislative histories online through Westlaw, LEXIS, and LEGI-SLATE.

## Section S
# Monitoring Proposed Legislation

Occasionally, you will be asked to monitor a bill currently before the legislature that has relevance to the caseload of the law office where you work. To monitor a bill means to determine its current status in the legislature and to keep track of all the forces that are trying to enact, defeat, or modify the bill. See exhibit 11.51. If you work for a corporation, you may be asked to monitor bills that affect the business of the company. Large corporations often hire lobbyists whose sole function is to monitor and try to influence the content of proposed legislation.

| EXHIBIT 11.51 | Techniques for Monitoring Proposed legislation |
|---|---|

1. Begin with the legislature. Find out what committee in each chamber of the legislature (often called the Senate and House) is considering the proposed legislation. Also determine whether more than two committees are considering the entire bill or portions of it.

2. Ask committee staff members to send you copies of the bill in its originally proposed form and in its amended forms.

3. Determine whether the committees considering the proposed legislation have written any reports on it and, if so, whether copies are available.

4. Determine whether any hearings have been scheduled by the committees on the bill. If so, try to attend. For hearings already conducted, see if they have been transcribed (recorded word-for-word).

5. Find out the names of people in the legislature who are working on the bill: legislators "pushing" the bill, legislators opposed to it, staff members of the individual legislators working on the bill, and staff members of the committees working on the bill. Ask for copies of any position papers or statements.

6. The local bar association may have taken a position on the bill. Call the association. Find out what committee of the bar is involved with the subject matter of the bill. This committee may have written a report on the bar's position on the bill. If so, try to obtain a copy.

7. Is an administrative agency of the government involved with the bill? Identify the agency with jurisdiction over the subject matter of the bill. Find out who in the agency is working on the bill and whether any written reports of the agency are available. Determine whether the agency has a legislative liaison office.

8. Who else is lobbying for or against the bill? What organizations are interested in it? Find out if they have taken any written positions.

9. What precipitated consideration of the bill by the legislature? Was there a court opinion that prompted the legislative action? If so, you should know what the opinion said.

10. Are any other legislatures in the country contemplating similar legislation? Some of the ways of finding out include the following:
    (a) Look for legal periodical literature on the subject matter of the bill (see exhibit 11.35).
    (b) Check loose-leaf services, if any, covering the subject matter of the bill (see exhibit 11.34)—these services often cover proposed legislation in the various legislatures.
    (c) Check legal treatises on the subject matter of the bill (see exhibit 11.38).
    (d) Organizations such as bar associations, public interest groups, business associations, etc., often assign staff members to perform state-by-state research on what the legislatures are doing. Such organizations may be willing to share this research with you.
    (e) Find out if there is a council of governments in your area. It may have done the same research mentioned in (d) above.
    (f) Contact an expert for leads to what other legislatures are doing (see exhibit 11.39).

11. Check the Internet. See, for example:
    ■ www.llrx.com/columns/roundup13.htm
    ■ www.GalleryWatch.com
    Also check the Internet site for the legislature (exhibit 11.47). It will often give you links to information on the status of current bills in the legislature. Some of the sites also provide direct e-mail links to individual legislators from whom you can seek information about pending bills.

12. Check online bill-tracking services on Westlaw (e.g. US–BILLTRK) and LEXIS (e.g., BLTRCK). Also check LEGI–SLATE of the Washington Post Company, ELSS (Electronic Legislative Search System) of Commerce Clearing House, WASHINGTON ALERT of the Congressional Quarterly, GPO Access, online versions of CIS/Index, etc.

## Section T
# READING AND FINDING CONSTITUTIONAL LAW

### READING CONSTITUTIONAL LAW

The constitution sets out the fundamental ground rules for the conduct of the government in the geographical area over which the government has authority or jurisdiction. The constitution defines the branches of the government, establishes basic rights and obligations of citizens, and covers matters that the framers considered important enough (such as limitations on the power to tax) to be included in the constitution. (See exhibit 6.1 in chapter 6.) The United States Constitution does this for the federal government, and the state constitution does it for the state government. In reading the constitution, keep the following guidelines in mind:

1. *Thumb through the headings of all the sections or articles of the constitution, or glance through the table of contents.* How is the document organized? What subjects did the framers want covered by the constitution? A quick scanning of the section headings or table of contents is a good way to obtain an overview of the structure of the text.

2. *The critical sections or articles are those that establish and define the powers of the legislative, judicial, and executive branches of government in the geographic area covered by the constitution.* Who passes, interprets, and executes the law? For the United States constitution, "all legislative Powers granted herein shall be vested in a Congress" (art. I, § 1); "the judicial Power of the United States, shall be vested in one supreme Court, and in such inferior Courts as the Congress may from time to time ordain and establish" (art. III, § 1); and "the executive Power shall be vested in a President of the United States of America" (art. II, § 1). The exact scope of these powers, as enunciated elsewhere in the Constitution, has been and continues to be an arena of constant controversy and litigation.

3. *The amendments to the constitution change or add to the body of the text.* The main vehicle for changing the constitution is the amendment process, which itself is defined in the constitution. Some constitutions, for example, can be amended by a vote of the people in a general election. A condition for most amendments is that they must be approved by one or more sessions of the legislature. Constitutional amendments usually appear at the end of the document.

4. *Constitutions are written in very broad terms.* There are, of course, exceptions to this, particularly in state constitutions, which can contain very specific provisions. In the main, however, a common characteristic of constitutions is their broad language. How would you interpret the following section?

   Congress shall make no laws respecting an establishment of religion, or prohibiting the free exercise thereof; or abridging the freedom of speech, or of the press; or of the right of the people to assemble, and to petition the Government for a redress of grievances.

   How many words in this provision do you *not* understand? What is an "establishment"? If the school board requires a "moment of silence" at the beginning of each day, is the school board establishing a religion? What does "abridging" mean? If a government official leaks secret documents to the press and the government tries to sue the press to prevent publication of the documents, has the "freedom" of the press been abridged? If the people have a right to "assemble," could the government pass a law prohibiting all gatherings of three or more people at any place within 1,000 yards of the White House gates? The questions arising from the interpretation of constitutional law are endless; tens of thousands of court opinions exist on questions such as these. The broader the language, the more ambiguous it is, and, therefore, the greater the need for interpretation.

5. *One of the central questions for the interpreter of constitutional law is: what meaning did the authors intend?* Common sense dictates that when language is ambiguous, the ambiguity may be resolved in part by attempting to determine what the author of the language intended by it. What was the author's meaning? In what context was the author writing? Does the context shed any light on what was meant? This kind of analysis is fundamental to legal reasoning, whether the document is a constitution, a statute, a regulation, or a court opinion. It is particularly difficult to do, however, for a constitution written over a hundred years ago.

   Finding the *original intent* of the authors of the constitution, however, is not the only method used to interpret particular provisions of the constitution. Another approach is to view the constitution as a "living" document that must be interpreted in light of the needs of modern society. The danger in this view is that too much can be read into the constitution based on the personal philosophies of individual judges. The charge is that these individuals rewrite the constitution under the guise of interpreting it to fit modern society. This debate, of course, adds to the controversy and the volume of constitutional law.

## FINDING CONSTITUTIONAL LAW

The techniques for finding constitutional law are summarized in exhibit 11.52.

---

**EXHIBIT 11.52** **Techniques for Finding Constitutional Law**

1. Start with the text of the constitution itself. It is usually found at the beginning of the statutory code of the jurisdiction. (The federal Constitution is in U.S.C./U.S.C.A./U.S.C.S.)
2. Use the CARTWHEEL to help you use the general index of the statutory code and the separate index for the constitution itself. (See exhibit 11.16.) Also check the table of contents material for the constitution in the statutory code.
3. Following the text of individual constitutional provisions there are often *Notes of Decisions* containing summaries of cases interpreting the constitution. Some of these notes can run hundreds of pages. Check any available index or table of contents covering these notes.
4. Annotations. Find annotations in A.L.R. (A.L.R. 1st), A.L.R.2d, etc. on the constitutional provisions in which you are interested. (See exhibit 11.27 on finding and updating annotations.)
5. Digests. Go to West Group's *United States Supreme Court Digest* and the American Digest System, which covers all courts. Use the Descriptive Word Index (DWI) to locate relevant key numbers. (See exhibit 11.23 on using West Group digests.) (For cases on the U.S. Constitution, you can also go to the LEXIS Law Publishing digest—the *United States Supreme Court Digest, Lawyers' Ed.*)
6. Legal treatises. Find legal treatises on the entire constitution or on the specific portions of the constitution in which you are interested. Numerous such treatises exist. (See exhibit 11.38 on finding legal treatises.)
7. Legal periodical literature. Go to the two indexes to legal periodical literature: ILP and CLI. Use them to help you locate what you need among the vast periodical literature on the constitution. (See exhibit 11.35 on finding legal periodical literature.)
8. Loose-leaf services. Find out if there are loose-leaf services on the area of the constitution in which you are interested. (See exhibit 11.34 on loose-leaf services.)
9. Phone and mail research. Contact an expert. (See exhibit 11.39 on phone and mail research.)
10. *Words and Phrases*. Identify specific words or phrases within the constitutional provision you are examining. Find court definitions of these words or phrases in the multivolume legal dictionary *Words and Phrases*.
11. Legal encyclopedias. Find discussions of constitutional law in Am. Jur. 2d and in C.J.S. (See exhibit 11.37 on legal encyclopedias.)
12. Once you have found a constitutional provision relevant to your research, shepardize or KeyCite the provision to find case law interpreting it. The set of Shepard's you use to shepardize the constitution is the same set of Shepard's you would use to shepardize a statute. (See exhibits 11.8 and 11.32.) Also, any case that you find should be shepardized (see exhibit 11.30) or KeyCited to try to find additional cases.
14. LEXIS and Westlaw contain the full text of the United States Constitution and every state constitution. They also can lead you to extensive case law interpreting these constitutions and legal periodical literature analyzing them.
15. For a list of constitutions on the Internet, see:
    - www.constitution.org/cons/usstcons.htm
    - www.findlaw.com/11stategov/indexconst.html
    - www.prairienet.org/~scruffy/f.htm
    - www.lib.uchicago.edu/~llou/conlaw.html

    Also check the Internet site for the state statutes of your state. See exhibit 11.47. Most of these sites will also lead you to the constitution of your state.

---

### Assignment 11.28

(a) Go to your state constitution. Find any provision in it that grants powers to your governor. Select one of the powers. Quote a sentence from the provision and give its citation.

(b) Go to the set of Shepard's that will allow you to shepardize this constitutional provision. Pick any citing case. Go to the reporter that contains this citing case. Quote the sentence from the case that cites this provision. Give the citation of your quote. (If there are no citing cases, redo part (a) of this assignment until you find a constitutional provision that does have a citing case.)

(c) Go back to the set of books you used in part (a). Are there Notes of Decisions in this set? If so, find the case you used for part (b). Photocopy this page and circle the case in these notes.

(d) Go to your main state digest. In this digest, find the case you used for part (b). Under what key number(s) was this case digested? On what page(s) of the digest volume (or its supplement) did you find this case digested?

(e) Go to the American Digest System. Find the case you used for part (b). Under what key number(s) was this case digested? In what units of the American Digest System and on what page(s) did you find this case digested?

## Section U
# FINDING ADMINISTRATIVE LAW

Many agencies write administrative regulations, but few have coherent systems of organizing and distributing the regulations. See exhibit 6.1 in chapter 6. A major exception is the federal agencies, whose regulations are first published in the *Federal Register*. Many are then codified in the *Code of Federal Regulations*. A large number of states follow this pattern of a separate register and code for the regulations of state administrative agencies. The state register and code, however, are not as sophisticated as the *Federal Register* and the *Code of Federal Regulations*.

Normally, an agency does not have the power to write regulations unless it has specific statutory authority to do so. An examination of the statute giving the agency this authority can be helpful in understanding the regulations themselves. In theory, the statutes of the legislature establish the purpose of the agency and define its overall policies but leave to the agency (through its regulations) the task of filling in the specifics of administration. Regulations, therefore, tend to be very detailed.

The other major kind of administrative law is the administrative decision. This is a resolution of a controversy between a party and an administrative agency involving the application of the regulations, statutes, or executive orders that govern the agency. (It is also called an administrative ruling. See exhibit 6.1 in chapter 6.) Not many agencies publish their decisions in any systematic order; some agencies do not publish them at all. Regulatory agencies, such as the Federal Communications Commission and state environmental agencies, often do a better job at publishing their decisions than other agencies.

The federal government and most states have an Administrative Procedure Act (APA). This is a statute that governs the steps that an agency must take to write a regulation or issue an administrative decision. Examples of these steps include publishing a notice of a proposed regulation and allowing affected parties to participate in a hearing that leads to an administrative decision. Part of legal research in administrative law should address the question of whether the agency properly complied with the Administrative Procedure Act on such steps.

When looking for an administrative regulation, you must simultaneously be looking for the enabling statute that is the authority for the regulation. (An enabling statute is a statute that authorizes the agency to write regulations to perform other specific tasks.) With very few exceptions, agencies do not have their own independent power. In large measure, the very reason for the existence of the agency is to carry out the statutes of the legislature that created the agency and gave it specific responsibilities. Consequently, two questions always confront the researcher:

■ Is there an administrative regulation on point?
■ If so, does the regulation go beyond what its enabling statute authorizes the agency to do? In other words, is the administrative regulation within the scope of the enabling statute?

To answer the second question, of course, you need to find the enabling statute. Often the lead you need to find this statute will be within the administrative code that contains the regulation.

Assume that you have found a federal administrative regulation in the *Code of Federal Regulations* (C.F.R.) that is on point. You now want to check the authority for that regulation in the enabling statute, which for federal statutes would be within the *United States Code* (U.S.C.) or the *United States Code Annotated* (U.S.C.A.) or the *United States Code Service* (U.S.C.S.). To find the statute, you would check the "Authority" reference within the C.F.R. itself. Beneath the regulation you are reading (or at the beginning of the cluster of regulations of which your regulation is a part), find an "Authority" reference that will tell you what federal statutes are the authority for the regulation. See research link R.

Suppose you have not yet found any administrative regulations, but you have found a statute that is on point. You want to determine whether there are any administrative regulations based on that statute. To find out, check the "Parallel Table of Authorities and Rules" in the pamphlet called *CFR Index and Finding Aids* that is part of the C.F.R. set. See research link S.

| Administrative regulation in *Code of Federal Regulations* (C.F.R.) (Check "Authority" reference) | Enabling statute in *United States Code* (U.S.C.) or *United States Code Annotated* (U.S.C.A.) or *United States Code Service* (U.S.C.S.) |
|---|---|

### RESEARCH LINK R

If you have found a federal administrative regulation, and you now want to find the enabling statute that is the authority for that regulation, check the "Authority" reference beneath the regulation in C.F.R. (or at the beginning of the cluster of regulations of which your regulation is a part). There you will be given the cite in U.S.C. (or U.S.C.A. or U.S.C.S.) to the federal statute that is the authority for the regulation.

| Enabling statute in *United States Code* (U.S.C.) or *United States Code Annotated* (U.S.C.A.) or *United States Code Service* (U.S.C.S.) | Administrative regulation in *Code of Federal Regulations* (C.F.R.) (Check "Parallel Table of Authorities and Rules" in *CFR Index and Finding Aids*) |
|---|---|

### RESEARCH LINK S

You have found a federal statute in U.S.C. (or U.S.C.A. or U.S.C.S.) and you now want to know whether there are any administrative regulations in C.F.R. that are based on that statute. To find out, check the "Parallel Table of Authorities and Rules" in the pamphlet called *CFR Index and Finding Aids* that is part of the C.F.R. set. This pamphlet will tell you if your statute is an enabling statute for any administrative regulations.

| EXHIBIT 11.53 | Techniques for Finding Administrative Law |
|---|---|

1. Start with your law library. Ask where you can find the kind of administrative law you are seeking, e.g., federal administrative regulations, state administrative regulations. Also check the catalog. (See exhibit 11.21.)

2. Many university libraries in your area subscribe to the the *Code of Federal Regulations* (C.F.R.) and the *Federal Register* (Fed. Reg.). If these libraries are *federal depository libraries,* you must be given access to this set as well as to other subscriptions the library receives free from the federal government, e.g., the *United States Code* and the *Congressional Record.* If there is a university library that you want to use, call its reference desk and ask if it is a depository library. On finding law libraries, see section E.

3. Consider calling or, if practical, visiting the agency itself. (Check your local phone directory listings under state, county, and federal government.) There may be a regional or district office near you. Contact the library, the law department, or the public information section in the agency. Ask for a list of the agency's publications, such as regulations, decisions, and annual reports. Also ask where these materials are located. Find out if you can come to the agency and use the materials. Ask about brochures describing the agency's functions, which can be sent to you.

4. Many federal administrative regulations are printed in the *Code of Federal Regulations* (C.F.R.), which are usually printed first in their proposed

EXHIBIT 11.53    Techniques for Finding Administrative Law—*continued*

form in the *Federal Register* before they are enacted by the agency. The C.F.R. comes out in a new edition—and a new color—every year. See research link D in section H. There are six main ways to locate regulations in the C.F.R.

**(a)** The *C.F.R. Index and Finding Aids* volume. This is a single-volume pamphlet that is reissued every year.

**(b)** The *Index to the Code of Federal Regulations* published by Congressional Information Service (CIS).

**(c)** Loose-leaf services. As indicated earlier, there are numerous loose-leaf services covering many federal agencies and some state agencies. These services usually give extensive references to administrative regulations and decisions. (See exhibit 11.34.)

**(d)** The *Federal Register*. Use the indexes to the *Federal Register* to find proposed regulations that could lead you to regulations in the *Code of Federal Regulations* itself. The main index to the entire *Federal Register* is the *CIS Index to the Federal Register*. There is also an annual index to the *Federal Register*.

**(e)** LEXIS and Westlaw. These commercial online services act as online indexes to federal regulations.

**(f)** The Internet:
  ■ To find the *Code of Federal Regulations*, go to: www.access.gpo.gov/nara/cfr
  ■ To find the *Federal Register*, go to: www.gpo.gov/su_docs/aces/aces140.html
  ■ Many federal agencies have their own sites. For example, to find the Securities and Exchange Commission, go to: www.sec.gov
  ■ If you do not know the Internet site of the agency in which you are interested, check FedWorld, a massive online locator service for access to information disseminated by the federal government. To use this service, go to: www.fedworld.gov. (See exhibit 11.7 in section H.)

**5.** Once you have found a federal regulation on point in the C.F.R., do the following:

**(a)** Shepardize the regulation. (See exhibit 11.33 on shepardizing a regulation.)

**(b)** KeyCite the regulation on Westlaw to find information about the regulation comparable to what Shepard's would reveal.

**(c)** Find the enabling statute that is the authority for that regulation. Read this statute in U.S.C./U.S.C.A./U.S.C.S. Make sure the regulation does not contradict, go beyond the scope of, or otherwise violate the statute that the regulation is supposed to implement:

  ■ If you have a regulation and want to find out what statute is the authority for that regulation, look for the "Authority" reference beneath the regulation in the C.F.R. (or at the beginning of the cluster of regulations in C.F.R. of which your regulation is a part). See research link R.

  ■ If you have a statute and want to find out if there are any regulations implementing that statute, check the Parallel Table of Authorities and Rules in a volume called *CFR Index and Finding Aids* which accompanies the C.F.R. See research link S.

**(d)** Once you have found a regulation in the C.F.R., you must find out if the regulation has been affected in any way (changed, revoked, added to, renumbered) by subsequent material printed in the *Federal Register*. This is done by checking your C.F.R. cite in:

  ■ The monthly pamphlet called *LSA: List of Sections Affected*. This pamphlet is also available on the Internet. See www.access.gpo.gov/nara/lsa/ browslsa.html.

  ■ The "CFR Parts Affected" table in the daily *Federal Register* from the date of the latest *LSA* pamphlet to the current date. (The Reader Aids section of the *Federal Register* has this table in a cumulative list.) CFR Parts Affected is also available on the Internet. See www.access.gpo.gov/nara/lsa/curlist.html. The *LSA* pamphlet and the CFR Parts Affected will tell you what pages of the *Federal Register* contain material that affects your regulation in the C.F.R. (You need to do this only until the next annual edition of the C.F.R. comes out, because anything affecting the regulation during the preceding year will be incorporated in the next edition of C.F.R.)

**(e)** Find out if there is an annotation on your regulation. Shepardize the regulation. Annotations in A.L.R. (A.L.R.1st), A.L.R.2d, etc. are among the citing materials of Shepard's and of KeyCite on Westlaw. Also, check the Table of Laws, Rules, and Regulations in the last volume of the *ALR Index*. Finally, see the separate volume called *ALR Federal Tables* for annotations on federal regulations in the C.F.R. (See exhibit 11.27.)

| EXHIBIT 11.53 | Techniques for Finding Administrative Law—*continued* |
|---|---|

6. Most *states* have an administrative code and an administrative register comparable to the federal C.F.R. and the *Federal Register*. The exact titles of the administrative code and register for every state can be found in the two main citation guides:
   - *The Bluebook: A Uniform System of Citation* (see tables at the end of the book)
   - *AWLD Citation Manual* (see appendix at the end of the book)

7. LEXIS and Westlaw contain regulations and other administrative laws of every state.

8. Many state administrative codes are available on the Internet. To find out if your state's code (and register) is on the Internet, check:
   www.nass.org/acr/internet.html
   www.lawsource.com/also/usa.cgi?us1
   www.law.cornell.edu/states/listing.html
   www.findlaw.com/casecode/#state

www.rmis.com/db/lawlaws.htm
Also check links on the state sites for your state's statutory code. See exhibit 11.47.

9. The first step in obtaining the administrative decisions of a federal or state administrative agency is to go to the Internet site of that agency to find out if they are available online. (For a list of agencies, click on your state at www.washlaw.edu/uslaw/statelaw.html.)

10. Federal administrative decisions are printed in separate reporter volumes for each agency. Some federal administrative decisions can be shepardized. See, for example, *Shepard's United States Administrative Citations* and *Shepard's Labor Law Citations*. State administrative decisions are often much more difficult to locate. Loose-leaf services that cover a particular federal or state agency are a good source for finding administrative decisions. (See exhibit 11.34.)

---

*Assignment 11.29*

(a) What is the title of the administrative code of your state? Does your state have a register? If so, what is its title?

(b) Find and cite any state administrative regulation that covers when workers in your state are entitled to worker's compensation for injuries on the job.

(c) Select any regulation in the *Code of Federal Regulations* (C.F.R.). Give the citation of the regulation. Use the tables in the recent issues of the *Federal Register* to find out how that regulation has been affected within the last year. State how it has been affected and give the citation to the page(s) in the *Federal Register* that tells you how it was affected. (If the tables in the *Federal Register* tell you that the regulation you selected has not been affected, pick a different regulation in C.F.R.)

(d) Find any five regulations in the *Code of Federal Regulations*, written by five different agencies, that mention attorneys. Quote one sentence from each regulation and give its citation.

(e) Give the cite for the enabling statute for each of the regulations you picked in part (d).

(f) Find any federal statute on taking a home office deduction on your federal income tax return. What is the citation of this statute? Find one regulation that carries out this statute. What is the citation of this regulation? How did you find it? List another way you could have used to find it.

---

Section V

# FINDING LOCAL LAW

The local level of government consists of thousands of counties, cities, and towns throughout the country. They pass laws that deal with a wide variety of subjects, e.g., zoning, transportation, housing, sanitation. Among the most common kinds of local laws are charters and ordinances. (For their definitions, see exhibit 6.1 in chapter 6.) The techniques for finding such laws are summarized in exhibit 11.54.

| EXHIBIT 11.54 | Techniques for Finding Local Law |
|---|---|

1. Contact your city, county, or other local form of government. Call city hall, the local council, the board of supervisors, the county commissioner's office, etc. Ask what kind of *local* laws it passes, where those laws can be found (e.g., are they on the Internet?), how they are updated, etc.
2. Find out if your local public library has municipal codes and other local laws.
3. For charters and municipal codes on the Internet, see:
   - www.spl.org/selectedsites/municode.html
   - www.generalcode.com

   The links to your state's statutory code in exhibit 11.47 may also lead you to charters, municipal codes, and other local laws in your state.
4. There are charters and municipal codes for some cities on Westlaw and LEXIS.
5. Legal periodical literature exists on local issues such as zoning, municipal bonds, etc. (see exhibit 11.35 on legal periodical literature).
6. The Shepard's volumes for a particular state will enable you to shepardize local charters and ordinances.
7. Digests can be used to find case law in charters and ordinances (see exhibit 11.23 on digests).
8. To find annotations on local law in A.L.R. (A.L.R.1st), A.L.R.2d, etc., see exhibit 11.27 on finding annotations.
9. Check legal treatises on local law (see exhibit 11.38 on legal treatises).
10. Am. Jur. 2d and C.J.S. have discussions on local law (see exhibit 11.37 on legal encyclopedias).
11. Loose-leaf services cover aspects of local law (see exhibit 11.34 on loose-leaf services).
12. *Ordinance Law Annotations* (published by Shepard's) summarizes court opinions that have interpreted ordinances.

## Section W
# FINDING RULES OF COURT

You must always check the rules of court (also called *court rules* and *rules of procedure*) governing practice and procedure before a *particular* court. These rules govern the mechanics of litigation. They will tell you how to file a request for an extension of time, the number of days a defendant has to answer a complaint, the format of a complaint or appellate brief, etc. (See exhibit 11.55.)

| EXHIBIT 11.55 | Techniques for Finding Rules of Court |
|---|---|

**Rules of Court for State Courts:**
1. Check your state statutory code for the text of the rules.
2. Ask your librarian if there is a rules service company that publishes an updated edition of state rules of court.
3. Find out if the court itself publishes its own rules.
4. LEXIS and Westlaw contain the rules of court for most state courts.
5. To find rules of court for state courts on the Internet check the following sites:
   www.llrx.com/courtrules
   www.washlaw.edu/uslaw/statelaw.html
   www.piperinfo.com/state/index.cfm

6. Shepardize rules of court in the same set of Shepard's you use to shepardize a statute (see exhibit 11.32).
7. For case law on the rules of court, check the digests for your state (see exhibit 11.23).
8. Check local practice books, form books, or other legal treatises (see exhibit 11.38 on legal treatises).

**Rules of Court for Federal Courts:**
9. Check the U.S.C./U.S.C.A./U.S.C.S., such as title 18 (Appendix) and title 28 (Appendix).
10. To find rules of court governing specific federal courts, check *Federal Local Court Rules*, a loose-leaf published by Lawyers' Co-op.

| EXHIBIT 11.55 | Techniques for Finding Rules of Court |
| --- | --- |

**11.** LEXIS and Westlaw contain rules of court of federal courts. Many rules are also available on CD–ROM.

**12.** To find rules of court for federal courts on the Internet. check the following sites:
www.llrx.com/courtrules-gen/all.html
www.uscourts.gov/links.html
www.washlaw.edu/searchlaw.html
supreme.lp.findlaw.com(U.S.SupremeCourt)
www.law.cornell.edu/rules/frcp/overview.htm
(Federal Rules of Civil Procedure)
www.courtrules.org/fre.htm (Federal Rules of Evidence)
www.law.ukans.edu/research/frcriml.htm (Federal Rules of Criminal Procedure)

**13.** Shepardize federal rules of court in *Federal Statute Citations* (see exhibit 11.8). KeyCite them on Westlaw.

**14.** For case law on rules of court, check the digests, such as *Federal Practice Digest* 4th (see exhibit 11.23).

**15.** Check the *Federal Rules Service*, a Callaghan publication that contains cases interpreting the Federal Rules of Civil Procedure.

**16.** Check special treatises on the federal rules such as:
*Moore's Federal Practice*
Wright and Miller, *Federal Practice and Procedure*

**17.** Find annotations on the federal rules of court. Check the Table of Laws, Rules, and Regulations in the last volume of the *CFR Index* and the separate volume, *ALR Federal Tables* (see exhibit 11.27).

**18.** Check legal periodical literature on the federal rules of court (see exhibit 11.35).

**19.** Check Am. Jur. 2d and C.J.S. on the federal rules of court (see exhibit 11.37).

*Assignment 11.30*

Locate the rules of court governing the three courts listed below. For each court, find and quote from any rule that imposes a time limitation on one or more of the parties for litigation within that court (e.g., the time within which a party must file a particular motion or respond to a discovery request). Also give the name, address, and fax number, and Internet address of each of the three courts you select:

(a) any state trial court of your state
(b) any United States District Court sitting in your state
(c) any United States Bankruptcy Court sitting in your state

Section X
# FINDING INTERNATIONAL LAW

International law consists of the law that exists between nations. The primary kind of international law is the **treaty**, which is a formal agreement between two or more foreign governments. The president negotiates treaties with other nations, but the Senate must approve the treaty by at least a two-thirds vote. An **executive agreement**, in contrast, is a formal agreement between two or more foreign governments that does not require a vote of approval by the Senate. What can be covered in an executive agreement rather than a treaty is not clear and has always been the subject of considerable debate between the president and Congress.

The first step in researching international law is to read one or more legal periodical articles or sections of a legal treatise that cover the area of your research. Before you start reading the text of treaties, executive agreements, and case law interpreting them, you need an overview of the technical terms involved. Secondary sources such as legal periodicals and legal treatises will provide this. (For a summary of these and other techniques for finding international law, see exhibit 11.56.)

| EXHIBIT 11.56 | Techniques for Finding International Law |
| --- | --- |

1. In general, check:
   - *United States Treaties and Other International Acts*
   - *Treaties and Other International Acts Series* (T.I.A.S.)
   - *United States Treaties and Other International Agreements* (U.S.T.)
   - Westlaw's database: USTREATIES
   - LEXIS libraries: ITRADE, INLAW
   - The yearly *United States Statutes at Large*, which contain U.S. treaties (up to 1950)
   - Blaustein and Flanz, *Constitutions of the Countries of the World*
   - *CCH Tax Treaties*
   - *Treaties in Force*
   - *Department of State Bulletin*
   - *United Nations Treaty Series*
   - Catalog of U.S. publications
   - *International Legal Materials*
   - Szladits, *Bibliography on Foreign and Comparative Law: Books and Articles in English*

   For other texts summarizing and commenting on treaties and international law generally, see exhibit 11.38 on legal treatises.

2. Legal periodical literature. There is extensive periodical literature on international law, both in general legal periodicals and in specialty periodicals devoted to international law exclusively. (See exhibit 11.35)

3. Loose-leaf services, such as *CCH Tax Treaties*, mentioned above. (See exhibit 11.34 on loose-leaf services)

4. American case law on international law. Check the digests. (See exhibit 11.23 on digests.)

5. Case law and statutory law of other countries. Go to the international law section of a large law library.

6. Annotations on international law. (See exhibit 11.27 on annotations.)

7. Legal encyclopedias. For material on international law in Am. Jur. 2d and in C.J.S., see exhibit 11.37

8. *Martindale-Hubbell Law Dictionary*—Digest volume. Contains brief summaries of the law of many countries.

9. Phone and mail research. (See exhibit 11.39 on contacting experts).

10. See *Restatement (Second) of Foreign Relations Law of the United States*.

11. Shepardize all treaties. Use *Shepard's Federal Statute Citations*.

12. Sites to check on the Internet:
    www.loc.gov/law/guide/multi.html
    www.lib.uchicago.edu/~llou/forintlaw.html
    www.washlaw.edu/forint/forintmain.html
    www.asil.org
    www.state.gov
    www.un.org

## Section Y
# The Third Level of Legal Research: Validation

### INTRODUCTION

In section N, we introduced the three levels of legal research:

- Background research
- Specific fact research
- Validation research

Exhibit 11.18 examined the steps for conducting *background research* on an area of law that is new to you. Section O to X examined the techniques of *specific fact research* through a series of extensive checklists. If you have done a comprehensive job on the first two stages of research, you may also have completed most of the third stage—**validation research**. At the validation stage, you ensure that everything you want to use from your research is still good law. This means making sure that the law is current and has not been affected by any later laws that you have not yet found.

### WHY THERE IS A HIGH RISK THAT YOU WILL RELY ON INVALID LAW

The importance of validation research cannot be overestimated. It is easy to understand why you do not want to rely on a case that has been overruled or on a statute that has been amended, repealed, or declared unconstitutional. Surprisingly, however, it is relatively easy to fall into such potentially disastrous traps. This is because some invalid laws are never removed from the shelves. This means that while you are reading such laws, you are given no indication that they are invalid and, therefore, are tempted—very tempted—to rely on them.

For example, a reporter volume may contain several hundred court opinions. Some of their holdings may have been overruled or declared unconstitutional years after the reporter volume was published. Yet no one goes back to this volume to insert corrections or warnings. An invalid case will be printed right next to a valid case. You must perform validation research before you rely on any law. For cases, you must use paper or online citator services such as Shepard's and KeyCite.

The same danger exists with statutes. A code volume may contain several thousand statutory sections and subsections. Some of them may have been amended, repealed, or declared unconstitutional years after the code volume was published. Yet no one goes back to this volume to insert corrections or warnings. Eventually, however, statutory code volumes (unlike reporter volumes) *are* updated, so that the code volumes containing invalid statutes are replaced by volumes containing valid statutes. But for some codes, this replacement may take more than 10 years! Consequently, when you are reading a statute, there may be invalid statutes printed right next to valid statutes without any indication of which were rendered invalid by subsequent action of the legislature or courts. To find out which statutes fall into this category, you must perform validation research. For statutes, you check available pocket parts, supplementation volumes or pamphlets, and paper or online citator services such as Shepard's and KeyCite.

In short, appearances are deceptive. Don't fall into the inviting trap of relying on invalid law simply because the law looks valid. Perform validation research on everything you want to use.

If you are lucky enough to be able to use commercial research databases such as Westlaw and LEXIS, you will be alerted by flags or other warning signs that a particular law you have called up is no longer valid or is of questionable validity. But these databases are very expensive to use. Most of your research will probably be done in the traditional paper formats of bound volumes, pamphlets, and loose-leafs, where the danger of relying on invalid authority is very real.

Can you rely on the free sites on the Internet that provide the law? Sites run by legislatures, courts, and administrative agencies can be reliable, although they are not always kept current. If the site is not run by the government, be skeptical. Anyone can go on the Web and say just about anything on any topic. The safest course is to use the validation techniques described in this section for anything that you find on the Internet.

## PERSPECTIVE OF THE OTHER SIDE

A good way to approach validation research is to take the perspective of the other side. Suppose that you have helped do some of the research for an appellate brief. It has been filed in court and served on the attorney for the other side. Your brief is handed over to a researcher in the law office of your opponent. That person will do the following:

- Read the full text of all *primary authority* (see exhibit 6.1 in chapter 6) on which you rely to see if you have interpreted the statutes, cases, regulations, etc., properly; to see whether you have taken quotations out of context, etc.
- *Shepardize* and/or KeyCite the statutes, cases, regulations, etc., that you cite to find out whether the law is still valid.
- Read the *secondary authority* (see exhibit 11.10) that you cite to see whether you have interpreted the legal treatise, legal periodical article, etc., properly; to see whether you have taken quotations out of context, etc.
- Look for other applicable primary authority that you failed to mention.
- Look for other applicable secondary authority that you failed to mention.

Proper validation research means that you will be able to predict what this imaginary researcher will find when he or she checks your research through these steps. In short, at the validation stage of your research, you must ask yourself:

- Have I found everything I should have found?
- Is everything I found good law?
- Have I properly interpreted what I found?

The answer to the first two questions should be *no* if:

- You did an incomplete job of CARTWHEELing the indexes of all the sets of books mentioned in the checklists and techniques in this chapter (see exhibit 11.16).
- You failed to shepardize and/or KeyCite cases, statutes, constitutional provisions, rules of court, ordinances, treaties, etc. (see exhibits 11.30, 11.32, and 11.33).
- You failed to take other standard validation steps, such as updating regulations in C.F.R. through the *LSA* pamphlet and the proper tables in the *Federal Register*.

## RESEARCH AUDIT

The checklist in exhibit 11.57 is designed to help you achieve the comprehensiveness that is essential to all aspects of legal research, especially validation research. *Fill out a separate research audit for each issue you research.* Start by summarizing the issue in the box at the top of the form. The checklist should act as a self-audit to make sure that you have covered all bases. It consists of a series of reminders. They are needed because you have so many resources to check in a comprehensive law library. Note that part IV reminds you to keep a Research Log. You not only want to be comprehensive but also want to be able to tell others (and remind yourself) what steps you took along the way.

| EXHIBIT 11.57 | Research Audit |
| --- | --- |

ISSUE # _____ (briefly state issue researched)

### I. What I Have Checked: Legal Materials

A. *Primary Authority*

| | | |
| --- | --- | --- |
| ☐ federal court opinions | ☐ international law | ☐ ordinances |
| ☐ federal statutes | ☐ state court opinions | ☐ charter |
| ☐ federal constitution | ☐ state statutes | ☐ local rules of court |
| ☐ federal rules of court | ☐ state constitution | ☐ local administrative regulations |
| ☐ federal administrative regulations | ☐ state rules of court | ☐ local administrative decisions |
| ☐ federal administrative decisions | ☐ state administrative regulations | |
| | ☐ state administrative decisions | |

B. *Secondary Authority*

| | | |
| --- | --- | --- |
| ☐ legal periodicals | ☐ legal treatises | ☐ loose-leaf services |
| ☐ ALR annotations | ☐ legal encyclopedias | ☐ legal newsletters |
| ☐ *Words & Phrases* (legal dictionary) | | |

### II. What I Have Checked: Nonlegal Materials

When relevant to the research problem, I have checked nonlegal literature in the areas of:

| | | | |
| --- | --- | --- | --- |
| ☐ medicine | ☐ psychology | ☐ psychiatry | ☐ economics |
| ☐ statistics | ☐ accounting | ☐ sociology | ☐ other |
| ☐ biology | ☐ chemistry | ☐ business management | |

**EXHIBIT 11.57  Research Audit—*continued***

### III. What I Intend to Rely On in My Research Memo
For every primary authority I intend to use, I have:
- ☐ used paper citators to determine whether it is still valid (e.g., Shepard's).
- ☐ used CD-ROM or online citators to determine whether it is still valid (e.g., Shepard's, KeyCite, Auto-Cite)
- ☐ checked other standard updating features (e.g., pocket parts, supplement pamphlets, history tables)

### IV. Research Log
For each paper volume, CD-ROM, or online resource (e.g., Internet, Westlaw, LEXIS, Loislaw) I have made the following brief notations in my research notebook or log.
- ☐ the name of the resource
- ☐ the major words/phrases I have checked in the resource
- ☐ which library I used for this resource (if more than one)

### V. People Consulted for Guidance/Leads before Completion
People with whom I have shared my research strategy to determine whether they think I have omitted something:
- ☐ supervisor
- ☐ other attorney(s) in office
- ☐ law librarian
- ☐ law clerk
- ☐ experienced paralegal
- ☐ experts (see exhibit 11.39).
- ☐ other

## TIME TO STOP?

At the outset of your research, the difficulty you face is often phrased as "Where do I begin?" As you resolve this difficulty, another one emerges: "When do I stop?" Once the research starts flowing, you are sometimes faced with a mountain of material, and yet you do not feel comfortable saying to yourself that you have found everything there is to be found. Exhibit 11.58 presents some guidelines on handling this concern. With experience, you will begin to acquire a clearer sense of when it is time to stop, but it is rare for you to know this with any certainty. You will always have the suspicion that if you pushed on just a little longer, you would find something new and more on point than what you have come up with to date. Also, there is no way around the reality that comprehensive research requires a substantial amount of time. It takes time to dig. It takes more time to dig comprehensively.

**EXHIBIT 11.58  Guidelines for Determining When to End Your Legal Research**

1. *Instructions from your supervisor*. You must, of course, live within time guidelines imposed by your supervisor. You cannot spend the rest of your career in the law library working on one problem! If your supervisor has not set specific time guidelines for the research project, ask him or her to do so as soon as you determine that the project is going to take a significant amount of time. This may be an opportunity for the supervisor to narrow the focus of the project or to redirect your energies entirely. It may also be an opportunity for the supervisor to let you know that you misunderstood the question to be researched.
2. *Repetition*. If you find that all the different avenues you are taking in the law library appear to be leading to the same primary and secondary authority, it may be time to stop. This repetition may be a good indication that you have already found what there is to find. Many legal materials are designed to be finding aids to the same kind of law, as we saw in section O on the nine major search resources. Digests and ALR annotations, for example, are both massive indexes to case law. Shepard's is also an excellent case finder. Always try to use more than one finding aid to locate any particular category of primary authority you are checking. (Also try to use finding aids published by different companies because the same publisher will often repeat the same material in different formats.) When multiple finding aids keep turning up the same cases, statutes, or other laws, it is a sign that you can stop.
3. *Comprehensive via checklists*. Work with checklists to be sure that you are covering all the bases in the law library. One indication of when it is time to stop is when you are able to check off everything on your checklists, particularly the research audit in exhibit 11.57.

## Section Z
## Annotated Bibliography and More Research Problems

An annotated bibliography is a report giving a list of library material on a particular topic, with a brief description of how the material relates to the topic. An annotated bibliography on contributory negligence, for example, would list the major cases, statutes, periodical articles, etc., and would explain in a sentence or two what each says about contributory negligence. The same would be true of an annotated bibliography on a set of facts that you are researching. If the facts present more than one research issue, you would do an annotated bibliography for each issue, or you would subdivide a single annotated bibliography into sections so that it would be clear to the reader which issue you are covering at any given place in the bibliography. The annotated bibliography is, in effect, a progress report on your research. It will show your supervisor the status of your research. (The instructions in exhibit 11.59 mainly cover the preparation of an annotated bibliography for a topic that requires the application of state and local law. The same instructions, however, would be used when doing the bibliography on a federal topic. The exception would be instruction 9, which calls for local ordinances. For all other instructions, replace the word *state* with the word *federal* when researching a federal topic.)

| EXHIBIT 11.59 | **Instructions for Preparing an Annotated Bibliography** |
| --- | --- |

1.  CARTWHEEL the topic of your annotated bibliography. (See exhibit 11.16.)
2.  *Annotated* here simply means that you provide some description of everything you list in the bibliography—not a long analysis, just a sentence or two explaining why you included it. If you find no relevant material in any of the following sets of books, specifically say so in your report.
3.  Hand in a report that will cover what you find on the topic in the sets of books mentioned in the following instructions.
4.  Statutes. Go to your state code. Make a list of the statutes on the topic. For each statute, give its citation and a brief quotation from it to show that it deals with the topic.
5.  Constitutions. Go to your state constitution (usually found within your state code). Make a list of the constitutional provisions on the topic. For each provision, give its citation and a brief quotation from it to show that it deals with the topic.
6.  Cases. If you found statutes or constitutional provisions on the topic, check to see if there are any cases summarized in the Notes of Decisions (see exhibit 11.44) *after* these statutes or provisions. Select several cases that deal with the topic. For each case you select, give its citation and a brief quote from the case summary in the Notes of Decisions to show that it deals with the topic.

7.  Digests. Go to the Descriptive Word Index of digests. Make a list of key topics that deal with the topic.
8.  Rules of court. Go to the rules of court that cover courts in your state. Make a list of the rules, if any, that deal with the topic. For each rule, give its citation and a brief quotation from it to show that it deals with the topic.
9.  Ordinances. Go to the ordinances that cover your city or county. Make a list of the ordinances, if any, that deal with the topic. For each ordinance, give its citation and a brief quotation from it to show that it deals with the topic.
10. Administrative regulations. Are there any state agencies that have jurisdiction over any aspect of the topic? If so, list the agencies. If your library has the regulations of the agencies, make a list of the regulations, if any, that deal with the topic. For each regulation, give its citation and a brief quote from it to show that it deals with the topic.
11. A.L.R. (A.L.R.1st), A.L.R.2d, A.L.R.3d, A.L.R.4th, A.L.R.5th, A.L.R. Fed. Go to these six sets of books. Try to find one annotation in *each* set that deals with your topic. Give the citation of the annotation in each set. Flip through the pages of each annotation and try to find the citation of one case from a state court of your state, or from a federal court with jurisdiction over your state. Give the citation of the case.

| EXHIBIT 11.59 | Instructions for Preparing an Annotated Bibliography |
|---|---|

12. Legal periodical literature. Use the *Index to Legal Periodicals and Books* and the *Current Legal Index* to locate four legal periodical articles that deal with the topic. Try to find at least two relevant articles in each index. Give the citations of the articles. Put a check mark next to the citation if your library has the legal periodical in which the article is located.

13. Legal treatises. Go to your card or computer catalog. Find any two legal treatises that cover your topic. Give the citation of the treatises. Sometimes you may not find entire books on the topic. The topic may be one of many subjects in a broader treatise.

14. Loose-leafs. Are there any loose-leaf services on this topic? Check the card or computer catalog and ask the librarian. For each loose-leaf, give its citation and explain how it covers the topic.

15. *Words and Phrases*. Go to this multivolume legal dictionary. In this dictionary, locate definitions, if any, of the major words and phrases involved in your topic. Limit yourself to definitions from court opinions of your state, if any.

16. Shepardize and/or KeyCite every case, statute, or constitutional provision you find to make sure it is still valid.

17. Other material. If you come across other relevant material not covered in the above instructions, include it in the bibliography as well.

18. When in doubt about whether to include something in the bibliography, include it.

19. There is no prescribed format for the bibliography. One possible outline format you can use is as follows: Topic:
   A. Statutes (instructions 4 and 16)
   B. Constitutions (instructions 5 and 16)
   C. Cases (instructions 6, 7, 11, and 16)
   D. Digests (instruction 7)
   E. Rules of court (instruction 8)
   F. Ordinances (instruction 9)
   G. Administrative regulations (instruction 10)
   H. A.L.R.1st, A.L.R.2d, A.L.R.3d, A.L.R. 4th, A.L.R.5th, A.L.R. Fed. (instruction 11)
   I. Legal periodical literature (instruction 12)
   J. Legal treatises (instruction 13)
   K. Loose-leafs (instruction 14)
   L. *Words and Phrases* (instruction 15)
   M. Other material (instruction 17)

## RESEARCH PROBLEMS

*Assignment 11.31*

Prepare an annotated bibliography on one of the following topics:

(a) Common law marriage
(b) Negligence liability of a driver of a car to his or her guest passenger
(c) Negligence liability of paralegals
(d) Overtime compensation for paralegals
(e) Sex discrimination
(f) The felony-murder rule
(g) Default judgment
(h) Worker's compensation for injury on the way to work
(i) Fact situation assigned by your instructor

*Assignment 11.32*

In the problems that follow, include citations that support every position you take in your responses. In analyzing and researching some of the problems below, you may find it difficult to proceed unless you know more facts about the problem. In such situations, clearly state the missing facts that you need to know. In order to proceed with the analysis and research, you can assume that certain facts exist as long as you state what your factual assumptions are *and* your assumptions are reasonable given the facts that you have.

(a) In your state, what entity (e.g., legislature, committee, court, agency) has the authority to prescribe rules and regulations on who can and who cannot practice law?

(b) List the kinds (or levels) of courts (local, state, or federal) that sit in your state and identify the major powers of each court; i.e., indicate what kinds of cases each court can hear.

(c) In your state, find a statute or court opinion that defines the following words or phrases:
(i)   Summons
(ii)  In personam
(iii) Mandamus
(iv)  Exhaustion of administrative remedies
(v)   Judgment
(vi)  Jurisdiction
(vii) Warrant

(d) Using the statutory codes of five different states (one of which must be your own state), find out how old a male and female must be to marry without consent of parent or guardian in each of the states.

(e) Go to any statutory code that has a pocket part. Starting with the first few pages of the pocket part, identify any three statutes that have totally repealed or partially modified the corresponding three statutes in the body of the bound text. Describe what the repeal or modification was. (*Note*: You may have to compare the new section in the pocket part with the old section in the body of the text to describe the change.)

In the following problems, use the state law of your state whenever you determine from your research that state law governs the problem.

(f) John Jones was sent to a state mental hospital after being declared mentally ill. He has been institutionalized for the last five years. In his own view, he is not now mentally ill. The hospital disagrees. What can John do? What steps might he take to try to get out?

(g) Peter Thomas is convicted of petty larceny. At the time of sentencing, his attorney asks the court to grant probation in lieu of a prison term. The judge replies, "Since Mr. Thomas has had three prior felony convictions (and since one of them was for attempted rape), I could not grant him probation even if I wanted to. I sentence him to a year in prison." On appeal, the attorney argues that the judge was incorrect in ruling that she had no power to grant probation to Mr. Thomas. Is the attorney correct?

(h) Mrs. Peterson invites a neighbor to her house for dinner. Mrs. Peterson's dog bites the neighbor. Is Mrs. Peterson responsible for the injury?

(i) Sam, age 15, goes to a used car lot. He signs a purchase agreement on a used car: $500 down and $100 a month for the next 10 months. One day after the purchase, Sam allows a friend to drive the car. The friend demolishes the car in an accident. When Sam tells the used car dealer about the accident, he is told that he must still make all payments until the purchase price has been paid. Is the dealer right?

(j) Dorothy Rhodes and John Samualson are the parents of Susan Samualson. (Dorothy married Robert Rhodes after divorcing John Samualson.) Dorothy died after separating from Robert Rhodes. Susan's father (John) has disappeared.

Mr. and Mrs. Ford were neighbors of the Rhodes. Susan lived with the Fords for a long period of time while her mother was having martial difficulties. A court granted the Fords custody and guardianship in 1988. The Social Security Administration sent Susan the social security benefits she was entitled to on the death of her mother. In 1990, the Fords formally adopted Susan but did not inform the Social Security office of this; they did not know that they had to. When the Social Security office learned of the adoption, they terminated the payments for Susan and informed the Fords that the money she had received since the adoption would have to be returned.

The Fords and Susan want to know what substantive and procedural rights they have.

**(k)** Jane Smith owns a small shoe repair shop. The city sanitation department determines that Jane is a carrier of a typhoid germ. She herself does not have typhoid fever, but others could become infected with the fever by coming in contact with her. The city orders Jane's shop to be closed. She and her husband are not allowed to leave the shop until arrangements can be made to transfer them to a hospital.
  (i)   Can the city quarantine Jane and her husband?
  (ii)  If they enter a hospital quarantine, can they be forced to pay the hospital bill?
  (iii) Can they recover loss of profits due to the closing of their business?

**(l)** The Henderson family owns a $140,000 home next door to a small grocery store. The store catches fire. The firefighters decide that to get at the fire from all angles, they must break through the Henderson home, which is not on fire. Damage to the Henderson home from the activity of the firefighters comes to $40,000. Who pays for this damage?

**(m)** After a series of serious accidents in which numerous riders are hurt, a bill is placed before the city council that would require all motorcyclists to wear protective helmets whenever riding. Is the bill constitutional?

**(n)** As a measure to enforce a standard of dental care, a bill is proposed that all the drinking water in the state be fluoridated and that every citizen be required to visit a dentist at least once a year. Is this bill constitutional?

**(o)** Tom Jones has terminal lung cancer. Modern technology, however, can keep him alive indefinitely. Tom requests that the hospital no longer use the technology on him. He wants to die. What are his rights?

**(p)** In 1992, James Fitzpatrick died, leaving an estate of $50,000. The executor tried to locate the heirs. In 1993, the probate court closed the estate and distributed the money to the heirs who were known at the time. In 2001, an individual who says he is an heir appears. He wants to go to court to reopen the estate and claim his share of the inheritance. What result?

**(q)** Mary is the sole beneficiary of her father's will. Another sister is intentionally left out of the will by her father. There are no other heirs. Mary murders her father. Who gets his estate?

**(r)** Most kosher meat stores accept the United Kosher Butchers Association (UKBA) as the authoritative certifier that "all the religious requirements have been thoroughly observed." Associated Synagogues (AS) certifies caterers as authentic carriers of kosher food. AS refuses to certify caterers who buy meat from stores certified by the UKBA because the latter refuses to submit to supervision by the rabbinical committee of AS. Many caterers then withdraw their patronage from stores supervised by UKBA. What legal action, if any, can the UKBA take?

**(s)** Mary Perry belongs to a religion that believes that medical problems can be resolved through spiritual meditation. Her son Paul is 10 years old. One day Paul is rushed to a hospital after collapsing at school. Mrs. Perry is called at home. When she arrives at the hospital, she is told that Paul will require emergency surgery. She refuses to give her consent. The doctor tells her that if the operation is not performed within the next twenty-four hours, Paul will die. Mrs. Perry responds by saying that "God will cure my son." What legal action, if any, can be taken to protect Paul's rights and to protect Mrs. Perry's rights?

## ■ Chapter Summary

The law is changing every day. The only dependable way to find out about all of these changes is through legal research. Research skills will take time and determination to develop. A useful first step is to compile a list of definitions or functions of the major research terms (such as citation, citator, cumulative, and headnote) and the major sets of research materials (such as A.L.R., *Corpus Juris Secundum*, *Federal Reporter 3d*, U.S.C.A., and Westlaw).

You need to know where to find law libraries in your community, particularly federal depository libraries. Within these libraries, you will find the following kinds of authority that courts consider in reaching a decision: primary authority, which consists of laws such as statutes and cases; secondary authority, which consists of nonlaws such as legal periodical articles and legal encyclopedias; mandatory authority, which a court *must* rely on; and persuasive authority, which a court has discretion to accept or reject.

A citation is an "address" where authority can be found in a library. Citation rules and manuals tell you what to abbreviate in the citation, where spaces and commas must be inserted, in what order the information in the citation must be provided, when to include a parallel cite, etc. When cite checking, you identify inaccuracies in citation form, shepardize or KeyCite the authorities cited, check the accuracy of any quotations used, etc.

Many law books have standard features. Each time you come across a new law book or set of law books, you should check features such as the copyright page, which contains the latest copyright date, and the foreword or preface, which may give a general description of how to use the book. The tables or lists at the beginning of the book will help you understand terms, symbols, or signals used in the book. Check also for updating features (such as pocket parts), various tables of contents, and index features that may be available.

The CARTWHEEL is a technique that helps you use the often poorly organized indexes (and tables of contents) of law books. The technique assumes that the entry you first check in the index (or table) leads you nowhere and that you must now think of some other entries to check that might be more productive. The CARTWHEEL is designed to help you identify these other entries.

There are three levels of legal research: background research, in which you start identifying the basic vocabulary and the major principles of an area of the law that is relatively new to you; specific fact research, in which you look for primary and secondary authority covering the facts of a client's case; and validation research, in which you check the current validity of whatever authority you initially believed was relevant to the problem you are researching. Occasionally, aspects of all three levels of research will be going on simultaneously.

A competent legal researcher knows how to use the major search tools or resources:

- Card or computer catalog to find what is available in the library you are using
- Digests to find court opinions
- Annotations to find court opinions
- Shepard's to shepardize court opinions, statutes, and regulations in order to validate cited material and to find citing material such as court opinions
- Loose-leaf services to give you leads to, and explanations of, primary authority
- Legal periodical literature to give you leads to, and explanations of, primary authority
- Legal encyclopedias to give you leads to, and explanations of, primary authority
- Legal treatises to give you leads to, and explanations of, primary authority
- Phone and mail research to give you leads to, and explanations of, primary authority

The major CALR (computer assisted legal research) tools are Westlaw and LEXIS. (In chapter 13, we will cover them in greater detail.)

These major search tools or resources will often lead you to more than one kind of primary authority: court opinions, statutes (plus legislative history), constitutions, administrative law, local law, rules of court, and international law.

## KEY TERMS

federal depository library
virtual
Internet
CALR
loose-leaf
interfiling
online
public domain
CD–ROM
microform
abstract
digest
act
slip law
administrative code
advance sheet
reporter
legislative service
advance session law service
annotation
annotated reporter
legal encyclopedia
annotated
annotated statutory code
notes of decisions
Auto-Cite
bill
legislative history
blue book
appellate brief
amicus curiae brief
opinion
docket
official reporter
unofficial reporter
unpublished opinion
unreported opinion
star paging
regional reporter
special edition state reporter
headnote
casebook
citation
parallel cite
public domain citation
citator
CLE materials
code
codify
cumulative
deskbook
key number
regional digest
form book
hornbook
World Wide Web

hypertext
listserv
intranet
interstate compact
KeyCite
legal dictionary
legal newsletter
legal newspaper
legal periodical
legal thesaurus
LegalTrac
legal treatise
legislation
public law
private law
LEXIS
loose-leaf service
law directory
nutshell
outline
pattern jury instructions
pocket part
record
register
Restatement
rules of court
edition
series
session laws
shepardize
cited material
citing material
statutory code
slip opinion
official statutory code
unofficial statutory code
Total-Client Service Library
uniform state laws
preliminary prints
authority
primary authority
secondary authority
mandatory authority
persuasive authority
nonauthority
enacted law
legislative intent
analogous
on point
key facts
on all fours
overrule
stare decisis
precedent
conflicts of law
subject matter jurisdiction

| | |
|---|---|
| personal jurisdiction | copyright page |
| full faith and credit | table of cases |
| Supremacy Clause | table of statutes |
| dictum | CARTWHEEL |
| holding | terms of art |
| plagiarism | committee reports |
| first impression | trace a key number |
| short-form citation | DWI |
| consolidated litigation | reverse |
| et al. | overrule |
| litigation status | superscript |
| docket number | session law cite |
| writ of certiorari | codified cite |
| nominative reporter | enabling statute |
| pinpoint cite | case note |
| vendor-neutral citation | black letter law |
| popular name | construction |
| cite checking | ejusdem generis |
| table of authorities | treaty |
| *supra* | executive agreement |
| *infra* | validation research |
| *id.* | |

## ON THE NET: MORE ON MAJOR LEGAL RESEARCH GUIDES AND TUTORIALS

- www.loc.gov/law/guide/index.html
- lib.law.washington.edu/ref/guides.html
- www.virtualchase.com
- www.llrx.com/guide
- www.llrx.com/features/us_fed.htm
- www.law.cornell.edu
- www.hg.org
- www.CataLaw.com
- www.west.net/~smith/research.htm
- library.law.unc.edu/tutorial/intro.htm
- www.ll.georgetown.edu/tutorials

## ENDNOTES

1. Ancil Ramey, *West Publishing Company to Print West Virginia Reports*, 5 W. Va. Law. 7 (Oct. 1991).
2. Most reportèrs, such as those published by West Group, call these summaries *headnotes*. A few, however, call them *syllabi* (plural of syl-labus). West Group has a different meaning for *syllabus*. In West Group reporters, a syllabus is a one-paragraph summary of the entire case, which is printed just below the caption and just before the headnotes.

# Appendix 11 A

# BIBLIOGRAPHY OF LEGAL RESEARCH AND CITATION GUIDES ON STATE LAW

**Alabama**

L. Kitchens & T. Laws, *Alabama Practice Materials*, 82 Law Library Journal 703 (1990)

**Alaska**

A. Ruzicka, *Alaska Legal and Law Related Publications* (American Ass'n of Law Libraries, 1984).

**Arizona**

K. Shimpock-Vieweg & M. Alcorn, *Arizona Legal Research Guide* (Hein, 1992).

K. Fitzhugh, *Arizona Practice Materials*, 81 Law Library Journal 277 (1989).

**Arkansas**

K. Fitzhugh, *Arkansas Practice Materials II*, 21 University of Arkansas at Little Rock Law Review 363 (1999).

**California**

D. Martin, *Henke's California Law Guide*, 4th (Butterworth, 1998).

L. Dershem, *California Legal Research Handbook* (Rothman, 1999).

T. Dabagh, *Legal Research Guide for California Practice* (Hein, 1985).

R. Formichi, *California Style Manual*, 3d (1986).

J. Hanft, *Legal Research in California*, 3d (Bancroft-Whitney, 1999).

**Colorado**

M. Fontenot, *Colorado Practice Materials*, 88 Law Library Journal 427 (1996).

**Connecticut**

J. Saxon, *Connecticut Practice Materials*, 91 Law Library Journal 139 (1999).

L. Cheeseman & A. Bielefield, *Connecticut Legal Research Handbook* (Conn. Law Book Co., 1992).

**Delaware**

P. Charles & D. King, *Delaware Practice Materials*, 89 Law Library Journal 349 (1997).

**District of Columbia**

L. Chanin et al., *Legal Research in the District of Columbia . . .* (Hein, 1995).

**Florida**

S. Rowe et al., *Florida Legal Research* (Carolina Academic Press, 1998).

B. Stupshi *Guide to Florida Legal Research*, 5th (Fla. Bar, Cont. Legal Education, 1998).

**Georgia**

N. Johnson & N. Deel, *Researching Georgia Law*, 14 Georgia State University Law Review 545 (1998).

L. Chanin & S. Cassidy, *Guide to Georgia Legal Research and Legal History* (Harrison, 1990).

**Hawaii**

R. Kahle, *How to Research Constitutional, Legislative and Statutory History in Hawaii* (Hawaii Legislative Reference Bureau; 1997).

**Idaho**

L. Seeger, *Idaho Practice Materials*, 87 Law Library Journal 534 (1995).

**Illinois**

F. Houdek & J. McKnight, *An Annotated Bibliography of Legal Research Tools*, 16 Southern Illinois University Law Review 767 (1992).

**Indiana**

L. Fariss & K. Buckley, *An Introduction to Indiana State Publications for the Law Librarian* (American Ass'n of Law Libraries, 1982).

## Iowa

A. Secrest, *Iowa Legal Documents Bibliography* (American Ass'n of Law Libraries, 1990).

## Kansas

J. Custer, *Kansas Legal Research & Reference Guide, 2d* (Kansas Bar Ass'n, 1997).

## Kentucky

K. Metzmeier, *Kentucky Legal Research on the Internet*, 86 Kentucky Law Journal 971 (1997–98).

A. Torres, *Kentucky Practice Materials*, 84 Law Library Journal 509 (1992).

## Louisiana

W. Chiang, *Louisiana Legal Research, 2d* (Butterworth, 1990).

M. Cunningham, *Guide to Louisiana and Selected French Materials and Citation*, 67 Tulane Law Review 1305 (1993).

## Maine

W. Wells, *Maine Legal Research Guide* (Tower Publishing, 1989).

## Maryland

P. Gregory, *Legal Research in the District of Columbia, Maryland, and Virginia* (Hein, 1995)

## Massachusetts

V. Wise, *How to Do Massachusetts Legal Research* (1998).

## Michigan

R. Beer & J. Field, *Michigan Legal Literature, 2d* (Hein, 1991).

N. Bosh, *The Research Edge* (Institute of Continuing Legal Education, 1993).

D. Johnson, *Michigan Practice Materials*, 73 Law Library Journal 672 (1980).

## Minnesota

M. Baum & M. Nelson, *Guide to Minnesota State Documents . . .* (American Ass'n of Law Libraries, 1986).

A. Soderberg & B. Golden, *Minnesota Legal Research Guide* (Hein, 1985).

## Mississippi

B. Cole, *Mississippi Legal Documents . . .* (American Ass'n of Law Libraries, 1987).

## Missouri

M. Nelson, *Guide to Missouri State Documents . . .* (American Ass'n of Law Libraries, 1991).

## Montana

S. Johnson, *A Guide to Montana Legal Research, 6th* (1999).

F. Snyder, *The Citation Practices of the Montana Supreme Court*, 57 Montana Law Review 453 (1966).

S. Jordan, *Montana Practice Materials*, 84 Law Library Journal 299 (1992).

## Nebraska

P. Charles et al., *Lexis Publishing's Research Guide to Nebraska Law, 2d* (1999).

B. Smith, *Nebraska Practice Materials*, 79 Nebraska Law Review 118 (2000)

## Nevada

G. Fletcher, *Nevada Practice Materials*, 91 Law Library Journal 313 (1999).

A. Jarrell & G. Fletcher, *Nevada State Documents Bibliography . . ., 2d* (American Ass'n of Law Libraries, 2000).

## New Jersey

P. Axel-Lute, *New Jersey Legal Research Handbook, 4th* (N.J. Institute for Continuing Legal Education, 1998).

## New Mexico

M. Woodward, *New Mexico Practice Materials*, 84 Law Library Journal 84 (1992).

## New York

R. Carter, *New York State Constitution: Sources of Legislative Intent* (Rothman, 1988).

E. Gibson, *New York Legal Research Guide, 2d* (Hein, 1998).

Brown, *An Annotated Bibliography of Current New York State Practice Materials*, 73 Law Library Journal 28 (1980).

*New York Rules of Citation, 2d* (St. John's Law Review, 1991).

## North Carolina

J. McKnight, *North Carolina Legal Research Guide* (Rothman, 1994).

## North Dakota

*For All Intents and Purposes: Essentials in Researching Legislative Histories* (N.D. Legislative Council, 1981).

## Ohio

J. Leonard, *A Select, Annotated Bibliography of Ohio Practice Materials*, 17 Ohio Northern University Law Review 265 (1990).

*Ohio Legal Resources . . . 4th* (Ohio Library Council, 1996).

M. Putnam & S. Schaefgen, *Ohio Legal Research Guide* (Hein, 1997).

*Manual of the Forms of Citation Used in the Ohio Official Reports* (Ohio Supreme Court, 1992).

## Oklahoma

M. Nicely, *Oklahoma Legal and Law-Related Documents . . ., 2d* (1997).

## Oregon

K. Beck, *Oregon Practice Materials*, 88 Law Library Journal 288 (1996).

## Pennsylvania

J. Fishman, *Bibliography of Pennsylvania Law: Secondary Sources* (Pa. Legal Resources Institute, 1992).

J. Fishman, *An Introduction to Pennsylvania State Publications . . .* (American Ass'n of Law Libraries, 1986). *See also* 78 Law Library Journal 74 (1986).

**Rhode Island**

C. McConaghy, *Selective Bibliography for the State of Rhode Island* (American Ass'n of Law Libraries, 1993).
*Legal Research in Rhode Island* (R.I. Law Institute, 1989).

**South Carolina**

P. Benson & D. Davis, *A Guide to South Carolina Legal Research and Citation* (S.C. Bar Continuing Legal Education, 1991).

**South Dakota**

D. Jorgensen, *South Dakota Legal Research Guide*, 2d (Hein, 1999).
S. Etling, *A Primer on Citation* (South Dakota Law School Foundation, 1996).

**Tennessee**

L. Laska, *Tennessee Legal Research Handbook* (Hein, 1977).
L. Laska, *Tennessee Rules of Citation* (1982).

**Texas**

P. Tepper & P. Kerley, *Texas Legal Research*, 2d (1997).
L. Brandt, *Texas Legal Research: An Essential Lawyering Skill* (Texas Lawyer Press, 1995).
*Texas Law Review Manual on Style, 7th* (1992).
*Texas Rules of Form, 8th* (1992).

**Utah**

K. Staheli, *Utah Practice Materials*, 87 Law Library Journal 50 (1995).

**Vermont**

V. Wise, *A Bibliographic Guide to the Vermont Legal System*, 2d (American Ass'n of Law Libraries, 1991).

**Virginia**

J. Eure & R. Murphy, *A Guide to Legal Research in Virginia*, 3d (Va. Law Foundation, 1999).
S. Wiant, *Legal Research in the District of Columbia, Maryland, and Virginia* (Hein, 1995).

**Washington**

Penny Hazelton et al., *Washington Legal Researcher's Deskbook*, 2d (Gallagher Law Library, 1996).
M. Cerjan, *Washington Legal Research Deskbook* (Wash. Law School Foundation, 1994).

**West Virginia**

S. Stemple et al., *West Virginia Legal Bibliography* (American Ass'n of Law Libraries, 1990).

**Wisconsin**

M. Platt & M. Koshollek, *Wisconsin Practice Materials* (Hein, 1999). See also 90 Law Library Journal 219 (1998).

**Wyoming**

N. Greene, *Wyoming State Legal Documents* (American Ass'n of Law Libraries, 1985).

# Chapter 12

# LEGAL WRITING

## Chapter Outline

## Section A
# INTRODUCTION

Legal writing is an important skill in the practice of law. To a large extent, the legal profession lives by the written word. Any important task of an attorney, judge, or legislator is often heavily documented in writing. Everyone is very reluctant to rely on oral communication alone. Consequently, a busy law office generates a vast quantity of paper. This is true even in the computer age, when most writing is done on a word processor (see chapter 13). Once documents are prepared on a computer, they are almost always printed as hard copy, i.e., on paper.

Competent attorneys tend to be very particular about how something should be written. A paralegal who works for more than one attorney should not expect that they will all have the same style. This can sometimes be disconcerting. What pleases one attorney may upset another.

Before examining ways to cope in this environment, it is important to understand that the phrase *legal writing* can be used to describe different tasks:

- Preparing documents that require *legal analysis*
- Preparing documents that require *legal research*
- Making sure that legal documents conform to their *special formats*
- Using clear and precise language to *communicate* effectively in any legal document

Although these four tasks are often interrelated, our primary focus in this chapter will be the latter two tasks: an introduction to the special formats used in some of the documents commonly prepared in a law office and an overview of important general communication techniques that can improve writing in any legal document. Legal analysis is covered in chapter 7 as well as in the pleading and discovery sections of chapter 10. Legal research is covered in chapter 11.

We begin with suggestions that can be helpful in any writing assignment in a law office:

1. Obtain the basic parameters of the writing assignment:

   - What are you asked to write? (See "Kinds of Legal Writing" in the next section.)
   - Who will be reading it? Who is the audience?
   - When is it due? Does it have priority over other assignments? (If you have assignments from different supervisors, consider asking the supervisors to establish the priorities.)
   - What format should you use in the document you will be preparing?
   - What resources can you use? For example, if your assignment requires legal research, can you use electronic research, e.g., Westlaw, LEXIS, Loislaw (see chapters 11 and 13)?
   - Will the supervisor (or anyone else in the office) be available to provide feedback on a complete or partial draft of the assignment before the final draft is due?

2. Find out if the office has its own style manual. Someone in the office may have collected general format instructions for different kinds of writing the office often prepares. Everyone may be expected to follow these instructions. The style manual may also include sample documents that conform to these instructions. (If such a manual exists, it may be in a notebook or in a computer database.)

3. If the office does not have a style manual, ask your supervisor where in the office you can find copies of documents on other cases that you may be able to use as a model for the document you are asked to prepare.

4. Find out if the office uses any commercial texts as guides for commonly prepared documents. For example, does the office follow the Blue Book for citation format (see chapter 11)? Is there a bar practice manual or treatise that is considered the bible for the substantive area of law involved in the assignment? If so, it may contain sample documents.

5. Once you have a model, adapt it to the specific facts and instructions of the writing assignment you are given. See "How to Avoid Abusing a Standard Form" in exhibit 10.11 in chapter 10.

6. Seek feedback before submitting the final draft. (See guideline 1.) For example, prepare an outline of the document and ask for feedback on the outline to make sure you are on the right track. (This will not be needed for relatively simple documents or ones that you often prepare.)

7. Carefully proofread to make sure there are no grammar and spelling errors in your final draft. Quietly reading your text out loud to yourself might turn up errors that were overlooked by silent reading and re-reading. Also, reading your text backwards might help reveal glaring errors in spelling or punctuation. Spell checkers in word processing programs (see chapter 13) are sometimes helpful. Be careful, however, in using them. They will tell you if you misspelled the word *there*, but they will not tell you if you should have used the word *their*. If you asked your spell checker to check the sentence, "Due eye sense that you are a frayed?" you would be told that there are no spelling errors in the sentence. Spell checkers cannot check the meaning or proper use of correctly spelled words.

## Section B
# KINDS OF LEGAL WRITING

Most of the legal writing in a law office falls into the following categories:

- Letters
- Memoranda of law
- Appellate briefs
- Instruments
- Pleadings

We will discuss the first three in this chapter. Here is a brief overview of the other two:

> *Instruments*: An **instrument** is a formal written document that gives expression to a legal act or agreement. Examples of instruments include contracts, deeds, wills, and leases.
>
> *Pleadings*: A **pleading** is a formal document containing a statement of claims and responses to claims (such as defenses) exchanged between parties involved in litigation. The major pleadings are the complaint (see exhibit 10.12 in chapter 10) and the answer to the complaint.

**instrument** A formal written document that gives expression to a legal act or agreement.

**pleading** A formal document containing a statement of claims and responses to claims (such as defenses) exchanged between parties in litigation.

Instruments and pleadings are seldom drafted from scratch, particularly in law offices that have many clients with the same kind of case (e.g., a collections practice or a divorce practice). Form books and computer software often contain standard instruments or pleadings that the office can easily adapt to the facts of particular clients. Or the office can simply adapt instruments or pleadings already in its own computer files from prior client cases. Word processors can make needed adaptations with relative ease. If there are no instruments or pleadings already in the computer, the office can scan an old instrument or pleading into the computer for adaptation to a current client. (For more on scanning, see chapter 13.)

## Section C
# LETTER WRITING

A law office sends out different kinds of letters:

- Enclosure letter (cover letter)
- Demand letter
- Informational letter
- Status letter
- Confirmatory letter

There is overlap in these categories because a single letter may seek to accomplish more than one purpose. (Exhibit 12.1 presents the standard components of most letters.)

| EXHIBIT 12.1 | Standard Components of Most letters |

- **Heading** The heading at the top or beginning of the letter contains the firm's letterhead, which is often preprinted and centered. The letterhead identifies the law firm by full name, street address, and phone number. If available, a fax number, e-mail address, and World Wide Web home page address may also be provided.
- **Date** Give the full date (month, day, year) that the letter will be sent out. It is often placed at the left margin under the heading.
- **Recipient** This is the full name, title, and address of the person who will be receiving the letter. It is often placed at the left margin.
- **RE**: A reference line is a brief statement that indicates the case to which the letter pertains, and occasionally the major theme of the letter (e.g., "RE: Henderson v. Jones, Civ. 03.179. Request for Extension of Time to File Responsive Declaration"). The notation *RE* goes at the beginning of the reference line. RE means *in the matter of* or *concerning*. The reference line is placed at the left margin after the address of the recipient and just before the salutation.
- **Salutation** Here, you address the recipient: "Dear. . . : ." A colon (:) follows the last name of this person. If he or she is a doctor, professor, or important public official, use his or her title. The salutation often starts at the left margin on the line under the address.
- **Body** The body of the letter often includes:
  - *Identification line* In the first line of the letter, let the reader know who is sending the letter, unless this is already obvious to the recipient because of prior contact.
  - *Purpose line* Shortly after the identification line, briefly tell the reader the main purpose of the letter.
  - *Request line* If you are asking the recipient to do something, include a specific request line that makes this clear.
  - *Elaboration* As needed, elaborate on why you are writing the letter.
- **Closing** Here, you conclude the letter. In a separate paragraph, you could say something like "If you have any questions about this matter, please do not hesitate to contact me" or "Thank you for your consideration in this matter." On the next line, write, "Sincerely" or "Very truly yours." Place the name and title of the signer of the letter below the space for his or her signature. As we saw in chapter 5 on ethics, when nonattorneys sign letters, their title should clearly indicate their nonattorney status. The titles *paralegal* and *legal assistant* comply with this ethical obligation.
- **Copies Sent** If you are sending a copy of the letter to someone, indicate this by saying "cc:" followed by the name of the person(s) receiving the copy ("cc" stands for carbon copies; this abbreviation is still used even though carbon is seldom the method used today to make copies). Suppose you send out copies of the letter, but you do not want the recipient to know this. On the recipient's letter, you say nothing about copies. On the office copy of the letter, say "bcc:" (blind carbon copy) followed by the name of the person(s) receiving the copies. In this way, only your copy of the letter indicates who received copies. The main letter is silent ("blind") on this point.
- **Enclosures** If you are enclosing anything with the letter, say "Encl." If enclosing more than one item, say "Encls."
- **Initials** If someone else typed the letter for you, place your initials in capital letters, followed by a colon (:) and the initials (in lowercase) of the person who did the typing.

**enclosure letter** A letter that tells the recipient what physical items are being sent in the envelope or package.

An **enclosure letter** (also called a *cover letter*) tells the recipient what physical items (e.g., pleadings, photographs) are being sent in the envelope or package. The list of what is being sent should be detailed. If a response is expected, it should be clearly stated. For example:

Enclosed for your records are:

- a copy of the defendant's answer (4 pages) filed with the court on May 5, 2003
- a copy of our response to the answer (5 pages)

Also enclosed is:

- a letter of authorization that allows us to obtain your confidential employment records from the personnel department.

Please read the letter of authorization, sign it, and return it to us. We will need it within the next week. If you have any questions, don't hesitate to call us.

A **demand letter** is an advocacy letter that asks the recipient to take specific action (e.g., pay a debt owed to the client) or to refrain from taking specific action (e.g., not to terminate the client). The letter will often:

- Tell the recipient that the office represents the client,
- Specify what the recipient is being asked to do or to refrain from doing.
- Present essential facts and legal principles that are the basis of the demand, and

Since the recipient is often a nonattorney, citations to authority are relatively rare except when a single statute or regulation is central to the demand.

Sending a demand letter is usually considered the practice of law. A paralegal can prepare a draft of the letter for an attorney's signature, but it would probably be the unauthorized practice of law (see chapters 4 and 5) for the paralegal to send the letter under his or her own name. If the demand letter seeks the collection of money that is owed, the letter must conform to the Fair Debt Collection Practices Act. For example, the letter must not use any "false, deceptive, or misleading representation or means in connection with the collection of any debt."[1]

An **informational letter** provides information to the recipient, seeks information from the recipient, or both. See exhibit 12.2 for a sample informational letter. An example of an informational letter is a **status letter** written to a client to inform him or her of what has happened in the case thus far and to indicate what next steps are expected.

In a **confirmatory letter**, you confirm that something important has been done or said. For example:

> This is to confirm that you have agreed to accept $5,000 in full settlement of the contract dispute between . . . .
>
> Thank you for coming to the office on Tuesday to discuss the extension of insurance coverage for the employees in the Southeast region of your company's operations. I want to state my understanding of what took place at the meeting. Please let me know if the following summary is consistent with your understanding. . . .

This kind of letter is important because it provides written confirmation of matters that might be subject to misunderstanding with the passage of time. It is also a good way to provide a record for the file. In this sense, a confirmatory letter is similar to a "memo to the file," in which you communicate something about the case that has taken place, e.g., the substance of a recent telephone conversation or the result of some research in the law library. Confirmatory letters are different, of course, in that they are sent to specific individuals outside the office in an effort to remind them of something and to prompt them to voice any disagreements with the contents of the letter.

In an **opinion letter**, the office writes to its client to explain the application of the law and advise the client what to do. Such letters try to clarify technical material. Unlike a brief or memorandum, the opinion letter does not make extensive reference to court opinions or statutes. The client's need is for clear, concise, practical advice.

**demand letter** An advocacy letter that asks the recipient to take specific action or to refrain from taking specific action affecting the client.

**informational letter** A letter that provides or seeks information.

**status letter** A letter telling a client what has happened in the case thus far and what next steps are expected.

**confirmatory letter** A letter that verifies or confirms that something important has been done or said.

**opinion letter** A letter to a client explaining the application of the law and providing legal advice based on that explanation.

---

*Assignment 12.1*

Prepare a letter for each of the following situations. You will need more facts to complete the letters (e.g., the address of the recipient, your address, and more details on the purpose of the letter). You can make up any of these facts as long as they are reasonably consistent with the facts provided. In each case, your supervisor is an attorney who wants you to draft the letter for his or her signature.

(a) The office represents Richard Clemens, who is a plaintiff in an automobile accident case against George Kiley. The latter's insurance company has offered to settle for $10,000. Draft a letter to Richard Clemens in which you tell him about the offer and ask him to call you so that you can schedule an appointment with your supervisor to discuss the offer. Point out that the supervisor is not pleased with the low amount of the offer but that the decision on whether to accept it will be entirely up to the client.

**(b)** Draft a letter to a client who failed to appear at two meetings last month with her attorney (your supervisor) at the office to discuss her case. The client is Diane Rolark. She is very wealthy. The office hopes to keep her as a client in the future on other cases. Hence the office does not want to antagonize her. The letter should remind her of the next appointment with her attorney (three weeks from today).

**(c)** Write an opinion letter to a client, James Duband, in which you explain any legal concept that you have learned in another course. Assume that this concept is relevant to the case of this client and that the client has written the office asking your supervisor to explain the concept as it pertains to his case. The client is a construction worker who never finished high school.

| EXHIBIT 12.2 | Example of an Informational Letter |
|---|---|

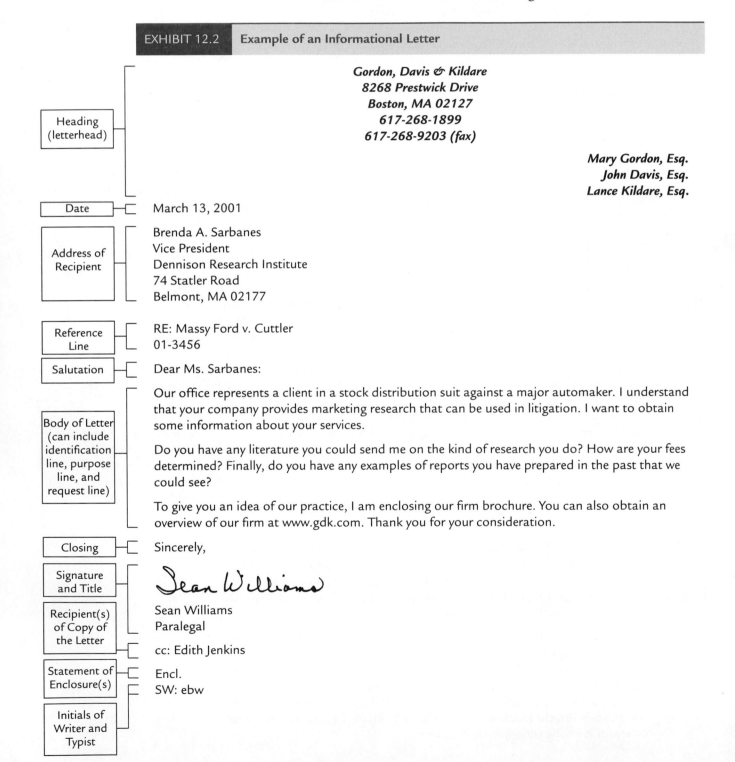

Heading (letterhead)

> ***Gordon, Davis & Kildare***
> ***8268 Prestwick Drive***
> ***Boston, MA 02127***
> ***617-268-1899***
> ***617-268-9203 (fax)***

> ***Mary Gordon, Esq.***
> ***John Davis, Esq.***
> ***Lance Kildare, Esq.***

Date

March 13, 2001

Address of Recipient

Brenda A. Sarbanes
Vice President
Dennison Research Institute
74 Statler Road
Belmont, MA 02177

Reference Line

RE: Massy Ford v. Cuttler
01-3456

Salutation

Dear Ms. Sarbanes:

Body of Letter (can include identification line, purpose line, and request line)

Our office represents a client in a stock distribution suit against a major automaker. I understand that your company provides marketing research that can be used in litigation. I want to obtain some information about your services.

Do you have any literature you could send me on the kind of research you do? How are your fees determined? Finally, do you have any examples of reports you have prepared in the past that we could see?

To give you an idea of our practice, I am enclosing our firm brochure. You can also obtain an overview of our firm at www.gdk.com. Thank you for your consideration.

Closing

Sincerely,

Signature and Title

Sean Williams
Paralegal

Recipient(s) of Copy of the Letter

cc: Edith Jenkins

Statement of Enclosure(s)

Encl.

Initials of Writer and Typist

SW: ebw

## Section D
# Memorandum of Law

A **memorandum of law** is a written analysis of a legal problem. (The plural is memoranda; the shorthand is memo.) More specifically, it is a written explanation of how the law might apply to the facts of a client's case. There are two main kinds of memoranda: (1) an internal or interoffice memorandum and (2) an external or advocacy memorandum. The differences are outlined in exhibit 12.3.

1. *Interoffice Memorandum of Law:* The main audience of your **interoffice memorandum of law** is your supervisor or someone else in the office; this memo is an internal document.[2] Your goal in the memo is to analyze the law in order to make a *prediction* of how a court or other tribunal will resolve the dispute in the client's case. It is extremely important that this memo present the strengths *and weaknesses* of the client's case. The supervisor must make strategy decisions based in part on what you say in the memo. Hence the supervisor must have a realistic picture of what the law is. Many students find it very difficult to present strengths and weaknesses in the same memo. They devote the vast majority of their memo to arguments that favor one side. This kind of writing is inappropriate in an interoffice memorandum of law. Force yourself to find arguments that support both sides—no matter which side is the client of your office and no matter which side you think should win. A hallmark of the professional is the ability to step back and assess a problem objectively. This means being able to analyze strengths and weaknesses of both sides.

2. *External or Advocacy Memorandum of Law:* The main audience of your **external memorandum of law** is someone outside the office, usually a judge or official in an administrative agency. An external memorandum might also be sent to an insurance company in support of a particular position (e.g., Memorandum in Support of the Life Insurance Claim of the Estate of George Samuelson). Your goal in this memo is to try to convince the reader to take a certain action in the client's case. Hence the memo is an *advocacy* document. In it, you are highlighting the strengths of the client's case and the weaknesses of the opponent's case.

   Different terminology is sometimes used for this kind of memo:

   ■ **Points and authorities memorandum:** An external memorandum submitted to a trial judge or hearing officer.
   ■ **Trial memorandum:** An external memorandum submitted to a trial judge. (A trial memorandum is sometimes referred to as a *trial brief*, although we will see later in the chapter that trial brief also has a very different meaning.)
   ■ **Hearing memorandum:** An external memorandum submitted to a hearing officer within an administrative agency.

When the document is submitted to an appellate court, it is called an *appellate brief*. The structure of the appellate brief is considered later in the chapter.

**memorandum of law** A written explanation of how the law might apply to the facts of a client's case.

**interoffice memorandum of law** A memorandum that objectively analyzes the law; the memo is written for your supervisor or for other individual(s) in your office.

**external memorandum of law** A memorandum that analyzes the law in order to convince someone outside your office to take a certain course of action.

---

| EXHIBIT 12.3 | Characteristics of Interoffice and External Memoranda of Law |
| --- | --- |

| INTEROFFICE MEMORANDUM OF LAW | EXTERNAL MEMORANDUM OF LAW |
| --- | --- |
| ■ Emphasizes both the strengths and the weaknesses of the client's position on each issue (objective) | ■ Emphasizes the strengths and minimizes or ignores the weaknesses of the client's position on each issue (advocacy) |
| ■ Emphasizes both the weaknesses and the strengths of the opposing party's known or anticipated position on each issue (objective) | ■ Emphasizes the weaknesses and minimizes or ignores the strengths of the opposing party's position on each issue (advocacy) |
| ■ Predicts the court's or the agency's probable decision on each issue | ■ Argues for a favorable decision on each issue |
| ■ Recommends the most favorable strategy for the client to follow | |

Most of the discussion that follows is on the internal interoffice memo. The external advocacy memo is mentioned only when there are significant differences.

## STRUCTURE OF AN INTEROFFICE MEMORANDUM OF LAW

What is the format or structure of an interoffice memorandum of law? The cardinal guideline is as follows: find out what format your supervisor prefers. There may be office memos in old files that you can use as models. If your supervisor does not express a preference, consider using the following format:

1. Heading
2. Statement of the assignment
3. Issues
4. Facts
5. Discussion or analysis
6. Conclusion
7. Recommendations
8. Appendix

### 1. Heading

The heading of the memo contains basic information about you and the nature of the memo:

**caption of memorandum**
The beginning of a memorandum containing its title or name.

a. A **caption of memorandum** centered at the top of the page stating the kind of document it is (Interoffice Memorandum of Law)
b. The name of the person to whom the memo is addressed (usually your supervisor)
c. Your name (the author of the memo)
d. The date the memo was completed and submitted
e. The name of the case (client's name and opponent, if any)
f. The office file number

**docket number** The number assigned to a case by the court.

g. The court **docket number** (if the suit has already been filed and the clerk of the court has assigned a docket number)
h. A very brief summary of the subject matter of the memo following the notation **RE:**, meaning "in the matter of" or "concerning"

**RE** In the matter of; concerning.

The example in exhibit 12.4 illustrates how this information might be set forth in a memo written on behalf of client Brown, who is suing Miller.

Note that the subject matter description (RE) in this example briefly indicates the nature of the question you are treating in the memorandum. This information is needed for at least two reasons. First, the average law office case file contains a large number of documents, often including several legal memoranda. A heading that at least briefly indicates the subject of the memorandum makes it easier to locate the memorandum in the client's file. Second, your memo might be examined sometime in the future, long after the case is over. Many offices keep copies of old office memoranda in files or in computer databases. They are cataloged by subject matter for reference in future cases. The subject matter heading on the memo facilitates the cataloging, filing, and retrieving of such memos.

---

| EXHIBIT 12.4 | Heading of Interoffice Memorandum |
| --- | --- |

**Interoffice Memorandum of Law**

TO: Jane Patterson, Esq.
FROM: John Jackson, Paralegal
DATE: March 13, 2003
CASE: Brown v. Miller
OFFICE FILE NUMBER: 03-1168
DOCKET NUMBER: C-34552-03

RE: Whether substituted service is allowed under Civil Code § 34–403(g)

Including the date on which the memorandum was completed and submitted is also important. Although your analysis and conclusions may have been accurate at the time the memorandum was written, the law may have changed by the time the memorandum is examined again. Hence a later reader will need to verify the current validity of every case, statute, or other authority you cited in the memorandum and determine whether totally new laws have been written since the date you wrote it.

### 2. Statement of the Assignment

Soon after you are given an interoffice memorandum assignment, you should write out what you were asked to do. State the parameters of the assignment. If limitations or restrictions were imposed, include them in your written statement. For example:

- You have asked me not to examine the issue of damages.
- You have asked me to spend no more than four hours on the assignment.
- You have asked me not to use fee-based online research services at this time.

Also list any assumptions that you have been asked to make. For example:

- You have asked me to assume that only New York law applies. (Or, you have asked me to discuss New York law only.)
- You have asked me to discuss the constitutionality of the client's statement to the police on the assumption that the state will be able to convince a trial judge that the statement was not privileged.

If you have any difficulty writing the statement of the assignment, consult with your supervisor immediately. The time to clarify what you are to do—and what you are not to do—is before you spend extensive time researching, analyzing, and writing. Here is another example:

> **Assignment** You have asked me to prepare a memorandum of law limited to the question of whether our client, Joan Davis, is required to return the overpayment she received from the Department of Revenue and Disbursements. You asked me to discuss Ohio law only.

Include this statement of the assignment after the heading. The value of clearly articulating the boundary lines of the memo cannot be overemphasized. Note that the statement of the assignment is a more elaborate presentation of what was briefly summarized as the topic of the memo in the heading after the notation RE.

### 3. Issues

The two critical components of an issue are as follows: (1) a brief quote from the element of the law in contention and (2) several of the important facts relevant to that contention. As we saw in chapter 7, an element is a portion of a rule that is a precondition of the applicability of the entire rule.

Assume, for example, that Mary Gallagher is suing Leo Grant, a store manager, for defamation. While trying to buy a coat at his store with her credit card, Grant told Gallagher, "Your credit card is bogus." The merchant denies that his statement was defamatory. The law being applied here is defamation tort law. One of the requirements or elements of this tort is proof that the defendant uttered a "defamatory statement." This is the **element in contention**. The phrasing of the issue in this case might be:

> Has a merchant made a "defamatory statement" when he tells a customer seeking to make a credit purchase that her "credit card is bogus"?

Note that the issue is made up of a quote from the element in contention and several of the important facts that are relevant to that element.

Let us look at another example. Assume that a taxpayer challenges a denial of a tax deduction under § 200.8 (a) of the state tax code. This statutory section says that an accelerated deduction can be taken for "equipment purchased for use primarily in areas of the state designated by the governor as economically blighted." Patricia Wallace has a restaurant in a section that the governor has designated as blighted. Wallace sought a § 200.8 (a) deduction for a refrigerator she leased for the restaurant with an option to buy

**element in contention** That portion of a rule about which the parties cannot agree. The disagreement may be over the definition of the element, how the element applies to the facts, or both.

after three years. The tax department has denied the deduction, asserting that a lease is not a purchase. Wallace claims that the lease with an option to buy within three years qualifies as a purchase, especially since she expects to exercise the option after three years of the lease. The law being applied here is § 200.8 (a) of the state tax code. The element of this law in contention is the requirement that the equipment be "purchased." The phrasing of the issue in this case might be:

> Has a taxpayer "purchased" a refrigerator entitling her to a deduction under § 200.8 (a) of the tax code when she leased the refrigerator with an option to buy after three years, which she intends to exercise?

Note again that the issue consists of a quote from the element in contention and several of the important facts that are relevant to that element.

For more on how to phrase issues, see the issue-statement skill in section D of chapter 7 on legal analysis.

Often you must state and discuss certain issues *on the assumption* that the court or agency will decide against you on prior issues that you discuss early in the memorandum. Suppose that the client is a defendant in a negligence action. The first issue may concern the liability of the defendant: Was the defendant negligent? The memorandum will cover the liability question and will attempt to demonstrate in the discussion or analysis of this issue why the defendant is *not* liable. All the evidence and authority supporting non-liability will be examined under this issue. At the time the memorandum is written, of course, this issue will not have been resolved. Hence you must proceed *on the assumption* that the client will lose the first issue and be prepared for other issues that will then arise. For example, all issues concerning damages (how much money must be paid to a plaintiff who has successfully established liability) should be anticipated and analyzed in the event that the liability issue is lost. The statement of the damagees issue in the memorandum should be prefaced by language such as:

> In the event that we lose the first issue, then we must discuss the issue of . . . .

*or*

> On the assumption that the court finds for [the other party] on the liability issue, the damages question then becomes whether . . . .

No matter how firmly you believe in your prediction of what a court or agency will do on an issue, be prepared for what will happen in the event that your prediction eventually proves to be erroneous. This must be done in an internal memorandum, in an external memorandum (hearing or trial), and in an appellate brief.

### 4. Facts

Your statement of the facts of the client's case is one of the most important components of the memorandum. You should take great pains to see that it is concise, highly accurate, and well organized.

    a. *Conciseness*: An unduly long fact statement only frustrates the reader. Try to eliminate any unnecessary facts from the statement. One way of doing this is to carefully review your fact statement *after* you have completed your analysis of the issues. If your statement contains facts that are not subsequently referred to in your analysis, it may be that those facts are not particularly relevant to your memorandum and can be eliminated in your final draft. Otherwise, go back and discuss them in your analysis.

    b. *Accuracy*: In many instances, you will be drafting the memorandum for an attorney who is preparing to go before a court or agency for the first time; there may be no prior proceedings. Hence there will be no record and no official findings of fact. The temptation will be to indulge in wishful thinking—to ignore adverse facts and to assume that disputed facts will be resolved in favor of the client. Do not give in to this temptation. You must assess the legal consequences of both favorable *and* unfavorable facts. If a particular fact is presently unknown, put aside your writing, if possible, and investigate whatever evidence exists to prove the fact one way or the other. If it is not practical to conduct an investigation at the present time, then you should provide an analysis of what law will apply based on your most reasonable estimate of what an investigation may uncover. (When you get to the recommendations section of the memo, be sure to include investigation that the office should undertake later.) The need for accuracy does not mean that you should fail to state the facts in the light most favorable to the client. It simply means that you must be careful to avoid making false or misleading statements of fact.

c. *Organization*: A disorganized statement of facts not only prevents the reader from understanding the events in question but also interferes with an understanding of your subsequent analysis. If the statement of facts is fairly long, you might begin with a one- or two-sentence summary of the facts. For example:

Facts

During 12 years of employment at Sinclair Chemicals, Inc., Mary Kiley was subjected to numerous instances of sexual harassment. When she began work there in 1990, she . . . .

Then provide a *chronological* statement of the detailed facts. Occasional variations from strict chronological order can be justified as long as they do not interfere with the flow of the story.

## 5. Discussion or Analysis

Here, you present the law and explain its applicability to the facts. In other words, you try to answer questions raised in the issues. For memos that require interpretation of statutes, the following organizational structure is suggested:

- Quote the section or subsection of the statute you are analyzing. Include only what must be discussed in the memo. If the section or subsection is long, you may want to place it in an appendix to the memo. If you are going to discuss more than one section or subsection, treat them separately in different parts of the memo unless they are so interrelated that they must be discussed together.
- Break the statute into its elements. List each element separately. (See "Organizing a Memorandum of Law" in exhibit 7.1 in chapter 7.)
- Briefly tell the reader which elements will be in contention and why. In effect, you are telling him or her why you have phrased the issue(s) the way you did earlier in the memo.
- Go through each element you have identified, one at a time, spending most of your time on the elements that are most in contention.
- For the elements not in contention, simply tell the reader why you think there will not be any dispute about them. For example, you anticipate that both sides probably will agree that the facts clearly support the applicability or nonapplicability of the element.
- For the elements in contention, present your interpretation of each element; discuss court opinions that have interpreted the statute, if any; discuss administrative regulations and administrative decisions that have interpreted the statute, if any; discuss the legislative history of the statute, if available; discuss scholarly interpretation of the statute, if any, in legal periodicals and legal treatises (see chapter 11).
- Give opposing viewpoints for the elements in contention. Try to anticipate how the other side will interpret these elements. For example, what counterarguments will the other side probably make through court opinions or legislative history?

The last point is particularly important. Too often student memos fail to provide a counteranalysis. They present only one side: either the side they think should, in fairness, win or the side their law office represents. To counteract this deficiency, use the **STOP** technique:

**STOP**

- after you write a Sentence of your analysis
- Think carefully

**STOP** A writing technique alerting you to the need for a counteranalysis: after writing a Sentence, Think carefully about whether the Other side would take a Position that is different from the one you took in the sentence.

- about whether the Other side
- would agree with the Position you have just taken in that sentence

If you conclude (once you STOP yourself) that the other side would not agree with what you have written, a counteranalysis to your position will be needed somewhere in the memo. The counteranalysis does not have to occur immediately after the sentence you wrote. You may decide to present the counteranalysis in a separate paragraph or in a separate section of the memo. STOP is simply a technique to remind you that your analysis will not be complete until you have covered every position the other side will probably raise.

### 6. Conclusion

Give your personal opinion as to which side has the better arguments. Do not state any new arguments in the conclusion. Simply state your own perspective on the strengths and weaknesses of your arguments.

### 7. Recommendations

State recommendations you feel are appropriate in view of the analysis and conclusion you have provided. For example, further facts should be investigated (specify which ones), further research should be undertaken (identify each issue in need of further research), a letter should be written to the government agency involved in the dispute (summarize or submit a draft of the proposed letter), the case should be settled or litigated (summarize why you think so), etc.

### 8. Appendix

At the end of the memo, include special items, if any, that you referred to in the memo, such as photographs, statistical tables, or the full text of statutes.

What follows is an interoffice memorandum of law that conforms with this structure. Assume that the supervisor wants this memorandum within a few hours after the assignment is given to you. You are asked to provide a preliminary analysis of a statute. Hence, at this point there has been no time to do any research on the statute, although the memo should indicate what research will be needed.

---

### SAMPLE INTEROFFICE MEMORANDUM OF LAW: THE DONALDSON CASE

#### INTEROFFICE MEMORANDUM OF LAW

To: Timothy Farrell, Esq.                     RE: Whether Donaldson has
FROM: Paul Vargas, Paralegal                          violated § 17
DATE: March 23, 2002
CASE: Department of Sanitation v. Jim Donaldson
OFFICE FILE NUMBER: 02-114
DOCKET NUMBER: (none at this time; no action has been filed)

#### A. ASSIGNMENT

You have asked me to do a preliminary analysis of 23 State Code Ann. § 17 (1980) to assess whether our client, Jim Donaldson has violated this statute. No research on the statute has been undertaken thus far, but I will indicate where such research might be helpful.

#### B. ISSUE

When a government employee is asked to rent a car for his agency, but uses the car for personal business before he signs the lease, has this employee violated

**SAMPLE INTEROFFICE MEMORANDUM OF LAW: continued**

§ 17, which prohibits the use of "property leased to the government" for nonofficial purposes?

## C. FACTS

Jim Donaldson is a government employee who works for the State Department of Sanitation. On February 12, 2002, he is asked by his supervisor, Fred Jackson, to rent a car for the agency for a two-year period. At the ABC Car Rental Company, Donaldson is shown several cars available for rental. He asks the manager if he could test drive one of the cars for about 15 minutes before making a decision. The manager agrees. Donaldson then drives the car to his home in the area, picks up a TV, and takes it to his sister's home. When he returns, he tells the manager that he wants to rent the car for his agency. He signs the lease and takes the car to the agency. The supervisor, however, finds out about the trip that Donaldson made to his sister with the TV. He is charged with a violation of § 17. Because Donaldson is a new employee at the agency, he is fearful that he might lose his job.

## D. ANALYSIS

Donaldson is charged with violating 23 State Code Ann. § 17 (1980), which provides as follows:

> §17. Use of Government Property
> An employee of any state agency shall not directly or indirectly use government property of any kind, including property leased to the government, for other than officially approved activities.

To establish a violation of this statute, the following elements must be proven:

(1) An employee of any state agency
(2) (a) shall not directly use government property of any kind including property leased to the government or
    (b) shall not indirectly use government property of any kind including property leased to the government.
(3) for other than officially approved activities.

The main problem in this case will be the second element.

(1) Employee of a state agency
    Donaldson works for the State Department of Sanitation, which is clearly a "state agency" under the statute.

(2) Use of property leased to the government.
    The central issue is whether Donaldson used property leased to the government. There should be no dispute that when Donaldson drove the car to his sister's, he directly used property. (He did not "indirectly" use property such as by causing someone else to drive the car.) The question is whether the car was "property leased to the government" within the meaning of § 17.
    Donaldson's best argument is a fairly strong one. His position will be that when he made the trip to his sister, he had not yet signed the lease. He will argue that "leased" means contractually committed to rent. Under this definition, the car did not become property leased to the government until after he returned from his sister's house. No costs were incurred by the government because of the test drive. Rental payments would not begin until the car was rented through the signing of the lease.
    The supervisor, on the other hand, will argue for a broader definition of "leased"—that it means the process of obtaining a contractual commitment to

**SAMPLE INTEROFFICE MEMORANDUM OF LAW: continued**

rent, including the necessary steps leading up to that commitment. Under this definition, the car was "leased" to Donaldson when he made the unauthorized trip. The test drive was arguably a necessary step in making the decision to sign a long-term leasing contract.

The supervisor will stress that the goal or purpose of the legislature in enacting § 17 should be kept in mind when trying to determine the meaning of any of the language of § 17. The legislature was trying to avoid the misuse of government resources. Public employees should not take advantage of their position for private gain. To do so would be a violation of the public trust. Yet this is what Donaldson did. While on the government payroll, he obtained access to a car and used it for a private trip. Common sense would lead to the conclusion that leasing in § 17 is not limited to the formal signing of a leasing contract. Anything that is necessarily part of the process of signing that contract should be included. The legislature wanted to prevent the misuse of government resources in all necessary aspects of the leasing of property.

It is not clear from the facts whether the manager of the ABC Rental Company knew that Donaldson was considering the rental on behalf of a government agency when he received permission to take the test drive. The likelihood is that he did know it, although this should be checked. If the manager did know, then Donaldson probably used the fact that he was a government employee to obtain the permission. He held himself out as a reliable individual because of the nature of his employment. This reinforces the misuse argument under the broader definition of "leased" that the supervisor will present.

I have not yet checked whether there are any court opinions or agency regulations interpreting § 17 on this point. Nor have I researched the legislative history of the statute. All this should be done soon.

(3) Officially Approved Activities

Nothing in the facts indicates that Donaldson's supervisor gave him any authorization to make the TV trip. Even if the supervisor had authorized the trip, it would probably not be "officially" approved, since the trip was not for official (i.e., public) business.

### E. CONCLUSION

Donaldson has the stronger argument based on the language of the statute. The property simply was not "leased" at the time he made the TV trip. I must admit, however, that the agency has some good points in its favor. Unlike Donaldson's technical argument, the agency's position is grounded in common sense. Yet on balance, Donaldson's argument should prevail.

### F. RECOMMENDATIONS

Some further investigation is needed. We should find out whether the ABC Rental Company manager knew that Donaldson was a government employee at the time he asked for the test drive. In addition, legal research should be undertaken to find out if any court opinions and agency regulations exist on the statute. A check into the legislative history of § 17 is also needed.

Finally, I recommend that we send a letter to Donaldson's supervisor, Fred Jackson, explaining our position. I have attached a draft of such a letter for your signature in the event you deem this action appropriate.

There is one matter that I have not addressed in this memo. Donaldson is concerned that he might lose his job over this incident. Assuming for the moment that he did violate § 17, it is not at all clear that termination would be an appropriate sanction. The statute is silent on this point. Let me know if you want me to research this issue.

## DRAFT OF PROPOSED LETTER IN THE DONALDSON CASE

**Farrell, Grote, & Schweitzer**
**Attorneys at Law**
**724 Central Plaza Place**
**West Union, Ohio 45693**
**513-363-7159**

*Timothy Farrell, Esq.*
*Angela Grote, Esq.*
*Clara Schweitzer, Esq.*

March 25, 2002

Frederick Jackson
Field Supervisor
Department of Sanitation
3416 34th St. NW
West Union, Ohio 45693

RE: James Donaldson
02-114

Dear Mr. Jackson:

Our firm represents Mr. James Donaldson. As you know, a question has arisen concerning Mr. Donaldson's use of a car prior to his renting it for your agency on February 12, 2002. Our understanding is that he was asked to go to the ABC Car Rental Company in order to rent a car that was needed by your agency, and that he did so satisfactorily.

Your agency became responsible for the car at the moment Mr. Donaldson signed the lease for the car rental. What happened prior to the time the lease was signed is not relevant. The governing statute (§ 17) is quite explicit. It forbids nonofficial use of property "leased" to the government. Such use did not occur in this case. No one has questioned Mr. Donaldson's performance of his duty once he "leased" the car.

If additional clarification is needed, we would be happy to discuss the matter with you further.
Sincerely,

Timothy Farrell, Esq.

TF: ps

---

### Assignment 12.2

The Pepsi Cola Bottling Company is authorized to do business in Florida. It wishes to prevent another Florida company from calling itself the Pepsi Catsup Company because this name violates § 225.25. The Pepsi Catsup Company denies that its name is in violation of this statute. The Secretary of State has the responsibility of enforcing this statute.

**48 State Code Ann. § 225.25 (1979).** The name of a company or corporation shall be such as will distinguish it from any other company or corporation doing business in Florida.

Your supervisor asks you to prepare a preliminary memorandum of law on the applicability of this statute. The office represents the Pepsi Catsup Company. You do not need to know trademark law or any other area of the law. Simply analyze the language of the statute (§ 225.25) in a manner similar to the analysis of the statute (§ 17) in the sample interoffice memorandum of law. Do no legal research at this time, although you should point out what research might be helpful. After you complete the memo, draft a letter to the Secretary of State giving the position of your office on the applicability of the statute. (You can make up the names and addresses of the people involved as well as any dates that you need.)

## Section E
# Appellate Brief

The word *brief* has several meanings.

First, to *brief* a case is to summarize its major components, such as key facts, issues, reasoning, and disposition. (See exhibit 7.2 in chapter 7.) Such a brief is your own summary of a court opinion for later use.

Second, a **trial brief** is an attorney's set of notes on how he or she will conduct the trial. The notes will be on the opening statement, witnesses, exhibits, direct and cross-examination, closing argument, etc. The trial brief is not submitted to the court or to the other side. A *trial memorandum* on points of law might be submitted but not the trial brief, which contains counsel's strategy. (This trial memorandum, however, is sometimes referred to as a trial brief. In such instances, the trial brief consists of arguments of law rather than the tactical blueprint for the conduct of the trial.)

Third, the **appellate brief** is the formal written argument to a court of appeals on why a lower court's decision should be affirmed (approved), modified, or reversed. It is submitted to the appellate court and to the other side. The appellate brief is one of the most sophisticated kinds of legal writing in a law office.

The first appellate brief that is usually submitted is the *appellant's* brief. The **appellant** is the party initiating the appeal. Then the *appellee's* brief is filed in response. The appeal is taken against the **appellee** (sometimes called the **respondent**). Finally, the appellant is often allowed to submit a **reply brief** to counter the position taken in the appellee's brief.

Occasionally, a court will permit a nonparty to the litigation to submit an appellate brief. This is referred to as an **amicus curiae** (friend of the court) brief. The *amicus* brief presents the nonparty's view on whether the appellate court should affirm, modify, or reverse what the lower court has done.

Not all appellate briefs have the same structure. Rules of court often specify what structure or format the brief should take, the print size, the maximum number of pages or words that can be used, the number of the copies to be submitted, etc. The following are the major components of many appellate briefs:

(a) *Caption:* The caption of an appellate brief states the names of the parties, the name of the court, the court file or docket number, and the kind of appellate brief it is. The caption goes on the front cover of the brief. (For a photograph of a caption, see the margin exhibit next to the word *Brief* in section H of chapter 11.)

(b) *The Statement of Jurisdiction:* In this section of the brief, there is a short statement explaining the subject matter jurisdiction of the appellate court. (Subject matter jurisdiction is the power of a court to resolve a particular category or kind of dispute. Subject matter jurisdiction is usually conferred by statute.) For example:

This Court has jurisdiction under 28 U.S.C. § 1291 (1997).

The jurisdiction statement may point out some of the essential facts that relate to the jurisdiction of the appellate court, such as how the case came up on appeal. For example:

On January 2, 1998, a judgment was entered by the U.S. Court of Appeals for the Second Circuit. The U.S. Supreme Court granted certiorari on February 6, 1998. 400 U.S. 302.

Later in the brief, there is a statement of the case that often includes more detailed jurisdictional material.

(c) *Table of Contents:* The table of contents is an outline of the major components of the brief, including **point headings**, and the pages in the brief on which everything begins. (A point heading is the party's conclusion it wants the court to adopt for a particular issue.) The function of the table of contents is to provide the reader with quick and easy access to each portion of the brief. Because the page numbers will not be known until the brief is completed, the table of contents is the last section of the brief to be written. The following excerpt from the respondent's brief

---

**trial brief** An attorney's set of notes on the strategy he or she proposes to follow in conducting a trial.

**appellate brief** A document in which a party gives reasons why an appellate court should affirm (approve), modify, or reverse what a lower court has done.

**appellant** The party bringing an appeal.

**appellee** The party against whom an appeal is brought. Also called respondent.

**respondent** The party against whom an appeal is brought. Also called appellee.

**reply brief** An appellate brief of the appellant that replies to the appellate brief of the appellee.

**amicus curiae** Friend of the court; a nonparty in the litigation.

**point heading** A conclusion that a party wants a court to accept on one of the issues in the case.

illustrates the structure of a table of contents that includes the point headings as part of the "argument."

---

## TABLE OF CONTENTS

---

(d) *Table of Authorities:* The **table of authorities** lists all the cases, statutes, regulations, administrative decisions, constitutional provisions, charter provisions, ordinances, rules of court, and secondary authority (e.g., legal periodical articles and legal treatises) cited in the brief. All the cases are listed in alphabetical order, all the statutes are listed in alphabetical and numerical order, etc. The page numbers on which each of these authorities is discussed in the brief are presented so that the table acts as an index to these authorities, as shown in the following excerpt:

**table of authorities** A list of primary authority (e.g., cases and statutes) and secondary authority (e.g., legal periodical articles and legal treatises) that a writer has cited in an appellate brief or other document. The list includes page numbers where each authority is cited in the document.

---

## TABLE OF AUTHORITIES

CASES:                                                                 Page
*Smith v. Jones*, 24 F.2d 445 (5th Cir, 1974) . . . . . . . . . . . . . . . . . . . . . . . 2, 4, 12
*Thompson v. Richardson*, 34 Miss. 650, 65 So. 109 (1930) . . . . . . . . . . . . . 3, 9

Etc.

CONSTITUTIONAL PROVISIONS
Art. 5, Miss. Constitution . . . . . . . . . . . . . . . . . . . . . . . . . . . . . . . . . . . 12, 17
Art. 7, Miss. Constitution . . . . . . . . . . . . . . . . . . . . . . . . . . . . . . . . . . . . . . 20

Etc.

STATUTES
Miss. Code Ann. § 23(b) (1978) . . . . . . . . . . . . . . . . . . . . . . . . . . . . . 2, 8, 23
Miss. Code Ann. § 779 (1978)

LEGAL PERIODICAL ARTICLES
Samuel Warren & Louis Brandeis, *The Right to Privacy*, 4 Harvard
Law Review 193 (1890) . . . . . . . . . . . . . . . . . . . . . . . . . . . . . . . . . . . . 6, 18
Thomas Cramer, *Government Controls Run Amok*, 84 American
Bar Association Journal 449 (November 1990) . . . . . . . . . . . . . 7

Etc.

**questions presented**  A statement of the legal issues in an appellate brief that a party wants the appellate court to resolve.

**statement of the case**  That portion of an appellate brief that summarizes the dispute and lower court proceedings to date, presents the essential facts, and often includes jurisdictional data.

(e) *Questions Presented:* The label used for the **questions presented** section of the brief varies. Other names for it include "Points Relied on for Reversal," "Points in Error," "Assignments of Error," and "Issues Presented." Regardless of the label, its substance is essentially the same: it is a statement of the legal issues that the party wishes the appellate court to consider and decide.

(f) *Statement of the Case:* In the **statement of the case**, the dispute and lower court proceedings to date are summarized, the essential facts of the case are presented, and often jurisdictional data are included. Here is an example:

---

### Statement of The Case

These are actions based upon the Federal Tort Claims Act, 28 U.S.C. §1346 (b), initiated by the appellants, Garrett Freightlines, Inc., and Charles R. Thomas in the United States District Court for the District of Idaho. The appellant alleged that appellee's employee, Randall W. Reynolds, while acting within the scope of his employment, negligently caused injury to appellants. The United States denied that the employee was acting within the scope of his employment.

On March 27, 2001, appellant Garrett made a motion for limited summary judgment on whether Reynolds was acting within the scope of his employment when the collision occurred. The actions of Garrett and Thomas were consolidated by order of the court, and appellee later moved for summary judgment (see trial transcript, page 204).

The District Court held, under the authority of *Berrettoni v. United States*, 436 F. 2d 1372 (9th Cir. 1970), that Reynolds was not within the scope of his employment when the accident occurred and granted appellee's motion for summary judgment. It is from that order and judgment that the injured now appeals.

Staff Sergeant Reynolds was a career soldier in the United States Military and, until November 9, 1998, stationed at Fort Rucker, Alabama. On or about July 30, 1998, official orders directed that Reynolds be reassigned to Japan. . . .

---

(g) *Summary of Argument:* The major points to be made in the brief are summarized in this section.

(h) *Argument:* Here, the attorney explains the legal positions of the client presented in the order of the point headings listed in the table of contents. All the primary and secondary authority relied on is analyzed.

(i) *Conclusion:* The conclusion states what action the attorney is asking the appellate court to take.

(j) *Appendixes:* The appendixes contain excerpts from statutes or other primary authority, excerpts from the trial **transcript,** charts, descriptions of exhibits entered into evidence at the trial, etc.

**transcript**  A word-for-word account.

---

## Section F
# SOME WRITING GUIDELINES

I believe that [the legal profession does] not use plain language for two reasons: time and fear. Time is the enemy of brevity as evidenced by a quotation I am certain many of us remember: "Please excuse the length of this letter; I did not have time to be brief." Fear, however, is an unavoidable concern to lawyers—we tremble at the thought of saying it differently than it has been said for years. Thus, "in the event that" still prevails [over] "if." William Nussbaum, *Afraid to Change?*, 69 The Florida Bar Journal 6 (December 1995).

Lawyers like to throw around jargon and flowery language because it makes them feel self-important and prestigious. Debbie Laskey, *Legalese . . . Is It English?*, 20 At Issue 14 (San Francisco Ass'n of Legal Assistants, May 1993).

1. *Do not use circumlocutions.*

A **circumlocution** is the use of more words than are needed to express something. An example is the use of a pair of words that have the same effect. Here is a list of circumlocutions commonly found in the law. Avoid using them. Pick one of the words and discard the other.

| *Do not say:* | *Say:* | *Or say:* |
|---|---|---|
| alter and change | alter | change |
| any and all | any | all |
| by and with | by | with |
| each and every | each | every |
| final and conclusive | final | conclusive |
| full and complete | full | complete |
| made and entered into | made | entered |
| null and void | null | void |
| order and direct | order | direct |
| over and above | over | above |
| sole and exclusive | sole | exclusive |
| type and kind | type | kind |
| unless and until | unless | until |

If language adds nothing to the sentence, don't use it. There is an easy test to find out if your phrase, clause, or sentence uses language that adds nothing. Remove it and ask yourself whether you have altered the meaning or emphasis desired. If not, keep it out.

Compare the sentences in these two columns:

| | |
|---|---|
| Your maximum recovery is $100 under the provisions of the Warsaw Convention. | Your maximum recovery is $100 under the Warsaw Convention. |

When we remove "the provisions of" from the first sentence, we lose neither meaning nor emphasis. Hence we don't need it.

Use the language in the second column unless you have a valid reason to use the language in the first column:

| *Do not say:* | *Say:* |
|---|---|
| (1) all of the | (1) all the |
| (2) by means of | (2) by *or* with |
| (3) does not operate to | (3) does not |
| (4) during the course of | (4) during |
| (5) in the time of | (5) during |
| (6) in order to | (6) to |
| (7) or in the alternative | (7) or |
| (8) period of time | (8) period *or* time |
| (9) provision of law | (9) law |
| (10) State of New Jersey | (10) New Jersey |
| (11) until such time as | (11) until |

2. *Use shorter words when longer ways of expressing the same idea add nothing.*

Use the language in the second column unless you have a valid reason to use the language in the first column:

| *Do not say:* | *Say:* |
|---|---|
| (1) adequate number of | (1) enough |
| (2) prohibited from | (2) shall not |
| (3) at such time as | (3) when |
| (4) during such time as | (4) while |

**circumlocution** The use of more words than are needed to express something.

|     |                              |      |                    |
|-----|------------------------------|------|--------------------|
| (5) | enter into a contact         | (5)  | contract (verb)    |
| (6) | for the duration of          | (6)  | during             |
| (7) | for the purpose of           | (7)  | for                |
| (8) | for the purpose of entering  | (8)  | to enter           |
| (9) | for the reason that          | (9)  | because            |
| (10)| give consideration to        | (10) | consider           |
| (11)| give recognition to           | (11) | recognize          |
| (12)| have need of                  | (12) | need               |
| (13)| in case                       | (13) | if                 |
| (14)| in a number of                | (14) | in some            |
| (15)| in cases in which             | (15) | when               |
| (16)| in connection with            | (16) | in *or* on         |
| (17)| in regard to                  | (17) | about              |
| (18)| in relation to                | (18) | about *or* toward  |
| (19)| in the case of                | (19) | if *or* in         |
| (20)| in the event of               | (20) | if                 |
| (21)| in the matter of              | (21) | in *or* on         |
| (22)| in the majority of instances  | (22) | usually            |
| (23)| in view of                    | (23) | because *or* since |
| (24)| is able to                    | (24) | can                |
| (25)| is applicable                 | (25) | applies            |
| (26)| is binding on                 | (26) | binds              |
| (27)| is dependent on               | (27) | depends on         |
| (28)| is entitled to                | (28) | may                |
| (29)| is permitted to               | (29) | may                |
| (30)| is required to                | (30) | shall              |
| (31)| is unable to                  | (31) | cannot             |
| (32)| is directed to                | (32) | shall              |
| (33)| it is your duty to            | (33) | you shall          |
| (34)| make an appointment of        | (34) | appoint            |
| (35)| make a determination of       | (35) | determine          |
| (36)| make application              | (36) | apply              |
| (37)| make payment                  | (37) | pay                |
| (38)| make provision for            | (38) | provide for        |
| (39)| on a few occasions            | (39) | occasionally       |
| (40)| on behalf of                  | (40) | for                |
| (41)| on the part of                | (41) | by *or* among      |
| (42)| provided that                 | (42) | if                 |
| (43)| subsequent to                 | (43) | after              |
| (44)| with reference to             | (44) | on                 |

3. *Use a less complicated or less fancy way of expressing the same idea.*
   Use the language in the second column unless you have a valid reason to use the language in the first column:

|      | *Do not say:*        |      | *Say:*                   |
|------|----------------------|------|--------------------------|
| (1)  | accorded             | (1)  | given                    |
| (2)  | afforded             | (2)  | given                    |
| (3)  | cause it to be done  | (3)  | have it done *or* do it  |
| (4)  | contiguous to        | (4)  | touching                 |
| (5)  | deem                 | (5)  | consider                 |
| (6)  | endeavor (as a verb) | (6)  | try                      |
| (7)  | evince               | (7)  | show                     |
| (8)  | expiration           | (8)  | end                      |
| (9)  | expires              | (9)  | ends                     |
| (10) | have knowledge of    | (10) | know                     |
| (11) | forthwith            | (11) | immediately              |

| | |
|---|---|
| (12) in accordance with | (12) under |
| (13) in the event of | (13) if |
| (14) in the event that | (14) if |
| (15) in the interest of | (15) for |
| (16) is applicable | (16) applies |
| (17) is authorized to | (17) may |
| (18) is directed to | (18) shall |
| (19) is empowered to | (19) may |
| (20) is entitled (for a name) | (20) is called |
| (21) is hereby authorized | (21) may |
| (22) is not prohibited | (22) may |
| (23) per annum | (23) per year |
| (24) provided that | (24) if |
| (25) render service | (25) give service |

---

**Assignment 12.3**

Rewrite any of the following sentences that contain language that can be simplified without interfering with the effectiveness of the sentence.

**(a)** You are required to pay the fine.

**(b)** The period of time you have to render assistance is three months.

**(c)** For the duration of construction, it shall be unlawful for a person to enter or to attempt entry.

**(d)** If you are unable to enter into a contract with him for the materials, the oral commitment is still binding on you.

**(e)** She consulted with a lawyer with respect to possible litigation.

**(f)** She accepted the appointment due to the fact that she was qualified.

**(g)** It is green in color.

**(h)** Ask the witness questions about the bills.

**(i)** Judge Jones is currently on the bench.

---

4. *Use action verbs and adjectives.*

Avoid **nominalizations**, which are nouns formed from verbs or adjectives. Examples include the noun *consideration* from the verb *consider* and the noun *effectiveness* from the adjective *effective*. Nominalizations are not grammatically incorrect. In most cases, however, they weaken a sentence. Unfortunately, the legal profession is addicted to nominalizations. Avoid this addiction yourself.

Compare the sentences in these two columns:

| A | B |
|---|---|
| He realizes the effort is futile. | He came to the realization that the effort is futile. |
| She decided to retire. | She made the decision to retire. |
| The court determined who should pay. | A determination of who should pay was made by the court. |

The nominalizations in column B are *realization, decision,* and *determination.* The sentences in column A using verbs (*realizes, decided,* and *determined*) are more forceful and direct. The sentences in column B using the nominalizations are more stilted and verbose. Using nominalizations often leads to longer words and longer sentences. It also encourages the use of the passive voice (in the third example), which should be avoided, as we will see.

| *Do not say:* | *Say:* |
|---|---|
| (1) give consideration to | (1) consider |
| (2) give recognition to | (2) recognize |

**nominalization** A noun formed from a verb or adjective.

| | |
|---|---|
| (3) have knowledge of | (3) know |
| (4) have need of | (4) need |
| (5) in the determination of | (5) determine |
| (6) is applicable | (6) applies |
| (7) is dependent on | (7) depends on |
| (8) is in attendance at | (8) attends |
| (9) make an appointment of | (9) appoint |
| (10) make application | (10) apply |
| (11) make payment | (11) pay |
| (12) make provision for | (12) provide for |

5. *Use active voice.*

**active voice** The grammatical verb form in which the subject or thing performing or causing the action is the main focus.

**passive voice** The grammatical verb form in which the object of the action is the main focus. The emphasis is on what is being done rather than on who or what is performing or causing the action.

Use **active voice** rather than **passive voice** by making the doer of the action the subject and main focus of the sentence. Compare the sentences in the following two columns:

| A (passive voice) | B (active voice) |
|---|---|
| The decision was announced by the judge. | The judge announced the decision. |
| The report will be prepared. | I will prepare the report. |
| The court was cleared. | The clerk cleared the court. |
| By Friday, the bridge will have been blown up by the workers. | By Friday, the workers will have blown up the bridge. |
| The strike was ended by the injunction. | The injunction ended the strike. |

The verbs in the sentences in the "A" column are in the passive voice. The verbs in the sentences in the "B" column are in the active voice. What are the differences between these two kinds of sentences?

Sentences with verbs in the *passive voice* have the following characteristics:

- The doer of the action is either unknown or given less emphasis than what was done.
- The doer of the action, if referred to at all, is mentioned after the action itself.
- The subject of the sentence receives the action. The subject is acted upon.

**truncated passive** A form of passive voice in which the doer or subject of the action is not mentioned.

If you do not mention the doer of the action in the sentence, the verb form is a **truncated passive**. In the following sentence, for example, you don't know who fired Jim:

Jim was fired at noon.

Sentences with verbs in the *active voice* have the following characteristics:

- The doer of the action is the important focus.
- The doer of the action is mentioned before the action itself.
- The subject of the sentence performs the action. The subject is the doer of the action.

The passive voice is often less effective because it is less direct and often less clear. It can dilute the forcefulness of a statement.

**Weak**: It is no longer allowed to take law library books overnight.
**Better**: The law library no longer allows you to take books overnight.
**Or**: The law library no longer allows borrowers to take books overnight.

The action in these sentences is the prohibition on taking books overnight. In the rewrite, we know who has performed this action—the law library. In the first sentence, we are not sure. The subject (and center of attention) in the rewrite is the law library; the subject (and center of attention) in the first sentence is the prohibition—the action.

> **Assignment 12.4**
> Rewrite any of the following sentences that use the passive voice. If you need to add any facts to the sentences to identify the doer of the action, you may make them up.
>
> **(a)** As the semester came to a close, the students prepared for their exams.
> **(b)** Examinations are not enjoyed.
> **(c)** No drugs were prescribed after the operation.
> **(d)** It has been determined that your license should be revoked.
> **(e)** Consideration is being given this matter by the attorney.
> **(f)** It is believed by district officials that the expense is legal.
> **(g)** The fracture was discovered by the plaintiffs in 1998.

6. *Use positive statements.*

   Phrase something positively rather than negatively whenever possible.

   | *Do not say:* | *Say:* |
   |---|---|
   | It is not difficult to imagine. | It is easy to imagine. |
   | The paper is not without flaws. | The paper has flaws. |

   When asked about the fundraising activities of a supporter, President Bill Clinton said,

   I had no reason to believe that he didn't know what the law was and wouldn't follow it.[3]

   Unless the president wanted to give a convoluted answer, he could have simply said, "I expected him to follow the law."

7. *Avoid verbosity.*

   Avoid unnecessary words.[4] Compare the following versions of the same sentence:

   | | |
   |---|---|
   | He consulted *with* a doctor *in regard* to his injuries. | He consulted a doctor *about* his injuries. |
   | He drove to the left *due to the fact* that the lane was blocked. | He drove to the left *because* the lane was blocked. |
   | This product is used for *hair-dyeing purposes.* | This product is used to *dye hair.* |
   | The continuance was requested *in order to obtain the presence of a witness who was not then available.* | The continuance was requested *because a witness was unavailable.* |

   Read the following sentences, with and without the italicized words.

   > The court directed a verdict in favor of the defendant *and against the plaintiff.* (Verdicts for defendants usually are against the plaintiff.)
   > The car was green *in color.* (This distinguishes it from the car that was green in size!)
   > A delivery was made every Tuesday *on a regular weekly basis.* (What does *every Tuesday* mean if not weekly and regularly?)

8. *Use shorter sentences.*

   There is no rule on how long a sentence must be. Yet in general we can say that the longer a sentence is, the more difficult it is to follow. Too many long sentences ask too much of the reader. This is not to say that a reader cannot understand such sentences. It simply means that you are taxing the patience of readers when you subject them to long, involved sentences. As a general guideline, try to avoid sentences longer than 25 words.

   Unfortunately, sentences are almost always too long in legal writing. Here is an example from a legal memorandum. In the rewrite, we have broken a 57 word sentence into four smaller, more readable sentences.

**Weak:** Claims for child support were not fully and finally adjudicated pursuant to a North Carolina divorce judgment where the North Carolina court did not have personal jurisdiction over the husband and could not adjudicate any child support claims without this kind of jurisdiction and therefore Florida is not precluded from collecting monies from the husband toward arrearages.

**Better:** The North Carolina divorce judgment did not fully and finally adjudicate the claims for child support. The court in this state did not have personal jurisdiction over the husband. It could not adjudicate any child support claims without this kind of jurisdiction. Florida is therefore not precluded from collecting monies from the husband toward arrearages.

Other examples:

**Weak:** In May of 1999, a district personnel administrator informed Mary Miller that the district had decided to transfer her to a different school which was a decision that was based on information Miller provided, however the administrator had never talked to Miller in person prior to the decision.

**Better:** In May of 1999, a district personnel administrator informed Mary Miller that the district decided to transfer her to a different school. The district based its decision on information Miller provided. The administrator, however, never talked to Miller in person prior to the decision.

**Weak:** Her new job at the firm as the legal administrator in charge of personnel and finances was enjoyable, lucrative, educational, and challenging, but confusing and frightening at times.

**Better:** Her new job at the firm as legal administrator in charge of personnel and finances was enjoyable, lucrative, educational, and challenging. It was also confusing and frightening at times.

**Weak:** The final issue for discussion concerns the status of the national and international parties that has been the main stumbling block in the contract negotiations thus far.

**Better:** The final issue for discussion is the status of the national and international parties. This issue has been the main stumbling block in contract negotiations thus far.

**Weak:** There is no need for you to submit a revised report to the Board unless you wish to include new matter which should have been included in an earlier report provided that the new matter covers only procedural issues except for those procedural issues that have already been resolved by the commission.

**Better:** You do not have to submit a revised report to the Board. An exception is when you wish to include new matter on procedural issues that should have been included in an earlier report. These procedural issues must not be ones that the commission has already resolved.

---

### Assignment 12.5
Rewrite any of the following sentences that are too long.

**(a)** The board can, within 60 days of the receipt of a certification from the secretary, take action to return ownership to persons of corporations certified as owners from whom the property was acquired by expropriation or by purchase under threat of expropriation.

**(b)** A short time later, as George approached the intersection of Woodruff and Fuller, someone in the middle of the street started shooting, but George kept driving when he heard about 15 shots that sounded like different guns firing, one of which hit his Pontiac, damaging the front windshield and dashboard.

**(c)** By way of illustration, presidential candidate Ross Perot and basketball player Michael Jordan arguably may have achieved such pervasive fame as to have become public figures for all purposes, while Dr. Jack Kevorkian may have voluntarily placed himself into the public controversy over euthanasia and physician-assisted suicide so as to have become a public figure for a limited range of issues.

9. *Be careful with pronoun references.*

Use pronouns only where the nouns to which the pronouns refer are unmistakably clear. Using pronouns with ambiguous referents can confuse the meaning of a sentence. If the pronoun could refer to more than one person or object in a sentence, repeat the name of the person or object to avoid ambiguity.

**Do Not Say:** After the administrator appoints a deputy assistant, he shall supervise the team. [Who does the supervising? The administrator or the deputy? If the latter is intended, then:]

**Say:** After the administrator appoints a deputy assistant, the deputy assistant shall supervise the team.

10. *Avoid sexism in language.*

Avoid gender-specific language when the intent is to refer to both sexes. If neutral language is not available, rewrite the sentence to avoid the problem.

| *Gender-Specific Language* | *Gender-Neutral Alternatives* |
|---|---|
| (1) businessman | (1) executive, member of the business community |
| (2) chairman | (2) chairperson, chair, moderator, head, presiding officer |
| (3) draftsman | (3) drafter, writer |
| (4) man | (4) person, human, humankind |
| (5) man-hours | (5) worker hours |
| (6) mankind | (6) humanity, human race, people |
| (7) manpower | (7) work force, personnel |
| (8) fireman | (8) firefighter |
| (9) policeman | (9) officer, police officer |
| (10) mailman | (10) letter carrier, postal worker |
| (11) salesman | (11) seller, sales representative |
| (12) clergyman | (12) minister, priest, rabbi, member of the clergy |
| (13) actress | (13) actor |
| (14) foreman | (14) supervisor, manager |
| (15) reasonable man | (15) reasonable person |
| (16) waitress, waiter | (16) server |

11. *Use plain English (even if the law does not require it).*

In the 1970s, the plain English movement began. The federal government and more than half the states passed laws requiring certain documents (e.g., insurance contracts, securities disclosure statements) to be written in plain English. In general, the components of plain English are those that we have been discussing in this chapter:

- Avoid long sentences.
- Use the active voice rather than the passive voice.
- Use strong verbs rather than nominalizations.
- Avoid superfluous words.
- Phrase things positively; avoid multiple negatives.

Some of the laws impose readability levels based in part on the number of words used in sentences. The lower the number of words a document uses in its sentences, on average, the better the overall readability score the document will have. (Readability refers to the ease with which someone can read a passage.) One way to force writers to use shorter sentences is to mandate that the document have a specified readability score.

Plain English laws do not apply to the kind of writing prepared in a law office such as a memorandum of law or appellate brief. The laws are designed to help citizens understand written materials prepared by government and by businesses. Yet the writing principles proposed by the plain English movement can be applied to *any* writing. It would be a high compliment to say of any document prepared by an attorney or paralegal (particularly a document that covers complex legal material) that it was written in plain English.

# ■ Chapter Summary

Legal writing is critical in the practice of law. The phrase *legal writing* can refer to preparing documents that require legal analysis or legal research. It can also refer to special formats for legal documents and general communication techniques. When given a writing assignment, determine basics such as the audience, due date, models to use, and availability of feedback before the due date.

A law office prepares many different kinds of writing. Instruments such as deeds, contracts, and other agreements are formal written documents that give expression to a legal act or agreement. Pleadings such as complaints and answers state claims, defenses, and other positions of parties in litigation. Enclosure letters tell the recipient what is being sent in the letter or package. Demand letters are advocacy letters that ask the recipient to do or to refrain from doing something. Informational letters provide or seek information. A status letter is an informational letter that tells the client what has happened in the case thus far and what is expected next. Confirmatory letters seek verification that something important has been done or said. Opinion letters provide legal advice to a client. An interoffice memorandum of law analyzes the law for other members of the office. An external memorandum of law (for example, a "points and authorities" memorandum) analyzes the law for someone outside the office, such as a hearing officer. The major components of a memorandum of law are the heading, statement of the assignment, issues (based on the elements in contention), facts, discussion or analysis (including a counteranalysis), conclusion, recommendations, and appendix. A case brief is a summary of the major parts of a court opinion. A trial brief is an attorney's set of notes on how he or she intends to conduct a trial. An appellate brief is an argument submitted to an appellate court on why the decision of a lower court should be affirmed, modified, or reversed.

The major components of an appellate brief are the caption, the statement of jurisdiction, the table of contents, the table of authorities, the questions presented, the statement of the case, the summary of the argument, the argument, the conclusion, and the appendixes.

Following a number of important guidelines will increase the clarity and effectiveness of any kind of writing. Avoid circumlocutions, omit excess language, use action verbs and adjectives, use active voice, express something positively whenever possible, use shorter sentences, make pronoun referents clear, and avoid sexist language. Following guidelines such as these will help produce a more readable document that might be classified as one written in plain English.

## KEY TERMS

| | |
|---|---|
| instrument | caption of memorandum |
| pleadings | docket number |
| enclosure letter | RE |
| demand letter | element in contention |
| informational letter | STOP |
| status letter | trial brief |
| confirmatory letter | appellate brief |
| opinion letter | appellant |
| memorandum of law | appellee |
| interoffice memorandum of law | respondent |
| external memorandum of law | reply brief |
| points and authorities memorandum | amicus curiae |
| trial memorandum | point heading |
| hearing memorandum | table of authorities |

questions presented
statement of the case
transcript
circumlocution

nominalization
active voice
passive voice
truncated passive

## ON THE NET

**Legal Writing Resources**
www.ualr.edu/~cmbarger/otherpeople.html
www.law.cornell.edu/topics/legal_writing.html
www.alwd.org

**Practitioner's Handbook for Appeals**
www.ca7.uscourts.gov/rules/handbook.htm

**Letter Writing**
www.business-letters.com/business-letters.htm
www.writinghelp-central.com/letter-writing.html

**Sample Appellate Briefs**
supreme.lp.findlaw.com/supreme_court/briefs/index.html
www.shapirolaw.com/briefs/index.html
www.briefreporter.com

**Commercial Brief Writing Service**
www.briefhelp.com

**Online Writing Resources: Usage, Grammar, Style, and Composition**
webster.commnet.edu/grammar
www.bartleby.com/usage
www.k-state.edu/artsci/write.html
www.rpi.edu/web/writingcenter/online.html
www.ipl.org/teen/aplus/referenceweb.htm
www.efuse.com/Design/wa-more_better_writing.html

**Plain English**
www.sec.gov/news/extra/handbook.htm
www.plainlanguagenetwork.org
www.plainlanguagenetwork.org/Organizations/michigan.html
204.254.113.225/main.htm
www.web.net/~plain/PlainTrain
www.plainenglish.co.uk
www.adler.demon.co.uk/clarity.htm

## ENDNOTES

1. 15 U.S.C. § 1962e.
2. Sometimes the interoffice memorandum of law is referred to as an intraoffice memorandum of law because it stays within the office.
3. Mark Gladstone and Allan Miller, *Gore Called 38 Donors on White House Phone*, Los Angeles Times, August 8, 1997, at A.9.
4. L. Gray, *Writing a Good Appellate Brief*, 88 Case and Comment 44, 48–50 (No. 6, November/December 1983). Reprinted by special permission. Copyrighted © 1983 by the Lawyers Cooperative Publishing Co.

# Chapter 13

# AN INTRODUCTION TO THE USE OF COMPUTERS IN A LAW OFFICE

## Chapter Outline

A. Introduction

B. Terminology: A Review of Some of the Basics

C. Software in a Law Firm

D. Computer-Assisted Legal Research

E. Internet

F. Intranet and Extranet

## Section A
# Introduction

Computers dominate many aspects of the practice of law. Therefore, paralegals need to learn as much as they can about computers in general and how they are used in a law office. In your first job interview, don't be surprised if you are asked questions such as:

- What are your computer skills?
- What do you know about networks?
- What litigation support software have you studied or used?
- Are you familiar with Word or WordPerfect?[1]

In addition, prospective employers often pay special attention to the computer experience you list on your résumé.

You can learn a great deal about computers on your own. Don't wait for someone to explain it all to you. Take the initiative by pursuing an aggressive program of self-education. Exhibit 13.1 presents an overview of steps you can begin now and continue after you graduate. Indeed, you will probably need to be a student of computers for the remainder of your career.

We have already covered different aspects of computers elsewhere in this book. At the end of most chapters, for example, there is a section called "On the Net," which refers you to Internet sites that contain resources on topics covered in the chapter. In addition, a variety of computer-related materials can be found throughout the chapters. For example:

- Internet sites of the major national paralegal associations (chapter 1)
- Internet sites of major law firms in the country, of the state personnel office in every state, and of organizations relevant to finding paralegal employment (chapter 2)
- Internet sites of organizations relevant to the regulation of paralegals (chapter 4)
- Internet sites on ethics and software programs used to conduct conflicts-of-interest checks (chapter 5)
- Fact investigation resources on commercial databases and on the Internet (chapter 9)
- Internet sites relevant to litigation (chapter 10)
- Legal research resources on commercial databases and on the Internet (chapter 11)
- Software programs on timekeeping and filing systems (chapter 14)

In this chapter, our focus will be on some of the basics of computer use. This material will supplement what you will learn elsewhere. It will also serve as a review of the fundamentals.

## Section B
# Terminology: A Review of Some of the Basics

Before examining specific computer programs, we will briefly review of some of the essential terminology that will be helpful in understanding these programs.

**Hardware** is the physical equipment (i.e., devices) of a computer system that is used by programs to process data. Hardware is what you take out of the box and plug together when you buy a computer system. Examples include the keyboard, central processing unit (CPU), monitor, cables, mouse, and printer. **Software** is a computer program that tells the hardware what to do. There are two main categories of software: (a) operating or systems software and (b) applications software. The **operating system** software tells the computer how to operate. It acts as the central control over the computer's hardware and software. The major operating system in use today is Windows, developed by Microsoft. (Others include UNIX, Macintosh, and OS/2.) **Applications software** consists of programs that perform specific tasks that consumers (i.e., end users) ask computers to

---

**hardware** The physical equipment of a computer system that is used by programs to process data.

**software** A computer program that tells the hardware what to do.

**operating system** The software that tells the computer how to operate.

**applications software** A computer program that performs specific tasks directly for the consumer or end user.

| EXHIBIT 13.1 | Developing Your Computer Skills: Things to Do On Your Own |
|---|---|

**Courses, Meetings, Groups**

- *Courses*. Take computer courses. Find out what is available at your school. Also check if free or low-cost computer courses exist in your community, e.g., adult education courses. Some may last no more than an afternoon. Call your local public library for leads. Once you know what is available, ask your instructor what courses would be most relevant to someone working in a law office. Anything on the basics of operating systems (e.g., Windows), word processing (e.g., Word), and the Internet will probably be valuable.
- *Computer events at paralegal associations*. Contact your local paralegal association to find out what upcoming events will cover computer use. There may, for example, be a continuing legal education (CLE) session on the Internet. (For a list of paralegal associations in your state, see appendix B.) Ask if you can attend as a paralegal student. If there is a fee, ask if a reduced rate is available for students. Some of the meetings and sessions may be geared to experienced paralegals. Nevertheless, you should consider attending because the more exposure you have to computer topics, the more you will eventually absorb. It is worthwhile to take detailed notes, even if you will not fully understand all of them until later. Furthermore, any contact you have with a paralegal association can be an excellent networking opportunity. (See the end of chapter 3 for networking techniques.)
- *Computer events at bar associations*. Your state and local bar association may also have CLE sessions that cover computer basics for attorneys. Find out if you can attend at a reduced rate. Go to the Internet sites of these associations to find out what programs are scheduled. (For the Internet addresses of the bar associations in your state, see appendix C).

**Internet**

- *Law firm of the day*. Spend five minutes a day surfing Internet sites of law firms. (See appendix 2.A at the end of chapter 2 for a list of sites.) Conduct your own informal survey of the variety of features contained on the sites of different law firms.
- *Search engine of the week*. Every week, pick one search engine to study. It can be a general search engine or a legal search engine. (See exhibit 13.10 later in the chapter for a list of search engines.) During the week, spend ten minutes a day (a) reading the online tips often provided by the search engine on how to use it effectively and (b) trying out specific searches. For topics to search, open any of your paralegal textbooks at random and select topics. As you study different search engines, enter the same search terms in each search engine. Conduct your own informal survey on the effectiveness of each engine. (Do the same for the directories listed in exhibit 13.10.)
- *Online tutorial of the week*. Every week, work on a tutorial. The Internet has many tutorials available. They cover topics such as understanding the Internet, using search engines, and learning word processors such as Word. To find these tutorials, type "computer tutorial" in the search box of any general search engine (e.g., www.google.com or www.altavista.com). See also the sites of tutorials listed at the end of this chapter in the section called On The Net.

**Miscellaneous**

- *Exchanging tutorials*. Most people know how to do something on a computer, e.g., insert footnotes in Word or WordPerfect, copy a file to a disk, create a macro, edit a macro, find recent supreme court opinions on the Internet. As you meet your fellow students, find out what they know how to do on a computer. When they list a task that is new to you, ask them to teach it to you in exchange for your teaching them something you know that they do not. Once every two weeks, try to arrange a half-hour of mutual hands-on teaching of this kind. Use your own computers or those available in public places such as neighborhood libraries.
- *Read, read, read*. Every week, pick a major computer topic such as word processing, spreadsheets, databases, presentation graphics, litigation support, case management, Westlaw, LEXIS, and any aspect of the Internet. During that week, devote some time reading about that topic. Don't wait to be assigned the topic for class. Begin reading on your own. To find the readings, start with your paralegal textbooks. Go to the index in all of them and check entries such as *computer* and *Internet*. In addition, ask your instructor and a librarian where you can find additional readings on the topic. Most public libraries have a large section of computer books. They will be very helpful for general computer topics. Find your topic in the index of books published within the last two years.
- *Typing Skills*. Brush up on your typing skills. In many law offices, there is a keyboard at every desk. At one time, legal professionals considered typing to be beneath their dignity. This is no longer true. Although you will not need the typing skill of a secretary, you should be able to type with moderate speed. There are online typing courses available (e.g., www.easytype.com and www.typing-tutorial.com). To find such courses, enter "typing tutorial" in the search box of any general search engine.

perform. Some of the major kinds of applications software are word processing, database, and spreadsheet programs.

To place information into a computer, you need an input device. The most commonly used input device is the keyboard. When you type something on the keyboard, text is entered at the **cursor** on the screen of the monitor. (The cursor is the marker or pointer that indicates where the next letter or other character will be displayed on the screen.) Other input devices include the mouse, speech recognition programs, and scanners, all of which can be used along with the keyboard. A **mouse** is a hand-held pointing device used to move the cursor by rolling, clicking, and dragging motions. For example, you can glide the mouse over a small picture (i.e., icon) of a printer, click on the mouse, and activate the printer connected to the computer. **Speech recognition** programs allow you to enter information by speaking rather than by typing on the keyboard. As you speak words and commands into a small microphone, the computer enters the words on the screen or executes the commands. A **scanner** is an input device that converts text and images into an electronic or digital format that a computer can recognize. In a process called **imaging** (or document imaging), the scanner captures an image of the text, photograph, graph, or whatever you are scanning and inserts it into the computer.

The **central processing unit (CPU)** is the "brain" of the computer that controls all of its parts. It performs operations and carries out software commands. In most computer systems, the CPU is the unit that contains the on/off switch and the slots for inserting and taking out floppy disks.

Computers can hold a great deal of data. The internal storage capacity of a computer is called its **memory**. There are two main kinds of memory: read-only and random access. **Read-only memory (ROM)** is memory that stores data that cannot be altered, removed, or added to; the data can only be read. When you shut the computer off, the data in ROM are not erased. ROM contains critical data such as the program needed to boot the computer. **Random access memory (RAM)** is memory that stores temporary data in an arbitrary or random manner. When you shut the computer off, these data vanish—unless you have properly saved the data. Data in RAM include applications software (e.g., your word processor) and whatever you have typed on the screen using this software (e.g., a letter or your résumé). Newer applications require increasing amounts of RAM. At times, you may be running more than one application at the same time, e.g., a word processor, a spreadsheet, your Internet connection, and the game of solitaire. As more applications are created by manufacturers, the temptation is to run them simultaneously. This may create problems if you do not have enough RAM. (Inadequate RAM is such a common problem that RAM is humorously referred to as Rarely Adequate Memory.)

The amount or quantity of memory is measured by units called **bytes**. A byte is the storage equivalent of one space or character of the alphabet typed into a computer. Bytes are expressed in the following quantities:

|  | Abbreviation | Approximate Number of Bytes |
|---|---|---|
| Kilobyte | K | one thousand |
| Megabyte | Mb | one million |
| Gigabyte | Gb | one billion |
| Terabyte | Tb | one trillion |

One megabyte (1 Mb) can hold the equivalent of a 600-page novel. One gigabyte (1 Gb) can hold approximately 300,000 single-sided pages of text.

A number of different devices exist to store bytes of data. Most of these storage devices have read/write capability, while others are read-only. **Read/write** means that the computer can read the data on the device *and* you can write (i.e., insert) additional data onto the device. If a device is writable, you can save and store data on it. As we saw earlier, **read-only** means that the computer can read the data on the device but not alter, remove, or add to the data.

If a storage device is read-only, it usually contains systems or applications software that the manufacturer does not want the user to be able to add to or otherwise modify.

**cursor** The marker or pointer on the screen that indicates where the next letter or other character will be displayed on the screen.

**mouse** A hand-held input device that moves the cursor by rolling, clicking, and dragging motions.

**speech recognition** An input program that enables one to enter information into a computer by talking into a microphone.

**scanner** An input device that converts text and images into an electronic or digital format that a computer can recognize.

**imaging** Converting text or an image into a format that a computer can read and display.

**central processing unit (CPU)** The part of the computer that controls all of its parts.

**memory** The internal storage capacity of a computer.

**read-only memory (ROM)** Memory that stores data that cannot be altered, removed, or added to. The data can be read only.

**random access memory (RAM)** Memory that stores temporary data in an arbitrary or random manner.

**byte** The storage equivalent of one space or character of the alphabet typed into a computer.

**read/write** Able to read data on a device *and* write or insert additional data into it.

**read-only** Able to read data on a device but not to alter, remove, or add to the data.

When you create your own document (e.g., a letter, a memorandum of law), it first goes into RAM. If you shut the computer off without saving and storing the document, it is lost. To prevent the loss of documents that you create, you must send them to a storage device that has read/write capability.

Here is a brief overview of some of the major storage devices that exist:

- *Hard disk*: A rigid magnetic disk that stores data. The **hard disk** is located within a disk drive called a hard drive. (In many computer systems, the hard drive is the C drive.) Hard disks have read/write capability.
- *Floppy disk*: A floppy magnetic disk that stores data. It is inserted into and taken out of its own disk drive, called a floppy drive. (In many computer systems, the floppy drive is the A drive.) Floppy disks have a much smaller storage capacity than hard disks. Floppy disks have read/write capability.
- *Magnetic tape system*: A device that stores data on tape reels or tape cartridges. Although tape systems can store a great deal of data, they are often slower than disk systems. Magnetic tape systems have read/write capability.
- *CD–ROM drive*: A device that can read data on a **CD–ROM**, which means compact disk read-only memory. A CD–ROM is a compact disk that uses optical technology or laser beams to store data. The disk looks similar to the disks that contain most popular music purchased today. Because of their large storage capacity, CD–ROMs are widely used. (One CD–ROM can store up to 650 Mb of data.) When you purchase software, it is usually contained on a CD–ROM. Most primary authority (e.g., court opinions, statutes, and administrative regulations) can also be purchased on CD–ROM. CD–ROM drives have read-only capability.
- *DVD–ROM drive*: A device that can read data on a DVD–ROM and on a CD–ROM. DVD means digital versatile disk. A DVD holds considerably more data than a CD–ROM. DVD–ROM drives (often used to play DVD video disks) have read-only capability.
- *CD–RW drive*: A device that can read and store data on compact disks. CD–RW means compact disk ReWritable. CD–RW drives have read/write capability.

If you want a **hard copy** of a document prepared on a computer, you need a printer to print that document. Printers use different technologies to produce characters and other images on a sheet of paper. Among the most popular are *ink-jet* printers, which use a spray of ionized ink, and *laser* printers, which use a laser beam.

Most printers allow you to print letters of the alphabet, punctuation marks, or other characters in different sizes (measured in **points**) and in different designs or styles (called **fonts**). Here are some examples:

This sentence is printed in a 10 point Arial font (regular).

## This sentence is in a 15 point Arial font (bold).

*This sentence is printed in a 10 point Serifa BT font (italics).*

This sentence is printed in a 12 point Times New Roman font (regular).

Drafters of documents may occasionally want to print tables, headings, or titles in a point size or font that is different from what they use in the body of the document. Exhibit 13.2 contains an example of a document that prints the title (motion for summary judgment) in a point size that is larger than the rest of the page.

Computers at different locations can exchange data by using communications devices. A **modem** is a communications device that allows computers to use telephone lines to send and receive data to and from each other. Other communication devices include cable modems (that connect computers by coaxial cable) and digital phone lines such as ISDN (integrated services digital network) and ADSL (asymmetric digital subscriber line). These other communication devices can transmit text, voice, and video (e.g., for real-time video-conferencing) at high speeds.[2]

**Real time** means occurring now, as you are watching. Suppose, for example, you are on the Internet watching a witness answer questions in a deposition in another city. You would be watching in real time if the witness is talking at the same time you are watching this witness on your computer screen. If, however, you are watching a deposition that

---

**hard disk** A rigid magnetic disk that stores data.

**CD–ROM** (compact disk read-only memory). A compact disk that uses optical technology or laser beams to store data.

**hard copy** A printed copy (usually on paper) of what has been prepared on a computer. Also called a printout.

**points** A measure of the size of printed letters of the alphabet, punctuation marks, or other characters.

**fonts** The design or style of printed letters of the alphabet, punctuation marks, or other characters.

**modem** A communications device that allows computers at different locations to use telephone lines to exchange data.

**real-time** Occurring now; happening as you are watching; able to respond immediately.

| EXHIBIT 13.2 | Computer Screen Showing Text with a Font in Different Point Sizes |
| --- | --- |

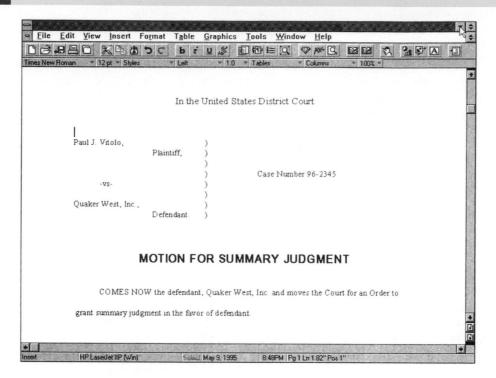

**videoconferencing** A meeting that occurs in more than one location between individuals who can hear and see each other on a computer screen.

**local area network (LAN)** A multiuser system linking computers that are in close proximity to each other so that they can share data and resources.

**groupware** A program that allows computers on a network to work together.

**shareware** Software that users receive without cost and are expected to purchase if they want to keep it after trying it out.

**wide area network (WAN)** A multiuser system linking computers over a large geographical area so that they can share data and resources.

**stand-alone computer** A computer that is not connected to a network.

was recorded earlier, you would not be experiencing the deposition in real time. Similarly, you are communicating in real time if what you type on your screen appears on the screen of others *as you type*. **Videoconferencing** is a meeting that occurs in more than one location between individuals who can hear and see each other on a computer screen.

Computers in a busy law office need to be connected with each other for a variety of reasons. They may need to share the same data (e.g., a client file) or the same equipment (e.g., a laser printer). If the computers are relatively close to each other, such as within the same building, they can be connected by a **local area network (LAN)**. Once connected (i.e., networked), **groupware** allows the computer users to share calendars, have meetings, exchange e-mail, and work on files together. (Groupware is not the same as **shareware**; the latter is software that users pay for only after deciding to keep it after trying it out.) Examples of groupware include Lotus Notes and Microsoft Exchange. If the computers are not geographically close, they can still be networked on what is called a **wide area network (WAN)**. Large law firms with branches in different cities, for example, can be linked on a WAN. (Computers that are not connected to a network are called **stand-alone computers**.)

## Section C
## SOFTWARE IN A LAW FIRM

We turn now to an overview of some of the major software programs used in many law firms, particularly applications software. Later in the chapter, we cover software for legal research and the Internet. Here, we will examine programs that perform the following tasks:

Word processing
Spreadsheet calculation
Database management
Presentation graphics
Litigation support
Case management

(Exhibit 13.3 presents an overview of these and other software programs used in a law office.) Some programs are suites or integrated packages that allow the user to perform multiple tasks such as word processing, spreadsheet calculations, and database management.

| EXHIBIT 13.3 | Software Used in Law Firms |
|---|---|
| **Software** | **Function** |
| Word processing | Enter and edit data in documents, e.g., letters, briefs, and memos. |
| Spreadsheet | Performs calculations on numbers and values entered by the user. Organizes, compiles, tracks, and calculates numerical data. |
| Database management | Organizes, searches, retrieves, and sorts information or data, e.g., conflict of interest records, client lists, and index to legal research performed to date. |
| Presentation graphics | Enhances the communication of data through the use of charts, graphs, video, and sound. |
| Litigation support | Stores, retrieves, and tracks documents, testimony, and other case-related information. |
| Case management | Helps maintain control over schedules, e.g., appointments and case deadlines. |
| CALR (computer-assisted legal research) | Performs legal research in computer databases, e.g., Westlaw, LEXIS, Loislaw, CD-ROM libraries, and Internet sites. |
| Web browser | Allows users to read pages on the World Wide Web. |
| Electronic mail (e-mail) | Sends and receives mail electronically. |
| Timekeeping and billing | Tracks time and expenses; prepares client invoices. |
| Accounting | Tracks financial information needed for the operation of a law firm. |
| Project management | Helps manage large projects. |
| Groupware | Allows computer users on a network to work together, e.g., to share documents and work on the same information at the same time. |
| Specialized legal software | Meets particular needs of a specialized practice. |
| Operating system | Tells the computer how to operate. Manages the hardware and other software of the computer. |

Source: Adapted from Brent Roper, *Computers in the Law*, 60 (3d ed. 2000).

## WORD PROCESSING

A **word processor** is a software program that allows you to enter and edit data in documents. Word processors are enormous improvements over standard typewriters. When you make an error on a word processor, for example, you do not reach for a bottle of "white out" to take out the error. Instead, you simply press the backspace or delete key

**word processor** Application software that allows you to enter and edit data in documents.

over the error and type your new text. If you left something out of a paragraph, you point the cursor to where the additional text should go and insert what you want to add. When you are in insert mode, the line opens up to make room for the new text. (See exhibit 13.4 for the definition of insert mode and other features of word processors.) With relative ease,

| EXHIBIT 13.4 | Word Processing Terms and Functions |
| --- | --- |

| TERM | Function |
| --- | --- |
| Backspace | The key that allows you to delete the character to the left of the cursor. |
| Block move | To copy, delete, or change the position of text you identify. |
| Bold | Heavy or dark type. **This sentence is printed in bold**. |
| Character | A letter, number, or symbol. |
| Character enhancement | Altering the appearance of characters such as by underlining, bolding, or italicizing them. |
| Default setting | The value used by the word processor when it is not instructed to use any other value. |
| Editing | Adding to, subtracting from, or otherwise changing text. |
| Endnote | A numbered citation or explanatory text printed at the end of a document or chapter. If printed at the bottom of the page, the citation or text is called a footnote. |
| Footer | The same text that is printed at the bottom of each page. |
| Format | The layout of a page, e.g., the margin settings. |
| Global | Pertaining to the entire document. |
| Grammar checker | The identification of possible grammatical errors in a document with suggested corrections. |
| Header | The same text that is printed at the top of each page. |
| Insert mode | When new text is typed in a line that already has text, the line opens to receive the new text. Nothing is erased or overtyped. |
| Justification | Every line is even (i.e., is aligned) at the left margin, at the right margin, or at both margins. |
| Macro | An automated way to insert frequently used text or to perform other repetitive tasks. |
| Paginate | To insert consecutive page numbers on text. |
| Print preview | A screen presentation of what the text will look like once it is printed. |
| Scroll | To move a line of text onto or off the screen. |
| Spell checker | The identification of possible spelling errors in a document with suggested corrections. |
| Status line | A message line that can state the current position of the cursor and provide other formatting information. |
| Subscript | A character that prints below the usual text baseline. For example, the number 7 in the following text is in subscript: Court$_7$. |
| Superscript | A character that prints above the usual text baseline. For example, the number 7 in the following text is in superscript: Court$^7$. |

| EXHIBIT 13.4 | Word Processing Terms and Functions—*continued* |
|---|---|

| TERM | Function |
|---|---|
| Table | A feature that allows the creation of a table of information using rows and columns. |
| Text file | A file containing text that you you create. A file containing a program is called a systems file. |
| Thesaurus | The identification of word alternatives that a user can substitute for words initially used or considered. |
| Tool bar | A list of shortcuts (often represented by icons) that can quickly execute commonly used functions. |
| Typeover mode | When new text is typed in a line that already has text, the old text is erased or overtyped with each keystroke. |
| Word wrap | When a word would extend beyond the right margin, the word is automatically sent to the beginning of the next line. |
| WYSIWYG | What You See (on the screen) is What You will Get (when the screen is printed). |

Source: Adapted from S. Mandell, *Introduction to Computers . . .*, 216 (3d ed. 1991).

you can copy, save, and paginate your text; insert footnotes or endnotes; underline or italicize text; and create tables or charts. Sophisticated word processors also allow you to spell check and grammar check your writing. (See the beginning of chapter 12, however, on the danger of overreliance on computer spell checkers.)

If you want to justify your margins, the word processor will allow you to do so quickly. In the language of printers and typesetting, justification means alignment of each line of text along a margin. Lines are aligned if they come out even—as opposed to being ragged—at the margin. Left justified means that every line on the left margin is aligned (except for the first line of a paragraph if the first line is indented). **Right justified** means that every line on the right margin is aligned except for the last line if it ends before the margin. Full justification means that every line of the paragraph is aligned on both margins—with the possible exception of the first and last lines. (See exhibit 13.5 for examples of justification and various indentation formats.)

One of the special features of word processors (and of other programs) is the ability to create **macros** that allow you to perform repetitive tasks without extensive retyping. Suppose, for example, that when you prepare a letter, you always type a heading at the top of the sheet containing your name, street address, city, state, zip code, phone number, and e-mail address. As you type the heading, you carefully center each line. Assume that this task consists of 100 keystrokes and takes about a minute to complete. An alternative is to create a macro to perform the task. Within the word processor's macro feature, you go through the steps of creating a macro. First, you name the macro—let's call our example *head*. Next, you type the repetitive text (all 100 strokes). You have now created a macro called *head*. From now on, every time you are preparing a new letter, you simply tell the word processor that you want to run the head macro. This is done by typing (or clicking) the word *head* within the macro feature of the word processor. In less than a second, all 100 keystrokes appear on the screen. If you type many letters, you can save a lot of time by using this macro.

Let's look at another example. Suppose you are typing a memorandum of law that frequently uses the phrase *federal subject-matter jurisdiction*. To avoid constantly retyping this phrase, you could create a macro called *fsmj* (or you could call it *f*). Now every time you run the *fsmj* macro (or the *f* macro if you used the shorter name), the full phrase automatically goes into your memorandum wherever you want it to appear.[3]

**right justified** Every line of a paragraph on the right margin is aligned (except for the last line if it ends before the margin).

**macro** An automated way to insert frequently used text or to perform other repetitive functions.

| EXHIBIT 13.5 | Arranging Text with a Word Processor |
| --- | --- |

| | |
| --- | --- |
| Here is an example of text created on a word processor that is *left justified* only. Note that the text is straight along the left margin but ragged along the right margin. | Left justification |
| Here is an example of text created on a word processor that is *right justified* only. Note that the text is ragged along the left margin, but straight along the right margin. | Right justification |
| Here is an example of text created on a word processor that has *full justification*. Note that the text is straight along both the left margin and the right (except for the last line). | Full justification |
| Here is an example of text created on a word processor that uses the *left indent* feature. Note that the entire text is indented from the left margin. (The text is also left justified only.) | Left indent |
| Here is an example of text created on a word processor that uses the *double indent* feature. Note that the entire text is indented the same amount from both the left margin and the right margin. (The text is also left justified only.) | Double indent |
| Here is an example of text created on a word processor that uses the *hanging indent* feature. Note that the first line hangs or "sticks out" to the left. (The text is also left justified only.) | Hanging indent |
| Here is an example of text created on a word processor that uses *first line indent*. Note that only the first line is indented in traditional paragraph format. (The text is also left justified only.) | First line indent |

**table of authorities** A list of primary authority (e.g., cases and statutes) and secondary authority (e.g., legal periodical articles and legal treatises) that a writer has cited in an appellate brief or other document. The list includes page numbers where each authority is cited in the document.

The two main word processors on the market are Word by Microsoft and WordPerfect by Corel. Both have features or editions that are geared to specific needs of attorneys in the practice of law. For example, they allow you to create a **table of authorities.** (This is a list of primary and secondary authority referred to in a document with the page number of each reference.) As an extra service to attorneys, Microsoft has written a *Legal User's Guide* on one of its Internet sites: *www.officeupdate.microsoft.com/legal.*

At one time, the most popular word processor in law firms was WordPerfect. Attorneys began to shift to Word, however, when many of their clients adopted Word. This made it easier to exchange electronic files between law firms and their clients. It is easier to read a document sent to you on a disk when your word processor is the same as the word processor on which the document was created. If you are using WordPerfect, it is not impossible for you to read a Word document, or vice versa, but communication is much simpler if sender and recipient are using the same word processor.

### SPREADSHEETS

**spreadsheet** Application software that automatically performs calculations on numbers and values that you enter.

**Spreadsheets** are programs that automatically perform calculations on numbers and values that you insert. A spreadsheet can perform many kinds of number-crunching tasks such as calculating future damages, tax liability, and mortgage payments. The spreadsheet lets you create many groups of interrelated numbers within a series of rows and columns. Once this is done, you can play "what if" by changing one of the numbers to see what happens to the other numbers. The spreadsheet will quickly recalculate all numbers that are dependent on the one that was changed. Suppose, for example, you are considering a loan to purchase a building and want to know what the monthly payments will be. Among the factors that will determine the amount of these payments are the interest rate, length of the mortgage, and amount of the loan. Entering these three numbers into a spreadsheet will give you the amount of the monthly payments. You can then change one or more of the numbers (e.g., enter a lower interest rate) to see what happens to the monthly payments.

What-if calculations can also be used in settlement negotiations. In a structured settlement, for example, the payment of damages will be spread over a period of time rather than paid in a lump sum. To calculate what these payments will be, the attorneys must make certain assumptions about the rate of inflation over this period. A spreadsheet will allow the attorneys to try different assumptions in order to see what impact they would have on the amounts to be paid over the period.

Commonly used spreadsheet programs such as Lotus 1–2–3 and Microsoft Excel can create charts that graphically illustrate the results of these calculations.

### DATABASE MANAGEMENT

A **database program** allows you to organize, search, retrieve, and sort information or data. Such programs are sometimes called database management systems (DBMSs). For example, a law firm can create a database containing a list of all of its past and present clients. Within this database, the categories of data could include:

| | |
|---|---|
| ■ Client's name | ■ Name of opponent |
| ■ Street address | ■ Names of other parties |
| ■ Phone | ■ Dates provided representation |
| ■ E-mail address | ■ Attorney who brought the case to firm |
| ■ Internet site | ■ Fees billed |
| ■ Type of case | ■ Fees collected |
| ■ Case number | |

**database program**
Application software that allows you to organize, search, retrieve, and sort information or data.

This database will allow the firm to accomplish a number of useful tasks. For example, it can be used to check for possible conflicts of interest. When the firm is considering a new client, it needs to find out if the firm has ever represented the opponent of the prospective client. One way to find out is to search that opponent's name in the firm's client database. (For a database used for conflicts checking, see exhibit 5.7 in chapter 5.) In addition, the database in our example can:

- Generate a list of every probate and estate client in order to send them a mailing on a new tax law
- Generate a list of every case that the firm closed in 2001
- Generate a list of every client who has bills that have not been paid for more than 60 days since they were sent
- Name the attorney who brought in clients with the largest billing totals in 2002.

Major database software used by law firms includes Microsoft's Access, Lotus's Approach, and Corel's Paradox.

### PRESENTATION GRAPHICS

In many settings, a law firm communicates a client's version of the facts. For example, during negotiations with opposing counsel or in a closing argument before a jury, an attorney may want to demonstrate:

- An injured plaintiff's loss of income for the months immediately after the accident
- The expenses of a parent who is seeking sole custody of a child in a divorce case
- The share of the market controlled by a company accused of antitrust violations
- The chemical components of a lake into which a manufacturing plant allegedly dumped pollutants over a 10-year period

The attorney can use **presentation graphics** (also called business graphics) to help communicate such facts forcefully by combining text with charts, graphs, video, and sound. In a courtroom, a trial judge might allow an attorney to use a laptop computer to project charts or graphs as a slide show on a large screen in front of the jury. To demonstrate the costs of caring for a particular child, for example, the attorney could prepare a pie chart that uses different colors and fonts to illustrate the percentage of the budget that each expense consumes. Visually appealing graphics of this kind can be very effective, particularly in cases where the facts are numerous and relatively complicated.

**presentation graphics**
Application software used to present text data with charts, graphs, video, and sound in order to communicate the data more effectively.

Presentation graphics programs are not limited to use in litigation. A law firm manager might use the software to report on expenses, billable hours, fee collection, cash flow, and other budget matters before a committee of senior partners. The software can also be effectively used by speakers at seminars or by instructors in office training programs. Examples of presentation graphics software used in law firms include Microsoft's PowerPoint, Corel's Presentations, and Lotus's Freelance Graphics. (For examples of computer-generated charts and graphs, see exhibits 14.4, 14.8, and 14.9 in chapter 14.)

## LITIGATION SUPPORT

Lawsuits often involve numerous documents, e.g., correspondence, memoranda, transcripts of depositions, interrogatories, requests for admissions, medical reports, investigation reports, complaints, answers, motions, briefs, and business records. In complex litigation such as product liability, consumer fraud, and environmental law, the quantity of documents can be enormous. In a recent tobacco case, the attorney representing Lorillard Tobacco Company told the court:

> Lorillard has produced approximately 1.8 million pages of documents in this lawsuit. If you were to take those documents and stack them . . . one on top of the other, they would be 666 feet high. That's the equivalent of a 66-story office building.[4]

**litigation support**
Application software used to help a law office store, retrieve, and track facts and documents that pertain to a lawsuit.

**Litigation support** software is designed to help a law firm manage the large number of facts and documents that can be involved in representing clients in litigation. The software can be used in large cases such as this tobacco case and in cases that are considerably less complex.

A major advantage of litigation support software is the time it can save when searching for information in documents, particularly when you need to search the full text (i.e., every word) of those documents. In a medical malpractice case, for example, suppose you wanted to locate every document in the litigation that mentions Dr. Daniel Summers, one of the primary witnesses in the case. If the full text of every document was in the computer database, you would conduct a **full-text search** of these documents. The software would search every word in every document to find those that mention Dr. Daniel Summers. Of course, to be able to conduct such searches, the complete text of every document must be in the database. (The primary method of entering complete documents is scanning.) If entering the full text of every document is not practical, the office may be able to create summaries or abstracts of every document and then conduct a search of these abstracts. The search would find every document whose abstract mentioned Dr. Daniel Summers.

**full-text search** A search of every word in every document in a database.

If computers were not available, the searches would have to be done manually. A recent study by a bar association found that a manual search of 10,000 documents took 67 paralegal hours and produced 15 relevant documents, while the same search conducted with litigation support software took a few seconds and produced 20 relevant documents.[5]

Numerous litigation support programs exist. Examples include Summation, CaseSoft, Lawpro, and Zylab.

## CASE MANAGEMENT

A law office cannot practice law without managing the clock. Representing clients often involves numerous appointments and deadlines. The calendar is filled with scheduled interviews, strategy meetings, negotiating sessions, hearing dates, and filing deadlines. For example:

- The date of a client meeting
- The date of a meeting with opposing counsel to discuss settlement options
- The date a lease must be renewed
- The date a stock option must be exercised
- The date a complaint must be filed
- The number of days within which the answer to the complaint must be filed
- The number of days within which answers to interrogatories must be served
- The date of a deposition
- The date of the trial

- The number of days within which an appeal of a judgment must be filed
- The date client bills are due

**Case management** software (also called docket control software) is designed to help a law office meet these time commitments. Any system that reminds the office of important dates is called a **tickler**—it prods or tickles the memory about what must be done by certain dates. The consequences of missed deadlines can be devastating. A nightmare of every plaintiff's attorney, for example, is the dismissal of an action because of the failure to file a complaint before the **statute of limitations** barred the action; a nightmare of every defendant's attorney is the entry of a **default judgment** because of a failure to file an answer to the complaint within the time allotted by law. Surprisingly, such devastating lapses are not uncommon. When an insurance company is considering an application for malpractice insurance by a law firm, one of the primary concerns of the company is whether the firm has effective case management systems in place for calendar control.

Commonly used case management software includes Abacus by Abacus Data Systems and Outlook by Microsoft.

## Section D
# Computer-Assisted Legal Research

### INTRODUCTION
**Computer-assisted legal research (CALR)** is one of the great inventions in the practice of law. What once took hours poring through library volumes can now be accomplished in seconds by CALR. A vast amount of legal material is available **online** 24 hours a day. (By online, we mean connected to a host computer system or information service—usually through telephone lines.) The major commercial online databases, for which users pay a fee, are Westlaw and LEXIS. Both are available through special software and on the Internet. In addition, there are numerous free resources on the Internet.

We begin our study of CALR with the commercial or fee-based online databases.

**Westlaw** is a product of West Group. **LEXIS**, the legal unit of the LEXIS–NEXIS service, is a product of Reed Elsevier. Upon request, each company sends customers its special software for downloading on personal computers. Access to both services can also be purchased on the Internet at *www.westlaw.com* (see exhibit 13.6) and *www.lexis.com* (see exhibit 13.7). Whether you want to use Westlaw and LEXIS through their special software or through the Internet, the steps are the same. You set up a billing account, enter your password, select the part of the service you want to search, and type your search terms. Westlaw calls its parts databases; LEXIS call its parts libraries. For example, there is a database in Westlaw and a library in LEXIS that contain all the court opinions of Pennsylvania. Similarly, there is a database in Westlaw and a library in LEXIS that contain all the federal statutes passed by Congress. (For convenience, the following discussion will refer to the resources in both services as databases.)

### SCOPE OF WESTLAW AND LEXIS
Westlaw and LEXIS allow you to search the full text of **primary authority** such as:

- Federal and state constitutions
- Federal and state statutes
- Federal and state court opinions
- Federal, state, and local administrative regulations
- Federal, state, and local administrative decisions
- Federal, state, and local rules of court
- Federal treaties and executive agreements
- Local charters and municipal codes

You can also conduct full-text searches of **secondary authority** such as:

- Legal periodicals
- Legal treatises
- Legal newsletters

**case management**
Application software used to help a law office maintain control over its appointments and deadlines.

**tickler** A system designed to provide reminders of important dates.

**statute of limitations** A law that designates the period within which a lawsuit must be commenced or it can never be brought.

**default judgment** A judgment against a defendant because of a failure to file a required pleading or otherwise to take necessary steps to respond to the plaintiff's claim.

**computer-assisted legal research (CALR)** Performing legal research in computer databases.

**online** Connected to a host computer system or information service—usually through telephone lines.

**Westlaw** A fee-based system of computer-assisted legal research owned by West Group.

**LEXIS** A fee-based system of computer-assisted legal research owned by Reed Elsevier.

**primary authority** Any law that a court could rely on in reaching its decision.

**secondary authority** Any nonlaw that a court could rely on in reaching its decision.

| EXHIBIT 13.6 | Example of a Westlaw Screen |
| --- | --- |

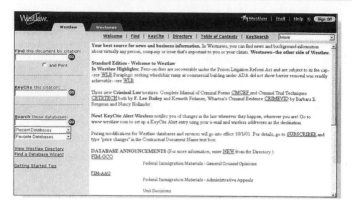

The Internet version of Westlaw (www.westlaw.com)

| EXHIBIT 13.7 | Example of a LEXIS Screen |
| --- | --- |

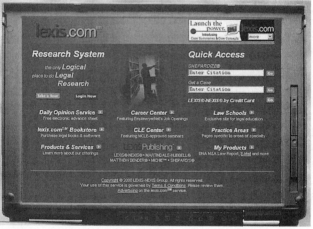

The Internet version of LEXIS (www.lexis.com)

In addition, Westlaw and LEXIS give you access to a large variety of factual information such as:

- The status of pending lawsuits in federal, state, and local courts
- Records of judgments in bankruptcy courts, federal district courts, other federal courts, state courts, county courts, and other local courts
- Statistics on jury awards for specific kinds of injuries
- Mechanic's lien filings
- Uniform Commercial Code (UCC) filings
- Business and personal addresses
- Names of key personnel in particular companies (e.g., officers, members of the board of directors)
- Major properties (e.g., land, stock, commercial equipment) owned by particular individuals and businesses
- Financial status of companies based on sales data, stock market prices, and property holdings

- Financial details and status of proposed mergers and acquisitions
- Chain of title records on specific property
- Medical research (e.g., side effects of particular drugs)
- News stories on particular topics, companies, or individuals in newspapers and other media throughout the world
- Birth and death records
- Social science studies

## SEARCH QUERIES

The first step in searching any computer database is to enter your search terms. When you do so, you are asking the database a question, called a **query**. There are two methods of phrasing search queries on Westlaw and LEXIS: (1) natural language and (2) terms and connectors.

### Natural-Language Searching

**Natural-language** searching uses everyday speech to phrase questions. LEXIS calls its natural-language method *Freestyle*; Westlaw calls its natural-language method *Natural Language*. Here are some examples of natural-language questions:

What is the statute of limitations for embezzlement?
When can a minor enter a contract?
Can strict liability be imposed for harm caused by smoking?

You type the query in the same way that you would ask a question in plain English to a friend or colleague.

### Terms-and-Connectors Searching

A more precise method of phrasing queries on Westlaw and LEXIS uses **terms and connectors**. (This method is based on rules of search logic referred to as Boolean logic.) In a terms-and-connectors search, you specify relationships between terms in a search query in order to identify the documents you want included in or excluded from the search. The relationships are indicated by powerful connectors such as *and*, *&*, *or*, and *not*.

Here is an example of a terms-and-connectors search in Westlaw:

marijuana & arrest

Let us assume you want to use this query to search for opinions in a database that contains opinions of your state courts. The query tells the computer to find every opinion in the database that contains the term *marijuana* anywhere in the opinion and that also contains the term *arrest* anywhere in the opinion. The terms being searched are marijuana and arrest. The AND connector (phrased in Westlaw by using the ampersand, &) tells the computer that you want to be given every opinion in the database that contains both terms.

Of course, if your search query consists of a single term, you do not need connectors. You are simply telling the computer to find every document that contains that term. Single-term searches, however, are usually unproductive because they produce too many documents. Suppose, for example, you entered the following search query:

law

This query would probably identify hundreds of thousands of documents because of the large number of documents that contain this term. In fact, Westlaw will quickly flash a message on the screen telling you to change your query because the one you are using is likely to generate too many documents. Hence, unless your single term is a unique legal term (e.g., asportation) or an unusual surname (e.g., Wyzinski), your query should include more than one term. When it does, connectors are needed to state the relationship between the terms. Although in the following discussion we will use some single-term queries for purposes of highlighting a particular search technique, keep in mind that multiple-term searches are usually more effective than single-term searches.

**query** A question that is used to try to find something in a computer database.

**natural language** Plain English as spoken or written every day as opposed to language that is specially designed for computer communication.

**terms and connectors** Relationships between terms in a search query that specify documents that should be included in or excluded from the search.

We turn now to a closer examination of terms-and-connectors searching in Westlaw and LEXIS. Here are the topics we will be covering:

Universal character (*) in Westlaw and LEXIS
Root expander (!) in Westlaw and LEXIS
Plurals in Westlaw and LEXIS
Formulating queries in Westlaw
Formulating queries in LEXIS

Before we begin, it should be pointed out that not all online search resources use terms and connectors in the same way. For example, we will see that Westlaw and LEXIS phrase the AND connector differently. The same is true of the free Internet search sites we will examine later in the chapter. They also use terms-and-connectors searching but not always in the same way.

**Universal Character (*) in Westlaw and LEXIS.**    Both Westlaw and LEXIS use the asterisk (*) as a **universal character** that stands for any single character such as a letter of the alphabet. A universal character is useful when you are not sure of the spelling of a term you want to search. For example, in the drug arrest example we just examined, suppose you were not sure whether the drug was spelled marijuana or marihuana. You could enter the search as:

**universal character** An asterisk (*) that stands for one character within a term you are searching in Westlaw or LEXIS.

> mari*uana & arrest

This query will find any document that spells the term as marijuana, marihuana, mariiuana, marizuana, etc. Because the asterisk stands for *any* single letter or character, it is called the universal character. You are not limited to one universal character per term. The following query:

> int**state

will find every document that contains the term *interstate* anywhere in the document and every document that contains the term *intrastate* anywhere in the document.
Similarly, the query:

> s****holder

will find:

- ■ Every document that contains the term *shareholder* anywhere in the document, and
- ■ Every document that contains the term *stockholder* anywhere in the document, and
- ■ Every document that contains the term *stakeholder* anywhere in the document.

The query:

> w**nst**n

will find any document that contains words with the following spellings (or misspellings) anywhere in the document: *Weinstein, Weinstien, Weinsteen, Wienstein, Wienstien, Wiensteen.*

**Root Expander (!) in Westlaw and LEXIS.**    Both Westlaw and LEXIS use the exclamation point (!) as a **root expander**. When added to the root of any term, the ! acts as a substitute for one or more characters. You simply insert the exclamation point at the end of a term (or at the end of a fragment of a term) in order to broaden the scope of the search. If your query is:

**root expander** An exclamation mark (!) that stands for one or more characters added to the root of a term you are searching in Westlaw or LEXIS.

> litig!

you will find every document that contains any of the following terms anywhere in the document: *litigable, litigate, litigated, litigating, litigation, litigator, litigious, litigiousness.* The root expander is quite powerful and can be overused. The query:

> tax!

will find every document that contains any of the following terms anywhere in the document: *tax, taxability, taxable, taxation, taxational, taxer, Taxco, taxeme, taxes, tax-deductible, tax-exempt, tax-free, taxi, taxicab, taxidermy, taxidermist, taxied, taximeter, taximetrics, taxing, taxis, taxiway, taxman, taxol, taxon, taxonomist, taxonomy, taxpayer, tax-shelter, taxy, taxying.* Hence, if you use *tax!* as a search query in a large database, you are likely to find documents that are far beyond the scope of your research problem.

**Plurals in Westlaw and LEXIS.**　In Westlaw and LEXIS searches, it is not necessary to use the universal character or the root expander to search for the plural of a term. The query:

prosecutor

will give you every document that contains the term *prosecutor* or the term *prosecutors* anywhere in the document. The same is true of irregular plurals:

- The query *child* will give you every document that contains the term *child* or the term *children* anywhere in the document.
- The query *memorandum* will give you every document that contains the term *memoranda* or the term *memorandums* anywhere in the document.

Entering the singular form of a term will automatically result in a search for the plural form of that term also.

Thus far we have examined the universal character (*) and root expander (!). Again keep in mind that this discussion applies only to Westlaw and LEXIS. When you are searching in other databases (e.g., on Internet search engines), you may find that these notations (* and !) serve related but different functions.

**Formulating Queries in Westlaw.**　To understand terms-and-connectors searches in Westlaw, we need to examine:

- The OR connector
- The AND connector (&)
- The sentence connector (/s) (+s)
- The paragraph connector (/p) (+p)
- The BUT NOT connector (%)
- The numerical connector (/n) (+n)
- Phrase searching ("")

### OR connector

The simplest connector in WESTLAW is OR, which is expressed by leaving a blank space between search terms. Westlaw interprets the blank space in the query to mean OR. This connector tells Westlaw to treat the terms as alternatives and to find every document that contains either term or both terms anywhere in the document. Hence the query:

doctor physician

will find:

- Every document that contains the term *doctor* and the term *physician* anywhere in the document
- Every document that contains the term *doctor* anywhere in the document even if it does not contain the term *physician*
- Every document that contains the term *physician* anywhere in the document even if it does not contain the term *doctor*

### AND connector (&)

As we have seen, the AND connector in Westlaw is expressed by typing the ampersand (&) between terms. The query:

paralegal & fee

will find every document that contains the term *paralegal* and the term *fee* anywhere in the document. If a particular document mentions *paralegals* 100 times but never mentions *fee*, the document will not be found by this query. The query requires both terms to be in the document. If you want documents that mention either term, the query would have to use Westlaw's OR connector (a blank space):

paralegal fee

### Sentence connector (/s) (+s)

The sentence connector in Westlaw is expressed by typing /s or +s between terms. When you type /s between terms, you want the terms to appear anywhere in the same sentence in the document. The query:

child /s support

will find every document in which the terms *child* and *support* appear in any sentence in the document. The query would find:

- A document containing the sentence "The payment of *child support* is a state function."
- A document containing the sentence "*Children* are entitled to the *support* of their school teachers."
- A document containing the sentence "Objections to the petitioner's attempt to *support* his first wife cannot be made by the attorney appointed to represent the *child*."
- A document containing the sentence "He would not *support* the decision to send the *child* to jail."

All of these sentences fit the query even though the meaning of the term *support* is hardly the same in each. Your research problem probably does not involve all of these meanings. Later we will see how to use other connectors that narrow the focus of your search in order to avoid this problem.

In the first and second documents, note that the term *child* (and its plural *children*) appear before the term *support* in the sentence. In the third and fourth documents, however, the order of the terms is reversed. The /s connector does not require that the terms appear in the sentence in the order in which you type them in the query. All that is required is that all the terms separated by /s appear anywhere in the sentence.

If you want the terms to appear in the sentence in the order you type them in the query, use the +s version of the sentence connector. Hence the query:

child +s support

will find only those documents in which the term *child* appears before the term *support* in any sentence in the document. This query would find the first and second documents above. It would not find the third and fourth documents because *child* does not appear before *support* in the sentences of these documents.

### Paragraph connector (/p) (+p)

The paragraph connector in Westlaw is expressed by typing /p or +p between terms. When you type /p between terms, you want the terms to appear anywhere (in any order) in the same paragraph in the document. When you type +p between terms, you want the terms to appear in the paragraph in the same order that you type the terms in the query. The query:

paralegal /p certif!

would find a document in which the term *paralegal* appears anywhere in a paragraph and one of the following terms also appears anywhere in the same paragraph: *certify, certified, certifying,* or *certification.* The query does not require that the term *paralegal* appear first. If you want to limit your search to documents in which the term *paralegal* appears first in the paragraph, the query would be:

paralegal +p certif!

### BUT NOT connector (%)

The BUT NOT connector in Westlaw is expressed by typing the percent symbol (%) between terms. When you type % after a term, everything after % is excluded from your search. The BUT NOT connector is helpful to narrow, your search. Assume, for example, that you are looking for opinions involving robbery with a gun. You try this query:

gun & robbery

You find that most of the documents found by this query involve bank robberies. If your research problem has nothing to do with banks, you could try the query:

gun & robbery % bank

This query will find every document in which the terms *gun* and *robbery* appear anywhere in the document so long as the term *bank* does not also appear anywhere in the document. For example, the query will not lead you to a document that mentions *gun* ten times, *robbery* twenty times, and *bank* once. Any mention of *bank* disqualifies the document from fitting within the query.

### Numerical connector (/n) (+n)

The numerical connector in Westlaw is expressed by typing /n or +n between terms. You use this connector when you want to specify how close you want the terms to appear to each other in the document. Closeness is measured by a specified number (n) of words. The query:

paralegal /5 license

would find every document in which the term *paralegal* appears within five words of the term *license*. Here is an example of text in a document that this query would find:

". . .the *paralegal* had no *license* from the state."

This document fits the query because our search terms are two words apart, well within the five-word limit (/5) set by the query. Here is an example of text in a document that this query would not find because the terms are more than five words apart:

". . .*paralegals* as well as notaries and process servers are not required to have a *license*."

The /n connector does not require that the terms in the document appear in the order in which you type them in the query. Hence our query would find a document containing the following text:

"The driver's *license* was found on the *paralegal*."

If you want to restrict your search to those documents in which the terms appear in the order you type them in the query, use the +n version of the numerical connector in the same manner that +s and +p are used in the sentence and paragraph connectors. Hence a document containing the sentence in the above example would not be found by the following query:

paralegal +5 license

### Phrase searching (" ")

There are many technical phrases in the law, e.g., habeas corpus, due process of law, search and seizure, beyond a reasonable doubt. You need to be careful when entering phrases in Westlaw queries. If, for example, your query was the phrase:

legal malpractice

the space between the terms would be interpreted by Westlaw as an OR connector, so that the query would find:

- Every document that contains the term *legal* and the term *malpractice* anywhere in the document
- Every document that contains the term *legal* anywhere in the document even if it does not contain the term *malpractice*
- Every document that contains the term *malpractice* anywhere in the document even if it does not contain the term *legal*

This query could lead to an enormous number of documents, many of which having nothing to do with legal malpractice. When searching for phrases, therefore, you need to tell Westlaw not to interpret a space as an OR connector. This is done by placing the phrase within quotation marks. Hence our query should read:

"legal malpractice"

Later we will see that LEXIS does not require quotation marks when conducting a phrase search because LEXIS does not interpret every space as an OR connector.

**Formulating Queries in LEXIS.**      To understand terms-and-connectors searches in LEXIS, we need to examine:

- The OR connector
- The AND connector
- The sentence connector (/s) (w/s)
- The paragraph connector (/p)
- The AND NOT connector
- The numerical connector (w/n)
- Phrase searching

As we examine each of these topics, we will see that there are similarities and differences between LEXIS and Westlaw search queries.

### OR connector

In LEXIS, the OR connector is expressed by typing the word OR between search terms. The query:

doctor OR physician

will find:

- Every document that contains the term *doctor* and the term *physician* anywhere in the document
- Every document that contains the term *doctor* anywhere in the document even if it does not contain the term *physician*
- Every document that contains the term *physician* anywhere in the document even if it does not contain the term *doctor*

Note that the phrasing of the OR connector is substantially different in LEXIS and West-law. In LEXIS, you use the word OR, whereas in Westlaw, you simply leave a space between the search terms. The use of OR in LEXIS (doctor OR physician) serves the same function as a space in Westlaw (doctor physician).

### AND connector

Another difference between Westlaw and LEXIS is the phrasing of the AND connector. As we have seen, the AND connector in Westlaw is expressed by typing an ampersand (&) between terms. In LEXIS, however, this connector is expressed by typing AND between terms. The query:

paralegal AND fee

in LEXIS will find every document that contains the term *paralegal* and the term *fee* anywhere in the document. The query will not find any document that mentions only one of these terms. The use of AND in LEXIS (paralegal AND fee) serves the same function as an ampersand in Westlaw (paralegal & fee).

### Sentence connector (/s) (w/s)

The sentence connector in LEXIS is expressed by typing /s between terms. When you type /s between terms, you want the terms to appear in the same sentence in the document. The query:

overdose /s drug

will find every document in which the terms *overdose* and *drug* appear in any sentence in the document. The sentence connector (/s) in LEXIS works the same as the sentence connector (/s) in Westlaw. (Unlike Westlaw, however, LEXIS does not have the +s option described earlier.) Another way to phrase the sentence connector in LEXIS is w/s.

### Paragraph connector (/p) (w/p)

The paragraph connector in LEXIS is expressed by typing /p between terms. When you type /p between terms, you want the terms to appear in the same paragraph in the document. The query:

international /p ship!

will find every document in which the term *international* appears anywhere in a paragraph and one of the following terms also appears anywhere in the same paragraph: *ship, shipbuilding, shipload, shipmate, shipment, shipper, shipworm, shipwreck, shipyard*.

The paragraph connector (/p) in LEXIS works the same as the paragraph connector (/p) in Westlaw. (Unlike Westlaw, however, LEXIS does not have the +p option described earlier.) Another way to phrase the paragraph connector in LEXIS is w/p.

### AND NOT connector

The AND NOT connector in LEXIS is expressed by typing AND NOT between terms. Every term after AND NOT is excluded from your search. The query:

cruelty AND NOT divorce

will find every document in which the term *cruelty* appears anywhere in the document so long as the term *divorce* does not also appear anywhere in the document. The query will not lead you to a document that mentions *cruelty* ten times and *divorce* once. Any mention of *divorce* disqualifies the document from fitting within the query. The AND NOT connector in LEXIS works the same as the BUT NOT (%) connector in Westlaw.

### Numerical connector (w/n) (PRE/n)

The numerical connector in LEXIS is expressed by typing either w/n or PRE/n between terms. You use this connector when you want to specify how close you want the terms to appear to each other in the document. Closeness is measured by a specified number (n) of words. Assume you wanted to find documents on the appointment of Chief Justice Rehnquist of the United States Supreme Court. The query:

Rehnquist w/4 appointment

would find every document in which the term *Rehnquist* appears within four words of the term *appointment*. If you want the terms to appear in the document in the order you type them in the query, use the PRE/n version of the numerical connector. The query:

Rehnquist PRE/4 appointment

- Will find a document containing the sentence "Justice *Rehnquist* received his *appointment* during the session."
- Will not find a document containing the sentence "The *appointment* of Justice *Rehnquist* had not been anticipated."

The second sentence is disqualified because *Rehnquist* does not appear before *appointment* as required by the PRE/n numerical connector.

The numerical connector (w/n) (PRE/n) in LEXIS works the same as the numerical connector (/n) (+n) in Westlaw.

### Phrase searching

Recall that phrase searching in Westlaw requires the use of quotation marks because Westlaw interprets a space between terms to mean OR. This is not so in LEXIS. To search for a phrase in LEXIS, you simply type that phrase. The query:

equal employment opportunity commission

would find any document in which the phrase *equal employment opportunity commission* appears anywhere in the document. The same search in Westlaw would have to be phrased:

"equal employment opportunity commission"

**Combination Queries.**　Most of the examples of queries we have examined thus far have involved one of the connectors. The exception was the example of the Westlaw query that combined the AND and the BUT NOT connectors in one query (gun & robbery % bank). You can use many connectors in a query in order to narrow your search. Here is another example of a Westlaw query that contains multiple connectors:

> bankruptcy /25 discharg! & student
> college education % foreign
> international

In LEXIS, this same query would be written:

> bankruptcy w/25 discharg! AND
> student OR college OR education AND
> NOT foreign OR international

For a document to fit either of these queries, it would have to meet all of the following criteria:

- The document must contain the term *bankruptcy*.
- This term *bankruptcy* must be found within 25 words of any of the following terms: *discharge, discharged, dischargeable,* or *dischargeability*.
- The document must also contain one or more of the following terms: *student, college, education*.
- The terms *foreign* and *international* must not appear anywhere in the document.

You might use this query if you were looking for documents on whether domestic student loans can be discharged in bankruptcy.

---

### Assignment 13.1

(a) Here are five separate queries. If they were run in either Westlaw or LEXIS, what terms in documents would they find?
 (1) para!
 (2) assign!
 (3) crim!
 (4) legis!
 (5) e****e
(b) You are looking for cases in which a paralegal is charged with unauthorized practice of law.
 (1) Write a query for Westlaw.
 (2) Write a query for LEXIS.
(c) You are looking for cases in which a law firm illegally failed to pay overtime compensation to its paralegals.
 (1) Write a query for Westlaw.
 (2) Write a query for LEXIS.
(d) You would like to know what your state courts have said about paralegals.
 (1) Write a query for Westlaw.
 (2) Write a query for LEXIS.
(e) Here is a query to be entered in Westlaw:

> cigar! tobacco smok! /p product strict! /5 liab!

Explain this query. State what the symbols and spaces mean. State what the query is designed to find.

---

### FIELD AND SEGMENT SEARCHING

When searching for documents such as court opinions in Westlaw and LEXIS, you probably want to find your search terms anywhere in documents. As we saw earlier, such searches are called full-text searches. Yet it is also possible to limit your search to part of each document. Westlaw calls these parts **fields**; LEXIS calls them **segments**. For example, one of the fields in the court opinion databases of Westlaw is title (ti), which covers the names of the parties. Assume that you wanted to obtain the name of every opinion in which General Motors was a party. Instead of doing a full-text search in Westlaw, you could restrict your search to the title of every opinion. The field query would be:

ti ("General Motors")

This query would ask for a list of every opinion in which General Motors was a party (e.g., a plaintiff or defendant). The comparable segment in LEXIS is called *name*. The segment query would be:

name (General Motors)

Here is a summary of the major field searches in Westlaw and segment searches in LEXIS when the documents you are searching are court opinions:

### Westlaw

*title* (ti): The names of the parties in the opinion.
Example: ti(Miranda)
*attorney* (at): The names of the attorneys litigating the case.
Example: at("Clarence Darrow")
*synopsis* (sy): The short summary of the entire opinion.
Example: sy("double jeopardy")
*le* (lead): The full text of the majority or plurality opinion.
Example: le(lead): (unconstitutional) This query would not search any concurring and dissenting opinions in the case.

### LEXIS

*name*: The name of the parties in the opinion.
Example: name(Miranda)
*counsel*: The names of the attorneys litigating the case.
Example: counsel(Clarence Darrow)
*syllabus*: The short summary of the entire opinion.
Example: syllabus(double jeopardy)
*opinion*: The full text of the majority or plurality opinion.
Example: opinion(unconstitutional) This query would not search any concurring and dissenting opinions in the case.

### CITATORS IN WESTLAW AND LEXIS

As we saw in chapter 11, a **citator** helps you assess the current validity of a law (e.g., opinion, statute) and gives you leads to other relevant materials. The online citator in Westlaw is called *KeyCite*. The online citator in LEXIS is called *Shepards*. (The latter is the electronic version of the bound volumes called *Shepard's Citations*.) Suppose, for example, you want to know whether a particular court opinion is still good law. Has the opinion been reversed on appeal? Have any other courts followed it or criticized it? Has the opinion been overruled? One of the ways to answer such questions is by using the online citators of Westlaw and LEXIS.

### LOCATING A DOCUMENT ONLINE WHEN YOU HAVE ITS CITATION

The most common reason you use Westlaw and LEXIS is to search for documents that you do not have. Suppose, however, that you already have the citation to a document and you simply want to read that document. You could take the citation to a law library and read the document in a traditional volume from the shelf. Alternatively, you could take your citation to Westlaw or LEXIS and read the document online.

To retrieve the document on Westlaw, type the citation in a box called "Enter Citation" or "Find this document by citation" and click "GO." (See exhibit 13.6.) Westlaw also

**field** A portion of a document in Westlaw that can be separately searched.

**segment** A portion of a document in LEXIS that can be separately searched.

**citator** A book, CD–ROM, or online service containing lists of citations that can (1) help you assess the current validity of an opinion, statute, or other item and (2) give you leads to other relevant materials.

allows you to retrieve the document by using a find (fi) command with the citation. Here, for example, are find commands for a court opinion and a statute:

fi 5 F3d 1412
fi 42 usca 12101

To retrieve a court opinion on LEXIS, type the citation in a box called "Enter Citation" and click "Go." (See exhibit 13.7.) LEXIS also allows you to:

■ Retrieve a court opinion by typing the citation of the court opinion in the *lexsee* feature of LEXIS and

■ Retrieve a statute by typing the citation of the statute in the *lexstat* feature of LEXIS.

## Section E
# INTERNET

### INTRODUCTION

Hundreds of millions of people around the world use the **Internet**, a self-governing network of networks, popularly known as the information superhighway. A network is two or more computers (or other devices) that are connected by telephone lines, fiber-optic cables, satellites, or other systems in order to share hardware, software, messages, and other data. These different networks can communicate with each other because they all follow a set of specifications called *protocols* that make the communication possible.

The Internet was developed in the 1960s by the U.S. Department of Defense to link a handful of computers in the event of a nuclear attack.[6] The idea was to design a system that would allow communication over a number of routes between linked computers. Thus, a message sent from a computer in Boston to a computer in Seattle might first be sent to a computer in Philadelphia, and then be forwarded to a computer in Pittsburgh, and then to Chicago, Denver, and Salt Lake City, before finally reaching Seattle. If the message could not travel along that path (because of military attack, technical malfunction, or other reason), the message would automatically be rerouted, perhaps, from Boston to Richmond, and then to Atlanta, New Orleans, Dallas, Albuquerque, and Los Angeles, and finally to Seattle. This type of transmission, and rerouting, could occur in a matter of seconds without human intervention or knowledge.

When the government no longer needed this link, it turned the system over to the public. Hence no single governmental, corporate, or academic entity owns or administers the Internet. It exists and functions because hundreds of thousands of separate operators of computers and computer networks independently decided to use common data transfer protocols to exchange communications and information with other computers (which in turn exchange communications and information with still other computers). There is no centralized storage location, control point, or communications channel for the Internet. Indeed, it would not be technically feasible for a single entity to control everything that is conveyed on the Internet.

To connect to the Internet, you need a company or organization that provides access, called an **Internet service provider** (e.g., America Online, Microsoft Network). Once connected, most of your online time will be spent on the "web"—the **World Wide Web (www).** The web is a system of sites using **hypertext** to enable you to display and link information in different locations on the same site or on different sites. When you are on a web page, you will see words, pictures, or buttons that are highlighted in some way, often with the use of color. If the words, pictures, or buttons on a site are highlighted (i.e., hypertexted), you can click on them and you will be taken to another section of the site or to another site. Suppose, for example, you are on the Legal Resources page of the Internet site of the National Federation of Paralegal Associations (see exhibit 13.8). Note the 15 resource buttons on this page. By clicking on any of these buttons, you will be led to thousands of other web sites on the Internet that will help you do factual and legal research. Do you want to find federal statutes? Click the option called "Federal Laws, Codes, Statutes" at the top of the second column of buttons. Do you want information on the

**Internet** A self-governing network of networks to which millions of computer users all over the world have access.

**Internet service provider** A company that provides access to the Internet, usually for a monthly fee.

**World Wide Web (www)** A system of sites on the Internet that can be accessed through hypertext links.

**hypertext** A method of displaying and linking information found in different locations on the same site or on different sites of the World Wide Web.

| EXHIBIT 13.8 | Legal Resources Site of the National Federation of Paralegal Associations (NFPA) |
|---|---|

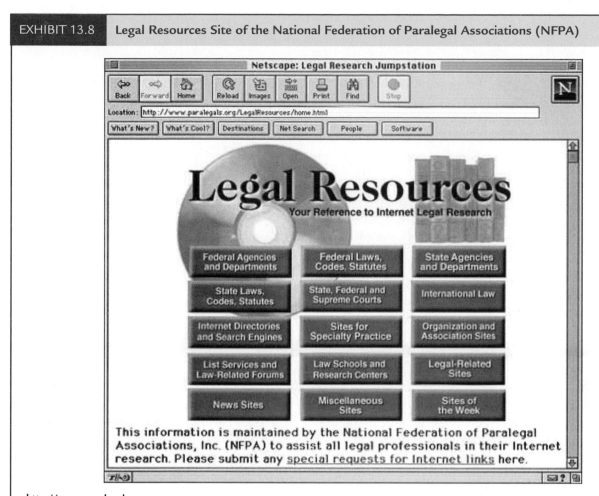

**http://www.paralegals.org**
Web Site of the National Federation of Paralegal Associations

Federal Trade Commission? Click the option called "Federal Agencies and Departments" at the top of the first column.

A great deal of legal and factual information is available on the Internet for free. Much of this information is also available for a fee from the major commercial online services, Westlaw and LEXIS. (See exhibits 13.6 and 13.7.) Neither of these giants, however, is likely to go out of business because of competition from the free resources on the Internet. Westlaw and LEXIS spend a great deal of editorial time ensuring the currentness and accuracy of the information they make available. No comparable control mechanisms exist for much of the even larger quantity of free information found on the Internet. The reliability of free information is increasing, but it has not yet reached the stage where it can satisfy the legal community's need for online information to the exclusion of the major fee-based services. There are, however, a number of smaller and cheaper fee-based online research companies on the Internet (e.g., *www.loislaw.com*) that are beginning to provide some competition to Westlaw and LEXIS.

### INTERNET ADDRESSES

The address of a resource on the World Wide Web (e.g., a document or an image) is called the **uniform resource locator (URL)**. Here is an example of a URL:

*http://www.loc.gov*

Http means hypertext transfer protocol. As we saw earlier, the protocol is the set of specifications or standards that allow computers to communicate with each other. Because most **web browsers** assume you are using the http protocol, you do not need to type http://. (A web browser is simply a program that allows you to read pages on the World Wide Web. The most popular browsers are Microsoft's Internet Explorer

**uniform resource locator (URL)** The address of a resource on the Internet.

**web browser** The program that allows you to read pages on the World Wide Web.

**server** A computer program that provides resources or services to other computers.

and Netscape's Navigator.) After the protocol in our URL example comes the address of the **server** *(www.loc.gov)* on which the resource is located. (A server is a computer program that provides resources or services, e.g., access to data, to other computers.) Typing the address of the server will usually lead you to its opening or home page. The last three digits of the server address (.gov) are the domain name or identifier, which indicates the category or type of server. Our example *(www.loc.gov)* will lead you to a government agency, the Library of Congress (loc). Here are the main categories of domain names:

> .com (commercial entity)
> .gov (government office)
> .org (organization, often nonprofit)
> .edu (educational institution)
> .mil (military institution)
> .net (network provider)

Other categories have been approved or are being planned, such as:

> .pro (for attorneys, physicians, and accountants)
> .coop (for cooperatives)
> .aero (for the air transport industry)
> .biz (for businesses)
> .name (for individuals)

After the URL's server name, you may find additional characters. For example:

*http://www.loc.gov/global/state/stategov.html*

The additional characters (/global/state/stategov.html) bypass the home page and take you directly to specific documents, images, or links available on the site.

## INTRODUCTION TO SEARCHING THE INTERNET

According to some estimates, over 5.5 billion World Wide Web pages are on the Internet. Every second, 25 new web pages are added. In light of this extraordinary volume of material, finding what you need can sometimes be a challenge. Exhibit 13.9 presents guidelines for using search engines and directories, two of the major Internet finding tools you can use.

**search engine** A search tool that will find sites on the Internet that contain terms you enter on any subject.

A **search engine** is a search tool that will find sites on the Internet that contain terms you enter on any subject. The terms you enter are sometimes called keywords. Another major search tool is the **directory**, which allows for a more focused search. When you use a directory, you first select a broad subject from a short list that you think fits the category of information you want. Here are some of the commonly used subject categories in directories:

**directory** A search tool in which you select from a list of broad subject categories and then enter the terms you want contained in sites that are part of the subject category you select.

| | | | |
|---|---|---|---|
| Art | Entertainment | Law and government | Shopping |
| Business | Fitness | Lifestyle | Sports |
| Careers | Games | News | Travel |
| Computers | Health | Reference | Weather |
| Education | International | Science | |

Once you select the subject, you then enter the search terms you want contained in sites that are part of that subject category.

There are a large number of search engines and directories on the Internet. Here are some of the variations that exist among them:

**metasearch** A search for terms in more than one search engine simultaneously.

- Some search sites are a combination of search engine and directory.
- Some search sites allow you to conduct **metasearches**, which search for your terms in more than one search engine simultaneously.
- Some search engines and directories allow you to search in natural language; in these sites, you type your queries in everyday sentences (e.g., *Where can I find the address of the IRS?*).

| EXHIBIT 13.9 | Internet Search Techniques |
| --- | --- |

1. Decide whether you want to use a search engine (on which you search by keywords on any subject) or a directory (in which you search by subject area and then by keywords). If you are not sure, try both. For a list of both categories of search resources, see exhibit 13.10.
2. Be ready to try more than one search engine or directory.
3. Every search engine or directory has its own help section that gives instructions and suggestions on how to search effectively within it. The section may be called Help, How to Search, Advanced Search, etc. Read this section carefully for every search engine or directory you try.
4. Here are six of the most important questions you want answered about every search engine or directory you use. Try to answer these questions by checking its help section. The questions are as follows:
   - How do you search for phrases? Do you need to add quotation marks around the phrase, e.g., "capital punishment"?
   - How do you search for plurals (e.g., vehicles, children)? Does the engine or directory automatically search for plurals when you enter the singular form of a search term?
   - Does the engine or directory have an AND connector? When your search query has more than one term (e.g., battery woman), how do you indicate that you want to limit your search to sites that contain all of your terms? Do you add AND between the terms (*battery AND woman*) or do you place a plus sign (+) immediately in front of each term (*+battery +woman*) that must appear in the site?
   - Does the engine or directory have an OR connector? How do you express alternative terms in your search query? Do you add OR between the terms (e.g., *zoning OR easement*) or does the engine/directory automatically treat every space between search terms as an OR so that OR does not have to be typed?
   - Does the engine or directory have a BUT NOT or AND NOT connector? How do you tell the engine/directory to avoid specific categories of sites? For example, how do you tell the engine/directory that you want sites on penicillin for adults only? Do you use the BUT NOT connector (*penicillin BUT NOT child*), the AND NOT connector (e.g., *penicillin AND NOT child*), or do you place a minus sign (–) immediately in front of any term that must not appear (*+penicillin +adult –child*)?
   - If you are not sure how to spell a term (e.g., Gieco? Geico?), can you use any universal characters or wildcards such as * (G**co) or ! (G!!co)?
5. Be specific in your use of search terms. For example, if you are looking for attorney fee cases in litigation involving the Ojibwa tribe in Maine, type *+attorney +fee +Ojibwa +Maine* (or *attorney AND fee AND Ojibwa AND Maine*); do not simply type *+attorney +fee* (or *attorney AND fee*).
6. Use synonyms in your search (e.g., *+divorce +dissolution*) or (*divorce AND dissolution*). To help you think of synonyms and other search-term options, use the CARTWHEEL technique discussed in exhibit 11.16 of chapter 11.
7. Refine your search terms as you continue to search. Some of the early sites you come across may not be what you need, but these sites may suggest new search terms to try. Also, watch for hyperlinks in every site you visit. A less-than-productive site may allow you to "jump" to a productive one.
8. If you have more than one search term, type the most important terms first. For example, if you are looking for sites on the incompatibility ground of divorce, your query might be *+divorce +incompatibility +grounds* (or *divorce AND incompatibility AND grounds*).
9. Type your search terms in lower case except for connectors such as AND and OR (*incarceration AND sentencing*).
10. Search the invisible Web to try to find materials that are not picked up by regular search engines or directories. For sites that help you search the invisible Web, see exhibit 13.10.
11. Once you are in a site, you can sometimes use the find command (e.g., ctrl-F) to try to find your search terms within the pages of the site.

- Some search sites allow you to search the **invisible Web**, which consists of sites that contain specialized databases or formats that are not reached by traditional search engines and directories.

**invisible web** That part of the Internet that is not found by traditional search engines and directories.

Exhibit 13.10 contains a list of some of the most important search engines, directories, and their variations.

| EXHIBIT 13.10 | Search Engines and Directories |
| --- | --- |

**MAJOR SITES**

**Lists of Available Search Engines and Directories**
www.searchengineshowdown.com/features
www.siteowner.com/dgdefault.cfm
cui.unige.ch/meta-index.html
www.allsearchengines.com
www.searchenginecolossus.com
www.gogettem.com

**Glossary of Search Engine Terms**
www.searchenginewatch.com/facts/glossary.html
www.cadenza.org/search_engine_terms
www.cs.jhu.edu/~weiss/glossary.html

**General Search Engines**
www.google.com
www.teoma.com
www.altavista.com
www.excite.com
www.lycos.com
www.webcrawler.com
search.msn.com

**Metasearch Engines** (searches more than one search engine simultaneously)
www.dogpile.com
www.metacrawler.com/index.html
vivisimo.com
ixquick.com
www.highway61.com
www.search.com
www.metor.com
www.profusion.com

**Directories: Searches by Subjects or Topics**
www.yahoo.com
www.looksmart.com
about.com
www.lii.org
infomine.ucr.edu
vlib.org

**Natural Language Searching**
www.askjeeves.com
www.northernlight.com/docs/search_help_natural.html

**Searching the Invisible Web**
www.invisibleweb.com
www.lib.berkeley.edu/TeachingLib/Guides/Internet/InvisibleWeb.html

## LEGAL RESEARCH ON THE INTERNET

In chapter 11, we covered some of the important Internet sites for legal research. See, for example:

- Exhibit 11.43 Finding Case Law on the Internet
- Exhibit 11.47 Finding Statutes on the Internet

In exhibit 13.11, you will find additional Internet sites that are important for legal research.

| EXHIBIT 13.11 | Legal Research on the Internet |
|---|---|

**Comprehensive General Legal Sites**
www.findlaw.com
www.hg.org
www.law.cornell.edu
www.catalaw.com
www.law.indiana.edu/v-lib
www.alllaw.com
www.ilrg.com
www.llrx.com/sources.html
www.washlaw.edu/reflaw/reflaw.html
www.legalengine.com

**Sites Covering Specific Areas of the Law** (e.g., bankruptcy, women's rights, etc.)
jurist.law.pitt.edu/subj_gd.htm
www.lii.org/search/file/law
www.ilrg.com/subject_ref.html
dir.yahoo.com/Government/Law/Web_Directories
www.academicinfo.net/law.html

**Legal Forms**
forms.lp.findlaw.com
www.ilrg.com/forms.html
www.lectlaw.com//form.html
www.formsguru.com

**State Cases and Statutes**
www.loc.gov/global/state/stategov.html
www.prairienet.org/~scruffy/f.htm
www.piperinfo.com/state/index.cfm
www.romingerlegal.com
www.washlaw.edu/reflaw/refstates.html
www.ncsconline.org/Information/info_court_web_sites.html

**Federal Law**
firstgov.gov
www.washlaw.edu/reflaw/reflawfed.html
www.legal.gsa.gov
www.fedworld.gov

**Court Rules (Rules of Court)**
www.llrx.com/courtrules

**Legal News**
www.washlaw.edu/reflaw/reflegalnews.html
www.news.findlaw.com
www.law.com

---

*Assignment 13.2*

For each of the following questions, use general search engines, directories, or legal search sites. (You can check the sites listed in exhibits 13.10 and 13.11, although you are not limited to these sites. You can also use the sites in the section called "On The Net" at the end of the chapter.) For each answer, give the complete uniform resource locator (URL) you used, the name of the site, and the date you visited it.

**(a)** List any three civil rights organizations. What is the cost of an annual membership in each?

(b) In any three states, find an attorney or law firm with experience in bank mergers.

(c) In any three states, find an independent paralegal who represents clients at social security hearings.

(d) How many legal abortions were performed in the United States in 1980, 1990, and 2000?

(e) In any three states, what is the minimum age someone must be to enter a valid marriage without the consent of his or her parents or guardians?

(f) Where can you obtain copies of appellate briefs filed with any three state or federal appellate courts?

(g) In any three states, what is the name of the presiding judge of the highest state court?

(h) In these same three states, what is the name of the presiding judge of the highest state court in 1990?

(i) Identify every paralegal listserv on the Internet and give instructions on how to subscribe to each one. (See the next section on listservs.)

## LISTSERVS

**listserv** A program that manages computer mailing lists automatically.

A **listserv** is a program that manages computer mailing lists automatically. These lists consist of individuals interested in receiving and sending **e-mail** (electronic mail) to each other on a topic of mutual interest. Thousands of topics are covered on listservs, e.g., travel, hobbies, job searching, cancer. Numerous *legal listservs* cover a large variety of law and law-related topics, e.g., bankruptcy, law office management, job hunting, the law of a particular state. (For sites that will tell you how to subscribe to listservs on legal topics, including those devoted to paralegal issues, see "On the Web" at the end of the chapter.) Once you have subscribed to a list, you can read the comments, questions, and replies sent by everyone else on the list. By reading these messages, you can keep abreast of developments in the subject matter of the group.

**e-mail** A message sent electronically.

Here are examples of the kinds of questions that might be posed on different listservs. On a paralegal listserv, a paralegal asks:

> I'm thinking about taking either NALA's certification exam (CLA) or NFPA's certification exam (PACE). Have any of you taken both so that you can give me some comparison?

A California paralegal member of a real estate listserv asks:

> We have a client who bought and sold land in Georgia in 1985, I'm trying to find a copy of the standard purchase agreement used by the Georgia Association of Real Estate Agents in the 1970s before they substantially changed the format of the contract. Anyone in Georgia who can help me? If you can fax me a copy, I'd appreciate it. Help!

At the beginning of the week, a New York attorney, in immediate need of locating Mississippi regulations on nursing homes, sends out the following urgent e-mail to the members of his listserv:

> I'm looking for the Mississippi Department of Health regulations on nursing homes. I didn't find them on Westlaw or LEXIS. The Department tells me it can't supply them until Friday. Anyone willing to FedEx the sections I need using my firm's account number?

Someone who uses the Word 2002 word processor sends this e-mail to members of a Word users listserv:

> I just got the upgrade and I can't get it to hook up with my HP 6620 printer. Are any of you out there using the upgrade with this printer? Were you able to get the two to work together?

Depending on the number of members in the listserv, you could receive scores of replies. Many members who have had their questions answered send "thanks-for-saving-my-life" messages to the group. Even if you do not send any questions yourself, you will probably find it instructive—and fun—to read the questions and answers others are sending to each other on topics that are relevant to your work.

Listservs are not the only way for computer users to communicate on the Internet. *Usenet* is a network of computers that offers news and discussion groups (also called newsgroups). *Internet relay chats* allow users to communicate in real time. One user types a message on the screen, and the other users can see the message on their screens as it is typed.

---

Section F
# Intranet and Extranet

Some organizations such as businesses and associations are able to set up the equivalent of a mini-Internet for internal use. It is called an **intranet**. Surfers around the globe would not have access to it. A law firm's intranet, for example, could give its employees access to:

- Vacation schedules
- Court dates of current cases
- Client databases, including current litigation documents
- **Brief banks** and legal forms
- A staff directory (with pictures)
- The personnel manual of the firm
- Lists of law library purchases
- Training manuals and continuing legal education (CLE) programs available at the firm

The employees can be in the same office or in branch offices around the world. (There are many similarities between an intranet and the local area network (LAN) and wide area network (WAN) discussed earlier.) An organization can allow selected outsiders to have online access to its intranet. (Such access converts the intranet to an **extranet**.) A law firm, for example, could permit a client to read the documents being prepared for the client on the firm's intranet.

**intranet** A private network of computers within a particular company or organization, established so that the computers can share information online, often using features similar to those of the World Wide Web.

**brief bank** A collection of appellate briefs and other legal documents drafted in prior cases that might be used as a model for drafting similar documents in the future.

**extranet** That part of an intranet to which selected outsiders have been given access.

---

### Assignment 13.3

Each student will make a presentation in front of the class on a computer product used in a law office. You can select your own product. (The instructor must approve the product in advance to ensure that it is suitable for a presentation and that no other student has selected that product.) You can select any product mentioned in this chapter, although you are not limited to the products discussed in the chapter. The product must meet the following characteristics:

- It is a hardware or software product that is offered for sale, lease, or subscription.
- It is extensively (although not necessarily exclusively) used by law offices.
- You can find at least two vendors on the Internet that sell their own version of the product, each with its own features.

The setting for your presentation will be a mock staff meeting of the law office where you work. You have been asked to research the product and give a presentation at the meeting. Your presentation will cover:

- A description of the function of the product, including how it is used
- The pros and cons of the two versions offered by the two vendors you have found
- Your recommendation of which vendor to select

If you can, download and print photographs or drawings of the two versions of the product in order to pass them around the room while you are making your presentation. If needed, you can make any reasonable assumptions about the office where you work such as what equipment it already has.

While you are making your presentation, the staff members in the room (i.e., your fellow students) will be asking you questions about the product. To be able to answer such questions, your research on the product must be substantial. You may need to check information sources beyond what is on the Internet. For example, if a vendor has a toll-free number, ask that some descriptive literature on the product be sent to you. Also, ask your instructor or a librarian where you can find magazine articles (e.g., reviews) on the product.

In addition to your presentation, prepare a written report on the two versions of the product. This will be for staff members who could not be present at your presentation but who will need the same information.

## ▮ CHAPTER SUMMARY

The computer plays a major role in the practice of law. You need to take every opportunity to learn as much as you can about computers. Take short-term computer courses available in the community, attend computer events at paralegal and bar associations, peruse the Internet sites of law firms, try out different search engines, take tutorials, etc.

Hardware is the physical equipment of a computer system. Software is a computer program that tells the hardware what to do. The two main categories of software are operating or systems software (programs that tell the computer how to operate all its parts) and applications software (programs that perform specific tasks for end users). Input devices that place information in a computer include the keyboard, the mouse, speech recognition programs, and scanners. The central processing unit (CPU) is the hardware that controls all of the computer's parts. The two main kinds of memory are read-only memory (ROM) and random access memory (RAM). Data in memory are measured in bytes. Storage devices with read/write capability allow users to read the data on the device and write additional data on the device. You cannot write data on a read-only device. Major storage devices include hard drives, floppy drives, magnetic tape storage systems, CD–ROM drives, DVD–ROM drives, and CD–RW drives. A paper or hard copy of a computer-created document is made on a printer that often can print text in different point sizes and fonts. Computers at different locations can exchange data by using communications devices such as modems. Computers can be connected by a local area network (LAN) (if they are relatively close to each other) or by a wide area network (WAN) (if they are not close).

A word processor is a software program that allows you to enter and edit data in documents. Special formatting features and shortcuts using macros make the creation of documents relatively easy. A spreadsheet is a software program that automatically performs calculations on numbers and values that you enter. Database software allows you to organize, search, retrieve, and sort information or data. Presentation graphics software is used to present text data with charts, graphs, video, and sound in order to communicate the data most effectively. Litigation support software helps a law office store, retrieve, and track the potentially large volume of data involved in litigation. Case management or docket control software helps a law office maintain control over its appointments and deadlines.

The main fee-based sources of computer-assisted legal research (CALR) for primary and secondary authority are Westlaw and LEXIS. Numerous business, medical, and social data are also available on both systems. There are two methods of phrasing search queries: natural language (using everyday sentences) and terms and connectors (stating relationships between the terms of the search). The universal character (*) stands for any character in a search term. The root expander (!) stands for any one or more characters added to the root of a word. Typing the singular form of a word in Westlaw and LEXIS will also find its plural. The connectors include the OR connector [space in Westlaw, OR in LEXIS]; the AND connector [& in Westlaw, AND in LEXIS]; the sentence connector [/s in Westlaw and in LEXIS]; the paragraph connector [/p in Westlaw and in LEXIS]; the BUT NOT or AND NOT connector [% in Westlaw, AND NOT in LEXIS]; and the numerical connector [(/n) (+n) in Westlaw, (w/n) (PRE/n) in LEXIS]. To search for a phrase in Westlaw, use quotation marks; in LEXIS, simply type the phrase. It is possible to limit a search to a portion of a document (fields in Westlaw, segments in LEXIS). Both Westlaw and LEXIS have on-line citators and allow you to retrieve a document if you already know its citation.

The Internet is a self-governing network of networks to which millions of computer users all over the world have access. The hypertext features of the World Wide Web allow relatively easy access to a vast quantity of data. Two of the major search tools are search engines and directories. Check their help feature to identify their unique search techniques. A listserv (a program that manages computer mailing lists automatically) can be a useful way to keep current on specialty topics. Intranets use Internet technology to allow members of a single company or organization to communicate with each other. When selected outsiders are allowed to have access to an intranet, it becomes an extranet.

## KEY TERMS

| | |
|---|---|
| hardware | litigation support |
| software | full-text search |
| operating system | case management |
| applications software | tickler |
| cursor | statute of limitations |
| mouse | default judgment |
| speech recognition | computer-assisted legal research (CALR) |
| scanner | online |
| imaging | Westlaw |
| central processing unit (CPU) | LEXIS |
| memory | primary authority |
| read-only memory (ROM) | secondary authority |
| random access memory (RAM) | query |
| byte | natural language |
| read/write | terms and connectors |
| read-only | universal character |
| hard disk | root expander |
| CD-ROM | field |
| hard copy | segment |
| points | citator |
| fonts | Internet |
| modem | Internet service provider |
| real-time | World Wide Web (www) |
| videoconferencing | hypertext |
| local area network (LAN) | uniform resource locator (URL) |
| groupware | web browser |
| shareware | server |
| wide area network (WAN) | search engine |
| stand-alone computer | directory |
| word processor | metasearch |
| right justified | invisible web |
| macro | listserv |
| table of authorities | e-mail |
| spreadsheet | intranet |
| database program | brief bank |
| presentation graphics | extranet |

## ON THE NET: MORE ON COMPUTERS IN THE LAW

**Online Dictionary of Computer Terms**
www.ora.com/reference/dictionary
www.webopedia.com
foldoc.doc.ic.ac.uk/foldoc/index.html

www.computeruser.com/resources/dictionary
www.learnthenet.com/english/glossary/glossary.htm

### Law Office Technology Resources
www.abanet.org/tech/ltrc
www.lawinfo.com/biz/lawproducts.html
www.lawofficecomputing.com
www.peertopeer.org

### Tutorials
www.henzinger.com/monika/icde/icde-final_files/v3_document.htm
www.netskills.ac.uk/TonicNG/cgi/sesame?tng
www.searchenginewatch.com/resources/tutorials.html
www.lib.berkeley.edu/TeachingLib/Guides/Internet/FindInfo.html

### Software Manufacturers
www.abacuslaw.com
www.lotus.com
www.clswin.com
www.microsoft.com
www.compulaw.com
www.corel.com

### Intranets
www.hotoffice.com
www.intranetjournal.com

### Legal Listservs
www.hg.org/listservs.html
www.lib.uchicago.edu/cgi-bin/law-lists
www.washlaw.edu/listserv.html

### Paralegal Listservs
www.paralegals.org/Forums/listsubscribe.html
www.legalassistanttoday.com/lat-forum

## ENDNOTES

1. C. Estrin & S. Hunt, *The Successful Paralegal Job Search Guide* 71, 236 (2001).
2. B. Roper, *Using Computers in the Law Office* 26 (2d ed. 2000).
3. Within a macro, you can also insert certain commands such as saving the document or inserting a number from another software application.
4. *State of Minnesota and Blue Cross and Blue Shield of Minnesota v. Philip Morris, Inc.*, Trial Transcript, Closing Argument, 1998 WL 242426 (D. Minn. May 7, 1998).
5. Roper, *supra* note 2, at 333.
6. See the historical overview in *American Civil Liberties Union v. Reno*, 929 F. Supp. 824, 832–34 (E.D. Pa. 1996).

# Chapter 14

# INTRODUCTION TO LAW OFFICE ADMINISTRATION*

## Chapter Outline

A. The Practice of Law in the Private Sector

B. The Legal Administrator and the Legal Assistant Manager

C. Expenses

D. Timekeeping

E. Kinds of Fees

F. Billing

G. Client Trust Accounts

H. Administrative Reports

I. Client File Management

*Portions of this chapter were originally written with Robert G. Baylor, Business Manager at Manatt, Phelps, Rothenberg, and Tunney, Los Angeles. Others who have reviewed this chapter and provided valuable commentary include Dorothy B. Moore, Kathleen M. Reed, Michele A. Coyne, Patsy R. Pressley, Deborah L. Thompson, and Shawn A. Jones.

## Section A
# The Practice of Law in the Private Sector

We begin our examination of how attorneys manage their practices with some statistics. In 1983, there were 612,000 attorneys in the United States. By 1999, the number had grown to 923,000.[1] In 1998, the median annual earnings of all attorneys was $78,170. The middle half of the occupation earned between $51,450 and $114,520. The bottom tenth earned less than $37,310.[2]

About 70 percent of attorneys practice in private law offices. Another 10 percent work for corporations in corporate practice. The remainder practice in the public sector for government, for legal aid and legal service offices, or for organizations such as unions, trade associations, and public interest groups, or they do not practice law at all. In this chapter, our primary focus will be on attorneys who practice law in relatively large private offices, although we will also look at other kinds of practice as well.

In the private sector, law is practiced in a variety of settings:

- Sole proprietorship
- Office-sharing arrangement
- Partnership
- Professional corporation
- Limited liability entity
- Corporate law department

### SOLE PROPRIETORSHIP

Any business can be operated as a **sole proprietorship,** which means that one person—the sole proprietor—owns all the assets of the business and assumes all its debts. Because this person has **personal liability**, debtors can reach his or her personal assets (e.g., a family checking account, a vacation home) *in addition to* his or her business assets (e.g., a business bank account, office furniture). If sole proprietors had limited liability, a debtor would be limited to their business assets. The liability of sole proprietors, however, is not limited; it is personal.

Many attorneys begin their practice of law as sole proprietorships. If they practice alone, they are **sole practitioners**, also called solo practitioners. (They are said to be "going solo.") Some owner-attorneys, however, employ other attorneys. If so, the latter receive a salary rather than a share of the profits.

An attorney in a sole proprietorship can be a generalist or a specialist. A generalist is the equivalent of a doctor in general practice. An attorney who is a **general practitioner** often tries to handle all kinds of cases. If, however, the case is unusually complex or if the attorney is very busy with other cases, he or she might consult with an attorney in another office or refer the case to another attorney. Other sole practitioners specialize. Their practice might be limited, for example, to tax, criminal, or patent and trademark cases, or—more commonly—to personal injury cases.

Most sole proprietorships have very few employees. There is a secretary, who often performs many paralegal functions along with the traditional clerical responsibilities of typing, filing, and reception work. He or she may also perform bookkeeping chores. The most common job title of this individual is *legal secretary*, although occasionally he or she will be known as a *legal assistant* or a *paralegal/secretary*. You will sometimes find job ads for small offices seeking paralegals with clerical skills. These skills are often phrased more positively as administrative or word processing skills, but they are, in essence, clerical. In recent years, however, more small offices have begun to hire one or more paralegals who are given minimal or no clerical duties. The office may also have a **law clerk.** This is a full- or part-time law office employee who is studying to be an attorney or who has graduated from law school and is waiting to pass the bar examination. Students in the office seeking practical experience, sometimes called *legal interns*, may or may not be paid.

### OFFICE-SHARING ARRANGEMENT

It can be very expensive to start a practice, particularly in high-rent areas of the country. One cost-saving alternative is **office sharing,** in which two or more attorneys with independent practices share the use and **overhead** costs of an office. For example, each pays a portion of the monthly office rent and also shares the cost of buying or leasing com-

---

**sole proprietorship** A business in which one person owns all the assets of the business and assumes all of its debts or liabilities.

**personal liability** Liability that can be satisfied out of an individual's personal assets.

**sole practitioner** An attorney who practices alone—without partners or associates in the office.

**general practitioner** A professional who handles any kind of case.

**law clerk** An employee who is still in law school or who has completed law school and is awaiting bar examination results.

**office sharing** Attorneys who are sole practitioners share the use and overhead costs of an office.

**overhead** The operating expenses of a business (e.g., office rent, furniture, insurance, clerical staff) for which clients are not charged a separate fee.

puters or other equipment. If the office has a secretary/receptionist, each attorney pays a part of this person's salary. The attorneys do not practice together as a partnership or corporation; in most office-sharing arrangements, each attorney practices alone in a sole proprietorship. To avoid the conflict-of-interest and confidentiality problems discussed in chapter 5, the attorneys (and their employees) must be careful in selecting clients and discussing their cases with each other.

### PARTNERSHIP

A **partnership** is an association of two or more individuals who jointly own a business. Each partner has personal liability for the debts of the partnership. (In this respect, a partnership is similar to a sole proprietorship.) Furthermore, one partner is liable for the torts or other wrongdoing committed by another partner.

**partnership** An association of two or more individuals who jointly own a business.

In a law partnership, the attorneys share the profits and losses of the law practice that they jointly own. If their partnership is relatively large, it will probably be organized into a series of departments (such as an antitrust department and a litigation department) based on client needs and will be managed through a series of committees (such as a recruitment committee, a library committee, and a records committee) based on the variety of support services available to the attorneys. See exhibit 14.1 for an example of the organization structure of a large law firm.

---

**EXHIBIT 14.1**  **Large Law Firm Organization Chart: An Example**

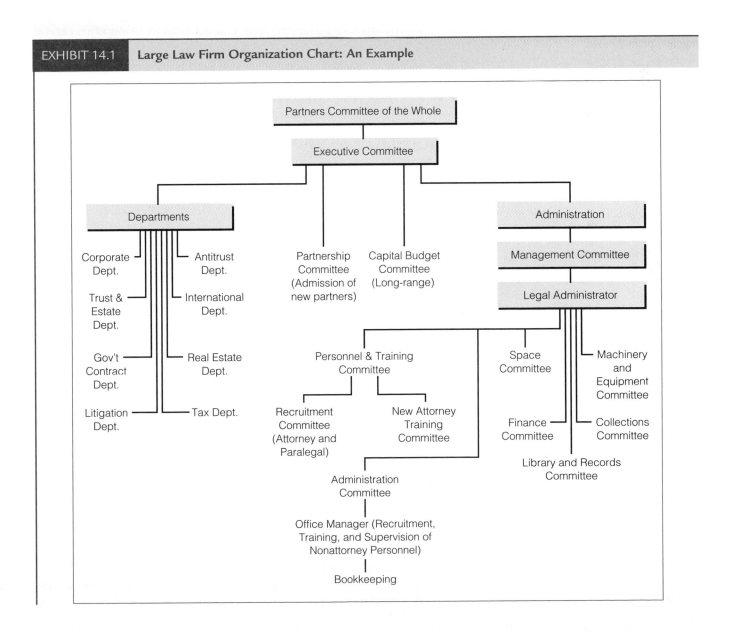

A large partnership can include a number of different categories of attorneys, the most common of which are:

- Partners
- Associates
- Staff attorneys
- Of counsel
- Contract attorneys

### 1. Partners

The founding partners contribute the capital that is needed to create the firm and to expand it as needed. They share the profits and losses of the firm pursuant to an elaborate partnership agreement. In a system referred to as "eat what you kill," the amount paid to partners often depends in large part on how much new business they generate for the firm. (Any attorney who attracts business is called a **rainmaker**.) Partners decide how the firm should be managed; when to take on new partners; whether to merge with another firm; what attorneys, paralegals, and other employees to hire; etc. Most of this is done through a variety of administrative staff. In short, the partners own the firm. A firm may have different categories of partners (for example, senior partner and junior partner) depending on such factors as the amount of capital the attorney contributed to the firm and how involved he or she is in the firm's management. As we will see, a distinction also exists between equity and nonequity partners.

Generally, partners are not on salary in the traditional sense, although they do receive a periodic **draw**, which is an advance against profits (or net income) in some firms and an overhead expense in others.

### 2. Associates

**Associates** are attorney employees of the firm who are hoping to become partners. Often they are hired right out of law school while studying for the bar examination. As students, they may have worked for the firm as a law clerk. Other associates, however, are hired from other law firms. They are known as **lateral hires**. (When partners and paralegals switch law firms, they also are referred to as lateral hires.) After a certain number of years at the firm, e.g., seven, associates are usually considered for partnership. If they are *passed over* for partner, they often leave the firm to practice elsewhere, although a few may be invited to stay as a **senior associate**. This person, in effect, becomes a permanent associate.

Some firms are moving away from the "up-or-out" system that adds great tension to the ranks of associates. To encourage good people to stay, the firms have created different tiers of partners. For example, a firm might create the category of **nonequity partner** (also called an income partner), to be distinguished from an **equity partner** (also called a capital partner). An equity partner is a full partner in the sense of owning the firm and sharing in its profits and losses. At the other end of the partner spectrum is the nonequity or income partner who has not made, or who does not aspire to become, a full partner. In effect, he or she is a permanent associate with a more inviting title.

Hence paralegals are not the only workers who are concerned by a lack of career ladders in the legal profession. As we saw in chapters 1 and 3, the paralegal field has been slowly developing career ladders, e.g., from case clerk to paralegal to senior paralegal to paralegal supervisor. Attorneys also want career ladders beyond the traditional associate-partner regime. Equally slowly, the profession has been responding to this need.

### 3. Staff Attorneys

**Staff attorneys** (sometimes called second-tier attorneys) are employees hired with the understanding that they will never be considered for partnership. This is what distinguishes them from associates.

### 4. Of Counsel

There is no fixed definition of this category of attorney. He or she is not a full partner or associate but has a special relationship at the firm. An attorney who is **of counsel** may be a semiretired partner or may work on a mixture of firm cases and his or her own

---

**rainmaker** An attorney who brings fee-generating cases into the office due to his or her extensive contacts and/or reputation as a skilled attorney.

**draw** A partner's advance against profits or net income.

**associate** An attorney employee of a partnership who hopes eventually to become a partner.

**lateral hire** Anyone hired from another law firm.

**senior associate** An attorney who has been passed over for partner status but who remains at the firm.

**nonequity partner** A special category of partner who does not own the firm in the sense of an equity or capital partner.

**equity partner** A full owner-partner of a law firm.

**staff attorney** A full-time attorney employee who has no expectation of becoming a full partner.

**of counsel** An attorney who is semiretired or has some other special status in the law firm.

cases. Not all firms use the title "of counsel." Some prefer "special counsel" or simply "counsel."

### 5. Contract Attorneys

**Contract attorneys** (sometimes called project attorneys) are hired when the firm has a temporary shortage of attorneys or needs expertise in a certain area for a limited period. Often paid on an hourly basis, the contract attorney is not a full-time employee.

### PROFESSIONAL CORPORATION

In most states, it is possible for attorneys to incorporate their practice of law as a **professional corporation** (P.C.), e.g., "Jamison & Jamison, P.C." From a tax and estate-planning perspective, it is often more advantageous to organize as a corporation than as a partnership. Another important feature of a corporation is **limited liability**. As we saw earlier, if the owner of a business has limited liability, his or her business debts are satisfied out of business assets, not out of personal assets. (If the owner has personal liability, his or her personal as well as business assets can be reached to satisfy business debts.) Like any corporation, a professional corporation has shareholders who are the owners of the corporation. The shareholders elect a board of directors who in turn appoint officers. Shareholders, directors, and officers of a professional corporation must be attorneys. The day-to-day operation of a professional corporation is practically identical to the operation of a traditional partnership. A client would hardly notice the difference.

### LIMITED LIABILITY ENTITY

Recently, a new form of organization has been developed—the **limited liability entity.** It can be a limited liability company (LLC) or a limited liability partnership (LLP). These entities are hybrid structures in that they combine features of a corporation and a partnership. Among the advantages of limited liability entities are special tax treatment and a limitation on the liability of one owner or partner for the wrongdoing of another owner or partner.

### CORPORATE LEGAL DEPARTMENT

Many large corporations have a **corporate legal department** (sometimes called the *law department*) headed by a **general counsel** (sometimes called *corporate counsel*) who may also be a vice-president of the company. Other attorneys in this office can include deputy or associate general counsel, senior attorneys, staff attorneys, etc. They are the in-house attorneys who handle the day-to-day tasks of advising the company on legal matters. They have one client—the corporation that hires them and that pays them a salary. Frequently, paralegals work with these attorneys. Other personnel may include legal administrators, legal secretaries, word processing and data processing operators, clerks, librarians, and record managers. There are, of course, no client fees. Funds to operate the department come directly from the corporate treasury. When expertise is needed, such as trial experience in a certain specialty, the general counsel will hire "outside" attorneys from law firms if the expertise is not available "in-house."

**contract attorney** An attorney hired to work for a relatively short period of time, usually on specific cases or projects.

**professional corporation** A law office that is organized as a corporation rather than as a partnership or sole proprietorship.

**limited liability** Liability that can be satisfied only out of business assets; liability that cannot be satisfied out of personal assets; restricted liability.

**limited liability entity** A company or partnership that is given special tax treatment and in which there are limits on the liability of one owner or partner for the wrongdoing of another owner or partner.

**corporate legal department** A law office within a corporation containing salaried attorneys (called in-house attorneys) who advise and represent the corporation.

**general counsel** The chief attorney in a corporate law department.

---

Section B

# The Legal Administrator and the Legal Assistant Manager

The practice of law is a profession, but it is also a business. The larger the practice, the more likely its business component will be managed by individuals whose main or sole responsibility is administration. Although the owners of a law firm have ultimate responsibility for administration, they often delegate this responsibility to others. For example, there may be a **managing partner**, often an attorney with a small case load or none at all. More and more firms are hiring new categories of management personnel who are not

**managing partner** A partner whose primary responsibility is management of the law firm.

**legal administrator** An individual, usually a nonattorney, who has responsibility for the day-to-day administration of a law office.

**legal assistant manager** A paralegal who helps recruit, train, and supervise all paralegals in a law office.

attorneys. We will focus on two such individuals: the **legal administrator** and the **legal assistant manager**. Each has a national association: the Association of Legal Administrators (*www.alanet.org*) and the Legal Assistant Management Association (*www.lamanet.org.*) One way to obtain an overview of law office management is to examine the job description of the legal administrator and the legal assistant manager.

The legal administrator works under the supervision of the managing partner or of an executive committee of the firm. The range of this person's responsibility, and of the business component of the practice of law, can be seen in the job description in exhibit 14.2.

| EXHIBIT 14.2 | Legal Administrator: Job Description (Association of Legal Administrators) |
|---|---|

**Summary of Responsibilities**

The legal administrator manages the planning, marketing, and business functions, as well as the overall operations, of a law office. He or she reports to the managing partner or the executive committee and participates in management meetings. In addition to having general responsibility for financial planning and controls, personnel administration (including compensation), systems, and physical facilities, the legal administrator also identifies and plans for the changing needs of the organization, shares responsibility with the appropriate partners for strategic planning, practice management, and marketing, and contributes to cost-effective management throughout the organization.

**WHETHER DIRECTLY OR THROUGH A MANAGEMENT TEAM, THE LEGAL ADMINISTRATOR IS RESPONSIBLE FOR MOST OR ALL OF THE FOLLOWING:**

**Financial Management:**
- ☐ Planning
- ☐ Forecasting
- ☐ Budgeting
- ☐ Variance analysis
- ☐ Profitability analysis
- ☐ Financial reporting
- ☐ Operations analysis
- ☐ General ledger accounting
- ☐ Rate analysis
- ☐ Billing and collections
- ☐ Cash flow control
- ☐ Banking relationships
- ☐ Investment
- ☐ Tax planning and reporting
- ☐ Trust accounting
- ☐ Payroll and pension plans
- ☐ Other related functions

**Systems Management:**
- ☐ Systems analysis
- ☐ Operational audits
- ☐ Procedures manual
- ☐ Cost-benefit analysis
- ☐ Computer systems design
- ☐ Programming and systems development
- ☐ Information services
- ☐ Records and library management
- ☐ Office automation
- ☐ Document construction systems

- ☐ Information storage and retrieval
- ☐ Telecommunications
- ☐ Litigation support
- ☐ Conflict-of-interest docket systems
- ☐ Legal practice systems
- ☐ Other related services

**Facilities Management:**
- ☐ Lease negotiations
- ☐ Space planning and design
- ☐ Office renovation
- ☐ Purchasing and inventory control
- ☐ Reprographics
- ☐ Reception/switchboard services
- ☐ Telecommunications
- ☐ Mail messenger services
- ☐ Other related functions

**Human Resource Management:**
- ☐ Recruitment, selection, and placement
- ☐ Orientation, training, and development
- ☐ Performance evaluation
- ☐ Salary and benefits administration
- ☐ Employee relations
- ☐ Motivation and counseling
- ☐ Discipline
- ☐ Termination
- ☐ Workers' compensation
- ☐ Personnel data systems
- ☐ Organization analysis
- ☐ Job design, development of job descriptions
- ☐ Resource allocation
- ☐ Other human resource management functions for the legal and support staff

| EXHIBIT 14.2 | Legal Administrator: Job Description (Association of Legal Administrators)—*continued* |
|---|---|

**AS A MEMBER OF THE LEGAL ORGANIZATION'S MANAGEMENT TEAM, THE LEGAL ADMINISTRATOR MANAGES AND/OR CONTRIBUTES SIGNIFICANTLY TO THE FOLLOWING:**

**General Management:**
- ☐ Policymaking
- ☐ Strategic and tactical planning
- ☐ Business development
- ☐ Risk management
- ☐ Quality control
- ☐ Organizational development
- ☐ Other general management functions

**Practice Management:**
- ☐ Attorney recruiting
- ☐ Attorney training and development
- ☐ Legal assistant supervision
- ☐ Work-product quality control
- ☐ Professional standards
- ☐ Substantive practice systems
- ☐ Other related functions

**Marketing:**
- ☐ Management of client-profitability analysis
- ☐ Forecasting of business opportunities
- ☐ Planning client development
- ☐ Marketing legal services: enhancement of the firm's visibility and image in the desired markets

**Job Requirements**

**Knowledge:** Has familiarity with legal or other professional service organizations, and experience in managing business operations, including planning, marketing, financial and personnel administration, and management of professionals.

**Skills and Abilities:** Able to identify and analyze complex issues and problems in management, finance, and human relations, and to recommend and implement solutions. Able to manage office functions economically and efficiently, and to organize work, establish priorities, and maintain good interpersonal relations and communications with attorneys and support staff. Excellent supervisory and leadership skills, as well as skills in written and oral communication. Demonstrated willingness and ability to delegate.

**Education:** Graduation from a recognized college or university with major coursework in business administration, finance, data processing, or personnel management, or comparable work experience.

Again, the job description of the legal administrator in exhibit 14.2 fits an individual who works for a law office that is fairly large. The support staff for such an office can also be quite extensive. Here are some examples:[3]

**Administrative Support Staff in a Large Law Office**

| | |
|---|---|
| Legal Administrator | Secretaries |
| Legal Assistant Manager | Data Processing Operators |
| Personnel Manager | Word Processing Supervisor |
| Records Information Manager | Word Processors |
| Employee Benefits Manager | Proofreaders |
| Recruiter | Docket Clerks |
| Director of Marketing | Computer Specialists |
| Facilities Manager | Equipment Managers |
| Risk Manager | File Room Clerks |
| Office Manager | Librarian |
| Financial Manager | Library Aides |
| Credit/Collections Manager | Messengers/Pages |
| Chief Financial Officer/Comptroller | Copy Room Clerks |
| Bookkeepers | Mail Clerks |
| Analysts | Purchasing Clerks |
| Payroll Specialists | Receptionists |
| Accounts Payable Clerk | Telephone Operators |
| Accounts Receivable Clerk | Reservation Clerks |
| Time and Billing Assistants | |

Prominent on this list is the legal assistant manager, whose job description is presented in exhibit 14.3.

| EXHIBIT 14.3 | Legal Assistant Manager: Job Description (Legal Assistant Management Association) |
|---|---|

**POSITION DESCRIPTION**

POSITION TITLE:        Legal Assistant Manager

DEPARTMENT:          Legal Assistant Administration

DATE:                6/01

A.  Summary

Responsible for supervision of the legal assistant staff, including recruiting, coordinating work assignments, and administering all firm policies regarding the legal assistant staff.

B.  Primary Duties and Responsibilities

■  Recruits, hires, and orients new and temporary legal assistants. When appropriate, assists in disciplinary actions and terminations.
■  Provides continuing legal education (CLE) by presenting in-house training programs and suggesting attendance at outside seminars.
■  Assigns projects to legal assistants, coordinates work flow, and monitors billable and nonbillable hours.
■  Prepares financial and statistical reports including a yearly budget for the Legal Assistant Program, periodic employee status reports, work assignment statistics, and profitability analyses.
■  Participates in periodic and yearly salary reviews and evaluations of legal assistants.
■  Participates in long-range planning of the firm, with a focus on legal assistant staffing.

C.  Secondary Duties and Responsibilities

■  Performs other administrative duties, including solving personnel problems; proposing new legal assistant policies and administering existing firm policies; complying with labor laws; and acting as a liaison between the legal assistants, attorneys, and the firm's Legal Assistant Committee to promote effective utilization of legal assistants.

D.  Reporting Relationship

1.  Reports directly to:     Legal Assistant Committee [or to Personnel Director, Executive Director of Administration, etc.].
2.  Also works with:        Internal—Litigation Support Staff; Personnel Manager, various personnel at all levels. External—Consultants, placement offices, vendors.
3.  Supervises:             Directly—All legal assistants, secretary. Indirectly—Project clerks, other nonattorney personnel on a project-oriented basis.

E.  Minimum Qualifications

1.  Education: College Degree, Post-graduate degree or paralegal certificate preferred.
2.  Experience: At least 3–5 years' experience as legal assistant. Previous management background preferred.
3.  Special Skills: Computer skills, public speaking skills, financial reporting skills.

## Section C
# EXPENSES

How does a large law firm spend the fee income that it receives? A number of organizations conduct surveys to answer this question. One of the largest is the Altman Weil Survey of Law Firm Economics. Its 2001 survey of 399 law firms covered just under 26,000 attorneys and 6,000 paralegals.[4] The average gross receipts of the law firms for the year were $338,167. To obtain these receipts, here are the billing rates and hours worked for the major fee earners in the firms:

*Standard hourly billing rates*

- $246 billed by equity partners/shareholders
- $164 billed by associates
- $83 billed by legal assistants
- $104 billed by paralegal supervisors

*Average annual billable hours worked*

- 1,754 by equity partners/shareholders
- 1,838 by associates
- 1,400 by legal assistants
- 1,486 by paralegal supervisors

How did the firms spend the $338,167 that they received? On average, the law firms spent:

- $8,460 per attorney for equipment. (This constituted 2.5% of gross receipts.)
- $25,629 per attorney for occupancy expenses. (This constituted 7.6% of gross receipts.)
- $5,865 per attorney for promotional expenses. (This constituted 1.7% of gross receipts.)
- $4,184 per attorney for library/reference expenses. (This constituted 1.2% of gross receipts.)
- $14,923 per attorney for paralegal expenses. (This constituted 4.4% of gross receipts.)
- $50,842 per attorney for staff expenses. (This constituted 15% of gross receipts.)

- $3,014 per attorney for malpractice insurance and settlement of malpractice claims. (This constituted .9% of gross receipts.)

These and other expenses totaled $144,568 per firm. The income available to the attorneys in the firm after paying these expenses was $193,599 (calculated by substracting $144,568 from gross receipts of $338,167). Attorney income constituted 57.2% of gross receipts. (See exhibit 14.4.)

| EXHIBIT 14.4 | Average Expenses and Attorney Income as a Percentage of Gross Receipts |
| --- | --- |

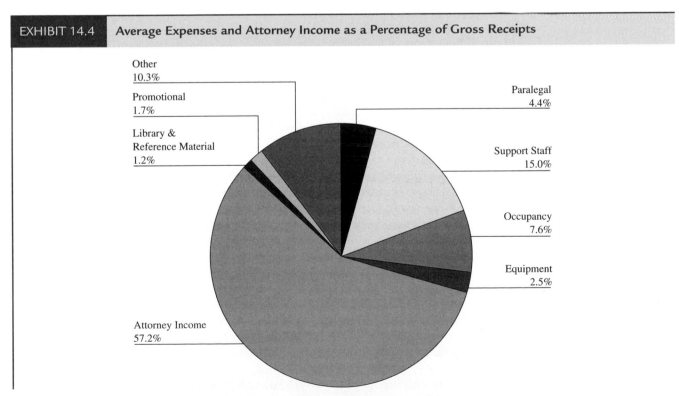

Other 10.3%
Promotional 1.7%
Library & Reference Material 1.2%
Paralegal 4.4%
Support Staff 15.0%
Occupancy 7.6%
Equipment 2.5%
Attorney Income 57.2%

Source: Altman Weil, Inc., *2001 Survey of Law Firm Economics*. (www.altmanweil.com/home.cfm)

## Section D
# TIMEKEEPING

Abraham Lincoln's famous statement that a "lawyer's time is his stock in trade" is still true today. Effective **timekeeping** is critical to the success of a law firm. In some firms, it is an obsession, as typified by the following story. A senior partner in a very prestigious Wall Street law firm walked down the corridor to visit the office of another senior partner. Upon entering the room, he was startled to find his colleague on the floor writhing in pain, apparently due to a heart attack. Standing there, he could think of only one thing to say to him: "Howard, are your time sheets in?"[5]

In some firms, the pressures of the clock on timekeepers (e.g., attorneys and paralegals) can be enormous:

> [Y]oung lawyers often are shocked to discover their new employer's time expectations. Many firms in major cities require as many as 2,400 billable hours per year. When one considers that many full-time employees outside of the law only *work* 2,000 hours per year, the time commitment required by these firms is staggering[6]

> The cry for billable hours is thought by many to be at the heart of much of the problem. Many legal assistants as well as attorneys have quotas of billable hours. Zlaket [the President of the State Bar of Arizona] stated that some firms require 2,200 hours a year and he deems this to be outrageous. He suggested that this only leads to padding of bills and time sheets, and it leads to unnecessary work that will be paid by somebody.[7]

The ethical dimensions of this problem are considered in chapter 5. Here, our concern is the administration of the timekeeping and billing system.

To gain an understanding of how a timekeeping and billing system might work in many large law firms, we will now trace the accounting route taken by a client's *case* (sometimes called a *matter*) within a law firm. After the initial client interview, the accounting starting point can be a **new file worksheet** (see exhibit 14.5). It is also sometimes referred to as a *new matter sheet* or a *new business sheet*. The new file worksheet becomes the source document for the creation of all the necessary accounting records involved in working on a new client case or matter. As the example in exhibit 14.5 demonstrates, the new file worksheet can also be used to record data that will help identify possible conflicts of interest. (See chapter 5 for the ethical rules on conflicts of interest.)

As timekeepers, attorneys and paralegals must keep an account of the time they spend on behalf of a client. Time records are needed for accurate billing of every client who is charged by the hour. Of course, all clients do not pay by the hour. A firm may be charging its client a flat fee under arrangements we will examine later in the chapter. Yet even in flat-fee cases, there are management reasons for keeping accurate time records. One of the ways to determine whether a particular case or client is profitable is to know how much time was needed to complete the work involved. Accurate time records are valuable management tools even in corporations where the corporate law office is financed out of the corporate treasury rather than out of fees. Decisions on whether to hire additional staff or to lay off present staff depend, in part, on knowing how much time is needed to complete certain tasks and who is and is not meeting those expectations.

As we saw in chapter 1, a losing party can be forced to pay the attorney and paralegal fees of the winning party in special statutory fee cases such as those alleging civil rights or environmental violations. To claim such fees, the winning side must be prepared to give the court detailed records of the time spent on these cases.

There are two main ways that time is recorded: by using paper forms or by using the computer. Some firms initially ask their timekeepers to record their time on paper forms, which are then coded into (i.e., transferred to) the computer for assessment and billing.

A commonly used paper form is the **daily time sheet** (see exhibit 14.6). This form becomes the journal from which all time entries are posted to individual clients. Suppose,

---

**timekeeping** Recording time spent on a client matter for purposes of billing and productivity assessment. Individuals who must record their time (e.g., attorneys and paralegals) are called timekeepers.

**new file worksheet** A form used by some law firms that is the source document for the creation of all necessary accounting records that are needed when a law firm begins working on a new client case or matter.

**daily time sheet** A paper form on which timekeepers record how much time they spend on particular client matters.

**EXHIBIT 14.5** | New File Worksheet

## NEW CLIENT/MATTER/CONFLICT FORM

Client Number:  Matter Number:  *Client Phone:*
*Client Fax:*
*Client E-Mail Address:*

Client Name and Address:  Billing Name and Address:

**Attn:**  **Attn:**

| Biller | | | Originator | | | Responsible | | |
|---|---|---|---|---|---|---|---|---|
| Name | Net ID | Pct | Name | Net ID | Pct | Name | Net ID | Pct |
| | | % | | | % | | | % |
| | | % | | | % | | | % |
| | | % | | | % | | | % |
| | | % | | | % | | | % |
| (Percent must = 100%) | | 100% | | | 100% | | | 100% |

*MATTER NAME:*
*CASE SYNOPSIS/COMMENTS:*
*PARENT/RELATED CLIENT:*
*CLIENT'S REF. NUMBER:*
*BUSINESS TYPE:*
*PRACTICE GROUP CODE:*
*INVOICE STYLE CODE:*
*COUNTRY CODE:*
*SIC CODE:*
*CASE CODE:*

[NONSTANDARD FEE ARRANGEMENTS (OTHER THAN CONTINGENT) REQUIRE THE WRITTEN APPROVAL OF THE PRACTICE GROUP CHAIR. CONTINGENT FEE ARRANGEMENTS REQUIRE THE COMPLETION OF A CONTINGENT FEE INTAKE INFORMATION FORM AND WRITTEN APPROVAL OF THE CONTINGENT FEE COMMITTEE.]

| FEE ARRANGEMENT | BILLING CYCLE |
|---|---|
| | |
| | |

Billing Attorney: _____ Practice Group Chair: _____

September 17, 2001  Completed by : _____ /

## CONFLICT CHECK

Billing Attorney:
Client Name:
Client Number, if not new:

Matter Name:

Matter Address (if matter name is a company different from client:

Standard Industrial Code (SIC), if known:

**Case Synopsis/Comments:** _____

These questions are designed to identify potential conflicts of interest. Examples given are for illustration only. Please be complete in responcing to the questions. Additional Name/Relationship information may be added after the form is assembled by adding rows to the existing table.

CLIENT IDENTIFICATION (new clients only):
If the client is a corporation, please provide, to the extent possible, the name(s) of all corporate parents and subsidiaries (including sister subsidiaries):
If there is a different "real party in interest," e.g., the beneficiary of our trustee or other fiduciary client, or the client of the law firm or accounting firm for whom we provide local or special representation, please provide, to the extent possible, the name of each such person or entity.

POTENTIALLY ADVERSE PARTIES:
In **litigation**, please identify, to the extent possible, all other parties, including co-defendants, co-plaintiffs, intervenors and third parties.
In **enforcement of remedies cases**, please identify, to the extent possible, all other lien claimants, etc.
In **commercial or corporate transactions**, please identify, to the extent possible, all potentially adverse individuals or entities, such as the purchaser when we represent the seller; the lessee when we draft a lease for the lessor, etc.
Please identify, to the extent possible, all other potentially adverse individuals or entities.

\*\*\*\*\*\*\*\*\*\*\*\*\*\*\*\*\*\*\*\*\*\*\*\*\*\*\*\*\*\*\*\*\*\*\*\*\*\*\*\*\*\*\*\*\*\*\*\*\*\*\*\*\*\*\*\*\*\*\*

FOR ADMINISTRATIVE USE

**New Business Department:**

_____ Conflict check performed and report attached — no potential conflicts found.

Signature _____

Date _____

OR

_____ Potential conflicts found and report sent to Billing Attorney.

Signature _____

Date _____

**Billing Attorney:**

Sign only _after_ resolving potential conflicts and forward to New Business Department.

Billing Attorney's Signature _____

Printed Name _____

Date _____

| EXHIBIT 14.6 | Daily Time Sheet |
|---|---|

**DAILY SERVICE REPORT OF:**                                                                 **DATE:**

| | | | | | | | | |
|---|---|---|---|---|---|---|---|---|
| ANS | –Answer | DEPO | –Deposition | K | –Contract | O | –Order | RES | –Research |
| APP | –Appearance or Attending | DIC | –Dictation | L | –Legal | OP | –Opinion | REV | –Revision |
| ARG | –Argue or Argument | DOC | –Document | LT | –Letter to | P | –Preparation | S | –Settlement |
| BR | –Brief | DR | –Drafting | LF | –Letter from | PL | –Plaintiff | TF | –Telephone from |
| COMP | –Complaint | F | –Facts | MT | –Memorandum to | PR | –Praecipe | TT | –Telephone to |
| CW | –Conference–Office | FL | –File | MF | –Memorandum from | PRT | –Pretrial | TR | –Trial |
| CWO | –Conference–Outside Office | H | –Hearing | MOT | –Motion | R | –Reading and Review | TRV | –Travel |
| DEF | –Defendant | INV | –Investigation | NEG | –Negotiation | REL | –Release | W | –Witness |
| DEM | –Demurrer | INT | –Interview | | | | | | |

| CLIENT (State billing division or department) | MATTER | DESCRIPTION OF WORK (Use abbreviations above) | TIME | |
|---|---|---|---|---|
| | | | Hours | 10ths |
| | | | | |
| | | | | |
| | | | | |
| | | | | |
| | | | | |
| | | | | |
| | | | | |
| | | | | |
| | | | | |
| | | | | |

for example, that a paralegal spends some time summarizing or digesting a deposition. Using the abbreviations at the top of the daily time sheet, the "Description of Work" in the third column of exhibit 14.6 might be "digesting DEPO."

Note that the last column of exhibit 14.6 asks for the amount of time taken for each task. Law firms often use tenths of an hour (increments of six minutes) as the base unit for the measurement of time, although a few firms use one-fourth of an hour as their base. Time is recorded in fractions of an hour as follows:

| Tenths of an Hour as Base | One-Fourth of an Hour as Base |
|---|---|
| 6 minutes = .10 of an hour | 15 minutes = .25 of an hour |
| 12 minutes = .20 of an hour | 30 minutes = .50 of an hour |
| 18 minutes = .30 of an hour | 45 minutes = .75 of an hour |
| 24 minutes = .40 of an hour | 60 minutes = 1.0 hour |
| 30 minutes = .50 of an hour | |
| 36 minutes = .60 of an hour | |
| 42 minutes = .70 of an hour | |
| 48 minutes = .80 of an hour | |
| 54 minutes = .90 of an hour | |
| 60 minutes = 1.0 hour | |

If, for example, the paralegal spends an hour and 30 minutes digesting the deposition in an office that records time in tenths of an hour, his or her time for this task would be entered as 1.50. Suppose the paralegal spent an hour and 44 minutes on the project. Forty-four minutes does not evenly divide into tenths of an hour. In most offices, timekeepers are instructed to round up or down to the nearest increment. The nearest 6-minute increment is 42 minutes. Hence an hour and 44 minutes would be recorded as 1.70. Other office policies may also exist on how to record travel time or short telephone conversations.

If computers are used for this task, time and billing software automatically records time once the timekeeper clicks the start-and-stop buttons on the screen. Menus on the screen allow the timekeeper to tell the computer the client or matter being worked on, whether the time is billable, and the nature of the work being performed. For an example of such a screen, see exhibit 14.7. Time and billing software also helps the office generate the bills and administrative reports that we will examine later in the chapter.

If you have never kept close track of your time, you will find that the task requires a great deal of effort and discipline; it does not come naturally to most of us. The key to per-

| EXHIBIT 14.7 | Computer-Assisted Timekeeping |
| --- | --- |

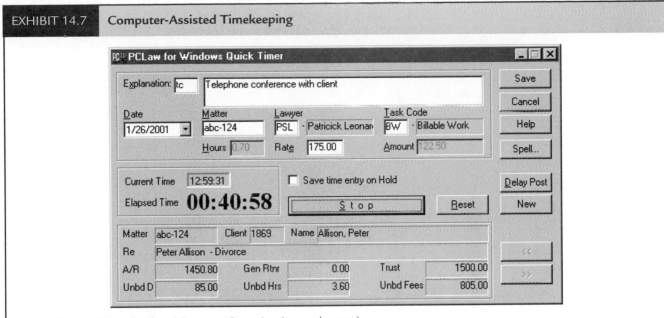

Source: Courtesy PCLaw by Alumni Computer Group, Inc. (www.pclaw.com)

forming the task effectively is to do it consistently and comprehensively until it becomes second nature.

Tory Barcott, a certified legal assistant in Anchorage, makes a number of important points about timekeeping:

> It "sometimes scares me a little to contemplate clients paying" $10.00 or more "for every six minutes of our time." To survive in this world, the legal assistant must possess the accuracy and efficiency of a Swiss watch. "I keep one of those small, cheap, adhesive digital clocks where it can't be missed or covered with paperwork. Sticking it to my phone, in the middle of my desk, works best for me. The first step in performing any task is to record the time on my time sheet. I do this before retrieving the file, making a phone call," or going to meet a supervising attorney. The clock is also helpful in recording the time when a task is interrupted by anything unrelated to the current client matter. "I take notes on the start and stop times exactly as displayed on my digital clock." Some Saturdays, while absently attending to household chores, I'll glance at the clock and catch myself thinking, "that floor took only 0.4 to clean." This is a sure sign that the discipline of timekeeping has been internalized![8]

Time spent by paralegals and attorneys on tasks for which clients cannot be asked to pay is called **nonbillable time**. Examples of such tasks include general file maintenance, learning to operate a new data processing program that the firm is implementing throughout the office, helping to develop standard forms, and taking lunch breaks. **Pro bono** work is also nonbillable. This consists of legal services provided without cost, usually for an **indigent** individual or for a public interest organization such as the Red Cross or a local group of community artists. (Someone is indigent if he or she does not have sufficient funds to hire a private attorney.) A firm's regular clients cannot be asked to pay for pro bono work the office does for others.

The firm needs to know how many billable and nonbillable hours paralegals and attorneys have accumulated over a particular period of time. Computer programs are very helpful in allowing timekeepers such as paralegals and attorneys to indicate which tasks fall into which category. They can also produce clear graphs that present this information in summary form. An example is the chart in exhibit 14.8.

Law firms also set *targets* on how many billable hours they hope to obtain from partners, associates, and paralegals. Exhibit 14.9 shows different formats that computers can help generate to provide a graphic presentation of these expectations.

**nonbillable time** Time spent on tasks for which clients cannot be asked to pay.

**pro bono** Performed for the public good without fee or compensation (pro bono publico).

**indigent** Impoverished; without funds to hire a private attorney.

| EXHIBIT 14.8 | Chart Showing Billable versus Unbillable Hours for Each Timekeeper |
|---|---|

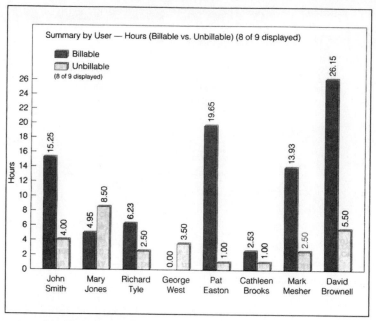

Source: Courtesy Timeslips Corporation (www.timeslips.com)

## Section E
## KINDS OF FEES

Most fees are based on the amount of time spent in providing legal services. Yet there are alternatives. Here is an overview of fee arrangements.

### CLOCK-BASED FEES

**1. Hourly Rate**

An hourly rate fee is based on the number of attorney hours worked. Paralegals have a separate hourly rate covering their time.

**2. Blended Hourly Rate**

A partner and an associate who have different hourly rates may work on the same case. The bill to the client could break the fee down by rates. For example: $600 for two hours spent by Smith (a partner who bills at $300 an hour) and $450 for three hours spent by Jacob (an associate who bills at $150 an hour). An alternative is to charge a **blended hourly rate**. This is a single hourly rate that is based on a blend or mix of partner and associate rates. For example, to calculate the blended hourly rate, the firm might take the average of the normal rates charged by the partner and associate working on the case. In some states, the firm is allowed to add a paralegal's time into this blended hourly rate.

**blended hourly rate** A single hourly rate based on a blend or mix of the rates normally charged by different individuals, e.g., a partner, a senior associate, a junior associate, and sometimes a paralegal.

### ALTERNATIVES

Many individuals are not happy with billing that is controlled by the clock, as reflected in the following comments made by a business client who often hires attorneys:

[We] have to look not only at the service and quality of law firms with which we do business but also at the linkage between price and performance. Hourly billing provides no such linkage. It is

| EXHIBIT 14.9 | Billable Hour Expectations: Timekeeper Productivity Report |
|---|---|

### AVERAGE BILLABLE HOURS BY TIMEKEEPER

|  | Jan | Feb | Mar | Apr | May | Jun |
|---|---|---|---|---|---|---|
| Partners | 128 | 132 | 127 | 134 | 144 | 141 |
| Associates | 170 | 163 | 175 | 170 | 159 | 179 |
| Paralegals | 118 | 111 | 120 | 119 | 121 | 108 |

### YEAR-TO-DATE SUMMARY

|  | Target | Average Year-to-Date | Variance |
|---|---|---|---|
| Partners | 140 | 134 | −4% |
| Associates | 165 | 169 | +2% |
| Paralegals | 125 | 116 | −7% |

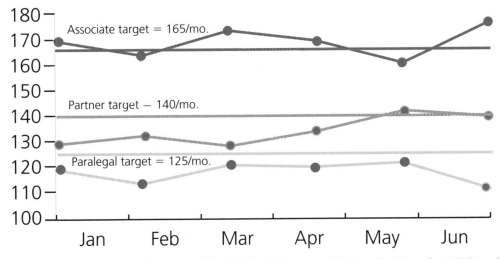

**Source:** Jeff Coburn, *Creating Financial Reports That Partners Will Read*, 14 Legal Management 40 (November/December, 1995), reprinted with permission from the Association of Legal Administrators, Vernon Hills, Illinois (www.alanet.org).

an accounting device. There is no credible economic theory underlying the hourly billing method, and for that reason, we no longer accept it as the sole, or even predominant, method of pricing legal services. In fact, hourly billing pushes the economic incentives in the wrong direction—weakening rather than strengthening the bonds between performance and pay. It also pushes law firms to near-obsession with billable hours. And this in turn supports the great unwritten rule of all law practices: those who want to get ahead must tally up the hours. This is first and foremost dubious economics. The number of hours spent on a matter is no measure of productivity. Productivity is better measured by results, including both outcome and time-frame. Linking the economic structure . . . to true measures of productivity—or value—will benefit both the firms and the client.[9]

Although billing by the hour is likely to remain an important method of financing legal services in most kinds of cases, there are alternatives, as suggested by this client. These

**value billing** A method of charging for legal services based on factors such as the complexity of the case or the results achieved rather than solely on the number of hours spent on the client's case.

alternatives are either to abandon the clock or to use it as only one factor in determining the fee.

A great deal of discussion centers on what is called **value billing**. This means that the fee is not based solely on the time required to perform the work but also takes into account factors such as the following.[10]

- The nature of the services provided.
- The complexity, novelty, and difficulty of the question.
- The time pressure under which the services were provided.
- The time limitations imposed by the client.
- The amount of responsibility assumed by the firm.
- The extent to which the services provided precluded the firm from taking other clients.
- The amount of money involved in the matter.
- The nature and length of the firm's relationship with the client.
- The efficiency with which the services were performed.
- The results achieved.

Using factors such as these, a number of different fee arrangements have been devised. Here is an overview of these arrangements, some of which overlap.

### 1. Fixed Fee

**fixed fee** A flat fee for services regardless of the amount of time needed to complete the task.

A **fixed fee** is a flat fee for the service—a set figure regardless of the amount of time needed to complete the service. The fixed fee can be a specific sum or a percentage of the recovery.

### 2. Capped Fee

**capped fee** An hourly rate leading to a final bill that will not exceed a predetermined amount.

Under a **capped fee**, the firm bills an hourly rate, but the total bill will not exceed a predetermined budgeted amount.

### 3. Task-Based Billing

**bundled legal services** All tasks needed to represent a client; all-inclusive legal services.

**pro se** Self-representation.

**unbundled legal services** Discrete task representation.

**task-based billing** Charging a specific amount for each legal task performed.

Most attorney services consist of a mix or bundle of tasks such as legal advice, investigation, document preparation, document review, document filing, legal research, negotiation, and court representation. Collectively, these tasks are called **bundled legal services**. Suppose, however, that a client does not want the full range of attorney services. The client might be representing him or herself (**pro se**) but would like the attorney to perform specific tasks such as reviewing a document the client has prepared or making a phone call on the client's behalf. Attorneys who agree to provide discrete task representation of this kind are providing **unbundled legal services**. Charging for such services is called **task-based billing**. (It is also referred to as *unit billing* or *project billing*.) There are different ways the attorneys can charge clients for such services:

- A set or fixed fee per task, regardless of how long it takes to perform the task,
- The same hourly rate the attorney charges for full (bundled) legal services, or
- A special hourly rate referred to as an unbundled rate.

Task-based billing for legal services is becoming increasingly popular as more consumers use the Internet to find attorneys willing to provide such services.

### 4. Hourly Plus Fixed Fee

**hourly plus fixed fee** An hourly rate charged until the nature and scope of the legal problem are known, at which time fixed fees are charged for services provided thereafter.

With an **hourly plus fixed fee**, the firm charges an hourly rate until the nature and scope of the legal problem are identified; thereafter, a fixed fee is charged for services provided.

### 5. Volume Discounts

The hourly or fixed fee might be reduced if the client gives the office a large amount of business, particularly when the office is able to reduce its own costs by standardization of work. A bill reduced for such reasons is called a **discounted hourly fee** or a volume discount.

### 6. Contingency Billing

The traditional **contingent fee** is a fee that is dependent—contingent—on the outcome of the case. The fee could be a fixed amount (e.g., $25,000) or a percentage (e.g., 33 percent) of the amount the plaintiff wins in the litigation or settlement. This kind of fee is most often used in personal injury litigation. Contingency billing, however, can also be used in many other kinds of cases. Suppose, for example, an attorney is hired to handle a contract dispute the client is having with one of its suppliers. Under a contingent billing arrangement with the attorney, "the law firm takes on part of the risk of the transaction. If the transaction fails to go through, the law firm bills the client either a pre-negotiated sum or a small portion of the actual billable hours. Conversely, if the deal is successful, the firm bills the client either a higher pre-negotiated sum or a premium."[11] A premium is sometimes referred to as **incentive billing** (or a *performance bonus*). The attorney receives an increased fee for achieving an exceptional result such as settling a case for an amount that exceeds a target set by the plaintiff-client and attorney.

Most contingent fees are earned by the plaintiff's attorney. A **defense contingent fee** (also called a *negative contingency*) is a fee for the defendant's attorney that is dependent on the outcome of the case. Most often the fee is a fixed amount.

Contingent fees are not allowed in every case. See chapter 5 for a discussion of when such fees are unethical in criminal and divorce cases.

### 7. Retroactive Negotiated Fee

Occasionally, a client and attorney might agree to finalize the fee *after* the services are provided. This is called a **retroactive negotiated fee**. When the case is over, the attorney and client agree on the value of the services provided and set the fee accordingly.

## Section F
## BILLING

In addition to fees for services, a law firm usually recovers out-of-pocket expenses that the firm incurs while working on the case. Examples include witness fees, long-distance phone calls, and out-of-town travel for the attorney or paralegal. The client also pays **court costs** imposed by the court. They include filing fees, jury fees, and special court taxes. Each time attorneys or paralegals incur such expenses, they often fill out an **expense slip** (see exhibit 14.10), which goes into the office's accounting system. In some cases, a court might order a party to pay court costs incurred by an *opposing* party. For example, if a defendant is forced to litigate what the court determines to be a frivolous claim of the plaintiff, the court might order the plaintiff to pay all court costs associated with the litigation of that claim.

The fees, expenses, and costs to be paid by the client should be spelled out in the **retainer**. Unfortunately, not everyone uses this word in the same way. In a general sense, a retainer is the contract of employment that covers the scope of services to be rendered

---

**discounted hourly fee** An hourly or fixed fee that is reduced because of the volume of business the client gives the office.

**contingent fee** A fee that is dependent on the outcome of the case (the fee is also called a contingency).

**incentive billing** A fee that is increased if a designated target is met; an increased fee for achieving an exceptional result.

**defense contingent fee** A fee received by the defendant's attorney that is dependent on the outcome of the case.

**retroactive negotiated fee** A client bill that is finalized *after* the services are rendered.

**court costs** Charges or fees imposed by the court directly related to litigation in that court.

**expense slip** A form used by an office to indicate that an expense has been incurred for which the client can be billed.

**retainer** (1) A contract between an attorney and a client that covers the scope of services, fees, expenses, and costs of legal services. (2) An amount of money (or other property) paid by a client as a deposit or advance against future fees, expenses, and costs of legal services.

---

| EXHIBIT 14.10 | Example of an Expense Slip |
|---|---|

Client name _____ File number _____
Nature of expense incurred _____
_____

Billable or nonbillable _____
Expense code _____ Date incurred _____ Amount paid or due _____
Name/address of vendor _____
Person incurring the expense _____
Approved by _____

and the fees, expenses, and costs of these services. (For a sample retainer, see exhibit 8.1 in chapter 8.) More specifically, it sometimes refers to an amount of money (or other property) paid by the client as a deposit or advance payment against future fees, expenses, and costs. Additional money is paid only when the deposit or advance runs out. The agreement should specify whether such money or other assets from the client are refundable if the client terminates the relationship because he or she fires the attorney or simply decides not to pursue the matter.

The actual billing process differs from firm to firm, and occasionally differs from case to case within the same firm. Client billing sometimes occurs only after the matter is completed. More commonly, a client is billed monthly, quarterly, or semiannually. An administrator in the firm usually works with the billing attorney to prepare the bill. When a matter is called for billing, the administrator may prepare a billing memorandum (the **draft bill**), which specifies the out-of-pocket expenses and costs incurred by the firm in connection with the matter, plus the amount of time each attorney and paralegal has spent on the matter (along with the billing rate of each). For example:[12]

- *Attorney Jones: $1,000.* This attorney, who has a billing rate of $200 an hour, spent 5 hours on the matter (5 × $200 = $1,000).
- *Attorney Sampson: $1,200.* This attorney, who has a billing rate of $150 an hour, spent 8 hours on the matter (8 × $150 = $1,200).
- *Paralegal Kelly: $600.* This paralegal, who has a billing rate of $60 an hour, spent 10 hours on the matter (10 × $60 = $600).

The billing attorney has three choices: (1) Bill the total of the actual amounts. In our example, this would produce a bill of $2,800 ($1,000 + $1,200 + $600). (2) **Write down** the matter by subtracting a certain amount, e.g., $300. This would produce a bill of $2,500. (3) **Write up** the matter by adding an amount, e.g., $600. This would produce a bill of $3,400. This adjustment downward or upward is known as **valuing the bill**. An increase is sometimes called a *premium adjustment*; a decrease, a *discount adjustment*. The decision to adjust is based on factors such as the potential liability exposure of the firm (leading to a write-up) and the relative inexperience of an attorney or paralegal working on the matter (leading to a write-down). If, for example, recently hired attorneys or paralegals take an unusually long time to complete a task they have not performed before, a write-down may be appropriate so that the client does not have to bear the full cost of their on-the-job training.

See exhibit 14.11 for an example of a bill sent to a client covering work of attorneys and paralegals on a matter.

Of course, not all client bills are paid immediately upon receipt. Collection problems can sometimes be substantial, as we will see later in the chapter when we discuss the aged accounts receivable report.

Furthermore, more and more clients are carefully scrutinizing the bills that they receive. Business clients that frequently hire attorneys may use outside auditors to review attorney bills before paying them. The auditor will look for potential problems that should be brought to the attention of the client. Law Audit Services, for example, reviews an average of $60,000 in bills a day from over 5,100 law firms hired by different insurance companies. Here are some of the more egregious irregularities flagged by this auditor:[13]

- An attorney bills for a 38-hour workday
- An attorney charges 31¢ a mile for a rental car with unlimited mileage
- An attorney bills 4.5 hours to look up addresses at a library

When the law firm employs paralegals, clients sometimes have asked the law firm to explain:

- Why a particular task performed by an attorney (and billed at attorney rates) was not delegated to a paralegal
- Why paralegal fees are sought for clerical tasks performed by the paralegal

Questions such as these are often asked in statutory fee cases in which the court has authority to order the losing side to pay the attorney fees (including paralegal fees) of the winning side. To find out whether these questions have been raised in your state, see the case

---

**draft bill** A billing memorandum prepared by a law office on a particular client case stating expenses, costs, time spent, and billing rates of attorneys and paralegals working on the case.

**write down** Deduct an amount from the bill.

**write up** Add an amount to the bill.

**valuing the bill** Determining whether there should be a write-down or a write-up of a bill to be sent to the client.

| EXHIBIT 14.11 | Bill Sent to Client Involving Attorney and Paralegal Services |
|---|---|

Rubin, Rinke, Pyeumac & Craigmoyle
1615 Broadway, Suite 1400
Oakland, California 94612–2115
(415) 444–5316
Tax ID 94–2169491

April 10, 2002

IBM Corporation
Norm Savage
3133 Northside Parkway
Atlanta GA 33033

Statement for Professional Services Rendered

Re:  Chapter 11                                                                    (IBM-1)
      Reorganization

Description of services

| Date | Description | | |
|---|---|---|---|
| 04/17/02 | Receipt and review of contracts regarding Armonk home office liquidation. | | |
| 04/18/02 | Meeting with opposing attorney regarding court appearance in Atlanta. | | |
| 04/21/02 | Receipt and preliminary review of depositions from seven hundred forty three (743) claimants to Austin plant parking facilities. | | |
| 04/22/02 | Meeting with officers of the corporation to discuss liquidation of office furniture in all branch offices. Scheduling of 2,000 simultaneous garage sales in marketing managers' driveways to be advertised during next year's Super Bowl. | | |

|  | Total for legal services rendered | | $1,797.50 |
|---|---|---|---|
|  | Hours | Rate | |
| Partners | 6.00 | 250 | 1,500.00 |
| Paralegals | 3.50 | 85 | 297.50 |

Reimbursable expenses and costs

| Date | Description | |
|---|---|---|
| 04/17/02 | Lunch meeting with three opposing attorneys. | 185.17 |
| 04/27/02 | Atlanta Bankruptcy Court filing fee due September 1, 2002 | 55.00 |
| 04/29/02 | Photocopies | 5.69 |
| 04/29/02 | Long-distance telephone charges | 36.90 |
|  | Total expenses | $282.76 |
|  | Total current charges. | $2,080.26 |

Source: Computer Software for Professionals, Inc., LEGALMASTER (www.legalmaster.com).

summaries in appendix F. (See also the discussion of *Missouri v. Jenkins* and statutory fees in chapter 1.)

Even if a client does not use an outside auditor, it is wise to assume that someone in the client's office will be scrutinizing law firm bills for potential problems. Furthermore, the rules of ethics must always be kept in mind. For an overview of the major fee and billing ethical violations, see chapter 5.

Section G
# CLIENT TRUST ACCOUNTS

Law firms must keep two separate checking accounts. One is the office account from which the office pays general operating expenses such as salaries, utility bills, and other

**client trust account** A bank account controlled by an attorney that contains client funds that may not be used for office operating expenses or for any personal purpose of the attorney.

**commingling** Mixing general law firm funds with client funds in a single account.

overhead items. The second is the **client trust account** (also called a client account or escrow account), which contains client funds that may not be used to cover office expenses or the attorney's personal expenses. Each client does not need its own client trust account. There can be one client trust account into which the funds of all office clients are deposited.[14] When deposits and withdrawals are made, careful records must indicate the client for which a particular deposit and withdrawal is made. Occasionally, however, an office may have separate client trust accounts for those clients whose cases involve large amounts of money.

There must be no **commingling** or mixing of office funds and client funds. It is unethical for the office to place everything in one account, no matter how meticulous the office may be about recording which funds in the single account belong to the office and which belong to clients. Furthermore, it is equally unethical for the attorney to use any client funds for a personal purpose (e.g., paying the attorney's home mortgage bill) or for an office purpose (e.g., paying the office rent) during a time when the attorney is experiencing a temporary cash flow problem. This is unethical even if the attorney returns the client funds with interest. When attorneys are audited by the bar association, the auditor (or monitor) often pays careful attention to the accounting records in the office to determine whether these rules on separate accounts are being followed.

What funds must go into a client trust account? Here are some examples:

- A settlement check from an opposing party (or from its insurance company) when a case is settled
- A court award of damages paid by an opposing party (or its insurance company) when a case is not settled
- Escrow funds from the sale of real property
- Prepayment of costs
- Unearned attorney fees

The last category is particularly important. Where attorney fees must be deposited depends on what the fees are for and whether they have been earned. Suppose, for example, an attorney agrees to take a divorce case for a fee of $200 an hour if the client pays an advance of $25,000. If this advance is a deposit against future fees (which is often the case), it must be deposited in the client trust account because it has not yet been earned by the attorney. It is still the client's money; the attorney is holding it "in trust" for the client. Once the attorney earns the right to be paid by working on the case, funds can be transferred from the client trust account to the office account. For example, if the attorney spends 20 hours on the divorce case, he or she can bill the client for $4,000 (20 × $200) and instruct the bank to transfer this amount from the client trust account into the office account. This leaves $21,000 in the client trust account. If the client decides to discharge the attorney or wants to drop the case, the attorney must refund all unearned cash remaining in the client fund.

Some attorney fees, however, are not advances against future legal services. They may constitute a nonrefundable sign-up bonus that commits the attorney to be available to the client as needed over a designated period of time. Such fees can be deposited directly into the attorney's office account because they are considered earned when received.

To avoid disputes, the contract of employment (the retainer) between an attorney and client should clarify the purpose and nature of fees to be paid. Are they advances? Are they refundable or nonrefundable? When are they considered earned? Such questions should be answered and the answers understood by the client before the attorney-client relationship begins. The ethical rules of each state must also be carefully checked in this area of practice. Some states, for example, place restrictions on an attorney's right to nonrefundable fees, even if the client agrees to pay them.

## Section H
# Administrative Reports

The managers of a law firm need to know what everyone in the firm is doing. Many attorneys routinely complete a form similar to that illustrated in exhibit 14.12, the work

| EXHIBIT 14.12 | Work Summary |
| --- | --- |

[ ] Can Handle More Work
[ ] Have All the Work
    I Can Handle
[ ] Need Help
Report of:

\* C   (Work Completed
        since Last Report)
WP  (Work in Progress)
IA   (Matter Is Inactive)
Date:

| Client | Matter | Description of Work [Designate Specialty Work by Symbol (S)] | Date Assgnd | Part-ner | Sta-tus |
| --- | --- | --- | --- | --- | --- |
| | | | | | |

summary. It can be filled out by computer or on a paper form provided by the office. Paralegals also fill out work summary reports, depending on the nature of the work they're doing. If they are working for many attorneys in one department, the department head and the paralegal supervisor, if any, often require copies of the work summary report in order to keep track of the work being done.

There are different types of administrative reports based on timekeeping, billing, and work summary data. Some of the more common reports used by law firms are outlined in exhibit 14.13

Of particular interest to paralegals are reports generated from timekeeping records that analyze how much time paralegals are investing in client matters. This analysis is similar to the analysis the firm performs on the time invested by attorneys. Management uses these data to evaluate where the profit centers are, whether costs need to be contained, whether work is properly allocated among attorneys and among paralegals, which attorneys and paralegals are in line for salary increases and bonuses, etc.

## Section I
## CLIENT FILE MANAGEMENT

When you begin work in a law office, one of your early tasks will be to learn the office's system for organizing, locating, and storing client files. In some offices, particularly small ones, paralegals are given considerable responsibility for maintaining this system. Efficient file management is of critical importance. "Files are the nerve center of any office. Therefore, the proper storage, safekeeping, and expeditious retrieval of information from the files is the key to . . . efficient operation."[15] Attorneys and paralegals will tell you that few experiences are more frustrating than coping with a lost document or a missing file. "But the damage can run even deeper." Lost and misplaced files can cause deadlines to be missed, "leading to one of the most common causes of malpractice claims against attorneys."[16]

| EXHIBIT 14.13 | Administrative Reports |
|---|---|

- *Aged Accounts Receivable Report*. A report showing all cases that have outstanding balances due and how long these balances are past due. For example, the report may state how many of the total receivables (i.e., accounts due and payable) are less than 30 days old, how many are 30–59 days old, how many are 60–90 days old, and how many are more than 90 days old. (Also called a firm utilization report.) (See exhibit 14.14)
- *Timekeeper Productivity Report*. A report showing how much billable and nonbillable time is being spent by each timekeeper. (See exhibits 14.8 and 14.9.)
- *Case-Type Productivity Report*. A report showing which types of cases in the firm (e.g., bankruptcy, personal injury, criminal) are most profitable. (Also called a practice analysis report.)
- *Fee Analysis Report*. A report on the fees generated by client, by area of law, by law firm branch office, and by individual attorney. The report helps the firm identify which cases, offices, and attorneys are profitable and which are not.
- *Work-in-Progress Report*. A report that provides the details of unbilled hours and costs per timekeeper, including client totals.
- *Cash Receipts Report*. A report that describes the income received in a day, week, month, quarter, or year. The cash receipts can be compared with the amount of projected income for a specific time period.
- *Client Investment Summary Report*. A report of the total amount billed and unbilled, with a calculation of the actual costs of providing legal services for a particular client.
- *Budget Performance Report*. A report that compares a firm's actual income and expenditures with budgeted or projected income and expenditures.

**Sources**: Brent Roper, *Practical Law Office Management*. (2d ed. West Group 2002); Pamela Everett, *Fundamentals of Law Office Management* (2d ed. West Group 2000).

| EXHIBIT 14.14 | Accounts Receivable (A/R)—Bills Not Yet Collected |
|---|---|

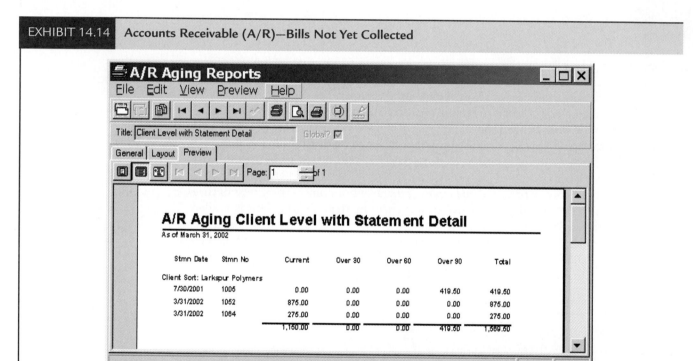

**Source**: ProLaw Software (www.prolaw.com).

Once an office accepts a client, its file soon begins to collect many documents. They are often placed in separate folders within the file. On the right side of one of the folders, you may find all incoming correspondence and copies of all outgoing correspondence. They will be in reverse chronological order, with the most recent correspondence always placed on top. To keep them all together, they will probably be two-hole punched and clipped to right side of the folder. All other documents (e.g., copies of pleadings) might be similarly clipped to the left side of the folder. Large documents such as transcripts of depositions will probably be kept in separate folders.

Almost every law office has multiple clients. The location of the files of these clients will depend on factors such as the kind and size of cases the office handles, the number of attorneys in the office, the use of computers, and the availability of storage space. Large law firms often have a centralized filing area where all or most files are located. File clerks (under the direction of a **record information manager**) file, check out, and keep track of every file. Smaller offices tend to be more decentralized, allowing files to be located in or near the office of the attorney working on those files.

There are two major kinds of filing systems: alphabetical and numerical.

In an **alphabetical filing system**, files are arranged in alphabetical order by client surname or by organization name. For example, the file of George Bellman would go in front of the file of Kelly Motor Corp., which would go in front of the file of Cheryl Thompson, etc. This system works relatively well if the office does not have a large number of clients. The more clients in the office, however, the more likely their names will be confusingly similar. Suppose, for example, that an office has the following clients, each with separate cases (or matters) handled by different attorneys in the office:

A–1 Norths Appliance Center (a tax case)
North Central Bank (a securities case)
Jason North (a divorce case)
Sam North (Jason's father) (a landlord-tenant case)
Northern Light, Inc. (a trademark case)

In an alphabetical filing system, there are rules that determine the order in which the files of these five clients would be kept in the file cabinet. Yet filing mistakes are fairly common in spite of the rules. Busy office workers do not always take the time to find out what the rules are. As documents in these files are used, returned, and reused throughout the day, the danger of misfiling is increased because of the similarity of some file names. A bank statement in Jason North's divorce case, for example, might end up as one of the financial records in the unrelated North Central Bank's securities case.

Color coding can help. To speed up the retrieval and return of files, the office can use colored file folders, colored file labels, or colored stickers. If, for example, colors are assigned to a particular area of the law, the folders and labels for all corporate law cases might be blue; those for all tax cases, orange; those for all family law cases, white; etc.[17] Alternatively, an office may use one color for every folder and file opened in a particular year regardless of the kind of case it is. When a new year arrives, new client cases go into folders and files of a different color.

A **numerical filing system** is substantially different from an alphabetical filing system. Numerical filing systems use numbers or letter-number combinations (rather than surnames) to identify files. Many varieties of numerical filing systems are in use. Here are five examples of how files might be identified in five different law offices:

- 02–778. The first two characters indicate the year the case was opened (02 = the year 2002) (778 is the number assigned to a particular client).
- LA01–55113. The first two letters indicate which branch office is handling the case (LA = the Los Angeles branch; 01 = the year 2001).
- PB–552. The first two letters indicate the type of case (PB = a probate case) (other examples: TX = a tax case; WC = a workers' compensation case).
- JH.02.111. The first two letters indicate the particular attorney in charge of the case (JH = Jane Harrison, Esq.).
- 37.007. The initial numbers indicate particular clients (37 = Avon Electronics, Inc.), and the following numbers indicate how many matters are being handled for those clients (007 = the seventh matter the office has handled for Avon).[18]

Some offices will assign a range of numbers to a particular type of case or matter, e.g., all estate and trust cases will use the numbers 001–999; all tax cases will use the numbers 1,000–1,999; and all criminal cases will use the numbers 2,000–2,999. Other variations are also possible.

Index cards can be used to help locate particular files organized under a numerical filing system. For example, Avon Electronics, Inc., would have its own card on which every

**record information manager** Someone in charge of files in a large office.

**alphabetical filing system** A method of storing client files in alphabetical order by the client's surname or organization name.

**numerical filing system** A method of storing client files by numbers or letter-number combinations.

file number assigned to it would be placed (37.007, 37.008, 37.009, etc.). These index cards would be kept in alphabetical order. If you want to read the file of a particular client, you would go to the index cards, find that client's name, jot down the numbers of the files that pertain to that client, and go to the file cabinets to locate those numbers. Additional cards allow for cross-indexing. For example, individual attorneys could have their own cards that contain all the case numbers they are handling or have handled. Also, cards for specific topics could be created (e.g., medical malpractice interrogatories, patent applications) on which the numbers for every case file containing documents on those topics would be written. If you want to look at medical malpractice interrogatories that the office has used in the past, go to the "m" cards, find the card on medical malpractice interrogatories, and jot down the number of every case containing such interrogatories.

Some large offices use bar coding to facilitate file management. Every file is assigned a **bar code**, which is a sequence of numbers and vertical lines that can be read by an optical scanner. Most supermarkets use this technology at checkout to record prices and provide inventory data to managers. Similarly, whenever you want to use a file that has been bar coded, you simply scan the bar code and take the file to your office. This is also done when you return the file to the file cabinet or storage room. The office thereby obtains an efficient computer record of who has which files, how long they have had them, or when they were returned.

In a bar code system, you scan the bar code into a computer. Suppose you are also able to scan the contents of *every document in every file* into the computer. This amounts to a fully automated file management system. Every attorney, paralegal, and secretary in the office can then be given instant computer access to any document in the files. Finding documents becomes substantially easier than combing through file drawers or boxes and carrying what you need to your desk. Search software allows you to define what you are looking for (e.g., the Ellerson deposition or all personal injury complaints filed in Suffolk Superior Court after 1997). Not many law offices are sophisticated enough to have every document on computer. We have not yet reached the paperless office, although we are clearly moving in this direction.

Once the office completes its work on a case, the file becomes a **closed file**, also called a dead file or a retired file. Some offices give the file a new number (e.g., a CF, closed file, number) to differentiate it from active files.[19] The file might be placed in storage boxes or transferred to microfilm or microfiche. Important original documents (e.g., wills, estate plans, deeds, tax returns) are usually returned to the client. The office keeps a copy.

The cost of storing client files can be substantial, particularly for law firms with many clients. Firms do not want the burden of keeping old files forever. Ethical rules in the state may impose an obligation to keep specified files for designated periods of time. "Firms should have policies on retention of files, turning files over to clients, destroying files, and security for files maintained in off-site storage. Since the client file is the property of the client, the attorney cannot destroy old files without informing the client and getting permission and/or giving the client the chance to keep the file.[20]

Finally, closed case files can often be of help to an office in future cases. To avoid reinventing the wheel, offices like to have closed case files accessible. Whenever work on a current case involves the drafting of a document, for example, examining the same or a similar document prepared for a prior case can often be a good starting point.

**bar code** A sequence of numbers and vertical lines of different shapes that can be read by an optical scanner.

**closed file** The file of a client whose case is no longer active in the firm.

---

### Assignment 14.1

(a) In the practice of law, time is money. Hence you must develop the discipline of recording your time. Supervisors will later decide what portions of your time are billable—and to what clients. Step one is to compile a record of your time.

To practice this discipline, fill out a daily time sheet for a day that you select. On *one* sheet of paper, record (in a chart form that you design) everything (approximately) that you do *in six-minute* intervals over a continuous eight-hour period. Once you design your chart, *it should take you no more than about 15 minutes to fill it out* during the eight-hour period. You do not, however, fill it out at one time; you fill it out contemporaneously as you go through the tasks you are keeping track of throughout the eight hours.

Select an eight-hour period in which you are engaged in a fairly wide variety of activities. If possible, avoid an eight-hour period that contains any single activity lasting over two hours. Draw a chart covering the eight-hour period. At the top of the chart, place your name, the date of the eight-hour period that you used, and the starting/ending times of the eight-hour period. The period can be within a school day, a workday, a day of leisure, etc.

Using abbreviations, make specific entries on your activities within the eight hours—in six-minute intervals. For example, "Reading a chapter in a real estate school text" might be abbreviated as RE-R. "Driving to school" might be abbreviated as D-Sch. "Purely personal matters" (such as taking a shower) might be abbreviated as PPM. You decide what the abbreviations are. On the back of the sheet of paper containing the chart, explain what the abbreviations mean. When an activity is repeated in more than one six-minute interval, simply repeat the abbreviation.

One format for the chart might be a series of vertical and horizontal lines on the sheet of paper. This will give you a small amount of space on which to insert your abbreviations for each six-minute interval. Design the chart any way that you want, keeping in mind the goal of the exercise: to enable someone else to know what you did within the eight-hour period.

In exhibit 14.6, there is an example of a daily time sheet used in a law office. *Do not* follow the format in exhibit 14.6. Use the guidelines listed here, e.g., place your abbreviations on the other side of the sheet of paper that you submit.

**(b)** Repeat this assignment for a period of a week. Your instructor will tell you which week to select. For each of the seven days of that week, fill out a daily time sheet.

---

### Assignment 14.2

Call a private law firm in the area that is large enough to have an office manager or legal administrator. Ask this person if you can interview him or her on the phone or in person for several minutes. Explain that you are taking a paralegal course that requires you to interview a manager. Ask this person about the following topics:

- How the office is organized (partnership, sole proprietorship, other)
- Major duties of the manager or administrator (use exhibit 14.2 as a guide to some of the areas to cover)
- Categories of attorneys and other staff in the office, their duties, and the chain of command among them
- Kinds of fees
- Timekeeping methods
- How work is delegated and evaluated
- Filing system
- Law library size

Prepare a report on what you learned from this interview.

---

## CHAPTER SUMMARY

Our examination of law office administration began with an overview of the different settings in which attorneys practice law in the private sector in the United States and of the different kinds of attorneys found in each setting.

A sole practitioner may operate a sole proprietorship, in which a single attorney owns the practice even if he or she employs other attorneys. The others do not share in the profits of the firm. To save on expenses, several sole practitioners may enter into an office-sharing arrangement under which the attorneys share expenses for office space, secretarial help, etc.

In a partnership, the equity or capital partners share in the profits and losses of the firm and control its management, often through a committee or department structure. Associates are attorneys in the firm who hope one day to be invited to become partners. There are, however, special categories of associates created for those who do not become partners, such as senior associate.

Other categories of attorneys who might be hired by a law firm include staff attorneys, of-counsel attorneys, and contract attorneys. For tax and estate-planning purposes, many states allow attorneys to practice law as a professional corporation. There is little practical difference, however, between the administration of a partnership and a professional corporation. The newest formats for law firms are the limited liability company (LLC) and the limited liability partnership (LLP). They combine features of a corporation and a partnership.

Finally, some attorneys practice law in the legal departments of corporations. They are employees of the corporation, which is their sole client.

Large law offices may have many nonattorney employees to help manage the office. Among the most prominent is the legal administrator. Also, if there are more than a few paralegals in the office, a legal assistant manager is often hired to help administer the office's system for recruiting, hiring, training, and monitoring the progress of paralegals.

The accounting foundation for new clients or matters is the new matter worksheet. There is considerable pressure on attorneys and paralegals to keep precise track of their time. The accounting records and financial health of the law firm depend on it. Time is recorded by using handwritten paper forms and/or by using the computer. A number of different fee arrangements exist: clock-based (e.g., hourly rate, blended hourly rate), and alternatives that stress value billing (e.g., fixed fee, capped fee, task-based billing, hourly plus fixed fee, discounted hourly fee, contingent fee, and retroactive negotiated fee). The method of paying the bill (including expenses and court costs) should be spelled out in the retainer. The amount actually paid by a client is not determined until there has been a valuing of the bill, which might result in a write-up, a write-down, or no change. Some business clients use an outside auditor to help them monitor law firm bills, particularly to identify irregularities.

Law firms must keep two separate checking accounts: the office account and the client trust account. The latter contains funds that belong to the clients such as settlement checks and unearned attorney fees. There must be no commingling (mixing) of office and client funds.

An efficient law firm uses administrative reports to help it keep track of and manage the practice. Examples include the aged accounts receivable report and the timekeeper productivity report.

Correspondence in client folders is often filed in reverse chronological order, with the most recent item placed on top. Correspondence is clipped to the right of the folder and all other documents are clipped on the left.

The location of client files in an office will be either centralized (often with the use of special filing personnel) or decentralized. The two major kinds of filing systems are the alphabetical system and the numerical system accompanied by a card index. An alphabetical system arranges files in alphabetical order by client surname or by organization name. A numerical system uses numbers or letter-number combinations (rather than surnames) to identify files. Offices can have the numbers and letters mean different things. Index cards help locate particular files and allow for cross-indexing. Some large offices use bar coding to facilitate file management. Once the office completes its work on a case, the file becomes a closed file. Practical considerations and the rules of ethics determine how long a firm must keep closed files. Important documents are returned to the client.

## KEY TERMS

sole proprietorship
personal liability

sole practitioner
general practitioner

law clerk
office sharing
overhead
partnership
rainmaker
draw
associate
lateral hire
senior associate
nonequity partner
equity partner
staff attorney
of counsel
contract attorney
professional corporation
limited liability
limited liability entity
corporate legal department
general counsel
managing partner
legal administrator
legal assistant manager
timekeeping
new file worksheet
daily time sheet
nonbillable time
pro bono
indigent

blended hourly rate
value billing
fixed fee
capped fee
bundled legal services
pro se
unbundled legal services
task-based billing
hourly plus fixed fee
discounted hourly fee
contingent fee
incentive billing
defense contingent fee
retroactive negotiated fee
court costs
expense slip
retainer
draft bill
write down
write up
valuing the bill
client trust account
commingling
record information manager
alphabetical filing system
numerical filing system
bar code
closed file

## ON THE NET: MORE ON LAW OFFICE MANAGEMENT

**Legal Administrator's Role**
www.alanet.org/jobs/samplejob.html

**Law Office Management Resources**
www.ioma.com
www.weilandco.com/manage.html
www.lexisone.com/practicemanagement/index.html
www.hornbook.com
www.LawMarketing.com
www.altmanweil.com

**Time and Billing Software**
www.timeslips.com
www.pclaw.com
www.prolaw.com
www.legalmaster.com

**"Greedy" Associates**
www.infirmation.com/bboard/clubs-top.tcl

## ENDNOTES

1. U.S. Census Bureau, *Statistical Abstract of the United States*, tbl. 669 (2000), *at* (www.census.gov/statab/www).
2. Bureau of Labor Statistics, U.S. Department of Labor, *Occupational Outlook Handbook*, Lawyers and Judicial Workers (2000–2001), *at* (www.stats.bls.gov/oco/ocos053.htm).
3. R. Green, ed., *The Quality Pursuit* 69 (American Bar Association, 1989).
4. Altman Weil, Inc., *2001 Survey of Law Firm Economics*, *at* (www.altmanweil.com/products/surveys/slfe/annual.cfm).
5. J. Margolis, *At the Bar* N.Y. Times, September 7, 1990, at B13.
6. A. Walljasper, *I Quit!*, Wisconsin Lawyer 16 (March 1990).
7. Morris, *Join the Effort to Restore Respect to the Legal Profession*, The Digest 3 (Arizona Paralegal Ass'n, April 1989).
8. T. Barcott, *Time Is Money*, AALA News (Alaska Ass'n of Legal Assistants, April 1990).

9. S. Matteucci, *What the Heck Is "Value Billing" Anyway?*, 18 The Montana Lawyer 2 (November 1992). See also D. Ricker, *The Vanishing Hourly Fee*, 80 American Bar Ass'n Journal 66 (March 1994); F. Marcotte, *Billing Choices* 75 American Bar Ass'n Journal 38 (November 1989).

10. G. Emmett Raitt, *What If Your Client Used Value Billing?*, Orange County Lawyer 37 (April 1992).

11. Michele Coyne, *Alternatives to Customary Billing Practices*, The LAMA Manager 19 (Legal Assistant Management Ass'n, Summer 1991).

12. Darby, *Of Firms and Fees: The Administrator's Role*, 8 Legal Management 34, 39 (March/April 1989).

13. M. Geyelin, *If You Think Insurers Are Tight, Try Being One of Their Lawyers*, Wall Street Journal, Feb 9, 1999, at Al.

14. In most states, some or all of the interest earned by these accounts is used for grants to foundations that help finance legal services for low-income clients. These grants are called IOLTA (Interest on Lawyers Trust Account) programs.

15. P. Hoffman, *Law Office Economics and Management Manual* § 41 : 04, at 4 (1986).

16. T. Light, *The Procedure Manual*, 26 The Practical Lawyer 71 (January 1980).

17. P. Everett, *Fundamentals of Law Office Management* 445 (2d ed. 2000).

18. B. Roper, *Practical Law Office Management* 387 (1995).

19. *Id.* at 393.

20. T. Cannon, *Ethics and Professional Responsibility for Legal Assistants* 258 (3d ed. 1999).

# Chapter 15

# INFORMAL AND FORMAL ADMINISTRATIVE ADVOCACY

## Chapter Outline

# Section A
# The Nature of Advocacy

**advocacy** The process by which you attempt to influence the behavior of others, often according to predetermined goals.

**Advocacy** is the process by which an individual attempts to influence the behavior of others, often according to predetermined goals. Advocacy is a basic component of everyday life; we are frequently advocates for ourselves and for others. Note, for example, the advocacy involved, or potentially involved, in the following circumstances:

1. At a supermarket checkout counter, a clerk tells a customer that the price of tomatoes is 99¢ a pound. The customer replies, "But the sign back there said 89¢ a pound." The clerk says, "I'm sorry, but the price is 99¢."
2. A student goes to the teacher to say that a term paper should have been graded "A" rather than "B."
3. A tenant tells the landlord that a $500 a month rent increase is ridiculous because the building has been steadily deteriorating.
4. A homeowner has been away on a vacation. Upon his return, he finds that his house has been burglarized. When he goes to the police station to report the crime, he asks the desk sergeant why his neighborhood has not been receiving better protection in view of all the burglaries that have been occurring in the area lately. The sergeant replies that there are not enough police available to patrol the neighborhood adequately. The homeowner is not satisfied with this response and asks to see the precinct captain.

The customer, student, tenant, and homeowner all have complaints. They are *complainants*. They are not satisfied with something. Their natural response is to make an argument for better service. In so doing, they become advocates for the goals or objectives that they are seeking. Advocacy does not always require courtrooms, judges, and attorneys; all that is needed is a complaint, a complainant, and someone who should be able to act on the complaint.

The distinction between *formal* and *informal advocacy* is primarily one of degree. Generally, the more the setting looks like a court procedure (for example, with a hearing officer present, evidence or testimony taken, or written decisions issued), the more formal it is. As we saw in chapter 6, an administrative agency's quasi-judicial powers are often exercised through hearings that have many similarities to courtroom proceedings. A **quasi-judicial proceeding** is one in which the agency acts much like a court when resolving a dispute between a citizen and the agency (such as between a social security recipient and the Social Security Administration) or between two or more citizens under the control of the agency (e.g., two students in the same school or two inmates in the same prison who are having a dispute). If you are representing yourself or someone else at such a hearing, you are engaged in formal advocacy, even if all of the formal procedures of a court proceeding are not followed.

**quasi-judicial proceeding** A proceeding within an administrative agency that seeks to resolve a dispute in a manner that is similar to a court (i.e., judicial) proceeding to resolve a dispute.

Our first concern in this chapter is *in*formal advocacy that occurs (a) in connection with administrative agencies not involving formal hearings or (b) outside the realm of administrative agencies altogether, as in the supermarket example at the beginning of this chapter. Our primary focus will be the informal advocacy techniques that can be used when confronting employees of *any* organization—for example, a public agency such as a workers' compensation office or a private business such as an insurance company.

Paralegals often have contact with organizations that require the application of informal advocacy techniques. Here are several examples:

- Determining the names and addresses of the principal shareholders of a corporation
- Gaining access to the records of an agency or of a company
- Obtaining copies of forms from the Securities and Exchange Commission on the disclosure and reporting requirements of a corporation
- Writing to or visiting an agency or company to obtain its position on a matter involving a client

■ Trying to convince a caseworker or a social worker that the action the agency has taken (or that it proposes to take) is illegal or ill-advised

A paralegal can meet resistance in any and all of these situations. The basic techniques of informal advocacy should help in handling this resistance.

## Section B
## THE TECHNIQUES OF INFORMAL ADVOCACY

Exhibit 15.1 presents a summary of 19 techniques of informal advocacy that are sometimes useful when trying to obtain action from an administrative agency or from any large organization. The techniques are listed in the approximate order of effectiveness. Of course, whether a particular technique will be effective depends on what you are trying to accomplish, whom the technique is directed against, and how well you execute the technique. In general, though, the techniques at the beginning of exhibit 15.1 are more likely to be effective than those at the end. Do you agree?

| EXHIBIT 15.1 | Techniques of Informal Advocacy |
| --- | --- |

1. *Put your cards on the table.* Be direct and completely aboveboard in telling the agency official what your position is and what you want.
2. *Insist on adequate service.* Point out to the agency official that the purpose of the agency is service and that this principle should guide the official's actions.
3. *Ask for authorization.* Insist that the agency official show you the regulation, law, or other authority that supports the action taken or proposed by the agency.
4. *Climb the chain of command.* Normally, everyone has a boss who can overrule decisions made by those beneath him or her. When you are dissatisfied with the decision or action of an employee, "appeal," or complain, "up the chain of command" to the employee's supervisor and to the supervisor's supervisor, if needed.
5. *Insist on common sense.* Convey to the agency official the impression that common sense supports your position—in addition to or despite regulations or technicalities that might be cited against you.
6. *Take the role of the tired, battered, helpless citizen.* Do not insist on anything. Play dumb; act exhausted; act in such a way that the agency official will think. "This person needs help"; act as if everyone else has given you the runaround and you are praying that this official (whom you have not dealt with before) will finally give you a sympathetic ear—and some help.
7. *Cite a precedent.* Point out to the agency official (if it is true) that your case is not unusual because the agency has granted what you want to others under the same or similar circumstances in the past.

8. *Find the points of compromise.* Ferret out the negotiable points in the dispute and determine whether you can bargain your way to a favorable result.
9. *Uncover the realm of discretion.* Those in authority often want you to believe that their hands are tied, that there is only one way to apply the rule. In fact, some discretion is often involved in the application of all rules. You need to find the realm of discretion and try to fit your case within it. The goal is to show that the discretion provides the agency official enough flexibility to give you what you are seeking.
10. *Demonstrate the exception.* Insist on the uniqueness of your client's situation. Show agency officials that the general rule they are using to deny your client a benefit is inapplicable.
11. *Cite the law.* Show the agency official that you know what administrative regulations apply to the case. Also cite statutes and other laws to demonstrate your point.
12. *Be a buddy.* Show agency officials that you are not an enemy, that you respect and like them, and that you are aware how difficult their job is.
13. *Make clear that you and your office are going to fight this case all the way up.* Make the agency official aware of how important the case is. Point out that you are thinking about taking the case to a formal agency hearing and that your office may go to court, if necessary.
14. *Redefine the problem.* If you can't solve a problem, redefine it—as long as you can still achieve the essentials of what the client seeks. For example, stop trying to qualify the client for program "Z" if program "Y" will serve the client equally well (or almost so) and the problems of qualifying the

**EXHIBIT 15.1    Techniques of Informal Advocacy—continued**

client for "Y" are not as great as you'll face by continuing to insist on "Z."

15. *Do a favor to get a favor.* Be willing to do something (within reason) for the person from whom you are seeking something.

16. *Seek the support of third persons.* Before you make your position known, gather the support of individuals or groups within and outside the agency so you can demonstrate that you are not alone.

17. *Preach.* Lecture the agency official about his or her responsibilities within the agency. Elaborate on

the mission of the agency, making clear that the denial of what you want violates or is inconsistent with that mission.

18. *Embarrass the official.* Show the agency official that you do not respect him or her. Do it in such a way that the official is made to look silly.

19. *Demonstrate anger.* Be completely open about the hostility you feel concerning what is being done or proposed

---

Effective advocacy involves other concerns as well:

**Advocacy**

   I. *Threshold Concerns*
      1. Define your goals in order of priority.
      2. Decide when to intervene.
  II. *Self-Evaluation of Techniques Used*
      1. Are you making yourself clear?
      2. Are you creating more problems than you are solving?
      3. Are you accomplishing your goal?
 III. *Adaptation.* Are you flexible enough to shift your techniques as needed?
 IV. *Recording*
      1. Describe what you saw.
      2. Describe what you did.

The focus of the first threshold concern is the priority of goals. This concern, of course, would not be applicable if the assignment you are given contains only one goal, such as obtaining a copy of a record at the agency or organization. Sometimes, however, an assignment contains a variety of objectives at the outset, or a single-objective assignment subsequently blossoms into tasks involving more than one goal. In that case, priorities must be set. If you try to do everything, you may end up accomplishing nothing. Every technique of informal advocacy will probably fail if you have unrealistic expectations of what can be accomplished.

The second threshold issue is to decide when to intervene with the advocacy techniques. The decision to intervene involves a strategic judgment about when it would be most appropriate to seek what you are after at the agency or organization. In most situations, a sense of timing is very important. For example, suppose that you must contact the complaint bureau of an agency that is relatively new to you. One approach would be simply to walk up to the complaint bureau and delve right into the matter that brought you there. Another approach would be to try to find out something about the bureau *before* going to it. There may be some literature available on the structure of the agency that will provide you with at least a general idea of what to expect. You may be able to talk to attorneys or other paralegals who have had prior contact with the bureau. Suppose you learn that two agency employees rotate their work at the bureau and that one employee has a reputation of being more cooperative than the other. You may decide not to go to the bureau until this employee is on duty. In short, you decide to postpone your contact with the bureau until circumstances are most favorable to the objective you are seeking.

As you use any of the techniques in exhibit 15.1, you must simultaneously judge the *effectiveness* of the technique in light of what you are trying to accomplish. Are you making yourself clear? Are you complicating rather than resolving the problem? Are you getting through? Are you comfortable with the technique you are using? Does it clash with your personality? Are you pacing yourself properly? Is your insistence on immediate success interfering with proceeding step-by-step along the road toward progress?

One of the major signs of ineffective advocacy is becoming so involved in the case that you begin to take roadblocks and defeat *personally*. Everyone agrees that objectivity is a good quality—and most of us claim to possess this quality in abundance. The unfortunate fact, however, is that *we tend to lose objectivity as friction increases*. We allow our careers and our lifestyles to be threatened when someone says to us, "You can't do that." We rarely admit that we can be so threatened. We justify our response by blaming someone else for insensitivity, unfairness, or stupidity.

Once you have disciplined yourself to identify the techniques you are using and to evaluate their effectiveness, you must be flexible enough to *adapt* your techniques and shift to more effective ones when needed.

Finally, the paralegal usually will have a recording responsibility. Almost every case you work on must be heavily documented in the office files. Your efforts at informal advocacy should be included in those files.

---

### Class Exercise 15.A

In each role-playing exercise, there are two characters: C (the complainant) and E (the agency employee). Students from the class will be assigned one or the other role. In each setting, C is seeking something from E. E is uncooperative. The objective of E is to antagonize C (within reason) to the point where C loses objectivity. The objective of C is to use effective advocacy techniques without losing objectivity.

**(a)** At 4:30 P.M., C goes to the Department of Motor Vehicles to apply for a license. E tells C that the office closes at 5:00 P.M. and the application procedure takes 45 minutes. E refuses to let C apply.

**(b)** C is filing a document at the clerk's office. The filing fee is $6. E tells C that the fee must be paid by check or the exact amount in cash. All C has is a $100 bill and must use some of it to take a long cab ride back to the office.

**(c)** C goes to the Bureau of Vital Statistics and requests a copy of his mother's birth certificate. E tells C that no citizen can obtain the birth certificate of another person without the written permission of the person. C's mother is ill in a hospital a thousand miles away. C wants the record without going through the bother of obtaining this permission.

Those members of the class who are not participating in the role-playing exercises should identify and evaluate the techniques of informal advocacy that C uses.

---

We now examine informal advocacy techniques in the context of the following fact situation:

> You are in your own home or apartment. You receive a letter from the gas company stating that your gas will be shut off in 10 days if you do not pay your bill. Your spouse tells you that all the bills have already been paid. You call the gas company, and when you question the clerk, she says to you, "I'm sorry sir; our records reflect an unpaid bill. You must pay the bill immediately." To try to straighten matters out, you take a trip to the utilities office.

In the dialogue that follows, the complainant is his own advocate. "C" is the complainant and "E" is a gas company employee. As you read the dialog, ask yourself how effective is C's informal advocacy.

E: Can I help you?

C: Yes, I want to see someone about a problem with my bill.

E: I'm sorry, sir, but the customer complaint division closed at 2 P.M. You'll have to come back or call tomorrow.

C: Closed! Well, let me see someone about terminating the gas service altogether.

E: All right, would you step right over to the desk?

TECHNIQUE: *If you can't solve a problem, redefine the problem* to manageable proportions if, on balance, it is consistent with your objectives. (See exhibit 15.1.) The client is taking a risk. He cannot get to the complaint division so he is going to try to achieve his objective through the termination division. He has substituted one problem (getting to the termination division) for another problem (getting to the complaint division) in the hope of expressing his grievance.

E:   Can I help you?

C:   Yes, I want to terminate my gas if I can't get this problem straightened out.

E:   You'll have to go over to the bill complaint division, sir.

C:   Look, stop sending me somewhere else! This has got to be straightened out immediately!

TECHNIQUE: *Demonstrate anger.* This is a dangerous tactic to employ. It is a fact of life, however, that some people respond to this kind of pressure.

C:   Aren't you here to serve the public?

TECHNIQUE: *Insist on adequate service.* Point out that the organization exists to serve and that you need better service.

E:   There are rules and procedures that we all must abide by and . . .

C:   Your responsibility is to take care of the public!

TECHNIQUE: *Preach.* Perhaps the most common way people try to change other people is to lecture them, to tell them what they should or should not be doing.

TECHNIQUE: *Embarrass the official.* Make the agency official look silly and unworthy of respect. At this point, has the complainant lost all objectivity? What risks are being taken? Do you think the complainant is aware of what he is doing? If you asked him whether he's being effective, what do you think his response would be? Is he more involved with the "justice" of his case than with the effectiveness of his approach?

C:   I'd like to speak to your supervisor. Who is in charge of this office?

E:   Well, Mr. Adams is the unit director. His office is in Room 307.

C:   Fine.

TECHNIQUE: *Climb the chain of command.* Everyone has a boss who can overrule his or her subordinate's decisions. If you're unhappy about a decision, complain "up the chain of command," to the top if necessary.

E:   Can I help you?

C:   I want to speak to Mr. Adams about a complaint. Tell him that it is very important.

E:   Just a moment. *[She goes into Mr. Adams's office for a few moments and then returns.]* You can go in, sir.

C:   Mr. Adams?

E:   Yes, what can I do for you? I understand you are having a little problem.

C:   It's about this bill. I have been talking to person after person in this office without getting any response. I'm going in circles. I need to talk to someone who is not going to send me to someone else!

TECHNIQUE: *Take the role of the tired, battered, helpless citizen.*

E:   Well, let me see what I can do. I've asked the secretary to get your file. . . . Here it is. The records say that you haven't paid several months' bills. Our policy here is to terminate utility service if payment is delinquent 60 days or more.

C:   What policy is that? Could I see a copy of this policy and what law it is based on?

TECHNIQUE: *Ask for authorization.* Make the agency show you the regulation, law, or authority that allegedly backs up the action it has taken or says it will take. What risk is the complainant taking by resorting to this technique? Is the complainant suggesting to Mr. Adams that he does not trust him? How would you have asked for authorization in this situation? Does the request for authorization always have to be made in a hostile manner?

E:   Well, I'll be glad to show you the brochure.

C:   I would like to see it and also the law it is based on. My position, Mr. Adams, is that my wife has paid the bills.

E:   Well, our records don't reflect it.

C:   The canceled checks have not all come back from the bank yet. I would like a photocopy of your file on me. Under the law, I am entitled to it.

TECHNIQUE: *Cite the law*. Demonstrate that you know what regulations and other laws apply to the case.

E:   You do have this right, but only if you make the request in writing.

C:   Let's be reasonable. I'm making the request in person. That should be sufficient.

TECHNIQUE: *Insist on common sense*. Show the agency official that your position makes good common sense, even if regulations or technicalities go against you.

C:   Surely, your rule calling for a written request can't apply when the person making the request is right in front of you.

TECHNIQUE: *Interpret the law*. Regulations, statutes, and cases often are susceptible to more than one meaning; identify and argue for the meaning most favorable to your cause.

TECHNIQUE: *Demonstrate the exception*. Insist that your situation is unique, not governed by the general rule.

C:   Don't you have the power to waive this rule in such a case?

TECHNIQUE: *Uncover the realm of discretion*. Argue that rules do not exist until they are applied and that in the application of rules, agency officials often have some latitude in interpreting them in spite of their claim that their hands are tied by the rules.

E:   Well, all right, I'll see if I can get a copy run off for you while you are here, but it will take a little time and I must point out that it's highly irregular.

C:   Now, Mr. Adams, I understand that you are a very busy man and that you have responsibilities more demanding than listening to people like me all day.

TECHNIQUE: *Be a buddy*. Show the agency official that you are not his enemy and that you respect and like him and that you are aware of how difficult his job is. Here the complainant has obviously shifted his tactic; he is no longer antagonistic. Consciously or unconsciously, he has made an evaluation of how successful his techniques have been thus far and has decided on a different course of action. What risk is he running in making this shift?

C:   All I want is a two-week extension of time so that I can collect the proof needed to show you that the bill has been paid.

TECHNIQUE: *Put your cards on the table*. Tell the agency official, directly and openly, what your position is and what you want.

E:   Well, we seldom give extensions. The situation must be extreme. I don't know . . .

C:   Mr. Adams, suppose we forget my request for a copy of the records for the time being. All I want is two weeks.

TECHNIQUE: *Find the points of compromise*. Look for the negotiable points and figure out whether you can bargain your way to a good result.

E:   I don't think so.

C:   Well, Mr. Adams, it's either that or I'm going to go to court. All I'm asking for is some fair treatment. There's a principle involved and I intend to fight for it.

TECHNIQUE: *Make clear that you are going to fight this case "all the way up"*. Make the agency official aware of how important this case is. When you have grounds to back you, point out that you are thinking about taking the case to a formal hearing and, if necessary, to court.

E:   I'm sorry you feel that way, but we have our rules here. It would be chaos if we broke them every time someone asked for it.

C:   Good day, Mr. Adams. *[You leave the office, resolved not to come back alone.]*

TECHNIQUE: *Seek the support of third persons.* Gather the support of individuals or groups within and outside the agency so that you can demonstrate that you are not alone.

Has the complainant failed? Was he a "bad" advocate? Has he accomplished anything? Should he give up? Do you think he will? If he does not, do you think he has learned (or that he should have learned) enough about the utility company to come back next time better equipped to handle his problem? If he comes back, what approach should he take and whom should he see? Should he see the supervisor of Mr. Adams, for example?

## Section C
# PROCEDURAL DUE PROCESS

Where paralegals are authorized by law to engage in *formal advocacy* by representing clients at administrative hearings (see chapter 4 and appendix E), it is one of the great challenges that they enjoy. In the remainder of the chapter, we will explore some of the skills required to perform this task effectively.

The subject matter of a hearing, as well as its procedure, can range from the very simple to the very complex. Our approach will be to examine a relatively simple hearing, after identifying the components of procedural due process.

When a government agency and a citizen have a serious dispute, basic fairness may require a number of procedural safeguards for the citizen. These safeguards are known as **procedural due process**. Let's look at an example:

> Tom is a civilian employee of the army. One day he receives a call from the manager of the division, who says, "I have just finished reading the report of the assistant manager. Based on my own observations and on this report, it is clear to me that you have been using the agency car for your own personal use. I have decided to fire you."

**procedural due process**
Procedural protections that are required before the government can take away or refuse to grant liberty or a public benefit.

As a matter of fairness and common sense, what is wrong with the manager's approach? Assume that Tom denies the charge and that this is the first time he has heard anything about an alleged improper use of an agency car. The *substantive* question is whether Tom used the car improperly. The *procedural* question is whether the agency's method of resolving this problem is fair. The latter is a question of procedural due process.

In exhibit 15.2, you will find some of the visceral responses that Tom or any citizen might make, plus their legal translation in terms of procedural safeguards.

As a matter of constitutional law, a citizen is not entitled to all 10 components of procedural due process outlined in exhibit 15.2 in every dispute with a government agency. What procedural safeguards are required? The answer depends primarily on the seriousness of the dispute. In a hearing on terminating public assistance, for example, all 10 safeguards are required when the recipient is challenging the termination. This is so because of the extreme consequences that could result from termination. The more extreme the possible consequences, the more procedural safeguards the law imposes on the conduct of hearings to determine whether those consequences should be imposed.

## Section D
# FORMAL ADMINISTRATIVE ADVOCACY

> "What would it be like to stand before a judge, and it would be you—yes, you—standing (without a law degree) before a judge representing a client? A person in need would be depending on your ability as a representative to help win the case. What would it be like?" Jeffrey S. Wolfe, United States Administrative Law Judge[1]

We turn now to a paralegal's role in formal administrative advocacy. As we saw in chapter 1, there are a number of state and federal administrative agencies that allow paralegals

**EXHIBIT 15.2** **Procedural Due Process: Procedural Safeguards**

| VISCERAL RESPONSE | LEGAL TRANSLATION |
|---|---|
| "Before I was fired, I should have been told the agency thinks I used the car illegally." | 1. *Notice.* To enable you to prepare a response, you should be given adequate advance **notice** of the charge against you. |
| "Show me the report the assistant manager wrote on me so that I can see what he's talking about. And tell me what observations you [the manager] made to arrive at this conclusion." | 2. *Examination of evidence.* In order to respond to the evidence against you, you should be able to see what that evidence is. |
| "Before you fire me, give me a chance to explain myself." | 3. *Hearing.* You should be given a formal meeting or **hearing**, where you can present your case. |
| "I want to present my case before someone other than the assistant manager or the manager." | 4. *Hearing officer free of bias.* The hearing officer should be uninvolved—free of **bias**. The person making the charge against you, or giving any evidence against you, should not be making the final decision as to whether the charge is true. (The accuser should not be the executioner.) |
| "If someone has something to say against me, I want to hear it from this person's own mouth, and I want to be able to ask him questions myself." | 5. *Confrontation and cross-examination.* Whoever is accusing you or giving any evidence against you should be required to do so in your presence **(confrontation)**. You should be able to ask this person questions about his or her allegations **(cross-examination).** |
| "I want to be able to bring my own counsel to help me." | 6. *Legal representation.* You should have the right to representation by an attorney or an attorney-substitute of your own choosing. |
| "I've had some unrelated troubles on the job in the past, plus some personal problems at home, but that has nothing to do with my use of the car." | 7. *Relevancy of evidence.* The hearing officer should consider only relevant evidence. **Relevancy** refers to anything reasonably related to establishing the truth or falsity of the charge. |
| "My co-worker knows everything about my use of agency cars. I want to bring him to the hearing." | 8. *Presentation of own witnesses.* You should be given the opportunity to present your own witnesses and any other evidence that supports your position. |
| "I want to see the decision in writing." | 9. *Written decision with reasons.* To enable you to prepare an appeal, you should be given the decision in writing as well as the reasons for the decision. |
| "I want to be able to appeal." | 10. *Appeal.* You should be given the right to **appeal** the decision to another individual or body |

**notice** Information about a fact; knowledge of something.

**hearing** A proceeding convened to resolve a dispute during which parties in the dispute can present their case.

**bias** An inclination or tendency to think and to act in a certain way. A danger of prejudgment. (A person without a bias is objective, dispassionate, or disinterested.)

**confrontation** Being present when others give evidence against you and having the opportunity to question them.

**cross-examination** Questioning of a witness at a hearing by an opponent after the other side has conducted a direct examination of that witness.

**relevancy** Having a reasonable relationship to the truth or falsity of a fact; that which reasonably tends to make the existence of a fact more probable or less probable.

**appeal** (1) A formal request that a higher authority examine or review a decision made by another body. (2) An examination or review by a higher authority of a decision made by another body.

to provide a full range of legal services, including representation of their own clients at administrative hearings. (See also appendix E.) One of the largest agencies where this occurs is the Social Security Administration (SSA). Although formal administrative advocacy differs from agency to agency, an examination of a paralegal's role at SSA can help us understand what is possible at many agencies.

One of SSA's largest programs provides disability benefits to individuals who suffer from an "inability to engage in any substantial gainful activity by reason of any medically determinable physical or mental impairment."[2] Every year 2.5 million people apply for social security disability benefits under one of two programs:

- Disability Insurance Benefits (DIB) for individuals who have a qualifying work history and
- Supplemental Security Income (SSI) for individuals who may have never worked.

Approximately 1.7 million of these applications are denied. The denials lead to a staggering 600,000 annual appeals handled by federal **administrative law judges (ALJ)** throughout the country. "The Social Security Administration . . . adjudicates more cases than all federal courts combined."[3] Social security law, as many citizens know from first-hand experience, can be complicated. This is particularly true of disability law. Consequently, the need for legal assistance in the 600,000 annual disability hearings is enormous.

Unfortunately, not enough attorneys practice social security law, although a growing number take social security cases under the broader practice of elder law. Part of the reason many attorneys stay away from disability cases is that they do not generate enough revenue. In most cases, a representative can collect $4,000 or 25 percent of back-due disability benefits, whichever is less. The fee cannot be higher even if the client agrees to pay more. Nationally, the average fee collected is $2,500.[4] This is not enough to interest many attorneys. Fortunately, claimants seeking legal representation have an alternative. Congress has specifically provided that persons:

"other than attorneys" may represent "claimants before the Social Security Administration."[5]

Hence paralegals have a federal mandate to practice law before SSA, including the right to charge fees for their services. Some attorneys may not want to refer to paralegal representation as practicing law, but that's what it is. This is not to say, however, that attorneys and paralegals are treated alike in social security cases. They both have the same responsibilities as representatives, but they are treated differently in the crucial area of fees. When attorneys win a disability case, their fee is deducted from the claimant's award by SSA and sent directly to the attorneys. When nonattorney representatives win a case, however, they must collect their fee on their own from the client.

The first step in being a representative is to be appointed by the client. (See exhibit 4.2 in chapter 4 for the form that a social security applicant must use to appoint a representative.) There is no examination, license, or registration requirement imposed by SSA to be a representative. Yet there is a requirement "that a representative know the significant issue(s) in a claim and have a working knowledge" of social security statutes, regulations, and rulings.[6]

### SAMPLE CASE

To gain a greater appreciation of paralegal representation at SSA disability hearings, we will examine a sample case. It involves a dispute over an overpayment to a recipient of disability payments under the Supplemental Security Income (SSI) program. Here are the major participants in the case:

Mary O'Brien:  SSI recipient and claimant
George O'Brien:  Mary's husband
John Powell:  paralegal representative of Mary
Helen Davis:  witness for Mary
Alex Bolton:  administrative law judge at SSA

### Background

Mary O'Brien is disabled. She suffers from depression, an affective disorder, and receives $531 a month in SSI. This amount assumes a total income of $3,600 a year in the

**administrative law judge (ALJ)** A government official at an administrative agency who presides over a hearing to resolve a legal dispute.

O'Brien household. Benefits under SSI are, in part, dependent on available income in the recipient's home. When Mary applied for SSI benefits, she told SSA that her husband, George O'Brien, earns $3,600 a year from a part-time job as a night watchman.

Mary and George have a strained relationship, although they continue to live together. She is not aware of what he does during the day. Indeed, when she questions him about his activities, he becomes hostile. He can be violent. On June 1, 2000, she called the police when he went into a rage. The police referred Mary to the County Domestic Violence Center. She went there and met with a counselor, Helen Davis. After describing what happened, Davis advised Mary to obtain a restraining order against her husband. Mary, however, did not want to involve the courts, since she felt this would enrage her husband all the more. Hence she did not file for a restraining order, although she continued to come to the Center to attend counseling sessions for abused women.

On September 1, 2001, SSA sends Mary a Notice of Overpayment. It states that according to information received from the Internal Revenue Service, George O'Brien reported taxable earnings of $12,000 during the year 2000. Her payment of $531 a month was based on a household income of $3,600. Since her husband was in fact earning considerably more, her 2000 entitlement has been recalculated. The SSA has concluded that Mary received an overpayment of $3,250 during 2000. To recoup this amount, SSA will deduct $53.10 a month from her disability check until the overpayment of $3,250 has been repaid.

This notice is quite distressing for Mary. She calls the local Neighborhood Legal Services Office for help. On the phone, a receptionist determines that she is eligible for free legal services because of her low income. The receptionist tells Mary to come in the next day for an appointment with John Powell, a paralegal in the office who handles social security cases.

John conducts an extensive interview of Mary. She tells John that her husband admits that he earned the extra money in 2000 but that it was "none of your business." He works as a night guard for a security firm that is managed by his cousin. She also describes his anger and violence over anything that questions or challenges his authority or that is considered an interference in his affairs.

### Prehearing Advocacy

John points out to Mary that if the extra money was earned, the only way she can avoid making the repayment is to file a Request for Waiver of Overpayment on the ground that she is without fault in causing the overpayment or in failing to report it and that requiring repayment will be a hardship and is against equity and good conscience. Furthermore, if they act quickly, they might prevent SSA from starting the deductions from her monthly disability check. Mary begins to feel relieved. She signs the SSA form appointing John as her representative (see exhibit 4.2 in chapter 4) and asks him to take whatever steps are necessary to try to avoid the repayment. He explains that if the request for waiver is denied, they can ask for a conference to explain their side and ultimately they can ask for a hearing before an administrative law judge.

In the weeks following the meeting between John and his client, a number of events occur:

- John helps Mary fill out the Request for Waiver of Overpayment. The basis of the request is that Mary is without fault because she knew nothing about her husband's side job, he is secretive about his finances, and he is abusive, particularly when she questions him about anything he does outside the home.
- John sends this request to SSA along with a cover letter asking SSA not to begin deductions from Mary's monthly payment until the appeal process is complete. He makes this request as a precaution even though SSA's policy is not to begin "adjustment action" until the waiver issue is resolved.
- A month later SSA sends Mary and John its response. The request for waiver is denied.
- John then asks the SSA field office for a personal conference during which he and Mary will explain their case before an SSA official who has not been involved in the initial decision to require the repayment of the overpayment. This request is granted.
- Five days before the personal conference, John exercises Mary's right to go to the SSA

office in order to examine the file that contains the records used by SSA to demand the return of the overpayment. He photocopies the records that he does not already have.
- By studying the SSA records in Mary's file, John identifies further evidence he will pursue to be better prepared to respond to the SSA's case against Mary.
- The personal conference takes place at the SSA office. It lasts about an hour. John goes over the details of what happened during 2000 and why Mary knew nothing about her husband's extra income. One of the reasons the conference is valuable (even if it does not result in a decision in Mary's favor) is that it gives John a clearer understanding of the SSA's case against her.
- A month later Mary and John receive a notice from SSA reaffirming the decision not to grant her the waiver.
- Further efforts to resolve the case (including use of reconsideration procedures) are unsuccessful. John then files a Request for Hearing before an administrative law judge.
- Several weeks later, John receives a call from the Office of Hearings and Appeals to arrange a date for the hearing. After consulting with Mary, a date for the hearing is set. John and Mary receive a formal Notice of Hearing indicating that the hearing will be held before United States Administrative Law Judge Alex Bolton on the agreed-upon date.

### Characteristics of Disability Hearings

A disability hearing in SSA's Office of Hearings and Appeals is **nonadversarial** because it is a one-party proceeding. At a hearing, the following participants might be present:

**nonadversarial** Pertaining to a conflict-resolution proceeding in which all parties to the conflict or dispute are not present.

- The claimant
- His or her representative (e.g., a paralegal)
- One or more witnesses (e.g., a vocational counselor, a relative)
- A reporter (often an SSA secretary) who makes a voice recording of the hearing
- The presiding administrative law judge (ALJ)

(See exhibit 15.3 for a typical arrangement of a SSA hearing room.) An official representing the SSA is not present. The only party at the hearing is the claimant.

This does not mean, however, that the claimant's representative will have an easy time establishing the position of the claimant. The ALJ is not an advocate, but he or she has an obligation to "develop the record." To fulfill this duty, the ALJ might take an affirmative role at the hearing such as by actively questioning the claimant and arranging for a vocational expert to be present to give testimony. The representative must convince the ALJ that the claimant's case fits within the guidelines of eligibility for disability benefits. This is done primarily through the testimony of the claimant and the introduction of documentary evidence such as medical and vocational records. Medical records can be lengthy, complicated, incomplete, confusing, and, at times, contradictory. Nevertheless, most ALJs will not tolerate a sloppy presentation; they will hold a representative's feet to the fire by insisting on a coherent presentation of the claimant's case. The representative must be able to anticipate possible questions from the ALJ and provide answers by citing information on specific pages of exhibits in the record. Competent representation can be a challenge even though the other side is technically absent and unrepresented.

A disability hearing is similar to a court trial in that both are on-the-record proceedings in which testimony is given under oath. A recorder is present at the disability hearing to tape-record everything that is said. Yet unlike court trials, the rules of evidence do not apply to disability hearings. The ALJ will consider any evidence that is relevant (broadly defined) to the issues in the case.

To a large extent, the conduct of a hearing depends on the style and personality of the presiding ALJ. Some ALJs will let the representative take the lead by making an opening statement, introducing documentary evidence, and questioning witnesses. The ALJ might ask his or her own questions after the representative has finished. Other ALJs take a more aggressive role. They might not allow the representative to take over until they ask questions of the claimant or other witnesses.

| EXHIBIT 15.3 | Typical Social Security Hearing Room |
| --- | --- |

An administrative law judge presides over a social security hearing. Present to the judges' left are the paralegal representative, the claimant, a witness, and a court reporter. Before the paralegal begins asking questions of the witness, the judge swears in the witness as the reporter prepares a transcript of the proceeding.

### Preparation for the Hearing

To prepare for Mary's hearing, John does the following:

- Asks Helen Davis to come to the hearing as a witness for Mary. Davis is the counselor at the County Domestic Violence Center where Mary went for assistance during 2000.
- Obtains a letter from Mary's doctor, David Stepps, Ph.D., that describes the medication he prescribed for her due to the tension she was under at home.
- Researches this medication on the Internet and finds a report from the National Institute of Mental Health on the reasons the medication is prescribed and its side effects of lethargy and extreme sensitivity to conflict. John downloads this report and prints the pertinent section for use at the hearing.
- Researches the battered women syndrome on the Internet and finds a medical study on the helplessness experienced by women faced with severe abuse from their husbands and boyfriends. He downloads and prints the study for use at the hearing.
- Researches SSA's policy manual on the Internet (*policy.ssa.gov/poms.nsf/aboutpoms*) to make sure he has a full grasp of all of the procedures that SSA should be following in Mary's case.
- Prepares a complete summary of all Mary's assets and liabilities, showing monthly household income and expenses.
- Obtains copies of the O'Briens' federal and state tax returns for 2000.
- Compiles Mary's medical history, which will be relevant to the hardship issue (particularly the amounts she must pay for drugs and other medical care) and to her ability to handle stress and understand household finances.
- Prepares a set of notes in which he identifies Mary's theory of the case, together with citations to applicable regulations and supporting facts in the exhibits.

■ Meets with Mary in his office to go over what is likely to happen at the hearing and to role-play her responses to the questions that he plans to ask her and that the ALJ might ask her. John comments on each of her responses, pointing out the importance of telling the truth and of giving detailed answers. He tells her that the hearing will be tape-recorded so she should speak clearly and answer questions verbally. The tape recorder will not know if she answers a question with a nod of her head.

### The O'Brien Hearing

Judge Bolton begins the hearing by introducing himself and letting everyone know that a reporter will be recording the proceeding. He then asks everyone to identify themselves for the record:

> Mary O'Brien: SSI recipient and claimant
> John Powell: paralegal representative of Mary
> Helen Davis: witness for Mary

Judge Bolton turns his attention to the reports and other exhibits already in the file and those that anyone wants considered. They are all identified with an exhibit number. He asks John if he has any objections to any of the exhibits. John responds that he does not but that he hopes to have the chance during the hearing to comment on some of the SSA reports in the file.

Judge Bolton administers the oath to tell the truth to all witnesses who will be giving testimony (Mary O'Brien and Helen Davis) and tells John to present his case.

John begins by summarizing the position of his client that she is without fault in receiving the overpayment because she had no knowledge of the extra earnings of her husband and that he has been physically abusive to her whenever she tries to question him about any financial matters. He also says that forcing a repayment will be a severe hardship on Mary.

John then asks Mary a series of questions to elaborate on these and other relevant points. For example:

> Who takes care of the finances in the household?
> Is your name on any bank accounts with your husband?
> Describe the living expenses you and your husband have in the home.
> Explain whether it will be a hardship to have to repay the overpayment.
> Has your husband told you what he does during the day?
> When do you see him during the course of the day?
> Did your husband hit you during 2000?
> Did you call the police?
> Why have you stayed living with a husband who is abusive?
> Are any other living arrangements available to you if you leave your husband?
> Describe your health during 2000.
> Were you taking any medication?
> What effect did the medication have on you?

While asking such questions, John refers to specific exhibits such as the letter of Doctor David Stepps on why he prescribed the medication, the report on the side effects of the medication, and the study on the battered women syndrome.

When John finishes questioning Mary, Judge Bolton asks her several questions about her educational background and about the times at home when she is able to get along with her husband. After Mary answers, John asks her some follow-up questions designed to reinforce her inability to understand financial matters and her fear of her husband.

Finally, John begins questioning Helen Davis, the counselor at the County Domestic Violence Center. John asks her to explain the services of the Center and the level of agitation and fear Mary expressed when she came there for help. He asks her whether it is common for abused women to remain with their abusers. Finally, he asks her to explain why she recommended that Mary obtain a restraining order against her husband and whether it is unusual for an abused woman to be afraid to do so.

At the conclusion of all the testimony, Judge Bolton thanks everyone and says that he will render a decision as soon as possible.

Before leaving, John has one final request of Judge Bolton. He asks if he can submit a memorandum to the judge in which he presents the facts in the light of the applicable law. Judge Bolton says he will be glad to receive such a memorandum. John knows that ALJs hold many hearings and a memorandum of this kind might help influence the outcome of his case. Preparing it after the hearing gives John the opportunity to highlight those facts and legal matters that appeared to be of concern to the ALJ at the hearing.

Seven months after submitting the memorandum, John and Mary receive the decision of Judge Bolton. Mary is found to have been without fault in causing the overpayment and it would be an undue hardship to require repayment. Victory!

### Further Appeals

If the decision had gone against Mary, the next step would have been a Request for Review by the Appeals Council. This is an appeal within the SSA. The claimant submits a brief to the Appeals Council indicating why the decision of the administrative law judge should be reversed. John would prepare the brief for Mary. A paralegal representative can write and sign these briefs. In the vast majority of cases, neither the party nor his or her representative makes a personal appearance before the Appeals Council. A decision is rendered on the record.

If a claimant was dissatisfied by the decision of the Appeals Council, the next step would be an appeal to the United States District Court. The case could be taken to court because the party had **exhausted administrative remedies**. At this point, an attorney would have to take over the case, although a paralegal could assist the attorney, as in any court case. The attorney could ask a competent paralegal to prepare the pleadings and briefs that would be submitted to the court, but only an attorney could sign them. The federal authorization for paralegals to represent claimants within SSA does not include court representation.

**exhaust administrative remedies** To go through all dispute-solving avenues that are available in an administrative agency before asking a court to review what the agency did.

### Conclusion

As you can see from John Powell's role as a representative before the SSA, formal administrative advocacy by paralegals, where it is allowed, can be a major undertaking. Although most paralegals do not have the opportunity to engage in such advocacy in their everyday work, you might consider **pro bono** work where such advocacy is needed. (See the list of pro bono work in section C of chapter 2.) There are neighborhood legal service offices, legal aid societies, and homeless projects in many cities that would welcome part-time volunteer work on social security cases. Perhaps you could inquire about teaming with an experienced paralegal whom you could assist until you felt comfortable enough to venture out on your own cases. The need for legal help in this area is enormous.

**pro bono** Performed for the public good without fee or compensation (pro bono publico).

## ◼ CHAPTER SUMMARY

Advocacy takes place all the time. It is an everyday process by which all citizens—not just attorneys—attempt to influence or change the actions of others at one time or another. Informal advocacy occurs outside of courts or other tribunals where hearings are held to resolve controversies that the participants have not been able to resolve informally.

Advocates try many techniques of informal advocacy, with varying degrees of success. Among the most common are the following: placing your cards on the table; insisting on adequate service; seeking the support of third parties; being a buddy; finding the points of compromise; insisting on common sense; demonstrating the exception; uncovering the realm of discretion; asking for authorization; citing the law; redefining the problem; showing anger; preaching; climbing the chain of command; embarrassing the official; making clear that you will fight the case; taking the role of the tired, battered, helpless citizen; doing a favor to get a favor; and citing a precedent. While using any of these techniques, you need to evaluate your effectiveness and modify the techniques based on this evaluation.

Whenever the government takes an action that seriously affects a citizen, such as denying or removing a benefit, basic fairness may require a number of procedural safeguards. These requirements are referred to as *procedural due process*. While not applicable to every situation, the safeguards include notice, a hearing, a personal appearance at the hearing, the absence of bias, representation, relevance of the evidence, an opportunity to examine the evidence, an opportunity to present your own witnesses, a decision in writing, and an opportunity to appeal.

At some state and federal administrative agencies, paralegals are authorized to provide a full range of legal services, including representation of their own clients at administrative hearings. A major example of such an agency is the Social Security Administration, particularly in the representation of applicants at disability hearings. Competent representation at such hearings requires extensive preparation and skill in marshalling facts and coherently presenting them at the hearing in light of the applicable law.

## KEY TERMS

| | |
|---|---|
| advocacy | cross-examination |
| quasi-judicial proceeding | relevancy |
| procedural due process | appeal |
| notice | administrative law judge (ALJ) |
| hearing | nonadversarial |
| bias | exhaust administrative remedies |
| confrontation | pro bono |

## ON THE NET: MORE ON ADMINISTRATIVE ADVOCACY

**Administrative Advocacy Training**
www.mnlegalservices.org/train/admin_adv.shtml

**Social Security Representation**
www.ssa.gov/representation
www.ssa.gov/pubs/10075.html

**National Organization of Social Security Claimants' Representatives**
www.nosscr.org

## ENDNOTES

1. Jeffrey S. Wolfe, *Professional Service to the Beat of a Different Drum: Non-Lawyer Representation before Social Security's Office of Hearings and Appeals*, Facts & Findings 37 (May 2000). The assistance of Judge Wolfe and of Christopher J. Holly, RP (an Indiana independent paralegal), in the preparation of the social security materials in this chapter is gratefully acknowledged. See Judge Wolfe's book *Social Security and the Legal Professional* (Delmar, 2003) and Christopher Holly's Internet site, (www.medicaidguide.com.)

2. 42 U.S.C. § 416(i)(1)(A).
3. Milton Carrow, *A Tortuous Road to Bureaucratic Fairness*, 46 Administrative Law Review 297 (Summer 1994).
4. Wolfe, *supra* note 1, at 39.
5. 42 U.S.C. § 406(a)(1).
6. 20 C.F.R. § 404.1740(b)(3)(I).

# Appendix A

# BIBLIOGRAPHY

## AAA

*AARP'S Legal Services Network: Expanding Legal Services to the Middle Class* by W. Moore, 32 Wake Forest Law Review 503 (1997).

*ABA Formal Opinion 93–379: Double Billing, Padding and Other Forms of Overbilling* by S. Chan, 9 Georgetown Journal of Legal Ethics 611 (1996).

*ABA Report Debates Nonlawyers' Role in Providing Legal Services*, 23 Montana Lawyer 11 (May 1998).

*Accounting Firms and the Unauthorized Practice of Law: Who Is the Bar Really Trying to Protect?* by E. Farrell, 33 Indiana Law Review 599 (2000).

*Activities of Insurance Adjusters as Unauthorized Practice of Law*, 29 A.L.R.4th 1156 (1984).

*Activities of Law Clerks as Illegal Practice of Law*, 13 A.L.R.3d 1137 (1967).

*Activities of Stock or Securities Broker Constitute Unauthorized Practice of Law*, 34 A.L.R.3d 1305 (1970).

*The Adventures of a Paralegal* by G. Stephens, 28 Colorado Lawyer 33 (Apr. 1999).

*Alternative Staffing Option: Freelance Paralegals* by E. Siemek, 27 Colorado Lawyer 49 (Apr. 1998).

*Another First for State Bar of Texas: Specialty Certification of Legal Assistants* by L. Thomas & D. Hardin, 57 Texas Bar Journal 58 (Jan. 1994).

*Another Perspective on Employing Disbarred or Suspended Attorneys* by C. Simpson, 2 The Lawyers Journal 5 (Oct. 2000) (Pennsylvania).

*Approaches for Continuing Legal Education for Paralegals*, 7 Journal of Paralegal Education & Practice 43 (1990).

*Are Organizations That Provide Free Legal Services Engaged in the Unauthorized Practice of Law?* by W. Moore, 67 Fordham Law Review 2397 (1999).

*The Art of Managing Your Support Staff* (American Bar Association Section of Economics of Law Practice, 1986).

*Asserting Confidentiality: The Need for a Lay Representative–Claimant Privilege* by J. Kaufman, 15 Pacific Law Journal 245 (1984) (administrative hearings).

*Assisting Clients in Achieving the American Dream* by M. Burgner, 75 Michigan Bar Journal 44 (Jan. 1996) (paralegals in real estate).

*Attorneys' Fees: Cost of Services Provided by Paralegals*, 73 A.L.R.4th 938 (1987).

*Attorney's Guide to Practicing with Legal Assistants*, 2d ed. (State Bar of Texas, 1992).

*Attorney's Splitting Fees with . . . Laymen as Grounds for Disciplinary Proceeding*, 6 A.L.R.3d 1446 (1966).

*The Attorney Timesaver: Records Requests and the Legal Assistant* by E. Moulton, 6 Nevada Lawyer 20 (Apr. 1998).

*The Authorized Practice of Legal Reference Service* by M. Mosley, 87 Law Library Journal 203 (1995).

## BBB

*Bankruptcy Paralegal Regulation* by M. Testerman, 23 California Bankruptcy Journal 37 (1996).

*Bar Seeks to Protect Public with Non-Lawyer Practice Rules*, 30 Arizona Attorney 10 (Mar. 1994).

*Better Resumes for Attorneys and Paralegals* by A. Lewis (Barron's, 1986).

*To Bill, or Not to Bill?* by A. Altman, 11 Georgetown Journal of Legal Ethics 203 (1998) (ethical billing practices).

*Blue-Chip Bilking: Regulation of Billing and Expense Fraud by Lawyers* by L. Lerman, 12 Georgetown Journal of Legal Ethics 205 (1999).

*Building a Strong Attorney-Paralegal Team* by N. Cattie, 27 Trial 24 (Jan. 1991).

## CCC

*Calculating Profit from Associates and Paralegals*, 58 Journal of the Kansas Bar Association 5 (Apr. 1989).

*California Paralegal's Guide*, 5th ed., by Z. Mack (LEXIS Publishing, 1998).

*Call the ~~Doctor~~ Nurse!: The Role of the Legal Nurse Consultant*, 19 San Francisco Attorney Magazine 20 (Dec. 1993/ Jan. 1994).

*The Certified Legal Assistant Credential* by the National Association of Legal Assistants, 11 Maine Bar Journal 376 (Nov. 1996).

*The Changing Role of Legal Secretaries* by J. Mitchell, 25 Montana Lawyer 15 (Dec. 1999).

*Chinese Walls* by M. Moser, 3 Georgetown Journal of Legal Ethics 399 (1990) (conflict of interest).

*Choice for Legal Services: Consumer Need for Legal Technicians Increasing* by R. Smith, 52 Oregon State Bar Bulletin 26 (June 1992).

*Civil Legal Assistance for the Twenty-First Century: Achieving Equal Justice for All* by A. Houseman, 17 Yale Law & Policy Review 369 (1998).

*The Client's Viewpoint on Paralegals* by W. Redd, 8 West Virginia Lawyer 19 (Apr. 1995).

*Code Crackdown: Bankruptcy Trustees Use Law to Police (Nonlawyer) Petition Preparers* by H. Samborn, 82 American Bar Association Journal 18 (May 1996).

*Collection Agencies and the Unauthorized Practice of Law* by K. Folts, 77 Nebraska Law Review 365 (1998).

*Colloquium on Nonlawyer Practice before Administrative Agencies*, 37 Administrative Law Review 359 (1985).

*Colorado Paralegals: Proposed Guidelines* by S. Davis, 25 The Colorado Lawyer 63 (Oct. 1996) (see also 25 The Colorado Lawyer 33 (Nov. 1996)).

*Community Courts* by W. Statsky, 3 Capital University Law Review 2 (1974).

*Computer Programs and Systems Optimize Legal Assistant Productivity* by M. Bjorkman, 70 Michigan Bar Journal 1154 (Nov. 1991).

*Conflicts and Confidences: Codes Address Ethics for Paralegals* by H. Samborn, 82 American Bar Association Journal 24 (June 1996).

*Could Your Office Use a Paralegal?* by R. Blount, 44 Advocate 23 (Jan. 2001) (Idaho).

*Court Interpreters: Standards of Practice and Standards for Training* by F. Salimbene, 6 Cornell Journal of Law & Public Policy 645 (1997).

*Criminal Defendant's Representation by Person Not Licensed to Practice Law as Violation of Right to Counsel*, 19 A.L.R.5th 351 (1994).

*Criteria for Recovering Legal Assistant Fees* by C. Embry, 5 Nevada Lawyer 30 (Feb. 1997).

## DDD

*Dances with Nonlawyers: A New Perspective on Law Firm Diversification* by G. Munneke, 61 Fordham Law Review 559 (1992).

*A Day with a Legal Assistant* by N. Stecker, 80 Michigan Bar Journal 58 (Mar. 2001).

*Defining Mediation and Its Use for Paralegals* by A. Chasen, 9 Journal of Paralegal Education & Practice 61 (1993).

*Defining the Unauthorized Practice of Law* by A. Morrison, 4 Nova Law Journal 363 (1980).

*Delawyerizing Labor Arbitration* by R. Alleyne, 50 Ohio State Law Journal 93 (1989).

*Delegate to Your Legal Assistant* by M. Gaige, 5 Maine Bar Journal 98 (Mar. 1990).

*The Delivery of Legal Services by Non-Lawyers* by D. Rhode, 4 Georgetown Journal of Legal Ethics 209 (1990).

*Deregulation of the Practice of Law* by M. Munro, 42 Hastings Law Journal 203 (1990).

*Developments in the Law of Professional Responsibility*, "Use of Legal Assistants" by C. Kidd, 28 Indiana Law Review 1013, 1015 (1995).

*Directions in Legal Assistant Training and Education* by L. Jevahirian, 75 Michigan Bar Journal 38 (Jan. 1996).

*Disciplinary Action against Attorney for Aiding or Assisting Another Person in Unauthorized Practice of Law*, 41 A.L.R.4th 361 (1985).

*Disorder in the People's Court: Rethinking the Role of Non-Lawyer Judges* by C. Mansfield, 29 New Mexico Law Review 119 (Winter 1999).

*Disqualified: Switching Sides by Legal Assistants in Litigation*, 77 American Bar Association Journal 88 (Oct. 1991).

*Divorce Litigants without Lawyers* by R. Yegge, 28 Family Law Quarterly 407 (1994).

*DOJ [Department of Justice] Probes Law Firms: Paralegal Who Copied Tobacco Company Documents Subpoenaed* by M. Curriden, 80 American Bar Association Journal 14 (June 1994).

*Domestic Violence Advocates' Exposure to Liability for Engaging in the Unauthorized Practice of Law* by M. Brown, 34 Columbia Journal of Law & Social Problems 279 (2001).

*Do Nonlawyer Justices Dispense Justice?* by C. Fieman, 69 New York State Bar Journal 20 (Jan. 1997).

*Don't Let Your Staff Do Wrong* by D. Walther, 13 Family Advocate 40 (Spring 1991).

*Do Your Confidences Go out the Window When Your Employees Go out the Door?* by K. Rendall, 42 Hastings Law Journal 1667 (1991).

*Drafting of Will or Other Estate Planning Activities as Illegal Practice of Law*, 22 A.L.R.3d 1112 (1968).

## EEE

*The Education and Utilization of Paralegals in . . . Immigration* by A. Wernick, 7 Journal of Paralegal Education & Practice 23 (1990).

*Education for the Practice of Law: The Times They Are A-Changin'* by R. Stuckey, 75 Nebraska Law Review 648 (1996).

*The Education of Legal Paraprofessionals: Myths, Realities, and Opportunities* by W. Statsky, 24 Vanderbilt Law Review 1083 (1971).

*Effective Use of Legal Assistants Equates to Greater Profit* by K. Libman, 23 Law Practice Management 40 (July/Aug. 1997).

*Ensuring Attorney/Paralegal Team Excellence* by G. Green, 38 The North Carolina State Bar Quarterly 33 (Winter 1991).

*Ensuring Meaningful Jailhouse Legal Assistance: The Need for a Jailhouse Lawyer–Inmate Privilege* by J. Nobel, 18 Cardozo Law Review 1569 (Jan. 1997).

*Ethical Considerations for Law Clerks and Paralegals* by E. Peterson, 23 Journal of the Legal Profession 235 (1999).

*Ethical Responsibility of Lawyers for Deception by Undercover Investigators* by D. Isbell, 8 Georgetown Journal of Legal Ethics 791 (1995).

*Ethical Standards for Legal Assistants* by V. Voisin, 70 Michigan Bar Journal 1178 (Nov. 1991).

*The Ethical Utilization of Paralegals in Ohio* by W. Wills, 45 Cleveland State Law Review 711 (1997).

*Ethics and Professional Responsibility for Legal Assistants*, 3d ed., by T. Cannon (Aspen, 1999).

*Ethics and the Legal Assistant* by Candace Jones, 6 Nevada Lawyer 13 (July 1998).

*Ethics for the Legal Assistant*, 4th ed., by D. Orlik (Marlin Hill, 1998).

*The Ethics of Giving Legal Advice: Legal Assistants Must Be Wary of Crossing the Line with Clients* by E. Lockwood, 27 Montana Lawyer 22 (Sept. 2001).

*The Evolving Role of the Paralegal* (New Jersey State Bar Association, 1991).

*Evolving Standards of Nonlawyer Liability* by C. Honchar, 6 Professional Lawyer 14 (May 1995).

*Examining the Issue of Paralegal Regulation* by R. Sova, 75 Michigan Bar Journal 34 (Jan. 1996).

*Exempt from Overtime Pay* by D. Ridgway, 8 West Virginia Lawyer 16 (Feb. 1995).

## FFF

*Fake Lawyers: Unauthorized Practice Issue Is Coming to a Head* by S. Hilander, 22 Montana Lawyer 3 (May 1997).

*To Fee or Not to Fee: The Tenth Anniversary of Missouri v. Jenkins* by K. Rute, 16 Journal of Paralegal Education & Practice 85 (2000).

*Filing, Handling, Perfecting and Foreclosing Oil and Gas Liens, Oil and Gas Law: For Legal Assistants and Attorneys* by S. Stinnett (State Bar of Texas, 1984).

*Finding, Interviewing, Hiring, and Retaining the Best Paralegal for Your Practice* by A. Dunkin, 63 Texas Bar Journal 276 (Mar. 2000).

*Fixed Salary for Paralegal Indicated Employee Status*, 80 Journal of Taxation 183 (Mar. 1994).

*The Florida Bar Advisory Opinion on Nonlawyer Representation in Securities Arbitration Adopted by Florida Supreme Court*, 696 Southern Reporter 2d 1178 (Florida Supreme Court 1997).

*The Florida Bar v. American Senior Citizens Alliance: Is "Gathering the Necessary Information" the Unlicensed Practice of Law?* by A. Bromfield, 12 Quinnipiac Probate Law Journal 523 (1998).

*FLSA: Exempting Paralegals from Overtime Pay* by A. Engel, 74 Washington University Law Quarterly 253 (1996).

*Focus on Corporate Practice: Legal Assistants and Legal Opinion Due Diligence* by C. Drozd, 7 Journal of Paralegal Education & Practice 63 (1990).

*Folly by Fiat: Pretending That Death Row Inmates Can Represent Themselves in State Capital Post-Conviction Proceedings* by C. Smith, 45 Loyola Law Review 55 (Spring 1999).

*The Freelance Legal Assistant* by P. Davidson, 70 Michigan Bar Journal 1184 (Nov. 1991).

*From the Reference Desk to the Jailhouse: Unauthorized Practice of Law and Librarians* by Y. Brown, 13 Legal Reference Services Quarterly 31 (1994).

*Functional Division of the American Legal Profession: The Legal Paraprofessional* by C. Selinger, 22 Journal of Legal Education 22 (1969).

*Functional Overlap between the Lawyer and Other Professionals: Its Implications for the Privileged Communications Doctrine*, 71 Yale Law Journal 1226 (1962).

*Fundamentals of Law Office Management* by P. Everett (West, 2000).

*The Future of the Legal Profession: The Delivery of Legal Services to Ordinary Americans* by R. Cramton, 44 Case Western Reserve Law Review 531 (1994).

## GGG

*Gender and Emotional Labor in the Contemporary Law Firm* by C. Franklin, 7 UCLA Women's Law Journal 131 (1996) (paralegal roles and gender).

*General Guidelines for the Utilization of the Services of Legal Assistants by Attorneys*, 63 Texas Bar Journal 280 (Mar. 2000).

*Going Global* by G. Avramov, 80 Michigan Bar Journal 46 (Mar. 2001) (paralegals in immigration law).

*The Golden Age of Paralegals and Risk Managers* by R. Martin, 9 West Virginia Lawyer 18 (Nov. 1995).

*A Guide for Legal Assistants: Roles, Responsibilities, Specializations*, 2d ed. (Practicing Law Institute, 1991).

## HHH

*Handling, Preparing, Presenting, or Trying Workmen's Compensation Claims or Cases as Practice of Law*, 2 A.L.R.3d 724 (1966).

*Hawaii Paralegals Head toward Certification through Federal Court* by V. Nakaahiki, 2 Hawaii Bar Journal 22 (Aug. 1998).

*Hawaii Paralegals to Make History* by V. Nakaahiki, 46 Federal Lawyer 24 (June 1999).

*The Hawaii Supreme Court Considers Adopting a Comprehensive System of Paralegal Certification* by R. LeClair, 5 Hawaii Bar Journal 23 (Jan. 2001).

*Help! . . . Can My Office Use a Legal Assistant?* by J. Work, 57 Texas Bar Journal 42 (Jan. 1994).

*History of the American Bar* by C. Warren (Little Brown, 1911).

*How Legal Assistants Can Aid You with Real Estate Foreclosures* by C. Burns, 63 Journal of the Kansas Bar Association 18 (May 1994).

*How Many Non-Lawyers Does It Take to Run a Law Firm?* by E. Freedman, 23 Pennsylvania Lawyer 32 (Mar./Apr. 2001).

*How Paralegals Make Money for Law Firms* by M. McClane, 46 St. Louis Bar Journal 28 (Summer 1999).

*How Should We Determine Who Should Regulate Lawyers?* by D. Wilkins, 65 Fordham Law Review 465 (1996).

*How to Evaluate the Qualifications of Legal Assistants* by T. Clarke, 30 Arizona Attorney 28 (May 1994).

*How to Get the Most Out of Your Support Staff* by S. Meyerowitz, 23 Pennsylvania Lawyer 40 (Mar./Apr. 2001).

*How to Use Legal Assistants to Enforce Commercial Secured Claims* by J. Verellen, 33 Practical Lawyer 9 (Dec. 1987).

### III

*The Impact of Antitrust Law on the Legal Profession* by T. Mogan, 67 Fordham Law Review 415 (1998).

*Inadvertent Waiver of the Attorney-Client Privilege and Work Product Doctrine in the First Circuit* by F. Libby, 41 Boston Bar Journal 16 (Nov./Dec. 1997).

*Income Tax Practice and Certified Public Accountants: The Case for a Status Based Exemption from State Unauthorized Practice of Law Rules* by M. Melone, 11 Akron Tax Journal 47 (1995).

*Increasing Access to Justice: Expanding the Role of Nonlawyers* by M. Lock, 72 University of Colorado Law Review 459 (2001).

*Independent Paralegals: Friends in Need or Foes at the Gate?* by J. Middlemiss, 17 Canadian Lawyer 26 (Feb. 1993).

*The Independent Paralegal's Handbook: How to Provide Legal Services without Becoming a Lawyer*, 5th ed., by C. Elias-Jermany (Nolo Press, 1999).

*Inmate Access to Prison Computers for Legal Work and the Right of Access to the Courts* by J. Snyder, 72 North Carolina Law Review 1697 (1994).

*Interstate Practice and the Unauthorized Practice of Law: Uncertainties Mandate Professional Caution* by David Curtis Glebe, 14 Delaware Lawyer 20 (Spring 1996).

*Introduction to Legal Nurse Consulting* by C. Weishapple (West Legal Studies, 2001).

*Is Regulation Necessary for the Legal Assistant?* by M. Marsh, 5 Nevada Lawyer 28 (Aug. 1997).

*Is Self-Representation a Reasonable Alternative to Attorney Representation in Divorce Cases?* by B. Sales, 37 St. Louis University Law Journal 553 (1993) (court hires full-time paralegal to provide procedural assistance to self-represented litigants).

*Issues in Paralegalism: Education, Certification, Licensing, Unauthorized Practice* by P. Haskell, 15 Georgia Law Review 631 (1981).

*It's a Good Idea to Let Paralegals Join the State Bar*, 23 Montana Lawyer 4 (May 1998).

*It's Time to Open the Legal Profession* by J. Scalone, 49 Washington State Bar News 41 (Mar. 1995).

### JJJ

*Jailhouse Lawyer: Nuisance or Necessity?* by A. Love, The Philadelphia Lawyer 31 (Sept. 1993).

*A Jailhouse Lawyer's Manual*, 5th ed. (Columbia Human Rights Law Review, 2000).

*Judging Credentials: Nonlawyer Judges and the Politics of Professionalism* by D. Provine (University of Chicago Press, 1986).

### KKK

*Kicking the Unethical Billing Habit* by W. Ross, 50 Rutgers Law Review 2199 (1998).

### LLL

*Law Clerks and the Unauthorized Practice of Law*, 46 Chicago-Kent Law Review 214 (1969).

*Law Clerks as Independent Contractors: A Cost-Saver You Can't Afford* by J. Ellis, 85 Illinois Bar Journal 436 (Sept. 1997).

*Law Firm Diversification and Affiliation between Lawyers and Nonlawyer Professionals* by D. Pitofsky, 3 Georgetown Journal of Legal Ethics 885 (1995).

*Law Firm Life for the Legal Assistant: Practical Guidance from a Veteran* by J. Dwight (Professional Education Systems, 2001).

*Law Firms on the Big Board?: A Proposal for Nonlawyer Investment in Law Firms* by E. Adams, 86 California Law Review 1 (1998).

*The Lawyer from Antiquity to Modern Times* by R. Pound (West, 1953).

*Lawyers, Accountants, and the Battle to Own Professional Services* by G. Munneke, 20 Pace Law Review 73 (1999).

*Lawyers as Monopolists, Aristocrats, and Entrepreneurs* by M. Osiel, 103 Harvard Law Review 2009 (1989).

*Lawyers, Foreign Lawyers, and Lawyer-Substitutes: The Market for Regulation in Japan* by J. Ramseyer, 27 Harvard International Law Journal 499 (1986).

*The Lay Advocate* by E. Sparer, 43 University of Detroit Law Journal 493 (1966).

*Layman's Assistance to Party in Divorce Proceeding as Unauthorized Practice of Law*, 12 A.L.R.4th 656 (1982).

*Laymen Cannot Lawyer, but Is Mediation the Practice of Law?* by J. Schwartz, 20 Cardozo Law Review 1715 (1999).

*Lay Practice before Administrative Tribunals: Clarification Needed*, 66 Michigan Bar Journal 675 (1987).

*Learning Styles and Paralegal Studies* by B. Nagle & P. Lechman-Woznick, 11 Journal of Paralegal Education & Practice 67 (1995).

*The Least Best Hope of Legal Services for the Poor in the Eighties: The Need for Public Sector Lay Advocates with Confidential Communications* by T. Siporin, 10 San Fernando Valley Law Review 21 (1982).

*Legal Advocacy: Lawyers and Nonlawyers at Work* by H. Kritzer (University of Michigan Press, 1998) (reviewed at 73 Wisconsin Lawyer 26 (Feb. 2000)).

*Legal Aid Community Law Centre: Empowering Rural South African Communities* by C. Baekey, 5 Maryland Journal of Contemporary Legal Issues 399 (1994) (paralegals in South Africa).

*Legal and Paralegal Services on Your Home-Based PC* by K. Hussey (Windcrest/McGraw-Hill, 1994).

*Legal Assistant Ethics for Attorneys* by E. Lockwood, 63 Texas Bar Journal 270 (Mar. 2000).

*The Legal Assistant in a Small Law Firm* by D. Holiday, 63 Journal of the Kansas Bar Association 7 (June/July 1994).

*Legal Assistant Professional, Educational and Career-Related Organizations* by G. Schrader, 8 Journal of Paralegal Education & Practice 63 (1991).

*Legal Assistants: A Growing Role in the Practice of Law in Alabama* by K. Rasmussen, 52 The Alabama Lawyer 214 (1991).

*Legal Assistants as Law Office Managers* by L. Kreiper, 59 Journal of the Kansas Bar Association 19 (July 1990).

*Legal Assistants: Has the Time Arrived for State-by-State Licensing?* by H. Samborn, 78 American Bar Association Journal 42 (Dec. 1992).

*Legal Assistants Listed on Letterheads?* by B. Kent, 60 Journal of the Kansas Bar Association 15 (Feb./Mar. 1991).

*Legal Assistants: Look What They Can Do for You* by C. Given, 9 West Virginia Lawyer 22 (Mar. 1996).

*Legal Assistants Provide Responsible Services for Nevada Government* by K. Swain, 6 Nevada Lawyer 27 (Mar. 1998).

*The Legal Assistant's Role in Automated Litigation Support* by A. Huffman, 44 Am. Jur. Trials 79 (1992).

*Legal Assistants Well-Suited for Malpractice Cases* by E. Moulton, 5 Nevada Lawyer 36 (Dec. 1997).

*Legal Education for the Pro Se Litigant: A Step towards a Meaningful Right to Be Heard* by H. Kim, 96 Yale Law Journal 1641 (1987).

*Legal Ethics for Paralegals and the Law Office* by L. Morrison (West, 1995).

*Legal Nurse Consultants* by B. Faherty, 41 Medical Trial Technique Quarterly 228 (1994).

*Legal Nurse Consulting: Principles and Practice* (America Association of Legal Nurse Consultants, 1998).

*Legal Paraprofessionals and Unauthorized Practice* by J. Avila, 8 Harvard Civil Rights–Civil Liberties Law Review 104 (1973).

*Legal Profession Faces Rising Tide of Nonlawyer Practice* by J. Podgers, 79 American Bar Association Journal 24 (Mar. 1994).

*The Legal Profession in Medieval England: A History of Regulation* by J. Rose, 48 Syracuse Law Review 1 (1998).

*Legal Services for Inmates: Co-opting the Jailhouse Lawyer* by W. Bluth, 1 Capital University Law Review 59 (1972).

*Legal Software and the Unauthorized Practice of Law: Protection or Protectionism* by W. Brown, 36 California Western Law Review 157 (1999).

*Let the Consumer Choose: Does Government Protect or Harm Consumers by Allowing Them to Choose a Non-Lawyer?* by J. Stubenvoll, 52 Oregon State Bar Bulletin 21 (June 1992).

*Leveraging Human Assets in Law Firms: Human Capital Structures and Organizational Capabilities* by P. Sherer, 48 Industrial & Labor Relations Review 671 (July 1995).

*Leveraging with Legal Assistants*, A. Greene, editor (American Bar Association, 1993).

*Life outside the Law Firm: Non-Traditional Careers for Paralegals* by K. Treffinger (West, 1995).

*Litigation, Law Firms, and Legal Assistants* by Sandra A. Naro & Monica McCarthy, 46 St. Louis Bar Journal 20 (Summer 1999).

*The Litigation Legal Assistant: From Case Inception to Pretrial* by K. Gooze, 75 Michigan Bar Journal 50 (Jan. 1996).

*Litigation Legal Assistants: Saving Time and Money for the Litigator!* by L. Sifuentes, 4 Nevada Lawyer 24 (June 1996).

*The Litigation Paralegal*, 4th ed., by J. McCord (West, 2002).

*Living Trusts in the Unauthorized Practice of Law* by A. Vallario, 59 Maryland Law Review 595 (2000).

*Looking Closely at the Role of Paralegals: The California, New Jersey, and Wisconsin Experiences*, 80 Michigan Bar Journal 56 (Mar. 2001).

## MMM

*Managing Associates and Legal Assistants* by M. Magness, 40 Practical Lawyer 25 (June 1994).

*Manual for Legal Assistants*, 3d ed., by National Association of Legal Assistants (West, 1999).

*Massachusetts Paralegal Practice Manual* (Massachusetts Continuing Legal Education, 1999).

*Medical Advocates: A Call for a New Profession* by M. Mehlman, 1 Widener Law Symposium Journal 299 (Spring 1996).

*Meet Legal Needs with Nonlawyers: It is Time to Accept Law Practitioners—and Regulate Them* by D. Rhode, 82 American Bar Association Journal 104 (Jan. 1996).

*Midwifery Is Not the Practice of Medicine* by S. Suarez, 5 Yale Journal of Law & Feminism 315 (Spring 1993).

*Modern Legal Ethics* by C. Wolfram (West, 1986).

*Modifying Model Rule 5.4 to Allow for Minority Ownership of Law Firms by Nonlawyers* by B. Sharfman, 13 Georgetown Journal of Legal Ethics 477 (2000).

*More States Adopting Divorce Mediation: With Nonlawyer Mediators, Some Spouses Will Get Bad Deals, Critics Claim* by D. Trigoboff, 81 American Bar Association Journal 32 (Mar. 1995).

## NNN

*National Regulation of Nonlawyer Practice* by P. Young, 57 Texas Bar Journal 28 (Jan. 1994).

*Nature of Legal Services . . . Which May Be Performed by Disbarred or Suspended Attorney*, 7 A.L.R. 3d 279 (1978).

*The Nebraska "Bright Line" Rule: The Automatic Disqualification of a Law Firm Due to a New Lawyer's or Nonlawyer's Prior Affiliations* by A. Romshe, 28 Creighton Law Review 213 (1994).

*New Career Opportunities in the Paralegal Profession* by R. Berkey (Arco, 1983).

*New Health Professionals: The Physician Assistant and Advanced Nurse Practitioner in Texas* by R. Toth, 22 South Texas Law Journal 132 (1982).

*The New Massachusetts Rules of Professional Conduct: Ethical Responsibilities in Supervising Others* by J. Whitlock, 82 Massachusetts Law Review 289 (1997).

*Nonlawyer Activities in Law-Related Situations* (American Bar Association Commission on Nonlawyer Practice, 1995).

*Nonlawyer Assistance to Individuals in Federal Mass Justice Agencies* by Z. Hostetler, 2 Administrative Law Journal 85 (1988).

*Nonlawyer Legal Assistance and Access to Justice* by A. Hurder, 67 Fordham Law Review 2241 (1999).

*Non-Lawyer Legal Technicians* by D. Nuffer, 7 Utah Bar Journal 6 (Oct. 1994).

*The Nonlawyer Partner: Moderate Proposals Deserve a Chance* by S. Gilbert, 2 Georgetown Journal of Legal Ethics 383 (1988).

*Nonlawyer Practice: An Expanding Role* by D. Tenenbaum, 67 Wisconsin Lawyer 12 (Nov. 1994).

*Nonlawyer Practice before Administrative Agencies Should Be Discouraged* by R. Heiserman, 37 Administrative Law Review 375 (1985).

*Nonlawyer Practice before Administrative Agencies Should Be Encouraged* by J. Rose, 37 Administrative Law Review 363 (1985).

*Nonlawyer Practice before Immigration Agencies* by D. Holmes, 37 Administrative Law Review 417 (1985).

*Nonlawyer Practice: Will GP's [General Practitioners] Survive the Onslaught?* by A. Garwin, 10 The Compleat Lawyer 31 (Fall 1993).

*The Nonlawyer Provider of Bankruptcy Legal Services: Angel or Vulture* by A. Cristol, 2 American Bankruptcy Institute Law Review 353 (1994).

*Nonlawyers and the Unauthorized Practice of Law: An Overview of the Legal and Ethical Parameters* by D. Denckla, 67 Fordham Law Review 2581 (1999).

*Nonlawyers Are Not the Answer* by T. Curtin, 80 American Bar Association Journal 128 (Apr. 1994).

*Nonlawyers as Legal Practitioners* by C. Jones, 17 Journal of the Legal Profession 287 (1992).

*Nonlawyers Engaged in the Practice of Law Subject to Bankruptcy Court's Disgorgement*, 7 Inside Litigation 18 (Sept. 1993).

*Nonlawyers in the Business of Law* by T. Andrews, 40 Hastings Law Journal 577 (1989).

*Nonlawyers Should Not Practice Law* by R. Ostertag, 82 American Bar Association Journal 116 (May 1996).

*No Substitutions: Legal Aides Are Crucial, but Some Tasks Lawyers Should Not Delegate* by K. Maher, 86 American Bar Association Journal 66 (Oct. 2001).

*Notaries Public from the Time of the Roman Empire to the United States Today, and Tomorrow* by M. Closen, 68 North Dakota Law Review 873 (1992).

*Not Just for Lawyers* by M. Agius, 80 Michigan Bar Journal 30 (Mar. 2001) (ethics and paralegals).

*The Nursing Profession in the 1990's: Negligence and Malpractice Liability* by F. Cavico, 43 Cleveland State Law Review 557 (1995).

## OOO

*$100,000 a Year for Paralegals?* by P. Marcotte, 73 American Bar Association Journal 19 (Oct. 1987).

*On the Question of Negligence: The Paraprofessional* by B. Davis, 4 University of Toledo Law Review 553 (1973).

*Operations of Collection Agency as Unauthorized Practice of Law*, 27 A.L.R.3d 1152 (1969).

*Opportunities in Paralegal Careers* by A. Fins (VGM Career Horizons, 1985).

*Overtime for Law Firm Employees: The Fair Labor Standards Act* by B. Benrud, 28 Colorado Lawyer 99 (Sept. 1999).

## PPP

*Parajudges and the Administration of Justice* by T. Clark, 24 Vanderbilt Law Review 1167 (1971).

*Paralegal Adventures in the Non-Profit Corporation* by A. Brown, 26 Montana Lawyer 30 (Feb. 2001).

*Paralegal Advocacy before Administrative Agencies* by W. Statsky, 4 University of Toledo Law Review 439 (1973).

*(Para) Legal Aid: What Sort of Assignments Can You Delegate to Nonlawyer Assistants?* by A. Garwin, 79 American Bar Association Journal 101 (July 1993).

*Paralegal: An Insider's Guide to the Fastest-Growing Occupation in the 1990s*, 2d ed., by B. Bernardo (Peterson's Guides, 1993).

*The Paralegal as [Law Library] Patron* by K. Carlson, 84 Law Library Journal 567 (1992).

*The Paralegal Book of Letters* (Aspen/Wiley, 1995).

*Paralegal Career Guide*, 3d ed., by C. Estrin (Prentice Hall, 2001).

*Paralegal Careers* by W. Fry (Enslow, 1986).

*Paralegal Career Starter* by J. Southard (Learning Express, 1998).

*Paralegal Discovery: Procedures and Forms*, 3d ed., by P. Medina (Aspen, 1999).

*Paralegal Education* by R. Marquardt, 40 Mississippi Lawyer 13 (Nov./Dec. 1993).

*Paralegal Guide to Automobile Accident Cases* by J. Murvin (Aspen, 1995).

*The Paralegal in Army Legal Practice* by R. Black, 1990 Army Lawyer 70 (Nov. 1990).

*Paralegalism: A Still Evolving Profession* by W. Peters, 40 Mississippi Lawyer 18 (Nov./Dec. 1993).

*Paralegalism: The United Profession* by J. Farinacci, 8 Journal of Paralegal Education & Practice 148 (1991).

*Paralegal Litigation Forms and Procedures*, 3d ed., by M. Delesandri (Aspen, 2000).

*Paralegal Overtime: Yes, No, or Maybe* by X. Rodriguez, 63 Texas Bar Journal 266 (Mar. 2000) (see also 57 Texas Bar Journal 32).

*Paralegal Practice and Procedure*, 3d ed., by D. Larbalestrier (Prentice-Hall, 1994).

*The Paralegal Profession* by Brown, 19 Howard Law Journal 117 (1976).

*Paralegal Representation of Social Security Claimants* by E. Tackett, 16 Journal of Paralegal Education & Practice 67 (2000).

*Paralegals and Lawyers: A Team Approach* by K. Dulin, 32 Trial 62 (Jan. 1996).

*Paralegals and Sublegals: Aids to the Legal Profession* by H. Holme, 46 Denver Law Journal 392 (1969).

*Paralegals and the Imputed Disqualification Rule* by M. Schairer, 7 Journal of Paralegal Education & Practice 1 (1990).

*Paralegals Can Apply to Join the State Bar* by C. Bronson, 24 Montana Lawyer 28 (Mar. 1999).

*Paralegals Can Be More Profitable than Associates* by A. Jones, 16 Montana Lawyer 7 (Dec. 1990).

*Paralegals Can Play Major Role in Preparation of Criminal Case* by C. Embry, 6 Nevada Lawyer 26 (June 1998).

*Paralegals: Changing the Practice of Law* by J. Rasmussen, 44 South Dakota Law Review 319 (1999).

*Paralegals, Clients, Fees* by J. Honohan, 51 The Iowa Lawyer 23 (Aug. 1991).

*The Paralegal's Desk Reference* by S. Albrecht (Arco, 1993).

*Paralegals: Entitled to Overtime Rate* by C. Quasebarth, 5 West Virginia Lawyer 21 (Feb. 1992).

*Paralegals: Getting Everything in Order* by E. Coari, 39 Louisiana Bar Journal 265 (Nov. 1991).

*The Paralegal's Guide to U.S. Government Jobs*, 7th ed. (Federal Reports, 1996).

*Paralegals' Image and How to Improve It* by B. Kautz, 25 Montana Lawyer 16 (Jan. 2000).

*Paralegals in Rural Africa*, A. Dieng, editor (International Commission of Jurists, Switzerland, Feb. 1990).

*Paralegals: Powerful Performers in a Changing World* by J. Bourgoin, 24 Colorado Lawyer 2193 (1995).

*Paralegals: Progress and Prospects of a Satellite Occupation* by Q. Johnstone (Greenwood Press, 1985).

*Paralegals: Should Legal Technicians Be Allowed to Practice Independently?* by D. Chalfie, 77 American Bar Association Journal 40 (Mar. 1991).

*Paralegals Taking a Bite Out of Associates' Work* by H. Rosen, 134 New Jersey Law Journal 195 (May 17, 1993).

*Paralegals: The Good, the Bad, and the Ugly* by G. Mund, 2 American Bankruptcy Institute Law Review 337 (1994).

*Paralegal Success: Going from Good to Great in the New Century* by D. Bogen (Prentice Hall, 2000).

*Paralegals: Untapped Potential for Performance and Profit* by P. Potter, 40 North Carolina State Bar Quarterly 16 (Summer 1993).

*Paralegal Trial Handbook*, 2d ed., by B. Hudson (Aspen, 1995).

*Paraprofessionals: Expanding the Legal Service Delivery Team* by W. Statsky, 24 Journal of Legal Education 397 (1972).

*Permanent Injunctions: Unauthorized Practice of Law* by T. Byerley, 78 Michigan Bar Journal 458 (May 1999).

*Personal-Bankruptcy Bar Attacks Low-Cost Services by Paralegals* by M. Shao, Wall Street Journal, Nov. 20, 1989, at 36.

*A Piece of Your Business: Competition from Nonlawyer "Technicians": Cause for Alarm?* by G. Yuda, 15 The Pennsylvania Lawyer 6 (May 1993).

*Plain Language for the Legal Assistant: Preparing Enclosure Letters* by S. McIntyre, 75 Michigan Bar Journal 73 (Jan. 1996).

*Policing the Professional Monopoly: A Constitutional and Empirical Analysis of Unauthorized Practice Prohibitions* by D. Rhode, 34 Stanford Law Review 1 (1981).

*Post–Law School Job (of Attorney) May Be as Paralegal* by H. Samborn, 81 American Bar Association Journal 14 (May 1995).

*Poverty Law for the '90s: Business Is Booming for Storefront Paralegals on the Poor Side of Town* by T. Sisco, 15 California Lawyer 31 (June 1995).

*Practical Law Office Management*, 2d ed., by B. Roper (West, 2002).

*Practice before Administrative Agencies and the Unauthorized Practice of Law* by V. Baur, 15 Federal Bar Journal 103 (1955).

*Practice by Non-Lawyers before the National Labor Relations Board* by J. Gall, 15 Federal Bar Journal 222 (1955).

*Practice by Non-Lawyers before the U.S. Patent Office* by J. Bailey, 15 Federal Bar Journal 211 (1955).

*The Practice of Law by Laymen and Lay Agencies* by F. Hicks, 41 Yale Law Journal 69 (1931).

*The Practice of Law with Non-Lawyer Colleagues in Maine* by T. Shaffer, 14 Maine Bar Journal 202 (July 1999).

*Practicing Law at the Margins: Surveying Ethics Rules for Legal Assistants and Lawyers Who Mediate* by J. Beyer, 11 Georgetown Journal of Legal Ethics 411 (1998).

*Practicing Law without a License* by F. Apicella, 81 American Bar Association Journal 36 (Jan. 1995).

*Preliminary Thoughts on the Economics of Witness Preparation* by C. Silver, 30 Texas Tech Law Review 1383 (1999) (paralegal preparation of witnesses).

*Preventive Law and the Paralegal* by L. Brown, 24 Vanderbilt Law Review 1181 (1971).

*Pro Bono and Paralegals: Making a Difference* by J. Price, 30 Colorado Lawyer 55 (Sept. 2001).

*Professionalism in Perspective: Alternative Approaches to Nonlawyer Practice* by D. Rhode, 22 New York University Review of Law & Social Change 701 (1996).

*Professional Negligence, Paralegals and Modern Ethics* by H. Cohen, 11 Journal of the Legal Profession 143 (1986).

*The Professional Paralegal Job Search* by C. French (Aspen, 1995).

*Professional Paralegal Organizations in Nevada and Their Benefits to You* by H. Heck, 5 Nevada Lawyer 29 (Mar. 1997).

*Professional Paralegals Oppose Disciplinary Board Recommendation* by L. Mansell, 2 Lawyers Journal 6 (Feb. 25, 2000) (proposal on allowing disbarred attorneys to be paralegals).

*Proper Scope of Nonlawyer Representation in State Administrative Proceedings* by G. Stevens, 43 Vanderbilt Law Review 245 (1990).

*Propriety and Effect of Corporation's Appearance Pro Se through Agent Who Is Not Attorney*, 8 A.L.R.5th 653 (1992).

*Protecting the Public, Not Anyone's Turf: The Unlicensed Practice of Law in Securities Arbitration* by J. Cleary, 26 Pepperdine Law Review 543 (1999).

*Public Benefits Issues in Divorce Cases: A Manual for Lawyers and Paralegals* (Center for Law and Social Policy, 1994).

## QQQ

*Questions Concerning the Utilization of Legal Assistants/ Paralegals Answered*, 69 Journal of the Kansas Bar Association 3 (Aug. 2000).

## RRR

*Recoverability of Legal Assistant Time in Attorney Fee Applications* by S. Koran, 9 Journal of Paralegal Education & Practice 1 (1993).

*Recovery of Legal Assistant Fees in Litigation* by C. Smith, 30 Trial 59 (Sept. 1994).

*Recruiting, Interviewing, and Hiring Legal Assistants* by A. Dodds, 57 Texas Bar Journal 40 (Jan. 1994).

*Report of the Commission on Nonlawyer Practice* by H. Rosenthal, 7 Professional Lawyer 12 (1995).

*Report of the Working Group on the Use of Nonlawyers*, 67 Fordham Law Review 1813 (1999) (paralegals and legal services to the poor).

*Representation of Claimants at Unemployment Compensation Proceedings: Identifying Models and Proposed Solutions* by M. Emsellem, 29 University of Michigan Journal of Law Reform 289 (1995).

*Representation of Clients before Administrative Agencies: Authorized or Unauthorized Practice of Law?* by M. Remmert, 15 Valparaiso University Law Review 567 (1981).

*Restrictions on Attorney Contacts with Adversaries' Former Employees* by C. Lewis, 83 Illinois Bar Journal 242 (May 1995).

*The Retention of Limitations on the Out-of-Court Practice of Law by Independent Paralegals* by C. Selinger, 9 Georgetown Journal of Legal Ethics 879 (1996).

*Rethinking Barriers to Legal Practice* by H. Kritzer, 80 Judicature 100 (Nov./Dec. 1997).

*Revitalization of the Legal Profession through Paralegalism* by J. Wells, 30 Baylor Law Review 841 (1978).

*Right of Juvenile Court Defendant to Be Represented during Court Proceedings by Parent*, 11 A.L.R.4th 719 (1982).

*The Role of a Legal Assistant in Real Estate Practice* by E. Mahoney, 70 Michigan Bar Journal 1160 (Nov. 1991).

*The Role of the Legal Assistant in Family Law Matters* by B. Miller, 75 Michigan Bar Journal 54 (Jan. 1996).

*The Role of the Paralegal in the Civil Commitment Process* by R. Lockwood, 10 Capital University Law Review 721 (1981).

## SSS

*Sale of Books or Forms . . . As Unauthorized Practice of Law*, 71 A.L.R. 3d 1000 (1976).

*Scenes from a Law Firm* by L. Lerman, 50 Rutgers Law Review 2153 (1998) (reporting on the frequency of ethics violations).

*The Secretarial Advantage, Law Students, Paralegal Tasks* by B. Morgenstern, 81 American Bar Association Journal 75 (Jan 1995).

*Self-Presented Litigants and the Unauthorized Practice of Law* by B. James, 35 Arizona Attorney 18 (May 1999).

*Separate Fee Awards for Paralegals* by T. Wright, 44 Rhode Island Bar Journal 23 (May 1996).

*Shades of Regulation: State Bills Apply Sundry Standards to Independent Paralegals* by H. Samborn 83 American Bar Association Journal 26 (1997).

*Should Law Societies "Prosecute the Hell" Out of Independent Paralegal Firms?* by P. Pevato, 7 Journal of Law & Social Policy 215 (Fall 1991).

*Should Legal Assistants Be Exempt or Non-Exempt from Overtime Pay?* 5 Nevada Lawyer 29 (Jan. 1997).

*Should More Be Done to Credential Paralegals* by T. Flynn, 80 Michigan Bar Journal (Mar. 2001).

*Should Nonlawyers Provide Legal Services?* by M. Brockmeyer, 27 Maryland Bar Journal 12 (July/Aug. 1994).

*Should Social Workers Engage in the Unauthorized Practice of Law?* by A. Bertelli, 8 Boston University Public Interest Law Journal 15 (Fall 1998).

*The Side-Switching Staff Person in a Law Firm* by S. Kalish, 15 Hamline Law Review 35 (1991).

*Sign of Tough Times: Out-of-Work Lawyers Taking Paralegal Jobs* by R. Cammarere, The New Jersey Lawyer, Sept. 11, 1995, at 1.

*Software and Hard Choices: Interactive Software Should Be Considered before Independent Paralegals Are Licensed* by C. James, 52 Oregon State Bar Bulletin 15 (July 1992).

*Staying Out of the Briar Patch: Ethical Considerations and the Legal Assistant* by M. Wise, 57 Texas Bar Journal 30 (Jan. 1994).

*Stemming the Tide of Unauthorized Practice* by S. Kimmel, 13 Maine Bar Journal 164 (July 1998).

*Still Paralegals after All These Years* by C. Gilsinan, 46 St. Louis Bar Journal 10 (Summer 1999).

*Successful Paralegal Utilization* by R. Simkins, 21 Massachusetts Lawyers Weekly 2409 (Apr. 26, 1993).

*Supervising Lawyers, Supervised . . . Nonlawyer Assistants: Ethical Responsibilities* by E. Wilkinson, 64 Texas Bar Journal 452 (May 2001).

*Supervision of Non-Lawyer Employees* by W. Steele, 58 Texas Bar Journal 798 (Sept. 1995).

*Support Staff Conflicts of Interest* by J. Burman, 20 Wyoming Lawyer 12 (Oct. 1997).

*Systemization and the Legal Assistant in the Law Office* by R. Endacott, 54 Nebraska Law Review 46 (1975).

### TTT

*Taking Note of Notary Employees: Employer Liability for Notary Employee Misconduct* by N. Spyke, 50 Maine Law Review 23 (1998).

*Teaching Corrections Law to Corrections Personnel* by W. Statsky, 37 Federal Probation 42 (June 1972).

*Techniques for Supervising Paralegals* by W. Statsky, 22 Practical Lawyer 81 (Nov. 1976).

*Texas Makes Solicitation a Felony* by M. Hansen, 79 American Bar Association Journal 32 (Sept. 1993).

*There Goes the Monopoly: The California Proposal to Allow Nonlawyers to Practice Law* by K. Justice, 44 Vanderbilt Law Review 179 (1991).

*The Thin Red Line: An Analysis of the Role of Legal Assistants in the Chapter 13 Bankruptcy Process* by G. Sullivan, 23 Journal of the Legal Profession 15 (1998–99).

*A Tobacco Turncoat's Odyssey: Surprise Ending for Paralegal Who Was a Spy* by M. Orey, Wall Street Journal, Sept. 13, 1999, at B1.

*Too Many Hands in the Cookie Jar: The Unauthorized Practice of Law by Real Estate Brokers* by S. Goudey, 75 Oregon Law Review 889 (1996).

*Tort Liability of Paralegals and Lawyers Who Use Their Services* by J. Wade, 24 Vanderbilt Law Review 1133 (1971).

*To the Rescue: Paralegals/Legal Assistants* by R. Kerl, 35 Advocate 7 (Mar. 1992) (Idaho).

*The Training of Community Judges* by W. Statsky, 4 Columbia Human Rights Law Review 401 (1972).

*Trouble for Nonlawyers Who Furnish Estate Planning Services and for the Lawyers Who Help Them and Other Recent Developments* by D. Doerhoff, 52 Journal of the Missouri Bar 269 (Sept./Oct. 1996).

*Turf Battles and Professional Biases: An Analysis of Mediator Qualifications in Child Custody Disputes* by N. Schoenfield, 11 Ohio State Journal on Dispute Resolution 469 (1996) (nonlawyers as mediators).

### UUU

*Unauthorized Corporate Law Practices in Small Claims Court: Should Anybody Care?* by R. Smith, 33 Washburn Law Journal 345 (Spring 1994).

*Unauthorized Practice and Pro Se Divorce* by S. Williams, 86 Yale Law Journal 104 (1976).

*Unauthorized Practice Linked to Unmet Pro Bono Need* by S. Hilander, 23 Montana Lawyer 1 (Dec. 1997).

*Unauthorized Practice of Law: Does Anyone Know What It Is?* by K. Currier, 8 Journal of Paralegal Education & Practice 21 (1991).

*The Unauthorized Practice of Law in Immigration* by A. Ashbrook, 5 Georgetown Journal of Legal Ethics 237 (1991).

*Unauthorized Practice of Law: Protection or Protectionism?* by D. Tenenbaum, 67 Wisconsin Lawyer 14 (Sept. 1994).

*Under New Mismanagement: The Problem of Nonlawyer Equity Partnership in Law Firms* by C. Carson, 7 Georgetown Journal of Legal Ethics 593 (1994).

*Use of Lay Representatives*, 58 Michigan Law Review 456 (1960).

*Use of Legal Assistants in Client Representation at Hearings, Depositions or Administrative Proceedings* by the Colorado Bar Assn, Ethics Committee, 18 The Colorado Lawyer 1149 (1989).

*Use of Paralegal Assistants in Divorce Practice* by P. Grove, 4 American Journal of Family Law 41 (Spring 1990).

*Use of Paralegals in a Matrimonial Practice* by L. Gold-Bikin, 16 Fair$hare 9 (Sept. 1996).

*Using Computers in the Law Office*, 3d ed., by B. Roper (West, 2000).

### VVV

*Validity of Will Drawn by Layman*, 18 A.L.R.2d 918 (1951).

### WWW

*The War between Attorneys and Lay Conveyancers: Empirical Evidence Says "Cease Fire!"* by J. Palomar, 31 Connecticut Law Review 423 (1999).

*We Are Going to Build a Chinese Wall* by E. Moulton, CLA, 5 Nevada Lawyer 28 (Sept. 1997) (conflict of interest).

*We Can't All Be Lawyers . . . Or Can We? Regulating the Unauthorized Practice of Law in Arizona* by R. Talamante, 34 Arizona Law Review 873 (1992).

*What Activities of Stock or Securities Broker Constitute Unauthorized Practice of Law*, 34 A.L.R.3d 1305 (1970).

*What Is a Paralegal, Anyway?* by D. Taylor, 37 Advocate 22 (July 1994) (Idaho).

*What Is the Unauthorized Practice of Law and How Is It Regulated* by E. Holmes, 76 Michigan Bar Journal 580 (June 1997).

*What Your Office Support Staff and You Need to Know about Professional Responsibility for Nonlawyer Assistants* by D. O'Roark, 54 Kentucky Bench & Bar 40 (Fall 1993).

*What Your Paralegals Always Wanted to Tell You but Didn't Dare Because They Needed a Job* by F. Dowell, 60 Kentucky Bench & Bar 23 (1996).

*When Attorneys and Paralegals Change Firms* by M. Suglia, 8 Nevada Lawyer 18 (Aug. 2000).

*When Legal Assistants Change Jobs: Ethical Issues and Solutions* by D. Kowalski, 75 Michigan Bar Journal 42 (Jan. 1996).

*Where We Are Today: Non-Lawyer Practice in Arizona* by L. Shely, 30 Arizona Attorney 11 (Feb. 1994).

*Who Should Regulate Lawyers?* by D. Wilkins, 105 Harvard Law Review 799 (1992).

*Wisconsin's Elderlinks Initiative: Using Technology to Provide Legal Services to Older Persons* by M. Doremus, 32 Wake Forest Law Review 545 (1997) (paralegal benefit specialists, administrative advocacy).

*Working with Legal Assistants*, P. Ulrch, editor (American Bar Association, 1980).

*The Writ-Writers: Jailhouse Lawyers Right of Meaningful Access to the Courts* by J. Myers, 18 Akron Law Review 649 (1984).

# Appendix B

# Paralegal Associations and Related Organizations

## PARALEGAL ASSOCIATIONS (NATIONAL)
(Membership statistics, where known, are presented in brackets.)

National Association of Legal Assistants [18,000]
1516 South Boston, Suite 200
Tulsa, OK 74119–4013
918–587–6828
nalanet@nala.org
www.nala.org

National Federation of Paralegal Associations [15,000]
32 West Bridlespur Terrace
P.O. Box 33108
Kansas City, MO 64114–0108
816–941–4000
info@paralegals.org
www.paralegals.org

The National Association of Legal Assistants (NALA) and the National Federation of Paralegal Associations (NFPA) have numerous affiliated local paralegal associations. NALA affiliates are indicated by one asterisk (*) below; NFPA affiliates are indicated by two asterisks (**). Associations without an asterisk are unaffiliated at the present time. For other national associations, see the list after Wyoming.

## PARALEGAL ASSOCIATIONS (STATE)
CAUTION: The addresses of many local paralegal associations change often. Very few of the associations have business offices. Most rent a P.O. box number and keep all association files in the home of an active paralegal member or in an available file cabinet of the law office where he or she works. If one of the addresses below turns out to be unproductive, (1) check the Internet by typing the name of the association in any search engine, (2) check with your program director, (3) ask your classmates if they have a different address, (4) ask a working paralegal in your area, (5) contact the national office of NALA or the NFPA if the association is affiliated with either, and (6) contact the association that is geographically closest to the one you are trying to contact and ask if it knows the current address. Also follow these steps if an association is listed below with no address.

## ALABAMA

Alabama Association of Legal Assistants (*) [220]
P.O. Box 55921
Birmingham, AL 35255
www.aala.net

Gulf Coast Paralegal Association (**) [37]
P.O. Box 66705
Mobile, AL 36660
communities.msn.com/gcpa
paralegals.org/Members/alabama.html

Mobile Association of Legal Assistants
P.O. Box 1852
Mobile, AL 36633

Alabama Legal Secretaries Association
www.alabama-als.org

## ALASKA

Alaska Association of Paralegals (**) [71]
P.O. Box 101956
Anchorage, AK 99510–1956
907–646–8018
www.alaskaparalegals.org

Anchorage Legal Secretaries Association
www.aklsa.org

## ARIZONA

Arizona Association of Professional Paralegals (**) [51]
P.O. Box 430
Phoenix, AZ 85001
paralegals.org/Arizona

Arizona Paralegal Association (*) [350]
P.O. Box 392
Phoenix, AZ 85001
www.azparalegal.org

Legal Assistants of Metropolitan Phoenix (*)
P.O. Box 13005
Phoenix, AZ 85002
www.geocities.com/azlamp

Maricopa County Bar Association Paralegal Division
303 East Palm Lane
Phoenix, AZ 85004
602–257–4200
www.maricopaparalegals.org

Tucson Association of Legal Assistants (*) [121]
P.O. Box 257
Tucson, AZ 85702
www.azstarnet.com/nonprofit/tala

Legal Support Professionals of Arizona
www.arizonalegalsupport.com/default.htm

## ARKANSAS

Arkansas Association of Legal Assistants (*) [68]
400 West Capitol Avenue, Suite 2840
Little Rock, AR 72201
501–372–5800
www.aala-legal.org

Association for Arkansas Legal Support Professionals
www.angelfire.com/ar2/aals72401

Jonesboro Legal Support Association
www.angelfire.com/ar2/JLSA2001

## CALIFORNIA

California Alliance of Paralegal Associations
P.O. Box 2234
San Francisco, CA 94126
www.caparalegal.org

California Association of Legal Document Assistants [125]
39120 Argonaut Way, PMB114
Fremont, CA 94530
800–780–2247
www.calda.org

Central Coast Paralegal Association
P.O. Box 93
San Luis Obispo, CA 93406

Commission for Advanced Paralegal Specialization
P.O. Box 22433
Santa Barbara, CA 93121
www.cla-cas.org

Inland Counties Association of Paralegals [101]
P.O. Box 143
Riverside, CA 92502
909–369–2789
www.icaparalegal.org

Kern County Paralegal Association
P.O. Box 2673
Bakersfield, CA 93303

Los Angeles Paralegal Association (*) [1,034]
P.O. Box 71708
Los Angeles, CA 90071
310–921–3094
www.lapa.org

Orange County Paralegal Association (*) [500]
P.O. Box 8512
Newport Beach, CA 92658
714–744–7747
www.ocparalegal.org

Paralegal Association of Santa Clara County (*) [525]
P.O. Box 26736
San Jose, CA 95159
www.sccparalegal.org
www.sccba.com/pascco/welcome.htm

Redwood Empire Legal Assistants
P.O. Box 143
Santa Rosa, CA 95402
www.CAPAralegal.org/rela.html

Sacramento Valley Paralegal Association (**) [238]
P.O. Box 453
Sacramento, CA 95812
916-763-7851
www.paralegals.org/Sacramento/sala.htm
www.paralegals.org/Sacramento
www.svpa.org

San Diego Paralegal Association (**) [150]
P.O. Box 87449
San Diego, CA 92138
619-491-1994
www.sdparalegal.org

San Francisco Paralegal Association (**) [648]
P.O. Box 2110
San Francisco, CA 94126-2110
415-777-2390
www.sfpa.com

San Joaquin Association of Legal Assistants (*) [98]
P.O. Box 28515
Fresno, CA 93729
www.fresnoparalegal.org

Santa Barbara Paralegal Association (*) [91]
1224 Coast Village Circle, Suite 32
Santa Barbara, CA 93108
www.sbparalegals.org

Sequoia Paralegal Association
P.O. Box 3884
Visalia, CA 93278
www.caparalegal.org/spa.html

Ventura Association of Legal Assistants (*) [80]
P.O. Box 24229
Ventura, CA 93002
www.caparalegal.org/vala.html

California Association of Photocopiers and Process
  Servers
www.capps.org

NALS (Association for Legal Professionals) of California
www.NALSofCA.org

Sacramento Legal Secretaries Association
www.slsa.org

Southern California Background Investigators
  Association
www.scbia.com

**COLORADO**

Association of Legal Assistants of Colorado (*) [35]
P.O. Box 1678
Colorado Springs, CO 80901
719-268-4542
firms.findlaw.com/ALAC

Legal Assistants of the Western Slope (*) [20]
62778 Niagara Road
Montrose, CO 81401

Rocky Mountain Paralegal Association (**) [300]
P.O. Box 481864
Denver, CO 80248
303-370-9444
www.rockymtnparalegal.org/index.html

**CONNECTICUT**

Central Connecticut Paralegal Association (**) [350]
P.O. Box 230594
Hartfod, CT 06123
paralegals.org/CentralConnecticut

Connecticut Association of Paralegals (**) [98]
P.O. Box 134
Bridgeport, CT 06601
paralegals.org/Connecticut

New Haven County Association of Paralegals (**) [75]
P.O. Box 862
New Haven, CT 06504
paralegals.org/NewHaven

**DELAWARE**

Delaware Paralegal Association (**) [250]
P.O. Box 1362
Wilmington, DE 19899
302-426-1362
paralegals.org/Delaware/home.html

**DISTRICT OF COLUMBIA**

National Capital Area Paralegal Association (**) [336]
P.O. Box 27607
Washington, DC 20038
www.ncapa.com
paralegals.org/NationalCapital

**FLORIDA**

Central Florida Paralegal Association (*) [105]
P.O. Box 1107
Orlando, FL 32902
407-672-6372
www.CFPA.com

Dade Association of Legal Assistants (*)
P.O. Box 110603
Miami, Florida 33111
305-944-0204
www.dala.org

Florida Association of Paralegals (**) [35]
12825 Harbor View Drive
Seminole, FL 33776
paralegals.org/Florida/home.html
hometown.aol.fapemail

Gainesville Association of Paralegals (*)
P.O. Box 141164
Gainesville, FL 32614
904-462-2249
www.afn.org/~gala
geocities.com/gaparalegals

Jacksonville Legal Assistants (*) [110]
P.O. Box 52264
Jacksonville, FL 32201
904-366-8440
www.jaxla.org

Northwest Florida Paralegal Association (*) [100]
P.O. Box 1333
Pensacola, FL 32502
paralegalsofnorthwestflorida.org

Paralegal Association of Florida (*) [925]
P.O. Box 7073
West Palm Beach, FL 33405
800-433-4352
561-833-1408
www.pafinc.org

Southwest Florida Paralegal Association (*) [46]
P.O. Box 2094
Sarasota, FL 34230
www.lasf.com

Tampa Bay Paralegal Association (**) [55]
P.O. Box 2722
Tampa, FL 33602

Volusia Association of Paralegals (*) [30]
P.O. Box 15075
Daytona Beach, FL 32115
www.volusiaparalegals.com

## GEORGIA

Georgia Association of Paralegals (**) [608]
1199 Euclid Avenue NE
Atlanta, GA 30307
www.gaparalegal.org

Georgia Legal Assistants (*)
Contact NALA (www.nala.org) for current address

Southeastern Association of Legal Assistants (*)
   [29]
Savannah, GA
www.seala.cjb.net

South Georgia Association of Legal Assistants (*)
Contact NALA (www.nala.org) for current address

NALS (Association for Legal Professionals) of Atlanta
www.nalsofatlanta.org

## HAWAII

Hawaii Paralegal Association (**) [125]
P.O. Box 674
Honolulu, HI 96809
www.hawaiiparalegal.org

Hawaii Legal Support Professionals
hawaiilsp.org

## IDAHO

Gem State Association of Legal Assistants (*)
P.O. Box 1118
Burley, ID 83318

## ILLINOIS

Central Illinois Paralegal Association (*)
P.O. Box 1948
Bloomington, IL 61702
hometown.aol.com/cipainfo/myhomepage/club.html

Heart of Illinois Paralegal Association (*)
Peoria, IL
Contact NALA (www.nala.org) for current address.

Illinois Paralegal Association (**) [1,400]
P.O. Box 452
New Lenox, IL 60451
815-462-4620
www.ipaonline.org

## INDIANA

Hamilton County Paralegal Association
P.O. Box 1853
Carmel, IN 46032

Indiana Legal Assistants (*)
c/o Indiana State Bar Association
230 East Ohio Street, 4th Floor
Indianapolis, IN 47204
www.freeyellow.com/members/ila

Indiana Paralegal Association (**) [87]
P.O. Box 44518
Indianapolis, IN 46204
317-767-7798
paralegals.org/Indiana

Michiana Paralegal Association (**) [108]
P.O. Box 11458
South Bend, IN 46634
paralegals.org/Michiana

Northeast Indiana Paralegal Association (**) [82]
P.O. Box 13646
Fort Wayne, IN 46865
paralegals.org/NortheastIndiana

## IOWA
Iowa Association of Legal Assistants (*)
P.O. Box 93153
Des Moines, IA 50393
www.ialanet.org

## KANSAS
Heartland Association of Legal Assistants (*) [45]
P.O. Box 12413
Overland Park, KS 66282

Kansas Association of Legal Assistants (*) [80]
P.O. Box 47031
Wichita, KS 67201
316-291-9711
www.ink.org/public/kala

Kansas Paralegal Association (**) [191]
P.O. Box 1675
Topeka, KS 66601
www.accesskansas.org/ksparalegals

## KENTUCKY
Appalachian Paralegal Association
P.O. Box 1542
Prestonsburg, KY 41653

Greater Lexington Paralegal Association (**) [88]
P.O. Box 574
Lexington, KY 40586
www.paralegals.com/Members/kentucky.html

Kentucky Paralegal Association
P.O. Box 2675
Louisville, KY 40201
www.kypa.org

Louisville Association of Paralegals
P.O. Box 70265
Louisville, KY 40270
www.loupara.com

Northern Kentucky Paralegal Association
Covington, KY

Southeastern Paralegal Association
Barbourville, KY

Southern Kentucky Paralegal Association
Bowling Green, KY

Tri-State Association of Legal Assistants
Ashland, KY

Western Kentucky Paralegals (*) [32]
P.O. Box 2895
Paducah, KY 42002

## LOUISIANA
Baton Rouge Paralegal Association
Baton Rouge, LA
See Louisiana State Paralegal Association
    (www.la-paralegals.org)
    for current address.

Lafayette Paralegal Association
Lafayette, LA
See Louisiana State Paralegal Association
    (www.la-paralegals.org)
    for current address.

Legal Assistants of Northeast Louisiana (*)
Monroe, LA
Contact NALA (www.nala.org) for current address.

Louisiana State Paralegal Association (*) [83]
P.O. Box 219
Baton Rouge, LA 70821
www.la-paralegals.org

Mid-State Paralegal Association
Marksville, LA
See Louisiana State Paralegal Association
    (www.la-paralegals.org)
    for current address.

New Orleans Paralegal Association (**) [120]
P.O. Box 30604
New Orleans; LA 70190
504-467-3136
paralegals.org/NewOrleans

Northwest Louisiana Paralegal Association (*) [40]
P.O. Box 1913
Shreveport, LA 71166

Southwest Louisiana Paralegal Association [30]
P.O. Box 1143
Lake Charles, LA 70602
swlap.tripod.com

## MAINE
Maine Association of Legal Assistants (*)
P.O. Box 7554
Portland, ME 04112
www.msala.org/INDEX.html

## MARYLAND
Maryland Association of Paralegals (**) [230]
P.O. Box 13244
Baltimore, MD 21203
paralegals.org/Maryland

## MASSACHUSETTS
Central Massachusetts Paralegal Association (**) [100]
P.O. Box 444
Worcester, MA 01614

Massachusetts Paralegal Association (**) [560]
c/o Offtech Management Services
99 Summer Street, Suite L-150
Boston, MA 02110
800-637-4311; 617-439-8639
paralegals.org/Massachusetts

Western Massachusetts Paralegal Association (**) [65]
P.O. Box 30005
Springfield, MA 01103
www.paralegals.org/WesternMassachusetts/home.html

## MICHIGAN
Legal Assistants Association of Michigan (*) [100]
P.O. Box 1453
East Lansing, MI 48826
www.laamnet.org

Legal Assistants Section of the State Bar of Michigan
    [600]
State Bar of Michigan
306 Townsend Street
Lansing, MI 48933
www.michbar.org/sections/legalassist

Macomb County Bar Association
Legal Assistant Section
Mount Clemens, MI
www.macombbar.org/las_pg.html

Michiana Paralegal Association
[see Indiana]

Michigan Council of Private Investigators
www.mcpihome.com

NALS (Association of Legal Professionals) of Lansing
www.nalsoflansing.org

NALS (Association of Legal Professionals) of
    Michigan
www.nalsofmichigan.org

## MINNESOTA
Minnesota Paralegal Association (**) [1,104]
1711 West County Road B, #300N
Roseville, MN 55113
651-633-2778
mnparalegals.org

## MISSISSIPPI
Mississippi Association of Legal Assistants (*)
    [125]
P.O. Box 996
Jackson, MS 39205
www.mslawyer.com/mala

## MISSOURI
Kansas City Paralegal Association (**) [312]
P.O. Box 344
Lee's Summit, MO 64063-0344
816-524-6078
www.paralegals.org/KansasCity/home.html

Mid-Missouri Paralegal Association [25]
P.O. Box 1291
Jefferson City, MO 65102

Missouri Bar Paralegals Committee
www.mobar.org/member/paramain.htm

Missouri Paralegal Association [60]
P.O. Box 1016
Jefferson City, MO 65102
www.missouriparalegalassoc.org

St. Louis Association of Legal Assistants (*)
P.O. Box 69218
St. Louis, MO 63169

Missouri Association of Legal Secretaries
www.show-me-lsa.org/index.htm

## MONTANA
Montana Association of Legal Assistants (*) [84]
P.O. Box 9016
Missoula, MT 59807
www.malanet.org

NALS (Association of Legal Professionals) of Montana
www.nalsofmontana.org

## NEBRASKA
Nebraska Association of Legal Assistants (*) [153]
P.O. Box 24943
Omaha, NE 98124
www.neala.org

## NEVADA
Clark County Organization of Legal Assistants (*) [130]
302 East Carson, Suite 1100
Las Vegas, NV 89101

Sierra Nevada Association of Paralegals (*) [64]
P.O. Box 2832
Reno, NV 89505

## NEW HAMPSHIRE
Paralegal Association of New Hampshire (**) [180]
P.O. Box 728
Manchester, NH 03195
www.panh.org

## NEW JERSEY

Legal Assistants Association of New Jersey (*) [325]
P.O. Box 142
Caldwell, NJ 07006
www.geocities.com/CapitolHill/2716/old.html

South Jersey Paralegal Association (**) [175]
P.O. Box 355
Haddonfield, NJ 08033
paralegals.org/SouthJersey

Prudential Insurance Company of America—Paralegal
    Council
751 Broad Street
Newark, NJ 07102

## NEW MEXICO

Legal Assistants Division
State Bar of New Mexico
www.nmbar.org/divisions/legalassistdivision/LAD.htm

Southwestern Association of Legal Assistants (*)
Albuquerque, NM

## NEW YORK

Adirondack Paralegal Association
Ft. Edward, NY 12828

Capital District Paralegal Association
Albany, NY 12212
capitaldistrict@paralegals.org

Long Island Paralegal Association (**) [104]
1877 Bly Road
East Meadow, NY 11554

Manhattan Paralegal Association (**)
P.O. Box 4006
Grand Central Station
New York, NY 10163
212-330-8213
paralegals.org/Manhattan

Paralegal Association of Rochester (**) [180]
P.O. Box 40567
Rochester, NY 14604
585-243-5923
par.itgo.com
www.paralegals.com/Rochester

Southern Tier Paralegal Association (**)
P.O. Box 2555
Binghamton, NY 13903
www.paralegals.org/SouthernTier/home.html

Western New York Paralegal Association (**) [235]
P.O. Box 207
Buffalo, NY 14201
716-635-8250
www.wnyparalegals.org
www.paralegals.org/WesternNewYork/home.html

West/Rock Paralegal Association (**) [38]
P.O. Box 668
New City, NY 10956
914-786-6184
www.paralegals.org/WestRock/home.html

NALS (Association of Legal Professionals) of New York
www.nalsofnewyorkinc.org

## NORTH CAROLINA

Cumberland County Paralegal Association
Fayetteville, NC

Legal Assistants Division of the North Carolina Bar
    Association [674]
www.barlinc.org/divisions/lad/index.asp

Metrolina Paralegal Association (*) [192]
P.O. Box 36260
Charlotte, NC 28236
704-444-3525

North Carolina Paralegal Association (*) [515]
P.O. Box 36264
Charlotte, NC 28236
800-479-1905; 704-535-3363
www.ncparalegal.org

Pitt County Paralegal Association
Winterville, NC

Raleigh-Wake Paralegal Association
P.O. Box 1427
Raleigh, NC 27602

## NORTH DAKOTA

Red River Valley Legal Assistant Association [38]
P.O. Box 1954
Fargo, ND 58107
communities.msn.com/RedRiverValleyLegalAssistants/
    whatsnew.msnw

Western Dakota Association of Legal Assistants (*) [42]
P.O. Box 1000
Bismarck, ND 58702
www.wdala.org

## OHIO

Cincinnati Paralegal Association (**) [270]
P.O. Box 1515
Cincinnati, OH 45201
513-244-1266
www.cincinnatiparalegals.org

Cleveland Association of Paralegals (**) [206]
P.O. Box 14517
Cleveland, OH 44114-0517
216-556-5437
paralegals.org/Cleveland

Greater Dayton Paralegal Association (**) [115]
P.O. Box 515, Mid–City Station
Dayton, OH 45402
www.paralegals.org/GreaterDayton/home.html

Northeastern Ohio Paralegal Association (**) [47]
P.O. Box 80068
Akron, OH 44308
www.paralegals.org/NortheasternOhio/home.html

Ohio State Bar Association
Legal Assistant/Paralegal Membership
www.ohiobar.org/application/paraapp.html

Paralegal Association of Central Ohio (**) [257]
P.O. Box 15182
Columbus, OH 43215–0182
614–224–9700
www.pacoparalegal.org
www.paralegals.org/CentralOhio/home.html

Toledo Association of Legal Assistants (*) [71]
P.O. Box 1322
Toledo, OH 43603
www.tala.org

## OKLAHOMA

Oklahoma Paralegal Association (*) [30]
P.O. Box 5784
Enid, OK 73702
www.okparalegal.org

Tulsa Association of Legal Assistants (*) [130]
P.O. Box 1484
Tulsa, OK 74101
www.tulsatala.org

## OREGON

Oregon Paralegal Association (**) [363]
P.O. Box 8523
Portland, OR 97207
503–796–1671
paralegals.org/Oregon

Pacific Northwest Legal Assistants (*)
Eugene, OR

NALS (Association of Legal Professionals) of
    Oregon
www.nalsor.org

## PENNSYLVANIA

Central Pennsylvania Paralegal Association (**)
    [102]
P.O. Box 11814
Harrisburg, PA 17108
paralegals.org/CentralPennsylvania

Chester County Paralegal Association (**)
P.O. Box 295
West Chester, PA 19381

Keystone Legal Assistants Association (*) [60]
P.O. Box 25
Enola, PA 17025

Lycoming County Paralegal Association (**) [53]
P.O. Box 991
Williamsport, PA 17701

Montgomery County Paralegal Association (**) [86]
c/o HRMML
375 Morris Road
P.O. Box 1479
Lansdale, PA 19446
www.paralegals.org/Montgomery/home.html

Philadelphia Association of Paralegals (**) [522]
P.O. Box 59179
Philadelphia, PA 19102–9179
215–545–5395
www.philaparalegals.com

Pittsburgh Paralegal Association (**) [400]
P.O. Box 2845
Pittsburgh, PA 15230
412–344–3904
www.pghparalegals.org
paralegals.org/Pittsburgh

Lehigh–Northampton Counties Legal Secretaries
    Association
www.enter.net/~lisajames

## RHODE ISLAND
Rhode Island Paralegal Association (**) [161]
P.O. Box 1003
Providence, RI 02901
paralegals.org/RhodeIsland

## SOUTH CAROLINA
Charleston Association of Legal Assistants (*) [60]
P.O. Box 1511
Charleston, SC 29402

Grand Strand Paralegal Association (*)
743 Hemlock Avenue
Myrtle Beach, SC 29577
www.hor.tec.sc.us/paralegal/GSPA.htm

Greenville Association of Legal Assistants (*) [60]
P.O. Box 10491
Greenville, SC 29603

Palmetto Paralegal Association (**) [200]
P.O. Box 11634
Columbia, SC 29211
803–252–0460
paralegals.org/Palmetto

Tri–County Paralegal Association (*) [59]
P.O. Box 62691
North Charleston, SC 29419
www.concentric.net/~Tcpa

South Carolina Association of Legal Investigators
www.scalinv.com

## SOUTH DAKOTA

South Dakota Paralegal Association (*) [100]
P.O. Box 8381
Rapid City, SD 57709
www.sdbar.org/sdpa/index.htm

## TENNESSEE

Greater Memphis Paralegal Alliance (*) [65]
P.O. Box, 3846
Memphis, TN 38173
901-527-6254
www.memphisparalegals.org

Memphis Paralegal Association (**)
P.O. Box 3646
Memphis, TN 38173-0646
paralegals.org/Memphis

Middle Tennessee Paralegal Association (**) [168]
P.O. Box 198006
Nashville, TN 37219
paralegals.org/Members/tennessee.html

Tennessee Paralegal Association (*)
281 Waddell Road SW
Cleveland, TN 37311
423-479-7171
firms.findlaw.com/TPA

Memphis Legal Secretaries Association
www.memphisLSA.org

## TEXAS

Alamo Area Professional Legal Assistants [120]
P.O. Box 524
San Antonio, TX 78292
210-231-5791
www.aapla.org

Capitol Area Paralegal Association (*) [300]
P.O. Box 773
Austin, TX 78767
512-505-6822
www.capatx.org

Dallas Area Paralegal Association (**) [400]
P.O. Box 12533
Dallas, TX 75225
972-991-0853
www.dallasparalegals.org

El Paso Association of Legal Assistants (*) [64]
P.O. Box 6
El Paso, TX 79940
www.epala.org

Fort Worth Paralegal Association [381]
P.O. Box 17021
Fort Worth, TX 76102
817-336-3972
www.fwpa.org

Galveston Area Legal Assistants Association [40]
P.O. Box 1319
Galveston, TX 77553

Houston Legal Assistants Association [700]
440 Louisiana, Suite 900
Houston, TX 77002
713-236-7724
www.hlaa.net

Houston Paralegal Association [22]
P.O. Box 61863
Houston, TX 77208
www.houstonparalegal.homestead.com

Legal Assistant Association/Permian Basin (*) [48]
P.O. Box 10683
Midland, TX 79702

Legal Assistants Division [2,200]
State Bar of Texas
P.O. Box 12487
Austin, TX 78711
www.lad.org

Legal Assistants of North Texas Association
P.O. Box 131207
Dallas, TX 75313
www.lantaweb.org

Metroplex Association of Corporate Paralegals [135]
P.O. Box 201592
Arlington, TX 76006
www.macp.net

Northeast Texas Association of Legal Assistants (*) [50]
P.O. Box 2284
Longview, TX 75606
www.ntala.net

Nueces County Association of Legal Assistants
P.O. Box 2624
Corpus Christi, TX 78403

Southeast Texas Association of Legal Assistants (*) [69]
P.O. Box 813
Beaumont, TX 77704
www.setala.org

Texas Panhandle Association of Legal Assistants (*) [55]
P.O. Box 1127
Amarillo, TX 79105

Tyler Area Association of Legal Assistants (*) [75]
P.O. Box 2013
Tyler, TX 75710

West Texas Association of Legal Assistants (*) [26]
P.O. Box 93103
Lubbock, TX 79493

Houston Association of Legal Secretaries
www.houstonals.org

Texas Process Servers Association
www.ntpsa.net

## UTAH

Legal Assistants Association of Utah (*) [53]
P.O. Box 112001
Salt Lake City, UT 84147

Utah State Bar
Legal Assistant Division
www.utahbar.org/sites/lad

## VERMONT

Vermont Paralegal Organization (**) [80]
P.O. Box 5755
Burlington, VT 05402
paralegals.org/Vermont/home.html

## VIRGINIA

Central Virginia Paralegal Association [15]
P.O. Box 143
Lynchburg, VA 24505

Charlottesville Association of Legal Assistants
Charlottesville, VA

Fredericksburg Association of Legal Assistants (*)
Fredericksburg, VA
mhanson@tgblaw.com

Fredericksburg Paralegal Association (**) [21]
P.O. Box 7351
Fredericksburg, VA 22404

National Capital Area Paralegal Association
See District of Columbia

Peninsula Legal Assistants (*) [40]
115 Freemoor Drive
Poquoson, VA 23662

Richmond Association of Legal Assistants (*) [235]
P.O. Box 384
Richmond, VA 23218
geocities.com/CapitolHill/7082

Roanoke Valley Paralegal Association (*) [40]
P.O. Box 1505
Roanoke, VA 24007

Shenandoah Valley Paralegal Association [30]
P.O. Box 88
Harrisonburg, VA 22803

Southside Paralegal Association
P.O. Box 2751
Danville, VA 24541

Tidewater Association of Legal Assistants (*)
   [105]
P.O. Box 3566
Norfolk, VA 23514

Virginia Alliance of Legal Assistant Associations
P.O. Box 2125
Richmond, VA 23218
www.geocities.com/rala1982/guidelines.html

VALS—Association of Legal Professionals
www.geocities.com/eureka/boardroom/4608

## VIRGIN ISLANDS

Virgin Islands Association of Legal Assistants (*)
P.O. Box 70
St. Thomas, VI 00804

## WASHINGTON

Washington State Paralegal Association (**) [280]
P.O. Box 48153
Burien, WA 98148
800–288–9772
www.wspaonline.com
paralegals.org/Washington

NALS (Association of Legal Professionals) of
   Washington
www.nalsofwashington.org/directory/directory.html

## WEST VIRGINIA

Legal Assistants of West Virginia (*) [211]
www.geocities.com/~lawv

## WISCONSIN

Madison Area Paralegal Association (*) [71]
P.O. Box 2242
Madison, WI 53701
www.califex.com/mapa

Paralegal Association of Wisconsin (**) [370]
P.O. Box 510892
Milwaukee, WI 53203
414–272–7168
www.wisconsinparalegal.org

Wisconsin Association for Legal Professionals
www.wisconsin-alp.org

## WYOMING

Legal Assistants of Wyoming (*) [105]
P.O. Box 155
Casper, WY 82602
www.lawyo.com

## OTHER

American Association for Paralegal Education
408 Wekiva Springs Road
Longwood, FL 32779
407–834–6688
www.aafpe.org

Standing Committee on Legal Assistants
American Bar Association
541 North Fairbanks Court
Chicago, IL 60611
312–988–5522
www.abanet.org/legalassts

Legal Assistant Management Association
2965 Flowers Road South, Suite 105
Atlanta, GA 30341
770–457–7746
www.lamanet.org

*Legal Assistant Today*
James Publishing
3520 Cadillac Avenue, Suite E
Costa Mesa, CA 92636
800–394–2626
www.legalassistanttoday.com

Association of Trial Lawyers of America
Paralegal Affiliate Program
www.atlanet.org/members/parabro.ht

American Corporate Legal Assistants Association [157]
www.aclaa.org

American Association of Legal Nurse Consultants
www.aalnc.org

NALS: The Association of Legal Professionals
(formerly National Association of Legal Secretaries)
www.nals.org

Legal Secretaries International
www.legalsecretaries.org

National Paralegal Association
P.O. Box 406
Solebury, PA 18963
215–297–8333
www.nationalparalegal.org

National Organization of Legal Services Workers,
    AFL–CIO
www.geocities.com/~uaw2320

Association of Legal Administrators
www.alanet.org

National Organization of Social Security Claimants'
    Representatives
www.nosscr.org

National Association of Enrolled Agents
www.naea.org

American Institute of Certified Public Accountants
www.aicpa.org

National Association of Tax Professionals
www.natptax.com

National Court Appointed Special Advocate Association
www.casanet.org

American Disability Representation Specialists
    Association
www.adrsa.com

National Association of Patent Practitioners
www.napp.org

Alberta Association of Professional Paralegals
alberta-paralegal.com

Canadian Association of Legal Assistants
www.cala-acaj.com

Canadian Independent Paralegals Association
www.angelfire.com/nc2/cipa

Institute of Law Clerks of Ontario
www.ilco.on.ca

Paralegal Society of Ontario
paralegalsocietyont.org

Professional Paralegal Association of Ontario
    Toronto, Canada
www.ppao.on.ca

Institute of Legal Executives
www.ilex.org.uk

New Zealand Institute of Legal Executives
www.nz-lawsoc.org.nz/general/nzile/lebro.htm

Scottish Paralegal Association
Glasgow, Scotland
www.scottish-paralegal.org.uk

National Community-Based Paralegal Association
Johannesburg, South Africa
www.paralegaladvice.org.za/docs/chap15/02.html

International Association for Independent Paralegals
work-at-home-4-cipa.tripod.com

National Association of Professional Process Servers
www.napps.org

International Process Servers Association
www.iprocesservers.com

National Association of Litigation Support Managers
www.nalsm.org/index2.html

National Association of Legal Investigators
www.nalionline.org

National Association of Document Examiners
www.documentexaminers.org

American Pro Se Association
www.legalhelp.org/home.htm

Association of Record Managers and Administrators
www.arma.org

Legal Marketing Association
www.legalmarketing.org

National Court Reporters Association
www.ncraonline.org

HALT: An Organization of Americans for Legal Reform
800-FOR-HALT
www.halt.org

NOLO Press
(legal self-help materials)
www.nolo.com

American Video Reporters Association
www2.chtree.com/per/avra

National Resource Center for Consumers of Legal Services
www.nrccls.org

# Appendix C

# ASSOCIATIONS OF ATTORNEYS

There are several reasons you should check Internet sites presented in this appendix:

1. You need to become familiar with bar associations in your state as soon as possible. They will continue to have a major impact on your paralegal career. At each bar site, try to find out which committees or sections are involved with paralegals. (Also take a look at those on law office management and the practice of law.) If there is a search feature on the site, type in *paralegal* and/or *legal assistant*.
2. Check any information or links on ethics, professional responsibility, and unauthorized practice of law.
3. Explore different areas of the law. Almost all of the sites (either directly or through links) will provide information about what attorneys do in different areas of the law. This information will be valuable in helping you decide what areas of the law you might want to pursue.
4. When you have your first job interview, part of your preparation should be to find out what state and national organizations are relevant to the kind of law practiced where you will be interviewing. There is probably a bar association committee or section and a national organization that are relevant to every employment setting.

## STATE AND LOCAL BAR ASSOCIATIONS
(The first site under each state often has regulatory authority over attorneys in the state)

### ALABAMA
Alabama State Bar Association
www.alabar.org

Alabama Trial Lawyers Association
www.atla.net

Birmingham Bar Association
www.birminghambar.org

Mobile Bar Association
www.mobilebar.com

### ALASKA
Alaska Bar Association
www.alaskabar.org

Alaska Academy of Trial Lawyers
www.alaskatriallawyers.org

### ARIZONA
State Bar of Arizona
www.azbar.org

Arizona Trial Lawyers Association
www.aztla.org

Los Abogados
www.losabogados.org

Pima County Bar Association
www.pimacountybar.org

## ARKANSAS
Arkansas Bar Association
www.arkbar.com

Arkansas Trial Lawyers Association
www.arktla.org

## CALIFORNIA
California State Bar Association
www.calbar.org

Academy of California Adoption Lawyers
www.acal.org

Alameda County Bar Association
www.acbanet.org

Bar Association of Northern San Diego
www.bansdc.org

Bar Association of San Francisco
www.sfbar.org

Bay Area Lawyers for Individual Freedom
www.balif.org

Beverly Hills Bar Association
www.bhba.org

Black Women Lawyers Association of Los Angeles
www.bwlla.org

California Minority Counsel Program
www.cmcp.org

California Women Lawyers
www.cwl.org

Consumer Attorneys of California
www.caoc.com

Consumer Attorneys of San Diego
www.casd.org

Contra Costa County Bar Association
www.cccba.org

Korean American Bar Association of Northern California
www.kabanc.org

Lawyers Club of Los Angeles County
www.lawyersclub.org

Los Angeles County Bar Association
www.lacba.org

Marin County Bar Association
www.marinbar.org

National Lawyers Guild, Los Angeles Chapter
www.nlg-la.org

Orange County Bar Association
www.ocbar.org

Palo Alto Bar Association
www.lawscape.com/paaba

Placer County Bar Association
www.placerbar.org

Riverside County Bar Association
www.rcba.net

Sacramento Bar Association
www.sacbar.org

San Bernardino County Bar Association
www.sbcba.org

San Diego County Bar Association
www.sdcba.org

San Fernando Valley Bar Association
www.sfvba.org

San Mateo County Bar Association
www.smcba.org

Santa Clara County Bar Association
www.sccba.com

Sonoma County Bar Association
www.sonomacountybar.org

Tahoe-Truckee Bar Association
www.geocities.com/tahoetruckeebar

Ventura County Bar Association
www.vcba.org

Yolo County Bar Association
www.macattorney.com/ycba.html

## COLORADO
Colorado Bar Association
www.cobar.org

Boulder County Bar Association
www.boulder-bar.org

Colorado Criminal Defense Bar
www.ccdb.org

Colorado Trial Lawyers Association
www.ctlanet.org

Colorado Women's Bar Association
www.cwba.org

Denver Bar Association
www.denbar.org

El Paso County Bar Association
www.elpasocountybar.org

## CONNECTICUT
Connecticut Bar Association
www.ctbar.org

Connecticut Trial Lawyers Association
www.ct-tla.org

## DELAWARE
Delaware State Bar Association
www.dsba.org

Delaware Trial Lawyers Association
www.dtla.org

## DISTRICT OF COLUMBIA

District of Columbia Bar Association
www.dcbar.org

Bar Association of the District of Columbia
www.badc.org

Hispanic Bar Association, District of Columbia
www.hbadc.org

## FLORIDA

The Florida Bar
www.flabar.org

Academy of Florida Trial Lawyers
www.aftl.org

American Immigration Law Association, Central Florida
Chapter
www.ailacfc.org

Brandon Bar Association
www.brandonbar.org

Broward County Bar Association
www.browardbar.org

Central Florida Bankruptcy Law Association
www.cfbla.org

Clearwater Bar Association
www.clwbar.org

Collier County Bar Association
www.naples.net/clubs/ccba

Coral Gables Bar Association
www.coralgablesbar.org

Dade County Bar Association
www.dadecountybar.org

Dade County Trial Lawyers Association
www.dctla.org

Florida Academy of Professional Mediators
www.tfapm.org

Florida Association of Criminal Defense Attorneys
www.facdl.org

Florida Defense Lawyers Association
www.fdla.org

Florida Law Related Education Association
www.flrea.org

Jacksonville Bar Association
www.jaxbar.org

Indian River County Bar Association
www.irclaw.org

National Bar Association, Florida Chapter
www.fcnba.org

Orange County Bar Association
www.ocbanet.org

Palm Beach County Bar Association
www.palmbeachbar.org

St. Petersburg Bar Association
www.stpetebar.com

Sarasota County Bar Association
www.sarasotabar.com

Volusia County Bar Association
www.volusiabar.org

West Pasco Bar Association
www.wpba.net

## GEORGIA

State Bar of Georgia
www.gabar.org

Atlanta Bar Association
www.atlantabar.org

Georgia Association of Criminal Defense Attorneys
www.gacdl.org

Georgia Indigent Defense Counsel
www.gidc.com

Georgia Trial Lawyers Association
www.gtla.org

North Fulton Bar Association
northfultonbar.com

## HAWAII

Hawaii State Bar Association
www.hsba.org

Consumer Lawyers of Hawaii
www.clh.org

Hawaii's Women Lawyers
www.hsba.org/sections/HWL/hwl.html

Maui County Bar Association
www.hsba.org/mcba

## IDAHO

Idaho State Bar Association
www2.state.id.us/isb

Idaho Trial Lawyers Association
www.itla.org

## ILLINOIS

Illinois State Bar Association
www.illinoisbar.org

Appellate Lawyers Association
www.applawyers.org

Black Women Lawyers' Association of Greater Chicago
www.bwla.org

Champaign County Bar Association
www.ccba.org

Chicago Bar Association
www.chicagobar.org

Chicago Council of Lawyers
www.chicagocouncil.org

Decatur Bar Association
www.decaturbar.org

DuPage County Bar Association
www.dcba.org

Illinois Association of Defense Trial Counsel
www.iadtc.org

Illinois Trial Lawyers Association
www.iltla.com

Kane County Bar Association
www.kanebar.org

Peoria County Bar Association
www.peoriabar.org

Prosecutors Bar Association
www.ipba.net

Will County Bar Association
www.willcountybar.com

Winnebago County Bar Association
www.wcbarockford.org

## INDIANA
Indiana State Bar Association
www.inbar.org

Evansville Bar Association
www.evvbar.org

Indianapolis Bar Association
www.indybar.org

Indiana Trial Lawyers Association
www.i-t-l-a.org

Lake County Bar Association
www.lcbar.com

Monroe County Bar Association
www.monroecountybar.com

St. Joseph County Bar Association
www.sjcba.org

## IOWA
Iowa State Bar Association
www.iowabar.org

Iowa Trial Lawyers Association
www.iowatla.org

Linn County Bar Association
www.linncobar.org

## KANSAS
Kansas Bar Association
www.ksbar.org

Johnson County Bar Association
www.jocobar.org

## KENTUCKY
Kentucky Bar Association
www.kybar.org

Fayette County Bar Association
www.fcba.com

Kentucky Academy of Trial Attorneys
www.kata.org

## LOUISIANA
Louisiana State Bar Association
www.lsba.org

Baton Rouge Bar Association
www.brba.org

Jefferson Bar Association
www.jeffbar.org

Lafayette Parish Bar Association
www.lafayettebar.org

Louisiana Trial Lawyers Association
www.ltla.org

New Orleans Bar Association
www.neworleansbar.org

Shreveport Bar Association
www.ShreveportBar.com

Southwest Louisiana Bar Association
www.lsba.org/swlba

## MAINE
Maine State Bar Association
www.mainebar.org

Maine Association of Criminal Defense Attorneys
home.gwi.net/~macdl/index.html

Maine Trial Lawyers Association
www.mtla.org

## MARYLAND
Maryland State Bar Association
www.msba.org

Anne Arundel County Bar Association
www.aabar.org

Baltimore County Bar Association
www.bcba.org

Bar Association of Baltimore County
www.baltimorebar.org

Bar Association of Frederick County
www.frederickbar.org

Bar Association, Howard County
www.mdlaw.net/howard

Bar Association of Montgomery County
www.montbar.org

Maryland Trial Lawyers Association
www.mdtriallawyers.com

Prince George's County Bar Association
www.pgcba.com

St. Mary's County Bar Association
www.mdlaw.net/stmarys

## MASSACHUSETTS
Massachusetts Bar Association
www.massbar.org

Massachusetts Academy of Trial Lawyers
www.massacademy.com

Boston Bar Association
www.bostonbar.org

Boston Patent Lawyers Association
www.bpla.org

Hampden County Bar Association
www.hcbar.org

Hellenic Bar Association
www.hellenicbarassociation.com

Women's Bar of Massachusetts
www.womensbar.org

## MICHIGAN
Michigan Bar Association
www.michbar.org

Detroit Metropolitan Bar Association
www.detroitlawyer.org

Genesee County Bar Association
www.gcbalaw.org

Grand Rapids Bar Association
www.grbar.org

Macomb County Bar Association
www.macombbar.org

Michigan Defense Trial Counsel
www.mdtc.org

Michigan Trial Lawyers Association
www.MTLA.net

Oakland County Bar Association
www.ocba.org

Washtenaw County Bar Association
www.washbar.org

## MINNESOTA
Minnesota State Bar Association
www.mnbar.org

Hennepin County Bar Association
www.hcba.org

Minnesota American Indian Bar Association
www.maiba.org

Minnesota Association of Black Lawyers
www.mabl.org

Minnesota Defense Lawyers Association
www.mdla.org

Minnesota Trial Lawyers Association
www.mntla.com

Minnesota Women Lawyers
www.mwlawyers.org

## MISSISSIPPI
Mississippi Bar
www.msbar.org

Mississippi Defense Lawyers Association
www.msdefenselaw.org

Mississippi Lawyers
www.mslawyer.com

Mississippi Trial Lawyers Association
www.mstla.com

## MISSOURI
Missouri Bar Association
www.mobar.org

Bar Association of Metropolitan St. Louis
www.bamsl.org

Kansas City Metropolitan Bar Association
www.kcmba.com

Missouri Association of Trial Attorneys
www.matanet.org

## MONTANA
Montana Bar Association
www.montanabar.org

Montana Trial Lawyers Association
www.monttla.com

## NEBRASKA
Nebraska State Bar Association
www.nebar.com

Nebraska Association of Trial Attorneys
www.nebraskatrial.com

## NEVADA
Nevada Bar Association
www.nvbar.org/index.php3

Clark County Bar Association
www.ccba.net

Nevada Trial Lawyers Association
www.ntla.org

Tahoe-Truckee Bar Association
www.geocities.com/tahoetruckeebar

## NEW HAMPSHIRE
New Hampshire Bar Association
www.nhbar.org

New Hampshire Trial Lawyers Association
www.nhtla.org

## NEW JERSEY
New Jersey State Bar Association
www.njsba.com

Association of Trial Lawyers of America—New Jersey
www.atlanj.org

Gloucester County Bar Association
www.gcbanj.org

Middlesex County Bar Association
www.mcbalaw.com

Morris County Bar Association
www.morriscountybar.com

## NEW MEXICO
State Bar of New Mexico
www.nmbar.org

New Mexico Trial Lawyer Association
www.nmtla.org

## NEW YORK
New York State Bar Association
www.nysba.org

Albany County Bar Association
www.albanycountybar.com

Association of the Bar of the City of New York
www.abcny.org

Bar Association of Erie County
www.eriebar.org

Brooklyn Bar Association
www.bklynbar.org

Cortland County Bar Association
www.zeus.odyssey.net/subscribers/fvisco/bar

Delaware County Bar Association
www.hancock.net/%7Edcba/dcba.html

Dutchess County Bar Association
www.mhv.net/~dcba/dcba3.htm

Lesbian and Gay Law Association of Greater New York
www.le-gal.org

Nassau County Bar Association
www.nassaubar.org

New York County Lawyers' Association
www.nycla.org

New York State Association of Criminal Defense Lawyers
www.nysacdl.org

New York State Defenders Association
www.nysda.org

New York State Trial Lawyers Association
www.nystla.org

Onondaga County Bar Association
www.onbar.org

Richmond County Bar Association
www.richmondcountybar.org

Suffolk County Bar Association
www.scba.org

Women's Bar Association of the State of New York
www.wbasny.org

## NORTH CAROLINA
North Carolina State Bar
www.ncbar.com

North Carolina Bar Association
www.barlinc.org

American Academy of Matrimonial Lawyers, North Carolina Chapter
www.NC-AAML.com

Forsyth County Bar Association
www.forsythlawyers.com

North Carolina Academy of Trial Lawyers
www.ncatl.org

North Carolina Association of Women Attorneys
www.ncawa.org

North Carolina Gay and Lesbian Attorneys
www.ncgala.org

Wake County Bar Association
www.lawsight.com/wcba.htm

## NORTH DAKOTA
State Bar Association of North Dakota
www.sband.org

## OHIO
Ohio State Bar Association
www.ohiobar.org

Akron Bar Association
www.akronbar.org

Cincinnati Bar Association
www.cincybar.org

Cleveland Bar Association
www.clevelandbar.org

Columbus Bar Association
www.cbalaw.org

Cuyahoga County Bar Association
www.cuybar.org

Dayton Bar Association
www.daybar.org

Lake County Bar Association
www.lcba-ohio.org

Lorain County Bar Association
www.loraincountybar.org

Miami Valley Trial Lawyers Association
www.mvtla.org

Ohio Academy of Trial Lawyers
www.oatlaw.org

Ohio Association of Civil Trial Attorneys
www.oacta.org

Ohio Association of Criminal Defense Lawyers
www.oacdl.org

Ohio Women's Bar Association
www.owba.org

Toledo Bar Association
www.toledobar.org

## OKLAHOMA

Oklahoma Bar Association
www.okbar.org

Oklahoma Indian Bar Association
www.oiba.homestead.com/homepage.html

Oklahoma Trial Lawyers Association
www.otla.org

Tulsa County Bar Association
www.tulsabar.com

## OREGON

Oregon State Bar
www.osbar.org

Multnomah Bar Association
www.mbabar.org

## PENNSYLVANIA

Pennsylvania Bar Association
www.pa-bar.org

Allegheny County Bar Association
www.acba.org

Bar Association of Lehigh County
www.lehighbar.org

Berks County Bar Association
www.berksbar.com

Bucks County Bar Association
www.bucksbar.org

Chester County Bar Association
www.chescobar.org

Dauphin County Bar Association
www.dcba-pa.org

Erie County Bar Association
www.eriebar.com

Gay and Lesbian Lawyers of Philadelphia
www.libertynet.org/gallop

Lancaster Bar Association
www.lancasterbar.org

Lycoming Law Association
www.lycolaw.org

Monroe County Bar Association
www.monroebar.org

Montgomery Bar Association
www.montgomerybar.org

Northampton County Bar Association
www.norcobar.org

Pennsylvania Association of Criminal Defense Lawyers
www.pacdl.org

Pennsylvania Trial Lawyers Association
www.patla.org

Philadelphia Bar Association
www.philabar.org

Philadelphia Trial Lawyers Association
www.philatla.org

Schuylkill County Bar Association
www.schuylkillbar.org

Westmorland Bar Association
www.westbar.org

York County Bar Association
www.yorkbar.com

## RHODE ISLAND

Rhode Island Bar Association
www.ribar.com

## SOUTH CAROLINA

South Carolina Bar
www.scbar.org

Charleston County Bar Association
www.charlestonbar.org

South Carolina Trial Lawyers Association
www.sctla.org

## SOUTH DAKOTA
State Bar of South Dakota
www.sdbar.org

## TENNESSEE
Tennessee Bar Association
www.tba.org

Chattanooga Bar Association
www.chattbar.org

Knoxville Bar Association
www.knoxbar.org

Memphis Bar Association
www.memphisbar.org

Nashville Bar Association
www.nashbar.org

Tennessee Association for Criminal Defense Lawyers
www.pdknox.org/tacdl

Tennessee Trial Lawyers Association
www.ttla.org

## TEXAS
State Bar of Texas Bar
www.texasbar.com

Bexar County Women's Bar Association
www.netxpress.com/~bcwba

Corpus Christi Bar Association
www.corpusbar.com

Dallas Bar Association
www.dallasbar.com

Denton County Bar Association
dentonbar.com

Houston Bar Association
www.hba.org

Houston Intellectual Property Law Association
www.hipla.org

Houston Northwest Bar Association
www.hnba.org

Local Bar Associations of Texas
www5.law.com/tx/bar/associations.htm

San Antonio Bar Association
www.sanantoniobar.org

San Antonio Trial Lawyers Association
www.satla.org

Tarrant County Bar Association
www.tarrantbar.org

Texas Academy of Family Law Specialists
www.tafls.org

Texas Criminal Defense Lawyers Association
www.tcdla.com

Texas Trial Lawyers Association
www.ttla.com

Travis County Bar Association
www.travisbar.com

## UTAH
Utah State Bar
www.utahbar.org

Utah Trial Lawyers Association
www.utla.org

## VERMONT
Vermont Bar Association
www.vtbar.org

Vermont Trial Lawyers Association
www.vtla.org

## VIRGINIA
Virginia State Bar
www.vsb.org

Alexandria Bar Association
www.alexandriabarassoc.com

Fairfax Bar Association
www.fairfaxbar.org

Norfolk and Portsmouth Bar Association
www.itnsonline.com/npba

Virginia Association of Defense Attorneys
www.vada.org

Virginia College of Criminal Defense Attorneys
www.vccda.org

Virginia Trial Lawyers Association
www.vtla.com

## VIRGIN ISLANDS
Virgin Islands Bar Association
www.vibar.org

## WASHINGTON
Washington State Bar Association
www.wsba.org

King County Bar Association
www.kcba.org

Kitsap County Lawyers
www.kitsapbar.com

Snohomish County Bar Association
www.snobar.org

Spokane County Bar Association
www.spokanebar.org

Washington Defender Association
www.defensenet.org

Washington Defense Trial Lawyers
www.wdtl.org

Washington State Trial Lawyers Association
www.wstla.org

Washington Women Lawyers
www.wwl.org

Whatcom County Bar Association
www.viewit.com/WhatcomBar

## WEST VIRGINIA

West Virginia Bar Association
www.wvbarassociation.com

West Virginia Trial Lawyers Association
www.wvtla.org

## WISCONSIN

State Bar of Wisconsin
www.wisbar.org

Milwaukee Bar Association
www.milwbar.org

Tri-County Bar Association
www.wisbar.org/bars/tricounty

Wisconsin Academy of Trial Lawyers
www.watl.org

## WYOMING

Wyoming State Bar
www.wyomingbar.org

Wyoming Trial Lawyers Association
www.wytla.org

## OTHER ASSOCIATIONS OF ATTORNEYS

American Academy of Elder Care Attorneys
www.naela.org

American Academy of Estate Planning Attorneys
www.aaepa.com

American Agricultural Law Association
www.aglaw-assn.org

American Arbitration Association
www.adr.org

American Association of Attorney-Certified Public
    Accountants
www.attorney-cpa.com

American Association of Nurse Attorneys
www.taana.org

American Bar Association
www.abanet.org

American Civil Liberties Union
www.aclu.org

American College of Trust and Estate Counsel
www.actec.org

American Corporate Counsel Association
www.acca.com

American Health Lawyers Association
www.healthlawyers.org

American Immigration Lawyers Association
www.aila.org

American Intellectual Property Law Association
www.aipla.org

American Judicature Society
www.ajs.org

American Law Institute
www.ali.org

American Lawyers Public Image Association
www.ALPIA.org

American Society for Pharmacy Law
www.aspl.org

American Society of Comparative Law
www.comparativelaw.org

American Society of Law, Medicine and Ethics
www.aslme.org

Animal Legal Defense Fund
www.aldf.org

Association for Continuing Legal Education
www.aclea.org

Association of Attorney-Mediators
www.attorney-mediators.org

Association of Federal Defense Attorneys
www.afda.org

Association of Professional Responsibility Lawyers
www.aprl.net

Association of Trial Lawyers of America
www.atlanet.org

Black Entertainment and Sports Lawyers Association
www.besla.org

Christian Legal Society
www.clsnet.org

Computer Law Association
www.cla.org

Council on Law in Higher Education
www.clhe.org

Cyberspace Bar Association
www.cyberbar.net

Defense Research Institute
www.dri.org

Education Law Association
www.educationlaw.org

Federal Bar Association
www.fedbar.org

Federal Communications Bar Association
www.fcba.org

Federation of Defense and Corporate Counsel
www.thefederation.org

First Amendment Lawyers Association
www.fala.org

Greek-American Lawyers Association
www.firms.findlaw.com/gala

Hellenic Bar Association
www.hellenicbarassociation.com

Hispanic National Bar Association
www.hnba.com

Indian Law Resource Center
www.indianlaw.org

International Center for Not-For-Profit Law
www.icnl.org

International Lawyers Network
www.lawinternational.com

Internet and Computer Law Association
www.grove.ufl.edu/~cmplaw

Internet Bar Association
www.lawyers.org

Judge Advocate Association
www.jaa.org

Italian-American Lawyers Association
www.iala.lawzone.com

Jurist, the Legal Education Network
www.clsnet.org

Lambda Legal Defense and Education Fund
www.lambdalegal.org

Lawyer Pilots Bar Association
www.lpba.org

Lawyers Committee for Human Rights
www.lchr.org/home.htm

Legal Justice Reform Network
www.atps.com/uclr

Legal Marketing Association
www.legalmarketing.org

Lithuanian-American Bar Association
www.javadvokatai.org

NAACP Legal Defense Fund
www.ldfla.org

National Academy of Elder Law Attorneys
www.naela.com

National Asian Pacific American Bar Association
www.napaba.org

National Association of Assistant United States Attorneys
www.naausa.org

National Association of Attorneys General
www.naag.org

National Association of Bond Attorneys
www.nabl.org

National Association of College and University Attorneys
www.nacua.org

National Association of Consumer Bankruptcy Attorneys
www.nacba.com

National Association of Criminal Defense Lawyers
www.nacdl.org

National Association of Legal Employers
www.nalp.org

National Association of Legal Search Consultants
www.nalsc.org

National Association of Patent Practitioners
www.napp.org

National Association of Public Interest Law
www.napil.org/HOME.html

National Association of Retail Collection Attorneys
www.narca.com

National Association of Women Judges
www.nawj.org

National Association of Women Lawyers
www.abanet.org/nawl/home.html

National Bar Association (African American Attorneys)
www.nationalbar.org

National Board of Trial Advocacy
www.nbtanet.org

National Center for Lesbian Rights
www.nclrights.org

National Center for State Courts
www.ncsconline.org

National Crime Victim Bar Association
www.victimbar.org

National District Attorneys Association
www.ndaa-apri.org

National Employment Lawyers Association
www.nela.org

National Lawyers Association
www.nla.org

National Lawyers Guild
www.nlg.org

National Legal Aid & Defender Association
www.nlada.org

National Native American Bar Association
www.nativeamericanbar.org

National Organization of Bar Counsel
www.nobc.org

National Right to Work Legal Defense Foundation
www.nrtw.org

National Transportation Safety Board Bar Association
www.ntsbbar.org

National Whistleblower Center
www.whistleblowers.org

NSBA Council of School Attorneys
www.nsba.org/cosa

Phi Alpha Delta (Law Fraternity)
www.pad.org

Philippine American Bar Association
www.philconnect.com/paba
www.markskatz.com/PABA.htm

Rocky Mountain Mineral Law Foundation
www.rmmlf.org

Sports Lawyers Association
www.sportslaw.org

Ukrainian American Bar Association
www.uaba.net

# Federal Government Organization Chart

# THE GOVERNMENT OF THE UNITED STATES

## THE CONSTITUTION

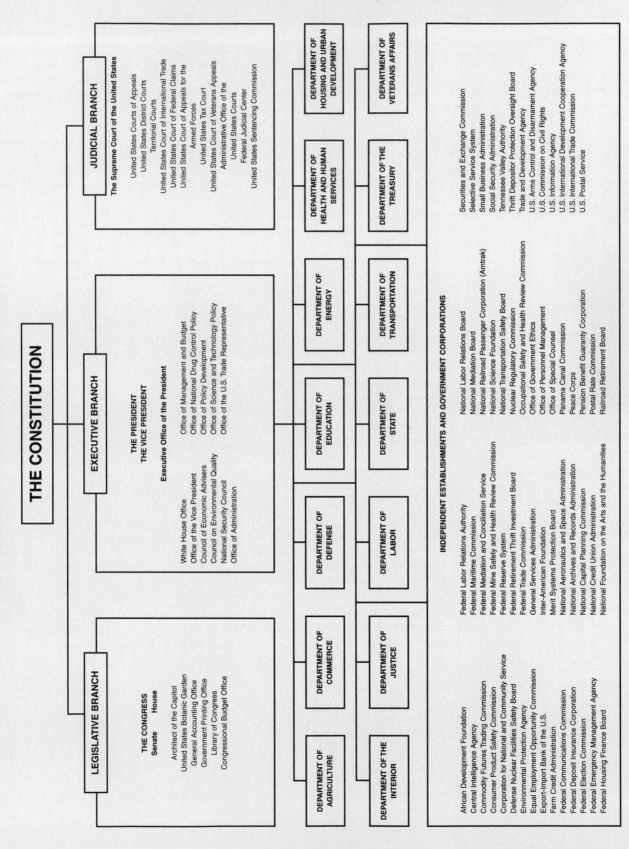

### LEGISLATIVE BRANCH

**THE CONGRESS**
**Senate    House**

Architect of the Capitol
United States Botanic Garden
General Accounting Office
Government Printing Office
Library of Congress
Congressional Budget Office

### EXECUTIVE BRANCH

**THE PRESIDENT**
**THE VICE PRESIDENT**

**Executive Office of the President**

White House Office
Office of the Vice President
Council of Economic Advisers
Council on Environmental Quality
National Security Council
Office of Administration

Office of Management and Budget
Office of National Drug Control Policy
Office of Policy Development
Office of Science and Technology Policy
Office of the U.S. Trade Representative

### JUDICIAL BRANCH

**The Supreme Court of the United States**

United States Courts of Appeals
United States District Courts
Territorial Courts
United States Court of International Trade
United States Court of Federal Claims
United States Court of Appeals for the
  Armed Forces
United States Tax Court
United States Court of Veterans Appeals
Administrative Office of the
  United States Courts
Federal Judicial Center
United States Sentencing Commission

DEPARTMENT OF AGRICULTURE

DEPARTMENT OF COMMERCE

DEPARTMENT OF DEFENSE

DEPARTMENT OF EDUCATION

DEPARTMENT OF ENERGY

DEPARTMENT OF HEALTH AND HUMAN SERVICES

DEPARTMENT OF HOUSING AND URBAN DEVELOPMENT

DEPARTMENT OF THE INTERIOR

DEPARTMENT OF JUSTICE

DEPARTMENT OF LABOR

DEPARTMENT OF STATE

DEPARTMENT OF TRANSPORTATION

DEPARTMENT OF THE TREASURY

DEPARTMENT OF VETERANS AFFAIRS

## INDEPENDENT ESTABLISHMENTS AND GOVERNMENT CORPORATIONS

African Development Foundation
Central Intelligence Agency
Commodity Futures Trading Commission
Consumer Product Safety Commission
Corporation for National and Community Service
Defense Nuclear Facilities Safety Board
Environmental Protection Agency
Equal Employment Opportunity Commission
Export-Import Bank of the U.S.
Farm Credit Administration
Federal Communications Commission
Federal Deposit Insurance Corporation
Federal Election Commission
Federal Emergency Management Agency
Federal Housing Finance Board

Federal Labor Relations Authority
Federal Maritime Commission
Federal Mediation and Conciliation Service
Federal Mine Safety and Health Review Commission
Federal Reserve System
Federal Retirement Thrift Investment Board
Federal Trade Commission
General Services Administration
Inter-American Foundation
Merit Systems Protection Board
National Aeronautics and Space Administration
National Archives and Records Administration
National Capital Planning Commission
National Credit Union Administration
National Foundation on the Arts and the Humanities

National Labor Relations Board
National Mediation Board
National Railroad Passenger Corporation (Amtrak)
National Science Foundation
National Transportation Safety Board
Nuclear Regulatory Commission
Occupational Safety and Health Review Commission
Office of Government Ethics
Office of Personnel Management
Office of Special Counsel
Panama Canal Commission
Peace Corps
Pension Benefit Guaranty Corporation
Postal Rate Commission
Railroad Retirement Board

Securities and Exchange Commission
Selective Service System
Small Business Administration
Social Security Administration
Tennessee Valley Authority
Thrift Depositor Protection Oversight Board
Trade and Development Agency
U.S. Arms Control and Disarmament Agency
U.S. Commission on Civil Rights
U.S. Information Agency
U.S. International Development Cooperation Agency
U.S. International Trade Commission
U.S. Postal Service

**Source:** United States Government Manual 2001/2002 (www.access.gpo/gov/nara/nara001.html).

# Appendix E

# SURVEY OF NONLAWYER PRACTICE BEFORE FEDERAL ADMINISTRATIVE AGENCIES

STANDING COMMITTEE ON LAWYERS' RESPONSIBILITY FOR CLIENT PROTECTION AND THE AMERICAN BAR ASSOCIATION CENTER FOR PROFESSIONAL RESPONSIBILITY (FEBRUARY 1985)

## 1. BACKGROUND

The American Bar Association Standing Committee on Lawyers' Responsibility for Client Protection disseminated this survey to thirty-three (33) federal administrative agencies in late August 1984. The survey was intended to provide background information on the experiences of agencies permitting nonlawyer practice (other than for purposes of self-representation). During September and October ninety-seven percent (97%) of the agencies responded either over the phone or by mail following initial contact with their Offices of General Counsel. The ABA Center for Professional Responsibility tabulated the results in October 1984.

## II. BRIEF ANALYSIS AND CONCLUSIONS

We found that the overwhelming majority of agencies studied permit nonlawyer representation in both adversarial and nonadversarial proceedings.* However, most of them seem to encounter lay practice very infrequently (in less than 5 percent of adjudications), while only a few encounter lay practice as often as lawyer practice. Thus, although universally permitted, lay practice before federal agencies rarely occurs.

Few of the responding agencies comprehensively monitor or control the lay practice that does occur. Only about twenty percent (20%) require nonlawyers to register with the agency before permitting them to practice. Registration procedures may range from simply listing nonlawyers'

* A proceeding is adversarial if there is an opposing side in the controversy whether or not the other side is represented. A proceeding is nonadversarial if only one side is appearing before the agency official.

names to more formalized certifying or licensing procedures, which may include testing and character reviews. Proceedings in most of these agencies tend to require highly technical or specialized knowledge. Registration insures that lay representation meets an appropriate level of quality and competence. In at least one agency, registration insures that nonlawyer representatives will charge only nominal fees or no fees at all.

No agencies indicated that they would discipline nonlawyers differently from lawyers, although they clearly have an additional ability to pursue sanctions against lawyers through external disciplinary mechanisms. Only a few agencies indicated any special need for nonlawyer discipline. Most reported they had not encountered any problems with misconduct by nonlawyers or any inability of nonlawyers to meet appropriate ethical standards (though fewer than a third of the agencies studied have actually defined any specific ethical standards). Of those that voiced complaints about nonlawyers' skills in representation, most indicated that the problem they encounter most frequently is nonlawyers' lack of familiarity with procedural rules and tactics. The majority of responses suggest that nonlawyers do not pose any special practice problems, nor do they receive any special disciplinary consideration. Overall, the concern for nonlawyers' competence and ethical conduct seems limited, perhaps because nonlawyer practice is not widespread.

## III. METHODOLOGY

Throughout the survey our questions focused on lay representation (other than self-representation) occurring in adjudicatory proceedings. In question 1, in which we asked whether agencies permitted nonlawyer representation, we attempted to distinguish between adversarial and nonadversarial proceedings. Our distinction did not prove particularly informative because all agencies permitting nonlawyer practice (97 percent) allow such practice in both arenas.

Question 2 sought the methods by which agencies control or limit those practicing before them. The responses vary considerably from agency to agency. Questions 3 and 4 requested statistics concerning the frequency of non-lawyer practice. Many of the agencies indicated that statistics were unavailable. These responses also vary considerably. The results of questions 1 through 4 are tabulated in Chart 1.

| CHART 1 | Regulations Governing Nonlawyer Representation Frequency and Type of Practice | | | | | | |
|---|---|---|---|---|---|---|---|
| Agency | Statute/ Regulation Permitting Appearance | Permits Nonlawyer Adversarial Representation? | Permits Nonlawyer Nonadversarial Representation? | Provisions Limiting or Governing Practice | Frequency of Nonlawyer Representation | Change in Frequency of Nonlawyer Rep. w/in Past 6 Years | Most Common Type(s) of Nonlawyer Representation |
| Board of Immigration Appeals: Immigration and Naturalization Serv. | 8 CFR § 292.1–3 | Yes | Yes | "Accredited representative"[1] working for "recognized organization"[2] may charge only nominal fees. "Reputable individual"[3] may not charge fees | No statistics available | No statistics available | One time only by family member/friend; charitable, religious, or social service organization |
| Civil Aeronautics Board | 14 CFR § 300.1–6 14 CFR § 302.11 | Yes | Yes | None | Fewer than 6 appearances per yr., less than 1% of appearances[4] | None | Economic consultants for corporations |
| Comptroller of the Currency | 12 CFR § 19.3 | Yes[5] | Yes | Nonlawyer may be required to file a power of attorney or show to the satisfaction of the Comptroller the possession of requisite qualifications | None | None | None |

[1] May become accredited by the Department of Immigration Appeals (D.I.A.) by submitting an application through a recognized organization for review of character and fitness and experience with and knowledge of immigration law. No formal testing requirement or licensing fee.

[2] Typically, a religious, charitable, or social service organization becomes recognized by submitting an application for approval to the D.I.A. assuring that it will charge only nominal fees and assess no representation charges.

[3] Typically, a family member or friend submits declaration that he or she charges no fee, has a preexisting relationship with immigrant-applicant, and appears only on individual basis at request of immigrant-applicant.

[4] Although nonlawyer practice [is] not discouraged, complexity of agency proceedings tends to require specialized legal practice. Typical parties, large corporations or businesses, tend to hire lawyers.

[5] Permitted but lay representation rare because of complex proceedings and substantial rights or amounts of money involved.

**CHART 1**    Regulations Governing Nonlawyer Representation Frequency and Type of Practice—continued

| Agency | Statute/Regulation Permitting Appearance | Permits Nonlawyer Adversarial Representation? | Permits Nonlawyer Nonadversarial Representation? | Provisions Limiting or Governing Practice | Frequency of Nonlawyer Representation | Change in Frequency of Nonlawyer Rep. w/in Past 6 Years | Most Common Type(s) of Nonlawyer Representation |
|---|---|---|---|---|---|---|---|
| Consumer Product Safety Comm'n | 16 CFR §1025.61 et seq. | Yes | Yes | Filing and approval of proof of qualifications See 16 CFR § 1025.65 | Very infrequent, 2–5% of appearances | None | Nonfee by industry rep., consultant, or private service agency |
| Dep't of Agric., Agricultural Marketing Serv. | 7 CFR § 50.27 | Yes | Yes | None | Fewer than 3 appearances per yr., less than 1% of appearances | Decreased,[6] no statistics available | Economist/ accountant providing assistance prior to appearance |
| Dep't of Commerce, Office of Secretary | Those of other agencies governing appearances before administrative bodies, e.g., MSPB, 5 CFR Part 1201 | Yes | Yes | Reasonable atty fees for litigated matters set by agency; maximum atty fees for settlement set at $75/hr. government pays fees to winning atty | No statistics available | No statistics available | Nonfee by union reps. |
| Dep't of Commerce, Patent and Trademark Office | 35 U.S.C. §§ 31–33 | Yes | Yes | Only registered[7] practitioners permitted to practice | Less than 16% of appearances[8] | None | Repeated practice for a fee by registered agents |
| Dep't of Health and Human Services, Food and Drug Admin. | 32 CFR §§ 12.40, 12.45 | Yes | Yes | None | No appearances in recent years | None | None |

| Agency | Citation | | | | | | |
|---|---|---|---|---|---|---|---|
| Dep't of Justice, Drug Enforcement Admin. | 21 CFR § 1316.50 | Yes | N/A, all proceedings adversarial | None | 2 to 3 appearances per yr., 5% of appearances[9] | None | One time only by officer/employee of small family-owned business |
| Dep't of Justice, Foreign Claims Settlement Comm'n | 45 CFR § 500.1–6 | No | No[10] | Lawyer's fees set by statute at 10% of claim award and deducted from award | N/A[11] | N/A[11] | Family member providing assistance prior to appearance |
| Dep't of Labor, Benefits Review Board | 20 CFR § 802.201(b) 20 CFR §802.202 | Yes | N/A, all proceedings adversarial | Employer pays fee for successful claimant represented by lawyer; claimant pays fee when represented by nonlawyer; lawyer may acquire lien against award; nonlawyers may not.[12] Professional status is criterion for determining fees.[13] | 2–4% of appearances | None | Repeated practice for fee |

[6] In agency's early history, economists provided a substantial amount of representation because of the economic nature of agency proceedings. As proceedings become more sophisticated, economists began aiding lawyers rather than assuming primary responsibility for legal representation. Representation by economists is now rare, and lawyers handle the bulk of representation.

[7] Nonlawyers become registered by passing a character and fitness review and an examination. Nonlawyers having served four years in the examining corps of the Patent and Trademark Office (P.T.O.) may waive the exam. See 57 CFR § 1.341.

[8] Nonlawyers comprise about 16% of registered practitioners, but not all registered practitioners appear before P.T.O., so that nonlawyers probably appear in less than 16% of patent applications filed with P.T.O.

[9] Appearances are by the employees or officers of small family-owned businesses, analogous to pro se appearances.

[10] The agency allows "representation" only by bar members. Family members may sometimes assist in preparation of claims or at oral hearings, typically where elderly parent has language barrier problems.

[11] No nonlawyer representation allowed.

[12] These policies may tend to discourage lay representation.

[13] Typically approved rates for nonlawyers are less than half of those attorneys receive.

| CHART 1 | Regulations Governing Nonlawyer Representation Frequency and Type of Practice—continued | | | | | | |
|---|---|---|---|---|---|---|---|
| Agency | Statute/ Regulation Permitting Appearance | Permits Nonlawyer Adversarial Representation? | Permits Nonlawyer Nonadversarial Representation? | Provisions Limiting or Governing Practice | Frequency of Nonlawyer Representation | Change in Frequency of Nonlawyer Rep. w/in Past 6 Years | Most Common Type(s) of Nonlawyer Representation |
| Dep't of Labor, Employees Compensation Appeals Board | 20 CFR § 501.11 | Yes | N/A, all proceedings adversarial | All fees approved by board | Appear as frequently as lawyers | None | One time only by family member/ friend; repeated practice for a fee |
| Dep't of Labor, National Railroad Adjustment Board | 45 U.S.C. § 3153 | Yes | N/A | Only entities identified in 45 U.S.C. § 151 allowed to practice | Almost 100% of appearances | None | Industry employees |
| Dep't of Labor, Wage and Appeals Board | 20 CFR § 725.362(a) 20 CFR § 725.365 20 CFR § 725.366(b) | Yes | N/A | Fees must be reasonably commensurate with services performed;[14] attorney's fee deducted from award; employer pays fee for successful claimant represented by lawyer; claimant pays fee when represented by nonlawyer; lawyer may require lien against award, while nonlawyers may not.[15] | 3% of appearances; as in 180 cases/yr. | Decrease due to investigations by Office of Inspector General into unauthorized receipt of fees | One time only by family member or friend; repeated practice for fee; assistance prior to appearance |

| Dep't of Transportation, Maritime Admin. | 46 CFR § 201.21 | Yes | Yes | Only registered nonlawyers permitted to practice | Very infrequent | None | |
| Federal Deposit Ins. Corp | 12 CFR § 308.04 | Yes | Yes | Only qualified nonlawyers permitted to represent | 10 to 20 appearances per yr., 5% of appearances | 50% decrease | One time only by family member/friend; nonlawyer assistance prior to appearance |
| Federal Energy Regulatory Comm'n | 18 CFR § 385.2101 | Yes | Yes | None | 1 or 2 per yr. | None | Engineering firm assisting in technical nonadversarial proceeding |
| Federal Maritime Comm'n | 46 CFR § 502.30 | Yes | Yes | Only registered nonlawyers permitted to appear[16] | .5 to 1% of appearances | None | One time only by family member/friend; nonfee by industry rep., consultant, or private service agency |
| Federal Mine Safety & Health Review Comm'n | 29 CFR § 2700.3(b) | Yes, at trial hearings before Administrative Law Judges (ALJ); at appellate reviews before commissioners | N/A | Nonlawyer may practice only if party, "representative of miners,"[17] or owner, partner, full-time officer or employee of party-business entity; otherwise permitted to appear for limited purpose in special proceedings | 5–10% of appearances | None | Nonfee by industry rep., consultant, or private service agency |

[14] See 20 CFR § 725.366(b) (black lung) and 20 CFR § 702.132 (longshore).
[15] These policies may tend to discourage lay representation.
[16] Certificates of registration are issued on payment of $13.00 processing fee and completion of application form indicating sufficient educational qualifications and recommendations. There is no testing or formal licensing.
[17] See generally 30 CFR § 40.1(b).

**CHART 1     Regulations Governing Nonlawyer Representation Frequency and Type of Practice—continued**

| Agency | Statute/Regulation Permitting Appearance | Permits Nonlawyer Adversarial Representation? | Permits Nonlawyer Nonadversarial Representation? | Provisions Limiting or Governing Practice | Frequency of Nonlawyer Representation | Change in Frequency of Nonlawyer Rep. w/in Past 6 Years | Most Common Type(s) of Nonlawyer Representation |
|---|---|---|---|---|---|---|---|
| General Accounting Office | 31 U.S.C. § 731–732; 4 CFR §§ 11 and 28; GAO Orders 2713.2, 2752.1, and 2777.1 | Yes, in adverse actions, grievance proceedings, and discrimination complaints | Yes | Nonlawyers not permitted fees; government pays fees to winning representatives[18] | Very infrequent | Not aware of any | |
| Internal Revenue Serv. | 13 CFR Part 10; 31 U.S.C. § 330; Treasury Dept. Circular 230 | Yes | Yes | Noncertified public accountant and nonlawyer must become enrolled agent[19] to practice | As frequent as lawyer representation.[20] | Increased, no statistics available | Repeated practice for fee by certified public accountant or enrolled agent |
| Interstate Commerce Comm'n | 49 CFR § 1103 | Yes | Yes | Fee limitations,[21] only registered nonlawyer permitted to practice,[22] however, self-representation is allowed without registration | 1,600 nonlawyers registered and account for 5% of appearances.[23] | Decreased,[24] no statistics available | Repeated practice for a fee |
| National Credit Union Admin. | 12 CFR § 747 | Yes | Yes | None | No statistics available | Decreased, no statistics available | Credit union representatives |
| National Labor Relations Board | | Yes | Yes | None | Infrequent | None | |

| | | | | | | | |
|---|---|---|---|---|---|---|---|
| National Mediation Board | None, agency governed by 29 CFR § 1200 et seq. | N/A, all proceedings adversarial | Yes | None | 200 appearances per yr., appear twice as frequently as lawyers | Decreased, no statistics available | Union representative |
| National Transportation Safety Board | 49 CFR § 821 49 CFR § 831 49 CFR § 845 | Yes | Yes | In adjudication, lawyer representation is encouraged; in investigation, lawyer participation is discouraged because technical expertise required; parties[25] participate in investigations | Very infrequent except at investigatory levels | None | Manufacturers at investigatory levels |
| Occupational Safety and Health Review Comm'n | 29 CFR § 2200.22 | Yes | N/A, all proceedings adversarial | Optional simplified procedures to encourage self-representation by small businesses | 20% of appearances[26] | 20% decrease[27] | Nonlegal employee representing employer; union representative |

[18] As provided in discrimination statutes, backpay act, and appeals authorized by law.

[19] Nonlawyers and noncertified public accountants become enrolled agents by (1) passing a character and fitness review and (2) successfully completing special enrollment examination testing on federal taxation and related matters, or (3) former employment with the IRS, provided duties qualify the individual. Lawyers and certified public accountants may practice without enrollment.

[20] Includes representation by certified public accountants as well as enrolled agents.

[21] Practitioners may not overestimate the value of services, accept compensation from party other than client, make contingent fee arrangements, or divide fees with laypersons. See 49 CFR § 1103.70.

[22] To become registered, applicant must (1) meet educational and experience requirements, (2) undergo character and fitness review, (3) pass exam administered by the agency testing knowledge in the field of transportation, and (4) take an oath. See 49 CFR § 1103.3.

[23] Figure includes appearances in rulemaking as well as adjudicatory proceedings.

[24] Deregulation has reduced the caseload, while proceedings have become more complex, creating a greater need for legal expertise.

[25] "Parties" includes manufacturers, unions, operators, and other regulatory agencies.

[26] Statistic includes pro se representation.

[27] Nonlawyer practice accounted in 1980 for 40% of the agency's caseload but decreased in 1982–83 to 20%. Decrease may result from increasing complexity in cases causing claimants to seek legal representation.

| CHART 1 | Regulations Governing Nonlawyer Representation Frequency and Type of Practice—continued | | | | | | | |
|---|---|---|---|---|---|---|---|---|
| Agency | Statute/ Regulation Permitting Appearance | Permits Nonlawyer Adversarial Representation? | Permits Nonlawyer Nonadversarial Representation? | Provisions Limiting or Governing Practice | Frequency of Nonlawyer Representation | Change in Frequency of Nonlawyer Rep. w/in Past 6 Years | Most Common Type(s) of Nonlawyer Representation |
| Small Business Admin. | 13 CFR § 121.11 13 CFR § 134.16 | Yes | N/A, all proceedings adversarial | None | Less than 1% of appearances[28] | None | |
| Social Security Admin. | 42 USC § 406(a) 29 CFR | Yes, tentatively as part of experiment; generally agency has no adversarial proceedings | Yes | Claimants advised of advantages of representation at hearing level;[29] fees set by agency;[30] attorney fees are withheld from awards[31] | Appear in 13% of total hearings or in 25–30% of hearings with representation | None, although lawyer representation increased by 56% since 1978. | One time only by family member/friend; repeated practice for fee; nonfee rep. by legal services paralegal |
| U.S. Customs Serv. | None | Yes | Yes | None | 5 to 15% of caseload volume | None | Repeated practice for fee by licensed customs brokers and former customs officials |
| U.S. Environmental Protection Agency | 40 CFR § 124 40 CFR § 164.30 40 CFR § 22.10 | Yes | N/A | None | No appearances | None | None |

[28] Figure excludes pro se appearances in size and Standard Industrial Classification (SIC) appeals. Approximately 50% of size and SIC appeals are conducted pro se by nonlawyers.

[29] When hearing request [is] filed, agency sends a letter to unrepresented claimant describing advantages of representation. Attached to letter is a list of organizations which may provide representation. The list includes lawyer referral services, legal aid groups, law schools, etc.

[30] The agency sets all fees based on criteria listed in 20 CFR § 404. 1725(b), including extent and type of services, complexity of case, level of skill and competence required in performing services, time spent, results achieved, level at which representative became involved, and amount requested.

[31] When decision is entered in favor of a claimant represented by a lawyer in a Title II or Black Lung case, normally 25% of the benefits awarded are withheld. After agency has set the fee, it forwards fee directly to the lawyer from the amount withheld, if attorney's fees exceed the amount withheld, the lawyer must seek the remainder from the claimant. If the attorney's fees are less than the amount withheld, the claimant receives the remainder. Nonlawyer representatives do not have this withholding benefit.

# Appendix F

# STATE SURVEY: OPINIONS, RULES, STATUTES, AND REPORTS ON PARALEGAL ETHICS AND RELATED TOPICS

The following summary of the 50 states and the District of Columbia covers paralegals and other nonattorneys. The purpose of the summary is to give an overview of the kinds of issues that have arisen. It is *not* meant to describe the current state of the law or provide the current ethics regulations of any particular state. Keep in mind that the rules governing paralegals are undergoing considerable change. See section F of chapter 5 on how to do legal research to determine the current ethics rules that apply to your state. You will occasionally see the abbreviation WL in this appendix. This abbreviation means Westlaw, the commercial online research service discussed in chapters 11 and 13. If you do not have access to Westlaw, check the Internet sources that are given for your state to determine whether the item is available to you on the Internet.

## ALABAMA

### ETHICAL RULES AND GUIDELINES IN ALABAMA

Under Rule 7.6 of the Rules of Professional Conduct, the title "Legal Assistant" is acceptable on a business card that also contains an attorney's or a law firm's name. The title of the nonattorney employee should be legibly and prominently displayed in close proximity to the employee's name. A casual observer of the card should not be misled into thinking that it is the card of an attorney. An earlier ethics opinion preferred the title *non-lawyer assistant*, since *paralegal* could be a misleading title. Alabama State Bar, *Opinion 86–04* (3/17/86). See also *Opinion 86–120* (12/2/86).

When a paralegal signs a letter to a nonattorney, the paralegal's name should be followed by one of these titles: *nonlawyer assistant, nonlawyer paralegal*, or *nonlawyer investigator*. Alabama State Bar, *Opinion 87–77* (6/16/87).

It is improper to include the name of a nonattorney assistant on the letterhead of law firm stationery. Alabama State Bar, *Opinion 83–87* (5/23/83).

The business card of a legal secretary can list the fact that she has been certified by passing an examination of the National Association of Legal Secretaries. Alabama State Bar, *Opinion 90–01* (1/17/90).

When a plaintiff's law firm hires an investigator who worked for a defense law firm, the plaintiff's law firm must withdraw from all cases in which the investigator previously worked unless the defense law firm consents and its clients consent. Screening the investigator from such cases is not enough. Alabama State Bar, *Opinion 89–41* (4/5/89). See also *Opinion 89–91* (8/7/89) on job switching by a secretary and the effectiveness of a Chinese Wall (screening) around her, and Alabama State Bar, *Opinion 91–01* (5/7/91) (reasonable measures to prevent the disclosure of confidential information *will* allow a law firm to continue to employ a part-time secretary/bookkeeper who is also employed by another firm).

An attorney cannot allow his paralegal to ask questions of debtors at meetings of creditors in bankruptcy cases. Alabama State Bar, *Opinion 89–76* (9/20/90).

Paralegals may draft documents if supervised by an attorney, but they cannot make court appearances or give legal advice. Alabama State Bar, *Opinion 86–120* (12/2/86).

An attorney engaged in collection work may not pay his lay employees on a commission basis. *Opinion of the General Counsel* (2/3/88, revised 2/14/90).

Nonattorney independent contractors who sell legal research services to attorneys are not engaged in the unauthorized practice of law. Alabama State Bar, *Opinion 90–04* (1/18/90).

An attorney who has been suspended or disbarred can work as a paralegal, law clerk, or legal assistant in a law firm if the attorney has no contact with the clients of the firm and operates under "continuous and regular" attorney supervision. *Opinions of the General Counsel (Disciplinary Commission of the Alabama State Bar)*, 58 Alabama Lawyer 106 (1997).

## DEFINING THE PRACTICE OF LAW IN ALABAMA

§ 34-3-6 (*Michie's Alabama Code*): . . . (b) For the purposes of this chapter, the practice of law is defined as follows: Whoever, (1) in a representative capacity appears as an advocate or draws papers, pleadings or documents, or performs any act in connection with proceedings pending or prospective before a court or a body, board, committee, commission or officer constituted by law or having authority to take evidence in or settle or determine controversies in the exercise of the judicial power of the state or any subdivision thereof; or (2) For a consideration, reward or pecuniary benefit, present or anticipated, direct or indirect, advises or counsels another as to secular law, or draws or procures or assists in the drawing of a paper, document or instrument affecting or relating to secular rights; or (3) For a consideration, reward or pecuniary benefit, present or anticipated, direct or indirect, does any act in a representative capacity in behalf of another tending to obtain or secure for such other the prevention or the redress of a wrong or the enforcement or establishment of a right; or (4) As a vocation, enforces, secures, settles, adjusts or compromises defaulted, controverted or disputed accounts, claims or demands between persons with neither of whom he is in privity or in the relation of employer and employee in the ordinary sense; is practicing law.

§ 6-5-573 (*Michie's Alabama Code*): Paralegals and legal assistants as legal service providers. Under the Alabama Legal Services Liability Act, the term "legal service provider" is defined as follows: Anyone licensed to practice law by the State of Alabama or engaged in the practice of law in the State of Alabama. The term legal service provider includes professional corporations, associations, and partnerships and the members of such professional corporations, associations, and partnerships and the persons, firms, or corporations either employed by or performing work or services for the benefit of such professional corporations, associations, and partnerships including, without limitation, law clerks, legal assistants, legal secretaries, investigators, paralegals, and couriers.

## ALABAMA ETHICS AND PRACTICE RULES ON THE INTERNET

www.law.cornell.edu/ethics/alabama.html
www.legalethics.com/ethics.law?state=Alabama
www.alabar.org/page.cfm?page=im_include/
    im_fopList.cfm
www.crossingthebar.com/AL-UPL.htm

## PARALEGALS (AND OTHER NONATTORNEYS) IN COURT

■ *Metropolitan Life Insurance Co. v. Akins*, 388 So. 2d 999 (Court of Civil Appeals of Alabama, 1980) (the fail-

ure of a "para-legal" to inform an attorney of a matter is not a sufficient excuse for the attorney's neglect of that matter).
■ *Black v. M.G.A. Inc.*, 51 F. Supp. 2d 1315, 1324 (U.S. District Court, M.D. Alabama, 1999) (a prevailing party may be compensated for work done by law clerks or paralegals only to the extent that such work is "traditionally done by an attorney"; organizing pleadings, correspondence, and unspecified documents is clerical work).
■ *Browder v. General Motors Corp.*, 5 F. Supp. 2d 1267, 1275 (U.S. District Court, M.D. Alabama, 1998) (the attorney's carelessness included the failure to review a proposed pretrial order drafted by a paralegal).
■ *Surge v. Massanari*, 155 F. Supp. 2d 1301 (U.S. District Court, M.D. Alabama, 2001) (hours claimed for paralegal time are reduced; there was duplication of effort between attorney and paralegal in working on a brief; also, the plaintiff has failed to submit any information regarding the paralegal's education, experience, or qualifications).
■ *Ex Parte Moody*, 681 So. 2d 276 (Court of Criminal Appeals of Alabama, 1996) (an indigent defendant representing himself in a criminal case does not have a constitutional right to the services of a paralegal).

# ALASKA

## ETHICAL RULES AND GUIDELINES IN ALASKA

A suspended attorney may work as a paralegal but only under the supervision of an attorney in good standing. He or she may not have a direct relationship with a client. Alaska Bar Ass'n, *Ethics Opinion 84-6* (8/25/84).

Under the supervision or review of an attorney, a legal assistant can investigate claims and have contact with insurance agents regarding the settlement of claims in worker's compensation cases. Alaska Bar Ass'n, *Ethics Opinion 73-1* (10/6/73).

Paralegal employees of attorneys may not conduct worker's compensation hearings. Alaska Bar Ass'n, *Ethics Opinion 84-7* (8/25/84). Note: this Opinion was *reversed* on 11/9/84.

## DEFINING THE PRACTICE OF LAW IN ALASKA

§ 08.08.230 (*Alaska Statutes*): Unlawful practice a misdemeanor. (a) A person not an active member of the Alaska Bar and not licensed to practice law in Alaska who engages in the practice of law or holds out as entitled to engage in the practice of law as that term is defined in the Alaska Bar Rules, or an active member of the Alaska Bar who wilfully employs such a person knowing that the person is engaging in the practice of law or holding out as entitled to so engage is guilty of a class A misdemeanor. (b) This section does not prohibit the use of paralegal personnel as defined by rules of the Alaska Supreme Court.

Rule 63. *Rules of the Alaska Bar Association*: For purposes of Alaska Statutes § 08.08.230 [making unauthorized practice of law a misdemeanor], "practice of law" is defined as: (a) representing oneself by words or conduct to be an attorney, and, if the person is authorized to practice law in another jurisdiction but is not a member of the Alaska Bar Association, representing oneself to be a member of the Alaska Bar Association; and (b) either (i) representing another before a court or governmental body which is operating in its adjudicative capacity, including the submission of pleadings, or (ii), for compensation, providing advice or preparing documents for another which effect legal rights or duties.

## RULES ON PARALEGAL FEES IN ALASKA

*Alaska Rules of Civil Procedure*: Rule 82 provides:

(a) Except as otherwise agreed to by the parties, the prevailing party in a civil case shall be awarded attorney's fees calculated under this rule. . . .

(b) (2) In cases in which the prevailing party recovers no money judgment, the court shall award the prevailing party in a case which goes to trial 30 percent of the prevailing party's reasonable actual attorney's fees which were necessarily incurred, and shall award the prevailing party in a case resolved without trial 20 percent of its actual attorney's fees which were necessarily incurred. The actual fees shall include fees for legal work customarily performed by an attorney but which was delegated to and performed by an investigator, paralegal or law clerk.

Title 8, § 45.180 *Alaska Administrative Code*: Costs and Attorney's Fees in Workers' Compensation Cases.

(f) The board will award an applicant the necessary and reasonable costs relating to the preparation and presentation of the issues upon which the applicant prevailed at the hearing on the claim. The applicant must file a statement listing each cost claimed, and must file an affidavit stating that the costs are correct and that the costs were incurred in connection with the claim. The following costs will, in the board's discretion, be awarded to an applicant: . . .

(14) fees for the services of a paralegal or law clerk, but only if the paralegal or law clerk

(A) is employed by an attorney licensed in this or another state;

(B) performed the work under the supervision of a licensed attorney;

(C) performed work that is not clerical in nature;

(D) files an affidavit itemizing the services performed and the time spent in performing each service; and

(E) does not duplicate work for which an attorney's fee was awarded.

## ALASKA ETHICS AND PRACTICE RULES ON THE INTERNET

www.law.cornell.edu/ethics/alaska.html
touchngo.com/lglcntr/ctrules/profcon/htframe.htm

www.alaskabar.org/793.cfm
www.legalethics.com/ethics.law?state=Alaska
www.crossingthebar.com/AK-UPL.htm

## PARALEGALS (AND OTHER NONATTORNEYS) IN COURT

■ *Nielson v. Benton*, 903 P.2d 1049 (Supreme Court of Alaska, 1995) (paralegal fees and Alaska Rule of Civil Procedure 82(b)(2)).

■ *Frontier Companies of Alaska v. Jack White Co.*, 818 P.2d 645 (Alaska Supreme Court, 1991) (paralegal fees).

■ *Pederson-Szafran v. Baily*, 837 P.2d 124 (Alaska Supreme Court, 1992) (paralegal in state government claims she was blacklisted).

# ARIZONA

## ETHICAL RULES AND GUIDELINES IN ARIZONA

The letterhead of an attorney or law firm can list nonattorney support personnel if their nonattorney status is made clear. State Bar of Arizona, *Ethics Opinion 90–03* (3/16/90). This overrules *Opinion 84–14* (10/5/84), which held to the contrary. The latter opinion also said that a separate letterhead for paralegals is not allowed).

A corporation consisting of independent contractor paralegals and a salaried attorney employee is impermissible. State Bar of Arizona, *Opinion 82–18* (12/1/82). It is unethical for an attorney to associate with a nonattorney-operated eviction service; there would be inadequate attorney supervision of the nonattorneys and improper sharing of fees with nonattorneys. State Bar of Arizona, *Ethics Opinion 93–01* (2/18/93).

A law firm can ethically compensate one of its nonattorney employees by a base monthly fee plus quarterly bonuses measured by a percentage of the firm's increased revenues derived from areas the nonattorney employee was hired to develop. State Bar of Arizona, *Ethics Opinion 90–14* (10/17/90).

A judge did not have to recuse himself where his daughter was employed as a paralegal in a law firm appearing in a case before him unless his daughter's work on the case was so extensive that a question might arise. Arizona Supreme Court Judicial Ethics Advisory Committee, *Opinion 77–1* (4/29/77).

Other State Bar of Arizona Opinions involving nonattorneys: *Ethics Opinion 86–7* (2/26/86) (it is ethically improper for an attorney to cooperate with a nonattorney "consulting service" that provided expert testimony to its customers for a contingent fee); *Ethics Opinion 82–18* (12/1/82) (it is ethically improper for an attorney to be a salaried employee—not an owner—of a paralegal-run corporation that contracted with attorneys to provide legal services on an as-needed basis).

## DEFINING THE PRACTICE OF LAW IN ARIZONA

*State Bar of Arizona v. Arizona Land Title and Trust Co.*, 366 P.2d 1, 8–9 (Supreme Court of Arizona, 1961): In the light of the historical development of the lawyer's functions, it is impossible to lay down an exhaustive definition of "the practice of law" by attempting to enumerate every conceivable act performed by lawyers in the normal course of their work. We believe it sufficient to state that those acts, whether performed in court or in the law office, which lawyers customarily have carried on from day to day through the centuries must constitute "the practice of law."

*In re Estate of Shumway*, 197 Ariz. 57, 61, 3 P.3d 977, 981 (Supreme Court of Arizona, 1999): Our supreme court has defined the "practice of law" as engaging in those tasks that "lawyers customarily have carried on from day to day through the centuries . . . [including] assisting or advising another in the preparation of [legal] documents . . . either with or without compensation.". . . This court has also recognized, however, that "[t]he line between what is and what is not the practice of law cannot be drawn with precision" and that "between the two, there is a region wherein much of what lawyers do every day in their practice may also be done by others without wrongful invasion of the lawyers' field." (Vacated in part, 9 P.3d 1062 (2000)).

Rule 31 (*Arizona State Supreme Court Rules*): 3. Privilege to practice. Except as hereinafter provided in subsection 4 of this section, no person shall practice law in this state or hold himself out as one who may practice law in this state unless he is an active member of the state bar. . . .

4. Exceptions. . . . B. An employee may . . . designate a representative, not necessarily an attorney, before any board hearing or any quasi-judicial hearing dealing with personnel matters, providing that no fee may be charged for any services. . . .

C. An officer of a corporation who is not an active member of the state bar may represent the corporation before a justice court or police court. . . .

D. A person who is not an active member of the State Bar may represent a party in small claims procedures in the Arizona Tax Court. . . .

G. A person who is not an active member of the state bar may represent a corporation in small claims procedures. . . .

## IMPORTANT ARIZONA LAWS ON PARALEGALS

§ 12–2234 (A) (*Arizona Revised Statutes Annotated*): In a civil action an attorney shall not, without the consent of his client, be examined as to any communication made by the client to him, or his advice given thereon in the course of professional employment. An attorney's paralegal, assistant, secretary, stenographer or clerk shall not, without the consent of his employer, be examined concerning any fact the knowledge of which was acquired in such capacity. . . .

R9-21-209 (B)(3) (*Arizona Administrative Code*): Mental Illness Records. An attorney, paralegal working under the supervision of an attorney, or other designated representative of the client shall be permitted to inspect and copy the record, if such attorney or representative furnishes written authorization from the client or guardian.

## ARIZONA ETHICS AND PRACTICE RULES ON THE INTERNET

www.law.cornell.edu/ethics/arizona.html
www.azbar.org/EthicsOpinions
www.crossingthebar.com/AZ-UPL.htm

## PARALEGALS (AND OTHER NONATTORNEYS) IN COURT

- *Styles v. Ceranski*, 916 P.2d 1164 (Court of Appeals of Arizona, 1996) (propriety of communication by a defense paralegal with an employee of the plaintiff without consent of the plaintiff's attorney).
- *In the Matter of Miller*, 872 P.2d 661 (Supreme Court of Arizona, 1994) (discipline of attorney for failure to supervise paralegals).
- *In Re Galbasini*, 789 P.2d 971 (Supreme Court of Arizona, 1990) (discipline of attorney for failure to supervise nonattorney employees.)
- *Smart Industries Corp. v. Superior Court*, 876 P.2d 1176 (Court of Appeals of Arizona, 1994) (disqualification of a plaintiff's attorney when he hired a legal assistant who once worked for the defendant's attorney).
- *Samaritan Foundation v. Goodfarb*, 862 P.2d 870 (Supreme Court of Arizona, 1993) (defendant's attorney hires a nurse paralegal who interviews hospital employees in a medical malpractice case; the statements of the employees are not within the hospital's attorney-client privilege).
- *Bustamonte v. Ryan*, 856 P.2d 1205 (Court of Appeals of Arizona, 1993) (paralegal assistance to prison inmates).
- *Aries v. Palmer Johnson, Inc.*, 735 P.2d 1373 (Court of Appeals of Arizona, 1987) (recoverability of paralegal fees).
- *State v. Murray*, 906 P.2d 542 (Supreme Court of Arizona, 1995) (becoming a paralegal is not a mitigating factor in a charge of murder!).

# ARKANSAS

## ETHICAL RULES AND GUIDELINES IN ARKANSAS

"The paralegal should never be placed in a position to decide what information takes priority over other information or to make decisions which affect the client." This function should never be delegated to a paralegal, even though "sometimes a fine line exists in the area of professional judgment." Paralegals need "specific guidelines," preferably in writing, in carrying out responsibilities. *The Paralegal in Practice* by A. Clinton, chairperson of the

Paralegal Committee of the Arkansas Bar Ass'n, 23 Arkansas Lawyer 22 (January 1989).

## DEFINING THE PRACTICE OF LAW IN ARKANSAS

§ 2.02 (*Arkansas Code of 1987 Annotated*): Defining the Practice of Law, Court Rules Regulations of the Arkansas Continuing Legal Education Board. Inactive Status.

(2) Definition: Practice of Law.—The practice of law shall be defined as any service rendered, regardless of whether compensation is received therefor, involving legal knowledge or legal advice. It shall include representation, provision of counsel, advocacy, whether in or out of court, rendered with respect to the rights, duties, regulations, liabilities, or business relations of one requiring the legal services.

§ 16–22–501 (*Arkansas Code of 1987 Annotated*): Unauthorized Practice of Law.

(a) A person commits an offense if, with intent to obtain a direct economic benefit for himself or herself, the person:

(1) Contracts with any person to represent that person with regard to personal causes of action for property damages or personal injury;

(2) Advises any person as to the person's rights and the advisability of making claims for personal injuries or property damages;

(3) Advises any person as to whether or not to accept an offered sum of money in settlement of claims for personal injuries or property damages;

(4) Enters into any contract with another person to represent that person in personal injury or property damage matters on a contingent fee basis with an attempted assignment of a portion of the person's cause of action;

(5) Enters into any contract, except a contract of insurance, with a third person which purports to grant the exclusive right to select and retain legal counsel to represent the individual in any legal proceeding; or

(6) Contacts any person by telephone or in person for the purpose of soliciting business which is legal in nature, as set forth above.

(b) This section does not apply to a person currently licensed to practice law. . . .

(e) This section shall not apply to a person who is licensed as an adjuster or employed as an adjuster by an insurer as authorized by § 23–64–101.

## ARKANSAS ETHICS AND PRACTICE RULES ON THE INTERNET

www.state.ar.us/arjudiciary/rules/index2.html#Model
www.courts.state.ar.us/rules/index2.html#Rules
www.arkansasethics.com/aec.htm
www.crossingthebar.com/AR-UPL.htm

## PARALEGALS (AND OTHER NONATTORNEYS) IN COURT

- *Fink v. Neal*, 328 Ark. 646, 945 S.W.2d 916 (Supreme Court of Arkansas, 1997) (the mistakes made by an attorney's paralegal do not constitute an excuse for the attorney's own negligence).
- *Brooks v. Central Arkansas Nursing Center*, 31 F. Supp. 2d 1151, 1154 (U.S. District Court, E.D. Arkansas, 1999) (award of attorney fees is reduced because "the Court is of the view these tasks could have been performed by a clerk or paralegal").
- *In re NWFX, Inc.*, 267 Bankruptcy Reporter 118 (U.S. Bankruptcy Court, Arkansas, 2001) (670 hours of paralegal fees awarded).
- *Herron v. Jones*, 637 S.W.2d 569 (Supreme Court of Arkansas, 1982) (conflict of interest allegation; an employee—a legal secretary—switches law firms in the same case; court refuses to disqualify current employer because confidentiality was not breached).
- *In re Anderson*, 851 S.W.2d 408 (Supreme Court of Arkansas, 1993) (attorney surrenders his license to practice law after a drug conviction and then goes to work as a paralegal in his father's law firm; readmission denied).
- *In re Lee*, 806 S.W.2d 382 (Supreme Court of Arkansas, 1991) (disbarred attorney as paralegal and investigator).
- *Carton v. Missouri Pacific Railroad Co.*, 865 S.W.2d 635 (Supreme Court of Arkansas, 1993) (juror did not have to be removed from a jury because she was a cousin of the paralegal for one of the attorneys).
- *Beech Abstract Guaranty Co. v. Bar Association of Arkansas*, 624 S.W.2d 900 (Supreme Court of Arkansas, 1959) (nonattorneys drafting real estate documents as the unauthorized practice of law).

# CALIFORNIA

## ETHICAL RULES AND GUIDELINES IN CALIFORNIA

See appendix G for the new law stating that the titles *paralegal* and *legal assistant* are restricted to those who work under attorney supervision. The law also imposes education and continuing legal education requirements. Appendix G also covers the position of legal document assistant for individuals formerly known as independent paralegals.

Attorneys not in practice together who share office space and paralegal services must take reasonable steps to protect each client's confidence and secrets. State Bar of California, *Opinion 1997–150* (1997) (1997 WL 240818).

When a paralegal is authorized to represent a client before the Workers' Compensation Appeals Board, a law firm can use its paralegal to represent a client of the firm before this Board if the client consents and the firm supervises the paralegal. State Bar of California, *Opinion 1988–103*.

Attorneys must take steps to ensure that nonattorney employees understand their obligation not to disclose client confidences and secrets. State Bar of California, *Opinion 1979–50.*

A nonattorney can use a business card if it is used for identification rather than for solicitation of business. Los Angeles County Bar Ass'n, *Opinion 381.*

A law firm can pay a bonus to its paralegal as long as the bonus does not involve a sharing of legal fees. Los Angeles Count Bar Ass'n, *Opinion 457* (11/20/89).

A nonprofit legal services center for the elderly cannot advertise in a local newspaper the availability of "legal help" from "para-legal aides" trained by a local attorney. Legal help implies legal services. San Diego Bar Ass'n, *Opinion 1976–9* (7/1/76).

A business that provides paralegal services to the public should have attorney supervision except for some purely ministerial tasks. San Diego Bar Ass'n, *Opinion 1983–7.*

## DEFINING THE PRACTICE OF LAW IN CALIFORNIA

*California v. Landlords Professional Services*, 264 Cal. Rptr. 548, 550 (Court of Appeals, 4th District, 1990): Business and Professions Code section 6125 states: "No person shall practice law in this State unless he is an active member of the State Bar." Business and Professions Code section 6126, subdivision (a), provides: "Any person advertising or holding himself or herself out as practicing or entitled to practice law or otherwise practicing law who is not an active member of the State Bar, is guilty of a misdemeanor." The code provides no definition for the term "practicing law." . . . "[A]s the term is generally understood, the practice of law is the doing and performing services in a court of justice in any manner depending therein throughout its various stages and in conformity with the adopted rules of procedure. But in a larger sense it includes legal advice and counsel and the preparation of legal instruments and contracts by which legal rights are secured although such matter may or may not be depending in court." . . . [N]onetheless . . . "ascertaining whether a particular activity falls within this general definition may be a formidable endeavor." . . . In close cases, the courts have determined that the resolution of legal questions for another by advice and action is practicing law "if difficult or doubtful legal questions are involved which, to safeguard the public, reasonably demand the application of a trained legal mind."

## IMPORTANT RECENT CALIFORNIA LAWS ON PARALEGALS

- § 6450, *West's Annotated California Business & Professions Code* (definition of paralegal; education and continuing legal education requirements) (for the text of this law, see appendix G).
- § 6400, *West's Annotated California Business & Professions Code* (legal document assistants and unlawful detailer assistants) (for the text of this law, see appendix G).
- Rule 10.140, *Los Angeles County Superior Court Rules, Probate Department.* The use of paralegals to perform services of an extraordinary nature is permitted. The court will require an itemized statement of services rendered by each paralegal, accompanied by allegations relating to the qualifications of the paralegal, as to both experience and training.

## CALIFORNIA ETHICS AND PRACTICE RULES ON THE INTERNET

www.law.cornell.edu/ethics/california.html
www.calbar.org/2pub/3eth/3ethndx.htm
www.calbar.org/pub250/index.htm
www.calbar.org/pub250/crpc.htm
www.crossingthebar.com/CA-UPL.htm

## PARALEGALS (AND OTHER NONATTORNEYS) IN COURT

- *In re Complex Asbestos Litigation*, 283 Cal. Rptr. 732 (California Court of Appeals, 1st District, 1991) (a paralegal who switches jobs might cause the disqualification of his or her new employer to represent clients about whom the paralegal obtained confidential information while working at a prior (opposing) law firm; a rebuttable presumption exists that the paralegal shared this information with the new employer; the most likely way for the new employer to rebut this presumption, and hence to avoid disqualification, is to show that when the paralegal was hired, a Chinese Wall was built around the paralegal with respect to any cases the paralegal worked on while at the prior employment). (See chapter 5.)
- *Devereux v. Latham & Watkins*, 38 Cal. Rptr. 2d 849 (California Court of Appeals, 2d District, 1995) (litigation paralegal sues her former law firm employer after the paralegal testified against the law firm in an overbilling case).
- *Saret-Cook v. Gilbert, Kelly, Crowley & Jennett*, 88 Cal. Rptr. 2d 732 (California Court of Appeals, 2d District, 1999) ("fatal attraction" case: paralegal loses sex harassment case against office attorney with whom she had an affair).
- *Insurance Co. of North America v. Superior Court*, 166 Cal. Rptr. 880 (California Court of Appeals, 1980) (memorandums and notes of paralegal in attorney's law office present at briefing were the work product of attorney's law firm and not discoverable).
- *In re Hessinger & Associates*, 192 Bankruptcy Reporter 211 (U.S. Bankruptcy Court, N.D. California, 1996) (law firm unethically allowed paralegals to complete bankruptcy petitions and to perform other work of legal character without adequate attorney supervision; the firm was organized much like a production line, with little or no review by attorneys; a persistent theme in appellant's position on the role of paralegals in its practice is the argument that "everybody does it"; that is, all large consumer bankruptcy firms rely on paralegals to perform a large amount of the work required for filing a bankruptcy petition, and in all such firms the paralegals do so with

only minimal attorney supervision; while this may well be true, the court will not condone an unethical practice merely because most consumer bankruptcy firms are engaging in it).

- *Oakland v. McCullough*; 53 Cal. Rptr. 2d 531 (California Court of Appeals, 1st District, 1996 (a claim for paralegal fees is rejected because of a failure to provide documentation in support of the claim).

# COLORADO

## ETHICAL RULES AND GUIDELINES IN COLORADO

The names of support personnel can be printed on law firm letterhead, and they can be given their own business card as long as they reveal clearly that they are not attorneys. Colorado Bar Ass'n, *Formal Ethics Opinion 84* (4/1990).

Paralegals must disclose their nonattorney status to everyone at the outset of any professional relationship. They should be given no task that requires the exercise of unsupervised legal judgment. They can write letters and sign correspondence on attorney letterhead as long as their nonattorney status is clear and the correspondence does not contain legal opinions or give legal advice. They can have their own business cards with the name of the law firm on them if their nonattorney status is made clear. The services performed by the paralegal must supplement, merge with, and become part of the attorney's work product. Colorado Bar Ass'n, *Guidelines for the Utilization of Legal Assistants* (1986).

Attorneys not in the same law firm sometimes share offices. To ensure confidentiality in such situations, the attorneys should avoid the sharing of staff to the extent possible, particularly secretaries and paralegals. Colorado Bar Assn, *Formal Ethics Opinion 89* (1999).

A law firm can use a paralegal to represent clients at administrative proceedings when authorized by statute and when the practice of law is not involved. To ensure competent representation, the attorney must train and supervise the paralegal. Colorado Bar Ass'n, *Opinion 79* (2/18/89).

An attorney shall continually monitor and supervise the work of assistants to assure that the services they render are performed competently and efficiently. Colorado Bar Ass'n, *Ethics Opinion 61* (10/23/82).

An attorney may not participate with nonattorneys in preparing and marketing estate planning documents when the venture consists of the unauthorized practice of law. Colorado Bar Ass'n, *Opinion 87* (7/14/90).

## DEFINING THE PRACTICE OF LAW IN COLORADO

*Unauthorized Practice of Law Committee of the Supreme Court of Colorado v. Prog,* 761 P.2d 1111, 1115 (Supreme Court of Colorado, 1988): The determination of what acts do or do not constitute the practice of law is a judicial function. . . . While recognizing the difficulty of formulating and applying an all-inclusive definition of the practice of law, we have stated that "generally

one who acts in a representative capacity in protecting, enforcing, or defending the legal rights and duties of another and in counseling, advising and assisting him in connection with these rights and duties is engaged in the practice of law."

Rule 201.3. *Court Rules Annotated (West's Colorado Revised Statutes Annotated)*: Rules Governing Admission to the Bar. . . .

(2) For purposes of this rule, "practice of law" means:

(a) the private practice of law . . .; or

(b) employment as a lawyer for a corporation . . . or other entity with the primary duties of:

(i) furnishing legal counsel, drafting documents and pleadings, and interpreting and giving advice with respect to the law, and/or

(ii) preparing, trying or presenting cases before courts, executive departments, administrative bureaus or agencies. . . .

## IMPORTANT COLORADO LAWS ON PARALEGALS

§ 13–90–107 (*West's Colorado Revised Statutes Annotated*):

(1) There are particular relations in which it is the policy of the law to encourage confidence and to preserve it inviolate; therefore, a person shall not be examined as a witness in the following cases: . . .

(b) An attorney shall not be examined without the consent of his client as to any communication made by the client to him or his advice given thereon in the course of professional employment; nor shall an attorney's secretary, paralegal, legal assistant, stenographer, or clerk be examined without the consent of his employer concerning any fact, the knowledge of which he has acquired in such capacity.

Rule 33.1. (*West's Colorado Revised Statutes Annotated*): Colorado Rules of Probate Procedure. Personal representatives and attorneys representing an estate are entitled to reasonable compensation. In setting attorneys' fees, the time expended by personnel performing paralegal functions under the direction and supervision of the attorney may be considered as an item separate from and in addition to the time spent by the attorney. In setting other fees, the time expended by personnel performing paraprofessional functions may be considered as a separate item.

## COLORADO ETHICS AND PRACTICE RULES ON THE INTERNET

www.law.cornell.edu/ethics/colorado.html
www2.law.cornell.edu/cgi-bin/foliocgi.exe/co-code?
www.cobar.org/comms/ethics/rulesprof/rulprofc.htm
www.cobar.org/comms/ethics/index.htm
www.crossingthebar.com/CO-UPL.htm

## PARALEGALS (AND OTHER NONATTORNEYS) IN COURT

- *Carr v. Fort Morgan School District*, 4 F. Supp. 2d 998 (U.S. District Court, Colorado, 1998) (fees involving paralegal time are reduced by 15% due to lack of detail as to the work done and apparent duplication of effort).

- *People v. Milner*, 35 P. 3d 670 (The Office of the Presiding Disciplinary Judge, Colorado, 2001) (Attorney's failure to adequately supervise her paralegal to assure that paralegal did not misrepresent status of matter to client violated disciplinary rules; although lacking in tact, paralegal's single impolite outburst toward a client, to "stop calling and bitching," would not be a separate basis for attorney discipline; attorney's alleged lack of awareness regarding her paralegal's activities could not be considered a mitigating factor.)
- *In re Gomez*, 259 Bankruptcy Reporter 379 (U.S. Bankruptcy Court, Colorado, 2001) (bankruptcy petition preparer, by its use of trade name that included the word "paralegals" on its letterhead and brochures, in answering telephone, and in its communications with prospective customers, violated Bankruptcy Code provision barring any petition preparer from using the word "legal" or "any similar term" in its advertisements).
- *People v. Fry*, 875 P.2d 222 (Supreme Court of Colorado, 1994) (failure of an attorney to supervise his paralegal as the unauthorized practice of law).
- *People v. Felker*, 770 P.2d 402 (Supreme Court of Colorado, 1989) (attorney disciplined for allowing nonattorney employee to give a client legal advice).
- *American Water Development v. City of Alamosa*, 874 P.2d 352 (Supreme Court of Colorado, 1994) (award of paralegal fees).

# Connecticut

## ETHICAL RULES AND GUIDELINES IN CONNECTICUT

*Definition:* A legal assistant is a person, qualified through education, training, or work experience, who is employed or retained by a lawyer, law office, governmental agency, or other entity in a capacity or function which involves the performance under the ultimate direction and supervision of an attorney, of specifically delegated substantive legal work, which work, for the most part, requires a sufficient knowledge of legal concepts that, absent such assistant, the attorney would perform the task.

A lawyer should take all reasonable supervisory measures to make sure the legal assistant acts in accordance with the lawyer's ethical obligations. (Guideline 1) Legal assistants can perform many tasks with lawyer supervision and review. They cannot give legal advice, accept cases, reject cases, or set legal fees. They may appear before adjudicatory bodies if authorized to do so. They may act as a witness at will executions. They may attend real estate closings alone but can act only as a messenger to deliver and pick up documents and funds. They cannot express any independent opinion or judgment about execution of the documents, changes in adjustments or price, or other matters involving documents or funds. (Guideline 2) The lawyer should take reasonable measures to ensure that all client confidences are protected by the legal assistant (Guideline 3) and that third persons are aware upon first contact with a legal assistant thatthe latter is not licensed to practice law (Guideline 4).The name and title of a legal assistant may appear on the lawyer's letterhead and on business cards identifying the lawyer's firm. (Guideline 5) A lawyer must take reasonable measures to ensure that the legal assistant does not create a conflict of interest due to current or prior employment, or to other business or personal interests. (Guideline 6) A lawyer shall not split legal fees with a legal assistant or pay a legal assistant for the referral of legal work. (Guideline 7) If a client consents, the lawyer can charge a reasonable and separate charge for legal assistant work. (Guideline 8) A lawyer shall not form a partnership with a legal assistant if any of the partnership's activities consist of the practice of law. (Guideline 9) A lawyer should encourage the legal assistant's participation in continuing education and pro bono publico activities. (Guideline 10) Connecticut Bar Association, *Guidelines for Lawyers Who Employ or Retain Legal Assistants* (1997) (*www.ctbar.org/public/committees/paralegals/guidelines.cfm*). See also *Lawyers' Professional Responsibility Obligations Concerning Paralegals*, 59 Connecticut Bar Journal 425 (1985).

Section 51-86 of *Connecticut General Statutes Annotated* covers solicitation by nonattorneys: "(a) A person who has not been admitted as an attorney in this state under the provisions of section 51-80 shall not solicit, advise, request or induce another person to cause an action for damages to be instituted, from which action or from which person the person soliciting, advising, requesting or inducing the action may, by agreement or otherwise, directly or indirectly, receive compensation from such other person or such person's attorney, or in which action the compensation of the attorney instituting or prosecuting the action, directly or indirectly, depends upon the amount of the recovery therein. (b) Any person who violates any provision of this section shall be fined not more than one hundred dollars or imprisoned not more than six months or both."

An attorney may use a paralegal as a messenger to deliver and pick up already prepared documents and funds required for a real estate closing. The supervising attorney does not have to be present. The paralegal can communicate information or questions from an attorney in the firm to the buyer's attorney. The paralegal, however, must not provide information or give an independent opinion regarding the legal implications or sufficiency of any of the documents. Connecticut Bar Ass'n, *Informal Opinion 96–16* (7/3/96) (1996 WL 405034).

A government attorney is not relieved of the obligation to exercise independent professional judgment simply because the attorney is under the supervision and direction of a government paralegal (a "supervisory paralegal specialist"). Connecticut Bar Ass'n, *Informal Opinion 00–9* (4/27/00) (2000 WL 1370788).

A law firm can take a new case even though one of its nonlawyer assistants worked on the other side of the same case while employed at a different firm so long as the employee has not already disclosed confidential information about the case learned while at the other firm and is screened from the case at the current firm. It is important that the paralegal not disclose, intentionally or inadvertently, information relating to representation of the former client and not otherwise work against the interest of the former client on the same or a substantially related matter. Connecticut Bar Ass'n, *Informal Opinion 00–23* (12/27/00) (2000 WL 33157218).

Other ethics opinions: Paralegals can have their own business card if their nonattorney status is clear, *Opinion 85–17* (11/20/85); it is unethical for an attorney to instruct a nonattorney to make misrepresentations to the public, *Informal Opinion 95–4* (1/6/95) (1995 WL 170147).

## DEFINING THE PRACTICE OF LAW IN CONNECTICUT

*In re Darlene C,* 717 A. 2d 1242, 1246 (Supreme Court of Connecticut, 1998): [while acknowledging that a]ttempts to define the practice of law have not been particularly successful, [the court nonetheless observed that] determining the legal theory of a case, drafting the papers necessary to commence a legal action, checking the various possible legal grounds, signing the pleadings and submitting them to the court [are] acts that are commonly understood to [constitute] the practice of law.

*State Bar Ass'n of Connecticut v. the Connecticut Bank and Trust Co.,* 140 A.2d 863, 870, 69 A.L.R.2d 394 (Supreme Court of Errors of Connecticut, 1958): The practice of law consists in no small part of work performed outside of any court and having no immediate relation to proceedings in court. It embraces the giving of legal advice on a large variety of subjects and the preparation of legal instruments covering an extensive field. Although such transactions may have no direct connection with court proceedings, they are always subject to subsequent involvement in litigation. They require in many aspects a high degree of legal skill and great capacity for adaptation to difficult and complex situations. No valid distinction can be drawn between the part of the work of the lawyer which involves appearance in court and the part which involves advice and the drafting of instruments.

## CONNECTICUT ETHICS AND PRACTICE RULES ON THE INTERNET

www.ctbar.org/public/committees/paralegals/
   guidelines.cfm
www.law.cornell.edu/ethics/connecticut.html
www2.law.cornell.edu/cgi-bin/foliocgi.exe/ct-code?
www.ctbar.org/public/ethics/cbaethics.shtml
www.ctbar.org/ethics/cbaethics.htm
www.crossingthebar.com/CT-UPL.htm

## PARALEGALS (AND OTHER NONATTORNEYS) IN COURT

- *Statewide Grievance Committee v. Harris,* 239 Conn. 256, 683 A. 2d 1362 (Supreme Court of Connecticut, 1996) (injunction against a paralegal charged with unauthorized practice of law in violation of General Statutes § 51–88; he ran an advertisement in the *Hartford Courant,* titled "Uncontested Pro se Divorce," in which he represented that "Paralegals prepare all papers for your signing and step you through the self-help divorce").
- *In re Darlene C,* 717 A.2d 1242 (Supreme Court of Connecticut, 1998) (nonlawyer representatives, who work for the state, prepare, sign, and file petitions for termination of parental rights; because a Connecticut statute authorizes these activities, they do not constitute the unauthorized practice of law).
- *Rivera v. Chicago Pneumatic Tool Co.,* 1991 WL 151892 (Connecticut Superior Court, 8/5/91) (trial court denies a motion to disqualify the plaintiff's attorney who hired a paralegal formerly employed by defendant's attorney even though the paralegal had been extensively involved in litigation concerning the defendant; there must be a sufficient Chinese Wall built around such a paralegal to ensure that confidences are not divulged).
- *Gazda v. Olin Corp.,* 5 CSCR 227 (1/18/90) (legal secretary switches firms; disqualification denied where reasonable efforts were taken to ensure that the nonattorney employee would not divulge any confidences she might have acquired).
- *Puglio v. Puglio,* 559 A.2d 1159 (Appellate Court of Connecticut, 1989) (a paralegal can testify in a foreclosure case on behalf of a mortgagee even though the paralegal had been involved in the preparation of the mortgagee's case).

# DELAWARE

## ETHICAL RULES AND GUIDELINES IN DELAWARE

A law firm cannot allow its paralegal to represent a client before the Industrial Accident Board on a worker's compensation case. Delaware State Bar Ass'n, *Opinion 1985–3.*

A nonattorney law clerk cannot work on a case where the other side is represented by the clerk's former employer. The clerk must be screened from involvement in the case. Delaware State Bar Ass'n, *Opinion 1986–1.*

## DEFINING THE PRACTICE OF LAW IN DELAWARE

*Delaware State Bar Ass'n v. Alexander,* 386 A.2d 652, 661, 12 A.L.R.4th 637 (Supreme Court of Delaware, 1978): In general, one is deemed to be practicing law whenever he furnishes to another advice or service under circumstances which imply the possession and use of legal knowledge and skill. The practice of law includes "all advice to clients, and all actions taken for them in matters connected with the law. . . . Practice of law includes the giving of legal advice and counsel, and the preparation of legal instruments and contracts [by] which legal rights are secured. . . . Where the rendering of services for another involves the use of legal knowledge or skill on his behalf where legal advice is required and is availed of or rendered in connection with such services these services necessarily constitute or include the practice of law." . . . "In determining what is the practice of law, it is well settled that it is the character of the acts performed and not the place where they are done that is decisive. The practice of law is not, therefore, necessarily limited to the conduct of cases in court but is engaged in whenever and wherever legal knowledge, training, skill and ability are required."

## DELAWARE ETHICS AND PRACTICE RULES ON THE INTERNET

www.law.cornell.edu/ethics/delaware.html
www.dsba.org/ethics.htm
www.crossingthebar.com/DE-UPL.htm

## PARALEGALS (AND OTHER NONATTORNEYS) IN COURT

- *In re Hull*, 767 A.2d 197 (Supreme Court of Delaware, 2001) (attorney disciplined for failure to supervise her legal assistant and for paying the latter an improper commission).
- *Spark v. MBNA Corp.*, 157 F. Supp. 2d 330 (U.S. District Court, Connecticut, 2001) (the request for paralegal fees did not set out information on the education and experience of the paralegals or on comparable billing rates for this professional in the market).
- *In re Arons*, 756 A.2d 867 (Supreme Court of Delaware, 2000) (it is the unauthorized practice of law for nonattorney lay advocates to represent families of children with disabilities in "due process" hearings held by Delaware Department of Public Instruction on federal disability issues; Congress did not authorize such lay representation).
- *In the Matter of the Estate of Ross*, 1996 WL 74731 (Court of Chancery of Delaware, 1996) ("In an age in which attorney fees are high, it is always welcome to see that good use is made of paralegals, with a resulting benefit to the client.").
- *McMackin v. McMackin*, 651 A.2d 778 (Family Court of Delaware, 1993) (award of paralegal fees).
- *In the Matter of Mekler*, 672 A.2d 23 (Supreme Court of Delaware, 1995) (suspended attorney can act as a paralegal but cannot have any contact with clients or prospective clients).

# District of Columbia

## ETHICAL RULES AND GUIDELINES IN THE DISTRICT OF COLUMBIA

A paralegal who switches firms must be screened from any cases involving clients represented by both firms. This will protect confidences and avoid imputed disqualification. D.C. Bar, *Opinion 227*, 21 Bar Report 2 (August/September 1992).

Nonattorneys can have a business card that prints the name of the law firm where they work as long as their nonattorney status is clear. D.C. Bar, *Opinion 19*. See also *Speaking of Ethics*, Bar Report 2 (February/March 1988).

A law firm can share a "success fee" with nonattorney experts on a case. *Opinion 233*, Bar Report 2 (June/July 1993).

A nonattorney *can* be a partner in a law firm. Hence a District of Columbia law firm *can* share fees with nonattorneys under the guidelines of Rule 5.4. For example, a lobbyist or an economist could form a partnership with an attorney. The nonattorney must agree to abide by the Rules of Professional Conduct. Rule 5.4, *Model Rules of Professional Conduct*.

A nonattorney who is an officer, director, or employee of a corporation can appear for that corporation in the settlement of any landlord-and-tenant case. If, however, the corporation files an answer, cross-claim, or counterclaim, the corporation must be represented by an attorney. D.C. Court of Appeals, Rule 49(c)(8), *Rules of the District of Columbia Court of Appeals*.

## DEFINING THE PRACTICE OF LAW IN THE DISTRICT OF COLUMBIA

Rule 49 (*Court Rules of the District of Columbia Court of Appeals*): (a) General Rule. No person shall engage in the practice of law in the District of Columbia or in any manner hold out as authorized or competent to practice law in the District of Columbia unless enrolled as an active member of the District of Columbia Bar . . . .

(b) (2) "Practice of Law" means the provision of professional legal advice or services where there is a client relationship of trust or reliance. One is presumed to be practicing law when engaging in any of the following conduct on behalf of another: (A) Preparing any legal document, including any deeds, mortgages, assignments, discharges, leases, trust instruments or any other instruments intended to affect interests in real or personal property, wills, codicils, instruments intended to affect the disposition of property of decedents' estates, other instruments intended to affect or secure legal rights, and contracts except routine agreements incidental to a regular course of business; (B) Preparing or expressing legal opinions; (C) Appearing or acting as an attorney in any tribunal; (D) Preparing any claims, demands or pleadings of any kind, or any written documents containing legal argument or interpretation of law, for filing in any court, administrative agency or other tribunal; (E) Providing advice or counsel as to how any of the activities described in sub-paragraph (A) through (D) might be done or whether they were done, in accordance with applicable law; . . . .

## DISTRICT OF COLUMBIA ETHICS AND PRACTICE RULES ON THE INTERNET

www.law.cornell.edu/ethics/dc.html
www2.law.cornell.edu/cgi-bin/foliocgi.exe/Dc-narr?
www.crossingthebar.com/DC-UPL.htm

## PARALEGALS (AND OTHER NONATTORNEYS) IN COURT

- *In re Meese*, 907 F.2d 1192, 1202 (U.S. Court of Appeals, D.C. Circuit, 1990) (the rates billed for paralegals are reasonable; however, we deduct $4253.75 for services billed at these rates that were of a purely clerical nature).
- *In Re Ryan*, 670 A.2d 375 (District of Columbia Court of Appeals, 1996) (attorney disciplined in part because of her overreliance on paralegals who had no paralegal training).
- *In Re Davis*, 650 A.2d 1319 (District of Columbia Court of Appeals, 1994) (disbarred attorney ordered to perform 250 hours of community service as a paralegal).
- *Hampton Courts Tenants Ass'n v. DC Rental Housing Commission*, 599 A.2d 1113, 1118 (District of Columbia Court of Appeals, 1991) ("Hours are not reasonably expended . . . if an attorney . . . performs tasks normally performed by paralegals. . . .").

# FLORIDA

## ETHICAL RULES AND GUIDELINES IN FLORIDA

Paralegals can have their own business cards. They may also be listed on a law firm's letterhead, but a title indicating their nonattorney status should appear beneath their name. Attorneys should not hold their paralegals out as "certified" if they are not. Florida Bar, *Opinion 86–4* (8/1/86). See also Florida Bar, *Opinion 71–39* (10/20/71) (nonattorney employee can use the law firm's name on his business card).

When a nonattorney changes jobs to an opposing law firm, the old and new employers must admonish him or her not to reveal any confidences or secrets obtained during prior employment, and the new employer must take steps to ensure there is no breach of confidentiality by this employee. Florida Bar, *Opinion 86–5* (8/1/86).

A law firm can allow a nonattorney to conduct a real estate closing if certain conditions are met, e.g., an attorney is available (in person or by telephone) to answer legal questions, the nonattorney performs only ministerial acts (he or she must not give legal advice or make any legal decisions),

and the client consents to having the closing handled by a nonattorney. Florida Bar, *Opinion 89–5* (11/1989) (overruling *Opinion 73–43*).

Preparing living trust documents constitutes the practice of law. It is the unauthorized practice of law for a nonattorney to decide whether a living trust is appropriate, and to prepare and execute the documents involved. *Florida Bar Re: Advisory Opinion on Nonlawyer Preparation of Living Trusts*, 613 So. 2d 426 (Supreme Court of Florida, 1992). See also *Florida Bar Re: Advisory Opinion on Nonlawyer Preparation of Residential Leases Up to One Year in Duration*, 602 So. 2d 914 (Supreme Court of Florida, 1992), and *Florida Bar Re: Nonlawyer Preparation of and Representation of Landlord in Uncontested Residential Evictions*, 605 So. 2d 868 (Supreme Court of Florida, 1992).

It is ethically improper for a law firm to delegate to nonattorneys the handling of negotiations with adjusters on claims of the firm's clients. Florida Bar, *Ethics Opinion 74–35* (9/23/74). But the nonlawyer employee can transmit information from the attorney. "For example, the nonlawyer employee may call the adjuster and inform the adjuster that the attorney will settle the matter for X. If the adjuster comes back with a counteroffer, the nonlawyer employee must inform the attorney. The employee cannot be given a range in which to settle." *Ethically Speaking*. The Florida Bar News, September, 15, 1991, at 15.

An attorney can allow a supervised nonattorney to conduct an initial interview of a prospective client if his or her nonattorney status is disclosed to the client and only factual information is obtained. Florida Bar, *Opinion 88–6* (4/15/88).

Other Florida Bar Opinions involving nonattorneys: *Opinion 88–15* (10/1/88) (sharing office space with nonattorneys); *Opinion 87–11* (4/15/88) (nonattorney signing pleadings); *Opinion 70–62* (2/12/71) (a law firm cannot delegate anything that requires personal judgment to a nonattorney employee); *Opinion 68–58* (1/17/69) (nonattorney employees of a law firm can be part of a retirement plan funded from firm profits); *Opinion 73–41* (3/11/74) (nonattorneys cannot take depositions); *Opinion 76–33* (3/15/77) (an attorney must not overbill for paralegal time).

## DEFINING THE PRACTICE OF LAW IN FLORIDA

*The Florida Bar v. Brumbaugh*, 355 So. 2d 1186, 1191–92 (Supreme Court of Florida, 1978). Although persons not licensed as attorney are prohibited from practicing law within this state, it is somewhat difficult to define exactly what constitutes the practice of law in all instances. This Court has previously stated that: ". . . if the giving of such advice and performance of such services affect important rights of a person under the law, and if the reasonable protection of the rights and property of those advised and served requires that the persons giving such advice possess legal skill and a knowledge of the law greater than that possessed by the average citizen, then the giving of such advice and the performance of such services by one for another as a course of conduct constitute the practice of law." This definition is broad and is given content by this Court only as it applies to specific circumstances of each case. We agree that "any attempt to formulate a lasting, all encompassing definition of 'practice of law' is doomed to failure for the reason that under our system of jurisprudence such practice must necessarily change with the ever changing business and social order."

Rule 10-2. 1, *Rules Regulating The Florida Bar* (West's Florida Statutes Annotated): (a) Unlicensed Practice of Law. The unlicensed practice of law shall mean the practice of law, as prohibited by statute, court rule, and case law of the State of Florida. For purposes of this chapter, it shall not constitute the unlicensed practice of law for a nonlawyer to engage in limited oral communications to assist a person in the completion of blanks on a legal form approved by the Supreme Court of Florida. Oral communications by nonlawyers are restricted to those communications reasonably necessary to elicit factual information to complete the blanks on the form and inform the person how to file the form.

## IMPORTANT FLORIDA RULES ON PARALEGALS

§ 57.104 (*West's Florida Statutes*): Computation of attorneys' fees. In any action in which attorneys' fees are to be determined or awarded by the court, the court shall consider, among other things, time and labor of any legal assistants who contributed nonclerical, meaningful legal support to the matter involved and who are working under the supervision of an attorney. For purposes of this section "legal assistant" means a person, who under the supervision and direction of a licensed attorney engages in legal research, and case development or planning in relation to modifications or initial proceedings, services, processes, or applications; or who prepares or interprets legal documents or selects, compiles, and uses technical information from references such as digests, encyclopedias, or practice manuals and analyzes and follows procedural problems that involve independent decisions.

Rule 4–5.3 (*Florida Rules of Professional Conduct*): A person who uses the title of paralegal, legal assistant, or other similar term when offering or providing legal services to the public must work for or under the direction of a lawyer. . . . (Rule change *proposed* to Florida Supreme Court by Florida Bar Association.)

## FLORIDA ETHICS AND PRACTICE RULES ON THE INTERNET
www.law.cornell.edu/ethics/florida.html
www2.law.cornell.edu/cgi-bin/foliocgi.exe/Fl-narr?
www.flabar.org/newflabar/memberservices/Ethics
www.crossingthebar.com/FL-UPL.htm

## PARALEGALS (AND OTHER NONATTORNEYS) IN COURT

- *Stewart v. Bee-Dee Neon & Signs, Inc.*, 751 So. 2d 196 (Florida District Court of Appeal, 2000) (disqualifi-

cation of law firm that hired paralegal of opposing firm was improper where no evidence was presented that the paralegal actually disclosed material confidential information to hiring firm, that the paralegal would necessarily work on case, or that screening measures would be ineffective) (compare *Koulisis v. Rivers*, 730 So. 2d 289 (Florida District Court of Appeal, 1999).
- *Wells Fargo Credit Corp. v. Martin*, 605 So. 2d 531 (Florida District Court of Appeal, 1992) (paralegal misreads her instructions and causes a $100,000 mistake).
- *Ramos v. Mast*, 789 So. 2d 1226 (Florida District Court of Appeal, 2001) (former attorney brought action against his former paralegal, alleging fraud, civil theft, racketeering, civil conspiracy, and libel in connection with paralegal's alleged embezzlement of funds from attorney's trust account).
- *The Florida Bar v. Miravelle*, 761 So. 2d 1049 (Florida Supreme Court, 2000) (legal form preparation service and the unauthorized practice of law).
- *The Florida Bar v. Florida Service Bureau*, 581 So. 2d 900 (Supreme Court of Florida, 1991) (it is not the unauthorized practice of law for nonattorneys to give assistance to landlords by explaining what the eviction procedure entails as long a they do not give legal advice; the "information given was no greater than that which anyone could glean from reading the eviction statute").
- *Florida Bar v. Lawless*, 640 So. 2d 1098 (Supreme Court of Florida, 1994) (attorney fails to supervise paralegal properly).
- *United States v. Pepper's Steel*, 742 F. Supp. 641 (U.S. District Court, S.D. Florida, 1990) (although a paralegal accidentally delivered documents to the opposing party[!], the documents are still protected by the attorney-client privilege).
- *Florida Bar v. Furman*, 376 So. 2d 378 (Florida Supreme Court, 1979) (see discussion of the *Furman* case in chapter 4).

# Georgia

## ETHICAL RULES AND GUIDELINES IN GEORGIA

It is the unauthorized practice of law for a law firm to allow a nonattorney to conduct a real estate closing. State Bar of Georgia, *Opinion 86–5* (5/12/89). It is not sufficient for the attorney to be available on the telephone during the course of the closing to respond to questions or to review documents. The lawyer's physical presence at a closing will assure that there is supervision of the work of the paralegal that is direct and constant. Supreme Court of Georgia, *Formal Advisory Opinion 00–3* (2/11/00).

An attorney aids a nonlawyer in the unauthorized practice of law when the attorney allows his or her paralegal to prepare and sign correspondence that threatens legal action or provides legal advice or both. Supreme Court of Georgia, *Formal Advisory Opinion 00–2* (2/11/00).

The payment of a monthly bonus by a lawyer to his nonlawyer employees based on the gross receipts of his law office in addition to their regular monthly salary constitutes the sharing of legal fees in violation of Standard No. 26. Accordingly, it would be ethically improper for a lawyer to pay his nonlawyer employees a monthly bonus based on the gross receipts of his law office. Supreme Court of Georgia, *Formal Advisory Opinion 91–3* (11/13/91).

An attorney should not allow a paralegal to correspond with an adverse party (or the latter's agents) on the attorney's letterhead if the letter discusses legal matters that suggest or assert claims. (Routine contacts with opposing counsel not involving the merits of the case are, however, permitted.) *Advisory Opinion 19* (7/18/75).

An attorney may delegate tasks to a paralegal that ordinarily comprise the practice of law, but only if the attorney has direct contact with the client and maintains "constant supervision" of the paralegal. The paralegal can render specialized advice on scientific or technical topics. The paralegal cannot negotiate with parties or opposing counsel on substantive issues. The paralegal's name may not appear on the letterhead or office door. The paralegal must not sign any pleadings, briefs, or other legal documents to be presented to a court. The paralegal can have a business card with the name of the firm on it if the word *paralegal* is clearly used to indicate nonattorney status. Unless previous contacts would justify the paralegal in believing that his or her nonattorney status is already known, the paralegal should begin oral communications, either face to face or on the telephone, with a clear statement that he or she is a paralegal employee of the law firm. Georgia, *Advisory Opinion 21* (9/16/77, revised 1983).

## DEFINING THE PRACTICE OF LAW IN GEORGIA

§ 15–19–50 (*Code of Georgia*): The practice of law in this state is defined as: (1) Representing litigants in court and preparing pleadings and other papers incident to any action or special proceedings in any court or other judicial body; (2) Conveyancing; (3) The preparation of legal instruments of all kinds whereby a legal right is secured; (4) The rendering of opinions as to the validity or invalidity of titles to real or personal property; (5) The giving of any legal advice; and (6) Any action taken for others in any matter connected with the law.

§ 15–19–51 (*Code of Georgia*): Unauthorized practice of law forbidden.

(a) It shall be unlawful for any person other than a duly licensed attorney at law: . . .

(4) To render or furnish legal services or advice; . . .

(6) To render legal services of any kind in actions or proceedings of any nature; . . .

(8) To advertise that . . . he has, owns, conducts, or maintains an office for the practice of law or for furnishing legal advice, services, or counsel.

## GEORGIA ETHICS AND PRACTICE RULES ON THE INTERNET

www.law.cornell.edu/ethics/georgia.html
www.abanet.org/cpr/links.html#States
www.gabar.org/partiv.htm
www.crossingthebar.com/GA-UPL.htm

## PARALEGALS (AND OTHER NONATTORNEYS) IN COURT

- *In re Arp*, 546 S.E.2d 486 (Supreme Court of Georgia, 2001) (attorney unethically pays a paralegal for the referral of cases and clients in violation of Standard 13 of Bar Rule 4–102, which prohibits an attorney from compensating a person or organization to recommend or secure employment by a client or as a reward for a recommendation).
- *In re Gaff*, 524 S.E.2d 728 (Supreme Court of Georgia, 2000) (attorney hires a disbarred attorney but fails to take any action to ensure that disbarred attorney, working as paralegal, had no contact with his clients after the State Bar had warned him of potential ethical problems that his employment of disbarred attorney might engender; one-year suspension was warranted).
- *Peters v. Hyatt Legal Services*, 469 S.E.2d 481 (Court of Appeals of Georgia, 1996) (a paralegal is sued for legal malpractice along with the law firm).
- *Jones v. Armstrong Cork Co.*, 630 F.2d 324 (U.S. Court of Appeals, 5th Circuit, 1980) (calling someone a "paralegal" does not necessarily mean he or she is a paralegal for purposes of awarding paralegal fees).
- *Cullins v. Georgia Dept. of Transportation*, 827 F. Supp. 756, 762 (U.S. District Court, M.D. Georgia, 1993) ("paralegal costs are recoverable as a part of . . . attorney's fees and expenses but only to the extent such work is the type traditionally performed by an attorney. Otherwise, paralegal expenses are separately unrecoverable overhead expenses").

# Hawaii

## ETHICAL RULES AND GUIDELINES IN HAWAII

An attorney may list a paralegal on professional cards, letterhead, and professional notices or announcement cards as long as the employee is identified as a paralegal or legal assistant. A paralegal can use a business card identifying him or her as an employee of the law firm. A paralegal can sign correspondence as a paralegal. Hawaii Supreme Court Disciplinary Board, *Formal Opinion 78–8–19* (6/28/84). See also *Opinion 78–8–19–Supp*.

The phrase "& Associates" cannot refer to nonlawyers, such as paralegals. Carole Richelieu, *Disciplinary Counsel's Report*, 1997 Hawaii Bar Journal 16 (March 1997).

## DEFINING THE PRACTICE OF LAW IN HAWAII

*Fought & Co., Inc. v. Steel Engineering and Erection, Inc.*, 951 P.2d 487, 496 (Supreme Court of Hawaii, 1998): The legislature has "expressly declined to adopt a formal definition of the term "practice of law," noting that "[a]ttempts to define the practice of law in terms of enumerating the specific types of services that come within the phrase are fruitless because new developments in society, whether legislative, social, or scientific in nature, continually create new concepts and new legal problems. . . . The legislature recognized that the practice of law is not limited to appearing before the courts. It consists, among other things of the giving of advice, the preparation of any document or the rendition of any service to a third party affecting the legal rights . . . of such party, where such advice, drafting or rendition of service requires the use of any degree of legal knowledge, skill or advocacy. Similarly, . . . this court has never formally defined the term 'practice of law'."

## HAWAII ETHICS AND PRACTICE RULES ON THE INTERNET

www.law.cornell.edu/ethics/listing.html
www2.law.cornell.edu/cgi-bin/foliocgi.exe/hi-code?
www.hawaii.gov/ethics/opinions/AO.htm

## PARALEGALS (AND OTHER NONATTORNEYS) IN COURT

- *Schefke v. Reliable Collection Agency, Ltd.*, 32 P.3d 52 (Hawaii Supreme Court, 2001) (courts should reduce an award of attorney's fees for excessive preparation time by a paralegal, duplicative efforts by the attorney and paralegal, and performance of clerical functions; where there is no documentation for paralegal time, courts can decline to make award for fees).
- *Blair v. Ing*, 31 P.3d 184 (Hawaii Supreme Court, 2001) (an award of paralegal fees is limited to charges for work performed that would otherwise have been required to be performed by a licensed attorney at a higher rate; this encourages cost-effective delivery of legal services; the fees will be for legal work, not for secretarial work the paralegal may perform).
- *Tirona v. State Farm Mutual Insurance Co.*, 821 F. Supp. 632 (U.S. District Court, Hawaii, 1993) (paralegal fees denied when most of the services performed by paralegals were clerical in nature).
- *Hawaii v. Liuafi*, 623 P.2d 1271 (Intermediate Court of Appeals of Hawaii, 1981) (paralegal assistance to prisoners).
- *Oahu Plumbing and Sheet Metal, Ltd. v. Kona Construction, Inc.*, 590 P.2d 570 (Hawaii, Supreme Court 1979) (with limited exceptions, it is the unauthorized practice of law for a nonattorney officer of a corporation to represent the corporation in litigation).

# Idaho

## ETHICAL RULES AND GUIDELINES IN IDAHO

An attorney must not share fees with nonattorneys. The attorney can request compensation for the work of a paralegal or other laypersons acting under his or her supervision as long as the request specifies that laypersons performed the work. Idaho State Bar, *Formal Ethics Opinion 125*.

A law firm cannot list legal assistants on its letterhead. Idaho State Bar, *Formal Opinion 109* (11/30/81).

Attorneys must not split fees with nonattorneys. Idaho State Bar Committee on Ethics, *Opinion 117* (3/14/86).

## DEFINING THE PRACTICE OF LAW IN IDAHO

*Idaho State Bar v. Meservy*, 335 P.2d 62, 64 (Idaho Supreme Court, 1959): The practice of law as generally understood, is the doing or performing services in a court of justice, in any matter depending [sic] therein, throughout its various stages, and in conformity with the adopted rules of procedure. But in a larger sense, it includes legal advice and counsel, and the preparation of instruments and contracts by which legal rights are secured, although such matter may or may not be depending [sic] in a court. . . . The drafting of . . . documents . . . or the giving of advice and counsel with respect thereto, by one not a licensed attorney at law, would constitute an unlawful practice of law, whether or not a charge was made therefor, and even though the documents or advice are not actually employed in an action or proceeding pending in a court. I.C. § 3-104.

## IMPORTANT IDAHO RULES ON PARALEGALS

Rule 54(e)(1), *Rules of Civil Procedure*, (*West's Idaho Rules of Court*): Attorney Fees. In any civil action the court may award reasonable attorney fees, which at the discretion of the court may include paralegal fees, to the prevailing party or parties as defined in Rule 54(d)(1)(B), when provided for by any statute or contract.

§ 19-2705 (*Idaho Code*): A paralegal, as an agent of the attorney of record, is allowed to visit a defendent who has been sentenced to death. (Historical note: "The Legislature further recognizes that under American jurisprudence an adequate defense of a death penalty inmate is an interdisciplinary endeavor requiring the skills of counsel, experts, investigators and paralegals working together on the convict's behalf.")

## IDAHO ETHICS AND PRACTICE RULES ON THE INTERNET

www.law.cornell.edu/ethics/idaho.html
www2.law.cornell.edu/cgi-bin/foliocgi.exe/rpc-idaho?
www2.state.id.us/isb/irpc.htm
www.crossingthebar.com/ID-UPL.htm

## PARALEGALS (AND OTHER NONATTORNEYS) IN COURT

- *Defendent A v. Idaho State Bar*, 25 P.3d 846 (Idaho Supreme Court, 2001) (attorney disciplined for overcharging for paralegal's work on a case).
- *In re Castorena*, 270 Bankruptcy Reporter 504 (U.S. Bankruptcy Court, Idaho, 2001) (bankruptcy attorneys may utilize paraprofessionals to assist them in rendering legal service to their clients but only if certain conditions are met: paralegals must be qualified, through training and experience, and capable of performing such services; must be adequately supervised; may not independently provide any legal advice; and may legitimately be delegated work only after attorney has first met with clients, determined what tasks need to be performed, and determined who may competently perform those tasks; also, neither attorneys nor paralegals may charge professional rates for clerical functions).
- *Perkins v. U.S. Transformer West*, 974 P.2d 73, 77 (Idaho Supreme Court, 1999) ("Fees for paralegal services clearly are not contemplated as awardable attorney's fees or costs under I.R.C.P. 54. Although the United States Supreme Court has approved an award for paralegal fees . . ., we conclude that the Supreme Court's reasoning is inapplicable to our Idaho Rule 54, I.R.C.P.").
- *Idaho State Bar v. Jenkins*, 816 P.2d 335 (Idaho Supreme Court, 1991) (an attorney was not sanctioned when his paralegal unethically solicited clients for the law firm, but without the knowledge or ratification of her attorney employer; hence there was no violation of Rule 5.3 of the code of ethics).
- *Kyle v. Beco Corp.*, 707 P.2d 378 (Idaho Supreme Court, 1985) (a party before the Industrial Commission must be represented by an attorney, if represented at all).
- *Coleman v. Idaho*, 762 P.2d 814, 817 (Idaho Supreme Court, 1988) (prison officials may not constitutionally prevent inmate paralegals from assisting illiterate inmates).
- *Idaho State Bar v. Williams*, 893 P.2d 202 (Idaho Supreme Court, 1995) (disbarred attorney as paralegal).

## Illinois

### ETHICAL RULES AND GUIDELINES IN ILLINOIS

Paralegal names can be printed on a firm's letterhead. The nonattorney status of the employee must be indicated. Illinois State Bar Ass'n, *Opinion 87–1* (9/8/87). This apparently overrules an earlier opinion that prohibited placing a nonattorney name on letterhead. *Opinion 350.*

Supervising attorneys must be sure their paralegals understand the rules of ethics governing attorneys. Paralegals can have contact with clients, but a direct attorney-client relationship remains primary. Paralegals must preserve confidentiality and make sure the paralegal's work does not benefit the client's adversaries. Attorneys may charge clients for paralegal services, but they may not form partnerships with paralegals. Illinois State Bar Ass'n, *Recommendations to Lawyers for the Use of Legal Assistants* (1988).

It is professionally improper to charge an hourly rate for a salaried paralegal as an expense in addition to a percentage of recovery on a contingent fee contract. Illinois State Bar Ass'n, *Opinion 86–1* (7/7/86).

A paralegal cannot handle phone calls involving legal matters of her law firm while at a collection agency that is one of the clients of the law firm. The law firm would not be able to supervise the paralegal. Illinois State Bar Ass'n, *Opinion 88–8* (3/15/89).

Attorney assistants can prepare standardized deeds and other real estate documents; correspond with any party, but only to obtain factual information; and assist at real estate closings, but only in the company of a supervising attorney. Illinois State Bar Ass'n, *Position Paper on Use of Attorney Assistants in Real Estate Transactions* (approved by Board of Governors, 5/16/84).

It is the unauthorized practice of law for a nonattorney to represent an employer before the Illinois Department of Employment Security in an unemployment compensation case in which the nonattorney prepares and presents evidence. The employer must be represented by an attorney. An attorney does not aid in the unauthorized practice of law by continuing to represent his client when the other side is represented by a nonattorney. Illinois State Bar Ass'n, *Advisory Opinion 93–15* (3/94).

Sharing fees with a nonattorney via profit-sharing is proper provided the sharing is based on a percentage of overall firm profit and is not tied to fees in a particular case. Illinois State Bar Ass'n, *Opinion 89–5* (7/17/89).

An attorney may not, pursuant to an arrangement with an organization that refers work to the attorney, employ the clerical or paralegal services of that organization. Illinois State Bar Ass'n, *Opinion 827* (4/1983). Also, it is professionally improper for a lawyer to participate in an arrangement with a nonlawyer whereby the lawyer obtains referrals in return for the payment of fees by the lawyer to the nonlawyer. Illinois State Bar Ass'n, *Advisory Opinion 99–02* (9/1999).

A paralegal can conduct a real estate closing without his or her attorney-supervisor present if no legal advice is given, if all the documents have been prepared in advance, if the attorney-supervisor is available by telephone to provide help, and if the other attorney consents. Chicago Bar Ass'n (1983).

Legal assistants can be listed on law firm letterhead or on the door as long as their nonattorney status is clear. Chicago Bar Ass'n, *Opinion 81–4.*

## DEFINING THE PRACTICE OF LAW IN ILLINOIS

*In re Howard*, 721 N.E.2d 1126, 1134 (Illinois Supreme Court, 1999): determining what conduct constitutes practicing law defies mechanistic formulation. It encompasses not only court appearances, but also services rendered out of court and includes the giving of any advice or rendering of any service requiring the use of legal knowledge.

§ 205/1, chapter 705 (*Illinois Compiled Statutes Annotated*): Nothing in this Act [which restricts the practice of law to licensed attorneys] shall be construed to prohibit representation of a party by a person who is not an attorney in a proceeding before . . . the Illinois Labor Relations Board, . . . the Illinois Educational Labor Relations Board, . . . the State Civil Service Commission, . . . the University Civil Service Merit Board, to the extent allowed pursuant to rules and regulations promulgated by those Boards and Commissions.

## IMPORTANT ILLINOIS LAWS ON PARALEGALS

§ 70/1.35, chapter 5 (*Illinois Compiled Statutes Annotated*): "Paralegal" means a person who is qualified through education, training, or work experience and is employed by a lawyer, law office, governmental agency, or other entity to work under the direction of an attorney in a capacity that involves the performance of substantive legal work that usually requires a sufficient knowledge of legal concepts and would be performed by the attorney in the absence of the paralegal. A reference in an Act to attorney fees includes paralegal fees, recoverable at market rates.

Rule 764 of the Supreme Court (*Illinois Compiled Statutes Annotated*): Disciplined Attorney. (b) Upon entry of the final order of discipline, the disciplined attorney shall not maintain a presence or occupy an office where the practice of law is conducted. The disciplined attorney shall take such action necessary to cause the removal of any indicia of the disciplined attorney as lawyer, counsellor at law, legal assistant, legal clerk, or similar title.

## ILLINOIS ETHICS AND PRACTICE RULES ON THE INTERNET

www.law.cornell.edu/ethics/illinois.html
www2.law.cornell.edu/cgi-bin/foliocgi.exe/Il-code?
www2.law.cornell.edu/cgi-bin//foliocgi.exe/Il-narr?
www.illinoisbar.org/CourtsBull/EthicsOpinions/
   home.html
www.crossingthebar.com/IL-UPL.htm

## PARALEGALS (AND OTHER NONATTORNEYS) IN COURT

■ *Becker v. Zellner*, 684 N.E.2d 1378 (Appellate Court of Illinois, 1997) (independent paralegals sue attorney for defamation for asserting that their work was worthless).

■ *In re Estate of Divine*, 635 N.E.2d 581 (Appellate Court of Illinois, 1994) (attorney supervisors are liable for the actions of their paralegals, but the latter should not be liable for the actions of their supervisors; a paralegal does not have an independent fiduciary duty to a law firm client).

■ *Kapco Mfg. Co., Inc. v. C&O Enterprises, Inc.*, 637 F. Supp. 1231 (U.S. District Court, N. D. Illinois, 1985) (disqualification of a law firm is not required simply because it hired a law office manager-secretary who had worked for opposing party at another law firm).

■ *Shortino v. Illinois Telephone Co.*, 665 N.E.2d 414, 419 (Appellate Court of Illinois, 1996) (just because an experienced attorney is paid $350 an hour while appearing in court, he or she should not also be paid $350 per hour for tasks that could easily be done by . . . paralegals . . . at a lower hourly rate).

■ *In re Marriage of Ahmad*, 555 N.E.2d 439 (Appellate Court of Illinois, 1990) (award of paralegal fees).

■ *Boettcher v. Fournie Farms, Inc.*, 612 N.E.2d 969 (Appellate Court of Illinois, 1993) (confidential communications made by a client to the paralegal of the client's attorney are protected by the attorney-client privilege).

■ *People v. Alexander*, 202 N.E.2d 841 (Appellate Court of Illinois, 1964) (a nonattorney can appear in court for purposes of handling ministerial acts such as submitting agreed or stipulated matters) (see discussion of this case in chapter 4).

# Indiana

## ETHICAL RULES AND GUIDELINES IN INDIANA

*Rules of Professional Conduct, Use of Legal Assistants* (1993). *Guideline 9.1*: An attorney must supervise the work of the legal assistant. Independent legal assistants, to wit, those not employed by a specific firm or by specific attorney are prohibited. *Guideline 9.2*: An attorney may delegate any task to a legal assistant so long as that task is not prohibited by law. The attorney must be responsible for the work product of the legal assistant. *Guideline 9.3*: An attorney cannot delegate to a legal assistant the tasks of establishing the attorney-client relationship, setting fees, or giving legal opinions to a client. *Guideline 9.4*: The attorney has the duty to make sure the client, the courts, and other attorneys know the legal assistant is not an attorney. *Guideline 9.5*: The legal assistant's name and title can appear on the attorney's letterhead and business card that also identifies the attorney's firm. *Guideline 9.6*: The attorney must take reasonable measures to ensure the legal assistant preserves client confidences. *Guideline 9.7*: The attorney can charge for the work performed by the legal assistant. *Guideline 9.8*: An attorney may not split fees with a legal assistant or pay legal assistants for referring legal business. An attorney may compensate a legal assistant based on the quantity and quality of the legal assistant's work and the value of that work to a law practice, but the legal assistant's compensation may not be contingent, by advance agreement, upon the profitability of the attorney's practice. *Guideline 9.9*: An attorney who employs a legal assistant should facilitate the legal assistant's participation in appropriate continuing legal education and pro bono publico activities. *Guideline 9.10*: All attorneys who employ legal assistants in the State of Indiana shall assure that such legal assistants conform their conduct to be consistent with the following ethical standards: (a) A legal assistant may perform any task delegated and supervised by an attorney so long as the attorney is responsible to the client, maintains a direct relationship with the client, and assumes full professional responsibility for the work product. (b) A legal assistant shall not engage in the unauthorized practice of law. (c) A legal assistant shall serve the public interest by the improvement of the legal system. (d) A legal assistant shall achieve and maintain a high level of competence, as well as a high level of personal and professional integrity and conduct. (e) A legal assistant's title shall be fully disclosed in all business and professional communications. (f) A legal assistant shall preserve all confidential information provided by the client or acquired from other sources before, during, and after the course of the professional relationship. (g) A legal assistant shall avoid conflicts of interest and shall disclose any possible conflict to the employer or client, as well as to the prospective employers or clients. (h) A legal assistant shall act within the bounds of the law, uncompromisingly for the benefit of the client. (i) A legal assistant shall do all things incidental, necessary, or expedient for the attainment of the ethics and responsibilities imposed by statute or rule of court. (j) A legal assistant shall be governed by the American Bar Association *Model Code of Professional Responsibility* and the American Bar Association *Model Rules of Professional Conduct*.

The above rules (particularly Guideline 9.1) on the *Use of Legal Assistants* do not prohibit the use of paralegals through temporary services, contract services, and leasing firms so long as the work on a given project is under the direct supervision of the lawyer. Indiana Bar Ass'n, *Opinion 4* (1994).

An attorney can utilize a paralegal to conduct a negotiation session where no lawsuit has been filed so long as the paralegal is not responsible for rendering any legal opinions to the client. The attorney cannot however, delegate to a paralegal the representation of the client in mediation. Legal Ethics Committee of the Indiana State Bar Ass'n, *Opinion 1* (1997) (40 Res Gestae 22 (April 1997)).

Paralegal names can be printed on a firm's letterhead if their nonattorney status is clear. The attorneys and nonattorneys must be distinguished clearly. Indiana Bar Ass'n, *Opinion 9* (1985) (overruling *Opinion 5*).

Paralegals may have a business card as long as their capacity is stated and the identity of their employing attorney is disclosed. Indiana Bar Ass'n, *Opinion 8* (1984).

An attorney aids an accountant in the unauthorized practice of law if the attorney prepares blank legal forms for the accountant who will help his clients fill them out without any attorney supervision. Indiana Bar Ass'n, *Opinion 2* (1995).

## DEFINING THE PRACTICE OF LAW IN INDIANA

*In the Matter of Fletcher*, 655 N.E.2d 58, 60 (Supreme Court of Indiana, 1995): It is the province of this Court to determine what acts constitute the practice of law. . . . The practice of law includes "the doing or performing services in a court of justice, in any matter depending therein, throughout its various stages . . . [b]ut in a larger sense it includes legal advice and counsel. . . ." The core element of practicing law is the giving of legal advice to a client and placing oneself in the very sensitive relationship wherein the confidence of the client, and the management of his affairs, is left totally in the hands of the attorney. . . . The practice of law includes the appearance in court representing another.

## IMPORTANT INDIANA LAWS ON PARALEGALS

§ 1–1–4–6 (*West's Annotated Indiana Code*): Attorney's fees as including paralegal's fees.

Sec. 6(a) As used in this section, "paralegal" means a person who is: (1) qualified through education, training, or work experience; and (2) employed by a lawyer, law office, governmental agency, or other entity; to work under the direction of an attorney in a capacity that involves the performance of substantive legal work that usually requires a sufficient knowledge of legal concepts and would be performed by the attorney in the absence of the paralegal. (b) A reference in the Indiana Code to attorney's fees includes paralegal's fees.

Rule 23 (*Indiana Rules for . . . the Discipline of Attorneys*): Sec. 26(b) Upon receiving notice of the order of suspension or disbarment, [an attorney] shall not maintain a presence or occupy an office where the practice of law is conducted. A respondent suspended for more than six (6) months or disbarred shall take such action as is necessary to cause the removal of any indicia of lawyer, counselor at law, legal assistant, law clerk or similar title.

## INDIANA ETHICS AND PRACTICE RULES ON THE INTERNET

www.law.cornell.edu/ethics/indiana.html
www.in.gov/judiciary/research/PR/section9.html
www.in.gov/judiciary/research/PR/toc.html
www.inbar.org/content/legalethics/legalethics2.asp
www.crossingthebar.com/IN-UPL.htm

## PARALEGALS (AND OTHER NONATTORNEYS) IN COURT

■ *Shell Oil Co. v. Meyer*, 684 N.E.2d 504, 525 (Court of Appeals of Indiana, 1997) ("When one considers that attorneys utilize paralegals to perform tasks which might otherwise have to be accomplished by a lawyer with a higher billing rate, recovery for a paralegal's fees is hardly unreasonable.").

- *Mayberry v. State*, 670 N.E.2d 1262 (Supreme Court of Indiana, 1996) (statement to paralegal is protected by attorney-client privilege).
- *Van Eaton v. Fink*, 697 N.E.2d 490 (Court of Appeals of Indiana, 1998) (paralegal admits to assisting attorney in fabricating evidence; paralegal sued for defamation).
- *Whitehead v. Indiana*, 511 N.E.2d 284 (Supreme Court of Indiana, 1987) (paralegal allowed to sit at counsel's table during trial).
- *Alston v. DeBruyn*, 13 F.3d 1036 (U.S. Court of Appeals, 7th Circuit, 1994) (paralegal assistance in prison).

## Iowa

### ETHICAL RULES AND GUIDELINES IN IOWA

A lawyer often delegates tasks required in performance of the client's legal services to clerks, secretaries and other nonlawyer personnel employed by the lawyer. Such delegation which extends beyond duties merely ministerial in nature is proper under the following circumstances:

(1) If it is for the purposes of (a) investigation of a factual situation or consultation with a lawyer's client for the purpose, only, of obtaining factual information; or (b) legal research; or (c) preparation or selection of legal instruments and documents, provided, however, that in each such situation the delegated work will assist the employer-lawyer in carrying the matter to a completed service either through the lawyer's personal examination and approval thereof or by other additional participation by the lawyer. However, the delegated work must be such as loses its separate identity and becomes the service or is merged in the service of the lawyer.

(2) The lawyer must maintain an initial, continuing and direct relationship with the client, directly supervise the delegated work, and assume complete professional responsibility for the work product. This requirement must not be ignored by a lawyer or given superficial recognition.

(3) The lawyer shall not permit employed laypersons to counsel the lawyer's clients about legal matters, appear in any court or administrative proceeding except to the extent authorized by court rule or administrative rule or regulation, or otherwise engage in the unauthorized practice of law. A lawyer should recognize the importance of being present, if practicable, when a client executes a will, contract, deed or other legal document, to insure that it is executed in compliance with the law and to answer the client's questions. A lawyer has a continuing affirmative duty to preserve and en-

hance the public's confidence in the legal profession. This is best accomplished when the client has direct access to a lawyer for the purpose of asking for and receiving legal advice prior to or at the time the client takes any contemplated legal action.

(4) A nonlawyer employed by a lawyer, law firm, agency or other employer may be referred to as a legal assistant if the majority of his or her job responsibilities include duties as defined in EC 3-6 (1). Such a legal assistant and the responsible supervising lawyer are at all times subject to all the provisions of EC 3-6. Such a legal assistant may be furnished with, and use, a professional card. The card must contain the following information on its face: Name; "Legal Assistant" centered immediately below the name; the name of the lawyer, law firm, agency or other employer whose lawyer is authorizing the issuance of the card; name of the employer or agency, if applicable; address and telephone number of the attorney, law firm, agency or other employer.

(5) When communicating with persons outside the law office, including other lawyers, a nonlawyer employed by a lawyer must disclose the nonlawyer's status. The disclosure must be made in a way that avoids confusion. With respect to oral communications, disclosure must be made at the outset of the conversation. It is permissible for layperson office personnel to sign letters on the firm's stationery as long as the nonlawyer status is clearly indicated.

(6) The supervising lawyer must exercise care to insure nonlawyer personnel comply with all applicable provisions of the Code of Professional Responsibility. This includes the obligation referred to in DR 4-101 (D) and EC 4-2 to see that such employees preserve and refrain from using the confidence and secrets of the lawyer's clients. Ethical Consideration 3-6, *Code of Professional Responsibility*. Rule 32.EC 3-6, *Iowa Code Annotated*.

A legal assistant who has passed the Certified Legal Assistant (CLA) exam of the National Association of Legal Assistants may *not* sign law firm correspondence with the designation "CLA, Legal Assistant" or "Certified Legal Assistant," since the public might be misled about his or her nonattorney status. A reader might think that *CLA* was a legal degree. Iowa State Bar Ass'n, *Opinion 88–5* (9/9/88), and *Opinion 88–19* (6/8/89). It is proper, however, to sign the letter with the title *Legal Assistant* or *Paralegal. Opinion 89–22* (12/8/89).

Paralegals and other nonattorney employees may not be listed on the law firm letterhead. Iowa State Bar Ass'n, *Opinion 87–18* (2/2/88). The office of the county public defender may not list the names of nonattorney personnel on its letterhead. *Opinion 89–35* (12/14/89).

A sign outside the door of a law firm may not list the name of nonattorney employees even though they are called *legal assistants*. Iowa State Bar Ass'n, *Opinion 89–23* (12/26/88). A law firm may not list its paralegals or other nonattorney employees in law directories such as *Martindale-Hubbell*. Iowa State Bar Ass'n, *Opinion 92–33* (5/27/93).

As an incentive, a law firm can pay a paralegal a percentage of the total income it earns as long as the compensation relates to the firm's profits and not the receipt of specific legal fees. Iowa State Bar Ass'n, *Opinion 90–9* (8/23/90).

It would be the unauthorized practice of law for a paralegal to represent a client in Small Claims Court. Iowa State Bar Ass'n, *Opinion 89–30* (12/8/89), and *Opinion 88–18* (2/20/89). Nor can a nonattorney represent someone before the city Civil Service Commission. *Opinion 92–18* (12/3/92).

It is unethical for an attorney to allow his or her paralegal to ask questions at a deposition even though the paralegal is supervised. Iowa Supreme Court Board of Professional Ethics and Conduct, *Opinion 96–03* (8/29/96).

In a Section 341 bankruptcy proceeding, a paralegal cannot sit with a debtor at the counsel table in the absence of the paralegal's supervising attorney. The paralegal can help the debtor find things in the schedule but cannot counsel the debtor. Iowa State Bar Ass'n, *Opinion 92–24* (2/28/93).

A retired attorney who is still licensed cannot function as a paralegal in a law office. Iowa State Bar Ass'n, *Opinion 94–1* (9/13/94).

## DEFINING THE PRACTICE OF LAW IN IOWA

Ethical Consideration 3-5, *Code of Professional Responsibility* (*Iowa Code Annotated*): It is neither necessary nor desirable to attempt the formulation of a single, specific definition of what constitutes the practice of law. However, the practice of law includes, but is not limited to, representing another before the courts; giving of legal advice and counsel to others relating to their rights and obligations under the law; and preparation or approval of the use of legal instruments by which legal rights of others are either obtained, secured or transferred even if such matters never become the subject of a court proceeding.

Court Rule 121.3(i)(5) (*Iowa Code Annotated*, chapter 602): Clients' security trust fund of the bar of Iowa. The practice of law as that term is employed in these rules includes the examination of abstracts, consummation of real estate transactions, preparation of legal briefs, deeds, buy and sell agreements, contracts, wills and tax returns as well as the representation of others in any Iowa courts, the right to represent others in any Iowa courts, or to regularly prepare legal instruments, secure legal rights, advise others as to their legal rights or the effect of contemplated actions upon their legal rights, or to hold oneself out to so do; or to be one who instructs others in legal rights. . . .

## IOWA ETHICS AND PRACTICE RULES ON THE INTERNET

www.law.cornell.edu/ethics/iowa.html

www.crossingthebar.com/IA-UPL.htm

## PARALEGALS (AND OTHER NONATTORNEYS) IN COURT

■ *Iowa Supreme Court Bd. of Professional Ethics and Conduct v. Herrera*, 626 N.W.2d 107 (Supreme Court of Iowa, 2001) (attorney disciplined for failure to supervise paralegal adequately).

■ *Committee on Professional Ethics . . . v. Lawler*, 342 N.W.2d 486 (Supreme Court of Iowa, 1984) (attorney disciplined for fee splitting with a nonattorney and failing to supervise his paralegal).

■ *Committee on Professional Ethics . . . v. Zimmerman*, 465 N.W.2d 288 (Supreme Court of Iowa, 1991) (attorney confused on how to bill for paralegal time; attorney disciplined for charging excessive and duplicative fees).

■ *Foxley Cattle Co. v. Grain Dealers . . .* 142 Federal Rules Decisions 677, 681 (U.S. District Court, S.D. Iowa, 1992) (attorney's claim for 8.8 hours to prepare a motion is excessive; "[t]his document easily could have been prepared by a legal assistant in two to three hours.").

# KANSAS

## ETHICAL RULES AND GUIDELINES IN KANSAS

Legal assistants may be listed on law firm letterhead if their nonattorney status is clear and they have achieved some minimal training as a legal assistant over and above that customarily given legal secretaries. Supervised nonattorney employees may also have their own business cards. Kansas Bar Ass'n, *Opinion 92–15* (12/2/92). This overrules *Opinion 88–02* (7/15/88), which did *not* allow legal assistant names on attorney letterhead. See also *Opinion 82–38* (11/4/82).

A legal assistant can use a business card that prints the name of his or her law firm if the legal assistant is identified as such. Kansas Bar Ass'n, *Opinion 85–4*. This overrules *Opinion 84–18*.

Clients must be fully informed that the legal assistant is not an attorney. An attorney shall not share legal fees with a legal assistant, meaning that no form of compensation must be tied to a particular fee. A legal assistant shall not be compensated for recommending an attorney. At the beginning of a professional contact, the legal assistant should disclose that he or she is not an attorney. A legal assistant can sign correspondence on law firm letterhead if the signature is followed by a designation that makes clear he or she is not an attorney. If an attorney accepts a case in which the legal assistant has a conflict of interest, the attorney should exclude the legal assistant from participating in that case. The client must be told of this conflict. Kansas Bar Ass'n Committee on Legal Assistants, *Standards and Guidelines for the Utilization of Legal Assistants in Kansas* (12/2/88).

## DEFINING THE PRACTICE OF LAW IN KANSAS

*Kansas v. Williams*, 793 P.2d 234, 240 (Supreme Court of Kansas, 1990): In determining what constitutes the "practice of law" no precise, all-encompassing definition is advisable, even if it were possible. Every matter asserting the unauthorized practice of law must be considered on its own facts on a case-by-case basis. . . . "As the term is generally understood, the practice of law is the doing or performing of services in a court of justice, in any matter depending therein, throughout its various stages, and in conformity to the adopted rules of procedure. But in a larger sense it includes legal advice and counsel, and the preparation of legal instruments and contracts by which legal rights are secured, although such matters may or may not be depending in a court." . . . [T]he practice of law [is] "the rendition of services requiring the knowledge and application of legal principles and technique to serve the interests of another with his consent." . . . "It is clearly the prerogative of the Supreme Court to define the practices of law: It is unnecessary here to explore the limits of judicial power conferred by [Article 3, Sec. 1, of the Kansas Constitution], but suffice it to say that the practice of law is so intimately connected and bound up with the exercise of judicial power in the administration of justice that the right to regulate the practice naturally and logically belongs to the judicial department of the government. . . . Included in that power is the supreme court's inherent right to prescribe conditions for admission to the Bar, to define, supervise, regulate and control the practice of law, whether in or out of court, and this is so notwithstanding acts of the legislature in the exercise of its police power to protect the public interest and welfare.

## KANSAS ETHICS AND PRACTICE RULES ON THE INTERNET

www.law.cornell.edu/ethics/kansas.html

www.kscourts.org/ctruls/atrul226.htm

www.crossingthebar.com/KS-UPL.htm

## PARALEGALS (AND OTHER NONATTORNEYS) IN COURT

- *Zimmerman v. Mahaska Bottling Co.*, 19 P.3d 784 (Supreme Court of Kansas, 2001) (when a nonlawyer moves from one private firm to another where the two firms are involved in pending litigation and represent adverse parties, a firm may avoid disqualification if (1) the nonlawyer employee has not acquired material and confidential information regarding the litigation or (2) if the client of the former firm waives disqualification and approves of the use of a screening device or Chinese Wall).
- *In re Arabia*, 19 P.3d 113 (Supreme Court of Kansas, 2001) (attorney gave his paralegals too little direction and supervision regarding the quantity of research they performed).
- *Hawkins v. Dennis*, 905 P.2d 678 (Supreme Court of Kansas, 1995) (attorney blames paralegal for errors).

- *In the Matter of Wilkinson*, 834 P.2d 1356 (Supreme Court of Kansas, 1992) (disbarred attorney can work as a paralegal or law clerk; the work must be exclusively of a preparatory nature).
- *Ortega v. City of Kansas City*, 659 F. Supp. 1201 (U.S. District Court, Kansas, 1987) (paralegal's presence at trial was not necessary; therefore, paralegal fees for time spent at trial are denied).

# Kentucky

## ETHICAL RULES AND GUIDELINES IN KENTUCKY

*Definition:* A paralegal is a person under the supervision and direction of a licensed lawyer, who may apply knowledge of law and legal procedures in rendering direct assistance to lawyers engaged in legal research; design, develop or plan modifications or new procedures, techniques, services, processes or applications; prepare or interpret legal documents and write detailed procedures for practicing in certain fields of law; select, compile and use technical information from such references as digests, encyclopedias or practice manuals; and analyze and follow procedural problems that involve independent decisions. Kentucky Paralegal Code, *Supreme Court Rule 3.700.*

The letterhead of an attorney can include the name of a paralegal. An attorney's name can appear on the business card of a paralegal if the latter's nonattorney status is clear. An attorney shall not share, on a proportionate basis, legal fees with a paralegal. When dealing with a client, a paralegal must disclose at the outset that he or she is not an attorney. This disclosure must be made to anyone who may have reason to believe that the paralegal is an attorney or is associated with an attorney. Kentucky Paralegal Code, *Supreme Court Rule 3.700.*

Kentucky Bar Association, *KBA U-47* (1994): A paralegal can be outside the office alone talking with clients if: (1) it is made clear that the paralegal is not a lawyer; (2) the lawyer discusses the specific issues with the paralegal both before the paralegal-client discussions and afterwards; and (3) the attorney accepts full responsibility for the paralegal's actions and advice.

Without client consent, it is unethical for an attorney to charge a client for paralegal services when the attorney's contract with the client calls for a statutory-set fee, a lump-sum fee, or a contingent fee. The attorney who charges an hourly rate *can* charge for paralegal services, which may be separately stated. Kentucky Bar Ass'n, *Opinion E-303* (5/1985).

To avoid disqualification, a law firm that hires a paralegal who brings a conflict of interest because of prior employment must screen the paralegal from the case in which the conflict arises and take other steps to avoid a breach of confidentiality. Kentucky Bar Ass'n, *Opinion E-308* (1985).

A suspended attorney may work in a law firm as a paralegal after the period of his suspension has expired, even if he has not been reinstated. Kentucky Bar Ass'n, *Opinion E-336* (9/1989).

A paralegal cannot appear in court on motion day or for the motion docket. Kentucky Bar Ass'n, *Opinion E-266* (11/1982).

A lay assistant cannot take (i.e., conduct) a deposition. Kentucky Bar Ass'n, *Opinion E-341* (1990).

Independent paralegals cannot provide legal services to the public without attorney supervision. Kentucky Bar Ass'n, *Opinion U-45* (1992).

A nonattorney cannot represent a corporation except in small claims court. Kentucky Bar Ass'n, *Opinion E-344* (1991).

A nonattorney nurse ombudsman cannot represent a nursing home patient before an administrative agency unless federal law allows it. Kentucky Bar Ass'n, *Opinion U-46* (1994).

## DEFINING THE PRACTICE OF LAW IN KENTUCKY

§ 3.020 (*Rules of the Kentucky Supreme Court*): The practice of law is any service rendered involving legal knowledge or legal advice, whether of representation, counsel or advocacy in or out of court, rendered in respect to the rights, duties, obligations, liabilities, or business relations of one requiring the services. But nothing herein shall prevent any natural person not holding himself out as a practicing attorney from drawing any instrument to which he is a party without consideration unto himself therefor. An appearance in the small claims division of the district court by a person who is an officer of or who is regularly employed in a managerial capacity by a corporation or partnership which is a party to the litigation in which the appearance is made shall not be considered an unauthorized practice of law.

## IMPORTANT KENTUCKY LAWS ON PARALEGALS

- Rule 6.24, *Kentucky Rules of Criminal Procedure* (*Kentucky Revised Statutes Annotated*): (Prior judicial approval for grand jury subpoena of an attorney or attorney's agent to obtain evidence concerning attorney's client.) A prosecutor shall not in comparable circumstances subpoena an agent of the attorney, such as an investigator or a paralegal, without prior judicial approval.
- Rule 18, *Rules of Court* (*Kentucky Revised Statutes Annotated*): Uniform Local Rules of the Circuit and District Courts of Boone, Campbell, Gallatin and Kenton Counties. B. Persons Permitted Inside the Bar of the Courtroom. Unless otherwise ordered by the Court, in all proceedings held in open Court, only the parties, the witnesses when actually testifying, the jury, if any, attorneys duly admitted to practice before the Court and paralegals or legal assistants working under their direction, the sheriff and/or deputies, the clerk and/or deputies, bailiffs; and

other officers and employees with the Court's permission shall be permitted inside the bar of the courtroom.

## KENTUCKY ETHICS AND PRACTICE RULES ON THE INTERNET

www.law.cornell.edu/ethics/kentucky.html
www2.law.cornell.edu/cgi-bin/foliocgi.exe/ky-code?
www.uky.edu/Law/kyethics
www.crossingthebar.com/KY-UPL.htm

## PARALEGALS (AND OTHER NONATTORNEYS) IN COURT

- *Turner v. Kentucky Bar Ass'n*, 980 S.W. 2d 560 (Supreme Court of Kentucky, 1998) (a statute authorizing nonlawyers to represent parties in worker's compensation proceedings violated constitutional principle of separation of powers; nonlawyer worker's compensation specialists did not engage in unauthorized practice of law when processing claims while supervised by an attorney; nonlawyers could not represent parties before any adjudicative tribunal).
- *Wal-Mart Stores, Inc. v. Dickinson*, 29 S.W.3d 796 (Supreme Court of Kentucky, 2000) (work product prepared by a paralegal is protected with equal force by attorney work product rule as is any trial preparation material prepared by an attorney in anticipation of litigation; the attorney-client privilege applies with equal force to paralegals).
- *Wyatt, Tarrant & Combs v. Williams*, 892 S.W.2d 584 (Supreme Court of Kentucky, 1995) (paralegal works on tobacco litigation at law firm; when the paralegal stopped working at the firm, he took copies of some of the tobacco litigation documents with him; law firm seeks injunction against the paralegal to prevent disclosure of the contents of these "stolen" documents). (See discussion of this case in chapter 5.)
- *Kentucky Bar Ass'n v. Legal Alternatives, Inc.*, 792 S.W.2d 368 (Supreme Court of Kentucky, 1990) (independent paralegals sued for unauthorized practice of law).
- *In re Belknap, Inc.*, 103 Bankruptcy Reporter 842, 844 (U.S. Bankruptcy Court, W.D. Kentucky, 1989) (in the award of fees: "Senior partners should not perform services which could be as competently performed by associates or paralegals; paralegals should not be used to perform tasks which are clerical in nature.").

# LOUISIANA

## ETHICAL RULES AND GUIDELINES IN LOUISIANA

An attorney may pay a paralegal or legal assistant a salary and charge clients for their services at a rate greater than their actual salary. *Docket: 96–00068.*

An attorney engaged in debt collection may not pay a nonlawyer a salary plus a bonus that is linked to increased revenues in the collections area. *Docket: 95–00098.*

## DEFINING THE PRACTICE OF LAW IN LOUISIANA

§ 37 : 212 (*West's Louisiana Statutes Annotated*): A. The practice of law means and includes: (1) In a representative capacity, the appearance as an advocate, or the drawing of papers, pleadings or documents, or the performance of any act in connection with pending or prospective proceedings before any court of record in this state; or (2) For a consideration, reward, or pecuniary benefit, present or anticipated, direct or indirect; (a) The advising or counseling of another as to secular law; (b) In behalf of another, the drawing or procuring, or the assisting in the drawing or procuring of a paper, document, or instrument affecting or relating to secular rights; (c) The doing of any act, in behalf of another, tending to obtain or secure for the other the prevention or the redress of a wrong or the enforcement or establishment of a right; or (d) Certifying or giving opinions as to title to immovable property or any interest therein or as to the rank or priority or validity of a lien, privilege or mortgage as well as the preparation of acts of sale, mortgages, credit sales or any acts or other documents passing titles to or encumbering immovable property.

B. Nothing in this Section prohibits any person from attending to and caring for his own business, claims, or demands; or from preparing abstracts of title; or from insuring titles to property, movable or immovable, or an interest therein, or a privilege and encumbrance thereon, but every title insurance contract relating to immovable property must be based upon the certification or opinion of a licensed Louisiana attorney authorized to engage in the practice of law. Nothing in this Section prohibits any person from performing, as a notary public, any act necessary or incidental to the exercise of the powers and functions of the office of notary public, as those powers are delineated in Louisiana Revised Statutes of 1950, Title 35, Section 1, et seq.

C. Nothing in this Section shall prohibit any partnership, corporation, or other legal entity from asserting any claim, not exceeding five thousand dollars, or defense pertaining to an open account or promissory note, or suit for eviction of tenants on its own behalf in the courts of limited jurisdiction on its own behalf through a duly authorized partner, shareholder, office, employee, or duly authorized agent or representative. No partnership, corporation, or other entity may assert any claim on behalf of another entity or any claim assigned to it.

## LOUISIANA ETHICS AND PRACTICE RULES ON THE INTERNET

www.law.cornell.edu/ethics/louisiana.html
www2.law.cornell.edu/cgi-bin/foliocgi.exe/la-code?
www.ladb.org/ladblp/lpext.dll/?f=templates&fn=main-j.htm
www.crossingthebar.com/LA-UPL.htm

## PARALEGALS (AND OTHER NONATTORNEYS) IN COURT

- *In re Watley*, 802 So. 2d 593 (Supreme Court of Louisiana, 2001) (an attorney's entry into a contract calling for fee splitting with an agency providing secretarial and paralegal support violated disciplinary rule prohibiting fee sharing with nonlawyers (see also *"We the People" Paralegal Services v. Watley* 766 So. 2d 744 (Court of Appeals of Louisiana, 2000)).
- *In re Cudzik*, 738 So. 2d 1054 (Supreme Court of Louisiana, 1999) (a disbarred attorney acting as a paralegal engages in the unauthorized practice of law).
- *State v. Diaz*, 708 So. 2d 1192 (Court of Appeal of Louisiana, 1998) (paralegal tells authorities of possible fraud committed by her attorney supervisor).
- *United States ex rel. Garibaldi v. Orleans Parish School Bd.*, 46 F. Supp. 2d 546 (U.S. District Court, Louisiana, 1999) (paralegal costs may fall into the category of attorney's fees if the work done by the paralegal was legal work and not clerical work).
- *Louisiana State Bar v. Edwins*, 540 So. 2d 294 (Supreme Court of Louisiana, 1989) (an attorney can be disbarred for delegating too much to a paralegal and for failing to supervise the paralegal).
- *Louisiana State Bar v. Lindsay*, 553 So. 2d 807 (Supreme Court of Louisiana, 1989) (an attorney charged with professional misconduct tries to shift the blame to his paralegal).
- *Salsbury v. Salsbury*, 658 So. zd 734 (Court of Appeal of Louisiana, 1995) (award of paralegal fees).
- *United States v. Cabra*, 622 F.2d 182 (U.S. Circuit Court, 5th Circuit, 1980) (it is improper to impound a paralegal's trial notes taken during a federal trial).

# Maine

## ETHICAL RULES AND GUIDELINES IN MAINE

The names of paralegals can be printed on a firm's letterhead as long as it is not misleading. Maine Board of Overseers of the Bar, *Opinion 34* (1/17/83).

An attorney cannot form a partnership or professional corporation with a nonattorney to provide legal and nonlegal services to clients. Maine Board of Overseers of the Bar, *Opinion 79* (5/6/87).

Other Opinions of the Maine Board of Overseers of the Bar involving nonattorneys: *69* (3/17/86); *99* (9/6/89); *102* (2/2/90).

## DEFINING THE PRACTICE OF LAW IN MAINE

Thomas Shaffer, *The Practice of Law with Non-Lawyer Colleagues in Maine*, 14 Maine Bar Journal 202, 203 (July 1999): [P]lease remember that the [Professional Ethics Commission of the Board of Overseers of the Maine State Bar Association] has had to cope with the fact that Maine law has never defined the practice of law.

§ 807 (*Maine Revised Statutes Annotated*): 1. Prohibition. No person may practice law or profess to practice law within the State or before its courts, or demand or receive any remuneration for those services rendered in this State, unless that person has been admitted to the bar of this State and has complied with section 806-A, or unless that person has been admitted to try cases in the courts of this State under Section 802. . . . 3. Application. This section shall not be construed to apply to: . . . B. A person pleading or managing that person's own cause in court; C. An officer or authorized employee of a corporation, partnership, sole proprietorship or governmental entity, who is not an attorney, but is appearing for that organization: (1) In an action cognizable as a small claim under Title 14, chapter 738. . . . G. A person who is not an attorney, but is representing a party in any hearing, action or proceeding before the Workers' Compensation Board as provided in Title 39-A, section 317; . . .

## IMPORTANT MAINE LAWS ON PARALEGALS

§ 921, title 4 (*Maine Revised Statutes Annotated*): 1. Paralegal and legal assistant. "Paralegal" and "legal assistant" mean a person, qualified by education, training or work experience, who is employed or retained by an attorney, law office, corporation, governmental agency or other entity and who performs specifically delegated substantive legal work for which an attorney is responsible.

§ 922, title 4 (*Maine Revised Statutes Annotated*):

1. Prohibition. A person may not use the title "paralegal" or "legal assistant" unless the person meets the definition in section 921, subsection 1.

2. Penalty. A person who violates subsection 1 commits a civil violation for which a forfeiture of not more than $1000 may be adjudged.

## MAINE ETHICS AND PRACTICE RULES ON THE INTERNET
www.law.cornell.edu/ethics/maine.html
www.mebaroverseers.org/recent.asp#A2
www.mebaroverseers.org/code.html
www.crossingthebar.com/ME-UPL.htm

## PARALEGALS (AND OTHER NONATTORNEYS) IN COURT

- *Maine v. DeMotte*, 669 A.2d 1331 (Supreme Judicial Court of Maine, 1996) (Chinese Wall built around paralegal to prevent disclosure of privileged communications and a conflict of interest).
- *First NH Banks Granite State v. Scarborough*, 615 A.2d 248, 251 (Supreme Judicial Court of Maine, 1992) (allows paralegal fees; we "adopt no talismanic formula with regard to the inclusion of paralegal fees").
- *Wilcox v. Stratton Lumber, Inc.*, 921 F. Supp. 837, 847 (U.S. District Court, Maine, 1996) (parties "seek to bill an excessive amount of paralegal time for unnecessary effort").

# MARYLAND

## ETHICAL RULES AND GUIDELINES IN MARYLAND
Legal assistants can have business cards as long as their legal assistant status is designated. Maryland Bar Ass'n, *Ethics Opinion 77–28* (10/18/76).

An attorney can list the names of paralegals on office letterhead or on the office door as long as their nonattorney status is designated. Maryland Bar Ass'n, *Ethics Opinion 81–69* (5/29/81).

A nonattorney once worked for attorney #A. She now works for attorney #B. These attorneys are opponents on a case in litigation. This case was underway when the nonattorney worked for attorney #A. If effective screening (i.e., a "Chinese Wall") is used to insulate the nonattorney from the case, attorney #B does not have to withdraw from the litigation. Maryland Bar Ass'n, *Ethics Docket 90–17* (1990).

An attorney can hire a freelance paralegal as long as the latter is supervised at all times by the attorney who takes steps to ensure there is no disclosure of client confidences. Maryland Bar Ass'n, *Opinion 86–83* (7/23/86).

It is unethical to pay a bonus to a paralegal for bringing business to the office. Maryland State Bar Ass'n, *Ethics Docket 86–57* (2/12/86).

An attorney cannot divide a fee with a nonattorney. Maryland Bar Ass'n, *Opinion 86–59* (2/12/86).

A legal assistant cannot be paid a percentage of the recovery in a case on which the assistant works. Maryland Bar Ass'n, *Ethics Opinion 84–103* (1984).

An attorney can rent office space to a nonattorney as long as confidentiality of the attorney's clients is not compromised. Maryland Bar Ass'n, *Ethics Opinion 89–45* (6/12/89).

It is unethical for a sole practitioner to hire as a paralegal his disbarred former associate. The public would think the paralegal is an attorney. Maryland State Bar Ass'n, *Ethics 79–41*. On the same issue, see *Attorney Grievance Commission of Maryland v. James*, 666 A.2d 1246 (Court of Appeals of Maryland, 1995).

## DEFINING THE PRACTICE OF LAW IN MARYLAND

§ 10-101 (*Annotated Code of Maryland, Business Occupations & Professions Code*): Lawyers.

(h) (1) "Practice law" means to engage in any of the following activities:

(i) giving legal advice;

(ii) representing another person before a unit of the State government or of a political subdivision; or

(iii) performing any other service that the Court of Appeals defines as practicing law.

(2) "Practice law" includes:

(i) advising in the administration of probate of estates of decedents in an orphans' court of the State;

(ii) preparing an instrument that affects title to real estate;

(iii) preparing or helping in the preparation of any form or document that is filed in a court or affects a case that is or may be filed in a court; or

(iv) giving advice about a case that is or may be filed in a court.

*Opinion 95–056* (Office of the Attorney General of the State of Maryland (December 19, 1995)): The opinion discusses the scope of the practice of law in Maryland and the distinction between giving legal advice and providing legal information; for the text of this opinion, see chapter 4.

## MARYLAND ETHICS AND PRACTICE RULES ON THE INTERNET

www.law.cornell.edu/ethics/maryland.html
www2.law.cornell.edu/cgi-bin/foliocgi.exe/md-code?
www2.law.cornell.edu/cgi-bin/foliocgi.exe/md-narr?
www.crossingthebar.com/MD-UPL.htm

## PARALEGALS (AND OTHER NONATTORNEYS) IN COURT

- *Attorney Grievance Commission v. Brennan*, 714 A.2d 157 (Court of Appeals of Maryland, 1998) (it is permissible for a disbarred or suspended lawyer to work as a paralegal, provided that proper procedures and constraints are in place to assure that no one is confused as to the person's status as a paralegal) (work performed by a paralegal does constitute the practice of law; whether it is the unauthorized practice of law depends on the extent to which it is supervised by the lawyer).
- *Attorney Grievance Commission of Maryland v. Wright*, 507 A.2d 618, 622, 623 (Court of Appeals of Maryland, 1986) (tasks were performed by paralegals "without detailed direction and under minimal supervision by way of review of the final product"; the dollar value of non-legal work "is not enhanced just because a lawyer does it").
- *Sheppard v. Riverview Nursing Centre, Inc.*, 870 F. Supp. 1369, 1380 (U.S. District Court, Maryland, 1994) (paralegal fees reduced; "[t]he Court regards the 33.7 hours [the paralegal] spent outlining and summarizing various depositions to be excessive and unnecessary in this straightforward case").
- *In re Ward*, 190 Bankruptcy Reporter 242, 248 (U.S. Bankruptcy Court, Maryland, 1995) ("[w]hen seeking compensation for clerical services performed by an attorney or a paralegal, an applicant must provide sufficient information enabling the court to make a determination as to why such services were performed by an attorney or paralegal as opposed to a paralegal or secretary, respectively").

- *Attorney Grievance Commission of Maryland v. Hallmon*, 681 A.2d 510 (Court of Appeals of Maryland, 1996) (attorney charged with aiding the unauthorized practice of law by one of his nonattorney employees).

# MASSACHUSETTS

## ETHICAL RULES AND GUIDELINES IN MASSACHUSETTS

It is unethical for an insurance company attorney to delegate tasks to paralegals without first determining that they are competent to perform those tasks even if the attorney's supervisor/boss requires such delegation. Massachusetts Bar Ass'n, *Opinion 00–4* (9/29/00).

Paralegal names can be printed on a firm's letterhead if their nonattorney status is clear. Massachusetts Bar Ass'n, *Ethics Opinion 83–10* (11/29/83).

A paralegal can sign his or her name on law firm letterhead. Massachusetts Bar Ass'n, *Ethics Opinion 73–2*.

A law firm cannot pay its office administrator (a nonattorney) a percentage of the firm's profits in addition to his fixed salary. Massachusetts Bar Ass'n, *Opinion 84–2* (1984).

## DEFINING THE PRACTICE OF LAW IN MASSACHUSETTS

*In re Opinion of the Justices*, 194 N.E. 313, 317, 318 (Supreme Judicial Court of Massachusetts, 1935): Practice of law under modern conditions consists in no small part of work performed outside of any court and having no immediate relation to proceedings in court. It embraces conveyancing, the giving of legal advice on a large variety of subjects, and the preparation and execution of legal instruments covering an extensive field of business and trust relations and other affairs. Although these transactions may have no direct connection with court proceedings, they are always subject to become involved in litigation. They require in many aspects a high degree of legal skill, a wide experience with men and affairs, and great capacity for adaptation to difficult and complex situations. These "customary functions of an attorney or counsellor at law . . . bear an intimate relation to the administration of justice by the courts. No valid distinction, so far as concerns the questions set forth in the order, can be drawn between that part of the work of the lawyer which involves appearance in court and that part which involves advice and drafting of instruments in his office. The work of the office lawyer is the groundwork for future possible contests in courts. It has profound effect on the whole scheme of the administration of justice. It is performed with that possibility in mind, and otherwise would hardly be needed. In this country the practice of law includes both forms of legal service; there is no separation, as in England, into barristers and solicitors. It is of importance to the welfare of the public that these manifold customary functions be performed by persons possessed of adequate learning and skill, of sound moral character, and acting at all times under the heavy trust obligation to clients which rests upon all attorneys. . . .

Individuals have been permitted to manage, prosecute or defend their own actions, suits, and proceedings, and to defend prosecutions against themselves except when the public welfare demanded otherwise, and this does not constitute the practice of law. . . . The occasional drafting of simple deeds, and other legal instruments when not conducted as an occupation or yielding substantial income may fall outside the practice of the law. The gratuitous furnishing of legal aid to the poor and unfortunate without means in the pursuit of any civil remedy, as matter of charity, the search of records of real estate to ascertain what may there be disclosed without giving opinion or advice as to the legal effect of what is found, the work of an accountant dissociated from legal advice, do not constitute the practice of law. There may be other kindred pursuits of the same character. All these activities, however, lie close to the border line and may easily become or be accompanied by practice of the law. The giving of advice as to investments in stocks, bonds and other securities, in real or personal property, and in making tax returns falls within the same category.

## MASSACHUSETTS ETHICS AND PRACTICE RULES ON THE INTERNET

www.law.cornell.edu/ethics/massachusetts.html
www.massbar.org/ethics
www.crossingthebar.com/MA-UPL.htm

## PARALEGALS (AND OTHER NONATTORNEYS) IN COURT

- *Matter of Eisenhauer*, 689 N.E.2d 783 (Supreme Judicial Court of Massachusetts, 1998) (attorney disciplined for charging attorney rates for paralegal time).
- *Britt v. Rosenberg*, 665 N.E.2d 1022, 1023 (Appeals Court of Massachusetts, 1996) (paralegal lies to court and opposing counsel about why the plaintiff failed to appear).
- *DeVaux v. American Home Assurance Co.*, 444 N.E.2d 355 (Supreme Judicial Court of Massachusetts, 1983) (nonattorney employee negligently misfiles a letter seeking legal assistance; client sues attorney for legal malpractice after the statute of limitations runs out on her claim).
- *Crance v. Commissioner of Public Welfare*, 507 N.E.2d 751, 753 (Supreme Judicial Court of Massachusetts, 1987) (award of paralegal fees where the paralegal's work was not merely ministerial but required the exercise of judgment).
- *In re Smuggler's Beach Properties*, 149 Bankruptcy Reporter 740, 743 (U.S. Bankruptcy Court, District for Massachusetts, 1993) (failure to delegate appropriate tasks to paralegals may warrant reduction in attorney fees).
- *In re Cumberland Farms, Inc.*, 154 Bankruptcy Reporter 9, 11 (U.S. Bankruptcy Court, District for Massachusetts, 1993) (attorney rewarded for efficiency in using paralegals).

# MICHIGAN

## ETHICAL RULES AND GUIDELINES IN MICHIGAN

State Bar Board of Commissioners, *Michigan Guidelines for the Utilization of Legal Assistant Services* (1993) (72 Michigan Bar Journal 563 (June 1993)). *Guideline 1:* An attorney must take reasonable steps to ensure that his or her legal assistant complies with the ethical rules governing Michigan attorneys. *Guideline 2:* The attorney must directly supervise and evaluate assigned tasks. A legal assistant may not convey to persons outside the law firm the legal assistant's opinion on the applicability of laws to particular cases. Legal documents on which a legal assistant works must be signed by an attorney. *Guideline 3:* An attorney cannot delegate to legal assistants the task of establishing an attorney-client relationship or the fee to be paid. *Guideline 4:* A legal assistant may be identified on attorney letterhead and on business cards that mention the law firm's name. *Guideline 5:* The attorney should take reasonable measures to ensure that no conflict of interest is presented arising out of the legal assistant's current or prior employment, or from the legal assistant's other business or personal interests. *Guideline 6:* An attorney can charge a client for legal assistant time if the client consents. *Guideline 7:* An attorney must not split fees with a legal assistant nor pay a legal assistant for referring legal business. A legal assistant can be included in a firm's retirement plan even if based on a profit-sharing arrangement. *Guideline 8:* The attorney should facilitate the legal assistant's participation in continuing legal education and public service activities.

---

Where a paralegal has had access during prior employment to confidential or secret information concerning a legal matter substantially related and materially adverse to a matter in which the new law firm employer is representing a client, the law firm must promptly and adequately screen the nonlawyer from the matter in order to avoid disqualification. State Bar of Michigan, *Opinion RI-285* (12/11/96). See also *Opinion CI-1168* (12/10/86) and *Opinion RI-115* (1/31/92).

Business cards and law firm letterhead can list the name of nonattorney employees with titles such as *legal assistant* or *paralegal*. The public must not be confused as to their nonattorney status. State Bar of Michigan, *Opinion RI-34* (10/25/89).

A law firm may pay a legal assistant compensation based on a set salary and a percentage of the net profits of the practice area in which the legal assistant is involved as long as no payments are made based on fees generated from particular clients. State Bar of Michigan, *Opinion RI-143* (8/25/92).

It is not possible for an attorney to give quality supervision to 24 paralegals located at six separate sites in the state. State Bar of Michigan, *Opinion R-1* (12/16/88).

An attorney's paralegal can represent clients in administrative hearings where authorized by law. The attorney must make sure that this paralegal acts ethically in providing this representation. State Bar of Michigan, *Opinion RI-125* (4/17/92). See also *Opinion RI-103* (10/9/91).

An attorney may not establish a business employing a paralegal who will sell will and trust forms where the paralegal will probably provide consultation and advice to clients. State Bar of Michigan, *Opinion RI-191* (2/14/94).

An attorney cannot avoid all direct client contact by obtaining all information about and from the client through the attorney's paralegal. State Bar of Michigan, *Opinion RI-128* (4/21/92).

When nonattorney employees with access to the files move to another law firm, a Chinese Wall may have to be built around them to prevent the imputed disqualification of the new firm. State Bar of Michigan, *Opinion R-4* (9/22/89).

An attorney is prohibited from representing a client if one of his nonattorney employees will become a witness who will give testimony that is not consistent with the interests of the attorney's client. State Bar of Michigan, *Opinion RI-26* (7/19/89).

Information collected by a legal assistant during an interview is protected against disclosure by the attorney-client privilege. State Bar of Michigan, *Opinion RI-123* (3/13/92).

## DEFINING THE PRACTICE OF LAW IN MICHIGAN

*State Bar of Michigan v. Cramer*, 249 N.W.2d 1, 6–7 (Supreme Court of Michigan, 1976): [T]he Legislature has not seen fit to define what constitutes the "practice of law", and, accordingly, "[t]he formidable task of constructing a definition of the practice of law has largely been left to the judiciary. . . ." We are still of the mind that any attempt to formulate a lasting, all encompassing definition of "practice of law" is doomed to failure "for the reason that under our system of jurisprudence such practice must necessarily change with the ever changing business and social order. . . ." No essential definition of the practice of law has been articulated and the descriptive definitions which have been agreed upon from time to time have only permitted disposition of specific questions. These definitions have been relatively helpful in counseling conduct but have provided no sure guide for the public's protection. A broad definition of the "practice of law" embraces virtually all commercial areas of human endeavor. This, of course, will not do. "It cannot be urged, with reason, that a lawyer must preside over every transaction where written legal forms must be selected and used by an agent for one of the parties. Such a restriction would so paralyze business activities that very few transactions could be expeditiously consummated. . . ." The result of this inability to fashion a definition of "practice of law" to fit every situation "has been a line of decisions consistent only in their inconsistency as the courts have sought to accommodate the need for public protection through restricting the practice of law to members of the bar with the economic and practical realities of modern society."

## IMPORTANT MICHIGAN RULE ON PARALEGALS

Rule 2.626 (*West's Michigan Rules of Court*): An award of attorney fees may include an award for the time and labor of any legal assistant who contributed nonclerical, legal support under the supervision of an attorney, provided the legal assistant meets the criteria set forth in Article 1, § 6 of the Bylaws of the State Bar of Michigan [governing eligibility to become an affiliate member of the State Bar of Michigan].

Article 1, § 6 (*Bylaws of the State Bar of Michigan*): Eligibility for Bar affiliate membership. Any person currently employed or retained by a lawyer, law office, governmental agency or other entity engaged in the practice of law, in a capacity or function which involves the performance under the direction and supervision of an attorney of specifically-delegated substantive legal work, which work, for the most part, requires a sufficient knowledge of legal concepts such that, absent that legal assistant, the attorney would perform the task, and which work is not primarily clerical or secretarial in nature. . . .

## MICHIGAN ETHICS AND PRACTICE RULES ON THE INTERNET

www.law.cornell.edu/ethics/michigan.html
www2.law.cornell.edu/cgi-bin/foliocgi.exe/mi-code?
www.michbar.org/sections/legalassist
www.michbar.org/opinions/ethics
www.crossingthebar.com/MI-UPL.htm

## PARALEGALS (AND OTHER NONATTORNEYS) IN COURT

■ *Michigan v. Hurst*, 517 N.W.2d 858, 862–63 (Court of Appeals of Michigan, 1994) (the "defendant's supplemental appellate brief . . . prepared by an apparently competent legal assistant, sufficiently apprised this court of the finer points of defendant's arguments").

■ *In the Matter of Bright*, 171 Bankruptcy Reporter 799, 802 (U.S. Bankruptcy Court, E.D. Michigan, 1994) (bankruptcy trustee charges paralegal with the unauthorized practice of law in helping the debtor; a disclaimer that one is "only providing 'scrivener' or 'paralegal' services is irrelevant if the nonlawyer in fact engages in the unauthorized practice of law).

■ *State Bar of Michigan v. Cramer*, 249 N.W.2d 1 (Supreme Court of Michigan, 1976) (the unauthorized practice of law and the sale of do-it-yourself divorce kits).

■ *Cobb Publishing Co. v. Hearst Corp.*, 907 F. Supp. 1038 (U.S. District Court, E. D. Michigan, 1995) (Chinese Wall to prevent disqualification of law firm due to conflict of interest; memo sent to all attorneys, paralegals, and other staff to stay away from the contaminated employee).

■ *Kearns v. Ford Motor Co.*, 114 Federal Rules Decisions 57 (U.S. District Court, E.D. Michigan, 1987) (paralegal gives copy of privileged litigation documents to someone with whom she was having a romantic relationship).

## MINNESOTA

### ETHICAL RULES AND GUIDELINES IN MINNESOTA

Paralegal names can be printed on a firm's letterhead, business cards, professional announcement cards, office signs, telephone directory listings, law lists, and legal directory listings if their nonattorney status is clear. Paralegals, so identified, may sign correspondence on behalf of the law firm if acting under an attorney's direction. But they cannot be named on pleadings under any identification. Minnesota Bar Ass'n, *Ethics Opinion 8* (6/26/74; amended 6/18/80 and 12/4/87). On letterheads, see also *Opinion 93* (6/7/84).

It is improper for a lawyer to permit any nonattorney employee to accept a gratuity offered by a court reporting service or other service for which the client is expected to pay unless the client consents. Minnesota Lawyers Professional Responsibility Board, *Opinion 17* (6/18/93).

### DEFINING THE PRACTICE OF LAW IN MINNESOTA

§ 481.02 (*Minnesota Statutes Annotated*): Subdivision 1. Prohibitions. It shall be unlawful for any person or association of persons, except members of the bar of Minnesota admitted and licensed to practice as attorneys at law, to appear as attorney or counselor at law in any action or proceeding in any court in this state to maintain, conduct, or defend the same, except personally as a party thereto in other than a representative capacity, or, by word, sign, letter, or advertisement, to hold out as competent or qualified to give legal advice or counsel, or to prepare legal documents, or as being engaged in advising or counseling in law or acting as attorney or counselor at law, or in furnishing to others the services of a lawyer, or lawyers, or, for a fee or any consideration, to give legal advice or counsel, perform for or furnish to another legal services, or, for or without a fee or any consideration, to prepare, directly or through another, for another person, firm, or corporation, any will or testamentary disposition or instrument of trust serving purposes similar to those of a will, or, for a fee or any consideration, to prepare for another person, firm, or corporation, any other legal document, except as provided in subdivision 3. . . .

Subdivision 3. Permitted actions. The provisions of this section shall not prohibit: . . . (2) a person from drawing a will for another in an emergency if the imminence of death leaves insufficient time to have it drawn and its execution supervised by a licensed attorney-at-law. . . . (5) any bona fide labor organization from giving legal advice to its members in matters arising out of their employment. . . . (14) the delivery of legal services by a specialized legal assistant in accordance with a specialty license issued by the supreme court before July 1, 1995. . . .

Subdivision 3a. Real estate closing services. Nothing in this section shall be construed to prevent a real estate broker, a real estate salesperson, or a real estate closing agent, as defined in section 82.17, from drawing or assisting in drawing papers incident to the sale, trade, lease, or loan of property, or from charging for drawing or assisting in drawing them, except as hereafter provided by the supreme court. . . .

Subdivision 7. Lay assistance to attorneys. Nothing herein contained shall be construed to prevent a corporation from furnishing to any person lawfully engaged in the practice of law, such information or such clerical service in and about the attorney's professional work as, except for the provisions of this section, may be lawful, provided, that at all times the lawyer receiving such information or such services shall maintain full, professional and direct responsibility to the attorney's clients for the information and services so received. . . .

### MINNESOTA ETHICS AND PRACTICE RULES ON THE INTERNET

www.law.cornell.edu/ethics/minnesota.html
www.courts.state.mn.us/lprb/opinions.html
www.crossingthebar.com/MN-UPL.htm

### PARALEGALS (AND OTHER NONATTORNEYS) IN COURT

- *In Re Rubin*, 484 N.W.2d 786 (Supreme Court of Minnesota, 1992) (attorney disciplined for permitting a legal assistant to back-date a signature on a deed).
- *Minnesota v. Richards*, 456 N.W.2d 260 (Supreme Court of Minnesota, 1990) (a county attorney's office is not disqualified from prosecuting the defendant merely because the office hired a paralegal who had previously interviewed for a job with defense counsel).
- *In re Mille Lacs County Attorney Salary and Budget v. County Board of Commissioners*, 422 N.W.2d 291 (Court of Appeals of Minnesota, 1988) (comparison of the role of a legal secretary and a paralegal).
- *Rose v. Neubauer*, 407 N.W.2d 727 (Court of Appeals of Minnesota, 1987) (paralegal files complaint and interrogatories without knowledge of attorney).
- *Narum v. Eli Lilly*, 914 F. Supp. 317 (U.S. District Court, Minnesota, 1996) (affidavit of paralegal, who was also a nurse, is inadmissible because of its unsupported conclusions).
- *Diocese of Winona v. Interstate Fire and Casualty Company*, 916 F. Supp. 923 (U.S. District Court, Minnesota, 1995) (award of paralegal fees).

## MISSISSIPPI

### ETHICAL RULES AND GUIDELINES IN MISSISSIPPI

Paralegal names can be printed on a firm's letterhead if their nonattorney status is clear. The paralegal should not be called a *paralegal associate*, since in common usage the term *associate* carries a connotation of being an attorney in a law firm. Mississippi Bar Ass'n, *Opinion 93* (6/7/84).

An attorney can pay a paralegal a bonus based on the number of her hours billed and collected in excess of a designated minimum. A nonattorney compensation or retirement plan can be based in whole or in part on a profit-sharing arrangement. Mississippi State Bar, *Opinion 154* (9/12/89).

Legal assistants can use the initials *CLA* (Certified Legal Assistant) or *CLAS* (Certified Legal Assistant Specialist) after their names on law firm letterhead as long as the designation is accompanied by language indicating that the legal assistant is not an attorney. These initials indicate the legal assistant has passed the test and met the other requirements of the National Association of Legal Assistants. Mississippi State Bar, *Opinion 223* (1/19/95).

A disbarred or suspended attorney cannot work as a paralegal. Mississippi State Bar, *Opinion 96* (6/7/84). See also *Opinion 171* (6/22/90).

## DEFINING THE PRACTICE OF LAW IN MISSISSIPPI

*Darby v. Mississippi State Board of Bar Admissions*, 185 So. 2d 684, 687 (Supreme Court of Mississippi, 1966): The practice of law includes the drafting or selection of documents, the giving of advice in regard to them, and the using of an informed or trained discretion in the drafting of documents to meet the needs of the person being served. So any exercise of intelligent choice in advising another of his legal rights and duties brings the activity within the practice of the legal profession. . . . The element of compensation for such services may be a factor in determining whether specified conduct constitutes the practice of law, but it is not controlling. The character of the service and its relation to the public interest determines its classification, not whether compensation is charged for it. . . . The objective of both the legislature and the courts in supervising admissions to the bar is the protection of the public against injuries from acts or services, professional in nature, constituting the practice of law, and done or performed by those not deemed to be qualified to perform them. A gratuitous service by a licensed doctor or lawyer is none the less professional. The welfare of the public is the principal consideration. . . . A statute makes it . . . unlawful for any person to engage in the practice of law without a license, stating that any person "who shall for a fee or reward or promise, directly or indirectly," write any paper to be filed in a proceeding or dictate a bill of sale, deed, deed of trust, mortgage, contract, or will, or make or certify to any abstract of title, "shall be held to be engaged in the practice of law." *Miss. Code Ann.* § 8682 (1956).

## MISSISSIPPI ETHICS AND PRACTICE RULES ON THE INTERNET

www.law.cornell.edu/ethics/mississippi.html
www2.law.cornell.edu/cgi-bin/foliocgi.exe/ms-code?

www.msbar.org/opinidx.html
www.crossingthebar.com/MS-UPL.htm

## PARALEGALS (AND OTHER NONATTORNEYS) IN COURT

- *Ivy v. K.D. Merchant*, 666 So. 2d 445 (Supreme Court of Mississippi, 1995) (inmate paralegal assistance; paralegal fined $25 for assisting an inmate who filed a frivolous lawsuit).
- *Williams v. Mississippi State Bar Ass'n*, 492 So. 2d 578 (Supreme Court of Mississippi, 1986) (a disbarred attorney should not act as a paralegal).
- *Minnick v. Mississippi*, 551 So. 2d 77, 101 (Supreme Court of Mississippi, 1988) (lawyer should not use a paralegal "to do his dirty work" in communicating with the other side).
- *Mississippi State Chapter Operation Push v. Mabus*, 788 F. Supp. 1406, 1421 (U.S. District Court, N.D. Mississippi, 1992) (award of paralegal fees criticized: it "is unnecessary to have three paralegals assisting at trial"; "using three paralegals when one would be sufficient").
- *In re White*, 171 Bankruptcy Reporter 554 (U.S. Bankruptcy Court, S.D. Mississippi, 1994) (attorney fees reduced; "too many lawyers are spending too much time on this case"; they "used paralegals to perform secretarial tasks").
- *Martin v. Mabus*, 734 F. Supp. 1216 (U.S. District Court, S.D. Mississippi, 1990) (award of paralegal fees).

# MISSOURI

## ETHICAL RULES AND GUIDELINES IN MISSOURI

*Missouri Bar Guidelines for Practicing with Paralegals. Definition:* A paralegal or legal assistant is a person qualified through education in legal studies, training and/or work experience in a law environment, who is employed or retained by a lawyer, law office, corporate in-house counsel, government agency, or other entity in a capacity or function which involves the performance, under the ultimate direction and supervision of an attorney, of specifically delegated substantive legal work that, for the most part, requires a sufficient knowledge of legal concepts that, absent the paralegal, the attorney would perform.

*Guideline I:* A lawyer is responsible for the professional and ethical conduct of a paralegal under his or her supervision. *Guideline II:* A lawyer shall not assist a paralegal in the performance of an activity that constitutes the unauthorized practice of law (UPL). A lawyer must supervise nonlawyer employees and ensure that their conduct is compatible with the professional obligations of the lawyer. When responding to client questions, paralegals can provide factual and procedural information that does not constitute legal advice. A paralegal can, however, relay advice specifically given to the paralegal by his or her supervising attorney. The lawyer must explain to clients and others what the role of the paralegal is. Paralegal assistance to a lawyer may include (a) researching cases and other legal authority, (b) factual investigation, (c) preparing legal documents, (d) reviewing and organizing case files, (e) assisting at and preparing a case for trial, (f) assisting at depositions, (g) summarizing depositions, (h) drafting interrogatory questions and answers, (i) interviewing clients and witnesses, (j) assisting in court, (k) handling administrative matters, and (l) communicating information to clients and other people. Paralegals cannot take a deposition, but may assist a lawyer at a deposition. *Guideline III:* A lawyer shall not share legal fees with a paralegal, but may include paralegals in a compensation or retirement plan that is based on profit-sharing. To avoid fee-splitting, paralegal compensation cannot be directly tied to particular legal fees or to the outcome of a case, although it can be tied to the profitability of the firm. To preserve a lawyer's independence, a lawyer and a paralegal cannot form a partnership that practices law. Nor can a lawyer practice law with a company or corporation in which a paralegal has an ownership interest or is a director or officer. *Guideline IV:* A lawyer must (a) develop policies that clearly define tasks paralegals can perform, (b) directly supervise the paralegal, (c) be responsible for the paralegal's work product, (d) give the paralegal copies of governing ethical rules and policies, (e) instruct the paralegal on ethical conduct, particularly the need to preserve client confidentiality, (f) check that the paralegal does not create a conflict of interest, and (g) check that the paralegal is qualified by education, training, or experience to act as a paralegal. *Guideline V:* A lawyer must (a) instruct the paralegal to disclose his or her paralegal status in all dealings with any other persons, (b) use the paralegal's title on all communications such as business cards and letterheads, and (c) instruct the paralegal to identify his/her title on written communications to others. A paralegal may sign correspondence on the law firm letterhead provided the signature is followed by an appropriate identifying designation as a paralegal. A paralegal's name can also appear on the letterhead of an office if clearly identified as a paralegal.

---

A paralegal cannot answer a docket call of an attorney. Missouri Bar Ass'n, *Informal Opinion 1* (7/9/82)

It would be an improper splitting of a fee with a paralegal if an attorney agrees not to pay a paralegal unless an entire particular fee is collected. Missouri Bar Ass'n, *Informal Opinion 20* (6/16/78).

## DEFINING THE PRACTICE OF LAW IN MISSOURI

§ 484.010 (*Vernon's Annotated Statutes*): 1. The "practice of the law" is hereby defined to be and is the appearance as an advocate in a representative capacity or the drawing of papers, pleadings or documents or the performance of any act in such capacity in connection with proceedings pending or prospective before any court of record, commissioner, referee or any body, board, committee or commission constituted by law or having authority to settle controversies.

2. The "law business" is hereby defined to be and is the advising or counseling for a valuable consideration of any person, firm, association, or corporation as to any secular law or the drawing or the procuring of or assisting in the drawing for a valuable consideration of any paper, document or instrument affecting or relating to secular rights or the doing of any act for a valuable consideration in a representative capacity, obtaining or tending to obtain or securing or tending to secure for any person, firm, association or corporation any property or property rights whatsoever.

## MISSOURI ETHICS AND PRACTICE RULES ON THE INTERNET

www.mobar.org/pamphlet/pracpara.htm
www.law.cornell.edu/ethics/missouri.html
www2.law.cornell.edu/cgi-bin/foliocgi.exe/mo-code?
www.mobar.net/opinions
www.crossingthebar.com/MO-UPL.htm

## PARALEGALS (AND OTHER NONATTORNEYS) IN COURT

- *Winsor v. Terex-Telelect-Inc.*, 43 S.W.3d 460 (Missouri Court of Appeals, 2001) (default judgments entered after a recently hired paralegal fails to enter a case into the office database; default judgment set aside, however, when court rules the error was negligent, not reckless).
- *Logan v. Hyatt Legal Plans, Inc.*, 874 S.W.2d 548 (Missouri Court of Appeals, 1994) (paralegal works for a law firm that represents the wife in a divorce action; paralegal has an affair with the husband of this client(!); paralegal is charged with disclosing confidential strategy information to her lover).
- *Missouri v. Jenkins*, 491 U.S. 274, 109 S. Ct. 2463, 105 L.Ed. 2d 229 (U.S. Supreme Court, 1989) (award of paralegal fees; see discussion of this case in Chapter 1).
- *In re Kroh Brothers . . .*, 105 Bankruptcy Reporter 515, 529 (U.S. Bankruptcy Court, W.D. Missouri, 1989) (in a request for attorney fees, the attorney fails to explain why some of the tasks performed by attorneys "were not performed by a paralegal").
- *Buckman v. Buckman*, 857 S.W. 2d 313 (Missouri Court of Appeals, 1993) (award of paralegal fees).
- *In the Matter of Kinghorn*, 764 S.W.2d 939 (Supreme Court of Missouri, 1989) (an attorney charged with ethical violations cannot assert in mitigation his reliance on a paralegal).
- *Dudley v. Shaver*, 770 S.W.2d 712 (Missouri Court of Appeals, 1989) (inmate paralegals).

# Montana

## ETHICAL RULES AND GUIDELINES IN MONTANA

An attorney must not split a fee with a nonattorney. State Bar of Montana, *Opinion (1) (9/13/85)*.

It is unethical for a law firm to pay "runners" to recommend the law firm to injured railroad workers. State Bar of Montana, *Opinion 930927* (1994) (19 Montana Lawyer 15 (1/1994)).

Paralegals employed by law firms cannot appear on behalf of creditors at section 341 hearings in bankruptcy proceedings to question and examine debtors. The appearance would constitute an unauthorized practice of law. State Bar of Montana, *Ethics Opinion 871008*.

Attorneys are responsible for the work product of their paralegal employees. There is no need to establish a bureaucracy to provide additional regulation on who can be a paralegal and how they can be used. *In the Matter of the Proposed Adoption of Rules Relating to Paralegals and Legal Assistants*, No. 94–577 (Supreme Court of Montana, 7/17/95).

## DEFINING THE PRACTICE OF LAW IN MONTANA

§ 37–61–201 (*Montana Code Annotated*): Who is considered to be practicing law. Any person who shall hold himself out or advertise as an attorney or counselor at law or who shall appear in any court of record or before a judicial body, referee, commissioner, or other officer appointed to determine any question of law or fact by a court or who shall engage in the business and duties and perform such acts, matters, and things as are usually done or performed by an attorney at law in the practice of his profession for the purposes of parts 1 through 3 of this chapter shall be deemed practicing law.

## IMPORTANT MONTANA LAWS ON PARALEGALS

§ 37–61–101, chapter 60 (*Montana Code Annotated*): Private Investigators and Patrol Officers.

As used in this chapter, the following definitions apply: . . . (12) "Paralegal" or "legal assistant" means a person qualified through education, training, or work experience to perform substantive legal work that requires knowledge of legal concepts and that is customarily but not exclusively performed by a lawyer and who may be retained or employed by one or more lawyers, law offices, governmental agencies, or other entities or who may be authorized by administrative, statutory, or court authority to perform this work.

§ 27–2–206 (*Montana Code Annotated*): Actions for legal malpractice. An action against an attorney licensed to practice law in Montana or a paralegal assistant or a legal intern employed by an attorney based upon the person's alleged professional negligent act or for error or omission in the person's practice must be commenced within 3 years after the plaintiff discovers or through the use of reasonable diligence should have discovered the act, error, or omission, whichever occurs last, but in no case may the action be commenced after 10 years from the date of the act, error, or omission.

## MONTANA ETHICS AND PRACTICE RULES ON THE INTERNET

www.law.cornell.edu/ethics/montana.html
www.montanabar.org/attyrulesandregs/index.html
www.crossingthebar.com/MT-UPL.htm

## PARALEGALS (AND OTHER NONATTORNEYS) IN COURT

- *Sparks v. Johnson*, 826 P.2d 928 (Supreme Court of Montana, 1992) (nonattorneys cannot practice in the justice's court on a recurring basis even though § 25–31–601 of the *Montana Code* says "any person" may act as an attorney in this court; the statute is a "one-time only" grant of a privilege of lay representation).
- *State ex rel. Montana Dept. of Transportation v. Slack*, 29 P.3d 503 (Supreme Court of Montana, 2001 (award of paralegal fees; allegation of duplicative billing).
- *In re Sirefco, Inc.*, 144 Bankruptcy Reporter 495, 497 (U.S. Bankruptcy Court, Montana, 1992) (paralegal fees disallowed; the paralegal's work in this case was duplicative and not beneficial; the attorney failed to establish that the paralegal's work "was not merely secretarial in nature").
- *Harris v. Maloughney*, 827 F. Supp. 1488 (U.S. District Court, Montana, 1993) (nonattorney legal assistance to inmates).
- *In re Semenza*, 121 Bankruptcy Reporter 56 (U.S. Bankruptcy Court, Montana, 1990) (paralegals are not "professional persons" within the meaning of the Bankruptcy Code; paralegals do not have to be licensed in Montana).

# Nebraska

## ETHICAL RULES AND GUIDELINES IN NEBRASKA

Paralegals can be listed on law firm letterhead if their nonattorney status is clear. Nebraska State Bar Ass'n, *Opinion 88–2*.

Several attorneys who are not partners, associates, or otherwise affiliated with each other share office space and share nonattorney personnel. They represent clients who are opposite each other in cases. This is not improper if the clients are aware of and consent to the arrangement and if steps are taken to ensure confidentiality—such as preventing common access to case files and preventing the nonattorneys from working both sides on a case. Nebraska State Bar Ass'n, *Opinion 89–2*.

Hiring someone who has worked for an opposing law firm in matters related to a particular case automatically disqualifies the hiring firm from the case. A Chinese Wall or cone of silence erected around an attorney, law clerk, paralegal, secretary or other ancillary staff member is insufficient to prevent disqualification due to a conflict of interest and appearance of impropriety. Nebraska State Bar Ass'n, *Opinion 94–4*.

A suspended attorney may be employed as a paralegal if the employment is at a place and in such a manner as to not give the appearance of practicing law. A suspended attorney may not be employed as a paralegal at an office where he or she previously shared office space or practiced law. Nebraska State Bar Ass'n, *Opinion 96–1*.

## DEFINING THE PRACTICE OF LAW IN NEBRASKA

*Nebraska . . . v. Butterfield*, 111 N.W.2d 543 545 (Supreme Court of Nebraska, 1961): The Supreme Court of this state has the inherent power to define and regulate the practice of law in this state. . . . While an all-embracing definition of the term "practicing law" would involve great difficulty, it is generally defined as the giving of advice or rendition of any sort of service by a person, firm, or corporation when the giving of such advice or rendition of such service requires the use of any degree of legal knowledge or skill. . . . In an ever-changing economic and social order, the "practice of law" must necessarily change, making it practically impossible to formulate an enduring definition. . . . In determining what constitutes the practice of law it is the character of the act and not the place where the act is performed that is the controlling factor. . . . Whether or not a fee is charged is not a decisive factor in determining if one has engaged in the practice of law.

Rule 5 (*West's Nebraska Court Rules and Procedure*): Admission of Attorneys.

(3) For purposes of this rule, "practice of law" means: . . .

(b) Employment as a lawyer for a corporation, partnership, trust, individual, or other entity with the primary duties of:

(i) Furnishing legal counsel, drafting documents and pleadings, and interpreting and giving advice with respect to the law, or

(ii) Preparing cases for presentation to or trying before courts, executive departments, or administrative bureaus or agencies; . . .

## IMPORTANT RECENT NEBRASKA RULE INVOLVING PARALEGALS

DR 5–109 (*Nebraska Code of Professional Responsibility*): Support Personnel of a Law Firm—Conflict of Interest

(A) For purposes of this rule, a support person shall mean any person, other than a lawyer, who is associated with a lawyer or a law firm and shall include but is not necessarily limited to the following: law clerks, paralegals, legal assistants, secretaries, messengers, and other support personnel employed by the law firm. . . .

(B) A lawyer shall not knowingly allow a support person to participate or assist in the representation of a current client in the same or a substantially related matter in which another lawyer or firm with which the support person formerly was associated had previously represented a client:

(1) Whose interests are materially adverse to the current client; and

(2) About whom the support person has acquired confidential information that is material to the matter, unless the former client consents after consultation. The support person shall be considered to have acquired confidential information that is material to the matter unless the support person demonstrates otherwise.

(C) If a support person, who has worked on a matter, is personally prohibited from working on a particular matter under subsection (B), the lawyer or firm with which that person is presently associated will not be prohibited from representing the current client in that matter if:

(1) The former client consents, or

(2) There is no genuine threat that confidential information of the former client will be used with material adverse effect on the former client because the confidential client information communicated to the support person while associated with the former firm is not likely to be significant in the current client's case.

## NEBRASKA ETHICS AND PRACTICE RULES ON THE INTERNET

www.law.cornell.edu/ethics/nebraska.html
www.nebar.com/legalresources/code/index.htm
www.nebar.com/legalresources/opinions/index.htm
www.crossingthebar.com/NE-UPL.htm

## PARALEGALS (AND OTHER NONATTORNEYS) IN COURT

■ *State ex rel. Counsel for Discipline of Nebraska Supreme Court v. Huston*, 631 N.W.2d 913 (Nebraska Supreme Court, 2001) (charges attorney claimed for a legal assistant were excessive, given that much of the itemized work was more secretarial in nature).

■ *State ex rel. Creighton University v. Hickman*, 512 N.W.2d 374 (Nebraska Supreme Court, 1994) (attorney works on a case and is disbarred; he then goes to work as a legal assistant to do discovery work for the opposing attorney on the same case; the new employer is disqualified from continuing on the case).

■ *Nebraska v. Thierstein*, 371 N.W.2d 746 (Nebraska Supreme Court, 1985) (a legal assistant must be supervised by an attorney).

■ *Nebraska v. Garvey*, 457 N.W.2d 297 (Nebraska Supreme Court, 1990) (suspended attorney ordered to perform 50 hours of pro bono paralegal work).

■ *Reutcke v. Dahm*, 707 F. Supp. 1121 (U.S. District Court, Nebraska, 1988) (legal training for inmate paralegals).

# Nevada

## DEFINITION OF PARALEGAL

State Bar of Nevada, Legal Assistants Division: Definition. A legal assistant (also known as a paralegal) is a person, qualified through education, training or work experience, who is employed or retained by a lawyer, law office, governmental agency or other entity in a capacity or function which involves the performance, under the ultimate direction and supervision of an attorney, of specifically delegated substantive legal work, which work, for the most part, requires sufficient knowledge of legal concepts that, absent such an assistant, the attorney would perform the task. (*www.nala.org/net.htm*)

## DEFINING THE PRACTICE OF LAW IN NEVADA

Rule 51.1 (*Supreme Court Rules*): Admission to practice.
2. Practice of law. For purposes of this rule, the term "practice of law" shall mean: . . .

(b) practice as an attorney for an individual, a corporation, partnership, trust, or other entity, with the primary duties of furnishing legal counsel, researching legal issues, drafting legal documents, pleadings, and memoranda, interpreting and giving advice regarding the law, or preparing, trying or presenting cases before courts, departments of government or administrative agencies. . . .

## NEVADA ETHICS AND PRACTICE RULES ON THE INTERNET

www.law.cornell.edu/ethics/nevada.html
www.nvbar.org/memberServices/indexEthicsOver.
   php3
www.leg.state.nv.us/other/cr/scr.html
www.crossingthebar.com/NV-UPL.htm

## PARALEGALS (AND OTHER NONATTORNEYS) IN COURT

■ *Ciaffone v. Eighth Judicial District Court of State of Nevada. in and for County of Clark*, 945 P.2d 950 (Supreme Court of Nevada, 1997) (if a nonlawyer employee changes law firms, the new employer need not in all cases be disqualified from matters on which employee's previous employer was also engaged as adverse party; if the employee never obtained confidential information, no ethical problem arises requiring disqualification, and even if employee had access to privileged information, the former employer and its client may waive disqualification if satisfied that the present employer is adequately screening the nonlawyer employee). See also *Brown v. Eighth Judicial District Court ex rel. County of Clark*, 14 P.3d 1266 (Supreme Court of Nevada 2000) (disqualification not warranted when legal secretary switches firms).

■ *In re Ginji*, 117 Bankruptcy Reporter 983, 993 (U.S. Bankruptcy Court, Nevada, 1990) (award of paralegal fees; work that "was done by an attorney which should have been done by a paralegal . . . shall be billed at a lower rate").

■ *Greenwell v. Paralegal Center*, 836 P.2d 70 (Supreme Court of Nevada, 1992) (injunction granted against a typing service for the unauthorized practice of law, but the court orders the state bar to investigate the alleged unavailability of legal services for low- and middle-income Nevadans).

■ *Pioneer Title v. State Bar*, 326 P.2d 408 (Supreme Court of Nevada, 1958) (some simple legal services may be so necessary that they could properly be provided by nonattorneys if they would otherwise be unavailable).

■ *Herbst v. Humana Health Insurance of Nevada*, 781 P.2d 762 (Supreme Court of Nevada, 1989) (award of paralegal fees; 359 hours of work performed by paralegals on the case).

■ *Housewright v. Simmons* 729 P.2d 499 (Supreme Court of Nevada, 1986) (inmate paralegals).

# New Hampshire

## ETHICAL RULES AND GUIDELINES IN NEW HAMPSHIRE

Rule 35 (*New Hampshire Supreme Court Rules*): *Definition*: A "legal assistant" shall mean a person not admitted to the practice of law in New Hampshire who is an employee of or an assistant to an active member of the New Hampshire Bar . . . and who, under the control and supervision of an active member of the New Hampshire Bar, renders services related to but not constituting the practice of law. *Rule 1:* Paralegals must not give legal advice, but they can, with adequate attorney supervision, provide information concerning legal matters. *Rule 2:* An attorney may not permit a legal assistant to represent a client in judicial or administrative proceedings unless authorized by statute, court rule or decision, administrative rule or regulation, or customary practice. *Rule 3:* A paralegal shall not be delegated any task that requires the exercise of professional legal judgment. The attorney must supervise the paralegal. *Rule 4:* An attorney must take care that the legal assistant does not reveal information relating to representation of a client or use such information to the disadvantage of the client. *Rule 5:* An attorney shall not form a partnership with a paralegal if any part of the partnership consists of the practice of law. *Rule 6:* An attorney shall not share fees with a paralegal but can include the paralegal in a retirement plan based on a profit-sharing arrangement. *Rule 7:* A paralegal's name may not be included on the letterhead of an attorney. A paralegal can have a business card that prints the name of the law firm where he or she works, if the card indicates the paralegal's nonattorney capacity and the firm does not use the paralegal to solicit business for the firm improperly. *Rule 8:* When dealing with clients, attorneys, or the public, the paralegal must disclose at the outset that he or she is not an attorney. *Rule 9:* An attorney must exercise care to prevent a legal assistant from engaging in conduct that would involve the attorney unethical conduct.

-------

A law firm cannot list legal assistants on its letterhead. New Hampshire Bar Ass'n, *Ethics Opinion 1982–3/20* (3/17/83).

Paralegals must avoid communications that involve the offering of legal advice, which is the exclusive function of the attorney. New Hampshire Bar Ass'n, *Successful Law Practice with Paralegals* (1992). See also New Hampshire Bar Ass'n, *Guidelines for the Utilization of the Services of Legal Assistants* (1977).

## DEFINING THE PRACTICE OF LAW IN NEW HAMPSHIRE

*New Hampshire v. Settle*, 480 A.2d 6, 8 (Supreme Court of New Hampshire, 1984): The only statutory definition of the unauthorized practice of law is provided in RSA 311:7 which states: "No person shall be permitted commonly to practice as an attorney in court unless be has been admitted by the court. . . ." The defendant argues that unless an individual is actually practicing in court, his conduct is not proscribed by the statute. We cannot read RSA 311:7 to limit the unauthorized practice of law to those instances in which an individual has physically appeared in the courtroom to represent a litigant. At the very least, this provision also encompasses the filling of documents in the court system. . . . There is no "single factor to determine whether someone is engaged in the unauthorized practice of law . . . [Rather, such a] determination must be made on a case-by-case basis."

## NEW HAMPSHIRE ETHICS AND PRACTICE RULES ON THE INTERNET
www.law.cornell.edu/ethics/nh.html
www.crossingthebar.com/NH-UPL.htm

## PARALEGALS (AND OTHER NONATTORNEYS) IN COURT
- *Tocci's Case*, 663 A.2d 88 (Supreme Court of New Hampshire, 1995) (§ 311:1 of the state code allows a party to "be represented by any citizen of good character"; this provision allows a nonlawyer to appear in an individual case; it does not allow persons "otherwise unable to practice law to act commonly, entering repeated appearances before the courts of this State").
- *Kalled's Case*, 607 A.2d 613 (Supreme Court of New Hampshire, 1992) (excessive billing by an attorney such as charging the client for 1,489 hours of paralegal time at $60 per hour).
- *Van Dorn Retail Management, Inc. v. Jim's Oxford Shop, Inc.*, 874 F. Supp. 476, 490 (U.S. District Court, New Hampshire, 1994) (paralegal fees reduced; "attorneys and paralegals duplicated their efforts"; paralegals "performed clerical functions").

# NEW JERSEY

## ETHICAL RULES AND GUIDELINES IN NEW JERSEY
New Jersey has added an additional subsection to Rule 5.3 of the *Model Rules of Professional Conduct* that is not is the ABA *Model Rules*. The N.J. addition is (c)(3): attorneys must make a "reasonable investigation of circumstances that would disclose past instances of conduct by the nonlawyer" that are "incompatible with the professional obligations of an attorney, which evidence a propensity for such conduct."

It is not the unauthorized practice of law for a nonattorney broker to conduct residential real estate closings and settlements without attorneys as long as the broker notifies the buyer and seller of the risk of not having attorney representation and of the conflicting interest that brokers and title companies have. *In re Opinion No. 26 of Committee on Unauthorized Practice of Law*, 1995 WL 121535.

It is unethical for attorneys to hire a paralegal to screen calls of prospective clients to determine whether the case involves "good liability and damages." The paralegal would discuss the claims of the callers and make a determination of whether to refer the case to an attorney. This is the unauthorized practice of law. New Jersey Supreme Court Advisory Committee on Professional Ethics, *Opinion 645* (10/4/90) (126 New Jersey Law Journal 894) (1990 WL 441602). In agreement: *Opinion 6* (10/4/90) of the New Jersey Supreme Court Advisory Committee on Attorney Advertising.

A paralegal can have a business card as long as the name of the employing law firm is also printed on it. New Jersey Supreme Court Advisory Committee on Professional Ethics, *Opinion 647* (1990) (126 New Jersey Law Journal 1525) (1990 WL 441612).

The names of paralegals may be printed on attorney letterhead and in advertisements. "[T]he respect accorded paralegals and the work they perform has increased immeasurably over the last 10 to 15 years." New Jersey Supreme Court Committee on Attorney Advertising, *Opinion 16* (1/24/94) (136 New Jersey Law Journal 375) (1994 WL 45949). This opinion superseded *Opinion 296* (1975).

Nonattorney employees of the country welfare agency may represent litigants before the Office of Administrative Law. New Jersey Supreme Court Advisory Committee on Professional Ethics, *Opinion 580* (2/27/86).

Paralegals can sign law firm correspondence concerning routine tasks such as gathering factual information and documents. They should not sign correspondence to clients, adverse attorneys, or tribunals. Minor exceptions are allowed such as "a purely routine request to a court clerk for a docket sheet." New Jersey Supreme Court Advisory Committee on Professional Ethics, *Opinion 611* (2/23/88) (121 New Jersey Law Journal 301) (1988 WL 356368).

A paralegal switches jobs between law firms that opposed each other in litigation. The paralegal worked on the litigation while at the former firm. The new employer is not disqualified if a Chinese Wall is built around the paralegal and she would work for an attorney who has no involvement in the litigation. Also, her office would be located in another end of the building. New Jersey Supreme Court Advisory Committee on Professional Ethics, *Opinion 665* (8/3/92) (131 New Jersey Law Journal 1074) (1992 WL 465626), modifying the per se prohibition announced in *Opinion 546* (11/8/84) (114 New Jersey Law Journal 496) (1984 WL 140946). See also *Opinion 633* (11/2/89) (a law firm litigating tobacco cases can hire a nonattorney who had been involved in tobacco litigation at another firm if the nonattorney had no substantial responsibility in the tobacco litigation at the other firm, obtained no confidential information concerning the litigation, and is screened from such litigation at the present firm).

## DEFINING THE PRACTICE OF LAW IN NEW JERSEY

*In re Opinion No. 24 of the Committee on the Unauthorized Practice of Law*, 607 A.2d 962, 966 (Supreme Court of New Jersey, 1992): No satisfactory, all-inclusive definition of what constitutes the practice of law has ever been devised. None will be attempted here. That has been left, and wisely so, to the courts when parties present them with concrete factual situations. . . . "What is now considered the practice of law is something which may be described more readily than defined." . . . Essentially, the Court decides what constitutes the practice of law on a case-by-case basis. . . . The practice of law is not subject to precise definition. It is not confined to litigation but often encompasses "legal activities in many non-litigious fields which entail specialized knowledge and ability." Therefore, the line between permissible business and professional activities and the unauthorized practice of law is often blurred. . . . There is no question that paralegals' work constitutes the practice of law. N.J.S.A. 2A:170–78 and 79 deem unauthorized the practice of law by a nonlawyer and make such practice a disorderly-persons offense. However, N.J.S.A. 2A:170–81 (f) excepts paralegals from being penalized for engaging in tasks that constitute legal practice if their supervising attorney assumes direct responsibility for the work that the paralegals perform. N.J.S.A. 2A:170–81(f) states: Any person or corporation furnishing to any person lawfully engaged in the practice of law such information or such clerical assistance in and about his professional work as, except for the provisions of this article, may be lawful, but the lawyer receiving such information or service shall at all times maintain full professional and direct responsibility to his client for the information and service so rendered. Consequently, paralegals who are supervised by attorneys do not engage in the unauthorized practice of law.

## NEW JERSEY ETHICS AND PRACTICE RULES ON THE INTERNET

www.law.cornell.edu/ethics/nj.html
www2.law.cornell.edu/cgi-bin/foliocgi.exe/nj-narr?
www.lawlibrary.rutgers.edu/ethics/search.html
www.crossingthebar.com/NJ-UPL.htm

## PARALEGALS (AND OTHER NONATTORNEYS) IN COURT

- *In re Opinion No. 24 of the Committee on the Unauthorized Practice of Law*, 607 A.2d 962 (Supreme Court of New Jersey, 1992) (see chapter 5) (attorneys may delegate tasks to paralegals whether the paralegal is employed by the attorney or is an independent paralegal who is retained by the attorney as long as the attorney maintains a direct relationship with his or her clients, supervises the paralegal's work, and is responsible for the paralegal's work product). This opinion overruled *Advisory Opinion 24* (1990) of the New Jersey Unauthorized Practice of Law Committee, which said that attorneys cannot hire paralegals as independent contractors because of the difficulty of providing them with needed day-to-day supervision and the danger of conflict-of-interest because the paralegals work for different attorneys.
- *Infante v. Gottesman*, 558 A.2d 1338 (Superior Court of New Jersey, 1989) (it is unethical for an attorney to form a partnership and split fees with a paralegal/investigation service).
- *Argila v. Argila*, 607 A.2d 675, 679 (Superior Court of New Jersey, 1992) (the application for paralegal fees failed to provide the qualifications of the paralegals and data on the prevailing market rate for paralegals).
- *Hawkins v. Harris*, 661 A.2d 284 (Supreme Court of New Jersey, 1995) (statements made by investigators can be privileged).
- *Buccilli v. Timby, Brown, Timby*, 660 A.2d 1261 (Superior Court of New Jersey, 1995) (New Jersey paralegal who worked for a Pennsylvania law firm claims she was fired because she told the firm she was subjected to sexual harassment, she intended to file a workers' compensation claim, and she objected to the lack of attorney supervision of her work and being asked to forge her attorney's name to court documents).
- *Prisoners' Legal Association v. Robertson*, 822 F. Supp. 185 (U.S. District Court, New Jersey, 1993) (inmate paralegals); *Jones v. Lilly*, 37 F.3d 964 (U.S. Court of Appeals, 3d Circuit, 1994) (inmate paralegal).
- *Valentine v. Beyer*, 850 F.2d 951 (U.S. Court of Appeals, 3d Circuit, 1988) (inmates challenge adequacy of paralegal program).
- *United States v. Barber*, 808 F. Supp. 361 (U.S. District Court, New Jersey, 1992) (disbarred attorney acts as paralegal).

# New Mexico

## ETHICAL RULES AND GUIDELINES IN NEW MEXICO

A paralegal shall disclose to all persons with whom he or she communicates—at the beginning of any dealings with them—that the paralegal is not an attorney. The word *associate* should not be used when referring to a paralegal, since it might be interpreted as an attorney-associate. A lawyer must ensure that the paralegal preserves the confidences and secrets of a client and that no personal, social, or business interest of the paralegal creates a conflict of interest with a client. Paralegals should not recommend that their law firm be retained. An attorney shall not share fees or form a partnership with a paralegal. The compensation of a paralegal shall not include a percentage of profits or fees received from clients referred to the attorney by the paralegal. A paralegal's name cannot be printed on the letterhead of an attorney. A paralegal can have a business card that prints the name of the law firm as long as his or her nonattorney status is clear. A paralegal can sign correspondence on attorney letterhead as long as his or her nonattorney status is disclosed by a title such as *legal assistant* or *paralegal*. An attorney should not assign tasks beyond the competence of a paralegal. "In addition, a lawyer should explain to the legal assistant that the legal assistant has a duty to inform the lawyer of any assignment which the assistant regards as beyond his capability." New Mexico Supreme Court, *Rules Governing Legal Assistant Services*, Rules 20-101 to 20-114 (1986); Judicial Pamphlet 16; State Bar of New Mexico, *Guidelines for the Use of Legal Assistant Services* (1980).

Attorneys must tell clients how much services to be rendered by office nonattorneys will cost. Advisory Opinions Committee of the State Bar of New Mexico, *Opinion 1990–4* (6/9/90).

Other opinion of the Advisory Opinions Committee of the State Bar of New Mexico involving nonattorneys: *Opinion 1983–3*.

## DEFINING THE PRACTICE OF LAW IN NEW MEXICO

*State Bar of New Mexico v. Guardian Abstract and Title Company, Inc.*, 575 P.2d 943, 948 (Supreme Court of New Mexico, 1978): The authority of the Supreme Court to define and regulate the practice of law is inherently contained in the grant of judicial power to the courts by the Constitution. . . . There is no comprehensive definition of what constitutes the practice of law in our basic law or the cases. This Court has specifically declined to take on the onerous task. . . . We have declined to define what constitutes the practice of law because of the infinite number of fact situations which may be presented, each of which must be judged according to its own circumstances. . . . "[R]endering a service that requires the use of legal knowledge" or "preparing instruments and contracts by which legal rights are secured" would be indicia of the practice of law. . . . Defining the practice of law is an extremely difficult task, which we find unnecessary to undertake at this time. The line between what constitutes practicing law and what is permissible business and professional activity by non-lawyers is indistinct. . . . The answer may be determined only from a consideration of the acts or service performed in each case. Generally, . . . courts hold that whenever, as

incidental to another transaction or calling, a layman, as part of his regular course of conduct resolves legal questions for another at his request and for a consideration by giving him advice or by taking action for and in his behalf, the layman is "practicing law," but only if difficult or doubtful legal questions are involved, which, to safeguard the public, reasonably demand the application of a trained legal mind. . . . What is a difficult or doubtful question of law demanding the application of a trained legal mind is not to be measured by the comprehension of a trained legal mind but by the understanding thereof which is possessed by a reasonably intelligent layman who is reasonably familiar with similar transactions. The test must be applied in a common-sense way which will protect primarily the interest of the public and not hamper or burden such interest with impractical and technical restrictions which have no reasonable justification.

Rule 20–102 (*New Mexico Rules of Court*): Definitions
As used in these guidelines:

A. A "legal assistant" is a person, qualified through education, training or work experience, who is employed or retained by a lawyer, law office, governmental agency or other entity in a capacity or function which involves the performance, under the ultimate direction and supervision of an attorney, of a specifically-delegated substantive legal work, which work, for the most part, requires a sufficient knowledge of legal concepts that, absent such assistant, the attorney would perform the task; and

B. practice of law, insofar as court proceedings are concerned, includes:

(1) representation of parties before judicial or administrative bodies; (2) preparation of pleadings and other papers, incident to actions and special proceedings; (3) management of such actions and proceedings; and (4) noncourt-related activities, such as: (a) giving legal advice and counsel; (b) rendering a service which requires use of legal knowledge or skill; and (c) preparing instruments and contracts by which legal rights are secured.

## NEW MEXICO ETHICS AND PRACTICE RULES ON THE INTERNET

www.law.cornell.edu/ethics/nm.html
www.nmbar.org/statebar/advisoryopinions/advopin.htm
www.crossingthebar.com/NM-UPL.htm

## PARALEGALS (AND OTHER NONATTORNEYS) IN COURT

■ *In re Houston*, 985 P.2d 752 (New Mexico Supreme Court, 1999) (having a legal assistant conduct all meetings with the clients, during which the clients' objectives and the means for pursuing them are discussed and decided, raises serious questions of unauthorized practice; the attorney needs instruction on the proper division of duties between lawyers and legal assistants and the ethical limits of the functions of a legal assistant).

- *In the Matter of Martinez*, 754 P.2d 842 (New Mexico Supreme Court, 1988) (attorney suspended for failing to supervise a paralegal to ensure that the conduct of the paralegal comported with the ethical obligations of the attorney).
- *In the Matter of Rawson*, 833 P.2d 235 (New Mexico Supreme Court, 1992) (disbarred attorney can act as paralegal).
- *Aragon v. Westside Jeep/Eagle*, 876 P.2d 235 (New Mexico Supreme Court, 1994) (law firm failed to file a notice of appeal and the appeal was dismissed; the firm alleges that the failure to file was caused by a "clerical difficulty" of its paralegal who had a heavy workload and was busy training a new employee when the notice of appeal should have been filed).

# NEW YORK

## ETHICAL RULES AND GUIDELINES IN NEW YORK

New York State Bar Association, *Guidelines for the Utilization by Lawyers of the Services of Legal Assistants* (1997). *Definition:* A legal assistant/paralegal is a person who is qualified through education, training or work experience to be employed or retained by a lawyer, law office, governmental agency, or other entity in a capacity or function that involves the performance, under the ultimate direction and supervision of, and/or accountability to, an attorney, of substantive legal work, that requires a sufficient knowledge of legal concepts such that, absent such legal assistant/paralegal, the attorney would perform the task. *Guideline I:* An attorney can permit a paralegal to perform services in the representation of a client if the attorney retains a direct relationship with the client, supervises the paralegal, and is fully responsible for the paralegal. *Guideline II:* An attorney must not assist a paralegal in engaging in the unauthorized practice of law. *Guideline III:* A paralegal may perform certain functions otherwise prohibited only to the extent authorized by law. An example would be a law that allows nonlawyer advocacy of clients at particular administrative agencies. *Guideline IV:* An attorney must take reasonable measures to ensure that all client confidences are preserved by paralegals and take appropriate measures to avoid conflicts of interest arising from their employment. *Guideline V:* An attorney shall not form a partnership with a paralegal if any part of the firm's activity consists of the practice of law, nor shall an attorney share legal fees with a paralegal. *Guideline VI:* An attorney shall require that a paralegal, when dealing with a client, disclose at the outset that the paralegal is not an attorney. The attorney shall also require such disclosure at the outset when the paralegal is dealing with a court, an administrative agency, attorneys, or the public if there is any reason for their believing that the paralegal is an attorney or associated with an attorney. *Guideline VII:* An attorney should promote the professional development of the paralegal. Examples include providing opportunities for continuing legal education, pro bono projects, and participation in professional associations.

––––––––––

Paralegal names *can* be printed on a firm's letterhead if their nonattorney status is clear. New York State Bar Ass'n, *Ethics Opinion 500* (12/6/78) (1978 WL 14163).

The titles *paralegal* and *senior paralegal* are acceptable, but the following titles are unacceptable because they are ambiguous: *paralegal coordinator, legal associate, public benefits advocate, legal advocate, family law advocate, housing law advocate, disability benefits advocate*, and *public benefits specialist*. The public might be misled about the non-attorney status of the people with these titles. New York State Bar Ass'n, *Ethics Opinion 640* (1992) (1992 WL 450730).

An attorney may include on letterhead and other materials the identification of a nonlegal employee as a "Certified Legal Assistant," provided that term is accompanied by the statement that the certification is afforded by the National Association of Legal Assistants (NALA), and provided further that the attorney has satisfied himself or herself that NALA is a bona fide organization that provides such certification to all who meet objective and consistently applied standards relevant to the work of legal assistants. New York State Bar Ass'n, *Opinion 695* (8/25/97).

There are circumstances in which an attorney can send his or her paralegal to attend a real estate closing alone. The attorney must determine that the closing calls for "merely ministerial" as opposed to discretionary duties, must be sure the background of the paralegal makes him or her suitable to attend, and must have a plan to cope with the unforeseen such as being available by telephone to the paralegal. "[F]rom an ethical standpoint, the lawyer who assigns a non-lawyer to work on a client's matter had better be right about the suitability of that task for delegation, and the suitability of that employee for the task at hand." New York State Bar Ass'n, *Opinion 677* (12/12/95) (1995 WL 870964).

A paralegal cannot conduct a deposition or supervise the execution of a will. New York State Bar Ass'n, *Ethics Opinion 304* (1973) and *Ethics Opinion 343*.

An attorney can give credit or recognition to a nonattorney for work performed in the preparation of a brief as long as his or her nonattorney status is clear. New York State Bar Ass'n, *Ethics Opinion 299*.

An attorney cannot allow a nonattorney to engage in settlement negotiations or to appear at a pretrial conference. Bar Ass'n of Nassau County, *Opinion 86–40* (9/12/89).

A nonattorney can attend a real estate closing to perform ministerial functions involving only formalities. His or her nonattorney status must be disclosed at the closing. Bar Ass'n of Nassau County, *Opinion 86–43* (10/21/86); reaffirmed in *Opinion 90–13 (3/18/90)*.

As attorney cannot divide a fee with a paralegal who brings clients to the attorney. Bar Ass'n of Nassau County, *Opinion 87–37* (10/1/87).

Nonattorneys cannot be referred to as *associates* of an attorney. Bar Ass'n of Nassau County, *Opinion 88–34* (9/29/88).

Nonattorneys can be listed on attorney letterhead if such employees are clearly described and identified as nonattorneys. Bar Ass'n of Nassau County, *Opinion 91–32* (1991) (accountants); *Opinion 87–14* (1987) (paralegals).

An attorney may not represent a defendant in a criminal case when the complainant in the case is an investigator whom the attorney used in an unrelated case. There would be an appearance of impropriety in such a representation. Bar Ass'n of Nassau County, *Opinion 89–1* (1/18/89).

An attorney cannot form a partnership with a nonattorney to practice law. An attorney who shares an office with a nonattorney must avoid misleading the public into believing the nonattorney is an attorney. Ass'n of the Bar of the City of New York, *Opinion 1987–1* (2/23/87).

A law firm may issue an announcement that it has hired a law student or other nonattorney. Ass'n of the Bar of the City of New York, *Opinion 1996–2* (2/26/96) (1996 WL 93063).

Attorneys must effectively supervise their nonattorney employees, refrain from aiding or encouraging them to engage in the unauthorized practice of law, and be sure that they maintain client confidences and that the public is not misled by their nonattorney status. Ass'n of the Bar of the City of New York, *Opinion 1995–1* (7/6/95) (1995 WL 607778).

Paralegals can be listed on the letterhead of a law firm and on a business card that prints the name of the law firm (without printing the name of the supervising attorney) as long as their nonattorney status is indicated. New York County Lawyers' Ass'n, *Opinion 673* (12/23/89).

## DEFINING THE PRACTICE OF LAW IN NEW YORK

*Gemayel v. Seaman*, 533 N.E.2d 245, 248, 536 N.Y.S.2d 406, 409 (Court of Appeals of New York, 1988): The "practice" of law reserved to duly licensed New York attorneys includes the rendering of legal advice as well as appearing in court and holding oneself out to be a lawyer. . . . Additionally, such advice or services must be rendered to particular clients. This is the essential of legal practice—the representation and the advising of a particular person in a particular situation.

§ 118.1 (*McKinney's New York Rules of Court*): Registration of attorneys.

(g) For purposes of this section, the "practice of law" shall mean the giving of legal advice or counsel to, or providing legal representation for, [a] particular body or individual in a particular situation in either the public or private sector in the State of New York or elsewhere, it shall include the appearance as an attorney before any court or administrative agency.

## NEW YORK ETHICS AND PRACTICE RULES ON THE INTERNET

www.law.cornell.edu/ethics/ny.html
www2.law.cornell.edu/cgi-bin//foliocgi.exe/ny-narr?
www.nysba.org/opinions/opinions.html
www.crossingthebar.com/NY-UPL.htm

## PARALEGALS (AND OTHER NONATTORNEYS) IN COURT

■ *People v. Mitchell*, 461 N.Y.S.2d 267 (Supreme Court, Appellate Division, 4th Dept., 1982) (statements made in a law office waiting room to a paralegal in the attorney's absence are not privileged).

■ *Fine v. Facet Aerospace Products Co.*, 133 Federal Rules Decisions 439 (U.S. District Court, S.D. New York, 1990) (handwritten notes made by a paralegal on a document in the course of discovery in another case are protected from disclosure under the work product doctrine).

■ *Glover Bottled Gas Corp. v. Circle M. Beverage Barn*, 514 N.Y.S.2d 440 (Supreme Court, Appellate Division, 2d Dept., 1987) (attorney is disqualified after hiring a paralegal who worked on specific litigation while previously employed by the opposing counsel in the litigation).

■ *First Deposit Nat'l Bank v. Moreno*, 606 N.Y.S.2d 938 (City Court of the City of New York, New York County, 1993) (a claim for paralegal fees must itemize what was done and how much time was spent by attorneys and by others; "paralegals often competently perform certain services equivalent to those done by attorneys, while generally charging their time at a lesser rate than attorneys, thus benefitting those who pay the fees").

■ *Day v. Morgenthau*, 909 F.2d 75 (U.S. Court of Appeals, 2d Circuit, 1990) (paralegal arrested and incarcerated for being in the wrong area of the criminal court; paralegal sues for false arrest and malicious prosecution).

■ *United States v. Hooper*, 43 F.3d 26 (U.S. Court of Appeals, 2d Circuit, 1994) (a paralegal's mistake on the deadline for filing a criminal appeal is not "excusable neglect" justifying permission to file the appeal late; the paralegal thought she had 30 days to file rather than 10).

■ *In the Matter of Saltz*, 536 N.Y.S.2d 126 (Supreme Court, Appellate Division, 2d Dept, 1988) (attorney disciplined for lying when he claimed that his paralegal "doctored" divorce papers).

■ *Paralegal Institute, Inc. v. American Bar Ass'n*, 475 E. Supp. 1123 (U.S. District Court, S.D. New York, 1979) (paralegal school charges ABA with antitrust violations).

■ *Perez v. Chater*, 77 F.3d 41 (U.S. Court of Appeals, 2d Circuit, 1996) (paralegal represents client at social security disability hearing).

## NORTH CAROLINA

### ETHICAL RULES AND GUIDELINES IN NORTH CAROLINA

*Guidelines for Use of Non-Lawyers in Rendering Legal Services,* North Carolina State Bar (1986, revised 1998). *Definition:* A legal assistant (or paralegal) is a person, qualified through education, training or work experience, who is employed or retained by a lawyer, law office, corporation, governmental agency, or other entity, and who performs specifically delegated substantive legal work for which a lawyer is responsible. *Guideline 1:* A lawyer shall not permit an assistant to engage in the practice of law. A lawyer may, however, allow an assistant to perform legally-related tasks, provided the lawyer and the assistant comply with these guidelines. *Guideline 2:* A lawyer shall not permit an assistant to appear on behalf of a client in a deposition, in court or before any agency or board, in person or on the record, unless permitted by the North Carolina General Statutes and a rule of a particular court, agency or board. *Guideline 3:* A lawyer shall require that an assistant disclose that he or she is not a lawyer when necessary to avoid misrepresentation. This is so even if the assistant is authorized to represent a client under Guideline 2. Common sense suggests a routine disclosure at the outset of a conference or any type of communication. The lawyer has an obligation to ensure that his or her assistant does not communicate directly with a party known to be represented by an attorney, without that attorney's consent. *Guideline 4:* A partner in a law firm shall make reasonable efforts to ensure that the firm has in effect measures giving reasonable assurance that the assistant's conduct is compatible with the professional obligations of the lawyer. See Rule 5.3(a). Lawyers with management responsibility for the firm must familiarize legal assistants with all relevant provisions of the Rules of Professional Conduct, particularly the obligation to maintain the confidentiality of information received incident to the representation of clients. A lawyer should ensure that a non-lawyer is properly educated or trained to perform any delegated task. When the assistant is not working as an employee of the lawyer, but instead contracts independently to perform legally-related tasks, the lawyer is still responsible for the assistant's work product and ethical conduct. Special care must be taken by the lawyer to make sure that the assistant performs both competently and ethically before entrusting services to an independent assistant. A lawyer who discovers that a non-lawyer has misappropriated money from the attorney's trust account must inform the State Bar. *Guideline 5:* A lawyer having direct supervisory authority over an assistant shall make reasonable efforts to ensure that the assistant's conduct is compatible with the professional obligations of the lawyer. See Rule 5.3(c). *Guideline 6:* A lawyer

shall maintain an active, direct, and personal relationship with the client, supervise the assistant's performance of duties, and remain fully responsible for the work performed. An assistant should inform the responsible lawyer of all significant actions and services performed by the assistant. Only by thorough supervision of the assistant can the lawyer ensure that the assistant is neither engaging in the unauthorized practice of law nor involving the lawyer in any violation of the lawyer's professional responsibilities. *Guideline 7:* A lawyer shall ensure that no interest or relationship of the assistant impinges upon the services rendered to the client. If the interests of a legal assistant might materially limit or otherwise adversely affect the lawyer's representation of a prospective or current client, the lawyer must decline or discontinue the representation. If a lawyer accepts a matter in which the assistant has a conflict of interest that does not affect or limit the lawyer's representation of the client, the lawyer should totally screen the assistant from participation in the case. In addition, the lawyer should inform the client that a non-lawyer employee has a conflict of interest which, were it the lawyer's conflict, might prevent further representation of the client in connection with the matter. The nature of the conflict should be disclosed. *Guideline 8:* A lawyer may charge a client for legal work performed by a legal assistant but shall not form a partnership or other business entity with an assistant for the practice of law. A lawyer cannot share fees with a non-lawyer. Compensation of an assistant may not include a percentage of the fees received by the lawyer, nor should the assistant receive any remuneration, directly or indirectly, for referring matters of a legal nature to the lawyer. *Guideline 9:* A lawyer's letterhead or a business card may include the name of a non-lawyer assistant if the assistant's capacity is clearly indicated and the document is otherwise neither false nor misleading. An assistant may also sign correspondence on a lawyer's or a law firm's letterhead, subject, however, to the same requirements. *Guideline 10:* A lawyer may use a non-lawyer, non-employee freelance legal assistant if the lawyer adequately supervises the non-lawyer's work and inquires into the freelance assistant's potential conflicts of interest. The lawyer should disclose to the client the use of a freelance assistant, the name of the freelance assistant and how the freelance assistant's services will be charged to the client, if the client inquires.

---

A lawyer or law firm shall not employ a disbarred or suspended lawyer as a law clerk or legal assistant if that individual was associated with such lawyer or law firm at any time on or after the date of the acts which resulted in disbarment or suspension through and including the effective date of disbarment or suspension. [The firm may not accept new clients who were clients of the disbarred lawyer's former firm during the period of misconduct.] Rule 3.1 (c) & (d). *Rules of Professional Conduct.*

A paralegal switches jobs. She now works for an attorney whose client opposes a party represented by the paralegal's former employer who says the paralegal worked on the case while there. The former employer seeks the disqualification of the current employer on the case. The request is denied. The imputed disqualification rules in Rule 5.11 do not apply to nonlawyers. But the current employer "must take extreme care" to ensure the paralegal is "totally screened" from the case even if her involvement in the case at the prior employment was negligible. North Carolina State Bar, *RPC 176* (7/21/94) (1994 WL 899356). In agreement: *RPC 74* (10/20/89) (1989 WL 550603).

An attorney may not pay a paralegal a percentage of fees as a bonus. A bonus for productivity can be given, but not as a percentage of fees. North Carolina State Bar, *RPC 147* (1/15/93) (1992 WL 753129).

A legal assistant can communicate and negotiate with a claims adjuster if directly supervised by an attorney. However, "[u]nder no circumstances should the legal assistant be permitted to exercise independent legal judgment regarding the value of the case, the advisability of making or accepting any offer of settlement or any other related matter." North Carolina State Bar, *RPC 70* (10/20/89).

An attorney can represent a client in an action to abate a nuisance even though his paralegal may be called as a witness against the opponent. North Carolina State Bar, *Revised RPC 213* (10/20/95) (1995 WL 853891).

An attorney may not permit his paralegal to examine or represent a witness at a deposition. North Carolina State Bar, *RPC 183* (10/21/94) (1994 WL 901318).

## DEFINING THE PRACTICE OF LAW IN NORTH CAROLINA

§ 84-2.1 (General Statutes of North Carolina): The phrase "practice law" as used in this chapter is defined to be performing any legal service for any other person, firm or corporation, with or without compensation, specifically including the preparation or aiding in the preparation of deeds, mortgages, wills, trust instruments, inventories, accounts or reports of guardians, trustees, administrators or executors, or preparing or aiding in the preparation of any petitions or orders in any probate or court proceeding; abstracting or passing upon titles, the preparation and filing of petitions for use in any court, including administrative tribunals and other judicial or quasi-judicial bodies, or assisting by advice, counsel, or otherwise in any legal work; and to advise or give opinion upon the legal rights of any person, firm or corporation: Provided, that the above reference to particular acts which are specifically included within the definition of the phrase "practice law" shall not be construed to limit the foregoing general definition of the term, but shall be construed to include the foregoing particular acts, as well as all other acts within the general definition.

## NORTH CAROLINA ETHICS AND PRACTICE RULES ON THE INTERNET

www.ncbar.com/home/non_lawyer_guidelines.asp
www.law.cornell.edu/ethics/nc.html
www.aoc.state.nc.us/www/public/aoc/barrules.html
www.ncbar.com/eth_op/ethics_o.asp
www.crossingthebar.com/NC-UPL.htm

## PARALEGALS (AND OTHER NONATTORNEYS) IN COURT

- *North Carolina v. Cummings*, 389 S.E.2d 66, 74 (Supreme Court of North Carolina, 1990) (paralegal allowed to testify about hearsay statement of victim made during intake interview).
- *Lea Co. v. North Carolina Board of Transportation*, 374 S.E.2d 868 (Supreme Court of North Carolina, 1989) (paralegal fees denied; the paralegal work in this case was largely clerical in nature and therefore part of ordinary office overhead to be subsumed in the hourly attorney rate).
- *Spell v. McDaniel*, 852 F.2d 762 (U.S. Court of Appeals, 4th Circuit, 1988) (award of paralegal fees challenged).
- *Bounds v. Smith*, 97 S. Ct. 1491 (U.S. Supreme Court, 1977) (inmate paralegals).
- *In re Grand Jury Investigation*, 142 Federal Rules Decisions 276 (U.S. District Court, M.D. North Carolina, 1992) (paralegal part of team that allegedly turns over documents protected by attorney-client privilege).

# North Dakota

## ETHICAL RULES AND GUIDELINES IN NORTH DAKOTA

"Legal Assistant" (or paralegal) means a person who assists lawyers in the delivery of legal services, and who through formal education, training, or experience, has knowledge and expertise regarding the legal system and substantive and procedural law which qualifies the person to do work of a legal nature under the direct supervision of a licensed lawyer. *North Dakota Rules of Professional Conduct.*

A lawyer may charge for work performed by a legal assistant. A lawyer may not split legal fees with a legal assistant or pay a legal assistant for the referral of legal business. A lawyer may compensate a legal assistant based on the quantity and quality of the legal assistant's work and value of that work to a law practice. The legal assistant's compensation may not be contingent, by advance agreement, upon the outcome of a case or upon the profitability of the lawyer's practice. Rule 1.5(f) & (g), *North Dakota Rules of Professional Conduct.* The lawyer should disclose to the client, either at the outset of the representation or at the point during the representation when the lawyer determines a legal assistant should be used, that the lawyer proposes to use a legal assistant and obtain the client's agreement to any separate charges for legal assistant services. A legal assistant may not be compensated on a contingent basis for a particular case or paid for "signing up" clients for a legal practice. The linchpin of the prohibition is the lawyer's obligation to pay the legal assistant regardless of the outcome of the case. Comment to Rule 1.5.

With respect to a nonlawyer employed or retained by or associated with a lawyer, the lawyer shall make reasonable efforts to put into effect measures giving reasonable assurance that the nonlawyer's conduct is compatible with the professional obligations of the lawyer. A lawyer may not delegate to a legal assistant: (i) responsibility for establishing an attorney-client relationship; (ii) responsibility for establishing the amount of a fee to be charged for a legal service; (iii) responsibility for a legal opinion rendered to a client; or (iv) responsibility for the work product. The lawyer shall make reasonable efforts to ensure that clients, courts, and other lawyers are aware that a legal assistant is not licensed to practice law. Rule 5.3, *North Dakota Rules of Professional Conduct*. The key to appropriate delegation is proper supervision, which includes adequate instruction when assigning projects, monitoring of the project, and review of the project. Comment to Rule 5.3.

A lawyer may identify a legal assistant on the lawyer's letterhead and on business cards identifying the lawyer's firm, provided the legal assistant's status is clearly identified. Rule 7.2 (e), *North Dakota Rules of Professional Conduct*.

## DEFINING THE PRACTICE OF LAW IN NORTH DAKOTA

*Ranta v. McCarney*, 391 N.W.2d 161, 162, 163 (Supreme Court of North Dakota, 1986): Practice of law under modern conditions consists in no small part of work performed outside of any court and having no immediate relation to proceedings in court. It embraces conveyancing, the giving of legal advice on a large variety of subjects, and the preparation and execution of legal instruments covering an extensive field of business and trust relations and other affairs. Although these transactions may have no direct connection with court proceedings, they are always subject to become involved in litigation. They require in many aspects a high degree of legal skill, a wide experience with men and affairs, and great capacity for adaptation to difficult and complex situations. These "customary functions of an attorney or counsellor at law" . . . bear an intimate relation to the administration of justice by the courts. No valid distinction . . . can be drawn between that part which involves appearance in court and that part which involves advice and drafting of instruments in his office. The work of the office lawyer is the ground work for future possible contests in courts. It has profound effect on the whole scheme of the administration of justice. It is performed with that possibility in mind, and otherwise would hardly be needed. . . . It is of importance to the welfare of the public that these manifold customary functions be performed by persons possessed of adequate learning and skill, of sound moral character, and acting at all times under the heavy trust obligation to clients which rests upon all attorneys. The underlying reasons which prevent corporations, associations and individuals other than members of the bar from appearing before the courts apply with equal force to the performance of these customary functions of attorneys and counsellors at law outside of courts. . . . If compensation is exacted either directly or in-

directly, "all advice to clients, and all action taken for them in matters connected with the law," constitute practicing law.

## NORTH DAKOTA ETHICS AND PRACTICE RULES ON THE INTERNET
www.law.cornell.edu/ethics/nd.html
www2.law.cornell.edu/cgi-bin/foliocgi.exe/nd-code?
www.crossingthebar.com/ND-UPL.htm

## PARALEGALS (AND OTHER NONATTORNEYS) IN COURT
■ *In the Matter of Nassif*, 547 N.W.2d 541 (Supreme Court of North Dakota, 1996) (attorney disciplined for allowing untrained "paralegals" to recruit and advise clients, negotiate fees, and perform unsupervised legal work for clients).
■ *In the Matter of Johnson*, 481 N.W.2d 225 (Supreme Court of North Dakota, 1992) (disbarred attorney is not allowed to practice as a paralegal).
■ *Nat'l Farmers Union . . . v. Souris River Telephone . . .*, 75 F.3d 1268 (U.S. Court of Appeals, 8th Circuit, 1996) (award of paralegal fees).
■ *Gassler v. Rayl*, 862 F.2d 706 (U.S. Court of Appeals, 8th Circuit, 1988) (inmate paralegal assistance).

# OHIO

## ETHICAL RULES AND GUIDELINES IN OHIO
It is improper for an insurance defense attorney to abide by an insurance company's litigation management guidelines (e.g., on when to delegate tasks to a paralegal) in the representation of an insured when the guidelines directly interfere with the professional judgment of the attorney. Board of Commissioners on Grievances and Discipline, *Opinion 2000–3* (6/1/00) (2000 WL 1005223).

A legal assistant can sign law firm correspondence on law firm stationery as long as his or her nonattorney status is clearly indicated. Board of Commissioners on Grievances and Discipline *Opinion 89–11* (4/14/89) (1989 WL 535016).

Nonattorneys *cannot* be listed on law firm letterhead. They can, however, have business cards as long as their nonattorney status is clear. Board of Commissioners on Grievances and Discipline, *Opinion 89–16* (6/16/89) (1989 WL 535021).

A retired or inactive attorney may not perform the duties of a paralegal, since such attorneys "may not render any legal service for an attorney" in active status. Board of Commissioners on Grievances and Discipline, *Opinion 92–4* (2/14/92) (1992 WL 739414). But a suspended or disbarred attorney can act as a paralegal. *Opinion 90–06* (4/20/90) (1990 WL 640501).

Law firm letterhead can print the names and titles of nonattorney employees as long as their nonattorney status is clear and they are listed separately from the attorneys. Columbus Bar Ass'n, *Opinion (6)* (11/17/88).

Law firm letterhead can list the names and titles of nonattorney employees, and the latter can also have their own business card as long as their nonattorney status is made clear. Cleveland Bar Ass'n, *Opinion 89–1* (2/25/89).

## DEFINING THE PRACTICE OF LAW IN OHIO

*Cincinnati Bar Ass'n v. Estep*, 657 N.E.2d 499, 500 (Supreme Court of Ohio, 1995): The practice of law is not limited to the conduct of cases in court. It embraces the preparation of pleadings and other papers incident to actions and special proceedings and the management of such actions and proceedings on behalf of clients . . . and in general all advice to clients and all action taken for them in matters connected with the law. . . . One who gives legal advice to others with the expectation of being compensated therefore engages in the practice of law.

## OHIO ETHICS AND PRACTICE RULES ON THE INTERNET

www.ohiobar.org/members/paralegal
www.law.cornell.edu/ethics/ohio.html
www2.law.cornell.edu/cgi-bin/foliocgi.exe/oh-narr?
www.sconet.state.oh.us/Rules/professional
www.crossingthebar.com/OH-UPL.htm

## PARALEGALS (AND OTHER NONATTORNEYS) IN COURT

- *Columbus Bar Ass'n v. Plymale*, 745 N.E.2d 413 (Supreme Court of Ohio, 2001) (sharing legal fees with a paralegal).
- *Cincinnati Bar v. Estep*, 657 N.E.2d 499 (Supreme Court of Ohio, 1995) (it is the unauthorized practice of law for a nonattorney to represent a client before the Ohio Bureau of Workers' Compensation).
- *Office of Disciplinary Counsel v. Ball*, 618 N.E.2d 159 (Supreme Court of Ohio, 1993) (attorney disciplined for failing to supervise secretary/paralegal).
- *In re Oakes*, 135 Bankruptcy Reporter 511 (U.S. Bankruptcy Court, N.D. Ohio, 1991) (paralegal fees reduced to the extent that fees were sought for doing work of a clerical nature).
- *Bowling v. Pfizer*, 922 F. Supp. 1261 (U.S. District Court, S.D. Ohio 1996) (award of paralegal fees).
- *Palmer v. Westmeyer*, 549 N.E.2d 1202 (Court of Appeals of Ohio, 1988) (a paralegal cannot be charged with legal malpractice, since she is not an attorney).

# OKLAHOMA

## ETHICAL RULES AND GUIDELINES IN OKLAHOMA

*Definition*: a legal assistant/paralegal is a person qualified by education, training, or work experience who is employed or retained by a lawyer, law office, corporation, governmental agency, or other entity who performs specifically delegated legal work for which a lawyer is responsible, and, absent such assistant, the lawyer would perform the task. Oklahoma Bar Ass'n, *Minimum Qualification Standards for Legal Assistants/Paralegals* (9/15/00).

Education and experience requirements for a qualified paralegal: *www.okbar.org/news/legalasst.htm*.

## DEFINING THE PRACTICE OF LAW IN OKLAHOMA

*Edwards v. Hert*, 504 P.2d 407, 416, 417 (Supreme Court of Oklahoma, 1972): [P]ractice of law: the rendition of services requiring the knowledge and the application of legal principles and technique to serve the interests of another with his consent. . . . [A] service which otherwise would be a form of the practice of law does not lose that character merely because it is rendered gratuitously. . . . "[I]t is not a prerequisite that a fee should be paid before the relation of attorney and client may exist" . . . [A]n unlicensed practitioner's performance of legal service is not sanctified by his failure to require pay. . . . It has been urged upon us that acts which properly are part of the lawyer's work also may form an integral part of the legitimate activity of another calling, and that, for performance of these acts by an unlicensed person, incidental to such an independent vocation, penalties should not be inflicted upon the theory that thereby he practices law. To a certain extent, this contention is sound. "There is authority for the proposition that the drafting of documents, when merely incidental to the work of a distinct occupation, is not the practice of law, although the documents have legal consequences." . . . If the practitioner of the "distinct occupation" goes beyond the determination of legal questions for the purpose of performing his special service, and, instead, advises his patron as to the course to be taken to secure a desired legal status, he is engaged in the practice of law. The title searcher is exempt if he performs his task "without giving opinion or advice as to the legal effect of what is found." . . . The work of the accountant is exempt only if it is "dissociated from legal advice." One who, in the exercise of a commission to draw a conveyance, selects language designed to create a certain effect is practicing law. . . . So is one who draws estate plans, involving legal analysis. . . . A layman who draws a will for another necessarily is practicing law. . . . So is one who draws legal instruments or contracts. . . . A layman who evaluates a claim, and undertakes to settle it, based upon applicable legal principles, is practicing law. . . . A bank which furnishes "legal information or legal advice with respect to investments, taxation, stocks, bonds, notes or other securities or property" is involved in "a considerable practice of law," despite the argument that this is an incident to the investment trade.

## OKLAHOMA ETHICS AND PRACTICE RULES ON THE INTERNET

www.law.cornell.edu/ethics/oklahoma.html
www.okbar.org/ethics
www.crossingthebar.com/OK-UPL.htm

## PARALEGALS (AND OTHER NONATTORNEYS) IN COURT

- *Taylor v. Chubb Group of Insurance Companies*, 874 P.2d 806, 809 (Supreme Court of Oklahoma, 1994) (award of paralegal fees is for substantive legal work, not for copying documents or for performing other secretarial tasks; a party must "prove that the charges made for nonattorney's time covered work that a lawyer would have had to perform but for the performance of such services by a legal assistant" at a lower total charge than a lawyer would have charged; a legal assistant may interview clients; draft pleadings and other documents; carry out conventional and computer legal research; research public documents; prepare discovery requests and responses; schedule depositions and prepare notices and subpoenas; summarize depositions and other discovery responses; coordinate and manage document production; locate and interview witnesses; organize pleadings, trial exhibits and other documents; prepare witness and exhibit lists; prepare trial notebooks; prepare for attendance of witnesses at trial; and assist lawyers at trials).
- *State ex rel. Oklahoma Bar Ass'n v. Simank*, 19 P.3d 860 (Supreme Court of Oklahoma, 2001) (failure to supervise a nonattorney employee).
- *Brown v. Ford*, 905 P.2d 223 (Supreme Court of Oklahoma, 1995) (paralegal alleges sexual harassment by attorney at work).
- *Ritter v. Shalala*, 1993 WL 332306 (U.S. Court of Appeals, 10th Circuit, 1993) (duties of administrative law judge when claimant for supplemental security income is represented at the hearing by a paralegal).
- *Battle v. Anderson*, 457 F. Supp. 719 (U.S. District Court, Oklahoma, 1978) (inmate paralegals).

# Oregon

## ETHICAL RULES AND GUIDELINES IN OREGON

An attorney can list nonattorneys (e.g., a legal assistant, an office manager) on the law firm's letterhead. Oregon State Bar Ass'n, *Formal Opinion 1991–65 (7/91)* (1991 WL 279132).

Two law firms who oppose each other on cases can employ the same nonattorney part-time if he or she has no access to the confidences or secrets of either firm. An example would be the mutual employment of a messenger. If they both hired the same legal assistant, however, this access would probably exist. Oregon State Bar Ass'n, *Formal Opinion 1991–44 (7/91)* (1991 WL 279229).

An attorney can hire a suspended or disbarred attorney as a paralegal as long as the person does not practice law and

there is no sharing of fees with him or her. Oregon State Bar Ass'n, *Formal Ethics Opinion 1991–24* (1991 WL 279165).

It is unethical for an attorney to let his legal assistant draft pleadings that the attorney would sign but not review prior to filing. Oregon State Bar Ass'n, *Formal Opinion 1991–20 (7/91)* (1991 WL 279161).

Nonattorneys in an estate-planning service are engaged in the unauthorized practice of law when they give legal advice to clients in connection with the service, even if an attorney reviews and executes the documents involved. Oregon State Bar, *Opinion 523* (3/89).

Nonattorney employees can have their own business cards that contain the name of their attorney-employer. Oregon State Bar, *Opinion 295* (7/75).

A paralegal can write and sign letters on attorney letterhead. Oregon State Bar, *Opinion 349* (6/77) and *Opinion 295* (7/75).

A paralegal cannot take (i.e., conduct) depositions. Oregon State Bar, *Opinion 449* (7/80).

A well-trained legal assistant can do almost anything an attorney can do. However, a legal assistant cannot accept a case, set a fee, give legal advice, or represent a client in judicial proceedings. The Legal Assistants (Joint) Committee of the Oregon State Bar, *The Lawyer and the Legal Assistant* (1988).

## DEFINING THE PRACTICE OF LAW IN OREGON

*Oregon State Bar v. Security Escrows, Inc.*, 377 P.2d 334, 337 (Supreme Court of Oregon, 1962): There have been numerous attempts elsewhere to define the practice of law. None has been universally accepted. The Arizona Supreme Court has said that an exhaustive definition is impossible. Perhaps it is. . . . Documents creating legal rights abound in the business community. The preparation of some of these documents is the principal occupation of some lawyers. The preparation of business documents also occupies part of the time of accountants, automobile salesmen, insurance agents, and many others. The practice of law manifestly includes the drafting of many documents which create legal rights. It does not follow, however, that the drafting of all such documents is always the practice of law. The problem, as is frequently the case, is largely one of drawing a recognizable line. Here the line must be drawn between those services which laymen ought not to undertake and those services which laymen can perform without harm to the public. . . . [A footnote of the court quotes from] Black's Law Dictionary (1957): "Practice of law. Not limited to appearing in court, or advising and assisting in the conduct of litigation, but embracing the preparation of pleadings, and other papers incident to actions and special proceedings, conveyancing, the preparation of legal instruments of all kinds, and the giving of all legal advice to clients. . . . It embraces all advice to clients and all actions taken for them in matters connected with the law."

Rule 9.700 (Oregon State Bar, *Rules of the Unlawful Practice of Law Committee*): The practice of law includes, but is not limited to, any of the following: . . . appearing, personally or otherwise, on behalf of another in any judicial or administrative proceeding; 3) providing advice or service to another on any matter involving the application of legal principles to rights, duties, obligations or liabilities.

## OREGON ETHICS AND PRACTICE RULES ON THE INTERNET

www.law.cornell.edu/ethics/oregon.html

www.osbar.org/Ethics/home.cfm

www.osbar.org/Programs/GeneralCounsel/
    EthicsAdvice.html

www.crossingthebar.com/OR-UPL.htm

## PARALEGALS (AND OTHER NONATTORNEYS) IN COURT

- *Mendoza v. SAIF*, 859 P.2d 582 (Court of Appeals of Oregon, 1993) (an attorney does not establish "good cause" for failure to file a request for a hearing by arguing that he told his legal assistant twice to file it but she failed to do so).
- *Richmark Corp. v. Timber Falling Consultants*, 126 Federal Rules Decisions 58 (U.S. District Court, Oregon, 1989) (paralegal mistakenly sends privileged documents to opposing counsel; attorney failed to supervise paralegal properly).
- *In the Matter of Griffith*, 913 P.2d 695 (Supreme Court of Oregon, 1995) (disbarred attorney acts as paralegal at his old law firm).
- *In re Conduct of Morin*, 878 P.2d 393 (Supreme Court of Oregon, 1994) (it is not the unauthorized practice of law for paralegals to give seminars on living trusts and answer general questions about living trust packages; it is the unauthorized practice of law for the paralegal to advise clients or potential clients on legal matters specific to them or to help them select among the legal forms available).
- *Robins v. Scholastic Book Fairs*, 928 F. Supp. 1027 (U.S. District Court, Oregon, 1996) (paralegal fees reduced; 210 hours spent by paralegals were excessive in a straightforward case).

# PENNSYLVANIA

## ETHICAL RULES AND GUIDELINES IN PENNSYLVANIA

Pennsylvania Bar Ass'n, *Ethical Considerations in the Use of Nonlawyer Assistants*, Formal Opinion Number 98–75 (12/4/98) (1998 WL 988168). A nonlawyer assistant who arrives with a disqualifying conflict of interest may be employed if she is screened and the client is notified. A nonlawyer assistant cannot appear before a court or an administrative tribunal unless such appearance is authorized by statute, court rule or administrative regulation. This includes even routine matters such as seeking a post-

ponement. A nonlawyer assistant cannot conduct a deposition even with predetermined approval by the lawyer. Attendance at a real estate settlement in the capacity of representing either the seller or the purchaser by anyone other than a lawyer constitutes the unauthorized practice of law. Lawyers and their nonlawyer assistants should make certain that clients and other persons dealing with them are aware that the nonlawyer assistant is not a lawyer and cannot give legal advice. Nonlawyers may not sign engagement letters, set fees, or solicit legal business for the lawyer or law firm. However, the name of a nonlawyer assistant may appear on the lawyer's or law firm letterhead if her status is properly revealed. Nonlawyer assistants may sign letters on firm stationery, again, if they are properly identified, and the letters do not contain legal advice. They may also have business cards with the name of the firm on it if they are properly identified and the information on the card conforms to the ethical rule on advertising. A lawyer may not share particular fees with a nonlawyer. It would be proper to compensate a nonlawyer on the basis of a fixed salary plus a percentage of the firm's net profits. The fees and expenses of legal assistants may be billed to a client who has consented to the arrangement. A suspended or disbarred lawyer may be engaged as a nonlawyer assistant.

---

Philadelphia Bar Ass'n, Professional Responsibility Committee, *Professional Responsibility for Nonlawyers* (1989). *Guideline 1:* Consider all work of the office confidential, even public knowledge about a client. Do not discuss the business of your office or your firm's clients with any outsider unless you have specific authorization from an attorney. It is illegal and unethical to disclose or to use any information about a company that might be of significance to the securities market in financial transactions such as the purchase or sale of stocks, bonds or other security. *Guideline 2:* A paralegal may not sign papers to be filed in court, ask questions at a deposition, or handle court appearances. A client with whom the paralegal has developed rapport will often ask the paralegal questions such as, "What do you think my chances of recovery are?" Such questions seek advice and the paralegal should refer them to an attorney. *Guideline 3:* If an attorney allows a nonattorney to sign letters on law firm stationery, a descriptive title such as *legal assistant* should be used to clearly indicate the nonattorney's position. *Guideline 4:* If you interview a witness who does not have his or her own attorney, explain who you are and who your office represents. You cannot give the witness any advice except to secure his or her own attorney. If the opposing party has an attorney, you cannot talk with that party without his or her attorney's permission. You might also need this permission to talk to any employees of the opposing party. *Guideline 5:* A paralegal must be truthful when dealing with others on behalf of a client. *Guideline 6:* If the law firm has possession of a client's money or other property, it must be kept completely separate from the attorney's or law firm's money or property, and a proper accounting must be maintained.

## DEFINING THE PRACTICE
## OF LAW IN PENNSYLVANIA

*Vohlman v. Western Pennsylvania Hospital*, 652 A.2d 849, 851, 852 (Superior Court of Pennsylvania, 1994): While the rules and laws proscribing the unauthorized practice of law are clear, defining the abstract boundaries of the "practice of law" would be an elusive, complex task, "more likely to invite criticism than to achieve clarity." . . . This is so because the practice of law may well be used in a different sense for various purposes. "Where . . . a judgment requires the abstract understanding of legal principles and a refined skill for their concrete application, the exercise of legal judgment is called for. While at times the line between lay and legal judgments may be a fine one, it is nevertheless discernible. Each given case must turn on a careful analysis of the particular judgment involved and the expertise that must be brought to bear on its exercise. . . . (See *7 American Jurisprudence 2d*, Attorneys at Law § 1 (1980) ("practice of law . . . embraces the preparation of pleadings and other papers incident to actions and special proceedings, the management of such actions and proceedings on behalf of clients before judges and courts").

§ 2524, title 42 (*Pennsylvania Consolidated Statutes Annotated*): [A]ny person, including, but not limited to, a paralegal or legal assistant, who within this Commonwealth shall practice law, or who shall hold himself out to the public as being entitled to practice law, or use or advertise the title of lawyer, attorney at law, attorney and counselor at law, counselor, or the equivalent in any language, in such a manner as to convey the impression that he is a practitioner of the law of any jurisdiction, without being an attorney at law or a corporation complying with 15 Pa.C.S. Ch. 29 (relating to professional corporations), commits a misdemeanor of the third degree upon a first violation. A second or subsequent violation of this subsection constitutes a misdemeanor of the first degree.

## PENNSYLVANIA ETHICS AND PRACTICE
## RULES ON THE INTERNET

www.law.cornell.edu/ethics/pennsylvania.html
www2.law.cornell.edu/cgi-bin/foliocgi.exe/Pa-code?
www.philabar.org/public/proresponsibility.asp
www.philabar.org/public/ethics.asp
www.crossingthebar.com/PA-UPL.htm

## PARALEGALS (AND OTHER
## NONATTORNEYS) IN COURT

- *Brown v. Hammond*, 810 F. Supp. 644 (U.S. District Court, E.D. Pennsylvania, 1993) (paralegal dismissed for disclosing illegal billing practices) (see text of case in chapter 5).
- *In re Busy Beaver Building Centers*, 19 F.3d 833 (U.S. Court of Appeals, 3d Circuit, 1994) (award of paralegal fees in bankruptcy case; extensive discussion of the role of the litigation paralegal as opposed to a legal secretary; amicus brief filed by the National Federation of Paralegal Associations; trial court disallowed compensation for those services performed by paralegals that it considered "purely clerical functions" and therefore part of an attorney's overhead for which there can be no separate payment; on appeal this decision was reversed; page 838: "if the court were to disallow paralegal assistance on such matters, the paralegal profession would suffer a major setback, and attorneys would instead perform those services but at greater expense" to the client; the standard on what paralegal services are compensable will be whether such services are compensable in nonbankruptcy cases: whether nonbankruptcy attorneys typically charge and collect from their clients fees for the kind of services in question, and the rates charged and collected therefor; the case was sent back to the lower court to apply this standard).

# RHODE ISLAND

## ETHICAL RULES AND GUIDELINES
## IN RHODE ISLAND

*Definition*: A legal assistant is one who under the supervision of a lawyer, shall apply knowledge of law and legal procedures in rendering direct assistance to lawyers, clients and courts; design, develop and modify procedures, techniques, services and processes; prepare and interpret legal documents; detail procedures for practicing in certain fields of law; research, select, assess, compile and use information from the law library and other references; and analyze and handle procedural problems that involve independent decisions. In contacts with clients, courts, agencies, attorneys, or the public, paralegals must disclose at the outset that they are not attorneys. They can assist at a real estate closing. They can sign correspondence as long as their nonattorney status is clear and the letter does not give legal advice or substantive instructions to a client. They can use a business card with the name of the law firm on it if their nonattorney status is disclosed. An attorney shall not form a partnership with a paralegal if any part of the partnership involves the practice of law. A paralegal cannot share legal fees or be compensated for referring matters to an attorney. An attorney cannot hire a suspended or disbarred attorney as a paralegal (or an attorney who has resigned because of a breach of ethics). Rhode Island Supreme Court, *Provisional Order No. 18* (2/1/83), revised 10/31/90.

A law firm's letterhead must place the title *legal assistant* after the name of an attorney who is licensed in another state but who is ineligible to sit for the Rhode Island bar examination because he was graduated from an unaccredited law school. Ethics Advisory Panel of the Rhode Island Supreme Court, *Opinion 93–28* (5/12/93). See also *Opinion 92–6* (1992), where the term *legal assistant* is preferred over *paralegal* for nonattorney employees.

An attorney may not hire a suspended or disbarred attorney as a paralegal. Ethics Advisory Panel of the Rhode Island Supreme Court, *Opinion 90–12* (2/27/90); *Opinion 91–64* (9/19/91).

## DEFINING THE PRACTICE OF LAW IN RHODE ISLAND

§ 11-27-2 (*Rhode Island Statutes*): The term "practice law" as used in this chapter shall be deemed to mean the doing of any act for another person usually done by attorneys at law in the course of their profession, and, without limiting the generality of the foregoing, shall be deemed to include the following: (1) The appearance or acting as the attorney, solicitor, or representative of another person before any court, referee, master, auditor, division, department, commission, board, judicial person, or body authorized or constituted by law to determine any question of law or fact or to exercise any judicial power, or the preparation of pleadings or other legal papers incident to any action or other proceeding of any kind before or to be brought before the court or other body; (2) The giving or tendering to another person for a consideration, direct or indirect, of any advice or counsel pertaining to a law question or a court action or judicial proceeding brought or to be brought; (3) The undertaking or acting as a representative or on behalf of another person to commence, settle, compromise, adjust, or dispose of any civil or criminal case or cause of action; (4) The preparation or drafting for another person of a will, codicil, corporation organization, amendment, or qualification papers, or any instrument which requires legal knowledge and capacity and is usually prepared by attorneys at law.

## RHODE ISLAND ETHICS AND PRACTICE RULES ON THE INTERNET

www.law.cornell.edu/ethics/ri.html

www.courts.state.ri.us/supreme/ethics/
    ethicsadvisorypanelopinions.htm

www.crossingthebar.com/RI-UPL.htm

## PARALEGALS (AND OTHER NONATTORNEYS) IN COURT

- *Schroff, Inc. v. Taylor-Peterson*, 732 A.2d 719 (Supreme Court of Rhode Island, 1999) (award of paralegal fees; utilizing services of paralegals should result in reducing, rather than enhancing, attorney fees).
- *Donovan v. Bowling*, 706 A.2d 937 (Supreme Court of Rhode Island, 1998) (paralegal can be called as a witness to give testimony on possible prior inconsistent statements by a witness).
- *In re Almacs*, 178 Bankruptcy Reporter 598 (U.S. Bankruptcy Court, Rhode Island, 1995) (some of the paralegal charges are for tasks that are clerical in nature and should be treated as overhead rather than as separate paralegal fees).

# SOUTH CAROLINA

## ETHICAL RULES AND GUIDELINES IN SOUTH CAROLINA

South Carolina Bar, *Guidelines for the Utilization by Lawyers of the Services of Legal Assistants* (12/11/81). *Guideline I:* An attorney shall not permit his or her legal assistant to engage in the unauthorized practice of law. *Guideline II:* A legal assistant may perform certain functions otherwise prohibited when and to the extent permitted by court or administrative agency. *Guideline III:* A legal assistant can perform services for the lawyer if (a) the client understands that the legal assistant is not an attorney, (b) the attorney supervises the legal assistant, and (c) the attorney is fully responsible for what the legal assistant does or fails to do. *Guideline IV:* The attorney must instruct the legal assistant to preserve the confidences and secrets of a client and shall exercise care that the legal assistant does so. *Guideline V:* An attorney shall not form a partnership with a legal assistant if any part of the partnership consists of the practice of law. Nor shall an attorney share, on a proportionate basis, legal fees with a legal assistant. The legal assistant, however, can be included in a retirement plan even though based in whole or in part on a profit-sharing arrangement. A legal assistant shall not be paid, directly or indirectly for referring legal matters to an attorney. *Guideline VI:* The letterhead of an attorney may not include the name of a legal assistant, but a legal assistant can have a business card that prints the name of his or her attorney as long as the legal assistant's capacity or status is clearly indicated. A legal assistant can sign letters on an attorney's letterhead as long as the legal assistant's signature is followed by an appropriate designation (e.g., "legal assistant") so that it is clear the signer is not an attorney. *Guideline VII:* An attorney shall require a legal assistant, when dealing with a client, to disclose at the outset that he or she is not an attorney. This disclosure is also required when the paralegal is dealing with a court, administrative agency, attorney, or the public if there is any reason for their believing the legal assistant is an attorney or is associated with an attorney. This guideline applies even in administrative agencies where the legal assistant is allowed to represent clients. *Guideline VIII:* Except as otherwise provided by law, any grievances or complaints of the use of legal assistants by attorneys shall be referred for action to the Board of Commissioners on Grievances and Discipline.

---

A compensation system in which a paralegal receives a bonus based on the charges billed to a client is a profit-sharing arrangement and expressly permitted under Rule 5.4(a)(3). A law firm, however, may run afoul of fee-splitting rules if the bonus is based on a percentage of a particular fee earned. South Carolina Bar, *Ethics Advisory Opinion 97–02* (3/1997).

A lawyer may employ the services of an independent paralegal assistance service provided the lawyer adequately supervises the work of the paralegals and remains responsible for their work product. In billing for the paralegal organization's services, the lawyer should comply with his fiduciary duty to disclose to his clients the basis of his fee and expenses. South Carolina Bar, *Ethics Advisory Opinion 96–13* (1996).

A lawyer may not bill a client for paralegal services rendered by an individual who is not performing paralegal services. The issuance of paralegal certificates to a lawyer's staff does not transform all of the duties of those individuals into paralegal services. South Carolina Bar, *Ethics Advisory Opinion 94–37* (1/1995).

A nonattorney switching jobs raises the possibility of disqualification of her new employer because of a conflict of interest. South Carolina Bar, *Ethics Advisory Opinion 93–29* (10/1993).

A lawyer who is disbarred, suspended, or transferred due to incapacity to inactive status shall not be employed by a member of the South Carolina Bar as a paralegal, as an investigator, or in any other capacity connected with the law. Appellate Court Rule 413, Lawyer Disciplinary Enforcement Rule 34.

Nonattorney employees can have their own business cards as long as the title *legal assistant* is used on the card. The name of the law firm can also be printed on the card but only if the legal assistant performs significant duties outside the law office. South Carolina Bar, *Opinion 88–6*.

An attorney can hire nonattorneys to fill in preprinted real estate forms and do title searches as long as they are supervised by the attorney and the attorney maintains direct contact with clients. South Carolina Bar, *Opinion 88–2* (6/1988). On title searches, see also *Opinion 78–26* (10/1978).

It is the unauthorized practice of law for a nonattorney to have an ownership interest, along with an attorney, in a corporation that drafts and provides real estate documents if the nonattorney controls any of the legal services provided. South Carolina Bar, *Opinion 84–3* (9/1985).

## DEFINING THE PRACTICE OF LAW IN SOUTH CAROLINA

*The South Carolina Medical Malpractice Joint Underwriting Association v. Froelich*, 377 S.E.2d 306, 307 (Supreme Court of South Carolina, 1989): Conduct constituting the practice of law includes a wide range of activities. It is too obvious for discussion that the practice of law is not limited to the conduct of cases in courts. According to the generally understood definition of the practice of law in this country, it embraces the preparation of pleadings and other papers incident to actions and special proceedings and the management of such actions and proceedings on behalf of clients before judges and courts, and in addition conveyancing, the preparation of legal instruments of all kinds, and in general all advice to clients and all action taken for them in matters connected with the law.

## SOUTH CAROLINA ETHICS AND PRACTICE RULES ON THE INTERNET

www.law.cornell.edu/ethics/sc.html
www2.law.cornell.edu/cgi-bin/foliocgi.exe/sc-code?
gandalf.scbar.org/ethics
www.crossingthebar.com/SC-UPL.htm

## PARALEGALS (AND OTHER NONATTORNEYS) IN COURT

■ *In re Konohia*, 550 S.E.2d 318 (Supreme Court of South Carolina, 2001) (attorney disciplined for failing to supervise paralegal).

■ *Doe v. Condon*, 532 S.E. 2d 879 (Supreme Court of South Carolina, 2000) (paralegals and the unauthorized practice of law).

■ *Lucas v. Guyton*, 901 F. Supp. 1047, 1059 (U.S. District Court, South Carolina, 1995) (the "court observed Ms. Pope to be a diligent and very able paralegal who assisted in many respects during the trial including reading the depositions of Plaintiff's death row witnesses, taking notes throughout the proceeding and, on numerous occasions, conferring with counsel during his presentation of the case").

■ *Andersdon v. Tolbert*, 473 S.E.2d 456 (Court of Appeals of South Carolina, 1996) (award of paralegal fees).

■ *In re Unauthorized Practice of Law Rules Proposed by the South Carolina Bar*, 422 S.E. 2d 123 (Supreme Court of South Carolina, 1992) (a business can be represented by a nonattorney employee in civil magistrate's court proceedings; a South Carolina state agency may authorize nonattorneys to appear and represent clients before the agency; an arresting police officer—a nonattorney—may prosecute traffic offenses in magistrate's court and in municipal court).

■ *In re Easler*, 272 S.E.2d 32, 32–33 (Supreme Court of South Carolina, 1980) (the activities of a paralegal do not constitute the practice of law as long as they are limited to work of a preparatory nature).

■ *South Carolina v. Robinson*, 468 S.E.2d 290 (Supreme Court of South Carolina, 1996) (injunction against paralegal who advertises in Yellow Pages—"If your civil rights have been violated, call me"—as a paralegal and represents clients in court; § 40–5–80 of the *South Carolina Code Annotated* allows a nonattorney to represent another in court if the permission of the court is first obtained—"with leave of the court"—but the paralegal in this case did not always obtain this permission).

■ *In the Matter of Jenkins*, 468 S.E.2d 869 (Supreme Court of South Carolina, 1996) (attorney disciplined for asking her paralegal to notarize a forged signature).

# South Dakota

## ETHICAL RULES AND GUIDELINES IN SOUTH DAKOTA

*Definition*: Legal assistants (also known as paralegals) are a distinguishable group of persons who assist licensed attorneys in the delivery of legal services. Through formal education, training, and experience, legal assistants have knowledge and expertise regarding the legal system, substantive and procedural law, the ethical considerations of the legal profession, and the Rules of Professional Conduct as stated in chapter 16–18, which qualify them to do work of a legal nature under the employment and direct supervision of a licensed attorney. This rule shall apply to all unlicensed persons employed by a licensed attorney who are represented to the public or clients as possessing training or education which qualifies them to assist in the handling of legal matters or document preparation for the client. An attorney must assure that a legal assistant is trained and competent to perform assigned tasks. The status of a legal assistant must be disclosed. The tasks assigned a legal assistant must not require the exercise of unsupervised legal judgment. An attorney must instruct the legal assistant about the standards of confidentiality and the other ethical standards governing attorneys. A legal assistant can write and sign correspondence on attorney letterhead as long as no legal opinion or advice is given. Legal assistants may be mentioned by name and title on attorney letterhead and on business cards that identify the attorney's firm. An attorney must take reasonable measures to prevent conflicts of interest created by the legal assistant's personal interests and other employment. There must be no splitting of fees with legal assistants nor paying them for a referral of legal business. A legal assistant's pay cannot, by advance agreement, be contingent on the profitability of the attorney's practice. To be a legal assistant in South Dakota, a person must meet minimum educational qualifications or a designated number of years of experience and in-house training. A disbarred or suspended attorney shall not serve as a paralegal without the approval of the Supreme Court of South Dakota. *South Dakota Codified Laws* § 16–18–34.

It is unethical for an attorney to give 5% of the fees collected from clients referred by a nonattorney. State Bar of South Dakota, *Opinion 94–12*.

A law firm can list paralegals on their letterhead (referring to graduates of law school who have not yet passed the bar exam). State Bar of South Dakota, *Opinion 90–10* (9/22/90).

## DEFINING THE PRACTICE OF LAW IN SOUTH DAKOTA

*Persche v. Jones*, 387 N.W.2d 32, 36 (Supreme Court of South Dakota, 1986): Practicing law "is not limited to conducting litigation, but includes giving legal advice and counsel, and rendering services that require the use of legal knowledge or skill and the preparing of instruments and contracts by which legal rights are secured, whether or not the matter is pending in a court."

## SOUTH DAKOTA ETHICS AND PRACTICE RULES ON THE INTERNET

www.law.cornell.edu/ethics/sd.html
www.sdbar.org/members/ethics/default.htm
www.crossingthebar.com/SD–UPL.htm

## PARALEGALS (AND OTHER NONATTORNEYS) IN COURT

■ *In re Discipline of Mines*, 612 N.W.2d 619 (Supreme Court of South Dakota, 2000) (disbarment of at-

torney warranted due in part to improper use of legal assistant and improper billing).

■ *In re French*, 162 Bankruptcy Reporter 541 (U.S. Bankruptcy Court, South Dakota, 1994) (disclosures by a debtor to a paralegal of the debtor's attorney are not protected by the attorney-client privilege).

■ *In re Yankton College*, 101 Bankruptcy Reporter 151, 159 (U.S. Bankruptcy Court, South Dakota, 1989) ("Paraprofessional Billing": if paralegal work is to be compensated, the qualifications of the paralegal should be established to justify the charge; "[s]imply classifying a secretary as a paralegal for billing purposes does not justify compensating secretary time" which should be part of overhead).

■ *Cody v. Hillard*, 599 F. Supp. 1025 (U.S. District Court, South Dakota, 1984) (inmates as paralegals).

# TENNESSEE

## ETHICAL RULES AND GUIDELINES IN TENNESSEE

If appropriate screening devices are in place and Client "A" consents, an entire law firm need not be disqualified from representing Client "A" simply because a "tainted" attorney in the firm once worked at another firm that represented Client "B" in a case adverse to Client "A." Furthermore, "the disqualification rules and screening procedures are applicable to lawyer, law clerk, paralegal, and legal secretary." Board of Professional Responsibility of the Supreme Court of Tennessee, *Formal Ethics Opinion 89-F-118* (3/10/89). Note: this Opinion may overrule *Formal Ethics Opinion 87-F-110* (6/10/87), which disqualified a law firm because of a "tainted" paralegal who switched jobs even though screening mechanisms were in place. The validity of *Opinion 89-F-110* is also in doubt because of *King v. King* (see discussion below).

It is the unauthorized practice of law for an attorney to allow his or her paralegal to appear at a section 341 meeting of creditors in bankruptcy cases to ask questions of debtors unless a court expressly authorizes it. Board of Professional Responsibility of the Supreme Court of Tennessee, *Advisory Ethics Opinion 92-A-473(a)* (5/12/92), confirming *Opinion 92-A-475* (1/1991). See *In re Kincaid* below, which *does* authorize it.

It is the unauthorized practice of law for an attorney to allow his or her paralegal to appear in court at docket calls on behalf of the attorney to schedule cases. Board of Professional Responsibility of the Supreme Court of Tennessee, *Formal Ethics Opinion 85-F-94* (5/6/85).

A suspended attorney should not act as a paralegal. Board of Professional Responsibility of the Supreme Court of Tennessee, *Ethics Opinion 83-F-50* (8/12/83).

It is the unauthorized practice of law for an unsupervised independent paralegal to provide the public with the service of filling out legal documents such as bankruptcy petitions, uncontested divorce petitions, wills, and premarital agreements for a fee. Attorney General of Tennessee, *Opinion 92–01* (1/9/92).

## DEFINING THE PRACTICE OF LAW IN TENNESSEE

§ 23-3-101 (*Tennessee Code Annotated*): (1) "Law business" means the advising or counseling for a valuable consideration of any person, firm, association, or corporation, as to any secular law, or the drawing or the procuring of or assisting in the drawing for a valuable consideration of any paper, document or instrument affecting or relating to secular rights, or the doing of any act for a valuable consideration in a representative capacity, obtaining or tending to secure for any person, firm, association or corporation any property or property rights whatsoever, or the soliciting of clients directly or indirectly to provide such services; and (2) "Practice of law" means the appearance as an advocate in a representative capacity or the drawing of papers, pleadings or documents or the performance of any act in such capacity in connection with proceedings pending or prospective before any court, commissioner, referee or any body, board, committee or commission constituted by law or having authority to settle controversies, or the soliciting of clients directly or indirectly to provide such services.

## TENNESSEE ETHICS AND PRACTICE RULES ON THE INTERNET

www.law.cornell.edu/ethics/tennessee.html
www.tba.org/Committees/Conduct/index.html
www.crossingthebar.com/TN-UPL.htm

## PARALEGALS (AND OTHER NONATTORNEYS) IN COURT

- *Clinard v. Blackwood*, 46 S.W. 3d 177 (Supreme Court of Tennessee, 2001) (screening involving office paralegals when an attorney's job switch creates a conflict of interest).
- *King v. King*, 1989 WL 122981 (Court of Appeals of Tennessee, 1989) (motion to disqualify the defendant's law firm is denied; the defendant hired a person who was once a secretary for the plaintiff's attorney, but there were no breaches of confidentiality by the secretary at the new firm; the court relied on *Ethics Opinion 87-F-110* but pointed out differences in the positions of legal secretaries and paralegals).
- *Moncier v. Ferrell*, 990 S.W.2d 710 (Supreme Court of Tennessee, 1998) (paralegal expenses were not authorized under supreme court rule permitting appointment of two attorneys for one defendant in capital cases).
- *In re Kincaid*, 146 Bankruptcy Reporter 387 (U.S. Bankruptcy Court, W.D. Tennessee, 1992) (a nonattorney regularly employed by a corporate-creditor could appear on behalf of the employer at a creditors' meeting in a bankruptcy case and question debtors without engaging in unauthorized practice of law).
- *Alexander v. Inman*, 903 S.W.2d 686, 704 (Court of Appeals of Tennessee, 1995) (the request to the court for an award of fees for paralegal services explained the services they provided in such general terms "that no finder of fact would be able to determine whether they were required or reasonable").
- *Tuggle v. Barksdale*, 641 F. Supp. 34 (U.S. District Court, W.D. Tennessee, 1985) (use of inmate paralegals—jailhouse lawyers).

# TEXAS

## ETHICAL RULES AND GUIDELINES IN TEXAS

State Bar of Texas, *General Guidelines for the Utilization of the Services of Legal Assistants by Attorneys* (January 22, 1993). *Guideline I:* An attorney should ensure that a legal assistant does not give legal advice or otherwise engage in the unauthorized practice of law. *Guideline II:* The attorney must take reasonable measures to ensure that the legal assistant's conduct is consistent with the Texas rules of ethics. *Guideline III:* An attorney may, with the client's consent, perform supervised functions authorized by law and ethics. *Guideline IV:* When dealing with others, the status of the legal assistant must be disclosed at the outset. *Guideline V:* The attorney must not assign functions to a legal assistant that require the exercise of independent professional legal judgment. The attorney must maintain a direct relationship with the client. The attorney is responsible for the actions taken and not taken by a legal assistant. *Guideline VI:* An attorney may not delegate to a legal assistant responsibility for establishing the attorney-client relationship, setting fees, or giving legal advice to a client. *Guideline VII:* An attorney must instruct the legal assistant to preserve the sanctity of all confidences and secrets and take reasonable measures to ensure that this is done. *Guideline VIII:* The attorney should take reasonable measures to prevent conflicts of interest resulting from a legal assistant's other employment or interests. *Guideline IX:* An attorney can charge and bill for a legal assistant's time but may not share legal fees with a legal assistant. *Guideline X:* An attorney may not split legal fees with a legal assistant nor pay a legal assistant for the referral of legal business. A legal assistant's compensation cannot be contingent, by advance agreement, upon the profitability of the attorney's practice. *Guideline XI:* The legal assistant can have a business card that names the firm as long as the status of the legal assistant is included on the card. The attorney must take reasonable measures to ensure that the card is not used in a deceptive way for unethical solicitation. See also State Bar of Texas, Legal Assistant Division, *Code of Ethics for Legal Assistants* (Texas Center for Legal Ethics and Professionalism) at *www.txethics.org/reference_ethics.asp*.

---

Law firm letterhead can print the name of legal assistants and can indicate that they have been certified (with a notation that they are legal assistants and are not licensed to practice law). State Bar of Texas, *Opinion 436* (6/20/86), which overrules *Opinion 390*.

A legal assistant can write a letter on the law firm's letterhead as long as he or she signs as a legal assistant. The letter should not contain legal advice, judgment, strategy, or settlement negotiations. Such letters should be signed by an attorney. State Bar of Texas, *Opinion 381* (3/1975).

A legal assistant may have a business card with the law firm's name appearing on it provided the status of the legal assistant is clearly disclosed. State Bar of Texas, *Opinion 403* (1982).

The name of an employee can be printed on an outdoor sign of a law firm as long as the nonattorney status of the employee is clear on the sign. Professional Ethics Committee of the State Bar of Texas, *Opinion 437* (6/20/86).

It is unethical for attorneys to take a case in which they know or believe that they may have to call their nonattorney employee as an expert witness. State Bar of Texas, *Opinion 516* (6/2/95).

A legal assistant switches sides between law firms who are opposing each other on a case. The new employer is not disqualified if he takes steps to ensure there will be no breach of confidentiality by the legal assistant. State Bar of Texas, *Opinion 472* (6/20/91).

When an attorney fails to supervise his paralegal, the attorney is responsible for the malpractice of the paralegal, such as the theft of client funds by the paralegal. "In the future, you should establish greater controls over your paralegals." Dallas Bar Ass'n, *Opinion 1989–5*.

## DEFINING THE PRACTICE OF LAW IN TEXAS

§ 81.101 (*Vernon's Texas Statutes and Codes Annotated*): (a) In this chapter the "practice of law" means the preparation of a pleading or other document incident to an action or special proceeding or the management of the action or proceeding on behalf of a client before a judge in court as well as a service rendered out of court, including the giving of advice or the rendering of any service requiring the use of legal skill or knowledge, such as preparing a will, contract, or other instrument, the legal effect of which under the facts and conclusions involved must be carefully determined.

## TEXAS ETHICS AND PRACTICE RULES ON THE INTERNET

www.law.cornell.edu/ethics/texas.html
www.tbls.org/Cert/Las.asp
www.txethics.org/reference_opinions.asp
www.txethics.org/reference_ethics.asp
www.lawlib.uh.edu/ethics/EC/index.html
www.crossingthebar.com/TX-UPL.htm

## PARALEGALS (AND OTHER NONATTORNEYS) IN COURT

- *Phoenix Founders, Inc. v. Marshall*, 887 S.W.2d 831, 834 (Supreme Court of Texas, 1994) (there is a rebuttable presumption that a nonattorney who switches sides in ongoing litigation, after having gained confidential information at the first firm, will share the information with members of the new firm; but the presumption may be rebutted to avoid disqualification upon a showing of sufficient precautions, e.g., building a Chinese Wall, to guard against any disclosure of confidences). See also *In re American Home Products Corp.*, 985 S.W.2d 68 (Supreme Court of Texas, 1998).
- *State Bar of Texas v. Faubion*, 821 S.W.2d 203 (Court of Appeals of Texas, 1991) (it was unethical for an attorney to pay a paralegal/investigator up to one-third of the fees generated from particular cases on which the paralegal worked; a bonus is proper if it is not based on a percentage of the law firm's profits or on a percentage of particular legal fees).
- *Secretary of Labor v. Page & Addison* (U.S. District Court, N.D. Texas, 1994) (overtime pay). See discussion of this case in chapter 4.
- *Stewart Title Guaranty Co. v. Aiello*, 911 S.W.2d 463 (Court of Appeals of Texas, 1995) (award of paralegal fees).
- *In re Witts*, 180 Bankruptcy Reporter 171, 173 (U.S. Bankruptcy Court, E.D. Texas, 1995) (attorney cannot recover paralegal rates for such clerical tasks as organizing files, proofreading and revising documents, faxing and copying).
- *Petroleos Mexicanos v. Crawford Enterprises, Inc.*, 826 F.2d 392 (U.S. Court of Appeals, 5th Circuit, 1987) (court appoints paralegal as a special master to monitor a company's discovery compliance).
- *Rea v. Cofer*, 879 S.W.2d 224 (Court of Appeals of Texas, 1994) (former client sues attorney and paralegal for legal malpractice).

# UTAH

## ETHICAL RULES AND GUIDELINES IN UTAH

*Definition.* A legal assistant is a person, qualified through education, training, or work experience, who is employed or retained by a lawyer, law office, governmental agency, or the entity in the capacity of function which involves the performance, under the ultimate direction and supervision of an attorney of specifically delegated substantive legal work, which work, for the most part, requires a sufficient knowledge of legal concepts that absent such assistance, the attorney would perform. A legal assistant or "paralegal" includes a paralegal on a contract or free-lance basis who works under the supervision of a lawyer or who produces work directly for a lawyer for which a lawyer is accountable. V. Creation of Legal Assistant Division of the Utah State Bar (Legal Assistant Affiliates). *West's Utah Rules of Court, Utah Code of Judicial Administration*, chapter 16, Utah State Bar Rules for Integration and Management.

A lawyer who negotiates or otherwise communicates with an opposing party's legal assistant representative on substantive matters affecting the rights of parties to a particular matter is not assisting in the unauthorized practice of law if that representative is supervised by a lawyer. Utah State Bar, *Opinion 99–02* (4/30/99).

A lawyer may not use the word "associate" in its name if there are no associated attorneys in the firm even if it "employs one or more associated nonattorneys such as paralegals or investigators." Utah State Bar, *Opinion 138* (1/27/94).

A law firm may not split fees with nonattorneys, but may include nonattorney employees in a compensation or retirement plan as long as compensation is not tied to particular fees and the nonattorney has no controlling interest in the firm. Utah State Bar, *Opinion 139* (1/27/94).

A nonattorney may be listed on the letterhead of an attorney as long as the nonattorney's status is clear. Utah State Bar, *Opinion 131* (5/20/93).

## DEFINING THE PRACTICE OF LAW IN UTAH

*Utah State Bar v. Summerhayes & Hayden*, 905 P.2d 867, 869, 870 (Supreme Court of Utah, 1995): The practice of law, although difficult to define precisely, is generally acknowledged to involve the rendering of services that require the knowledge and application of legal principles to serve the interests of another with his consent. . . . It not only consists of performing services in the courts of justice throughout the various stages of a matter, but in a larger sense involves counseling, advising, and assisting others in connection with their legal rights, duties, and liabilities. . . . It also includes the preparation of contracts and other legal instruments by which legal rights and duties are fixed. . . . This Court has the exclusive authority to regulate the practice of law in Utah. . . . This authority includes the power to determine what constitutes the practice of law and to promulgate rules to control and regulate that practice. There is little in Utah case law that assists the determination of which specific acts, beyond the representation of another's legal interests in a court of law, constitute the practice of law. What constitutes the practice of law in any given situation requires a case-by-case decision, and therefore, each case must be evaluated to determine whether the particular acts involved constitute the practice of law.

## UTAH ETHICS AND PRACTICE RULES ON THE INTERNET

www.law.cornell.edu/ethics/utah.html
www2.law.cornell.edu/cgi-bin/foliocgi.exe/ut-code?
www.utahbar.org/rules/index.html
www.utahbar.org/opinions/index.html
www.crossingthebar.com/UT-UPL.htm

## PARALEGALS (AND OTHER NONATTORNEYS) IN COURT

- *Barnard v. Utah State Bar*, 857 P.2d 917 (Supreme Court of Utah, 1993) (attorney charged with unauthorized practice of law for using paralegals to help clients file their own divorces).
- *Utah v. Long*, 844 P.2d 381 (Court of Appeals of Utah, 1992) (attorney disciplined for failing to supervise his legal assistant who gave a client incorrect legal advice).
- *Anderson v. Secretary of Health and Human Services*, 80 F.3d 1500 (U.S. Court of Appeals, 10th Circuit, 1996) (paralegal costs denied where no documentation—other than the statement of the lead attorney—was submitted on what the paralegal did).
- *Baldwin v. Burton*, 850 P.2d 1188, 1200 (Supreme Court of Utah, 1993) ("allowing recovery for legal assistant fees promotes lawyer efficiency and decreases client litigation costs").
- *Gold Standard, Inc. v. American Barrick Resources Corp.*, 805 P.2d 164, 169 (Supreme Court of Utah, 1990) (a nonattorney's work in preparation for litigation is protected by the attorney work-product rule).

# VERMONT

## ETHICAL RULES AND GUIDELINES IN VERMONT

A paralegal may not sign court pleadings with an attorney's name and the paralegal's initials after the attorney's name. Vermont Bar Ass'n, *Opinion 01–5* (2001).

With client consent, a supervising attorney may permit a paralegal to conduct a loan closing on behalf of a lender client where the client consents, the paralegal's role is ministerial in nature, and the attorney is available for questions, at least by telephone. Vermont Bar Ass'n, *Opinion 99–3* (1999).

Law Firm A may employ a paralegal who formerly was employed by Law Firm B, despite the fact that the two firms are engaged in litigation against each other in a matter in which the paralegal participated for Law Firm B. However, Law Firm A must now screen the paralegal from involvement in the pending litigation and any matter in which the interests of Law Firm B's client are adverse to those of any client of Law Firm A. Further, Law Firm A must ensure that no information relating to the representation of the client of Law Firm B is revealed by the paralegal to any person in Law Firm A. Vermont Bar Ass'n, *Opinion 97–9* (1997).

A law firm cannot continue to represent a defendant in a civil case after hiring a nonattorney employee who had previously performed extensive work on the same case while employed by the law firm representing the plaintiff. Vermont Bar Ass'n, *Opinion 85–8* (1985). For other disqualification cases involving paralegals, see also *Opinion 89–4* (1989), *Opinion 87–15* (1987), and *Opinion 78–2* (1978).

In a conversation with a nonattorney employee, if a prospective client threatens to kill someone, the employee who believes the threat can warn the potential victim. Vermont Bar Ass'n, *Opinion 86–3.*

## DEFINING THE PRACTICE OF LAW IN VERMONT

*In re Welch*, 185 A.2d 458, 459 (Supreme Court of Vermont, 1962): In general, one is deemed to be practicing law whenever he furnishes to another advice or service under circumstances which imply the possession and use of legal knowledge and skill. The practice of law includes "all advice to clients, and all actions taken for them in matters connected with the law." . . . Practice of law includes the giving of legal advice and counsel, and the preparation of legal instruments and contracts [by] which legal rights are secured. . . . Where the rendering of services for another involves the use of legal knowledge or skill on his behalf—where legal advice is required and is availed of or rendered in connection with such services—these services necessarily constitute or include the practice of law. . . . We cannot over-emphasize the necessity of legal training in the proper drafting of legal documents and advice relating thereto. The absence of such training may result in legal instruments faulty in form and contents, and also lead to a failure of purpose, litigation, and expense.

## VERMONT ETHICS AND PRACTICE RULES ON THE INTERNET

www.law.cornell.edu/ethics/vermont.html

www.vtbar.org/AdvisoryEthicsOpinions/index.htm

www.crossingthebar.com/VT-UPL.htm

## PARALEGALS (AND OTHER NONATTORNEYS) IN COURT

- *In re S.T.N. Enterprises, Inc.*, 70 Bankruptcy Reporter 823 (U.S. Bankruptcy Court, Vermont, 1987) (court will reduce an attorney's rate of compensation for performing tasks that could have been performed by a paralegal at a lower rate).
- *McSweeney v. McSweeney*, 618 A.2d 1332 (Supreme Court of Vermont, 1992) (it is not the unauthorized practice of law for nonattorney employees of the Office of Child Support to prepare and file complaints and motions in child support cases before a magistrate [4 V.S.A. § 464,] but they cannot handle URESA cases involving interstate support issues before a magistrate).
- *Nash v. Coxon*, 583 A.2d 96 (Supreme Court of Vermont, 1990) (court refuses to order payment of inmate's paralegal correspondence course).
- *Hohman v. Hogan*, 458 F. Supp. 669 (U.S. District Court, Vermont, 1978) (paralegal assistance to inmates).
- *Berry v. Schweiker*, 675 F.2d 464 (U.S. Court of Appeals, 2d Circuit, 1982) (paralegal represents client at disability benefits hearing).

# Virginia

## ETHICAL RULES AND GUIDELINES IN VIRGINIA

*Definition.* A legal assistant (or paralegal) is a specially trained individual who performs substantive legal work that requires a knowledge of legal concepts. Legal assistants either work under the supervision of an attorney, who assumes responsibility for the final work product, or work in areas where lay individuals are explicitly authorized by statute or regulation to assume certain law-related responsibilities. Recommended by the Virginia State Bar Standing Committee on Unauthorized Practice of Law by Resolution adopted March 8, 1995. See *www.geocities.com/rala1982/guidelines.html.*

A nonlawyer employee working under the direct supervision of a Virginia attorney may participate in gathering information from a client during an initial interview (a client intake), provided that this involves nothing more than the gathering of factual data and the nonlawyer renders no legal advice. In contrast, a nonlawyer employee may not determine the validity of the client's legal claim, as that determination appears to directly involve the application of legal principles to facts, purposes, or desires and is therefore considered the practice of law. The nonlawyer employee may transmit the attorney/client fee agreement to the client and obtain the client's signature on the document. While a nonlawyer employee is permitted to answer straightforward, factual questions regarding the fee agreement, such answers must not include any advice as to the legal ramifications of the contract provisions. Concerning settlement negotiations, a nonlawyer employee may transmit information and documents between the attorney and the client. For example, the employee could share with the client the latest settlement offer. However, it would not be permissible for the employee to evaluate the offer or to recommend to the client whether or not to accept an offer. In contrast, it would be permissible for the nonlawyer to communicate with the client the lawyer's evaluation or recommendation. Unauthorized Practice of Law Committee of the Virginia State Bar, *Opinion 191 (9/29/98).*

A paralegal shall not communicate with clients, outside attorneys, or the public without disclosing his or her nonattorney status. *Code of Professional Responsibility*, DR 3-104(E).

An attorney is not required to withdraw from a case as long as a nonattorney employee does not disclose confidential information learned while she worked for an opposing attorney. Standing Committee on Legal Ethics of the Virginia State Bar, *Opinion 745* (1985).

An attorney represents a client in a case in which the attorney's former nonattorney employee will testify against this client. The attorney is not disqualified from representing this client as long as the client is informed of this situation and still wants the attorney to represent him. Standing Committee on Legal Ethics of the Virginia State Bar, *Opinion 891 (4/1/87).*

A law firm can print the names of nonattorney employees on its letterhead as long as their nonattorney status is clear. These employees can participate in a profit-sharing plan of the firm as part of a compensation or retirement program. Standing Committee on Legal Ethics of the Virginia State Bar, *Opinion 762* (1/29/86). See also *Opinion 970* (9/30/87) (attorney may list name and title of firm's chief investigator as long as listing includes affirmative statement that investigator is not licensed to practice law).

An attorney must not split fees with nonattorneys, but they can be paid a bonus that is based on profit-sharing. Standing Committee on Legal Ethics of the Virginia State Bar, *Opinion 806* (6/25/86).

A law firm engaged in collection work can pay its nonattorney employee a percentage of profits from the collections received plus a salary. Standing Committee on Legal Ethics of the Virginia State Bar, *Opinion 885* (3/11/87).

It is unethical for a nonattorney employee of a law firm to contact prospective collections clients in order to suggest that they hire the law firm for their collections work. Standing Committee on Legal Ethics of the Virginia State Bar, *Opinion 1290* (10/25/89).

A "real estate paralegal company" can provide assistance to an attorney in closing real estate loans that have been referred to this company by the closing attorney. This is not the unauthorized practice of law as long as designated procedures are followed. Unauthorized Practice of Law Committee, *Opinion 147* (4/19/91).

It is not the unauthorized practice of law for a nonattorney to give a judicial officer information (present facts) that concerns the weight of the evidence in bail cases. Unauthorized Practice of Law Committee, *Opinion 186* (9/7/95).

It is not the unauthorized practice of law for a paralegal to appear in court to collect monies resulting from a garnishment as long as this appearance involves only a ministerial or clerical act. Unauthorized Practice of Law Committee, *Opinion 72* (12/12/84).

A lawyer employing a lawyer as a legal assistant when that lawyer's license is suspended or revoked for professional misconduct shall not represent any client represented by the disciplined lawyer or by any lawyer with whom the disciplined lawyer practiced on or after the date of the acts that resulted in suspension or revocation. Rule 5.5, *Rules of Professional Conduct, Virginia Rules of Court*.

A paralegal's name can be printed on the door of the paralegal's private office as long as it does not create the impression that the paralegal is an attorney. Unauthorized Practice of Law Committee, *Opinion 225* (5/21/73) and *Opinion 326* (6/19/79).

A private law firm employs a paralegal whose husband is an attorney who represents the government in cases against clients of the law firm. The law firm can continue to employ this paralegal, but it must tell its clients and the court of the relationship between the paralegal and the government attorney. Unauthorized Practice of Law Committee, *Opinion 358* (3/10/80).

An attorney can instruct his paralegal to call a prospective defendant to ask if it manufactures a particular product. This does not violate the rule against contacting the other side, since there is no litigation under way. The call is part of proper investigation. Unauthorized Practice of Law Committee, *Opinion 1190* (1/4/89). See also *Opinion 1504* (12/14/92) (paralegal can contact opponent to obtain information under Virginia Freedom of Information Act) and *Opinion 1639* (4/24/95) (OK for paralegal to contact the other side to provide information as a courtesy).

## DEFINING THE PRACTICE OF LAW IN VIRGINIA

*Virginia Rules of Court, Rules of the Supreme Court of Virginia*: Part 6. Section I. Unauthorized Practice Rules and Considerations. [O]ne is deemed to be practicing law whenever—

(1) One undertakes for compensation, direct or indirect, to advise another, not his regular employer, in any matter involving the application of legal principles to facts or purposes or desires.

(2) One, other than as a regular employee acting for his employer, undertakes, with or without compensation, to prepare for another legal instruments of any character, other than notices or contracts incident to the regular course of conducting a licensed business.

(3) One undertakes, with or without compensation, to represent the interest of another before any tribunal—judicial, administrative, or executive—otherwise than in the presentation of facts, figures, or factual conclusions, as distinguished from legal conclusions, by an employee regularly and bona fide employed on a salary basis, or by one specially employed as an expert in respect to such facts and figures when such representation by such employee or expert does not involve the examination of witnesses or preparation of pleadings.

## VIRGINIA ETHICS AND PRACTICE RULES ON THE INTERNET

www.law.cornell.edu/ethics/virginia.html
www.vsb.org/profguides/index.html
www.vacle.org/leos.htm
www.crossingthebar.com/VA-UPL.htm
www.crossingthebar.com/VA-UPLOPS.htm

## PARALEGALS (AND OTHER NONATTORNEYS) IN COURT

- *Mullins v. Va. Lutheran Homes, Inc.*, 44 Va. Cir. 156, 1997 WL 1070493 (Circuit Court of Virginia, 1997) ("It may markedly aid the lawyer to have his paralegal assistant present. However, in my view, neither the client nor, in this case, the opposing party, should have to expect to pay an additional sum, over and above the lawyer's hourly fee, for this aid.")
- *Musselman v. Willoughby Corp.*, 337 S.E.2d 724 (Supreme Court of Virginia, 1985) (paralegal negligence asserted in legal malpractice case brought by client against attorney).

- *EEOC v. American Nat'l Bank*, 625 F.2d 1176 (U.S. Court of Appeals, 4th Circuit, 1981) (role of paralegal in racial discrimination case).
- *Kaufhold v. Bright*, 835 F. Supp. 294 (U.S. District Court, W.D. Virginia, 1993) (inmate who attended paralegal correspondence school sues the parole board for impeding his potential employment as a paralegal).
- *Tanksley v. Garrett*, 175 Bankruptcy Reporter 434 (U.S. Bankruptcy Court, W.D. Virginia, 1994) (United States Trustee seeks to enjoin a law firm from allowing a paralegal to represent clients at section 341 bankruptcy hearing).
- *Trimper v. City of Norfolk*, 58 F.3d 68 (U.S. Court of Appeals, 4th Circuit, 1995) (award of paralegal fees).
- *Martin v. Cavalier Hotel Corp.* 48 F.3d 1343, 1360 (U.S. Court of Appeals, 4th Circuit, 1995) (paying for 30 hours of paralegal time for "jury observation" is excessive; there was no reasonable necessity for other paralegals to attend 47 hours of trial proceedings).

## WASHINGTON STATE

### ETHICAL RULES AND GUIDELINES IN WASHINGTON STATE

A disbarred attorney cannot be employed as a paralegal. Washington State Bar Ass'n, *Opinion 184* (1990).

An attorney cannot let a collection agency use his name on court documents unless the attorney provides legal assistance on each particular case. Rubber-stamping legal papers of nonattorneys is unethical. Washington State Bar Ass'n, *Opinion 18* (1952) and *Opinion 76* (1960).

### DEFINING THE PRACTICE OF LAW IN WASHINGTON STATE

Rule 24 (*West's Washington Court Rules*): Part I, General Rules (GR).

(a) General Definition. The practice of law is the application of legal principles and judgment with regard to the circumstances or objectives of another entity or person(s) which require the knowledge and skill of a person trained in the law. This includes but is not limited to:

(1) Giving advice or counsel to others as to their legal rights or the legal rights or responsibilities of others for fees or other consideration.

(2) Selection, drafting, or completion of legal documents or agreements which affect the legal rights of an entity or person(s).

(3) Representation of another entity or person(s) in a court, or in a formal administrative adjudicative proceeding or other formal dispute resolution process or in an administrative adjudicative proceeding in which legal pleadings are filed or a record is established as the basis for judicial review.

(4) Negotiation of legal rights or responsibilities on behalf of another entity or person(s).

(b) Exceptions and Exclusions. Whether or not they constitute the practice of law, the following are permitted:

(1) Practicing law authorized by a limited license to practice pursuant to Admission to Practice Rules 8 (special admission for: a particular purpose or action; indigent representation; educational purposes; emeritus membership; house counsel), 9 (legal interns), 12 (limited practice for closing officers), or 14 (limited practice for foreign law consultants).

(2) Serving as a court house facilitator pursuant to court rule.

(3) Acting as a lay representative authorized by administrative agencies or tribunals.

(4) Serving in a neutral capacity as a mediator, arbitrator, conciliator, or facilitator.

(5) Participation in labor negotiations, arbitrations or conciliations arising under collective bargaining rights or agreements.

(6) Providing assistance to another to complete a form provided by a court for protection under RCW chapters 10.14 (harassment) or 26.50 (domestic violence prevention) when no fee is charged to do so.

(7) Acting as a legislative lobbyist.

(8) Sale of legal forms in any format.

(9) Activities which are preempted by Federal law.

(10) Such other activities that the Supreme Court has determined by published opinion do not constitute the unlicensed or unauthorized practice of law or that have been permitted under a regulatory system established by the Supreme Court.

(c) Nonlawyer Assistants. Nothing in this rule shall affect the ability of nonlawyer assistants to act under the supervision of a lawyer in compliance with Rule 5.3 of the Rules of Professional Conduct.

(d) General Information. Nothing in this rule shall affect the ability of a person or entity to provide information of a general nature about the law and legal procedures to members of the public.

(e) Governmental Agencies. Nothing in this rule shall affect the ability of a governmental agency to carry out responsibilities provided by law.

For the guidelines of the Supreme Court of Washington on limited licensing, see exhibit 4.3 in chapter 4.

### WASHINGTON ETHICS AND PRACTICE RULES ON THE INTERNET

www.law.cornell.edu/ethics/washington.html
www2.law.cornell.edu/cgi-bin/foliocgi.exe/wa-code?
www.wsba.org/barnews/ethicsandthelaw//ethics-non-lawyers.html
www.wsba.org/c/RPC/fo
www.wsba.org/rpc/ifo/default.htm
www.crossingthebar.com/WA-UPL.htm

### PARALEGALS (AND OTHER NONATTORNEYS) IN COURT

- *Trainer v. Kitsap County*, 107 Wash. App. 1035, 2001 WL 873826 (Court of Appeals of Washington, 2001) (relevant criteria for determining whether legal assistant services should be compensated: (1) the services performed by the nonlawyer personnel must be legal in nature; (2) the performance of these services must be supervised by an attorney; (3) the qualifications of the person performing the services must be specified in the request for fees in sufficient detail to demonstrate that the person is qualified by virtue of education, training, or work experience to perform substantive legal work; (4) the nature of the services performed must be specified in the request for fees in order to allow the reviewing court to determine that the services performed were legal rather than clerical; (5) as with attorney time, the amount of time expended must be set forth and must be reasonable; and (6) the amount charged must reflect reasonable community standards for charges by that category of personnel (citing *Absher Construction v. Kent School District*, 917 P. 2d 1086 (Court of Appeals of Washington, 1995)).

- *Tegman v. Accident & Medical Investigations, Inc.*, 30 P.3d 8, 11 (Court of Appeals of Washington, 2001) (paralegals charged with unauthorized practice of law and negligence; "[w]hen a paralegal performs legal services with knowledge that there is no supervising attorney responsible for the case, the paralegal will be held to an attorney's standard of care"; "[n]on-attorneys who attempt to practice law will be held to the same standards of competence demanded of attorneys and will be liable for negligence if these standards are not met").

- *State v. S.M.*, 996 P.2d 1111 (Court of Appeals of Washington, 2000) (paralegal gives wrong legal advice).

- *Richards v. Jain*, 168 F. Supp. 2d 1195, 1200 (U.S. District Court, W.D. Washington, 2001) (Law firm is disqualified when its paralegal viewed privileged documents of the opponent. The supervising attorney failed to take reasonable steps to ensure that its nonlawyer employees complied with ethical rules. Paralegal are not held to a lower standard of ethical behavior than attorneys. "[N]onlawyers and lawyers are bound by the same ethical duties.").

- *In the Matter of Gillingham*, 896 P.2d 656 (Supreme Court of Washington, 1995) (discipline of attorney for failure to supervise paralegal).

- *Storseth v. Spellman*, 654 F.2d 1349 (U.S. Court of Appeals, 9th Circuit, 1981) (paralegal assistance to inmates; jailhouse lawyers).

- *In re Berglund Construction Co.*, 142 Bankruptcy Reporter 947 (U.S. Bankruptcy Court, E.D. Washington, 1992) (compensation of paralegal in bankruptcy case).

# West Virginia

## ETHICAL RULES AND GUIDELINES IN WEST VIRGINIA

*Definition.* A legal assistant is a person, qualified through education, training or work experience, who is employed or retained by a lawyer, law office, governmental agency, or other entity, in a capacity or function which involves the performance, under the ultimate direction and supervision of an attorney, of delegated substantive legal work, which work, for the most part, requires a sufficient knowledge of legal concepts that, absent such assistance, the attorney would perform the task. West Virginia State Bar, Board of Governors Meeting (July 16–17, 1999).

Anything delegated to a nonattorney must lose its separate identity and be merged in the service of the attorney. When communicating with persons outside the office, a paralegal "must disclose his status as such." Nonattorneys can sign letters on law firm stationery as long as their nonattorney status is clearly indicated. *Legal Ethics Inquiry 76–7* (3 W.Va. State Bar Journal (Spring 1977)).

A corporation can be represented by a nonattorney in Magistrates Court. "Any party to a civil action in a magistrate court may appear and conduct such action in person, by agent or by attorney. . . . [T]he appearance by an agent shall not constitute the unauthorized practice of law. . . ." (*W. Va. Code* § 50-4-4a). West Virginia State Bar Committee on Unlawful Practice, *Advisory Opinion 93–001*.

## DEFINING THE PRACTICE OF LAW IN WEST VIRGINIA

Court Rules, *Michie's West Virginia Code Annotated* 535 (1996). "Practice of Law Definitions": In general, one is deemed to be practicing law whenever he or it furnishes another advice or service under circumstances which imply the possession or use of legal knowledge and skill. More specifically but without purporting to formulate a precise and completely comprehensive definition of the practice of law or to prescribe limits to the scope of that activity, one is deemed to be practicing law whenever (1) one undertakes, with or without compensation and whether or not in connection with another activity, to advise another in any matter involving the application of legal principles to facts, purposes or desires; (2) one undertakes, with or without compensation and whether or not in connection with another activity, to prepare for another legal instruments of any character; or (3) one undertakes, with or without compensation and whether or not in connection with another activity, to represent the interest of another before any judicial tribunal or officer, or to represent the interest of another before any executive or administrative tribunal, agency or officer otherwise than in the presentation of facts, figures or factual conclusions as distinguished from legal conclusions in respect to such facts and figures. Nothing in this paragraph shall be deemed to prohibit a lay person from appearing as agent before a justice of the peace or to prohibit a bona fide full-time lay employee from performing legal services for his regular employer (other than in connection with representation of his employer before any judicial, executive or administrative tribunal, agency or officer) in matters relating solely to the internal affairs of such employer, as distinguished from such services rendered to or for others. Quoted in *Lawyer Disciplinary Bd. v. Allen*, 479 S.E. 2d 317, 333 (Supreme Court of Appeals of West Virginia, 1996).

## WEST VIRGINIA ETHICS AND PRACTICE RULES ON THE INTERNET

www.law.cornell.edu/ethics/wv.html

www.wvbar.org/BARINFO/wvlegalresearch/ethics/
   ethics.htm

www.wvbar.org/BARINFO/rulesprofconduct/index.htm

www.crossingthebar.com/WV-UPL.htm

## PARALEGALS (AND OTHER NONATTORNEYS) IN COURT

- *Office of Disciplinary Counsel v. Battistelli*, 465 S.E.2d 644 (Supreme Court of Appeals of West Virginia, 1995) (suspended attorney can work as a paralegal but must have no contact with clients).
- *Stacy v. B.O. Stroud*, 845 F. Supp. 1135, 1145 (U.S. District Court, S.D. West Virginia, 1993) (award of attorney fees; "Delegating appropriate tasks to paralegals reduces the overall costs of . . . litigation.").
- *In re Heck's, Inc.*, 112 Bankruptcy Reporter 775 (U.S. Bankruptcy Court, S.D. West Virginia, 1990) (objections filed to claims for paralegal fees).

# WISCONSIN

## ETHICAL RULES AND GUIDELINES IN WISCONSIN

Wisconsin State Bar, Paralegal Task Force, *Proposed Ethics Rules for Paralegals*. See *www.wisbar.org/sections/comm/ commpages/ptf/ethics.html*.

A paralegal can attend a real estate closing on behalf of a client without a supervising attorney being present if the paralegal is trained and the client consents, but the paralegal cannot give legal advice or legal opinions at the closing. Wisconsin State Bar, *Opinion E-95-3* (7/1998).

An attorney whose license to practice law is suspended or revoked or who is suspended from the practice of law may not engage in the practice of law or in any law work activity customarily done by paralegals. Supreme Court Rule 20:5.5(2). *Rules of Professional Conduct for Attorneys*. See also Rule 22.26(f)(2).

Law firm letterhead can include the names of paralegals as long as their nonattorney status is made clear. State Bar of Wisconsin, *Opinion E-85-6* (10/1985).

The office of the district attorney and the office of a circuit judge can share the services of a paralegal as long as the paralegal is supervised so as to maintain the confidentiality of each office. State Bar of Wisconsin, *Opinion E-86-13* (9/24/86).

A paralegal can have a business card containing the law firm's name but cannot be listed on the law firm's letterhead. State Bar of Wisconsin, *Opinion E-75-22*. (Note: *Opinion E-85-6* changes the letterhead portion of *E-75-22*.)

A paralegal can be listed on law firm letterhead. State Bar of Wisconsin, *Opinion E-85-6*.

A paralegal who is a licensed real estate broker cannot appear at a real estate closing. "If a paralegal from the attorney's office appears at the closing, it will *seem* that he is there in a legal capacity." State Bar of Wisconsin, *Opinion E-80-2*.

A law firm can hire a litigation paralegal who will also provide court reporting services to other attorneys. State Bar of Wisconsin, *Opinion E-86-19* (12/12/86).

## DEFINING THE PRACTICE OF LAW IN WISCONSIN

§ 757.30 (*Wisconsin Statutes Annotated*): (2) Every person who appears as agent, representative or attorney, for or on behalf of any other person, or any firm, partnership, association or corporation in any action or proceeding in or before any court of record, court commissioner, or judicial tribunal of the United States, or of any state, or who otherwise, in or out of court, for compensation or pecuniary reward gives professional legal advice not incidental to his or her usual or ordinary business, or renders any legal service for any other person, or any firm, partnership, association or corporation, shall be deemed to be practicing law within the meaning of this section.

## WISCONSIN ETHICS AND PRACTICE RULES ON THE INTERNET

www.law.cornell.edu/ethics/wisconsin.html

www2.law.cornell.edu/cgi-bin/foliocgi.exe/wi-code?

www.wisbar.org/ethop

www.wisbar.org/sections/comm/commpages/ptf/
   ethics.html

www.crossingthebar.com/WI-UPL.htm

## PARALEGALS (AND OTHER NONATTORNEYS) IN COURT

- *In the Matter of Hinnawi*, 549 N.W.2d 245 (Supreme Court of Wisconsin, 1996) (a suspended or disbarred attorney may not work as a paralegal, SCR 22.26).
- *In re Webster*, 120 Bankruptcy Reporter 111 (U.S. Bankruptcy Court, E.D. Wisconsin, 1990) (injunction against nonattorney for engaging in unauthorized practice of law in providing bankruptcy services).
- *In the Matter of Leaf*, 476 N.W.2d 13 (Supreme Court of Wisconsin, 1991) (attorney assists a nonattorney associate in the unauthorized practice of law).
- *Wisconsin v. Town of Turtle Lake*, 526 N.W.2d 784 (Court of Appeals of Wisconsin, 1994) (award of paralegal fees).
- *Hutchison v. Amateur Electronic Supply*, 42 F.3d 1037, 1048 (U.S. Court of Appeals, 7th Circuit, 1994) (fee award reduced for "failure to utilize paralegals").
- *EEOC v. Accurate Mechanical Contractors, Inc.*, 863 F. Supp. 828 (U.S. District Court, E.D. Wisconsin, 1994) (paralegal fees are limited to work performed

by paralegals that would otherwise be performed by an attorney).

- *Purdy v. Security Savings . . .*, 727 F. Supp. 1266, 1270 (U.S. District Court, E. D. Wisconsin, 1989) (it is "clearly excessive" to claim six and a half hours of paralegal time to cite check a document with only 40 citations in it).
- *Piper v. Popp*, 482 N.W.2d 353 (Supreme Court of Wisconsin, 1992) (inmate paralegal assistance).

# Wyoming

## ETHICAL RULES AND GUIDELINES IN WYOMING

It is professional misconduct for a lawyer to (g) knowingly employ any person in the practice of law who has been disbarred or is under suspension from the practice of law in any position or capacity as a paralegal. Rule 8.4. *Wyoming Court Rules*. Rules of Professional Conduct for Attorneys.

Attorney responsibilities regarding nonattorney assistants. Rule 5.3, *Wyoming Court Rules*. Rules of Professional Conduct for Attorneys. See discussion of Rule 5.3 in chapter 5.

## DEFINING THE PRACTICE OF LAW IN WYOMING

Rule 11 (*Wyoming Rules of Court*): (a)(1) "Practice of law" means advising others and taking action for them in matters connected with law. It includes preparation of legal instruments and acting or proceeding for another before judges, courts, tribunals, commissioners, boards or other governmental agencies.

## WYOMING ETHICS AND PRACTICE RULES ON THE INTERNET

www.secure.law.cornell.edu/ethics/wyoming.html
www.courts.state.wy.us/RULES/Professional
　　%20Conduct%20for%20Attorneys.html
www.crossingthebar.com/WY-UPL.htm

## PARALEGALS (AND OTHER NONATTORNEYS) IN COURT

- *Brooks v. Zebre*, 792 P.2d 196, 220 (Supreme Court of Wyoming, 1990) (a "lawyer who approaches a represented third party without going through counsel should be severely punished. And this is so though the lawyer uses a law representative or paralegal to do his dirty work.").
- *Mendicino v. Whitchurch*, 565 P.2d 460, 478 (Supreme Court of Wyoming, 1977) (a suspended attorney shall not participate in the practice of law as an attorney or paralegal).
- *Van Riper v. Wyoming*, 882 P.2d 230 (Supreme Court of Wyoming, 1994) (felony defendant with paralegal training defends himself).
- *Wyoming v. Brown*, 805 P.2d 830 (Supreme Court of Wyoming, 1991) (award of paralegal fees).
- *Baker v. Bowen*, 707 F. Supp. 481 (U.S. District Court, Wyoming, 1989) (award of paralegal fees).

# Appendix G

# CALIFORNIA LEGISLATION

One of the most dramatic events in the last decade has been the enactment of a law in California on who can be called a paralegal or legal assistant. The law also created the position of legal document assistant (LDA), an independent contractor who sells services to the public without attorney supervision. The law governing the LDA also applies to the unlawful detainer assistant (UDA), a position created earlier in the state. These developments are described in detail in Chapter 4. Given the importance of these developments, the text of the new California law is reprinted here from *West's Annotated California Business & Professions Code*.

## § 6450. Paralegal; Defined; Prohibitions; Certifications

(a) "Paralegal" means a person who holds himself or herself out to be a paralegal, who is qualified by education, training, or work experience, and who either contracts with or is employed by an attorney, law firm, corporation, governmental agency, or other entity, and who performs substantial legal work under the direction and supervision of an active member of the State Bar of California, as defined in Section 6060, or an attorney practicing law in the federal courts of this state, that has been specifically delegated by the attorney to him or her. Tasks performed by a paralegal may include, but are not limited to, case planning, development, and management; legal research; interviewing clients; fact gathering and retrieving information; drafting and analyzing legal documents; collecting, compiling, and utilizing technical information to make an independent decision and recommendation to the supervising attorney; and representing clients before a state or federal administrative agency if that representation is permitted by statute, court rule, or administrative rule or regulation.

(b) Notwithstanding subdivision (a), a paralegal shall not do any of the following:
   (1) Provide legal advice.
   (2) Represent a client in court.
   (3) Select, explain, draft, or recommend the use of any legal document to or for any person other than the attorney who directs and supervises the paralegal.
   (4) Act as a runner or capper, as defined in Sections 6151 and 6152.
   (5) Engage in conduct that constitutes the unlawful practice of law.
   (6) Contract with, or be employed by, a natural person other than an attorney to perform paralegal services.
   (7) In connection with providing paralegal services, induce a person to make an investment, purchase a financial product or service, or enter a transaction from which income or profit, or both, purportedly may be derived.
   (8) Establish the fees to charge a client for the services the paralegal performs, which shall be established by the attorney who supervises the paralegal's work. This paragraph does not apply to fees charged by a paralegal in a contract to provide paralegal services to an attorney, law firm, corporation, governmental agency, or other entity as provided in subdivision (a).

(c) A paralegal shall possess at least one of the following:
   (1) A certificate of completion of a paralegal program approved by the American Bar Association.
   (2) A certificate of completion of a paralegal program at, or a degree from, a postsecondary institution that requires the successful completion of a min-

imum of 24 semester, or equivalent, units in law-related courses and that has been accredited by a national or regional accrediting organization or approved by the Bureau for Private Postsecondary and Vocational Education.

(3) A baccalaureate degree or an advanced degree in any subject, a minimum of one year of law-related experience under the supervision of an attorney who has been an active member of the State Bar of California for at least the preceding three years or who has practiced in the federal courts of this state for at least the preceding three years, and a written declaration from this attorney stating that the person is qualified to perform paralegal tasks.

(4) A high school diploma or general equivalency diploma, a minimum of three years of law-related experience under the supervision of an attorney who has been an active member of the State Bar of California for at least the preceding three years or who has practiced in the federal courts of this state for at least the preceding three years, and a written declaration from this attorney stating that the person is qualified to perform paralegal tasks. This experience and training shall be completed no later than December 31, 2003.

(d) All paralegals shall be required to certify completion every three years of four hours of mandatory continuing legal education in legal ethics. All continuing legal education courses shall meet the requirements of Section 6070. Every two years, all paralegals shall be required to certify completion of four hours of mandatory continuing education in either general law or in a specialized area of law. Certification of these continuing education requirements shall be made with the paralegal's supervising attorney. The paralegal shall be responsible for keeping a record of the paralegal's certifications.

(e) A paralegal does not include a nonlawyer who provides legal services directly to members of the public or a legal document assistant or unlawful detainer assistant as defined in Section 6400.

(f) If a legal document assistant, as defined in subdivision (c) of Section 6400, has registered, on or before January 1, 2001, as required by law, a business name that includes the word "paralegal," that person may continue to use that business name until he or she is required to renew registration.

(g) This section shall remain in effect only until January 1, 2004, and as of that date is repealed, unless a later enacted statute, which is enacted before January 1, 2004, deletes or extends that date.

## § 6451. Paralegal; Unlawful Practices; Services for Consumers

It is unlawful for a paralegal to perform any services for a consumer except as performed under the direction and supervision of the attorney, law firm, corporation, government agency, or other entity that employs or contracts with the paralegal. Nothing in this chapter shall prohibit a paralegal who is employed by an attorney, law firm, governmental agency, or other entity from providing services to a consumer served by one of these entities if those services are specifically allowed by statute, case law, court rule, or federal or state administrative rule or regulation. "Consumer" means a natural person, firm, association, organization, partnership, business trust, corporation, or public entity.

## § 6452. Paralegal; Unlawful Practices; Persons Identifying Themselves as Paralegals

(a) It is unlawful for a person to identify himself or herself as a paralegal on any advertisement, letterhead, business card or sign, or elsewhere unless he or she has met the qualifications of subdivision (c) of Section 6450 and performs all services under the direction and supervision of an attorney who is an active member of the State Bar of California or an attorney practicing law in the federal courts of this state who is responsible for all of the services performed by the paralegal. The business card of a paralegal shall include the name of the law firm where he or she is employed or a statement that he or she is employed by or contracting with a licensed attorney.

(b) An attorney who uses the services of a paralegal is liable for any harm caused as the result of the paralegal's negligence, misconduct, or violation of this chapter.

## § 6453. Duty of Paralegal; Confidentiality

A paralegal is subject to the same duty as an attorney specified in subdivision (e) of Section 6068 to maintain inviolate the confidentiality, and at every peril to himself or herself to preserve the attorney-client privilege, of a consumer for whom the paralegal has provided any of the services described in subdivision (a) of Section 6450.

## § 6454. Definitions

The terms "paralegal," "legal assistant," "attorney assistant," "freelance paralegal," "independent paralegal," and "contract paralegal" are synonymous for purposes of this chapter.

## § 6455. Injured Consumers; Filing of Complaints; Violations and Punishment

(a) Any consumer injured by a violation of this chapter may file a complaint and seek redress in any municipal or superior court for injunctive relief, restitution, and damages. Attorney's fees shall be awarded in this action to the prevailing plaintiff.

(b) Any person who violates the provisions of Section 6451 or 6452 is guilty of an infraction for the first violation, which is punishable upon conviction by a fine of up to two thousand five hundred dollars ($2,500) as to each consumer with respect to whom a violation occurs, and is guilty of a misdemeanor for the second and each subsequent violation, which is punishable upon conviction by a fine of two thousand five hundred dollars ($2,500) as to each consumer with respect to whom a violation occurs, or imprisonment in a county jail for not more than one year, or by both that fine and imprisonment. Any person convicted of a violation of this section shall be ordered by the court to pay restitution to the victim pursuant to Section 1202.4 of the Penal Code.

### § 6456. Exemptions from Chapter

An individual employed by the state as a paralegal, legal assistant, legal analyst, or similar title, is exempt from the provisions of this chapter.

### § 6400. Definitions

(a) "Unlawful detainer assistant" means any individual who for compensation renders assistance or advice in the prosecution or defense of an unlawful detainer claim or action, including any bankruptcy petition that may affect the unlawful detainer claim or action.

(b) "Unlawful detainer claim" means a proceeding, filing, or action affecting rights or liabilities of any person that arises under Chapter 4 (commencing with Section 1159) of Title 3 of Part 3 of the Code of Civil Procedure and that contemplates an adjudication by a court.

(c) "Legal document assistant" means:

   (1) Any person who is not exempted under Section 6401 and who provides, or assists in providing, or offers to provide, or offers to assist in providing, for compensation, any self-help service to a member of the public who is representing himself or herself in a legal matter, or who holds himself or herself out as someone who offers that service or has that authority. This paragraph shall not apply to any individual whose assistance consists merely of secretarial or receptionist services.

   (2) A corporation, partnership, association, or other entity that employs or contracts with any person not exempted under Section 6401 who, as part of his or her responsibilities, provides, or assists in providing, or offers to provide, or offers to assist in providing, for compensation, any self-help service to a member of the public who is representing himself or herself in a legal matter or holds himself or herself out as someone who offers that service or has that authority. This paragraph shall not apply to an individual whose assistance consists merely of secretarial or receptionist services.

(d) "Self-help service" means all of the following:

   (1) Completing legal documents in a ministerial manner, selected by a person who is representing himself or herself in a legal matter, by typing or otherwise completing the documents at the person's specific direction.

   (2) Providing general published factual information that has been written or approved by an attorney, pertaining to legal procedures, rights, or obligations to a person who is representing himself or herself in a legal matter, to assist the person in representing himself or herself. This service in and of itself, shall not require registration as a legal document assistant.

   (3) Making published legal documents available to a person who is representing himself or herself in a legal matter.

   (4) Filing and serving legal forms and documents at the specific direction of a person who is representing himself or herself in a legal matter.

(e) "Compensation" means money, property, or anything else of value.

(f) A legal document assistant, including any legal document assistant employed by a partnership or corporation, shall not provide any self-help service for compensation after January 1, 2000, unless the legal document assistant is registered in the county in which his or her principal place of business is located and in any other county in which he or she performs acts for which registration is required.

(g) A legal document assistant shall not provide any kind of advice, explanation, opinion, or recommendation to a consumer about possible legal rights, remedies, defenses, options, selection of forms, or strategies. A legal document assistant shall complete documents only in the manner prescribed by paragraph (1) of subdivision (d).

### § 6401. Chapter Application Exceptions

This chapter does not apply to any person engaged in any of the following occupations, provided that the person does not also perform the duties of a legal document assistant in addition to those occupations:

(a) Any government employee who is acting in the course of his or her employment.

(b) A member of the State Bar of California, or his or her employee, paralegal, or agent, or an independent contractor while acting on behalf of a member of the State Bar.

(c) Any employee of a nonprofit, tax-exempt corporation who either assists clients free of charge or is supervised by a member of the State Bar of California who has malpractice insurance.

(d) A licensed real estate broker or licensed real estate salesperson, as defined in Chapter 3 (commencing with Section 10130) of Part 1 of Division 4, who acts pursuant to subdivision (b) of Section 10131 on an unlawful detainer claim as defined in subdivision (b) of Section 6400, and who is a party to the unlawful detainer action.

(e) An immigration consultant, as defined in Chapter 19.5 (commencing with Section 22441) of Division 8.

(f)  A person registered as a process server under Chapter 16 (commencing with Section 22350) or a person registered as a professional photocopier under Chapter 20 (commencing with Section 22450) of Division 8.

(g)  A person who provides services relative to the preparation of security instruments or conveyance documents as an integral part of the provision of title or escrow service.

(h)  A person who provides services that are regulated by federal law.

(i)  A person who is employed by, and provides services to, a supervised financial institution, holding company, subsidiary or affiliate.

### § 6402.1. Registration Eligibility

To be eligible to apply for registration under this chapter as a legal document assistant, the applicant shall possess at least one of the following:

(a)  A high school diploma or general equivalency diploma, and either a minimum of two years of law-related experience under the supervision of a licensed attorney, or a minimum of two years experience, prior to January 1, 1999, providing self-help service.

(b)  A baccalaureate degree in any field and either a minimum of one year of law-related experience under the supervision of a licensed attorney, or a minimum of one year of experience, prior to January 1, 1999, providing self-help service.

(c)  A certificate of completion from a paralegal program that is institutionally accredited but not approved by the American Bar Association, that requires successful completion of a minimum of 24 semester units, or the equivalent, in legal specialization courses.

(d)  A certificate of completion from a paralegal program approved by the American Bar Association.

(e)  This section shall remain in effect only until January 1, 2003, or the date the director suspends the requirements of this chapter applicable to legal document assistants pursuant to Section 6416, whichever first occurs, and as of that date is repealed, unless a later enacted statute, that is enacted before that date, deletes or extends that date.

### § 6410. Written Contracts Required; Contents; Rescinding and Voiding

(a)  Every legal document assistant or unlawful detainer assistant who enters into a contract or agreement with a client to provide services shall, prior to providing any services, provide the client with a written contract, the contents of which shall be prescribed by regulations adopted by the Department of Consumer Affairs.

(b)  The written contract shall include provisions relating to the following:

(1)  The services to be performed.

(2)  The costs of the services to be performed.

(3)  There shall be printed on the face of the contract in 12-point boldface type a statement that the legal document assistant or unlawful detainer assistant is not an attorney and may not perform the legal services that an attorney performs.

(4)  The contract shall contain a statement in 12-point boldface type that the county clerk has not evaluated or approved the registrant's knowledge or experience, or the quality of the registrant's services.

(5)  The contract shall contain a statement in 12-point boldface type that the consumer may obtain information regarding free or low-cost representation through a local bar association or legal aid foundation and that the consumer may contact local law enforcement, a district attorney, or a legal aid foundation if the consumer believes that he or she has been a victim of fraud, the unauthorized practice of law, or any other injury.

(6)  The contract shall contain a statement in 12-point boldface type that a legal document assistant or unlawful detainer assistant is not permitted to engage in the practice of law, including providing any kind of advice, explanation, opinion, or recommendation to a consumer about possible legal rights, remedies, defenses, options, selection of forms, or strategies.

(c)  The provisions of the written contract shall be stated both in English and in any other language comprehended by the client and principally used in any oral sales presentation or negotiation leading to execution of the contract. The legal document assistant or the unlawful detainer assistant shall be responsible for translating the contract into the language principally used in any oral sales presentation or negotiation leading to the execution of the contract.

(d)  Failure of a legal document assistant or unlawful detainer assistant to comply with subdivisions (a), (b), and (c) shall make the contract or agreement for services voidable at the option of the client. Upon the voiding of the contract, the legal document assistant or unlawful detainer assistant shall immediately return in full any fees paid by the client.

# Appendix H

# PARALEGAL BUSINESS CARDS

Most paralegals have their own business cards. As indicated in chapter 5 and in appendix F, it is ethical for an attorney to allow a paralegal employee to have a business card that also prints the name of the employer. Here are several examples of such cards in use today:

---

BURR & FORMAN LLP

MICHAEL CARL IVEY, CLA
CERTIFIED LEGAL ASSISTANT

3100 SOUTHTRUST TOWER
420 NORTH 20TH STREET, BIRMINGHAM, AL 35203
DIRECT: (205) 458-5380    MAIN: (205) 251-3000
FACSIMILE: (205) 458-5100    INTERNET: MIVEY@BURR.COM

BIRMINGHAM • HUNTSVILLE • ATLANTA

---

**Deborah Baer McKinney, RP**
PACE Registered Paralegal

Cors & Bassett, LLC
ATTORNEYS AT LAW

537 East Pete Rose Way
Suite 400
Cincinnati, Ohio 45202-3502
*telephone* (513) **852-8218**
*facsimile* (513) **852-8222**
dbm@corsbassett.com

---

BYH | BENJAMIN, YOCUM & HEATHER, LLC
ATTORNEYS AT LAW

JOSÉ PEDRO SANTOS
SENIOR PARALEGAL

312 ELM STREET
SUITE 1850
CINCINNATI, OHIO 45202-2763

TELEPHONE: (513) 721-5672
FAX: (513) 562-4388
WEB SITE: byhlaw.com
E-MAIL: jpsantos@byhlaw.com

---

**Pamela R. Horn**
Senior Paralegal
Board Certified Legal Assistant
Civil Trial Law - Texas Bd. of Legal Specialization

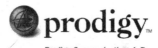**prodigy**™

**Prodigy Communications L.P.**
6500 River Place Blvd., Bldg. III, Austin, TX 78730-1111
Tel 512-527-1161  Fax 512-527-1199
Email  phom@corp.prodigy.com

---

**CELIA C. ELWELL, RP**
PACE Registered Paralegal
Legal Assistant II

**The City of**
**OKLAHOMA CITY**
OFFICE OF THE MUNICIPAL COUNSELOR
200 N. WALKER, SUITE 400
OKLAHOMA CITY, OK 73102
**405/297-2695**
**FAX 405/297-2118 •297-3851**
**email: celia.elwell@ci.okc.ok.us**

---

corvette@qnis.net

**Robin J. Schumacher, LDA**
Document Preparation & Filing
Registration # X20011000000 Exp. 01-31-03

(559) 442-4969
Fax (559) 264-5010
3045 W. Lincoln Ave.
Fresno, CA 93706

Bonded and Licensed
Bankruptcy, Divorce,
Child Support, Wills,
Trusts & Misc.

---

        Divorce with Dignity
a Divorce Planning Service

Cindy Elwell
CEO

1150 Ballena Blvd. Suite 100
Alameda CA 94501
510-523-7290
Fax: 510-523-0183

dwdignity@aol.com
www.dwdignity.com
LDA No. 17, Alameda County

# Appendix I

# STATE RESOURCES

## ABBREVIATIONS

AG: attorney general
BA: bar associations in the state (see also appendix C)
CS: court system of the state
GO: governor's office
LF: law firms in the state
LL: law library of the state (or alternative)
LR: legal research sources on state law
MV: motor vehicle laws of the state
SF: state forms, e.g., summons, will, probate
SL: state legislature
SS: secretary of state (or equivalent office)
WC: workers' compensation in the state

## ALABAMA

AG: www.ago.state.al.us
BA: www.findlaw.com/11stategov/al/associations.html
CS: www.judicial.state.al.us
www.findlaw.com/11stategov/al/courts.html
GO: www.governor.state.al.us/flash/gov2.html
LF: www.attorneylocate.com/scripts/city.asp?city_statecode=AL
www.directory.findlaw.com/lawyer/servlet/SCityFirm?state=AL
LL: www.alalinc.net/library
LR: www.law.cornell.edu/states/alabama.html
www.findlaw.com/11stategov/al/index.html
MV: www.ador.state.al.us/motorvehicle/MVD_MAIN.html
SF: www.alllaw.com/state_resources/alabama/forms
forms.lp.findlaw.com/states/al.html
SL: www.legislature.state.al.us
SS: www.sos.state.al.us
WC: www.dir.state.al.us/wc/index.htm

## ALASKA

AG: www.law.state.ak.us
BA: www.findlaw.com/11stategov/ak/associations.html

CS:   www.state.ak.us/courts
GO:   www.gov.state.ak.us
LF:   www.attorneylocate.com/scripts/city.asp?city_statecode=AK
      www.directory.findlaw.com/lawyer/servlet/SCityFirm?state=AK
LL:   www.state.ak.us/courts/libinfo.htm
      www.state.ak.us/courts/libhrs.htm
LR:   www.findlaw.com/11stategov/ak/index.html
      www.loc.gov/law/guide/us-ak.html
MV:   www.state.ak.us/dmv
SF:   www.alllaw.com/state_resources/alaska/forms
      forms.lp.findlaw.com/states/ak.html
SL:   www.legis.state.ak.us
SS:   www.gov.state.ak.us/ltgov
WC:   www.labor.state.ak.us/wc/wc.htm

## ARIZONA

AG:   www.ag.state.az.us
BA:   www.findlaw.com/11stategov/az/associations.html
CS:   www.supreme.state.az.us/nav2/sitemap.htm
      www.ncsconline.org/Information/info_court_web_sites.html
GO:   www.governor.state.az.us
LF:   www.attorneylocate.com/scripts/city.asp?city_statecode=AZ
      www.directory.findlaw.com/lawyer/servlet/SCityFirm?state=AZ
LL:   www.lib.az.us/law/index.html
LR:   www.findlaw.com/11stategov/az/index.html
      www.loc.gov/law/guide/us-az.html
MV:   www.dot.state.az.us/MVD/mvd.htm
SF:   www.alllaw.com/state_resources/arizona/forms
      forms.lp.findlaw.com/states/az.html
SL:   www.azleg.state.az.us
SS:   www.sosaz.com
WC:   www.ica.state.az.us

## ARKANSAS

AG:   www.ag.state.ar.us
BA:   www.findlaw.com/11stategov/ar/associations.html
CS:   www.courts.state.ar.us
      www.findlaw.com/11stategov/ar/courts.html
GO:   www.state.ar.us/governor
LF:   www.attorneylocate.com/scripts/city.asp?city_statecode=AR
LR:   www.findlaw.com/11stategov/ar/index.html
      www.loc.gov/law/guide/us-ar.html
MV:   www.state.ar.us/dfa/motorvehicle
SF:   www.alllaw.com/state_resources/arkansas/forms
      forms.lp.findlaw.com/states/ar.html
SL:   www.arkleg.state.ar.us
SS:   www.sosweb.state.ar.us
WC:   www.awcc.state.ar.us

## CALIFORNIA

AG:   www.caag.state.ca.us
BA:   california.lp.findlaw.com/ca03_associations/cabar.html
CS:   www.courtinfo.ca.gov
      www.appellatecases.courtinfo.ca.gov
GO:   www.governor.ca.gov/state/govsite/gov_homepage.jsp

LF:   www.attorneylocate.com/scripts/city.asp?city_statecode=CA
      www.directory.findlaw.com/lawyer/servlet/SCityFirm?state=CA
LL:   www.cccll.org/cccll-cll.htm
LR:   california.lp.findlaw.com
      www.loc.gov/law/guide/us-ca.html
MV:   www.dmv.ca.gov
SF:   www.alllaw.com/state_resources/california/forms
      forms.lp.findlaw.com/states/ca.html
SL:   www.leginfo.ca.gov
SS:   www.ss.ca.gov
WC:   www.dir.ca.gov/DWC/dwc_home_page.htm


## COLORADO

AG:   www.ago.state.co.us
BA:   www.findlaw.com/11stategov/co/associations.html
CS:   www.courts.state.co.us
GO:   www.state.co.us/gov_dir/governor_office.html
LF:   www.attorneylocate.com/scripts/city.asp?city_statecode=CO
      www.directory.findlaw.com/lawyer/servlet/SCityFirm?state=CO
LL:   www.state.co.us/courts/sctlib
LR:   www.findlaw.com/11stategov/co/index.html
      www.loc.gov/law/guide/us-co.html
MV:   www.state.co.us/gov_dir/revenue_dir/MV_dir/mv.html
SF:   www.alllaw.com/state_resources/colorado/forms
      forms.lp.findlaw.com/states/co.html
SL:   www.state.co.us/dleg.html
SS:   www.sos.state.co.us
WC:   www.coworkforce.com/DWC


## CONNECTICUT

AG:   www.cslib.org/attygenl
BA:   www.findlaw.com/11stategov/ct/associations.html
CS:   www.jud.state.ct.us
GO:   www.state.ct.us/governor
LF:   www.attorneylocate.com/scripts/city.asp?city_statecode=CT
      www.directory.findlaw.com/lawyer/servlet/SCityFirm?state=CT
LL:   www.jud.state.ct.us/LawLib
LR:   www.findlaw.com/11stategov/ct/index.html
      www.loc.gov/law/guide/us-ct.html
      www.jud.state.ct.us/lawlib/state.htm
MV:   www.dmvct.org
SF:   www.alllaw.com/state_resources/connecticut/forms
      forms.lp.findlaw.com/states/ct.html
SL:   www.cga.state.ct.us/default.htm
SS:   www.sots.state.ct.us
WC:   wcc.state.ct.us


## DELAWARE

AG:   www.state.de.us/attgen/index.htm
BA:   www.findlaw.com/11stategov/de/associations.html
CS:   courts.state.de.us
GO:   www.state.de.us/governor/index.htm
LF:   www.attorneylocate.com/scripts/city.asp?city_statecode=DE
      www.directory.findlaw.com/lawyer/servlet/SCityFirm?state=DE

LR:  www.findlaw.com/11stategov/de/index.html
     www.loc.gov/law/guide/us-de.html
MV:  www.delaware.gov/yahoo/DMV
SF:  www.alllaw.com/state_resources/delaware/forms
     forms.lp.findlaw.com/states/de.html
SL:  www.legis.state.de.us/Legislature.nsf/?Opendatabase
SS:  www.state.de.us/sos
WC:  www.delawareworks.com/divisions/industaffairs/workers.comp.htm

## DISTRICT OF COLUMBIA
AG:  www.occ.dc.gov/main.shtm
BA:  www.findlaw.com/11stategov/dc/associations.html
CS:  www.dcsc.gov
     www.ncsconline.org/Information/info_court_web_sites.html
GO:  www.dc.gov/mayor/index.htm
LF:  www.attorneylocate.com/scripts/city.asp?city_statecode=DC
     www.directory.findlaw.com/lawyer/servlet/SCityFirm?state=DC
LL:  www.dc-legal.com/legal_lib.htm
LR:  www.findlaw.com/11stategov/dc/index.html
     www.loc.gov/law/guide/us-dc.html
MV:  www.dmv.washingtondc.gov/main.shtm
SF:  www.alllaw.com/state_resources/dc/forms
     forms.lp.findlaw.com/states/dc.html
SL:  www.dccouncil.washington.dc.us
WC:  www.does.ci.washington.dc.us/services/wkr_comp.shtm

## FLORIDA
AG:  legal.firn.edu
BA:  www.findlaw.com/11stategov/fl/associations.html
CS:  www.flcourts.org
GO:  www.myflorida.com/myflorida/governorsoffice/index.html
LF:  www.attorneylocate.com/scripts/city.asp?city_statecode=FL
     www.directory.findlaw.com/lawyer/servlet/SCityFirm?state=FL
LL:  library.flcourts.org
LR:  www.findlaw.com/11stategov/fl/index.html
     www.loc.gov/law/guide/us-fl.html
MV:  www.hsmv.state.fl.us
SF:  www.alllaw.com/state_resources/florida/forms
     forms.lp.findlaw.com/states/fl.html
SL:  www.leg.state.fl.us/Welcome/index.cfm
SS:  www.dos.state.fl.us
WC:  www2.myflorida.com/les/wc/index.html

## GEORGIA
AG:  www.ganet.org/ago
BA:  www.findlaw.com/11stategov/ga/associations.html
CS:  www.georgiacourts.org/index.html
GO:  www.ganet.org/governor
LF:  www.attorneylocate.com/scripts/city.asp?city_statecode=GA
     www.directory.findlaw.com/lawyer/servlet/SCityFirm?state=GA
LL:  gsll.home.mindspring.com
LR:  www.findlaw.com/11stategov/ga/index.html
     www.loc.gov/law/guide/us-ga.html
MV:  www.dmvs.ga.gov

SF: www.alllaw.com/state_resources/georgia/forms
forms.lp.findlaw.com/states/ga.html
SL: www2.state.ga.us/Legis
SS: www.sos.state.ga.us/default1024.asp
WC: www.ganet.org/sbwc

## HAWAII
AG: www.hawaii.gov/ag/index.html
BA: www.findlaw.com/11stategov/hi/associations.html
CS: www.state.hi.us/jud ·
GO: gov.state.hi.us
LF: www.attorneylocate.com/scripts/city.asp?city_statecode=HI
www.directory.findlaw.com/lawyer/servlet/SCityFirm?state=HI
LL: www.hawaii.edu/law(click UI I Law Library)
www.hsba.hostme.com/index2.htm
LR: www.findlaw.com/11stategov/hi/index.html
www.loc.gov/law/guide/us-hi.html
www.legalhawaii.com/lawlinks.htm
MV: www.hawaii.gov/dot
SF: www.alllaw.com/state_resources/hawaii/forms
forms.lp.findlaw.com/states/hi.html
SL: www.capitol.hawaii.gov
SS: www.hawaii.gov/icsd/test2.htm
WC: www.dlir.state.hi.us

## IDAHO
AG: www2.state.id.us/ag/index.html
BA: www.findlaw.com/11stategov/id/associations.html
CS: www2.state.id.us/judicial/judicial.html
GO: www2.state.id.us/gov/index.htm
LF: www.attorneylocate.com/scripts/city.asp?city_statecode=ID
www.directory.findlaw.com/lawyer/servlet/SCityFirm?state=ID
LL: www2.state.id.us/lawlib/lawlib.html
LR: www.findlaw.com/11stategov/id/index.html
www.loc.gov/law/guide/us-id.html
MV: www2.state.id.us/itd/dmv/dmv.htm
SF: www.alllaw.com/state_resources/idaho/forms
forms.lp.findlaw.com/states/id.html
SL: www2.state.id.us/legislat/legislat.html
SS: www.idsos.state.id.us
WC: www2.state.id.us/iic/index.html

## ILLINOIS
AG: www.ag.state.il.us
BA: www.findlaw.com/11stategov/il/associations.html
CS: www.state.il.us/court
GO: www100.state.il.us/gov
LF: www.attorneylocate.com/scripts/city.asp?city_statecode=IL
www.directory.findlaw.com/lawyer/servlet/SCityFirm?state=IL
LL: www.law.siu.edu/lawlib/illaw/general/index.htm
LR: www.findlaw.com/11stategov/il/index.html
www.loc.gov/law/guide/us-il.html
MV: www.sos.state.il.us/depts/vehicles/veh_home.html
SF: www.alllaw.com/state_resources/illinois/forms
forms.lp.findlaw.com/states/il.html
SL: www.state.il.us/government/gov_legislature.cfm

SS:   www.sos.state.il.us
WC:   www.state.il.us/agency/iic


## INDIANA
AG:   www.IN.gov/attorneygeneral
BA:   www.findlaw.com/11stategov/in/associations.html
CS:   www.ai.org/judiciary
GO:   www.state.in.us/gov
LF:   www.attorneylocate.com/scripts/city.asp?city_statecode=IN
       www.directory.findlaw.com/lawyer/servlet/SCityFirm?state=IN
LL:   www.indylaw.indiana.edu/library/library.htm
LR:   www.findlaw.com/11stategov/in/index.html
       www.loc.gov/law/guide/us-in.html
MV:   www.state.in.us/bmv/index.html
SF:   www.alllaw.com/state_resources/indiana/forms
       forms.lp.findlaw.com/states/in.html
SL:   www.state.in.us/legislative
SS:   www.state.in.us/sos
WC:   www.state.in.us/wkcomp/index.html


## IOWA
AG:   www.state.ia.us/government/ag/index.html
BA:   www.findlaw.com/11stategov/ia/associations.html
CS:   www.judicial.state.ia.us
GO:   www.state.ia.us/governor
LF:   www.attorneylocate.com/scripts/city.asp?city_statecode=IA
       www.directory.findlaw.com/lawyer/servlet/SCityFirm?state=IA
LL:   www.silo.lib.ia.us/lawlibrary.htm
LR:   www.findlaw.com/11stategov/ia/index.html
       www.loc.gov/law/guide/us-ia.html
MV:   www.dot.state.ia.us/sitemap.htm
SF:   www.alllaw.com/state_resources/iowa/forms
       forms.lp.findlaw.com/states/ia.html
SL:   www.legis.state.ia.us
SS:   www.sos.state.ia.us
WC:   www.state.ia.us/iwd/wc/index.html


## KANSAS
AG:   www.ink.org/public/ksag
BA:   www.findlaw.com/11stategov/ks/associations.html
CS:   www.kscourts.org
GO:   www.accesskansas.org/governor
LF:   www.attorneylocate.com/scripts/city.asp?city_statecode=KS
       www.directory.findlaw.com/lawyer/servlet/SCityFirm?state=KS
LL:   www.kscourts.org/ctlib
LR:   www.findlaw.com/11stategov/ks/index.html
       www.loc.gov/law/guide/us-ks.html
MV:   www.ksrevenue.org/kdorvehicle.html
SF:   www.alllaw.com/state_resources/kansas/forms
       www.law.ukans.edu/research/prac_forms.html
SL:   www.kslegislature.org/cgi-bin/index.cgi
SS:   www.kssos.org
WC:   www.hr.state.ks.us/wc/html/wc.htm

## KENTUCKY

AG: www.law.state.ky.us
BA: www.findlaw.com/11stategov/ky/associations.html
CS: www.kycourts.net
GO: gov.state.ky.us
LF: www.attorneylocate.com/scripts/city.asp?city_statecode=KY
www.directory.findlaw.com/lawyer/servlet/SCityFirm?state=KY
LL: www.uky.edu/Law/library
LR: www.findlaw.com/11stategov/ky/index.html
www.loc.gov/law/guide/us-ky.html
MV: www.kytc.state.ky.us/DrLic/home.htm
SF: www.alllaw.com/state_resources/kentucky/forms
forms.lp.findlaw.com/states/ky.html
SL: www.lrc.state.ky.us/home.htm
SS: www.sos.state.ky.us
WC: www.dwc.state.ky.us

## LOUISIANA

AG: www.ag.state.la.us
BA: www.findlaw.com/11stategov/la/associations.html
CS: www.state.la.us/gov_judicial.htm
GO: www.gov.state.la.us
LF: www.attorneylocate.com/scripts/city.asp?city_statecode=LA
www.directory.findlaw.com/lawyer/servlet/SCityFirm?state=LA
LL: www.lasc.org/lawlib/lawlib.html
LR: www.findlaw.com/11stategov/la/index.html
www.loc.gov/law/guide/us-la.html
MV: www.dps.state.la.us/dpsweb.nsf
SF: www.alllaw.com/state_resources/louisiana/forms
forms.lp.findlaw.com/states/la.html
SL: www.legis.state.la.us
SS: www.sec.state.la.us
WC: www.ldol.state.la.us/sec2owca.asp

## MAINE

AG: www.state.me.us/ag/homepage.htm
BA: www.findlaw.com/11stategov/me/associations.html
CS: www.findlaw.com/11stategov/me/courts.html
GO: www.state.me.us/governor
LF: www.attorneylocate.com/scripts/city.asp?city_statecode=ME
www.directory.findlaw.com/lawyer/servlet/SCityFirm?state=ME
LL: www.state.me.us/legis/lawlib/homepage.htm
LR: www.findlaw.com/11stategov/me/index.html
www.loc.gov/law/guide/us-me.html
MV: www.state.me.us/sos/bmv
SF: www.alllaw.com/state_resources/maine/forms
www.parasec.com/maine.html
SL: janus.state.me.us/legis
SS: www.state.me.us/sos
WC: www.state.me.us/wcb

## MARYLAND

AG: www.oag.state.md.us
BA: www.findlaw.com/11stategov/md/associations.html

CS:   www.courts.state.md.us
GO:   www.gov.state.md.us
LF:   www.attorneylocate.com/scripts/city.asp?city_statecode=MD
      www.directory. findlaw.com/lawyer/servlet/SCityFirm?state=MD
LL:   www.lawlib.state.md.us
LR:   www.findlaw.com/11stategov/md/index.html
      www.loc.gov/law/guide/us-md.html
MV:   www.mva.state.md.us
SF:   www.alllaw.com/state_resources/maryland/forms
      www.parasec.com/maryland.html
SL:   www.mlis.state.md.us
SS:   www.sos.state.md.us
WC:   www.charm.net/~wcc

## MASSACHUSETTS

AG:   www.ago.state.ma.us
BA:   www.findlaw.com/11stategov/ma/associations.html
CS:   www.state.ma.us/courts
GO:   www.state.ma.us/gov
LF:   www.attorneylocate.com/scripts/city.asp?city_statecode=MA
      www.directory.findlaw.com/lawyer/servlet/SCityFirm?state=MA
LL:   www.socialaw.com
LR:   www.findlaw.com/11stategov/ma/index.html
      www.loc.gov/law/guide/us-ma.html
MV:   www.state.ma.us/rmv/index.html
SF:   www.alllaw.com/state_resources/massachusetts/forms
      forms.lp.findlaw.com/states/ma.html
SL:   www.state.ma.us/legis
SS:   www.state.ma.us/sec
WC:   www.state.ma.us/dia

## MICHIGAN

AG:   www.ag.state.mi.us
BA:   www.findlaw.com/11stategov/mi/associations.html
CS:   www.supremecourt.state.mi.us/searchengine.htm
      www.ncsconline.org/Information/info_court_web_sites.html
GO:   www.michigan.gov/gov
LF:   www.attorneylocate.com/scripts/city.asp?city_statecode=MI
      www.directory.findlaw.com/lawyer/servlet/SCityFirm?state=MI
LL:   www.libofmich.lib.mi.us/law/lawlib.html
LR:   www.findlaw.com/11stategov/mi/index.html
      www.loc.gov/law/guide/us-mi.html
MV:   www.sos.state.mi.us/dv/index.html
SF:   www.alllaw.com/state_resources/michigan/forms
      forms.lp.findlaw.com/states/mi.html
SL:   www.michiganlegislature.org
SS:   www.sos.state.mi.us
WC:   www.cis.state.mi.us/wkrcomp/bwdc/home.htm

## MINNESOTA

AG:   www.ag.state.mn.us
BA:   www.findlaw.com/11stategov/mn/associations.html
CS:   www.courts.state.mn.us/home/ndefault.asp?msel=1
GO:   www.governor.state.mn.us

LF:  www.attorneylocate.com/scripts/city.asp?city_statecode=MN
     www.directory.findlaw.com/lawyer/servlet/SCityFirm?state=MN
LL:  www.lawlibrary.state.mn.us
LR:  www.findlaw.com/11stategov/mn/index.html
     www.loc.gov/law/guide/us-mn.html
MV:  www.dps.state.mn.us/dvs/index.html
SF:  www.alllaw.com/state_resources/minnesota/forms
     www.parasec.com/minne.html
SL:  www.leg.state.mn.us/leg/legis.htm
SS:  www.sos.state.mn.us
WC:  www.doli.state.mn.us/workcomp.html


## MISSISSIPPI

AG:  www.ago.state.mn.us
BA:  www.findlaw.com/11stategov/ms/associations.html
CS:  www.mssc.state.ms.us
     www.ncsconline.org/Information/info_court_web_sites.html
GO:  www.governor.state.ms.us
LF:  www.attorneylocate.com/scripts/city.asp?city_statecode=MS
     www.directory.findlaw.com/lawyer/servlet/SCityFirm?state=MS
LL:  www.mssc.state.ms.us/library/default.asp
LR:  www.findlaw.com/11stategov/ms/index.html
     library.law.olemiss.edu
     www.loc.gov/law/guide/us-ms.html
MV:  www.dps.state.ms.us/dps/dps.nsf/main?OpenForm
SF:  www.alllaw.com/state_resources/mississippi/forms
     www.parasec.com/mississ.html
SL:  www.ls.state.ms.us
SS:  www.sos.state.ms.us
WC:  www.mwcc.state.ms.us


## MISSOURI

AG:  www.ago.state.mo.us/index.htm
BA:  www.findlaw.com/11stategov/mo/associations.html
CS:  www.osca.state.mo.us/index.nsf
GO:  www.gov.state.mo.us
LF:  www.attorneylocate.com/scripts/city.asp?city_statecode=MO
     www.directory.findlaw.com/lawyer/servlet/SCityFirm?state=MO
LL:  www.law.missouri.edu/library
LR:  www.findlaw.com/11stategov/mo/index.html
     www.loc.gov/law/guide/us-mo.html
MV:  www.dor.state.mo.us
SF:  www.alllaw.com/state_resources/missouri/forms
     www.parasec.com/missouri.html
SL:  www.moga.state.mo.us
SS:  www.sos.state.mo.us
WC:  www.dolir.state.mo.us/wc/index.htm


## MONTANA

AG:  www.doj.state.mt.us/ago
BA:  www.findlaw.com/11stategov/mt/associations.html
CS:  www.lawlibrary.state.mt.us
     www.ncsconline.org/Information/info_court_web_sites.html
GO:  www.discoveringmontana.com/gov2/css/default.asp

LF: www.attorneylocate.com/scripts/city.asp?city_statecode=MT
www.directory.findlaw.com/lawyer/servlet/SCityFirm?state=MT
LL: www.lawlibrary.state.mt.us
LR: www.findlaw.com/11stategov/mt/index.html
www.loc.gov/law/guide/us-mt.html
MV: www.doj.state.mt.us/mvd/index.htm
SF: www.alllaw.com/state_resources/montana/forms
forms.lp.findlaw.com/states/mt.html
SL: www.leg.state.mt.us/index.htm
SS: www.sos.state.mt.us/css/index.asp
WC: www.wcc.dli.state.mt.us

## NEBRASKA

AG: www.ago.state.ne.us
BA: www.findlaw.com/11stategov/ne/associations.html
CS: court.nol.org
GO: gov.nol.org
LF: www.attorneylocate.com/scripts/city.asp?city_statecode=NE
www.directory.findlaw.com/lawyer/servlet/SCityFirm?state=NE
LL: court.nol.org/library/lawlibindex.htm
LR: www.findlaw.com/11stategov/ne/index.html
www.loc.gov/law/guide/us-ne.html
MV: www.nol.org/home/DMV
SF: www.alllaw.com/state_resources/nebraska/forms
forms.lp.findlaw.com/states/ne.html
SL: www.unicam.state.ne.us/index.htm
SS: www.nol.org/home/SOS
WC: www.nol.org/home/WC

## NEVADA

AG: www.ag.state.nv.us
BA: www.findlaw.com/11stategov/ne/associations.html
CS: www.clan.lib.nv.us/polpac/nsc/nevadacourts.htm
GO: www.gov.state.nv.us
LF: www.attorneylocate.com/scripts/city.asp?city_statecode=NV
www.directory.findlaw.com/lawyer/servlet/SCityFirm?state=NV
LL: www.clan.lib.nv.us/polpac/nsc/nscl.htm
LR: www.findlaw.com/11stategov/nv/index.html
www.loc.gov/law/guide/us-nv.html
MV: www.nevadadmv.state.nv.us/tocdmvps.htm
SF: www.alllaw.com/state_resources/nevada/forms
www.parasec.com/nevada.html
SL: www.leg.state.nv.us
SS: www.sos.state.nv.us
WC: www.dirweb.state.nv.us

## NEW HAMPSHIRE

AG: www.state.nh.us/nhdoj/index.html
BA: www.findlaw.com/11stategov/nh/associations.html
CS: www.state.nh.us/courts/default.htm
GO: www.state.nh.us/governor
LF: www.attorneylocate.com/scripts/city.asp?city_statecode=NH
www.directory.findlaw.com/lawyer/servlet/SCityFirm?state=NH
LL: www.state.nh.us/courts/lawlib/services.htm

LR:  www.findlaw.com/11stategov/nh/index.html
     www.loc.gov/law/guide/us-nh.html
MV:  www.state.nh.us/dmv
SF:  www.alllaw.com/state_resources/new_hampshire/forms
     forms.lp.findlaw.com/states/nh.html
SL:  www.gencourt.state.nh.us/ns
SS:  webster.state.nh.us/sos
WC:  labor.state.nh.us

## NEW JERSEY

AG:  www.state.nj.us/lps
BA:  www.findlaw.com/11stategov/nj/associations.html
CS:  www.judiciary.state.nj.us
GO:  www.state.nj.us
LF:  www.attorneylocate.com/scripts/city.asp?city_statecode=NJ
     www.directory.findlaw.com/lawyer/servlet/SCityFirm?state=NJ
LL:  www.njstatelib.org/aboutus/SGIS/liblaw.htm
LR:  www.findlaw.com/11stategov/nj/index.html
     www.loc.gov/law/guide/us-nj.html
MV:  www.state.nj.us/mvs
SF:  www.alllaw.com/state_resources/new_jersey/forms
     forms.lp.findlaw.com/states/nj.html
SL:  www.njleg.state.nj.us
SS:  www.state.nj.us/state
WC:  www.state.nj.us/labor/wc/Default.htm

## NEW MEXICO

AG:  www.ago.state.nm.us
BA:  www.findlaw.com/11stategov/nm/associations.html
CS:  www.nmcourts.com
GO:  www.governor.state.nm.us
LF:  www.attorneylocate.com/scripts/city.asp?city_statecode=NM
     www.directory.findlaw.com/lawyer/servlet/SCityFirm?state=NM
LL:  www.fscll.org
LR:  www.findlaw.com/11stategov/nm/index.html
     www.loc.gov/law/guide/us-nm.html
MV:  www.state.nm.us/tax/mvd/mvd_home.htm
SF:  www.alllaw.com/state_resources/new_mexico/forms
     forms.lp.findlaw.com/states/nm.html
SL:  www.legis.state.nm.us
SS:  www.sos.state.nm.us
WC:  www.state.nm.us/wca

## NEW YORK

AG:  www.oag.state.ny.us
BA:  www.findlaw.com/11stategov/ny/associations.html
CS:  www.courts.state.ny.us
GO:  www.state.ny.us/governor
LF:  www.attorneylocate.com/scripts/city.asp?city_statecode=NY
     www.directory.findlaw.com/lawyer/servlet/SCityFirm?state=NY
LL:  www.courts.state.ny.us/ucslib.html
LR:  www.findlaw.com/11stategov/ny/index.html
     www.loc.gov/law/guide/us-ny.html
MV:  www.nydmv.state.ny.us

SF:  www.alllaw.com/state_resources/new_york/forms
     forms.lp.findlaw.com/states/ny.html
SL:  www.assembly.state.ny.us
     www.senate.state.ny.us
SS:  www.dos.state.ny.us
WC:  www.wcb.state.ny.us

## NORTH CAROLINA

AG:  www.jus.state.nc.us
BA:  www.findlaw.com/11stategov/nc/associations.html
CS:  www.nccourts.org
GO:  www.governor.state.nc.us
LF:  www.attorneylocate.com/scripts/city.asp?city_statecode=NC
     www.directory.findlaw.com/lawyer/servlet/SCityFirm?state=NC
LL:  www.aoc.state.nc.us/www/public/html/sc_library.htm
LR:  www.findlaw.com/11stategov/nc/index.html
     www.loc.gov/law/guide/us-nc.html
MV:  www.dmv.dot.state.nc.us
SF:  www.alllaw.com/state_resources/north_carolina/forms
     forms.lp.findlaw.com/states/nc.html
SL:  www.ncga.state.nc.us
SS:  www.secstate.state.nc.us
WC:  www.comp.state.nc.us

## NORTH DAKOTA

AG:  www.ag.state.nd.us
BA:  www.findlaw.com/11stategov/nd/associations.html
CS:  www.court.state.nd.us
GO:  www.governor.state.nd.us
LF:  www.attorneylocate.com/scripts/city.asp?city_statecode=ND
     www.directory.findlaw.com/lawyer/servlet/SCityFirm?state=ND
LL:  www.law.und.nodak.edu/lawweb/thormodsgard/library/html
LR:  www.findlaw.com/11stategov/nd/index.html
     www.loc.gov/law/guide/us-nd.html
MV:  www.state.nd.us/dot/dnv.html
SF:  www.alllaw.com/state_resources/north_dakota/forms
     forms.lp.findlaw.com/states/nd.html
SL:  www.state.nd.us/lr
SS:  www.state.nd.us/sec
WC:  www.ndworkerscomp.com

## OHIO

AG:  www.ag.state.oh.us
BA:  www.findlaw.com/11stategov/oh/associations.html
CS:  www.sconet.state.oh.us/Web_Sites/courts
GO:  www.state.oh.us/gov
LF:  www.attorneylocate.com/scripts/city.asp?city_statecode=OH
     www.directory.findlaw.com/lawyer/servlet/SCityFirm?state=OH
LL:  www.sconet.state.oh.us/lawlibrary
LR:  www.findlaw.com/11stategov/oh/index.html
     www.loc.gov/law/guide/us-oh.html
MV:  www.ohio.gov/odps/division/bmv/bmv.html
SF:  www.alllaw.com/state_resources/ohio/forms
     www.parasec.com/ohio.html
SL:  www.legislature.state.oh.us

SS:  www.state.oh.us/sos
WC:  www.ohiobwc.com

## OKLAHOMA

AG:  www.oag.state.ok.us/explorer.index.html
BA:  www.findlaw.com/11stategov/ok/associations.html
CS:  www.oscn.net/applications/oscn/start.asp
GO:  www.governor.state.ok.us
LF:  www.attorneylocate.com/scripts/city.asp?city_statecode=OK
     www.directory.findlaw.com/lawyer/servlet/SCityFirm?state=OK
LL:  www.odl.state.ok.us/lawinfo/index.htm
LR:  www.findlaw.com/11stategov/ok/index.html
     www.loc.gov/law/guide/us-ok.html
     www.law.ou.edu/library/oklahoma-noframes.shtml
MV:  www.dps.state.ok.us/dls
SF:  www.alllaw.com/state_resources/oklahoma/forms
     forms.lp.findlaw.com/states/ok.html
SL:  www.lsb.state.ok.us
SS:  www.sos.state.ok.us
WC:  www.oklaosf.state.ok.us/~okdol/workcomp/index.htm

## OREGON

AG:  www.doj.state.or.us
BA:  www.findlaw.com/11stategov/or/associations.html
CS:  www.ojd.state.or.us
GO:  www.governor.state.or.us
LF:  www.attorneylocate.com/scripts/city.asp?city_statecode=OR
     www.directory.findlaw.com/lawyer/servlet/SCityFirm?state=OR
LL:  www.ojd.state.or.us/library
LR:  www.findlaw.com/11stategov/or/index.html
     www.loc.gov/law/guide/us_or.html
MV:  www.odot.state.or.us/dmv
SF:  www.alllaw.com/state_resources/oregon/forms
     www.parasec.com/oregon.html
SL:  www.leg.state.or.us
SS:  www.sos.state.or.us
WC:  www.cbs.state.or.us/wcd

## PENNSYLVANIA

AG:  www.attorneygeneral.gov
BA:  www.findlaw.com/11stategov/pa/associations.html
CS:  www.courts.state.pa.us
GO:  sites.state.pa.us/PA_Exec/Governor/overview.html
LF:  www.attorneylocate.com/scripts/city.asp?city_statecode=PA
     www.directory.findlaw.com/lawyer/servlet/SCityFirm?state=PA
LL:  www.law.upenn.edu/bll
LR:  www.findlaw.com/11stategov/pa/index.html
     www.loc.gov/law/guide/us-pa.html
MV:  www.dmv.state.pa.us
SF:  www.alllaw.com/state_resources/pennsylvania/forms
     forms.lp.findlaw.com/states/pa.html
SL:  www.legis.state.pa.us
SS:  www.dos.state.pa.us
WC:  www.dli.state.pa.us/landi/cwp/browse.asp?A=198

## RHODE ISLAND
AG: www.riag.state.ri.us
BA: www.findlaw.com/11stategov/ri/associations.html
CS: www.courts.state.ri.us
GO: www.governor.state.ri.us
LF: www.attorneylocate.com/scripts/city.asp?city_statecode=RI
www.directory.findlaw.com/lawyer/servlet/SCityFirm?state=RI
LL: www.courts.state.ri.us/library
LR: www.findlaw.com/11stategov/ri/index.html
www.loc.gov/law/guide/us-ri.html
MV: www.dmv.state.ri.us
SF: www.alllaw.com/state_resources/rhode_island/forms
forms.lp.findlaw.com/states/ri.html
SL: www.rilin.state.ri.us
SS: www.state.ri.us
WC: www.state.ri.us/bus/wkcomp.htm

## SOUTH CAROLINA
AG: www.scattorneygeneral.org/index.asp
BA: www.findlaw.com/11stategov/sc/associations.html
CS: www.judicial.state.sc.us
GO: www.state.sc.us/governor
LF: www.attorneylocate.com/scripts/city.asp?city_statecode=SC
www.directory.findlaw.com/lawyer/servlet/SCityFirm?state=SC
LL: www.law.sc.edu/lawlib.htm
LR: www.findlaw.com/11stategov/sc/index.html
www.loc.gov/law/guide/us-sc.html
MV: www.scdps.org/dmv
SF: www.alllaw.com/state_resources/south_carolina/forms
www.parasec.com/sc.html
SL: www.lpitr.state.sc.us
SS: www.scsos.com
WC: www.wcc.state.sc.us

## SOUTH DAKOTA
AG: www.state.sd.us/attorney/index.htm
BA: www.findlaw.com/11stategov/sd/associations.html
CS: www.state.sd.us/state/judicial
GO: www.state.sd.us/governor/index.htm
LF: www.attorneylocate.com/scripts/city.asp?city_statecode=SD
www.directory.findlaw.com/lawyer/servlet/SCityFirm?state=SD
LL: www.usd.edu/lawlib
LR: www.findlaw.com/11stategov/sd/index.html
www.loc.gov/law/guide/us-sd.html
MV: www.state.sd.us/revenue/motorvcl.htm
SF: www.alllaw.com/state_resources/south_dakota/forms
www.parasec.com/sd.html
SL: legis.state.sd.us/index.cfm
SS: www.state.sd.us/sos/sos.htm
WC: www.state.sd.us/dol/dlm/dlm-home.htm

## TENNESSEE
AG: www.attorneygeneral.state.tn.us
BA: www.findlaw.com/11stategov/tn/associations.html
CS: www.tsc.state.tn.us

GO:  www.state.tn.us/governor
LF:  www.attorneylocate.com/scripts/city.asp?city_statecode=TN
      www.directory.findlaw.com/lawyer/servlet/SCityFirm?state=TN
LL:  www.law.utk.edu/admin/library
LR:  www.findlaw.com/11stategov/tn/index.html
      www.loc.gov/law/guide/us-tn.html
MV:  www.state.tn.us/safety
SF:  www.alllaw.com/state_resources/tennessee/forms
      forms.lp.findlaw.com/states/tn.html
SL:  www.legislature.state.tn.us
SS:  www.state.tn.us/sos/index.htm
WC:  www.state.tn.us/labor-wfd/wcomp.html


## TEXAS

AG:  www.oag.state.tx.us
BA:  www.findlaw.com/11stategov/tx/associations.html
CS:  www.courts.state.tx.us
GO:  www.governor.state.tx.us
LF:  www.attorneylocate.com/scripts/city.asp?city_statecode=TX
      www.directory.findlaw.com/lawyer/servlet/SCityFirm?state=TX
LL:  www.sll.state.tx.us
LR:  www.findlaw.com/11stategov/tx/index.html
      www.loc.gov/law/guide/us-tx.html
      suefaw.home.texas.net/texas.html
MV:  www.dot.state.tx.us/vtrinfo/vtrinfo.htm
SF:  www.alllaw.com/state_resources/texas/forms
      forms.lp.findlaw.com/states/tx.html
SL:  www.capitol.state.tx.us
SS:  www.sos.state.tx.us
WC:  www.twcc.state.tx.us


## UTAH

AG:  www.attygen.state.ut.us
BA:  www.findlaw.com/11stategov/ut/associations.html
CS:  courtlink.utcourts.gov
GO:  www.governor.state.ut.us
LF:  www.attorneylocate.com/scripts/city.asp?city_statecode=UT
      www.directory.findlaw.com/lawyer/servlet/SCityFirm?state=UT
LL:  courtlink.utcourts.gov/appellate/lawlib.htm
LR:  www.findlaw.com/11stategov/ut/index.html
      www.loc.gov/law/guide/us-ut.html
MV:  www.dmv-utah.com
SF:  www.alllaw.com/state_resources/utah/forms
      forms.lp.findlaw.com/states/ut.html
SL:  www.le.state.ut.us
SS:  www.elections.utah.gov
WC:  www.ind-com.state.ut.us


## VERMONT

AG:  www.state.vt.us/atg
BA:  www.findlaw.com/11stategov/vt/associations.html
CS:  www.state.vt.us/courts/vtcourts.htm
GO:  www.gov.state.vt.us
LF:  www.attorneylocate.com/scripts/city.asp?city_statecode=VT
      www.directory.findlaw.com/lawyer/servlet/SCityFirm?state=VT

LL:   www.vermontlaw.edu/library/index.cfm
LR:   www.findlaw.com/11stategov/vt/index.html
      www.loc.gov/law/guide/us-vt.html
MV:   www.aot.state.vt.us/dmv/dmvhp.htm
SF:   www.allaw.com/state_resources/vermont/forms
      www.parasec.com/vermont.html
SL:   www.leg.state.vt.us
SS:   www.sec.state.vt.us
WC:   www.state.vt.us/labind/wcindex.htm

## VIRGINIA

AG:   www.agelect.state.va.us
BA:   www.findlaw.com/11stategov/va/associations.html
CS:   www.courts.state.va.us/opin.htm
GO:   www.governor.state.va.us
LF:   www.attorneylocate.com/scripts/city.asp?city_statecode=VA
      www.directory.findlaw.com/lawyer/servlet/SCityFirm?state=VA
LL:   www.courts.state.va.us/library/library.htm
LR:   www.findlaw.com/11stategov/va/index.html
      www.loc.gov/law/guide/us-va.html
MV:   www.dmv.state.va.us
SF:   www.alllaw.com/state_resources/virginia/forms
      forms.lp.findlaw.com/states/va.html
SL:   legis.state.va.us
SS:   www.soc.vipnet.org
WC:   www.vwc.state.va.us

## WASHINGTON

AG:   www.wa.gov/ago
BA:   www.findlaw.com/11stategov/wa/associations.html
CS:   www.courts.wa.gov
GO:   www.governor.wa.gov
LF:   www.attorneylocate.com/scripts/city.asp?city_statecode=WA
      www.directory.findlaw.com/lawyer/servlet/SCityFirm?state=WA
LL:   www.courts.wa.gov/library
LR:   www.findlaw.com/11stategov/wa/index.html
      www.loc.gov/law/guide/us-wa.html
MV:   www.wa.gov/dol
SF:   www.alllaw.com/state_resources/washington/forms
      www.forms.lp.findlaw.com/states/wa.html
SL:   www.leg.wa.gov/wsladm/default.htm
SS:   www.secstate.wa.gov
WC:   www.lni.wa.gov/insurance

## WEST VIRGINIA

AG:   www.state.wv.us/wvag
BA:   www.findlaw.com/11stategov/wv/associations.html
CS:   www.state.wv.us/wvsca/wvsystem.htm
GO:   www.state.wv.us/governor
LF:   www.attorneylocate.com/scripts/city.asp?city_statecode=WV
      www.directory.findlaw.com/lawyer/servlet/SCityFirm?state=WV
LL:   www.state.wv.us/wvsca/library/menu.htm
LR:   www.findlaw.com/11stategov/wv/index.html
      www.loc.gov/law/guide/us-wv.html
MV:   www.wvdot.com/6_motorists/dmv/6G_DMV.HTM

SF:  www.alllaw.com/state_resources/west_virginia/forms
     forms.lp.findlaw.com/states/wv.html
SL:  www.legis.state.wv.us
SS:  www.wvsos.com
WC:  www.state.wv.us/bep/WC/default.HTM

## WISCONSIN
AG:  www.doj.state.wi.us
BA:  www.findlaw.com/11stategov/wi/associations.html
CS:  www.courts.state.wi.us
GO:  www.wisgov.state.wi.us
LF:  www.attorneylocate.com/scripts/city.asp?city_statecode=WI
     www.directory.findlaw.com/lawyer/servlet/SCityFirm?state=WI
LL:  www.wsll.state.wi.us
LR:  www.findlaw.com/11stategov/wi/index.html
     www.loc.gov/law/guide/us-wi.html
MV:  www.dot.state.wi.us/dmv/dmv.html
SF:  www.alllaw.com/state_resources/wisconsin/forms
     forms.lp.findlaw.com/states/wi.html
SL:  www.legis.state.wi.us
SS:  www.state.wi.us/agencies/sos
WC:  www.dwd.state.wi.us/wc/default.htm

## WYOMING
AG:  attorneygeneral.state.wy.us
BA:  www.findlaw.com/11stategov/wy/associations.html
CS:  www.courts.state.wy.us
GO:  www.state.wy.us/governor/governor_home.html
LF:  www.attorneylocate.com/scripts/city.asp?city_statecode=WY
     www.directory.findlaw.com/lawyer/servlet/SCityFirm?state=WY
LL:  www.courts.state.wy.us/state_law_library.htm
LR:  www.findlaw.com/11stategov/wy/index.html
     www.loc.gov/law/guide/us-wy.html
MV:  wydotweb.state.wy.us
SF:  www.alllaw.com/state_resources/wyoming/forms
     www.parasec.com/wyoming.html
SL:  legisweb.state.wy.us
SS:  soswy.state.wy.us/election/election.htm
WC:  wydoe.state.wy.us/doe.asp?ID=9

# Appendix J

# Starting a Freelance Paralegal Business

## INTRODUCTION

Sometime during their career, most paralegals wonder what it would be like to own their own business and be their own boss as a freelance paralegal.

There are two major kinds of businesses that paralegals have formed:

1. A business that offers legal and law-related services directly to the public without attorney supervision. The service providers are independent contractors who are sometimes called freelance paralegals, independent paralegals, or legal technicians. (In California, however, they have titles such as legal document assistant because only individuals who work under attorney supervision can be called paralegals.)

2. A business that offers services to attorneys. The service providers are independent contractors who are sometimes called freelance paralegals, independent paralegals, or contract paralegals. They perform their services under attorney supervision even though they are not employees of attorneys.

Our focus in this appendix is primarily on the freelance paralegal who offers services to attorneys, although much of what is said will apply as well to the first category of business. (See also chapter 4 for a discussion of the legal issues involved when nonattorneys sell services directly to the public and chapter 15 for a description of an independent paralegal who represents clients in social security hearings.)

Running your own business is a major undertaking. Veteran freelance paralegals frequently comment on the time commitment that they must make. "You need to understand that you'll never work harder than when you own your own business"[1] If you become successful, nine-to-five work days will probably be rare. "There are no 'normal' work hours," reports a freelance paralegal in California

who once had an attorney client show up on Sunday, December 24, 2000, "with paperwork that had to be prepared before the rules changed on January 1, 2001."[2] Another freelancer cautions that you need to subscribe to the "old adage that you work 80 hours a week just so you don't have to work 40 hours a week for someone else."[3]

Yet the rewards of success in this endeavor can be substantial. In an article called *Following My Dream*, a freelance paralegal exclaimed, upon receiving her first check as a freelance paralegal, "I thought I had died and gone to entrepreneurial paralegal heaven."[4]

## SHOULD I DO IT?

Is owning a freelance business a realistic option for you? Should you do it? Not many paralegals are in business as freelance paralegals. Surveys show that they constitute between 1 and 2 percent of paralegals in the state,[5] although the percentage who have tried to start such a business without success is higher. The two most important questions you need to ask yourself when deciding whether to start your own freelance business are as follows: Do have the expertise that attorneys want? Can you survive without a steady cash flow during your first year in business?

### Expertise

Attorneys expect you to be an expert in what they are asking you to do. They will take the time to tell you what they want done; they will almost never take the time to explain to you how to do it. You are expected to know. Consequently, the vast majority of successful freelance paralegals do not go into business until they have had years of experience, primarily as traditional paralegals employed by attorneys. Here are some examples of tasks commonly performed by freelance paralegals that you will need to know how to do *before* anyone is likely to hire you to perform them:

- Digest the transcript of depositions or other litigation documents
- Collect and digest medical records
- Prepare the 706 federal estate tax return and other applicable federal and estate returns
- Prepare all the documents needed to probate an estate
- Prepare trial exhibits
- Incorporate a business
- Conduct an asset search and other public record searches
- Conduct a due-diligence search
- Compile a chain of title to real property
- Prepare and file trademark and patent applications

Which of these tasks you are able to perform will, of course, depend on what specialties you developed while you were an employed paralegal. There are some freelance assignments that do not require great skill. For example:

- Bates stamp litigation documents
- Encode litigation documents in a computer database
- Complete service of process
- File pleadings in court

Yet these assignments usually pay the least, and there may not be enough of them to keep a full-time business running. You need to be able to offer specialized skills. If the tasks to be done did not require such skills, the attorney would not need a competent paralegal. A temporary secretary would be sufficient for most of them.

### Cash Flow

If you need the security of a steady flow of income every week or month, it is too soon to start your freelance business. You need to have a cash reserve that will keep you in minimum survival mode until you find out whether your business will work. How long will it take to find this out? Although circumstances will differ from person to person, as a rule of thumb, you should have enough savings to sustain your personal life and your new business for six months to a year.

The cash flow problem is not simply due to the fact that it will take time to develop attorney clients for your business. Payment delays also cause cash flow headaches. A freelance paralegal may not be paid immediately upon completing an assignment. Law firms have their own cash flow problems. An attorney might take the position that the freelance paralegal will be paid when the attorney is paid. In some cases, the attorney must wait months for payment. This, of course, can place great strains on the finances of a paralegal's business. You need to know at the outset whether you may have to wait an extended period to be paid. If a special payment arrangement cannot be established with the attorney on such a case (e.g., a monthly payment schedule), you may have to decline the work. Many freelance paralegals require monthly payment in the agreement they sign with their attorney clients. (See the discussion of agreements below.) This, however, does not always eliminate the cash flow problem.

### BEGIN MODESTLY

Given these economic realities, you are strongly advised to begin modestly. Do not give up your day job too soon. Consider starting on a part-time basis. Find out if your current employer would have any objections to your taking some freelance cases from other law firms in the evening, on the weekend, or during your vacation. Your employer needs to know because of the conflict of interest issues to be discussed later.

Keep your overhead low. Work out of your home if possible. The expenses of renting an office and paying a new set of utility bills can be substantial. At a minimum, you will need:

- A phone line dedicated to your business
- An answering machine
- E-mail communication
- A computer, word processing software, and a printer
- A basic accounting program such as Quicken
- A fax machine
- Business cards
- A flyer or brochure that lists your services

If you need a copier, start by purchasing one of the smaller ones without the expensive bells and whistles. If you can set up a World Wide Web page for little or no cost, do so. Find out if your Internet service provider will allow you to set one up at no additional charge. Many freelance paralegals, however, say their Internet site is not very useful for generating business, although they like to have it in order to project a professional image.

Do not hire employees at the outset. You will have enough to do in getting your business off the ground and in sorting out the myriad of problems that you have probably never faced before. Even if you have enough work to justify bringing on help, it would be unwise to do so until you feel confident that the business is running smoothly. Obtaining good help is not always easy. You will have to supervise anyone who joins your staff. Too often the time required to train and monitor a new person outweighs the benefit that person provides as an assistant. Hence you need to choose carefully. Consider these options when you are ready for help:

- Contact area paralegal schools to find out if they would be interested in having any of their students intern at your office. If you are unable to pay an intern, ask the school if an unpaid internship is possible.
- If you can pay someone, consider offering part-time employment at the outset. This will give you an opportunity to assess the person's competence and the extent to which your personalities match. Terminating a full-time employee can be a wrenching experience.

## LEGALITIES

You need to know the rules and regulations that govern businesses. To find out what they are, consult then information available from the Small Business Administration (*www.sba.gov*), the Service Corps of Retired Executives (*www.score.org*), and your local chamber of commerce. Organizations such as these can often send you a packet or kit on starting a new business or can tell you where you can obtain one, often at no cost. The organizations can also give you guidance on writing a business plan. Specialty groups in the area (e.g., professional women's groups, minority rights associations) may also be able to give you leads to available assistance for new businesses.

If you are starting out on your own, you will probably operate your business as a sole proprietorship, the simplest kind of business entity. In a sole proprietorship, one person owns all of the assets of the business and assumes all of its debts or liabilities. As a sole proprietor, you cannot separate your business debts from your personal debts. If you default on your business debts, your creditors can reach your personal assets (e.g., a car). Similarly, your business assets (e.g., a computer) can be reached to satisfy your personal debts. Other business formats exist such as the corporation, partnership, and limited liability company. Although you should find out what the requirements, advantages, and disadvantages are for these other formats in your state, the simpler sole-proprietorship format will usually be sufficient to start a modest, one-person freelance business.

If you operate as a sole proprietorship and conduct a business under a name that does not include your surname, you may need to register your assumed or fictitious name with the state.[6]

One of your first steps should be to go to the phone book and look up the names and numbers of the agencies in your state, county, and city that have jurisdiction over businesses. They might be called the Department of Economic Development, Bureau of Licenses, Secretary of State, etc. You want to obtain information on starting a business. For example:

- Do you need a business license from the local or state government? From both?
- As a business, what reporting requirements do you have?
- Can you operate your business out of your home? Are there any zoning restrictions on such businesses?

Almost all governments have agencies that provide literature on the legal requirements for operating a business. The literature may also give you suggestions on the different kinds of business formats you can choose. Most of these agencies have Internet sites that provide the same information.

Also contact the tax departments of the federal, state, and local governments. You want to know what kind of tax returns you will have to file for your business. Don't wait until the end of the year (or until April) to find out. As a sole proprietorship, for example, you will probably report your income on Schedule C of your federal return. As a self-employed individual, you must make estimated tax payments every three months. Substantial social security taxes will have to be paid on your self-employment income. You may also have to pay personal property taxes on your business property. Obtain all the necessary forms and instructions well before filing time. Hiring a tax accountant to do your returns can be expensive. Even if you eventually use an accountant or other tax preparer, the best way to work intelligently with him or her is to know how to do the returns yourself.

The Internal Revenue Service (IRS) has pamphlets on tax obligations and record keeping for small businesses. They are also available on its Internet site (*www.irs.gov*). Find out if your state and local tax authorities have similar material available for mailing and on the Internet.

One of the tax issues faced by attorneys is whether they are trying to avoid paying employment taxes by using freelance paralegals who are not really independent contractors. The IRS may consider you to be an employee even if you have your own business license, have a home office, and are not on anyone's payroll. The test is not what your title is. The more control the attorney has over the "manner and means" of the work assigned to you, the greater the likelihood that the IRS will treat you as an employee. The IRS uses 20 factors to decide whether someone is an employee as opposed to an independent contractor. For more on this issue, type *independent contractor* in the search feature at *www.irs.gov*. Also call the IRS 800 number (see the federal government pages in your local phone book) and ask for publications on independent contractors such as Publication 15-A.

## INSURANCE

Ask every attorney for whom you work whether you are covered by the firm's malpractice liability insurance policy. These policies usually cover independent contractors the attorney hires such as freelance paralegals, but you should check. Because these policies often provide such coverage, not many freelance paralegals have purchased their own policy.

If you work out of your home, you may have a homeowners policy that covers fire, theft, and liability arising out of the property. Although such insurance will not cover malpractice liability, you need to know to what extent it does cover your business. For example, if any of your business equipment is stolen, is it covered? Do you need to tell your insurance carrier what equipment you have? How is portable equipment covered, e.g., a laptop computer that you take with you wherever you go? Does the policy cover the suit that is brought against you because your dog bites the crosstown delivery person who comes to your home to deliver a deposition you will be digesting?

## MARKETING

How do you market yourself? Where do you find attorney clients who will hire you? The most important initial source of clients will be the network of attorneys that you developed while you worked as a traditional paralegal. When you decide to leave your current employment, one of the first questions you should ask your employer is:

> After I leave, would you be interested in having me do some work for you on a freelance basis?

Many attorneys will see the advantages of such an arrangement. They lower their overhead costs (e.g., no full salary, benefits, or employment taxes to be paid) and are able to continue to work with someone who has proven his or her competence—you. Once this new arrangement proves to be successful, the attorney will often help you find additional attorney clients in the area's legal community. As mentioned earlier, you should explore the possibility of taking some freelance assignments from other law firms on your own time with the knowledge and cooperation of your employer. You want to try to line up as many attorney clients as possible before you quit your current job.

Find out if your state or local bar association allows paralegals to become associate or affiliate members. If so, join. Even if such membership is not allowed, you may be able to attend continuing legal education (CLE) sessions of the bar in the areas of your specialty. You want to meet as many attorneys as possible who might be interested in the kind of services you offer. You cannot be shy. Walk up to attorneys at these sessions, introduce yourself, and hand them your card or a flyer that lists your services. Extensive networking at such functions is a must.

Some paralegals place brief ads in the magazine or newsletter that the bar association sends to all its members. The cost of such an ad, however, may be prohibitive. Furthermore, ads may not be as effective a marketing tool as the networking you do on your own and the referrals obtained from the attorneys with whom you have worked.

When you meet with new attorneys who want to know more about your services, be prepared to show them (1) samples of the kind of work you can do, e.g., the first page of a deposition digest, and (2) a list of references. Have a portfolio of samples readily available. If any of your writing samples comes from a real client document, be sure that actual names and other identifying information are blocked out to preserve confidentiality. The list of references should consist primarily of your present and prior attorney clients who have told you that you can list them as references.

Develop a network among fellow freelance paralegals in the state. They can be a source of mutual referrals. A freelance paralegal may be willing to refer an attorney client to you because of a busy schedule, a conflict of interest, or a lack of expertise in the work sought by the client. You, of course, must be willing to make similar referrals. Where can you meet other freelance paralegals? Find out if there is a freelance section of your paralegal association. If one does not exist, organize one. Whenever you are in the company of paralegals, ask them if they know of any freelance paralegals in the area. With persistence, you'll soon know the names of most of them. Some may be reluctant to talk with you because you might be viewed as a competitive threat. If, however, your willingness to share what you know becomes clear, many fellow freelance paralegals will be receptive to the idea of helping to create a mutual support network.

Some paralegal associations have placement services that allow freelance members to list their availability for hire. Find out if your association has such a service. Also, join paralegal listservs. Freelance paralegals are often members of such listservs. You can direct questions to them. For example, on one listserv, someone could post the following question: "I'm trying to start a freelance business and want to write a promotional brochure to give out to attorneys. Have any of you had any luck with such brochures? I'd appreciate any suggestions." As a result of this e-mail message, scores of responses might materialize from all over the country. You will also occasionally see messages posted such as the following: "Anyone know a good freelancer in Springfield who can track down some real property records for us at the county courthouse? If so, please contact me ASAP." A number of paralegal listervs exist. For example, check the ones sponsored by Legal Assistant Today (*www.legalassistanttoday.com*) and the National Federation of Paralegal Associations at (*www.paralegals.org*). Also, if you are a member of the National Association of Legal Assistants (*www.nala.org*), check its bulletin board for freelance paralegals.

### FEES

How much should you charge attorneys for your services? Experienced paralegals determine their fees primarily on the basis of the complexity of the task and their own experience. Most bill by the hour, although a flat fee may be charged for some tasks, particularly those that can be completed within a predictable amount of time, e.g., filing papers in court. You need to find out what the market will bear. What is the competition charging? Do any of the freelance paralegals in your area have billing rate sheets that you can examine? Freelancers sometimes send fliers to attorneys advertising their services. Ask your attorney contacts if they have any in their files that you could examine. Some freelance paralegals charge two-thirds of the hourly rate that attorneys charge their clients for the time of their traditional paralegals.[7] Others try to charge one-half of the attorney's hourly rate.

Out-of-pocket costs are usually paid in addition to hourly or flat fees. For example, if a freelance paralegal is asked to use an overnight shipping service or to take a cab to file a pleading in court, the costs of doing so should be separately charged to the attorney. Long-distance calls are also normal cost items. This needs to be made clear in the freelancer's agreement with the attorney. The agreement that both the freelance paralegal and the attorney sign should state:

- The tasks to be performed
- Due dates

- Fees and costs to be paid
- Time of payment

In your networking contacts with fellow freelance paralegals, find out if any standard service contracts are in use. If they are, you should consider adapting them to your own needs.

## ETHICS

A freelance paralegal has the same ethical responsibilities as a traditional paralegal. Phrased another way, attorneys have the same ethical responsibilities working with freelance paralegals as they do working with their salaried paralegal employees.

The ethical duty of supervision is particularly important. An attorney must supervise the paralegal—traditional or freelance. This is not always easy, particularly in a busy office. Some attorneys do an inadequate job of supervising the paralegal employees they work with in the office every day. Supervising freelance paralegals who may work at their own office or at home can be an even greater challenge. At one time, New Jersey considered making it unethical for attorneys to use freelance paralegals because of the great difficulty of supervising them from a distance. Although the New Jersey Supreme Court eventually rejected this extreme position, the court did caution attorneys that extra care was needed to fulfill their duty of supervising paralegals who do not work in the same office.[8]

Busy attorneys who have great confidence in the ability of freelance paralegals are likely to give them minimal supervision. Of course, you can't control the conduct of the attorneys who hire you. Yet, to protect yourself, you need to reinforce the importance of supervision whenever you can. Some freelance paralegals insert a clause in their agreement for hire stating that the attorney will provide adequate supervision on all assignments. Ask for feedback as often as possible. "Have you looked at the deposition digest I prepared?" "What did you think of the complaint I drafted for you?" "I want to keep improving my skills, so I hope you'll let me know how it could have been better." Focusing on your need for feedback will probably be more productive than pointing out the attorney's ethical duty to supervise you.

Be careful about the unauthorized practice of law (UPL). Friends, relatives, clients, and strangers *regularly* ask freelance paralegals for legal advice or other help that only an attorney can provide. You may find it awkward to refuse their requests, particularly if you are an expert in the area of their need. Yet you must refuse. Your integrity and professionalism are on the line. If you have a list of attorneys that you feel comfortable recommending, have their phone numbers readily available to give out. If you do not have such a list, memorize the phone number of the local bar association's lawyer referral service so that you can give it to the large number of people who will be asking you questions that should be directed to attorneys.

Disclose your status. Busy freelance paralegals often have contact with many people. You may think that someone you meet for the first time already knows you are not an attorney. Avoid making this assumption. Let everyone know that you are not an attorney. A clear communication might be as follows: "I am a paralegal. I am not an attorney, but I work under the supervision of one."

Preserve client confidentiality. Treat everything you learn about an attorney's client the same way you would treat personal information about yourself that you do not want anyone to know. If you travel from office to office, be scrupulous about not letting strangers see your files, including the names of the parties on the front cover of any of the files. Carelessness in this area not only is an ethical violation but also can lead to a waiver of the attorney-client privilege. What a paralegal learns about a client may be covered by the attorney-client privilege. If, however, the information protected by the privilege is disclosed or inadvertently revealed, the privilege may be lost.

Avoid conflicts of interest. Freelance paralegals who work for more than one attorney run the risk of creating a disqualifying conflict of interest. Attorney X, for example, may hire you for a project on a client's case without knowing that you now work or once worked on the case of Attorney Y's client whose interests are adverse to Attorney X's client. To avoid a conflict of interest:

- Keep a detailed list of parties and attorneys involved in all your present and prior paralegal work; for every case on which you have worked, the list should contain the names of the parties and attorneys for both sides, what you did on the case, and the dates of your involvement.
- Before you take a new assignment, ask for the names of the parties on both sides and all of their attorneys.
- Be ready to refuse to take the assignment if you once worked in opposition to the party you are now being asked to help or if you once worked for the party on the other side, even if it was on a different case.
- Allow the attorney hiring you to see your list of parties and attorneys so that he or she can make an informed decision on whether hiring you might create a conflict of interest.

Also let the attorney know of any personal connection you might have to the case, e.g., your brother works or once worked for the opponent of a current client or you recently bought stock in the company of a client. Let the attorney decide whether these personal facts raise conflicts issues.

## KEEPING CURRENT

You need to maintain your expertise. The main vehicle for doing so is continuing legal education (CLE). Often, CLE sessions will discuss the latest cases, statutes, and regulations that you need to know about in your specialty. In the middle of an assignment, a freelance paralegal never wants to have to say, "I didn't know the law changed on that." To maintain your expertise:

- Attend CLE sponsored by paralegal associations.
- Attend CLE sponsored by bar associations.
- Join the specialty section of your paralegal association; if one does not exist in your area of expertise, organize one.
- Take advanced courses offered by area paralegal schools.
- Read (and consider subscribing to) specialty magazines and other periodicals in your area of expertise.

## RESOURCES

### Articles and Books

- Katrina Bakke, *Freelance/Contract Paralegals: How Can They Help?*, (www.wsba.org/DeNovo/2000/novdec2000/bakke.htm).
- Susan Daugherty, *Freelancing Paralegal Services to Small Firms and Solos*, 24 National Paralegal Reporter (National Federation of Paralegal Associations, Summer 2000) (www.paralegals.com/Reporter/Summer00/freelanc.htm).
- Cathy Heath, *Paralegal Services: How to Manage Your Own Firm* (Rimrock, 2000) (www.rimrockpublishing.com).
- Cathy Heath, *Ethics for the Freelance Paralegal*, Part I (www.paralegals.org/Reporter/Fall00/ethics.htm), and Part II (www.paralegals.com/Reporter/Winter00/ethics.htm).
- Dorothy Secol, *Starting and Managing Your Own Business: A Freelancing Guide for Paralegals* (Aspen, 1997) (www.aspenpub.com).

## MORE ON THE INTERNET

### Service Corps of Retired Executives
www.score.org

### Resource Center for Freelancers
www.freelanceonline.com

**Independent Contractor Resource**
www.guru.com

**Internal Revenue Service**
www.irs.gov

**National Association for the Self-Employed**
www.nase.org

**Colorado Freelance Paralegal Network**
www.paralegalsfreelance.com

**Massachusetts Freelance Paralegal Network**
www.freelanceparalegals.homestead.com

**Freelancers on the Internet**
www.paralegalonassignment.com [see exhibit 2.2 in chapter 2]
www.medicalguide.com
www.ipparalegal.com/paralegals.htm
www.earmyhq.com/vps
www.paralegalserv.com
www.paralegalpartners.com
www.aaslegal.com

## ENDNOTES

1. Cathy Heath, *Paralegal Services: How to Manage Your Own Firm* vii (Rimrock, 2000) (www.rimrockpublishing.com).
2. *They Do It Their Way*, 15 National Paralegal Reporter 32 (April/May 2001).
3. Chere Estrin, *When to Say "No (Thank You)" to Your Dream Job*, Recap 12 (California Alliance of Paralegal Associations, Spring 1999).
4. Lee Davis, *Following My Dream*, 25 National Paralegal Reporter 5 (April/May 2001).
5. See, for example, the *2000 Michigan Legal Assistant Survey* (www2.oakland.edu/contin-ed/legalassistant/2000survey.htm).
6. Mary Willard, *Is It Time to Freelance?*, 28 Facts & Findings 18, 20 (National Association of Legal Assistants, May 2001).
7. Mary Uriko, *Freelancing 101*, 18 Legal Assistant Today 83, 84 (September/October 2000).
8. See *In re Opinion No. 26 of Committee on Unauthorized Practice of Law*, 654 A.2d 1344 (N.J. 1995), and *In re Opinion 24 on Unauthorized Practice of Law*, 607 A.2d 962 (N.J. 1992).

# Appendix K

# "PARALEGAL DAY"

In many states, governors and mayors have issued proclamations that set aside a particular day or week to honor paralegals. Here are two examples:

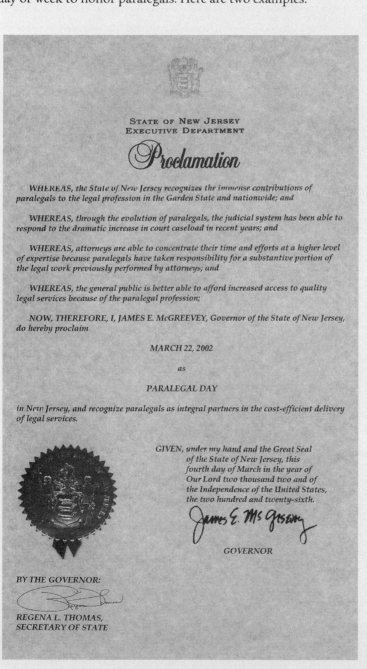

STATE OF NEW JERSEY
EXECUTIVE DEPARTMENT

*Proclamation*

WHEREAS, the State of New Jersey recognizes the immense contributions of paralegals to the legal profession in the Garden State and nationwide; and

WHEREAS, through the evolution of paralegals, the judicial system has been able to respond to the dramatic increase in court caseload in recent years; and

WHEREAS, attorneys are able to concentrate their time and efforts at a higher level of expertise because paralegals have taken responsibility for a substantive portion of the legal work previously performed by attorneys; and

WHEREAS, the general public is better able to afford increased access to quality legal services because of the paralegal profession;

NOW, THEREFORE, I, JAMES E. McGREEVEY, Governor of the State of New Jersey, do hereby proclaim

MARCH 22, 2002

as

PARALEGAL DAY

in New Jersey, and recognize paralegals as integral partners in the cost-efficient delivery of legal services.

GIVEN, under my hand and the Great Seal of the State of New Jersey, this fourth day of March in the year of Our Lord two thousand two and of the Independence of the United States, the two hundred and twenty-sixth.

*James E. McGreevey*

GOVERNOR

BY THE GOVERNOR:

REGENA L. THOMAS,
SECRETARY OF STATE

OFFICIAL MEMORANDUM
STATE OF TEXAS
OFFICE OF THE GOVERNOR

The legal assistant is a vital part of the operations of any office or organization. He or she must perform a variety of duties in an efficient, professional manner and have a broad knowledge of many subjects.

The legal assistant strives to maintain a high standard of professionalism with continued educational growth and development. These individuals understand the importance of their position and take great pride in their performance.

The State Bar of Texas also realizes the invaluable contributions of these assistants to the legal system in our state. The Legal Assistants Division of the State Bar was created to better facilitate and coordinate the services these individuals provide; October 23, 1990 marks the ninth anniversary of the establishment of that division.

Therefore, I, William P. Clements, Jr., Governor of Texas, do hereby find it fitting and proper to designate October 23rd, 1990 as:

**LEGAL ASSISTANTS DAY**

in Texas and urge the appropriate recognition thereof.

In official recognition whereof, I hereby affix my signature this

____10th____ day of __October__ , 19 _90_ .

_____
Governor of Texas

# Appendix L

# News Stories, War Stories, and Parting Shots

## Legal Assistant Elected Probate Judge

In November 1987, Arleen G. Keegan, a legal assistant, was elected Probate Judge in the town of Litchfield, Connecticut. A law degree is not required to be a Probate Judge in Connecticut. Judge Keegan handles a wide variety of cases. In one case, for example, family members argued that their mother was incompetent when she prepared her will. "It was a tough decision because I had to get in the middle of a situation with family members pulling against a close friend of the decedent." "I get to deal with a lot of people, and I find people totally intriguing." Howard, *A*

*Legal Assistant Is Elected Probate Judge*, 5 Legal Assistant Today 32 (March/April 1988).

## Paralegal Appointed Chairman of Bar Association Committee

The Colorado Bar Association has appointed Joanna Hughbanks "to serve as chairman of the Legal Assistants Committee of the Colorado Bar Association." Ms. Hughbanks is an independent paralegal in Denver. She is believed to be the first nonattorney to chair a standing committee of a bar association. Letter from Christopher R.

Probate Judge (and former legal assistant) Arleen Keegan, at the courthouse in Litchfield, Connecticut.

Brauchi, President of the Colorado Bar Association, to Joanna Hughbanks, June 27, 1989. As more and more bar associations allow paralegals to become associate or affiliate members (see chapter 4), leadership roles for paralegals on bar committees are becoming increasingly common. A recent dramatic example is paralegal Karen McLead, who served in the sensitive and high-profile position of chair of the Florida Bar's Unlicensed Practice of Law Committee between 1998 and 2000. Mary Micheletti, *Karen McLead Serving with Distinction*, 17 Legal Assistant Today 52 (September/October 1999).

## Paralegal Appointed Bankruptcy Trustee

A Fort Worth paralegal, Twalla Dupriest, was appointed by the Bankruptcy Court as trustee for the estate of T. Cullen Davis, who was one of the wealthiest men in the United States. Twalla was responsible for gathering all of Davis's assets for the purpose of repaying creditors and presided at the meetings of creditors. *Paralegal Appointed Trustee to Cullen Davis Estate*, Newsletter (Dallas Ass'n of Legal Assistants, September 1987).

## Paralegal Runs for the Legislature

Rosemary Mulligan, an Illinois paralegal, ran for a seat in the Illinois House of Representatives in 1990 against an incumbent. The election was held in a district in a suburb of Chicago. The vote was so close that it was declared a tie. By law, such elections are decided by lottery—a toss of the coin. Although the paralegal won the toss, a court later declared her opponent the victor after reviewing some disputed ballots. *Toss of Coin to Decide Race in Illinois*, New York Times, July 18, 1990, at A12. In 1992, Ms. Mulligan ran again, and this time she won outright. The biography on her Web site says, "Prior to her election as a State Representative, Rosemary was a paralegal with a specialty in municipal land development and family law." State Representative Rosemary Mulligan, *www.repmulligan.org/biography.html* (visited January 23, 2002).

## Paralegal Charged with Insider Trading

A 24-year-old paralegal was charged with insider trading by the Securities and Exchange Commission. The complaint against the paralegal alleged that she had access to confidential information pertaining to the proposed merger of a client of the firm where she worked. She "tipped" her friends by giving them confidential information. The friends then used this information to earn $823,471 through the purchase of 65,020 shares. A civil complaint sought damages of $3.29 million. The paralegal was fired by the law firm. *Securities and Exchange Commission v. Hurton*, 43 S.E.C. Docket 1422, 1989 WL 991581 (May 16, 1989).

## A $90,000,000 Mistake!

A paralegal for Prudential Insurance Company inadvertently left off the last three zeros on a mortgage used to secure a $92,885,000 loan made by Prudential to a company that is now bankrupt. As a result of the mistake, Prudential was left with only a $92,885 lien. Prudential's attorneys have asked the U.S. Bankruptcy Court in New York City to ignore the mistake—and restore the zeros. *17 At Issue* (San Francisco Legal Assistants Ass'n, Dec. 1990).

## Paralegal Convicted

Mershan Shaddy was an independent paralegal in San Diego. He charged clients $180 to handle uncontested divorces, plus $50 if property had to be divided, and $30 for each child. He was arrested after an undercover investigator posed as a divorce client and secretly recorded him giving legal advice in violation of the California law against the unauthorized practice of law. He was convicted and sentenced to 45 days in jail. *Paralegal's Role in Legal System Stirs a Debate*, San Diego Union, March 29, 1990, at B-1.

## Billionaire Paralegal Prefers Prison to Filling Out Time Sheets

Michael Milken, the billionaire "junk bond king," went to prison for illegal activities stemming from his Wall Street career. While still under the jurisdiction of federal prison and parole authorities, Milken worked for three weeks as a "paralegal" in a law firm. He did not enjoy the experience. Comparing prison to the law firm, he told reporters that he would rather have other people keep track of his time than to have to "fill out those . . . time sheets every day." *News across the Country*, KLAS Action (Kansas Legal Assistants Society, December/January 1994).

## Did the Paralegal Work 43 Hours on January 10?

Hotel magnate Leona Helmsley (infamous for her wealth and her comment that "only little people pay taxes") sued a New York law firm for $35 million because she claimed they submitted fraudulent bills for fees and expenses. Among the allegedly fraudulent items cited in the suit was a bill for 43 hours of work charged by a paralegal for one day—January 10. Andrew Blum, *The Empress*

*Strikes Back*, The National Law Journal, July 11, 1994, at A6.

## DON'T BE PHOTOGRAPHED IN THAT T-SHIRT

An insurance company challenged a bill for attorney and paralegal time submitted by the Los Angeles law firm of Latham & Watkins. During a court proceeding on the dispute, the company embarrassed the firm by introducing into evidence a photograph of the paralegal working on the case while wearing a T-Shirt that read "Born to Bill." *Take Note of This*, California Paralegal 9 (January/March 1992)

## LAW FIRM SUES ITS FORMER PARALEGAL

Richard Trotter once worked as a paralegal for a Denver law firm. He wrote a book called *A Toothless Paper Tiger* about his experiences at the law firm. The book alleged that the firm improperly authorized him and other paralegals at the firm to perform the work of attorneys. The law firm sought an injunction to prevent the release of the book. Hicks, *Law Firm Fights Book by Former Employee*, National Law Journal, August 6, 1990, at 39.

## PARALEGAL ORDERED TO PAY $925,000 IN ATTORNEY FEES

Los Angeles Superior Court Judge Arnold Gold dismissed the sexual harassment lawsuit brought by a paralegal, Elizabeth Saret-Cook, against her former law firm employer, Gilbert, Kelly, Crowley & Jannett. She alleged that she had been harassed after getting pregnant with the child of an attorney at the firm, Clifford Woosley. Calling her suit "frivolous" and "completely without merit," the judge ordered the paralegal to pay $925,000 in attorney fees to the law firm and to Woosley. This decision was affirmed on appeal. *Saret-Cook v. Gilbert, Kelly, Crowley & Jennett*, 88 Cal. Rptr. 2d 732 (Cal. App. 2d Dist. 1999). According to court documents, the law firm had earlier offered to settle the suit for $400,000, but Saret-Cook refused the offer. Rebecca Liss, *Paralegal Ordered to Pay Fees in Harassment Case*, Los Angeles Daily Journal, September 27, 1996, at 2.

## LAW FIRM SETTLES SUIT BROUGHT BY PARALEGALS

A class action was brought by paralegals and clerical workers who claimed that the Oakland firm where they worked failed to pay them overtime compensation. The case was eventually settled for $170,000, which was distributed among the paralegals and clerical workers. Ziegler, *Firm Settles Suit on Overtime for Paralegals*, San Francisco Banner Daily Journal, January 25, 1989.

## "WILL THE LEGAL ASSISTANT PLEASE TELL THE COURT THE FACTS OF THE CASE?"

At a paralegal association meeting in Houston, Judge Lynn Hughes, a federal district court judge, drew a "big laugh" concerning an incident in her courtroom. During a hearing, she watched a "Big Gun" senior partner constantly turn to his associate for information on the facts of the case. This associate, in turn, would ask his legal assistant for this information. Finally, Judge Hughes asked the legal assistant to stand up and tell the court the facts of the case! *National News . . . Houston Legal Assistants Association*, 21 Outlook 5 (Illinois Paralegal Ass'n, Spring 1991).

## "THEN YOU SHOULD HAVE USED A PARALEGAL!"

At oral argument before the United States Supreme Court in a case on paralegal fees, an attorney was interrupted by Justice Thurgood Marshall during the attorney's description of the custom of billing in New Orleans. In the following fascinating excerpt from the transcript of the oral argument, a clearly irritated Justice Marshall suggested that the attorney was unprepared because he did not have a paralegal working with him on the case:

| | |
|---|---|
| JUSTICE MARSHALL: | Is all that in the record? |
| ATTORNEY: | I'm sorry . . . |
| JUSTICE MARSHALL: | Is that in the record? |
| ATTORNEY: | I'm not . . . |
| JUSTICE MARSHALL: | What you've just said, that the custom of billing and all in New Orleans, is that in the record? |
| ATTORNEY: | I think it is Justice Marshall. |
| JUSTICE MARSHALL: | You think? Didn't you try the case? |
| ATTORNEY: | I tried the case, but whether or not that particular item is in the record, it is certainly in the briefs, but . . . |
| JUSTICE MARSHALL: | Then you should have used a paralegal! |

*Official Transcript Proceedings before the Supreme Court of the United States, Arthur J. Blanchard, Petitioner v. James Bergerson, et al.*, Case 87–1485, at 25 (November 28, 1988).

## THE PERFECT RECIPE

"To one paralegal, add a pound of variety, eight ounces of flexibility, four ounces of creativity, and a healthy sense of humor. The result? One cost-effective, efficient litigation paralegal." Vore, *A Litigation Recipe*, On Point (Nat'l Capital Area Paralegal Ass'n, November 1990).

## Paralegal Trapped

A paralegal, on his way to an assignment on another floor, became trapped in an elevator just after getting on. Fellow employees gathered around the elevator door. The time-conscious paralegal called out from inside the elevator, "Is this billable or nonbillable time?" *A Lighter Note*, MALA Advance 15 (Summer 1989).

## Suspense Novel about a Paralegal by a Paralegal

E. P. Dalton has published *Housebreaker*, a novel by David Linzee, who has worked as a litigation paralegal. It is about Megan Lofting. "Megan used to be a probate paralegal at a Connecticut law firm. She used to try hard never to do something wrong. But then she was unjustly fired. Now a big-time criminal is offering her a chance to make a fortune, and to strike back at the client who got her fired, and the lawyer—once her lover—who let it happen." *The First Suspense Novel Ever about a Paralegal . . . by a Former Paralegal*, 4 Viewpoint 10 (Massachusetts Paralegal Ass'n, July/August 1987). See David Linzee, *Housebreaker* (E.P. Dalton, 1987) (PS 3562.I56 H68 1987) (*authors.missouri.org/linzee-d.html*).

## The Cost of What?

Recently, a paralegal was given an unusual assignment by her supervising attorney. She was asked to determine how much it would cost to purchase a penguin! *How Much Does a Penguin Cost?*, SJPA Reporter 3 (South Jersey Paralegal Ass'n September 1990).

## Paralegal Watches Exorcism

Kevin McKinley is a paralegal at a West Palm Beach law firm that represented a defendant in a murder case. While working on the case, Kevin found an urn in the room of the defendant where the latter allegedly practiced voodoo and black magic. The family of the defendant was concerned that if the urn was opened in the courtroom, the spirit within it would harm those attending the trial. Hence an exorcism was performed to remove the defendant's control over this spirit. Kevin's assignment was to be a witness at this exorcism. *Columbus Dispatch* (January 6, 1991).

## The Paralegal Floral Strategy

A litigation legal assistant was given the task of serving a subpoena on a defendant who was unlikely to open the door. She came up with a creative approach. On her way to the defendant's house, she stopped at a flower shop and picked up a plant. Upon her arrival, she rang the doorbell. The defendant looked out, saw a person with flowers, opened the door, and was presented with a plant . . . and a subpoena! Anderson, *In the Line of Duty*, MALA Advance 17 (Minnesota Ass'n of Legal Assistants, Spring 1991).

## Wanted: Adventurous Paralegal 107 Pounds or under

The following want ad appeared in the classified section of a San Francisco legal newspaper. "ADVENTUROUS PARALEGAL. Travel in pvt. aircraft around the country up to 3 wks/mo. investigating franchise cases. Duties incl: client interviews, lgl research & witness invest. Your weight max: 107 lbs. (flight requirement)." *Daily Journal Classifieds*, The Daily Journal, May 17, 1993, at 18.

## Wanted: Paralegal with Minimum of 203 Years of Experience

A paralegal placement agency is seeking a person "w/at least 203 yrs exp in paralegal field." The ad was either a typo or the first step in getting recognition in the next edition of the Guinness record book. *Employment Registry*, Reporter, 11 (Los Angeles Paralegal Ass'n, June 1993).

## I Don't Believe He Said That

- "I told him that I'm a paralegal. He thinks I am a lawyer who jumps out of planes"—in parachutes. *Compendium* (Orange County Paralegal Ass'n, Oct. 1990).
- When asked what to do for your secretary when she needs recognition but doesn't deserve a raise, the attorney answered, "Make her a paralegal!" *The Question of Paralegals*, 20 The Legal Investigator 35 (February 1991).
- At a cocktail party, Therese Carey was introduced to a middle-aged businessman. He asked her what she did for a living. Answering that she was a legal assistant, Therese enthusiastically explained her duties. After her response, the man turned to her and earnestly said, "Say, you know, with your background, have you ever considered becoming a paralegal?" Burdett, *Rodney Dangerfield: You're Not Alone*, Newsletter 2, (Rhode Island Paralegal Ass'n, (January 1987).

## BUMPER STICKER AWARD

The Alaska Association of Legal Assistants had a bumper sticker contest. The top three winners were as follows:

> **PARALEGALS KNOW THEIR MOTIONS**

> **PARALEGALS GET ON YOUR CASE**

> **PARALEGALS KNOW BRIEFS**

Reprinted with permission of Alaska Association of Paralegals.

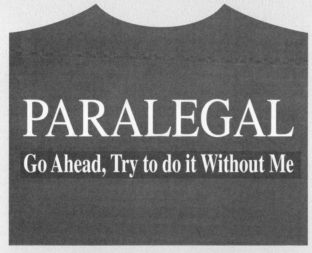

**PARALEGAL**
Go Ahead, Try to do it Without Me

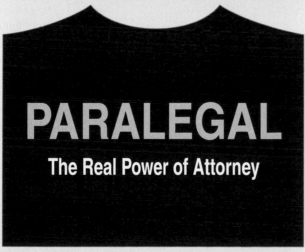

**PARALEGAL**
The Real Power of Attorney

For Counsel: Products and Gifts for Lawyers (*www.forcounsel.com*). Reprinted with permission of Now and Zen Productions, Inc.

## "What It Is That I Do"

A. Pergola, Newsletter, Rocky Mountain Legal Assistants Association (June 1980). Reprinted with permission of Anna M. Pergola.

## The World of Attorneys

■ "I served with General Washington in the legislature of Virginia before the revolution, and during it, with Dr. Franklin in Congress. . . . If the present Congress errs in too much talking, how could it do otherwise in a body to which the people send 150 lawyers, whose trade it is to question everything, yield nothing & talk by the hour?" *Autobiography 1743–1790*, Thomas Jefferson.

■ If a man were to give another man an orange, he would say, simply, "Have an orange." But if the transaction were entrusted to an attorney, he would say: "I hereby give, grant, bargain and sell to you, all my right, title and interest in, of, and to said orange, together with all its rind, skin, juice, pulp, and pips, and all rights and advantages therein, with full power to bite, cut, and otherwise eat of the same, or give the same away, with or without the rind, skin, juice, pulp, and pips, anything hereinbefore or hereinafter, or in any other deed or deeds, instrument or instruments, of whatever kind or nature whatsoever to the contrary in any wise notwithstanding." Hirsch, *Pittsburgh Legal Journal*.

■ A document recently filed in the United States Bankruptcy Court in Tennessee contained the following language: "Debtors hereby amend the Amendment to Second Amended and Restated Disclosure Statement, Third Amended and Restated Plan of Reorganization, and Amendment to Third Amended and Restated Plan of Organization as follows. Wherever the name 'Mortgage Company' appears in the Amendment to Second Amended and Restated Disclosure Statement, Third Amended and Restated Plan of Reorganization and Amendment to Third Amended and Restated Plan of Organization, the name 'Bank' shall be inserted in lieu thereof." *The Reporter* 15 (Delaware Paralegal Ass'n, May/June 1991).

■ Question: How many lawyers does it take to change a light bulb? Answer. Three senior partners to contemplate the history of light; two junior partners to check for conflicts of interest; ten associates to do the research on the antitrust implications of using a particular brand, on the cost-benefits of electric lighting versus candle light, on the health aspects of incandescent versus fluorescent bulb lighting, on the electric components that make light bulbs work, etc. And, of course, a paralegal to screw the bulb into the socket! *On the Lighter Side*, Par Spectives 5 (Paralegal Ass'n of Rochester, May 1990).

# Murphy's Laws for Paralegals

1. The day you wear comfortable, ugly old shoes is the day you are called into the managing partner's office or have to meet with an important client.

2. The day you wear attractive, stylish pumps that pinch your toes, bite your instep, and chafe your heels is the day that you have to serve papers at Nick Tahou's in an unpaved part of the county.

3. The night when you have a date, theater tickets, or fifteen dinner guests due at 7:30 is the night you are asked to stay late.

4. The day your car is in the garage and you carpooled is the day that you receive a 15-hour project that has to be done before you go home.

5. Your mother, your spouse, your significant other, or your bookie always calls when the boss is standing in your office.

6. Clients that work near you never have to sign anything. The number of documents that need to be signed by a client increases in proportion to the number of miles between their home or office and your office.

7. Whatever you lost is what everyone must have immediately.

8. Whatever can't be found was last in the possession of a paralegal.

9. Whatever needs to be hand delivered or picked up is always beyond the messenger's responsibility.

10. The day you have liverwurst and onion for lunch is the day that you have to attend an unscheduled meeting with an important client or another attorney.

11. The volume of Carmody-Wait 2nd that you require to prepare a motion is always missing from the library.

12. Nobody ever asks you about subjects with which you are familiar. If you are an expert on the mating habits of mosquitoes, you will be asked to digest a deposition or prepare research about the malfunction of the farabus and ullie pin connection in Yugoslavian lawnmowers.

Celeste E. Ciaccia, *Murphy's Laws for Paralegals,* 9 Newsletter 12 (Dallas Ass'n of Legal Assistants, September 1985).

## A SUIT TO COMPENSATE A TREE

In one of the oddest court opinions ever written, a three-judge panel in Michigan affirmed a lower court decision that denied relief for damage caused by the defendant's Chevrolet to the plaintiff's tree. The opinion is *Fisher v. Lowe*, 333 N.W.2d 67 (Mich. Ct. App. 1983). Here is the opinion:

We thought that we would never see
A suit to compensate a tree.
A suit whose claim in tort is prest
Upon a mangled tree's behest;
A tree whose battered trunk was prest
Against a Chevy's crumpled crest;
A tree that faces each new day
With bark and limb in disarray;
A tree that may forever bear
A lasting need for tender care.
Flora lovers though we three,
We must uphold the court's decree.
Affirmed.

# AND FINALLY:
# Truth in Advertising

---

*The remnants of the once proud firms of*
*DAZZLE & DROWN*
*and*
*BETTEROFF, SOMEWHERE & ELSE*
*are pleased to announce the merger*
*of what is left of their practices. They will*
*continue under the name of*
*BETTEROFF & DROWN*

*The firm will continue to specialize*
*in whatever it takes to survive.*

---

**DREAMS BEE & DASHED**

*A Professional Corporation*

is pleased to announce
the relocation of its office to

**Grant Avenue Safeway FoodMart**

1001 Grant Avenue
Collegial, AZ
Telephone (393) 422-9987

*The Firm will continue to seek subtenants for*
*its penthouse suite in the Palace Tower*

---

HAPPY & BLIND

*is pleased to announce that*

Truman R. Rightwig

*formerly a partner for 27 years before being let go by*

Shining, Star & Nomore

*has joined the firm as a Contract Attorney*

Mr. Rightwig *will continue to specialize in litigating*
Nixon's 1971 Price Control Act

---

*The Law Firm of*
**HURTING & SMARTING**
*is pleased to announce*
*the terminations of*

Harvey Notgood, Partner
Constance Reminder, Partner
Cynthia Snorz, Partner
Frederick Grating, Associate
Mildred Muddle, Associate
Eric Tomorrow, Paralegal
Janet Time, Secretary
Raymont Rabbit, Messenger

*as part of its strategic plan to*
*fit the size of the firm to its*
*level of business.*

---

**GARGLE,**
**MUMBLE & NUMB**
*Attorneys at Law*

is pleased to announce
the cessation of its
recruiting program and
the decrease in its
first year associate starting
salary to $32,000

Applicants can
take it or leave it.

---

Jim Cowan, Truth in Advertising, 10 ALA Newsletter 30
(Association of Legal Administrators, August/September 1991)
(Reprinted with permission)

# GLOSSARY

**AAfPE** American Association for Paralegal Education.

**ABA** American Bar Association.

**Abstract** A summary of something; an overview. *See also* Digest.

**Accounts Receivable** A list of who owes money to the office, how much, how long the debt has been due, etc.

**Accreditation** The process by which an organization evaluates and recognizes an institution or a program of study as meeting specified qualifications or standards.

**Acquit** To find not guilty.

**Act** *See* Statute.

**Active Voice** The grammatical verb form in which the subject or thing performing or causing the action is the main focus.

**Ad Damnum** The amount of damages claimed in the complaint.

**Add-On Question** A question that stacks one or more additional questions within it.

**Ad Hoc** For the specific or special purpose at hand.

**Adjudicate** To use a court or other tribunal to resolve a legal dispute through litigation. The noun is *adjudication*; the adjective is *adjudicative*. *See also* Quasi-adjudication.

**Ad Litem** For the purposes of this litigation.

**Administrative Agency** A governmental body whose primary function is to carry out or administer statutes passed by the legislature, executive orders issued by the governor or other chief executive, and administrative regulations issued by the agency itself.

**Administrative Code** A collection of administrative regulations organized by subject matter rather than by date.

**Administrative Decision** A resolution of a controversy between a party and an administrative agency involving the application of the regulations, statutes, or executive orders that govern the agency. Sometimes called a *ruling*.

**Administrative Hearing** A proceeding at an administrative agency presided over by a hearing officer (e.g., an administrative law judge) to resolve a controversy.

**Administrative Law Judge (ALJ)** A government official at an administrative agency who presides over a hearing to resolve a legal dispute.

**Administrative Procedure Act (APA)** The statute that governs procedures before federal administrative agencies. Many states have their own APA for procedures before state administrative agencies.

**Administrative Regulation** A law of an administrative agency designed to explain or carry out the statutes and executive orders that govern the agency. Also called a *rule*.

**Administrative Rule** *See* Administrative Regulation.

**Admiralty Law** An area of the law that covers accidents and injuries on navigable waters. Also called *maritime law*.

**Admissible Evidence** Evidence that the court will allow the trier of fact (usually the jury) to consider.

**Admission** A voluntary acknowledgment of a fact that an opponent wants to prove.

**Admission by a Party Opponent** An earlier statement by a party that is now offered in court by an opponent. (An exception to the hearsay rule.)

**Admonition** A nonpublic declaration that the attorney's conduct was improper. This does not affect his or her right to practice. Also called a *private reprimand*.

**ADR** *See* Alternative Dispute Resolution.

**Advance Session Law Service** *See* Legislative Service.

**Advance Sheet** A pamphlet that comes out before (in advance of) a later volume.

**Adversarial** Involving conflict or adversaries.

**Adversarial Memorandum** *See* External/Adversary Memorandum, Memorandum of Law.

**Adversarial System** A method of resolving disputes based on the principle that justice and truth have a greater chance of being achieved when the parties to a dispute appear (alone or through an advocate) before a neutral judge who will resolve the dispute after hearing their conflicting positions.

**Adversary Hearing** A hearing at which all parties to a dispute are present before the judge or presiding officer to argue their positions.

**Adverse Interests** Opposing purposes or claims.

**Adverse Judgment** A judgment or decision against you.

**Advice** *See* Professional Judgment.

**Advocacy** The process by which you attempt to influence the behavior of others, often according to predetermined goals.

**Affiant** *See* Affidavit.

**Affidavit** A written statement of fact in which a person (called the *affiant*) swears that the facts in the statement are true.

**Affiliate Member** *See* Associate Member.

**Affirmative Defense** A defense that is based on new factual allegations by the defendant not contained in the plaintiff's allegations.

**Aged Accounts Receivable Report** A report showing all cases that have outstanding balances due and how long these balances are past due. (Also called *firm utilization report.*)

**Agency Practitioner** An individual authorized to practice before an administrative agency. This individual often does not have to be an attorney.

**ALA** Association of Legal Administrators.

**Allegation** A claimed fact.

**Alphabetical Filing System** A method of storing client files in alphabetical order by the client's surname or organization name.

**Alternate** An extra juror who will take the place of a regular juror if one becomes incapacitated during the trial.

**Alternative Dispute Resolution (ADR)** A formal method of resolving a legal dispute without litigating it in a court or before an administrative agency.

**ALWD Citation Manual** The citation guide published by the Association of Legal Writing Directors. It is the major competitor to the *Bluebook*.

**Ambulance Chasing** Approaching accident victims (or others with potential legal claims) to encourage them to hire a particular attorney. If the attorney uses someone else to do the soliciting, the latter is called a *runner*. If this other person uses deception or fraud in the solicitation, he or she is sometimes called a *capper* or a *steerer*. *See also* Court Runner.

**Amicus Curiae** Friend of the court, a nonparty in the litigation.

**Amicus Curiae Brief** An appellate brief submitted by a friend of the court. *See also* Amicus Curiae.

**Analogous** Sufficiently similar to justify a similar result. Being on point with facts that are similar to the facts before you, although there may be some fact differences.

**Analogy** A comparison of similarities and differences.

**Annotate** To provide notes or commentary. A text is annotated if such notes and commentary are provided along with the text.

**Annotated Bibliography** A bibliography that briefly states why you included each entry in the bibliography.

**Annotated Reporter** A set of books that contains the full text of court opinions plus commentary on them (annotations).

**Annotated Statutory Code** A collection of statutes organized by subject matter rather than by date, along with notes and commentary.

**Annotation** A set of notes or commentaries on something; for example, the research notes found within the annotated reporter, *American Law Reports*.

**Answer** The pleading that responds to or answers the allegations of the complaint.

**Antitrust Law** The law governing unlawful restraints of trade, price fixing, and monopolies.

**APA** *See* Administrative Procedure Act.

**Appeal** (1) A formal request that a higher authority examine or review a decision made by another body. (2) An examination or review by a higher authority of a decision made by another body.

**Appeal as a Matter of Right** The appeal of a case that an appellate court must hear; it has no discretion on whether to take the appeal.

**Appearance** Going to court to act on behalf of a party to the litigation. The first time this is done, the attorney files a *notice of appearance*.

**Appellant** The party bringing an appeal because of dissatisfaction with something the lower tribunal did.

**Appellate Brief** A document in which a party gives reasons why an appellate court should affirm (approve), modify, or reverse what a lower court has done.

**Appellate Jurisdiction** The power of a court to hear an appeal of a case from a lower tribunal (e.g., a lower court or administrative agency) to determine whether the lower tribunal committed any errors of law.

**Appellee** The party against whom an appeal is brought. Also called the *respondent*.

**Appendixes** Additions to a volume or document printed after the body of the text.

**Applications Software** A computer program that performs specific tasks directly for the consumer or end user.

**Apprentice** A person in training for an occupation under the supervision of a full member of that occupation.

**Approval** The recognition that comes from accreditation, certification, licensure, or registration. The ABA uses *approval* as a substitute for the word *accreditation*.

**Arbitration** A method of alternative dispute resolution in which the parties submit their dispute to a neutral third person who renders a decision that resolves the dispute. It is an alternative to litigation.

**Arraignment** A court proceeding in which the defendant is formally charged with a crime and enters a plea.

**Arrest** To take someone into custody in order to bring him or her before the proper authorities.

**Assertive** Confident, prepared, and tactfully demonstrative about one's accomplishments and needs.

**Assigned Counsel** A private attorney appointed by the court to represent an individual who cannot afford to hire an attorney. If the attorney is a government employee handling criminal cases, he or she is often called a *public defender*.

**Associate** An attorney employee of a partnership who hopes eventually to become a partner.

**Associated** Pertaining to an attorney who is an associate in a law firm.

**Associate Member** A nonattorney who is allowed to become part of—but not a full member of—a bar association. Sometimes called *affiliate member*.

**At Common Law** All the case law and statutory law in England and in the American colonies before the Revolution. The phrase also sometimes means judge-made law that existed before it was changed by statute. *See also* Common Law.

**Attentive Listening** Taking affirmative, ongoing steps to let an interviewee know that you have heard what he or she has said and that you consider the meeting with him or her to be important.

**Attestation Clause** A clause stating that a person saw someone sign a document or perform other tasks related to the validity of the document.

**Attorney Attestation** A signed statement by an attorney that a paralegal applying for membership in an association meets one or more of the criteria of the association.

**Attorney-Client Privilege** A client and an attorney can refuse to disclose any communication between them if its purpose was to facilitate the provision of legal services for the client.

**Attorney General** The chief attorney for the government. *See also* Opinion of the Attorney General.

**Attorney of Record** The attorney who has filed a notice of appearance. *See also* Appearance.

**Attorney Work Product** *See* Work-Product Rule.

**At-Will Employee** An employee who can quit or be terminated at any time and for any reason. An employee with no contract protection.

**Authentication** Evidence that a writing or other physical item is genuine and is what it purports to be.

**Authority** Any source that a court could rely on in reaching its decision.

**Authorized Practice of Law** Services constituting the practice of law that a nonattorney has authorization to provide. *See also* Practice of Law, Professional Judgment.

**Auto-Cite** An online program of LEXIS that tells you whether an opinion you are checking is still good law. *See also* Citator.

**Automatic Pagination** A feature that enables a word processor to number printed pages automatically.

**Baby Attorney** A condescending term for an attorney with little or no experience, usually a first-year associate.

**Background Research** Checking secondary sources to give you a general understanding of an area of law that is new to you.

**Backspace** The key that allows you to delete the character to the left of the cursor.

**Backup** To copy information.

**Bail** A sum of money or other property deposited with the court to ensure that the defendant will reappear in court at designated times.

**Bailiff** A court employee who keeps order in the courtroom and renders general administrative assistance to the judge.

**Bankruptcy Petition Preparer (BPP)** A nonattorney who is authorized to charge fees for preparing (without attorney supervision) a bankruptcy petition or any other bankruptcy document that a debtor will file in a federal court.

**Bar**  Prevent or stop.

**Bar Code**  A sequence of numbers and vertical lines of different shapes that can be read by an optical scanner.

**Barratry**  The crime of stirring up quarrels or litigation; persistently instigating lawsuits, often groundless ones. The illegal solicitation of clients.

**Barrister**  A lawyer in England who represents clients in the higher courts.

**Bar Treaties**  Agreements between attorneys and other occupations that identify the law-related activities of these other occupations that will not be considered the unauthorized practice of law.

**Bates Stamp**  A desk tool used to place a sequential number on a page. After using the stamp on a page, it automatically advances to the next number, ready to stamp the next page.

**Below**  (1) The lower tribunal that heard the case before it was appealed. (2) Later in the document.

**Bene**  In proper legal form; legally sufficient.

**Best Evidence Rule**  To prove the contents of a private writing, the original writing should be produced unless it is unavailable.

**Beyond a Reasonable Doubt**  There is no reasonable doubt that every element of the crime has been established. Reasonable doubt is such doubt as would cause prudent persons to hesitate before acting in matters of importance to themselves.

**Bias**  An inclination or tendency to think and to act in a certain way. A danger of prejudgment. A person without a bias is objective, dispassionate, or disinterested.

**Bicameral**  Having two houses in the legislature. If there is only one house, it is *unicameral*.

**Bill**  A proposed statute.

**Billable Hours Quota**  A minimum number of hours expected from a timekeeper on client matters that can be charged (billed) to clients per week, month, year, or other time period.

**Billable Tasks**  Those tasks requiring time that can be charged to a client. A *billable hour* is time spent on a client's case for which the client can be charged.

**Billing Memorandum**  A draft of a client bill that states disbursements, time expended, and billing rates of those working on the matter. *See also* Portable Billings.

**Black Letter Law**  A statement of a fundamental or basic principle of law.

**Blended Hourly Rate**  A single hourly rate based on a blend or mix of the rates normally charged by different in-dividuals, e.g., a partner, a senior associate, a junior associate, and sometimes a paralegal. *See also* Fee.

**Blind Ad**  A want ad that does not print the name and address of the prospective employer. The contact is made through a third party, e.g., the newspaper.

**Block**  A group of characters, e.g., a word, a sentence, a paragraph. Block movement is a feature of a word processor that allows the user to define a block of text and then do something with that block, e.g., move it, delete it.

**Bluebook**  (also called Blue Book)  (1) The *Uniform System of Citation*, the bible of citation form. (2) The *National Reporter Blue Book*, a source for parallel cites. (3) The *A.L.R. Bluebook of Supplemental Decisions*, a set of books that allows you to update the annotations in *A.L.R. 1st.*

**Board of Appeals**  The unit within an administrative agency to which a party can appeal a decision of the agency.

**Boilerplate**  Standard language that is commonly used in a certain kind of document. Standard verbiage.

**Boldface**  Heavier or darker than normal type.

**Bona fide**  Good faith.

**Bond**  A sum of money deposited in court to ensure compliance with a requirement.

**Bonus**  A payment beyond one's regular salary, usually as a reward or recognition. *See also* Incentive Billing.

**Boolean Search**  A search that allows words to be specifically included or excluded through operatives such as AND, OR, and NOT.

**Boutique Law Firm**  A firm that specializes primarily in one area of the law.

**Breach of Contract**  A cause of action in which a party seeks a court remedy for the alleged failure of a party to perform the term(s) of an enforceable contract.

**Brief**  (1) Shorthand for appellate brief. A document submitted to an appellate court in which a party seeks to affirm (approve), modify, or reverse what a lower court has done. A party's written argument to a court of appeals covering the issues that relate to claimed errors that occurred during the trial or other lower court proceeding. (2) A document submitted to a trial court in support of a particular position. (3) A summary of the main or essential parts of a court opinion. (4) Shorthand for a trial brief, which contains an attorney's personal notes on how to conduct a trial.

**Brief Bank**  A collection of appellate briefs and other legal documents drafted in prior cases that might be used as a model for drafting similar documents in the future.

**Brief of a Case**  A set of notes on the essential parts of a court opinion, e.g., facts, issues, holding, reasoning.

**Broadband** A service that provides high-speed data communication.

**Budget Performance Report** A report that compares a firm's actual income and expenditures with budgeted or projected income and expenditures.

**"Bugs"** Manufacturing or design errors that exist in products such as computer hardware or software.

**Bulletin Board** A user-run, relatively inexpensive version of a commercial computer information service.

**Bundled Legal Services** All tasks needed to represent a client; all-inclusive legal services. *See also* Unbundled Legal Services.

**Burden of Proof** The responsibility of proving a fact at trial.

**Business Entry** An out-of-court statement found in business records made in the regular course of business by someone whose duty is to make such entries. (An exception to the hearsay rule.)

**Byte** The storage equivalent of one space or character of the alphabet typed into a computer.

**CALR** Computer-assisted legal research.

**Capital Partner** *See* Equity Partner.

**Capped Fee** An hourly rate leading to a final bill that will not exceed a predetermined amount. *See also* Fee.

**Capper** *See* Ambulance Chasing, Runner.

**Caption of Appellate Brief** The front of an appellate brief that prints the name of the parties, the name of the court, the docket number, and the kind of appellate brief it is.

**Caption of Complaint** The beginning (usually the top) of a complaint that provides identifying information such as the names of the parties, the court in which the action is being brought, and the docket number assigned to the case by the court.

**Caption of Memorandum** The beginning of a memorandum containing its title or name.

**Caption of Opinion** The title of an opinion (usually consisting of the names of the parties), the name of the court that wrote it, the docket number, and the date of decision—all printed just before the opinion begins.

**Career Ladder** A formal promotion structure within a company or office.

**CARTWHEEL** A technique designed to help you think of a large variety of words and phrases to check in indexes, tables of contents, and online search engines.

**CAS** California Advanced Specialist, a person who has passed the California Advanced Specialty Exam.

**Case** (1) A court's written explanation of how it applied the law to the facts to resolve a legal dispute. *See also*

Opinion. (2) A pending matter on a court calendar. (3) A client matter handled by a law office.

**Casebook** A law-school textbook containing numerous edited court opinions.

**Case Clerk** An assistant to a paralegal; an entry-level paralegal.

**Case Management** Application software used to help a law office maintain control over its appointments and deadlines.

**Case Manager** An experienced legal assistant who can coordinate or direct legal assistant activities on a major case or transaction.

**Case Note** A relatively brief commentary on a recent court opinion.

**Case-Type Productivity Report** A report showing which types of cases in the firm (e.g., bankruptcy, personal injury, criminal) are most profitable. (Also called a *practice analysis report*.)

**Cash Receipts Report** A report that describes the income received in a day, week, month, quarter, or year. The cash receipts can be compared with the amount of projected income for a specific time period.

**Cause of Action** A legally acceptable reason for suing. Facts that give a party the right to judicial relief.

**CD–ROM** (compact disk read-only memory). A compact disk that uses optical technology or laser beams to store data.

**CEB** Continuing education of the bar.

**Censure** A formal disapproval or declaration of blame. *See also* Reprimand.

**Central Processing Unit (CPU)** The part of the computer that controls all of its parts.

**Certificated** Having met the qualifications for certification from a school or training program.

**Certification** The process by which a nongovernmental organization grants recognition to a person who has met the qualifications set by that organization. *See also* Specialty Certification.

**Certified** Having complied with or met the qualifications for certification.

**Certified Legal Assistant (CLA)** The credential bestowed by the National Association of Legal Assistants for meeting its criteria such as passing a national, entry-level certification exam.

**Certified Legal Assistant Specialist (CLAS)** The credential bestowed by the National Association of Legal Assistants for meeting its criteria such as passing an advanced national certification exam.

**Certified PLS**  A Certified Professional Legal Secretary. This status is achieved after passing an examination and meeting other requirements of NALS, the National Association of Legal Secretaries.

**Certiorari**  *See* Writ of Certiorari.

**CFLA**  Certified Florida Legal Assistant. To earn this title, a paralegal must first pass the CLA (Certified Legal Assistant) exam of NALA and then pass a special exam on Florida law.

**Challenge for Cause**  A request to exclude someone from a jury for a specified reason. *See also* Peremptory Challenge.

**Champerty**  Promoting someone else's litigation, often by helping to finance the litigation in exchange for a share in the recovery.

**Character**  A letter, number, or symbol. Character enhancement includes underlining, boldfacing, subscripting, and superscripting.

**Chargeable Hour Schedule**  A report that summarizes hours invested by attorneys and paralegals; usually on a monthly basis.

**Charge to Jury**  Instructions to the jury on how to go about determining the facts and reaching its verdict.

**Charter**  The fundamental law of a municipality or other local unit of government authorizing it to perform designated governmental functions.

**Checks and Balances**  An allocation of governmental powers whereby one branch of government can block, check, or review what another branch wants to do (or has done) in order to maintain a balance of power among the legislative, executive, and judicial branches.

**Chinese Wall**  Steps taken to prevent a tainted employee (attorney or paralegal) from having any contact with the case of a particular client in the office. The employee is tainted because he or she has a conflict of interest with that client. A Chinese Wall is also called an *ethical wall* and a *cone of silence*. A tainted employee is also called a *contaminated employee*. Once the Chinese Wall is set up around the tainted employee, the latter is referred to as a *quarantined employee*.

**Chronological Résumé**  A résumé that presents biographical data on education and experience in a chronological sequence starting with the present and working backward.

**Churning**  Providing services beyond what the circumstances warrant for the primary purpose of generating fees and commissions.

**Circumlocution**  The use of more words than are needed to express something.

**Circumstantial Evidence**  Evidence of one fact (not based on personal knowledge or observation) from which another fact can be inferred.

**Citation**  A reference to any material printed on paper or stored in a computer database. It is the "address" where you can locate and read the material. *See also* Parallel Cite, Pinpoint Cite, Public Domain Citation.

**Citator**  A book, CD–ROM, or online service containing lists of citations that can (1) help you assess the current validity of an opinion, statute, or other item and (2) give you leads to other relevant materials.

**Cite**  (1) A citation. (2) To give the volume number, page number, or other information that will enable you to locate written material in a library.

**Cite Checking**  Examining every citation in a document to determine, for example, whether the format of the citation is correct, whether quoted material is accurate, and whether the law cited is still valid (as determined by checking standard citators).

**Cited Material**  The case, statute, regulation, or other document that you are shepardizing.

**Citing Material**  The case, article, or annotation that mentions whatever you are shepardizing, i.e., that mentions the cited material.

**Civil**  Pertaining to a private right or matter.

**Civil Dispute**  A legal controversy in which (1) one private person or business sues another, (2) a private person or business sues the government, or (3) the government sues a private person or business for a matter other than the commission of a crime.

**Civil Law**  (1) The law governing Civil disputes. Any law other than criminal law. *See also* Civil Dispute. (2) The law that applies in many Western European countries other than England.

**Civil Law System**  The legal system of many Western European countries (other than England) that place a greater emphasis on statutory or code law than do countries (such as England and the United States) whose common law system places a greater emphasis on case law.

**CLA**  *See* Certified Legal Assistant.

**Claims-Made Policy**  Insurance that covers only claims actually filed (i.e., made) during the period in which the policy is in effect.

**CLAS**  *See* Certified Legal Assistant Specialist.

**CLE**  Continuing legal education. Undertaken after an individual has received his or her primary education or training in a law-related occupation.

**CLE Materials**  Continuing legal education texts, video, or other materials prepared for attorneys after they have completed law school.

**Clergy-Penitent Privilege** A member of the clergy and a penitent can refuse to disclose communications between them that relate to spiritual counseling or consultation.

**Clerk** The court employee who assists judges with record keeping and other administrative duties. *See also* Law Clerk.

**Client Investment Summary Report** A report of the total amount billed and unbilled, with a calculation of the actual costs of providing legal services for a particular client.

**Client Trust Account** A bank account controlled by an attorney that contains client funds that may not be used for office operating expenses or for any personal purpose of the attorney.

**Clinical Education** A training program in which students work on real cases under attorney supervision.

**Closed-Ended Question** A narrowly structured question that usually can be answered in one or two words, often yes or no. Also called a *directed question*.

**Closed File** The file of a client whose case is no longer active in the firm. Also called a *dead file* or a *retired file*.

**Closing** The event during which steps are taken to finalize the transfer of an interest in property.

**Code** A set of rules, organized by subject matter.

**Codefendants** More than one defendant sued in the same civil case. More than one defendant prosecuted in the same criminal case.

**Code of Ethics and Professional Responsibility** A statement of the ethical guidelines of the National Association of Legal Assistants.

**Codified Cite** The citation to a statute (or other enacted law) that has been printed in a code and, therefore, is organized by subject matter.

**Codify** To arrange laws by subject matter regardless of when they were enacted.

**Combination Question** A question that has more than one part.

**Command** An instruction typed into a computer.

**Commingling** Mixing general law firm funds with client funds in a single account.

**Committee Report** A summary of a bill and a statement of the reasons for and against its enactment by the legislature.

**Common Law** (1) Court opinions, all of case law. (2) The legal system of England and of those countries such as the United States whose legal system is based on England's. (3) The case law *and* statutory law in England and in the

American colonies before the American Revolution. (4) Judge-made law in the absence of controlling statutory law or other higher law. *See also* At Common Law, Enacted Law.

**Common Representation** *See* Multiple Representation.

**Competent** (1) Using the knowledge and skill that are reasonably necessary to represent a particular client. (2) Allowed to give testimony because the person understands the obligation to tell the truth, has the ability to communicate, and has knowledge of the topic of his or her testimony.

**Complaint** The pleading (sometimes called a *petition*) filed by the plaintiff that tries to state a claim or cause of action against the defendant.

**Computer-Assisted Legal Research (CALR)** Performing legal research in computer databases.

**Concurrent Jurisdiction** The power of a court to hear a particular kind of case, along with other courts that could also hear it.

**Concurring Opinion** An opinion written by less than a majority of the judges on the court that agrees with the *result* reached by the majority but not with all of its reasoning.

**Conference Committee** A committee made up of members of both houses of the legislature that meets to try to resolve differences in the versions of a bill that each house passed.

**Confidential** That which should not be revealed; pertaining to information that others do not have a right to receive.

**Confirmatory Letter** A letter that verifies or confirms that something important has been done or said.

**Conflict of Interest** Divided loyalty that actually or potentially harms someone who is owed undivided loyalty.

**Conflicts Check** A determination of whether a conflict of interest exists that might disqualify a law office from representing a client or from continuing the representation. The person performing this check full-time is also called a *conflicts specialist* or a *conflicts technician*.

**Conflicts of Law** An area of the law that determines what law applies when a choice must be made between the laws of different, coequal legal systems, e.g., those of two states.

**Conflicts Specialist** A law firm employee, often a paralegal, who helps the firm determine whether a conflict of interest exists between prospective clients and current or former clients. Also called a *conflicts technician*.

**Confrontation** Being present when others give evidence against you and having the opportunity to question them.

**Connectors** Characters, words, or symbols used to show the relationship between the words and phrases in a query.

**Consent** To waive a right; to agree.

**Consolidated Litigation** More than one lawsuit being resolved in the same litigation.

**Constitution** The fundamental law that creates the branches of government and that identifies basic rights and obligations.

**Construction** Interpretation (the verb is *construe*).

**Contaminated** Pertaining to an employee who brings a conflict of interest to the office. *See also* Chinese Wall.

**Contest** To challenge.

**Contingent Fee** A plaintiff's fee that is dependent on the outcome of the case (the fee is also called a *contingency*). A *defense contingent fee* (also called a *negative contingency*) is a fee for the defendant's attorney that is dependent on the outcome of the case.

**Continuance** The adjournment or postponement of a proceeding until a later date.

**Continuing Legal Education (CLE)** Training in the law (usually short term) that a person receives after completing his or her formal legal training. *See also* CLE Materials.

**Contract Attorney** An attorney hired to work for a relatively short period of time, usually on specific cases or projects. Also called a *project attorney*.

**Contract Paralegal** A self-employed paralegal who often works for several different attorneys on a freelance basis. *See also* Freelance Paralegal.

**Control Character** A coded character that does not print but is part of the command sequence in a word processor.

**Copyright Page** The page in a book that provides the year(s) in which the book was protected by copyright.

**Corporate Counsel** An in-house attorney, often the chief attorney, of a corporation. Sometimes called *general counsel*.

**Corporate Legal Department** A law office within a corporation containing salaried attorneys (called *in-house attorneys*) who advise and represent the corporation. Also called a *law department*.

**Counterclaim** A claim or cause of action against the plaintiff stated in the defendant's answer.

**Court Costs** Charges or fees imposed by the court directly related to litigation in that court.

**Court of First Instance** A trial court; a court with original jurisdiction.

**Court Runner** A messenger used primarily to deliver and pick up documents and files from the courts. *See also* Ambulance Chasing.

**Credentialization** A form of official recognition based on one's training or employment status.

**Credible** Believable.

**Criminal Dispute** Legal controversy in which the government alleges the commission of a crime.

**Cross-claim** Usually, a claim by one codefendant against another.

**Cross-Examination** Questioning of a witness at a hearing by an opponent after the other side has conducted a direct examination of that witness.

**Cumulative** That which repeats earlier material and consolidates it with new material. A cumulative supplement contains new supplemental material and repeats earlier supplemental material.

**Cure** To correct or overcome.

**Curriculum Vitae** A résumé.

**Daily Time Sheet** A paper form on which timekeepers record how much time they spend on particular client matters.

**Damages** An award of money paid by the wrongdoer to compensate the person who has been harmed.

**Data** Information that can be used by a computer.

**Database Program** Application software that allows you to organize, search, retrieve, and sort information or data.

**Decision** *See* Administrative Decision, Opinion.

**Declarant** A person who makes a statement.

**Declaration against Interest** An out-of-court statement made by a nonparty to the litigation that is against the interest of that nonparty. (An exception to the hearsay rule.)

**Declaration of Bodily Feelings** An out-of-court statement or utterance made spontaneously about the person's present bodily condition. (An exception to the hearsay rule.)

**Declaration of Present Sense Impression** An out-of-court statement that describes an event while it is being observed by the person making the statement. (An exception to the hearsay rule.)

**Declaration of State of Mind** An out-of-court statement made about the person's present state of mind. (An exception to the hearsay rule.)

**Declaratory Judgment** A court decision establishing the rights and obligations of the parties but not ordering them to do or to refrain from doing anything.

**Declination Letter** *See* Letter of Disengagement.

**Deep Pocket** An individual, business, or other organization with resources to pay a potential judgment. *See also* Shallow Pocket.

**De Facto** In fact; actually. Exercising power even though not by law or formal authority.

**Default Judgment** A judgment against a defendant because of a failure to file a required pleading or otherwise to take necessary steps to respond to the plaintiff's claim.

**Defense** A response to a claim of the other party, setting forth reason(s) the claim should be denied. The response may be an allegation of facts and/or a presentation of a legal theory.

**Defense Contingent Fee** A fee received by the defendant's attorney that is dependent on the outcome of the case. Also called a *negative contingency*.

**De Jure** Lawful; in compliance with the requirements of the law.

**"Delegatitis"** An inordinate fear of delegating tasks to others.

**Demand Letter** An advocacy letter that asks the recipient to take specific action or refrain from specific action affecting the client.

**Demonstrative Evidence** Physical evidence that can be seen and inspected.

**Demurrer** Even if the plaintiff proved all the facts stated in the complaint, a cause of action would not be established.

**De Novo** Anew; starting over.

**Denturist** A nondentist who produces and dispenses removable dentures directly to the public.

**Deponent** *See* Deposition.

**Deposition** A method of discovery by which parties and their prospective witnesses are questioned outside the courtroom before trial. A pretrial question-and-answer session to help parties prepare for trial. The person questioned is called the *deponent*.

**Depository Library** *See* Federal Depository Library.

**Depo Summarizer** An employee whose main job is digesting discovery documents, particularly depositions.

**Deskbook** A single-volume collection of the rules of court for one or more courts, often within the same judicial system.

**Detainer** Keeping something in one's custody. *See also* Unlawful Detainer Assistant.

**Dictum** A statement made by a court that was not necessary to resolve the specific legal issues before the court. The plural of dictum is dicta.

**Digest** (1) A summary of something. (2) Volumes that contain summaries of court opinions. These summaries are sometimes called *abstracts* or *squibs*. (3) Volumes that contain summaries of annotations in A.L.R., A.L.R.2d, A.L.R.3d, etc.

**Digest by Person** A summary of the information in a document organized around every mention of a particular person.

**Digest by Subject Matter** A summary of the information in a document organized around every mention of a particular topic.

**Digesting** Summarizing discovery documents. *See also* Depo Summarizer.

**Directed Question** *See* Closed-Ended Question.

**Directed Verdict** An order by the court that the jury reach a verdict for the party making the motion on the ground that the other side, which has just rested its case, has failed to produce enough convincing evidence to establish a cause of action.

**Direct Evidence** Evidence (based on personal knowledge or observation) that tends to establish an alleged fact (or to disprove an alleged fact) without the need for an inference.

**Direct Examination** Questioning of a witness at a hearing by the side that called the witness.

**Directory** A search tool in which you select from a list of broad subject categories and then enter the terms you want contained in sites that are part of the subject category you select.

**Disbarment** The temporary or permanent termination of the right to practice law.

**Disbursements** Out-of-pocket expenses.

**Disciplinary Rule (DR)** *See* Model Code of Professional Responsibility.

**Discount Adjustment** A write-down (decrease) in the bill.

**Discounted Hourly Fee** An hourly or fixed fee that is reduced because of the volume of business the client gives the office. *See also* Fee.

**Discoverable** Obtainable through one of the devices of pretrial discovery such as interrogatories or deposition.

**Discovery** Compulsory pretrial disclosure of information related to litigation by one party (and its prospective witnesses) to another party. Discovery can also be used in post-judgment enforcement proceedings. *See also* Deposition, Interrogatories, Request for Admission.

**Discretionary Statute** A statute that permits something to be done but does not require or mandate it.

**Disengagement** *See* Letter of Disengagement.

**Disinterested** Not working for one side or the other in a controversy; not deriving benefit if one side of a dispute wins or loses; objective.

**Dismissal without Prejudice** A dismissal based on procedural, not substantive, grounds. The party can try to bring the case again.

**Disqualification** *See* Vicarious Disqualification.

**Dissenting Opinion** An opinion that disagrees with the result and the reasoning used by the majority.

**District Court** *See* United States District Court.

**Diversity of Citizenship** The parties to the litigation are citizens of different states, and the amount in controversy exceeds the amount specified by federal statute. This diversity gives jurisdiction to a United States District Court.

**Divided Loyalty** *See* Conflict of Interest.

**Docket** A list of cases on a court's calendar.

**Docket Number** The consecutive number assigned to a case by the court.

**Doctor-Patient Privilege** A doctor and a patient can refuse to disclose any confidential (private) communications between them that relate to medical care.

**Document Clerk** An individual whose main responsibility is to organize, file, code, or digest litigation or other client documents.

**Double Billing** Fraudulently charging a client twice for the same service.

**DR Disciplinary Rule.** *See* Model Code of Professional Responsibility.

**Draft** (1) To write. (She *drafted* a memorandum.) (2) A document in one of its preliminary stages. (I was asked to proofread a *draft* of a contract before it was printed.)

**Draft Bill** A billing memorandum prepared by a law office on a particular client case stating expenses, costs, time spent, and billing rates of attorneys and paralegals working on the case.

**Draw** A partner's advance against profits or net income.

**Duty of Loyalty** The obligation to protect the interests of a client without having a similar obligation to anyone else that would present an actual or potential conflict.

**DWI** Descriptive Word Index, an index to the digests of West Group.

**Dying Declaration** An out-of-court statement concerning the causes or circumstances of death made by a person whose death is imminent. (An exception to the hearsay rule.)

**EC** Ethical Consideration. *See* Model Code of Professional Responsibility.

**Edition** A version of a text that is usually a revision of an earlier version.

**EEOC** *See* Equal Employment Opportunity Commission.

**E-filing** Electronic filing of court pleadings and other documents.

**Ejusdem Generis** A rule of construction that a general word or phrase should be interpreted as being of the same kind as the specific words or phrases that the general one follows.

**Electronic Citation** *See* Public Domain Citation.

**Element** A portion of a rule that is a precondition of the applicability of the entire rule. *See also* Element in Contention.

**Element in Contention** That portion of a rule about which the parties cannot agree. The disagreement may be over the definition of the element, how the element applies to the facts, or both.

**E-mail** A message sent electronically.

**Empaneled** *See* Impaneled.

**Employment at Will** *See* At-Will Employee.

**Enabling Statute** A statute that authorizes an agency to write regulations or to perform other specific tasks.

**Enacted Law** Law written by a deliberative body such as a legislature or constitutional convention after it is proposed and often debated and amended; law that is not created within litigation.

**En Banc** The entire membership of the court; by the entire court.

**Enclosure Letter** A letter that tells the recipient what physical items are being sent in the envelope or package.

**Encrypted** Converted into a code that renders the data incomprehensible until they are reconverted to a readable format by an authorized recipient.

**Encyclopedia** *See* Legal Encyclopedia.

**Endnote** A numbered citation or explanatory text that is printed at the end of a document or chapter. If printed at the bottom of the page, the citation or text is a footnote.

**Enrolled Agent** An individual authorized to represent taxpayers at all administrative proceedings within the Internal Revenue Service—this person does not have to be an attorney.

**Enrollment** *See* Registration.

**Entry-Level Certification** Certification of individuals who have just begun their careers.

**Equal Employment Opportunity Commission (EEOC)** The federal agency that investigates employment discrimination that violates federal law.

**Equity Partner** A full owner-partner of a law firm. Also called a *capital partner*.

**Estate** All of the property left by a decedent, from which any debts of the decedent must be paid. When we say that an estate brings a suit or is sued, we are referring to the decedent's representative, who is authorized to resolve claims involving the decedent's assets and debts.

**Et al.** And others.

**Ethical Consideration (EC)** *See* Model Code of Professional Responsibility.

**Ethical Wall** *See* Chinese Wall.

**Ethics** Rules that embody standards of behavior to which members of an organization are expected to conform.

**Et Seq.** And following.

**Evidence** Anything that is offered to help establish or disprove a factual position. A separate determination must be made on whether a particular item of evidence is relevant or irrelevant, admissible or inadmissible.

**Excited Utterance** An out-of-court statement relating to a startling event or condition made while the declarant was under the stress of excitement caused by the event or condition. (An exception to the hearsay rule.)

**Exclusive Jurisdiction** The power of a court to hear a particular kind of case, to the exclusion of other courts.

**Execution** Carrying out or enforcing a judgment.

**Executive Agreement** An agreement between the United States and other nations or sovereigns that does not require the approval of the United States Senate.

**Executive Branch** The branch of government with primary responsibility for carrying out, executing, or administering the laws.

**Executive Department Agency** An administrative agency that exists within the executive branch of government, often at the cabinet level.

**Executive Order** A law issued by the chief executive pursuant to specific statutory authority or to the executive's inherent authority to direct the operation of governmental agencies.

**Executor** The person named in a will who has the responsibility of carrying out the terms of the will. (Called the *executrix*, if a woman.)

**Exempt Employee** An employee who is not entitled to overtime compensation under the Fair Labor Standards Act because the employee is a professional, administrative, or executive employee.

**Exhaust Administrative Remedies** To go through all dispute-solving avenues that are available in an administrative agency before asking a court to review what the agency did.

**Exhibit** An item of physical or tangible evidence offered to the court for inspection.

**Existing Physical or Mental Condition, Statement of** An out-of-court statement of a then-existing physical or mental condition.

**Ex Parte** Involving one party only.

**Ex Parte Hearing** A hearing at which only one party is present. A court order issued at such a hearing is an *ex parte order*.

**Expense Slip** A form used by an office to indicate that an expense has been incurred for which the client can be billed.

**Ex Post Facto** After the fact.

**External/Adversary Memorandum of Law** A memorandum written primarily for individuals outside the office to convince them to take a certain course of action. *See also* Memorandum of Law.

**Extranet** That part of an intranet to which selected outsiders have been given access. *See* Intranet.

**Fact** Something that actually exists. A statement that can be objectively established as true or false. An opinion is a value judgment that cannot be objectively verified.

**Fact Particularization** A fact-gathering technique used to generate a list of numerous factual questions that will help you obtain a specific and a comprehensive picture of all available facts that are relevant to a legal issue.

**Fact Pleading** A statement of every ultimate fact. A fact is ultimate if it is essential to establish an element of a cause of action.

***Facts & Findings*** A periodical of the National Association of Legal Assistants.

**Failure to State a Cause of Action** Failure of a party to allege enough facts that, if proved, would entitle the party to judicial relief.

**Fair Labor Standards Act** The federal statute that regulates conditions of employment such as when overtime compensation must be paid. *See also* Exempt Employee.

**Federal Depository Library** A public or private library that receives free federal government publications to which it must allow access by the general public.

**Federalism** The division of powers between the federal government and the state governments.

**Federal Question** A legal question that arises from the application of the United States Constitution, a statute of Congress, or a federal administrative regulation.

**Fee** The amount charged for services rendered. An *hourly rate fee* is based on the number of hours worked. A *blended* *hourly rate* is a single hourly rate that is based on a blend or mix of partner, associate, and sometimes paralegal rates. A *fixed fee* is a flat fee for the service regardless of the amount of time needed to complete it. A *capped fee* is an hourly rate leading to a total bill that will not exceed a predetermined amount. An *hourly plus fixed fee* is an hourly rate charged until the nature and scope of the legal problem are identified, at which time a fixed fee is charged for services provided thereafter. *See also* Contingent Fee, Fee-Generating Case, Fee Splitting, Incentive Billing, Task-Based Billing, Value Billing.

**Fee Analysis Report**  A report on the fees generated by client, by area of law, by law firm branch office, and by individual attorney.

**Fee-Generating Case**  The case of a client who can pay a fee out of the damages awarded or from his or her independent resources.

**Fee Splitting**  A single client bill covering the fees of two or more attorneys who are not in the same firm.

**Felony**  A crime punishable by a sentence of one year or more.

**Field**  A portion of a document in Westlaw that can be separately searched.

**File**  To deposit a pleading, motion, or other formal document with an official, often a court clerk. What is filed frequently becomes a public record.

**Firm Utilization Report**  *See* Aged Accounts Receivable Report.

**First Impression**  New; that which has come before the court for the first time.

**First Instance, Court of**  A trial court; a court with original jurisdiction.

**Fixed Fee**  A flat fee for services, regardless of the amount of time needed to complete the task. *See also* Fee.

**Font**  The design or style of printed letters of the alphabet, punctuation marks, or other characters.

**Footer**  The same text that is printed at the bottom of every page.

**Forensic**  Pertaining to the use of science to help resolve a legal question. Used in arguments or public debate.

**Format**  In word processing the layout of the page, e.g., the number of lines and margin settings.

**Form Book**  A collection of sample forms, often with practical guidance on how to use them. Also called a *practice manual*.

**Forum**  The court where the case is to be tried.

**Forwarding Fee**  A fee received by one attorney from another to whom the first attorney referred a client. Also called a *referral fee*.

**FRCP**  Federal Rules of Civil Procedure.

**Freedom of Information Act**  A statute that gives citizens access to certain information in the possession of the government.

**Freelance Paralegal**  An independent contractor (1) who sells his or her services to one or more attorneys or (2) who sells his or her services directly to the public without attorney supervision. Also called an *independent paralegal*.

**Friendly Divorce**  A divorce proceeding in which the parties have no significant disputes between them.

**Frivolous Position**  A position taken on behalf of a client that the attorney cannot support by a good-faith argument based on existing law or on the need for a change in the law.

**Full Faith and Credit**  One state must recognize and enforce valid public acts of other states, e.g., a valid court judgment.

**Full-Text Search**  A search of every word in every document in a database.

**Functional Résumé**  A résumé that clusters skills and experience together regardless of when they were developed or occurred.

**General Counsel**  An in-house attorney, often the chief attorney, of a corporation. Sometimes called *corporate counsel*.

**General Jurisdiction**  The power of the court (within its geographic boundaries) to hear any kind of case, with certain exceptions.

**General Practitioner**  A professional who handles any kind of case.

**General Schedule (GS)**  The pay-scale system used in the federal government.

**Generic Citation**  A citation to material based on a system that is not dependent on traditional volume and page numbers. Also called a *public domain citation*. It is medium neutral. If the references are to documents online, it is called an *electronic citation*.

**Geographic Jurisdiction**  The area of the state or country over which a court has power to render decisions.

**Gigabyte**  One billion bytes (approximate).

**Global**  In word processing, an instruction that will be carried out throughout the document.

**Go Bare**  To engage in an occupation or profession without malpractice insurance.

**GOD**  The Great Overtime Debate. *See* Exempt Employee.

**Government Corporation**  An entity that is a mixture of a corporation and a government agency created to serve a predominantly business function in the public interest.

**Grammar Checker** A computer software program that identifies possible grammatical errors in a document with suggested corrections.

**Grand Jury** A special jury whose duty is to hear evidence of felonies presented by the prosecutor to determine whether there is sufficient evidence to return an indictment against the defendant and cause him or her to stand trial on the charges.

**Ground** A reason that is legally sufficient to obtain a remedy or other result.

**Group Legal Services** A form of legal insurance in which members of a group pay a set amount on a regular basis, for which they receive designated legal services. Also called *prepaid legal services*.

**Groupware** A program that allows computers on a network to work together.

**GS** *See* General Schedule.

**Guideline** Suggested conduct that will help an applicant obtain accreditation, certification, licensure, registration, or approval.

**HALT** Help Abolish Legal Tyranny, an organization that seeks to reform the legal profession, primarily by eliminating the monopoly of attorneys over the practice of law.

**Handbook** *See* Form Book.

**Harassment** *See* Hostile Environment Harassment, Quid Pro Quo Harassment.

**Hard Copy** A printed copy (usually on paper) of what has been prepared on a computer. Also called a *printout*.

**Hard Disk** A rigid magnetic disk that stores data.

**Hardware** The physical equipment of a computer system that is used by programs to process data.

**Header** The same text that is printed at the top of every page.

**Headhunter** Someone who tries to locate people to work in a particular office.

**Heading of Memorandum** The beginning of a memorandum that lists who the memo is for, who wrote it, what it is about, etc.

**Headnote** A small-paragraph summary of a portion of a court opinion, written by a private publisher.

**Hearing** A proceeding convened to resolve a dispute during which parties in the dispute can present their case.

**Hearing Examiner** One who presides over an administrative hearing.

**Hearing Memorandum** A memorandum of law submitted to a hearing officer.

**Hearsay** An out-of-court statement offered to prove the truth of the matter asserted in the statement.

**Historical Note** Information on the legislative history of a statute printed after the text of the statute.

**Holding** A court's answer to one of the legal issues in the case. Also called a *ruling*.

**Hornbook** A legal treatise (that summarizes an area of the law that is often covered within a single law school course) designed primarily for the law school student.

**Hostile Environment Harassment** Pervasive unwelcome sexual conduct or sex-based ridicule that unreasonably interferes with an individual's job performance or creates an intimidating, hostile, or offensive working environment.

**Hourly plus Fixed Fee** An hourly rate charged until the nature and scope of the legal problem are known, at which time fixed fees are charged for services provided thereafter. *See also* Fee.

**Hypertext** A method of displaying and linking information found in different locations on the same site or on different sites of the World Wide Web.

**Hypothetical** Not actual or real but presented for purposes of discussion or analysis; based on an assumed set of facts; based on a hypothesis.

**Hypothetical Question** A question in which the interviewee is asked to respond to a set of assumed facts provided by the interviewer.

**Icon** A picture or graphic that is "clicked" on with a mouse in order to execute it.

**id.** The same as the immediately preceding authority cited.

**Imaging** Converting text or an image into a format that a computer can read and display. Creating a computer-readable image of a document.

**Impaired Attorney** An attorney with a drug or alcohol problem.

**Impaneled** Selected and sworn in (referring to a jury) (also spelled *empaneled*).

**Impeach** To challenge, to attack the credibility of.

**Imputed Disqualification** All attorneys in the same firm are ineligible to represent a client because one of the attorneys or other employees in the firm has a conflict of interest with that client. Also called *vicarious disqualification*.

**Incentive Billing** A fee that is increased if a designated target is met; an increased fee for achieving an exceptional result. Also called a *performance bonus*.

**Income Partner** *See* Nonequity Partner.

**Incremental Spacing** In word processing, a method by which the printer inserts spaces between words and letters to produce margins that are justified. Also called *microspacing*.

**Independent Contractor** One who operates his or her own business and contracts to do work for others who do not control the details of how that work is performed.

**Independent Paralegal** *See* Freelance Paralegal.

**Independent Regulatory Agency** An administrative agency (often existing outside the executive department) created to regulate an aspect of society.

**Index** An alphabetical list of topics covered in a document with page or section numbers where those topics are covered in the document.

**Indictment** A formal document issued by a grand jury accusing the defendant of a crime. *See also* Grand Jury.

**Indigent** Impoverished; without funds to hire a private attorney.

**Inferior Court** A lower court of limited or special jurisdiction.

**Information** A document accusing the defendant of a crime (used in states without a grand jury).

**Informational Interview** A interview whose primary purpose is to find out information about a particular kind of employment.

**Informational Letter** A letter that provides or seeks information.

**Information and Belief** To the best of one's knowledge; a good-faith understanding.

**Infra** Below, mentioned or referred to later in the document.

**In-house Attorney** An attorney who is an employee of a corporation. *See* Corporate Legal Department.

**In Issue** In dispute or question.

**Initial Appearance** The first criminal court appearance by the accused during which the court informs him or her of the charges, makes a decision on bail, and determines the date of the next court proceeding.

**In Personam Jurisdiction** *See* Personal Jurisdiction.

**In Propria Persona** (In Pro Per) In one's own proper person. *See also* Pro Se.

**In Re** In the matter of.

**In Rem Jurisdiction** The court's power over a particular thing (rem) located within the territory over which the court has authority.

**Insert Mode** When new text is typed in a line that already has text, the line opens to receive the new text. Nothing is erased or overtyped.

**Insider Trading** Improperly using material, nonpublic information to trade in the shares of a company.

**Instrument** A formal written document that gives expression to a legal act or agreement, e.g., contract, mortgage.

**Intake Memo** A memorandum that summarizes the facts given by a client during the initial client interview.

**Integrated Bar Association** A state bar association to which an attorney must belong in order to practice law in the state. Also called a *mandatory* or *unified bar association*.

**Intellectual Property Law** The law governing patents, copyrights, trademarks, and trade names.

**Interfiling** Inserting pages anywhere they belong in an existing text such as a loose-leaf volume.

**Interim Suspension** A temporary suspension, pending the imposition of final discipline.

**Interlocutory Appeal** An appeal of a trial court ruling before the trial court reaches its final judgment.

**Intermediate Appellate Court** A court with appellate jurisdiction to which parties can appeal before they appeal to the highest court in the judicial system.

**Intern** *See* Legal Intern.

**Internal Memorandum of Law** *See* Interoffice Memorandum of Law.

**Internet** A self-governing network of networks to which millions of computer users all over the world have access.

**Internet Service Provider** A company that provides access to the Internet, usually for a monthly fee.

**Interoffice Memorandum of Law** A memorandum that objectively analyzes the law; the memo is written for your supervisor or for other individual(s) in your office. *See also* External/Adversary Memorandum of Law, Memorandum of Law.

**Interrogatories** A method of discovery consisting of written questions sent by one party to another to assist the sender in preparing for trial.

**Interstate Compact** An agreement between two or more states governing a problem of mutual concern.

**Intra-agency Appeal** An appeal within an administrative agency, before the case is appealed to a court.

**Intranet** A private network of computers within a particular company or organization, established so that the computers can share information online, often using features similar to those of the World Wide Web.

**Investigation** *See* Legal Investigation.

**Invisible Web** That part of the Internet that is not found by traditional search engines and directories.

**IOLTA** (Interest on Lawyers Trust Account) Under IOLTA programs, designated client funds held by an attorney are deposited in a bank account. The interest income from the account is paid to foundations that help finance legal services for low-income clients.

**IRAC** An acronym that stands for the components of legal analysis: issue (I), rule (R), application of the rule to the facts (A), and conclusion (C). A structure for legal analysis.

**Irrebuttable** Conclusive; evidence to the contrary is inadmissible. Nonrebuttable.

**Jailhouse Lawyer** An incarcerated paralegal, usually self-taught, who has a limited right to provide other inmates with legal services if the institution does not provide adequate alternatives to such services. Also called a *writ writer*.

**Jargon** Technical language; language that does not have an everyday meaning.

**Job Bank** A service that lists available jobs, usually available only to members of an organization.

**Joint and Several Liability** Legally responsible together and individually.

**Judgment** The final conclusion of a court. The judgment will resolve the legal dispute before the court, or will decide what further proceedings are needed to resolve the dispute.

**Judgment Creditor** The person to whom a court-awarded money judgment (damages) is owed.

**Judgment Debtor** The person ordered by a court to pay a money judgment (damages).

**Judgment NOV (Notwinstanding the Verdict)** A judgment by the trial judge that is contrary to the verdict reached by the jury.

**Judgment on the Merits** A decision on the substance of the claims raised.

**Judicial Branch** The branch of government with primary responsibility for interpreting laws by resolving disputes that arise under them.

**Judicial Notice** A court's acceptance of a well-known fact without requiring proof of that fact.

**Judicial Review** The power of a court to determine the constitutionality of a statute or other law, including the power to refuse to enforce it if the court concludes that it violates the constitution.

**Jump Cite** *See* Pinpont Cite.

**Jurisdiction** Power or authority to act. *See also* In Rem Jurisdiction, Personal Jurisdiction, Subject Matter Jurisdiction.

**Jury Panel** *See* Panel.

**Justification** In word processing, a feature for making lines of text even at the margins.

**K** A measure of capacity in a computer system.

**Kardex** A file in which the library records the volume numbers and dates of incoming publications that are part of subscriptions.

**KeyCite** An online citator available on Westlaw. *See also* Citator.

**Key Fact** A critical fact; a fact that is essential or very important to the decision (holding) reached by the court.

**Key Number** A general topic and a number of a subtopic. It is the heart of the system used by West Group to organize the millions of small-paragraph summaries of court opinions in its digests.

**Key-Word Search** A search through a list of specified words that functions like an index to a database.

**Kilobyte** One thousand bytes (approximately).

**LAMA** Legal Assistant Management Association.

**Landmen** Paralegals who work in the area of oil and gas law. Also called *land technicians*.

**Laser Printer** A printer that uses a laser beam of light to reproduce images.

**Lateral Hire** An attorney, paralegal, or other employee who has been hired from another law office.

**Law Clerk** (1) An attorney's employee who is in law school studying to become an attorney or who has graduated from law school and is waiting to pass the bar examination. (2) In Ontario, Canada, a law clerk is a trained professional doing independent legal work, which may include managerial duties, under the direction and guidance of a lawyer, and whose function is to relieve a lawyer of routine and administrative matters and to assist a lawyer in the more complex ones.

**Law Department** *See* Corporate Legal Department.

**Law Directory** A list of attorneys.

**Law Review** A legal periodical published by a law school. Sometimes called a *law journal*.

**Lay Opinion Evidence** The opinion of someone who is not an expert.

**LCP** Louisiana Certified Paralegal, a person who has passed the Louisiana Certified Paralegal Exam.

**Leading Question** A question that suggests an answer within the question.

**Legal Administrator** An individual, usually a nonattorney, with broad management responsibility for a law office.

**Legal Advice** The application of laws or legal principles to the facts of a particular person's legal problem. *See also* Professional Judgment.

**Legal Analysis** The application of one or more rules to the facts of a client's case in order to answer a legal question that will help (1) keep a legal dispute from arising, (2) resolve a legal dispute that has arisen, or (3) prevent a legal dispute from becoming worse.

**Legal Assistant** *See* Paralegal.

**Legal Assistant Clerk** A person who assists a legal assistant in clerical tasks such as document numbering, alphabetizing, filing, and any other project that does not require substantive knowledge of litigation or of a particular transaction. *See also* Document Clerk.

**Legal Assistant Division** A few state bar associations, e.g., Texas, have established special divisions that paralegals can join as associate members.

**Legal Assistant Manager** A person who is responsible for recruiting, interviewing, and hiring legal assistants and spends little or no time working on client cases as a legal assistant. He or she may also be substantially involved in other matters pertaining to legal assistants, e.g., training, monitoring work assignments, designing budgets, and overseeing the billing of paralegal time. Also known as a *paralegal manager*.

**Legal Bias** *See* Bias.

**Legal Dictionary** An alphabetical list of legal terms that are defined.

**Legal Document Assistant (LDA)** A nonattorney in California who is authorized to charge fees for providing "self-help" service (without attorney supervision) to anyone representing himself or herself in a legal matter.

**Legal Encyclopedia** A multivolume set of books that alphabetically summarizes almost every major legal topic.

**Legal Executive** A trained and certified employee of a solicitor in England; the equivalent of an American paralegal but with more training and credentials.

**Legal Insurance** *See* Group Legal Services.

**Legal Intern** A student in a law office seeking practical experience.

**Legal Investigation** The process of verifying presently known facts and gathering additional facts in order to advise a client about solving or avoiding a legal problem.

**Legal Issue** A question of law; a question of what the law is, or what the law means, or how the law applies to a set of facts. If the dispute is over the truth or falsity of the alleged facts, it is referred to as a *question of fact* or a *factual issue*.

**Legally Relevant** Contributing to the resolution of a legal problem or issue.

**Legalman** A nonattorney in the Navy who assists attorneys in the practice of law.

**Legal Newsletter** A special interest report (published daily, weekly, etc.) covering practical suggestions and current developments in a particular area of the law.

**Legal Newspaper** A newspaper (published daily, weekly, etc.) devoted primarily to legal news.

**Legal Periodical** A publication on legal topics that is issued at regular intervals. The major examples are law reviews and bar journals.

**Legal Technician** A self-employed paralegal who works for several different attorneys, or a self-employed paralegal who works directly for the public. Sometimes called an *independent paralegal* or a *freelance paralegal*.

**Legal Thesaurus** A volume of word alternatives for words used in the law.

**LegalTrac** A CD–ROM index to legal periodical literature. It is the CD–ROM version of the *Current Law Index*.

**Legal Treatise** A book written by a private individual (or by a public individual writing as a private citizen) that provides an overview, summary, or commentary on a legal topic.

**Legislation** (1) The process of making statutory law. (2) A statute.

**Legislative Branch** The branch of government with primary responsibility for making or enacting the law.

**Legislative History** All of the events that occur in the legislature before a bill is enacted into a statute.

**Legislative Intent** The purpose of the legislature in enacting a particular statute.

**Legislative Service** A publication that prints recently enacted session laws. Also called *session law service* or *advance session law service*. In addition, the service may print bills, which are proposed statutes.

**Letterhead** The top part of stationery, which identifies the name and address of the office (often with the names of selected employees).

**Letter of Disengagement** A letter sent to a client formally notifying him or her that the law office will no longer be representing the client. The letter severs the attorney-client relationship. Also called a *declination letter*.

**Letter of Nonengagement** A letter sent to a prospective client that explicitly states that the law office will not be representing him or her.

**Leverage** The ability to make a profit from the income-generating work of others.

**LEXIS** The fee-based legal research computer service of Reed Elsevier Co.

**Liable** Legally responsible.

**Licensure** The process by which an agency of government grants permission to persons meeting specified qualifications to engage in an occupation and often to use a particular title.

**Limited Jurisdiction** The power of a court to hear only certain kinds of cases. Also called *special jurisdiction*.

**Limited Liability** Restricted liability; liability that can be satisfied only out of business assets; liability that cannot be satisfied out of personal assets.

**Limited Liability Entity** A company or partnership that is given special tax treatment and in which there are limits on the liability of one owner or partner for the wrongdoing of another owner or partner.

**Limited Licensure** The process by which an agency of government grants permission to persons meeting specified qualifications to engage in designated activities that are now customarily (although not always exclusively) performed by another license holder, i.e., that are part of someone else's monopoly.

**Limited Practice Officer** A nonattorney in Washington State who has the authority to select and prepare designated legal documents pertaining to real estate closings.

**Lis Pendens** A pending suit.

**Listserv** A program that manages computer mailing lists automatically, including the receipt and distribution of messages from and to members of the list.

**Litigation** The formal process of resolving a legal dispute through special tribunals such as courts; a lawsuit.

**Litigation Status** The procedural category of a party during any stage of litigation, e.g., plaintiff, defendant, appellant.

**Litigation Support** Application software used to help a law office store, retrieve, and track facts and documents that pertain to a lawsuit.

**Litigious** Inclined to resolve disputes through litigation; quarrelsome.

**Local Area Network (LAN)** A multiuser system linking computers that are in close proximity to each other so that they can share data and resources.

**Lodestar** A method of calculating an award of attorney fees authorized by statute. The number of reasonable hours spent on the case is multiplied by a reasonable hourly rate. Other factors might also be considered above the lodestar in setting the fee, e.g., the quality of representation, any delay in receiving payment, and the risk at the outset of the litigation that the prevailing attorney will receive no fee.

**Loose-Leaf** Containing pages that can be inserted and removed easily, often using a three-ring binder.

**Loose-Leaf Service** A loose-leaf containing current information on a broad or narrow topic. In law, the service might contain recent court opinions, relevant legislation, administrative regulations, etc.

**Macro** An automated way to insert frequently used text or to perform other repetitive functions.

**Magistrate** A judicial officer having some but not all the powers of a judge.

**Majority Opinion** The opinion whose result and reasoning are supported by at least half plus one of the judges on the court.

**Malpractice** Professional misconduct or wrongdoing such as an ethical violation, crime, negligence, battery, or other tort.

**Managing Partner** The partner of a firm who has day-to-day responsibility for running the administrative aspects of the firm.

**Mandate** The order of the court.

**Mandatory Authority** Whatever source a court must rely on in reaching its decision.

**Mandatory Bar Association** *See* Integrated Bar Association.

**Mandatory Statute** A statute that requires something to be done.

**Marital Communications** A husband and a wife can refuse to disclose communications between them during the marriage.

**Maritime Law** *See* Admiralty Law.

**Market Rate** The prevailing rate in the area.

***Martindale-Hubbell Law Directory*** A national directory of attorneys.

**Med-Arb** A method of alternative dispute resolution in which the parties first try mediation, and if it does not work, they try arbitration. It is an alternative to litigation.

**Mediation** A method of alternative dispute resolution in which the parties submit their dispute to a neutral third person who helps the parties reach their own decision to resolve the dispute. It is an alternative to litigation.

**Megabyte** One million bytes (approximately).

**Memorandum of Law** A written explanation of how the law might apply to the fact situation of a client.

**Memorandum Opinion** A court opinion, usually a short one, that does not name the judge who wrote the opinion. Also called a *per curiam* opinion.

**Memory** The internal storage capacity of a computer.

**Mental Condition** *See* Declaration of State of Mind; Existing Physical or Mental Condition.

**Menu**  In word processing and other programs, a list of commands or prompts on the display screen.

**Metasearch**  A search for terms in more than one search engine simultaneously.

**Microfiche**  *See* Microform.

**Microform**  Images or photographs that have been reduced in size. Microforms can be *Microfilms*, which store material on reels or cassettes, or *microfiche* and *ultrafiche*, which store material that has been reduced by a factor of 100 or more on a single sheet of film.

**Minimum-Fee Schedule**  A bar association list of the lowest fees an attorney can charge for specific kinds of legal services.

**Misdemeanor**  A crime punishable by a sentence of less than a year.

**Model Code of Ethics and Professional Responsibility**  A statement of ethical guidelines of the National Federation of Paralegal Associations.

**Model Code of Professional Responsibility**  An earlier edition of the ethical rules governing attorneys recommended by the American Bar Association. The *Model Code* consisted of Ethical Considerations (ECs), which represented the objectives toward which each attorney should strive, and Disciplinary Rules (DRs), which were mandatory statements of the minimum conduct below which no attorney could fall without being subject to discipline.

**Model Guidelines for the Utilization of Legal Assistant Services**  Ethical guidelines recommended by the American Bar Association for the ethical use of paralegals by attorneys.

**Model Rule 5.3**  The rule in the ABA *Model Rules of Professional Conduct* governing the responsibility of different categories of attorneys for the misconduct of paralegals and other nonattorney assistants in a law firm.

**Model Rules of Professional Conduct**  The current set of ethical rules governing attorneys recommended by the American Bar Association. These rules revised the ABA's earlier rules found in the *Model Code of Professional Responsibility*.

**Modem**  A communications device that allows computers at different locations to use telephone lines to exchange data.

**Monitor**  A display screen; a TV-like device used to display what is typed at the keyboard and the response of the computer.

**Monitoring Legislation**  Finding current information on the status of a proposed statute in the legislature.

**Mouse**  A hand-held input device that moves the cursor by rolling, clicking, and dragging motions.

**Movant**  The party who formally requests a court to do something.

**Multidisciplinary Practice (MDP)**  A partnership consisting of attorneys and nonlegal professionals that offers legal and nonlegal services.

**Multiple-Choice Question**  A question that asks the interviewee to choose among two or more options stated in the question.

**Multiple Representation**  Representing more than one side in a legal matter or controversy. Also called *common representation*.

**Multitasking**  Having the capacity to run several large programs simultaneously.

**NALA**  National Association of Legal Assistants.

**NALS**  National Association of Legal Professionals, an association consisting primarily of legal secretaries, many of whom consider themselves legal assistants. The Association was once called the National Association of Legal Secretaries.

**National Paralegal Reporter**  A periodical of the National Federation of Paralegal Associations.

**Natural Language**  Plain English as spoken or written every day as opposed to language that is specially designed for computer communication.

**Negative Contingency**  *See* Contingent Fee.

**Negligence**  Harm caused by the failure to use reasonable care.

**Neighborhood Justice Center (NJC)**  A government or private center where disputes can be resolved by mediation or other method of alternative dispute resolution.

**Neighborhood Legal Service Office**  A law office that serves the legal needs of the poor, often publicly funded.

**Network**  A group of computers that are linked or connected together.

**Networking**  Establishing contacts with people who might become personal or professional resources.

**New File Worksheet**  A form used by some law firms that is the source document for the creation of all necessary accounting records that are needed when a law firm begins working on a new client case or matter. Also called a *new matter sheet* or *new business sheet*.

**NFPA**  National Federation of Paralegal Associations.

**NJC**  Neighborhood Justice Center.

**Nolle Prosequi**  A statement by the prosecutor that he or she is unwilling to prosecute the case.

**Nominalization**  A noun formed from a verb or adjective.

**Nominative Reporter**  A reporter volume that is identified by the name of the person reponsible for compiling and printing the opinions in the volume.

**Nonadversarial** Pertaining to a conflict-resolution proceeding in which all parties to the conflict or dispute are not present. *See also* Adversarial, Adversary Hearing.

**Nonauthority** Any primary or secondary authority that is not on point, any primary authority that is invalid, or any materials that are solely finding aids.

**Nonbillable Time** Time spent on tasks for which clients cannot be asked to pay.

**Nonengagement** *See* Letter of Nonengagement.

**Nonequity Partner** A special category of partner who does not own the firm in the sense of an equity or capital partner. Also called an *income partner*.

**Nonexempt Employee** An employee who must be paid overtime compensation.

**Nonrebuttable** *See* Irrebuttable.

**Notary Public** A person who witnesses (i.e., attests to the authenticity of) signatures, administers oaths, and performs related tasks. In Europe, a notary often has more extensive authority.

**Notes of Decision** Summaries of opinions that have interpreted a statute, usually printed beneath the text of the statute.

**Notice** Information about a fact; knowledge of something.

**Notice of Appearance** *See* Appearance.

**Notice Pleading** A short and plain statement of the claim showing that the pleader is entitled to relief.

**NOV** *See* Judgment NOV.

**Numerical Filling System** A method of storing client files by numbers or letter-number combinations.

**Nutshell** A legal treatise (written in pamphlet form) that summarizes a topic that is covered in a law school course.

**Oath** A sworn statement that what you say is true.

**Objectivity** The state of being dispassionate; the absence of a bias. *See also* Bias.

**Occurrence Policy** Malpractice insurance that covers all occurrences (e.g., a negligent error or omission) during the period the policy is in effect, even if the claim is not actually filed until after the policy expires.

**Occurrence Witness** Someone who actually observed an event or incident.

**Of Counsel** An attorney who is semiretired or has some other special status in the law firm.

**Office Sharing** Attorneys who are sole practitioners share the use and overhead costs of an office.

**Official Reporter** A reporter printed under the authority of the government, often by a government printing office.

An unofficial reporter is a reporter printed by a commercial publishing company without special authority from the government.

**Official Statutory Code** A statutory code published by the government or by a private company with special permission or authority from the government. *See also* Unofficial Statutory Code.

**Offprint Reporter** *See* Special Edition State Reporter.

**OJT** On-the-job Training.

**On All Fours** The facts are exactly the same, or almost so.

**Online** Being connected to a host computer system or information service—usually through the telephone lines.

**On Point** Raising or covering the same issue as the one before you.

**Open-Ended Question** A broad, unstructured question that rarely can be answered in one or two words.

**Operating System** The software that tells the computer how to operate.

**Opinion** A court's written explanation of how it applied the law to the facts before it to resolve a legal dispute. Also called a *case*. Opinions are printed in volumes called *reporters*.

**Opinion Letter** A letter to a client explaining the application of the law and providing legal advice based on that explanation.

**Opinion of the Attorney General** Formal legal advice given by the chief law officer of the government to another government official or agency.

**Oral Argument** A spoken presentation before an appellate court on why the rulings of a lower tribunal were valid or invalid. The presentation is usually made by the attorney for the appellant or appellee.

**Ordinance** A law passed by the local legislative branch of government (e.g., city council) that declares, commands, or prohibits something.

**Original Jurisdiction** The power of a court to hear a particular kind of case initially. A trial court has original jurisdiction.

**Outline** A pamphlet that summarizes a legal subject in the form of a detailed outline.

**Outside Counsel** An attorney used by a company who is not an employee of the company.

**Outstanding** Still unresolved; still unpaid.

**Overhead** The operating expenses of a business (e.g., office rent, furniture, insurance, clerical staff) for which customers or clients are not charged a separate fee.

**Override** To supersede or change a result. To approve a bill over the veto of the chief executive.

**Overrule** To change the holding of a prior opinion in the same litigation. *See also* Reverse.

**Overview Question** A question that asks for a summary of an event or condition.

**PACE** *See* Paralegal Advanced Certification Exam.

**PACER** Public Access to Court Electronic Records.

**Padding** Adding something without justification; adding unnecessary material in order to make something larger.

**Page 52 Debate** A debate on whether there should be limited licensing for paralegals (based on a recommendation in favor of such licensing on page 52 of a report of an American Bar Association commission).

**Panel** (1) A group of judges, usually three, who decide a case. The group is often part of a court that consists of a larger number of judges. (2) A list of individuals summoned for jury duty; from this list, juries for particular trials are selected. (3) A group of attorneys available in a group legal services plan. (4) Members of a commission.

**Paralegal** A person with legal skills who works under the supervision of an attorney or who is otherwise authorized to use those skills; this person performs tasks that do not require all the skills of an attorney and that most secretaries are not trained to perform. Synonymous with *legal assistant*.

**Paralegal Advanced Certification Exam (PACE)** The credential bestowed by the National Federation of Paralegal Associations for meeting its criteria such as passing a national certification exam for experienced paralegals.

**Paralegal Code** Rules and guidelines covering ethical issues involving paralegals.

**Paralegal Fees** Fees that an attorney can collect for the nonclerical work of his or her paralegal on a client case.

**Paralegal Manager** *See* Legal Assistant Manager.

**Paralegal Specialist** The major civil service job classification for paralegals who work for the federal government and for some state governments.

**Parallel Cite** An additional citation where you can find the same written material in the library.

**Parallelism** Using a consistent (i.e., parallel) grammatical structure when phrasing logically related ideas in a list.

**Paraphrase** To phrase something partly or entirely in your own words.

**Parol Evidence** Oral evidence.

**Parol Evidence Rule** Oral evidence cannot be introduced to alter or contradict the contents of a written document if the parties initially intended the written document to be a complete statement of the agreement.

**Partner, Full** An attorney who contributes the capital to create the firm and to expand it, who shares the profits and losses of the firm, who controls the management of the firm, and who decides whether the firm will go out of existence.

**Partnership** An association of two or more individuals who jointly own a business.

**Passive Voice** The grammatical verb form in which the object of the action is the main focus. The emphasis is on what is being done rather than on who or what is performing or causing the action.

**Pattern Jury Instructions** Suggested instructions to a jury that can be adapted to specific trials.

**People** The state or government as a party.

**Percentage Fee** The fee is a percentage of the amount involved in the transaction or award.

**Per Curiam** By the court. A per curiam opinion is a court opinion, usually a short one, that does not name the judge who wrote the opinion. Also called a *memorandum opinion*.

**Peremptory Challenge** A request to exclude someone from a jury without stating a reason for the request. *See also* Challenge for Cause.

**Performance Bonus** *See* Incentive Billing.

**Personal Jurisdiction** The court's power over a particular person. Also called *in personam jurisdiction*.

**Personal Liability** Liability that can be satisfied out of an individual's personal assets. *See also* Limited Liability.

**Personal Recognizance** The release of an accused solely on the basis of his or her promise to return at designated times. No bond or bail is required.

**Persuasive Authority** Whatever source a court relies on in reaching its decision that it is not required to rely on.

**Petition** (1) A formal request or motion. (2) A complaint.

**Physical Evidence** That which can be seen or touched. Also called *tangible evidence*.

**Physician Assistant** An individual who is qualified by academic and clinical training to provide patient care services under the supervision and responsibility of a doctor of medicine or osteopathy.

**PI Cases** Personal injury (tort) cases.

**Pinpoint Cite** A reference to material on a specific page number in a document, e.g., a case, as opposed to the page number where the document begins. In some documents, the pinpoint reference is to a specific paragraph number in the document. Also called a *jump cite*.

**Pirated Software** Software that has been placed ("loaded") in a computer that is not authorized by the terms of the purchase or lease of the software.

**Plagiarism** Use of someone else's writing without appropriate citation.

**Plaintiff** The party initiating the lawsuit.

**Plea Bargaining** An attempt to avoid a criminal trial by negotiating a plea, e.g., the defendant agrees to plead guilty to a lesser charge than initially brought.

**Plead** To deliver a formal statement or response.

**Pleading** A formal document containing a statement of claims and responses to claims (such as defenses) exchanged between parties in litigation. The major pleadings are the complaint and answer.

**PL Number** Public Law number.

**PLS** Professional Legal Secretary.

**Pocket Part** An insert that fits into a small pocket built into the inside back (and occasionally front) cover of a hardcover volume usually containing text that updates the material in the volume.

**Pocket Veto** The chief executive's "silent" rejection of a bill by not acting on it within 10 weekdays of receiving it if the legislature adjourns during this period.

**Point Heading** A conclusion that a party wants a court to accept on one of the issues in the case. The conclusion is written as a heading at the beginning of the argument on that issue.

**Points** A measure of the size of printed letters of the alphabet, punctuation marks, or other characters.

**Points and Authorities Memorandum** A memorandum of law submitted to a judge or hearing officer. Sometimes called a *trial memorandum*.

**Poll** (1) To ask each member of a body (e.g., a jury) that has just voted how he or she individually voted. (2) To seek a sampling of opinions.

**Popular Name** A phrase or short title identifying a particular statute.

**Portable Billings** Fees that an attorney brings with him or her when he or she changes law firms.

**Post-occurrence Witness** Someone who did not observe an event or incident but who can give a firsthand account of what happened after the event or incident.

**Practical Manual** *See* Form Book.

**Practice Analysis Report** *See* Case-Type Productivity Report.

**Practice of Law** Using legal skills to assist a person resolve his or her specific legal problem.

**Praecipe** A formal request to the court (usually made through the clerk) that something be done.

**Prayer for Relief** The request for damages or other form of judicial relief.

**Precedent** A prior decision that can be used as a standard in a later similar case.

**Pre-evaluation Memo** A memorandum sent to a supervisor before a formal evaluation in which the employee lists the following information (since the last formal evaluation): major projects, functions on those projects, names of co-workers on the projects, evidence of initiative, quotations on the quality of work, etc.

**Preliminary Hearing** A hearing during which the state is required to produce sufficient evidence to establish that there is probable cause to believe the defendant committed the crimes charged.

**Preliminary Prints** The advance sheets for *United States Reports*.

**Premium Adjustment** A write-up (increase) of a bill.

**Pre-occurrence Witness** Someone who did not observe an event or incident but who can give a firsthand account of what happened before the event or incident.

**Prepaid Legal Services** *See* Group Legal Services.

**Preponderance of the Evidence** It is more likely than not that the fact is as alleged.

**Presentation Graphics** Application software used to present text data with charts, graphs, video, and sound in order to communicate the data more effectively.

**Present Sense Impression, Statement of** An out-of-court statement describing or explaining an event or condition made while the declarant was perceiving the event or condition or immediately thereafter. (An exception to the hearsay rule.)

**Presumption** An assumption or inference that a certain fact is true once another fact is established.

**Pretrial Conference** A meeting between the judge (or magistrate) and the attorneys to prepare the case for trial and perhaps to make one last effort to settle the case.

**Prima Facie** On the face of it; that which would be legally sufficient, if believed, to support a verdict.

**Primary Authority** Any *law* that a court could rely on in reaching its decision.

**Print Review** In word processing, a feature that enables you to view a representation on the screen of how the document will look when printed.

**Private Law** A statute that applies to specifically named individuals or groups and has little or no permanence or general interest.

**Private Law Firm** A law firm that generates its income from the fees of individual clients.

**Private Reprimand** *See* Admonition.

**Private Sector** Offices in which operating funds come from client fees or the corporate treasury. *See also* Public Sector.

**Privilege** A special benefit, right, or protection. In the law of evidence, a privilege is the right to refuse to testify or to prevent someone else from testifying.

**Privilege against Self-Incrimination** Persons cannot be compelled to testify in a criminal proceeding or to answer incriminating questions that directly or indirectly connect themselves to the commission of a crime.

**Probable Cause** A reasonable basis to believe that the defendant is guilty of the crime(s) charged.

**Probate** (1) To bring a will before the proper court to prove it is genuine. (2) The act of proving that a will is genuine.

**Probation** Supervised punishment in the community in lieu of incarceration. In the field of ethics, probation means to allow an attorney to continue to practice, but under specified conditions, e.g., submit to periodic audits, make restitution to a client.

**Pro Bono** Performed for the public good without fee or compensation (pro bono publico).

**Procedural Due Process** Procedural protections that are required before the government can take away or refuse to grant liberty or a public benefit.

**Procedural Law** The rules that govern the mechanics of resolving a dispute in court or in an administrative agency, e.g., a rule on the time a party has to respond to a complaint.

**Process** *See* Service of Process.

**Professional Corporation** A law office that is organized as a corporation rather than as a partnership or sole proprietorship.

**Professional Judgment** Relating or applying the general body and philosophy of law to a specific legal problem. When communicated to a client, the result is known as *legal advice.*

**Project Attorney** *See* Contract Attorney.

**Project Billing** *See* Task-Based Billing.

**Pro. Per.** *See* Pro Se.

**Pro Se** Appearing or representing oneself; acting without representation. This person is said to be proceeding *in propria persona*—in one's own proper person. The abbreviation is *pro. per.*

**Prosecution** (1) Bringing and processing criminal proceedings against someone. (2) The attorney representing the government in a criminal case, also called the *prosecutor.* (3) Bringing and processing civil proceedings against someone.

**Prosecutor** The attorney representing the government in a criminal case.

**Prospective** Applying only to facts that arise after the effective date. *See also* Retroactive.

**Public Benefits** Government benefits.

**Public Censure** *See* Reprimand.

**Public Defender** A government attorney who represents indigent (i.e., low-income) people charged with crimes. *See also* Assigned Counsel.

**Public Domain** Free; accessible to anyone at no cost.

**Public Domain Citation** A citation that is medium neutral. To find the material in the citation, you do not have to use the traditional volume and page numbers of a commercial publisher such as West Group. Also called a *generic citation.* If the reference is to documents online, the public domain citation is called an *electronic citation.*

**Public Law** A statute that applies to the general public or to a segment of the public and has permanence or general interest.

**Public Sector** Offices in which operating funds come from charity or the government. *See also* Private Sector.

**Quasi-Adjudication** An administrative decision written by an administrative agency that has some characteristics of an opinion written by a court.

**Quasi-Independent Agency** An administrative agency that has characteristics of an executive department agency and of an independent regulatory agency.

**Quasi-judicial Proceeding** A proceeding within an administrative agency that seeks to resolve a dispute in a manner that is similar to a court (i.e., judicial) proceeding to resolve a dispute.

**Quasi-legislation** An administrative regulation enacted by an administrative agency that has some characteristics of the legislation (i.e., statutes) enacted by the legislature.

**Quarantined** Isolated; kept away from information that would disqualify the firm. *See also* Chinese Wall.

**Query** A question used to try to find something in a computer database.

**Question of Law/Question of Fact** *See* Legal Issue.

**Quid Pro Quo Harassment** Using submission to or rejection of unwelcome sexual conduct as the basis for making employment decisions affecting an individual.

**Rainmaker** An attorney who brings fee-generating cases into the office due to his or her extensive contacts and/or reputation as a skilled attorney.

**Random Access Memory (RAM)** Memory that stores temporary data in an arbitrary or random manner.

**RE** Concerning.

**Read-Only** Able to read data on a device but not to alter, remove, or add to the data.

**Read-Only Memory (ROM)** Memory that stores data that cannot be altered, removed, or added to. The data can be read only.

**Read/Write** Able to read data on a device *and* write or insert additional data into it.

**Real-Time** Occurring now; happening as you are watching; able to respond immediately.

**Reasonable Doubt** Such doubt as would cause prudent persons to hesitate before acting in matters of importance to themselves.

**Reasonable Fee** A fee that is not excessive in light of the amount of time and labor involved, the complexity of the case, the experience and reputation of the attorney, the customary fee charged in the locality for the same kind of case, etc.

**Reasoning** An explanation of why the court resolved a legal issue the way it did—why it reached that particular holding.

**Rebuttable** Not conclusive; evidence to the contrary is admissible.

**Receivables** Accounts due and payable.

**Record** (1) The official collection of all the trial pleadings, exhibits, orders, and word-for-word testimony given during the trial. (2) A collection of data fields that constitute a single unit, e.g., employee record.

**Record Information Manager** Someone in charge of files in a large office.

**Redirect Examination** Questioning your own witness (i.e., one you called) after cross-examination of that witness by the other side.

**Referendum** A vote by the electorate on a proposed constitutional provision or statute. A direct vote by voters in the general public on proposed laws.

**Referral Fee** *See* Forwarding Fee.

**Regional Digest** A digest that summarizes court opinions that are printed in full in its corresponding regional reporter.

**Regional Reporter** A reporter that contains state court opinions of states within a region of the country.

**Register** A set of books that contain administrative regulations.

**Registered Agent** An attorney or nonattorney authorized to practice before the United States Patent Office.

**Registration** The process by which individuals or institutions list their names on a roster kept by an agency of government or by a nongovernmental organization. The agency or organization will often establish qualifications for the right to register and determine whether applicants meet these qualifications. Also called *enrollment*.

**Regulation** Any governmental or nongovernmental method of controlling conduct. *See also* Administrative Regulation.

**Relevancy** Having a reasonable relationship to the truth or falsity of an alleged fact; that which reasonably tends to make the existence of a fact more probable or less probable.

**Relevant Evidence** Evidence that has a reasonable relationship to the truth or falsity of an alleged fact; evidence that reasonably tends to make the existence of a fact more probable or less probable than it would be without that evidence; evidence that has the tendency to prove or disprove a fact in issue.

**Remand** Send the case back to a lower tribunal with instructions from the appellate court.

**Rent-a-Judge** A method of alternative dispute resolution in which the parties hire a retired judge to arbitrate their dispute. An alternative to litigation.

**Reply Brief** An appellate brief of the appellant that responds to the appellate brief of the appellee.

**Reporter** A set of law books that contains the full text of court opinions. *See also* Annotated Reporter, Official Reporter.

**Reprimand** A public declaration that an attorney's conduct was improper. This does not affect his or her right to practice. Also called a *censure* and a *public censure*.

**Request for Admission** A method of discovery consisting of a statement of fact that the other side is asked to affirm or deny.

**Res Gestae Exceptions** Exceptions to the hearsay rule that consist of statements or utterances closely connected to or concurrent with an occurrence.

**Res Judicata** A judgment on the merits will prevent the same parties from relitigating the same cause of action on the same facts.

**Respondeat Superior** Let the master (boss) answer. An employer is responsible (liable) for the wrongs committed by an employee within the scope of employment.

**Respondent** *See* Appellee.

**Restatements** A series of volumes that attempt to formulate existing law in a given area.

**Retainer** (1) The contract between an attorney and a client that covers the scope of services, fees, expenses, and costs of legal services. (2) An amount of money (or other property) paid by a client as a deposit or advance against future fees, expenses, and costs of legal services.

**Retroactive** Applying to facts that arise before as well as after the effective date. *See also* Prospective.

**Retroactive Negotiated Fee** A client bill that is finalized *after* the services are rendered.

**Reverse** To change the holding of an opinion in a different litigation.

**Review** To examine in order to determine whether any errors of law were made. *See also* Appellate Jurisdiction.

**Right Justify** Every line of a paragraph on the right margin is aligned.

**Root Expander** An exclamation mark (!) that stands for one or more characters added to the root of a term you are searching in a Westlaw or LEXIS database.

**Rule** *See* Administrative Regulation, Rules of Court.

**Rule-Making Function** Writing administrative regulations.

**Rule of Three** A general guideline used by some law firms to identify budget expectations from hiring paralegals: gross revenue generated through paralegal billing should equal three times a paralegal's salary.

**Rules of Court** The procedural laws that govern the mechanics of litigation before a particular court. Also called *court rules.*

**Ruling** The outcome of a decision of a court, administrative agency, or other body exercising judicial or quasi-judicial power. *See also* Administrative Decision, Holding.

**Run** To cause a program to (1) be loaded into the computer from a disk drive and (2) begin to perform its task.

**Runner** Someone who solicits clients, usually personal injury clients, for an attorney. If this person uses deception or fraud in the solicitation, he or she is sometimes called a *capper* or a *steerer.*

**Sanction** (1) Penalty or punishment imposed for unacceptable conduct. (2) Permission or approval.

**Satisfy** To comply with a legal obligation.

**Save** To cause a program or data in the computer memory to be moved or stored on a diskette or hard drive.

**Scanner** An input device that converts text and images into an electronic or digital format that a computer can recognize.

**Scienter** Knowingly.

**Scope Note** The summary of coverage of a topic within a West Group digest.

**Scope of Employment** That which is done by an employee in furtherance of the business of the employer.

**Screen Formatting** In word processing and other programs, a feature that controls how the text will appear on the screen.

**Scrivener** A professional copyist; a document preparer.

**Scrolling** In word processing and other programs, moving a line of text onto or off the screen.

**Search and Find** In word processing and other programs, a routine that searches for and places the cursor at a specified string of characters.

**Search and Replace** In word processing and other programs, a routine that searches for a specified string of characters and replaces it with another string.

**Search Engine** A search tool that will find sites on the Internet that contain terms you enter on any subject.

**Search Query** A computer research question; what you ask the computer in order to find something in a database.

**Secondary Authority** Any *nonlaw* that a court could rely on in reaching its decision.

**Second Chair** A seat at the counsel's table in the courtroom used by an assistant to the trial attorney during the trial.

**Second-Tier Attorney** *See* Staff Attorney.

**Section (§)** A portion of a statute, regulation, or book.

**Segment** A portion of a document in LEXIS that can be separately searched.

**Self-Interest** *See* Statement against Self-Interest.

**Self-Regulation** A process by which members of an occupation or profession establish and administer the rules on who can become a member and when members should be disciplined.

**Senior Associate** An attorney who has been passed over for partner status but who remains at the firm.

**Senior Legal Assistant** An experienced legal assistant with the ability to supervise or train other legal assistants. He or she may have developed a specialty in a practice area.

**Series** A set of books with its own internal volume-numbering system. When a new series in the set begins, the volume number starts again with 1.

**Service Company** A business that sells particular services, usually to other businesses.

**Service of Process** *Process* is the means used by the court to acquire or exercise its power or jurisdiction over a person. *Service of process* is the formal notification given to a defendant that a suit has been initiated against him or her and that he or she must respond to it.

**Session Law Cite** The citation to a statute that has not yet been printed in a code and therefore is organized chronologically. *See also* Codified.

**Session Laws** The uncodified statutes of the legislature printed chronologically.

**Settlement** An agreement to end a dispute before it is resolved by all available agencies or courts.

**Settlement Work-Up** A summary of the major facts in the case presented in a manner designed to encourage the other side (or its liability insurance company) to settle the case. Also called a *settlement brochure.*

**Sexual Harassment** *See* Hostile Environment Harassment, Quid Pro Quo Harassment.

**Shadow Trial** A mock trial conducted by one side in order to give its attorneys practice and feedback from individuals playing the role of jurors.

**Shallow Pocket** An individual who does not have resources with which to pay a potential judgment. *See also* Deep Pocket.

**Shareware** Software that a user receives without cost and is expected to purchase only after trying and deciding to keep it.

**Shepardize** To use Shepard's citations (in book form, on CD–ROM, or online) to obtain validation and other data on whatever you are Shepardizing.

**Short-Form Citation** An abbreviated citation format of an authority for which you have provided a complete citation elsewhere in what you are writing.

**Situs** Location.

**Skiptracing** Efforts to locate individuals, particularly debtors, and their assets.

**Slip Law** A single act passed by the legislature and printed separately, often in a small pamphlet. It is the first official publication of the act.

**Slip Opinion** A single court opinion, which for many courts is the first printing of the case.

**Software** A computer program that tells the hardware what to do.

**Sole Practitioner** An attorney who practices alone. There are no partners or associates in the office.

**Sole Proprietorship** A business in which one person owns all the assets of the business and assumes all of its debts or liabilities.

**Solicitation** A request; a step taken to obtain something.

**Solicitor** (1) A lawyer in England who handles day-to-day legal problems of clients with only limited rights to represent clients in certain lower courts. *See also* Barrister. (2) In the United States, some high government attorneys are called solicitors, e.g., the solicitor general of the United States, who argues cases before the United States Supreme Court for the federal government.

**Special Edition State Reporter** A reporter that prints the court opinions of one state, which are also printed within

the regional reporter that covers that state. Also called *offprint reporter.*

**Special Interest Group** An organization that serves a particular group or cause.

**Special Jurisdiction** *See* Limited Jurisdiction.

**Specialty Certification** Official recognition of competency in a particular area of law. The National Association of Legal Assistants, for example, has a specialty certification program to recognize a person as a Certified Legal Assistant Specialist (CLAS). A paralegal must first become a Certified Legal Assistant (CLA) and then pass one of NALA's specialty exams. *See also* Certified Legal Assistant, Certified Legal Assistant Specialist.

**Speech Recognition** A program that enables one to enter information into a computer by talking into a microphone.

**Spell Checker** The identification of possible spelling errors in a document with suggested corrections.

**Spontaneous Declaration** An out-of-court statement or utterance made spontaneously during or immediately after an exciting event by an observer. (An exception to the hearsay rule.)

**Spreadsheet** Application software that automatically performs calculations on numbers and values that you enter.

**Squibs** *See* Digest.

**Staff Attorney** A full-time attorney employee who has no expectation of becoming a full partner. Sometimes called a *second-tier* attorney.

**Staffing Agency** An employment agency providing part-time employees for businesses. Often the business pays the agency, which in turn pays the employee.

**Stand-Alone Computer** A computer that is not connected to a network.

**Standard Form** A preprinted form used for commonly prepared documents.

**Standard of Proof** A statement of how convincing a version of a fact must be before the trier of facts can accept it as true.

**Stare Decisis** Courts should decide similar cases in the same way unless there is good reason for the court to do otherwise. A reluctance to reject precedent—prior opinions.

**Star-Paging** A notation (e.g., an asterisk or star) next to text within a page of an unofficial reporter that indicates where the same text is found in an official reporter. *See also* Official Reporter.

**Statement against Self-Interest** An out-of-court statement made by a nonparty (who is now unavailable as a witness) if the statement was against the financial interest of the declarant at the time it was made. (An exception to the hearsay rule.)

**Statement of Principles** Guidelines that try to identify the activities of specified law-related occupations that do not constitute the unauthorized practice of law.

**State Question** A legal question that arises from the application of the state constitution, a state statute, or a state administrative regulation.

**State-Specific** Covering the law of one state; pertaining to the law and practice of an individual state.

**Stating a Cause of Action** Including in a pleading those facts which, if proved at trial, would entitle the party to win (assuming the other party does not plead and prove any defenses that would defeat the effort).

**Status Letter** A letter telling a client what has happened in the case thus far and what next steps are expected.

**Status Line** A message line that can state the current position of the cursor and provide other formatting information.

**Statute** A law passed by the legislature declaring, commanding, or prohibiting something. The statute is contained in a document called an *act*. *See also* Private Law, Public Law.

**Statute in Derogation of the Common Law** A statute that changes the common law. *See* Common Law.

**Statute of Limitations** A law that designates the period within which a lawsuit must be commenced or it can never be brought.

**Statutory Code** A collection of statutes organized by subject matter rather than by date.

**Statutory Fee Case** A case applying a special statute that gives a judge authority to order the losing party to pay the winning party's attorney and paralegal fees.

**Stay** To delay enforcement or execution of a judgment.

**Steerer** *See* Ambulance Chasing, Runner.

**Stipulation** An agreement between opposing parties about a particular matter.

**STOP** A writing technique alerting you to the need for a counteranalysis: after writing a Sentence, Think carefully about whether the Other side would take a Position that is different from the one you took in the sentence.

**Sua Sponte** Voluntarily; of its own will.

**Subject Matter Jurisdiction** The power of the court to resolve a particular category of dispute.

**Subpoena** A command to appear at a certain time and place.

**Subpoena ad Testificandum** A command to appear at a certain time and place to give testimony.

**Subpoena Duces Tecum** A command that a witness appear at a certain time and place and bring specified things such as documents or records.

**Subscript** In word processing and other programs, a character that prints below the usual text baseline. *See also* Superscript.

**Subscription** A signature; the act of signing one's name.

**Substantive Law** The nonprocedural rules that define or govern rights and duties.

**Summary** Quick, expedited, without going through a full adversarial hearing.

**Summary Judgment** A judgment of the court that is rendered without a full trial because of the absence of conflict on any of the material facts.

**Summary Jury Trial** A method of alternative dispute resolution in which the parties present their evidence to an advisory jury, which renders a nonbinding verdict.

**Summons** A formal notice from the court ordering the defendant to appear and answer the plaintiff's complaint. *See also* Service of Process.

**Superior Court** Usually a trial court.

**Superscript** A number (or other character) that is printed above the usual text baseline. *See also* Subscript.

**Superseded** Outdated and replaced.

**Supervising Legal Assistant** Someone who spends about 50 percent of his or her time supervising other legal assistants and about 50 percent on client cases as a legal assistant.

**Supplemented** Added to.

**Supra** Above; mentioned earlier in the document.

**Supremacy Clause** The clause of the United States Constitution that says federal law controls over state law whenever a federal question is raised. (U.S. Const. art. VI, cl. 2.)

**Supreme Court** The highest court in a judicial system. (In New York, however, the supreme court is a trial court.)

**Surrogate Court** A special court with subject matter jurisdiction over wills, probate, guardianships, etc.

**Suspension** The removal of an attorney from the practice of law for a specified minimum period, after which the attorney can apply for reinstatement.

**Sustain** To affirm the validity of.

**"Swoose" Syndrome** Being recognized as part of the clerical staff in some respects and as part of the professional staff in others.

**Syllabus** (1) A one-paragraph summary of an entire court opinion, usually written by a private publisher rather than by the court. (2) In *Shepard's Citations*, the syllabus refers to the headnotes of an opinion that summarize a portion of the opinion.

**System** An organized method of performing a recurring task.

**Table** A feature that allows the creation of a table of information using rows and columns.

**Table of Authorities** A list of primary authority (e.g., cases and statutes) and secondary authority (e.g., legal periodical articles and legal treatises) that a writer has cited in an appellate brief or other document. The list includes page numbers where each authority is cited in the document.

**Table of Cases** An alphabetical list of all the opinions printed or referred to in the volume, and where they are found in the volume.

**Table of Statutes** A list of all the statutes printed or referred to in the volume, and where they are found in the volume.

**Tainted** Having or causing a conflict of interest; contaminated. *See also* Chinese Wall.

**Tainted Paralegal** A paralegal who brings a conflict of interest to a law firm because of the paralegal's prior work at another law firm.

**TANF** Tempory Assistance for Needy Families.

**Tangible Evidence** Evidence that can be seen or touched; physical evidence; evidence that has a physical form.

**Task-Based Billing** Charging a specific amount for each legal task performed. Also called *unit billing* or *project billing. See also* Fee.

**Template** A set of formulas created to perform a designated task.

**Term of Art** A word or phrase that has a special or technical meaning.

**Terms and Connectors** Relationships between terms in a search query that specify documents that should be included in or excluded from the search.

**Testimony** Evidence given by a witness during a trial, deposition, or other formal proceeding.

**Thesaurus** A volume of word alternatives for words initially used.

**Third-Party Complaint** A complaint filed by the defendant against a third party.

**Tickler** A system designed to provide reminders of important dates.

**Timekeeper Productivity Report** A report showing how much billable and nonbillable time is being spent by each timekeeper.

**Timekeeping** Recording time spent on a client matter for purposes of billing and productivity assessment.

**Time Line** A chronological presentation of significant events, often organized in a straight line or linear arrangement.

**Title Page** A page at the beginning of a book that lists the name of the book, the author(s), publisher, etc. On this page, or on the next page, the latest copyright date of the book is printed.

**Tool Bar** A list of shortcuts (usually represented by icons) that can quickly execute commonly used functions.

**Topic and Key Number** *See* Key Number.

**Tort** A civil wrong (other than a breach of contract) that causes injury or other damage for which our legal system deems it just to provide a remedy such as compensation.

**Total-Client Service Library** A chart that leads you to additional materials on the legal topic of the chart.

**Trace a Key Number** To find out what case law, if any, is digested (summarized) under a particular key number in different digests of West Group.

**Traditional Paralegal** A paralegal who is an employee of an attorney.

**Transactional** Pertaining to the preparation and interpretation of contracts, leases, mergers, incorporations, estate plans, patent applications, and other transactions; involving anything other than litigation.

**Transactional Paralegal** A paralegal who helps an attorney provide legal representation in client transactions such as contracts and corporate matters. *See also* Transactional.

**Transcribed** Copied or written out, word for word.

**Transcript** A word-for-word account.

**Treatise** *See* Legal Treatise.

**Treaty** An agreement between two or more nations or sovereigns that requires the approval of the United States Senate. Also called a *convention. See also* Executive Agreement.

**Trial Book** *See* Trial Brief.

**Trial Brief** An attorney's set of notes on the strategy he or she proposes to follow in conducting a trial. Sometimes called a *trial book, trial manual,* or *trial notebook.*

**Trial de Novo** A totally new fact-finding hearing.

**Trial Manual** *See* Trial Brief.

**Trial Memorandum** *See* Points and Authorities Memorandum.

**Trial Notebook** A collection of documents, arguments, and strategies that an attorney plans to use during a trial. Sometimes referred to as the *trial brief*. (It can mean the notebook in which the trial brief is placed)

**Truncated Passive** A form of passive voice in which the doer or subject of the action is not mentioned. *See also* Active Voice, Passive Voice.

**Typeover Mode** When new text is typed in a line that already has text, the old text is erased or overtyped with each keystroke. *See also* Insert Mode.

**Ultrafiche** *See* Microform.

**Unauthorized Practice of Law** Engaging in acts that require either a license to practice law or other special authorization by a person who does not have the license or special authorization.

**Unbundled Legal Services** Discrete task representation. *See also* Bundled Legal Services.

**Uncodified** Organized chronologically rather than by subject matter.

**Uncontested** Unchallenged; without opposition.

**Unicameral** *See* Bicameral.

**Unified Bar Association** *See* Integrated Bar Association.

**Uniform State Law** A proposed statute presented to all the state legislatures by the National Conference of Commissioners on Uniform State Law.

**Unit Billing** *See* Task-Based Billing.

**United States Court of Appeals** The main federal appellate court just below the United States Supreme Court.

**United States District Court** The main federal trial court.

**United States Supreme Court** The highest court in the federal judicial system.

**Universal Character** An asterisk (*) that stands for one character within a term you are searching in a Westlaw or LEXIS database.

**Unlawful Detainer Assistant (UDA)** A nonattorney in California who is authorized (without attorney supervision) to charge fees for helping landlords or tenants bring or defend actions for the possession of land.

**Unofficial Reporter** *See* Official Reporter.

**Unofficial Statutory Code** A statutory code published by a private company without special permission or authority from the government. *See also* official Statutory Code.

**Unpublished Opinion** An opinion that the court decides is not important enough for general publication. Also called an *unreported opinion*.

**Unreported Opinion** *See* Unpublished Opinion.

**Utterance** *See* Excited Utterance.

**Vacate** (1) To annul or put an end to. (2) To move out.

**Validation Research** Using citators and other legal materials to check the current validity of every primary authority (case, statute, etc.) you intend to rely on in the memorandum of law, appellate brief, or other document you are helping to prepare.

**Value Billing** A method of charging for legal services based on factors such as the complexity of the case or the results achieved rather than solely on the number of hours spent on the client's case. *See also* Fee.

**Valuing the Bill** Determining whether there should be a write-down or a write-up of a bill to be sent to the client. *See also* Write Down, Write up.

**Vendor-Neutral Citation** *See* Public Domain Citation.

**Venue** The place of the trial.

**Verdict** The final conclusion of the jury.

**Verification** An affidavit stating that a party has read the pleading (e.g., a complaint) and swears that it is true to the best of his or her knowledge.

**Veto** A rejection by the chief executive of a bill passed by the legislature. *See also* Pocket Veto.

**Vicarious Disqualification** *See* Imputed Disqualification.

**Vicarious Liability** Being responsible (liable) solely because of what someone else has done or failed to do.

**Videoconference** A meeting that occurs in more than one location between individuals who can hear and see each other on a computer screen.

**Videosynchronization** The word-for-word text of what someone is saying on a video is printed on the screen as he or she speaks.

**Virtual** Existing in a computer-generated environment.

**Voir Dire** The oral examination of prospective jurors for purposes of selecting a jury.

**Volume Discount** *See* Discounted Hourly Fee; Fee.

**Wage and Hour Division** The unit within the U.S. Department of Labor that administers the Fair Labor Standards Act, which governs overtime compensation and related matters. *See also* Exempt Employee, Fair Labor Standards Act.

**Waiver** The loss of a right or privilege because of an explicit rejection of it or because of a failure to claim it at the appropriate time.

**Warrant** An order from a judicial officer authorizing an act, e.g., the arrest of an individual, the search of property.

**Web Browser** The program that allows you to read pages on the World Wide Web.

**Westlaw** The fee-based legal research computer service of West Group.

**Wide Area Network (WAN)** A multiuser system linking computers over a large geographical area so that they can share data and resources.

**Word Processor** Application software that allows you to enter and edit data in documents.

**Word Wrap** A word is automatically moved to the next line if it goes past the right margin.

**Work-in-Progress Report** A report that provides the details of unbilled hours and costs per timekeeper, including client totals.

**Work-Product Rule** Notes, working papers, memoranda, and similar documents and tangible things prepared by the attorney in anticipation of litigation are not discoverable. *See also* Discoverable.

**World Wide Web** A system of sites on the Internet that can be accessed through hypertext links.

**Write Down** Deduct an amount from the bill. Also called a *discount adjustment.*

**Write Up** Add an amount to the bill. Also called a *premium adjustment.*

**Writ of Certiorari** An order by an appellate court requiring a lower court to certify the record of a lower court proceeding and send it up to the appellate court, which has decided to accept an appeal of the decision reached in the lower court proceeding.

**Writ Writer** *See* Jailhouse Lawyer.

**WYSIWYG** What You See (on the screen) Is What You Get (when the screen is printed).

# INDEX

**Credits and Acknowledgments** (page numbers are in boldface type) **7** (left) screen capture. Reproduced with permission of the National Federation of Paralegal Associations; (right) screen capture. Reproduced with permission of the National Association of Legal Assistants. **37** Screen capture. Reproduced with permission of Julie J. Chandler. **77** © Martindale-Hubbell, a division of Reed-Elsevier Inc. **78** Screen capture. Reproduced with permission of FindLaw West Legal Directory. **88, 89** Screen capture. Reproduced with permission of Proskauer Rose LLP. **167** Reprinted with permission of Gamble in the Florida Times-Union. **175** Photo courtesy of Anne Dowie. **185** © Susan Spann. **190** Reprinted with permission of Tamara Parker. **260** Reprinted with permission of Hinckley, Allen & Snyder LLP. **261** Reprinted with permission of Holland & Hart LLP. **390, 391** Reprinted with permission of TRIAL (February 1991). Copyright the Association of Trial Lawyers of America. **415** © James L. Shaffer **445** Reprinted with permission of Bindertek. **447** Reproduced with permission of Kathleen Young, Litigation Visuals, Inc. **455** Michael Newman/PhotoEdit. **467** Photos courtesy of WestGroup. **470, 471, 472** (top & middle) Reprinted with the permission of LexisNexis, a division of Reed Elsevier Inc. (bottom) Photos courtesy of WestGroup. **475, 476** Photos courtesy of WestGroup. **477** Photo courtesy of WestGroup. Map reprinted with permission of WestGroup. **478, 479** Photo courtesy of WestGroup. **481** Photos courtesy of WestGroup. United States code box courtesy of West-Group. **482, 483** Key numbers boxes courtesy of WestGroup. **484, 485, 488, 489** Photos courtesy of WestGroup. **492** (1st photo): Photo courtesy of WestGroup. (2nd photo): Reprinted with permission of American Lawyer Media. (3rd photo): Reprinted with permission of Marquette Law Review. (4th photo): Reprinted with permission of Yale Law Journal. **493** Photo courtesy of WestGroup. **494** (top): Reproduced with permission from *Environment Reporter.* Copyright 2002 by the Bureau of National Affairs, Inc. (800-372-1033) http://www.bna.com (middle): Reprinted with the permission of LexisNexis, a division of Reed Elsevier Inc. (bottom): Photo courtesy of WestGroup. **495, 496** Photo courtesy of West-Group. **497** Reprinted with the permission of LexisNexis, a division of Reed Elsevier Inc. **499, 500** (left col.) Photos courtesy of WestGroup. (right col.) Reprinted with the permission of LexisNexis, a division of Reed Elsevier Inc. **501** (top) Reprinted with the permission of LexisNexis, a division of Reed Elsevier Inc. (bottom) Photo courtesy of West-Group. **502, 503, 504** Photos courtesy of WestGroup. **519** (top) Courtesy of WestGroup. (bottom) Reprinted with the permission of LexisNexis, a division of Reed Elsevier Inc. **520** (top) Reprinted with the permission of LexisNexis, a division of Reed Elsevier Inc. (bottom) Courtesy of WestGroup. **537** Reprinted with the permission of LexisNexis, a division of Reed Elsevier Inc. **538** Courtesy WestGroup. **542** Courtesy of WestGroup. **544** Courtesy of WestGroup. **550** Courtesy of WestGroup. **556** Photo and page excerpt courtesy of WestGroup. **559** Excerpts courtesy of WestGroup. **562** Reprinted with the permission of LexisNexis, a division of Reed Elsevier Inc. **563, 564, 565** Reprinted with the permission of LexisNexis, a division of Reed Elsevier Inc. **568** Courtesy of WestGroup. **570, 576** Reprinted with the permission of LexisNexis, a division of Reed Elsevier Inc. **578** Photo courtesy of WestGroup. **581** (left) Photo courtesy of H. W. Wilson Co. (right) Photo courtesy of The Gale Group. **584, 585** Photo courtesy of WestGroup. **593** Courtesy of WestGroup. **595, 596** Courtesy of WestGroup. **668** (top) Reproduced courtesy of WestGroup. (bottom) Reproduced with the permission of LexisNexis, a division of Reed Elsevier Inc. **679** Reproduced with the permission of the National Federation of Paralegal Associations. **699** Reproduced with permission of Oppenheimer, Wolff & Donnelly. **701** Reprinted with permission of ProLaw Software (www.prolaw.com). **702** Reproduced courtesy of TIMESLIPS Corporation. **707** Reproduced courtesy of Computer Software for Professionals, Inc., LEGALMASTER (www.legalmaster.com). **710** Reproduced with permission of ProLaw Software (www.prolaw.com). **729** Photo of hearing room recreation with permission of West/Thomson Learning. **865** Reprinted with permission of the State of New Jersey, Office of the Governor. **867** Photo with permission from Arleen G. Keegan. **871** (top) Reprinted with permission of Alaska Association of Paralegals. (bottom) Reprinted with permission of Now and Zen Productions, Inc. **872** Reprinted with permission of Anna M. Pergola. **874** Reprinted with permission of the Association of Legal Administrators.

# PARALEGAL ASSOCIATIONS: LOCAL

1. Determine how many paralegal associations exist in your state (or in any state where you hope to work). See appendix B.

2. Photocopy the following form, fill out one form for each association you identify in step 1, and mail the form to each association.

---

Date: _____

Dear Paralegal Association:

I am a student at the following paralegal school:

_____

Would you be kind enough to answer the following questions:

1. Can paralegal students be members of your association? If so, what are the dues for students?

2. Does your association have a mentor program where an experienced paralegal member provides guidance or advice to new members?

3. Do you have a student rate for subscriptions to your newsletter?

4. Does your association have a job bank service? If so, can student members take advantage of this service?

5. Would your association consider conducting a "Career Day" in which experienced paralegal members of your association describe work in different employment settings in the state?

Any other information you can send me about the association would be greatly appreciated.

I hope to hear from you.

Sincerely,

_____

My Address: _____

_____

_____

Source: Statsky, *Introduction to Paralegalism* (Delmar Learning)

---

# PARALEGAL ASSOCIATIONS: NATIONAL

Please send me information about the Federation.

My Name and Address:

_____

_____

_____

_____

Clip this form and mail to:

National Federation of Paralegal
   Associations
2517 Eastlake Avenue East
Suite 200
Seattle, WA 98102

Statsky, *Introduction to Paralegalism* (Delmar Learning)

---

Please send me information about NALA.

My Name and Address:

_____

_____

_____

Clip this form and mail to:

National Association of
   Legal Assistants
1516 South Boston, Suite 200
Tulsa, OK 74119-4013

Statsky, *Introduction to Paralegalism* (Delmar Learning)